T0191667

Lecture Notes in Computer Science 12890

More information about this subseries at http://www.springer.com/series/7412

Yuxin Peng · Shi-Min Hu ·
Moncef Gabbouj · Kun Zhou ·
Michael Elad · Kun Xu (Eds.)

Image
and Graphics

11th International Conference, ICIG 2021
Haikou, China, August 6–8, 2021
Proceedings, Part III

Springer

Editors
Yuxin Peng
Peking University
Beijing, China

Shi-Min Hu
Tsinghua University
Beijing, China

Moncef Gabbouj
Tampere University
Tampere, Finland

Kun Zhou
Zhejiang University
Hangzhou, China

Michael Elad
Technion – Israel Institute of Technology
Haifa, Israel

Kun Xu
Tsinghua University
Beijing, China

ISSN 0302-9743   ISSN 1611-3349   (electronic)
Lecture Notes in Computer Science
ISBN 978-3-030-87360-8   ISBN 978-3-030-87361-5   (eBook)
https://doi.org/10.1007/978-3-030-87361-5

LNCS Sublibrary: SL6 – Image Processing, Computer Vision, Pattern Recognition, and Graphics

This Springer imprint is published by the registered company Springer Nature Switzerland AG
The registered company address is: Gewerbestrasse 11, 6330 Cham, Switzerland

Preface

These are the proceedings of the 11th International Conference on Image and Graphics (ICIG 2021), which was supposed to be held in Haikou, China, during August 6–8, 2021, but was postponed due to COVID-19.

The China Society of Image and Graphics (CSIG) has hosted the series of ICIG conferences since 2000. ICIG is the biennial conference organized by the CSIG that focuses on innovative technologies of image, video, and graphics processing and fosters innovation, entrepreneurship, and networking. This time, the conference was organized by Hainan University. Details about the past conferences are as follows:

Conference	Place	Date	Submitted	Proceeding
First (ICIG 2000)	Tianjin, China	August 16–18	220	156
Second (ICIG 2002)	Hefei, China	August 15–18	280	166
Third (ICIG 2004)	Hong Kong, China	December 17–19	460	140
4th (ICIG 2007)	Chengdu, China	August 22–24	525	184
5th (ICIG 2009)	Xi'an, China	September 20–23	362	179
6th (ICIG 2011)	Hefei, China	August 12–15	329	183
7th (ICIG 2013)	Qingdao, China	July 26–28	346	181
8th (ICIG 2015)	Tianjin, China	August 13–16	345	170
9th (ICIG 2017)	Shanghai, China	September 13–15	370	172
10th (ICIG 2019)	Shanghai, China	August 23–25	384	183

For ICIG 2021, 421 submissions were received and 198 papers were accepted. To ease the search of a required paper in these proceedings, the accepted papers have been arranged into different sections according to their topic.

We sincerely thank all the contributors, who came from around the world to present their advanced work at this event. We would also like to thank all the reviewers, who carefully reviewed all submissions and made their valuable comments for improving the accepted papers. The proceedings could not have been produced without the invaluable efforts of the members of the Organizing Committee, and a number of active members of CSIG.

August 2021

Yuxin Peng
Shi-Min Hu
Moncef Gabbouj
Kun Zhou
Michael Elad
Kun Xu

Organization

Organizing Committee

General Chairs

Yaonan Wang	Hunan University, China
Laurence T. Yang	Hainan University, China
Ming Lin	University of Maryland at College Park, USA

Technical Program Chairs

Yuxin Peng	Peking University, China
Shi-Min Hu	Tsinghua University, China
Moncef Gabbouj	TUT, Finland
Kun Zhou	Zhejiang University, China

Organizing Committee Chairs

Mingming Cheng	Nankai University, China
Zhaohui Wang	Hainan University, China
Faouzi Alaya Cheikh	NTNU, Norway

Sponsorship Chairs

Rongrong Ji	Xiamen University, China
Yafeng Deng	Qihoo 360 Technology Co., Ltd., China

Finance Chair

Jing Dong	Institute of Automation, CAS, China

Special Session Chairs

Ioan Tabus	Tampere University, Finland
Jian Cheng	Institute of Automation, CAS, China

Award Chairs

Yirong Wu	Aerospace Information Research Institute, CAS, China
Ridha Hamila	Qatar University, Qatar
Jieqing Feng	Zhejiang University, China

Publicity Chairs

Sid Ahmed Fezza	INTTIC, Algeria
Zhi Jin	Sun Yat-sen University, China
Jimin Xiao	Xi'an Jiaotong-Liverpool University, China

Exhibits Chairs

Jinjian Wu	Xidian University, China
Drahansky Martin	Brno University of Technology, Czech Republic
Dong Wang	Dalian University of Technology, China

Publication Chairs

Michael Elad	Israel Institute of Technology, Israel
Kun Xu	Tsinghua University, China

Oversea Liaison Chairs

Yubing Tong	University of Pennsylvania, USA
Azeddine Beghdadi	University Sorbonne Paris Nord, France

Local Chair

Xiaozhang Liu	Hainan University, China

Tutorial Chairs

Hongkai Xiong	Shanghai Jiao Tong University, China
Yo-Sung Ho	GIST, South Korea
Zhanchuan Cai	MUST, Macau, China

Workshop Chairs

Yunchao Wei	UTS, Australia
Joaquín Olivares	University of Cordoba, Spain
Cheng Deng	Xidian University, China

Symposium Chairs

Chia-wen Lin	Tsing Hua University, Taiwan, China
Frederic Dufaux	CNRS, France

Website Chair

Zhenwei Shi	Beihang University, China

Area Chairs

Weihong Deng	Meina Kan	Huimin Lu	Hang Su
Jing Dong	Weiyao Lin	Wanli Ouyang	Hao Su
Hu Han	Risheng Liu	Jinshan Pan	Nannan Wang
Gao Huang	Jiaying Liu	Houwen Peng	Shuhui Wang
Di Huang	Si Liu	Xi Peng	Yunhai Wang
Xu Jia	Zhilei Liu	Boxin Shi	Xinchao Wang

Limin Wang   Baoyuan Wu   Shiqi Yu   Liang Zheng
Dong Wang   Yong Xia   Shanshan Zhang   Xiaobin Zhu
Yunhai Wang   Guisong Xia   Xi Sheryl Zhang Chao Zuo
Yingcai Wu   Junchi Yan   Xiaoyu Zhang

Additional Reviewers

Haoran Bai   Jiajun Deng   Songfang Han   Zeren Jiang
Xiaoyu Bai   Weijian Deng   Xinzhe Han   Zhiying Jiang
Zhidong Bai   Shangzhe Di   Yahong Han   Lianwen Jin
Bingkun Bao   Jian Ding   Yizeng Han   Zhuochen Jin
Daniel Barath   Hao Du   Zheng Han   Yongcheng Jing
Chunjuan Bo   Heming Du   Zhenjun Han   Meina Kan
Jintong Cai   Peiqi Duan   Shuai Hao   Yongzhen Ke
Zewei Cai   Yuping Duan   You Hao   Jianhuang Lai
Zhanchuan Cai   Jiahao Fan   Zhongkai Hao   Nan Lai
Anqi Cao   Yao Fan   Xiangyang He   Xing Lan
Jian Cao   Yongxian Fan   Richang Hong   Hyeongmin Lee
Jianhui Chang   Zejia Fan   Yuchen Hong   Baohua Li
Di Chen   Zhenfeng Fan   Chenping Hou   Boyun Li
Han Chen   Sheng Fang   JieBo Hou   Fenghai Li
Hao Chen   Xianyong Fang   Yunzhong Hou   Guozhang Li
Jinsong Chen   Jieqing Feng   Yuxuan Hou   Han Li
Shuaijun Chen   Qianjin Feng   Donghui Hu   Hangyu Li
Wenting Chen   Xiaomei Feng   Fuyuan Hu   Hongjun Li
Xiaojun Chen   Zunlei Feng   Lanqing Hu   Jiaji Li
Xin Chen   Chenping Fu   Peng Hu   Ping Li
Xiu Chen   Jiahui Fu   Qingyong Hu   Ruihuang Li
Yang Chen   Xueyang Fu   Ruimin Hu   Shuang Li
Yuanyuan Chen   Jingru Gan   Shishuai Hu   Wenbin Li
Yuqing Chen   Difei Gao   Yang Hu   Wenhao Li
Zhibo Chen   Guangshuai Gao   Zhenzhen Hu   Yi Li
Zhihua Chen   Jiaxin Gao   Yan Hu   Yifan Li
De Cheng   Jun Gao   Bao Hua   Yixuan Li
Yu Cheng   Ruochen Gao   Haofeng Huang   Yunfan Li
Zhanglin Cheng   Shang Gao   Jun Huang   Zekun Li
Xiangtong Chu   Ziteng Gao   Shaofei Huang   Zhuoshi Li
Yang Cong   Zhang Ge   Yan Huang   Zhuoxiao Li
Hengfei Cui   Yuanbiao Gou   Zhenghua Huang   Hao Liang
Yutao Cui   Heng Guo   Zhenyu Huang   Min Liang
Zhaopeng Cui   Jie Guo   Xiaopeng Ji   Zhifang Liang
Enyan Dai   Senhui Guo   Haozhe Jia   Xin Liao
Ju Dai   Xuyang Guo   Mengxi Jia   Zehui Liao
Congyue Deng   Yingkai guo   Muwei Jian   Yijie Lin
Dazhen Deng   Chunrui Han   Xinrui Jiang   Chang Liu

Chenglin Liu
Hao Liu
Jie Liu
Jinyuan Liu
Liu Liu
Min Liu
Minghua Liu
Pengbo Liu
Qingshan Liu
Risheng Liu
Ruijun Liu
Shiguang Liu
Shuaiqi Liu
Si Liu
Wenyu Liu
Xuan Liu
Xuejing Liu
Yaohua Liu
Yaqi Liu
Yiguang Liu
Yipeng Liu
Yong Liu
Yu Liu
Yuchi Liu
Yunan Liu
Zhenguang Liu
Zimo Liu
Yang Long
Hongtao Lu
Hu Lu
Kaiyue Lu
Linpeng Lu
Tao Lu
Bin Luo
Weiqi Luo
Kai Lv
Youwei Lyu
Huimin Ma
Lizhuang Ma
Long Ma
Tengyu Ma
Xiaorui Ma
Xinzhu Ma
Yuhao Ma
Qirong Mao
Shitong Mao

Yongwei Miao
Weidong Min
Zhou Ning
Xuesong Niu
Weihua Ou
Xuran Pan
Guansong Pang
Bo Peng
Sida Peng
Xi Peng
Zhaobo Qi
Jiaming Qian
Rui Qian
Zhenxing Qian
Qingyang Wu
Jiayan Qiu
Xinkuan Qiu
Zelin Qiu
Zhong Qu
Wenqi Ren
Tushar Sandhan
Hanbo Sang
Nong Sang
Cai Shang
Shuai Shao
Zhiwen Shao
Chunhua Shen
Linlin Shen
Qian Shen
Yuefan Shen
Shurong Sheng
Haichao Shi
Jun Shi
Yongjie Shi
Zhenghao Shi
Zhenwei Shi
Shizhan Liu
Jaskirat Singh
Guoxian Song
Sijie Song
Bowen Sun
Haomiao Sun
Jiande Sun
Jianing Sun
Shitong Sun
Xiaoxiao Sun

Bin Tan
Haoteng Tang
Hong Tang
Shixiang Tang
Jun Tao
Zhou Tao
Yadong Teng
Zhan Tong
Jun Tu
Kurban Ubul
Thomas Verelst
Fang Wan
Renjie Wan
Beibei Wang
Bowen Wang
Ce Wang
Chengyu Wang
Di Wang
Dong Wang
Feipeng Wang
Fudong Wang
Guodong Wang
Hanli Wang
Hanzi Wang
Hongyu Wang
Hu Wang
Huiqun Wang
Jinwei Wang
Kaili Wang
Kangkan Wang
Kunfeng Wang
Lijun Wang
Longguang Wang
Mei Wang
Meng Wang
Min Wang
Qiang Wang
Runzhong Wang
Shengjin Wang
Shuhui Wang
Shujun Wang
Tao Wang
Dongsheng Wang
Wei Wang
Weizheng Wang
Wenbin Wang

Xiaoxing Wang
Xingce Wang
Xinhao Wang
Xueping Wang
Xun Wang
Yifan Wang
Yingqian Wang
Yongfang Wang
Yuehuan Wang
Zhengyi Wang
Zhihui Wang
Ziming Wang
Hongyuan Wang
Jinjia Wang
Jie Wei
Xiushen Wei
Ziyu Wei
Weifan Guan
Ying Wen
Di Weng
Shuchen Weng
Zhi Weng
Wenhua Qian
Kan Wu
Runmin Wu
Yawen Wu
Yicheng Wu
Zhongke Wu
Zizhao Wu
Zhuofan Xia
Fanbo Xiang
Tao Xiang
Wei Xiang
Wenzhao Xiang
Qinjie Xiao
Jingwei Xin
Xiaomeng Xin
Bowen Xu
Fang Xu
Jia Xu
Qian Xu
Shibiao Xu
Mingliang Xue
Xiangyang Xue
Xinwei Xue
Zhe Xue

Zhenfeng Xue
Ziyu Xue
Xuejuan Wu
Bin Yan
Xin Yan
Bangbang Yang
Hongyu Yang
Mouxing Yang
Qisen Yang
Shuo Yang
Xue Yang
Yiding Yang
Yifang Yang
Yuansheng Yao
Yue Yao
Jingwen Ye
Shuainan Ye
Yiwen Ye
Zhichao Ye

Wei Yin
Yongkai Yin
Zhaoxia Yin
Zhenfei Yin
Chengyang Ying
Di You
Baosheng Yu
Hongyuan Yu
Nenghai Yu
Zhenxun Yuan
Yuzhang Hu
Jiabei Zeng
Geng Zhan
Yinwei Zhan
Bohua Zhang
Boyuan Zhang
Cuicui Zhang
Jialin Zhang
Jianguo Zhang

Jiawan Zhang
Jie Zhang
Jing Zhang
Junxing Zhang
Kaihua Zhang
Pengyu Zhang
Pingping Zhang
Runnan Zhang
Shaoxiong Zhang
Shizhou Zhang
Songyang Zhang
Xiaoshuai Zhang
Xinfeng Zhang
Xinpeng Zhang
Xinyu Zhang
Yanan Zhang
Yanfu Zhang
Yanhao Zhang
Yaru Zhang

Yifan Zhang
Zhanqiu Zhang
Zhexi Zhang
Ziwei Zhang
Jie Zhao
Tianxiang Zhao
Wenda Zhao
Yan Zhao
Qian Zheng
Weishi Zheng
Chengju Zhou
Chu Zhou
Dawei Zhou
Guijing Zhu
Jianqing Zhu
Mingrui Zhu
Zijian Zhu
Yunzhi Zhuge
Junbao Zhuo

Contents – Part III

Computational Photography

Computer Graphics and Visualization

Motion and Tracking

Video Analysis and Understanding

3D Computer Vision

Efficient Depth-Included Residual Refinement Network for RGB-D Saliency Detection

Jinhao Yu, Guoliang Yan, Xiuqi Xu, Jian Wang, Shuhan Chen[✉],
and Xuelong Hu

School of Information Engineering, Yangzhou University, Yangzhou, China
shchen@yzu.edu.cn

Abstract. RGB-D saliency detection aims to segment eye-catching objects from images with the help of depth. Although many excellent methods raised, it is still difficult to locate salient objects accurately and efficiently, which lies in two challenges: (1) It is difficult to seamlessly and efficiently integrate cross-modal features from RGB-D inputs; (2) Low-quality depth maps have a serious negative impact on the final prediction results. The existing methods use two backbone networks to extract saliency features, which also introduce much redundancy. To address issues, we propose a simple and efficient deep feature refinement module to extract complementary depth features. We also design a depth correction module to filter out noisy depth input adaptively. Experiments with 13 recently proposed methods on 7 datasets demonstrate the effectiveness of the proposed approach both quantitatively and qualitatively, especially in efficiency and compactness.

Keywords: RGB-D saliency detection · Efficient deep feature extraction · Guided residual refinement · Depth correction

1 Introduction

Salient object detection (SOD) is a binary segmentation task and has been widely studied in computer vision, which can be applied in re-identification [33], image understanding [29], object tracking [11], video object segmentation [26] and so on. In recent years, with the development of deep learning, there are more and more new methods proposed for SOD, among them, CNN-based methods [17,25,28,34] have achieved excellent performances due to its powerful feature extraction capabilities. Nevertheless, it is still difficult for them to accurately locate the salient object in complex scenarios.

RGB images are easily affected by shooting environment, lighting, and the clothing texture of the actor. Fortunately, with the development of depth cameras, it is easy for us to get depth information complementary to RGB image, which is of great help to SOD [7,10,20,23,30,37] for accurate detection.

© Springer Nature Switzerland AG 2021
Y. Peng et al. (Eds.): ICIG 2021, LNCS 12890, pp. 3–14, 2021.
https://doi.org/10.1007/978-3-030-87361-5_1

As shown in Fig. 1, there are two typical architectures in existing RGB-D SOD. One uses two backbone networks to respectively extract features from the RGB image and the depth map at the cost of increasing model parameters. The other one directly concatenates RGB and depth together to feed into the same backbone for efficiency. However, RGB and depth information do not belong to the same modal, and using the same network may causes incompatible problem due to their inherent modality differences. Since the depth map itself contains rich spatial information, we design a simple and efficient branch for depth feature extraction, as illustrated in the right of Fig. 1, which does not require a complex backbone network to extract depth information. Compared with the previous methods, our proposed architecture can reduce model parameters and calculation cost while keeps accuracy.

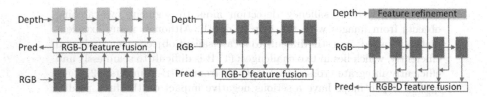

Fig. 1. The left one shows a two-stream architecture by using two backbones. The one in the middle indicates that RGB images and depth images use the same backbone. The right structure is proposed by us, which designs a lower-complexity feature refinement module instead of a backbone in depth branch.

As mentioned above, the depth maps can provide a wealth of spatial information for the network. However, the quality of depth maps is uneven and the low-quality depth maps have a negative impact on the prediction result. The existing methods usually pay equal attention on the RGB feature and depth feature, but ignore the quality of the depth maps. In order to reduce the influence of low-quality depth maps, we design a depth correction module (DCM), which adds adaptive weights into the depth inputs. As a result, low-quality depth maps will get relatively low weights, thus can reduce the negative impact of the low-quality depth maps. In addition, we embed a Multi-Scale Localization Module (MSLM) on top of the backbone to increase the receptive field for more accurate localization. Furthermore, Residual Refinement Module (RRM) is proposed to remedy the missing object parts and boundary details in a top-down manner.

In summary, our main contributions are listed as follows:

(1) We propose a simple and efficient depth feature extraction branch to replace the backbone network used in the previous methods.
(2) We design a depth correction module to add adaptive weights to the depth map to reduce its negative impact to the final result.
(3) Experimental results show competitive performance against 13 state-of-the-art methods on 7 datasets, especially in advantages of efficiency (82 FPS) and compactness (108 MB).

2 Related Work

2.1 RGB Salient Object Detection

Recent years, we have witnessed the rapid development of SOD for the RGB images. Su et al. [25] proposed a boundary-aware network with successive dilation to enhance the feature selectivity at boundaries; Zhao et al. [34] employed pyramid feature attention network to focus on effective high-level context features; Zheng et al. [28] used multi-source weak supervision for sailency detection; Liu et al. [17] expanded the role of pooling in Convolutional Neural Networks (CNNs) to detect saliency. However, in the face of SOD in the challenge and complex scenes, such as low contrast, multi salient objects, etc., the single-modal SOD models did not perform well.

2.2 RGB-D Salient Object Detection

The pioneering work for RGB-D SOD was produced by Niu et al. [20], who introduced disparity contrast and domain knowledge into stereoscopic photography to measure stereo saliency. After Niu's work, various handcrafted features are originally applied for RGB SOD were extended to RGB-D.

In the past five years, deep learning-based RGB-D methods have achieved outstanding performance in salient target detection. Many methods begin to use two backbone networks (e.g. VGG, ResNet) to explore the mining and fusion of the cross-modal RGB-D information. Zhu et al. [37] employed an independent encoder network to take advantage of spatial structural information in depth maps and assist the RGB-stream network. Chen et al. [4] exploited the cross-modal complement across all the levels by a complementarity-aware fusion module based on a two-stream structure. Chen et al. [5] proposed a multi-scale multi-path fusion network with cross-modal interactions to enable sufficient and efficient fusion.

Recently, Piao et al. [23] proposed an adaptive and attentive depth distiller to transfer depth information from depth-stream to RGB-stream. Hence, their network needed no more depth maps when testing, which promotes the practical application of RGB-D SOD approaches. Fu et al. [10] consumed that RGB data and depth information are common and propose a single backbone network to learn from both RGB and depth inputs. Chen et al. [7] introduced depth potentiality-aware mechanism to explicitly model the potentiality of the depth map and effectively integrate the cross-modal complementarity of RGB-D data. Zhang et al. [30] were inspired by the saliency data labeling process and propose probabilistic RGB-D saliency detection network via conditional variational autoencoders to model human annotation uncertainty and generate multiple saliency maps for each input image by sampling in the latent space.

However, most of the above RGB-D approaches [4,5,7,20,23,30,37] use an additional backbone network to extract depth feature. Different from them, we improve two-stream network by designing a simpler and efficient depth branch, which achieved with less computation cost and memory consumption than a traditional two-stream network.

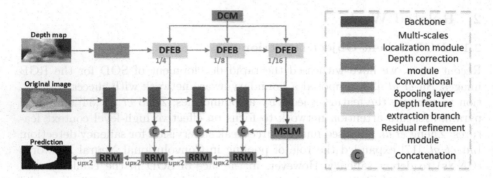

Fig. 2. The schematic illustration of our proposed network. Compared with traditional two-stream architectures, we design a deep feature refining module to refine depth information, which reduces the model parameter quantity.

3   The Proposed Network

3.1   Architecture Overview

As shown in Fig. 2, our proposed network employs ResNet-50 [4] as the RGB branch and used multi-scales localization module to expand the receptive field to obtain more significant information. We adopt a depth feature extraction branch to replace a backbone network in the original dual-stream structure. Finally, we obtain the saliency result maps after using residual refinement module to fuse the cross-modal RGB and depth salient feature maps.

Deep Feature Extraction Branch. The existing dual-stream structure uses backbone networks such as VGG to extract depth information, which leads to the problem of large model size and large number of parameters. As the left figure shown in Fig. 3, we propose a simple and efficient depth feature extraction branch (DFEB) to solve the problems, using only four 3 × 3 convolutions. We adopt DFEB to replace the backbone network in the deep branch. DFEB is an operation of extracting feature map, which lets them divide into four parts, add and convolute each other, and finally put them together. Compared with other backbone network structures, such as VGG16 [24], our DFFM module has fewer convolutional layers and lower complexity. Because the depth map itself contains rich spatial information, our simple DFEB can also extract feature maps with rich information, which is verified in a later ablation study.

3.2   Depth Correction Module

In the past, the RGB feature maps and depth feature maps were fused indiscriminately. And because of the different methods of obtaining depth images, the quality of depth images is uneven. Low-quality depth maps negatively affect the final prediction results.

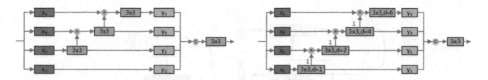

Fig. 3. The left structure is deep feature refining module and the other one is multi-scales localization module. "C" denotes concatenation operation. "3 × 3" means convolution kernel size is 3. "d" represents dilation rate.

We design a depth correction module (DCM) to alleviate the negative effects of low quality depth maps. Generally, the higher the quality of the depth maps, the more similar they are to the GT maps, so we take the GT map as the standard to judge the quality of the depth map, by using Peak Signal to Noise Ratio (PSNR) [27] function as a calculation method. Low-quality depth maps will get lower PSNR weights, indicating that it has less information involved in deep learning. We add the result calculated by the PSNR function as an adaptive weight to the depth branch to obtain an optimized depth image. PSNR is an objective measurement method to evaluate image quality, which is defined as:

$$PSNR(X,Y) = 20 \cdot \log_{10}(\frac{2^n - 1}{\sqrt{MSE}}) \tag{1}$$

where n is the number of bits per pixel, MSE is the mean square error of the current image X and the reference image Y. MSE is defined as:

$$MSE(X,Y) = \frac{1}{H \times W} \sum_{i=1}^{H} \sum_{j=1}^{W} (X(i,j) - Y(i,j))^2 \tag{2}$$

where H and W are the height and width of the image respectively.

3.3 Multi-scales Localization Module

Salient object detection (SOC) is a kind of semantic annotation task at pixel level. In order to improve the performance of SOC, the last layer of the backbone network is usually used as the output layer of the saliency prediction map because of its strong semantic capture ability.

As the right figure shown in Fig. 3, We divide the channel numbers of the image into 4 parts to save memory and each branch has only one convolutional layer. The convolution dilation rates of each convolution layer are 1, 2, 4 and 6 respectively. In addition to the first branch, the second-level input of each branch has to add the output result of the previous branch. Finally, the results of the four branches are connected together, restore the number of channels, and input into the 3 × 3 convolution, and finally a rough predicted result image is output.

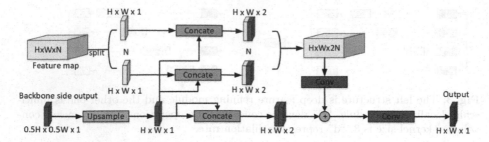

Fig. 4. The construction of RRM. "Upsample" represents upsampling operation with a factor of 2 and "Concate" means concatenation operation. H × W × N means images with length H and width W with N channels.

3.4   Residual Refinement Module

The low-level feature map includes rich details such as boundary, texture and space. The high-level contains rich semantic information. there is an unavoidable problem that the characteristic information of the high-level layer is diluted when it is transferred to the low-level layer.

Therefore, we design a residual refinement module (RRM) to solve this dilution problem. As shown in Fig. 4, the function of RRM is to divide the input feature map with N channels into N non-overlapping one-channel feature maps. Then, the output feature map of the corresponding layer of the backbone network is used as a guide feature map, and it is spliced with the N segmented one-channel feature maps to obtain a total of 2N channel feature maps. Then the module uses several 3 × 3 convolutional layers for guided learning to obtain a 1-channel feature map, which is added together with the input guided map as a new prediction result map. RRM can well alleviate the dilution problem of high-level semantic information in the U-shaped structure.

4   Experiments

4.1   Experimental Setup

Datasets. We evaluate the proposed approach on 7 public RGB-D SOD datasets, namely NJUD [12], NLPR [4], STERE [20], LFSD [16], SSD [15], DUT [22] and SIP [8]. These datasets contain different objects and complex backgrounds, so it is a challenge for SOD task.

Implementation Details. Training dataset is the same as [22], which selects 1487 images from NJUD [12], 700 images from NLPR [4] and 800 images from DUT [22]. To prevent the overfitting, we augment the training set by flipping, cropping, rotating, and light changing. In this work, we train two versions which employ VGG-16 [24] and ResNet-50 [4] as backbone network respectively. The RGB branch is initialized by VGG-16 and ResNet-50, and the others are using the default setting of the PyTorch. We implement the proposed network with

Pytorch on a PC with an Intel i7 6700K CPU, 16GB RAM, and an NVIDIA TiTan Xp GPU. All the experiments are performed using the Adam [13] optimizer with an initial learning rate of 5e-5 which is divided by 10 after 20 epochs. Our network is trained for 30 epochs in total. Finally, we use the sum of binary cross entropy (BCE) loss [1] and intersection over union (IoU) loss [19] as a standard for evaluating network performance.

Evaluation Metrics. We employ F-measure [2], S-measure [5,32], E-measure [8,9], and mean absolute error (MAE) for quantitative evaluations.

Table 1. Quantitative measures: S-measure (S_α), F-measure (F_β), E-measure (E_ε), MAE (M) of SOTA methods on seven RGB-D datasets. The best result is highlighted in bold.

Metric		TANet [3]	CPFP [32]	DMRA [22]	D3Net [8]	ICNet [14]	S2MA [18]	SSF [31]	UCNet [30]	JLDCF [10]	PGAR [6]	HDFN [21]	DANet [36]	GateNet [35]	Our (Vgg)	Our (Res)
DUT	$S_\alpha\downarrow$	0.808	0.749	0.889	-	0.852	0.903	0.916	-	0.905	0.920	0.907	0.899	-	0.920	**0.928**
	$F_\beta\uparrow$	0.779	0.736	0.884	-	0.830	0.866	0.914	-	0.883	0.914	0.864	0.889	-	0.922	**0.929**
	$E_\varepsilon\uparrow$	0.866	0.815	0.927	-	0.897	0.921	0.946	-	0.931	0.944	0.938	0.937	-	0.948	**0.953**
	$M\downarrow$	0.093	0.100	0.048	-	0.072	0.044	0.034	-	0.043	0.035	0.041	0.043	-	0.033	**0.030**
LFSD	$S_\alpha\uparrow$	0.801	0.828	0.847	0.832	0.868	0.837	0.859	0.864	0.861	0.853	0.854	-	-	0.879	**0.880**
	$F_\beta\uparrow$	0.794	0.813	0.849	0.801	0.861	0.820	0.867	0.859	0.854	0.852	0.806	-	-	0.885	**0.887**
	$E_\varepsilon\uparrow$	0.845	0.867	0.899	0.833	0.891	0.863	0.895	0.897	0.882	0.889	0.891	-	-	0.904	**0.911**
	$M\downarrow$	0.111	0.088	0.075	0.099	0.071	0.094	0.066	0.066	0.070	0.074	0.076	-	-	0.061	**0.059**
NJUD	$S_\alpha\uparrow$	0.878	-	0.886	0.895	0.894	0.894	0.898	0.897	0.902	0.909	0.908	0.899	0.902	0.906	**0.914**
	$F_\beta\uparrow$	0.844	-	0.872	0.840	0.868	0.865	0.885	0.889	0.885	0.893	0.877	0.871	0.879	0.897	**0.906**
	$E_\varepsilon\uparrow$	0.893	-	0.908	0.892	0.905	0.896	0.912	0.903	0.913	0.916	**0.932**	0.922	0.922	0.915	0.926
	$M\downarrow$	0.060	-	0.051	0.051	0.052	0.053	0.043	0.043	0.041	0.042	0.038	0.045	0.047	0.041	**0.036**
NLPR	$S_\alpha\uparrow$	0.886	0.888	0.899	0.906	0.923	0.915	0.914	0.919	0.925	**0.930**	0.923	0.915	0.910	0.925	**0.930**
	$F_\beta\uparrow$	0.796	0.822	0.854	0.834	0.870	0.852	0.873	0.890	0.878	0.885	0.882	0.870	0.854	0.901	**0.902**
	$E_\varepsilon\uparrow$	0.916	0.924	0.941	0.932	0.944	0.937	0.949	0.953	0.953	0.955	0.957	0.949	0.942	**0.960**	0.960
	$M\downarrow$	0.041	0.036	0.031	0.034	0.028	0.030	0.026	0.025	0.022	0.024	0.023	0.028	0.032	0.022	**0.021**
SIP	$S_\alpha\uparrow$	0.835	0.850	0.806	0.864	0.854	0.690	0.874	0.875	0.880	0.876	0.886	0.875	0.874	0.883	**0.887**
	$F_\beta\uparrow$	0.809	0.819	0.819	0.831	0.836	0.615	0.861	0.868	0.873	0.854	0.848	0.855	0.856	0.870	**0.887**
	$E_\varepsilon\uparrow$	0.893	0.899	0.863	0.902	0.899	0.796	0.916	0.913	0.921	0.908	**0.924**	0.915	0.914	0.919	0.922
	$M\downarrow$	0.075	0.064	0.085	0.063	0.060	0.150	0.052	0.051	0.049	0.055	0.047	0.051	0.057	0.047	**0.040**
SSD	$S_\alpha\uparrow$	0.839	0.807	0.857	0.866	-	0.868	0.844	-	-	-	**0.879**	0.864	0.870	0.861	0.870
	$F_\beta\uparrow$	0.767	0.726	0.821	0.793	-	0.818	0.812	-	-	-	0.821	0.827	0.822	0.835	**0.845**
	$E_\varepsilon\uparrow$	0.879	0.832	0.892	0.888	-	0.891	0.889	-	-	-	0.911	0.911	0.901	0.901	**0.913**
	$M\downarrow$	0.063	0.082	0.058	0.058	-	0.052	0.058	-	-	-	0.045	0.050	0.055	0.053	**0.044**
STERE	$S_\alpha\uparrow$	0.871	0.879	0.834	0.891	0.903	0.890	0.893	0.903	0.903	0.907	0.900	-	-	0.907	**0.911**
	$F_\beta\uparrow$	0.835	0.830	0.844	0.833	0.865	0.855	0.880	0.885	0.869	0.880	0.853	-	-	0.893	**0.894**
	$E_\varepsilon\uparrow$	0.906	0.903	0.899	0.904	0.915	0.907	0.923	0.922	0.919	0.919	**0.931**	-	-	0.925	0.927
	$M\downarrow$	0.060	0.051	0.066	0.054	0.045	0.051	0.044	0.039	0.040	0.041	0.041	-	-	0.037	**0.036**

4.2 Compared with the State-of-the-arts

We compare our network with other 13 state-of-the-art methods, including TANet [3], CPFP [32], DMRA [22], D3Net [8], ICNet [14], S2MA [18], SSF [31], UCNet [30], JLDCF [10], PGAR [6], PCAN [4], DANet [36], GateNet [35]. For fair comparisons, we use their released saliency maps or adopt the released code and their default parameters to reproduce their results.

Quantitative Evaluation. We present the quantitative comparison results in Table 1. We can clearly find that our method consistently outperforms the other methods on all the seven datasets with respect to S-measure, F-measure, E-measure and MAE scores. Thus, the above quantitative evaluation demonstrates the effectiveness and superiority of our proposed method on detecting salient objects.

Qualitative Evaluation. In order to show our results more intuitively, we provide some visual representative saliency maps of different methods to demonstrate the superiority of our proposed network. As can be seen in Fig. 5, the salient regions are highlighted more accurately by our method even in some challenging cases. And our results have more clear boundaries compared to other methods.

Table 2. Running speed and model size comparisons with recent models

Method	CPFP	DMRA	S2MA	SSF	Our (Vgg)	Our (Res)
Platform	Caffe	Pytorch	Pytorch	Pytorch	Pytorch	Pytorch
FPS↑	20	16	61	26	**92**	85
MS(MB)↓	291.9	238.8	346.8	134.8	**108.0**	**108.0**

Complexity Evalution. Moreover, we further compare the FPS (Frames Per Second) and model size with other models for complexity evalution as shown in Table 2. It can be observed that both running speed and model size of our proposed model performs better than other models.

Table 3. Quantitative evaluation for ablation studies about the effectiveness of DCM, MSLM and RRM.

Method	LFSD				NLPR			
	S_α ↑	F_β ↑	E_ε ↑	M↓	S_α ↑	F_β ↑	E_ε ↑	M↓
DCM	0.845	0.842	0.886	0.080	0.908	0.860	0.946	0.028
MSLM	0.847	0.841	0.875	0.080	0.911	0.863	0.947	0.028
RRM	0.851	0.853	0.885	0.075	0.923	0.898	0.957	0.025
DCM+MSLM	0.850	0.842	0.883	0.076	0.908	0.857	0.944	0.028
DCM+RRM	0.874	0.878	0.906	0.062	0.923	0.896	0.955	0.023
MSLM+RRM	0.879	0.884	0.901	0.062	0.925	0.897	0.955	0.023
DCM+MSLM+RRM	**0.880**	**0.887**	**0.911**	**0.059**	**0.927**	**0.898**	**0.957**	**0.021**

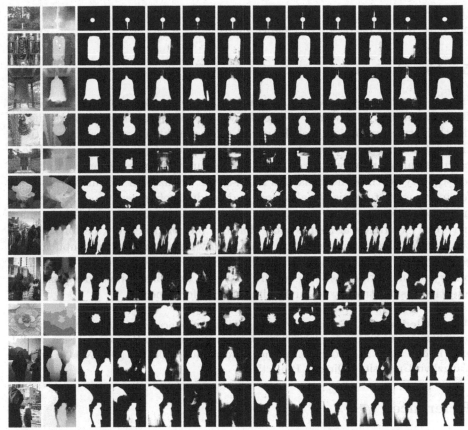

Image Depth   GT DMRA D3Net ICNet S2MA   SSF   UCNet JLDCF HDFN DANet Ours

Fig. 5. Visual comparisons of ERN with SOTA RGB-D saliency models.

4.3   Ablation Study

In this section, we carry out the ablation studies to demonstrate the effectiveness of the proposed module components. We use ResNet-50 as backbone for RGB branch in the following experiments.

To verify the effectiveness of the modules proposed in this paper, we conduct some experiments to evaluate their performance with different combinations. We select the network which removes DCM, MSLM and RRM as baseline. In the baseline, RRMs are replaced with element-wise summation and 3×3 convolution operation. As shown in Table 3, we can conclude that when using a single module, RRM has the best network performance, which shows that RRM can indeed solve the dilution problem very well. When using two modules, MSLM+RRM achieves the best performance, indicating that MSLM expands receptive field to obtain more advanced semantic information. When all modules are used, the network performance is further improved, indicating that DCM reduces the negative impact of low-quality depth maps.

5   Conclusion

In this paper, we propose an efficient and compact convolutional network for RGB-D saliency detection. Specifically, we first proposed a simple and efficient depth feature extraction branch to replace the backbone network in the traditional dual-stream based methods. Then, we design a depth correction module to calculate an adaptive weight on the depth feature to reduce the negative effect of low-quality depth input. Finally, a multi-scales localization module is embedded for more accurate initial localization, and residual refinement module is applied into each side-output to remedy the missing object parts in a top-down manner. The experimental results show that our proposed network performs better than other 13 state-of-the-art methods, and with advantages in simplicity and compactness. We think that our network can be applied to other cross-modal binary segmentation tasks. In our future works, we will continue to explore more effective fusion strategy to further improve performance.

Acknowledgement. Supported by the Natural Science Foundation of China (No. 61802336 No. 61806175 No. 62073322), Jiangsu Province 7th Projects for Summit Talents in Six Main Industries, Electronic Information Industry (DZXX-149, No.110), Yangzhou University "Qinglan Project".

References

1. Boer, P.T.D., Kroese, D., Mannor, S., Rubinstein, R.: A tutorial on the cross-entropy method. Ann. Oper. Res. **134**, 19–67 (2002)
2. Borji, A., Cheng, M., Jiang, H., Li, J.: Salient object detection: a benchmark. IEEE Trans. Image Process. **24**(12), 5706–5722 (2015)
3. Chen, H., Li, Y.: Three-stream attention-aware network for rgb-d salient object detection. IEEE Trans. Image Process. **28**(6), 2825–2835 (2019)
4. Chen, H., Li, Y.: Progressively complementarity-aware fusion network for rgb-d salient object detection, pp. 3051–3060 (06 2018)
5. Chen, H., Li, Y., Su, D.: Multi-modal fusion network with multi-scale multi-path and cross-modal interactions for rgb-d salient object detection. Pattern Recogn. **86**, 376–385 (2018)
6. Chen, S., Fu, Y.: Progressively guided alternate refinement network for RGB-D salient object detection. CoRR abs/2008.07064 (2020)
7. Chen, Z., Cong, R., Xu, Q., Huang, Q.: Dpanet: Depth potentiality-aware gated attention network for rgb-d salient object detection. IEEE Trans. Image Process. **1**, 7012–7024 (2020)
8. Fan, D.P., Lin, Z., Zhang, Z., Zhu, M., Cheng, M.M.: Rethinking rgb-d salient object detection: models, data sets, and large-scale benchmarks. IEEE Trans. Neural Netw. Learn. Syst. **1**, 2075–2089 (2020)
9. Fan, D.P., Gong, C., Cao, Y., Ren, B., Cheng, M.M., Borji, A.: Enhanced-alignment measure for binary foreground map evaluation (2018)

10. Fu, K., Fan, D.P., Ji, G.P., Zhao, Q.: Jl-dcf: Joint learning and densely-cooperative fusion framework for rgb-d salient object detection. In: 2020 IEEE/CVF Conference on Computer Vision and Pattern Recognition (CVPR), pp. 3049–3059 (2020)
11. Hong, S., You, T., Kwak, S., Han, B.: Online tracking by learning discriminative saliency map with convolutional neural network (2015)
12. Ju, R., Ge, L., Geng, W., Ren, T., Wu, G.: Depth saliency based on anisotropic center-surround difference. In: 2014 IEEE International Conference on Image Processing (ICIP), pp. 1115–1119 (2014)
13. Kingma, D.P., Ba, J.: Adam: a method for stochastic optimization (2017)
14. Li, G., Liu, Z., Ling, H.: Icnet: Information conversion network for rgb-d based salient object detection. IEEE Trans. Image Process. **29**, 4873–4884 (2020)
15. Li, G., Zhu, C.: A three-pathway psychobiological framework of salient object detection using stereoscopic technology. In: 2017 IEEE International Conference on Computer Vision Workshops (ICCVW), pp. 3008–3014 (2017)
16. Li, N., Ye, J., Ji, Y., Ling, H., Yu, J.: Saliency detection on light field. In: Proceedings of the 2014 IEEE Conference on Computer Vision and Pattern Recognition, CVPR 2014, pp. 2806–2813. IEEE Computer Society, USA (2014)
17. Liu, J., Hou, Q., Cheng, M., Feng, J., Jiang, J.: A simple pooling-based design for real-time salient object detection. In: 2019 IEEE/CVF Conference on Computer Vision and Pattern Recognition (CVPR), pp. 3912–3921 (2019)
18. Liu, N., Zhang, N., Han, J.: Learning selective self-mutual attention for rgb-d saliency detection. In: 2020 IEEE/CVF Conference on Computer Vision and Pattern Recognition (CVPR), pp. 13753–13762 (2020)
19. Máttyus, G., Luo, W., Urtasun, R.: Deeproadmapper: extracting road topology from aerial images. In: 2017 IEEE International Conference on Computer Vision (ICCV), pp. 3458–3466 (2017)
20. Niu, Y., Geng, Y., Li, X., Liu, F.: Leveraging stereopsis for saliency analysis. In: 2012 IEEE Conference on Computer Vision and Pattern Recognition, pp. 454–461 (2012)
21. Pang, Y., Zhang, L., Zhao, X., Lu, H.: Hierarchical dynamic filtering network for rgb-d salient object detection (2020)
22. Piao, Y., Ji, W., Li, J., Zhang, M., Lu, H.: Depth-induced multi-scale recurrent attention network for saliency detection. In: 2019 IEEE/CVF International Conference on Computer Vision (ICCV), pp. 7253–7262 (2019)
23. Piao, Y., Rong, Z., Zhang, M., Ren, W., Lu, H.: A2dele: adaptive and attentive depth distiller for efficient rgb-d salient object detection. In: 2020 IEEE/CVF Conference on Computer Vision and Pattern Recognition (CVPR), pp. 9057–9066 (2020)
24. Simonyan, K., Zisserman, A.: Very deep convolutional networks for large-scale image recognition (09 2014)
25. Su, J., Li, J., Zhang, Y., Xia, C., Tian, Y.: Selectivity or invariance: boundary-aware salient object detection. In: 2019 IEEE/CVF International Conference on Computer Vision (ICCV), pp. 3798–3807 (2019)
26. Wang, W., Shen, J., Yang, R., Porikli, F.: Saliency-aware video object segmentation. IEEE Trans. Pattern Anal. Mach. Intell. **40**(1), 20–33 (2018)
27. Wang, Z., Simoncelli, E.P., Bovik, A.C.: Multiscale structural similarity for image quality assessment. In: 2003 The Thrity-Seventh Asilomar Conference on Signals, Systems Computers, vol. 2, pp. 1398–1402 (2003)
28. Zeng, Y., Zhuge, Y., Lu, H., Zhang, L., Qian, M., Yu, Y.: Multi-source weak supervision for saliency detection. In: 2019 IEEE/CVF Conference on Computer Vision and Pattern Recognition (CVPR), pp. 6067–6076 (2019)

29. Zhang, F., Du, B., Zhang, L.: Saliency-guided unsupervised feature learning for scene classification. IEEE Trans. Geosci. Remote Sens. **53**(4), 2175–2184 (2015)
30. Zhang, J., et al.: Uc-net: Uncertainty inspired rgb-d saliency detection via conditional variational autoencoders. In: 2020 IEEE/CVF Conference on Computer Vision and Pattern Recognition (CVPR), pp. 8579–8588 (2020)
31. Zhang, M., Ren, W., Piao, Y., Rong, Z., Lu, H.: Select, supplement and focus for rgb-d saliency detection. In: 2020 IEEE/CVF Conference on Computer Vision and Pattern Recognition (CVPR), pp. 3469–3478 (2020)
32. Zhao, J., Cao, Y., Fan, D., Cheng, M., Li, X., Zhang, L.: Contrast prior and fluid pyramid integration for rgbd salient object detection. In: 2019 IEEE/CVF Conference on Computer Vision and Pattern Recognition (CVPR), pp. 3922–3931 (2019)
33. Zhao, R., Ouyang, W., Wang, X.: Unsupervised salience learning for person re-identification. In: 2013 IEEE Conference on Computer Vision and Pattern Recognition, pp. 3586–3593 (2013)
34. Zhao, T., Wu, X.: Pyramid feature attention network for saliency detection (2019)
35. Zhao, X., Pang, Y., Zhang, L., Lu, H., Zhang, L.: Suppress and balance: a simple gated network for salient object detection (2020)
36. Zhao, X., Zhang, L., Pang, Y., Lu, H., Zhang, L.: A single stream network for robust and real-time rgb-d salient object detection (2020)
37. Zhu, C., Cai, X., Huang, K., Li, T.H., Li, G.: Pdnet: prior-model guided depth-enhanced network for salient object detection. In: 2019 IEEE International Conference on Multimedia and Expo (ICME), pp. 199–204 (2019)

Learning Cross-Domain Descriptors for 2D-3D Matching with Hard Triplet Loss and Spatial Transformer Network

Baiqi Lai, Weiquan Liu(✉) (iD), Cheng Wang (iD), Xuesheng Bian, Yanfei Su,
Xiuhong Lin, Zhimin Yuan, Siqi Shen, and Ming Cheng

Fujian Key Laboratory of Sensing and Computing for Smart Cities,
School of Informatics, Xiamen University, Xiamen 361005, China
laibaiqi@stu.xmu.edu.cn, {wqliu,cwang}@xmu.edu.cn

Abstract. The 2D-3D matching determine the spatial relationship between 2D and 3D space, which can be used for Augmented Reality (AR) and robot pose estimation, and provides support for multi-sensor fusion. Specifically, the cross-domain descriptor extraction between 2D images and 3D point clouds is a solution to achieve 2D-3D matching. Essentially, the 3D point cloud volumes and 2D image patches can be sampled based on the keypoints of 3D point clouds and 2D images, which are used to learn the cross-domain descriptors for 2D-3D matching. However, it is difficult to achieve 2D-3D matching by using handcrafted descriptors; meanwhile, the cross-domain descriptors based on learning is vulnerable to translation, scale, rotation of cross-domain data. In this paper, we propose a novel network, HAS-Net, for learning cross-domain descriptors to achieve 2D image patch and 3D point cloud volume matching. The HAS-Net introduces the spatial transformer network (STN) to overcome the translation, scale, rotation and more generic warping of 2D image patches. In addition, the HAS-Net uses the negative sample sampling strategy of hard triplet loss to solve the uncertainty of randomly sampling negative samples during training, thereby improving the ability to distinguish hardest samples. Experiments demonstrate the superiority of HAS-Net on the 2D-3D retrieval and matching. To demonstrate the robustness of the learned descriptors, the 3D descriptors of cross-domain descriptors learned by HAS-Net are applied in 3D global registration.

Keywords: Cross-domain descriptor · 2D-3D Matching · Spatial transformer · Point cloud · Image

1 Introduction

With the development of the computer vision, machines perceive the surrounding environment through sensor information and respond accordingly. In sensor data, camera images and 3D point cloud are the mainstream sensor data structures in 2D and 3D data, respectively. On the one hand, 2D camera image is a

© Springer Nature Switzerland AG 2021
Y. Peng et al. (Eds.): ICIG 2021, LNCS 12890, pp. 15–27, 2021.
https://doi.org/10.1007/978-3-030-87361-5_2

2D grid composed of pixels, usually containing single-channel grayscale images, three-channel RGB images, and RGB-D images including depth information. In terms of deep feature extraction, 2D camera image uses convolution neural network (CNN) to extract local descriptors, which are widely used in industrial projects. However, 2D camera image is difficult to reflect the real 3D world due to its dimensional limitation. On the other hand, 3D point cloud is a point set that contains spatial information. However, due to the disorder of 3D point cloud, it is difficult to effectively extract the internal local relationships. With the development of deep learning, the PointNet [16] solves the problem of point cloud disorder and applies end-to-end neural network to point cloud feature extraction.

Cross-domain data is captured from different sensors. Due to the different imaging principles and data generation methods of different types of sensors, the data varies greatly. The domain gap makes it difficult to extract common features from cross-domain data [1]. Specifically, by learned cross-domain descriptors, the spatial relationship between 2D and 3D space will be established, which provides the promotion and reference significance in the development of 2D and 3D computer vision applications, e.g. AR and robot pose estimation. Using the robust local cross-domain feature descriptors of 2D images and 3D point clouds for 2D to 3D retrieval is a solution to match 2D images and 3D point clouds.

In computer vision-based pose estimation, the popular methods usually use 2D image matching to obtain the camera pose. Nowadays, the 2D-3D matching method has slow progress and poor performance, because of the following problems: 1) There are dimensional differences between 2D and 3D data. 2D image represents the 2D projection of the 3D real world under a certain camera pose, which is different from the spatial information contained of the 3D point cloud. 2) There is a data structure difference between the image and point cloud. The image is a 2D grid with strong domain relations and rich texture information; the point cloud is a collection of discrete 3D points with a better spatial expression, but its discrete type limits the perception of the domain relationship of points. By manually designing descriptors, it is difficult to directly express the common characteristics of these two data types. 3) The feature extraction network designed in the previous work aims at the feature extraction of the same domain descriptors. In the learning of cross-domain descriptors, the previous feature extraction methods expand domain gap between different data types.

In this paper, we propose a novel network, HAS-Net, to jointly learn the robust local cross-domain feature descriptors. The HAS-Net introduces a spatial transformer network (STN) [25] to modify the translation, scale, rotation and more generic warping of patches. In addition, the training process of HAS-Net uses the negative sample sampling strategy of hard triplet loss to solve the uncertainty of randomly sampling negative samples, thereby improving the ability of network to discriminate hardest samples. The contributions are as follows:

1) We propose a novel network, HAS-Net, to jointly learn cross-domain descriptors of 2D image patches and 3D point cloud volumes. Meanwhile, the STN module is embedded to solve translation, scale, rotation and more generic warping between 2D image patches and 3D point cloud volumes.
2) The local cross-domain feature descriptor learned by the proposed HAS-Net has been applied in 2D-3D retrieval and 3D global registration tasks, and has been demonstrated that 2D-3D retrieval achieves state-of-the-art performance.

The remainder of the paper is organized as follows. We firstly introduce the related works of 2D matching, 3D matching and cross-domain matching in Sect. 2. In Sect. 3, we describe the proposed HAS-Net framework as well as STN module and hard triplet loss. In Sect. 4, we introduce the experiments and analyze the results from 2D-3D retrieval task and 3D global registration. Finally, we conclude this paper in Sect. 5.

2   Related Works

2.1   2D Feature Descriptors

2D feature descriptors are designed as a local feature vector of the 2D grid in the images. Previous 2D handcrafted feature descriptors, such as SIFT [2], SURF [3], BRIEF [4], DAISY [5], etc. have been widely used in the feature description and feature detection of images. With the development of computer vision, several 2D feature descriptors of deep learning have been proposed, DeepDesc [6], H-net [7], L2-Net [8], FaceNet [9], DOAP [10], DDSAT [11], etc., which have been demonstrated the performance outperform handcrafted feature descriptors.

2.2   3D Feature Descriptors

3D feature descriptors are designed as a local feature vector of the 3D volumes in the point cloud. Handcrafted 3D feature descriptors, such as PFH [12,13], FPFH [14] and ROPS [15] are defined by geometric relationships between points. Recently, deep learning methods are proposed to measure point cloud, such as PointNet [16], PointNet++ [17], PointSIFT [18] and PointCNN [19], etc., which also have been demonstrated the performance outperform the handcrafted feature descriptors.

2.3   Deep Similarity Learning Networks

Deep similarity learning networks are used to learn data features and the similarity between different data. Through the similarity of data in the high-level feature space, the data matching and data retrieval are completed. Siamese networks and triplet networks are popular deep similarity learning networks [20].

2.4   2D-3D Cross-Domain Feature Descriptors

Recently, several neural networks have tried to jointly learn the local feature descriptors of 2D image patches and 3D point cloud volumes, such as 2D3D-MatchNet [21], Siam2D3D-Net [22] and LCD [23]. Cross-domain descriptors are used in 2D-3D retrieval task. However, the previous work failed to consider the existence of translation, scale, rotation and more generic warping between 2D patches sampled from camera images and 3D volumes sampled from point cloud, which interfere with system working process.

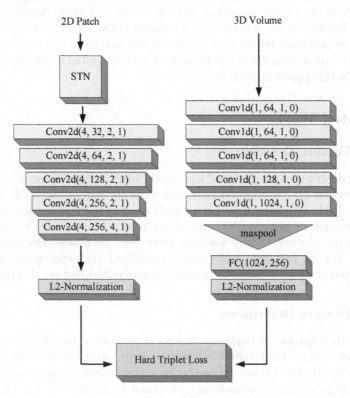

Fig. 1. The HAS-Net framework with network parameters. Feature descriptors are measured by hard triplet loss.

3   Methodology

In this section, we describe our proposed HAS-Net which efficiently learn cross-domain descriptors of 2D patches (image) and 3D volumes (point cloud). In addition, we also introduce the spatial transformer network (STN) [25] module and hard triplet loss that we use to optimize the HAS-Net.

3.1 Network Architecture

HAS-Net is a Siamese network with two branches, 2D branch and 3D branch (Fig. 1), which are designed for extracting 2D patch and 3D volume features. The inputs of HAS-Net are the matching pairs of 2D patches and 3D volumes, whereas the non-matching pairs are generated during the training process.

The 2D branch architecture is composed of CNN and STN. The input of 2D branch are 2D patches with size of $64 \times 64 \times 3$, and the output of 2D branch are 256-dimensional descriptors. Except for the last layer, Batch Normalization (BN) is added after each layer of convolutional layer. The parameter of network are shown in Fig. 1.

The 3D branch architecture adopts the network structure of PointNet [16], the parameters of network are shown in Fig. 1. The 3D volumes is a spherical point set containing 1024 points, the input of 3D branch is 3D volumes with 1024×6. After feeding into 3D branch, each volume outputs a 256-dimensional feature descriptor.

For each matching pairs, hard triplet loss [26] is introduced for optimizing network and Euclidean distance is applied for measuring similarity of descriptors.

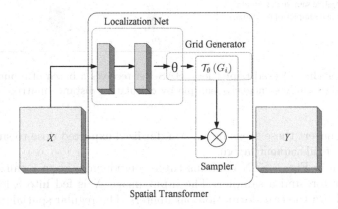

Fig. 2. The detailed structure of spatial transformer network (STN). The input image X is fed into modual and the output map Y is generated.

3.2 Spatial Transformer Network

Spatial Transformer Network (STN) [25] are introduced in HAS-Net to learn invariance to translation, scale, rotation and more generic warping of 2D patches. The Pooling layers make the receptive fields fixed and local. The STN transforms an image by producing an appropriate transformation for each input sample, then performs a transformation on the image, including scaling, cropping, rotation, and non-rigid deformation. This mechanism allows the network including the spatial transformer to not only select the most relevant areas in the image,

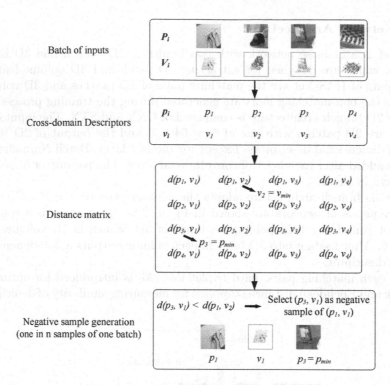

Fig. 3. The pipeline of hrad triplet loss. HAS-Net receives a batch of inputs and generates hardeset sample as negative sample by calculating distance matrix.

but also to convert these areas into a standardized expected pose to simplify the recognition of subsequent layers.

As shown in Fig. 2, STN contains three components, i.e. a localization net, a grid generator, and a sampler. The input image X is fed into a localization network to learn the transformation parameters. The regular spatial grid G over X is used to generate sampling points from the input image X, and outputs map Y:

$$\begin{pmatrix} x_i^s \\ y_i^s \end{pmatrix} = \mathcal{T}_\theta (G_i) = M_\theta \begin{pmatrix} x_i^t \\ y_i^t \\ 1 \end{pmatrix} \tag{1}$$

where (x_i^s, y_i^s) is the source pixel point in the input image X, while (x_i^t, y_i^t) is the target point in the map Y. M_θ is a 2×3 affine transformation matrix with 6 parameters. The two fully connected layers each have 32 neurons, which are used to locate the network to regress 6 parameters. The sampler samples the input feature map X according to the grid $\mathcal{T}_\theta (G_i)$ generated by the grid generator to generate the final output feature map Y.

3.3   Hard Triplet Loss

In training process, we use hard triplet loss [26] provides negative sample generator and loss function for optimizing the proposed HAS-Net. Hard triplet loss works as follow: 1) For a batch of input $\mathcal{X} = (P_i, V_i)_{i=1..n}$, P_i is the 2D patch and V_i means the 3D correspondence. n 2D patches and n 3D volumes of $\mathcal{X}$ are fed into the 2D branch and 3D branch network, respectively. Then, we make the L2 pairwise distance matrix of output cross-domain descriptors $D = [d(p_i, v_j)]$, where $d(p_i, v_j) = \sqrt{2 - 2p_i v_j}, i = 1..n, j = 1..n$, where p_i means the descriptor of 2D patch P_i and v_i means the descriptor of 3D volume V_i. 2) We choose the hardest negative sample of each pair by calculating the 2nd nearest neighbor, as shown in Fig. 3. $v_{j_{min}}$ is the closest non-matching descriptor to p_i, where $j_{min} = \arg\min_{j=1...n, j \neq i} d(p_i, v_j)$. $p_{k_{min}}$ is the closest non-matching descriptor to v_i, where $k_{min} = \arg\min_{k=1...n, k \neq i} d(p_k, v_i)$. For each pair descriptors (p_i, vi), we generate a quadruplet of descriptors $(p_i, v_i, v_{j_{min}}, p_{k_{min}})$. 3) The triplet margin loss function are made of n quadruplets of descriptors:

$$L = \frac{1}{n} \sum_{i=1,n} \max\left(0, 0.2 + d(p_i, v_i) - \min\left(d(p_i, v_{j_{min}}), d(p_{k_{min}}, v_i)\right)\right) \quad (2)$$

where $\min\left(d(p_i, v_{j_{min}}), d(p_{k_{min}}, v_i)\right)$ are chosen during training process.

4   Experiments

4.1   Dataset

The 2D-3D correspondence dataset used in this paper is generated from the 3DMatch [24] dataset by using the sampling strategy of LCD [23]. The sub-datasets are chosen to collect 2D-3D correspondences from 54 RGB-D scans in 3DMatch dataset. A total of 60,000 pairs of corresponding 2D image patches and 3D point cloud volumes were collected, several samples are shown in Fig. 4. In this paper, we use 580,000 pairs as training data, and 20,000 pairs correspondences are set as testing data in 2D-3D retrieval task. The training data and testing data don not intersect each other.

Fig. 4. The data samples of 2D image patches and 3D point cloud volumes, each column are corresponding matching cross-domain data.

4.2   2D-3D Retrieval Task

2D-3D retrieval task is to evaluate cross-domain descriptor performance of HAS-Net. In testing process, we use 20,000 2D-3D correspondences as testing data. The TOP1 and TOP5 retrieval accuracy on the testing dataset has been set to evaluate HAS-Net and comparative networks. In detail, the 2D feature descriptor is set as query to retrieve 3D feature descriptor to calculate the TOP1 and TOP5 retrieval accuracy. The successful TOP1 retrieval is that the 2D feature descriptor finds the corresponding 3D feature descriptor of the nearest L2-distance neighbor; the successful TOP5 retrieval is that the 2D feature descriptor finds the corresponding 3D feature descriptor in the 5-nearest L2-distance neighbor.

Table 1. Retrieval accuracy of HAS-Net and comparative networks.

Method	TOP1	TOP5
2D3D-MatchNet [21]	0.2097	0.4318
Siam2D3D-Net [22]	0.2123	0.4567
LCD [23]	0.7174	0.9412
HAS-Net	**0.7637**	**0.9645**

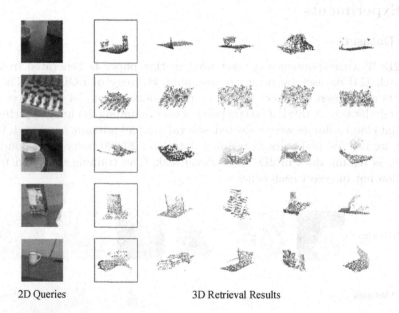

2D Queries   3D Retrieval Results

Fig. 5. The visualization of retrieval results. Each row includes a 2D query and corresponding 5-nearest neigbors 3D volumes of the 2D query. 3D volumes with red bounding box is ground truth of 2D queries.

2D Patches Query 3D Volumes Results. Based on testing data, we use 20,000 2D patches as query to retrieve 3D volumes, and calculate the TOP1 and TOP5 retrieval accuracy, as shown in Table 1. The HAS-Net and all comparative networks output 256-dimensional descriptors in experiments. Result shows that HAS-Net achieves the state-of-art retrieval performance, and verifies the performance of cross-domain feature descriptors learned by HAS-Net are superior than LCD [23], Siam2D3D-Net [22] and 2D3D-MatchNet [21]. In addition, we visualize the 2D-3D retrieval result in Fig. 5. Each 2D image patch shows the 5-nearest L2-distance neighbors of 3D point cloud volumes. The 3D point cloud volume with red bounding box is the ground truth of 2D image patch query. The 5-nearest neighbors have similar structure and texture, which demonstrates the validity of cross-domain in 2D-3D retrieval task.

Visualization of Cross-Domain Descriptors. In order to further study the quality of cross-domain matching of 2D image patches and 3D point cloud volumes, we visualize the cross-domain descriptors of 2D image patches and 3D point cloud volumes learned by HAS-Net, as shown in Fig. 6. In the visualization histogram, x-axis represents the dimension of cross-domain descriptor, y-axis represents the value of the cross-domain descriptor in dimensions. It can be viewed that the distribution trend and the salient area of the matching feature histogram are similar, which demonstrates the similarity of the cross-domain feature descriptors learned by HAS-Net.

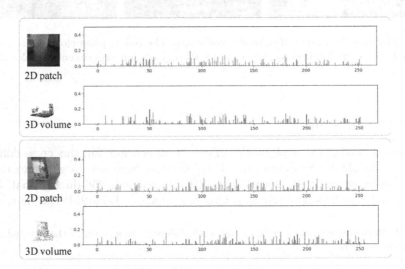

Fig. 6. The visualization of HAS-Net descriptors. x-axis and y-axis represents the dimension of cross-domain descriptor and their value of each dimensions, respectively.

4.3 3D Global Registration

In order to explore the robustness and multitasking capabilities of cross-domain descriptors, we use cross-domain descriptors of 3D point cloud volums for 3D Global registration. Several sences of 3DMatch dataset have been sampled for 3D registration tasks. It should be emphasized that since the network is designed for cross-domain matching tasks, only its feasibility is verified on 3D global registration, not its superior performance. In 3D global registration process, two fragments are first downsampled to get keypoints. Second, taking 3D volume with 30 cm radius for each keypoint. Third, each volume is fed to HAS-Net to obtain 3D feature descriptor. Finally, all keypoints are matched by descriptor nearest search and the transformation matrix is estimated with RANSAC.

The 3D global registration results are shown in Fig. 7. The blue point cloud and yellow point cloud are two fragments of a indoor scene. The cross-domain descriptors of 3D volumes work steadily on the point cloud registration, which proves the robustness and multitasking capabilities of cross-domain descriptors of HAS-Net.

Fig. 7. The visualization of 3D global registration. The yellow point cloud set as source and the blue point cloud set as target in our 3D registration experiments. (Color figure online)

4.4 Ablation Study

In ablation study, we explore the effect of dimension for the cross-domain descriptor in 2D-3D retrieval task. HAS-Net has been set to generate cross-domain descriptors of 64-dimensional, 128-dimensional, 256-dimensional, 512-dimensional. The 2D-3D retrieval results are shown in Table 2. It can be viewed

Table 2. Retrieval accuracy of HAS-Net with different dimension of the learned ross-domain descriptors.

Dimension	TOP1	TOP5
64	0.7352	0.9551
128	0.7565	0.9623
256	0.7637	0.9645
512	**0.7810**	**0.9684**

that the 512-dimensional cross-domain descriptors have the best retrieval accuracy, because 512-dimensional descriptors have more feature information than others.

In order to explore the impact of hardest triplet loss and STN on network performance, we have trained HAS-Net without STN, HAS-Net without hardest triplet loss and HAS-Net without both STN and hardest triplet loss. Experiments show that Has-Net has the better performance than the other three networks, and hardest triplet loss improves the performance the most (Table 3).

Table 3. Comparison of HAS-Net with or without hard triplet loss and STN.

Network	TOP1	TOP5
HAS-Net w/o both	0.5034	0.8193
HAS-Net w/o STN	0.6873	0.9348
HAS-Net w/o hard triplet loss	0.7096	0.9420
HAS-Net	**0.7810**	**0.9684**

5   Conclusion

In this paper, we propose a 2D-3D matching network, HAS-Net, which jointly learn cross-domain descriptor of 2D image patches and 3D point cloud volumes. In HAS-Net, Spatial Transformer Network (STN) has been introduced to learn the translation, scale, rotation and more generic warping between 2D-3D correspondences. To strengthen the ability of network to distinguish hardest samples, HAS-Net uses hard triplet loss to measure cross-domain descriptors and the negative samples are generated during training process. Experiments show that the corss-domain descriptors learned by HAS-Net achieve state-of-the-art results in 2D-3D retrieval tasks. In addition, the descriptors of 3D volumes are successfully used in 3D global registration to verify the robustness and representativeness.

Acknowledgements. This work was funded by China Postdoctoral Science Foundation (No. 2021M690094).

References

1. Liu, W., Wang, C., Bian, X., et al.: Learning to match ground camera image and uav 3-d model-rendered image based on siamese network with attention mechanism. IEEE Geosci. Remote Sens. Lett. **17**(9), 1608–1612 (2019)
2. Lowe, D.G.: Distinctive image features from scale-invariant keypoints. Int. J. Comput. Vision **60**(2), 91–110 (2004)
3. Bay, H., Tuytelaars, T., Van Gool, L.: SURF: speeded up robust features. In: Leonardis, A., Bischof, H., Pinz, A. (eds.) ECCV 2006. LNCS, vol. 3951, pp. 404–417. Springer, Heidelberg (2006). https://doi.org/10.1007/11744023_32

4. Calonder, M., Lepetit, V., Strecha, C., Fua, P.: BRIEF: binary robust independent elementary features. In: Daniilidis, K., Maragos, P., Paragios, N. (eds.) ECCV 2010. LNCS, vol. 6314, pp. 778–792. Springer, Heidelberg (2010). https://doi.org/10.1007/978-3-642-15561-1_56

5. Tola, E., Lepetit, V., Fua, P.: Daisy: An efficient dense descriptor applied to wide-baseline stereo. IEEE Trans. Pattern Anal. Mach. Intell. **32**(5), 815–830 (2009)

6. Simo-Serra, E., Trulls, E., Ferraz, L., et al.: Discriminative learning of deep convolutional feature point descriptors. In: Proceedings of the IEEE International Conference on Computer Vision, pp. 118–126 (2015)

7. Liu, W., Shen, X., Wang, C., et al.: H-Net: neural network for cross-domain image patch matching. In: IJCAI, pp. 856–853 (2018)

8. Tian, Y., Fan, B., Wu, F.: L2-net: deep learning of discriminative patch descriptor in euclidean space. In: Proceedings of the IEEE Conference on Computer Vision and Pattern Recognition, pp. 661–669 (2017)

9. Schroff, F., Kalenichenko, D., Philbin, J.: Facenet: a unified embedding for face recognition and clustering. In: Proceedings of the IEEE Conference on Computer Vision and Pattern Recognition, pp. 815–823 (2015)

10. He, K., Lu, Y., Sclaroff, S.: Local descriptors optimized for average precision. In: Proceedings of the IEEE Conference on Computer Vision and Pattern Recognition, pp. 596–605 (2018)

11. Keller, M., Chen, Z., Maffra, F., et al.: Learning deep descriptors with scale-aware triplet networks. In: Proceedings of the IEEE Conference on Computer Vision and Pattern Recognition, pp. 2762–2770 (2018)

12. Rusu, R.B., Blodow, N., Marton, Z. C., et al.: Aligning point cloud views using persistent feature histograms. In: EEE/RSJ International Conference on Intelligent Robots and Systems, pp. 3384–3391 (2008)

13. Rusu, R.B., Marton, Z.C., Blodow, N., et al.: Learning informative point classes for the acquisition of object model maps. In: 2008 10th International Conference on Control, Automation, Robotics and Vision, pp. 643–650 (2008)

14. Rusu, R.B., Blodow, N., Beetz, M.: Fast point feature histograms (fpfh) for 3d registration. In: 2009 IEEE International Conference on Robotics and Automation, pp. 3212–3217 (2009)

15. Guo, Y., Sohel, F., Bennamoun, M., et al.: Rotational projection statistics for 3d local surface description and object recognition. Int. J. Comput. Vision **105**(1), 63–86 (2013)

16. Qi, C.R., Su, H., Mo, K., et al.: Pointnet: deep learning on point sets for 3d classification and segmentation. In: Proceedings of the IEEE Conference on Computer Vision and Pattern Recognition (CVPR), pp. 652–660 (2017)

17. Qi, C.R., Yi, L., Su, H., et al.: Guibas: Pointnet++: deep hierarchical feature learning on point sets in a metric space. In: Advances in Neural Information Processing Systems, pp. 5099–5108 (2017)

18. Jiang, M., Wu, Y., Zhao, T., et al.: Pointsift: A sift like network module for 3d point cloud semantic segmentation. arXiv preprint arXiv:1807.00652 (2018)

19. Li, Y., Bu, R., Sun, M., et al.: Pointcnn: convolution on x-transformed points. In: Advances in Neural Information Processing Systems, pp. 820–830 (2018)

20. Liu, W., Lai, B., Wang, C., et al.: Ground camera image and large-scale 3D image-based point cloud registration based on learning domain invariant feature descriptors. IEEE J. Sel. Topics Appl. Earth Obs. Remote Sens. **14**, 997–1009 (2021)

21. Feng, M., Hu, S., Ang, M.H., et al.: 2d3d-matchnet: Learning to match keypoints across 2d image and 3d point cloud. In: 2019 International Conference on Robotics and Automation (ICRA), pp. 4790–4796 (2019)

22. Liu, W., Lai, B., Wang, C., et al.: Learning to match 2d images and 3d lidar point clouds for outdoor augmented reality. In: 2020 IEEE Conference on Virtual Reality and 3D User Interfaces Abstracts and Workshops (IEEE VR), pp. 655–656 (2020)
23. Pham, Q.-H., Uy, M.A., Hua, B.-S., et al.: LCd: learned cross-domain descriptors for 2d–3d matching. In: Proceedings of the AAAI Conference on Artificial Intelligence (AAAI), pp. 11 856–11 864 (2020)
24. Zeng, A., Song, S., Nießner, M., et al.: 3dmatch: Learning local geometric descriptors from rgb-d reconstructions. In: Proceedings of the IEEE Conference on Computer Vision and Pattern Recognition (CVPR), pp. 1802–1811 (2017)
25. Jaderberg, M., Simonyan, K., Zisserman, A., et al.: Spatial transformer networks. In: Advances in Neural Information Processing Systems 28: Annual Conference on Neural Information Processing Systems 2015, 7–12 December 2015, Montreal, Quebec, Canada, pp. 2017–2025 (2015)
26. Mishchuk, A., Mishkin, D., Radenovic, F., et al.: Working hard to know your neighbor's margins: local descriptor learning loss. In: Proceedings of Advances in Neural Information Processing Systems (NIPS), pp. 4826–4837 (2017)

A Stereo Matching Method
for Three-Dimensional Eye Localization
of Autostereoscopic Display

Bangpeng Xiao, Shenyuan Ye, Xicai Li, Min Li, Lingyu Zhang,
and Yuanqing Wang^(✉)

School of Electronic Science and Engineering, Nanjing University, Nanjing 210023, China
yqwang@nju.edu.cn

Abstract. In order to reduce crosstalk and support dynamic viewing, the mainstream autostereoscopic display technology requires high-precision three-dimensional eye localization. Due to the need of displaying high frame rate video images, higher requirements are put forward on the real-time performance of the three-dimensional eye localization algorithm. The three-dimensional measurement of the distance of the eye is particularly complicated, and stereo matching usually needs to be done with the help of binocular cameras. Aiming at the problem of low efficiency in conventional stereo matching, this paper improves and optimizes the ZNCC stereo matching algorithm from two aspects. On one hand, the operation logic of the matching algorithm is improved. It uses computer memory to save the intermediate results of the operation and uses a dynamic programming method to reduce the computational complexity of the matching cost function. On the other hand, the scanning strategy is optimized based on the application scenarios of stereoscopic display. Using the characteristics of the application scenarios and the additional constraints information of stereoscopic display, the search area is narrowed to reduce the frequency of the matching cost calculation. Various comparative experiments show that the method has the characteristics of strong real-time performance, strong robustness, and high accuracy, and can achieve great application effects in actual autostereoscopic display systems.

Keywords: Stereoscopic display · Eye localization · Three-dimensional localization · Stereo matching · Dynamic programming · ZNCC

1 Introduction

Stereoscopic display technology, compared with the traditional flat-panel display, can deliver additional depth information, restore real scenes more comprehensively and bring unique viewing effects and visual impact, so it has been widely concerned by the industry. As a research hotspot, the stereoscopic display technology has extremely extensive application prospects in the fields of military equipment, medical surgery, media entertainment, and design modeling [1]. Resulting from continuous progress and development in the evolution of needs in various fields, multiple research directions

© Springer Nature Switzerland AG 2021
Y. Peng et al. (Eds.): ICIG 2021, LNCS 12890, pp. 28–43, 2021.
https://doi.org/10.1007/978-3-030-87361-5_3

has been derived based on different realization principles. Among them, the display technology through which the three-dimensional effect can be directly obtained by the observer viewing with the naked eye is collectively referred to as autostereoscopic display technology [2].

2 Autostereoscopic Display and Eye Localization

Take the mainstream autostereoscopic display technology based on disparity views as an example. In principle, the lights needs to be controlled by a specific optical structure before the display, so that the two views with disparity enter the eye of the observer separately at the corresponding positions to achieve a three-dimensional effect [3]. Due to the limitation of the optical structure, the traditional implementation can only support static viewing.

Figure 1 takes a five-viewing-zones autostereoscopic display system based on lenticular lenses [3] as an example to show the principle of optical separation of autostereoscopic display technology based on disparity barrier. Among the viewing zones, the adjacent numbered pixels come from different views with disparity, and the lights are projected to different areas through the lenticular lenses. At the distance of d, five viewing zones with the best separation effect will be formed in real-time and the distance d is called the current optimal viewing distance. When the observer's left and right eyes are located at the adjacent viewing zones with decreasing serial numbers, a fine stereoscopic effect can be observed. However, during the actual display process of stereoscopic video images, the observer's real-time observation position is uncertain. If the observer moves to the viewing zones with increasing serial numbers or moves along the depth direction of the display to distance dx, crosstalk will occur and even form anti-stereoscopic effects, affecting the viewing experience [4].

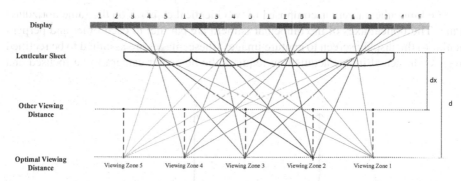

Fig. 1. The principle of optical separation of autostereoscopic display technology based on disparity barrier.

In order to enable a continuous stereoscopic visual effect during the movement in different areas, it is often necessary to cooperate the display technology with the eye localization technology to projecting corresponding disparity images to the left and right eyes quickly and accurately [5]. In addition, due to the limitation of the persistence of vision and the display requirements of high frame rate video images, which are extremely sensitive to the screen refresh interval, the autostereoscopic display system brings great challenges to the accuracy and real-time performance of the three-dimensional eye localization method. Since various kinds of two-dimensional eye localization algorithms are relatively mature, this article focuses on the process of three-dimensional eye localization and proposes a stereo matching method for three-dimensional eye localization of autostereoscopic display.

3   Stereo Matching and 3D Localization

3.1   The Principle of Binocular Stereo Vision

The framework for the development of stereo matching is shown in Fig. 2. The most critical principle is the same as the principle of the stereo effect produced by the human brain's visual center, which is to find the matching pixels of different targets in the left and right views through the comparison of the two views, calculate the horizontal disparity, and then obtain the corresponding depth information through the geometric relation conversion [6]. The difference is that the brain's visual center acquires the pair of left and right views through the eyes, while that acquisition of the stereo matching method is completed by the binocular camera.

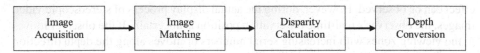

Fig. 2. The framework for the development of stereo matching.

The binocular camera is composed of two identical cameras on the same horizontal plane. The optical axes of the binocular camera are parallel to each other and perpendicular to the display screen to capture images (these images are assumed to be rectified images and actual image acquisition requires the binocular camera to be focused and

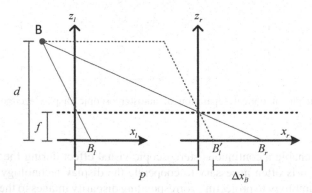

Fig. 3. The ideal optical model of binocular camera and the principle of depth calculation.

calibrated [7]). The ideal optical model of binocular camera and the principle of depth calculation is shown in Fig. 3.

As shown in the figure, an independent coordinate system is established, where the intersection of the optical axes and the two camera sensor planes are defined as the origin. The optical axes z_l and z_r are kept parallel in the depth direction of the left and right cameras. The object B is on the left side of the binocular camera. Through the left and right camera lenses, it is imaged at B_l of x_l and B_r of x_r on the sensor plane respectively by pinhole imaging. The distance between the optical axes is p, the focal length of the camera is f, and the distance from eyes to the image plane of the binocular camera, that is, the depth is d. The position of B_l in the left view coordinate system corresponds to the position of B_l' in the right view coordinate system, so the disparity of the object B in the left and right view coordinate systems is $\Delta x_B = x_{B_r} - x_{B_l}'$. It is easy to infer from the similar relations in the figure that

$$\frac{\Delta x_B}{p} = \frac{f}{d} \tag{1}$$

Thus, the depth d of object B can be obtained as

$$d = \frac{p \cdot f}{\Delta x_B} \tag{2}$$

Under normal circumstances, the camera focal length f and the distance between optical axes p are constant, so the depth d of the object B is inversely proportional to the disparity Δx_B.

The imaging plane of the binocular camera usually overlaps with the display plane of the autostereoscopic display system. Combining the plane pixel coordinate information in the two-dimensional view and the calculated depth, the eyes can be positioned three-dimensionally.

3.2 Image Matching Algorithm

The stereo matching process, different from the process in the visual center of the brain, must locate matching pixels of object from the left and right views through an image matching algorithm before the computation of the corresponding disparity. Implementations of image matching algorithms are mainly based on geometric constraints and scene constraints of stereo matching. However, due to naturally existing problems such as weak texture, occlusion problem, tilt problem, uneven illumination, depth discontinuity issues, etc. [8], the accuracy and robustness of the algorithm are facing varying degrees of challenges. Generally, image matching algorithms can be divided into two kinds according to the principle of implementation: local image matching algorithms and global image matching algorithms [9].

Traditional local image matching algorithms usually need to compute the matching cost based on local information, that is to calculate the degree of correlation between the corresponding regions of two views, using the WTA (Winner-take-all) algorithm to aggregate matching cost to determine the final matched pixel coordinates. Common matching cost functions include SAD (Sum of absolute difference), SSD (Sum of squared difference), and NCC (Normalized cross-correlation). Using the surrounding pixels to remove the DC offset can enhance the algorithm's robustness to changes in brightness and obtain the corresponding functions: ZSAD (Zero-mean SAD), ZSSD (Zero-mean SSD), and ZNCC (Zero-mean NCC). In addition, other non-parametric methods such as rank transform and census transform are also used for matching cost computation. Local stereo matching algorithms are usually faster in computation, and their accuracy and robustness mainly depend on the matching cost function [9].

Global image matching algorithms usually do not require matching cost aggregation. Common algorithms include matching algorithms based on dynamic programming, image segmentation, belief propagation, and neural networks, etc. Global image matching algorithms generally have higher accuracy, but less computational efficiency [9].

The three-dimensional eye localization in the autostereoscopic display system is based on the stereo matching process of face detection and alignment, which means it has local characteristics. Combined with the characteristics of the viewing scene of the stereo display, this paper adopts a local image matching algorithm based on ZNCC to complete the stereo matching process for three-dimensional eye localization.

4 An Eye Stereo Matching Algorithm Based on ZNCC

4.1 Algorithm Overview

The stereo matching algorithm based on ZNCC is a classic area-based stereo matching algorithm. The actual matching process needs to use the window area which contains eyes in the right (left) view as a template and make a scan in the left (right) view. In this way, the area with the highest matching degree can be found through matching cost computation and aggregation. Just as the name implies, the ZNCC algorithm uses the zero-mean normalized cross-correlation coefficient V_{ZNCC} as the matching cost to determine the correlation degree of the corresponding windows of the left and right views.

The ZNCC coefficient V_{ZNCC} is given by Eq. (3), where the size of the template window in the right view and the corresponding scan window in the left view size are both $M \times N$. Using $p_l(x, y)$ and $p_r(x, y)$ to denote the pixel value of the coordinate position at (x, y) of two windows respectively, d_x and d_y to denote the horizontal coordinate difference and the vertical coordinate difference of two windows respectively. And using $\overline{p_l}$ and $\overline{p_r}$ to indicate the average value of two windows respectively. Obviously, the value range of the V_{ZNCC} is $-1 \leq V_{ZNCC} \leq 1$. The closer the V_{ZNCC} value is to 1, the higher correlation of two windows is and the better the matching effect is.

$$
V_{ZNCC} = \frac{\sum_{m=0}^{M-1} \sum_{n=0}^{N-1} \left[(p_r(x+m, y+n) - \overline{p_r}) \cdot (p_l(x+d_x+m, y+d_y+n) - \overline{p_l}) \right]}{\sqrt{\sum_{m=0}^{M-1} \sum_{n=0}^{N-1} (p_r(x+m, y+n) - \overline{p_r})^2} \cdot \sqrt{\sum_{m=0}^{M-1} \sum_{n=0}^{N-1} (p_l(x+d_x+m, y+d_y+n) - \overline{p_l})^2}}
$$
(3)

It should be noted that, ideally, the horizontal baselines of the left and right views are the same, and the depth computation of the target is only related to the horizontal disparity. So the conventional ZNCC algorithm only needs to consider the horizontal coordinate difference d_x. In practice, however, it is inevitable that the lenses of the binocular camera will tilt horizontally during the process of moving, placing and assembling the stereoscopic display system, which leads to inconsistent horizontal baselines of the disparity views even if the binocular camera has been baseline-corrected in advance.

Figure 4 shows the principle of stereo matching in the eyes area based on the disparity views using the ZNCC algorithm. using *Pattern* in the right view as a template (the same way as selecting the eyes area in the left view, in which the scanning direction is opposite). If only considering the horizontal coordinate difference d_x, the conventional ZNCC algorithm needs to scan the area of *Search Area 1* in the left view (the rectangular dashed area which coincides with the left edge of the corresponding area of *Pattern*, has the same height with *Pattern*, and extends to the right edge of the image) and calculate the matching cost V_{ZNCC}. According to the WTA algorithm, the window with the highest matching degree (the window with the V_{ZNCC} value closest to 1) is selected as the matched target for subsequent disparity calculation and depth conversion. However, when the horizontal baselines of two views are inconsistent, the real target area *Target* may not be within the range of the *Search Area 1*, which leads to deviations in the matching results and errors in the three-dimensional eye localization results. In order to avoid this problem, the window scanning should take the vertical coordinate difference d_y into consideration and expand the scanning area to *Search Area 2* in the vertical range, so that the target area Target falls into it. The details of the selection for the search area will be discussed below.

Fig. 4. The principle of eye stereo matching based on the binocular view.

Illumination has a great influence on the brightness of the skin area in the visible light image. The ZNCC algorithm not only has relatively great robustness to changes of brightness [6], but also has strong anti-noise ability, which is very suitable for completing the matching work of the eyes area. However, the ZNCC algorithm has low computational efficiency and poor real-time performance, which makes it difficult to meet the needs of real-time three-dimensional eye localization of autostereoscopic display. Therefore, it is necessary to improve the traditional ZNCC algorithm in combination with the application scenarios of autostereoscopic display.

4.2 Improvement Based on the Operation Logic of Matching Algorithm

The improvement based on the operation logic of matching algorithm is mainly divided into two aspects. Firstly, it uses computer memory to save the intermediate results of the calculation process, in order that it can avoid the repeated calculation of frequently used data and obtain these data by addressing access within the time complexity of $O(1)$, which is a strategy of space-for-time. Secondly, it optimizes the operation logic and uses ideas such as dynamic programming to reduce the time complexity of the algorithm.

By analyzing Eq. (3), we find that the ZNCC algorithm has low computational efficiency, which is mainly derived from the large frequency of summing operations involved in the calculation process of each scan and the matching cost value V_{ZNCC}. For the calculation logic of the ZNCC algorithm, Eq. (3) is simplified and the matching calculation process is improved as follows.

The template area *Pattern* in the right view has been determined to be located at (x, y) after two-dimensional eye localization, so part of the calculation result in the template area of the right view can be regarded as constants and stored in the memory to avoid repeated calculations. We suppose

$$\begin{cases} V_r = \sqrt{\sum_{m=0}^{M-1} \sum_{n=0}^{N-1} (p_r(x+m, y+n) - \overline{p_r})^2} \\ P_{m,n} = p_r(x+m, y+n) - \overline{p_r} \end{cases} \tag{4}$$

Substitute the constants V_r and $P_{m,n}$ into the Eq. (3), and simplify it to

$$V_{ZNCC} = \frac{\sum_{m=0}^{M-1} \sum_{n=0}^{N-1} \left[P_{m,n} \cdot \left(p_l(x+d_x+m, y+d_y+n) - \overline{p_l}\right)\right]}{V_r \cdot \sqrt{\sum_{m=0}^{M-1} \sum_{n=0}^{N-1} \left(p_l(x+d_x+m, y+d_y+n) - \overline{p_l}\right)^2}} \tag{5}$$

In the left view, using $s_1(x, y)$ to denote the sum of window pixels, and $s_2(x, y)$ to indicate the sum of squares of window pixels. Then

$$\begin{cases} s_1(x, y) = \sum_{m=0}^{M-1} \sum_{n=0}^{N-1} p_l(x+m, y+n) \\ s_2(x, y) = \sum_{m=0}^{M-1} \sum_{n=0}^{N-1} p_l(x+m, y+n)^2 \end{cases} \tag{6}$$

Then expand the quadratic term in the root sign in the denominator, there is

$$\sum_{m=0}^{M-1} \sum_{n=0}^{N-1} \left(p_l(x+d_x+m, y+d_y+n) - \overline{p_l}\right)^2 = s_2(x+d_x, y+d_y) - \frac{s_1(x+d_x, y+d_y)^2}{M \cdot N} \tag{7}$$

Thus, the Eq. (3) can be rewritten as

$$V_{ZNCC} = \frac{\sum_{m=0}^{M-1} \sum_{n=0}^{N-1} \left[P_{m,n} \cdot \left(p_l(x+d_x+m, y+d_y+n) - \frac{s_1(x+d_x, y+d_y)}{M \cdot N}\right)\right]}{V_r \cdot \sqrt{s_2(x+d_x, y+d_y) - \frac{s_1(x+d_x, y+d_y)^2}{M \cdot N}}} \tag{8}$$

Inspired by the thought of incremental computation from other improvement methods [10–12], the summation operation during the window scanning process can be quickly calculated through the dynamic programming algorithm. Regard the window pixel sum

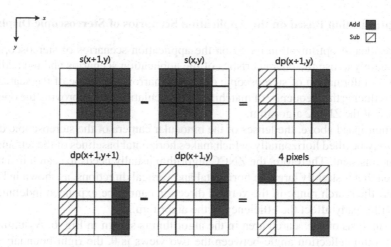

Fig. 5. The principles of dynamic programming algorithm.

$s_1(x, y)$ and the window pixel square sum $s_2(x, y)$ as a kind of summation problem $s(x, y)$. The principle of the dynamic programming algorithm is shown in Fig. 5.

Using $p(x, y)$ to denote the pixel value corresponding to coordinate (x, y), and $dp(x, y)$ is defined as the horizontal increment of $s(x, y)$ relative to $s(x - 1, y)$ during the window scanning process, which can be described as

$$dp(x, y) = s(x, y) - s(x - 1, y) \tag{9}$$

Assuming that the window size is $M \times N$ (for a brief analysis, the window in the figure is set to $M = N = 3$), then the dynamic transfer equation of $dp(x, y)$ is

$$dp(x, y) = dp(x, y - 1) + p(x + M - 1, y + N - 1) + p(x - 1, y - 1) \\ -p(x + M - 1, y - 1) - p(x - 1, y + M - 1) \tag{10}$$

Save dp during the calculation process into the computer memory and use Eq. (11) to perform dynamic incremental calculation on $s(x, y)$ during the window movement process. The result can be directly obtained without a complete summation process.

$$s(x, y) = s(x - 1, y) + dp(x, y) \tag{11}$$

For the search area of $W \times H$ and the window size of $M \times N$, the dynamic programming algorithm only needs to calculate the summation of the starting window, the incremental summation of the first column of the window, and the incremental sum of the first row of the window as the initial input of the algorithm. The times of summations can be reduced from $W \times H$ to $W + H - 1$, and the complete summation of $M \times N$ level only needs to be done once. The extension of the dynamic programming to the case of other area-based stereo matching algorithms is straightforward.

Apply the dynamic programming algorithm to Eq. (8), the denominator term and part of the numerator term of the matching cost V_{ZNCC} can be optimized as dynamic incremental computation. Comparing with Eq. (3), the number of operations with the level of $M \times N$ in each calculation can theoretically be reduced from 4 times (average calculation and summation operation) to 1 time at most.

4.3 Optimization Based on the Application Scenarios of Stereoscopic Display

The core idea of optimization based on the application scenarios of stereoscopic display is mainly to use the characteristics of the application scenarios and the additional constraints information of stereoscopic display to narrow the scope of the search area, thereby reducing the frequency of matching cost calculation and improving the operating efficiency of the ZNCC algorithm.

As mentioned above, the lenses of the binocular camera of the stereoscopic display system may be tilted horizontally, which makes horizontal baselines of the left and right views inconsistent. Therefore, the ZNCC algorithm usually needs to search in a rectangular area that is slightly larger in horizontal and vertical directions, as shown in Eq. (3). However, the search range in the vertical direction cannot be expanded indefinitely or else it will greatly affect the efficiency of the algorithm.

The analysis of the search area in the algorithm is shown in Fig. 6. Assuming that the maximum deflection angle between the two views is θ, the right boundary of the search area of the left view is *Edge*, and the size of the template *Pattern* in the right view is $M \times N$. The search area is shown in the figure. The actual calculation area of the matching cost shapes as an isosceles trapezoid with an upper base of N, a lower base of $N + 2 \cdot (Edge - x - M) \tan \theta$, and a height of $Edge - x - M$. The search area of this shape is smaller than the rectangular area by $(Edge - x - M)^2 \tan \theta$.

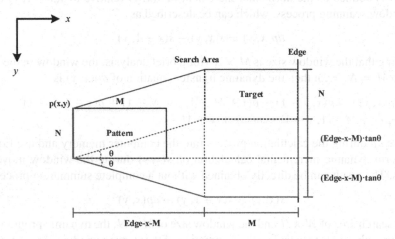

Fig. 6. The analysis of the search area in the algorithm.

The common ZNCC algorithm without other auxiliary information needs to search till reaching the boundary of the view in the horizontal direction, that is, the *Edge* is the right border of the image. The stereo matching algorithm based on eye localization has already obtained the position of the key points of eyes through face detection and alignment before execution, and the interpupillary distance of the detection target can be calculated through these key points. The relative width of the interpupillary distance in the view coordinate system (in pixels) is mainly related to the distance between the eyes and the camera. As shown in Fig. 7 and from the given geometric relations, we can find that the relative width g of the same interpupillary distance l in the view is inversely proportional to the depth d. And it can be inferred from the Eq. (1) that the interpupillary distance is directly proportional to the disparity.

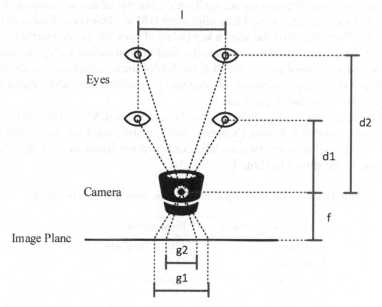

Fig. 7. The relative width of the interpupillary distance in the view at different depths.

The average interpupillary distance is 65 mm. It can usually be considered that the interpupillary distance of different people only changes within a small absolute range of width. Therefore, the area search strategy of the stereo matching algorithm can be optimized by using the interpupillary distance information provided by the two-dimensional eye localization. Using g to denote the horizontal width of the interpupillary distance in the view, w to denote the weight coefficient related to the binocular camera parameters, and e to indicate the error introduced by the change of the interpupillary distance (affected by the size and angle of face area), and then the search range of the window in the horizontal direction can be optimized from $0 \leq d_x \leq Edge - x$ to $wg - e \leq d_x \leq wg + e$.

Concluding the discussion above, the range of the search area of ZNCC algorithm can be optimized to

$$
\begin{cases}
wg - e \leq d_x \leq wg + e \\
-(wg + e) \tan \theta \leq d_y \leq (wg + e) \tan \theta + N
\end{cases}
\tag{12}
$$

The same optimization method is also applicable to other regional search strategies of stereo matching based on two-dimensional eye localization.

5 Experiment and Discussion

Since various kinds of research on image-based two-dimensional eye localization algorithms are relatively mature and are not in the main scope of this paper, the experiment directly uses the open-source face recognition engine SeetaFace to complete the process of face detection [13, 14] and face alignment [15] to obtain coordinates of the key point of eyes. Then, based on the known key points of eyes, the stereo matching method proposed in this paper is used to complete the final three-dimensional eye localization.

The three-dimensional eye localization module of the autostereoscopic display system developed in this paper is mainly divided into two parts: a binocular camera module and an embedded computing platform.

The binocular camera module is designed based on LenaCV® CAM-AR0135-3T16 made by Lena Computer Vision Company and is mainly used for the collection and transmission of visible video images. The configuration parameters of the binocular camera module are shown in Table 1.

Table 1. The configuration parameter of the binocular camera module.

Configuration parameters	Parameter value
Resolution	1280 × 480 pixels
Frame rate	90 fps
Image Sensor	AR0135
Sensor size	1/3"
Single pixel size	3.75 μm × 3.75 μm
Photosensitive spectrum range	380 – 1060 nm
Focal length	3.6 mm
Distance between lenses	65 mm
Camera angle of view	Horizontal 71°, Vertical 55°
Transmission interface	USB 3.0

The embedded computing platform is designed and retrofitted on the motherboard of M7 made by IRU. It is mainly used for the reception and processing of video images from the binocular camera module, the execution of three-dimensional eye localization algorithms, and the transmission of execution results. The configuration parameters of embedded computing platform are shown in Table 2.

Table 2. The configuration parameter of embedded computing platform.

Configuration parameters	Parameter value
CPU	Intel(R) Core (TM) i7-10510U@ 1.80 GHz
Memory	16 GB
Hard disk	1TB SSD
Operating system	Windows 10

The physical objects of the binocular camera module and the embedded computing platform are shown in Fig. 8 (a) and (b) are the front-view and upward-view images of the binocular camera module. The two lenses of the binocular camera are on both sides of the module and the acquired images are transmitted to the embedded computing platform through the bottom interface; (c) is the motherboard of the embedded computing platform, which receives the video images from the binocular camera through the interface on the right side. The motherboard executes the three-dimensional eye localization algorithm, and sends the real-time calculated coordinates of eyes to the photoelectric control module of the stereo display system through the interface on the left side, completing the final real-time opto-mechatronics adjustment and display.

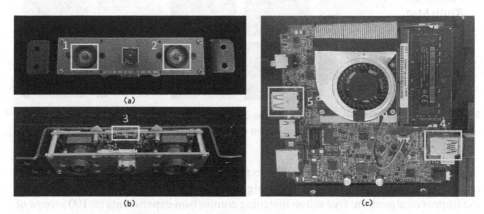

Fig. 8. The physical image of binocular camera module and embedded computing platform. (a) Front-view of binocular camera module; (b) Upward view of binocular camera module; (c) Embedded computing platform; (1) Right camera lens; (2) Left camera lens; (3) Image data sending interface; (4) Image data receiving interface; (5) the calculated coordinates of eyes sending interface.

Due to the distinctiveness of the need of eye stereo matching, there are no corresponding open evaluation datasets with a large amount of data. Thus, the stereo matching experiment first uses the open evaluation datasets from the Middlebury stereo vision database (http://vision.middlebury.edu/) to preliminarily verify the calculation logic of the matching algorithm through experiment (not including the optimization based on the application scenarios of stereoscopic display), and then use the actual collected images for the subsequent experiment on eye stereo matching.

The ZNCC-based stereo matching algorithm is used to calculate the disparity of the full image from the open data set of the Middlebury stereo vision database. Part of the dense disparity map calculated from the experiment is shown in Fig. 9. The average error rate of the algorithm is 8.038% and the average error of the algorithm is 0.986 pixels. The result of preliminary experimental verification shows that the ZNCC-based stereo matching algorithm is of high accuracy, small average error, strong robustness to lighting and other factors, and can be used for the three-dimensional eye stereo matching algorithm.

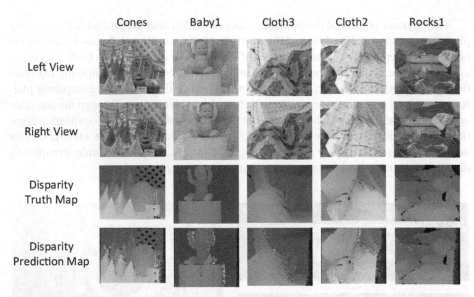

Fig. 9. Part of the experimental effect of the ZNCC-based stereo matching algorithm on the evaluation datasets of Middlebury stereo vision database.

In order to further test the actual effect of the algorithm, this paper compares and analyzes the traditional stereo matching algorithm, the traditional ZNCC algorithm and the improved algorithm. Eye stereo matching comparison experiments on 100 groups of left and right views actually collected by the three-dimensional eye localization module are executed in various methods (the template window size is 20 × 20, and the initial search area size is 300 × 40, The number of repeated executions is 10,000 times), and the results are shown in Table 3. After comparative analysis, the following conclusions can be drawn: (a) The average error of the ZNCC algorithm is slightly smaller than that of ZSAD and ZSSD. The overall effect is similar, but the average time consumption is relatively long and the efficiency is relatively low. (b) Due to the improvement based on the operation logic, the average time consumption is reduced to about one-third compared with the traditional ZNCC algorithm, which means the improvement

Table 3. The result of eye stereo matching experiment.

Technical index	ZSAD	ZSSD	ZNCC	Improvement based on the operation logic	Optimization based on the application scenarios	Comprehensive improved algorithm
Average error (pixel)	0.46	0.45	0.41	0.41	0.41	0.41
Average time (ms)	9.24	9.27	13.22	4.47	0.95	0.41

is relatively effective. (c) Due to the optimization based on the application scenarios, the average time consumption is reduced to about one-fourteenth while maintaining the accuracy compared with the traditional ZNCC algorithm. This means that the optimization effect is excellent. (d) The comprehensive improved algorithm with the two improvement schemes applied, whose efficiency has been increased by about 31.24 times compared with the traditional ZNCC algorithm, has higher accuracy, and better real-time performance.

The experiment mentioned above involves multiple scenarios such as different distances, multi-face targets, changes of brightness, and changes of face angle. The comprehensive improved algorithm is applied to the three-dimensional eye localization module of the autostereoscopic display system, and part of the experimental renderings is shown in Fig. 10. The module performs three-dimensional eye localization in real-time and marks the specific position (the two-dimensional pixel coordinates and the depth value of the left eye) above the area of eyes (the blue rectangular frame). Experiments show that the algorithm can adapt to various scenarios and has strong robustness.

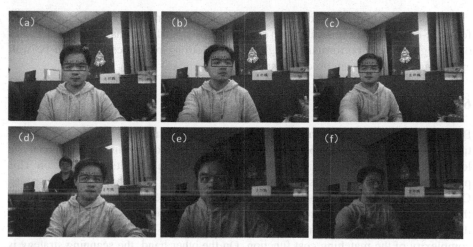

Fig. 10. Part of the experimental renderings of the three-dimensional eye localization module. (1) Positive face; (2) Slight change of face angle; (3) Change of distance; (4) Multi-face targets & Change of distance; (5) Change of brightness; (5) Change of brightness & Change of face angle. (Color figure online)

The autostereoscopic display system equipped with the three-dimensional eye localization module is shown in Fig. 11. The system can work normally and display naked-eye stereoscopic images and provide corresponding stereoscopic images according to the real-time position of the observer. The dynamic resolution of the exit pupil is 20 mm at the general optimal viewing distance of 1000 mm of the stereoscopic display system, while the depth measurement error of the eye localization module is of ±10 mm. It means that the module can theoretically adapt to the dynamic changes of the observer during the viewing process. In the actual experience feedback of the 20 test subjects, a continuous great three-dimensional effect was produced.

Fig. 11. The autostereoscopic display system equipped with the three-dimensional eye localization module. (a) Front-view of the system; (b) Rear-view of the internal system; (1)–(2) Binocular camera module; (3) Embedded computing platform; (4) Optomechanical control module; (5) Display screen that playing naked-eye stereoscopic images.

The overall experiment shows that the stereo matching method proposed in this paper for three-dimensional eye localization of autostereoscopic display has the characteristics of strong real-time performance, high accuracy, strong robustness, and can be well applied in actual autostereoscopic display systems.

6 Conclusion

Based on the ZNCC stereo matching algorithm and combined with the specific application scenarios, this paper proposes a stereo matching method for three-dimensional eye localization of autostereoscopic display, which achieves great results in application. This paper improves and optimizes the ZNCC stereo matching algorithm from two aspects. On one hand, the optimization is based on the improvement of the operation logic of the matching algorithm. It uses computer memory to save the intermediate results of the operation and uses the dynamic programming method to reduce the computational complexity of the matching cost function. On the other hand, the scanning strategy is optimized based on the application scenarios of stereoscopic display. Using the characteristics of the application scenarios and the additional constraints information of stereoscopic display, the search area is narrowed to reduce the frequency of the matching cost calculation. Tested in the actual scene, the average time of this method is 0.41 ms and the average error of this method is 0.41 pixel. Compared with the traditional ZNCC algorithm, the computational efficiency is increased by about 31.24 times while maintaining the original accuracy and robustness. The method also has significant advantages compared with other traditional algorithms. The dynamic resolution of the exit pupil is 20 mm at the general optimal viewing distance of 1000 mm of the stereoscopic display system, while the depth measurement error of the eye localization module is of ±10 mm. It means that the module can theoretically adapt to the dynamic changes of the observer during the viewing process. Various comparative experiments show that the method has the characteristics of strong real-time performance, strong robustness and high accuracy, and can achieve great application effects in actual autostereoscopic display systems.

References

1. Yuanqing, W.: Application and technology status of auto-stereoscopic display. Adv. Display. **01**, 38–41 (2003)
2. Urey, H., et al.: State of the art in stereoscopic and autostereoscopic displays. Proc. IEEE **99**(4), 540–555 (2011)
3. Yuanqing, W.: Research on the optical principle auto-stereo display base on grid. Adv. Display. **03**, 29–32 (2003)
4. Woods, A.J.: Crosstalk in stereoscopic displays: a review. J. Electron. Imaging. **21**(4), 0409 (2012)
5. Xicai, L., et al.: High-speed and robust infrared-guiding multiuser eye localization system for autostereoscopic display. Appl. Opt. **59**(14), 4199–4208 (2020)
6. Brown, M.Z., Burschka, D., Hager, G.D.: Advances in computational stereo. IEEE Trans. Pattern Anal. Mach. Intell. **25**(8), 993–1008 (2003)
7. Xicai, L., Qinqin, W., Yuanqing, W.: Binocular vision calibration method for a long-wavelength infrared camera and a visible spectrum camera with different resolutions. Opt Express. **29**(3), 3855–3872 (2021)
8. Hamzah, R.A., Ibrahim, H.: Literature survey on stereo vision disparity map algorithms. J. Sensors **2016**, 1–23 (2016)
9. Lazaros, N., Sirakoulis, G.C., Gasteratos, A.: Review of stereo vision algorithms: from software to hardware. Int. J. Optomechatron. **2**(4), 435–462 (2008)
10. Yoo, J.-C., Han, T.H.: Fast normalized cross-correlation. Circ. Syst. Signal Process. **28**(6), 819–843 (2009)
11. Briechle, K., Hanebeck, U.D.: Template matching using fast normalized cross correlation. In: Optical Pattern Recognition XII. International Society for Optics and Photonics, p. 4387 (2001)
12. Tsai, D.-M., Lin, C.-T.: Fast normalized cross correlation for defect detection. Pattern Recogn. Lett. **24**(15), 2625–2631 (2003)
13. Wu, S., et al.: Funnel-structured cascade for multi-view face detection with alignment-awareness. Neurocomputing **221**, 138–145 (2017)
14. Yan, S., et al.: Locally assembled binary (LAB) feature with feature-centric cascade for fast and accurate face detection. In: 2008 IEEE Conference on Computer Vision and Pattern Recognition. IEEE (2008)
15. Zhang, J., Shan, S., Kan, M., Chen, X.: Coarse-to-fine auto-encoder networks (cfan) for real-time face alignment. In: Fleet, David, Pajdla, Tomas, Schiele, Bernt, Tuytelaars, Tinne (eds.) ECCV 2014. LNCS, vol. 8690, pp. 1–16. Springer, Cham (2014). https://doi.org/10.1007/978-3-319-10605-2_1

Scaling Invariant Harmonic Wave Kernel Signature for 3D Point Cloud Similarity

Dan Zhang[1,2][✉], Na Liu[3], Yuhuan Yan[1], Xiujuan Ma[1], Zhuome Renqing[1], Xiaojuan Zhang[1], and Fuxiang Ma[1]

[1] The Computer College of Qinghai Normal University, Xining 810008, P.R. China
[2] Academy of Plateau Science and Sustainability, Xining 81017, P.R. China
danz@mail.bnu.edu.cn
[3] School of Artificial Intelligence of Beijing Normal University, Beijing, China
lna@mail.bnu.edu.cn

Abstract. In recent years, the analysis tasks of 3D point cloud models have also attracted wide attention from researchers. The most basic and important research work of 3D point cloud model analysis is the similarity measurement of 3D models. The similarity measurement of 3D point cloud models are generally calculated by shape descriptors, which can capture the most unique features for 3D point cloud models. However, the traditional feature extraction methods for 3D point cloud models are less robust, only focus on rigid deformation and less attention to non-rigid deformation. Recent publications introduce the Laplace-Beltrami operator to define shape descriptors and analysis the non-rigid deformation of models. In this paper, a concise 3D point cloud descriptor is defined to describe the internal structure of 3D point cloud models: scaling invariant harmonic wave kernel signature (SIHWKS). SIHWKS is a shape descriptor involving in the Laplace-Beltrami operator, which can effectively extract geometric and topological information from 3D point cloud models. Based on SIHWKS, the modified Hausdorff distance between SIHWKS values of 3D point cloud model is calculated as similarity measurement, which provides an effective method for 3D point cloud model analysis. Lastly, experiments conducted on public 3D shape datasets show the SIHWKS has the advantages of isometric invariance, scaling invariance and it is robust to topology, sampling and noise.

Keywords: 3D point cloud model · Shape feature · Laplace-Beltrami operator · Shape similarity

1 Introduction

Measuring the difference of 3D models is an important topic in the fields of computer graphics and computer vision. To define the similarity measure of 3D point

Supported by The Natural Science Foundation of Qinghai Province in China (NO. 2018−ZJ−777) and National Natural Science Foundation of China(No.62007019).

cloud models, researchers use shape features to capture geometric shape information. Therefore, feature extractions of 3D point cloud models have important theoretical significance for 3D point cloud models similarity measurement. The feature of 3D point cloud model is represented by the shape descriptor, which is a compact digital representation method of shape that can be understood and recognized by computer. The efficient shape descriptors should invariant to structure-preserving non-rigid deformations, particularly isometric, topological and sampling deformation. At the same time, the similarity measurement between the captured shape descriptors should be easy to define and calculate. Due to the Laplace-Beltrami operator for feature extraction of 3D mesh model has good performance and invariance. Therefore in this paper, we present a 3D point cloud models similarity measurement framework based on Laplace-Beltrami operator which, achieves the state-of-the-art performance in shape analysis tasks. By calculating the modified Hausdorff distance between the scaling invariant harmonic wave kernel signature, the proposed framework is used to measure the similarity between the 3D point cloud models.

2   Related Works

3D point cloud model, the common and basic representation of 3D shapes, contains more geometric information than triangular mesh model. However, compared with triangular mesh model, 3D point cloud model lacks clear topological connection structure and point connection information. Therefore, the existing feature extraction methods for 3D point cloud models include two types:

(1) **Based on shape geometry features**: estimate the geometric structure of 3D point cloud model and extract some geometric features, such as principal curvature [1], normal vector or [2] principal direction [3], to extract geometric discontinuous points of the 3D point cloud models. Most of these methods are devoted to the estimation of geometric information of 3D point cloud models, such as normal vector estimation [4]. Bao L et al. [5] proposed a method of normal estimation on un-organized point cloud. By using robust statistical method to detect the best local section of each point, the algorithm can deal with the points located in high curvature region or complex sharp features, and has strong robustness to noise and outliers. Pei et al. [6] presented a clustering based method for normal estimation which preserves sharp features. These above methods are very dependent on the estimation of geometric information and the accuracy of those method is not high.

(2) **Based on shape statistical features**: In this class, the 3D point cloud model is regarded as a matrix, and the statistical features of the model are extracted on the basis of statistics. For example, feature extraction is based on statistical shape models (SSMs) [7,8], principal component analysis (PCA) [9] and based on model histogram [10,11]. Rahmani H et al. [10] proposed a descriptor at a point by encoding the Histogram of Oriented Principal Components (HOPC) within an adaptive spatio-temporal support volume around that point. Iqbal M Z et al. [11] proposed a fuzzy logic

and Histogram of Normal Orientation (HoNO) based 3D keypoint detection scheme for 3D point cloud models. Most of those methods consider the rigid deformation of 3D point cloud models, and few methods consider the non-rigid deformation.

Shape descriptors based on Laplace-Beltrami operator, called spectral shape descriptors, have been widely used in computational shape analysis in recent years. Spectral shape descriptors try to exploit the geometry arising from the eigenvalues λ_i and eigenvectors φ_i of the LBO [12]. The heat kernel signature (HKS) was proposed by Sun et al. [13] based on the fundamental solutions of the heat equation. Based on the HKS, Brosten proposed the scale-invariant heat kernel signature (SIHKS) that removes the sensitivity of the shape to scaling changes [14]. The wave kernel signature (WKS) uses a bandpass filter to clearly separate different sets of frequencies on the shape and allows access to high-frequency information and does not rely on the time parameter [15]. Li et al. [16] added the scaling invariance for wave kernel signature to design scale-invariant wave kernel signature (SIWKS) for Non-Rigid 3D Shape Retrieval. However, the performance of HKS, WKS, SIHKS and SIWKS depends largely on the parameters selection and have multi-parameters, researchers usually give a single parameter or select several parameters as multi-parameter sequences of those descriptors. In order to describe the local and global information of shape, our previous work [17] provide the harmonic wave kernel (HWKS) by introducing two energy parameters, HWKS can effectively extract geometric and topological information from 3D mesh skulls and faces.

2.1 Contribution

Although the HWKS can describe the detail differences of shapes, and can express the local and global attributes of shapes. It has rigid invariance, isometric invariance, topological robustness and so on, but the HWKS is sensitive to scaling deformation and it is defined on triangular meshes. When calculating the similarity based on the HWKS, it is necessary to normalize the model to eliminate scaling. In order to avoid shape preprocessing, a 3D point cloud descriptor based on the HWKS is proposed, which is invariant to scale deformation. Thus, the contributions of our study as follows:

- We propose a novel 3D point cloud descriptor SIHWKS, which describes the local and global properties of the 3D point cloud models at the same time by selecting two different energy parameters and it is invariant to scale deformation by introducing eigenvalues of the LBO;
- By calculating the modified Hausdorff distance between SIHWKS of a pair of 3D point cloud models, this paper proposes a method to directly measure the similarity of 3D point cloud models without shape registration and finding corresponding points.

The remainder of this paper is organized as follows. In Sect. 2, we introduce the fundamentals and pipeline of our framework. In Sect. 3, we present the definition and calculation of SIHWKS, discuss the invariance of SIHWKS and introduce the similarity calculation based on SIHWKS. In Sect. 4, we show our experimental results. Finally, we draw conclusions in Sect. 5.

3   Fundamentals and Pipeline

In this section, we introduce the fundamentals and pipeline of our method, which is based on the Laplace-Beltrami operator (LBO). The LBO is a well-known intrinsic operator that is decomposed by spectral decomposition. This section first gives the definition and the discrete calculation of the LBO and then gives the general framework for the 3D point cloud models similarity measurement.

3.1   3D Point Cloud Laplace-Beltrami Operator

To effectively represent the intrinsic information and geometric features of the shape, we consider the 3D non-rigid shape as a manifold M. For a compact manifold M, we apply the LBO to define shape descriptors. According to the definitions of gradient and divergence on a Riemannian manifold, if g is the metric tensor on M and G is the determinant of the matrix g_{ij}, then the LBO can be expressed as [18]:

$$\Delta f = \nabla \cdot \nabla f = \frac{1}{\sqrt{G}} \sum_{i,j=1}^{n} g^{ij} \frac{\partial}{\partial x^i} (\sqrt{G} g^{ij} \frac{\partial f}{\partial x^j}) \tag{1}$$

The LBO on the M is decomposed into the matrix product of the eigenvalue and eigenfunction: $\Delta_M \phi_i = \lambda_i \phi_i$, where λ_i is the $i-th$ eigenvalue and ϕ_i is the corresponding eigenfunction. The smallest non-zero eigenvalue is λ_2. The LBO eigenfunctions are intrinsic to the manifold.

In discrete mathematics, the finite-dimensional discrete LBO is typically called the discrete Laplace-Beltrami matrix. On a 3D point cloud model with the vertex number of n, the discrete LBO at the p_i of the point on 3D point cloud M can be calculated [19]:

$$L(i,j) = \frac{1}{nt(4\pi t)^{3/2}} \begin{cases} \exp(-\frac{\|i-p_j\|_2}{4t}), i \neq j \\ -\sum_{k \neq i} \exp(-\frac{\|p_i-p_k\|_2}{4t}), i = j \end{cases} \tag{2}$$

To guarantee the sparsity of the Laplacian matrix, for each point p_i we consider only the entries $L(i,j)$ related to the points $p_j = \{p_j, j \in N_{pi}\}$ that are closest to p_i with respect to the Euclidean distance. In this case, the author select either the k-nearest neighbor or the points that belong to a sphere centered at p_i and with radius r. In this paper, we use K nearest neighbors (KNN) algorithm [20] to construct k-nearest neighbors on 3D point cloud models and calculate the LBO.

3.2   Pipeline

In this paper, we propose a pipeline for 3D point cloud models similarity measurements. Figure 1 schematically describes the generic framework for measuring the similarity of 3D point cloud models based on the SIHWKS. The specific pipeline is shown in the following steps:

A. Input 3D point cloud models: The first step is to select a pair of 3D point cloud models;

B. Calculate the LBO of models: Given a pair of 3D point cloud models, a real-valued function f is defined on its surface. We calculate the spectral decomposition of the LBO of 3D point cloud models;

C. Calculate the SIHWKS of 3D point cloud models: According to the spectral decomposition of the LBO, we can calculate the SIHWKS of 3D point cloud models by choosing efficient energy parameters;

D. Output the 3D point cloud models similarity: Based on the SIHWKS values of 3D point cloud models, we define a measurement to measure the similarity based on the modified Hausdorff distance.

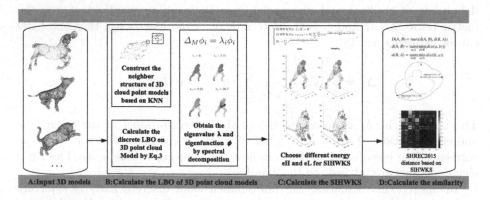

Fig. 1. The 3D point cloud models similarity based on the SIHWKS

4   Scaling Invariant Harmonic Wave Kernel Signature

In this section, we introduce the wave kernel signature involving the LBO, and we propose a way to construct a scaling invariant harmonic wave kernel signature that is used for describing the feature of 3D point cloud models and measuring the models similarity.

4.1   Wave Kernel Signature

For each point on a shape, a shape descriptor called the wave kernel signature (WKS) operator is defined by measuring the average probability distribution of quantum particles with different energy levels. The evolution of the quantum particles is governed by the wave function, which is obtained by solving the Schrödinger equation [15]:

$$\frac{\partial \phi}{\partial t}(x,t) = i\Delta\phi(x,t) \tag{3}$$

The wave function expresses the energy oscillation, where x is a point on a manifold, Δ is the LBO, and i is an imaginary number; the product of the LBO and i ensures that the energy will not decay after oscillating at different frequencies. $\phi(x,t)$ is the wave function, when t is 0, the expectation of the function $\phi(x,t)$ is E, and the probability distribution is λ_k. If only the energy parameters was consider, the WKS is define as a particle whose energy is E at point x and the WKS can be described as follow:

$$WKS(x,E) = \sum_{k=0}^{\infty} \phi_k(x)^2 f_E(\lambda_k) \tag{4}$$

To facilitate this calculation, the above formula is concretely expressed, and the detailed derivation process can be observed [15]. When e_N is the energy scale parameter, where $e_N = log(E)$, λ_k is the $k-th$ eigenvalue of LBO, σ is the variance, and $C_e = (\sum_k e^{\frac{-(e_N - \log \lambda_k)^2}{2\sigma^2}})^{-1}$ is the regularized WKS function. Then, the wave function $WKS(x, e_N)$ of the particle is given by

$$\begin{cases} WKS(x,\cdot) : R \rightarrow R; \\ WKS(x,e_N) = C_e \sum_k \phi_k^2(x) e^{\frac{-(e_N - \log \lambda_k)^2}{2\sigma^2}} \end{cases} \tag{5}$$

In this function, the energy parameter has been replaced by the energy, which is a very useful aspect because the energy is directly related to the eigenvalues of the LBO.

4.2 Scaling Invariant Harmonic Wave Kernel Signature

For WKS, if quantum particles with higher energy levels are selected, the shorter the wavelength is, the closer it is to the point on the shape. In this case, the local characteristics of the shape are reflected. Conversely, the quantum particles with lower energy levels reflects the global characteristics of the shape.

In paper [17], we constructed a shape descriptor which reflects the global and local features of shapes at the same time. Based on the method of synthetic feature in machine learning, we introduce the concept of the feature quotient and define a new harmonic wave kernel signature (HWKS), we simultaneously simulate the process of high energy particles and low energy particles oscillating in the shape:

$$\begin{cases} HWKS(x,\cdot) : R \to R; \\ HWKS(x,e_H,e_L) = H_e \sum_k \phi_k^2(x) e^{\frac{-(e_H - e_L)(e_H + e_L - 2\log \lambda_k)}{2\sigma^2}} \\ H_e = \sum_k e^{\frac{-(e_H - e_L)(e_H + e_L - 2\log \lambda_k)}{2\sigma^2}} \end{cases} \qquad (6)$$

where e_L and e_H stand for the low energy and high energy levels, and σ is the Gaussian variance. H_e is the regularized HWKS. We introduce two energy levels to balance the global and local feature of shapes. And the relationship of higher energy H and lower energy L can be written as:

$$\begin{aligned} e_H - e_L &= (e_{min} + (H-1)d) - (e_{min} + (L-1)d) \\ &= (H-L)d \end{aligned} \qquad (7)$$

where d is a constant. Aim to balance the global and local features and describe more local differences of 3D models, we choose the higher energy H and the larger the difference of $(H-L)$, the result shows better. Note that the value of L cannot be too small which can maintain global property of the shape. For the values of L and H, we give empirical values in the paper [17].

A significant disadvantage of HWKS is that it is not robust to scaling deformation. When a point cloud model is scaled, the value of HWKS will change. In this paper, to overcome this disadvantage, we propose an efficient 3D point cloud descriptor which is robust to scaling deformation. From the paper [16], the author thought that when given a shape M and its scaled vision $M' = \beta M$, the scaled eigenvalues and eigenfunctions would satisfy $\lambda' = \beta\lambda$ and $\phi' = \beta\phi$. And the scaled HWKS of M an be written as:

$$\begin{cases} HWKS(x,\cdot) : R \to R; \\ HWKS(x,e_H,e_L) = H_e \sum_k \beta^2 \phi_k^2(x) e^{\frac{-(e_H - e_L)(e_H + e_L - 2\log \lambda_k)}{2\sigma^2}} \\ H_e = \sum_k e^{\frac{-(e_H - e_L)(e_H + e_L - 2\log \lambda_k)}{2\sigma^2}} \end{cases} \qquad (8)$$

In order to remove the scaling deformation, the paper [16] introduced the Green's function and normalized the WKS by eigenvalues, and the effect of scaling deformation is eliminated by normalization. Therefore, in this paper, we also introduce the eigenvalues of LBO to remove the scaling deformation of the HWKS in Eq. 8. Then ,the scaling invariance HWKS is defined as:

$$\begin{cases} SIHWKS(x,\cdot) : R \to R \\ SIHWKS(x,e_H,e_L) = H_e \sum_k \frac{\phi_k^2}{\lambda_k}(x) e^{\frac{-(e_H - e_L)(e_H + e_L - 2\log \lambda_k)}{2\sigma^2}} \\ H_e = \sum_k e^{\frac{-(e_H - e_L)(e_H + e_L - 2\log \lambda_k)}{2\sigma^2}} \end{cases} ; \qquad (9)$$

where λ_k is the $k-th$ eigenvalues of LBO, e_L and e_H stand for the low energy and high energy levels, and σ is the Gaussian variance. H_e is the regularized SIHWKS.

4.3   Invariance of the Harmonic Wave Kernel Signature

The SIHWKS has good invariances under different deformation, which has the following characteristics:

Scale Invariance: SIHWKS is scale invariance. Therefore, if we calculate the SIHWKS before and after the scale change of the shape separately, the SIHWKS value remains unchanged. $S : X \rightarrow Y$ is an scaling deformation, $SIHWKS(S(x), e_H, e_L) = SIHWKS(x, e_H, e_L)$ for all $x \in M$;

Isometric Invariance: The SIHWKS has isometric invariance; $T : X \rightarrow Y$ is an isometric deformation, $SIHWKS(T(x), e_H, e_L) = SIHWKS(x, e_H, e_L)$ for all $x \in M$;

Topological Robustness: In many real scenarios, the shape also suffers from "topological noise". Due to the high robustness of the wave diffusion distance to topological changes, the SIHWKS is also robust to topological changes.

Sampling Robustness: For the 3D point cloud model M, if the vertices of of M are sampled, including upsampling and downsampling, the resampled SIHWKS value is very close to the original SIHWKS value.

Noise Robustness: When scanning 3D point cloud, the 3D point cloud model will appear noise due to the accuracy of scanning equipment. Because the LBO has robustness and stability, the SIHWKS has noise robustness.

4.4   3D Point Cloud Models Similarity Measure

Without finding the corresponding points of a pair of shapes, a similarity measurement method is immediate given. The 3D point cloud models similarity measurement is defined based on the modified Hausdorff distance(MHD) [21]. Marie-Pierre et al. proposed the MHD, studied 24 types of Hausdorff distances between two point sets, and found an optimal MHD through experiments.

When calculating $d(A, B)$, the mean value of the minimum distance between each point in set A $(a \in A)$ and set B is used to replace the single maximum-minimum distance, and vice versa for $d(B, A)$ is the same. In this way, the influence of abnormal points on the distance calculation is weakened, and the accuracy of the distance calculation is improved. When calculating the $MHD(A, B)$ between two point sets, the same number of points in the two point sets and pre-process of corresponding points are all not essential. The MHD between a pair of 3D point cloud models M and N based on $SIHWKS$ can be defined as:

$$
\begin{aligned}
D(M, N) &= \max(d(M, N), d(N, M)) \\
d(M, N) &= \max_{a \in A}(\min_{b \in B}(\|d(SIHWKS(M) - SIHWKS(N)\|))) \\
d(N, M) &= \max_{b \in B}(\min_{a \in A}(\|d(SIHWKS(N) - SIHWKS(M)\|)))
\end{aligned} \tag{10}
$$

The modified Hausdorff distance based on $SIHWKS$ for a pair of 3D point cloud models M and N calculates the maximum value of the orientation distance $d(M, N)$ and $d(N, M)$, which measures two the maximum degree of mismatch of a point set: if the value of $D(M, N)$ is smaller, M and N are more matched, and vice versa; if $D(M, N)$ is equal to zero, then the 3D point cloud models M and N match exactly.

5   Experiments

We use a subset of SHREC 2010 databases [23] and the SHREC2015 canonical forms database [22], which provide a large number of 3D shapes for non-rigid deformation shape analysis. The query sets of SHREC 2010 include 13 shape classes. For each shape, deformations are split into 12 classes (isometric, topology, scaling, noise, and so on). The SHREC2015 canonical forms database contains a training set and a test set(there are 10 different types of models,each class has 10 models, a total of 100 models).

5.1   Effectiveness of the SIHWKS

After many experiments, we obtain the values of the energy parameters for the SIHWKS. We can see from the Fig. 2, when the value of high energy is too large, the global attributes of the shape will be displayed at this time, ignoring the description of local attributes, and the effective energy parameter values are the low energy is about $s = (1/10) * e_{max} = 10$ and the high energy is about $s = (3/5) * e_{max} = 60$.

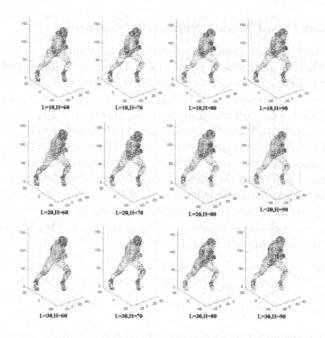

Fig. 2. Choosing the values of the energy parameters for SIHWKS

After obtaining the parameter value of the SIHWKS, we also describe the different point cloud models by using HKS, WKS, SIHKS, SIWKS and our proposed

SIHWKS which shown in Fig. 3, compared with the other four spectral descriptors, the band region of the models can be clearly separated using SIHWKS, which has superior feature localization and can distinguish different regions of the 3D point cloud, which is very suitable for describing the 3D point cloud models.

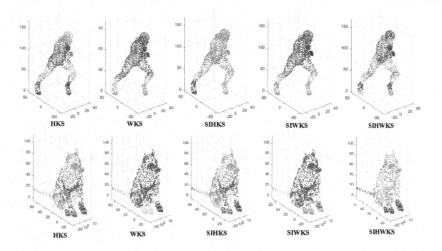

Fig. 3. The models describing by using HKS, WKS, SIHKS, SIWKS and SIHWKS

5.2   Robutness of the SIHWKS and Similarity Results

This section compares the robustness of SIHWKS descriptors through shrec 2010, which is selected to compare the isometric and scaling invariance, topology, sampling and noise robustness of SIHWKS in Fig. 4, it can be seen that the SIHWKS has isometric and scaling invariance, topology, sampling and robustness, and it can describe more details of the point cloud model. Especially, when the models have the isometric deformation, a small part of SIHWKS changed due to using KNN algorithm, but it is not affect its performance by showing in Fig. 5.

To compare the sampling robustness and scale invariance of different SIHWKS and rapid calculation, this section compares the robustness and efficiency of SIHWKS through the SHREC2015 database. Figure 5 shows the thermodynamic diagram of the distance matrix of SIWKS and SIHWKS based on shrec2015. It can be seen from the Fig. 5 that SIHWKS has better performance than SIWKS, showing more blocking levels. And based on the distance, the SIHWKS can be applied to different shape analysis tasks.

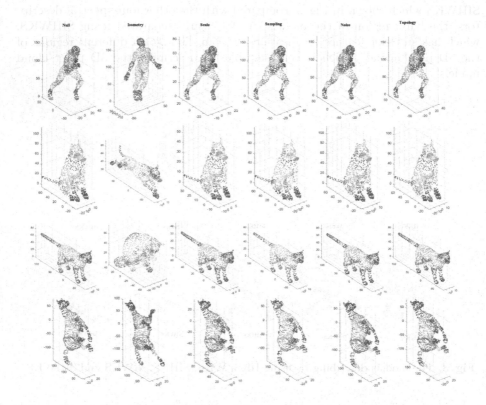

Fig. 4. Visual diagram of the different deformation models describing by SIHWKS

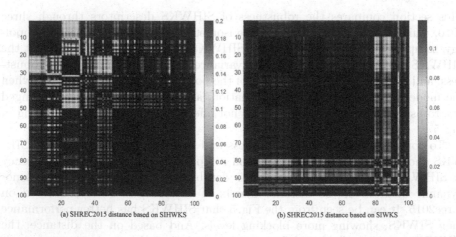

(a) SHREC2015 distance based on SIHWKS

(b) SHREC2015 distance based on SIWKS

Fig. 5. Visual thermodynamic diagram of the model similarity results using SIHWKS and SIWKS based on the SHREC2015 database

6   Conclusion

In this article, we provides a 3D point cloud models similarity measurement pipeline by defining an efficient shape descriptor SIHWKS. Our pipeline is more ubiquitous for measuring the similarity of 3D point cloud models, which is the most important work for shape classification, shape retrieval and so on. The experiment results based on SHREC2010 and SHREC2015 show that our proposed measurement pipeline can effectively and accurately measure the 3D point cloud models similarity.

References

1. Deng, H., Wei, Z., Mortensen, E.N., et al.: Principal curvature-based region detector for object recognition. In: CVPR 2007, pp. 18–23 (2007)
2. Huangfu, Z., Yan, L., Zhang, S.: A new method for estimation of normal vector and curvature based on scattered point cloud. J. Comput. Inf. Syst. **8**(19), 7937–7945 (2012)
3. Ke, Y.L., Li, A.: Rotational surface extraction based on principal direction Gaussian image from point cloud. J. Zhejiang Univ. (Eng. Sci.) **40**(6), 942–946 (2006)
4. Sanchez, J., Denis, F., Coeurjolly, D., et al.: Robust normal vector estimation in 3D point clouds through iterative principal component analysis. ISPRS J. Photogrammetry Remote Sens. **163**, 18–35 (2020)
5. Bao, L., Schnabel, R., Klein, R., et al.: Robust normal estimation for point clouds with sharp features. Comput. Graph. **34**(2), 94–106 (2010)
6. Pei, L., Wu, Z., Xia, C., et al.: Robust normal estimation of point cloud with sharp features via subspace clustering. In: International Conference on Graphic & Image Processing (2014)
7. Srivastava, A., Kurtek, S., Klassen, E.: Statistical Shape Analysis. In: Ikeuchi, K. (eds) Computer Vision. Springer, Boston (2014). https://doi.org/10.1007/978-0-387-31439-6_778
8. Srivastava, A., Joshi, S.H., Mio, W., et al.: Statistical shape analysis: clustering, learning, and testing. IEEE Trans. Pattern Anal. Mach. Intell. **27**(4), 590 (2005)
9. Bezerra, M.A., Bruns, R.E., Ferreira, S.: Statistical design-principal component analysis optimization of a multiple response procedure using cloud point extraction and simultaneous determination of metals by ICP OES. Analytica Chimica Acta **580**(2), 251–257 (2006)
10. Rahmani, H., Mahmood, A., Q Huynh, D., Mian, A.: HOPC: histogram of oriented principal components of 3D pointclouds for action recognition. In: Fleet, D., Pajdla, T., Schiele, B., Tuytelaars, T. (eds.) ECCV 2014. LNCS, vol. 8690, pp. 742–757. Springer, Cham (2014). https://doi.org/10.1007/978-3-319-10605-2_48
11. Iqbal, M.Z., Bobkov, D., Steinbach, E.: Fuzzy logic and histogram of normal orientation-based 3D keypoint detection for point clouds. Pattern Recogn, Lett. **136**, 40–47 (2020)
12. Fan, D., Liu, Y., Ying, H.: Recent progress in the Laplace-Beltrami operator and its applications to digital geometry processing. J. Comput. Aided Des. Comput. Graph. **27**, 559–569 (2015)
13. Sun, J., Ovsjanikov, M., Guibas, L.: A concise and provably informative multiscale signature based on heat diffusion. Comput. Graph. Forum **28**(5), 1383–1392 (2010)

14. Bronstein, M.M., Kokkinos, I.: Scale-invariant heat kernel signatures for non-rigid shape recognition. In: 2010 IEEE Conference on Computer Vision and Pattern Recognition (CVPR), pp. 1704–1711. IEEE (2010)
15. Aubry, M., Schlickewei, U., Cremers, D.: The wave kernel signature: a quantum mechanical approach to shape analysis. In: IEEE International Conference on Computer 588 Vision Workshops, pp. 1626–1633 (2011)
16. Li, H., Li, S., Wu, X., et al.: Scale-invariant wave kernel signature for non-rigid 3D shape retrieval. In: 2018 IEEE International Conference on Big Data and Smart Computing. IEEE (2018)
17. Zhang, D., Wu, Z., Wang, X., et al.: 3D skull and face similarity measurements based on a harmonic wave kernel signature. Visual Comput. (7) (2020)
18. Rustamov, R.M.: Laplace-Beltrami eigenfunctions for deformation invariant shape representation. In: Proceedings of the 5th Eurographics Symposium on Geometry Processing, pp. 225–233 (2007)
19. Patané, G.: STAR Laplacian spectral kernels and distances for geometry processing and shape analysis. In: Proceedings of the Computer Graphics Forum, pp. 599–624 (2016)
20. Zhang, S., Zong, M., Sun, K., Liu, Y., Cheng, D.: Efficient kNN algorithm based on graph sparse reconstruction. In: Luo, X., Yu, J.X., Li, Z. (eds.) ADMA 2014. LNCS (LNAI), vol. 8933, pp. 356–369. Springer, Cham (2014). https://doi.org/10.1007/978-3-319-14717-8_28
21. Dubuisson, M.P., Jain, A.K.: A modified Hausdorff distance for object matching. In: 600 International Conference on Pattern Recognition (2002)
22. Pickup, D., Sun, X., Rosin, P.L., et al.: SHREC 2015 track: canonical forms for non-rigid 3D shape retrieval. In: Eurographics Workshop on 3D Object Retrieval (2015)
23. Bronstein, A.M., Bronstein, M.M., Castellani, U., et al.: SHREC 2010: robust large-scale shape retrieval benchmark. In: Proceedings of the EUROGRAPHICS Workshop on 3D Object Retrieval (3DOR) (2010)

PST-NET: Point Cloud Sampling via Point-Based Transformer

Xu Wang⬚, Yi Jin(✉)⬚, Yigang Cen⬚, Congyan Lang, and Yidong Li⬚

School of Computer and Information Technology, Beijing Jiaotong University, Beijing, China
{xu.wang,yjin,ygcen,cylang,ydli}@bjtu.edu.cn

Abstract. Sampling is widely used for point cloud processing tasks, especially in autonomous driving domain with multiple 3D sensors to gather extensive point sets. However, geometric relations among points are rarely considered in sampling. Inspired by the recent advances in vision domain, the point-based transformer is introduced to process the point cloud with the inherent permutation invariance characteristic. We develop Point Sampling Transformer Network (PST-NET), including data augmentation, self-attention and local feature extraction, to generate optimal resampling distribution that is excellent for a particular point cloud application. PST-NET with characteristics of permutation-invariant, task-specific and noise-insensitive, is thus exactly suitable for point cloud sampling. Experiments verified that PST-NET successfully downsamples point cloud and captures more detailed information, with remarkable improvement for shape classification. Also various combinations of relation functions for self-attention are analyzed based on controlled experiments. The result shows that concatenation is more suitable for self-attention in sampling.

Keywords: Point cloud · Sampling · Transformer

1 Introduction

With the rapid development of 3D devices, 3D sensors play an important role in perception of visual scene for many intelligent transportation tasks, such as autonomous driving and environment understanding. Actually, 3D sensors, e.g., LiDAR, need to capture highly-accurate and information-rich data in intelligent transportation tasks. Especially in the domain of self-driving [9], multiple 3D sensors with 360° shooting mode will be equipped to ensure that enough redundant information is captured for a deep neural network (DNN) to make it more accurate and robust. However, limited by energy consumption and computation capability of mobile devices and terminals, point cloud is expected to shrunk the size of point set to enhance computational timeliness and energy efficiency. In many large-scale point cloud processing tasks, sampling uniformly has been widely used as a preprocess step. Traditional sampling approaches have

© Springer Nature Switzerland AG 2021
Y. Peng et al. (Eds.): ICIG 2021, LNCS 12890, pp. 57–69, 2021.
https://doi.org/10.1007/978-3-030-87361-5_5

been successfully applied in point cloud tasks, such as Farthest Point Sampling (FPS) [16] and randomly sampling [2], but they are based on non-learned predetermined rule which agnostic to downstream applications [5]. Meanwhile, data acquisition in complicated scene would generate noise inevitably. As we know, sampled points from non-learned approaches are a subset of original point cloud, and hence are noise sensitive.

In recent years, artificial intelligence techniques have been widely and successfully used in point cloud learning. With the introduction of various DNN architectures, such as multi-layer perceptron [5,19] and convolutional neural network [13], DNN can realize learned point cloud sampling. However, unlike 2D structured image data, point clouds are unordered and irregular. The above sampling networks attempt to reorder or voxelize the point cloud to obtain a structured domain. Transforming the point clouds will lead to the loss of shape information as geometric relations between points are removed. Additionally, traffic participants in self-driving are very important that must be reliably recognized and localized in order to take subsequent action. However, distant or small size objects only represent by sparse points, it is hard to extract sufficient information. Consequently, we need to design a new sampling network to overcome above problems: (1) variant to permutation of the input point clouds; (2) task agnostic for sampling strategy; (3) sensitive to noise; (4) coarse-grained feature extraction from sparse point cloud.

Inspired by the recent advances in point transformer architectures [6,8,15,30], point-based transformer is suitable for sampling because the main component of self-attention (SA) has inherently permutation invariant for point cloud learning and able to extract refined global features for its input features based on context. Therefore, draw upon the ideas of point-based transformer, we introduce Point Sampling Transformer Network (PST-NET), a point cloud sampling architecture to learn a simplified point cloud that is optimized for a downstream task. In traditional transformers, positional encoding is a crucial infrastructure that gives extra information about the position of the input points. Due to unorder structure of input points, we use for reference the Guo *et al.* [8]'s work of coordinate-based input embedding to replace positional encoding. To attack the local feature extracting problem, we design a local feature extraction mechanism to achieve both robustness and detail capture. First, we introduce a sampling and grouping (SG) layer to partition the set of input points into overlapping local regions by the distance metric of the underlying space [19]. Second, we combine the point clouds into a two-dimensional form, one dimension represents the number of subsets and the other represents the number of neighborhood points. Then, we leverage a convolutional network to progressively capture local features at increasingly larger scales along a multi-resolution hierarchy. In summary, the main contributions of this paper are as follows:

1. To our knowledge, this paper is a pioneering effort that directly introduces point-based transformer in point sampling. PST-NET is invariant to permutation, task-specific and noise insensitive and is thus exactly suitable to point cloud sampling.

2. Based on the work of exploring self-attention with multiple relation functions for 2D structured data [29], we assess variety relation functions effectiveness as the basic operation to 3D point cloud sampling for self-attention models.
3. Extensive experiments demonstrate the improved performance for point cloud sampling. The controlled experiments also indicate that the relation function of concatenation is more suitable to self-attention in sampling.

2 Related Work

2.1 Point Cloud Sampling

For compressing irregular point clouds, an intuitive way is based on non-learned predetermined rule[1, 26]. Moenning et al. [16] develop a Fast Marching farthest point sampling for point cloud simplification, called FastFPS algorithm, in a uniform and feature-sensitive manner. Chen et al. [2] present a randomized sampling strategy to find optimal resampling distribution of original point cloud. This approach is based on graph signal processing with random-walk graph Laplacian matrix to digest local dependencies among point sets. The non-learned methods we described above aim to find a sparse point distribution that preserve information in the original point cloud as possible. However, They are noise sensitively and task agnostic, or without the consideration of the spatial distribution of original points.

In recent years, learned point cloud sampling techniques which subject to a subsequent mission objective have been proposed. Yang et al. [28] present an learnable, but task-agnostic sampling approach that uses a self-attention mechanism on learning relations between points. This approach only samples at high-dimension embedding space which neglects the spatial distribution. Dovrat et al. [5] combine the architecture of PointNet with nearest neighbour matching to generate a simplified network, called S-NET, to produce a smaller point set that is optimized for a particular task. Similar, Lang et al. [10] propose a differentiable relaxation of nearest neighbor selection strategy for point cloud sampling, called SampleNet. Unlike SampleNet, differentiable operation to the matching step is not introduced in our work. As we know, S-NET is the first data-driven-based sampling approach, subject to subsequent task objective. Therefore, we draw upon the ideas of S-NET and transformer architecture to design a learned PST-NET for point cloud sampling.

2.2 Point-Based Deep Learning

Driven by the breakthroughs brought by DNN and the accessibility of point clouds, point-based deep learning approaches have been proposed. Voxel-based representation of point clouds makes the 3D convolution can be directly utilized in voxel grids [21, 27]. Maturana et al. [14] using 3D convolution filters and fully connected layers to conduct 3D object recognition based on volumetric points representation. Qi et al. [18] pioneered combines the merits of both Multilayer Perceptron (MLP) and max-pooling to consuming point clouds directly for 3D tasks. Thereafter, Qi *et al.* [19] design a sampling and grouping module to enhance the capability of fine-grained local information extraction for PointNet. Despite the availability of point cloud processing, the above approaches may disrupt the spatial distribution between points.

Recently, inspired by the success of transformer architectures in natural language processing [3], transformers have been proven to be suitable for vision tasks, and the performance is better than traditional MLP and CNN networks [4,25]. Engel *et al.* [6] design a network, named Point Transformer (PT), that processes directly on point clouds without spatial deformation. To capture fine-grained shape and context information of the point cloud, they introduce a local-global attention mechanism. In other work, Guo *et al.* [8] develop a point cloud learning network called Point Cloud Transformer (PCT) to extract semantic information directly from a point cloud. Therefore, we draw upon the above ideas of PT and PCT, to design a point cloud sampling architecture, PST-NET, to produce a optimal dowmsampling distribution for point cloud.

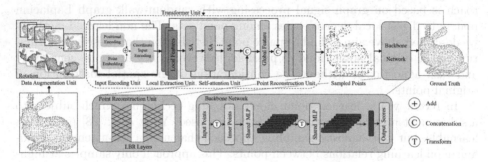

Fig. 1. Overview of the Point Sampling Transformer Network (PST-NET)

3   Network

Our goal is downsampling the input point cloud while producing an optimal resampling distribution to original geometric information. To achieve this goal, we propose PST-NET, a permutation invariant, task specific and noise insensitive network, to learn a simplified point cloud. The fundamental architecture of the sampling network is similar to the S-NET [5], namely, we utilize PST-NET to learn a set of points, then the learned points are matched with the input to obtain a point cloud subset. Moreover, we further combine data augmentation and local feature extraction modules into an sampling system based on point-based transformer. The overall architecture of PST-NET is present in Fig. 1. We describe our network in a top-down approach at following sections.

3.1   Data Augmentation

DNN for point cloud processing aims to model objective function F that approximate the true distribution D for given data $P = \{p_i \in R^{3+f}, i = 1, 2, \cdots, n\}$, where n is the number of points and f is feature dimension except for the xyz-dimension, such as color, reflectance, normal etc. The formula is as follows:

$$\min |F(P) - D(P)| < \varepsilon \tag{1}$$

Thus, the trained task network tends to be overfitted regardless of the data domain. One way to alleviate overfitting is data augmentation, which enriches the diversity of the training samples [11,20]. For this reason, we introduce general conventional methods of data augmentation for point cloud input, such as rotation and jittering, to improve diversity of the training samples while preserving the shape of original data.

3.2 Transformer

Coordinate-Based Positional Encoding. In a transformer, positional encoding gives additional information about the position of the input tokens in order [22]. In general, standard positional encoding mechanism falls into two categories: the fixed and trainable [7]. Noteworthily, point clouds do not have a fixed order, they are disordered and unstructured. Several point-based transformer works have been proven that the 3D points coordinate themselves are a natural candidate for position encoding. We follow the method of coordinate-based input embedding [8], which uses point's coordinate instead general positional encoding.

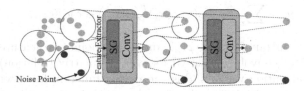

Fig. 2. Local point set feature extraction

Local Feature Extraction Unit. The ability to extract local features or structure for convolutional networks have effectively proved that it can recognize detail patterns and generalizability to complex scenes. Traditional convolutional operation requires highly regular input data format. Since point cloud is irregular and unordered, convolutional architectures certainly will obscure natural invariances of the data. Followed works of [6,8,19], we design a local feature extraction mechanism to achieve both robustness and detail capture. As shown in Fig. 2, our local feature extraction module include sampling and grouping (SG) layer, and convolutional layer. The SG layer aims to build a hierarchical sets of input point cloud. Then, progressively abstract larger and larger local regions along the hierarchy by accumulate multiple convolutional layers. In this paper, we only use single-layer convolution structure to reduce the network complexity.

More specifically, given input point cloud P with N points, the output of SG layer is M subsets $P_K^M = \{p_k^m \in P, p_k \in R^{3+f}, m = 1, 2, ..., M, k = 1, 2, ..., K\}$, where each set P^m corresponds to a local region with K neighborhood points of centroid points P_c^M. During the sampling operation, we adopt FPS algorithm to select M centroid points $P_c^M = \{p_c^m \in R^{3+f}, m = 1, 2, ..., M\}$. In 3D point cloud grouping, the neighborhoods of each centroid point are defined by metric distance [19]. Normally, adjacent points may represent the same object. Therefore, we use k-nearest neighbors (KNN) to aggregate points from local neighbor, each point in a subset satisfied with Euclidean Metric ρ:

$$\sqrt{(x_k^m - x_c^m)^2 + (y_k^m - y_c^m)^2 + (z_k^m - z_c^m)^2} < \rho \tag{2}$$

Then, we use convolutional layer to encode local region patterns into output feature f', where we expand P into a 2D form $[M,K]$. Finally, the local feature extraction layer output subsampled points with new feature f'. Ultimately, the local feature extraction unit in PST-NET is an effective mechanism for fine-grained feature extraction from input point clouds.

Self-attention Unit. Self-attention modules have demonstrated impressive results in point cloud processing tasks [6,24,30]. In PST-NET, we introduce a self-attention (SA) mechanism to extract refined global features for its input features based on context. An example of self-attention is illustrated in Fig. 3, has the following form:

$$y_i = \sum_{x_i \in X} \theta[\rho(\gamma(\varphi(x_i)^T, \beta(x_j)) + \delta)\alpha(x_j), x] \tag{3}$$

where y_i is new output feature. φ, β and α are pointwise feature transformations, such as 1×1 convolution or MLPs. γ is the matrix (relation) function for producing the attention weights, θ is the matrix function for attention weights and input x. δ is a position encoding function and ρ is a normalization function, such as softmax.

Zhao et al. [29]'s work indicate that different matrix function may impact output results of 2D image tasks, such as recognition. Inspired by Guo et al. [8]'s work, they introduce offset-attention layer to calculate the difference between the self-attention features and input features, we move to explore multiple forms for the matrix function θ in 3D point cloud sampling task:

Summation: $\theta(SA(x_i), x) = SA(x_i) + x$
Subtraction: $\theta(SA(x_i), x) = SA(x_i) - x$
Concatenation: $\theta(SA(x_i), x) = [SA(x_i), x]$
Hadamard product: $\theta(SA(x_i), x) = SA(x_i) \odot x$
Dot product: $\theta(SA(x_i), x) = SA(x_i) \cdot x$

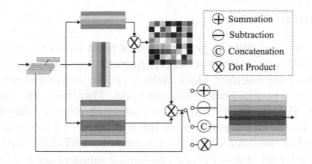

Fig. 3. Our self-attention block

3.3 Loss

For input point cloud $P = \{p_i \in R^{3+f}, i = 1, 2, \cdots, n\}$, the goal of sampling is to learn a subset P_s through deep neural network, with $s < n$, such that the task sampling loss L can maintain or even lower than the original point clouds which may affected by noise points. Denoting the objective function L as:

$$
\begin{cases}
P_s = [p_1, p_2, \cdots, p_s] \\
s.t. \quad s - n < 0 \\
\min_{P_s} \frac{1}{s} \sum_{i=1}^{s} L(p_i, (3+f)_i, t_i)
\end{cases}
\tag{4}
$$

where t_i is the ground truth. However, this optimization problem exposes a challenge due to the non-differentiability of the sampling operation [17]. Dovrat *et al.* [5] proposed a sampling loss function, which makes sampled points is optimal for the task and its points are close to the original P. The sampling regularization loss is:

$$
\begin{aligned}
L_{\text{sampling}}(P, P_s)_i &= L_f(P, P_s)_i + \alpha L_m(P, P_s)_i + (\gamma + \delta|G|)L_b(P_s, P)_i \\
&= \min \|P - P_S\|_2^2 + \alpha(\max \min \|P - P_S\|_2^2) + (\gamma + \delta|G|)(\min \|P_S, P\|_2^2)
\end{aligned}
\tag{5}
$$

where L_f and L_m are average and maximal nearest neighbor loss respectively, and L_b is the matching loss. Finally, the total training loss needs to be combined with the task loss of backbone network:

$$
L_{total}(P, P_S) = L_{task}(P_s) + \beta L_{sampling}(P - P_S)
\tag{6}
$$

Table 1. Controlled comparison of different relation functions on self-attention

Method		Points	Accuracy	Params
PST-NET	Summation	32	63.23	5.53M
	Subtraction	32	60.31	5.53M
	Concatenation	32	**64.65**	5.66M
	Had. product	32	56.74	5.53M
	Dot product	32	56.45	5.53M

4   Experiments

In this section, we evaluate the performance of point cloud sampling with PST-NET on public dataset ModelNet40 [27]. Actually, our sampling network is an adaptive point cloud learning block, which can be combined with any point cloud processing networks under different tasks. Therefore, we chose a popular network named PointNet [18], which is a pioneering effort to directly processes point sets, as the backbone network. In inference time, we use nearest neighbor matching to match the sampled points generated by PST-NET with the original input point cloud, and utilize FPS to fine-tuning sampled points. For controlled experiments on self-attention networks, we test 5 relation function, summation, subtraction, concatenation, hadamard product and dot product, with same network architecture and hyperparameters to ensure a fair comparison.

4.1   ModelNet40

ModelNet40 is widely used dataset in robotics, cognitive science, and computer vision tasks. It provides 3D CAD models for objects, and contains 40 most common object categories in the real world, such as airplane, bed, bench and door. We apply the official split strategy with 9840 samples for training, and 2468 sampling for testing. To facilitate the point cloud sampling, each sample only retains 1024 uniformly distribute points as original point set. The pretrained backbone network, PointNet, also trained by the same preprocessed point sets.

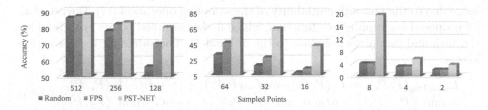

Fig. 4. PST-NET for classification.

4.2   Implementation Details

We trained all models in TensorFlow on a single TITAN Xp GPU. We use exponential learning rate schedule with base learning rate 0.005. To alleviate overfitting, we apply general data augmentation methods on ModelNet40, including point clouds rotation and jittering. We select Adam optimizer with batch size 32 for 600 epochs. We trained 10 models under different sampled point [1024, 512, 256, ...,4, 2]. For the backbone network of PointNet, we refer to the original network architecture and hyperparameters without any modification. In comparative experiments on self-attention, we select the model with 32 sampled points to assess the effectiveness of different relation functions. This choice ensures that architectural and hyperparameter are made on the same set.

Table 2. Comparison of PointNet (backbone) and sampled point clouds

Sampled points	1024	512	256	128	64	32	16	8
S-Net [5]	89.2	87.8	82.3	77.5	70.3	60.7	36.1	14.5
ProgressiveNet [5]	89.2	85.0	82.0	77.9	74.1	60.7	39.6	15.2
PST-NET (ours)	89.2	**87.9**	**83.2**	**80.1**	**76.1**	**64.6**	**42.3**	**19.3**

4.3 Controlled Experiments of Relation Function

Table 1 shows the comparative results of different relation functions on the point cloud sampling. Different from the result in 2D structured data [29], concatenation function achieves the top accuracy which is slightly higher than summation, about 1.42%. Meanwhile, we find that the accuracy of subtraction, same as the offset-attention in PCT [8], is 4.34% lower than that of concatenation. A simplified point cloud must preserve similarity to the original shape, but subtraction operation may lead to increased context information loss. Instead, concatenation function aggregates with input features and attention features, which makes the output have sufficient context for next learning, making the network more robust. The concatenation function outperforms Hadamard product and dot product, 7.91% and 8.2% respectively. Therefore, the latter experiments adopt the concatenation-based self-attention structure.

Table 3. Comparison of different backbones and sampled point clouds

Sampled points	1024	512	256	128
DGCNN [23]	92.9	86.9	53.9	–
EC-GDP [23]	**93.2**	**87.9**	57.5	–
PointCNN [12]	87.8	75.5(614)	50.2(410)	19.7(204)
PST-NET (ours)	89.2	**87.9**	**83.2**	**80.1**

Table 4. Ablation study: the impact of self-attention operator in different forms

Method		Points	Accuracy	Params
Vector attention	Summation	32	62.4	5.82M
	Subtraction	32	64.4	5.82M
	Concatenation	32	62.6	5.85M
	Had. product	32	61.6	5.92M
	Dot product	32	61.2	5.82M
Scalar attention (ours)	Concatenation	32	**64.6**	**5.66M**

Table 5. Ablation study: the impact of local feature extraction unit

Method	Points	Accuracy
PST-NET(1SA)	32	61.7
PST-NET(2SA)	32	**64.6**
PST-NET(3SA)	32	52.0
PST-NET(4SA)	32	48.5

Table 6. Ablation study: the impact of local feature extraction unit

Method	Points	Accuracy
PST-NET (only SA)	32	59.5
PST-NET (only Local)	32	64.4
PST-NET (SA + Local)	32	**64.6**

4.4 Classification

Experimental results of classification accuracy on ModelNet40 dataset are shown in Fig. 4. Based on PointNet network, it is trained on original point cloud with 1024 points per object and tested on sampled point sets of different size. We compared traditional sampling strategies of random and FPS [5] with our PST-NET approach. PST-NET achieves the best classification accuracy around all sample rates. For learned sampling strategies, Table 2 compares the same backbone, PointNet, under sampled point clouds. Compared to S-NET, the best margin of up is around 6.2% under 16 sampled points. Therefore, employing Point-based transformer sampling allows us to better maintain PointNet's accuracy under small size point sets. The comparison of sampled point clouds for different algorithms are reported in Table 3, where the number in brackets represents the real number of downsampling point clouds. Also, Fig. 5 shows the sampled point cloud of 64 points, provided by S-NET and PST-NET. We see that both approaches achieve good results and our approach achieves superior results since it contains more detailed information. Our results indicate the potential of using a transformer in point cloud sampling.

To probe the validity of the components in PST-NET, we conduct an ablation study on ModelNet40 dataset. First, we investigate the form of attention module used in point transformer layer. The results are shown in Table 4. Compared with [30], scalar attention with concatenate function is expressive than the vector attention with subtraction function. Although the highest accuracy is similar, vector attention with extra two linear layers leads to the increase of memory costs. Second, we explore the impact of classification accuracy with different attention layers. The number X in XSA refers to the number of scalar attention layers. As depicted in Table 5, the best accuracy of 64.6% is obtained by a two-layer attention. The reason might be that increasing the number of attention layers may brings some difficulty for PST-NET training. Therefore, we set the size of scalar attention layer to 2 as our default for all models. Finally, we look into the effectiveness of the local feature extraction unit in PST-NET. The results are summarized in Table 6. With the combination of scalar self-attention and local feature extraction unit, accuracy is significantly improved.

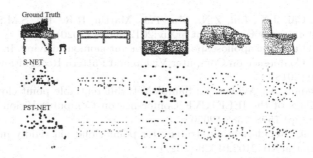

Fig. 5. Sampled point cloud from S-NET, PST-NET and Ground Truth

5   Conclusion

This paper presents a Point Sampling Transformer Network (PST-NET), a permutation-invariant, task-specific and noise-insensitive neural network that samples on unordered and irregular point clouds. We introduce point-based transformer with a global-local feature extraction and augmentation strategy to generate a more robust subset data distribution. Besides, we probe into the influence of relation functions on self-attention module. Finally, experiments indicate that PST-NET is more powerfully and robustly outperforms non-learned sampling approaches, and achieves the state-of-the-art performance.

Acknowledgement. This work was supported by the National Natural Science Foundation of China under grant No. 61972030.

References

1. Aichholzer, O., et al.: Recovering structure from r-sampled objects. In: Computer Graphics Forum, pp. 1349–1360 (2009)
2. Chen, S., Tian, D., Feng, C., Vetro, A., Kovačević, J.: Fast resampling of three-dimensional point clouds via graphs. IEEE Trans. Signal Process. **66**(3), 666–681 (2017)
3. Dai, Z., Yang, Z., Yang, Y., Carbonell, J.G., Le, Q., Salakhutdinov, R.: Transformer-XL: attentive language models beyond a fixed-length context. In: Proceedings of the 57th Annual Meeting of the Association for Computational Linguistics, pp. 2978–2988 (2019)
4. Dosovitskiy, A., et al.: An image is worth 16 × 16 words: transformers for image recognition at scale. arXiv preprint arXiv:2010.11929 (2020)
5. Dovrat, O., Lang, I., Avidan, S.: Learning to sample. In: Proceedings of the IEEE/CVF Conference on Computer Vision and Pattern Recognition, pp. 2760–2769 (2019)
6. Engel, N., Belagiannis, V., Dietmayer, K.: Point transformer. arXiv preprint arXiv:2011.00931 (2020)
7. Gehring, J., Auli, M., Grangier, D., Yarats, D., Dauphin, Y.N.: Convolutional sequence to sequence learning. In: International Conference on Machine Learning, pp. 1243–1252 (2017)

8. Guo, M.H., Cai, J.X., Liu, Z.N., Mu, T.J., Martin, R.R., Hu, S.M.: PCT: point cloud transformer. arXiv preprint arXiv:2012.09688 (2020)
9. Huang, X., et al.: The apolloscape dataset for autonomous driving. In: Proceedings of the IEEE Conference on Computer Vision and Pattern Recognition Workshops, pp. 954–960 (2018)
10. Lang, I., Manor, A., Avidan, S.: SampleNet: differentiable point cloud sampling. In: Proceedings of the IEEE/CVF Conference on Computer Vision and Pattern Recognition, pp. 7578–7588 (2020)
11. Lee, D., et al.: Regularization strategy for point cloud via rigidly mixed sample. arXiv preprint arXiv:2102.01929 (2021)
12. Li, X., Yu, L., Fu, C.W., Cohen-Or, D., Heng, P.A.: Unsupervised detection of distinctive regions on 3D shapes. ACM Trans. Graph. **39**(5), 1–14 (2020)
13. Liu, Y., Fan, B., Xiang, S., Pan, C.: Relation-shape convolutional neural network for point cloud analysis. In: Proceedings of the IEEE/CVF Conference on Computer Vision and Pattern Recognition, pp. 8895–8904 (2019)
14. Maturana, D., Scherer, S.: VoxNet: A 3D convolutional neural network for real-time object recognition. In: 2015 IEEE/RSJ International Conference on Intelligent Robots and Systems, pp. 922–928 (2015)
15. Mikuni, V., Canelli, F.: Point cloud transformers applied to collider physics. arXiv preprint arXiv:2102.05073 (2021)
16. Moenning, C., Dodgson, N.A.: A new point cloud simplification algorithm. In: Proceedings of Interenational Conference on Visualization, Imaging and Image Processing, pp. 1027–1033 (2003)
17. Nezhadarya, E., Taghavi, E., Razani, R., Liu, B., Luo, J.: Adaptive hierarchical down-sampling for point cloud classification. In: Proceedings of the IEEE/CVF Conference on Computer Vision and Pattern Recognition, pp. 12956–12964 (2020)
18. Qi, C.R., Su, H., Mo, K., Guibas, L.J.: PointNet: deep learning on point sets for 3D classification and segmentation. In: Proceedings of the IEEE Conference on Computer Vision and Pattern Recognition, pp. 652–660 (2017)
19. Qi, C.R., Yi, L., Su, H., Guibas, L.J.: PointNet++: deep hierarchical feature learning on point sets in a metric space. In: Neural Information Processing Systems, pp. 5099–5108 (2017)
20. Shorten, C., Khoshgoftaar, T.M.: A survey on image data augmentation for deep learning. J. Big Data **6**, 1–48 (2019). https://doi.org/10.1186/s40537-019-0197-0
21. Tatarchenko, M., Dosovitskiy, A., Brox, T.: Octree generating networks: efficient convolutional architectures for high-resolution 3D outputs. In: Proceedings of the IEEE International Conference on Computer Vision, pp. 2088–2096 (2017)
22. Vaswani, A., et al.: Attention is all you need. In: Neural Information Processing Systems (2017)
23. Wang, J., Zhao, Y., Liu, T., Wei, S.: GDS: global description guided down-sampling for 3D point cloud classification. In: Proceedings of the 2020 4th International Conference on Vision, Image and Signal Processing, pp. 1–6 (2020)
24. Wang, X., Jin, Y., Cen, Y., Wang, T., Li, Y.: Attention models for point clouds in deep learning: a survey. arXiv preprint arXiv:2102.10788 (2021)
25. Wu, B., et al.: Visual transformers: token-based image representation and processing for computer vision. arXiv preprint arXiv:2006.03677 (2020)
26. Wu, J., Kobbelt, L.: Optimized sub-sampling of point sets for surface splatting. In: Computer Graphics Forum, pp. 643–652 (2004)
27. Wu, Z., et al.: 3D ShapeNets: a deep representation for volumetric shapes. In: Proceedings of the IEEE Conference on Computer Vision and Pattern Recognition, pp. 1912–1920 (2015)

28. Yang, J., et al.: Modeling point clouds with self-attention and Gumbel subset sampling. In: Proceedings of the IEEE/CVF Conference on Computer Vision and Pattern Recognition, pp. 3323–3332 (2019)
29. Zhao, H., Jia, J., Koltun, V.: Exploring self-attention for image recognition. In: Proceedings of the IEEE/CVF Conference on Computer Vision and Pattern Recognition, pp. 10076–10085 (2020)
30. Zhao, H., Jiang, L., Jia, J., Torr, P., Koltun, V.: Point transformer. arXiv preprint arXiv:2012.09164 (2020)

Bird Keypoint Detection via Exploiting 2D Texture and 3D Geometric Features

Tingting Zhang[1], Qijun Zhao[1], and Pubu Danzeng[2(✉)]

[1] College of Computer Science, Sichuan University, Chengdu, China
[2] School of Information Science and Technology, Tibet University, Lhasa, China
pbdz@utibet.edu.cn

Abstract. Keypoint detection can help fine-grained bird recognition by aligning the bird with the detected keypoints. Most of the existing bird keypoint detection methods have poor performance on symmetric keypoints, because they mainly use texture features only, which usually can not distinguish between symmetric keypoints, such as the keypoints on left and right legs. Besides, these methods cannot deal well with the complex image background. Therefore, we propose a two-branch keypoint detection network that combines both 2D texture and 3D geometric features to tackle these problems. In the 2D branch, we use anchor loss to distinguish between foreground and background to alleviate the influence of complex background on keypoint detection. In the 3D branch, we introduce a 3D deformable mesh model to provide geometric information of symmetric keypoints. The prediction results of the two branches are fused to obtain the final keypoint detection results. We demonstrate the effectiveness of our proposed method on the widely-used CUB200-2011 [23] dataset. The experimental results show that our method can achieve superior accuracy in comparison with the state-of-the-art approaches.

Keywords: Bird keypoint detection · Symmetric keypoint · 3D geometric information

1 Introduction

Semantic keypoints play an important role in object detection [10,21] and classification [26,29]. For example, in fine-grained image classification (e.g., for birds [4,18,26] or dogs [12,15]), keypoints are used to align objects and capture discriminative information to distinguish subcategories. Generally, the accuracy of keypoint detection has a significant impact on the effectiveness of extracted features representing the objects. In this paper, we focus on bird keypoint detection across different bird species.

Bird keypoint detection is challenging because the appearance of birds could vary largely across different species and poses. For example, hummingbirds have thin and long beaks, while parrots have hard and hooked beaks; flying birds and perching birds look quite different especially in their wings. To

© Springer Nature Switzerland AG 2021
Y. Peng et al. (Eds.): ICIG 2021, LNCS 12890, pp. 70–82, 2021.
https://doi.org/10.1007/978-3-030-87361-5_6

Input   Our Results   PAIRS [4] Results   Groundtruth

Fig. 1. Our proposed method can detect the keypoints of birds with more reasonable results. It has a significantly better performance on the symmetric keypoints and complex background. For easy comparison, we circle the areas with considerable prediction differences between our method and state-of-the-art with red circles. And we use circles with white boundary to emphasize the keypoints with considerable prediction differences. (Color figure online)

conquer these challenges, early works [1,2,11,13,27] usually use handcrafted features to model the appearance, combining with a pictorial structure model to capture the geometric position relationship between bird parts. Recently, convolutional neural networks (CNNs) have obtained impressive results in keypoint detection thanks to their powerful capabilities of feature learning and implicit spatial modeling [4,7,8,14,18,28]. However, they still suffer from the following two challenges (see Fig. 1): ambiguous keypoints like those symmetric keypoints on left and right legs or wings of birds that have similar appearance, and protective coloration [6] that makes it hard to distinguish birds from the background. Particularly, existing CNN-based methods often confuse the ambiguous keypoints due to ignorance of the geometric structure among keypoints. Although some approaches use pictorial structure models to constrain the relative positions of keypoints, they still suffer the ambiguity about symmetric parts caused by ignoring the 3D properties of birds.

To tackle these problems, we propose a two-branch bird keypoint detection network that combines texture information from a 2D branch and geometric information from a 3D branch. The 2D branch mainly extracts the texture information to detect keypoints by stacked hourglass network [16]. Simultaneously, in this branch, we use anchor loss [17] to deal with complex background through hard negative example mining. In the 3D branch, we introduce a 3D deformable mesh model to provide the geometric information of keypoints explicitly, avoiding the ambiguous position of symmetric parts in 2D images. The 3D branch produces the 3D keypoints by predicting the vertex deformation of the mesh and then projecting 3D keypoints to the image plane to get the 2D keypoints. Finally, the prediction results of the two branches are fused through a fusion module.

Our contributions can be summarized as follows:

- We propose a two-branch network combining the 2D texture and 3D geometric information to detect bird keypoints.
- We use anchor loss to deal with complex background through hard negative example mining.
- Experimental results demonstrate that the proposed method outperforms the other state-of-the-art approaches, validating the effectiveness of the method.

2   Related Work

Existing bird keypoint detection methods can be roughly divided into two categories: traditional methods and deep learning methods. In this section, we briefly review these existing methods, and highlight the motivation of our method.

2.1   Traditional Methods

Most early works use template matching with handcrafted features. They can be divided into two types: one is to build powerful part detectors, and the other is to design expressive pictorial structure models.

The former focuses on utilizing more expressive image features. For example, Farrell et al. [2] propose the birdlets, using color SIFT descriptor [22] to locate object parts in different poses and viewpoints. However, this method requires expensive filter combinations and extensive supervision. The latter models the appearance and shape of birds. Liu et al. [11,13] propose an exemplar-based model to locate parts by imposing geometric constraints between parts. In addition to the geometric constraints between parts, some works focus on a wider range of constraints. For example, some researchers extend the deformable part model (DPM) [3] to learn the holistic and local positional relationship via combining strong supervision [1,27] or segmentation masks [2].

2.2   Deep Learning Methods

Recently, CNN-based methods have been increasingly used for bird keypoint detection. According to the supervision of the network, these methods can be divided into two categories: coordinate-based methods, and heatmap-based methods.

The coordinate-based methods regress the keypoint coordinates directly. Shih et al. regress coordinates based on AlexNet [9], significantly improving the keypoint detection accuracy [18]. However, this method requires a good initialization and does not consider the geometric information. Therefore, Xiang et al. suggest learning a group of shape basis, and roughly estimating the position of keypoints through the shape basis combination [25]. Then they use thin-plate spline transformation to predict local deformation to get the final position. Liu et al. [14] propose a method that does not require keypoint annotations. Instead, they use the strong correlation between attributes and parts to learn the location of keypoints. These methods are heavily dependent on the distribution of training data and lacking generalization ability. The heatmap-based methods represent keypoints with heatmaps and use CNN to predict heatmaps. Zhang et al. use VGGNet [19] to regress the Gaussian heatmaps and calculate the location of maximum likelihood as the keypoint position [28]. However, they generate low-resolution heatmaps, which would lead to significant errors when performing the coordinate transformation. Huang et al. predict higher-resolution heatmaps [8]. At the same time, they adopt a coarse-to-fine detection strategy [8], using multi-level supervision to achieve precise detection of keypoints. Guo et al. utilize the classic stacked hourglass network [16] to predict the gaussian heatmaps and achieve the best keypoint detection result by fusing multi-scale information through repeated bottom-up and top-down inference [4].

2.3 Motivation of Our Method

The above approaches mainly focus on the texture information of images. They cannot handle symmetric parts with similar appearances. Although some approaches use pictorial structure models to constrain the relative positions of keypoints, they still have some drawbacks. [1,2,11,13,27] use multiple pictorial structure models to describe the geometric position relationship of bird keypoints across different poses. Unfortunately, the effectiveness of these approaches across different bird poses depends on whether the pose is in the template library. [25] uses all training birds as a template library to alleviate this problem. It precomputes shape bases by principal component analysis, then uses the linear combination of shape bases to represent bird keypoints. However, it directly uses an overall weight rather than the weights for different base parts. Therefore, the expressive power of the model is limited. It can not deal well with the bird parts with large deformation. In addition, the geometric information of the keypoints in pictorial structure models is derived from the image plane without considering 3D properties of birds. Consequently, these approaches are also easily confused about the positions of symmetric parts.

Our method proposes a two-branch bird keypoint detection network that combines 2D texture information and 3D geometric information. In the 3D branch, we introduce a 3D deformable mesh model to represent the overall shape of a bird. This 3D model provides the relative spatial position information of keypoints, avoiding the ambiguous position of symmetric parts in 2D images. Simultaneously, we learn the deformation of each vertex on the 3D deformable mesh without the limitation of views. So it can better deal with the deformation of birds across various poses.

3 Proposed Method

The overall framework of our method is shown in Fig. 2. The input of the network is a single RGB image of a bird, and the output is the detected keypoints. The entire network adopts a two-branch structure. The 2D branch mainly utilizes texture information to generate keypoint predictions. The 3D branch uses 3D geometric information to predict keypoints. Finally, the fusion module combines the two predictions to get the final keypoint detection results.

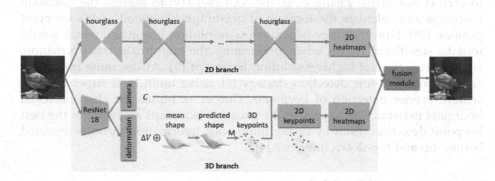

Fig. 2. The framework of the proposed method.

3.1 2D Branch

The 2D branch uses the stacked hourglass network, which has been successfully applied in many keypoint detection tasks. In each hourglass, the high-resolution image is first down-scaled to low resolution by pooling operation. When reaching the lowest resolution, the network starts up-sampling and combining features across scales through skip connections to recover the image resolution. After reaching the output resolution, the network uses two 1-1 convolutional layers to produce the final prediction. The output of this branch is a set of heatmaps. Each heatmap represents a keypoint. Each pixel value in the heatmaps encodes the confidence that a particular keypoint occurs. Besides, we stack eight hourglasses and use intermediate supervision to address vanishing gradients.

However, there is always a sample imbalance problem when using heatmaps for training. The ground-truth heatmaps are generated by placing a 2D Gaussian distribution centered at each keypoint. It contains foreground pixels, simple background pixels, and difficult background pixels. Here, foreground pixels represent the pixels with positive values. Simple background pixels and difficult background pixels are the pixels with zero values. Additionally, simple background pixels are far away from the keypoint and easy to distinguish from the foreground. Difficult background pixels are close to keypoint and look similar to the foreground. Unfortunately, simple background pixels in heatmaps have a large proportion. In contrast, difficult background and foreground regions with a more significant impact on prediction have a small proportion. We discover that when directly using cross-entropy (CE) or mean squared error (MSE) constraints, the loss will be dominated by simple background regions because these constraints deal with each pixel equally. It makes the network pay more attention to learning simple background rather than the foreground and difficult background. Thus, it may lead the network to think that difficult background regions are also part of the foreground, making the prediction results shift to the background. Inspired by [17], we use anchor loss to solve this problem. It essentially reweights the loss values of the background area according to prediction difficulty. Specifically, simple background pixels have small weights, while difficult background pixels have large weights. We measure the difficulty of prediction by the maximum value of the target prediction. If the background pixel has a greater score than the maximum value, it will be considered as a difficult background pixel. Otherwise, it is a simple background pixel. The anchor loss function is as follows:

$$L_{2D} = M(p) * (1 + q - q_{max})^{\gamma} * L_{BCE}(p,q) + [1 - M(p)] * L_{BCE}(p,q) \qquad (1)$$

Here, p and q denote the ground-truth value and prediction value of the pixel, respectively. $M(p)$ is the mask of the background area. Specifically, if $p = 0$, $M(p) = 1$; otherwise, $M(p) = 0$. q_{max} is the maximum value of the prediction result corresponding to the foreground area whose ground-truth value is greater than 0.5. L_{BCE} is the standard binary cross-entropy loss. $\gamma \geq 0$ is a hyper-parameter that controls the weight range of the loss function.

Through the 2D branch, we obtain the keypoint detection results that are robust to complex background. The symmetric keypoints of birds have similar texture information in the image. Therefore, the geometric information is vital to distinguish them. However, the 2D branch mainly uses texture information to detect keypoints, lacking the understanding of the geometric structure information of birds. Therefore, the 2D branch has poor performance on symmetric keypoints, which may produce inverse prediction results (see Fig. 3).

3.2 3D Branch

In the 3D branch, we use a 3D deformable mesh model to provide the relative spatial position information of the keypoints. The 3D deformable mesh model enables the network to understand the approximate geometric structure of the bird, reducing inaccurate predictions of symmetric keypoints. Specifically, we represent the bird shape as a 3D deformable mesh model $M \equiv (V; F)$, which is defined by vertices $V \in \mathbb{R}^{|V| \times 3}$ and triangular faces F. We pre-determine and fix the vertices connectivity, then use the faces F corresponding to a spherical mesh. Therefore, the predicted 3D vertices are semantically consistent. We use a keypoint assignment matrix $M \in \mathbb{R}^{|K| \times |V|}$ s.t. $\sum_v M_{k,v} = 1$ to describe the correspondence between the 3D mesh vertices and the 2D keypoints. Each row M_k in the matrix defines a probability distribution over the mesh vertices corresponding to a particular 2D keypoint. We consider the vertices with maximum value in each row as 3D keypoints. The final predicted 3D vertices V are obtained by adding the predicted deformations $\triangle V$ to mean vertex locations $\bar{V}$, $V = \bar{V} + \triangle V$.

In general, we first produce 3D keypoints by predicting the vertex deformation of the mesh and then project 3D keypoints to the image plane to get the 2D keypoints. Specifically, we use ResNet18 [5] to learn the deformation of mesh vertexes from the mean shape and then apply it to the mean shape to obtain the predicted 3D shape. The 3D keypoints are then projected to the image plane to obtain the 2D keypoints through a keypoint assignment matrix and the predicted camera parameters. In this way, we can get the keypoint prediction results with a reasonable geometric structure. Finally, we convert the 2D keypoints into heatmaps to integrate with the 2D branch. Additionally, we use the structure-from-motion algorithm on the annotated 2D keypoints to calculate the convex hull of the mean 3D keypoint position and then project an icosphere onto this convex hull to get the 3D mean shape of the bird.

To determine the parameters in the network, we use the constraints in [20] for supervision. The objective function is

$$L = L_{kp} + L_{edge} + L_{sil} + L_{sidemask} + L_{cam} + L_{vert2kp} + L_{def} + L_{smooth} \qquad (2)$$

Here, L_{kp}, L_{edge}, L_{sil}, $L_{sidemask}$, and L_{cam} are defined as the MSE loss between ground-truth and prediction of keypoints, the topology consistency of keypoints, silhouettes, side output mask and camera parameters, respectively. $L_{vert2kp}$ is an entropy loss that encourages the keypoint assignment matrix to be a peaked distribution. L_{smooth} is discrete Laplace-Beltrami operator, and L_{def} is a regularization term to discourage arbitrarily large deformation.

3.3 Fusion Module

In the fusion module, we fuse the detection results of two branches to get the final prediction. We first concatenate the heatmap predictions of two branches, then use three 3 * 3 convolutions to extract features. Eventually, we use a 1 * 1 convolution to generate heatmaps, from which the final prediction of keypoints is obtained.

4 Experiments

4.1 Implementation Details

The entire network is implemented in PyTorch and optimized using Adam. Our training divides into two stages. The first stage is to train the 2D and 3D branches, respectively. The second stage is training the fusion module while fixing the 2D and 3D branches. We set the value of the hyperparameter in Eq. (1) as 2. Besides, we perform data augmentation by randomly cropping and flipping images and keypoints. The entire network uses a 256 * 256 RGB image as input and 64 * 64 resolution heatmaps as intermediate outputs.

4.2 Dataset and Evaluation Metrics

We evaluate our method on the challenging dataset CUB200-2011 [23]. It contains 11,788 images of 200 subcategories belonging to birds. Each image has detailed annotations: a subcategory label, 15 keypoints, 312 binary attributes, and a bounding box. We use the standard dataset split, where 5,994 images are used for training and the remaining 5,794 for testing.

We use the popular percentage of correct keypoints (PCK) [24] metric to evaluate bird keypoint detection accuracy, which reports the percentage of keypoint detection falling within a normalized distance to the ground-truth. It defines a candidate keypoint to be correct if it satisfies the following condition:

$$\|y^i_{pred} - y^i_{gt}\|_2 \leq \alpha D \tag{3}$$

where y^i_{pred} is the prediction of i-th keypoint, y^i_{gt} is the ground-truth. D is the reference normalizer, using the maximum of the height and width of the bounding box. The parameter α is the relative threshold for correctness.

Table 1. Comparison with other methods that report per-keypoint PCK (%), the average PCK (%) of symmetric keypoints, and the average PCK (%) of all keypoints on CUB200-2011. The abbreviated keypoint names from top to bottom are: Back, Beak, Belly, Breast, Crown, Forehead, Left Eye, Left Leg, Left Wing, Nape, Right Eye, Right Leg, Right Wing, Tail, and Throat.

Keypoint	PNR [28]	DDN [25]	DPS [8]	CFN [7]	PAIRS (FCN) [4]	PAIRS (SHN) [4]	Ours
Ba	85.6	94.0	89.0	88.3	91.3	–	96.2
Bk	94.9	82.5	95.0	94.5	96.8	–	97.2
Be	81.9	92.2	92.2	87.0	89.0	–	94.5
Br	84.5	83.0	93.2	91.0	91.5	–	96.0
Cr	94.8	92.2	95.2	93.0	96.9	–	98.0
Fh	96.0	91.5	94.2	92.7	97.6	–	97.8
Le	95.7	93.3	90.5	93.7	96.9	–	98.4
Ll	64.6	69.7	73.2	76.9	80.2	–	88.3
Lw	67.8	68.1	81.5	80.5	76.8	–	88.2
Na	90.7	86.0	94.4	93.2	94.6	–	96.5
Re	93.8	93.8	91.6	94.0	97.6	–	97.8
Rl	64.9	74.2	75.5	81.2	80.3	–	88.6
Rw	69.3	68.9	82.3	79.2	75.3	–	86.2
Ta	74.7	77.4	83.2	79.7	83.6	–	87.0
Th	94.5	93.4	95.8	95.1	97.4	–	97.8
Eyes	94.8	93.6	91.1	93.9	97.3	–	98.1
Legs	64.8	72.0	74.4	78.7	80.3	–	88.5
Wings	68.6	69.0	81.9	79.9	76.1	–	87.2
Total	83.6	84.7	85.5	88.0	90.5	92.5	93.9

4.3   Comparison with State-of-the-arts

We report our keypoint detection results using PCK@0.1 in Table 1. Our method attains an accuracy of 93.9%, 1.4% higher than the current state-of-the-art result. We compare with the two results of PAIRS [4], one is PAIRS with fully convolutional network (FCN), another is PAIRS with stacked hourglass network (SHN). Because they only report the per-keypoint result of PAIRS (FCN) without the better result of PAIRS (SHN). Especially, previous works show the poor performance of the 'leg' and 'wing' keypoint detection. Our method achieves up to 10.2% and 14.6% improvements for the two parts over PAIRS (FCN) [4]. It shows that our method can deal with symmetric keypoints detection well. Additionally, we find that using semantic keypoints to represent bird parts does not have a unified standard. It is a controversial issue for different birds to determine which position can represent these parts well, especially the belly, back, wings, and tail, which correspond to large areas. The CUB dataset determines the keypoint position as the average of the five annotators' results.

We also report PCK with $\alpha \in \{0.02, 0.05\}$ to evaluate our method under more hard criteria in Table 2. Our method achieves the best performance across different values of α. It also shows that when using stricter standards, our method improves the keypoint detection results even more. Notably, our method obtains a 63.7% improvement over [7] using the strictest PCK metric.

Table 2. Average PCK scores (%) of legs, wings, eyes, other keypoints, and all keypoints with different α on CUB200-2011.

Method	a = 0.02					a = 0.05				
	Eyes	Legs	Wings	Others	Total	Eyes	Legs	Wings	Others	Total
PNR [28]	11.9	7.6	6.5	10.8	9.9	65.1	35.0	32.5	52.2	49.0
DDN [25]	19.3	6.8	8.5	14.1	13.0	66.6	33.7	36.5	57.0	52.4
CFN [7]	47.5	20.5	13.8	27.3	27.3	90.0	60.3	51.0	73.6	70.9
Ours	76.1	36.0	21.1	45.0	44.7	95.3	73.9	62.9	84.2	81.5

Table 3. Alation study results with PCK@0.1(%). Here, 'baseline' is the 2D branch with BCE loss, 'anchor' means using anchor loss to supervision, '3D' denotes 3D branch and fusion module.

Keypoint	Baseline	Baseline+anchor	Baseline+anchor+3D
Ba	95.0	95.8	**96.2**
Bk	96.7	97.1	**97.2**
Be	93.9	93.6	**94.5**
Br	95.3	95.8	**96.0**
Cr	97.7	97.8	**98.0**
Fh	97.7	**97.8**	97.8
Le	97.9	98.3	**98.4**
Ll	85.6	87.2	**88.3**
Lw	85.4	87.0	**88.2**
Na	96.2	96.4	**96.5**
Re	97.7	97.6	**97.8**
Rl	86.1	86.6	**88.6**
Rw	85.2	85.0	**86.2**
Ta	85.5	86.6	**87.0**
Th	97.6	**97.9**	97.8
Eyes	97.8	98.0	**98.1**
Legs	85.9	86.9	**88.5**
Wings	85.3	86.0	**87.2**
Total	92.9	93.4	**93.9**

4.4 Ablation Study

In this experiment, we evaluate the contribution of different components to the performance gain of the proposed method. To this end, we gradually integrate the following components: anchor loss in the 2D branch (anchor), 3D branch with fusion module (3D). Table 3 gives the results of the ablation study. These results clearly prove that all the proposed components can effectively improve the accuracy of keypoint detection. Figure 3 shows some qualitative results on the CUB200-2011 testing set. It also demonstrates the effectiveness of using 3D geometric information to constrain the relative position of symmetric keypoints.

| Groundtruth | 2D branch prediction | 3D branch prediction | Final prediction |

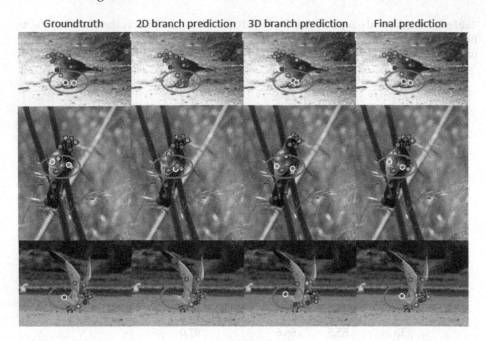

Fig. 3. Keypoint detection results of our method on CUB200-2011. For easy comparison, we circle the areas with considerable prediction differences between different branches and the fusion module with orange circles. And we use circles with white and red boundary to emphasize the keypoints with crucial prediction differences. White boundary means the detected keypoint is correct, while red boundary represents the detected keypoint is incorrect. (Color figure online)

5   Conclusion

In this paper, we propose a two-branch network for bird keypoint detection, which exploits both 2D texture and 3D geometric information. The 2D branch mainly uses image texture information to detect keypoints. In this branch, we adopt anchor loss to make the network robust to the complex background. The 3D branch utilizes the 3D geometric information of birds to generate predictions. Simultaneously, in this branch, we use a 3D deformable mesh model of birds to provide relative spatial position information of keypoints. The combination of the two branches can better cope with the symmetric keypoints and complex background. Our method achieves state-of-the-art performance on the challenging dataset CUB200-2011, which proves the vital importance of 3D geometric information for bird keypoint detection.

Acknowledgement. This work is supported by the National Natural Science Foundation of China (61773270, 61971005).

References

1. Branson, S., Perona, P., Belongie, S.: Strong supervision from weak annotation: interactive training of deformable part models. In: Proceedings of the International Conference on Computer Vision, pp. 1832–1839. IEEE (2011)
2. Farrell, R., Oza, O., Zhang, N., Morariu, V.I., Darrell, T., Davis, L.S.: Birdlets: subordinate categorization using volumetric primitives and pose-normalized appearance. In: Proceedings of the International Conference on Computer Vision, pp. 161–168. IEEE (2011)
3. Felzenszwalb, P.F., Girshick, R.B., McAllester, D., Ramanan, D.: Object detection with discriminatively trained part-based models. IEEE Trans. Pattern Anal. Mach. Intell. $32(9)$, 1627–1645 (2009)
4. Guo, P., Farrell, R.: Aligned to the object, not to the image: a unified pose-aligned representation for fine-grained recognition. In: Proceedings of the Winter Conference on Applications of Computer Vision (WACV), pp. 1876–1885. IEEE (2019)
5. He, K., Zhang, X., Ren, S., Sun, J.: Deep residual learning for image recognition. In: Proceedings of the Computer Vision and Pattern Recognition, pp. 770–778 (2016)
6. Hill, G.E., Hill, G.E., McGraw, K.J., Kevin, J., et al.: Bird Coloration: Function and Evolution, vol. 2. Harvard University Press (2006)
7. Huang, S., Gong, M., Tao, D.: A coarse-fine network for keypoint localization. In: Proceedings of the International Conference on Computer Vision, pp. 3028–3037 (2017)
8. Huang, S., Tao, D.: Real time fine-grained categorization with accuracy and interpretability. arXiv preprint arXiv:1610.00824 (2016)
9. Krizhevsky, A., Sutskever, I., Hinton, G.E.: ImageNet classification with deep convolutional neural networks. In: Advances in Neural Information Processing Systems, vol. 25, pp. 1097–1105 (2012)
10. Law, H., Deng, J.: CornerNet: detecting objects as paired keypoints. In: Ferrari, V., Hebert, M., Sminchisescu, C., Weiss, Y. (eds.) Computer Vision – ECCV 2018. LNCS, vol. 11218, pp. 765–781. Springer, Cham (2018). https://doi.org/10.1007/978-3-030-01264-9_45
11. Liu, J., Belhumeur, P.N.: Bird part localization using exemplar-based models with enforced pose and subcategory consistency. In: Proceedings of the IEEE International Conference on Computer Vision, pp. 2520–2527 (2013)
12. Liu, J., Kanazawa, A., Jacobs, D., Belhumeur, P.: Dog breed classification using part localization. In: Fitzgibbon, A., Lazebnik, S., Perona, P., Sato, Y., Schmid, C. (eds.) ECCV 2012. LNCS, vol. 7572, pp. 172–185. Springer, Heidelberg (2012). https://doi.org/10.1007/978-3-642-33718-5_13
13. Liu, J., Li, Y., Belhumeur, P.N.: Part-pair representation for part localization. In: Fleet, D., Pajdla, T., Schiele, B., Tuytelaars, T. (eds.) ECCV 2014. LNCS, vol. 8690, pp. 456–471. Springer, Cham (2014). https://doi.org/10.1007/978-3-319-10605-2_30
14. Liu, X., Wang, J., Wen, S., Ding, E., Lin, Y.: Localizing by describing: attribute-guided attention localization for fine-grained recognition. In: Proceedings of the AAAI Conference on Artificial Intelligence, vol. 31 (2017)
15. Meena, S.D., Agilandeeswari, L.: An efficient framework for animal breeds classification using semi-supervised learning and multi-part convolutional neural network (MP-CNN). IEEE Access 7, 151783–151802 (2019)
16. Newell, A., Yang, K., Deng, J.: Stacked hourglass networks for human pose estimation. In: Leibe, B., Matas, J., Sebe, N., Welling, M. (eds.) ECCV 2016. LNCS, vol. 9912, pp. 483–499. Springer, Cham (2016). https://doi.org/10.1007/978-3-319-46484-8_29

17. Ryou, S., Jeong, S.G., Perona, P.: Anchor loss: modulating loss scale based on prediction difficulty. In: Proceedings of the International Conference on Computer Vision, pp. 5992–6001 (2019)
18. Shih, K.J., Mallya, A., Singh, S., Hoiem, D.: Part localization using multi-proposal consensus for fine-grained categorization. In: Proceedings of the British Machine Vision Conference, pp. 128.1–128.12 (2015)
19. Simonyan, K., Zisserman, A.: Very deep convolutional networks for large-scale image recognition. In: Proceedings of the International Conference on Learning Representations (2015)
20. Sun, S., Zhu, Z., Dai, X., Zhao, Q., Li, J.: Weakly-supervised reconstruction of 3D objects with large shape variation from single in-the-wild images. In: Proceedings of the Asian Conference on Computer Vision (2020)
21. Tian, Z., Shen, C., Chen, H., He, T.: FCOS: fully convolutional one-stage object detection. In: Proceedings of the International Conference on Computer Vision, pp. 9627–9636 (2019)
22. Van De Sande, K., Gevers, T., Snoek, C.: Evaluating color descriptors for object and scene recognition. IEEE Trans. Pattern Anal. Mach. Intell. **32**(9), 1582–1596 (2009)
23. Wah, C., Branson, S., Welinder, P., Perona, P., Belongie, S.: The caltech-UCSD birds-200-2011 dataset. Technical report (2011)
24. Yang, Y., Ramanan, D.: Articulated pose estimation with flexible mixtures-of-parts. In: CVPR 2011, pp. 1385–1392. IEEE (2011)
25. Yu, X., Zhou, F., Chandraker, M.: Deep deformation network for object landmark localization. In: Leibe, B., Matas, J., Sebe, N., Welling, M. (eds.) ECCV 2016. LNCS, vol. 9909, pp. 52–70. Springer, Cham (2016). https://doi.org/10.1007/978-3-319-46454-1_4
26. Zhang, H., et al.: SPDA-CNN: unifying semantic part detection and abstraction for fine-grained recognition. In: Proceedings of the Computer Vision and Pattern Recognition, pp. 1143–1152 (2016)
27. Zhang, N., Farrell, R., Iandola, F., Darrell, T.: Deformable part descriptors for fine-grained recognition and attribute prediction. In: Proceedings of the International Conference on Computer Vision, pp. 729–736 (2013)
28. Zhang, N., Shelhamer, E., Gao, Y., Darrell, T.: Fine-grained pose prediction, normalization, and recognition. arXiv preprint arXiv:1511.07063 (2015)
29. Zhu, P., Wang, H., Saligrama, V.: Generalized zero-shot recognition based on visually semantic embedding. In: Proceedings of the Computer Vision and Pattern Recognition, pp. 2995–3003 (2019)

Rotation Aware 3D Point Cloud Vehicle Detection

Hongchao Feng, Yunqian He, and Guihua Xia[✉]

College of Intelligent Systems Science and Engineering,
Harbin Engineering University, Harbin 150001, People's Republic of China
xiaguihua@hrbeu.edu.cn

Abstract. 3D point cloud object detection is an important task of environment perception in autonomous driving. However, the point cloud data collected by LiDAR is limited in angle. In order to solve this problem, we propose a Rotation Aware Detection Network. We apply an augmentation method of angle transformation in the original scenes to obtain the corresponding derivative scenes. We propose an auxiliary network to learn the difference between the two scenes we designed. Our method can effectively enhance the detection capability of the network without additional inference cost. Our approach can improve the performance in the car detection task on the KITTI dataset.

Keywords: Point cloud · Object detection · Auxiliary network

1 Introduction

With the development of 3D sensors, the point cloud data collected by LiDAR has become an important data comparable to camera images in the field of 3D vision. Unlike other regular data, point cloud is sparse and disordered. So mature 2-dimension methods are difficult to be directly applied on it in 3-dimension. Therefore, many scholars have begun to devote themselves to the research of point clouds, and object detection task based on 3D point clouds are the cornerstone of further 3D tasks.

In recent studies, 3D object detection methods are mainly divided into two types according to the pre-processing methods of point cloud: point-based and voxel-based. Aiming at the characteristics of point cloud data, PointNet [8] and PointNet++ [9] proposed by Qi are used to directly extract features from the original point cloud data. In the three-dimensional detection task, PointRCNN [11] and F-PointNet [7] use the network in PointNet as the backbone to obtain the features of the scene. Among them, PointRCNN uses the two-stage structure as faster-RCNN [10] to refine the predicted bounding boxes. F-PointNet integrates image features and predicts the three-dimensional boxes in the three-dimensional frustum projected by the image detection result. Different from the limitations of point-based methods, the voxel-based series of methods are more influential. VoxelNet [16] first divides the entire scene into regular voxels, then uses 3D CNN

© Springer Nature Switzerland AG 2021
Y. Peng et al. (Eds.): ICIG 2021, LNCS 12890, pp. 83–93, 2021.
https://doi.org/10.1007/978-3-030-87361-5_7

to extract the features of the scene. Finally it uses the anchor-based method to generate the detection predictions. Later SECOND [12] and PointPillar [5] further improved the speed and accuracy of the method by introducing sparse convolution and pillar, respectively.

Although the Point-based method can adaptively learn features from the point cloud, the voxel-based method can extract dense high-level feature maps more efficiently. Our work is also based on the voxel structure. In the point cloud object detection task, the current point cloud data collected based on lidar is limited in view. Therefore, many occluded and truncated targets are difficult to predict in most methods.

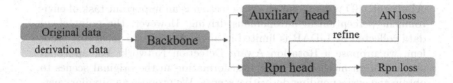

Fig. 1. The rotation aware detection structure with auxiliary network.

We propose a Rotation Aware Detection Network as shown in Fig. 1 that utilizes the incompleteness of the target point cloud in the scene and the consistency of the target shape to construct an auxiliary network. We form a derivative scene by rotating the target in the original scene, and the auxiliary network is used to assist in learning the difference between the two scenes to enhance the network. In addition, the auxiliary network is only used in the training stage to assist the parameter learning of the main network, and will be removed in the inference stage without affecting the actual detection efficiency.

2   Related Work

We will review related works about 3D object detection including point-based methods and voxel-based methods.

2.1   Point-Based Methods

PointRCNN [11] uses PointNet as the backbone and consists of two stages. The first stage is used for bottom-up 3D region proposal, and the second stage is used to refine the proposal in the standard coordinate system to obtain the final detection result. The F-PointNet [7] method proposed by Qi uses two different types of data. First, according to the results of object detection on the picture, the point cloud of the corresponding object is projected in the three-dimensional space. After obtaining the point cloud of each object, PointNet is used to extract the entire feature of the object point cloud. 3DSSD [13] analyzes the time cost of the point-based method and eliminates the redundant upsampling and refinement stage. It propose a fusion sampling method to solve the problem of fewer foreground points, while using voting [6] to move the surface points of the foreground to the center of the target.

2.2 Voxel-Based Methods

VoxelNet [16] expresses the point cloud in the form of voxel, and then uses the VFE block to perform feature extraction on the points in each voxel. The backbone uses three-dimensional convolution on the obtained regularized voxels for feature extraction, and constructs an RPN network for object detection. SECOND [12] made key improvements to the pain points of low computational efficiency caused by the sparsity of VoxelNet. It introduces a sparse convolution layer and performed sparse convolution processing on voxels in the Z direction. While extracting features, the network gradually thins the three-dimensional voxels in space, and the finally obtained BEV map is processed by a two-dimensional object detection network. PointPillars [5] simplifies SECOND and directly represented the point cloud as "Pillar". Then this method uses VFE to extract the features and directly obtains the pseudo-image, omitting the sparse convolution operation in SECOND.

3 Method

3.1 Backbone and Detection Networks

The voxel-based methods with 3d sparse convolution networks can efficiently extract scene features in 3D point cloud detection. Therefore, we use a similar structure as the backbone and the region proposal network in our work, as shown in Fig. 2. And we create derivative scenes according to the original scenes to enhance the data, which is the foundation of the auxiliary network.

Backbone. The input point cloud is divided into a voxel set of size $L \times W \times H$ by a fixed voxel size in the Euclidean space of the entire scene. And it uses the mean operation to aggregate the points in each non-empty voxel as the initial feature $[x, y, z, r]$, where $[x, y, z]$ is the three-dimensional coordinates of the point cloud, and r is the reflection intensity. The network applies sparse convolution and submanifold convolution to stack and extract the 3D features of the point cloud. It utilize four convolution blocks and the last three blocks contain a sparse convolution layer with $stride = 2$. The feature map is downsampled by $1\times, 2\times, 4\times,$ and $8\times$ in the four blocks respectively. Finally, the 3D feature map is stacked along the z-axis by channels to obtain a 2D BEV feature map with a scale of $\frac{L}{8} \times \frac{W}{8}$.

Region Proposal Network. The RPN further extract the 2D features obtained from the backbone. There are two convolution blocks in the region proposal network, and each block contains 5 convolution layers and 1 deconvolution layer. The two deconvolution layers of blocks keep the sizes of the output feature maps consistent at $\frac{L}{8} \times \frac{W}{8}$, and the two output features combine together within the channels. Finally, each super pixel on the feature map outputs anchor-based predictions for classification and regression tasks.

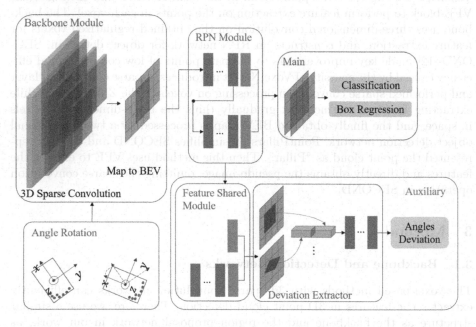

Fig. 2. Overall of the proposed framework of Rotation Aware Detection Network.

Derivative Scenes. In order to apply the auxiliary network, we automatically construct a set of derivative scenes for each training. The derivative scenes and the original scenes share the same background, and perform random rotation operations on the angle of each target. Corresponding scenes are jointly transmitted to the backbone for prediction to enhance the robustness of the network.

3.2 Auxiliary Network

The auxiliary network uses a customized RoI operation to extract the features of the corresponding target in the original scene and the derivative scene respectively. It determines the change of the target direction according to the difference of the features from the two scenes.

Feature Proposals. The corresponding features $\left(F^{ori}, F^{aux}\right)$ extracted from the original scenes and the derivative scenes perform additional predictions in the auxiliary network, and these feature pairs come from the RPN modules. The two-dimensional RPN features reduce the further computational complexity comparing to the sparse three-dimensional features from the backbone. At the same time, every single super-pixel contains more target information after feature aggregations in the RPN network.

Suppose the set $S = \left\{s_j = \left(P_j^{ori}, P_j^{aux}\right) | k = 1, 2, ..., N\right\}$ is the target pair of the original scenes and the derivative scenes, where s_j is the $j - th$ pair extracted from $\left(F^{ori}, F^{aux}\right)$. Let $g_j^{ori} = [x_c, y_c, z_c, l, w, h, \alpha]$ and $g_j^{aux} = [x_c, y_c, z_c, l, w, h, \alpha + \theta_j]$ respectively represents the ground true boxes of the $j - th$ targets in the original scene and derivative scene. And the ground true boxes pair set is $G = \left\{g_j = \left(g_j^{ori}, g_j^{aux}\right)\right\}$.

We proposed a customized RoI operation that is different from the RoI in the two-stage method, which uses the prediction from the RPN stage as proposals to extract the feature of each target. It is difficult to determine whether the proposals generated from the two scenes in the RPN stage have the same correspondence with s_j. Also when $\lim_{N_{iter} \to \infty} Loss_{RPN} \to 0$, $\lim_{N_{iter} \to \infty} Prop_j \to g_j$. So in this work we use g_j as the proposals of s_j.

RoI Pooling. The projection $\hat{g}_j$ of g_j on the BEV map is divided into a grid of size $N_{grid} \times N_{grid}$, and the coordinates of the grid is mapped to the 2D features from feature shared layers. Then we use the bilinear interpolation method to obtain the features of each grid. Define the four corners of each grid as $(x_1, y_1, f(x_1, y_1)), (x_1, y_2, f(x_1, y_2)), (x_2, y_1, f(x_2, y_1))$ and $(x_2, y_2, f(x_2, y_2))$ and the interpolation estimation $f(x, y)$ is calculated by:

$$
\begin{aligned}
f(x, y_1) &= f(x_1, y_1) \frac{x_2 - x}{x_2 - x_1} + f(x_2, y_1) \frac{x - x_1}{x_2 - x_1}, \\
f(x, y_2) &= f(x_1, y_2) \frac{x_2 - x}{x_2 - x_1} + f(x_2, y_2) \frac{x - x_1}{x_2 - x_1}, \\
f(x, y) &= f(x, y_1) \frac{y_2 - y}{y_2 - y_1} + f(x, y_2) \frac{y - y_1}{y_2 - y_1}.
\end{aligned}
\tag{1}
$$

After interpolation, the feature pair $\left(\hat{f}_j^{ori}, \hat{f}_j^{aux}\right)$ corresponding to s_j is obtained as shown in Fig. 3, where $\hat{f}_j^{ori}, \hat{f}_j^{aux} \in R^{N_{grid} \times N_{grid} \times C}$.

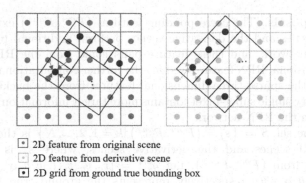

☑ 2D feature from original scene
☑ 2D feature from derivative scene
☑ 2D grid from ground true bounding box

Fig. 3. The bilinear interpolation in ground ture in auxiliary network.

Finally, we encode $\hat{f}_j^{ori} and \hat{f}_j^{aux}$ within the channel to obtain the deviation feature $f_d = \left[\hat{f}_j^{ori}; \hat{f}_j^{aux} \right]$ corresponding to s_j, where $f_d \in R^{N_{grid} \times N_{grid} \times 2C}$). We predict the orientation deviation between the original scene and the derivative scene by:

$$\theta_j = \phi(f_d), \tag{2}$$

where ϕ represents a 2D convolution layers.

Angle Deviation Prediction. For the angle deviation prediction between each scene pair, we apply a hybrid of classification and regression formulation for θ. Specifically, we define N_a equally split orientation angle bins classify the proposal orientation angle into different bins $\hat{bin}_{cls}$. Residual $\hat{bin}_{reg}$ is regressed with respect to the bin value.

3.3   Loss Function

In our network, only original scene is predicted by the main network during each training. For training the main network, we define the loss function with three parts including classification loss, regression loss and direction loss. We define the ground true box as $(x_g, y_g, z_g, w_g, l_g, h_g, \theta_g)$, and a positive anchor as $(x_a, y_a, z_a, w_a, l_a, h_a, \theta_g)$. Thus, we define the target vector as follows:

$$\Delta x = \frac{x_g - x_a}{d_a}, \Delta y = \frac{y_g - y_a}{d_a}, \Delta z = \frac{z_g - z_a}{h_a},$$

$$\Delta w = \log(\frac{w_g}{w_a}), \Delta l = \log(\frac{l_g}{l_a}), \Delta h = \log(\frac{h_g}{h_a}), \tag{3}$$

$$\Delta \theta = \sin(\theta_g - \theta_a),$$

where x, y, z are the center coordinates; w, l, h are the width, length and height respectively; θ is the yaw rotation around the z-axis; subscripts g and a are ground truth and anchor; $d_a = \sqrt{(l_a)^2 + (w_a)^2}$ is the diagonal of the base of the anchor box.

For the classification loss function in our network, we use the focus loss function to reduce the extreme imbalance between positive and negative samples. For the regression loss function, we use the $SmoothL1$ function to minimize the target vector $(\Delta x, \Delta y, \Delta z, \Delta w, \Delta l, \Delta h, \Delta \theta)$. At the same time, we use $\sin(\theta_g - \theta_a)$ to solve the problem of excessive loss when the prediction is opposite to the target position. The direction loss follows the cross-entropy loss function. We combine these functions to get the total main network loss function as follows:

$$L_{main} = \alpha L_{cls} + \beta L_{reg} + \gamma L_{dir} \tag{4}$$

where L_{cls} denotes the loss of the classification, L_{reg} denotes the loss of the regression, and L_{dir} denotes the loss of the direction. The regression and direction values jointly make up the bounding box predictions. And α, β, γ are coefficients of these components.

In our work, we propose a auxiliary network to enhance the prediction, while bring a joint prediction loss function for the entire network. For the auxiliary loss function, we define the ground true of the angle deviation between two scenes as bin_{cls}, bin_{reg}. Then the auxiliary loss function is:

$$L_{aux} = L_{cls}^{bin}\left(bin_{cls}, \hat{bin}_{cls}\right) + L_{reg}^{bin}\left(bin_{reg}, \hat{bin}_{reg}\right) \tag{5}$$

where the L_{cls}^{bin} is cross-entropy classification loss, and L_{reg}^{bin} is $Smooth - L1$ loss. Overall, we jointly optimize the main network and the auxiliary one by applying a gradient descent method to minimize the weighted sum of the following losses:

$$L = L_{main} + \eta L_{aux} \tag{6}$$

4   Experiment

We train and test the proposed network on the KITTI dataset [2] with only LiDAR data for 3D object detection benchmark. KITTI contains 7481 training data and 7518 testing data including car, pedestrian, and cyclist. For each category, the detection task is divided into three difficulty levels: easy, moderate, and hard, according to the size of object, occlusion, and truncation. We divided the training set equally into two complementary parts and selected one set for training and the other for validation testing. So validation set and testing set has no duplicate samples with the training set.

We follow the official KITTI evaluation protocol, where the IoU threshold is 0.7 for class Car in both BEV and 3D detection. We compare methods by using the average precision (AP).

4.1 Implementation Details

Firstly, we keep the points within the range of $[-3, 1] \times [-40, 40] \times [0, 70.4]$ meters along $z \times y \times x$ axis respectively. The voxel size is $[0.1, 0.05, 0.05]$ meters, and the maximum number of the randomly sampled points is 5 for each non-empty voxel. After the sparse convolutional neural networks, the output shape of the high-level feature is $64 \times 2 \times 200 \times 176$. Then we down-sample the feature map along the z-axis to 1 and resize the final map size to $128 \times 200 \times 176$ for the RPN network. The size of the car is fixed and the point cloud has no multi-scale issues, so we use fixed-size anchor points to represent the bounding box. According to the typical car size, we set the anchor size to $w = 1.6, l = 3.9, h = 1.56$ m and the center to $z = -1.0$ m. Also, The angle bin division N_a is 12.

We used stochastic gradient descent (SGD) and applied Adam optimizer during training. The initial learning rate is 0.003 and the decay weight is 0.01. Every inference is conducted by PyTorch framework on a single NVIDIA 2080Ti GPU card.

4.2 Evaluation on KITTI Validation Set

We compared the state-of-the-art LiDAR-based methods in the validation set of car categories. The 3D results and BEV results are shown in Table 1.

Fig. 4. Results on the test set. And the detection results are indicated by a green box. (Color figure online)

Our method in both results shows significantly superior to the other methods in the three modes of easy, moderate (mod.) and hard. All results performs in 11 recall according to the detection metrics of the other proposed methods.

The Fig. 4 shows some results for detecting car categories on the test set. From the figure we would find that our proposed framework estimate accurate locations by using only point cloud, which enhanced by the auxiliary network.

4.3 Ablation Studies

In this section we study the effect of proposed auxiliary network and the effect of the parameter η. All of the ablation experiments were trained on a training set consisting of 3712 samples and tested on the validation set. All results perform in 11 recall.

According to the Table 2, we can compare the effect of η to detection results. Specially, (a) method represents the auxiliary network does not make an impact on the main network with $\eta = 0$. (b)–(d) method represents the refinement ability of auxiliary network is increasing, where reflects the results of main network are better when η within a certain range. Therefore, it proves that the auxiliary

Table 1. Performance comparison in detection AP (%) on KITTI val set for the car class

Method	3D			BEV		
	Easy	Mod.	Hard	Easy	Mod.	Hard
MV3D [1]	71.29	62.68	56.56	86.55	78.10	76.67
F-PointNet [7]	83.76	70.92	63.65	88.16	84.02	76.44
AVOD-FPN [3]	84.41	74.44	68.65	–	–	–
VoxelNet [16]	81.97	65.46	62.85	89.60	84.81	78.57
IPOD [14]	84.10	76.40	75.30	88.30	86.40	84.60
SECOND [12]	87.43	76.48	69.10	89.96	84.81	78.57
Voxel-FPN [4]	88.42	77.70	76.03	–	–	–
PointRGCN [15]	88.37	78.54	77.60	89.61	87.35	85.43
PointRCNN [11]	88.88	78.63	77.38	–	–	–
Our method	**89.04**	**78.96**	**77.74**	**90.01**	**88.42**	**87.30**

Table 2. The performance (AP_{3D}) of our method with different η on KITTI val set for car class.

Methods	η	Moderate
(a)	0	78.62
(b)	0.2	78.96
(c)	0.8	78.68
(d)	1.4	78.50

network is beneficial to improve the detection precision by setting a rational hyper-parameter $\eta = 0.2$.

5 Conclusions

The point cloud data collected by LiDAR is limited in angle and view. Therefore, we propose a Rotation Aware Detection Network to solve this angle issue. We apply an augmentation method of angle transformation in the original scenes to obtain the corresponding derivative scenes. We propose an auxiliary network to learn the deviation between the two scenes in training. Our method can effectively enhance the detection capability of the network without additional inference cost. Our approach can improve the performance in the car detection task on the KITTI dataset.

References

1. Chen, X., Ma, H., Wan, J., Li, B., Xia, T.: Multi-view 3D object detection network for autonomous driving. In: Proceedings of the IEEE Conference on Computer Vision and Pattern Recognition, pp. 1907–1915 (2017)
2. Geiger, A., Lenz, P., Urtasun, R.: Are we ready for autonomous driving? The kitti vision benchmark suite. In: 2012 IEEE Conference on Computer Vision and Pattern Recognition, pp. 3354–3361. IEEE (2012)
3. Ku, J., Mozifian, M., Lee, J., Harakeh, A., Waslander, S.L.: Joint 3D proposal generation and object detection from view aggregation. In: 2018 IEEE/RSJ International Conference on Intelligent Robots and Systems, pp. 1–8. IEEE (2018)
4. Kuang, H., Wang, B., An, J., Zhang, M., Zhang, Z.: Voxel-FPN: multi-scale voxel feature aggregation for 3D object detection from lidar point clouds (2020)
5. Lang, A.H., Vora, S., Caesar, H., Zhou, L., Yang, J., Beijbom, O.: PointPillars: fast encoders for object detection from point clouds. In: Proceedings of the IEEE Conference on Computer Vision and Pattern Recognition, pp. 12697–12705 (2019)
6. Qi, C.R., Litany, O., He, K., Guibas, L.J.: Deep hough voting for 3D object detection in point clouds. In: Proceedings of the IEEE/CVF International Conference on Computer Vision, pp. 9277–9286 (2019)
7. Qi, C.R., Liu, W., Wu, C., Su, H., Guibas, L.J.: Frustum pointnets for 3D object detection from RGB-D data. In: Proceedings of the IEEE Conference on Computer Vision and Pattern Recognition, pp. 918–927 (2018)
8. Qi, C.R., Su, H., Mo, K., Guibas, L.J.: PointNet: deep learning on point sets for 3D classification and segmentation. In: Proceedings of the IEEE Conference on Computer Vision and Pattern Recognition, pp. 652–660 (2017)
9. Qi, C.R., Yi, L., Su, H., Guibas, L.J.: PointNet++: deep hierarchical feature learning on point sets in a metric space. In: Advances in Neural Information Processing Systems, pp. 5099–5108 (2017)
10. Ren, S., He, K., Girshick, R., Sun, J.: Faster R-CNN: towards real-time object detection with region proposal networks. IEEE Trans. Pattern Anal. Mach. Intell. **39**(6), 1137–1149 (2016)
11. Shi, S., Wang, X., Li, H.: PointRCNN: 3D object proposal generation and detection from point cloud, pp. 770–779 (2019)

12. Yan, Y., Mao, Y., Li, B.: Second: sparsely embedded convolutional detection. Sensors **18**(10), 3337 (2018)
13. Yang, Z., Sun, Y., Liu, S., Jia, J.: 3DSSD: point-based 3D single stage object detector. In: Proceedings of the IEEE/CVF Conference on Computer Vision and Pattern Recognition, pp. 11040–11048 (2020)
14. Yang, Z., Sun, Y., Liu, S., Shen, X., Jia, J.: IPOD: intensive point-based object detector for point cloud. arXiv preprint arXiv:1812.05276 (2018)
15. Zarzar, J., Giancola, S., Ghanem, B.: PointRGCN: graph convolution networks for 3D vehicles detection refinement. arXiv preprint arXiv:1911.12236 (2019)
16. Zhou, Y., Tuzel, O.: VoxeLNet: end-to-end learning for point cloud based 3D object detection. In: Proceedings of the IEEE Conference on Computer Vision and Pattern Recognition, pp. 4490–4499 (2018)

Improved 3D Morphable Model for Facial Action Unit Synthesis

Minghui Wang and Zhilei Liu[✉] iD

College of Intelligence and Computing, Tianjin University, Tianjin 300350, China
{wangminghfly,zhileiliu}@tju.edu.cn

Abstract. To overcome the limitation of the conventional 3D face model on the synthesis of local facial expression movements, this paper proposes an improved 3D face model that combines facial action coding system (FACS) and 3D morphable model (3DMM). Our proposed 3D face model can be used for 3D facial expression synthesis with local action units (AUs). To be specific, AUs are introduced as prior knowledge into the 3D face model to capture the anatomically defined muscle movements of different facial expressions. Our proposed model extracts the parameters of a single AU, which can also be used to represent AU information to facilitate AU recognition. The qualitative and quantitative experimental results demonstrate that our proposed model can generate 3D faces with specific AU labels. These AU parameters of our proposed model perform better in AU classification than the global expression parameters of conventional 3DMM.

Keywords: FACS · 3DMM · Action unit synthesis · 3D Face

1 Introduction

In recent years, 3D facial expression analysis has attracted more and more attention in computer graphics and computer vision due to its wide application in animation and games. The Facial Action Coding System (FACS) [8] is a well-known system for recognizing and labeling facial expressions by describing the movement of muscles of the face. According to anatomical knowledge, it divides facial muscles into independent and interconnected muscle actions called Action Units (AUs), each of which has an intensity at a six-point ordinal scale [26]. Although FACS provides a method to represent facial expressions accurately, some open challenges still affect its widespread applications [12,13]. First of all, AU annotation is a highly time-consuming task, even for AU experts, and this problem has resulted in a small number of publicly available 3D facial expression datasets containing AU labels. Secondly, the specific expressions rarely appear in the datasets, and this problem has caused an extreme imbalance between the various AUs in current datasets.

To alleviate these problems, recent studies [6,13,15] have focused more on generating a large-scale 3D face dataset with specific AU labels. 3DMM [3] is a

© Springer Nature Switzerland AG 2021
Y. Peng et al. (Eds.): ICIG 2021, LNCS 12890, pp. 94–105, 2021.
https://doi.org/10.1007/978-3-030-87361-5_8

parametric model that divides face attributes into several different parts, such as identity, expression, texture. Different components of face attributes can be generated through a set of parameters using 3DMM and then combined to obtain a 3D face. In facial expression analysis, 3DMM can usually be used to separate the facial expression information globally. However, generating a specific expression requires local control of the expression. Because of the above reasons, this paper aims to decompose the expression information further to realize control of facial expressions locally.

In this paper, an improved 3D morphable model is proposed for AU synthesis based on 3DMM and FACS. In particular, the proposed 3D model captures the local variations of each AU from faces with different expressions according to the definition of AU. The contributions of this paper are threefold. First, we propose a framework to decompose the expression information of the 3D face to realize the control of a single AU. To the best of our knowledge, this has not been done before. Second, with the help of our proposed framework, a large number of 3D face data with specific AU labels can be synthesized, which can effectively alleviate the lack of available data in 3D face expression analysis. Third, both quantitative and qualitative experiments are conducted on the FaceWarehouse dataset [4] to verify that the AU parameters of our model have a good effect on the task of AU classification.

2 Related Work

Action Unit Synthesis. Each AU can represent the local muscle movement of a specific facial region, and Table 1 lists some AU descriptions and the corresponding muscle movements. The AU label can either use a binary classification to indicate whether the AU is activated or not or use the intensity value to indicate the intensity of the activated AU.

Table 1. List of AUs and the corresponding description

Action unit	Description	Facial muscle
10	Upper lip raiser	Levator labii superioris, caput infraorbitalis
14	Dimpler	Buccinator
17	Chin raiser	Mentalis
20	Lip stretcher	Risorius
23	Lip tightener	Orbicularis oris
25	Lips part	Depressor labii, orbicularis oris
28	Lip suck	Orbicularis oris
43	Eyes closed	Relaxation of levator palpebrae superioris

According to previous research, it has been proved that AU labels are more helpful for facial expression recognition than landmarks [16,24]. Therefore, the recognition of AU has always been an essential topic in facial expression analysis. AUs inherently have a relatively fixed position on the face. Therefore, Li et al. [9] added an attention map to the AU location area in the middle layer of the neural network to force the model to pay more attention to AU interest regions on face images. Shao et al. [18] learned an adaptive attention network to determine the attention distribution of each AU's ROI with the help of face alignment results. In addition, according to facial anatomy information, strong relationships exist among different AUs under different facial expressions, e.g., a smile is usually a combination of AU6 (Cheek Raiser) and AU12 (Lip Corner Puller). Therefore, Liu et al. [11] tried to model the relationship between AUs through graph convolutional networks to improve the overall recognition accuracy of AUs. However, these works are all carried out using 2D face images, and 3D faces is easier to capture subtle deformations. Chen et al. [5] combined the 2D image and the 3D face mesh model as the input of the AU recognition network.

The methods described above are all limited by the amount of available AU data. In the commonly used benchmark datasets, BP4D [28] and BP4D+ [29] contain videos of more than one hundred subjects under specific multiple tasks and the corresponding 3D face models and let AU experts perform AU annotations on some of the sequences. However, building a large AU data set is time-consuming and labor-intensive work, so the synthesis of AUs has gradually become an important research work. Liu et al. [12] divided the face into multiple small patches according to the AU locations and then conditional GAN [14] to edit the AU separately. Liu et al. [13] made use of 3DMM to extract a low-dimensional representation of the 3D face, and then the conditional generative adversarial network (CGAN) was adopted to achieve AU synthesis on the 3D face. However, this model that uses CGAN to synthesize AU has a problem that when the model changes the state of one AU, other AUs may also change at the same time.

3D Face Model. 3D Morphable Model (3DMM) is currently the most widely used 3D face statistical model [17,21], which is built from 3D scans of data and densely corresponding face models [2]. It reduces the dimensionality of the 3D face data and uses parameters to represent the 3D face. Therefore, some works use 3DMM as the dimensionality reduction representation of 3D human faces and then perform subsequent expression analysis and other works [19,20]. An intuitive application of the 3DMM is to use 3DMM parameters to fit a 3D face or regress 3DMM parameters from a face image [10,30]. Tewari et al. [22] proposed a model-based deep convolutional network to regress 3DMM parameters from the image and further reconstruct the 3D face. Tran et al. [23] used deep neural networks to learn a nonlinear 3DMM model with better representation capabilities than conventional linear models.

As a representation of a 3D face, 3DMM can facilitate the 3D face reconstruction process and control the attributes of the face by adjusting the 3DMM parameters. In addition, face attributes in 3D space are easier to control or edit, such as illumination, expression, and pose [27]. Consequently, another important application of 3DMM is to change the attributes of face images by changing 3DMM parameters. Ververas et al. [25] proposed SliderGAN, which can change the expression attributes of face images by utilizing 3DMM parameters. Deng et al. [7] introduced imitative learning and contrastive learning to ensure that the facial expression or illumination is changed without changing the identity attributes of the face image. However, using 3DMM to edit the attributes of a human face is limited by the global expression of the 3DMM. It cannot edit the local expression of the human face, which is an inherent defect of the 3DMM. Our model is inspired by the fact that multiple AUs can decompose facial expressions and solves this problem.

3   Proposed Method

3.1   3D Morphable Model

Blanz et al. [3] aligns the 3D scan data of 200 human faces and then stacks the aligned data into two matrices: texture and shape. The 3D shape $\hat{S}$ and texture $\hat{T}$ of a face are represented as

$$\hat{S} = \bar{S} + B_s \cdot diag(\sigma_s) \cdot \alpha_s, \tag{1}$$

$$\hat{T} = \bar{T} + B_t \cdot diag(\sigma_t) \cdot \beta_t, \tag{2}$$

where $\bar{S}$ and $\bar{T}$ are the average face shape and texture, B_s, and B_t are the PCA bases of shape, and texture, respectively, σ_s, σ_t are corresponding eigenvalues, and α_s, β_t are corresponding 3DMM parameters.

In Eq. 1, a set of parameters is defined to describe the shape of the face. On this basis, the neutral face is regarded as the identity attribute of the face. The difference between the expression face and the neutral face is regarded as the expression attribute of the face. The shape $\hat{S}$ of the face can be further expressed as

$$\hat{S} = \bar{S} + B_{id} \cdot diag(\sigma_{id}) \cdot \alpha_{id} + B_{exp} \cdot diag(\sigma_{exp}) \cdot \alpha_{exp}, \tag{3}$$

where B_{exp} is the result of the principal component analysis of the deformation matrix of the relatively neutral face. As can be seen from Eq. 3, the parameter α_{exp} describes the variation of the facial expression within the span of the training data. The eigenvalue of the corresponding matrices scales the coefficients.

3.2   Improved 3DMM for AU Synthesis (AU-3DMM)

The expression parameters of the conventional 3DMM are representation on the global level, lacking semantic information, and cannot control the expression locally. Our goal is to build a face model that can locally control the expression attributes of a 3D face, so we propose an improved 3D face model over the conventional 3DMM. Our proposed method of combining AUs and 3DMM is a very natural and suitable way to improve conventional 3DMM. The improved model can activate single or multiple AUs of the 3D face while keeping the identity attributes of the 3D face unchanged.

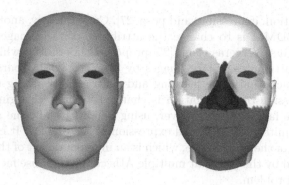

Fig. 1. Visualization of average face and AU-related mask

3D Face Data. In our work, we use the FaceWarehouse dataset [4], which contains 150 individuals aged 7–80. For each person, the dataset includes its neutral expression and 19 other expressional 3D mesh models, all of which have been densely corresponded to meet the conditions for constructing a 3DMM. Each mesh model includes 11,510 points and 11,400 faces. As for the AU labels, we use an open-source AU detection tool, OpenFace [1], to perform AU detection on the RGB images corresponding to all 3D faces in the data. In order to capture a more physical variance of AUs, we select AUs with a high occurrence rate from the data. In this work, we finally selected 8 primary AUs, namely AU10, AU14, AU17, AU20, AU23, AU25, AU28, AU43.

Parameterization of AUs. First, we get the average face $\bar{S}$ and the PCA bases of the identity attribute from 150 faces. Next, we need to obtain the PCA bases of each AU. Considering that the location of muscle movement represented by AU is relatively fixed, so we utilize a region mask to obtain the deformation of the face shape represented by the area where the AU is located and perform PCA on the deformation matrix of each AU to obtain the PCA basis B_i and eigenvalues σ_i for a single AU. Finally, our 3D face model can be expressed as:

$$\hat{S} = \bar{S} + B_{id} \cdot diag(\sigma_{id}) \cdot \alpha_{id} + \sum_{i \in U} f \cdot M_i \cdot B_i \cdot diag(\sigma_i) \cdot \alpha_i, \qquad (4)$$

where U is a set of AUs, i is the index of AU, f is a parameter that controls the intensity of AU, and M_i is the mask of the i-th AU. We divide the face into several regions according to the AU positions and get the corresponding region mask in this work. As shown in Fig. 1, we show the average face $\bar{S}$ of the model and the mask area on the average face.

Smooth Processing. At this point, we can randomly generate a set of AU parameters to generate the corresponding 3D face according to Eq. 4. However, the face we generated in this way will appear a little unnatural at the mask's boundary, so we added a smoothing operation to make a face more realistic. First, we use the normalized Gaussian weighted Euclidean distance as the weight for the interpolation:

$$W = N(exp(-d^2/2\sigma^2)) \tag{5}$$

where d is the Euclidean distance from the point in the region to the regional center, and $N(\cdot)$ is the normalization operation. Then, a more natural result is obtained by linear interpolation.

$$\hat{P} = W \cdot P + (1 - W) \cdot P', \tag{6}$$

where $\hat{P}$ is the smoothed final position, P is the origin position, P' is the position before smoothing.

4 Experiments

In this section, we evaluate our proposed model from multiple aspects. Our model can edit the state of 8 AUs, namely AU10, AU14, AU17, AU20, AU23, AU25, AU28, AU43. We analyze our proposed model qualitatively and quantitatively and show our experimental results as below.

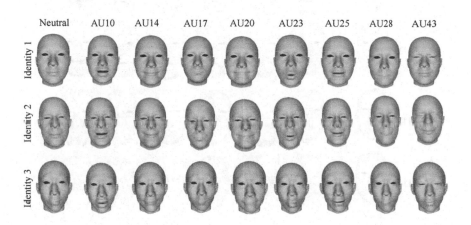

Fig. 2. Synthetic results of different AUs under different identities

Qualitative Results. Our proposed improved 3DMM model can change one of the identity attribute and the AU attribute of the 3D face without changing the other attribute. As shown in Fig. 2, we ensure that one attribute remains unchanged and displays the 3D face after another attribute is changed. Each row represents the result of changing different AU with a fixed identity parameter. In addition, we can observe that the same AU parameters show similar shape deformations on different 3D faces, which also verifies our model's control ability over a single AU.

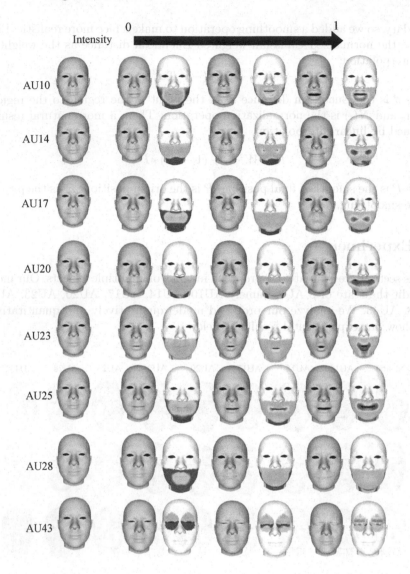

Fig. 3. Synthetic results of different AUs under different intensities

The same AU may also have different intensities, so we show the changes of facial expressions under different AU intensities, as shown in Fig. 3. These results demonstrate that the AU parameters in our improved 3DMM can capture a variety of AUs intensities.

AU10   AU14   AU17   AU20   AU23   AU25   AU28 AU43

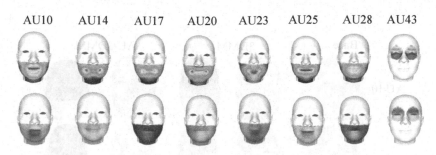

Fig. 4. Visualization of deformation caused by AU change

In order to prove that the AU controlled by our improved 3DMM model conforms to the description of AU definition, we calculate the deformation intensity and displacement that occurs when AUs are activated and then visualize the results, as shown in Fig. 4. The first row of the figure illustrates that deformation's intensity distribution before and after AU be activated. The second row of the figure demonstrates the displacement of a single AU before and after activation. These two visualization results demonstrate that the control of AU by our improved 3DMM is consistent with the definition of AU by FACS.

Finally, we compared AU-3DMM and conventional 3DMM and the results are shown in Fig. 5. We change the status of a single AU on a 3D face and display the changed 3D face and the corresponding deformation. Since a traditional 3DMM model cannot change a single AU, we present two 3D faces of the same person that differ only in the state of a single AU. It can be seen from the comparison results that our proposed model can change the state of a single AU while ensuring that the state of other AUs remains unchanged.

Quantitative Results. To verify the facial expression representation ability of the expression parameters in 3DMM and our proposed AU-3DMM, quantitative evaluations for AU detection using expression parameters of both models are performed on the FaceWarehouse [4] dataset. We use 80% of the data set as the training set to train an SVM and FCN as the AU classifier. We set the radial basis function as the kernel function of SVM and FCN is a 3-layer fully connected network, $lr = 0.0001$, $epochs = 30$. The expression parameters of conventional 3DMM and AU parameters of our improved AU-3DMM are taken as input, respectively, and the AU detection results evaluated using accuracy and F1-score are shown in Table 2. It can be observed that our AU-3DMM model achieves better AU detection performance on both accuracy and F1-score, which verifies the effectiveness of our proposed model on AU modeling.

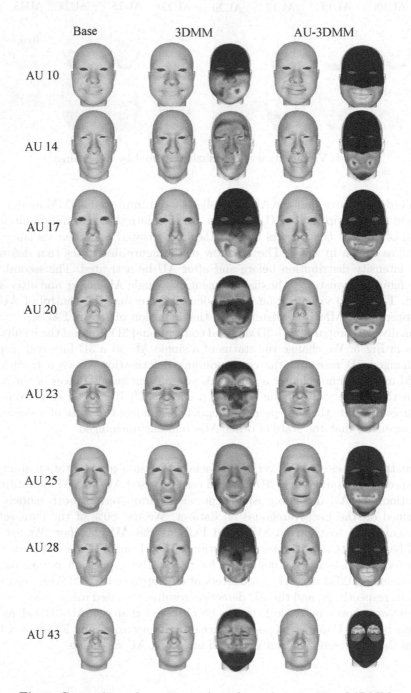

Fig. 5. Comparison of experimental results with conventional 3DMM

Table 2. Performance comparison of models for the different classifier

Classifier	AU	Metrics			
		Accuracy		F1-score	
		3DMM	AU-3DMM	3DMM	AU-3DMM
SVM	AU10	79.12	84.41	78.25	70.97
	AU14	62.81	86.67	62.46	86.03
	AU20	53.25	85.26	51.63	80.66
	AU25	80.61	88.42	78.25	87.55
	AU28	67.89	71.93	66.32	65.81
	AU43	63.77	88.07	67.02	87.31
	AVG	67.91	**84.13**	67.32	**79.72**
FCN	AU10	83.51	86.67	64.44	85.61
	AU14	74.74	87.02	70.54	89.23
	AU20	70.26	88.77	73.05	88.22
	AU25	93.68	95.09	86.67	79.81
	AU28	74.01	78.75	54.44	75.34
	AU43	71.93	95.09	77.13	93.81
	AVG	78.02	**88.57**	71.05	**85.34**

5   Conclusion

In this paper, we propose an improved 3DMM model (AU-3DMM) by combining FACS and 3DMM. The proposed AU-3DMM realizes the expression modeling of facial movements at the local AU level so that parameters can be used to control the AU state. Moreover, the model can generate many 3D faces with specific AU annotations, which is of great help to the study of 3D facial expressions. In addition, AU parameters can also be used as a low-dimensional representation of facial expression information, combined with deep neural networks can further improve the performance of the model, which is also our future research direction. Another future direction for our research is to introduce more AUs so that we can control the generated 3D facial expressions beyond the 8 AU combinations used in this paper.

Acknowledgment. This work is supported by the National Natural Science Foundation of China (No. 61503277).

References

1. Amos, B., Ludwiczuk, B., Satyanarayanan, M.: Openface: a general-purpose face recognition library with mobile applications. Tech. rep., CMU-CS-16-118, CMU School of Computer Science (2016)

2. Basso, C., Vetter, T., Blanz, V.: Regularized 3D morphable models. In: First IEEE International Workshop on Higher-Level Knowledge in 3D Modeling and Motion Analysis, 2003. HLK 2003, pp. 3–10. IEEE (2003)
3. Blanz, V., Vetter, T.: A morphable model for the synthesis of 3D faces. In: Proceedings of the 26th Annual Conference on Computer Graphics and Interactive Techniques, pp. 187–194 (1999)
4. Cao, C., Weng, Y., Zhou, S., Tong, Y., Zhou, K.: FaceWarehouse: a 3D facial expression database for visual computing. IEEE Trans. Visual. Comput. Graph. **20**(3), 413–425 (2013)
5. Chen, Y., Song, G., Shao, Z., Cai, J., Cham, T.J., Zheng, J.: GeoConv: geodesic guided convolution for facial action unit recognition. arXiv preprint arXiv:2003.03055 (2020)
6. Cosker, D., Krumhuber, E., Hilton, A.: A FACS valid 3D dynamic action unit database with applications to 3D dynamic morphable facial modeling. In: 2011 International Conference on Computer Vision, pp. 2296–2303. IEEE (2011)
7. Deng, Y., Yang, J., Chen, D., Wen, F., Tong, X.: Disentangled and controllable face image generation via 3D imitative-contrastive learning. In: Proceedings of the IEEE/CVF Conference on Computer Vision and Pattern Recognition, pp. 5154–5163 (2020)
8. Ekman, P., Friesen, W.V.: Manual for the Facial Action Coding System. Consulting Psychologists Press (1978)
9. Li, W., Abtahi, F., Zhu, Z., Yin, L.: EAC-Net: a region-based deep enhancing and cropping approach for facial action unit detection. In: 2017 12th IEEE International Conference on Automatic Face & Gesture Recognition (FG 2017), pp. 103–110. IEEE (2017)
10. Lin, J., Yuan, Y., Shao, T., Zhou, K.: Towards high-fidelity 3D face reconstruction from in-the-wild images using graph convolutional networks. In: Proceedings of the IEEE/CVF Conference on Computer Vision and Pattern Recognition, pp. 5891–5900 (2020)
11. Liu, Z., Dong, J., Zhang, C., Wang, L., Dang, J.: Relation modeling with graph convolutional networks for facial action unit detection. In: Ro, Y.M., et al. (eds.) Relation modeling with graph convolutional networks for facial action unit detection. LNCS, vol. 11962, pp. 489–501. Springer, Cham (2020). https://doi.org/10.1007/978-3-030-37734-2_40
12. Liu, Z., Liu, D., Wu, Y.: Region based adversarial synthesis of facial action units. In: Ro, Y.M., et al. (eds.) MMM 2020. LNCS, vol. 11962, pp. 514–526. Springer, Cham (2020). https://doi.org/10.1007/978-3-030-37734-2_42
13. Liu, Z., Song, G., Cai, J., Cham, T.J., Zhang, J.: Conditional adversarial synthesis of 3D facial action units. Neurocomputing **355**, 200–208 (2019)
14. Mirza, M., Osindero, S.: Conditional generative adversarial nets. arXiv preprint arXiv:1411.1784 (2014)
15. Niinuma, K., Ertugrul, I.O., Cohn, J.F., Jeni, L.A.: Synthetic expressions are better than real for learning to detect facial actions. In: Proceedings of the IEEE/CVF Winter Conference on Applications of Computer Vision, pp. 1248–1257 (2021)
16. Pham, T.T.D., Kim, S., Lu, Y., Jung, S.W., Won, C.S.: Facial action units-based image retrieval for facial expression recognition. IEEE Access **7**, 5200–5207 (2019)
17. Roth, J., Tong, Y., Liu, X.: Adaptive 3D face reconstruction from unconstrained photo collections. In: Proceedings of the IEEE Conference on Computer Vision and Pattern Recognition, pp. 4197–4206 (2016)

18. Shao, Z., Liu, Z., Cai, J., Ma, L.: Deep adaptive attention for joint facial action unit detection and face alignment. In: Ferrari, V., Hebert, M., Sminchisescu, C., Weiss, Y. (eds.) ECCV 2018. LNCS, vol. 11217, pp. 725–740. Springer, Cham (2018). https://doi.org/10.1007/978-3-030-01261-8_43
19. Shi, T., Yuan, Y., Fan, C., Zou, Z., Shi, Z., Liu, Y.: Face-to-parameter translation for game character auto-creation. In: Proceedings of the IEEE/CVF International Conference on Computer Vision, pp. 161–170 (2019)
20. Song, X., et al.: Unsupervised learning facial parameter regressor for action unit intensity estimation via differentiable renderer. In: Proceedings of the 28th ACM International Conference on Multimedia, pp. 2842–2851 (2020)
21. Suwajanakorn, S., Kemelmacher-Shlizerman, I., Seitz, S.M.: Total moving face reconstruction. In: Fleet, D., Pajdla, T., Schiele, B., Tuytelaars, T. (eds.) ECCV 2014. LNCS, vol. 8692, pp. 796–812. Springer, Cham (2014). https://doi.org/10.1007/978-3-319-10593-2_52
22. Tewari, A., et al.: MOFA: model-based deep convolutional face autoencoder for unsupervised monocular reconstruction. In: Proceedings of the IEEE International Conference on Computer Vision Workshops, pp. 1274–1283 (2017)
23. Tran, L., Liu, X.: Nonlinear 3D face morphable model. In: Proceedings of the IEEE Conference on Computer Vision and Pattern Recognition, pp. 7346–7355 (2018)
24. Vemulapalli, R., Agarwala, A.: A compact embedding for facial expression similarity. In: Proceedings of the IEEE/CVF Conference on Computer Vision and Pattern Recognition, pp. 5683–5692 (2019)
25. Ververas, E., Zafeiriou, S.: SliderGAN: synthesizing expressive face images by sliding 3D blendshape parameters. Int. J. Comput. Vis. **128**(10), 2629–2650 (2020)
26. Walecki, R., Rudovic, O., Pavlovic, V., Schuller, B., Pantic, M.: Deep structured learning for facial action unit intensity estimation. In: 2017 IEEE Conference on Computer Vision and Pattern Recognition (CVPR) (2017)
27. Wu, R., Lu, S.: LEED: label-free expression editing via disentanglement. In: Vedaldi, A., Bischof, H., Brox, T., Frahm, J.-M. (eds.) ECCV 2020. LNCS, vol. 12357, pp. 781–798. Springer, Cham (2020). https://doi.org/10.1007/978-3-030-58610-2_46
28. Zhang, X., et al.: BP4D-spontaneous: a high-resolution spontaneous 3D dynamic facial expression database. Image Vis. Comput. **32**(10), 692–706 (2014)
29. Zhang, Z., et al.: Multimodal spontaneous emotion corpus for human behavior analysis. In: Proceedings of the IEEE Conference on Computer Vision and Pattern Recognition, pp. 3438–3446 (2016)
30. Zhu, W., Wu, H., Chen, Z., Vesdapunt, N., Wang, B.: ReDa: reinforced differentiable attribute for 3D face reconstruction. In: Proceedings of the IEEE/CVF Conference on Computer Vision and Pattern Recognition, pp. 4958–4967 (2020)

Semantic Guided Multi-directional Mixed-Color 3D Printing

Lifang Wu[✉], Tianqin Yang, Yupeng Guan, Ge Shi, Ye Xiang, and Yisong Gao

Faculty of Information Technology, Beijing University of Technology, Beijing, China
lfwu@bjut.edu.cn

Abstract. Fused deposition model (FDM) 3D printing technology, which directly manufactures physical objects from digital 3D models, has become a research hotspot in the manufacturing field in recent years. The current 3D printing has problems such as single printing direction and monotonous printing color. These problems usually waste more human and material resources. To address this problem, this paper studies multi-directional mixed-color FDM 3D printing technology. By introducing a five-axis mechanical system, the model is divided into multiple components that can be printed in different direction to realize multi-directional printing; furthermore, a extrusion head with color mixing function is designed to realize colorful printing, combined with the color mixing algorithm, it can mix the three colors of filament according to a certain proportion to achieve the desired color; and then combined with semantic-guided model segmentation to realize printing with user assigned colors. Finally, a control scheme is designed for clean color boundary.

Keywords: 3D printing · Model segmentation · Semantic information · Color mixing · Multi direction printing

1 Introduction

Fused deposition modeling (FDM) is one of the most popular 3D printing technologies. It has a wide range of applications due to its simple principle, low cost, non-polluting, and no special requirements for the printing environment. However, most FDM 3D printers are unidirectional, which print the model in a fixed direction. It is challenging to deal with the printing of some complex shapes. In some cases, it is needed to add the extra supporting structure or to divide the model into several parts and to print and manually assemble all the parts separately. Furthermore, the existing FDM printers prints the object using a kind of material, and the color of the object is monotonous.

To address this problem, Wu L. et al. [1] proposed a multi-directional 3d printing scheme. It replaces the 3-axis mechanical system (Including three translation axes) with a 5-axis system (Including three translation axis and two rotation axes), so that the printing platform can not only translate but also rotate. Furthermore, Gao Y. et al. [2] and Chengkai D. et al. [3] proposed a novel multi-directional 3D printing model decomposition method that enables printing with minimal support material cost. For model segmentation, the

Y. Peng et al. (Eds.): ICIG 2021, LNCS 12890, pp. 106–117, 2021.
https://doi.org/10.1007/978-3-030-87361-5_9

commonly used methods are skeleton extraction based on mesh shrinkage [4], skeleton extraction based on the mean curvature flow of the model surface [5], skeleton extraction, and segmentation based on shape diameter function [6], and so on. Strictly speaking, the segmentation results of these methods are printable, but do not contain semantic information directly. After the model is decomposed into several components, each of which could be printed in a single direction. Moreover, the components are printed sequentially in different directions.

Furthermore, the color printing is suitable for multi-directional printing. However, the existed color printing is implemented by changing the material of different colors. And the color types are limited by the material colors. In the real application scenarios, different users possibly like different colors to the different parts of the model and users like to assign the color layout for the model by themselves. It is obvious that the color of printing material is far from enough. If we could composite color on demand in the printing process, it will raise the level of 3D printing and extend the application.

Motivated by the above, this paper proposes a semantics-guided multi-directional mixed color FDM 3D printing scheme. It can print the objects with the user assigned color. The system is composed of hardware and software. The hardware includes a 5-axis mechanical system, a three-input extruder, and the printing platform. The software is composed of user assigned model semantics and colors, semantics-guided model segmentation algorithm, color mixing control and color switching control scheme. Using the prototype system, some example objects are printed. The experimental results show that the proposed scheme can print the objects with the user assigned colors.

The main contributions of this paper are as follows.

1) A multi-directional mixed color FDM 3D printing scheme is proposed and the hardware is designed. It is composed of a 5-axis mechanical system, a 3-input extruder and a printing platform. And a color mixing control scheme is designed for mixing color in proportion. A color switching control scheme is designed for clear color boundary.
2) A semantic guided model segmentation algorithm is proposed. The model is firstly segmented and the color is assigned by users. Furthermore, the printability of each component from the user segmentation is analyzed and it is re-segmented if it is not printable in single direction.
3) A prototype system is established to integrating the designed hardware and the software. And some samples are printed with the color user assigned.

2   The System

2.1   The Hardware

The hardware is shown in Fig. 1. It includes four parts: five-axis mechanical system, 3-input extruder the printing platform and computer. The five-axis mechanical system can adjust the position and direction of the printing platform, the 3-input extruder can mix three colors of PLA filament into the desired color on demand, and the objects are printed on the platform. Computer is the interaction tool between the user and the printer.

The five-axis mechanical unit is proposed to include three translation axes (X-axis, Y-axis and Z-axis) and two rotation axes (A-axis, B-axis), A-axis rotates around X-axis, B-axis rotates around Z-axis. The printing direction can be extended by the five-axis mechanical system to meet the need of printing in any direction. In order to avoid the collision between the extruder and the printing platform, the printing work range in this paper is the upper hemispherical surface with the printing platform in the horizontal state as the demarcation. So, before each component starts printing convert the normal vector of its bottom surface to the vertical upward direction.

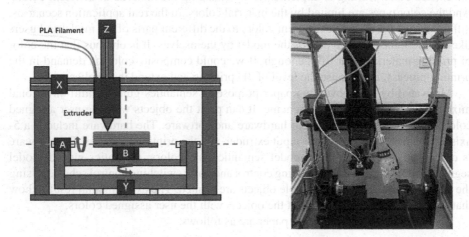

Fig. 1. Multi-directional FDM 3D printer.

2.2 The Software

The block diagram of the software is shown in Fig. 2. Among them, color mixing control and color switching control are described in detail in Sect. 3; user assigned model semantics and colors, and semantics-guided model segmentation will be described in detail in Sect. 4. After this, the printable G-code is generated.

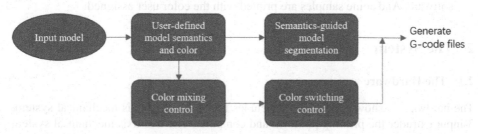

Fig. 2. Software system flow chart.

3   Color Mixing Scheme

3.1   Extruder with Multiple Inputs

The color mixing printhead adopts the structure of three inputs and one output, which can mix up to three colors of PLA materials at the same time. The printhead contains cooling fan, heat sink, heating module, temperature sensor, nozzle and other major parts (see Fig. 3). Three kinds of material are input into the heating module for mixing, then the material with the mixed colored is extruded from the nozzle.

Printing materials of 3 colors is feed into the extruder in proportion so that the specific user assigned color could be obtained. The proposed remote extrusion design for this part, with three MK8 extruders installed away from the printhead, can greatly reduce the weight on the printhead, reduce the inertia of movement during printing, and improve accuracy.

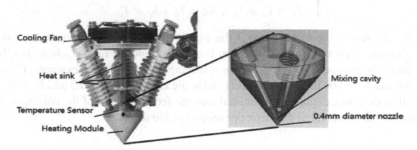

Fig. 3. The structure schematic of the 3-input extruder.

3.2   Color Mixing Control

Usually we choose three basic materials with the color of red, yellow and blue as the three inputs for the extrusion head (see Fig. 4). If the user wants to print the object using a color different from the three colors, the color should be composited by mixing the three filaments in proportion.

Fig. 4. Three kinds material with the basic colors (Color figure online).

We first measure the RGB component of the basic material and then obtain the corresponding CMY components could be obtained, as shown in Table1.

Table 1. Color information for red, yellow and blue filaments.

Basic material	RGB components	CMY components
Red	216,10,28	0,100,97
Yellow	224,206,0	0,8,100
Blue	17,87,237	93,63,0

Suppose the ratios of three basic material with color (a, b, c) are k_a, k_b, k_c respectively. The mixed color x, can be represented as the CMY components in Eq. (1).

$$\begin{cases} C_x = k_a \times C_a + k_b \times C_b + k_c \times C_c \\ M_x = k_a \times M_a + k_b \times M_b + k_c \times M_c \\ Y_x = k_a \times Y_a + k_b \times Y_b + k_c \times Y_c \end{cases} \quad (1)$$

In this Equation, the mixed color is the weighted summation of three basic colors, in other words, if a set of CMY component is assigned, and the ratio $(k_a, k_b, k_c,)$ of three basic materials are could be computed by resolving the Eq. (1). For example, $C_x = 0$, $M_x = 54$ and $Y_x = 98$, the corresponding ratios are $k_a = 0.5$, $k_b = 0.5$ and $k_c = 0$.

Finally, the ratios could be transmitted into the feeding speed of the corresponding material, which is related to the steps per second of the motor.

3.3 Removing the Material with Transition Color

The printed traffic cone with alternated red and white color (see Fig. 5). We can see that there is 3–5 layer whose colors are not white or red, it is mixing of red and white. We named them the transition color. It results that the color switching is not clear. Three kinds of material are mixed in the heating module. In other word, it is a kind of material buffer. When the printed material has been changed, there is still remaining of the mixed material in the chamber. Therefore, the extrude material is mixing of two kinds of materials, which represents the transit color from the color of the material just printed to the color of existing printed material.it is obvious that the material with transition color should be removed to obtain the clean color change.

Fig. 5. Traffic cones with a clear color transition zone (Color figure online).

In order to remove the material with the transition color, it is first needed to estimate the volume of such material. It can be obtained by measuring the size of the chamber. The inner structure of the extruder is shown below (see Fig. 6). the diameter of feeding pipe is 2 mm and length is 21 mm. the feeding pipe is connected with the extruder by using a tubule with diameter 0.4 mm and length 2 mm. the extruder is also with diameter 0.4 mm and length 2 mm. considering the interfacing of different materials, the region between the feeding pipe and the extruder is chamber, its size is about 2 mm^3. Considering the complex structure of the extruder and the liquid printing material is very sticky, the volume of material with the transition color is measured by experiment. And the volume of material with transit color is transmitted into the length of extruder moving. By experiments if the extruder moves about 60 mm, the material with transition color could be squeezed out completely.

In order to remove the material with transition color in the printing process, a printing control scheme with a switching tower is designed. Its main idea is to print a switching tower using the filament with transition color. After the material with transition color is squeezed out completely, the model will be printed with the true desired color. The switching tower is a cuboid. Its height is same as that of the printed model and its length and width both are 6 mm. the inner structure is the ZigZag path with 100% filling (see Fig. 7). By printing a layer of the switching tower, the length of the extruded material

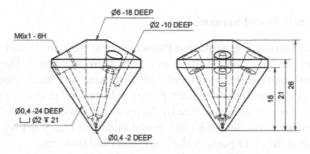

Fig. 6. The internal structure of the extruder.

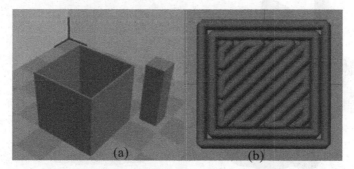

Fig. 7. Illustration of the switching tower. (a): The printed model and the switching tower. (b): The structure of a layer in the switching tower.

is longer than 60 mm, which make sure that the material with transition color could be squeezed out completely.

4 Semantic Guided Model Segmentation

The block diagram of model segmentation is as follows (see Fig. 8). Firstly, the user assigns the segmentation plane and color of different components. And then, all these semantic information are used as input to model segmentation algorithm. Secondly, all the segmentation plane is ranked by the printing sequence. Thirdly, each component is further segmented based on the printability. Then the corresponding components are printed using the user assigned color.

Fig. 8. The block diagram of the semantic guided model segmentation system.

4.1 User Assigned Model Semantics

User Interaction Setting Segmentation Plane. In our system, the model is loaded first, and then the user can freely add multiple planes by their preference. The user controls the translation and rotation of these planes with the mouse, and finally places the planes in the desired segmentation position. Each plane can be resized to ensure the accuracy of the segmentation. The model segmented by the user-selected facet is usually segmented with semantic information, let's take the model bunny in Fig. 9 (a) for example, the bunny is segmented into four parts of the body, head and two ears.

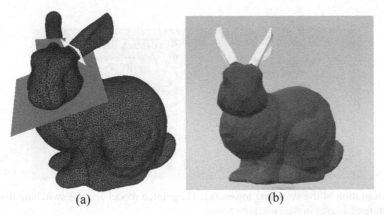

(a)   (b)

Fig. 9. (a)User-inserted segmentation plane. (b)Diagram defining the color of each part (Color figure online).

User Assigned Model Colors. Further, user could continue to assign the color of each component by their preference. For example, here the bunny's body is set to red, its head to blue and its ears to yellow (see Fig. 9 (b)).

4.2 Print Sequence Planning

The user assigned segmentation plane is unordered, we know the model is segmented into four components (see Fig. 10), but their location relation is unknown. In this section, the components are ranked by the printable order.

Fig. 10. Model original sequence.

First, all of the components are marked. The components are marked as 1, 2, 3 and 4 respectively (see Fig. 10). Secondly, the printing process can be represented as a tree structure due to the fixed printing base, and traversing with breadth-first strategy can better avoid the extrusion head colliding with the already printed component.

A method is proposed to quickly build a print hierarchy tree based on trial cutting (see Fig. 12). For an unordered sequence containing n partitioned planes, two planes are extracted according to an ordered permutation to obtain $n(n-1)/2$ sets of plane pairs. For each plane pair, set as $\{pl_i, pl_j\}$, use the method of keeping the lower half of the partition line and removing the upper half of the partition line, first try to cut according to pl_i and then keep the lower half, and then try to cut the lower half of the model according to pl_j; if there is no intersection line when trying to cut according to pl_j, the method is considered unreasonable and marked as 1 for the time being, otherwise marked as 0; after that, flip the order of plane pairs and try to cut again, that is, first try to cut according to pl_j and then try to cut according to pl_i. If there is no intersection line in the test cut according to pl_j, then it is considered unreasonable and marked as 1. If $\{pl_i, pl_j\} = 1$ and $\{pl_j, pl_i\} = 0$, it means that pl_j should be segment before pl_i, add 1 to the level of pl_j and add pl_j to the set of subnodes of pl_i; conversely, add 1 to the level of pl_i and add pl_i to the set of subnodes of pl_j; if $\{pl_i, pl_j\} = \{pl_j, pl_i\} = 0$, then means that the order of the two segmented planes do not affect each other and the hierarchy is maintained. When all the $n(n-1)/2$ pairs of segmentation planes have completed the trial cut, a printed hierarchy tree can be built based on the set of hierarchies and sub-nodes, and then the segmentation order can be obtained.

Four components are ranked by the printing order, and the print hierarchy tree has been created (see Fig. 11).

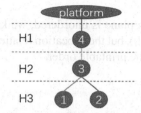

Fig. 11. Printing hierarchy tree for multi-directional 3D printing.

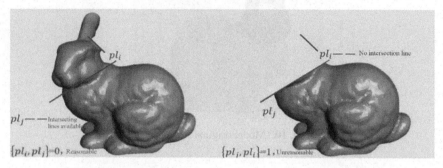

Fig. 12. Fast print hierarchy tree building based on inverse trial cut.

4.3 Subdivision of Components

After the print hierarchy tree is built, the overhang area of each component in its print direction could be estimated. The model is allowed to have a small amount of overhang. When the overhang area of a component is greater than a threshold (25 mm^2 is used in this paper), the component should be further segmented. Here, a genetic algorithm-based optimization method proposed by Gao et al. [2] is used to find the solution with

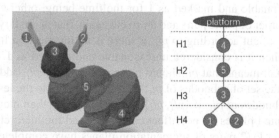

Fig. 13. The result of model sub-division and the new print hierarchy tree.

the least overhanging area. To prevent over-segmentation of the model, an upper limit is set for each component, and special attention should be paid here to treat the segmented plane of the current component as the bottom surface (platform) to prevent collisions in the printing process due to cutting the bottom surface. Finally, the segmentation plane generated by subdivision is supplemented to the hierarchy tree (see Fig. 13).

5   Experiment

In this section, two experiments are conducted. The first one is to compare the printed objects using the printing control scheme with or without a switching tower. Then some models with user assigned colors and the printed objects are demonstrated.

5.1   Effectiveness of Color Switching Scheme

In order to test the effectiveness of the color switching scheme, a model cubic of size 20 mm × 20 mm × 20 mm with three colors red, yellow and blue (see Fig. 14) is printed. One is the printed object with the switching tower as shown in Fig. 14 (a), and the other is printed without the switching tower as shown in Fig. 14 (b). It is obvious that the color transition in the model printed by adding the switching tower is clear, while in Fig. 14(b) there is transition color as marked in the rectangle with red dash line. This experiment demonstrates that the accurate color control could be implemented by using the switching tower.

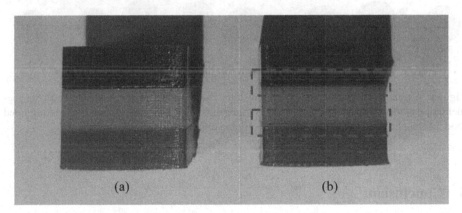

Fig. 14.   Printed test model. (a) With switch tower. (b) Without switch tower (Color figure online).

5.2   Some Examples

In this Section, some objects are printed with the used assigned colors. We printed models of bunny, squirrel and Mickey Mouse head (see Fig. 15). The color of the bunny was set as a red body, blue head and yellow ears. The squirrel was set as a white lower body and tail, light blue upper limbs and head, and yellow ears. Mickey Mouse's head is set to green, and the ears are set to dark red and purple respectively. The first column is the user segmentation, the second column is the user assigned color and the third column is the results of semantic guided model segmentation. In the first row, the body of the bunny is not printable and it should be further segmented into two components. And the last column is the printed object with the user assigned colors.

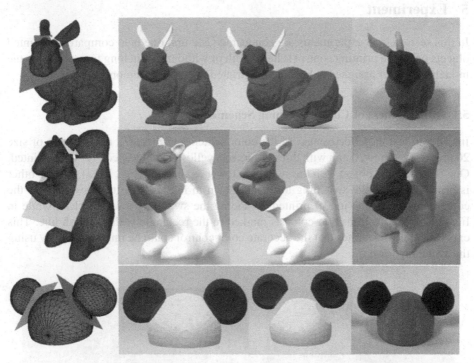

Fig. 15. Model segmentation and printing results. The first column: the model and user-set segmentation planes. The second column: the user assigned colors. The third column: semantic guided model segmentation. The forth column: the printed objects (Color figure online).

6   Conclusion

In this paper we propose and implement a multi-directional mixed color 3D printing scheme. It can print the model with the color user assigned. It realizes the functions including the users segment the model by themselves and assign the color of each component of the model by their preference. And a switching color control scheme is proposed to make sure that the color is clearly switched.

Acknowledgments. This work is supported in part by Beijing Municipal Education Committee Science Foundation (KZ202110005007).

References

1. Wu, L., Yu, M., Gao, Y., Yan, D., Liu, L.: Multi-DOF 3D printing with visual surveillance. In: SIGGRAPH Asia 2017 Posters, pp.1–2 (2017)
2. Gao, Y., Wu L., Yan, D., Nan, L.: Near support-free multi-directional 3D printing via global-optimal decomposition. In: Graphical Models (2019)
3. Dai, C., Wang, C., Wu, C., Lefebvre, S., Fang, G., Liu, Y.: Support-free volume printing by multi-axis motion. ACM Trans. Graphics 37(4), 1–14 (2018)
4. Au, O.K.: Skeleton extraction by mesh contraction. ACM Trans. Graphics 27(3), 1–10 (2008)
5. Tagliasacchi, A., Alhashim, I., Olson, M., Zhang, H.: Mean curvature skeletons. Eurographics Assoc. Blackwell Publishing Ltd 31(5), 1735–1744 (2012)
6. Shapira, L., Shamir, A., Cohen-Or, D.: Consistent mesh partitioning and skeletonization using the shape diameter function. Vis. Comput. 24(4), 249 (2008)

KeypointNet: Ranking Point Cloud for Convolution Neural Network

Zuodong Gao⬡, Yanyun Qu(✉)⬡, and Cuihua Li

Xiamen University, Xiamen, China
yyqu@xmu.edu.cn

Abstract. In recent years, convolutional neural networks on point clouds have greatly improved the performance of point cloud classification and segmentation. However, the irregularity and disorder of point clouds make the convolution operation ill-suited to preserve the spatial-local structure and make the existing convolution networks very shallow. In order to solve the problems, we propose a novel pre-processor network named KeypointNet which ranks the point cloud according to the contribution to the final task, such as classification and segmentation. With the ordered point cloud, a convolution neural network on point clouds goes as deeper as possible similar to that on images. Two scoring mechanisms: directly scoring (DS) and gradually scoring (GS), are designed based on a pre-trained PointNet which is easily and fast trained. Both scoring mechanisms score a point depending on its contribution to the output of PointNet. The former scores the point cloud only one time and the later scores the point cloud on grade level. KeypointNet can be unified with any existing convolution neural networks on point clouds. Extensive experiments demonstrate that our method is effective and efficient and achieves SOTA classification results and comparable segmentation results, while greatly reducing space consumption.

Keywords: Point cloud · Classification · Segmentation.

1 Introduction

With the rising of modern 3D sensors such as laser scanners, point clouds are easily obtained and widely used in indoor navigation [29], self-driving vehicles [13], robotics [27], and so on. Convolution neural networks on point clouds have achieved promising performance on some visual tasks such as classification and segmentation. EdgeConv [21] uses the coordinates concatenating its pairwise distance as the edge feature and uses multiple layer perception as the filter. X-Conv [9] learns a transformation, which projects the local information of a point into a potential space, and then performs standard convolution. Most existing convolution neural networks on point clouds pay more attention to the spatial correlation per point while neglecting the ordering of point cloud data, and in order to reduce the recourse consumption, they have to select some points

© Springer Nature Switzerland AG 2021
Y. Peng et al. (Eds.): ICIG 2021, LNCS 12890, pp. 118–129, 2021.
https://doi.org/10.1007/978-3-030-87361-5_10

according to some presetting rules which are unordered and independent. Thus, they are ill-suited to use the spatial local correlation. Due to the sparseness, irregularity and disorder of point cloud, the convolution neural networks on point clouds do not go as deeper as those on images in depth and they consume large computational recourses.

Draw lessons from convolutional neural networks on 2D images, which are grid-like data, the ordering and regularity make the convolution operator on images effective in exploiting the spatial correlation. Thus, the ordered point cloud data favor for the convolution operator. There are some methods dealing with the ordering for point clouds. Most deep models for 3D point cloud need a pre-processing operation, such as transforming irregular point clouds into either voxel representations [16,20,23] or 2D images by view projection [2,3,26]. However, they result in the loss of fidelity of the local shape or the loss of the natural invariance of the point cloud.

In order to solve the ordering problem, unlike the mentioned voxel representation methods and view projection methods, we design the ranking network named KeypointNet, which ranks the point cloud data according to their contribution to the final task. Take the classification task as an example, the output of a classifier is closely related to the features. Because PointNet is widely used for point cloud classification and easy and fast to train, we measure the importance of a point to the output as the criteria of ranking. We design two score mechanisms: directly scoring (DS) and gradually scoring (GS). Both score mechanisms depend on a pre-trained PointNet. The former scores the point cloud only one time and the later scores the point cloud on grade level. According to the scores, we rank the points.

With the ordered point cloud data, we design the downsampling layer, that is, the top k points are treated as the Keypoints. KeypointNet can be treated as a pre-processor which presents the ordered points and uses only one time during testing. Moreover, we form the representation feature with the keypoints by combining the local point features in the neighbor of Keypoints. Thus the keypoints and their local structural information make the convolution neural networks go deeper without large spatial recourse consumption on searching critical points. With the usage of KeypointNet, the downsampling method and aggregation of keypoints, each step is based on the contribution to the final result, so our method is interpretable and result-guided.

2   Method

2.1   KeypointNet

KeypointNet is designed for ranking the point cloud data, and its backbone is PointNet without the transformation layers, which is pre-trained on the corresponding task, and after that, the score block (Scorer) is added behind the last max-pooling layer of PointNet. The scorer outputs the ordered point cloud data. The architecture of KeypointNet is shown in Fig. 1 a). The unordered points are

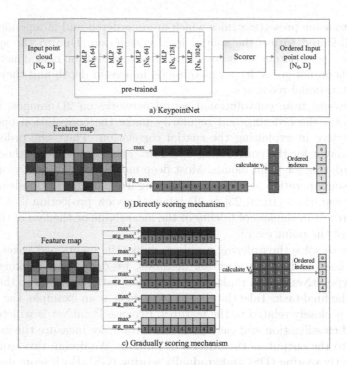

Fig. 1. a) The architecture of KeypointNet b) Directly scoring mechanism c) Gradually scoring mechanism.

fed into KeypointNet and pass through five multi-layer perceptions (MLP) followed by the Scorer. And KeypointNet outputs the ordered point cloud. In the Scorer, we design two novel score mechanisms which measure the importance of a point: Directly Scoring (DS) and Gradually Scoring (GS). In order to detail the two score mechanisms, let us represent the features of the point cloud with N_0 points as $P = \{p_i \in \mathbb{R}^D, i = 1, 2, \cdots, N_0\}$, which concatenates the coordinates and RGB vector of a point. Let us denote the operation of MLP as $MLP()$, so the output of the last MLP in KeypointNet is formulated as follows:

$$F_i = MLP(p_i), \forall p_i \in P, \tag{1}$$

where $F_i = \{f_{i1}, f_{i2}, \cdots, f_{iM}\}$ is the M-dimensional feature of the i-th point, and f_{ij} is the element. We compute the importance of a point with the output of the features by the last MLP in KeypointNet.

Directly Scoring (DS): In order to evaluate the importance of a point, DS computes the contribution of a point to the label prediction. As we know, the last pooling layer follows the MLP of PointNet, and the output is fed into the activation layer which outputs the label prediction. The score mechanism of DS is shown in Fig. 1 b). The features F_i form a matrix, and the pooling operation is to find the maximum of each column, which is formulated as:

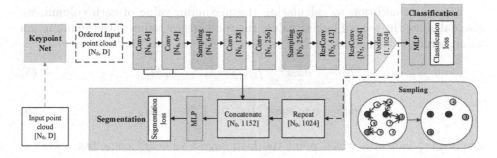

Fig. 2. The architecture of Instantiation Network.

$$f_j = \max_{i=1,2,\cdots,N_0} f_{ij}, \ j = 1, 2, \cdots, M, \tag{2}$$

$$idx_j = \arg\max_{i=1,2,\cdots,N_0} f_{ij}, \ j = 1, 2, \cdots, M, \tag{3}$$

where idx_j indicates the point which has the maximum value in the j-th dimension. $idx = [idx_1, idx_2, \cdots, idx_M]$ is a vector of these values. And the importance of a point is defined as its frequency in the vector idx which can be formulated as:

$$v_i = \sum_{j=1}^{M} \mathbb{1}(idx_j == i), \ i = 1, 2, \cdots, N_0, \tag{4}$$

where v_i is the score of each point and $\mathbb{1}(x)$ an indicator and it is equal to 1 when x is true, otherwise 0. In downsampling operation, we choose N_1 points with the highest value of v_i as the keypoints.

However this method has a disadvantage: Keypoints may degenerate to only a small part of the points. In fact, not all the points scores are positive. For those points without contributions to the pooling operation, their v_i are zero. In our experiments, it is observed that there are only about 20% in the 1024-D features whose importance v_i are greater than zero. In the sampling layer, the presetting number of points may be 50% of the points. That means the number of keypoints is much smaller than the presetting number of points in the downsampling layer, which results in the lose of information.

To avoid this disadvantage, the simplest way is to generate the higher dimension features. Obviously, the larger the dimension M is, the more points scores are positive values. In our experiments, the dimension M is experimentally set to 2800, which leads to at least 50% v_i are not zero. This means that the relation between the dimension M and the number of points whose score is positive is not linear.

The disadvantages of this method are obvious. It can be only used when N_0 is 1024, but in fact, the number of points in the segmentation tasks is 2048 or 4096, so it requires M unachievable large.

Gradually Scoring(GS): In order to mitigate the disadvantage of DS, we pave another way to calculate the importance of point, see Fig. 1 c).

Firstly, in addition to calculating the maximum value of each column, we also calculate the second largest value, the third largest value until the minimum value, which is formulated as:

$$f_j^k = \max_{i=1,2,\cdots,N_0}^{k} f_{ij}, \ j = 1, 2, \cdots, M, \tag{5}$$

$$idx_j^k = \arg\_max_{i=1,2,\cdots,N_0}^{k} f_{ij}, \ j = 1, 2, \cdots, M, \tag{6}$$

where idx_j^k indicates which point the k-th largest value f_j^k come from. $idx^k = [idx_1^k, idx_2^k, \cdots, idx_M^k]$ is a vector that records the source of the k-th largest value of each column. The importance of each point will be defined by its frequency from idx^1 to idx^{N_0}. This can be formulated as:

$$v_i^k = \sum_{j=1}^{M} \mathbb{1}(idx_j^k == i), \ i = 1, 2, \cdots, N_0, \tag{7}$$

where v_i is all the contributions of each point to the k-th largest value. $Vi = [v_i^1, v_i^2, \cdots, v_i^{N_0}]$ is the score of the i-th point.

Since the score of each point is a vector but not a scalar, we need to redefine the comparison rules. If V_i is greater than V_j, then there must be a t such that V_i^k is equal to V_j^k for all k less than t, and V_i^t is greater than V_j^t. Then we can select N_1 points with the highest score as the keypoints.

Because the score of each point is a vector, and it is obvious that there is no point whose score vector is zero, so GS overcomes the shortcomings of DS. GS can be applied to any size point cloud. The disadvantage of this method is that it is not as interpretable as DS. Because in PointNet, except the maximum value of each column is used for the final task, other values are not used. We use other values to evaluate the score of a point, which is not convincing.

Relationship between DS and GS: In fact, GS is related to DS. We can directly implement GS by DS, which makes GS also interpretable. Let the initial feature matrix denoted by F, which contains N_0 features with M dimensions corresponding to N_0 points. We firstly conduct DS on the feature matrix F. Then we take out the points whose v_i is not 0 according to v_i from large to small, and get new feature matrix F by setting these points to 0 in the old F. Then, repeat the above operation until feature matrix F is 0 matrix, that is, all points are taken out. We determine the importance of the points in the order in which they are taken out. The earlier points are taken out, the more important they are.

Algorithm 1 summarizes the process. In the third step of the algorithm, the indexes obtained by DS are vi not 0 and arranged from large to small. This implementation is different from the previous GS implementation, but the result is exactly the same. This implementation exposes the relationship between DS and GS and increases our trust in GS.

Table 1. Classification results on ScanObjectNN.

	OBJ_ONLY	OBJ_BG	PB_T25	PB_T25_R	PB_T50_R	PB_T50_RS
3DmFV [1]	73.8	68.2	67.1	67.4	63.5	63.0
PointNet [14]	79.2	73.3	73.5	72.7	68.2	68.2
SpiderCNN [25]	79.5	77.1	78.1	77.7	73.8	73.7
PointNet++ [15]	84.3	82.3	82.7	81.4	79.1	77.9
DGCNN [21]	86.2	82.8	83.3	81.5	80.0	78.1
PointCNN [9]	85.5	86.1	83.6	82.5	78.5	78.0
Random+EdgeConv	87.1	86.9	86.3	84.3	80.8	81.2
FPS+EdgeConv	87.2	87.7	86.6	85.5	81.4	80.2
Gpool+EdgeConv	81.2	78.6	82.9	81.0	76.6	76.5
WCPL+EdgeConv	82.6	82.2	80.2	79.4	75.7	74.5
DS+EdgeConv(DGCNN)	**88.8**	**90.5**	**87.9**	**86.3**	82.6	**82.8**
GS+EdgeConv(DGCNN)	88.6	89.2	87.5	86.1	**82.8**	82.2
DS+MSG(PointNet++)	86.8	89.1	86.2	84.4	82.1	82.4
GS+MSG(PointNet++)	86.6	88.3	85.4	84.3	81.6	82.3

Algorithm 1. Using DS to implement GS.

Require:
  input feature, F;
  Directly Scoring, DS;
1: ordered_indexes=[];
2: **while** F is not 0 matrix **do**
3:    indexes=DS(F)
4:    keypoin_indexes.append(index)
5:    F[indexes]=0
6: **end while**
7: **return** keypoin_indexes

2.2 KeypointNet Instantiation for CNN

We embed KeypointNet which is used in downsampling layers with convolution neural networks. The architecture of the instantiation network is shown in Fig. 2, which contains three components: KeypointNet, convolutional layers, and sampling layers. The convolution layer can be instantiated by the convolution of Point Cloud, such as EdgeConv [21], MSG [15], etc. KeypointNet, which relies on a pre-trained PointNet [14], takes unordered point cloud as input, and outputs ordered point cloud. In the sampling layer, the keypoints are firstly selected and their local features are aggregated similar to the pooling operation in the 2D convolution neural network. As for the classification task, the output of the pooling layer is passed into MLP, and the label is obtained. As for the segmentation task, the output of the pooling layer is concatenated with the output of the first convolution module which is passed into MLP, and the segmentation output is obtained.

2.3 Sampling Layer

In the downsampling layer, the keypoints should be described by aggregating its neighbor features. The description method is somewhat like the standard 2D pooling operation, which regards the largest feature in its neighbor features as the keypoint feature. It is formulated as:

$$F_i^{'} = \max_{\forall F_j \in \mathcal{N}(i)} F_j, i = 1, 2, \cdots, N_1. \tag{8}$$

$\mathcal{N}(i)$ is a set of features of the i-th point neighbors and N_1 is $N_0/2$ or $N_0/4$. In this way, key points carry their own local information into the next layer, which makes the information of key points more abundant. At the same time, some non key points can also integrate their own information into the key points into the next layer, reducing information loss and improving network performance.

3 Experimental Results

3.1 Comparison on Classification

Datasets: ModelNet40 [23] contains 9843 training samples and 2468 testing samples with 40 categories. ScanObjectNN [19] contains six sub-datasets: OBJ_ONLY, OBJ_BG, PB_T25, PB_T25R, PB_T50_R and PB_T50_RS.

Experiment Setting: The optimizer used in our experiments is stochastic gradient descent (SGD). The initial learning rate is 0.01, and it decays by 0.8 times every 20 epochs. Batch Normalization is used after each layer of convolution. Activation function is Leaky ReLU. And Dropout technology is applied to alleviate the over-fitting problem in the full connection layer. The number of downsampling points N_1 and N_2 in the KeypointNet instantiation are set to 512, 256, respectively.

Experimental Results: We report the overall accuracy on ModelNet40. In Table 2, we compare our method with other approaches. DS+EdgeConv achieves the best classification results, which is at least 0.4% higher than the other algorithms. In addition, compared with EdgeConv, we have gained 1.3% improvement. DS+MSG also exceeds PointNet++ 2.1%. Interestingly, DS method is usually better than GS method in the experiment. We think that it is because the maximum point cloud embedding as a reference can better reflect the importance of each point.

Evaluation performance on ScanObjectNN is reported in Table 1. Our methods exceed all the comparison models. Especially the result of DS+EdgeConv on PB_T50_RS reaches 82.8% which outperforms the previous best method by 4.7%. Specifically, except PointCNN [9] and ours, all methods performed worse on OBJ_BG compared with OBJ_ONLY. It demonstrates that our model is more robust to the disturbance caused by confusion between foreground and background points. Just because our method can select the keypoints by Keypoint-Net, it automatically removes the noise points in the downsampling, it will be

Table 2. Classification results on ModelNet40.

	Input	Acc.
PointwiseCNN [6]	1024 points	86.1
PointNet [14]	1024 points	89.2
PointNet++ [15]	1024 points	90.7
PointNet++ [15]	5000 points+normal	91.9
Kd-Network [7]	1024 points	91.8
ShapeContextNet [24]	1024 points	90.0
KCNet [17]	1024 points	91.0
PointCNN [9]	1024 points	92.2
DGCNN [21]	1024 points	92.2
SO-Net [8]	2048 points	90.9
SpiderCNN [25]	1024 points+normal	92.4
Point2Seq [10]	1024 points	92.6
3Dcapsule [4]	1024 points	92.7
PointConv [22]	1024 points+normal	92.5
InterpCNN [11]	1024 points	93.0
ShellNet [28]	1024 points	93.1
KPConv [18]	1024 points	92.9
Random+EdgeConv	1024 points	92.8
FPS+EdgeConv	1024 points	92.6
Gpool+EdgeConv	1024 points	92.4
WCPL+EdgeConv	1024 points	92.5
DS+EdgeConv(DGCNN)	1024 points	**93.5**
GS+EdgeConv(DGCNN)	1024 points	93.1
DS+MSG(PointNet++)	1024 points	92.8
GS+MSG(PointNet++)	1024 points	92.7

robust to the background information. Moreover, compared with ModelNet40, our algorithm is significantly better than others in this more challenging and authentic dataset. This means that our methods are more anti-jamming than vanilla counterparts, more adaptable to complex environments, and have higher practical value.

Taking EdgeConv as an example, we do comparative experiments on ModelNet40 and ScanObjectNN to compare our methods with other downsampling methods. Please refer to the Table 2 and Table 1. Our downsampling methods are leading the way. Especially on ScanObjectNN, our methods are superior to others with a large margin. WCPL [12] is similar to DS, but its effect is very poor. For example, on OBJ_BG, the DS is more than WCPL 8.3%. This is because WCPL is to see the contribution of each point to the middle point cloud embedding, and this point cloud embedding is not related to the task,

Table 3. Segmentation results on ShapeNetPart.

	Mean	Air	Bag	Cap	Car	cCair	Ear.	Gui.	Knife	Lamp	Lap.	Motor	Mug	Pistol	Rocket	Skate	Table
PointNet [14]	83.7	83.4	78.7	82.5	74.9	89.6	73.0	**91.5**	85.9	80.8	95.3	65.2	93.0	81.2	57.9	72.8	80.6
PointNet++ [15]	85.1	82.4	79.0	87.7	77.3	**90.8**	71.8	91.0	85.9	83.7	95.3	**71.6**	94.1	**81.3**	58.7	**76.4**	82.6
Kd-Network [7]	82.3	80.1	74.6	74.3	70.3	88.6	73.5	90.2	87.2	81.0	94.9	57.4	86.7	78.1	51.8	69.9	80.3
SO-Net [8]	84.9	82.8	77.8	**88.0**	77.3	90.6	73.5	90.7	83.9	82.8	94.8	69.1	94.2	80.9	53.1	72.9	83.0
DGCNN [21]	**85.2**	84.0	**83.4**	86.7	77.8	90.6	74.7	91.2	87.5	82.8	**95.7**	66.3	**94.9**	81.1	**63.5**	74.5	82.6
GS+EdgeConv	85.1	**83.9**	82.6	84.5	**78.7**	90.5	**75.9**	91.4	86.4	83.7	95.5	67.0	94.6	80.8	57.4	73.7	**83.2**
GS+MSG	**85.2**	83.7	79.8	86.7	77.3	90.6	73.6	91.3	**87.6**	**83.9**	95.4	66.1	94.1	80.3	60.5	75.5	83.0

Table 4. Segmentation results on S3DIS.

Model	OA%	mAcc%	mIOU%
PointNet [14]	78.6	66.2	47.6
PointNet++ [15]	81.0	67.1	54.5
DGCNN [21]	**84.1**	–	56.1
GS+MSG	82.5	71.2	59.2
GS+EdgeConv	83.6	**72.3**	**59.8**

so the selected point not only does not contribute to the task, but also brings interference. Gpool [5] has learned a scorer, but it is doubtful whether the scorer can really select the more important points. The experimental results show that the points selected by it do not represent the original point cloud very well. Although FPS and Random are simple, they also get better results. But they are not as good as our methods.

3.2   Comparison on Segmentation

Datasets: ShapeNetPart contains 16,881 3D shapes from 16 object categories, annotated with 50 parts in total. S3DIS includes 3D scan point clouds for 6 indoor areas with 272 rooms in total.

Experiment Setting: The optimizer used is Adam. The initial learning rate is 0.001, and every 20 epochs changes to 0.5 times of the original on ShapeNetPart and 0.7 times on S3DIS. Batch Normalization is used after each layer of convolution. Activation function is Leaky ReLU. And Dropout technology is applied to alleviate the over-fitting problem in the full connection layer. N1 is 512 and N2 is 128 on ShapeNetPart. N1 is 1024 and N2 is 256 on S3DIS.

Experimental Results: The experimental results on ShapeNetPart are shown in the Table 3 and the results on S3DIS are shown in the Table 4. The result of our network segmentation is very similar to the mean result of baseline, but it is different in some small class segmentation. It shows that our network can give full play to the convolutions effect of baseline. Of course, due to the limitation of convolutions, our method still has a certain gap compared with some of the most latest methods.

In Table 5, we compare the model sizes of the convolution neural network with and without KeypointNet. It shows that KeypointNet make DGCNN or PointNet++ reduce the memory consumption while the instantiation network with KeypointNet achieve the comparable segmentation results. Among them, GS+MSG reduced memory consumption by 57.9% while GS+EdgeConv reduced memory consumption by 48.8% on ShapeNetPart. And GS+MSG reduced memory consumption by 64.1% while GS+EdgeConv reduced memory consumption by 40.5% on S3DIS. The above results show that our network structure is more practical.

Table 5. Model memory consumption.

Model	Dateset	Batch	Memory	↓
PointNet++	ShapeNetPart	16	9531	–
GS+MSG	ShapeNetPart	16	4012	**57.9%**
DGCNN	ShapeNetPart	32	8795	–
GS+EdgeConv	ShapeNetPart	32	4503	**48.8%**
PointNet++	S3DIS	8	9981	–
GS+MSG	S3DIS	8	3579	**64.1%**
DGCNN	S3DIS	16	10073	–
GS+EdgeConv	S3DIS	16	5989	**40.5%**

4   Conclusion

In this paper, we design KeypointNet to make the irregular and disorder points in order. Two new point cloud sorting methods, directly scoring(DS) and gradually scoring(GS), are proposed. The ordered point cloud favor for the downsampling layer to select more important points. Then instantiating with EdgeConv or MSG, we give two instantiation networks to implement the tasks of point cloud classification and segmentation. Extensive experiments are done and the experimental results show that our method makes the irregular point cloud orderly, which can keep more important points in downsampling layers. KeypointNet make the model size of CNN reduce while achieving superior performance on point cloud classification and comparable performance on point cloud segmentation.

References

1. Ben-Shabat, Y., Lindenbaum, M., Fischer, A.: 3dmfv: 3d point cloud classification in real-time using convolutional neural network. IEEE Robot. Autom. Lett. (99), 1 (2018)
2. Cao, Z., Huang, Q., Karthik, R.: 3d object classification via spherical projections. In: 2017 International Conference on 3D Vision (3DV), pp. 566–574. IEEE (2017)
3. Chen, S., Zheng, L., Zhang, Y., Sun, Z., Xu, K.: Veram: view-enhanced recurrent attention model for 3d shape classification. IEEE Trans. Visual. Comput. Graph. **25**(12), 3244–3257 (2018)
4. Cheraghian, A., Petersson, L.: 3dcapsule: Extending the capsule architecture to classify 3d point clouds. In: 2019 IEEE Winter Conference on Applications of Computer Vision (WACV), pp. 1194–1202. IEEE (2019)
5. Gao, H., Ji, S.: Graph u-nets. arXiv preprint arXiv:1905.05178 (2019)
6. Hua, B.S., Tran, M.K., Yeung, S.K.: Pointwise convolutional neural networks. In: Proceedings of the IEEE Conference on Computer Vision and Pattern Recognition, pp. 984–993 (2018)
7. Klokov, R., Lempitsky, V.: Escape from cells: deep kd-networks for the recognition of 3d point cloud models. In: Proceedings of the IEEE International Conference on Computer Vision, pp. 863–872 (2017)
8. Li, J., Chen, B.M., Hee Lee, G.: So-net: Self-organizing network for point cloud analysis. In: Proceedings of the IEEE Conference on Computer Vision and Pattern Recognition, pp. 9397–9406 (2018)
9. Li, Y., Bu, R., Sun, M., Wu, W., Di, X., Chen, B.: Pointcnn: convolution on x-transformed points. In: Advances in Neural Information Processing Systems, pp. 820–830 (2018)
10. Liu, X., Han, Z., Liu, Y.S., Zwicker, M.: Point2sequence: Learning the shape representation of 3d point clouds with an attention-based sequence to sequence network. In: Proceedings of the AAAI Conference on Artificial Intelligence, vol. 33, pp. 8778–8785 (2019)
11. Mao, J., Wang, X., Li, H.: Interpolated convolutional networks for 3d point cloud understanding. In: Proceedings of the IEEE International Conference on Computer Vision, pp. 1578–1587 (2019)
12. Nezhadarya, E., Taghavi, E., Liu, B., Luo, J.: Adaptive hierarchical down-sampling for point cloud classification. arXiv preprint arXiv:1904.08506 (2019)
13. Qi, C.R., Liu, W., Wu, C., Su, H., Guibas, L.J.: Frustum pointnets for 3d object detection from rgb-d data. In: Proceedings of the IEEE Conference on Computer Vision and Pattern Recognition, pp. 918–927 (2018)
14. Qi, C.R., Su, H., Mo, K., Guibas, L.J.: Pointnet: deep learning on point sets for 3d classification and segmentation. In: Proceedings of the IEEE Conference on Computer Vision and Pattern Recognition, pp. 652–660 (2017)
15. Qi, C.R., Yi, L., Su, H., Guibas, L.J.: Pointnet++: Deep hierarchical feature learning on point sets in a metric space. In: Advances in Neural Information Processing Systems, pp. 5099–5108 (2017)
16. Riegler, G., Osman Ulusoy, A., Geiger, A.: Octnet: learning deep 3d representations at high resolutions. In: Proceedings of the IEEE Conference on Computer Vision and Pattern Recognition, pp. 3577–3586 (2017)
17. Shen, Y., Feng, C., Yang, Y., Tian, D.: Mining point cloud local structures by kernel correlation and graph pooling. In: Proceedings of the IEEE Conference on Computer Vision and Pattern Recognition, pp. 4548–4557 (2018)

18. Thomas, H., Qi, C.R., Deschaud, J.E., Marcotegui, B., Goulette, F., Guibas, L.J.: Kpconv: Flexible and deformable convolution for point clouds. arXiv preprint arXiv:1904.08889 (2019)
19. Uy, M.A., Pham, Q.H., Hua, B.S., Nguyen, T., Yeung, S.K.: Revisiting point cloud classification: a new benchmark dataset and classification model on real-world data. In: Proceedings of the IEEE International Conference on Computer Vision, pp. 1588–1597 (2019)
20. Wang, P.S., Liu, Y., Guo, Y.X., Sun, C.Y., Tong, X.: O-cnn: octree-based convolutional neural networks for 3d shape analysis. Acm Trans. Graph. 36(4), 72 (2017)
21. Wang, Y., Sun, Y., Liu, Z., Sarma, S.E., Bronstein, M.M., Solomon, J.M.: Dynamic graph cnn for learning on point clouds. ACM Trans. Graph. (TOG) 38(5), 146 (2019)
22. Wu, W., Qi, Z., Fuxin, L.: Pointconv: deep convolutional networks on 3d point clouds. In: Proceedings of the IEEE Conference on Computer Vision and Pattern Recognition, pp. 9621–9630 (2019)
23. Wu, Z., et al.: 3d shapenets: a deep representation for volumetric shapes. In: Proceedings of the IEEE Conference on Computer Vision and Pattern Recognition, pp. 1912–1920 (2015)
24. Xie, S., Liu, S., Chen, Z., Tu, Z.: Attentional shapecontextnet for point cloud recognition. In: Proceedings of the IEEE Conference on Computer Vision and Pattern Recognition, pp. 4606–4615 (2018)
25. Xu, Y., Fan, T., Xu, M., Zeng, L., Qiao, Y.: Spidercnn: deep learning on point sets with parameterized convolutional filters. In: Proceedings of the European Conference on Computer Vision (ECCV), pp. 87–102 (2018)
26. Yavartanoo, M., Kim, E.Y., Lee, K.M.: SPNet: deep 3D object classification and retrieval using stereographic projection. In: Jawahar, C.V., Li, H., Mori, G., Schindler, K. (eds.) ACCV 2018. LNCS, vol. 11365, pp. 691–706. Springer, Cham (2019). https://doi.org/10.1007/978-3-030-20873-8_44
27. Zhang, K., et al.: Environmental features recognition for lower limb prostheses toward predictive walking. IEEE Trans. Neural Syst. Rehabil. Eng. 27(3), 465 476 (2019)
28. Zhang, Z., Hua, B.S., Yeung, S.K.: Shellnet: Efficient point cloud convolutional neural networks using concentric shells statistics. In: Proceedings of the IEEE International Conference on Computer Vision, pp. 1607–1616 (2019)
29. Zhu, Y., et al.: Target-driven visual navigation in indoor scenes using deep reinforcement learning. In: 2017 IEEE International Conference on Robotics and Automation (ICRA), pp. 3357–3364. IEEE (2017)

Geometric Context Sensitive Loss and Its Application for Nonrigid Structure from Motion

Fudong Nian[1,2], Shimeng Yang[3], Xia Chen[2,4(✉)], Jun Wang[1], and Gang Lv[1]

[1] School of Advanced Manufacturing Engineering, Hefei University,
Hefei 230601, China
[2] Anhui Provincial Key Laboratory of Multimodal Cognitive Computation,
Anhui University, Hefei 230601, China
[3] School of Computer Science and Technology, Anhui University, Hefei 230601, China
[4] School of Information and Computer, Anhui Agricultural University,
Hefei 230036, China
xiachen@ahau.edu.cn

Abstract. Coordinate prediction is an important signal processing task, which aims to predict 2D or 3D coordinates from a single image or a series of images. Previous techniques utilize Mean Square Error (MSE) loss function to measure the difference between the prediction coordinates and its corresponding ground-truth in training step, which usually assumes that coordinates are independent to each other without considering their correlations, neglecting the geometric context of the object. To address the issue, this paper presents a novel loss function named Geometric Context Sensitive (GCS) loss to model the geometric shape context of general objects by measuring the difference between any pair of prediction coordinates and their corresponding ground-truth coordinates. Our proposed method has several advantages: (1) The proposed GCS loss is trainable and can be optimized by Gauss-Newton in the traditional models. (2) GCS loss can be formulated in both 2D and 3D forms. Thus, the proposed GCS loss is easy to be implemented and can be integrated into current popular 2D/3D coordinates prediction models naturally and effectively, e.g., nonrigid structure from motion. (3) No additional learnable parameters. Though the proposed GCS loss is intuitive in theory, extensive experimental results on several public NRSFM datasets show that GCS loss can significantly boost the performance. We share the implementation code and models of our proposed methods at https://github.com/nianfudong/GCS/tree/master/NRSFM.

Keywords: Loss function design · Geometric context constraint · NRSFM

1 Introduction

Coordinate prediction (or detection) plays a major role in computer vision/ multimedia area, e.g., as illustrated in Fig. 1(a), facial landmark detection aims

© Springer Nature Switzerland AG 2021
Y. Peng et al. (Eds.): ICIG 2021, LNCS 12890, pp. 130–142, 2021.
https://doi.org/10.1007/978-3-030-87361-5_11

(a) The common coordinate prediction tasks.

(b) Illustration of the MSE loss and it's drawback.

Fig. 1. The illustration of the coordinate prediction task and the drawback of conventional MSE loss. (Color figure online)

to predict keypoint positions on face images, Nonrigid Structure from Motion (NRSFM) [11] is to recover the object's 3D shape and 3D pose when given multiple images of a deformable object with a set of corresponding 2D points. Accurate coordinate prediction can be used in a variety of applications such as virtual makeup, face verification, face retrieval and human pose estimation.

In most cases, the geometric shape context of objects can be an important knowledge in human vision to locate their key points. Keypoints of various objects, e.g. facial and body, have strong geometric correlation. From Fig. 1(a) we can realize that *"left mouse corner always on the left of right mouse corner"* or *"the neck always between the waist and the head"*. In this paper, we deem these phenomena as geometric context constraint, and model it can greatly boost the performance of coordinate prediction. It should be noted that considering geometric context is not new in coordinate prediction. For example, Zadeh *et al.* [17] assume that all facial landmarks follow a point distribution model. Liu *et al.* [9] present an adaptive cascade regression model. Similarly, utilizing cascade-based framework to model shape context are also introduced in [15,16]. Beyond 2D domain, there are several methods (e.g. [3,7,18]) being proposed addressing 3D geometric context modeling. Akhter *et al.* [1] demonstrate that gradual 3D shape deformation can be seen as the smooth time-trajectory of a single point within a low-dimensional shape space. But these methods are usually domain specific and complex to be implemented.

In coordinate prediction area, state-of-the-art methods usually put the emphasis on model structure rather than loss function. All methods mentioned above used Mean Square Error (MSE) as a criterion to measure the difference between the prediction and their corresponding ground-truth coordinates. Though effective, MSE only considers the local appearance of keypoints while neglects the geometric correlations among them. As illustrated in Fig. 1(b), we can observe that it may result in a common failure case in which each predicted landmark (green) is close to its corresponding ground-truth (red) but the relative positions between two landmarks are not appropriate. The reason is that MSE implicitly assumes all coordinates are independent and not take advantage of the geometric shape knowledge of the object.

Recently, various outstanding loss function designs demonstrate similar or better performance as complicated model structure. However, how to handle object's geometric context in loss function and how to optimize it while maintain the existing model architectures have been largely ignored previously.

In order to model object's geometric context in coordinate prediction tasks, we propose a general and powerful loss function named Geometric Context Sensitive (GCS) loss by explicitly measuring the correlations among all coordinates simultaneously, and integrate it into state-of-the-art coordinate prediction models naturally. Specifically, we consider the relative coordinates between any pairs of coordinates as a new supervision signal, which guarantees the relative position between any pairs of prediction coordinates is close to ground-truth object keypoints shape. We convert the shift of any two prediction coordinates equal to the shift of their corresponding two ground-truth coordinates rather than the Euclidean distance. By constraining the relative positions of all pairs of coordinates, every three-coordinates form a triangle to represent the geometric context of the object. With the joint supervision of MSE loss, which represents local appearance, and GCS loss for geometric shape, we can promise not only each individual prediction coordinate close to its ground-truth and each pair of prediction coordinates close to the ground-truth two coordinates, which therefore leads to high precision in coordinate prediction.

The proposed loss is general that can be applied to several 2D/3D tasks. Here we intensively evaluate it in a typical vision applications: NRSFM. We prove that GCS loss could be optimized by Gauss-Newton on the traditional models-based NRSFM task. The quantitative and qualitative results on benchmark datasets demonstrate the effectiveness of the proposed GCS loss.

The technical contributions of this paper are three folds:

- This paper introduces GCS loss, a novel, general and practical loss function, which works well for coordinate prediction task. GCS loss is the first effort to model object's geometric context from the perspective of loss function design. Moreover, GCS loss is cheap because parameters and computational complexity are not added in the inference phase.
- The proposed GCS loss is easy to be implemented and can be deemed as a powerful complementation for existing methods which can be integrated directly in existing architectures to improve their performance. We demonstrate that GCS loss is suitable for both 2D and 3D applications. And we prove that the proposed GCS loss function is trainable and can be optimized by Gauss-Newton in traditional models without changing model structures.
- We conduct extensive experiments on several public datasets using the proposed methods, and achieve superior performance to conventional methods with MSE loss on NRSFM task.

The rest of the paper is organized as follows. In Sect. 2, the related work is reviewed. Section 3 introduces the details of the proposed GCS loss. Application details in NRSFM task are described in Sect. 4. In Sect. 5, we report and analyze extensive experimental results. Finally, we conclude the paper in Sect. 6.

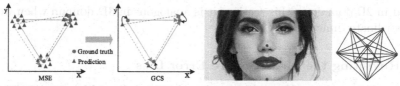

(a) The difference between MSE loss and GCS loss

(b) The geometry interpretation of the proposed GCS Loss.

Fig. 2. The illustration of the proposed GCS Loss.

2   Related Work

Most existing approaches attack NRSFM using either matrix factorization or EM algorithm, The key is to select a proper model or piror constraint in those pipelines. Torresani et al. [12,13] present a Gaussian prior to shape deformation and maximize the likelihood using the EM algorithm. Paladini et al. [10] propose an alternating optimization approach to deal with non-rigid and articulated objects. Dai et al. [4] use a rank minimization technique to indirectly impose the rank-3 constraint for rotations.

Meanwhile, many researchers deem NRSFM as a trajectory estimation problem. Akhter et al. [1] demonstrate gradual 3D shape deformation can be seen as the smooth time-trajectory of a single point within a low-dimensional shape space. Gotardo et al. [5] assume that the columns of the input observation matrix describe smooth 2D point trajectories over time, then derive a family of efficient methods that estimate the column space of observation matrix using compact parameterizations in the Discrete Cosine Transform (DCT) domain. To model the problem that no temporal relation is known, Hamsici et al. [6] consider deformations as spatial variations in shape space and then enforce spatial, smoothness. Recently, with the dramatic development of deep learning, Kong et al. [8] and Wang et al. [14] attempt addressing NRSFM problem via deep learning.

All existing NRSFM methods (whether it is traditional method or deep learning method) measure the difference between the prediction 3D shape and it's ground-truth by computing average of the mean squares of the errors each prediction coordinate with it's corresponding ground-truth, which neglect the correlations among these coordinates in final error loss function. In this paper, we demonstrate that these correlations could reflect the object's geometric context. Furthermore, we propose a novel and practical GCS loss to handle geometric context by modeling relative positions of all coordinates pairs. The proposed GCS loss is able to improve the precision of NRSFM significantly while maintain the traditional algorithm steps unchanged.

3   The Proposed GCS Loss Function

In this section, we first give a brief introduction of the conventional MSE loss function and then present our GCS loss function. Note that all formulations are derived in 2D domain in this section, it is analogous in 3D domain when we add one coordinate dimension.

3.1 Revisiting the Mean Square Error Loss

Suppose that we have N samples and each sample has M keypoints need to prediction, the prediction coordinates in each sample are $(\hat{x}_{ni}, \hat{y}_{ni})$ while it's corresponding ground-truth coordinates are (x_{ni}, y_{ni}), where $n = 1, 2, ..., N$ is the sample index and $i = 1, 2, ..., M$ is the coordinate index. Then the MSE loss is defined as follow:

$$MSE = \frac{1}{2NM} \sum_{n=1}^{N} \sum_{i=1}^{M} \|\hat{x}_{ni} - x_{ni}\|_2^2 + \|\hat{y}_{ni} - y_{ni}\|_2^2 \tag{1}$$

Though conventional methods utilize Eq. (1) and have achieved significant progress, it has a major drawback of MSE loss function for coordinate prediction. Due to Eq. (1) neglects the relative correlation between two coordinates and lacks of global shape consideration, it may result in a number of cases where each prediction coordinate is close to its ground-truth but the relative positions between some coordinates are false predicted.

One typical failure case is shown in Fig. 1(b), two prediction landmarks (green triangles) are close to their ground-truth (red circles). However, compared with the ground-truth, the relative coordinate between two prediction landmarks is wrong. A toy example in Fig. 2(a) (left) illustrates this situation, optimizing MSE loss function only guarantees the prediction coordinates around the corresponding ground-truth and not constraints the relative position relation of any two prediction coordinates, the coordinate prediction model achieve a sub-optimal state which results in the whole predicted shape is not accuracy. Since many objects (e.g. human/animal face, human body) has geometric context and link all coordinates can reflect this geometric context, it is natural to incorporate geometric context information to enhance the coordinate prediction performance. To this end, we propose a novel way to model object's geometric context.

3.2 The Proposed Geometric Context Sensitive Loss

At beginning, we first define two symbols, i.e. Δn_{ijx} and Δn_{ijy} to measure the correlation between two coordinates i and j of sample n, as shown in Eq. (2) and Eq. (3),

$$\Delta n_{ijx} = (\hat{x}_{ni} - \hat{x}_{nj}) - (x_{ni} - x_{nj}) \tag{2}$$

$$\Delta n_{ijy} = (\hat{y}_{ni} - \hat{y}_{nj}) - (y_{ni} - y_{nj}) \tag{3}$$

Here, x and y are abscissa and ordinate respectively. Then, we define the GCS loss function as in Eq. (4);

$$GCS = \frac{1}{2N} \sum_{n=1}^{N} (\sum_{1 \leqslant i < j} (\|\Delta n_{ijx}\|_2^2 + \|\Delta n_{ijy}\|_2^2)) \tag{4}$$

Apparently, Eq. (4) constrains the relative position of each coordinate with all the other coordinates. In fact, Eq. (4) can handle object's geometric context to model its global shape. To prove and illustrate why and how the proposed GCS loss function can address the drawback of traditional MSE loss function and is able to model geometric context, we define two virtual points $A(\hat{x}_{ni} - \hat{x}_{nj}, \hat{y}_{ni} - \hat{y}_{nj})$ and $B(x_{ni} - x_{nj}, y_{ni} - y_{nj})$ according Eq. (2) and Eq. (3).

Therefore, $\|\Delta n_{ijx}\|_2^2 + \|\Delta n_{ijy}\|_2^2$ in Eq. (4) can be deemed as the Euclidean loss of points A and B. From another point of view, A is the shift of two prediction coordinates, B is the shift of two ground-truth coordinates, as illustrated in Eq. (5) and Eq. (6):

$$A = (\hat{x}_{ni}, \hat{y}_{ni}) - (\hat{x}_{nj}, \hat{y}_{nj}) \tag{5}$$

$$B = (x_{ni}, y_{ni}) - (x_{nj}, y_{nj}) \tag{6}$$

Thus, the meaning of Eq. (4) is to make the shift of any two prediction coordinates equal to the shift of their corresponding two ground-truth coordinates, that is moving point A to point B. A toy example is shown in Fig. 2(a), which constraints the position of landmarks by the shifts of prediction and ground-truth. Naturally, when Eq. (4) arrives at an optimal value, the relative coordinates between any pairs of prediction are closed to the relative coordinates between their two ground-truth. Figure 2(b) gives a geometry interpretation of the proposed GCS Loss. By constraining the relative positions of all pairs of coordinates, every three coordinates form a stable triangle which is able to represent the geometric context of the object. Thus, our GCS loss is sensitive of the geometric context.

4   Applications of the GCS Loss in NRSFM

In this section, we investigate the potential of the proposed GCS loss in nonrigid structure-from-motion in 3D domain. Our GCS loss is easy to be integrated with all existing techniques. For all applications, we control the effect of the geometric context by a hyper parameter.

4.1   Basic Formulation

For a NRSFM problem with T images (cameras), the n input 2D point tracks are given in an input matrix $\mathbf{W} \in \mathbb{R}^{2T \times n}$; $[x_{t,v}, y_{t,v}]^T$ is the 2D projection of the vth 3D point observed on the tth image, $t = 1, 2, ..., T, v = 1, 2, ..., n$. For clarity of presentation, assume for now that: (1) $\mathbf{W}$ is complete, meaning that no 2D points became occluded during tracking; and (2) its mean column vector $\mathbf{t} \in \mathbb{R}^{2T}$ has been subtracted from all columns, making them zero-mean. With orthographic projection and a world coordinate system centered on the observed 3D object, $\mathbf{t}$ gives the observed 2D camera translations in each image.

The matrix factorization approach of [2] models $\mathbf{W} = \mathbf{MS}$ as a product of two matrix factors of low-rank $3K$, $\mathbf{M} \in \mathbb{R}^{2T \times 3K}$ and $\mathbf{S} \in \mathbb{R}^{3K \times n}$,

$$
\underbrace{\begin{bmatrix} x_{1,1} & x_{1,2} & \cdots & x_{1,n} \\ y_{1,1} & y_{1,2} & \cdots & y_{1,n} \\ \cdots & \cdots & \cdots & \cdots \\ x_{T,1} & x_{T,2} & \cdots & x_{T,n} \\ x_{T,1} & x_{T,2} & \cdots & x_{T,n} \end{bmatrix}}_{\mathbf{W}} = \underbrace{\begin{bmatrix} \widehat{\mathbf{R}}_1 & & & \\ & \widehat{\mathbf{R}}_2 & & \\ & & \ddots & \\ & & & \widehat{\mathbf{R}}_T \end{bmatrix}}_{\mathbf{D}} \left\{ \underbrace{\begin{bmatrix} c_{1,1} & \cdots & c_{1,K} \\ c_{2,1} & \cdots & c_{2,K} \\ \cdots & \ddots & \cdots \\ c_{T,1} & \cdots & c_{T,K} \end{bmatrix}}_{\mathbf{C}} \otimes \mathbf{I}_3 \right\} \underbrace{\begin{bmatrix} \widehat{\mathbf{S}}_1 \\ \vdots \\ \widehat{\mathbf{S}}_K \end{bmatrix}}_{\mathbf{S}}
$$

Factor $\mathbf{M} = \mathbf{D}(\mathbf{C} \otimes \mathbf{I}_3)$ comprises a block-diagonal rotation matrix $\mathbf{D} \in \mathbb{R}^{2T \times 3T}$ and a shape coefficient matrix $\mathbf{C} \in \mathbb{R}^{T \times K}$.

The goal is then to minimize the 2D reprojection error,

$$
e(\mathbf{M}) = \| \mathbf{W} - \mathbf{W}^* \|_F^2, \mathbf{W}^* = \mathbf{MS} = \mathbf{MM}^\dagger \mathbf{W} \tag{7}
$$

where, $\mathbf{M}$ is the function of model parameter matrix $\mathbf{X} \in \mathbb{R}^{d \times K}$, here d is the number of low-frequency DCT coefficients as in [6]. Moreover, $\mathbf{I}_n$ is the $n \times n$ identity matrix; $\mathbf{A} \otimes \mathbf{B}$ is the Kronecker product of two matrices; $\mathbf{A}^\dagger$ denotes the Moore-Penrose pseudo-inverse of $\mathbf{A}$; $\|\mathbf{A}\|_F$ is the Frobenius norm. Previous NRSFM techniques usually utilize Gauss-Newton algorithm to minimize Eq. (7) in terms of $\mathbf{X}$ only.

4.2   Leverage GCS Loss

At beginning, we first define a residual matrix $\overline{\mathbf{W}}$ to measure the difference of prediction and ground-truth coordinates.

$$
\overline{\mathbf{W}} = \mathbf{W} - \mathbf{W}^* \tag{8}
$$

We denote $\overline{\mathbf{W}}_*$ is the $*$-th column of matrix $\overline{\mathbf{W}}$, then the GCS loss function could be written as follows:

$$
\mathcal{L}_r = \frac{1}{2T} \sum_{1 \leqslant u < v}^{n} (\overline{\mathbf{W}}_u - \overline{\mathbf{W}}_v)^T (\overline{\mathbf{W}}_u - \overline{\mathbf{W}}_v) \tag{9}
$$

Therefore, the final optimization function is:

$$
\mathcal{L} = e(\mathbf{M}) + \lambda \mathcal{L}_r \tag{10}
$$

Similar as facial landmark detection, a scalar λ is used for balancing the two loss functions. Previous NRSFM methods' optimization target could be consider as a special case of Eq. (10), if λ is set to 0.

4.3   Optimization

In order to train with Eq. (7) in an unified framework, we also use Gauss-Newton algorithm to optimize Eq. (9). Therefore, we should calculate gradient matrix $\mathbf{G} \in \mathbb{R}^{(d*K) \times 1}$ and Hessian matrix $\mathbf{H} \in \mathbb{R}^{(d*K) \times (d*K)}$.

The first-order derivative of Eq. (9) is:

$$
\begin{aligned}
d\mathcal{L}_r =& \frac{1}{2T} \sum_{1 \leqslant u < v}^{n} [(d(\overline{\mathbf{W}}_u - \overline{\mathbf{W}}_v)^{\mathrm{T}})(\overline{\mathbf{W}}_u - \overline{\mathbf{W}}_v) \\
& + (\overline{\mathbf{W}}_u - \overline{\mathbf{W}}_j)^{\mathrm{T}}(d(\overline{\mathbf{W}}_u - \overline{\mathbf{W}}_v))] \\
=& \frac{1}{T} \sum_{1 \leqslant u < v}^{n} [(d(\overline{\mathbf{W}}_u - \overline{\mathbf{W}}_v)^{\mathrm{T}})(\overline{\mathbf{W}}_u - \overline{\mathbf{W}}_v)] \\
=& \frac{1}{T} \sum_{1 \leqslant u < v}^{n} [(\overline{\mathbf{W}}_u - \overline{\mathbf{W}}_v)^{\mathrm{T}}(d(\overline{\mathbf{W}}_u - \overline{\mathbf{W}}_v))]
\end{aligned}
\tag{11}
$$

The second-order derivative of Eq. (9) is:

$$
d^2 \mathcal{L}_r = \frac{1}{T} \sum_{1 \leqslant u < v}^{n} [(d(\overline{\mathbf{W}}_u - \overline{\mathbf{W}}_v)^{\mathrm{T}})(d(\overline{\mathbf{W}}_u - \overline{\mathbf{W}}_v))]
\tag{12}
$$

Thus, our objective is to calculate $d(\overline{\mathbf{W}}_u)$ and $d(\overline{\mathbf{W}}_v)$. Recall that $\mathbf{M}$ is the function of model parameter matrix $\mathbf{X} \in \mathbb{R}^{d \times K}$ and $\overline{\mathbf{W}}$ is the function of $\mathbf{M}$. Therefore, both $\overline{\mathbf{W}}_u$ and $\overline{\mathbf{W}}_v$ are the function of $\mathbf{X}$. We then denote two Jacobian matrixes: $\mathbf{J}_u \in \mathbb{R}^{2T \times (d*K)}$ and $\mathbf{J}_v \in \mathbb{R}^{2T \times (d*K)}$ to model the derivative of all variables in low-rank $3K$ condition[1]. Therefore, gradient matrix and Hessian matrix are calculated as follows:

$$
\mathbf{G} = - \sum_{1 \leqslant u < v}^{n} [(\mathbf{J}_u - \mathbf{J}_v)^{\mathrm{T}}(\overline{\mathbf{W}}_u - \overline{\mathbf{W}}_v)]
\tag{13}
$$

$$
\mathbf{H} = \sum_{1 \leqslant u < v}^{n} [(\mathbf{J}_u - \mathbf{J}_v)^{\mathrm{T}}(\mathbf{J}_u - \mathbf{J}_v)]
\tag{14}
$$

5   Experiments

We evaluate the proposed GCS loss on several public NRSFM datasets. In this section, we first introduce these datasets, evaluation metrics and our implementation details, and then compare the performance of GCS with baselines. Finally, we discuss the experimental results. It is worth noting that, the purpose of this section is to demonstrate the effective of the proposed GCS rather than achieve state-of-the-art results.

---

[1] Please refer [6] for details.

Table 1. Average 3D error (standard deviation) of NRSFM solutions on temporally ordered and randomly permuted (π) datasets. Parameters (d, K, λ) are also shown.

Algorithm	face1	stretch	pick-up	yoga	dance	walking
STA	0.056	0.068	0.228	0.147	0.172	0.105
	(0.037)	(0.043)	(0.176)	(0.119)	(0.171)	(0.141)
RIK	0.067	0.087	0.229	0.150	0.174	0.133
	(0.041)	(0.062)	(0.175)	(0.120)	(0.164)	(0.203)
RIK+ GCS	0.053	0.072	0.228	0.148	0.205	0.108
	(0.029)	(0.046)	(0.177)	(0.119)	(0.213)	(0.142)
STA$^\pi$	0.130	0.384	0.424	0.366	0.396	0.323
	(0.098)	(0.346)	(0.281)	(0.303)	(0.312)	(0.445)
RIK$^\pi$	0.067	0.087	0.229	0.150	0.229	0.133
	(0.041)	(0.062)	(0.175)	(0.120)	(0.241)	(0.203)
RIK$^\pi$+ GCS	0.053	0.072	0.228	0.148	0.205	0.108
	(0.029)	(0.046)	(0.177)	(0.119)	(0.213)	(0.142)
STA / STA$^\pi$ (d, K)	0.3T, 5	0.1T, 8	0.1T, 3	0.1T, 7	0.1T, 7	0.3T, 5
RIK / RIK$^\pi$ (d, K)	0.3T, 5	0.2T, 8	0.2T, 3	0.2T, 7	0.2T, 7	0.2T, 5
RIK / RIK$^\pi$+ GCS (d, K, λ)	0.3T, 5, 0.8	0.2T, 8, 1.5	0.2T, 3, 0.5	0.2T, 7, 0.5	0.2T, 7, 0.6	0.2T, 5, 0.9

5.1 Datasets

We consider a variety of motion capture 3D datasets widely used in previous work, with the number of frames and 3D points indicated as (T, n) after the dataset name: *face1*(74,37), *stretch*(370,41), *pick-up*(357,41), *yoga*(307,41), *dance*(264,75), *walking*(260,55).

5.2 Evaluation Metrics

For fair comparisons, we utilize 3D reconstruction error (average Euclidean distance to the 3D points of the ground truth shapes, normalized by average shape size) as evaluation metric as in [6].

5.3 Implementation Details

Our approach utilizes the same experimental settings as [6] and we implement the optimization process of Sect. 4.3 in MATLAB. Moreover, we vary λ from 0 to 1.5 to get optimized hyper parameter.

5.4   Baselines

To evaluate the effectiveness of the proposed GCS loss, we choose RIK-based NRSFM [6] as baseline. One reason is that [6] has demonstrated that the performance of RIK-based NRSFM is unaffected by permutations in the input data, while the performance of Shape Trajectory Approach (STA) decreases significantly. Another reason is that the core idea of this paper is to show that the proposed GCS loss can be used to handle geometric context of objects and improve the performance drastically compared against conventional loss function rather than achieving state-of-the-art performance in a certain dataset by all manner of means.

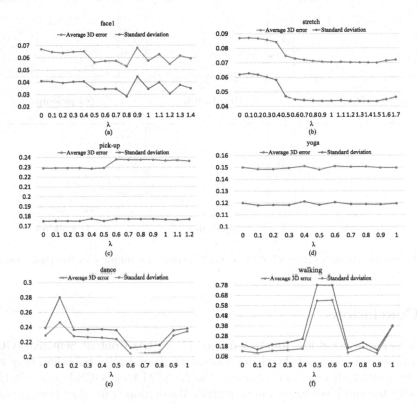

Fig. 3. Average 3D error (standard deviation) of NRSFM solutions on different datasets with different λ. d, K are fixed as in Table 1.

5.5   Results and Discussions

Figure 3 shows the effect of hyper parameter λ (with d, K fixed) in the NRSFM case, we can observe that different object has different optimal λ. Table 1 shows average 3D error (standard deviation) of NRSFM solutions on temporally ordered and randomly permuted (π) datasets. It is obvious that the proposed

GCS loss is able to improve the precision significantly, compared to the baseline. Note that our results are worse than baseline on *dance* dataset, though [6] reports 3D error is 0.174, we run their source code and get 0.229 3D error. Therefore, we can conclude that the proposed solution better than baseline on all datasets. Furthermore, the reconstruction errors of *RIK + GCS* versus the number of iterations on different datasets are shown in Fig. 4, which demonstrate that the GCS loss is easy to be optimized by Gauss-Newton algorithm. Based on the results of NRSFM datasets, we can conclude that our GCS loss can handle complex human body 3D geometric shape.

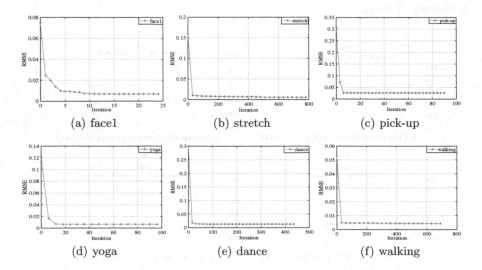

(a) face1   (b) stretch   (c) pick-up

(d) yoga   (e) dance   (f) walking

Fig. 4. Reconstruction errors of *RIK + GCS* versus the number of iterations on different datasets.

6   Conclusions

In this paper, a novel loss function named Geometric Context Sensitive (GCS) loss is proposed to model the shape context of general objects by handling correlations among all pairs of coordinates on NRSFM task. GCS loss is effective, generalizable and easy to be implemented. We demonstrate that the proposed GCS loss function is trainable and easy to be optimized by Gauss-Newton algorithm in the traditional models. In addition, GCS loss can be a convenient geometric complementation to various existing methods while maintain the model structure unchanged. We have conducted extensive experiments for NRSFM, and the results show that the proposed GCS loss can enhance the performance of coordinate prediction significantly.

Acknowledgements. This work was supported by National Natural Science Foundation (NSF) of China (No. 61902104), Anhui Provincial Natural Science Foundation (No. 2008085QF295), Natural Science Research Key Project of Anhui Provincial

Department of Education (No. KJ2020A0651), the Talent Research Foundation of Hefei University (No. 18-19RC54), and the Open Project of Anhui Provincial Key Laboratory of Multimodal Cognitive Computation, Anhui University (No. MMC202004).

References

1. Akhter, I., Sheikh, Y., Khan, S., Kanade, T.: Trajectory space: a dual representation for nonrigid structure from motion. IEEE Trans. Pattern Anal. Mach. Intell. **33**(7), 1442–1456 (2011)
2. Bregler, C., Hertzmann, A., Biermann, H.: Recovering non-rigid 3d shape from image streams. In: Proceedings IEEE Conference on Computer Vision and Pattern Recognition, 2000, vol. 2, pp. 690–696. IEEE (2000)
3. Bulat, A., Tzimiropoulos, G.: How far are we from solving the 2d & 3d face alignment problem? (and a dataset of 230,000 3d facial landmarks). In: International Conference on Computer Vision, vol. 1, p. 8 (2017)
4. Dai, Y., Li, H., He, M.: A simple prior-free method for non-rigid structure-from-motion factorization. Int. J. Comput. Vision **107**(2), 101–122 (2014)
5. Gotardo, P.F., Martinez, A.M.: Computing smooth time trajectories for camera and deformable shape in structure from motion with occlusion. IEEE Trans. Pattern Anal. Mach. Intell. **33**(10), 2051–2065 (2011)
6. Hamsici, O.C., Gotardo, P.F.U., Martinez, A.M.: Learning spatially-smooth mappings in non-rigid structure from motion. In: Fitzgibbon, A., Lazebnik, S., Perona, P., Sato, Y., Schmid, C. (eds.) ECCV 2012. LNCS, vol. 7575, pp. 260–273. Springer, Heidelberg (2012). https://doi.org/10.1007/978-3-642-33765-9_19
7. Jourabloo, A., Liu, X.: Large-pose face alignment via cnn-based dense 3d model fitting. In: Proceedings of the IEEE Conference on Computer Vision and Pattern Recognition, pp. 4188–4196 (2016)
8. Kong, C., Lucey, S.: Deep non-rigid structure from motion. In: Proceedings of the IEEE/CVF International Conference on Computer Vision, pp. 1558–1567 (2019)
9. Liu, Q., Deng, J., Yang, J., Liu, G., Tao, D.: Adaptive cascade regression model for robust face alignment. IEEE Trans. Image Process. **26**(2), 797–807 (2017)
10. Paladini, M., Del Bue, A., Stosic, M., Dodig, M., Xavier, J., Agapito, L.: Factorization for non-rigid and articulated structure using metric projections. In: 2009 IEEE Conference on Computer Vision and Pattern Recognition, CVPR 2009, pp. 2898–2905. IEEE (2009)
11. Rabaud, V., Belongie, S.: Re-thinking non-rigid structure from motion. In: 2008 IEEE Conference on Computer Vision and Pattern Recognition, CVPR 2008, pp. 1–8. IEEE (2008)
12. Torresani, L., Hertzmann, A., Bregler, C.: Nonrigid structure-from-motion: estimating shape and motion with hierarchical priors. IEEE Trans. Pattern Anal. Mach. Intell. **30**(5), 878–892 (2008)
13. Torresani, L., Hertzmann, A., Bregler, C.: Learning non-rigid 3d shape from 2d motion. In: NIPS, vol. 16, p. 2 (2003)
14. Wang, C., Lin, C.H., Lucey, S.: Deep nrsfm++: towards unsupervised 2d–3d lifting in the wild. In: 2020 International Conference on 3D Vision (3DV), pp. 12–22. IEEE (2020)
15. Yang, H., Zhang, R., Robinson, P.: Human and sheep facial landmarks localisation by triplet interpolated features. In: 2016 IEEE Winter Conference on Applications of Computer Vision (WACV), pp. 1–8. IEEE (2016)

142   F. Nian et al.

16. Yu, X., Zhou, F., Chandraker, M.: Deep deformation network for object landmark localization. In: Leibe, B., Matas, J., Sebe, N., Welling, M. (eds.) ECCV 2016. LNCS, vol. 9909, pp. 52–70. Springer, Cham (2016). https://doi.org/10.1007/978-3-319-46454-1_4
17. Zadeh, A., Baltrušaitis, T., Morency, L.P.: Deep constrained local models for facial landmark detection. arXiv preprint arXiv:1611.08657 (2016)
18. Zhu, X., Lei, Z., Liu, X., Shi, H., Li, S.Z.: Face alignment across large poses: A 3d solution. In: Proceedings of the IEEE Conference on Computer Vision and Pattern Recognition, pp. 146–155 (2016)

3D Reconstruction from Single-View Image Using Feature Selection

Bo Wang and Hongxun Yao[✉]

Faculty of Computing, Harbin Institute of Technology, Harbin, China
h.yao@hit.edu.cn

Abstract. Recovering the 3D shape of an object from single-view image with deep neural network has been attracting increasing attention in the past few years. Recent approaches based on convolutional neural networks have shown excellent results on single-view image. Most of them, however, have many model's parameters or fewer parameters with performance degradation. Therefore, in this work we propose a feature selection module to balance this problem. This module first calculates the uncertain degree map to obtain the feature coordinates which means some coarse parts needs to be corrected. Then using these coordinates, features in several feature maps are selected. Finally, use MLP Layer to obtain fine features by taking features selected as input. Training and Inference are slightly different in this module. Using this module, we achieve better performance with about 18% parameters addition and comparable performance with about 30% model's parameters decrease based on the Pix2Vox [1] framework.

Keywords: 3D reconstruction · Single-view image · Feature selection

1 Introduction

The problem of single-view 3D shape reconstruction can be framed as follows: Given a single image representation of the depicted object as faithfully as possible. This problem of reconstructing a 3D shape from a single 2D representation is ill-posed since there exists more than one solution for single view image, especially because the information lost in the original 3D shape models to 2D image projection.

Since the introduction of the 3D-R2N2 [2] methods, different methods based on recurrent neural networks have achieved great success in single-view or multiple-view 3D object reconstruction. Pix2Vox addressed long-term memory loss and order-inconsistency of these RNN-based approaches with a new unified framework. Pix2Vox proposed two versions named Pix2Vox-F and Pix2Vox-A. Compared to Pix2Vox-F, the Pix2Vox-A version has more parameters. While Pix2Vox-F has fewer parameters but the performance is worse than Pix2Vox-A. In the Pix2Vox framework, a context-aware fusion module adaptively selects high-quality reconstructions from different coarse 3D volumes across multiple views.

However, in a single view image, how can we select coarse quality parts and refine them to high quality parts? In this work, we present a way, feature selection module,

© Springer Nature Switzerland AG 2021
Y. Peng et al. (Eds.): ICIG 2021, LNCS 12890, pp. 143–152, 2021.
https://doi.org/10.1007/978-3-030-87361-5_12

to address this problem. We draw inspiration from Point Rend [14] which proposed a neural network module to adaptively selected points coordinates in feature maps based on an iterative subdivision algorithm. It is used in instance and semantic segmentation tasks. Our feature selection module is inserted into this framework using the framework's corresponding encoder and decoder without its context-aware fusion module, as shown in Fig. 1. Compared to Point Rend, our feature selection module exists three major differences in: (1) our point coordinates selection of feature is used in the 3D volumes while point rend is in the 2D images. (2) the uncertain degree map function is different both in training and inference time. (3) loss function of the selected feature vector is different.

The contributions can be summarized as follows:

1. We present feature selection module to select coarse quality parts from 3D generated feature map, and use them to generate fine volume in single view 3D reconstruction.
2. We achieve better performance than Pix2Vox-F and comparable performance with Pix2Vox-A using the same encoder and decoder in its framework.

2   Related Work

Predicting the complete 3D shape of an object from a single image is a challenging task. Conventionally, many attempts have been made to address this issue, such as Shape from X [3, 4], where X represent silhouettes [5], shading [6], or texture [7]. These methods require strong presumptions and abundant expertise in natural images. However, recently, convolution networks achieve great advance in single view 3D reconstruction.

Most of these methods follow an encoding-decoding frame. The image is encoded into a feature vector and then decoded into one representation of the 3D shape. 3D object reconstruction's output representation has voxel grid, point clouds, meshes or others. A 3D object can be represented as "a probabilistic distribution of binary variables" on a 3D voxel grid. Using voxel grids as an output is a popular approach, because convolutional operators can easily fit the voxel grids.

In this section, we first review methods based on voxel grid using deep neural networks and classify these methods into: (1) 32^3 resolution; (2) higher resolution. Secondly, we briefly introduce other representation of 3D object because the experiment using feature selection module is all based on voxel grid.

2.1   Voxel Grid

32^3 **Resolution.** Choy proposed 3D-R2N2 a Recurrent Neural Network to learn the mapping between image and its underlying 3D shapes. The main contribution of their work is the proposed 3D convolutional Long Short-Term Memory (3D-LSTM) which resides between the encoder and the decoder. With generative adversarial networks (GAN) [8] and variational autoencoders (VAE) [9], 3D-VAE-GAN [10] uses GAN and VAE to generate 3D shape by taking single view image as input. Pix2Vox present a unified framework for both single-view and multiple-view 3D reconstruction, which has a context-aware fusion module to adaptively select high-quality reconstructions for each part.

Higher Resolution. MarrNet [11] use 2.5D intermediate information by estimating depth, surface normal and silhouettes of 2D image. ShapeHD [12] incorporating a shape naturalness network based on the MarrNet to improve the reconstruction results. And IDCT [20] use inverse discrete cosine transform decoder. These methods lead to 128^3 resolution voxel. Matryoshka Network [13] recursively decomposes a 3D shape into nested shape layers which leads to 256^3 resolution voxel.

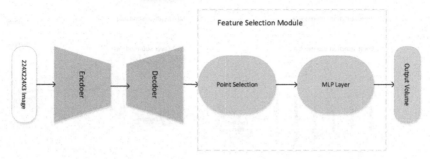

Fig. 1. Network structure. Feature Selection Module has Point Selection sub-module and MLP Layer sub-module. This module is insert into the Pix2Vox framework and get two versions of network using the same Feature Selection Module and corresponding encoder and decoder in the framework. The experiment section elaborates in detail.

2.2 Other Representation of 3D Object

OGN [15] and O-CNN [16] use octree to represent higher resolution volumetric 3D object. OGN uses octree to obtain a high-resolution result with memory budget. Compared to O-CNN, OGN representations are complex and consume more computational resources due to the complexity of octree representations.

DISN [17] predicts the underlying signed distance field given a single input image. PSG [18] firstly recovers a point cloud from a single image with deep neural networks. Pixel2Mesh [19] is reconstruct the 3D shape in a triangular mesh from a single image firstly.

3   The Proposed Module

In some voxel outputs corresponding to its single view, there may exists some detail parts lost, for example, a chair with thin legs which cannot recover well. Pix2Vox using context-aware fusion module to select high-quality parts. However, in single view image, we also want to select coarse parts. Motivated by this, we select these coarse parts in feature map and use them to feed into the module. Finally, the module outputs fine features corresponding to each point coordinate.

In this section, we elaboration the proposed feature selection module as shown in Fig. 2. This module can be divided into two sub-modules corresponding to the following two sub-sections.

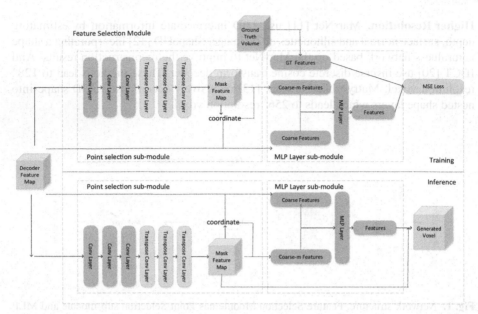

Fig. 2. Illustration of Feature Selection Module. It contains Point Selection submodule and MLP Layer submodule. Training and Inference are different. During training, it returns MSE Loss and the mask Feature Map for BCE Loss, while during inference, only generated Voxel is returned.

3.1 Point Selection in Inference and Training

At the core of our method is the idea of flexibly and adaptively selecting points in the generated voxel volume. Intuitively, these points should be located more densely near high-uncertainty degree areas, such as thin legs of chair. We develop this idea for inference and training.

Inference. Our selection strategy for inference is closely related to the threshold of voxel output. The threshold is used to make the generated voxel volume value zero or one, instead of float number. Compared to the inference in Point Rend, we do not use iterative way in a coarse-to-fine fashion. We calculate the uncertain degree map as the following formula which defines the coarse uncertain degree on the generated voxels.

$$Uncertain\,Degree\,Map = -\|g - \tau\| \tag{1}$$

Where g and τ represent the generated voxel volume and threshold. Considering that the final generated voxel result has to be compared with the threshold value, so the float number near the threshold in the generated voxels should be most uncertain. After selecting the N most uncertain points (e.g., those with probabilities closest to 0.3) on this grid, we compute the point-wise feature representation (described shortly in Subsect. 3.2). Noted that we select points on 3D grid while Point Rend selects on 2D grid.

Training. During training, this module also needs to select points at which to construct point-wise features for training. The sampling strategy selects N points on a feature map to train on. Similar to Point Rend, we also use the bias selection towards uncertain regions which retaining some degree of uniform coverage. More specifically, (I) Over generation: over-generate candidate points by randomly sampling kN points from a uniform distribution. (II Importance sampling: βN points are selected from the over-generate candidates. (III) the remaining (1-β) N points are sampled from a uniform distribution. β and k are the importance coefficient and oversampling coefficient, such as 0.8 and 3, respectively.

However, we use another formula to calculate the uncertain map during the training time.

$$Uncertain\ Degree\ Map = \|g - gt\| \tag{2}$$

Where g and gt represent the generated voxel volume and the ground truth voxel volume. Considering that ground truth voxel volumes are used as supervision, we have uncertain degree on each point coordinate, since we know whether it should be 0 or 1 at a specific coordinate. Using this uncertain degree map, features can be selected. At training time, loss functions on the N sampled points are computed as a part of the total training loss.

3.2 Point-Wise Features and MLP Layer Head

This subsection describes the selected features including coarse features and coarse-m features which are combined to feed into the MLP Layer Head.

Coarse-m Features. We extract a feature vector at each sampled point from the mask feature map. Because a point is a real-value 3D coordinate, we perform trilinear interpolation on the feature map to compute the feature vector.

Coarse Features. We extract a feature vector at each sampled point from the decoder's output feature map. In Pix2Vox framework, the generated voxel volume from decoder does not perform as well as adding a refiner behind it. Thus, we think the coarse features can be selected from it.

MLP Layer Head. With the point-wise features are selected, coarse features and coarse-m features are concatenated, and then feed into a multi-layer perceptron (MLP) with weights shared across all points. During training time, we also select vector from ground truth voxel volume using the same point coordinate. MSE Loss are computed and backward between ground truth vector and the MLP Layer output feature vector as a part of total training loss. While, during inference, the final voxel volume is scatter using the same point coordinate and the MLP Layer output feature vector.

4 Experiments

4.1 Datasets, Metrics and Loss Function

Datasets. We evaluate this feature selection module based on the Pix2Vox framework. Corresponding to the Pix2Vox-F and the Pix2Vox-A two versions, we also evaluate two versions named FS-F and FS-A.

Here, we just use the encoder and the decoder in the corresponding Pix2Vox-F and Pix2Vox-A versions. We use synthetic images of objects from the ShapeNet [21] dataset. More specifically, we use a subset of ShapeNet consisting of 13 major categories and 43,783 3D models following the settings of 3D-R2N2.

Evaluation Metrics. To evaluate the quality of the output from the FS-F and FS-A, we binarize the probabilities at a fixed threshold of 0.3 and use intersection over union (IoU) as the similarity measure between prediction and ground truth. More formally,

$$IoU = \frac{\sum_{i,j,k} I(\hat{p}_{(i,j,k)} > \tau) I(p_{(i,j,k)})}{\sum_{i,j,k} I[I(\hat{p}_{(i,j,k)} > \tau) + I(p_{(i,j,k)})]} \tag{3}$$

Where $\hat{p}_{(i,j,k)}$ and $p_{(i,j,k)}$ represent the predicted occupancy probability and the ground truth at (i, j, k), respectively. $I(\bullet)$ is an indicator function and τ denotes a voxelization threshold. Higher IoU values indicates better reconstruction results.

Loss Function. The total loss function of the network is defined as the mean value of the voxel-wise binary cross entropies between the ground truth and the generated voxel, the mean squared error between the ground truth vector and the MLP Layer output feature vector. More formally, it can be defined as

$$l = \frac{1}{N} \sum_{i=1}^{N} \left[gt_i \log(g_i) + (1 - gt_i) \log(1 - g_i) \right] + \frac{1}{Nx} \sum_{i=1}^{Nx} (gtv_i - gv_i)^2 \tag{4}$$

where N denotes the number of voxels in ground truth. gt_i and g_i represent the ground truth and the corresponding generated voxel. Nx denotes the length of vectors in extracted ground truth vector. gtv_i and gv_i represent the ground truth vector and the MLP Layer output feature vector.

4.2 Implementation Details

We use 224×224 RGB images as input to train the FS-F and FS-A with a shape batch size of 64. The output voxel reconstruction is 32^3 in size. The optimizer is Adam optimizer with a $\beta 1$ of 0.9 and a $\beta 2$ of 0.999. The initial learning rate is 0.001, same as the one in the framework. We select 64 feature points.

Table 1. Single-view reconstruction on ShapeNet compared using Intersection-over-Union (IoU). The best number of each category is highlighted in bold.

Category	3D-R2N2	Pix2Vox-F	Pix2Vox-A	FS-F	FS-A
Airplane	0.513	0.600	**0.684**	0.623	0.658
Bench	0.421	0.538	**0.616**	0.546	0.580

(continued)

Table 1. (*continued*)

Category	3D-R2N2	Pix2Vox-F	Pix2Vox-A	FS-F	FS-A
Cabinet	0.716	0.765	0.792	0.782	**0.793**
Car	0.798	0.837	**0.854**	0.842	0.849
Chair	0.466	0.535	**0.567**	0.545	0.562
Display	0.468	0.511	**0.537**	0.535	0.530
Lamp	0.381	0.435	0.443	0.449	**0.464**
Speaker	0.662	0.707	**0.714**	0.702	0.699
Rifle	0.554	0.598	0.615	0.605	**0.617**
Sofa	0.628	0.687	0.709	0.708	**0.727**
Table	0.513	0.587	0.601	0.597	**0.613**
Telephone	0.661	0.770	**0.776**	0.724	0.742
Watercraft	0.513	0.582	0.594	0.605	**0.619**
Overall	0.560	0.634	**0.661**	0.644	0.660

Table 2. Number of parameters on different network parts. FS-F and FS-A use the same Feature Selection Module. Inference time of networks are given.

#Parameters(M)	Pix2Vox-F	Pix2Vox-A	FS-F	FS-A
Encoder	4.66	7.77	4.66	7.77
Decoder	2.77	71.58	2.77	71.58
Merger	0.01	0.01	–	–
Refiner	–	34.88		
FS	–	–	1.35	1.35
Inference time	6.80 ms	8.35 ms	7.78 ms	7.80 ms

4.3   Reconstruction of Synthetic Images

To evaluate the performance of the FS-F and the FS-A in handing synthetic images, we compare methods against several methods on the ShapeNet testing set. All methods are compared with the same input images for all experiments to make a fair comparison. Table 1 shows the performance of single view reconstruction.

The reconstruction results of FS-F significantly outperform the Pix2Vox-F. Compared to Pix2Vox-A, FS-A has better performance in six categories. It is worth noting that we use the same Feature Selection Module and corresponding encoder and decoder network convolutional layers. See detail in Subsect. 4.4.

Figure 3 shows several reconstruction examples from the ShapeNet testing set. For better representation, we just show some examples using FS-A. Figure 4 shows the visualization of the generated voxel results on different methods.

Fig. 3. Several reconstruction examples from the ShapeNet on each category. The first column is the input single view image and the next column is the generated voxel result. As this interval, we show 13 category results.

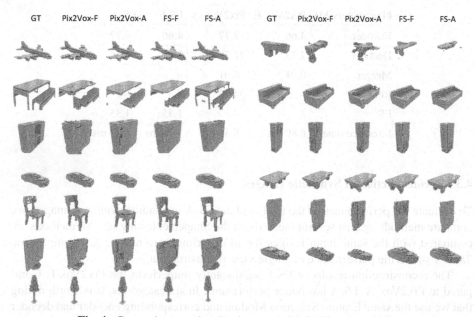

GT   Pix2Vox-F   Pix2Vox-A   FS-F   FS-A   GT   Pix2Vox-F   Pix2Vox-A   FS-F   FS-A

Fig. 4. Comparison on visualization example of different methods.

4.4 Space Complexity

Table 2 shows the numbers of parameters of different networks methods. We do not use the merger network in both FS-F and FS-A. Compared to the Pix2Vox-F, we just add about 18% parameters. As for FS-A, we reduce about 30% total parameters. And the refiner networks are replaced by the Feature Selection Module. We also test the inference time on the test datasets, and give the average inference time of single view image. Results show that FS-A method is 0.55 ms faster than Pix2Vox-A. During the experiments, we find that the main gap of inference time between the two versions of Pix2Vox lies in Refiner module, although decoder module' parameters are huge different. Noted that we test on NVIDIA 3080 GPU.

5 Conclusions

In this paper, we propose a feature selection module. Using this module, we select some coarse features parts in feature map and then use MLP Layer to adjust these feature vectors to generate fine feature vectors underlying the supervision of ground truth voxel volume feature vector. Based on Pix2Vox framework, we replace the refine network parts using this module, experiments results show that we achieve better performance than Pix2Vox-F with 18% parameters addition in FS-F version. Compared to Pix2Vox-A, we achieve comparable performance with about 30% total parameters reducing in FS-A version.

References

1. Xie, H., Yao, H., Sun, X., Zhou, S., Zhang, S.: Pix2Vox: context-aware 3D reconstruction from single and multi-view images. In: ICCV (2019)
2. Choy, C.B., Xu, D., Gwak, J., Chen, K., Savarese, S.: 3D-R2N2. a unified approach for single and multi-view 3D object reconstruction. In: ECCV (2016)
3. Barron, J.T., Malik, J.: Shape, illumination, and reflectance from shading. TPAMI 37(8), 1670–1687 (2015)
4. Savarese, S., Andreetto, M., Rushmeier, H.E., Bernardini, F., Perona, P.: 3D reconstruction by shadow carving: theory and practical evaluation. IJCV 71(3), 305–336 (2007)
5. Dibra, E., Jain, H., Oztireli, A.C., Ziegler, R., Gross, M.H.: Human shape from silhouettes using generative HKS descriptors and cross-modal neural networks. In: CVPR (2017)
6. Richter, S.R., Roth, S.: Discriminative shape from shading in uncalibrated illumination. In: CVPR (2015)
7. Witkin, A.P.: Recovering surface shape and orientation from texture. Artif. Intell. 17(1–3), 17–45 (1981)
8. Goodfeoolow, I.J., et al.: Generative adversarial nets. In: NIPS (2014)
9. Kingma, D.P., Welling, M.: Auto-encoding variational bayes. arXiv, abs/1312.6114 (2013)
10. Wu, J., Zhang, C., Xue, T., Freeman, B., Tenenbaum, J.: Learning a probabilistic latent space of object shapes via 3D generative-adversarial modeling. In: NIPS (2016)
11. Wu, J., Wang, Y., Xue, T., Sun, X., Freeman, B., Tenenbaum, J.: MarrNet: 3D shape reconstruction via 2.5D sketches. In: NIPS (2017)

12. Wu, J., Zhang, C., Zhang, X., Zhang, Z., Freeman, W.T., Tenenbaum, J.B.: Learning shape priors for single-view 3D completion and reconstruction. In: Ferrari, V., Hebert, M., Sminchisescu, C., Weiss, Y. (eds.) ECCV 2018. LNCS, vol. 11215, pp. 673–691. Springer, Cham (2018). https://doi.org/10.1007/978-3-030-01252-6_40

13. Richter, S.R., Roth, S.: Matryoshka networks: prediction 3D geometry via nested shape layers. In: CVPR (2018)

14. Kirillov, A., Wu, Y., He, K., et al.: PointRend: image segmentation as rendering. In: CVPR (2020)

15. Tatarchenko, M., Dosovitskiy, A., Brox, T.: Octree generating networks: efficient convolutional architectures for high-resolution 3D outputs. In: ICCV (2017)

16. Wang, P., Liu, Y., Guo, Y., Sun, C., Tong, X.: O-CNN: octree-based convolutional neural networks for 3D shape analysis. ACM Trans. Graph. **36**(4), 72:1–72:11 (2017)

17. Xu, Q., Wang, W., Ceylan, D., Mech, R., Neumann, U.: DISN: deep implicit surface network for high-quality single-view 3D reconstruction. In: NeurIPS (2019)

18. Fan, H., Su, H., Guibas, L.J.: A point set generation network for 3D object reconstruction from a single image. In: CVPR (2017)

19. Wang, N., Zhang, Y., Li, Z., Fu, Y., Liu, W., Jiang, Y.-G.: Pixel2Mesh: generating 3D mesh models from single RGB images. In: Ferrari, V., Hebert, M., Sminchisescu, C., Weiss, Y. (eds.) ECCV 2018. LNCS, vol. 11215, pp. 55–71. Springer, Cham (2018). https://doi.org/10.1007/978-3-030-01252-6_4

20. Johnston, A., Garg, R., Carneiro, G., Reid, I., van den Hengel, A.: Scaling cnns for high resolution volumetric reconstruction from a single image. In: ICCV (2017)

21. Wu, Z., et al.: 3D ShapeNets: a deep representation for volumetric shapes. In: CVPR (2015)

Computational Photography

Adaptive Steganography Based on Image Edge Enhancement and Automatic Distortion Learning

Enlu Li[2], Zhangjie Fu[1,2(✉)], and Junfu Chen[2]

[1] Engineering Research Center of Digital Forensics, Ministry of Education, Nanjing University of Information Secience and Technology, Nanjing 210044, China
[2] School of Computer and Software, Nanjing University of Information Secience and Technology, Nanjing 210044, China
fzj@nuist.edu.cn

Abstract. The research of steganography has been one of the hotspots in the field of information security. The automatic distortion learning steganographic method based on generative adversarial networks (GAN) has outperformed the hand-crafted steganographic algorithms. However, the detection accuracy of steganalysis networks keeps improving as they are continuously combined with the latest neural network structures. It poses a great threat to the security of steganographic algorithms. Therefore, how to enhance the imperceptibility of secret messages is an ongoing issue. In this paper, we propose an automatic distortion learning steganographic method with better security performance based on image edge enhancement. To reduce the search space and increase the training efficiency, we change the input of the network by feeding edge-enhanced images to generator. In addition, to make the pixel change probability map more accurate and hereby improve the abaility to resist steganalyzer, we add shallower connections to the U-Net structure to build the generator. After this, the generated pixel change probability map is further used to simulate information embedding. Under this framework, we use XuNet to judge the imperceptibility of secret messsages in time and adjust the pixel change probability. The experimental results on BOSS-Base dataset show that our proposed method performs better than the hand-crafted (S-UNIWARD) and GAN-based automatic steganographic algorithms (UT-GAN) on security against XuNet, SRNet and SRM.

Keywords: Adaptive steganography · Image edge enhancement · Automatic distortion learning · Generative adversarial networks · Steganalysis

Supported by the National Natural Science Foundation of China under grant U1836110, U1836208; by the Jiangsu Basic Research Programs-Natural Science Foundation under grant numbers BK20200039.

Y. Peng et al. (Eds.): ICIG 2021, LNCS 12890, pp. 155–167, 2021.
https://doi.org/10.1007/978-3-030-87361-5_13

1 Introduction

In the field of information security, image steganography can be used for secret transmission of important information. Image steganography achieves the purpose of information hiding by hiding secret messages in a cover image. Adaptive steganography methods hide the secret message in the high-frequency areas with complex texture to reduce abnormal variations in the image. Therefore, adaptive steganography is effectively resistant to detection. Based on this perception, different adaptive steganography methods design different distortion functions to measure the imapct of modifying cover image. The proposal of HUGO [10] marks the beginning of adaptive steganography. Since then, many advanced spatial adaptive steganography schemes have been proposed, such as WOW [6], S-UNIWARD [7], HILL [8], and MiPOD [13]. After obtaining the distortion function, the secret messages are usually embedded in the image using Syndrome-trellis code (STC) [3]. STC can approximate the minimum embedding distortion for a given embedding cost and payload.

However, it is pointed out that designing distortion functions based on heuristic principles without directly considering statistical undetectability is a common problem in adaptive steganography frameworks [15]. The hand-crafted distortion function design process should be reduced thus reducing human involvement in the steganography process. The design of distortion functions that measure statistical detectability was identified as one of the most important problems. Meanwhile, with the development of spatial rich model (SRM) [4] and neural network-based steganalysis [11,14,16,17,20], the security performance of the existing adaptive steganography is under threat.

To reduce human interference in the design of distortion function and improve the ability to resist steganalysis, the researchers use steganalysis network to measure the statistical undetectability of the image when designing the distortion function. Tang et al. [15] proposed an automatic steganographic distortion learning framework (ASDL-GAN). This method uses the framework of generative adversarial networks (GAN) [5]. Although ASDL has learned to embed secret messages in an adaptive manner, it is still inferior to the state-of-the-art hand-crafed steganographic algorithms, such as S-UNIWARD. Compared with ASDL-GAN, Yang et al. proposed UT-GAN [18,19] that surpasses the performance of S-UNIWARD. Due to limitations in the convergence speed of GAN and the development of steganalysis networks, the steganography method should further improve the computational efficiency and security performance.

How to improve the security performance of neural network-based image steganography methods and improve the training efficiency of the network is a major challenge. Theoretically, increasing the depth of the network and the number of trainable parameters can optimize the training effect of the network and improve the ability to resist steganalysis. However, trading training time for training performance is not very efficient and is easily limited by the training environment and equipment.

In this paper, we try to improve the training efficiency of the network, and the ability to resist steganalysis. It can be seen from most steganography and steganalysis methods that the use of domain knowledge can be very helpful in improving the efficiency of the model. Existed adaptive steganographic algorithms that take into account the image's own properties greatly improve the imperceptibility of steganography methods. The high accuracy of most steganalysis based on neural networks depends on using the KV kernels in the SRM. It illuminates that we can leverage existing domain knowledge to pre-process the images, rather than using the original images as input to the GAN-based steganographic algorithm. In this paper, we follow up the study and propose an adaptive steganography method based on image edge enhancement and automatic distortion learning. The main contributions of this paper can be summarized as follows:

1) We propose a new adaptive steganography method based on image edge enhancement and automatic distortion learning. It improves security performance and training efficiency of the steganographic algorithm.
2) We replace the raw image with a Laplacian-enhanced image as the input to the generator, which reduces search space and deceives steganalysis effectively in less training time.
3) We design a generator by adding shallow connections to the U-Net structure. It increases the reuse rate of effective features and makes the pixel change probability map generated by the generator more sophisticated.
4) Experimental results are detected by the conventional SRM, the most commonly used XuNet and the advanced SRNet. The experiment results show that the proposed method further improves the detection error rate of steganalyzer compared to S-UNIWARD and UT-GAN.

The rest of this paper is organized as followed. The related work is reviewed in Sect. 2. The proposed architecture is described in Sect. 3. Experimental results and discussions are shown in Sect. 4. The conclusion and future works are summarized in Sect. 5.

2 Related Work

In this section, to complete the paper, we first present the theoretical basis for the proposed method, which is the minimum distortion steganography framework for adaptive steganography. Then, we summarise the framework of several automatic distortion learning steganography methods using GAN, since our proposed method have made improvements based on this framework.

2.1 Distortion Minimization Framework

The distortion minimization framework for steganography is to minimize the overall distortion of the image caused by the embedding of secret message under a given embedding rate, which can be expressed as:

$$\min D, s.t. H = M \times N \times Q, \tag{1}$$

where D denotes the overall distortion of the image, M and N are the height and width of the cover image, Q represents the embedding bits per pixel, and H is the embedding capacity of the cover image during the process of steganography.

The additive distortion function is defined as follows:

$$D = \sum_{i=1}^{M} \sum_{j=1}^{N} \rho_{i,j} p_{i,j}, \tag{2}$$

where $\rho_{i,j}$ means the embedding cost at the position(i,j) , and $p_{i,j}$ represents the change probability between 0 and 0.5. The possible modification of each pixel includes three cases: $+1, -1$, 0. In other words, for one pixel, the corresponding change probability and embedding cost have three values.

Combining the function of entropy and the change probability of each pixel, in actual situations, the expectation is used to evaluate the average capacity of embedded information in the image. The function is defined as follows:

$$C = - \sum_{i=1}^{M} \sum_{j=1}^{N} p_{i,j} \log_2 p_{i,j}, \tag{3}$$

where C represents the embedding capacity computed based on the pixel change probability.

2.2   Automatic Distortion Learning Steganography Methods Using GAN

The automatic distortion learning steganography methods [15,18,19] learn reasonable pixel change probability maps through the adversarial training of generator and steganalyzer. The method replaces the process of designing the distortion function based on human experience in existed adaptive steganography. The training process of automatic distortion learning steganography can be summarized as the following steps.

Firstly, build a generative subnetwork that generates the change probability maps for cover images. Secondly, after obtaining the change probability map, calculate the pixel modification map under the optimal simulation embedding situation. Thirdly, combine the pixel modification map with the original cover image to obtain the corresponding stego image. Finally, the steganalysis subnetwork classifies the cover images and the generated stego images. Trains the overall network according to embedding capacity and the cross-entropy loss function used in the GAN network until the network converges.

In this framework, the network has been able to learn reasonable pixel change probability maps and obtain corresponding embedding distortions. The security performance of stego images can exceed that of traditional method S-UNIWARD. However, the network relies only on the raw image pixels and does not exploit the priori knowledge that secret messages are almost always concentrated in the high-frequency regions of the image. Therefore, in this paper, we propose a new adaptive steganography method, where the reconstructed generative network fed with enhanced images.

3   The Proposed Framework

In this section, we will present the proposed steganography method based on image edge enhancement in detail. We first briefly outline the overall framework. Then, we describe the application of image edge enhancement algorithms for automatic distortion learning. After that, We introduce the improved generator structure and the training strategy for the model.

3.1   The Overall Architecture

In this paper, we propose an adaptive steganography method based on image edge enhencement. Firstly, we use the edge enhencement algorithm to enhence the cover image. The areas where the pixel values are abruptly changed, i.e. the areas suitable for steganography, are highlighted. Then, We feed the enhanced image into the generator. Motivated by the ASDL-GAN and UT-GAN, we use the structure of the adversarial network to learn pixel change probability map. To make the generated pixel change probability more reasonable, we nested two shallower U-Net [12] networks on the basis of the original U-Net as the generator. The detailed structure of the generator is explained in Sect. 4.3. After this, we obtain the stego image according to the optimal embedding simulation function proposed in UT-GAN. In order to evaluate the reasonability of the generated pixel change probability map, we use steganalysis to discriminate the generated stego image in time. Finally, we boost the imperceptibility of image steganography according to adversarial loss and capacity loss. The overall framework of the proposed network is shown in Fig. 1.

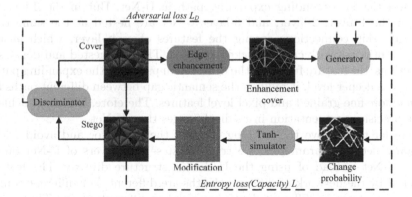

Fig. 1. The framework of the proposed network.

3.2   Image Edge Enhancement

In existed adaptive image steganography methods, the pixel change probability obtained by designing different steganography distortion functions is not the same. However, the pixels with higher change probability are distributed at the boundary that distinguishes the content of the image and the fine edge that depicts the details, because it is more difficult for the steganalysis to make accurate judgments on these areas. Therefore, we already know the approximate location of the pixel with higher change probability. This is the domain knowledge in image steganography. Although in the previous work, the network can accurately learn the pixel change probability value, domain knowledge-based learning processes can accelerate network convergence and improve the learning effect.

In the field of computer vision, researchers have studied a variety of edge detection methods to extract the edges of objects in images. The image after processing is similar to the pixel change probability map. Therefore, in our proposed method, edge detection is used to find areas with high change probability. The feasibility of this idea is verified experimentally in Sect. 4.2. We tried four commonly used image edge enhancement operators, namely Roberts, Prewitt, Sobel, and Laplacian. The detailed experiments are described in Sect. 4.2. In the proposed method, the Laplacian operator is finally used for image edge enhancement.

3.3   The Architecture of the Generator G

The article by Yang et al. has proved that the generator with U-Net as the network structure can effectively learn the pixel change probability of the carrier image. However, the U-Net structure does not combine enough different levels of feature information. In the structure of U-Net++ [23], each layer of feature information in the contracting path is up-sampled. We take the 3-layer U-Net and U-Net++ in Fig. 2(a) and 2(b) as a comparison. There is only one contraction path and the corresponding expanding path in U-Net. But in the 3-layer U-Net++, the 1-layer, 2-layer, and 3-layer U-Net are nested at the same time. There are skip connections among the features of each layer, which ensures that the entire network can be backpropagated. Through nested and dense skip connections, the feature fusion in the contraction path and the expanding path is richer. At a deeper level, it reduces the semantic gap between different paths and obtains more fine-grained and pixel-level features. Therefore, U-Net++ achieves higher-precision segmentation in medical images than U-Net.

In order to improve the learning effect of the generator and avoid adding too many network parameters, we try to nest several layers of U-Net on the 7-layer U-Net instead of using the U-Net++ structure directly. The features extracted by the network of different depths are different. For different content training sets, training different depth network has different effects. The number of extracted features and parameters is not necessarily positively correlated with the training effect of the model. We tried a variety of different network structures, and selected the structure suitable for the current task and data set according to the experimental results, as shown in Fig. 2(c). The choice of network structure will be further explained in Sect. 4.3.

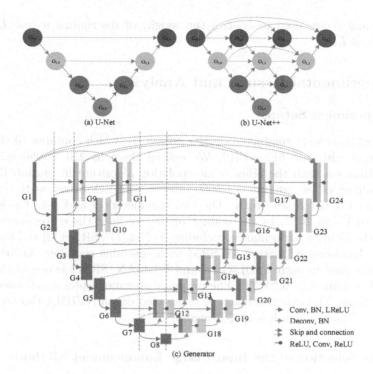

Fig. 2. The framework of the proposed network.

3.4   The Training Strategy

For given image size and embedding rate, the embedding capacity H of this image can be calculated according to function (1). According to the pixel change probability generated by the generator and function (2), the capacity C of the stego image in the current training process can be calculated. Therefore, the loss L is defined to ensure that the image under the current training situation can hide enough information.

$$L - (C - H)^2. \tag{4}$$

For the discriminator D, its task is to distinguish the cover image and the currently generated stego image. The loss L_D can be defined as:

$$L_D = -\sum_{i=1}^{2} y_i' \log(y_i), \tag{5}$$

where y_i' is the ground truths, y_i is the softmax output of the discriminator.

For the generator G, the pixel change probability it generates must not only ensure the capacity of the embedded information, but also ensure that the stego image obtained on this basis can deceive the discriminator. So the L_G can be defined as:

$$L_G = -\alpha \times L_D + \beta \times L, \tag{6}$$

where α and β are used to control the weight of discriminator loss L_D and capacity loss L.

4 Experimental Results and Analysis

4.1 Experiment Setups

The experiments were conducted on BOSSBase [1], which contains 10000 gray-scale images with size 512×512. We resized them to 256×256 using the imresize function with the bilinear interpolation algorithm in Matlab R2019b. In the training phase, we selected 6000 images from BOSSBase as the training set. We set the batch size to 24. The two parameters α and β in the loss L_G were set to 1 and 10^{-7}. In the testing phase, we used three steganalyzers to evaluate the security performance, including XuNet [17], SRNet [2] and the state-of-the-art hand-crafted feature set SRM with ensemble classifier. XuNet is the steganalysis used in both ASDL-GAN and UT-GAN. SRNet is one of the most advanced steganalysis [9,21,22]. The proposed steganography was implemented in TensorFlow. The experiments were conducted on an NVIDIA GeForce RTX 2080Ti GPU card which has 11 GB memory.

4.2 The Selection of the Image Edge Enhancement Methods

In order to find an image edge enhancement method suitable for our proposed method, we conduct experiments based on the UT-GAN structure on the basis of Laplacian, Sobel, Prewitt, and Roberts operator under 0.4bpp. To compare the proposed method with the previous work UT-GAN and S-UNIWARD, we use the detection accuracy of XuNet, SRNet and SRM to measure the security performance, which is the ratio of correctly judged samples to all samples. The experimental results of security performance are shown in Table 1. The embedded capacity of all methods is 0.4bpp. It can be found any method based on image edge enhancement shows the advantages over UT-GAN and S-UNIWARD. Among them, images processed by Laplacian show the best security performance.

To further demonstrate the higher training efficiency of the structure based on image edge enhancement, we compare the network with 20,000 iterations prepocessed by Laplacian to UT-GAN with 30,000 iterations and S-UNIWARD. The detection results of XuNet shows that the proposed method achieves similar security performance to UT-GAN, 4.22% lower detection accuracy than S-UNIWARD. The proposed method achieves 3.64% and 5.60% lower detection accuracy eveluted by SRNet compared to UT-GAN and S-UNIWARD. The detection accuracy of the proposed method is 0.83% and 2.03% lower than UT-GAN and S-UNIWARD, respectively, when using SRM to extract high-dimensional features and ensemble classifier for detection. As we expected, the proposed method is more efficient and enhances the safety performance.

According to the steganalysis detection accuracy in Table 1, we choose the image enhanced by Laplacian as the input of the generator.

Table 1. Security performance of different steganography schemes.

	Laplacian(20000)	Laplacian	Sobel	Prewitt	Roberts	UT-GAN	S-UNIWARD
XuNet	69.47	68.61	68.87	67.93	68.77	69.01	73.69
SRNet	79.10	78.08	78.51	78.76	81.53	82.74	84.70
SRM	76.01	74.88	75.28	75.69	76.01	76.84	78.04

4.3 Comparison of Different Generators

As mentioned in Sect. 3.3, it is difficult for us to confirm which layers of features extracted are particularly effective for our task. Therefore, we conducted many experiments on BOSSBase to find a network structure with faster training speed and better training effect. The experimental results are recorded in Table 2. All networks iterated 30,000 iterations. We first tried a 5-layer U-Net++ network as the generator and named it L-12345, which means that the network contains all the U-Net structures from the 1 to 5 layers. Experimental results show that security performance of 5-layer U-Net++ is inferior to the 7-layer U-Net, called L-7. It can be seen that only using shallow features cannot learn the appropriate pixel change probability map. Then we tried a different network structure on the basis of L-7. We up-sampled from different layers on the contraction path as shown in the Table 2. After comparing experimental data, it can be found that adding the structure L-1, L-2 and L-6 which upsampled from the second and sixth layers can achieve the best security performance.

It is not difficult to find from the Table 2 that the 7-layer U-Net++ does not show the advantages. The compact structure means that there are more parameters to be trained. We list the number of trainable parameters of all generator subnetworks in Table 3. It demonstrates that when learning appropriate pixel change probability maps, it is not the more parameters and features utilized that make network training effective. Too many parameters may cause problems such as overfitting and difficult convergence. For different tasks on different datasets, we need to select effective features to improve the efficiency of network training. In our proposed method, we use L-1267 as the generator.

Table 2. Security performance of different generator structure based on laplacian.

	L-12345	L-7	L-127	L-1237	L-1267	L-1357	L-1234567
XuNet	70.41	68.61	**68.60**	70.55	68.91	69.23	69.96
SRNet	81.09	79.08	79.54	82.29	**79.03**	81.03	82.21
SRM	76.91	74.88	75.38	76.45	**74.69**	75.88	76.21

Table 3. Comparison of the number of parameters in different generator.

	L-12345	L-7	L-127	L-1237	L-1267	L-1357	L-1234567
Number of parameters	2989272	4111144	4204200	4322168	4500472	4314040	6835352

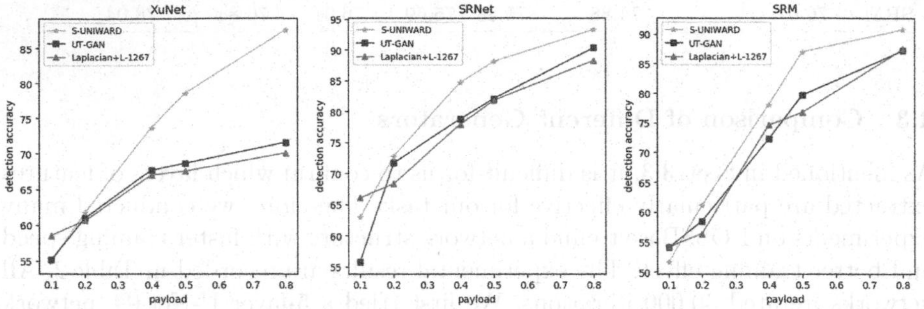

Fig. 3. Detection accyracy of different steganography methods on BOSSBase.

4.4   Comparison with State-of-the-Art Methods

In this part, we compare our proposed steganography method with existing state-of-the-art methods. We train the proposed network with different payloads for 60,000 iterations on the training set BOSSBase. We use the accuracy of XuNet, SRNet and SRM to evaluate the security performance and record the results in Fig. 3 and Table 4.

From Fig. 3 and Table 4, it can be seen that our proposed method has almost optimal security performance for different payloads. Taking the payload of 0.4bpp as an example. The proposed method achieves 6.69%, 5.82% and 3.45% lower detection accuracy rate than the conventional steganography method S-UNIWARD evaluted by XuNet, SRNet and SRM respectively. Compared with UT-GAN, the detection accuracy rate decreases by 0.69% and 0.89% evaluted by XuNet and SRNet.

However, it is difficult for the deep-learning based method to learn the effective pixel change probability map with low payload. We have analyzed the reasons for this phenomenon. One reason is that the current loss function simply reduces the difference between the stego image and the cover image in terms of pixel values. The loss function does not evaluate the impact of pixel modifications, instead this is taken into account by the hand-designed distortion function. Therefore, it is difficult for the network to precisely limit the image modifications when the embedding capacity is small. Another reason is that the model of GAN cannot be trained to an optimal state, which makes it difficult to break through on such a microscopic and delicate task as image steganography. Therefore, it is difficult but necessary to explore pixel change probability maps with fine-grained and high-precision accuracy.

To separately verify the effect of image edge enhancement and network structure tuning on the experimental performance, we tabulate the results in Table 5.

It can be seen that both methods are helpful in improving the security performence of steganography. However, the image edge enhancement method is more stable, and the combined use of these two methods is optimal. This indicates that the reasonable use of prior knowledge helps the network to learn effectively. In contrast, the process of network training has more uninterpretability and instability.

Table 4. Comparison of the proposed method and advanced methods in terms of security performence.

Steganalyzer	Steganography methods	0.1bpp	0.2bpp	0.4bpp	0.5bpp	0.8bpp
XuNet	S-UNIWARD	**54.91**	61.75	73.69	78.59	87.55
	UT-GAN	55.16	60.99	67.69	68.69	71.63
	Laplacian+L-1267	58.55	**60.02**	**67.00**	**67.60**	**70.14**
SRNet	S-UNIWARD	62.89	72.74	84.70	88.08	93.30
	UT-GAN	**55.76**	71.67	78.77	82.09	90.32
	Laplacian+L-1267	66.05	**68.30**	**77.88**	**81.79**	**88.26**
SRM	S-UNIWARD	**51.70**	61.16	78.04	86.94	90.78
	UT-GAN	54.11	58.52	**72.26**	79.60	**87.21**
	Laplacian+L-1267	54.21	**56.42**	74.59	**78.68**	87.44

Table 5. Comparison of each part of the proposed method in terms of safety performance.

	XuNet	SRNet	SRM
Laplacian	67.59	77.90	74.65
L-1267	67.15	78.46	75.03
Laplacian+L-1267	67.00	77.88	74.59

4.5 The Practical Application

In the actual embedding process, we use STC to embed secret messages. This approach can meet the actual embedding rate, and there is no need to consider the information extraction process. Because the information can be extracted accurately without loss. The only difference from the traditional adaptive steganography methods is the design of the embedding distortion. In practical application, we input the cover image into the generator to get the pixel change probability map. According to the function (7) proposed in the paper [13], the change probability can be converted into the embedding cost. According to the cover image, the embedding cost of the pixel, the secret message and the key, the STC encoding is performed to obtain the stego image. In the decryption process, the secret messages can be extracted based on the same key.

$$\rho_{i,j} = \ln\left(1/P_{i,j} - 2\right).\tag{7}$$

5   Conclusion

In this paper, we proposed a new steganography method combining image enhancement and automatic distortion learning. Before the generator generates change probability maps, we preprocess the image based on domain knowledge. This operation reduces the search space of the network and was shown to be beneficial for generator to generate more suitable change probability maps. In order to improve the utilization of features, we use a more compact network structure. Experimental results prove that this method can generate pixel change probability maps related to pixel distortion more efficiently and effectively, and further reduces the accuracy of steganalysis. Our approach is especially advantageous in the case of high embedding capacity. It achieves better security performance than S-UNIWARD and UT-GAN.

References

1. Bas, P., Filler, T., Pevný, T.: Break our steganographic system: the ins and outs of organizing BOSS. In: Filler, T., Pevný, T., Craver, S., Ker, A. (eds.) IH 2011. LNCS, vol. 6958, pp. 59–70. Springer, Heidelberg (2011). https://doi.org/10.1007/978-3-642-24178-9_5
2. Boroumand, M., Chen, M., Fridrich, J.: Deep residual network for steganalysis of digital images. IEEE Trans. Inf. Forensics Secur. **14**(5), 1181–1193 (2018)
3. Filler, T., Judas, J., Fridrich, J.: Minimizing additive distortion in steganography using syndrome-trellis codes. IEEE Trans. Inf. Forensics Secur. **6**(3), 920–935 (2011)
4. Fridrich, J., Kodovsky, J.: Rich models for steganalysis of digital images. IEEE Trans. Inf. Forensics Secur. **7**(3), 868–882 (2012)
5. Goodfellow, I., et al.: Generative adversarial nets. In: Advances in Neural Information Processing Systems, pp. 2672–2680 (2014)
6. Holub, V., Fridrich, J.: Designing steganographic distortion using directional filters. In: 2012 IEEE International workshop on information forensics and security (WIFS), pp. 234–239. IEEE (2012)
7. Holub, V., Fridrich, J., Denemark, T.: Universal distortion function for steganography in an arbitrary domain. EURASIP J. Inf. Secur. **2014**(1), 1–13 (2014). https://doi.org/10.1186/1687-417X-2014-1
8. Li, B., Wang, M., Huang, J., Li, X.: A new cost function for spatial image steganography. In: 2014 IEEE International Conference on Image Processing (ICIP), pp. 4206–4210. IEEE (2014)
9. Li, B., Wei, W., Ferreira, A., Tan, S.: Rest-net: diverse activation modules and parallel subnets-based cnn for spatial image steganalysis. IEEE Sig. Process. Lett. **25**(5), 650–654 (2018)

10. Pevný, T., Filler, T., Bas, P.: Using high-dimensional image models to perform highly undetectable steganography. In: Böhme, R., Fong, P.W.L., Safavi-Naini, R. (eds.) IH 2010. LNCS, vol. 6387, pp. 161–177. Springer, Heidelberg (2010). https://doi.org/10.1007/978-3-642-16435-4_13
11. Qian, Y., Dong, J., Wang, W., Tan, T.: Learning and transferring representations for image steganalysis using convolutional neural network. In: 2016 IEEE International Conference on Image Processing (ICIP), pp. 2752–2756. IEEE (2016)
12. Ronneberger, O., Fischer, P., Brox, T.: U-Net: convolutional networks for biomedical image segmentation. In: Navab, N., Hornegger, J., Wells, W.M., Frangi, A.F. (eds.) MICCAI 2015. LNCS, vol. 9351, pp. 234–241. Springer, Cham (2015). https://doi.org/10.1007/978-3-319-24574-4_28
13. Sedighi, V., Cogranne, R., Fridrich, J.: Content-adaptive steganography by minimizing statistical detectability. IEEE Trans. Inf. Forensics Secur. 11(2), 221–234 (2015)
14. Tan, S., Li, B.: Stacked convolutional auto-encoders for steganalysis of digital images. In: Signal and Information Processing Association Annual Summit and Conference (APSIPA), 2014 Asia-Pacific, pp. 1–4. IEEE (2014)
15. Tang, W., Tan, S., Li, B., Huang, J.: Automatic steganographic distortion learning using a generative adversarial network. IEEE Signal Process. Lett. 24(10), 1547–1551 (2017)
16. Xu, G., Wu, H.Z., Shi, Y.Q.: Ensemble of cnns for steganalysis: an empirical study. in: Proceedings of the 4th ACM Workshop on Information Hiding and Multimedia Security, pp. 103–107 (2016)
17. Xu, G., Wu, H.Z., Shi, Y.Q.: Structural design of convolutional neural networks for steganalysis. IEEE Signal Process. Lett. 23(5), 708–712 (2016)
18. Yang, J., Liu, K., Kang, X., Wong, E.K., Shi, Y.Q.: Spatial image steganography based on generative adversarial network. arXiv preprint arXiv:1804.07939 (2018)
19. Yang, J., Ruan, D., Huang, J., Kang, X., Shi, Y.Q.: An embedding cost learning framework using gan. IEEE Trans. Inf. Forensics Secur. 15, 839–851 (2019)
20. Ye, J., Ni, J., Yi, Y.: Deep learning hierarchical representations for image steganalysis. IEEE Trans. Inf. Forensics Secur. 12(11), 2545–2557 (2017)
21. Yedroudj, M., Comby, F., Chaumont, M.: Yedroudj-net: an efficient cnn for spatial steganalysis. In: 2018 IEEE International Conference on Acoustics, Speech and Signal Processing (ICASSP), pp. 2092–2096. IEEE (2018)
22. Zhang, R., Zhu, F., Liu, J., Liu, G.: Depth-wise separable convolutions and multi-level pooling for an efficient spatial cnn-based steganalysis. IEEE Trans. Inf. Forensics Secur. 15, 1138–1150 (2019)
23. Zhou, Z., Rahman Siddiquee, M.M., Tajbakhsh, N., Liang, J.: UNet++: a nested U-Net architecture for medical image segmentation. In: Stoyanov, D., et al. (eds.) DLMIA/ML-CDS -2018. LNCS, vol. 11045, pp. 3–11. Springer, Cham (2018). https://doi.org/10.1007/978-3-030-00889-5_1

No-Reference Image Quality Assessment via Broad Learning System

Jing Yue[1,2], Guojun liu[1(✉)], and Lizhuan Huang[1]

[1] School of Mathematics and Statistics, Ningxia University, Yinchuan, China
liugj@nxu.edu.cn
[2] School of Electrical and Control Engineering, Xi'an University of Science and Technology, Xi'an, China

Abstract. Deep Learning (DL) can be used to model the process of No Reference-Image Quality Assessment (NR-IQA), which has a great contribution to the field of image processing. Even though, a large number of super parameters make the computational complexity gradually increase. Surprisingly, Broad Learning System (BLS) can transform the deep structure of DL into a flat and visual network structure, which reduces the difficulty for practical applications. By applying BLS in NR-IQA, combining the structural and statistical features of the image to reflect the image quality, which expands the research of NR-IQA undoubtedly. In this paper, the mathematical relationship between the image and the score is modeled by BLS, the effectiveness of the proposed method is demonstrated in the numerical experiments.

Keywords: No-Reference Image Quality Assessment · Broad Learning System · Deep Learning · Neural network

1 Introduction

With the advance of digital communication and multimedia processing, machine learning and DL is used widely. NR-IQA based on DL is mainly designed by neural network. For example, the methods of supervised learning [1] combined the statistical gradient feature with BP neural network to construct blind IQA algorithm. In addition, Deep Neural Network (DNN) as showed in Fig. 1, Convolutional Neural Network (CNN) [2, 6], Deep Belief Network (DBN) [7], semantic network [7], or deep residual network [9], the depth similarity [10] used SSIM to evaluate the quality of image by using neural network. In order to overcome the dependence of the training characteristics on the content of the image, Yang et al. [11] used multiple Laplacian Of Gaussian (LOG) kernel convolve the image to extract the pixel sequence curve, and then fitted the parameters by the asymmetric generalized Gaussian distribution without depend only on the content of image. These works have made greatly contribution for the research of NR-IQA.

Unsupervised learning methods such as Lin et al. [12] generated an the illusion reference image to compensate for the lack of the real reference one. Pairing information of the illusion reference one with the distorted image and forwarded to the pre-set

Y. Peng et al. (Eds.): ICIG 2021, LNCS 12890, pp. 168–181, 2021.
https://doi.org/10.1007/978-3-030-87361-5_14

corrector to learn the perceived difference under the guidance of the implicit ordering. What is remarkable and practical about NR IQA is it that can generate images moving actively in the process actively breaking the barriers of traditional methods. In addition to generating a new reference image, Ren et al. [13] proposed a restorative generative network to imitate human visual system, extracting features from the recovered segments and taking the weighted sum of the recovered segment scores as the output. What's more, Lim et al. [14] proposed a novel virtual reality IQA method and Pan [15] applied the intermediate similarity map derived from the traditional full reference IQA method, predicting the similarity quality map only from the distorted image. It's observed that unsupervised learning methods have made great breakthrough compared with traditional DL methods.

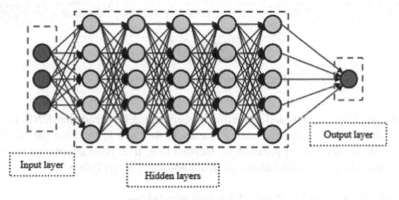

Fig. 1. Deep neural network

In this paper, we mainly discussed whether we could find a more efficient machine learning method can be used for the image quality evaluation such as BLS besides the DL method. The rest of the paper is developed into four sections. Section 2 gives the preliminaries of BLS. Section 3 illustrates the features for NR IQA and sets forth the details of the proposed algorithms. Section 4 contrasts the performance in NR IQA with various methods. Section 5 discusses the results and draws conclusions.

2 Broad Learning System

DL has received much attention and contributed a lot in image processing [16, 17]. Deep neural network has outstanding applicability but it has complex structure and too many hyper parameters which is difficult for the theoretical analysis. How to reduce the complexity while ensuring accuracy is the vital challenge. BLS can be used as an alternative way for IQA and it can learn incrementally. Fortunately, the random vector functional link neural network (RVFLNN) [18] in the 1990s, which can reduce the training time effectively and ensure the performance of the approximation.

Recently, Chen proposed a dynamic algorithm with step-by-step [21] to update the new input data and the output weight of the new enhanced node to solve the big data problems. On this basis, Broad Learning System (BLS) [22] was proposed as shown in Fig. 2. Later, authors extended BLS to the Fuzzy BLS [23] which can be applied to regression and classification. Firstly, BLS used the characteristics of the input data mapping as the "feature nodes" of the network. Secondly, the features of the mapping are enhanced to "enhanced nodes" that generate weight randomly. Finally, all mapped features and enhancement nodes are directly connected to the output, and the corresponding output coefficients can be derived from the pseudo-reverse of the courier.

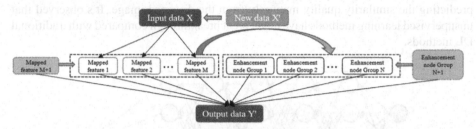

Fig. 2. Broad learning system [23]

The complex structure and numerous hyper parameters lead that DNN has long training time. To obtain higher testing accuracy, we have to increase the number of layers or add the number of parameters. Beyond that, BLS is an alternative method of DL network. The main contributions of this manuscript are as follows:

- A novel NR measure based on a flat neural network;
- A novel NR technique which used statistical distribution of gradient magnitude and the information of luminance;
- An effective fusion of the introduced NR measures;
- Avoiding excessive hyper parameters and deep layers.

3   NR IQA Based BLS

NR IQA is a critical measure in image processing. How to select various features that can describe the image logically is an important factor in IQA. The structure and contour of the image will be changed by extracting gradient features on the other hand the locally normalized luminance coefficients will be used to describe the statistical characteristics of the image.

3.1   Structure Features

Gradients can reflect the structural information of the image, such as Fig. 3. Considering the importance of the Gradient amplitude and LOG response of an image, we combine two common local contrast features and joint statistical normalized [24] as the first set of features. Given an image I,

$$G_I = \sqrt{[I \otimes h_x]^2 + [I \otimes h_y]^2} \tag{1}$$

$$L_I = I \otimes h_{LOG} \tag{2}$$

$$h_{LOG}(x, y|\sigma) = \frac{\partial^2}{\partial x^2} g(x, y|\sigma) + \frac{\partial^2}{\partial y^2} g(x, y|\sigma)$$

$$= \frac{1}{2\pi\sigma^2} \frac{x^2 + y^2 - 2\sigma^2}{\sigma^4} \exp\left(-\frac{x^2 + y^2}{2\sigma^2}\right) \tag{3}$$

where "$\otimes$" is a linear convolution operator, h_d, $d = \{x, y\}$ is Gaussian partial derivative filter along the horizontal and vertical direction

$$h_d(x, y|\sigma) = \frac{\partial}{\partial d} g(x, y|\sigma)$$

$$= -\frac{1}{2\pi\sigma^2} \frac{d}{\sigma^2} \exp(-\frac{x^2 + y^2}{2\sigma^2}), d \in \{x, y\} \tag{4}$$

In Eq. (4). $g(x, y|\sigma) = \frac{1}{2\pi\sigma^2} \exp\left(-\frac{x^2+y^2}{2\sigma^2}\right)$ is an isotropic Gaussian function with scale parameter σ. We use the Weibull distribution [25] and the generalized Gaussian distribution [26] to fit the gradient feature LOG response of image. Firstly, we set

$$F_I(i, j) = \sqrt{G_I^2(i, j) + L_I^2(i, j)} \tag{5}$$

Subsequently, we an add adaptive normalization factor at a local location (i, j)

$$N_I(i, j) = \sqrt{\sum \sum_{l,k \in \Omega_{i,j}} \omega(l, k) F_I(l, k)} \tag{6}$$

where $\Omega_{i,j}$ is a window, $\omega(l, k)$ is a weight which obeys Gaussian distribution, and satisfies $\sum_{l,k} \omega(l, k) = 1$. Normalizing the Eq. (1) and Eq. (2) as

$$\overline{G_I} = G_I/(N_I + \varepsilon) \tag{7}$$

$$\overline{L_I} = L_I/(N_I + \varepsilon) \tag{8}$$

where ε is a normal small number to prevent N_I being too small and resulting unstable values.

Then quantified $\overline{G_I}(i, j)$ and $\overline{L_I}(i, j)$ as m levels $\{g_1, g_2, g_3, ...g_m\}$ and n levels $\{l_1, l_2, l_3, ...l_n\}$, expressed as G and L respectively. The joint probability distribution, the marginal distribution and the independence of G and L are defined as follows

$$K_{m,n} = P(G = g_m, L = l_n), m = 1, ...M; n = 1, ...N \tag{9}$$

$$\begin{cases} P_G(G = g_m) = \sum_{n=1}^{N} K_{m,n} \\ P_L(L = l_n) = \sum_{m=1}^{M} K_{m,n} \end{cases} \tag{10}$$

$$D_{m,n} = \frac{K_{m,n}}{P(G = g_m) \times P(L = l_n)} \tag{11}$$

$D_{m,n} = 1$ for all m and n if G and L are independent. Hence

$$Q_G(G = g_m) = \frac{1}{N} \sum_{n=1}^{N} \frac{P(G = g_m, L = l_n)}{P(L = l_n)}$$

$$= \frac{1}{N} \sum_{n=1}^{N} P(G = g_m | L = l_n) \tag{12}$$

$$Q_L(L = l_n) = \frac{1}{M} \sum_{m=1}^{M} \frac{P(G = g_m, L = l_n)}{P(G = g_m)}$$

$$= \frac{1}{M} \sum_{m=1}^{M} P(L = l_n | G = g_m) \tag{13}$$

Equation (12) and Eq. (13) describe the independence between G and L. We set the ratio parameter of the filter as 0.5 which can capture more details in the feature maps, we extract 40 dimensional features.

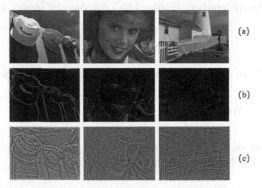

Fig. 3. (a) three example images; (b) the gradient magnitude of (a); (c) locally normalized luminance of (a)

3.2 Statistical Features

Using the scene statistics of the locally normalized luminance coefficients [31] to quantify the loss caused by the distortion. Which as follows

$$\hat{I}(i,j) = \frac{I(i,j) - \mu(i,j)}{\delta(i,j) + C} \tag{14}$$

where

$$\mu(i,j) = \sum_{s=-S}^{S} \sum_{t=-T}^{T} \varpi_{s,t} I_{s,t}(i,j) \tag{15}$$

$$\delta(i,j) = \sqrt{\sum_{s=-S}^{S}\sum_{t=-T}^{T} \varpi_{s,t}\big(I_{s,t}(i,j) - \mu(i,j)\big)^2} \tag{16}$$

and $\varpi = \{\varpi_{s,t}|s = -S, ..., S; t = -T, ..., T\}$. We fit the Mean Subtracted Contrast Normalized (MSCN) coefficient by Generalized Gaussian Distribution:

$$f(x; \alpha, \delta^2) = \frac{\alpha}{2\beta\Gamma(1/\alpha)} \exp-\left(-\left(\frac{|x|}{\beta}\right)^{\alpha}\right) \tag{17}$$

where $\beta = \delta\sqrt{\frac{\Gamma(1/\alpha)}{\Gamma(3/\alpha)}}$, $\Gamma(\bullet)$ is the Gamma function. The direction information of an image can fit by Asymmetric Generalized Gaussian Distribution (AGGD). Including horizontal H, vertical V, diagonal $D1$ and $D2$.

$$H(i,j) = \hat{I}(i,j)\hat{I}(i,j+1) \tag{18}$$

$$V(i,j) = \hat{I}(i,j)\hat{I}(i+1,j) \tag{19}$$

$$D1(i,j) = \hat{I}(i,j)\hat{I}(i+1,j+1) \tag{20}$$

$$D2(i,j) = \hat{I}(i,j)\hat{I}(i+1,j-1) \tag{21}$$

$$f(x; v, \delta_l^2, \delta_r^2) = \begin{cases} \dfrac{v}{(\beta_l + \beta_r)\Gamma(\frac{1}{v})} \exp\left(-(\dfrac{-x}{\beta_l})^v\right), x < 0 \\[3mm] \dfrac{v}{(\beta_l + \beta_r)\Gamma(\frac{1}{v})} \exp\left(-(\dfrac{-x}{\beta_r})^v\right), x \geq 0 \end{cases} \tag{22}$$

where

$$\beta_l = \delta_l\sqrt{\frac{\Gamma(\frac{1}{v})}{\Gamma(\frac{3}{v})}}, \ \beta_r = \delta_r\sqrt{\frac{\Gamma(\frac{1}{v})}{\Gamma(\frac{3}{v})}}, \ \eta = (\beta_r - \beta_l)\frac{\Gamma(\frac{2}{v})}{\Gamma(\frac{1}{v})} \tag{23}$$

In Eq. (22), the parameter v controls the ?shape? of fitting; δ_l^2 and δ_r^2 fitting the two sides of the distribution. The parameters $(\eta, v, \delta_l^2, \delta_r^2)$ of AGGD are fitted using moment matching.

Above all, there are 76 of features each image extraxted by our method. Figure 4 is the flow chart of the algorithm.

4 Numerical Experiments

In this section, we use LIVE [28], CSIQ [29], TID2008 [30], TID2013 [31] for experiments. LIVE, CSIQ and TID2008 are used for single database performance testing, and each one divided 80% for training and the rest 20% used for testing. We will compare the forecast and its corresponding subjective scores to calculate SROCC and PLCC and RMSE to measure the performance of the BLS-IQA algorithm. Besides, we use four databases test the performance of individual distortion types.

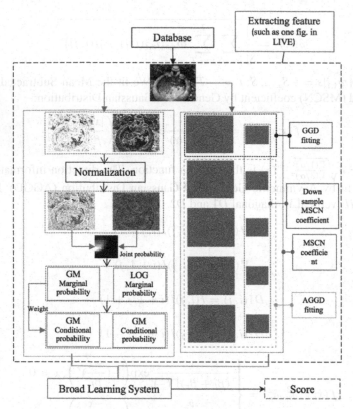

Fig. 4. The flow chart of BLS-IQA

4.1 Single Database Performance Comparisons

We will compare the BLS-IQA method with three full reference methods and six non-reference methods, which follows that Table 1.

Above Table 1, we marked the top three algorithms. It can be seen that the number of marked data of FSIM, GMLOG and BLS-IQA is mostly. We can find that in the last two columns the weighted average SROCC value of the algorithm reached 0.9408. From the above table, the analysis shows that themethod in this paper has certain competitiveness,and the performance is outstanding in some aspects such as the SROCC value of BLSIQA algorithm reached 0.9567 in TID2008, better than other full reference and no reference algorithm.

4.2 Single Distortion Type Performance Comparison

In this subsection, we use 23 types of distortion of the TID2013 database to demonstrate the performance of the BLS-IQA algorithm for better presentation which shown in Table 2. Each distortion type was divided into 80% for training and 20% for testing. We blacked out the best one. It can be seen that the BLS-IQA method perform best compared with the other six non-reference image quality evaluation algorithms. The SROCC can reach

Table 1. The comparison of performance with 10 algorithms on 3 databases

Algorithms	LIVE (779 images)			TID2008 (384 images)			CSIQ (600 images)			Weighted average	
	SROCC	PLCC	RMSE	SROCC	PLCC	RMSE	SROCC	PLCC	RMSE	SROCC	PLCC
PSNR[32]	0.8829	0.8821	12.898	0.8789	0.8611	0.8073	0.9292	0.8562	0.1444	0.8978	0.8687
SSIM[33]	0.9486	0.9464	8.804	0.9032	0.9087	0.6620	0.9362	0.9347	0.0990	0.9345	0.9342
FSIM[34]	0.9639	0.9612	7.546	0.9555	0.9539	0.4707	0.9629	0.9675	0.0710	0.9617	0.9617
BIQI[35]	0.8084	0.8250	15.388	0.8438	0.8704	0.7872	0.7598	0.8353	0.1542	0.7995	0.8384
DIIVINE[36]	0.8816	0.8916	12.329	0.8930	0.9038	0.6714	0.8697	0.9010	0.1249	0.8800	0.8974
BLIINDS2[37]	0.9302	0.9366	9.5185	0.8982	0.9219	0.6117	0.9003	0.9282	0.1028	0.9131	0.9305
CORNIA[38]	0.9466	0.9487	8.6969	0.8990	0.9347	0.5669	0.8845	0.9241	0.1054	0.9151	0.9373
BRISQUE[11]	0.9430	0.9468	8.7214	0.9357	0.9391	0.5442	0.9085	0.9356	0.0980	0.9298	0.9414
GMLOG[24]	0.9511	0.9551	8.0444	0.9369	0.9406	0.5377	0.9243	0.9457	0.0909	0.9390	0.9488
BLS-IQA	0.9301	0.9510	0.0748	0.9567	0.9569	0.0731	0.9445	0.9382	0.0991	0.9408	0.9479

above 0.9 through 15 types of distortion, and 0.8 through 18 types of distortion. Without chromaticity information and higher level semantic information, the distortion such as JPEG, NEPN, Block, MS, and CTC has been greatly improved on the basis of the original results, but still needs improvements.

In addition, the comparisons of the performance through individual distortion types are shown under three other databases. We use five types in LIVE database and four types in CSIQ and TID2008. The last line in Table 3 lists the average SROCC value of all types under each algorithm and the top two are marked black. Comparing with other non-reference quality evaluation algorithms, the BLS-IQA has black numbers up to 13, while other algorithms have less than 10, which shows that in LIVE, CSIQ, and TID2008, our algorithm can perform betterthan several types of distortions. Despite such good results, there are several points that should not be ignored such as the JPEG distortion type in LIVE database.

Besides, from Table 3 we can find that there are 15 performance evaluations of BLS-IQA above 0.95. Especially for the WN distortion type in LIVE database, the performance evaluation of BLS-IQA is as high as 0.9901, which is highly consistent with human visual perception system.

Table 2. The SROCC values of comparison of single distortion type of seven algorithms

Distortion types	BIQI[35]	BRISQUE[11]	BLIINEDII[37]	DIIVINE[36]	CORNIA[38]	CSIF	BLS-IQA
AGN	0.7842	0.8523	0.7226	0.8553	0.7561	0.9071	**0.9846**
ANC	0.5405	0.709	0.6497	0.712	0.7498	0.7928	**0.9685**
SCN	0.4653	0.4908	0.7674	0.4626	0.7265	0.0742	**0.9408**
MN	0.4938	0.5748	0.5127	0.6752	0.7262	0.3114	**0.8185**
HFN	0.8773	0.7528	0.8245	0.8778	0.7964	0.9179	**0.9502**
IN	0.748	0.6299	0.6501	0.8063	0.7667	0.7947	**0.9000**
QN	0.3894	0.7984	0.7816	0.165	0.0156	0.8687	**0.9092**
GB	0.7642	0.8134	0.8557	0.8344	0.9209	0.8630	**0.9457**
DEN	0.4094	0.5864	0.7116	0.7231	0.8315	0.3906	**0.8085**
JPEG	0.8567	0.8521	0.8643	0.6288	0.8743	0.8901	**0.9000**
JP2K	0.7327	0.8925	0.8984	0.8534	0.9103	0.9062	**0.9208**
JGTE	0.3035	0.315	0.117	0.2387	0.6856	0.3831	**0.7300**
J2TE	0.367	0.3594	0.6209	0.0606	0.6784	0.1700	**0.9308**
NEPN	0.0073	0.1453	0.0968	0.0598	0.2857	0.1532	**0.6563**
Block	0.0812	0.2235	0.2098	0.0928	0.2188	0.2731	**0.5992**
MS	0.0346	0.1241	0.1284	0.0104	0.0645	0.1557	**0.2435**
CTC	0.4125	0.0403	0.1505	0.4601	0.1823	0.0387	**0.6008**
MGN	0.6424	0.7242	0.7165	0.7873	0.6438	0.7962	**0.9517**
CN	0.2141	0.0081	0.0178	0.1156	0.5341	0.0038	**0.8715**

(continued)

Table 2. (*continued*)

Distortion types	BIQI[35]	BRISQUE[11]	BLIINEDII[37]	DIIVINE[36]	CORNIA[38]	CSIF	BLS-IQA
LCNI	0.5261	0.6852	0.7193	0.6327	0.8623	0.8559	**0.9285**
ICQD	0.6983	0.764	0.7358	0.4362	0.2717	0.8723	**0.9429**
CHA	0.5435	0.616	0.5397	0.6608	0.7922	0.6623	**0.9338**
SSR	0.7595	0.7841	0.8164	0.8334	0.8624	0.8751	**0.9723**

Table 3. Performance comparison of 7 algorithms on 3 databases for each type of distortion

Database	Distortion types	BIQI[35]	BLIINDS2 [37]	BRISQUE[11]	DIIVINE[36]	CORNIA [38]	GMLOG [24]	BLS-IQA
LIVE	JP2K	0.7849	0.9258	0.9175	0.8418	0.9271	**0.9283**	**0.9279**
	JPEG	0.8801	0.9500	**0.9655**	0.8926	0.9437	**0.9659**	0.8459
	WN	0.9157	0.9477	0.9789	0.9617	0.9608	**0.9853**	**0.9901**
	GB	0.8367	0.9132	0.9479	0.8792	**0.9553**	0.9395	**0.9690**
	FF	0.7023	0.8736	0.8854	0.8202	**0.9103**	0.9008	**0.9586**
CSIQ	WN	0.6000	0.8863	0.9310	0.8131	0.7980	**0.9406**	**0.9841**
	JPEG	0.8384	0.9115	0.9253	0.8843	0.8845	**0.9328**	**0.9711**
	JP2K	0.7573	0.8870	0.8934	0.8692	0.8950	**0.9172**	**0.9592**
	GB	0.8160	**0.9152**	0.9143	0.8756	0.9006	0.9070	**0.9492**
TID2008	WN	0.5368	0.7314	0.8603	0.7130	0.5941	**0.9068**	**0.9838**
	GB	0.8878	**0.9176**	0.9059	0.8824	0.8941	0.8812	**0.9647**
	JPEG	0.8996	0.8853	0.9103	0.9033	0.9099	**0.9338**	**0.9794**
	JP2K	0.8147	0.9118	0.9044	0.9103	**0.9290**	0.9263	**0.9618**
Mean		0.7900	0.8966	0.9185	0.8651	0.8848	**0.9281**	**0.9573**
Marked		0	2	1	0	3	9	13

4.3 Cross-Validation Performance

To reflect the generalization ability of BLS-IQA algorithm, we compare the performance of cross-validation on the three databases. Firstly, we train on LIVE database and test on CSIQ, TID2008. Then we train on CSIQ, using TID2008 and LIVE for test. Finally, we train on TID2008 and test on LIVE, CSIQ.

In Table 4, we calculate the standard deviation of all the scores of each algorithm after cross-validation which can reflect the robustness of the generalization ability of the algorithm and black out the lowest STD. Although the GMLOG performed well on the four cross sets, and the BLS-IQA only performs well on one case, BLS-IQA has the lowest STD value, which indicates that the algorithm has better robustness.

Table 4. The cross-validation performance comparison of 7 algorithms on 3 databases

Training database	Test database	BIQI[35]	BLIINDS2[37]	BRISQUE[11]	DIIVINE[36]	CORNIA[38]	GMLOG[24]	BLS-IQA
LIVE	CSIQ	0.7805	0.8878	0.8993	0.8571	0.8973	**0.9108**	0.8817
LIVE	TID2008	0.8194	0.9056	0.9050	0.8599	0.8932	**0.9204**	0.8733
CSIQ	LIVE	0.4538	0.9365	0.9311	0.8475	0.9279	**0.9459**	0.8987
CSIQ	TID2008	0.6977	0.8005	0.8986	0.8223	0.8704	**0.9051**	0.8956
TID2008	LIVE	0.7631	**0.9389**	0.9288	0.8658	0.9091	0.9336	0.9003
TID2008	CSIQ	0.8009	0.8747	0.8665	0.8481	0.8381	0.8393	**0.8758**
STD		0.1366	0.0511	0.0237	0.0153	0.0314	0.0373	**0.0121**

4.3 Cross-validation Performance

5   Conclusion

The experimental results show that BLS can be used as an alternative method of DL which can avoid the complexity of hyper parameters when modeling the affine function between image features and subjective scores. However, there are still some ideas that can provide directions for future research: 1) With chrominance information, whether the algorithm can be improved; 2) Whether the unsupervised learning method such as Generative Adversarial Nets can be used to learn the IQA; 3) Whether this efficient method can be applied to other image processing problems.

Acknowledgments. This work was supported in part by the National Natural Science Foundation of China (Grant No. 62061040, 51769026); the Major Innovation Projects for Building First-class Universities in China's Western Region (Grant No. ZKZD2017009); the Natural Science Foundation of Ningxia (Grant No. 2018AAC03014) and the Postgraduate Innovation Project of Ningxia University (No. GIP2019011).

References

1. Liu, L., Hua, Y., Zhao, Q., Huang, H, Bovik, A.C.: Blind image quality assessment by relative gradient statistics and AdaBoosting neural network[J]. Signal Process Image Commun. **40**(C), 1–15 (2016)
2. Bianco, S., Celona, L., Napoletano, P., Schettini, R.: On the use of deep learning for blind image quality assessment[J]. SIViP **12**(2), 355–362 (2018)
3. Gao, F., Yu, J.: Blind image quality prediction by exploiting multi-level deep representations[J]. Pattern Recogn. **81**, 432–442 (2018)
4. Fang, Y., Zhang, C., Yang, W., Liu, J., Guo, Z.: Blind visual quality assessment for image super-resolution by convolutional neural network[J]. Multimedia Tools Appl. **77**(22), 29829–29846 (2018)
5. Fang, Y.M., Yan, J.B.. Stereoscopic image quality assessment by deep convolutional neural network[J]. J. Vis. Commun. Image Represent. **58**, 400–406 (2019)
6. Jia, S., Zhang, Y.: Saliency-based deep convolutional neural network for no-reference image quality assessment[J]. Multimedia Tools Appl. **77**(12), 14859–14872 (2018)
7. Yang, J.C., Zhao, Y., Zhu, Y.H., Xua, H.F., Lu, W., Meng, Q.G.: Blind assessment for stereo images considering binocular characteristics and deep perception map based on deep belief network[J]. Inf. Sci. **474**, 1–17 (2019)
8. Ji, W.P., Wu, J.J., Shi, G.M., Wan, W.F., Xie, X.M.: Blind image quality assessment with semantic information[J]. J. Vis. Commun. Image Represent **58**, 195–204 (2019)
9. Wu, J., Zeng, J., Liu, Y., Shi, G.M.: Hierarchical feature degradation based blind image quality assessment[C]. In: IEEE International Conference on Computer Vision Workshop (2017)
10. Gao, F., Wang, Y., Li, P.P., Tan, M., Yu, J., Zhu, Y.: DeepSim: deep similarity for image quality assessment [J]. Neuro comput. **257**, 104–114 (2017)
11. Yang, Y., Cheng, G., Yu, D.H., Ye, R.Z.: Blind image quality assessment via content-invariant statistical feature[J]. Optik **138**, 21–32 (2017)
12. Lin, K.Y., Wang, G.: Hallucinated-IQA: no-reference image quality assessment via adversarial learning[J]. In: The IEEE Conference on Computer Vision and Pattern Recognition (CVPR), pp. 732–741 (2018)
13. Ren, H., Chen, D., Wang, Y.: RAN4IQA: Restorative adversarial nets for no-reference image quality assessment[C]. arXiv preprint arXiv:1712.05444 (2017)

14. Lim, H.T., Kim, H.G., Ro, Y.M.: VR IQA NET: deep virtual reality image quality assessment using adversarial learning[C]. In: IEEE International Conference on Acoustics Speech and Signal Processing (ICASSP), pp. 6737–6741 (2018)

15. Pan, D., Shi, P., Hou, M., Ying, Z.F., Fu, S.Z., Zhang, Y.: Blind predicting similar quality map for image quality assessment[C]. In: The IEEE Conference on Computer Vision and Pattern Recognition (CVPR), pp. 6373–6382 (2018)

16. Hinton, G.E., Osindero, S., Teh, Y.W.: A fast learning algorithm for deep belief nets[J]. Neural Comput. **18**(7), 1527–1554 (2006)

17. Hinton, G.E., Sejnowski, T.J.: Learning and relearning in Boltzmann Machines[J]. Parallel Distrib. Process. Explor. Microstruct. Cogn. **1**, 282–317 (1986)

18. Pao, Y.H., Takefuji, Y.: Functional-link net computing: theory, system architecture, and functionalities[J]. Computer **25**(5), 76–79 (1992)

19. Pao, Y.H., Park, G.H., Sobajic, D.J.: Learning and generalization characteristics of the random vector functional-link net[J]. Neurocomputing **6**(2), 163–180 (1994)

20. Igelnik, B., Pao, Y.H.: Stochastic choice of basis functions in adaptive function approximation and the functional-link net[J]. IEEE Trans. Neural Netw. Learn. Syst. **6**(6), 1320–1329 (1995)

21. Chen, C.L.P., Wan, J.Z.: A rapid learning and dynamic stepwise updating algorithm for flat neural networks and the application to time-series prediction[J]. IEEE Trans. Syst. Man Cybern. Part B (Cybernetics) **29**(1), 62–72 (1999)

22. Chen, C.L.P., Liu, Z.: Broad learning system: an effective and efficient incremental learning system without the need for deep architecture[J]. IEEE Trans. Neural Netw. Learn. Syst. **29**(1), 10–24 (2018)

23. Shuang, F., Chen, C.L.P.: Fuzzy broad learning system: a novel neuro-fuzzy model for regression and classification[J]. IEEE Trans. Cybern., 1–11 (2018)

24. Xue, W., Mou, X., Zhang, L., Bovik, A.C., Feng, X.C., et al.: Blind image quality assessment using joint statistics of gradient magnitude and Laplacian features[J]. IEEE Trans. Image Process. **23**(11), 4850–4862 (2014)

25. Geusebroek, J.M., Smeulders, A.: A six-stimulus theory for stochastic texture[J]. Int. J. Comput. Vision **62**(1–2), 7–16 (2005)

26. Huang, J.G., Mumford, D.: Statistics of natural images and models[C]. In: IEEE Computer Society Conference on Computer Vision and Pattern Recognition (1999)

27. Ruderman, D.L.: The statistics of natural images[J]. Netw. Comput. Neural Syst. **5**(4), 517–548 (1994)

28. Sheikh, H.R., Wang, Z., Cormack, L., Bovik, A.C.: LIVE image quality assessment database release 2. http://live.ece.utexas.edu/research/quality. 4 February 2015

29. Larson, E.C., Chandler, D.M.: Most apparent distortion: full reference image quality assessment and the role of strategy[J]. J. Electron. Imaging **19**(011006), 1–21 (2010)

30. Ponomarenko, N., Lukin, V., Zelensky, A.: TID2008 a database for evaluation of full-reference visual quality assessment metrics[J]. Adv. Modern Radio Electr. **1**(10), 30–45 (2009)

31. Ponomarenko, N., Jin, L., Leremeiev, O., Lukin, V., Egiazarian, K., Astola, J., et al.: Image database TID2013: peculiarities, results and perspectives[J]. Signal Process. Image Commun. **1**(30), 55–77 (2015)

32. Wang, Z., Bovik, A.C., Lu, L.G.: Why is image quality assessment so difficult?[C]. In: IEEE International Conference on Acoustics, Speech, and Signal Processing, pp. 3313–3316 (2002)

33. Wang, Z., Bovik, A.C., Sheikh, H.R., Simoncelli, E.P.: Image quality assessment: from error visibility to structural similarity[J]. IEEE Trans. Image Process. **13**(4), 600–612 (2004)

34. Zhang, L., Zhang, L., Mou, X.Q., Zhang, D.: FSIM: a feature similarity index for image quality assessment[J]. IEEE Trans. Image Process. **20**(8), 2378–2386 (2011)

35. Moorthy, A.K., Bovik, A.C.: A two-step framework for constructing blind image quality indices[J]. IEEE Signal Process. Lett. **17**(5), 513–516 (2010)

36. Moorthy, A.K., Bovik, A.C.: Blind image quality assessment: from natural scene statistics to perceptual quality[J]. IEEE Trans. Image Process. **20**(12), 3350–3364 (2011)
37. Saad, M.A., Bovik, A.C., Charrier, C.: Blind image quality assessment: a natural scene statistics approach in the DCT domain[J]. IEEE Trans. Image Process. **21**(8), 3339–3352 (2012)
38. Ye, P., Kumar, J., Kang, L., Doermann, D.: Unsupervised feature learning framework for no-reference image quality assessment[C]. In: IEEE Conference on Computer Vision and Pattern Recognition (2012)

Hindsight Curriculum Generation Based Multi-Goal Experience Replay

Xiaoyun Feng[✉]

University of Science and Technology of China, Hefei, Anhui, China

Abstract. In multi-goal tasks, an agent learns to achieve diverse goals from past experiences. Hindsight Experience Replay (HER)—which replays experiences with pseudo goals—has shown the potential to learn from failed experiences. However, not all the pseudo goals are well-explored to provide reliable value estimates. In view of value estimation, the agent should learn from achievable goals towards desired goals distribution progressively. To tackle the problem, we propose to generate a hindsight curriculum, which maintains a sequence of balancing distributions of achieved goals to replay. Based on the hindsight curriculum, the agent evaluates hindsight experiences with a batch of similar well-explored experiences, and strikes a dynamic balance between function approximation and task solving. We implement Hindsight Curriculum Generation (HCG) with the vanilla Deep Deterministic Policy Gradient (DDPG), and experiments on several multi-goal tasks with sparse binary rewards demonstrate that HCG improves sample efficiency of the state-of-the-art.

Keywords: Artificial intelligence · Game · Reinforcement learning

1 Introduction

Deep Reinforcement Learning (DRL) has shown great power in solving large sequential decision-making problems, such as Computer Go [1,2], Atari Games [3] and Robotic Control [4–6]. By interacting with the environment and maximizing the expected sum of rewards, a DRL agent optimizes its approximated value function and policy. In many real-world scenarios, the agent suffers from sparse rewards. For example, in Multi-Goal [7] tasks, it receives no extrinsic reward until reaches the position defined by the desired goal. It's impractical to carefully engineer a shaped reward function [8,9] that aligns with each task. Such a sparse rewards problem makes the objective problematic and difficult to optimize. To allow sample-efficient learning from sparse rewards, [10] presents Hindsight Experience Replay (HER) to relabel past experiences with pseudo goals, which is likely to turn failed experiences into successful ones with nonzero rewards. The enriched successful experiences are able to guide the policy optimization without further exploration. HER works better with goals that were

© Springer Nature Switzerland AG 2021
Y. Peng et al. (Eds.): ICIG 2021, LNCS 12890, pp. 182–194, 2021.
https://doi.org/10.1007/978-3-030-87361-5_15

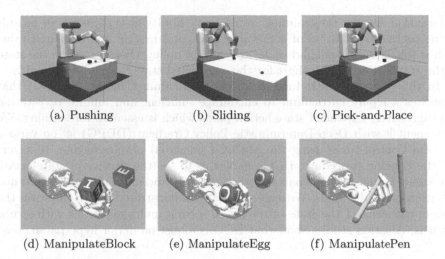

(a) Pushing   (b) Sliding   (c) Pick-and-Place

(d) ManipulateBlock   (e) ManipulateEgg   (f) ManipulatePen

Fig. 1. Tasks with sparse binary rewards. They include Pushing, Sliding and Pick-and-Place with a Fetch robotic arm as well as different in-hand object manipulations with a Shadow Dexterous Hand. The agent obtains a reward of 1 if it achieves the desired goal within some task-specific tolerance and 0 otherwise.

going to be achieved in the near future from the trajectories [10], which indicates that achievable goals contribute to efficient learning in different degrees.

Recent works focus on improving HER by resampling goals with various criteria. HER with Energy-Based Prioritization(EBP) [11] defines a trajectory energy function as the sum of transitions' physical energy of the target object over the trajectory. Curriculum-guided HER (CHER) [12] adaptively selects pseudo goals according to the proximity to the true goals and the curiosity of exploration over diverse goals with gradually changed proportion. Maximum Entropy-based Prioritization (MEP) [13] with HER proposes and optimizes a weighted entropy-based objective to encourage to maximize the expected return, as well as to achieve diverse goals. However, existing HER strategies ignore that the agent will not further explore most of the pseudo goals. When combining temporal difference learning with function approximation, updating the value at one state-goal pair creates a risk of inappropriately changing the values of other state-goal pairs, including the state-goal pair being bootstrapped upon.

Noticing that achieved goals are often biased towards behavior policies [13], state-goal pair with high likelihood will get credible estimate under the current policy, and vice versa. Meanwhile, it is critical for RL agent to revisit any goal sufficiently often. [14] If pseudo goals are not well-explored, it will lead to an unreliable estimate of the universal value function [15]. To address this challenge, we take advantage of relative goals, i.e. distances between the achieved goals and the desired goals, which are widely distributed and can be frequently revisited. Then we generate a hindsight curriculum that automatically shifts resample probability from achieved goals distribution towards the overall desired goals distribution. During the training, we resample hindsight experiences in pursuit of the overall distribution of achievable goals, and modify approximated value with state-action's likelihood under the current policy. (For simplicity, the state in the state-action pair is short for the augmented state, i.e. state-goal pair.)

In this paper, we introduce Hindsight Curriculum Generation (HCG) that generates a replay curriculum to encourage sufficient and infinite revisitation to progressively expanded state-action pairs, which is essential for learning. We implement it with Deep Deterministic Policy Gradient (DDPG) [4] on various Robotic Control tasks using the MuJoCo simulated physics engine [16]. During the training procedure, HCG enables us to see the density of state-action visitations for unexplored goals more conveniently and maintains a balanced distribution over valid goals. We experimentally demonstrated that it improves the sample efficiency of the state-of-the-art in solving multi-goal tasks with sparse rewards. Ablation studies show that HCG is robust on major hyperparameters.

2 Related Works

Hindsights in RL. HER introduces hindsight relabelling scheme to extract information from failures. Temporal Difference Model(TDM) [17] generalizes policy to not only unseen goals but also a multi-step temporal scale by relabelling. Hindsight Policy Gradient (HPG) [18] adopts the potential for goal-conditional policies to enable higher-level planning based on subgoals in policy gradient methods. Generalized Hindsight (GH) [19] converts the data generated from the policy under one task to a different task. Moreover, Exploration via Hindsight Goal Generation (HGG) [20] constructs a curriculum on goals guiding the exploration of the environment. Dynamic HER (DHER) [21] assembles successful experiences from relevant failures with dynamic goals.

Sparse Rewards. When signals indicating origin tasks solving are rare, most works rely heavily on additional tasks to help training. Some works assign the agent a set of general auxiliary tasks that rely on expert knowledge [22] or intrinsic motivation [23,24], and some works construct a series of sub-tasks [25] to guide exploration.

3 Background

In this section we briefly introduce the Multi-Goal RL framework, universal value function approximators and HER strategy used in the paper.

3.1 Multi-Goal RL

Consider an infinite-horizon discounted Markov decision process(MDP), defined by the tuple $(\mathcal{S}, \mathcal{A}, \mathcal{G}, P, r, \gamma)$, where $\mathcal{S}$ is a set of states, $\mathcal{A}$ is a set of actions, $\mathcal{G}$ is a set of goals, $P : \mathcal{S} \times \mathcal{A} \times \mathcal{S} \to \mathbb{R}$ is the transition probability distribution, $r : \mathcal{S} \times \mathcal{A} \times \mathcal{G} \to \mathbb{R}$ is the reward function, and $\gamma \in (0, 1)$ is the discount factor.

Algorithm 1. Hindsight Curriculum Generation

Require:
- an off-policy RL algorithm $\mathbb{A}$
- a distribution p for resampling goals for replay
- a reward function $r : \mathcal{S} \times \mathcal{A} \times \mathcal{G} \to \mathbb{R}$

Initialize $\mathbb{A}$, Replay buffer R, K, c, L, γ
for $episode = 1 \to M$ **do**
    Sample a goal g and an initial state s_0
    Step with behavioral policy $\mathbb{A}$ and store the transition in R
    Perform the K-means clustering in R as describe in Section 4.2
    for $t = 0 \to T - 1$ **do**
        Sample a set of additional goal for replay G with p in R
        for $g' \in G$ **do**
            $r' := r(s_t, a_t, g')$
            Store the transition $(s_t \| g', a_t, r', s_{t+1} \| g')$ in R
        end for
    end for
    for $t = 1 \to N$ **do**
        Sample a minibatch B from the replay buffer R
        Perform one step of optimization using $\mathbb{A}$ and minibatch B via Eq.(6)
    end for
    Update p with via Eq. (7) in Section 4.3
end for

In Multi-Goal RL, an agent interacts with its discounted MDP environment in a sequence of episodes. At the beginning of each episode, the agent receives a goal $g \in \mathcal{G}$. In this paper we set that each $g \in \mathcal{G}$ corresponds to a state $s_g \in \mathcal{S}$. Moreover, we assume that given a state s we can easily find a goal g which is satisfied in this state. At each timestep t, the agent observes a state $s_t \subset \mathcal{S}$, chooses and executes an action $a_t \in \mathcal{A}$. And the agent will receive a resulting reward $r(s_t, a_t, g)$ at the next timestep $t + 1$. (For simplicity, we denote $r_t = r(s_t, a_t, g)$.) In Multi-Goal RL, the reward function r is a binary sparse signal indicating whether the agent achieves the desired goal:

$$r_t = \begin{cases} 1, \|\phi(s_{t+1}) - g\|_2 \le \delta_g \\ 0, \quad otherwise \end{cases}$$

where $\phi : \mathcal{S} \to \mathcal{G}$, a known and tractable mapping, defines the corresponding goal representation of each state, and δ_g is a task-specific tolerance threshold [7].

3.2 Universal Value Function Approximators

Tasks following the Multi-Goal RL framework tell agent what to achieve by a goal in each episode, and goals vary across episodes. In continuous control tasks, the agent could not afford to learn a specific policy for each goal. Instead, the policy should generalize not just over states but also over goals via deep neural networks. Formally, Universal Value Function Approximators (UVFA) [15] factor observed values into separate embedding vectors for states and goals, then learn a mapping from (s, g) pairs to factored embedding vectors.

Let $\tau = s_1, a_1, s_2, a_2, \ldots, s_{T-1}, a_{T-1}, s_T$ denote a trajectory, which is also an episode, $R_t = \sum_{i=t}^{T} \gamma^{i-t} r_i$ denote its discounted return at every timestep $t \in [1, T]$. Let $\pi : \mathcal{S} \times \mathcal{G} \to \mathcal{A}$ denote a universal policy, $V^\pi : \mathcal{S} \times \mathcal{G} \to \mathbb{R}$ denote its value function. The objective of the agent is to learn a general value function parameterized by θ that represents the expected discounted return, i.e.

$$V^\pi(s_t, g) := \mathbb{E}\left[R_t | \theta\right],$$

or to learn a policy π that maximizes expected discounted return. The Q-function $Q^\pi : \mathcal{S} \times \mathcal{G} \times \mathcal{A} \to \mathbb{R}$ also depends on goals. UVFA trains an approximator to the Q-function using direct bootstrapping from the Bellman equation

$$Q^\pi(s_t, g, a_t) := \mathbb{E}_{s_{t+1}}\left[r_t + \gamma V^\pi(s_{t+1}, g)\right]. \tag{1}$$

The previous works [10–13] concatenate state s and goal g together as joint input for value function, so do we. As the deep neural network has a strong generalization ability, it learns a similar representation for similar augmented states, i.e. state-goal pairs. Providing sufficient revisitations for any augmented state is essential for a credible value estimation.

3.3 Hindsight Experience Replay

Experience replay is the key strategy of off-policy RL to remember and reuse past experiences. By resampling experiences for agent training, it makes better use of experiences than on-policy RL. Let $\mu : \mathcal{S} \times \mathcal{G} \to \mathcal{A}$ denote a universal behavior policy and π denote the target policy. In off-policy RL, the target policy can learn from experiences generated by any behavior policy as long as if $\mathbb{P}(a = \pi(s_t, g)) > 0$, we have $\mathbb{P}(a = \mu(s_t, g)) > 0$ at each t. If any state-action pair (s_t, g, a) is unavailable for behavior policy, there will be approximation error in the estimation of $Q^\pi(s_t, g, a_t)$.

Given that the transition probability distribution is independent of goals, Eq. (1) holds with another goal g',

$$Q^\pi(s_t, g', a_t) := \mathbb{E}_{s_{t+1}}\left[r_t + \gamma V^\pi(s_{t+1}, g')\right], \tag{2}$$

which makes it possible to relabel past experiences with additional goals. HER relabels the desired goals in the replay transitions to some achieved goals sampled from failed episodes. Specifically, it stores transitions not only with the original goal used for its episode but also with a subset of other goals. HER proposes various goal generation strategies, e.g. *future* strategy that replays with m random states which come from the same episode as the transition being replayed and were observed after it. The hyperparameter m controls the ratio of relabeled experiences to those coming from normal experience replay.

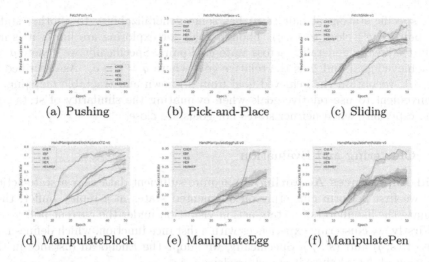

(a) Pushing   (b) Pick-and-Place   (c) Sliding

(d) ManipulateBlock   (e) ManipulateEgg   (f) ManipulatePen

Fig. 2. Learning curves for variants with multiple goals. It shows that at an early stage, our method (labeled HCG) can maintain a stable high success rate.

4 Hindsight Curriculum Generation

In this section, we analyze the challenges of HER and introduce a novel hindsight strategy to sample valuable experiences for replay, as well as to maintain credible value estimation. Then we incorporate our HCG with vanilla HER, aiming at accelerating the learning in multi-goal tasks with sparse binary rewards. During the process, the updated distributions $\{p_i, i = 1, 2, \dots\}$ automatically form a curriculum as the range of sampled goals progressively expands.

4.1 Challenges of Hindsight

Dealing with sparse rewards, HER relabels past experiences with achieved goals. The hindsight—the pseudo goal is going to be achieved along sampled trajectory—enables an agent to learn from failure. For (s_t, a, s_{t+1}, g) and a pseudo goal g', it estimates the value of relabelled experience via a variant of Eq. (2)

$$Q^\pi(s_t, g', a_t) = \mathbb{E}_{s_{t+1}}\left[r_t + \gamma Q^\pi(s_{t+1}, g', a)\right], \tag{3}$$

where a is sampled by π. However, there are challenges that 1) the current policy could not give crediable estimation for the new state-goal pair (s_{t+1}, g') in lack of sufficient exploration near pseudo goal g'; 2) though all the achieved goals can be replayed, the desired goals are distributed according to the target task.

Generalizing the policy to unseen state-action pairs requires a large number of samples, given the huge state and action spaces that characterize continuous robotic control problems. From the perspective of value generalization, approximating the value relies on the assumption that a value function of a policy π

for a specific state-goal pair (s, g) has some generalizability to another state-goal pair (s', g') close to (s, g). Though goals for exploring are finite, it is not costly to directly generalize across state-goal pairs. Specifically, we denote g_s as the achieved goal and $\tilde{g}$ as the relative goal where $\tilde{g} = g - g_s$. As described in Sect. 3.1, we obtain the achieved goal from a known and tractable mapping. It is convenient to use relative goals when evaluating the similarity of state-goal pairs, especially when neither states nor goals are close.

4.2   Clustering and Evaluation

Valid Experiences Acquiring. To acquire sufficient data near a state-action pair, we first perform clustering on augmented states in a replay buffer, then estimate the likelihood of a state-action visitation under the current policy.

Firstly, we clustering experiences with a distance function, which defines how close of $(s, \tilde{g})$ and $(s', \tilde{g}')$. Specifically, we adopt the Euclidean distance in the definition of $d(*, *)$ since it is task-irrelevant, i.e.

$$d((s, \tilde{g}), (s', \tilde{g}')) = c * d(s, s') + d(\tilde{g}, \tilde{g}'), \tag{4}$$

where the hyperparameter c ensures that the influence of each item won't be omitted. It partitions augmented states into K clusters in which each state belongs to the cluster with the nearest mean. It is trivial to sample similar states for a new state after finding the nearest clustering center. Formally, for each $(s, \tilde{g})$, there is $\{(s^i, \tilde{g}^i, a^i) | d((s, \tilde{g}), (s^i, \tilde{g}^i)) < \epsilon_1, i = 1, 2, \ldots, n\}$ where ϵ_1 is small.

Secondly, we estimate the likelihood of a $(s, \tilde{g})$ visitation with a batch of similar states. If $(s, \tilde{g})$ is well-explored by a policy, the policy will give reliable and stable value estimates for similar pairs. Hence we define that the likelihood $F(s, \tilde{g}, \pi(s, \tilde{g}))$ is inversely proportional to the max estimate difference, i.e.

$$\epsilon(s^i, \tilde{g}^i) = ||Q^\pi(s, \tilde{g}, \pi(s, \tilde{g})) - Q^\pi(s^i, \tilde{g}^i, \pi(s^i, \tilde{g}^i))||_2,$$

$$F(s, \tilde{g}, \pi(s, \tilde{g})) \propto \frac{1}{\max_{1 \leq i \leq n} \epsilon(s^i, \tilde{g}^i)}.$$

Evaluation. We suppose that the estimated value is more reliable for the state-action pair with a high likelihood score, and vice versa. Besides evaluating the likelihood of a state-action visitation, we accelerate the value approximating via modifying the Eq. (3) to give the value a bound related to similar states.

Assume that we have $(s, g) \sim \tau$, $(s', g') \sim \tau'$ and $d((s, g), (s', g')) < \epsilon_1$, where $d(*, *)$ defined in Eq. (4) evaluates the similarity between them and $\epsilon_1 > 0$ is small. Inspired by the generalizability assumption, as excuting the identical π, the value function can generalize from one to another. Formally, the generalizability can be specifically expressed as the Lipschitz continuity of value function [20]:

$$|Q^\pi(s, \tilde{g}, \pi(s, \tilde{g})) - Q^\pi(s', \tilde{g}', \pi(s', \tilde{g}'))| \leq L d((s, g), (s', \tilde{g}')), \tag{5}$$

where $L > 0$ is the Lipschitz coefficient and $d(*,*)$ defined in Eq. (4) evaluats the similarity between (s, g) and $(s', \tilde{g}')$. The bound Eq. (5) holds for most of the state-goal pairs when $d((s, \tilde{g}), (s', \tilde{g}'))$ is small.

As described in Sect. 3.3, unsufficient visitations lead to an unreliable estimate. When the likelihood of a state-action visitation is low, it is alternative to sample an action from the executed ones at the similar state. Therefore, we take the likelihood into account to sample the action a at the next state for the critic. After acquiring a batch of experiences with similar states for the $(s_{t+1}, \tilde{g})$ pair, $\{(s^i, \tilde{g}^i, a^i)|d((s, \tilde{g}), (s^i, \tilde{g}^i)) < \epsilon_1, i = 1, 2, \ldots, n\}$, we modify the approximated value $Q^\pi(s_{t+1}, \tilde{g}, \pi(s_{t+1}, \tilde{g}))$ in Eq. (3) to

$$\underline{Q}^\pi(s_{t+1}, \tilde{g}, a) = \begin{cases} Q^\pi(s_{t+1}, \tilde{g}, \pi(s_{t+1}, \tilde{g})), & F(s_{t+1}, \tilde{g}, \pi(s_{t+1}, \tilde{g})) > \epsilon_2 \\ \max_{1 \le i \le n} Q^\pi(s^i, \tilde{g}^i, a^i) - Ld((s_{t+1}, \tilde{g}), (s^i, \tilde{g}^i)), & otherwise \end{cases}$$

where $\epsilon_2 > 0$ is the threshold of the likelihood. It gives a reliable bound of Q value when the action generated by the policy is unfamiliar. Consequently, we perform the value update in Eq. (3) via

$$Q^\pi(s_t, \tilde{g}, a_t) = \mathbb{E}_{s_{t+1}} \left[r_t + \gamma \underline{Q}^\pi(s_{t+1}, \tilde{g}, a) \right]. \tag{6}$$

4.3 Goals Replay

In Robotic Control problems, $\mathcal{G}$ is a set of goals with finite volume. After the preprocessing, each $g \in \mathcal{G}$ leads to various relative goals. Maintaining a broad distribution of relative goals turns to mathematically maximize the entropy of the distribution. Since each relative goal is feasible, maximizing the entropy of the distribution may seem to maintain uniform distribution of achievable goals. Inspired by the skew-fit strategy in [26] that iteratively increases the entropy of a generative model, we propose a heuristic operator to manipulate a balanced distribution over valid relative goals.

Curriculum Generation. Let $\{p_i, i = 1, 2, \ldots\}$ be the distributions of relative goals to resample the hindsight experiences. At i-th iteration, we sample N augmented states from valid experiences with p_i. Since we have partitioned M states into clusters $\{C_k, k = 1, 2, \ldots, K\}$, it is trivial to construct empirical distributions of clusters for past valid experiences and sampled hindsight experiences. Formally, by classifying a state to the nearest cluster, we get p_{ve_i} for valid experiences and p_{he_i} for hindsight ones.

$$p_{ve_i}(C_k) = \frac{1}{M} \sum_1^M \mathbb{1}\{(s, \tilde{g}) \in C_k\}, \forall(s, \tilde{g}),$$

$$p_{he_i}(C_k) = \frac{1}{N} \sum_1^N \mathbb{1}\{(s, \tilde{g}) \in C_k\}, (s, \tilde{g}) \sim p_i.$$

Then we skew the p_{ve_i} with the p_{he_i} via

$$p_{skewed_i}(C_k) = \frac{1}{Z_\alpha} p_{ve_i}(C_k) p_{he_i}^\alpha(C_k), \alpha \in [-1, 0],$$

where Z_α is the normalization factor. Secondly, we estimate the Gaussian densities of clusters by calculating the mean μ_k and the covariance σ_k^2 of goals for each cluster. We expand p_{skewed_i} to a distribution of goals and fit p_{i+1} to it according to

$$p_{i+1} \leftarrow \sum_k p_{skewed_i}(C_k) \mathcal{N}(\tilde{g}|\mu_k, \sigma_k^2). \tag{7}$$

Repeat the process until we maintain uniform distribution over clusters or a broad distribution of relative goals. The Gaussian mixture model can be trained reasonably fast for RL agents and we take a lazy update on the clustering.

4.4   Multi-Goal Experience Replay

To give a reliable estimate for unseen goals, we make use of hindsight experiences as well as ensure the generalization over state-action pairs. In particular, it samples goals from experiences with a high likelihood of corresponding state-action pair under current policy and maintains a broad overall distribution of relative goals. The detailed algorithm is shown in Algorithm 1.

5   Experiments

We employ environments for multi-goal RL introduced in [7] and tasks shown in Fig. 1. As for goal replay, we compare with vanilla HER (labeled HER), HER with Energy-based Prioritization (labeled EBP), HER with Maximum Entropy-based Prioritization (labeled HERMEP), Curriculum-guided HER (labeled CHER), and our method (labeled HCG).

All the variants are implanted with the DDPG algorithm. Policies are represented as Multi-Layer Perceptrons (MLPs) with Rectified Linear Unit (ReLU) activation functions as in [10]. All the variant shares the same environment setting and experimental configuration, except for their private controlling parameters. The whole training procedure is performed in the simulation. For improved efficiency, we use 20 workers—each with 2 rollouts which average the parameters after every update. If the agent achieved the desired goal in an episode, we consider it a success. The results averages across 6 random seeds with shaded areas represent one standard deviation.

Learning Curve in Multi-Goal Setting. We show the learning cures of the median success rate of tasks in different settings. From the learning curve in Fig. 2, we can see the success rates during test rollouts increase along with the

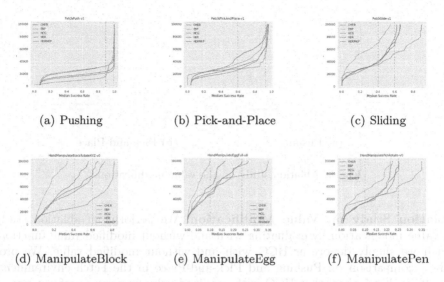

(a) Pushing   (b) Pick-and-Place   (c) Sliding

(d) ManipulateBlock   (e) ManipulateEgg   (f) ManipulatePen

Fig. 3. Sample efficient curves for variants with multiple goals. It shows that our method (labeled HCG) achieves high performance with less training samples.

training process. From the learning curve in Fig. 3, we can see the corresponding training batch for the current success rate. Our method improves the learning efficiency that exceeds most of the variants and also maintains a stable high success rate.

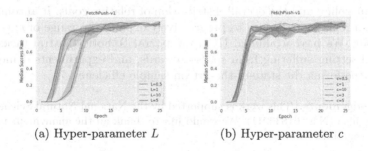

(a) Hyper-parameter L (b) Hyper-parameter c

Fig. 4. Ablation studies on hyper-parameter L and c.

Ablation Studies on Hyperparameters. In this section, we discuss key design choices for our HCG that provide substantially improved performance. The major hyperparameters are the Lipschitz coefficient L that controls the value generalization, and weight c that controls the distance. We provide a comparison on Pushing in the Fetch environment. Results in Fig. 4 indicates that the choice of L and c are robust. The number of the clusters, K, remains constant.

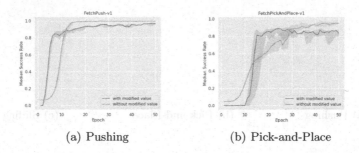

(a) Pushing   (b) Pick-and-Place

Fig. 5. Ablation study on the value modification.

Ablation Study on Value Modification. We perform an ablation study on value modification by evaluating with and without modified value function, which we simply denote as HCG with and without modified value. We provide a comparison on Pushing and Pick-and-Place in the Fetch environment. Results in Fig. 5 show that HCG with modified value improves performance at an early stage and keeps a stable success rate. The generalization assumption does improve the sample efficiency.

6   Conclusion

In this paper, we propose Hindsight Curriculum Generation (HCG) to sample hindsight experiences that guide the generalization of value function to unfamiliar goals. It utilizes the likelihood of the corresponding state-action pair under the current policy and the overall distribution of relative goals. It automatically generates a replay curriculum to progressively expand the range of experiences for training. We have evaluated HCG on several Robotic Control tasks in the multi-goal setting suffering from sparse rewards, and experiments demonstrate that it outperforms the state-of-the-art on sample efficiency.

Acknowledgements. This work is supported by the National Natural Science Foundation of China (Nos. 61836011). We would like to thank all the anonymous reviewers for their insightful comments.

References

1. Silver, D., et al.: Mastering the game of go with deep neural networks and tree search. Nature **529**, 484 (2016)
2. Silver, D., et al.: Mastering the game of go without human knowledge. Nature **550**(7676), 354–359 (2017)
3. Mnih, V., Kavukcuoglu, K., Silver, D.: Human-level control through deep reinforcement learning. Nature **518**, 529–533 (2015)

4. Lillicrap, T.P., et al.: Continuous control with deep reinforcement learning. In: 4th International Conference on Learning Representations, ICLR 2016, San Juan, Puerto Rico, 2–4 May 2016, Conference Track Proceedings (2016)
5. Schulman, J., Wolski, F., Dhariwal, P., Radford, A., Klimov, O.: Proximal policy optimization algorithms. CoRR abs/1707.06347 (2017)
6. Wu, Y., Mansimov, E., Grosse, R.B., Liao, S., Ba, J.: Scalable trust-region method for deep reinforcement learning using kronecker-factored approximation. In: Advances in Neural Information Processing Systems, vol. 30 (2017)
7. Plappert, M., et al.: Multi-goal reinforcement learning: challenging robotics environments and request for research. CoRR abs/1802.09464 (2018)
8. Ng, A.Y., Harada, D., Russell, S.: Policy invariance under reward transformations: theory and application to reward shaping. In: ICML, vol. 99, pp. 278–287 (1999)
9. Popov, I., et al.: Data-efficient deep reinforcement learning for dexterous manipulation. CoRR abs/1704.03073 (2017)
10. Andrychowicz, M., et al.: Hindsight experience replay. In: Advances in Neural Information Processing Systems, vol. 30. Curran Associates, Inc. (2017)
11. Zhao, R., Tresp, V.: Energy-based hindsight experience prioritization. In: Proceedings of The 2nd Conference on Robot Learning. Proceedings of Machine Learning Research, vol. 87, pp. 113–122. PMLR, 29–31 Oct 2018
12. Fang, M., Zhou, T., Du, Y., Han, L., Zhang, Z.: Curriculum-guided hindsight experience replay. In: Advances in Neural Information Processing Systems, vol. 32. Curran Associates, Inc. (2019)
13. Zhao, R., Sun, X., Tresp, V.: Maximum entropy-regularized multi-goal reinforcement learning. In: Proceedings of the 23rd International Conference on Machine Learning (2019)
14. Sutton, R.S., Barto, A.G.: Reinforcement Learning: An Introduction, 2nd edn. The MIT press, Cambridge (2018)
15. Schaul, T., Horgan, D., Gregor, K., Silver, D.: Universal value function approximators. In: ICML, pp. 1312–1320 (2015)
16. Todorov, E., Erez, T., Tassa, Y.: MuJoCo: a physics engine for model-based control. In: 2012 IEEE/RSJ International Conference on Intelligent Robots and Systems, pp. 5026–5033 (2012)
17. Pong, V., Gu, S., Dalal, M., Levine, S.: Temporal difference models: model-free deep RL for model-based control. CoRR abs/1802.09081 (2018)
18. Rauber, P., Ummadisingu, A., Mutz, F., Schmidhuber, J.: Hindsight policy gradients. In: International Conference on Learning Representations (2019)
19. Li, A., Pinto, L., Abbeel, P.: Generalized hindsight for reinforcement learning. ArXiv:abs/2002.11708 (2020)
20. Ren, Z., Dong, K., Zhou, Y., Liu, Q., Peng, J.: Exploration via hindsight goal generation. In: Advances in Neural Information Processing Systems, vol. 32. Curran Associates, Inc. (2019)
21. Fang, M., Zhou, C., Shi, B., Gong, B., Xu, J., Zhang, T.: DHER: Hindsight experience replay for dynamic goals. In: International Conference on Learning Representations (2019)
22. Riedmiller, M., et al.: Learning by playing - solving sparse reward tasks from scratch (2018)
23. Şimşek, O., Barto, A.G.: An intrinsic reward mechanism for efficient exploration. In: Proceedings of the 23rd International Conference on Machine Learning. pp. 833–840. ICML 2006. ACM, New York (2006)
24. Cameron, J., Pierce, W.D.: Reinforcement, reward, and intrinsic motivation: a meta-analysis. Rev. Educ. Res. 64(3), 363–423 (1994)

25. Florensa, C., Held, D., Geng, X., Abbeel, P.: Automatic goal generation for rein-
    forcement learning agents. In: Proceedings of the 35th International Conference on
    Machine Learning. Proceedings of Machine Learning Research, vol. 80, pp. 1515–
    1528. PMLR, Stockholmsmässan, 10–15 Jul 2018
26. Pong, V.H., Dalal, M., Lin, S., Nair, A., Bahl, S., Levine, S.: Skew-fit: state-covering
    self-supervised reinforcement learning. CoRR abs/1903.03698 (2019)

Gesture-Based Autonomous Diving Buddy for Underwater Photography

Hao Zhang[1,2], Fei Yuan[1,2], Jiajun Chen[1,2], Xinyu He[1,2], and Yi Zhu[1,2](✉)

[1] Key Laboratory of Underwater Acoustic Communication and Marine Information
Technology (Xiamen University), Ministry of Education, Xiamen, China
`zhuyi@xmu.edu.cn`
[2] Department of Communication Engineering, School of Information,
Xiamen University, Xiamen, China

Abstract. The working environment of divers under water is complex
and changeable, which is full of danger and needs effective monitoring
measures. This paper presents an Autonomous Diving Buddy to assist
divers and ensure their safety. In this paper, considering the limitations
of the previous underwater interaction, we proposed an algorithm based
on gesture recognition, assisted by underwater image enhancement and
target tracking, which can effectively complete the task of underwater
gesture recognition. Then we experimented on the algorithm and the
system. Experiments show that the algorithm performs well and the
proposed ADB can make corresponding actions correctly according to
gestures.

Keywords: Human-robot interaction · Gesture recognition ·
Underwater image enhancement

1 Introduction

In recent years, with the development of economy, the exploitation of oceans and
other waters has been intensified. At present, marine exploration is mainly based
on divers. However, the underwater environment is complex and changeable
which means difficult to monitor. Working under such conditions, to monitor
the status of divers in real time would be difficult. Once an emergency occurs,
it is hard to report for help in time, which is likely to cause serious harm to the
life of the divers.

With the rapid development of underwater robots, researchers have begun to
apply underwater robot technology to the diving industry to monitor the status
of divers and obtain underwater images. In the underwater operating environment of 'man-robot co-diving', effective and accurate interaction between man
and machine is of utmost importance. Good interaction methods can maximize
the role of underwater robots and promote cooperation between humans and
machines to achieve the goals of underwater tasks. Under the current technical framework, subject to the characteristics of the underwater communication

ⓒ Springer Nature Switzerland AG 2021
Y. Peng et al. (Eds.): ICIG 2021, LNCS 12890, pp. 195–206, 2021.
https://doi.org/10.1007/978-3-030-87361-5_16

environment, the most commonly used and most reliable way of underwater communication is to use acoustics. But there are still two main shortcomings: high equipment price and extremely low data transmission rate [1].

Inspired by the communication mechanism of underwater divers, human-robot interaction can take the most natural way: gestures. The underwater robot obtains the diver's intention by acquiring underwater gesture images for analysis and recognition, and then makes corresponding maneuvers. In this way, information can be effectively transmitted between man and robot, and existing problems such as redundant equipment and low transmission rate can be avoided, which has great application prospects.

Taking into account the complex and changeable underwater environment and the existing underwater image distortion [3], a single gesture interaction module may not perform well: Underwater robots cannot effectively capture gesture pictures, and gesture pictures may be severely distorted and cannot be accurately classified and recognized. An autonomous diving buddy for underwater photography system with gesture recognition as the main body, supplemented by target tracking and underwater image enhancement, can well overcome the above problems. Target tracking can ensure that the underwater robot can effectively accompany the diver and that the diver continues to appear in the photographic field of view; underwater image enhancement can effectively overcome the problem of image distortion, thereby ensuring the accuracy of gesture recognition. In this way, the role of human-robot gesture interaction can be exerted to the greatest extent. So as to achieve the purpose of effectively acquiring underwater images, ensuring the safety of divers, and assisting divers with completing underwater operations.

Based on previous studies, this paper proposes an gesture-based autonomous diving buddy system for underwater photography. The work structure is as follows: Sect. 2 mainly introduces the existing related research work; Sect. 3 mainly introduces the main application scenarios, workflow and overall description of the system; Sect. 4 introduces the design of gesture interaction and related theories; Sect. 5 shows the experimental verification results of related algorithms and the system; Sect. 6 explains our conclusions and prospects for future work.

2   Related Work

At present, most of the researches on ROV and AUV focuses on the ability of robots to complete tasks alone [5], lack of support and protection for divers, and lack of complete human-robot interaction functions.

Compared with other traditional interaction methods, gesture interaction has the advantages of lower user learning cost, lower equipment complexity, less impact on normal activities and large amount of information transmission, which has attracted the attention of many researchers. For example, Reference [6] proposed a human-robot interaction method based on gesture recognition. In [7], two methods of template method and neural network are used for gesture recognition. Most of these studies focus on use scenarios on land, and the test environment is mostly single background. The algorithms mentioned in [8] are all based on land design, and do not take into account the many influencing factors of the underwater environment in which underwater robots work. These methods have many problems in robustness and repeatability. In the paper [9], the author has carried out excellent research on underwater gesture interaction, and fully considered the underwater characteristics, designed a set of gesture language system for human-computer interaction, but limited to syntax, semantics and communication protocol, and considered underwater gesture recognition as a single language problem rather than an engineering problem.

There are few researches on underwater human-robot gesture interaction and very little work related to the underwater photographic robot system with gesture recognition as the main body, supplemented by target tracking and underwater image enhancement. So there is a lot of work to be done.

3 Application Scenarios and System Description

3.1 Applications Scenarios

The main work scene of Gesture Based Autonomous Diving Buddy (ADB) is to accompany divers in underwater survey, salvage and other tasks. These tasks usually take divers as the main body and require divers to perform long-term operations underwater. The operating environment is sometimes in dangerous environments such as low temperature, rapid water currents and even polluted waters [11]. This undoubtedly poses a challenge to the safety of divers. Using ADB can ensure the safety of divers to a large extent, effectively obtain underwater image information, and assist in completing underwater tasks. Similarly, ADB can also be used in entertaining scenes to record the beautiful moments of diving enthusiasts while ensuring the safety of divers.

First, the diver enters the water together with ADB. The diver activates and initializes ADB by making a preset gesture command to ADB. ADB will turn on the target tracking function to continuously track the diver. After the target tracking function is successfully turned on, ADB will use a specific light sequence as feedback, to remind the divers that the system is initialized successfully; in the next step, ADB will continue to track the divers and upload the underwater conditions to the platform in real time to supervise and protect the safety of the divers.

3.2 System Description

The basic structure of ADB system can be divided into control module, vision processing module, image acquisition module, lighting module and power module.

The image acquisition module is composed of a high-definition underwater camera, which continuously acquires underwater images and transmits them to the vision processing module. The vision processing module includes underwater image enhancement algorithm, target tracking algorithm, and gesture recognition algorithm. It is mounted on an embedded GPU computing platform. Through the real-time processing of the video stream, the processor integrates the gesture recognition results and the diver's coordinate information into a specific protocol, which is transmitted to the control module through USART. The control module is mounted on a microcontroller. On the one hand, according to different instructions, it sends 500 Hz–1000 Hz PWM control signal to the power module through 8 channels, that drives the motor to work, and sends signals to the lighting module to provide divers with feedback. On the other hand, according to the diver's situation information transmitted by the vision processing module, a real-time signal is sent to the platform to report the diver's situation. The power module is composed of an ESC and a brushless underwater thruster. According to the signal from the control module, it completes the corresponding maneuver and target tracking function.

4   Gesture-Based Control Design

In the application scenario as described above, ADB needs to follow the diver in real time and recognize the gestures that the diver may make. Our goal is to obtain the coordinate information of the diver in the real-time video stream and accurately recognize the preset gestures made by the diver. Taking into account the complex and changeable underwater environmental and imaging conditions, possible occlusion problems, limited embedded computing power and other issues, ADB uses a suitable method.

4.1   Framework

In order to solve the above-mentioned problems, we proposed a human-robot interaction method with gesture recognition as the main body, supplemented by underwater image enhancement and target tracking algorithms. The system block diagram is shown in Fig. 1.

After the original underwater video stream is collected, it is first processed by the underwater image enhancement algorithm to improve the imaging effect which lays the foundation for subsequent visual processing algorithms. Further, the target tracking algorithm is used for the video stream after the underwater image enhancement processing. First, the target detection algorithm is used to obtain the image coordinates of the diver; then transfers the image coordinate data to the target tracking algorithm to start tracking and evaluate the quality of the composition. If it is unable to track continuously due to occlusion and other problems, the object detection algorithm is used to locate the coordinates and recover the tracking algorithm. After that, the diver's coordinate information and video stream are transmitted to the gesture recognition algorithm. First, the video stream is cropped according to the coordinate information to reduce the amount of calculation; then the trained gesture recognition model is used to recognize and classify to obtain the gesture recognition result and transmit it to other modules.

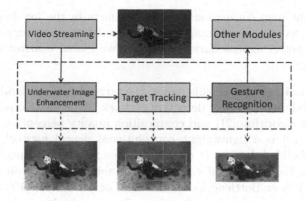

Fig. 1. Gesture-based control framework

4.2 Theory and Algorithm Design

Underwater Image Enhancement Algorithm. In this paper, we used white balance processing on images to correct the color cast. The brightness channel is equalized by the histogram, and then the edge is enhanced by the bilateral filter [24] which means the traditional enhancement result is obtained; on the other hand, the input is generated through the designed GAN to generate a confrontation. The network estimates the transmission map and restores the image through the underwater imaging model. The color cast can be corrected and clarified end-to-end to obtain the result of deep learning. Finally, the two parts are merged with the Laplace pyramid to obtain the final restored image. The structural block diagram is shown as in Fig. 2.

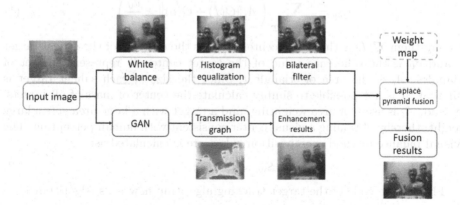

Fig. 2. Proposed underwater image enhancement framework

We combined the image processed by the traditional method and the image restored by the GAN network, and their related four weights. In order to avoid the sharp weight map conversion creating artifacts in the low-frequency components of the reconstructed image, a multi-level fusion strategy is used. Our algorithm can better expose dark areas, improve global contrast and enhance details and edges.

Target Tracking Algorithm. In this paper, the target tracking algorithm consists of the SSD-MobileNet-v3 object detection network [20], KCF (Kernel Correlation Filter) tracking algorithm [21] and composition quality perception algorithm.

MobileNet [18] is a lightweight convolutional neural network suitable for mobile and embedded devices. It uses Depthwise Separable Convolution, which greatly reduces the amount of calculation. MobileNet-v3 introduces Inverted Residuals and Linear Bottlenecks on the basis of MobileNet [19], which solves the problem of information loss that is easily caused when performing ReLU operations on low dimensions. It uses NAS (neural structure search) to search for network configuration and parameters, which improves the accuracy and further reduces the amount of parameters [20].

The KCF algorithm is a discriminative tracking algorithm. It uses the given samples to train a discriminative classifier, uses the rotation matrix to collect the samples, and uses the fast Fourier transform to accelerate the calculation of the algorithm [21].

In terms of composition quality perception algorithm, this paper uses a composition rule based on the "visual balance method" to evaluate the quality of the acquired image to ensure the quality of the image acquired by ADB. Under this rule, the overall visual center of all salient objects should be as close to the image center as possible, and the distance between the visual center of all salient objects and the image center is calculated as a standard to measure the quality of the image composition. "Visual Balance Error" E_{vb} is defined as [23]:

$$E_{vb} = \sum_{o \in O, t \in T} \left(A_t \| C(I) - C(o) \| \pm \frac{d_0}{2} \right) \tag{1}$$

Among them, $C(I)$ is the image center, $C(o)$ is the centroid of the salient target o, and d_0 is the difference value of the target center. T represent the set of triangles, A_t is the area of triangle t. Since the size of each salient target is different, it is not possible to simply calculate the center of mass of all targets. Instead, A_t is used for area weighting, and a target with a large area gets a large weight, thereby obtaining a visual center consistent with human perception. The "visual balance method" composition rule score is calculated as:

$$S_{vb} = 1 - E_{vb} \tag{2}$$

The pseudo code of the target tracking algorithm flow is as Algorithm 1.

Gesture Recognition Algorithm. The gesture recognition algorithm uses the SSD-MobileNet-v3 object detection network mentioned above. Through collection of underwater and onshore gesture pictures and network collection, a total of 5,000 gesture pictures were obtained, and the data was expanded using random cropping and affine transformation methods to create a data set (Fig. 3).

Algorithm 1. Target tracking algorithm

Input: Video stream after image enhancement I
Output: ADB command cmd
  Load trained Mobilenet weight, initialize $thre$
  for frame $F \in I$ **do**
    Inference frame F, get confidence score $conf$, bbox $cord$
    if $conf > thre$ **then**
      Enable KCF to track $cord$, get $flag$
      while $flag = true$ **do**
        According to (1) (2), get S_{vb}
        Calculate cmd
      end while
    end if
  end for

Fig. 3. Underwater image acquisition

5   Algorithm and System Experiment

5.1   Algorithm Experiment

We compared the underwater image enhancement algorithm in this article with the current methods for subjective and objective comparative analysis. The experimental results are shown in Fig. 4 and Table 1. It can be seen that the method in this paper has good effects in correcting color cast and deblurring.

Figure 5 shows the results of a set of composition quality perception methods. The visual quality center of picture (a) is close to the image center, and the visual quality center of picture (b), picture (c) and picture (d) deviate from the image center.

Table 2 shows the composition error value and composition scoring result of the "visual balance method" of each picture in Fig. 5. The higher the composition score, the higher the image quality. It can be seen from the results that the closer the visual quality center is to the image center, the higher the score; the further away the visual quality center is from the image center, the lower the score. The composition quality perception method in this paper is basically consistent with the human eye perception results.

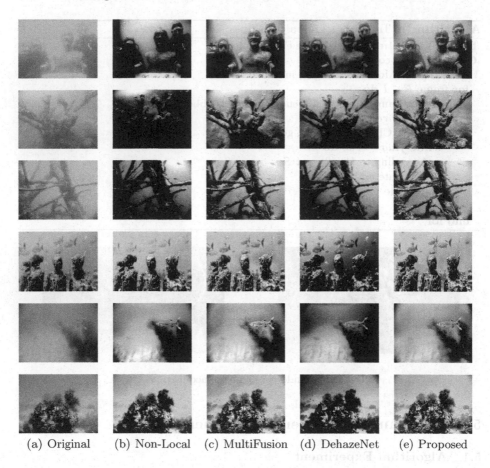

(a) Original   (b) Non-Local   (c) MultiFusion   (d) DehazeNet   (e) Proposed

Fig. 4. Underwater image enhancement effect

Gesture recognition algorithm tested in our test set, mAP (mean Average precision) reached 97.4% and the inferred speed reached 25FPS on embedded devices, basically met the needs of real-time processing. The model size is only 4.8M. Figure 6 shows some gesture recognition results.

5.2   System Experiment

In order to test the performance of the entire system, we conducted field experiments and commissioning in the swimming pool. The entire experimental scene is shown in Fig. 7. The pool is 50 m long, 20 m wide, and 2 m deep. Figure 7 also shows the shape of ADB prototype, with a camera and light on the front.

According to the system usage process mentioned above, the diver entered the water together with ADB. The diver activated and initialized the ADB by making a preset gesture command to it, and the ADB sent a light feedback to remind the diver that the initialization was successful, as shown in Fig. 8.

Table 1. Comparison of different obfuscations in terms of their transformation capabilities

	Non local [15]	MultiFusion [16]	DehazeNet [17]	Proposed
UIConM	0.5205	0.6702	0.6041	0.6283
GWH-GLBH	3.2932	3.2581	3.4329	3.4509
NIQE	3.2917	2.9088	3.5302	3.6438
SISBLIM	−9.6758	−11.6481	−10.8109	−6.0680
NFERM	9.5685	28.8690	28.5643	36.0594
BQMS	0.9224	0.8449	0.8620	0.9092
SIQE	0.7696	0.7701	0.7403	0.7711
LPSI	0.9330	0.9412	0.9347	0.9524
SSIM	0.2964	0.3200	0.3976	0.3994
FSIM	0.8798	0.8706	0.8705	0.9226
PSNR	15.2314	18.2947	16.0019	16.3866

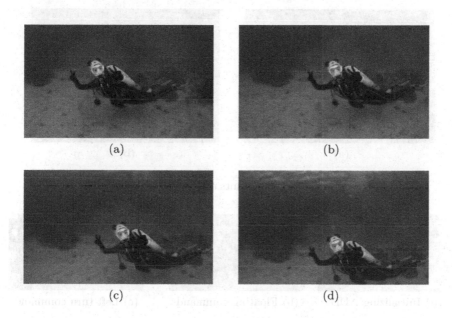

(a)　　　　　　　　　　　　(b)

(c)　　　　　　　　　　　　(d)

Fig. 5. Composition evaluation of visual balance method

Table 2. "Visual balance method" composition quality perception results

	(a)	(b)	(c)	(d)
Error value E_{vb}	0.0318	0.2236	0.2932	0.3704
Composition score S_{vb}	0.9682	0.7764	0.7068	0.6296

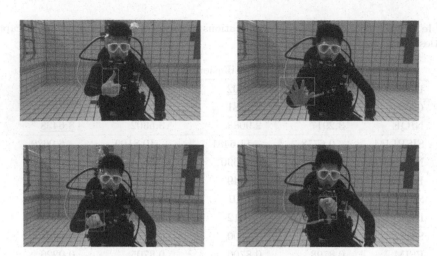

Fig. 6. Gesture recognition results

(a)   (b)

Fig. 7. Experiments scene and ADB

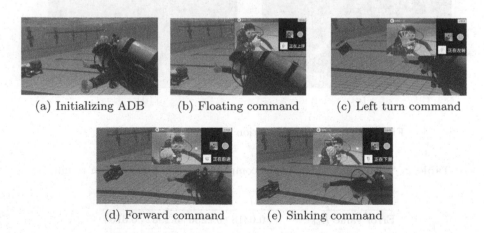

(a) Initializing ADB   (b) Floating command   (c) Left turn command

(d) Forward command   (e) Sinking command

Fig. 8. Gesture interaction experiment

Then, other preset gestures were tested, such as floating, diving and turning and the system can accurately recognize and make correct maneuvers, as shown in Fig. 8.

6 Conclusions

In this paper, a gesture-based autonomous diving buddy system for underwater photography is proposed. The proposed work is mainly focused on the underwater visual processing and gesture interaction. A prototype is produced for experimental verification and certain results have been achieved. Experiments have verified that the proposed algorithms perform well, that can run stably in real-time on embedded devices and obtain correct results.

However, most of our work is focused on the design and optimization of image algorithms and the work on the hardware structure is not yet complete. In future research, we will gradually improve the related hardware structure. Besides, we have fully considered the underwater environment and imaging characteristics in the algorithm design and tested the relevant experimental materials for each module. But due to the limitations of the experimental conditions, we have not yet placed the prototype in the marine environment for testing.

The next step of the research will be to continue to improve the robustness of the gesture interaction system and further improve the related hardware structure. On this basis, tests in real environments will be carried out, and the system is constantly revised to improve system performance.

References

1. Kilfoyle, D., Baggeroer, A.: The state of the art in underwater acoustic telemetry. IEEE J. Ocean. Eng. **25**, 4–27 (2000)
2. Neasham, J., Hinton, O.: Underwater acoustic communications-how far have we progressed and what challenges remain. In: Proceedings of the 7th European Conference on Underwater Acoustics, Delft, The Netherlands, 5–8 July 2004
3. Gorden, H.R.: Can the Lambert-Beer law be applied to the diffuse attenuation coefficient of ocean water? Limnol. Oceanogr. **34**(8), 1389–1409 (1989)
4. Shen, K., Yan, Y., Yan, H.: Research status and development trend of deep-sea work class ROV in China. Control Inf. Technol. **03**, 1–7 (2020)
5. Huang, Y., Li, Y., Jiancheng, Yu., Li, S., Feng, X.: State-of-the-art and development trends of AUV intelligence. Robot **42**(02), 215–231 (2020)
6. Xu, Y., Guillemot, M., Nishida, T.: An experiment study of gesture-based human-robot interface. In: Proceedings of the 2007 IEEE/ICME International Conference on Complex Medical Engineering, Beijing, China, 23–27 May 2007, pp. 457–463 (2007)
7. Waldherr, S., Romero, R., Thrun, S.: A gesture based interface for human-robot interaction. Auton. Rob. **9**, 151–173 (2000)
8. Rautaray, S.S., Agrawal, A.: Vision based hand gesture recognition for human computer interaction: a survey. Artif. Intell. Rev. **43**, 1–54 (2015)
9. Chiarella, D., Bibuli, M., et al.: A novel gesture-based language for underwater human-robot interaction. J. Mar. Sci. Eng. **6**, 91 (2018)

10. Wu, J.: Underwater work safety monitoring system for divers. Xiamen University
11. Yang, M., Sowmya, A.: An underwater color image quality evaluation metric. IEEE Trans. Image Process. **24**(12), 6062–6071 (2015)
12. Pan, P., Yuan, F., Cheng, E.: Underwater image de-scattering and enhancing using DehazeNet and HWD. J. Mar. Sci. Technol. **26**(4), 531–540 (2018)
13. Galdran, A.: Image dehazing by artificial multiple-exposure image fusion. Signal Process. **149**, 135–147 (2018)
14. Ancuti, C., Ancuti, C.O., Haber, T., Bekaert, P.: Enhancing underwater images and videos by fusion. In: 2012 IEEE Conference on Computer Vision and Pattern Recognition, pp. 81–88 (2012)
15. Berman, D., Treibitz, T., Avidan, S.: Non-local image dehazing. In: Proceedings of the IEEE Computer Society Conference on Computer Vision and Pattern Recognition, pp. 1674–1682 (2016)
16. Ancuti, C.O., Ancuti, C., De Vleeschouwer, C., Bekaert, P.: Color balance and fusion for underwater image enhancement. IEEE Trans. Image Process. **27**(1), 379–393 (2018)
17. Fu, X., Zhuang, P., Yue, H., et al.: A retinex-based enhancing approach for single underwater image. In: IEEE International Conference on Image Processing (ICIP). IEEE (2015)
18. Howard, A.G., Zhu, M., Chen, B., et al.: MobileNets: efficient convolutional neural networks for mobile vision applications. IEEE Access (2017)
19. Sandler, M., Howard, A., Zhu, M., et al.: Mobile NetV2: inverted residuals and linear bottlenecks. IEEE Access (2018)
20. Howard, A., Sandler, M., Chu, G., et al.: Searching for MobileNetV3 (2019)
21. Henriques, J.F., Caseiro, R., Martins, P., et al.: High-speed tracking with kernelized correlation filters. IEEE Trans. Pattern Anal. Mach. Intell. **37**(3), 583–596 (2015)
22. Wang, R., Wang, S., Wang, Y., et al.: Vision-based autonomous hovering for the biomimetic underwater robot-RobCutt-II. IEEE Trans. Industr. Electron. **66**(11), 8578–8588 (2019)
23. Islam, M.B., Wong, L.K., Low, K.L., et al.: Aesthetics-driven stereoscopic 3-D image recomposition with depth adaptation. IEEE Trans. Multimedia **20**(11), 2964–2979 (2018)
24. Tomasi, C., Manduchi, R.: Bilateral filtering for gray and color images. In: International Conference on Computer Vision. IEEE (2002)

Adaptive Underwater Image Enhancement via Color Channel Compensation Based on Optical Restoration and Fusion

Xiaojie Wang[1], Fei Li[1], Shujie Zhou[1], and Hong Du[2(✉)]

[1] Shanghai University, 99 Shangda Road, Baoshan, Shanghai, China
xiaojiewang@shu.edu.cn
[2] Jiangsu Shipping College, 185 Tongsheng Avenue, Economic and Technological Development Zone, Nantong, Jiangsu, China
du_hong_121@ntsc.edu.cn

Abstract. As human beings continue their way to find more and more resources beneath water and ocean, it becomes more urgent to have a very clear and detailed underwater image for us to explore the world unseen in the water. However, with the light propagating into the water, it is absorbed and scattered along the way which makes the underwater image unclear, hazy, detail-lost and color-shifted. Obviously, it is not the image we wish for. In the paper, the proposed method aims to enhance underwater image adaptively via color channel compensation based on optical image model. In the beginning the underwater image is restored only in green channel aiming to reduce the haze effect, then an adaptive color channel compensation is applied to correct the shifted color, lastly a multi-scale fusion is executed to show more image details after a white balance operation. Going for massive experiments, the proposed adaptive method fits in versatile scenes adaptively of greenish, bluish and turbid water body producing eye-friendly haze cover removed, color shift corrected, detail enhanced clear result image. Particularly the proposed method highly reduces the reddish effect after execution compared to many other state of art underwater image enhancement algorithm, while quantitatively the proposed method gives a better score too by underwater image quality measure (UIQM) and underwater color image quality evaluation (UCIQE).

Keywords: Underwater image enhancement · Adaptive color channel compensation

1 Introduction

As we all know, the world has long been catching eyes beneath the water and ocean where tremendous resources has been explored and exploited for the human beings such as raw oil, combustible ice, seafloor soil, and many kinds of

© Springer Nature Switzerland AG 2021
Y. Peng et al. (Eds.): ICIG 2021, LNCS 12890, pp. 207–217, 2021.
https://doi.org/10.1007/978-3-030-87361-5_17

fishes, corals and reefs. Following the developments of USV (unmanned surface vehicle), UUV (unmanned underwater vehicle), and AUV (automated underwater vehicle), more and more technologies have been deployed to serve us to see a real underwater environment among which the underwater image is the most important and vivid way to show it real.

However, things do not go as we wish, as we go deep and deep into the water, the image we captured underwater becomes color-shifted (greenish and bluish) and much more paler and bleacher because the image loses its color contrast and receives hazy cover with the object-reflected light absorbed and scattered. The degraded underwater image cannot fit well on the object recognition and track network which is a huge challenge for massive underwater application usage. So, there is a great impact on this field if we could process for a better eye-friendly and detail-clear underwater image.

1.1 Recent Method

There are already some existing methods to solve the problem we mentioned above. One direct way to make it is to use high-end hardware [4,7], for example, underwater camera which is of extremely expense and of high energy consumption. In this case many experts have developed different algorithms to tackle this issue. The following are some representative methods:

Multi-image Methods: Polarization method [16] is executed by using several images with varying polarization degrees. Other multi-image process methods like [12] is exploited by using several images captured in different conditions. But all these multi-image methods are not suitable for underwater environment because the water current changing rate, the particle concentration, sun angle, temperature are rarely varied in a short period of time which makes it hard for divers to capture different images belonging to different conditions. And sincerely these methods cannot restore and enhance the underwater images enough as we want which inspires more experts to develop more effective methods to tackle this problem.

Single-Image Methods: For convenience, some single image process methods come into our eyes. The most foundational method is DCP [5] which has initially been proposed for outdoor scenes dehazing. It assumes that the radiance of an object in a natural scene is small in at least one of three color components. Later UDCP [15] has been proposed and has a better transmission (It is part of object-reflected light that reaches the camera pane among all the object-reflected light) estimation of underwater image because it is considered that in underwater scene the dominant color spaces are green and blue since red is absorbed rapidly within 5m depth which is also why most underwater images show greenish and bluish. There are also some methods that do not estimate the scene transmission, for example, J. Tarel et al. [17] proposed a method which can fast restore the scene visibility and control the restoration percentage by only estimating the veiling light but not the transmission. C. O. Ancuti *et al.* [1] proposed a single image that does not require specialized hardware or knowledge about the underwater conditions or scene structure. It builds on the blending of two images that are directly derived from a color-compensated and white-balanced version of the original degraded image. Later based on the observation that under adverse conditions, the information contained in at least one color channel is close to completely lost, making the traditional enhancing techniques subject to noise and color shifting, they proposed a new pre-processing step for image enhancement [2] which reconstructs the lost channel based on the opponent color channel.

Deep-Learning Methods: Latterly, following the development of deep learning and machine learning, some network-based enhancement methods have been proposed, for example, C. Li *et al.* [8] constructed an Underwater Image Enhancement Benchmark (UIEB) and proposed an underwater image enhancement network (called WaterNet) trained on this benchmark as a baseline, which indicates the generalization of the proposed UIEB for training Convolutional Neural Networks (CNNs). But as the real underwater scene is never directly shown up there and rare datasets are available to use, the network-based underwater enhancement method has a long way to go before it really stimulates this field.

1.2 Underwater Image Formation Model

The most used underwater image formation model (B. L. McGlamery and J. S. Jaffe) [6,11] comes from Koschmieder's law. The simplified is as followed:

$$I(x,y) = R(x,y)e^{-kd(x,y)} + I_s\left(1 - e^{-kd(x,y)}\right) \tag{1}$$

(x, y) is the pixel coordinate, $I(x, y)$ is the pixel intensity we captured on the image plane, $R(x, y)$ is the pixel intensity without attenuation that we want to restore, $e^{-kd(x,y)}$ is the scene transmission, and $d(x, y)$ is distance along the light line between the image scene pixel (x, y) and the camera. $I_s\left(1 - e^{-kd(x,y)}\right)$ is the veiling light $V(x, y)$ of the underwater environment. That is $V(x,y) = I_s\left(1 - e^{-kd(x,y)}\right)$.

1.3 Strength and Weakness

Following the previous research, we found that there is not a method that can restore underwater images with different appearance taken in different conditions. Even though Ancuti *et al.* proposed a 3C [2] method that can fit in different image appearance, it cannot fit well in underwater image, and cannot solve problems adaptively which inspires us to make a new adaptive methods enhancing underwater image.

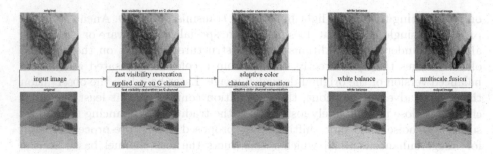

Fig. 1. Workflow of our proposed method (Color figure online)

The proposed method in this paper is executed one by one in below steps: first the input image is restored only in green channel based on the underwater image formation model, then it comes into the most important and innovative step, adaptive color channel compensation decided by image property of every channel intensity. Later it is white-balanced before going into the final multiscale fusion processing. Our method shows a great visual appearance of underwater image after enhancement and quantitatively our method shows an equal or higher score than the other state of art algorithm. However, in some particular cases like containing large sand area in the image, our method sometimes makes the enhanced image partly reddish which is a common phenomenon after enhancement of most other state of art algorithms. To be mentioned that even in this case our method still overtakes other methods of reducing the reddish problem after enhancement.

2   Restoration and Enhancement Details

As mentioned in Sect. 1, our proposed method follows below steps:

- First the input image is restored only in green channel based on the underwater image formation model
- Then it comes into the most important and innovative step, adaptive color channel compensation decided by image property of every channel intensity
- Later it is white-balanced before going into the final multiscale fusion processing

It is illustrated in Fig. 1 to have a better understanding for readers.

2.1   Fast Visibility Restoration Applied on Green Channel

As we analyze the U45 [10] underwater image data set, the green channel mean intensity of green images is 154.5958, the green channel mean intensity of blue images is 124.7431, the green channel mean intensity of hazy images is 133.9884. and the green channel mean intensity of all U45 images is 138.3413. So, the green channel is mostly a dominant channel in underwater images of this data set. Thus, we can deduce that the most haze effect is also caused by the green channel. We then think of removing the haze effect by fast visibility restoration on green channel.

From [17] we approach a fast visibility restoration applied only on green channel which is a foundational step for a more accurate adaptive color channel compensation in the next step as we want a natural and clear green channel without haze which is pivotal for the compensation. In this way the following compensation step will bring a better color enhancement of the underwater image.

From (1) we have:

$$I(x,y) = R(x,y) \left(1 - \frac{V(x,y)}{I_s} \right) + V(x,y) \tag{2}$$

The fast visibility restoration algorithm as introduced in [7] can thus be decomposed into several steps: estimation of I_s, inference of $V(x,y)$, restoration of $R(x,y)$ by inversing (2), smoothing to handle noise amplification and a tone mapping. So, we follow their method but keep in mind that we only restore the green channel. This is a pre-setup for the next adaptive color channel compensation step. And the green-restored image is referred to the second picture from the left of Fig. 1.

2.2 Adaptive Color Channel Compensation

After the former step, fast visibility restoration applied only on green channel, we move forward to the most key and innovative step, adaptive color channel compensation, which sets up the compensation factor automatically decided by image property of every channel intensity.

The statistically proven observation, that, under poor illumination, or in the presence of strong and non-uniform spectral attenuation, the color information from at least one color channel might be lost for the whole scene, especially for the underwater image. [2] Commonly, the red channel is attenuated and absorbed the most among the 3 color channels and almost disappears after 5–6 m depth, the following is yellow at around 10–15 m depth, the last is green at around 20 m depth, so if the image is captured at a depth larger than 20, it most probably appears blue. But this principle is for clear ocean waters, in turbid water, blue channel is disappeared first, that is why the inter-land river is always looking yellowish.

From [2] we know that working in the CIEL^*a* b* opponent space can facilitate the compensation of strong color shifts induced by common attenuation/lighting spectral distribution. We assume that the mean of each opponent channel is zero (neutral color) when a sufficiently large scene is considered. For example, in greenish pictures, since the loss of red induces an a* channel shift in favor of the green color, this loss could be offset/mitigated by bringing back the a* channel towards mean zero values. The same holds for the b* channel when dealing with blueish (loss of yellow) and yellowish (loss of blue) pictures. when one of the R, G, and B component is severely attenuated, it can be recovered by pushing the opponent colors towards a zero local mean.

Following [2], the level of color attenuation (and thus color shift) may vary spatially. Therefore, a local mean, estimated by a Gaussian filter with large spatial support, is subtracted from each opponent channel. Formally, the compensated opponent color channels I_{a*}^c and I_{b*}^c are computed in every pixel x as:

$$I_{a*}^c(x) = I_{a*}(x) - \kappa \cdot M(x) \cdot GI_{a*}(x)$$
$$I_{b*}^c(x) = I_{b*}(x) - \lambda \cdot M(x) \cdot GI_{b*}(x)$$

(3)

where I_{a*}, I_{b*} are the initial color opponent channels and GI_{a*} and GI_{b*} represent their Gaussian filtered versions. The parameters κ and λ are our adaptive color channel compensation factors for the two opponent channels. The mask M is a refinement that has been introduced to maintain significant illumination in light source locations. For a pixel location, the mask value is set to zero when mean(r, g, b) >0.85 and to 1 elsewhere. The mask is smoothed with a simple Gaussian with a medium kernel size (default size is set to 20).

After large scale experiments, we have some well-worked adaptive color channel compensation factor sets for the two pair of opponent channels:

- κ is set to 0.6 and λ is set to 0 by default because most time the heavily lost opponent color channels of underwater image are green and red.
- If the mean intensity of blue channel is larger than 145, κ is set to 0.3 and λ is set to 0.
- If the mean intensity of green channel is larger than 145, κ is set to 0.05 and λ is set to 0.
- If the mean intensity of blue channel is larger than 145 and meanwhile the mean intensity of green channel is larger than 145, κ is set to 0.9 and λ is set to −0.15.
- If the mean intensity of blue channel is larger than 200, κ is set to 0.8 and λ is set to 0.4.

After each inspection of above-mentioned conditions, if the latter one is true, it will cover the former one because we find that inspecting in green-red opponent color channels can always product satisfied result more commonly. And the last set is designed to tackle extreme blue underwater image which is a rare case so we put it in the last set. In this way, our proposed method can fit well in different underwater image appearance, and more innovatively it can solve problems adaptively.

The green-restored image after adaptive color channel compensation is referred to the middle picture of Fig. 1.

2.3   White Balance Before Multiscale Fusion

After adaptive color channel compensation, we convey the image into white balance procedure (Gray World Assumption) for a natural sub-sea appearance of underwater image without distorted illumination impact along the vertical depth before the final multiscale fusion which aims to level up the object edge sharpness and color contrast. [1] We conduct white balance procedure (Gray World Assumption) before final multiscale fusion, and the white balanced image is referred to the second picture from the right of Fig. 1. Last, we perform multiscale fusion of [1] to produce the final restored and enhanced underwater image with more details which is shown in the last picture of Fig. 1.

3   Experiments

Now we show our result comparison with some previous state of art methods qualitatively and quantitatively. From the comparison it is illustrated that our method gives a better or even result.

3.1   Qualitative Assessment

In the section our method is compared with these state of art methods, UDCP [15], GBDRC [9], UNDERHL [3], IBLA [14], and FUSION [1]. From Fig. 2, we see that UDCP, GBDRC and IBLA cannot restore the color appearance as we want which still shows greenish or bluish or turbid while the GBDRC and UNDERHL produce a color casted (unwanted red or yellow appearance) underwater image after restoration. FUSION method gives a good output image in which the color appearance is restored and image contrast is enhanced. It produces a very visual friendly result as we wish. Compared to FUSION method, our method gives an even better output image with more details removing more haze cover and looking clearer while restoring color appearance and enhancing image contrast. Considering the extreme blue images, our method outperforms other methods as it reduces the red appearance evidently.

From Fig. 3, we see that by our method the unwanted reddish appearance is removed from the circled object which enables a uniform color appearance compared to FUSION method.

From a broader viewpoint, our method is more scene-adaptive than other state of art methods. Our method works well in both greenish, bluish or turbid scenes which saves much time because we don't have to choose a particular state of art method depending on the particular scene.

Fig. 2. Experiments results of different state of art methods: from the first column to the last column: input underwater image, UDCP [15], GBDRC [9], UNDERHL [3], IBLA [14], FUSION [1], and Ours. (Color figure online)

3.2 Quantitative Comparison

Coming up next, we conduct a quantitative comparison of our method and other state of art methods. UIQM [13] comprises three underwater image attribute measures: the underwater image colorfulness measure (UICM), the underwater image sharpness measure (UISM), and the underwater image contrast measure (UIConM). UCIQE [18] is a linear combination of chroma, saturation, and contrast to quantify the non-uniform color cast, blurring, and low-contrast that

Fig. 3. Detail experiment: from first column to last: the input underwater image, FUSION [1], and Ours

characterize underwater images. We make a comparison of 10 underwater images captured in different scenes with FUSION by these measurements in Table 1 as other state of art methods cannot produce visual-friendly results. We see that our method outscores FUSION in most of these measurements.

4 Conclusion

After implementing comparative experiments, the proposed method produces an astonishing result as we would love to see. The restored underwater image shows a haze-removed, color cast-corrected and detail-enhanced as well as contrast-increased clear appearance which perfectly solves the light absorption and scattering problem when it propagating beneath the water. Meanwhile, the proposed method tackles the after-enhancement reddish problem (This problem commonly exists in many underwater image enhancement methods) beyond our imagination. As the quantitative analyses shows, the proposed method outscores the other state of art methods through underwater image quality measure (UIQM) and underwater color image quality evaluation (UCIQE). So, we believe that this proposed method will greatly boost the massive exploration of underwater resources by providing a visual-friendly clear underwater environment image with removed color shift and enhanced details. For the outlook we hope later we could modify this proposed method making it fitting into the inland yellowish

Table 1. Quantitative comparison result

Image	Measurements	FUSION	Ours	Image	Measurements	FUSION	Ours
diver.jpg	uciqe	26.286	**28.046**	coral.jpg	uciqe	27.920	**30.054**
	uicm	2.551	**2.779**		uicm	**5.085**	4.842
	uiconm	0.576	**0.629**		uiconm	0.622	**0.670**
	uiqm	**4.112**	4.003		uiqm	3.574	**4.171**
	uism	6.723	**6.803**		uism	6.665	**6.688**
shell.jpg	uciqe	25.284	**26.004**	ship.jpg	uciqe	**28.336**	28.166
	uicm	1.177	**1.327**		uicm	2.908	**3.074**
	uiconm	0.728	**0.760**		uiconm	0.518	**0.545**
	uiqm	**4.458**	4.373		uiqm	3.532	**3.810**
	uism	6.688	**6.940**		uism	6.493	**6.546**
statue.jpg	uciqe	26.296	**26.440**	seafloor.jpg	uciqe	**25.961**	25.360
	uicm	5.861	**6.328**		uicm	2.384	**2.495**
	uiconm	0.599	**0.652**		uiconm	0.327	**0.331**
	uiqm	**4.292**	4.085		uiqm	3.014	**3.409**
	uism	6.789	**6.884**		uism	6.796	**6.865**
rock.jpg	uciqe	27.475	**27.898**	sand.jpg	uciqe	26.531	**26.863**
	uicm	**1.493**	1.454		uicm	**1.034**	0.950
	uiconm	0.893	**0.920**		uiconm	0.877	**0.907**
	uiqm	4.708	**5.098**		uiqm	4.985	**5.019**
	uism	6.836	**6.856**		uism	7.060	**7.081**
fish.jpg	uciqe	727.114	**29.818**	stone.jpg	uciqe	23.257	**24.602**
	uicm	3.872	**4.583**		uicm	**1.126**	0.935
	uiconm	0.486	**0.570**		uiconm	0.587	**0.632**
	uiqm	3.445	**3.952**		uiqm	4.082	**4.330**
	uism	6.618	**6.653**		uism	**6.728**	6.725

river environment much more. Because we think it is very important for us to protect our Yangtze river and Yellow river biodiversity as well as the rest of the world if we could provide a clear image of this hostile underwater environment.

References

1. Ancuti, C.O., Ancuti, C., De Vleeschouwer, C., Bekaert, P.: Color balance and fusion for underwater image enhancement. IEEE Trans. Image Process. **27**(1), 379–393 (2017)
2. Ancuti, C.O., Ancuti, C., De Vleeschouwer, C., Sbert, M.: Color channel compensation (3C): a fundamental pre-processing step for image enhancement. IEEE Trans. Image Process. **29**, 2653–2665 (2019)
3. Berman, D., Levy, D., Avidan, S., Treibitz, T.: Underwater single image color restoration using haze-lines and a new quantitative dataset. IEEE Trans. Pattern Anal. Mach. Intell. (2020)
4. He, D.M., Seet, G.G.: Divergent-beam lidar imaging in turbid water. Opt. Lasers Eng. **41**(1), 217–231 (2004)

5. He, K., Sun, J., Tang, X.: Single image haze removal using dark channel prior. IEEE Trans. Pattern Anal. Mach. Intell. **33**(12), 2341–2353 (2010)
6. Jaffe, J.S.: Computer modeling and the design of optimal underwater imaging systems. IEEE J. Oceanic Eng. **15**(2), 101–111 (1990)
7. Levoy, M., Chen, B., Vaish, V., Horowitz, M., McDowall, I., Bolas, M.: Synthetic aperture confocal imaging. ACM Trans. Graph. (ToG) **23**(3), 825–834 (2004)
8. Li, C., et al.: An underwater image enhancement benchmark dataset and beyond. IEEE Trans. Image Process. **29**, 4376–4389 (2019)
9. Li, C., Quo, J., Pang, Y., Chen, S., Wang, J.: Single underwater image restoration by blue-green channels dehazing and red channel correction. In: 2016 IEEE International Conference on Acoustics, Speech and Signal Processing (ICASSP), pp. 1731–1735. IEEE (2016)
10. Li, H., Li, J., Wang, W.: A fusion adversarial underwater image enhancement network with a public test dataset. arXiv preprint arXiv:1906.06819 (2019)
11. McGlamery, B.: A computer model for underwater camera systems. In: Ocean Optics VI, vol. 208, pp. 221–231. International Society for Optics and Photonics (1980)
12. Narasimhan, S.G., Nayar, S.K.: Contrast restoration of weather degraded images. IEEE Trans. Pattern Anal. Mach. Intell. **25**(6), 713–724 (2003)
13. Panetta, K., Gao, C., Agaian, S.: Human-visual-system-inspired underwater image quality measures. IEEE J. Oceanic Eng. **41**(3), 541–551 (2015)
14. Peng, Y.T., Cosman, P.C.: Underwater image restoration based on image blurriness and light absorption. IEEE Trans. Image Process. **26**(4), 1579–1594 (2017)
15. Sathya, R., Bharathi, M., Dhivyasri, G.: Underwater image enhancement by dark channel prior. In: 2015 2nd International Conference on Electronics and Communication Systems (ICECS), pp. 1119–1123. IEEE (2015)
16. Schechner, Y.Y., Averbuch, Y.: Regularized image recovery in scattering media. IEEE Trans. Pattern Anal. Mach. Intell. **29**(9), 1655–1660 (2007)
17. Tarel, J.P., Hautiere, N.: Fast visibility restoration from a single color or gray level image. In: 2009 IEEE 12th International Conference on Computer Vision, pp. 2201–2208. IEEE (2009)
18. Yang, M., Sowmya, A.: An underwater color image quality evaluation metric. IEEE Trans. Image Process. **24**(12), 6062–6071 (2015)

A Fast Domain Adaptation Network
for Image Super-Resolution

Hongyang Zhou[1], Zheng Han[1], Wenli Zheng[1(✉)], Yifan Chen[2], and Fenghai Li[3]

[1] University of Science and Technology Beijing, Beijing, China
[2] Canvard College, Beijing Technology and Business University, Beijing, China
[3] Beijing Technology and Business University, Beijing, China

Abstract. Most previous super-resolution (SR) methods are based on high-resolution (HR) images and corresponding low-resolution (LR) images obtained artificially through bicubic downsampling. However, in real scenes, LR images are usually obtained with complex degradation functions, which may result in the domain gap between LR images. And we observe that this can sharply weaken the performance of the SR model. In this work, we propose a Fast Domain Adaptation Network for SR to solve this issue. First, we train a domain adaptation module to transform source LR images to the bicubic downsampled LR images. Then, we apply this module on the top of any SR model pretrained on bicubically downsampled images. Abundant experiments demonstrate the effectiveness of our proposed method and show that our network outperforms previous state-of-the-art works in terms of both qualitative and quantitative aspects on real-world dataset and synthetic dataset.

Keywords: Image super-resolution · Domain adaptation · Deep learning

1 Introduction

1.1 A Subsection Sample

The propose of single image super-resolution (SISR) is to reconstruct a visually natural high-resolution (HR) image using a single low-resolution (LR) image. SISR has been widely used in daily life, such as enhancing the images visual perception on high-resolution devices and improving the quality of other vision tasks [4]. It is a low-level computer vision task and inherently ill-posed since one LR image can generate multiple HR images. In order to solve this problem, a large number of SISR methods that are based on Deep Neural Networks (DNNs) have been proposed recently [6,14,17,19,26,29,40,41].

Although the performance of SISR has been greatly improved in recent years, it still needs further research. One of the problems is caused by the mismatch between the over-simple degradation models of the existing SISR methods and the unknown degradations of the real images [7]. Generally, the training data

© Springer Nature Switzerland AG 2021
Y. Peng et al. (Eds.): ICIG 2021, LNCS 12890, pp. 218–229, 2021.
https://doi.org/10.1007/978-3-030-87361-5_18

| (a) RCAN(BI) | (b) RCAN(RealSR) | (c) HR |

Fig. 1. Comparison RCAN (BI), RCAN (RealSR) and HR images for ×4 SR. (BI) means trained with bicubically downsampled dataset and (RealSR) means retrained with RealSR dataset. (a) and (b) show a huge performance difference caused by the dataset field mismatch.

of SISR methods are obtained by using a fixed known degradation process (e.g. bicubic), but the degradation process in real scenes are typically complicated and unavailable. As mentioned in [7,11], the performance of SISR methods will suffer severe drop when the pre-defined degradation process is different from the real one. Different degradation models lead to different data distributions, thus the problem with unknown data distribution largely limited their usage in real-world applications. Several recent SISR approaches have been introduced for alleviating the limitation of DNNs to the fixed degradation assumption made in the training phase. These methods include: integrating a set of predefined downscaling kernels during the input phase of the training process [11,39]; utilizing DNNs to learn prior knowledge of natural images which is separated from the SISR task [38]; or transforming the LR image to match one which is obtained by the bicubic kernel [13].

To solve this drawback and put SISR into more practical applications, we propose a fast data adaptation network to make the pre-trained SISR methods quickly adapt to the new dataset without retraining and our method is inspired by the kernel correction [11,13].

The major contribution of proposed method are summarized as follow:

- We propose a lightweight CNN-based LR-to-LR image adaptation module, which we call the Fast Domain Adaptation Module. This module can quickly convert a LR image to its corresponding target LR image obtained by bicubic downsampling. Applying this module to any pretrained SR model can produce huge performance gain, which solves the domain gap problem due to complex degenerations in reality.
- This module can quickly adapt to any SR model pretrained on bicubically downsampled LR images without retraining the entire model on new datasets. Thus the entire cost of training can be reduced.
- Abundant experiments demonstrate the effectiveness of our proposed model. The results on real-world dataset and synthetic dataset exceed previous state-of-the-art methods on both qualitative and quantitative aspects.

2   Related Works

2.1   Single Image Super Resolution

Recently, numerous methods have employed DNNs for the SISR task, Dong et al. [6] firstly proposed a three consecutive convolutional neural network in SISR to learn a complex LR-HR mapping. Kim et al. [14] increased the depth of the network and used a skip connection for stable training. Shi et al. [26] firstly proposed a real-time super-resolution algorithm ESPCNN by proposing the sub-pixel convolution layer. In order to make the network deeper and achieve significant performance, most of the methods adopt residual architecture [14]. SRGAN [17] first introduced residual blocks and the adversarial learning into SISR networks. EDSR [19] enhanced it by removing batch normalization layer in residual block and deepening the network depth. SRDenseNet [29] present an effective residual dense block and RDN [41] further use local/global residual dense block to improve the quality of SISR results. Zhang et al. [40] introduced the residual channel attention to the SISR framework. Zhang et al. [39] proposed a stretching strategy to integrate LR Image with degradation information in a SISR network.

However, existing approaches for SISR rely on the paired training data, HR images with their synthetic LR counterparts, while the distribution of real-world images is different from that of synthetic LR images obtained by a specific degradation method (e.g. bicubic). When the distribution of testing data mismatch training data, the result suffer from a huge performance drop as shown in Fig. 1. In this work, the Fast Domain Adaptation Network we propose can perfectly solve this problem.

2.2   Domain Adaptation

In order to alleviate the domain gap caused by different dataset distributions of training and testing data, a large number of domain adaptation methods have been proposed through the past decade [25,32]. In general, they can be categorized into three cases.

The first case is based on the discrepancy and aims to seek suitable measure criterions for the statistical distribution between the source domain and target domain. The most commonly used criterions for measuring and reducing domain gap are maximum mean discrepancy (MMD) [8,20,21,31,35], correlation alignment (CORAL) [27,42,43] and earth mover's distance (EMD) [5,36]. The second case can be referred to as an adversarial-based adaptation approach [22,30,34], which is analogical to the generative adversarial networks [10]. A domain classifier is trained to distinguish whether the training image is from the source domain or the target domain. The feature extracter is trained to minimize the classification loss and maximize the domain confusion loss. In this way, domain-invariant yet discriminative features are seemingly obtained through an adversarial training process between the feature extracter and the classifier. The last case is based on reconstruction and assumes that the reconstructor such as the variational autoencoder [16] can ensure both discernible intra-domain representations and confouded inter-domain representations [2,9]. These methods take the data reconstruction of source or target samples as an auxiliary task to construct a shared feature space where discriminative domain-invariant features are reserved.

In this work, we propose a novel domain adaptation module to learn the distribution of the degradated HR image. This module is hot-pluggable and can fast adapt to any SR model pretrained on bicubically downsampled data without retraining the entire model.

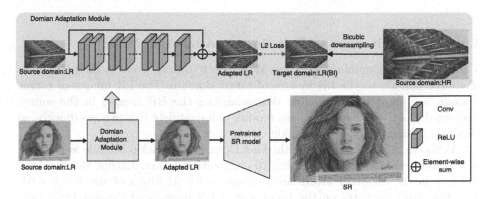

Fig. 2. The architecture of th Fast Domain Adaptation Network for SR. First, we transform source domain LR images to target domain LR images obtained by bicubic downsampling through our Domain Adapation Module. We then pass the adapted LR image as input to a pretrained SR model trained on bicubically downsampled images.

3 The Proposed Method

3.1 Overview of Fast Domain Adaptation Network

Our method consists of two steps: first, we use a fast domain adaptation module, whose purpose is to take the LR image of source domain as input and adapt it into an image of the same size and content, but which looks as if it had been downsampled bicubically. We call this output the adapted LR image. Second, we use any SR model pretrained on bicubically downsampled data to take the adapted LR image as input and output the SR image. Figure 2 shows an overview of our proposed method. In the following subsections, we describe each component of our method in more details.

Table 1. Quantitative results with RealSR testing set. Red color indicates the best performance, and blue color indicates the second best performance.

Method	Scale	PSNR/SSIM	Scale	PSNR/SSIM	Scale	PSNR/SSIM
Bicubic	×2	31.67/0.887	×3	28.63/0.808	×4	27.23/0.764
Bicubic+our method	×2	33.30/0.902	×3	30.11/0.848	×4	28.36/0.796
RCAN	×2	32.08/0.897	×3	28.98/0.821	×4	27.65/0.780
RCAN+our method	×2	33.80/0.921	×3	30.71/0.863	×4	29.02/0.820
SRFBN	×2	32.07/0.894	×3	28.98/0.821	×4	27.64/0.780
SRFBN+our method	×2	33.79/0.921	×3	30.70/0.863	×4	28.99/0.819

3.2 The Architecture of Fast Domain Adapation Module

The goal of Fast Domain Adapation Module is to quickly convert the LR images of source domain to the LR images of target domain. The LR images of target domain are obtained by bicubic downsampling the HR images in the source domain dataset. We hope that this module can complete this process quickly, so we design the module as lightweight as possible.

As shown in Fig. 2, we design the Fast Domain Adapation Module as a simple adapation network, which contains 16 convolution layers. Except the first and the last layers, all other layers are the same with 64 filters of size $3 \times 3 \times 64$. The first layer operates on the input source LR image and the last layer used for adapted LR image reconstruction, which consists of a single filter of size $3 \times 3 \times 64$. We use a residual connection to learn the details of the target image. The output of the last layer of convolution will be added with the input LR image to give the final image. Our loss layer takes three inputs: residual estimate, network input (source LR image) and target LR image. The loss is computed as the Euclidean distance between the reconstructed image and target LR images. This network is pretty light-weight and only operates between LR images, so brings low computational cost. Experiments show that this simple structure can already achieve satisfactory results.

For training, Let x denote a source LR image and y denote a source HR image. Given a new training dataset $\{x(i), y(i)\}_{i=1}^{N}$, our goal is to learn a model $D(\cdot)$ that predicts values $\bar{x} = D(x)$, where $\bar{x}$ is an estimate of the target LR image. In order to constrain the above process, we need to bicubic downsample y to get target LR image x_{BI}. We minimize the mean squared error $\frac{1}{2}\|x_{BI} - D(x)\|^2$ averaged over the training set is minimized.

3.3 Pretrained SR Model

Due to the difficulty of collecting HR-LR image pairs, most SR approaches usually adopt a simulated image degradation for training and testing, e.g., bicubic downsampling. However, when these models are applied to a new data domain that is different from bicubic degradation method, their performance will drop sharply. Although it is possible to retrain SR models on the new data domain to solve this problem, the previously trained model will not be usable, and retraining will cost a lot of time. Our method can perfectly solve this problem. Through our domain adaptation method, we can quickly adapt the LR image of source domain to the LR image of target domain obtained by bicubic downsampling. After obtaining the adapted LR image, we need the SR model to generate the HR image. We directly put it into any SR model trained on bicubic downsampled data to generate a satisfactory HR image. This process uses the existing trained SR model and does not need to be retrained.

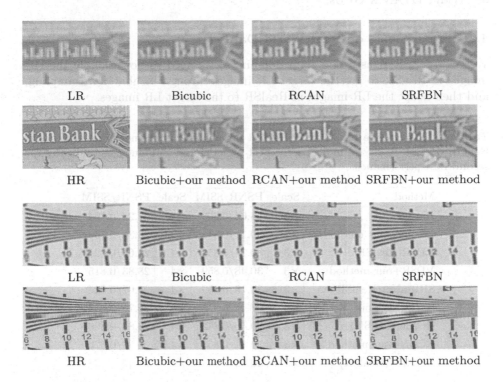

Fig. 3. Visual comparison of different methods for ×4 SR on image *Nikon_046* and image *Nikon_050* from RealSR.

4   Experiments

4.1   Experimental Details

To prove the effectiveness of our method, we mainly conduct experiments from real-world dataset and synthetic dataset. In terms of real-world dataset, we choose RealSR [3] as training and testing data. For the synthetic dataset, we take high-quality dataset DIV2K [28] as training data and use five standard benchmark datasets: Set5 [1], Set14 [37], BSDS100 [23], Urban100 [12] and Manga109

[24] as testing data. For comparison, we consider the peak signal-to-noise ratio (PSNR) and structural similarity index (SSIM) [33] on the Y channel of the transformed YCbCr color space. We train our network by minimizing L2 loss between the target LR images and corresponding source LR images. The optimizer is Adam [15] and the learning rate is initialized to 10^{-4} for all the layers. We set train patch size to 41×41, and batch size to 64. Data augmentation is performed by randomly rotating 90°, 180°, 270° and horizontally flipping the input. All of our experiments are conducted in PyTorch and train our network on Nvidia TITAN X GPUs.

4.2 Experiments on Real-World Dataset

We regard RealSR as a new data domain, so we need to downsample the HR images in RealSR to get the target LR images through bicubic downsampling, and then adapt the LR images in RealSR to the target LR images.

Table 2. Quantitative results with RealSR dataset. (RealSR) means retrained with RealSR dataset. Red color indicates the best performance, and blue color indicates the second best performance.

Method	Scale	PSNR/SSIM	Scale	PSNR/SSIM
Bicubic	×3	28.63/0.808	×4	27.23/0.764
Bicubic+our method	×3	30.11/0.848	×4	28.36/0.796
VDSR(RealSR)	×3	30.14/0.856	×4	28.63/0.821
VDSR+our method	×3	30.48/0.859	×4	28.83/0.815
SRResNet(RealSR)	×3	30.18/0.859	×4	28.67/0.824
SRResNet+our method	×3	-/-	×4	28.71/0.813
RCAN(RealSR)	×3	30.40/0.862	×4	28.88/0.826
RCAN+our method	×3	30.71/0.863	×4	29.02/0.820
LP-KPN(RealSR)	×3	30.42/0.868	×4	28.92/0.834

We compare our approach with two state-of-the-art SR methods: RCAN [40] and SRFBN [18]. The results are presented in Table 1 for the testset RealSR. It can be seen that the proposed fast domain adaptation network significantly improves the results of RCAN and SRFBN, which have been trained for the bicubic kernel. The RCAN equipped with our method notably improves the performance about 1.72 dB, 1.73 dB, 1.37 dB of PSNR for scaling factors ×2, ×3, ×4. Similar results are also reflected in Bicubic and SRFBN. Moreoever, note that Bicubic using our method also outperforms the plain applications of RCAN and SRFBN by about 1.22 dB, 1.13 dB, 0.71 dB of PSNR for scaling factors ×2, ×3, ×4.

We also conduct visual comparison to the several methods. Figure 3 visualizes SR results of the competing methods and ours. It is observed that the direct test result of existing SR methods are prone to generate detailed textures with visual aliasing and artifacts. In contrast, our proposed method can help these methods to reconstruct clear and natural details. The qualitative comparison proves that the domain adaptation method we proposed helps to improve the pre-existing model to quickly adapt to the new data domain without retraining.

To further validate challenge of our method, we compare our method with several state-of-the-art SR methods trained on RealSR, including VDSR [14], SRResNet [17], RCAN [40] and LP-KPN [3]. In Table 2, our method makes the PSNR of RCAN exceed LP-KPN in scale of ×3 and ×4. Similar to the RCAN using our method, our proposed method significantly improves the results of VDSR and SRResNet, validating the effectiveness of our method.

Table 3. Quantitative results with BD degradation model. Each cell displays PSNR [dB] (left) and SSIM (right). Red color indicates the best performance, and blue color indicates the second best performance.

Method	Scale	Set5	Set14	BSDS100	Urban100	Manga109
Bicubic	×2	29.06/0.843	26.74/0.745	26.59/0.709	23.78/0.705	25.82/0.831
	×3	28.79/0.832	26.46/0.730	26.34/0.693	23.52/0.687	25.47/0.816
	×4	27.76/0.792	25.62/0.691	25.67/0.655	22.81/0.645	24.42/0.777
Bicubic+our method	×2	33.19/0.923	30.01/0.859	29.28/0.831	26.70/0.832	30.46/0.928
	×3	30.27/0.867	27.52/0.774	27.15/0.736	24.42/0.734	26.87/0.855
	×4	28.33/0.810	26.98/0.705	25.92/0.669	23.11/0.659	24.86/0.788
RCAN	×2	29.52/0.857	27.17/0.765	31.51/0.883	24.20/0.729	26.36/0.850
	×3	30.72/0.882	27.99/0.786	29.18/0.808	25.27/0.773	28.00/0.886
	×4	31.16/0.883	28.00/0.770	27.55/0.740	25.79/0.783	29.23/0.897
RCAN+our method	×2	36.56/0.949	32.82/0.902	31.51/0.883	30.92/0.910	36.47/0.967
	×3	34.39/0.920	30.43/0.843	29.19/0.808	28.66/0.862	33.74/0.947
	×4	32.22/0.897	28.62/0.785	27.55/0.740	26.55/0.805	30.76/0.915
SRFBN	×2	29.52/0.857	27.17/0.765	26.95/0.730	24.20/0.729	26.36/0.850
	×3	30.67/0.881	27.96/0.785	27.47/0.745	25.19/0.770	27.91/0.884
	×4	30.99/0.880	27.87/0.766	27.20/0.721	25.54/0.774	29.00/0.894
SRFBN+our method	×2	36.53/0.949	32.71/0.901	31.49/0.882	30.76/0.908	36.49/0.967
	×3	34.34/0.927	30.31/0.842	29.12/0.805	28.38/0.857	33.53/0.945
	×4	32.10/0.896	28.55/0.783	27.52/0.737	26.36/0.798	30.66/0.913

4.3 Experiments on Synthetic Dataset

In order to simulate the new data domain, we degenerate the DIV2K to get the LR image through blur-down (BD) degradation model and construct a complete dataset. Similarly, we downsample the HR images in the new dataset to obtain the target LR images through bicubic sampling.

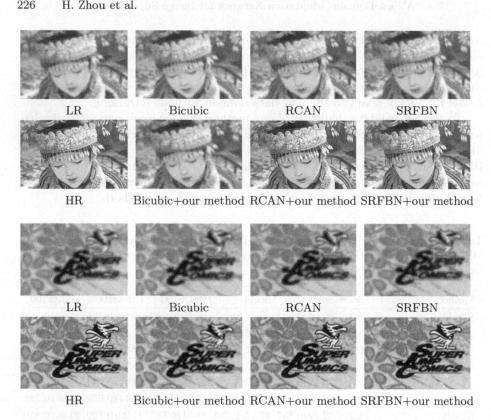

LR   Bicubic   RCAN   SRFBN

HR   Bicubic+our method   RCAN+our method   SRFBN+our method

LR   Bicubic   RCAN   SRFBN

HR   Bicubic+our method   RCAN+our method   SRFBN+our method

Fig. 4. Visual comparison of different methods for ×2 SR on image *comic* from Set14 and image *BurariTessenTorimonocho* from Manga109.

To evaluate the adaptation performance on our method, we conduct our method on synthetic datasets. The results for Set5, Set14, BSD100, Urban100, Manga109 are given in Table 3, respectively, and visual examples are presented in Fig. 4.

From Table 3, the model with our method consistently outperforms the baseline counterpart on all the datasets. What is unexpected is that the results in scale of ×2 tested directly using plain RCAN are lower than the results in scale of ×3 and ×4, some results are even lower than Bicubic. But the RCAN using our method still shows strong performance, which further demonstrates the effectiveness of our method. These results demonstrate the effectiveness of the proposed adaptation method.

5   Conclusion

Recently, the SISR task has benefited a lot from the developments in DNNs. However, the performance will suffer from a huge drop when the DNNs-driven methods are tested on images that are not mismatch for the assumptions of the acquisition process used in training phase. In this paper, We have introduced a novel method named Fast Domain Adaptation Network to address the issue that quickly adapt to a new dataset through a single model. The proposed method could quickly convert the data distribution of LR in the new dataset to the known data distribution. Then use the existing single image super-resolution methods to generate the desired HR image without retraining. Thanks to the process of rapid adaptation, we can maximize the performance of the existing pre-trained DNNs methods.

Acknowledgement. This work was supported by National Key R&D Program of China (2017Y FB1401000), National Natural Science Foundation of China (61806017, 62006018).

References

1. Bevilacqua, M., Roumy, A., Guillemot, C., Alberi-Morel, M.L.: Low-complexity single-image super-resolution based on nonnegative neighbor embedding (2012)
2. Bousmalis, K., Trigeorgis, G., Silberman, N., Krishnan, D., Erhan, D.: Domain separation networks. arXiv preprint arXiv:1608.06019 (2016)
3. Cai, J., Zeng, H., Yong, H., Cao, Z., Zhang, L.: Toward real-world single image super-resolution: a new benchmark and a new model. In: Proceedings of the IEEE International Conference on Computer Vision, pp. 3086–3095 (2019)
4. Dai, D., Wang, Y., Chen, Y., Van Gool, L.: Is image super-resolution helpful for other vision tasks? In: 2016 IEEE Winter Conference on Applications of Computer Vision (WACV), pp. 1–9. IEEE (2016)
5. Damodaran, B.B., Kellenberger, B., Flamary, R., Tuia, D., Courty, N.: DeepJDOT: deep joint distribution optimal transport for unsupervised domain adaptation. In: Ferrari, V., Hebert, M., Sminchisescu, C., Weiss, Y. (eds.) ECCV 2018. LNCS, vol. 11208, pp. 467–483. Springer, Cham (2018). https://doi.org/10.1007/978-3-030-01225-0_28
6. Dong, C., Loy, C.C., He, K., Tang, X.: Learning a deep convolutional network for image super-resolution. In: Fleet, D., Pajdla, T., Schiele, B., Tuytelaars, T. (eds.) ECCV 2014. LNCS, vol. 8692, pp. 184–199. Springer, Cham (2014). https://doi.org/10.1007/978-3-319-10593-2_13
7. Efrat, N., Glasner, D., Apartsin, A., Nadler, B., Levin, A.: Accurate blur models vs. image priors in single image super-resolution. In: Proceedings of the IEEE International Conference on Computer Vision, pp. 2832–2839 (2013)
8. Ghifary, M., Kleijn, W.B., Zhang, M.: Domain adaptive neural networks for object recognition. In: Pham, D.-N., Park, S.-B. (eds.) PRICAI 2014. LNCS (LNAI), vol. 8862, pp. 898–904. Springer, Cham (2014). https://doi.org/10.1007/978-3-319-13560-1_76
9. Ghifary, M., Kleijn, W.B., Zhang, M., Balduzzi, D., Li, W.: Deep reconstruction-classification networks for unsupervised domain adaptation. In: Leibe, B., Matas, J., Sebe, N., Welling, M. (eds.) ECCV 2016. LNCS, vol. 9908, pp. 597–613. Springer, Cham (2016). https://doi.org/10.1007/978-3-319-46493-0_36
10. Goodfellow, I.J., et al.: Generative adversarial networks. arXiv preprint arXiv:1406.2661 (2014)

11. Gu, J., Lu, H., Zuo, W., Dong, C.: Blind super-resolution with iterative kernel correction. In: Proceedings of the IEEE Conference on Computer Vision and Pattern Recognition, pp. 1604–1613 (2019)
12. Huang, J.B., Singh, A., Ahuja, N.: Single image super-resolution from transformed self-exemplars. In: Proceedings of the IEEE Conference on Computer Vision and Pattern Recognition, pp. 5197–5206 (2015)
13. Hussein, S.A., Tirer, T., Giryes, R.: Correction filter for single image super-resolution: robustifying off-the-shelf deep super-resolvers. In: Proceedings of the IEEE/CVF Conference on Computer Vision and Pattern Recognition, pp. 1428–1437 (2020)
14. Kim, J., Kwon Lee, J., Mu Lee, K.: Accurate image super-resolution using very deep convolutional networks. In: Proceedings of the IEEE Conference on Computer Vision and Pattern Recognition, pp. 1646–1654 (2016)
15. Kingma, D.P., Ba, J.: Adam: a method for stochastic optimization. arXiv preprint arXiv:1412.6980 (2014)
16. Kingma, D.P., Welling, M.: Auto-encoding variational Bayes. arXiv preprint arXiv:1312.6114 (2013)
17. Ledig, C., et al.: Photo-realistic single image super-resolution using a generative adversarial network. In: Proceedings of the IEEE Conference on Computer Vision and Pattern Recognition, pp. 4681–4690 (2017)
18. Li, Z., Yang, J., Liu, Z., Yang, X., Jeon, G., Wu, W.: Feedback network for image super-resolution. In: Proceedings of the IEEE/CVF Conference on Computer Vision and Pattern Recognition, pp. 3867–3876 (2019)
19. Lim, B., Son, S., Kim, H., Nah, S., Mu Lee, K.: Enhanced deep residual networks for single image super-resolution. In: Proceedings of the IEEE Conference on Computer Vision and Pattern Recognition Workshops, pp. 136–144 (2017)
20. Long, M., Zhu, H., Wang, J., Jordan, M.I.: Unsupervised domain adaptation with residual transfer networks. In: Proceedings of the 30th International Conference on Neural Information Processing Systems, NIPS 2016, pp. 136–144. Curran Associates Inc., Red Hook (2016)
21. Long, M., Zhu, H., Wang, J., Jordan, M.I.: Deep transfer learning with joint adaptation networks. In: International Conference on Machine Learning, pp. 2208–2217. PMLR (2017)
22. Ma, X., Zhang, T., Xu, C.: GCAN: graph convolutional adversarial network for unsupervised domain adaptation. In: Proceedings of the IEEE/CVF Conference on Computer Vision and Pattern Recognition, pp. 8266–8276 (2019)
23. Martin, D., Fowlkes, C., Tal, D., Malik, J.: A database of human segmented natural images and its application to evaluating segmentation algorithms and measuring ecological statistics. In: Proceedings Eighth IEEE International Conference on Computer Vision. ICCV 2001, vol. 2, pp. 416–423. IEEE (2001)
24. Matsui, Y., et al.: Sketch-based manga retrieval using manga109 dataset. Multimedia Tools Appl. **76**(20), 21811–21838 (2017)
25. Patel, V.M., Gopalan, R., Li, R., Chellappa, R.: Visual domain adaptation: a survey of recent advances. IEEE Signal Process. Mag. **32**(3), 53–69 (2015)
26. Shi, W., et al.: Real-time single image and video super-resolution using an efficient sub-pixel convolutional neural network. In: Proceedings of the IEEE Conference on Computer Vision and Pattern Recognition, pp. 1874–1883 (2016)
27. Sun, B., Feng, J., Saenko, K.: Correlation alignment for unsupervised domain adaptation. In: Csurka, G. (ed.) Domain Adaptation in Computer Vision Applications. ACVPR, pp. 153–171. Springer, Cham (2017). https://doi.org/10.1007/978-3-319-58347-1_8

28. Timofte, R., Agustsson, E., Van Gool, L., Yang, M.H., Zhang, L.: NTIRE 2017 challenge on single image super-resolution: methods and results. In: Proceedings of the IEEE Conference on Computer Vision and Pattern Recognition Workshops, pp. 114–125 (2017)

29. Tong, T., Li, G., Liu, X., Gao, Q.: Image super-resolution using dense skip connections. In: Proceedings of the IEEE International Conference on Computer Vision, pp. 4799–4807 (2017)

30. Tzeng, E., Hoffman, J., Saenko, K., Darrell, T.: Adversarial discriminative domain adaptation. In: Proceedings of the IEEE Conference on Computer Vision and Pattern Recognition, pp. 7167–7176 (2017)

31. Tzeng, E., Hoffman, J., Zhang, N., Saenko, K., Darrell, T.: Deep domain confusion: Maximizing for domain invariance. arXiv preprint arXiv:1412.3474 (2014)

32. Wang, M., Deng, W.: Deep visual domain adaptation: a survey. Neurocomputing **312**, 135–153 (2018)

33. Wang, Z., Bovik, A.C., Sheikh, H.R., Simoncelli, E.P.: Image quality assessment: from error visibility to structural similarity. IEEE Trans. Image Process. **13**(4), 600–612 (2004)

34. Xie, S., Zheng, Z., Chen, L., Chen, C.: Learning semantic representations for unsupervised domain adaptation. In: International Conference on Machine Learning, pp. 5423–5432. PMLR (2018)

35. Yan, H., Ding, Y., Li, P., Wang, Q., Xu, Y., Zuo, W.: Mind the class weight bias: weighted maximum mean discrepancy for unsupervised domain adaptation. In: Proceedings of the IEEE Conference on Computer Vision and Pattern Recognition, pp. 2272–2281 (2017)

36. Yan, Y., Li, W., Wu, H., Min, H., Tan, M., Wu, Q.: Semi-supervised optimal transport for heterogeneous domain adaptation. IJCAI **7**, 2969–2975 (2018)

37. Zeyde, R., Elad, M., Protter, M.: On single image scale-up using sparse-representations. In: Boissonnat, J.-D., et al. (eds.) Curves and Surfaces 2010. LNCS, vol. 6920, pp. 711–730. Springer, Heidelberg (2012). https://doi.org/10.1007/978-3-642-27413-8_47

38. Zhang, K., Zuo, W., Gu, S., Zhang, L.: Learning deep CNN denoiser prior for image restoration. In: Proceedings of the IEEE Conference on Computer Vision and Pattern Recognition, pp. 3929–3938 (2017)

39. Zhang, K., Zuo, W., Zhang, L.: Learning a single convolutional super-resolution network for multiple degradations. In: Proceedings of the IEEE Conference on Computer Vision and Pattern Recognition, pp. 3262–3271 (2018)

40. Zhang, Y., Li, K., Li, K., Wang, L., Zhong, B., Fu, Y.: Image super-resolution using very deep residual channel attention networks. In: Ferrari, V., Hebert, M., Sminchisescu, C., Weiss, Y. (eds.) ECCV 2018. LNCS, vol. 11211, pp. 294–310. Springer, Cham (2018). https://doi.org/10.1007/978-3-030-01234-2_18

41. Zhang, Y., Tian, Y., Kong, Y., Zhong, B., Fu, Y.: Residual dense network for image super-resolution. In: Proceedings of the IEEE Conference on Computer Vision and Pattern Recognition, pp. 2472–2481 (2018)

42. Zhang, Y., Wang, N., Cai, S., Song, L.: Unsupervised domain adaptation by mapped correlation alignment. IEEE Access **6**, 44698–44706 (2018)

43. Zhang, Z., Doi, K., Iwasaki, A., Xu, G.: Unsupervised domain adaptation of high-resolution aerial images via correlation alignment and self training. IEEE Geosci. Remote Sens. Lett. **18**, 746–750 (2020)

Using Conv-LSTM to Refine Features for Lightweight Image Super-Resolution Network

Jiangtao Zhang, Yanyun Qu$^{(\boxtimes)}$, and Liang Chen

School of Informatics, Xiamen University, Xiamen, China
yyqu@xmu.edu.cn

Abstract. In this paper, we propose a lightweight network that uses conv-LSTM for feature fusion (LFN) to improve image super-resolution performance and save the number of parameters. The network extracts features of different levels from the input image through a deep extraction block (DB) composed of two hourglass blocks (HB). HB progressively compresses and expands the channel of the input feature map to achieve compact feature aggregation and amplification, thereby making the information in the network more compact. The information at different levels in the network is regarded as a sequence, and Conv-LSTM is used to repeatedly fuse and extract more effective information from this sequence to obtain an effective expression. Experimental results show that our network can achieve a good balance between performance, number of parameters and amount of calculation.

Keywords: Single image super-resolution · Convolutional neural network · Conv-LSTM

1 Introduction

The purpose of single image super-resolution (SISR) is to give a low-resolution (LR) image and solve its corresponding high-resolution (HR) image. The SISR problem is an ill-posed problem with no unique solution. Recently, many CNN-based methods [7,14,22,24] have made breakthroughs on this issue. Most of these methods improve performance by stacking residual blocks or increasing the network width. However, it not only requires a large number of parameters, but also is often accompanied by a large number of calculations and memory consumption, which is not convenient for application in some practical scenarios. In order to solve this problem, some lightweight models [4,10,20,21] are proposed, which pay more attention to how to extract more effective feature information from the input and how to integrate these features more efficiently.

Many existing methods feed the input image to a module to extract features, which is composed of multiple convolutional layers with fixed channels. This design causes some redundant information to be generated in the network. Due to this problem, we propose a deep information extraction module composed of

© Springer Nature Switzerland AG 2021
Y. Peng et al. (Eds.): ICIG 2021, LNCS 12890, pp. 230–240, 2021.
https://doi.org/10.1007/978-3-030-87361-5_19

hourglass blocks, which can make the information extracted by the network more compact. To put it simply, the hourglass module compresses and expands the feature map to achieve the aggregation and amplification of effective information. As shown in Fig. 1, (a) is the LR image, (b)–(f) is the mean of the feature maps in channel dimension after two progressive channel compression and expansion (blue represents 0, red represents 1). (d) is the map with the largest compression rate of the number of channels. It can be seen that red color covers most of the area, which represents that its information attracts most attention. It is generated by (b) and then expanded through the channel to obtain (f). It acts as a bridge in the middle layer, condensing the network's concerns together and then spreading it out. More detailed explanation will be shown in Sect. 2.2.

For reducing the number of parameters, there are many ways to achieve this goal, but the simplest and most effective way is to use recursive networks. For example, [3,12] uses recursive networks to reduce redundant parameters. However, these methods have not done further research on feature fusion. For example, [20] only adopts a simple parameter sharing strategy, and does not filter the information of different recursive stages.

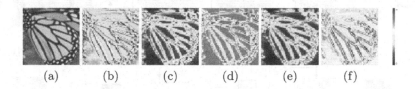

(a)   (b)   (c)   (d)   (e)   (f)

Fig. 1. Visualization of feature maps of HB module. (Color figure online)

Therefore, in order to better use the hidden state in the middle layers of network, we think of Long Short-Term Memory (LSTM) [8], a special type network of recurrent neural network (RNN). Since the difference between Conv-LSTM and LSTM is only the exchange of multiplication and convolution calculations, in the following we use LSTM to refer to Conv-LSTM. In previous work, LSTM is mostly used to process time series data. These data are continuously changing in the time dimension, showing a progressive relationship. Analogous to the SR problem, the feature maps from different layers of the network are obtained by transforming the previous layer, which also presents a progressive relationship. So they can be regarded as a sequence and it makes sense to send them to LSTM to extract more information. The last feature map contain the most effective information. We combine it with the initial extracted features and obtain the SR image through a pixel-shuffle [18] without parameters.

In summary, the main contributions of this work are:

– The DB composed of HB can make the information in the network more compact, thereby reducing the amount of parameters while enhancing the capabilities of the network.

- LSTM integrates different levels of feature maps and hidden state information more finely so that the information of different levels in the network can be expressed more efficiently.
- The network we propose can achieve a good balance between performance, number of parameters and amount of calculation.

2 Methodology

2.1 Network Architecture

The proposed network framework named LFN is shown in Fig. 2, which contains three parts: initial shallow feature extraction, LSTM feature refinement and HR image reconstruction.

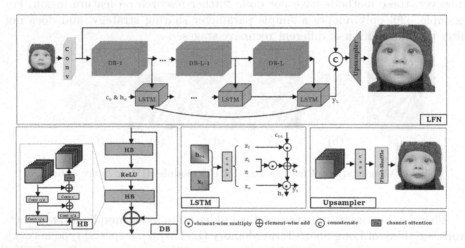

Fig. 2. LFN contains three parts: initial shallow feature extraction, LSTM feature refinement, HR image reconstruction. The first part is a convolution layer. The second part consists of L DBs and 1 LSTM. It can be used to update the state and refine the feature information. The last module uses pixel-shuffle to get a reconstructed SR image.

The initial shallow feature extraction includes a convolutional layer with a kernel size of 3×3, which is used to map the image from the image space to the feature space, which is formalized as:

$$F_0 = f_{FE}(I_{LR}) \tag{1}$$

Among them, I_{LR} is the LR image, f_{FE} is the convolution, and F_0 is the initial extracted feature. Then F_0 will go through the LSTM feature refinement module for extracting effective information. The LSTM feature refine module consists of L DB blocks and 1 LSTM, which is formalized as:

$$F_l = f_{DB_l}(F_{l-1}) \tag{2}$$

$$h_l, y_l, c_l = f_{LSTM}([h_{l-1}, F_l], c_{l-1}) \tag{3}$$

The Eq. (2) indicates that the feature F_{l-1} of the layer number $l-1$ is transformed by the l-th DB module f_{DB_l} to obtain the l-th feature F_l. Then the hidden state h_{l-1} and cell state c_{l-1} and F_l are sent to the LSTM together, as shown in Eq. (3), to update the state and refine the feature information. Square bracket represents the concatenation in the channel dimension and f_{LSTM} represents LSTM. Then we get the new state: h_l, c_l and the output y_l. The finally obtained y_L which is equal to h_L (In fact, h and y are equal at each stage) carries rich information of different layers in the network. In order to further combine with the features in the network, we recursively input it into the DB module. After many recursive processes, it carries more effectively. Finally, it will be further fused with the initial feature F_0 and be passed through channel conversion and pixel-shuffle to reconstruct SR image:

$$I_{SR} = f_{ps}(f_{cvt}(f_{fusion}([y_L, F_0]))) \tag{4}$$

Here, f_{fusion} represents feature fusion. f_{cvt} represents channel conversion. f_{ps} represents pixel-shuffle operation without parameters, and I_{SR} is the SR result we get.

2.2   Deep Feature Extraction

The low-rank approximation of a matrix is a sparse representation, that is, a matrix with a lower rank is used to approximate the original matrix, which not only retains the main characteristics of the original matrix, but also reduces the storage space and computational complexity of the data. For example, if a matrix $\mathbf{M}$ of size $m \times n$ can be decomposed into the multiplication form of two matrices: $\mathbf{M} = \mathbf{P} \times \mathbf{Q}$, where the size of $\mathbf{P}$ is $m \times k$ and the size of $\mathbf{Q}$ is $k \times n$. When $k < min(m, n)$, this operation can be regarded as a low-rank approximation to the matrix $\mathbf{M}$. Since the convolution operation and the matrix operation are both linear operations, we extend this idea to the convolution calculation. In order to make the convolution calculation more lightweight and maximize the transformation ability, we let $k = min(m, n)/2$, so that the network learns a capability that is closer to the original convolution and learns more compact features. We propose a deep extraction block, which extracts more effective information by compressing and expanding the network channel and reduces the amount of network parameters. It can be more effectively applied to SR. The DB block is also in the form of Residual-in-Residual (RIR), which contains two HBs. The outer layers of the two hourglass blocks are connected by a skip connection. The formula is:

$$F_{l+1} = F_l + f_{B_2}(f_{B_1}(F_l)) \tag{5}$$

Among them, f_{B_1} and f_{B_2} are the first and second HB respectively. In each HB, the process of compressing and expanding the channel is included. This process can not only reduce the amount of network parameters, but also enables the network to pass more important information to the next state. Assuming that the number of channels of the feature map we input is c, without loss of generality, we take the first HB as an example and compress the channels first:

$$F_{l,2} = f_{c \to c/2}(F_{l,1}) \tag{6}$$

$F_{l,1}$ represents the first feature map of the l-th layer. Then the resulting feature map will further compress and expand the channel through a residual structure, in the form:

$$F_{l,3} = F_{l,2} + f_{c/4 \to c/2}(f_{c/2 \to c/4}(F_{l,2})) \tag{7}$$

Through this operation, the effective information in the network will be gathered in the compressed channel. After that, we expand the number of channels to the original size, which distributes useful information to more channels. We scale the channels, which may damage the correlation of the channel and the importance of each channel. So we use the channel attention module(CA) used in RCAN [24] which consists of avgpool-reduction-expansion-multiply. Finally, the network obtains the final feature map through a residual connection:

$$F_{l,4} = f_{l,1} + f_{CA}(f_{c/2 \to c}(F_{l,3})) \tag{8}$$

By reducing and expanding the number of channels, the effective information in the network will be regrouped and reallocated, which enhances the expressive ability of network. From Fig. 1, we observe that after the number of channels is compressed, the attention area (red area in (d)) in the feature map becomes significantly larger, which shows that the effective information is gathered. Then we expand the number of channels and the information is redistributed, so that more attention is paid to the new feature map (yellow area in (f)).

2.3   LSTM Feature Refinement

Literature [15] shows that the shallow layer of the network contains more image details, and the deep layer contains more high-frequency and strong semantic information. Therefore, how to efficiently merge the shallow and deep features of the network is critical to the final reconstruction result. Common feature fusion methods include element-wise addition and concatenation. These methods are often mentioned in previous lightweight super-resolution networks, and can achieve better performance. However, they lack some judgments of feature maps and evaluation of importance, but directly stack them or add them directly, which may affect the final result.

LSTM [8] is often used in neural networks that processes sequence data [17, 19]. The feature maps from different levels of the neural network are converted from the feature map of the previous level through convolution or other modules, so it can be regarded as a kind of sequence data and feeding it to LSTM to refine information is meaningful. For reducing the amount of parameters and being suitable for SR tasks, we replace the activation function in LSTM, and we directly use a convolution operator to obtain the forget gate z_f, the input gate z_i, the output gate z_o and z:

$$z_f, z_i, z_o, z = f_{split}(Conv([h_{l-1}, x_l])) \tag{9}$$

f_{split} represents the split on the channel. LSTM can extract and filter the information of the input data through two states, so that the final output information is the most helpful to the result. When using LSTM to refine features, we input the result F_l of the DB output of the l-th layer as x_l and the hidden state h_{l-1} and cell state c_{l-1} of $l-1$-th layer into it. After transformation, we get new y_l, h_l, c_l. In this process, the cell state c_{l-1} firstly be filtered by the forget gate z_f. It "forgets" part of the previous information and adds some supplement information filtered by the input gate z_i, which is updated to c_l. Then we multiply c_l with the current output gate z_o to obtain the output feature y_l, which determines the information whether needs to be reduced and supplemented for this feature. The entire process is formalized as:

$$c_l = z_f * c_{l-1} + z_i * z \tag{10}$$
$$y_l = h_l = z_o * c_l \tag{11}$$

In order to further enhance the network's ability and reconstruction performance, we recursively input the obtained y_l into the network. After multiple times of this recursive process, the information in the network will become more effective. It should be noted that the multiple LSTMs shown in Fig. 2 are actually the same LSTM. In other words, they share the same parameters. When the final y_L is obtained, we concatenate it with the initial F_0, as shown in Eq. (4), to achieve a pseudo residual connection. Then we convert the feature to the corresponding channel number and use pixel-shuffle to get the reconstructed image I_{SR}.

Table 1. The comparison of EDSR-baseline, EDSR-HB w/ CA, and EDSR-HB w/o CA on scale 4× in 400 epochs.

Method	Set5	Set14	BSD100	Urban100	Params(K)	MultAdds(G)
EDSR-baseline [14]	32.08	28.53	27.55	25.96	1518	114.2
EDSR-HB w/ CA	32.08	28.50	27.51	25.88	1048	86.6
EDSR-HB w/o CA	32.05	28.50	27.52	25.86	1039	86.6

Table 2. The comparison of different feature map fusion methods on scale 4×. '*' stands for recursion. The best result is **highlighted** and the second best is <u>underlined</u>

Method	Params(K)	Set5 PSNR	Urban100 PSNR
Baseline	478	31.90	25.58
Baseline+addition	478	31.86	25.56
Baseline+concatenation	625	31.88	25.60
Baseline+LSTM	664	<u>32.01</u>	<u>25.75</u>
Baseline+LSTM*	664	**32.10**	**25.83**

3 Experiments and Results

3.1 Experiment Settings

Datasets. We train all networks with 800 training images from DIV2K dataset [1]. And for testing, we use the standard benchmark datasets: Set5 [2], Set14 [23], BSD100 [16], Urban100 [9]. We use peak signal-to-noise ratio (PSNR) and structure similarity index (SSIM) as the criteria. In order to prepare the training samples, we randomly sample 192 × 192 patches from HR images and then downscale them with the scaling factors (×2, ×3, ×4) by using bicubic interpolation method. And the batch size is set to 16. We augment the training data by randomly flipping horizontally or vertically and rotating 90°. Here, we set the number of recursive to 3, which can make the reconstruction effect better. We only adopt L_1 loss for training our network. The SR results are evaluated with PSNR and SSIM on Y channel (i.e., luminance) of transformed YCbCr space. Our models are trained with ADAM optimizer. The learning rate is initialized to 1×10^{-4} and decays by half at every 200 epochs. The activation function in each HB are ReLU. L is set to 4 and the number of channels c is set to 64. All experiments are implemented in PyTorch.

3.2 Ablation Studies

In this subsection, we will analyze the proposed hourglass blocks and the effectiveness of using LSTM to refine features.

Hourglass Blocks. In order to verify the effectiveness of the HB, we use the EDSR-baseline [14] model (abbreviated as EDSR) as our baseline, and replace the ResBlock (RB) in it with the proposed HB. As shown in Table 1, the number of EDSR-HB w/CA model parameters will reduce the number of EDSR parameters by 31.0%, but the PSNR value is the same on the Set5 dataset. Since there is a channel attention module (CA) in our HB module, in order to verify that the HB module is effective not just because of this module, we remove it and perform experiments. We can see that after removing the CA, the number of

Table 3. Quantitative evaluation of some light-weight SR methods at scale 2×, 3× and 4× for 4 datasets. Red color indicates the best and blue color indicates the second best performance

Method	Scale	Params	Multi-Adds	Set5 PSNR/SSIM	Set14 PSNR/SSIM	BSD100 PSNR/SSIM	Urban100 PSNR/SSIM
Bicubic	2	–	–	33.66/0.9299	30.24/0.8688	29.56/0.8431	26.88/0.8403
SRCNN [5]	2	8K	52.7G	36.66/0.9542	32.45/0.9067	31.36/0.8879	29.50/0.8946
FSRCNN [6]	2	12K	6.0G	37.05/0.9560	32.66/0.9090	31.53/0.8920	29.88/0.9020
VDSR [11]	2	665K	612.6G	37.53/0.9587	33.03/0.9124	31.90/0.8960	30.76/0.9140
DRCN [12]	2	1,774K	17974.3G	37.63/0.9588	33.04/0.9118	31.85/0.8942	30.75/0.9133
LapSRN [13]	2	813K	29.9G	37.52/0.9590	33.08/0.9130	31.80/0.8950	30.41/0.9100
DRRN [20]	2	297K	6,796.9G	37.74/0.9591	33.23/0.9136	32.05/0.8973	31.23/0.9188
IDN [10]	2	556K	124.6G	37.83/0.9600	33.30/0.9148	32.08/0.8985	31.27/0.9196
MemNet [21]	2	677K	2662.4G	37.78/0.9597	33.28/0.9142	32.08/0.8978	31.31/0.9195
LFN (ours)	2	644K	275.7G	37.88/0.9600	33.38/0.9158	32.04/0.8980	31.66/0.9233
LFN+ (ours)	2	644K	275.7G	37.97/0.9603	33.47/0.9166	32.10/0.8987	31.81/0.9247
Bicubic	3	–	–	30.39/0.8682	27.55/0.7742	27.21/0.7385	24.46/0.7349
SRCNN [5]	3	8K	52.7G	32.75/0.9090	29.30/0.8215	28.41/0.7863	26.24/0.7989
FSRCNN [6]	3	12K	5.0G	33.16/0.9140	29.43/0.8242	28.53/0.7910	26.43/0.8080
VDSR [11]	3	666K	612.6G	33.66/0.9213	29.77/0.8314	28.82/0.7976	27.14/0.8279
DRCN [12]	3	1,774K	17,974.3G	33.82/0.9226	29.76/0.8311	28.80/0.7963	27.15/0.8276
LapSRN [13]	3	502K	–	33.81/0.9220	29.79/0.8325	28.82/0.7980	27.07/0.8275
DRRN [20]	3	297K	6,796.9G	34.03/0.9244	29.96/0.8349	28.95/0.8004	27.53/0.8378
IDN [10]	3	553K	56.3G	34.11/0.9253	29.99/0.8354	28.95/0.8013	27.42/0.8359
MemNet [21]	3	678K	2,662.4G	34.09/0.9248	30.00/0.8350	28.96/0.8001	27.56/0.8376
LFN (ours)	3	652K	123.2G	34.20/0.9258	30.18/0.8386	28.98/0.8021	27.80/0.8444
LFN+ (ours)	3	652K	123.2G	34.34/0.9266	30.26/0.8398	29.04/0.8031	27.93/0.8466
Bicubic	4	–	–	28.42/0.8104	26.00/0.7027	25.96/0.6675	23.14/0.6577
SRCNN [5]	4	8K	52.7G	30.48/0.8628	27.50/0.7513	26.90/0.7101	24.52/0.7221
FSRCNN [6]	4	12K	4.6G	30.72/0.8660	27.61/0.7550	26.98/0.7150	24.62/0.7280
VDSR [11]	4	666K	612.6G	31.35/0.8838	28.01/0.7674	27.29/0.7251	25.18/0.7524
DRCN [12]	4	1,774K	17,974.3G	31.53/0.8854	28.02/0.7670	27.23/0.7233	25.14/0.7510
LapSRN [13]	4	502K	149.4G	31.54/0.8852	28.09/0.7700	27.32/0.7275	25.21/0.7562
DRRN [20]	4	297K	6,796.9G	31.68/0.8888	28.21/0.7720	27.38/0.7284	25.44/0.7638
IDN [10]	4	553K	32.3G	31.82/0.8903	28.25/0.7730	27.41/0.7297	25.41/0.7632
MemNet [21]	4	678K	2,662.4G	31.74/0.8893	28.26/0.7723	27.40/0.7281	25.50/0.7630
LFN(ours)	4	664K	198.9G	32.10/0.8937	28.48/0.7753	27.50/0.7334	25.83/0.7777
LFN+(ours)	4	664K	198.9G	32.21/0.8949	28.57/0.7770	27.55/0.7347	25.94/0.7805

network parameters has hardly been reduced, and performance has not been greatly affected. In this way, our HB module can be well applied to reduce the amount of network parameters. In addition, we visualized the HB module in the network. As shown in Fig. 1(d) is the heat map with the largest compression rate of the number of channels. The pixel in red area is larger, so it contains the most effective information. After integrating the information, the compact features will be separated by expanding the number of channel. It can be seen that the HB has the characteristics of aggregating effective information. So HB can extract more effective information and reduce the number of parameters in the network.

LSTM. In order to verify the effectiveness of LSTM for feature refinement, we compared the other two methods of fusing features in the experiment, namely concatenate and element-wise addition. Baseline is the structure of the mentioned LFN without LSTM. It can be seen from Table 2 that PSNR of the other two methods has almost no improvement compared with the baseline and the performance of using LSTM is higher than the other two methods. Compared

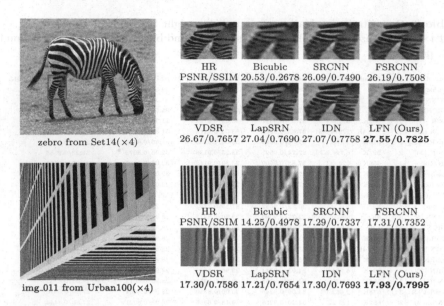

Fig. 3. The qualitative and quantitative comparisons of the other methods and our LFN on images from Set14 and Urban100 with the scale factor 4×. The best results are **highlighted**.

with baseline, using LSTM can increase the PSNR by 0.11 dB and 0.17 dB on the two datasets with a small number of parameters. This also shows that LSTM can refine more effective information from feature maps.

In addition, LSTM is often used in recursive modules, so it is effective to update it multiple times. To verify this idea, we can get a new $Y = [y_1, y_2, ..., y_L]$ sequence after one iteration and we send the final results y_L to the LSTM again, which can continue to participate the next step of information extraction. Experimental results show that multiple recursion is beneficial to the result. Compared with the case of no recursion, it can increase by 0.09 dB and 0.05 dB respectively.

3.3 Comparisons with Other Methods

We compare our method with eight state-of-the-art SR methods: SRCNN [5], FSRCNN [6], VDSR [11], DRCN [12], LapSRN [13], DRRN [20], MemNet [21] and IDN [10] on four public benchmark datasets. Mult-Adds is the number of composite multiply-accumulate operations for a single image. We assume the HR image size to be 720p (1280 × 720) to calculate Multi-Adds.

Qualitative Comparison. For the sake of fairness, we don't compare with some SR methods with larger amount of parameters. Our method has achieved a good balance between the amount of calculation and the amount of parameters. For example, the amount of parameters of the MemNet is close to ours, but the amount of calculation is larger. The amount of parameters of DRRN is small, but the amount of calculation is so huge. From Table 3, LFN+ is the self-ensemble results of LFN. We can see that the performance of LFN+ and LFN achieve the best results in benchmark datasets. When the scaling factors are big (e.g., 4×), our method performs the best. For example, on the Urban100 dataset, our method is superior to MemNet by 0.33 dB in PSNR. In general, it demonstrates that our method is superior to other SR methods in comprehensive performance.

Quantitative Comparison. We also compare the visual quality of the results with other methods, Fig. 3 provides a showcase of the images reconstructed by our proposed model and the other methods. It can be seen that our result has the correct texture structure, such as texture direction and texture continuity, which can be learned correctly through multiple recursion. For example, the diagonal texture in the image with the name 'img_011', other methods will be interfered by the surrounding pixels, which will cause the texture to be greatly distorted, and even faults. Our method can restore the continuous correctness. In addition, we can also see that our method not only has better visual fidelity, but also has better performance on objective indicators such as PSNR and SSIM.

4   Conclusions

In this paper, we propose a lightweight SR network that uses Conv-LSTM for feature refinement. In order to extract better features, we design a deep extraction block composed of two hourglass blocks, which can aggregate information well. For effectively integrating these features from different levels of network, we regard them as the sequence data due to their correlation. We modify the LSTM to save the amount of parameters and can better filter the useful information in the network. Experiments show that our method surpasses existing methods in performance, and has reached a rare balance in terms of parameter amount, calculation amount and performance.

References

1. Agustsson, E., Timofte, R.: NTIRE 2017 challenge on single image super-resolution: dataset and study. In: CVPR Workshops (2017)
2. Bevilacqua, M., Roumy, A., Guillemot, C., Alberi-Morel, M.L.: Low-complexity single-image super-resolution based on nonnegative neighbor embedding. In: BMVC (2012)
3. Choi, J.H., Kim, J.H., Cheon, M., Lee, J.S.: Lightweight and efficient image super-resolution with block state-based recursive network. arXiv preprint arXiv:1811.12546 (2018)
4. Chu, X., Zhang, B., Ma, H., Xu, R., Li, J., Li, Q.: Fast, accurate and lightweight super-resolution with neural architecture search. arXiv preprint arXiv:1901.07261 (2019)

5. Dong, C., Loy, C.C., He, K., Tang, X.: Learning a deep convolutional network for image super-resolution. In: Fleet, D., Pajdla, T., Schiele, B., Tuytelaars, T. (eds.) ECCV 2014. LNCS, vol. 8692, pp. 184–199. Springer, Cham (2014). https://doi.org/10.1007/978-3-319-10593-2_13

6. Dong, C., Loy, C.C., Tang, X.: Accelerating the super-resolution convolutional neural network. In: Leibe, B., Matas, J., Sebe, N., Welling, M. (eds.) ECCV 2016. LNCS, vol. 9906, pp. 391–407. Springer, Cham (2016). https://doi.org/10.1007/978-3-319-46475-6_25

7. Han, W., Chang, S., Liu, D., Yu, M., Witbrock, M., Huang, T.S.: Image super-resolution via dual-state recurrent networks. In: CVPR (2018)

8. Hochreiter, S., Schmidhuber, J.: Long short-term memory. Neural Comput. 9(8), 1735–1780 (1997)

9. Huang, J.B., Singh, A., Ahuja, N.: Single image super-resolution from transformed self-exemplars. In: CVPR (2015)

10. Hui, Z., Wang, X., Gao, X.: Fast and accurate single image super-resolution via information distillation network. In: CVPR (2018)

11. Kim, J., Kwon Lee, J., Mu Lee, K.: Accurate image super-resolution using very deep convolutional networks. In: CVPR (2016)

12. Kim, J., Kwon Lee, J., Mu Lee, K.: Deeply-recursive convolutional network for image super-resolution. In: CVPR (2016)

13. Lai, W.S., Huang, J.B., Ahuja, N., Yang, M.H.: Deep Laplacian pyramid networks for fast and accurate super-resolution. In: CVPR (2017)

14. Lim, B., Son, S., Kim, H., Nah, S., Lee, K.M.: Enhanced deep residual networks for single image super-resolution. In: CVPR Workshops (2017)

15. Lin, T.Y., Dollr, P., Girshick, R., He, K., Hariharan, B., Belongie, S.: Feature pyramid networks for object detection. In: 2017 IEEE Conference on Computer Vision and Pattern Recognition (CVPR) (2017)

16. Martin, D., Fowlkes, C., Tal, D., Malik, J., et al.: A database of human segmented natural images and its application to evaluating segmentation algorithms and measuring ecological statistics. In: ICCV, Vancouver (2001)

17. Merity, S., Keskar, N.S., Socher, R.: Regularizing and optimizing LSTM language models. arXiv preprint arXiv:1708.02182 (2017)

18. Shi, W., et al.: Real-time single image and video super-resolution using an efficient sub-pixel convolutional neural network. In: CVPR (2016)

19. Srivastava, N., Mansimov, E., Salakhutdinov, R.: Unsupervised learning of video representations using LSTMs. In: ICML (2015)

20. Tai, Y., Yang, J., Liu, X.: Image super-resolution via deep recursive residual network. In: CVPR (2017)

21. Tai, Y., Yang, J., Liu, X., Xu, C.: MemNet: a persistent memory network for image restoration. In: ICCV (2017)

22. Tong, T., Li, G., Liu, X., Gao, Q.: Image super-resolution using dense skip connections. In: ICCV (2017)

23. Zeyde, R., Elad, M., Protter, M.: On single image scale-up using sparse-representations. In: Boissonnat, J.-D., et al. (eds.) Curves and Surfaces 2010. LNCS, vol. 6920, pp. 711–730. Springer, Heidelberg (2012). https://doi.org/10.1007/978-3-642-27413-8_47

24. Zhang, Y., Li, K., Li, K., Wang, L., Zhong, B., Fu, Y.: Image super-resolution using very deep residual channel attention networks. In: Ferrari, V., Hebert, M., Sminchisescu, C., Weiss, Y. (eds.) ECCV 2018. LNCS, vol. 11211, pp. 294–310. Springer, Cham (2018). https://doi.org/10.1007/978-3-030-01234-2_18

No-Reference Image Quality Assessment for Contrast Distorted Images

Yiming Zhu, Xianzhi Chen, and Shengkui Dai[✉]

School of Information Science and Engineering, Huaqiao University, Xiamen 361000, China
d.s.k@hqu.edu.cn

Abstract. Image contrast distortion is a common type of distortion in digital images. However, there is almost no research on the no-reference image quality assessment (NR-IQA) algorithm for image contrast. Therefore, we propose a histogram-based NR-IQA algorithm for contrast distorted images. Firstly, we analyze the image sequence with gradually changing contrast, and the image features are extracted from two aspects: objective statistical attribute, subjective perception attribute. And then we propose three statistical features, including image local contrast, histogram shape and image brightness, which can describe the image quality more simply and intuitively. Furthermore, we introduce the Just noticeable difference (JND) model, which makes the proposed algorithm have a higher matching degree between the human vision system (HVS) and the objective features in the algorithm. Finally, the support vector regression (SVR) is utilized to obtain the mapping relationship between the quantified features and the subjective scores to predict the quality of contrast distorted images. The outstanding performance of the proposed algorithm have been proved on CSIQ, TID2013 and CCID2014 databases.

Keywords: Contrast distortion · Image sequence analysis · No-reference image quality assessment · JND · SVR

1 Introduction

Due to the influence of many factors in the process of acquisition, transmission, and processing of digital images, different types of distortion are prone to occur, such as blurring, noise, blocking, and contrast distortion. And such distortion makes it impossible for the HVS to get enough effective information from images. Therefore, for an image quality assessment algorithm aimed to effectively help HVS to distinguish the type or degree of distortion, an effective reference is in great need for image quality optimization.

Currently, the image quality assessment algorithms are divided into full-reference image quality assessment (FR-IQA), reduced-reference image quality assessment (RR-IQA) and no-reference image quality assessment (NR-IQA) according to the dependence degree of reference information [1]. Both FR-IQA and RR-IQA rely on the information of the reference image to evaluate the distorted image [2]. But in actual scenes, there is no reference image in most cases, which limits their practical application. As the blind

© Springer Nature Switzerland AG 2021
Y. Peng et al. (Eds.): ICIG 2021, LNCS 12890, pp. 241–252, 2021.
https://doi.org/10.1007/978-3-030-87361-5_20

image assessment algorithm, the NR-IQA algorithm can do the evaluation without the information from the reference image, which leads to the widest application in practice [3].

The FR-IQA needs all the information of the reference image. In detail, such an image quality assessment is realized by comparing the reference image and the distorted image pixel by pixel. In the FR-IQA, both Mean Square Error (MSE) and Peak Signal-to-Noise Ratio (PSNR) metrics are classic assessment algorithms. And then some structure-based algorithms were proposed, where structural similarity (Structural Similarity, SSIM) [4] is one of the most representative FR-IQA algorithms. In SSIM, the distortion of image quality is perceived by comparing image brightness, contrast, and structural character-istics. In addition, many new algorithms were proposed, such as multi-scale SSIM [5], information-weighted SSIM [6], gradient-based SSIM [7] and complex wavelet SSIM [8].

The RR-IQA selects part of the information from the reference information for assessment. Though the algorithm complexity is lower than that of the FR-IQA algo-rithm, it still cannot be widely applied due to part reliance on the reference information. Wang [9] proposed a Reduced-Reference image quality assessment based on Wavelet-domain natural Image Statistic Model (RR-WISM). Kusuma [10] proposed a hybrid image quality metric (Hybrid Image Quality Metric, HIQM) based on various artifact effects.

For the NR-IQA algorithm, Fang [11] designed the natural scene statistics (NSS) model of NR-IQA for contrast distorted images by using the mean, standard deviation, skewness, kurtosis, and entropy of the inherent attributes of the image. Gu [12] designed an NR-IQA that considers the local and global features of contrast distorted images. The local part calculates the maximum information entropy of a specific unpredicted area, and the global part compares the image histogram with the uniformly distributed histogram through the symmetric Kullbackleibler divergence. Nafchi [13] designed an NR-IQA to evaluate simple and complex types of contrast distortion using two features and entropy information based on Minkowski distance. Although low-level features are considered, they still cannot effectively reflect the subjective quality of contrast distorted images. Gu [14] proposed a framework for image quality detection without reference. The algorithm comprehensively considers the five influence factors, including image contrast, sharpness, brightness, colorfulness and naturalness.

In the past 30 years, researchers have conducted in-depth researches on the NR-IQA algorithms for diverse distortion types such as image blur, noise, blocking artifact et al. [15], and achieved satisfactory results. However, there is almost no research on the NR-IQA algorithm for contrast distorted images [16, 17], leaving work to do in pursuit of pleasant achievements. In this paper, we propose a histogram-based NR-IQA algorithm for contrast distorted images. By analyzing the change process of the image sequence with gradually changing contrast, the features are extracted from two aspects: objective statistical attributes and subjective perception attributes, including three statistical features of image local contrast, histogram shape and image brightness. Subsequently, SVR is applied to fuse the extracted image features to realize image quality assessment. According to the algorithm performance test on CCID2014, TID2013 and

CSIQ databases, and the comparison with other similar algorithms, the results reflect the superior performance of the proposed algorithm.

2 Proposed Method

2.1 Image Sequence

For image sequence with slowly changing contrast, it is often easier to grasp the changing characteristics of contrast distorted images. Therefore, we mainly introduce the generation method of image sequence with gradually changing contrast in this section. Each image in the image sequence is obtained by enhancing the original contrast distorted image which is achieved by an image enhancement algorithm. Herein, an image enhancement scheme based on histogram truncation and equal division is adopted, and multiple contrast distorted images are generated by adjusting the parameters in the image enhancement algorithm. Finally, an image sequence with gradually changing contrast is obtained. The specific implementation method is as follows:

Firstly, we select any original contrast distorted image to obtain the corresponding histogram h, and perform mean normalization processing to obtain the mean normalized histogram h_{norm} which is computed as follows:

$$h_{norm}(i) = \frac{h(i)}{N} \times (L_{max} - L_{min}), \ i \in [L_{min}, L_{max}] \tag{1}$$

where N denotes the number of pixels of the original image, i denotes the grayscale of the image, L_{min} denotes the minimum grayscale of the image, and L_{max} denotes the maximum grayscale of the image.

Then according to the current truncation threshold T, the histogram h_{norm} is truncated and equally divided to obtain the histogram h_D. The image histogram truncation and average model are described as follows:

$$h_T(i) = \begin{cases} T, & if \ h_{norm}(i) \geq T \\ h(i), & if \ h_{norm}(i) < T \end{cases}, \ T \in [0, T_{max}] \tag{2}$$

$$h_D(i) = h_T(i) + [\sum_{i=0}^{L-1} h_{norm}(i) - \sum_{i=0}^{L-1} h_T(i)]/L, \ i \in [0, L-1] \tag{3}$$

where i denotes the grayscale of the image, h_T denotes the histogram obtained by truncating h_{norm} based on the truncation threshold T, L denotes the maximum range of the image grayscale, and h_D denotes the average distribution of the data truncated from the histogram according to L.

Then we use the traditional histogram equalization to achieve image contrast enhancement. (I) the corresponding cumulative distribution function cdf is obtained by the histogram h_D, and cdf is normalized to the range of $[0, L]$. (II) according to the normalized cumulative distribution function cdf, the selected original contrast distorted image is mapped to the grayscale. (III) a contrast-enhanced image is finished.

According to the specified step length, the original histogram is truncated and equally divided by selecting different histogram truncation thresholds in order to achieve different degrees of contrast enhancement of the original image. Thereby, the image sequence with gradually changing contrast is obtained, and the calculation formula of the truncation threshold is as follows:

$$T = a^p \times \max(h) \tag{4}$$

where a denotes the selected truncation ratio, 21 contrast gradient images are selected for testing in this paper, so we set the parameter $a \in 0.05, 0.1, ..., 0.95, 1$. p denotes the correction parameter making the selected images obviously and visually different, we set the parameter $p = 0.5$. And h denotes the histogram of the original image. Therefore, the image sequence with gradually changing contrast selected for testing is shown in Fig. 1 below.

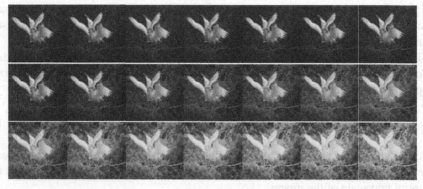

Fig. 1. Image sequence with gradually changing contrast

2.2 Objective Statistical Attributes

First, we analyze the changed characteristics of a set of image sequences with gradually changing contrast, and find that the overall contrast of the image gradually increases, and part of the histogram corresponding to the image area is continuously stretched. The increase of the grayscale difference will seriously affect the human eyes' perception of image quality.

Figure 2 shows an example of image sequence with gradually changing contrast. In Fig. 2(f)–(g), it is found that the difference between the main stem and the branches in the partial image is more obvious, and the details of the branches are more clearly visible. In the histogram area marked by the red box of Fig. 2(k)–(o), it is found that part of the grayscale is continuously stretched, which has a significant impact on the image quality. Therefore, we use it as one of the objective statistical characteristics of the image quality assessment algorithm, and establish a mathematical model for it.

The grayscales are stretched, which can be used to express the cumulative sum of the absolute differences of the grayscales corresponding to the number of non-zero pixels in the histogram. At the same time, the grayscales with more pixels are changed in the

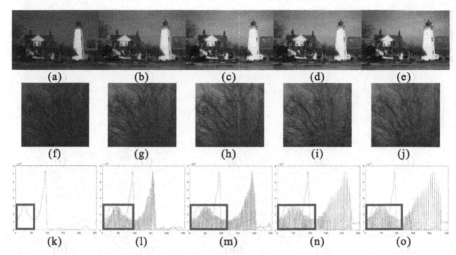

Fig. 2. From (a) to (e) are the selected partial images in the image sequence with gradually changing contrast. From (f) to (g) are the partial enlarged images corresponding to (a) to (e). From (k) to (o) are the image histograms corresponding to (a) to (e).

image, it has a greater impact on image quality, while the grayscales with the fewer pixel's changes in the image, it has a less impact on image quality. Thus, the number of pixels is changed. The ratio of the pixels number corresponding to the non-zero grayscale to the total number of pixels in the image is merged into the feature C_{part} as the weighting factor of D_k. Finally, the optimized objective statistical features are obtained.

$$C_{part} = \sum_{k=k_{\min}}^{k=k_{\max}} P_k \wedge \beta \times D_k, (D_k > 1) \tag{5}$$

where P_k denotes the ratio of the pixels number of the kth grayscale in the image histogram to the total number of pixels in the image, and β denotes the matching parameter between the objective feature and the subjective human eyes' intuitive perception. We set the parameter $\beta = 0.5$.

Figure 3 also shows an example of image sequence with gradually changing contrast. Based on the analysis of Fig. 3, it is found that the visibility of the gaps between the bricks on the wall is reduced, the details on the lighthouse are constantly disappearing, and the perception of the image area of the human vision is obviously different. As the overall contrast of the image continues to increase, another part of the grayscale in the image histogram is constantly being merged which also obviously affects the perception of image quality by human vision.

Therefore, we regard it as another objective statistical feature of the image quality assessment algorithm, and establish a mathematical model for it. In order to describe this process, we use the number of effective grayscales in the image as the objective statistical feature of the proposed NR-IQA algorithm in this paper to measure the degree to which the grayscales of the image are merged. The more grayscales are merged, the smaller the number of effective grayscales, the more serious the loss of details in the

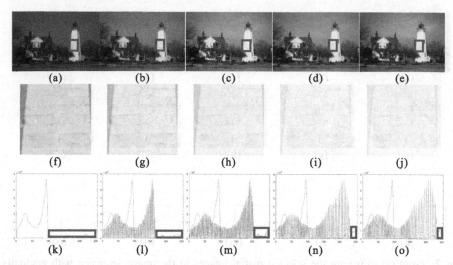

Fig. 3. From (a) to (e) are the selected partial images in the image sequence with gradually changing contrast. From (f) to (g) are the partial enlarged images corresponding to (a) to (e). From (k) to (o) are the image histograms corresponding to (a) to (e).

image. Conversely, the less the grayscales are merged, the more effectively grayscales will be retained, the more details it will be preserved in the image. At the same time, we use the ratio of the number of non-zero grayscale pixels in the image histogram to the total number of pixels in the image as the weighting factor in the algorithm feature to obtain the final local contrast merge feature H_{num}.

$$H_{num} = (\sum_{k=k_{\min}}^{k=k_{\max}} P_k \wedge \alpha)/D_{range}, P_k > 0 \tag{6}$$

where P_k denotes the ratio of the number of pixels in the kth grayscale in the image histogram to the total number of pixels in the image, and α denotes the matching parameter between the objective feature and the subjective human intuitive perception, and D_{range} denotes the absolute difference between the maximum grayscales and the smallest grayscales. We set the parameter $\alpha = 0.25$.

In addition, Since the histogram shape of an image is mainly determined by the distribution of grayscales, we introduce the concept of information entropy. The one-dimensional information entropy of the image describes the distribution degree of the adjacent grayscale difference in the direction of the grayscale of the image histogram (the abscissa of the image histogram). It can be formulated by:

$$E_x = \sum_{j=0}^{N} d_j \log d_j \tag{7}$$

where d_j denotes the absolute difference between the jth grayscale with a non-zero number of pixels and the $(j + 1)$th grayscale with a non-zero number of pixels (the image grayscale is sorted from small to large), and N denotes the total number of effective grayscales in the image.

At the same time, based on the one-dimensional information entropy of the image, the distribution degree of the number of grayscale pixel is described in the direction of the number of grayscale pixel (the ordinate of the image histogram) to express the shape of the image histogram. It can be formulated by:

$$E_y = \sum_{i=0}^{L} p_i \log p_i \tag{8}$$

where L denotes the maximum grayscale of the image, and p_i denotes the ratio of the number of pixels corresponding to the ith grayscale to the total number of pixels in the image.

2.3 Subjective Perception Attributes

As the image quality assessment algorithm results need to be as consistent as possible with the subjective perception of the HVS, we need to analyze the image features from the subjective perspective of the HVS to ensure that the assessment algorithm can predict image quality more comprehensively and accurately. In image sequence with gradually changing contrast, the shift of image brightness is also one of the important factors that affect the perception of image quality by human vision as shown in Fig. 4:

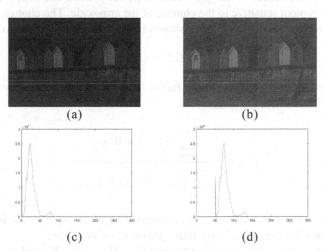

Fig. 4. (a) and (b) are brightness offset images. (c) and (d) are the image histograms corresponding to (a) and (b)

In Fig. 4, when the image grayscale shifts overall, the details of the house in the figure are more easily collected by the HVS, and the human eyes' perception of the content in the image changes significantly. Therefore, we regard the image brightness as one of the statistical features of the proposed NR-IQA algorithm in this paper, and quantify the image brightness features through the average gray value of the image. In the visual characteristics of HVS, low image brightness changes are not enough to for HVS to perceive sufficient image brightness changes; while a more moderate image brightness range changes are enough to for HVS to perceive sufficient image brightness changes. We introduce the JND [18] model:

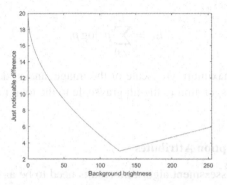

Fig. 5. JND model

It can be seen from Fig. 5 that when the image brightness is in the middle of the grayscale, the HVS is most sensitive to the change of the grayscale, and when the image brightness is on both sides of the grayscale, especially when the image brightness is dark, the HVS is most sensitive to the change of the grayscale. The change of grayscale is the least sensitive. The JND model is shown in Fig. 5 and normalized to get W_{JND}.

$$W_{JND} = (5.9 - 0.2 \times (JND - 1))/3.5 \tag{9}$$

Then we use W_{JND} as the weighting factor in the brightness feature, and finally get the image brightness feature L_{mean}.

$$L_{mean} = \frac{\sum_{i=0}^{L_{max}} (h_i \times i \times W_{JND})}{\sum_{i=0}^{L_{max}} (h_i \times W_{JND}) \times L_{max}} \tag{10}$$

where h_i denotes the number of pixels corresponding to the i grayscale in the image, and L_{max} denotes the theoretical maximum grayscale of the image.

In summary, we extract statical features C_{part}, H_{num}, E_x, E_y and L_{mean} from the perspective of subjective perception and objective statistics. These features are calculated based on the image histogram. All these features are empirically trained the SVR model, whose kernel function is the radial basis function (RBF), the margin of tolerance is set to 0.05 and the penalty factor is set to 1, to predict contrast distorted image quality.

3   Experimental Results

In order to verify the performance of the proposed NR-IQA algorithm, the algorithm is tested in a DELL laptop with a CPU frequency of 2.3 GHz, a memory of 8 GB, and a software level of Matlab 9.7.

On the one hand, based on the three image quality assessment databases of CSIQ [19], TID2013 [20] and CCID2014 [21], we calculate the four similarity indicators of RMSE, PLCC, SROCC, and KROCC for QAC [22], NIQMC [12], BIQME [14], CEIQ [23], HEFCS [24] and the proposed algorithm. The four similarity indicators compare the performance of the no-referenced image quality assessment algorithm in terms of accuracy and monotonicity. Before calculating RMSE and PLCC, a five-parameter logic function [25] is applied to map the objective result of the assessment algorithm to the subjective score. On the other hand, it takes time to test the algorithm in the CCID2014 database with the same image size.

Since the TID2013 and CSIQ databases contain multiple types of distortion, the contrast distorted images need to be selected, including: 125 global contrast change images and 125 average brightness displacement distortion images in TID2013; 116 contrast change images in CSIQ. For each image assessment database, 80% of the images are randomly selected according to the reference image as the training set, while the remaining images are used as the test set. Four similarity indicators are calculated, and 1000-time repetition is applied. Their median is selected as the algorithm performance test result. Table 1 and Table 2 are the four similarity indexes in the four databases of the NR-IQA algorithm. The number in bold indicates the optimal test index of the assessment algorithm under the corresponding database.

Table 1. Comparison of six metrics on the CSIQ database

Metric	SROCC	KROCC	PLCC	RMSE
Proposed	**0.9486**	**0.8261**	**0.9646**	**0.0434**
HEFCS	0.8711	0.7038	0.9068	0.0780
CEIQ	**0.9475**	**0.8182**	**0.9532**	**0.0415**
BIQME	0.7848	0.5983	0.8106	0.0860
NIQMC	0.8533	0.6689	0.8747	0.0796
QAC	0.0304	0.0177	0.1138	0.9744

where the optimal values in the metrics are highlighted in bold and red, the subprime values in the metrics are highlighted with bold. By observing the results in Tables 1, 2 and 3, the following conclusions can be drawn: The four algorithm performance metrics obtained by the proposed NR-IQA algorithm in this paper on the TID2013 and CCID2014 databases are better than the other algorithms in this test. The performance of the proposed algorithm is similar to the CEIQ algorithm in the CSIQ database, and the four indicators have their own advantages. It matches well between the prediction result of the algorithm and the result of the subjective perception of the HVS. We analyze the

Table 2. Comparison of six metrics on the TID2013 database

Metric	SROCC	KROCC	PLCC	RMSE
Proposed	**0.8353**	**0.6582**	**0.8880**	**0.4453**
HEFCS	0.7507	0.5780	0.8168	0.6008
CEIQ	**0.8193**	**0.6302**	**0.8718**	**0.4569**
BIQME	0.8149	0.6109	0.8524	0.6394
NIQMC	0.6458	0.4687	0.7225	0.5798
QAC	0.0304	0.0177	0.1138	0.9744

Table 3. Comparison of six metrics on the CCID2014 database

Metric	SROCC	KROCC	PLCC	RMSE
Proposed	**0.8542**	**0.6618**	**0.8789**	**0.3078**
HEFCS	**0.8426**	**0.6395**	**0.8650**	**0.3135**
CEIQ	0.8363	0.6362	0.8675	0.3155
BIQME	0.8363	0.6362	0.8675	0.3155
NIQMC	0.8368	0.6221	0.8719	0.3122
QAC	0.8309	0.6305	0.8588	0.3350

image sequence with gradually changing contrast, and compare the subtle differences between the different contrast distorted images, so the objective statistical characteristics of the image contrast is comprehensively extracted from an objective point of view. And as HVS is introduced in this paper, the visual characteristics make the proposed algorithm more in line with human visual perception.

In order to verify the complexity of the algorithm, the running time of the assessment algorithm is calculated in the CCID2014 database, including 655 pictures with each size of 768×512, and the test is repeated 100 times to obtain the average running time of each algorithm. Finally, we calculate the consumption time of each algorithm participating in the test to run a picture, and compare the average running time of the proposed algorithm in this chapter with the other comparison algorithm, as shown in Table 4:

Table 4. Computational complexity of three metrics on the CCID2014 database

Metric	QAC	NIQMC	BIQME	CEIQ	HEFCS	Proposed
Time(second/image)	0.450	2.537	0.719	**0.053**	0.287	**0.003**

As is known that the computational complexity of the NR-IQA algorithm mainly depends on the difficulty of the algorithm for extracting the features of the distorted image. From Table 4, it is found that the proposed algorithm takes the shortest time and NIQMC takes the longest time among all the tastes. The proposed algorithm is close to the time consumption of the CEIQ algorithm. The NIQMC and BIQME algorithms for extraction need a large amount of time for more complex local features. For CEIQ, HEFCS and the proposed algorithms in this paper, they mainly extract features from a global perspective, so the algorithm complexity is low.

4 Conclusion

Aimed at the contrast distorted image, we proposed a NR-IQA algorithm based on histogram by analyzing the image sequence with gradually changing contrast. Feature extraction is carried out from the aspects of image local contrast, histogram distribution and brightness, as well as the subjective characteristics of HVS. Based on these features, the SVR model is applied to understand the relationship between these features and MOS. Experimental results on the popular image quality assessment data set further prove the effectiveness and robustness of the proposed NR-IQA algorithm for contrast distorted images. Besides, the proposed algorithm has an advantage in complexity.

References

1. Zhou, W., Bovik, A.C., Sheikh, H.R., Simoncelli, E.P.: Image quality assessment: from error visibility to structural similarity. IEEE Trans. Image Process **13**(4), 600–612 (2004)
2. Anush, K.M., Kalpana, S., Rajiv, S., Alan, C.B.: Wireless video quality assessment: a study of subjective scores and objective algorithms. IEEE Trans. Circuits Syst. Video Technol. **20**(4), 587–599 (2010)
3. Lv, X., Wang, Z.J.: Reduced-reference image quality assessment based on perceptual image hashing. In: Proc. Int. Conf. Image Process, ICIP, pp. 4361–4364. IEEE Computer Society, Cairo (2009)
4. Wang, Z., Bovik, A.C., Sheikh, H.R., Simoncelli, E.P.: Image quality assessment: from error visibility to structural similarity. IEEE Trans. Image Process **13**(4), 600–612 (2004)
5. Wang, Z., Simoncelli, E.P., Bovik, A.C.: Multi-scale structural similarity for image quality assessment. In: Proc. 37th Asilomar Conf. Signals Syst, pp. 1398–1402. IEEE, Pacific Grove (2004)
6. Wang, Z., Li, Q.: Information content weighting for perceptual image quality assessment. IEEE Trans. Image Process **20**(5), 1185–1198 (2011)
7. Chen, G.H., Yang, C.L., Xie, S.L.: Gradient-based structural similarity for image quality assessment. In: Proc. Int. Conf. Image Process, ICIP, pp. 2929–2932. IEEE, Atlanta (2006)
8. Yang, C.L., Gao, W.R., Po, L.M.: Discrete wavelet transform-based structural similarity for image quality assessment. In: Proc. 15th IEEE Int. Conf. Image Process, pp. 377–380. IEEE, San Diego (2008)
9. Shi, Z., Chen, K., Pang, K., et al.: A perceptual image quality index based on global and double-random window similarity. Digit. Signal Process **60**, 277–286 (2017)
10. Zhou, W., Simoncelli, E.P.: Reduced-reference image quality assessment using a wavelet-domain natural image statistic model. In: Proceedings of SPIE-IS and T Electronic Imaging - Human Vision and Electronic Imaging X, pp. 149–159. SPIE, San Jose (2005)
11. Fang, Y., Ma, K., Wang, Z., et al.: No-reference quality assessment of contrast-distorted images based on natural scene statistics. IEEE Signal Process. Lett. **22**(7), 838–842 (2015)

12. Gu, K., Lin, W., Zhai, G., et al.: No-reference quality metric of contrast-distorted images based on information maximization. IEEE Trans. Cybern. **47**(12), 4559–4565 (2017)
13. Nafchi, H.Z., Cheriet, M.: Efficient no-reference quality assessment and classification model for contrast distorted images. IEEE Trans. Broadcast. **64**(2), 518–523 (2018)
14. Gu, K., Tao, D., Qiao, J., et al.: Learning a no-reference quality assessment model of en-hanced images with big data. IEEE Trans. Neural Netw. Learn. Syst. **29**(4), 1301–1313 (2018)
15. Gu, H., Zhai, G., Liu, M., et al.: Exploiting global and local information for image quality assessment with contrast change. In: IEEE International Symposium on Broad-band Multimedia Systems and Broadcasting, BMSB, pp. 1–5. IEEE, Ghent (2015)
16. Min, X., Zhai, G., Gu, K., Liu, Y., Yang, X.: Blind image quality estimation via distortion aggravation. IEEE Trans. Broadcast. **64**(2), 508–517 (2018)
17. Min, X., Gu, K., Zhai, G., Liu, J., Yang, X., Chen, C.: Blind quality assessment based on pseudo-reference image. IEEE Trans. Multimedia **20**(8), 2049–2062 (2017)
18. Nikil, J.: Signal compression: technology targets and research directions. IEEE J. Sel. Areas Commun. **10**(5), 796–818 (1992)
19. Larson, E.C., Chandler, D.M.: Most apparent distortion: full-reference image quality assessment and the role of strategy. Electron. Image **19**(1), 22–24 (2010)
20. Ponomarenko, N., Jin, L., Ieremeiev, O., et al.: Image database TID2013: Peculiarities, results and perspectives. Signal Process. Image Commun. **30**(12), 57–77 (2015)
21. Gu, K., Zhai, G., Lin, W., et al.: The analysis of image contrast: from quality assessment to automatic enhancement. IEEE Trans. Cybern. **46**(1), 84–97 (2016)
22. Xue, W., Zhang, L., Mou, X.: Learning without human scores for blind image quality assess-ment. In: Proceedings of the IEEE Conference on Computer Vision and Pattern Recognition, CVPR, pp. 995–1002. IEEE Computer Society, Portland (2013)
23. Yan, J., Li, J., Fu, X.: No-Reference Quality Assessment of Contrast-Distorted Images using Contrast Enhancement. arXiv e-prints (2019)
24. Khosravi, M.H., Hassanpour, H.: Blind quality metric for contrast-distorted images based on eigen decomposition of color histograms. IEEE Trans. Circuits Syst. Video Technol. **30**(1), 48–58 (2020)
25. Rohaly, A.M., Libert, J., Corriveau, P., et al.: Final report from the video quality experts group on the validation of objective models of video quality assessment. ITU-T Standards Contribution COM, 9–80 (2000)

Multi-scale Deformable Deblurring Kernel Prediction for Dynamic Scene Deblurring

Kai Zhu and Nong Sang[✉]

Key Laboratory of Image Processing and Intelligent Control, School of Artificial
Intelligence and Automation, Huazhong University of Science and Technology,
Wuhan, China
{m202072874,nsang}@hust.edu.cn

Abstract. Deblurring aims to restore clear images from blurred ones.
Recently deep learning are widely used. Previous methods regard deblurring as dense prediction problems and rarely consider the inverse operation of blur. In this paper, we propose a multi-scale deformable deblurring kernel prediction network for dynamic scene deblurring which uses
a coarse-to-fine method to predict the per-pixel deformable deblurring
kernel and uses the fusion weight to integrate the latent images in different scales. Since the spatially variable blur scatters pixel information to
surrounding sub-pixels and leads to the spatially and quantitively uneven
distribution of latent pixel information, the per-pixel deformable deblurring kernel can adaptively select the sub-pixels and linearly combine
them into the clean pixel for information aggregation. The multi-scale
architecture helps the deformable deblurring kernel enlarge the reception field. The residual image is added to convolution result in each scale
to supply refined edges when the kernel cannot cover the areas existing
latent pixel information. Besides, we add local similarity loss to constrain deformable deblurring kernel's weight and offset which boosts the
deblurring performance. Qualitative and quantitative experiments show
that our method can produce competitive deblurring performance.

Keywords: Dynamic scene deblurring · Deformable convolution ·
Dynamic convolution

1 Introduction

The deblurring task is highly ill-posed. Early deblurring methods use various
hand-craft image priors [8,14,15,24] to constrain the solution space. The quality
of the deblurring depends on the choice of the prior. Due to the combination of
camera shake, object movement, changes of depth, the real cause of blur is more
complicated than the model. Therefore, it is difficult for hand-craft image priors
to obtain good generalization ability on dynamic scene blurred images.

In recent years, with the development of deep learning, various dynamic scene
deblurring methods based on convolution neural networks have been proposed

© Springer Nature Switzerland AG 2021
Y. Peng et al. (Eds.): ICIG 2021, LNCS 12890, pp. 253–264, 2021.
https://doi.org/10.1007/978-3-030-87361-5_21

[3, 9, 12, 17, 18, 20, 26–28]. They are trained in an end-to-end way to learn the nonlinear mapping from blurred images to clear images. Benefiting from the proposed paired dynamic scene deblurring datasets [11,12,18], these methods show satisfactory deblurring performance and generalization ability.

However, the existing methods based on convolution neural networks still face challenges in solving dynamic scene blur. The network uses the same convolution kernel parameters at different locations. It is sub-optimal for spatially variable dynamic scene blur. Therefore, the previous methods usually need to stack numerous convolution layers to obtain a large reception field and strong non-linear mapping ability.

Actually, the dynamic scene blur's intensity and direction are spatially variable. The information on a pixel will be scattered to the surrounding sub-pixels and the distribution is usually not geometrically uniform but is related to the direction of camera shake and object movement. We need to aggregate latent pixel information of different directions and use different weights. Although Sim et al. [17] convert the deblurring problem into a deblurring kernel prediction problem, they only take the intensity of kernel into consideration and neglect the direction.

Inspired by deformable convolution [2,29], we propose a deformable deblurring kernel prediction network. As the inverse operator of blur, the deformable deblurring kernel consists of two parts: the per-pixel deblurring kernel and its offset. It linearly combines sampled sub-pixels which can aggregate the scattered latent pixel information and filter the interference of irrelevant pixels. The deformable deblurring kernel can be spatially variable not only in weight but also in shape which is no longer limited to the conventional regular-shaped convolution kernel so it can better deal with dynamic scene blur.

When the blur is severe, it will cause the latent pixel information to be scattered on too many pixels or too far away. In this case, the single-scale architecture cannot meet the requirements of deblurring. The multi-scale method can deal with large blur kernel by progressively removing blur and obtaining high-resolution deblurring results from a coarse to fine image pyramid. For this reason, we use multi-scale architecture to deal with various scales of blur and enlarge the reception field of deformable deblurring kernel. Additionally, our network learns the residual image and add it to convolution result. The predicted RGB pixels supply refined edges when the kernel cannot cover all the areas existing latent pixel information. Finally, we integrate the deblurring results of different scales to obtain a refined result.

The blur kernel of adjacent pixels are usually close. As the inverse operator of blur, the deformable deblurring kernels of adjacent pixels should be close. We add local similarity loss which constrains the weight and offset of the adjacent deformable deblurring kernels. Qualitative and quantitative experiments on the public GoPro dataset [12] demonstrate that our full model produces competitive deblurring performance.

Our contributions are summarized below:

- We introduce the per-pixel deformable deblurring kernel for dynamic scene deblurring which can adaptively select the sub-pixels.

- We propose a multi-scale architecture to further deal with the severe dynamic scene blur which can enlarge the reception field and remove blur progressively.
- We add local similarity loss to constrain adjacent deformable deblurring kernels which further boosts the performance.

2   Related Works

Dynamic Scene Deblurring. With the introduction of paired dynamic scene deblurring datasets [11,12,18] in recent years, convolution neural networks have been widely used to deal with complicated dynamic scene blur. Among them, the encoder-decoder architecture and multi-scale architecture achieve great success [3,9,12,17,18,20,26–28]. Nah et al. [12] use a coarse-to-fine multi-scale network which stacks 40 residual blocks in each scale and does not share parameters among all scales to remove blur gradually. Tao et al. [20] share the encoder-decoder network parameters between three scales which not only reduces the parameters but also allows the network to train stably and converge quickly. They use ConvLSTM [5,16] to transmit the information of three scales. Zhang et al. [27] analyze that deconvolution can be realized by RNNs [10]. To enlarge the reception field and fuse features in different directions, they add four RNNs followed by a convolution layer. An additional CNN is used to learn the weights for the RNN at every location.

Deformable Convolution. Dai et al. [2] firstly propose deformable convolution which learns the offset based on the convolution kernel. The deformable convolution kernel can capture the further and finer sub-pixels from the current regular neighborhood. Modulated deformable convolution [29] additionally learns a mask which modulates the input feature amplitudes from different locations. Deformable convolution has been applied to high-level vision tasks such as object detection [1,2], semantic segmentation [2], and human pose estimation [19], and low-level vision tasks such as video super-resolution [21,22], mainly for feature-level video frames alignment.

Dynamic Convolution. Recently dynamic convolution has been widely used in low-level vision tasks. Conventional convolution shares parameters for all locations, which is sub-optimal for spatially variable dynamic scene blur. Some methods [6,13,17,23,28] use dynamic convolution to adaptively remove blur. Sim et al. [17] learn the per-pixel deblurring kernel which is used to aggregate the scattered latent pixel information and filter the disturbing information. Zhou et al. [28] use dynamic convolution at the feature level to align and deblur the input frames respectively.

However, previous dynamic convolution's shape is fixed. The deformable deblurring kernel we proposed retains weight variability and obtains shape variability. In fact, our work is an improvement on [17].

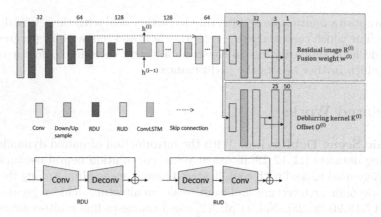

Fig. 1. Our proposed multi-scale deformable deblurring kernel prediction network architecture. Only one scale is shown. The network outputs per-pixel deblurring kernel, corresponding offset, residual image, fusion weight, and hidden state in each scale, where the deblurring kernel, offset, and residual image are used to construct the current scale deblurring result, and the hidden state is used for cross-scale information transmission. The final deblurring result is the integration of the deblurring results of three scales by using fusion weight.

3   Proposed Methods

3.1   Overview

The network architecture is shown in Fig. 1. It includes three scales, including 1/4 scale, 1/2 scale and the original scale. The three scales are denoted as 1, 2, and 3 respectively. Except for ConvLSTM among three scales, the rest architecture does not share parameters. The network takes three consecutive blurred frames B_{t-1}, B_t, B_{t+1} as input, where the subscript t represents the frame number. Bilinear downsampling is used to downsample the input frames twice to obtain the image pyramid. Downsampling is formulated as

$$B_{t-1}^{(3)}, B_t^{(3)}, B_{t+1}^{(3)} = B_{t-1}, B_t, B_{t+1} \tag{1}$$

$$B_{t-1}^{(i)}, B_t^{(i)}, B_{t+1}^{(i)} = (B_{t-1}^{(i+1)}, B_t^{(i+1)}, B_{t+1}^{(i+1)})^{\downarrow 2}, i = 1, 2 \tag{2}$$

where (i) represents scale, and $\downarrow 2$ the $2\times$ bilinear downsampling operation.

In $i-th$ scale, three frames of the corresponding scale are concatenated as the input. The network outputs are divided into two branches. One branch is deformable deblurring kernel branch, which outputs 25-channel per-pixel deblurring kernel $K^{(i)}$ and corresponding 50-channel $O^{(i)}$. Because offset includes horizontal and vertical directions, the channels of offset are twice that of the deblurring kernel. For each pixel of the blurred target frame $B_t^{(i)}$, deformable convolution is performed to aggregate local latent pixel information and filter irrelevant information. The other branch is residual image and fusion branch, which outputs 3-channel residual image $R^{(i)}$ and 1-channel fusion weight $w^{(i)}$. Then the residual image is added to the frame after deformable convolution to supply the refined edges for deblurring result $\hat{L}_t^{(i)}$. The fusion weight is used to integrate $\hat{L}_t^{(i)}$ and upsampled $\hat{L}_t^{(i-1)}$ to obtain refined deblurring result $L_t^{(i)}$. Because the deblurring kernel features are obviously different from the input image, we only connect skip connections to residual image and fusion branch.

The feature related to blur type, blur direction, and edges in coarse scale is helpful to the prediction of fine scale, so cross-scale information transmission is necessary. Similar to [20], we insert a ConvLSTM between the encoder and the decoder which transmits the 128-channel, 1/4 size of $i-th$ scale hidden state $h^{(i)}$. The output process is formulated as

$$B^{(i)} = cat(B_{t-1}^{(i)}, B_t^{(i)}, B_{t+1}^{(i)}) \tag{3}$$

$$K^{(i)}, O^{(i)}, R^{(i)}, w^{(i)}, h^{(i)} = f(B^{(i)}, h^{(i-1)\uparrow 2}|\theta^{(i)}, \theta_{LSTM}) \tag{4}$$

$$\hat{L}_t^{(i)} = deform(B_t^{(i)}, K^{(i)}, O^{(i)}) + R^{(i)} \tag{5}$$

$$L_t^{(i)} = w^{(i)} \cdot \hat{L}_t^{(i)} + (1 - w^{(i)}) \cdot L_t^{(i-1)\uparrow 2} \tag{6}$$

where cat represents the concatenation operation, f one scale of network architecture, $\uparrow 2$ the $2\times$ bilinear upsampling operation, $\theta^{(i)}$ the encoder and decoder parameters of $i-th$ scale, θ_{LSTM} the ConvLSTM parameters, $deform$ the deformable deblurring operation. We set $h^{(0)}$ to 0. See Sect. 3.2 for the detail implementation of deformable deblurring. It should be noted that there is no coarser $0-th$ scale. It means $L_t^{(0)}$ does not exist in Eq. (6). We directly set $w^{(1)}$ to 1 instead of learning it.

U-Net architecture changes the spatial resolution and channels of features. To prevent the loss of information, it adds skip connection between encoder and decoder. Recent researches [17,25] show that the operation of changing channels on the intermediate features can improve the restoration performance. Similar to [17], we use residual down up(RDU) and residual up down(RUD) blocks to replace the conventional residual blocks [4] in the encoder and decoder respectively which can take the advantage of U-Net architecture. In RDU block, input feature is fed into the convolution layer with stride 2 followed by the transposed convolution layer with stride 2. In RUD block, input feature is fed into the transposed convolution layer with stride 2 followed by the convolution layer with stride 2. The input feature is added to the output through skip connection to prevent the loss of detail information.

3.2   Deformable Deblurring

The deformable deblurring operation is shown in Fig. 2. When inputting a blurred frame $B_t^{(i)} \in \mathbb{R}^{C \times H \times W}$, the network outputs deblurring kernel $K^{(i)} \in \mathbb{R}^{\kappa^2 \times H \times W}$ and offset $O^{(i)} \in \mathbb{R}^{2\kappa^2 \times H \times W}$, where C represents the channels of input frames, H the input height, W the input width, and κ the deblurring kernel size. Taking $\kappa = 3$ as an example, the deformable deblurring kernel has 9 sampling

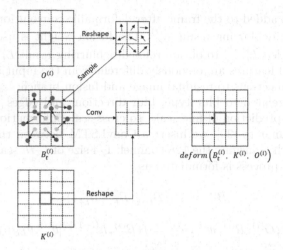

Fig. 2. A toy example of deformable deblurring. The deblurring kernel size κ shown in the figure is 3. The red box represents the location p_0 which needs deformable deblurring and the blue box represents the reception field of the conventional convolution kernel. We reshape the deblurring kernel $K^{(i)}$ and offset $O^{(i)}$ of all channels at location p_0. The offset guides the pixels sampled by the convolution operation to move from the original light green pixels to the current dark green sub-pixels. Finally, the sampled sub-pixels are convolved with the deblurring kernel to obtain a deformable deblurring pixel. The deblurring kernel size κ we actually adopt is 5. (Color figure online)

points. We set the fixed offset as $p_k \in \{(-1,-1), (-1,0), ..., (1,1)\}$. At location p_0, $K^{(i)}(p_0)$ is changed from the original dimension $(\kappa^2, 1, 1)$ to $(\kappa^2, 1)$ and repeats C times along the channel axis to (κ^2, C), $O^{(i)}(p_0)$ is changed from the original dimension $(2\kappa^2, 1, 1)$ to $(\kappa^2, 2)$. We denote them as $K_{p_0}^{(i)}$ and $O_{p_0}^{(i)}$ respectively which form the deformable deblurring kernel. The deformable deblurring operation is formulated as

$$deform(B_t^{(i)}, K^{(i)}, O^{(i)})(p_0) = \sum_{k=1}^{\kappa^2} K_{p_0}^{(i)}(k) \cdot B_t^{(i)}(p_0 + p_k + O_{p_0}^{(i)}(k)) \qquad (7)$$

Deformable deblurring uses bilinear interpolation when the sampling location is not an integer.

3.3 Local Similarity Loss

We add a loss function called local similarity loss to constrain the adjacent deformable deblurring kernel to be close. The loss function consists of two parts, one part called L_{kernel} is used to constrain the deformable deblurring kernel's weight and the other part called L_{offset} is used to constrain the deformable deblurring kernel's offset. The local similarity loss L_{LS} is formulated as

$$L_{LS} = L_{kernel} + \lambda_{offset} \cdot L_{offset} \qquad (8)$$

$$L_{kernel} = \sum_{i=1}^{3} \sum_{p \in \Omega} \left\| \partial_x K^{(i)}(p) \right\|_1 + \left\| \partial_y K^{(i)}(p) \right\|_1 \qquad (9)$$

$$L_{offset} = \sum_{i=1}^{3} \sum_{p \in \Omega} \left\| \partial_x O^{(i)}(p) \right\|_1 + \left\| \partial_y O^{(i)}(p) \right\|_1 \qquad (10)$$

where ∂_x and ∂_y respectively represent partial derivatives along horizontal and vertical directions, Ω the two-dimensional image plane, λ_{offset} the weight of L_{offset}.

Similar to previous methods [3,12,20,26], multi-scale content loss is applied to every scale of pyramid. To emphasize the importance of the fine-scale deblurring results, we add more loss functions to fine-scale. The multi-scale content loss L_{MS} is formulated as

$$L_{MS} = L_1 + L_2 + L_3 \qquad (11)$$

$$L_1 = L_C(L_t^{(1)}, S_t^{(1)}) \qquad (12)$$

$$L_2 = L_C(\hat{L}_t^{(2)}, S_t^{(2)}) + L_C(L_t^{(2)}, S_t^{(2)}) \qquad (13)$$

$$L_3 = L_C(\hat{L}_t^{(3)}, S_t^{(3)}) + L_C(L_t^{(3)}, S_t^{(3)}) + \lambda_{SSIM} \cdot L_{SSIM}(L_t^{(3)}, S_t^{(3)}) \qquad (14)$$

where L_C represents the Charbonnier loss, L_{SSIM} the SSIM loss, λ_{SSIM} the weight of SSIM loss. It is noted that ground truth frame S_t uses the same method as Eq. (1), (2) to construct the image pyramid. The final loss is formulated as

$$L = \lambda_{MS} \cdot L_{MS} + \lambda_{LS} \cdot L_{LS} \qquad (15)$$

where λ_{MS} and λ_{LS} are coefficients to balance the two terms.

4 Experiments

4.1 Dataset and Implementation Details

Nah et al. [12] use a high-speed camera to average the continuous clear frames to obtain a synthetic paired dataset called GoPro dataset. It contains 3214 pairs of images in 33 sequences and the resolution is 1280×720. Consistent with the setting of [12], we use 22 sequences for training and the remaining 11 sequences for testing.

During training, the cropping size is 256×256 and we randomly perform horizontal flip and rotation operations for data enhancement. We input three consecutive frames into the network. We use bilinear downsampling to construct the image pyramid of three scales. We set the batch size to 8 and the initial learning rate to $1e-4$. Cosine annealing is used until the learning rate drops to $1e-7$. The trade-off weights are set as: $\lambda_{offset} = 1$, $\lambda_{SSIM} = 1$, $\lambda_{MS} = 0.2$ and $\lambda_{LS} = 0.1$. Adam [7] is applied to optimize our network with the default settings $\beta_1 = 0.9$, $\beta_2 = 0.999$, $\varepsilon = 1e-8$. We train our network for 2000 epochs. We use the PyTorch framework and 4 NVIDIA TITAN XP GPUs.

Peak signal-to-noise ratio (PSNR) and structural similarity index (SSIM) are used as metrics in our experiments.

Table 1. Results of ablation study on our proposed network. If 'Multi-Frame' is unchecked, only one frame is used as input. If 'Multi-Scale' is unchecked, the single-scale architecture is applied. If 'Offset' is unchecked, the regular-shaped deblurring kernel is applied. If 'RDU and RUD' and 'ConvLSTM' are unchecked, we replace them with conventional residual block and single convolution layer respectively. 'LS Loss' is the proposed local similarity loss.

Design	Model 1	Model 2	Model 3	Model 4	Model 5	Model 6	Model 7	Model 8
Multi-Frame		✓	✓	✓	✓	✓	✓	✓
Multi-Scale				✓	✓	✓	✓	✓
Offset			✓			✓	✓	✓
RDU and RUD	✓	✓	✓		✓		✓	✓
ConvLSTM					✓		✓	✓
LS Loss								✓
PSNR	31.34	31.41	31.64	31.46	31.52	31.65	31.72	**31.90**
SSIM	0.9474	0.9475	0.9500	0.9486	0.9496	0.9500	0.9509	**0.9525**

Fig. 3. The sampling points of deformable deblurring kernel. From left to right are the optical flow of clear frame and the deblurring result $\hat{L}_t^{(i)}$ of $1-st$, $2-nd$ and $3-rd$ scale. The red points and the green points respectively represent the sampling points of two different pixels in deformable deblurring operation. (Color figure online)

4.2 Ablation Study

To demonstrate the effectiveness of our proposed method, we conduct experiments for each individual design. Table 1 summarizes the ablation study results. Our full model (Model 8) achieves the best deblurring performance on both PSNR and SSIM metrics.

By comparing Model 2 and Model 3, Model 5 and Model 7, it can be found that additionally learning the offset can significantly improve the deblurring performance which brings more than 0.2 dB improvement in terms of PSNR no matter in single-scale or multi-scale. Figure 3 visualizes the sampling points of deformable deblurring operation. Our network can perceive the movement of cameras and objects and generate different sampling patterns for different movements, which adaptively select appropriate sub-pixels for different dynamic

Fig. 4. The visualization of deblurring process. From left to right are the blurred frame $B_t^{(i)}$, residual image $R^{(i)}$, deblurring result $L_t^{(i)}$ and ground truth $S_t^{(i)}$. From top to bottom represent the $1-st$, $2-nd$ and $3-rd$ scale.

scenes and filter the influence of irrelevant pixels. At the same time, the multi-scale strategy enlarges the reception field of deformable deblurring kernel.

The progressive deblurring process of multi-scale network can be seen in Fig. 4. Among them, the residual image focuses on details which are not restored due to the limited reception field of the deformable deblurring kernel. Through the comparison of Model 2 and Model 5, Model 3 and Model 7, it shows the effectiveness of the multi-scale strategy. Benefiting from the strategy, our network can remove severe dynamic scene blur progressively and output fine deblurring results. As shown in Model 6 and Model 7, our network obtains 0.07 dB improvement on PSNR without significantly increasing network parameters by replacing conventional residual block and convolution layer with RDU and RUD block and ConvLSTM respectively.

The local similarity loss we proposed adds a constraint to the deformable deblurring kernel which constrains the adjacent kernels to be close. Experiments on Model 7 and Model 8 show that this prior constraint is very effective for deblurring which further boosts the deblurring performance of the network. The local similarity loss improves PSNR by 0.18 dB.

4.3   Comparison with State-of-the-Art Methods

Our proposed network is compared with the state-of-the-art methods, Nah et al. [12], Tao et al. [20], Gao et al. [3], Sim et al. [17]. For a fair comparison, only a single frame is input to our proposed network in both the training and testing phases. On the GoPro dataset, results are shown in Table 2. Our proposed network exhibited the best PSNR and SSIM performances. It is clear that our method outperforms all other methods by at least 0.4dB. Several test examples are visualized in Fig. 5. It shows that the existing methods cannot keep sharp edges and remove the dynamic scene blur well. With deformable deblurring

Fig. 5. Comparison of deblurring results of our proposed full model and other state-of-the-art methods. From left to right are input blurred frame, results of Tao et al. [20], results of Sim et al. [17], results of our network.

Table 2. PSNR and SSIM comparisons of our network and other state-of-the-art methods for the GoPro dataset [12].

	PSNR	SSIM	Time (s)
Nah et al. [12]	29.23	0.9162	6.0
Tao et al. [20]	30.10	0.9323	1.2
Gao et al. [3]	30.92	0.9421	1.0
Sim et al. [17]	31.34	0.9474	0.6
Ours	**31.75**	**0.9513**	2.5

kernel, our network performs the best and restores clearer images. All these results verify the effectiveness of our method.

5   Conclusion

We propose a multi-scale deformable deblurring kernel prediction network. The deformable deblurring kernel can adaptively generate different sampling patterns for different dynamic scenes. The flexible and effective deblurring kernel enables the network to sample appropriate sub-pixels and filter interference of irrelevant pixels which is conducive to removing dynamic scene blur. The multi-scale architecture helps the deformable deblurring kernel enlarge the reception field and remove blur progressively. The residual image supplies the refined edges when deblurring kernel cannot cover all blurred areas. Besides, the use of RDU and RUD blocks, and ConvLSTM improves the performance of the network. Finally, we add local similarity loss to constrain the weight and offset of deformable deblurring kernel which significantly boosts the deblurring performance. Our network produces competitive deblurring performance in both qualitative and quantitative experiments.

References

1. Bertasius, G., Torresani, L., Shi, J.: Object detection in video with spatiotemporal sampling networks. In: Proceedings of the European Conference on Computer Vision, pp. 331–346 (2018)
2. Dai, J., et al.: Deformable convolutional networks. In: Proceedings of the IEEE International Conference on Computer Vision, pp. 764–773 (2017)
3. Gao, H., Tao, X., Shen, X., Jia, J.: Dynamic scene deblurring with parameter selective sharing and nested skip connections. In: Proceedings of the IEEE Conference on Computer Vision and Pattern Recognition, pp. 3848–3856 (2019)
4. He, K., Zhang, X., Ren, S., Sun, J.: Deep residual learning for image recognition. In: Proceedings of the IEEE Conference on Computer Vision and Pattern Recognition, pp. 770–778 (2016)
5. Hochreiter, S., Schmidhuber, J.: Long short-term memory. Neural Comput. 9(8), 1735–1780 (1997)
6. Jo, Y., Oh, S.W., Kang, J., Kim, S.J.: Deep video super-resolution network using dynamic upsampling filters without explicit motion compensation. In: Proceedings of the IEEE Conference on Computer Vision and Pattern Recognition, pp. 3224–3232 (2018)
7. Kingma, D.P., Ba, J.: Adam: a method for stochastic optimization. arXiv preprint arXiv:1412.6980 (2014)
8. Krishnan, D., Tay, T., Fergus, R.: Blind deconvolution using a normalized sparsity measure. In: Proceedings of the IEEE Conference on Computer Vision and Pattern Recognition, pp. 233–240 (2011)
9. Kupyn, O., Budzan, V., Mykhailych, M., Mishkin, D., Matas, J.: Deblurgan: blind motion deblurring using conditional adversarial networks. In: Proceedings of the IEEE Conference on Computer Vision and Pattern Recognition, pp. 8183–8192 (2018)
10. Liu, S., Pan, J., Yang, M.H.: Learning recursive filters for low-level vision via a hybrid neural network. In: Proceedings of the European Conference on Computer Vision, pp. 560–576 (2016)
11. Nah, S., et al.: Ntire 2019 challenge on video deblurring and super-resolution: dataset and study. In: Proceedings of the IEEE Conference on Computer Vision and Pattern Recognition Workshops (2019)
12. Nah, S., Hyun Kim, T., Mu Lee, K.: Deep multi-scale convolutional neural network for dynamic scene deblurring. In: Proceedings of the IEEE Conference on Computer Vision and Pattern Recognition, pp. 3883–3891 (2017)
13. Niklaus, S., Mai, L., Liu, F.: Video frame interpolation via adaptive convolution. In: Proceedings of the IEEE Conference on Computer Vision and Pattern Recognition, pp. 670–679 (2017)
14. Pan, J., Hu, Z., Su, Z., Yang, M.H.: Deblurring text images via l0-regularized intensity and gradient prior. In: Proceedings of the IEEE Conference on Computer Vision and Pattern Recognition, pp. 2901–2908 (2014)
15. Pan, J., Sun, D., Pfister, H., Yang, M.H.: Blind image deblurring using dark channel prior. In: Proceedings of the IEEE Conference on Computer Vision and Pattern Recognition, pp. 1628–1636 (2016)
16. Shi, X., Chen, Z., Wang, H., Yeung, D.Y., Wong, W.K., Woo, W.C.: Convolutional lstm network: a machine learning approach for precipitation nowcasting. In: Advances in Neural Information Processing Systems, pp. 802–810 (2015)

17. Sim, H., Kim, M.: A deep motion deblurring network based on per-pixel adaptive kernels with residual down-up and up-down modules. In: Proceedings of the IEEE Conference on Computer Vision and Pattern Recognition Workshops (2019)
18. Su, S., Delbracio, M., Wang, J., Sapiro, G., Heidrich, W., Wang, O.: Deep video deblurring for hand-held cameras. In: Proceedings of the IEEE Conference on Computer Vision and Pattern Recognition, pp. 1279–1288 (2017)
19. Sun, X., Xiao, B., Wei, F., Liang, S., Wei, Y.: Integral human pose regression. In: Proceedings of the European Conference on Computer Vision, pp. 529–545 (2018)
20. Tao, X., Gao, H., Shen, X., Wang, J., Jia, J.: Scale-recurrent network for deep image deblurring. In: Proceedings of the IEEE Conference on Computer Vision and Pattern Recognition, pp. 8174–8182 (2018)
21. Tian, Y., Zhang, Y., Fu, Y., Xu, C.: Tdan: temporally-deformable alignment network for video super-resolution. In: Proceedings of the IEEE Conference on Computer Vision and Pattern Recognition, pp. 3360–3369 (2020)
22. Wang, X., Chan, K.C., Yu, K., Dong, C., Change Loy, C.: Edvr: video restoration with enhanced deformable convolutional networks. In: Proceedings of the IEEE Conference on Computer Vision and Pattern Recognition Workshops (2019)
23. Xu, Y.S., Tseng, S.Y.R., Tseng, Y., Kuo, H.K., Tsai, Y.M.: Unified dynamic convolutional network for super-resolution with variational degradations. In: Proceedings of the IEEE Conference on Computer Vision and Pattern Recognition, pp. 12496–12505 (2020)
24. Yan, Y., Ren, W., Guo, Y., Wang, R., Cao, X.: Image deblurring via extreme channels prior. In: Proceedings of the IEEE Conference on Computer Vision and Pattern Recognition, pp. 4003–4011 (2017)
25. Yu, J., Fan, Y., Yang, J., Xu, N., Wang, Z., Wang, X., Huang, T.: Wide activation for efficient and accurate image super-resolution. arXiv preprint arXiv:1808.08718 (2018)
26. Zhang, H., Dai, Y., Li, H., Koniusz, P.: Deep stacked hierarchical multi-patch network for image deblurring. In: Proceedings of the IEEE Conference on Computer Vision and Pattern Recognition, pp. 5978–5986 (2019)
27. Zhang, J., et al.: Dynamic scene deblurring using spatially variant recurrent neural networks. In: Proceedings of the IEEE Conference on Computer Vision and Pattern Recognition, pp. 2521–2529 (2018)
28. Zhou, S., Zhang, J., Pan, J., Xie, H., Zuo, W., Ren, J.: Spatio-temporal filter adaptive network for video deblurring. In: Proceedings of the IEEE International Conference on Computer Vision, pp. 2482–2491 (2019)
29. Zhu, X., Hu, H., Lin, S., Dai, J.: Deformable convnets v2: more deformable, better results. In: Proceedings of the IEEE Conference on Computer Vision and Pattern Recognition, pp. 9308–9316 (2019)

Structure Adaptive Filtering
for Edge-Preserving Image Smoothing

Wenming Tang[1](✉), Yuanhao Gong[1], Linyu Su[1], Wenhui Wu[1],
and Guoping Qiu[1,2]

[1] College of Information Engineering, Guangdong Key Laboratory of Intelligent
Information Processing, Shenzhen Institute of Artificial Intelligence and Robotics
for Society, Shenzhen University, Shenzhen, China
tangwenming@szu.edu.cn

[2] School of Computer Science, University of Nottingham, Nottingham NG8 1BB, UK

Abstract. In this paper, we propose a new edge-preserving image
smoothing technique. A simple and effective scheme that classifies a pixel
as situating on a corner, an edge or a plane has been developed. For the
central pixel to be processed, nine adjacent support regions are constructed, leading to nine dimensional variation. Then the selected support region is adaptively determined by the coefficient of variation and
variance, and finally the center pixel is updated iteratively according to
the selected support region. More specifically, we show that a pixel at
a location with very small variation is very likely situating on a plane
(a smooth region). Otherwise, When the coefficient of variation is larger
than the mean, then it is likely an edge pixel, otherwise it is a corner
pixel. We adaptively select the appropriate filtering windows based on
the local image structures to achieve excellent edge-preserving image
smoothing. We present experimental results to show the effectiveness of
our new technique.

Keywords: Adaptive image filter · Coefficient of variation ·
Smoothing · Edge-preserving

1 Introduction

Image filtering is one of the most common and basic operations in computer
vision. The main purposes include amongst others, image smoothing and noise
removal. There are many classical methods for image smoothing, such as mean
filter, box filter, Gaussian filter, median filter, etc. However, many algorithms
often blur important image features such as edges while removing noise. The
goal of image smoothing algorithms is to remove noise while preserving image
structures.

In order to achieve this goal, many edge-preserving smoothing algorithms
have been proposed, such as bilateral filter [14], guided filter [7], Rolling guidance
filter [18], kuwahara filter [9], curvature filter [3,4], side window filter [16], etc.

© Springer Nature Switzerland AG 2021
Y. Peng et al. (Eds.): ICIG 2021, LNCS 12890, pp. 265–276, 2021.
https://doi.org/10.1007/978-3-030-87361-5_22

It is worth noting that all the above are local optimization based algorithms while global optimization based algorithms include the total variation (TV) [11], weighted least squares [10], and iterative global optimization algorithm [20], etc. Local algorithms have become the mainstream of current research because they can be implemented in real-time compared to global algorithms.

Local-based edge-preserving filters are implemented by calculating the relationship between a pixel and its neighbors. The implementation of these algorithms involved setting parameters such as filtering window size (and shape), thresholds, and number of iterations. For example, the traditional Gaussian filter can achieve the edge-preserving effect with the help of the threshold parameter of the Gaussian kernel and the size of the window kernel. However, only consider the spatial relationship between the pixels is not enough, Tomasi et al. [14] designed bilateral filters. They designed filtering weights in two domains: intensity domain and spatial domain. The addition of the intensity domain has greatly enhanced the edge-preserving ability of the filter. Another direction is to implement filtering by analyzing the characteristics of the pixel value distribution in the neighborhood, such as the kuwahara filter [9], the side window filter [16] and the gradient analysis filter [5]. Filtering algorithms based on neighbouring pixel distribution characteristics can achieve very good edge-preserving, but they can create artificial boundaries when the algorithms are applied iteratively, such as kuwahara filter [9]. In general, achieving good noise removal while protecting important image features such as edges and corners is still an open and challenging problem.

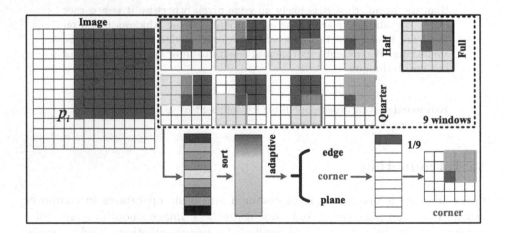

Fig. 1. The framework of adaptive filter for image smoothing.

This paper proposes a local filtering algorithm based on the coefficient of variation of adaptive neighborhood selection. Inspired by the kuwahara filter [9] and the side window filter [16], this paper constructs 9-dimensional variation obtained from 9 windows of center pixel and neighboring pixels, and realizes feature classification (corner, edge, plane) by the coefficient of variation and the variance. Our algorithm does not need to extract and analyze features, and to set additional parameters, and can adaptively achieve edge-preserving smoothing. The framework of our algorithm as show in Fig. 1.

The main contributions of this paper are: (1) We propose a new robust adaptive local image filter that can achieve edge-preserving smoothing. (2) Our algorithm analyzes the relationship between the center pixel and the neighboring pixels through the coefficient of variation, and adaptively classifies the center point pixel to the corner, edge or plane class. There is no need to manually adjust the parameters, which is very simple and robust.

The organization of the paper is as follows: Sect. 2 Review related work, mainly based on the development of local filters. Section 3 Introduce our algorithm design and principle. Section 4 Show the comparison experiment between our algorithm and existing edge-preserving smoothing algorithms. Section 5 Summarize the full text and outlook.

2   Related Work

Edge-preserving filters can be divided into explicit or implicit [5], local or global, linear approximation or non-linear approximation [16], traditional or deep learning, etc. In this part we mainly review local linear and nonlinear approximation algorithms.

2.1   Local Linear Approximation Algorithms

When the calculation of the filter on the pixels in the neighborhood is a linear operation, it is called a linear filter. For example, using a window function for weighted summation or convolution operation can be called linear filtering. Common linear filters are: mean filter [19], Gaussian filter [6], Laplacian filter [1], side window filter [16], etc.

Mean filter [19] is a typical linear filtering algorithm. It refers to giving a template to the target pixel on the image. This template includes neighboring pixels around it, and then the average value of all pixels in the template is used to replace the original pixel value. The advantage of mean filtering lies in its simple design and good real-time performance. The disadvantage is that it cannot preserve the details of the image very well. It also destroys the details of the image while smoothing the image, which makes the image blurry and cannot remove noise well. Gaussian filter [6] is also widely used since most of the noise in the image is Gaussian noise. The difference is that the template coefficients of the mean filter are all the same as constant 1, while for the template coefficient of the Gaussian filter, it decreases as the distance from the center of the template increases. Therefore, the Gaussian filter has a smaller degree of blurring of the image compared to the mean filter. Laplacian is a differential operator and is widely used for contour extraction and sharpening. Zhou et al. [1] used Laplacian filter to achieve edge-preserving filtering with invariant image scale. Zhang et al. [17] proposed an adaptive weighted mean filter for detecting and removing salt-and-pepper noise. It adjusts the window size adaptively to obtain the maximum and minimum values of the neighborhood pixels, and then determines whether it is noise. If it is noise, it is updated by the mean window value, otherwise it is not updated. Thus, the denoising ability of the mean filter is greatly improved. Yin et al. [16] proposed a side window filter. They designed multiple side windows to replace a box window. Compared the traditional box filter that has blurred boundaries, the side window filter cleverly selects a box window value closest to the center pixel to iteratively update, which greatly improves the edge-preserving ability.

2.2 Local Nonlinear Approximation Algorithms

Nonlinear filtering uses the relationship between the original image and the template to achieve filtering, such as maximum and minimum filter [15], median filter [8], kuwahara filter [9], bilateral filter [14], guided filter [7], and gradient analysis filter [5], etc.

The method of the maximum and minimum filter [15] is to sort the surrounding pixels and the center pixel value first, and then compare the center pixel value with the minimum and maximum pixel values. If it is smaller than the minimum value, the center pixel is replaced with the minimum value, and if the center pixel is larger than the maximum value, the center pixel is replaced with the maximum value. The maximum and minimum filter can effectively deal with salt-and-pepper noise, but the disadvantage is that there will be image boundary drift. The median filter [8] is a filtering method that uses the median of all pixel values within the filter range to replace the pixel value at the center of the filter. Kuwahara et al. [9] proposed a filter named Kuwahara to achieve edge-preserving smoothing. This method calculated the mean value and variance in the neighborhood of the image template, and select the mean value of the area with relatively uniform gray value of the image to replace the gray value of the center pixel of the template. The core idea is that the variance corresponding to the more uniform area in the image template is the smallest. Another classic edge-preserving filter is the bilateral filter proposed by Tomasi et al. [14]. The edge-preserving smoothing effect can be achieved because the filter is composed of two functions. One function is to determine the filter coefficients by the geometric spatial distance. The other is determined by the pixel difference value of the filter coefficient. Later, He et al. [7] proposed a guided filter. Guided filtering is called this name because the algorithm needs a guide image. The guide image can be a separate image or the input image itself. When the guide image is the input image, the guided filter becomes a filtering operation that preserves the edges. Guided filtering can be used for noise reduction, detail smoothing, HDR compression, matting, dehazing, and joint sampling. Singh et al. [13] proposed a notch-based guided filter and utilized it to achieve outdoor defogging tasks. Gudkov et al. [5] proposed an edge-preserving smoothing algorithm based on gradient analysis. It distinguishes texture and boundary by constructing magnitudes and directions gradient vectors, and realizes edge-preserving smoothing.

3 Method Overview

In this section, we first discuss the theoretical basis of edge-preserving smoothing algorithm, and then discuss the design of a new edge-preserving smoothing algorithm based on adaptive support regions.

3.1 Theoretical Basis of the Edge-Preserving Smoothing

A basic local linear image filter is the weighted sum of pixels in the center pixel's neighborhood, as in formula (1):

$$p'_i = \sum_{j \in N(i)} w(p_i, q_j) q_j \tag{1}$$

where p_i, p'_i, $N(i)$, q_j, $w(p_i, q_j)$ represent the i-th central pixel, the i-th central pixel after the weighted average summation, the neighborhood set of the i-th central pixel, the j-th pixel in the neighborhood set $N(i)$, and the local weight function, respectively. According to formula (1), if the local weight function is a constant value, and the neighborhood set is a local window containing the central pixel, it is a mean filter, which is difficult to achieve the edge-preserving smoothing effect. Therefore, in generally, local linear filters are designed from the neighborhood set $N(i)$ and the weight function $w(p_i, q_j)$.

The Kuwahara filter is an edge-preserving filter which analyzes the mean and variance of pixels in a sub-window around the central pixel p_i. The filter window is divided into four areas $N_{(i)}^{(k)}$, where $k \in \{0, 1, 2, 3\}$. The mean and variance of each sub-window are calculated according to formula as follow:

$$\mu_i^{(k)} = \frac{1}{|N_{(i)}^{(k)}|} \sum_{j \in N_{(i)}^{(k)}} q_j \tag{2}$$

$$\delta_k^2 = \frac{1}{|N_{(i)}^{(k)}|} \sum_{j \in N_{(i)}^{(k)}} (q_j - \mu_i^{(k)})^2 \tag{3}$$

The filtering result of the center pixel p_i is the average value of the pixels within the sub-window that has the smallest variance as shown in formula (4).

$$\delta_{min}^2 = min(\delta_k^2), \ k \in \{0, 1, 2, 3\} \tag{4}$$

The core of the side window filter is to construct 8 sub-windows of the central pixel $SW_i = \{L, R, U, D, NW, NE, SW, SE\}$. For specific definitions, see Sect. 2 of the paper [16]. The center pixel p_i is updated by the following formula:

$$p'_i = argmin \|p_i - \sum_{j \in SW_i^k} q_j\|_2^2, \ k \in \{L, R, U, D, NW, NE, SW, SE\} \tag{5}$$

that is, it selects the sub-window which has an average pixel value that is the closest to the current pixel as the filtering window.

The above two smoothing algorithms use different filtering windows based on the pixel structure in the neighbourhood of the center pixel p_i. Our new method is also based on a similar designing principle. Starting from the study of image structural features, we know that the image can be mainly divided into three main features: corner, edge, and plane as shown in Fig. 2(a), (b), (c). Therefore, we can design an algorithm to protect these three types of image features as much as possible for achieving edge-preserving smoothing.

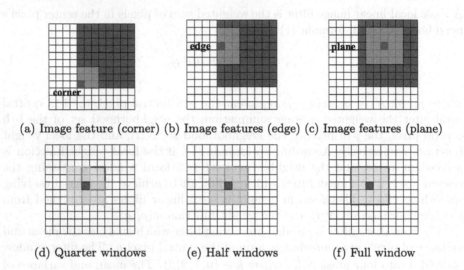

(a) Image feature (corner) (b) Image features (edge) (c) Image features (plane)

(d) Quarter windows   (e) Half windows   (f) Full window

Fig. 2. Image features and three windows. The smallest quarter window size shown in the figure is 3×3. (a), (b), (c), represent corner, edge and plane features. (d), (e), (f), respectively represent quarter windows, half windows, and the full window, respectively.

3.2 Algorithm Design

From the previous section, we designed 9 support regions for the central pixel p_i, they are $SR_i = \{Q_1, Q_2, Q_3, Q4, H_1, H_2, H_3, H_4, F\}$, which respectively represent 4 quarter windows, 4 half windows, and a full window, as shown in Fig. 2(d), (c), (e). We use the box filter framework to calculate the pixel values $p_{SR_i}^{(k)}$ corresponding to the SR support region set, as shown in formula (6).

$$p_{SR_i}^{(k)} = \frac{1}{|SR_{(i)}^{(k)}|} \sum_{j \in SR_{(i)}^{(k)}} q_j, \ k \in \{Q_1, Q_2, Q_3, Q_4, H_1, H_2, H_3, H_4, F\} \quad (6)$$

Then, we calculate the difference between $p_{SR_i}^{(k)}$ and the center pixel p_i, as shown in formula (7), whose absolute value is normalized as formula (8), and the value range of k is shown in formula (6).

$$\triangle p_i^{(k)} = p_i - p_{SR_i}^{(k)} \quad (7)$$

$$|\triangle \hat{p}_i^{(k)}| = \frac{|\triangle p_i^{(k)}|}{MAX}, MAX = max(|\triangle p_i^{(1)}|, \ldots, |\triangle p_i^{(9)}|), \ MAX \neq 0 \qquad (8)$$

Then we can find the corresponding mean, variance, and coefficient of variation [2], corresponding to formula (9), (10), (11).

$$\mu_i = \frac{1}{|SR_i|} \sum_{j \in SR_{(i)}^{(k)}} |\triangle \hat{p}_i^{(j)}| \qquad (9)$$

$$\delta_i = \frac{1}{|SR_i|} \sum_{j \in SR_{(i)}^{(k)}} (|\triangle \hat{p}_i^{(j)}| - \mu_i)^2 \qquad (10)$$

$$cv_i = \frac{\delta_i}{\mu_i}, \ \mu_i \neq 0 \qquad (11)$$

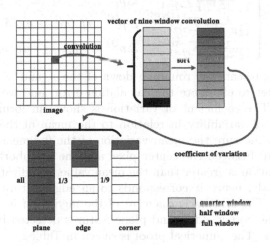

Fig. 3. Schematic diagram of our algorithm.

After that, we can use the coefficient of variation, mean, and variance of the center pixel p_i to distinguish which type of feature the pixel belongs to. We get the 9-dimensional variation set $\triangle P_i = \{\triangle p_i^{(1)}, \triangle p_i^{(2)}, \ldots, \triangle p_i^{(9)}\}$ and the normalized set of absolute value $|\triangle \hat{P}_i| = \{|\triangle \hat{p}_i^{(1)}|, |\triangle \hat{p}_i^{(2)}|, \ldots, |\triangle \hat{p}_i^{(9)}|\}$. First, we sort the 9-dimensional $|\triangle \hat{P}_i|$ from small to large $|\triangle \hat{P}_i^{(sort)}|$. Through the index of the sorted set $|\triangle \hat{P}_i^{(sort)}|$, we can get the corresponding new 9-dimensional variation set $\triangle P_i' = \{\triangle p_i^{(1)'}, \triangle p_i^{(2)'}, \ldots, \triangle p_i^{(9)'}\}$. Then, if the variance is small enough (generally we take a constant very close to 0), the pixel p_i is highly likely a plane feature. Otherwise, we will compare the coefficient of variation with the mean, and if it is larger, it is an edge feature, otherwise it is a

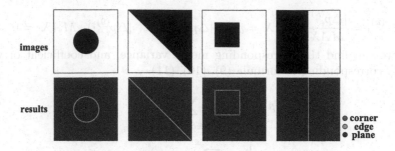

Fig. 4. Three types of feature detection (corner, edge, plane).

corner feature. Finally, we update the pixel p_i according to the feature selection and the variation set $\triangle P_i'$, as shown in formula (12).

$$p_i' = p_i + \begin{cases} \frac{1}{\lfloor|\triangle P_i'|\rfloor} \sum_{j=1}^{\lfloor|\triangle P_i'|\rfloor} \triangle p_i^{(j)'}, & if \ (\delta_i \leq \xi) \\ \frac{1}{\lfloor\frac{1}{3}|\triangle P_i'|\rfloor} \sum_{j=1}^{\lfloor\frac{1}{3}|\triangle P_i'|\rfloor} \triangle p_i^{(j)'}, & if \ (cv_i > \mu_i, \ \delta_i \geq \xi) \\ \frac{1}{\lfloor\frac{1}{9}|\triangle P_i'|\rfloor} \sum_{j=1}^{\lfloor\frac{1}{9}|\triangle P_i'|\rfloor} \triangle p_i^{(j)'}, & if \ (cv_i \leq \mu_i, \ \delta_i \geq \xi) \end{cases} \quad (12)$$

Where, $\lfloor x \rfloor$ represents the rounding down of the x, and ξ is generally not taken as 0 in order to eliminate the calculation error, and we set $\xi = 0.05$ in all experiments. The coefficient of variation is shown in formula (11), which shows the extent of variability in relation to the mean of the population [2]. Here we use it to measure the mean variation of the 9-dimensional data, that is, the relationship between the center pixel and the neighborhood. When the coefficient of variation is greater than the mean value, it indicates that the data has changed greatly, hence it corresponds to an edge feature, otherwise it is a corner feature. The schematic diagram of the algorithm is shown in Fig. 3. Figure 4 shows the corner, edge, and plane features detected by the algorithm in different images. The numerical proof is shown in Table 1.

Table 1. Numerical proof of our algorithm on ideal images. Using Fig. 2 (a), (b), (c) red box pixels to illustrate. For the convenience of calculation, suppose that the blue pixel value in the image is 0 and the white pixel value is 1.

Figure 2 (a) Corner	Figure 2 (b) Edge	Figure 2 (c) Plane
$p_i = 0$	$p_i = 0$	$p_i = 0$
$SR_i = \{0, 1, 1, 1, 0.5, 1, 1, 0.5, 0.75\}$	$SR_i = \{0, 1, 1, 0, 0.5, 1, 0.5, 0, 0.5\}$	$SR_i = \{0, 0, 0, 0, 0, 0, 0, 0, 0\}$
$|\triangle \hat{P}_i| = \{0, 0.5, 0.5, 0.75, 1, 1, 1, 1, 1\}$	$|\triangle \hat{P}_i| = \{0, 0, 0, 0.5, 0.5, 0.5, 1, 1, 1\}$	$|\triangle \hat{P}_i| = \{0, 0, 0, 0, 0, 0, 0, 0, 0\}$
$index = \{0, 4, 7, 8, 1, 5, 6, 2, 3\}$	$index = \{0, 6, 7, 1, 5, 8, 4, 2, 3\}$	$index = \{0, 1, 2, 3, 4, 5, 6, 7, 8\}$
$\triangle P_i' = \{0, 0.5, 0.5, 0.75, 1, 1, 1, 1, 1\}$	$\triangle P_i' = \{0, 0, 0, 0.5, 0.5, 0.5, 1, 1, 1\}$	$\triangle P_i' = \{0, 0, 0, 0, 0, 0, 0, 0, 0\}$
$\delta_i = 0.333$	$\delta_i = 0.408$	$\delta_i = 0$
$\mu_i = 0.75$	$\mu_i = 0.5$	$\mu_i = 0$
$cv_i = 0.444$	$cv_i = 0.816$	$cv_i = 0$
$\delta_i = 0.333 > \xi, \ cv_i < \mu_i$	$\delta_i = 0.408 > \xi, \ cv_i > \mu_i$	$\delta_i = 0 < \xi$
$p_i' = p_i + \frac{1}{\lfloor\frac{1}{9}|\triangle P_i'|\rfloor} \sum_{j=1}^{\lfloor\frac{1}{9}|\triangle P_i'|\rfloor} \triangle p_i^{(j)'}$	$p_i' = p_i + \frac{1}{\lfloor\frac{1}{3}|\triangle P_i'|\rfloor} \sum_{j=1}^{\lfloor\frac{1}{3}|\triangle P_i'|\rfloor} \triangle p_i^{(j)'}$	$p_i' = p_i + \frac{1}{\lfloor|\triangle P_i'|\rfloor} \sum_{j=1}^{\lfloor|\triangle P_i'|\rfloor} \triangle p_i^{(j)'}$
$p_i' = p_i + \sum_{j=1}^{1} \triangle p_i^{(j)'}$	$p_i' = p_i + \frac{1}{3} \sum_{j=1}^{3} \triangle p_i^{(j)'}$	$p_i' = p_i + \frac{1}{9} \sum_{j=1}^{9} \triangle p_i^{(j)'}$
$p_i' = 0 + 0 = 0$	$p_i' = 0 + (0 + 0 + 0)/3 = 0$	$p_i' = 0 + (0 + 0 + 0 + 0 + 0 + 0 + 0 + 0 + 0)/9 = 0$

4   Experiments

In this section, the proposed edge-preserving smoothing algorithm is compared with 6 edge-preserving smoothing algorithms, which include a box filter (opencv default, BF), a kuwahara filter (KF) [9], a bilateral filter (BIF) [14], a guided filter (GF) [7], a side window filter (SF) [16], a gradient analysis filter (GAF) [5].

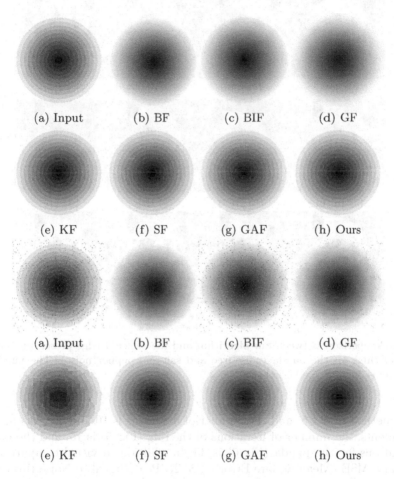

(a) Input   (b) BF   (c) BIF   (d) GF

(e) KF   (f) SF   (g) GAF   (h) Ours

(a) Input   (b) BF   (c) BIF   (d) GF

(e) KF   (f) SF   (g) GAF   (h) Ours

Fig. 5. Comparison between our algorithm and the selected edge-preserving smoothing algorithms on the ring (noise-free and Gaussian random noise). The number of iterations is 10, and the kernel size is 5 × 5.

In order to verify the performance of our algorithm, we will compare it with the above algorithm on noise-free and noisy images (Gaussian random noise, salt-and-pepper noise). For the sake of fairness, we set the kernel size of the

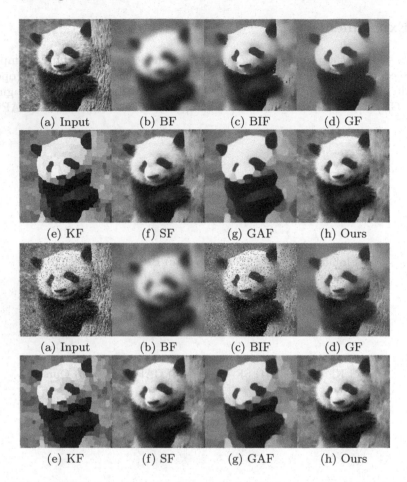

Fig. 6. Comparison between our algorithm and the selected edge-preserving smoothing algorithms on the panda (noise-free and salt-and-pepper noise). The number of iterations is 30, and the kernel size is 5 × 5.

above method to 5 × 5, and the number of iterations is 10 and 30. Among all of experiments, the number of iterations of the ring (Fig. 5) is 10, and the number of iterations for the panda (Fig. 6) is 30. In addition to visual comparison, we also chose MSE (Mean Square Error), PSNR (Peak Signal to Noise Ratio), and SSIM (Structural Similarity Index) [12] for quantitative comparison of results. The smaller the MSE, the closer it is to the ground truth, the larger the PSNR and SSIM, the stronger the ability to preserve the main structure.

Under the same conditions in Fig. 5 (rows 1–2, noise-free), BF, BIF, and GF are over-smoothed, and KF has artificial errors, but our method does not have these problems. It shows that our algorithm has achieved the best edge-preserving smoothing effect. Figure 5 (rows 2–4, Gaussian random noise) shows that our algorithm can obtain the best results of all comparison methods not only on noise-free image, but also on image with Gaussian random noise. Figure 6 shows that our algorithm can also achieve the best results on salt-and-pepper noise images. The specific qualitative comparison results are shown in Table 2.

Table 2. Quantitative comparison of edge-preserving smoothing performances with other methods.

Input	Methods	MSE	PSNR	SSIM	Input	Methods	MSE	PSNR	SSIM
Ring Fig. 5 (Rows 1-2)	BF	53.654	30.834	0.9999316	Ring Fig. 5 (Rows 2-4)	BF	57.539	30.5311	0.9995035
	BIF	20.004	35.119	0.99997843		BIF	21.289	34.849	0.9997776
	GF	31.036	33.212	0.9995574		GF	32.420	33.022	0.9993586
	KF	10.154	38.064	0.9999288		KF	21.396	34.827	0.9999357
	SF	1.828	45.509	0.999997		SF	3.619	42.544	0.9999861
	GAF	11.709	37.445	0.9999577		GAF	13.098	36.958	0.9998033
	Ours	**1.628**	**46.012**	**0.9999999**		Ours	**2.969**	**43.404**	**0.9999933**
Panda Fig. 6 (Rows 1-2)	BF	98.594	28.192	0.9832603	Panda Fig. 6 (Rows 2-4)	BF	99.947	28.133	0.962458
	BIF	78.293	29.193	0.9973552		BIF	78.058	29.206	**0.999888**
	GF	91.893	28.497	0.9902354		GF	91.939	28.495	0.9841815
	KF	76.415	29.299	0.9982965		KF	81.012	29.045	0.9992489
	SF	55.189	30.712	0.9987298		SF	59.904	30.356	0.9983071
	GAF	76.765	29.279	**0.9997370**		GAF	85.454	28.813	0.9986002
	Ours	**52.947**	**30.892**	0.9988239		Ours	**58.081**	**30.490**	0.9982481

5   Conclusion

In this paper, we propose a new adaptive edge-preserving smoothing algorithm. By studying the three main features in the image: corners, edges, and planes, 9 kinds of support regions are designed to construct a 9-dimensional variation corresponding to each pixel. The 9-dimensional variation is adaptively classified and selected by the coefficient of variation and the variance. From all comparative experiments in the paper, it can be found that our algorithm performs well on edge-preserving smoothing on noise-free or noisy images, and has only one iteration parameter, which is robust and easy to use.

In future work, we will study to improve the real-time performance of the algorithm, and explore the possibility of HD video processing and 3D graphics.

Acknowledgments. This work is partially supported by the Education Department of Guangdong Province, PR China, under project No 2019KZDZX1028, the National Natural Science Foundation of China under Grant 61907031, the University Stability Support Program of Shenzhen under Grant 20200810150732001, and the National Natural Science Foundation of China under Grant 62006158.

References

1. Aubry, M., Paris, S., Hasinoff, S.W., Kautz, J., Durand, F.: Fast local laplacian filters: theory and applications. ACM Trans. Graph. (TOG) **33**(5), 1–14 (2014)
2. Everitt, B., Skrondal, A.: The Cambridge Dictionary of Statistics, vol. 106. Cambridge University Press, Cambridge (2002)

3. Gong, Y., Goksel, O.: Weighted mean curvature. Signal Process. **164**, 329–339 (2019)
4. Gong, Y., Sbalzarini, I.F.: Curvature filters efficiently reduce certain variational energies. IEEE Trans. Image Process. **26**(4), 1786–1798 (2017)
5. Gudkov, V., Moiseev, I.: Image smoothing algorithm based on gradient analysis. In: 2020 Ural Symposium on Biomedical Engineering, Radioelectronics and Information Technology (USBEREIT), pp. 403–406. IEEE (2020)
6. Haddad, R.A., Akansu, A.N., et al.: A class of fast gaussian binomial filters for speech and image processing. IEEE Trans. Signal Process. **39**(3), 723–727 (1991)
7. He, K., Sun, J., Tang, X.: Guided image filtering. In: Daniilidis, K., Maragos, P., Paragios, N. (eds.) ECCV 2010. LNCS, vol. 6311, pp. 1–14. Springer, Heidelberg (2010). https://doi.org/10.1007/978-3-642-15549-9_1
8. Huang, T., Yang, G., Tang, G.: A fast two-dimensional median filtering algorithm. IEEE Trans. Acoustics Speech Signal Process. **27**(1), 13–18 (1979)
9. Kuwahara, M., Hachimura, K., Eiho, S., Kinoshita, M.: Processing of ri-angiocardiographic images. In: Preston, K., Onoe, M. (eds.) Digital Processing of Biomedical Images, pp. 187–202. Springer, Boston (1976). https://doi.org/10.1007/978-1-4684-0769-3_13
10. Min, D., Choi, S., Lu, J., Ham, B., Sohn, K., Do, M.N.: Fast global image smoothing based on weighted least squares. IEEE Trans. Image Process. **23**(12), 5638–5653 (2014)
11. Rudin, L.I., Osher, S., Fatemi, E.: Nonlinear total variation based noise removal algorithms. Physica D: Nonlinear Phenomena **60**(1–4), 259–268 (1992)
12. Sara, U., Akter, M., Uddin, M.S.: Image quality assessment through fsim, ssim, mse and psnr-a comparative study. J. Comput. Commun. **7**(3), 8–18 (2019)
13. Singh, D., Kumar, V.: Dehazing of outdoor images using notch based integral guided filter. Multimed. Tools Appl. **77**(20), 27363–27386 (2018)
14. Tomasi, C., Manduchi, R.: Bilateral filtering for gray and color images. In: Sixth International Conference on Computer Vision (IEEE Cat. No. 98CH36271), pp. 839–846. IEEE (1998)
15. Van Herk, M.: A fast algorithm for local minimum and maximum filters on rectangular and octagonal kernels. Pattern Recogn. Lett. **13**(7), 517–521 (1992)
16. Yin, H., Gong, Y., Qiu, G.: Side window filtering. In: Proceedings of the IEEE/CVF Conference on Computer Vision and Pattern Recognition, pp. 8758–8766 (2019)
17. Zhang, P., Li, F.: A new adaptive weighted mean filter for removing salt-and-pepper noise. IEEE Signal Process. Lett. **21**(10), 1280–1283 (2014)
18. Zhang, Q., Shen, X., Xu, L., Jia, J.: Rolling guidance filter. In: Fleet, D., Pajdla, T., Schiele, B., Tuytelaars, T. (eds.) ECCV 2014. LNCS, vol. 8691, pp. 815–830. Springer, Cham (2014). https://doi.org/10.1007/978-3-319-10578-9_53
19. Zhang, X., Xiong, Y.: Impulse noise removal using directional difference based noise detector and adaptive weighted mean filter. IEEE Signal Process. Lett. **16**(4), 295–298 (2009)
20. Zhou, Z., Wang, B., Ma, J.: Scale-aware edge-preserving image filtering via iterative global optimization. IEEE Trans. Multimed. **20**(6), 1392–1405 (2017)

Robust Image Cropping by Filtering Composition Irrelevant Factors

Zhiyu Pan, Ke Xian, Hao Lu, and Zhiguo Cao[✉]

National Key Laboratory of Science and Technology on Multispectral Information Processing, School of Artificial Intelligence and Automation, Huazhong University of Science and Technology, Wuhan, China
{zhiyupan,kexian,hlu,zgcao}@hust.edu.cn

Abstract. Numerous factors can impact the aesthetic quality of images: composition, resolution, exposure, color saturation and so on. Image cropping is to improve the aesthetic quality by recomposing the images. When the only consideration of an image cropping system is composition, the automatic image cropping algorithm should be single input single output system (SISOS). However, most of the existing approaches are multiple input multiple output systems (MIMOS) which consider image composition and image aesthetics synchronously. In these MIMOSs, cropping result may change when composition irrelevant factors (e.g., resolution, exposure, color saturation) varies, which is undesirable to users. Based on this observation, we try to discriminate image composition and aesthetics to get a SISOS based on composition by the saliency map. From our observation, although the saliency map is robust to the composition irrelevant factors, it is a less informative data format for composition. Hence, it is transformed to the salient cluster that is similar to point cloud. The salient points in salient cluster can directly describe the spatial structure of an image, so the salient cluster can be treated as an expression of composition and serves as the only input of the proposed model. Our model is designed based on PointNet and made up of content screening module (CSM) and composition regression module (CRM). CSM extracts the points of interest and CRM outputs a cropping box. The experimental results on public datasets shows that, compared with prior arts, our network is more robust to composition irrelevant factor with a comparable or better performance.

Keywords: Image cropping · Composition · Aesthetics · Pointnet

1 Introduction

With the popularity of portable photography equipment, acquiring digital images becomes easier and sharing them on social media comes into vogue. For social media users, images with high aesthetic quality are expected. Nevertheless, obtaining an image with high aesthetic quality needs expertise that common

© Springer Nature Switzerland AG 2021
Y. Peng et al. (Eds.): ICIG 2021, LNCS 12890, pp. 277–289, 2021.
https://doi.org/10.1007/978-3-030-87361-5_23

users may not have. In this case, automatic image cropping algorithm that can enhance the aesthetic quality is in great demand.

The arrangements of objects or region of interest in an image is known as composition. The composition is hardly altered during the transmission of images, however the composition irrelevant factors may change. Existing image cropping methods [3, 6, 21, 23] implicitly model the composition by introducing the concept of image aesthetics into image recomposition. The task of image cropping is transformed to pick up the cropping candidate with highest aesthetic score in predefined candidates. The cropping results of these methods may change when the composition irrelevant factors vary during the transmission, which is unacceptable to a multi-platforms ecosystem that requires consistency. The coupling of image aesthetics and composition in these multiple input multiple output systems (MIMOS) makes the cropping results sensitive to the change of composition irrelevant factors. To address this problem, it is necessary to filter the composition irrelevant factors in the input. Recently, some methods establish robust image cropping systems by laying emphasis on composition. They reduce the affect of composition irrelevant factor by enhancing the composition. These works [8, 19, 20] try to represent the composition explicitly with attention box, but their following-up operations are still based on aesthetics, which means that the coupling of image composition and image aesthetic evaluation still exists.

In this paper, we try to construct a single input single output system (SISOS) by filtering composition irrelevant factors. Efforts are made to learn composition directly from spatial information so that the influence of irrelevant factors is excluded. We still model composition based on saliency map but transform the saliency map to a point-cloud-like data format, which is defined as salient cluster. In this way, richer spatial information is expressed and composition irrelevant factors are filtered out. The salient cluster manifests spatial information directly in predefined coordinate system, which helps to search for the spatial correlation between salient points and cropping box. We present a PointNet based approach to generate a cropping box from salient cluster. More specifically, our two-stage framework is made up of a content screening module (CSM) and a composition regression module (CRM). The CSM filter out the points that are helpful for composition in salient cluster and CRM maps the spatial information to cropping box. The main contributions of this work are three fold:

- The coupling of image composition and aesthetics that exists in existing deep neural network based methods is revealed by experiments. The coupling makes the cropping results change when composition irrelevant factor varies. Hence, these methods are sensitive transmission operations (e.g., image compression) which are common in application.
- We proposed a framework with a novel data processing method that is designed for filtering the composition irrelevant factors. This data processing method transforms the saliency map into salient cluster so that most spatial information can be preserved. To the best of our knowledge, existing saliency based methods only transform the saliency map into a score or a bounding box. The input of our framework is only salient cluster rather than the whole

image. In this way, the influence of irrelevant factors can be avoided, which means that the coupling of image composition and aesthetics is alleviated.

- By filtering composition irrelevant factors, the experiments illustrates that our framework is more robust to composition irrelevant factor. Furthermore, the experimental results on public datasets shows that our network has a comparable or better performance than state-of-the-art regression approaches. This result demonstrates that filtering composition irrelevant factors is of great importance in image auto cropping system.

2   Related Works

In this section, we review the image cropping and spatial information learning from point cloud.

Automatic Image Cropping Methods. Conventional image cropping methods are based on artificially designed criteria. These cropping systems are basically SISOSs that delineate the composition by visual salient areas and models the relationship between composition and the cropping box. Most of these methods enhance the subject dominance to boost the visual quality by salient features (e.g., saliency detection [5], face detection [17], and eye fixation data [16]). Other predefined composition rules are also encoded into the energy function that is used to assess the cropping result [4,10]. Unfortunately, the results of these SISO cropping systems can not align well with the preference of the users, for the reason that the artificially designed criteria can hardly cover all the composition rules. Recently, the data-driven models that introduce the aesthetic evaluation into the system emerge. These models transform the image cropping task to a set of image aesthetics evaluation. Predefined candidate views are evaluated and ranked according to their aesthetic quality that modeled by self-supervision [3], knowledge distillation [21], and aesthetic feature fusion [23]. Introducing the aesthetics into cropping system is a double-edged sword that makes the cropping results align well with the preference of users but sensitive to the composition irrelevant factors. Our method constructs a SISO cropping system in data-driven manner, which makes our model robust to the composition irrelevant factors with good performance.

Learning from Point Cloud Data. In 3D tasks, point cloud can provide with rich spatial information. However, due to the characteristics of disorder, point cloud data is hard to process. Early works [7,9,14,18,22] convert point clouds to images or volumetric before feature encoding. Recently, Qi et al. [13,15] proposed the PointNets which can directly consumes raw point cloud. PointNets can be used to spatial perception tasks like 3D object classification, 3D semantic segmentation and 3D object detection [11,12], we explore how to model composition more exactly by the means of PointNet and extend this backbone to map spatial information in image recomposition to the cropping box.

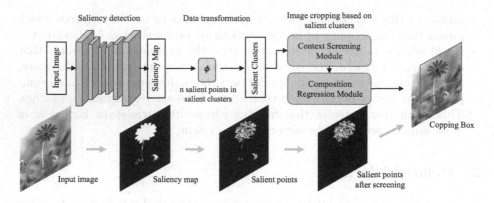

Fig. 1. The workflow of proposed SISO cropping system.

3 Problem Formulation and Proposed Approach

3.1 Overview

The input image I can be formulated as $\{A, C\} \subset I$, in which A represents the aesthetic factors (composition irrelevant factors) and C represents the composition factor. The output cropping box is denoted as R. Then, the SISO cropping system can be described as

$$R = f_s(\hat{C}),\tag{1}$$

where $\hat{C}$ is the composition features for C. $f(\cdot)$ is the cropping function. When it comes to the MIMO cropping system, it can be represented by

$$R = f_m\left(\begin{pmatrix} \hat{A} \\ \hat{C} \end{pmatrix}\right),\tag{2}$$

where $\hat{A}$ and $\hat{C}$ are aesthetic and composition features for A and C respectively. The goal of this paper is to filter the $\hat{A}$ and find a effective $f(\cdot)$ which can map $\hat{C}$ to R. In this way, the cropping results will be robust to $\hat{A}$. Hence, our image cropping system after filtering the composition irrelevant factors is

$$\begin{cases} R = f_s(\hat{C}) \\ \hat{C} = \gamma\left(\begin{pmatrix} A \\ C \end{pmatrix}\right), \end{cases}\tag{3}$$

where $\gamma(\cdot)$ is a function that can filter the composition irrelevant features from the combination of A and C.

To filter composition irrelevant factors and preserve image composition, as illustrated in Fig. 1, we propose a novel image cropping pipeline only based on composition. We firstly represent regions of interest as saliency map. Then the saliency map is transformed to salient cluster to get richer spatial information. The salient cluster is a point cloud similar data form which describes the visual

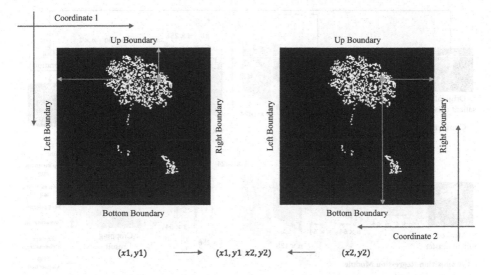

Fig. 2. The dual coordinate system of the salient points.

attractive region with salient points. The salient points are represented in a dual image coordinates. A PointNet based network that consists of a context screening module and a composition regression module is designed to process the salient cluster and generate the cropping result. Following this formulation, our approach shows obvious distinction of being the first SISO cropping system based on deep neural network.

3.2 Encoding Robust Composition Features

Due to the consistency between saliency and visual attractiveness, the saliency map is adopted to encode the composition. The utilization of saliency map in previous works is to draw a tight attention box with largest saliency value. However, processing saliency map in this way suffers huge loss of spatial information. For the sake of obtaining a more detailed expression of spatial information, we check the saliency value of every local area. If the saliency value is over the predefined threshold, the local area is compressed into a salient point that represented in image coordinate. The composition is about the spatial relation between the regions of interest and four image boundaries, one image coordinate system is not enough. Thus, as shown in Fig. 2, we express each salient point in a dual coordinate systems. When one salient point is denoted as $p_i = (x_1, y_1, x_2, y_2)$, in which, (x_1, y_1) and (x_2, y_2) are coordinates in two coordinate systems. Then the salient cluster is $P = \{p_i | i = 1, ..., n\}$ where n is the total points number of salient cluster.

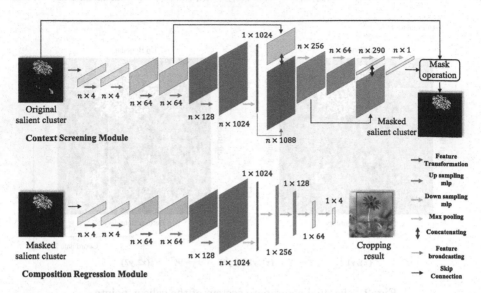

Fig. 3. The structure of context screening module and composition regression module.

3.3 Image Cropping Based on Composition Relevant Factors

Our cropping system is composed by two modules: the Context Screening Module (CSM) and the Composition Regression Module (CRM). The CSM is used to find the points of interest in the input salient cluster and the CRM can generate a cropping box based on the salient cluster which is masked by CSM.

Context screening module is used to mimic the focus action of human user when they try to crop an image. When cropping is treated as the task to discover the general relationship between subject of interest and cropping box, it is of great importance to locate the region of interest firstly. Although saliency map has a consistence with the region of interest, there exist some salient regions which makes minor sense to composition. Obviously, if the input of the composition regression module contained noise (salient but composition irrelevant information), the output cropping box will loss attention to the focus. Thus, it is necessary to filter out the composition irrelevant information. Under our formulation, the composition irrelevant information is instantiated as composition irrelevant points in original salient clusters. As shown in Fig. 3 (Context Screening Module), we design a PointNet based module with a $n \times 4$ input and a $n \times 1$ output representing the contribution for cropping of every point. Given a predefined threshold, the points whose contribution is under the threshold are filtered out. Intuitively, this segmentation module should care about the patterns between local information and high level content information. Hence, we merge the shallow features with high level features to determine the contribution of every points. The loss function of this module is

$$L_{seg} = -\sum_{i}^{N} \delta(p_i) \log c(q_i), \tag{4}$$

the $c(p_i)$ denotes the predicted contribution for cropping of point p_i and the $\delta(\cdot)$ can be represented as:

$$\delta(p) = \begin{cases} 1 & p \ in \ \dot{B} \\ 0 & p \ not \ in \ \dot{B} \end{cases}, \tag{5}$$

where $\dot{B}$ is the ground truth cropping box.

Composition regression module is designed to imitate the process of drawing the cropping box based on the region of interest. Similar to the context screening module, the composition regression module is also based on PointNet with a input of $m \times 4$ tensor. The $m \times 4$ tensor represents the salient points masked out from the original salient cluster. Different from the context screening module, generating a cropping box is about the distribution of high level visual feature in an image. So, we design the composition regression module in a straight forward encoding-decoding manner. Furthermore, the cropping box can not be too small for the purpose to avoid too much loss of image content [23]. Following this idea, we constrain the predicted cropping box in an area between the center and the boundaries of an image. In order to get a soft and robust result, we not only optimize this module with a typical $L1$ loss, but also adopt a $GIoU$ loss. Then, when the four boundaries of a cropping box B_i can be represented as $B_i = (l_i, r_i, u_i, b_i)$ and the $\dot{B}_i$ represents the ground truth cropping box, the loss function of this module is:

$$L_{reg} = \frac{1}{N} \sum_{i}^{N} \Big(\sum_{j=l_i, r_j, u_i, d_i} |j - \dot{j}| + 1 - \frac{\beta(\dot{B}_i \cap B_i)}{\beta(\dot{B}_i \cup B_i)} + \frac{A_c - \beta(\dot{B}_i \cup B_i)}{\beta(\dot{B}_i \cup B_i)} \Big), \tag{6}$$

where the $\beta(\cdot)$ denotes the area of the cropping box and A_c represent the minimum closure of B_i and $\dot{B}_i$.

We optimize the two modules simultaneously with the loss:

$$L = L_{seg} + \lambda L_{reg} + \mu L_{trans}, \tag{7}$$

where, the L_{trans} is the loss of the feature transformation loss. The λ and the μ are hyper parameters which can control the influence of L_{reg} and L_{trans}. Then the SISO cropping system can be optimized in an end-to-end way.

4 Experiments

4.1 Datasets and Implementation Details

We collect winning entries in photography competitions as the training examples. Given the winning entries in photography competitions, we simulate the distribution of user images by padding with noise. We treat the patch of salient cluster of other images as noise. By padding noise to our collecting data, we can get our training dataset. We perform our analysis experiments and test the performance of our model on two public datasets, including Flickr Cropping Dataset (FCD) [2], and Human Cropping Dataset (HCD) [4]. FCD is composed of 348 test images, and each image in FCD has only one ground truth cropping box. As for HCD, there are 500 test images, each of them has ten annotations. For definiteness and without loss of generality, we choose the FCD as our experimental environment when we perform our analysis experiments. As far as performance comparing, all these datasets are used for comparison. When we compare our model with previous works, we follow the same evaluation metrics which are the mean intersection over union ($mIoU$) and the mean boundary displacement ($mBDE$). The ground truth cropping box and the predicted cropping box of ith image are denoted as $\dot{B}_i$ and B_i respectively. Then, the $mIoU$ of one dataset that contains N images can be computed as

$$mIoU = \frac{1}{N} \sum_{i=1}^{N} \frac{\beta(\dot{B}_i \cap B_i)}{\beta(\dot{B}_i \cup B_i)}, \tag{8}$$

where $\beta(\cdot)$ denotes the area of the cropping box. When the length of original image boundaries is denoted as $(L(l_i), L(r_i), L(u_i), L(d_i))$, the $mBDE$ can be computed as

$$mBDE = \frac{1}{4N} \sum_{i=1}^{N} \sum_{j=l_i, r_j, u_i, d_i} \frac{|j - \dot{j}|}{L(j)}. \tag{9}$$

Nevertheless, due to that HCD has much more ground truth cropping box, the $mIoU$ and $mBDE$ is computationally intensive. Hence, metrics on this dataset are mean maximum intersection over union $mMIoU$ and mean maximum boundary displacement $mMBDE$. When the ground truth cropping boxes set of the ith image is $G = \{\dot{B}_i^j | j = 1, ..., 10\}$, the $mMIoU$ can be computed as

$$mMIoU = \frac{1}{N} \sum_{i=1}^{N} max(\frac{\beta(\dot{B}_i^j \cap B_i)}{\beta(\dot{B}_i^j \cup B_i)} | \dot{B}_i^j \in G). \tag{10}$$

The mean maximum boundary displacement $mMBDE$ can be calculated follow the similar way and so on.

In the trainin stage, $1,600$ images in our training set are augmented by padding to $16,000$ training examples. Our model is optimized by Adam optimizer with the learning rate of $1e-4$. The λ and the μ are set to 0.5 and 0.01 respectively. The batch size is set to 64. For every input salient cluster, we sample 1024 points.

4.2   Robustness Comparison

In this section, we study how much the predicted cropping box changes when composition irrelevant factors vary. Intuitively, we can measure the change by the drop of performance. The composition irrelevant factors taken into account

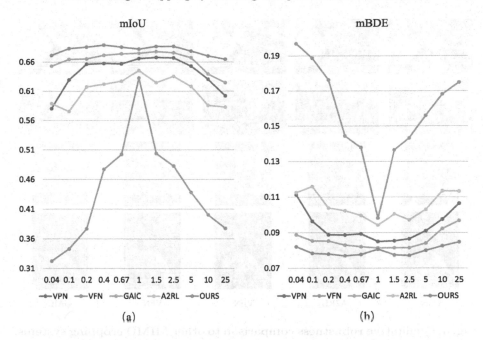

Fig. 4. Quantitative robustness comparison to other MIMO cropping systems. When the gamma varies from 0.04 to 25, the change of mIoU and mBDE performance on FCD dataset of different models are illustrate in (a) and (b) respectively.

are the brightness and saturation. For the original images, we change the composition irrelevant factors by performing gamma transformation. We set ten experimental scenarios with gamma of 0.04, 0.1, 0.2, 0.4, 0.67, 1.5, 2.5, 5, 10 and 25. The $mIoU$ and $mBDE$ performance on FCDB of different open source methods under different scenarios are shown in Fig. 4. Compared with other open source method, the proposed method is hardly disturbed with best performance. This illustrates that the MIMO cropping systems are obviously sensitive to composition irrelevant factors and our model is more robust. In Fig. 5, we show this by qualitative comparison. It is evident that the cropping results of our model shift slightly when composition irrelevant factors vary, but the cropping boxes from other methods change dramatically. Both of the quantitative and qualitative results demonstrate that the coupling of image composition and aesthetics exists in prior methods and makes the cropping system sensitive to the composition irrelevant factors.

4.3 Performance Comparison

In this section, we compare the cropping performance of our model with previous methods. The cropping performance is measured by the metrics of $mIoU$ and $mBDE$. Essentially, our model is in a regression manner which is similar to the AGDRN method [8]. The AGDRN methods directly predicts the cropping box

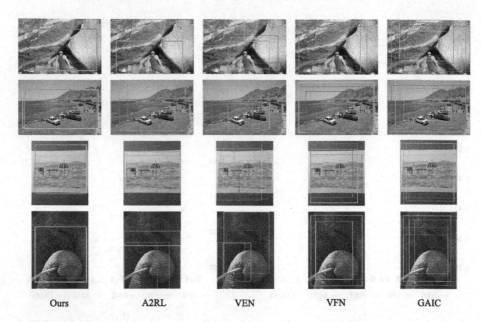

| Ours | A2RL | VEN | VFN | GAIC |

Fig. 5. Qualitative robustness comparison to other MIMO cropping systems. The cropping results disturbed by different gamma transformation are denoted by the boxes in different colors.

Table 1. Quantitative comparison on FCD dataset. The best performance is in boldface, and the second best performance is underlined.

Method	ATC [17]	AIC [1]	ABP_AA [19]	VFN [3]	A2RL [6]	AGDRN [8]	Ours
mIoU	0.580	0.470	0.650	<u>0.684</u>	0.663	0.659	**0.689**
mBDE	0.100	0.130	0.080	0.084	0.0892	**0.062**	<u>0.079</u>

Table 2. Quantitative comparison on HCD dataset. The best performance is in boldface, and the second best performance is underlined.

Method	ATC [17]	AIC [1]	ABP_AA [19]	VFN [3]	A2RL [6]	AGDRN [8]	Ours
mMIoU	0.720	0.640	0.810	<u>0.835</u>	0.820	**0.843**	<u>0.835</u>
mMBDE	0.063	0.075	0.057	0.044	-	**0.029**	<u>0.030</u>

based on the image patch in an attention box which is quit different form other ranking based methods. As far as I know, no other method is in the regression manner, hence we treat the AGDRN method as a baseline to show that our model can achieve even better performance with significant robustness. From another view, our method can be classified as saliency based method. So we also compare the performance of our model with some other saliency based methods. The results on FCD and HCD dataset are reported in Table 1 and Table 2 respectively. From the results, we can see that our model can achieve comparable

Fig. 6. The cropping results of our model. The annotated cropping boxes are in red, the predicted cropping boxes of our model are in green. (Color figure online)

or better performance compared with the prior MIMO cropping models. The dominance of landscape images in HCD may account for the relatively poor performance of our model on HCD dataset. The salient points of landscape images are sparse, which can not provide enough spatial information to our model. The cropping results of portraiture, landscape, still life images of our model are shown in Fig. 6. From which, we can see that our model can perform well under different situations.

5   Conclusion

In this paper, we argue that the coupling of image composition and aesthetics makes existing cropping methods sensitive to the composition irrelevant factors. We propose to filter the composition irrelevant factors by salient cluster that can provide rich spatial information. Context screening module and composition regression module are designed to encode the composition and predict the final cropping boxes. Experimental results demonstrate the robustness and the effectiveness of the proposed method. Which also shows that focusing on composition matters in automatic image cropping.

References

1. Chen, J., Bai, G., Liang, S., Li, Z.: Automatic image cropping: a computational complexity study. In: CVPR, pp. 507–515 (2016)
2. Chen, Y.L., Huang, T.W., Chang, K.H., Tsai, Y.C., Chen, H.T., Chen, B.Y.: Quantitative analysis of automatic image cropping algorithms: a dataset and comparative study. In: WACV, pp. 226–234. IEEE (2017)
3. Chen, Y.L., Klopp, J., Sun, M., Chien, S.Y., Ma, K.L.: Learning to compose with professional photographs on the web. In: MM, pp. 37–45 (2017)
4. Fang, C., Lin, Z., Mech, R., Shen, X.: Automatic image cropping using visual composition, boundary simplicity and content preservation models. In: MM, pp. 1105–1108 (2014)
5. Greco, L., La Cascia, M.: Saliency based aesthetic cut of digital images. In: Petrosino, A. (ed.) ICIAP 2013. LNCS, vol. 8157, pp. 151–160. Springer, Heidelberg (2013). https://doi.org/10.1007/978-3-642-41184-7_16
6. Li, D., Wu, H., Zhang, J., Huang, K.: A2-rl: aesthetics aware reinforcement learning for image cropping. In: CVPR, pp. 8193–8201 (2018)
7. Li, Y., Pirk, S., Su, H., Qi, C.R., Guibas, L.J.: Fpnn: field probing neural networks for 3d data. In: NIPS, pp. 307–315 (2016)
8. Lu, P., Zhang, H., Peng, X., Peng, X.: Aesthetic guided deep regression network for image cropping. Signal Processing: Image Communication, pp. 1–10 (2019)
9. Maturana, D., Scherer, S.: Voxnet: a 3d convolutional neural network for real-time object recognition. In: IROS, pp. 922–928. IEEE (2015)
10. Park, J., Lee, J.Y., Tai, Y.W., Kweon, I.S.: Modeling photo composition and its application to photo re-arrangement. In: ICIP, pp. 2741–2744. IEEE (2012)
11. Qi, C.R., Litany, O., He, K., Guibas, L.J.: Deep hough voting for 3d object detection in point clouds. In: ICCV, pp. 9277–9286 (2019)
12. Qi, C.R., Liu, W., Wu, C., Su, H., Guibas, L.J.: Frustum pointnets for 3d object detection from rgb-d data. In: CVPR, pp. 918–927 (2018)
13. Qi, C.R., Su, H., Mo, K., Guibas, L.J.: Pointnet: deep learning on point sets for 3d classification and segmentation. In: CVPR, pp. 652–660 (2017)
14. Qi, C.R., Su, H., Nießner, M., Dai, A., Yan, M., Guibas, L.J.: Volumetric and multi-view cnns for object classification on 3d data. In: CVPR, pp. 5648–5656 (2016)
15. Qi, C.R., Yi, L., Su, H., Guibas, L.J.: Pointnet++: deep hierarchical feature learning on point sets in a metric space. In: NIPS, pp. 5099–5108 (2017)
16. Santella, A., Agrawala, M., DeCarlo, D., Salesin, D., Cohen, M.: Gaze-based interaction for semi-automatic photo cropping. In: CHI, pp. 771–780 (2006)
17. Suh, B., Ling, H., Bederson, B.B., Jacobs, D.W.: Automatic thumbnail cropping and its effectiveness. In: UIST, pp. 95–104 (2003)
18. Wang, P.S., Liu, Y., Guo, Y.X., Sun, C.Y., Tong, X.: O-cnn: octree-based convolutional neural networks for 3d shape analysis. TOG 36(4), 1–11 (2017)
19. Wang, W., Shen, J.: Deep cropping via attention box prediction and aesthetics assessment. In: ICCV, pp. 2186–2194 (2017)

20. Wang, W., Shen, J., Ling, H.: A deep network solution for attention and aesthetics aware photo cropping. TPAMI **41**(7), 1531–1544 (2018)
21. Wei, Z., et al.: Good view hunting: Learning photo composition from dense view pairs. In: CVPR, pp. 5437–5446 (2018)
22. Wu, Z., et al.: 3d shapenets: a deep representation for volumetric shapes. In: CVPR, pp. 1912–1920 (2015)
23. Zeng, H., Li, L., Cao, Z., Zhang, L.: Grid anchor based image cropping: a new benchmark and an efficient model. arXiv preprint arXiv:1909.08989 (2019)

Robust Chinese License Plate Generation via Foreground Text and Background Separation

Yi-Fan Sun, Qi Liu, Song-Lu Chen, Fang Zhou$^{(\boxtimes)}$, and Xu-Cheng Yin

University of Science and Technology Beijing, Beijing, China
{yifansun,qiliu7}@xs.ustb.edu.cn, zhoufang@ies.ustb.edu.cn,
xuchengyin@ustb.edu.cn

Abstract. To solve data scarcity, generating Chinese license plates with Generative Adversarial Network becomes an efficient solution. However, many previous methods are proposed to directly generate the whole license plate image, which causes the mutual interference of the foreground text and background. This way, it may cause unclear character strokes and an unreal sense of the overall image. To solve these problems, we propose a robust Chinese license plate generation method by separating the foreground text and background of the license plate to eliminate mutual interference. The proposed method can generate any Chinese license plate image while maintaining the precise character stroke and background of the real license plate. Specifically, we substitute the foreground text of the real license plate with the target text. To provide supervision data for text substitution, we propose to synthesize them via foreground text and background separation. Firstly, we erase the text of the real license plate to obtain the corresponding background image. Secondly, we extract the foreground text of another real license plate and merge it with the background obtained above. Qualitative and quantitative experiments verify that the license plates generated by our method are more homogeneous with the real license plates. Besides, we enhance license plate recognition performance with the generated license plates, which validates the effectiveness of our proposed method. Moreover, we release a generated dataset (https://github.com/ICIG2021-187) with 1,000 license plates for each province, including all 31 provinces of the Chinese mainland.

Keywords: License plate generation · Generative adversarial network · License plate recognition

1 Introduction

As the license plate is the unique identification of a car, license plate recognition (LPR) is widely used in many applications, such as traffic control, parking charge, and criminal investigation. However, recent LPR approaches need massive data for training, and it is labor-intensive and costly to collect and annotate

© Springer Nature Switzerland AG 2021
Y. Peng et al. (Eds.): ICIG 2021, LNCS 12890, pp. 290–302, 2021.
https://doi.org/10.1007/978-3-030-87361-5_24

license plate images. Hence, generating license plates with Generative Adversarial Network (GAN) becomes an efficient solution for data augmentation.

Many GAN-based license plate generation methods [14–16,18] are proposed based on pix2pix [8] and CycleGAN [21], and these methods generate the whole license plate image directly. As shown in Fig. 1 (b)–(e), the character strokes of the generated license plates are unclear, especially the Chinese characters. Moreover, the foreground text and background are less distinct than the real license plates.

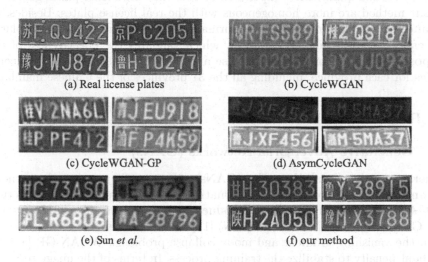

(a) Real license plates

(b) CycleWGAN

(c) CycleWGAN-GP

(d) AsymCycleGAN

(e) Sun *et al.*

(f) our method

Fig. 1. (a) Some examples of real license plates. Some examples generated by (b) CycleWGAN [15], (c) CycleWGAN-GP [16], (d) AsymCycleGAN [18], (e) Sun *et al.* [14], (f) our method.

These problems are mainly caused by the mutual interference of the foreground text and background, and the above GAN-based networks cannot generate both of them effectively. Specifically, background generation mainly focuses on texture features, such as background color, plate frame, space mark, rivets, and lighting factors. Meanwhile, the foreground text generation mainly focuses on the shape and stroke of the character. However, it is challenging for neural networks to generate them simultaneously. Hence, inspired by the modular approach [17], we propose to separate the foreground text and background of the license plate to eliminate mutual interference.

In this work, we propose a robust Chinese license plate generation method that can generate any Chinese license plate image while maintaining the precise character stroke and background of the real license plate. Specifically, we generate the license plate by substituting the foreground text of the real license plate with the target text, and the background texture is preserved appropriately. To provide supervision data for text substitution, we propose to synthesize them via foreground text and background separation. Firstly, we erase the text of the real license plate and fill this text region with appropriate background texture to obtain the corresponding background image. Secondly, we randomly select another license plate and extract its foreground text, then merge it with the background obtained above to obtain the merged license plate. The merged license plate and the real license plate with the same background are used as the input and output of the text substitution to supervise training. Compared with the existing license plate generation methods, our method can generate more clear and precise text stroke and a more real sense of the overall image. Qualitative and quantitative experiments prove that the license plates generated by our method are more homogeneous with the real license plates. Besides, we enhance license plate recognition performance with the generated license plates, especially for the Chinese characters, which validates the effectiveness of our proposed method. Moreover, we release a generated dataset with 1,000 license plates for each province, including all the 31 provinces of the Chinese mainland.

2 Related Work

2.1 Generative Adversarial Networks (GANs)

Generative Adversarial Networks (GANs) [3] generally consist of a generator and a discriminator, trained alternatively by an adversarial loss function. DCGAN [12] is the first work to introduce deep convolutional neural networks into GANs. Wasserstein GAN (WGAN) [1] presents Wasserstein distance loss to solve the vanishing gradient and mode collapse problems. WGAN-GP [4] adds gradient penalty to stabilize the training process. In terms of the image-to-image translation task, pix2pix [8] applies a conditional-GAN [11] to learn a mapping relationship from the input domain to the output domain but requires paired data. CycleGAN [21] designs a cycle consistency loss with unpaired training data to achieve cross-domain style transfer. However, these methods perform deficiently on text image generation due to the large variety of text shapes.

EnsNet [19] is an end-to-end GAN-based network to erase the scene text on the whole image, but it cannot deal with text image generation. Wu et al. [17] propose a style retention network to edit the text in natural images. However, the foreground text of the generated license plate is intertwined with background. To solve these problems, we separate the real license plate into the foreground text and background and finally fuse them.

2.2 License Plate Generation

With the development of GAN, using GAN for license plate generation is widely studied by researchers. Wang et al. [15] apply Wasserstein distance loss to CycleGAN [21] as CycleWGAN, which is the first work of using GAN-generated images for the license plate recognition task. Similarly, Wu et al. [16] present CycleWGAN-GP to improve license plate recognition performance. Huang et al. [7] conduct comparative experiments of GAN, WGAN, DCGAN, and CycleGAN on the license plate generation task and conclude that Cycle-GAN performs best. Sun *et al.* [14] employ a P-module for paired images and a U-module for unpaired images to solve the data imbalance problem. Zhang *et al.* [18] propose a robust framework for license plate recognition, in which a tailored CycleGAN model (called AsymCycleGAN) provides balanced data for plate recognition.

These methods are mainly based on CycleGAN [21], taking an entire image as the input. However, as shown in Fig. 1, these methods cannot generate precise character strokes, especially the Chinese characters, and the sense of the overall image is unreal. It is because foreground text and the background have different features, and they interfere with each other when trained together. Hence, we try to solve this problem by separating the foreground text and background of the license plate.

3 Methodology

We propose a Chinese license plate generation method to generate robust license plate images by separating the foreground text and background. As shown in Fig. 2, the overall architecture consists of background generation network, supervision synthesizing algorithm, and text substitution network.

3.1 Background Generation Network

The background generation network is a GAN-based network composed of a generator G and a discriminator D, which can obtain the corresponding background image of the real license plate. The generator G aims to generate an image, and the discriminator D judges whether the image is real. The input of the background generation network is a pair of images, i.e., the real license plate image x and its corresponding ground-truth background image z. The output is a generated license plate background image y. The above process is defined as a mathematical min-max problem, which can be regarded as optimization of the following formula. G and D are trained alternatively with the cross-entropy loss.

$$\min_{G} \max_{D} E_{x \sim p_{data(x)}, z}[\log(1 - D(x, G(x, z)))]$$
$$+ E_{x \sim p_{data(x,y)}, z}[\log D(x, y)] \tag{1}$$

The framework is an encoder-decoder based on Fully-Convolution-Network (FCN). The encoder uses a lightweight ResNet18 [6] network for feature extraction. The decoder is composed of five deconvolutional layers which expand the size of the feature map layer by layer to ensure that the generated license plate can be the same size as the input.

3.2 Supervision Synthesizing Algorithm

In this subsection, the supervision synthesizing algorithm can synthesize a set of supervision images for the text substitution network by the real license plate

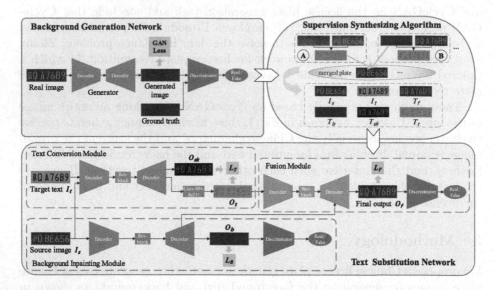

Fig. 2. Overall architecture. Firstly, the background generation network erases the text of the real license plate to obtain the background image. Secondly, the supervision synthesizing algorithm provides supervision data for the text substitution network. For example, it extracts the foreground text of the real license plate A and merges it with the background of another license plate B. The merged license plate I_s is the source image of the text substitution network, and the real license plate B is set as T_f to supervise the final output O_f. The target text I_t has the same text content with T_f. T_{sk} is the text skeleton of the real plate B. Finally, the text substitution network substitutes the foreground text of I_s with the target text I_t. T_{sk}, T_t, T_b, and T_f are the ground truth of O_{sk}, O_t, O_b, and O_f, respectively.

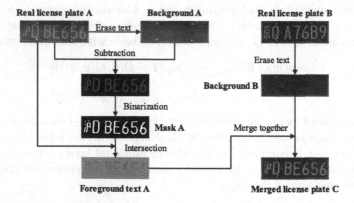

Fig. 3. The synthesizing process of the merged license plate. The merged license plate C is a synthetic image with the foreground text of real license plate A and the background of real license plate B.

image and its corresponding background image obtained before. The supervision images include the real license plate, background, foreground text, text skeleton, the standard format text, and the merged license plate.

The synthesizing process of the merged license plate is illustrated in Fig. 3. The background generation network outputs the background image of the input real license plate A. After subtraction and binarization, we get the mask image for extracting the foreground text. The foreground text A is obtained by the intersection of the real license plate A and its mask. Finally, the merged license plate C, a new image with the text of plate A and the background of plate B, is synthesized through conditional pixel-by-pixel traversal.

Correctly, we synthesize the supervision data via Algorithm 1. All the mathematical symbols are explained as follows, where I denotes input and T indicates target.

- I_s: the source image of the license plate;
- I_t: the target image with the target foreground text;
- T_f: the final output image;
- T_{sk}: the text skeleton of T_f;
- T_t: the foreground text of T_f with the grey background;
- T_b: the background of I_s and T_f;
- T_{mask}: the binary image of T_t.

T_f, T_{sk}, T_t, and T_b are the ground truth of O_f, O_{sk}, O_t, and O_b in Fig. 2, respectively.

Algorithm 1: Supervision Synthesizing Algorithm

Input: T_f, T_b;
Output: I_s, I_t, T_{sk}, T_t, T_b, T_f;

1 $T_{mask} = binarize(T_f - T_b)$;
2 $T_t = T_f \wedge T_{mask}$;
3 $T_{sk} = skeleton(T_{mask})$;
4 $I_t = drawIt(the\ text\ of\ T_f)$;
5 **for** $n = 1; n \leq 2000; n++$ **do**
6   **for** $m = 1; m \leq 15; m++$ **do**
7          $temp = randomly\ choose\ a\ T_t$;
8          $I_s^{nm} = T_b^n \vee temp$; // T_b^n is reused 15 times.
9   // Except for I_s^{nm}, others are copied 15 times.
10         $I_t^{nm} = I_t^n$;
11         $T_t^{nm} = T_t^n$;
12         $T_f^{nm} = T_f^n$;
13         $T_b^{nm} = T_b^n$;
14         $T_{sk}^{nm} = T_{sk}^n$;
15 **return** I_s^{nm}, I_t^{nm}, T_{sk}^{nm}, T_t^{nm}, T_b^{nm}, T_f^{nm};

From a real license plate T_f and its background T_b, the mask T_{mask} and the foreground text T_t are synthesized by the process illustrated in Fig. 3. The text skeleton T_{sk} is extracted from T_{mask} by image corrosion and expansion. The target text I_t is drawn by a standard format with the same text content as the real license plate T_f. After that, each real license plate T_f has its corresponding T_b, T_t, T_{sk}, and I_t. We randomly choose 15 different foreground texts T_t and respectively merge them with the same background T_b to synthesize 15 different I_s for each T_f. Except for I_s, others are copied 15 times. Hence, we can expand 2,000 pairs of real license plates and their background images to 30,000 sets of supervision data that the text substitution network requires.

3.3   Text Substitution Network

The text substitution network consists of three modules: text conversion module, background inpainting module, and fusion module.

Text Conversion Module. The text conversion module aims to generate the foreground text image by substituting the text content of the source license plate with the target text while keeping the original text style. This module is an encoder-decoder FCN, including three down-sampling convolutional layers, four residual blocks [6], three deconvolutional layers, and a Conv-BN-ReLU block. The text conversion loss is the combination of L1 loss and skeleton loss [10]. The target text skeleton T_{sk} is used to obtain more precise skeleton and stroke of the foreground text.

$$L_T = \|T_t - G_T(I_t, I_s)\|_1 + \alpha(1 - \frac{2\sum\limits_i^N (T_{sk})_i (O_{sk})_i}{\sum\limits_i^N (T_{sk})_i + \sum\limits_i^N (O_{sk})_i}), \qquad (2)$$

where G_T denotes the text conversion module. O_{sk} is the output text skeleton image. α is the regularization parameter, which is set to 1.0 by default.

Background Inpainting Module. The background inpainting module erases the text and fills the text region with appropriate texture. This module is similar to the text conversion module, but the decoder is composed of three up-sampling transposed convolutional layers. A generator G_B and a discriminator D_B are trained alternatively with adversarial loss and L1 loss, where β is set to 10.

$$
\begin{aligned}
L_B = \; & E_{(T_b, I_s)}[\log D_B(T_b, I_s)] + E_{I_s} \log[1 - D_B(G_B(I_s), I_s)] \\
& + \beta \|T_b - G_B(I_s)\|_1
\end{aligned}
\qquad (3)
$$

Fusion Module. The fusion module fuses the substituted foreground text with the background and generates a new license plate. It includes a generator G_F, a discriminator D_F, and an encoder-decoder FCN. The fusion loss function is the sum of adversarial loss and L1 loss.

$$L_F = E_{(T_f, I_t)}[\log D_F(T_f, I_t)] + E_{I_t} \log[1 - D_F(O_f, I_t)] + \theta \|T_f - O_f\|_1, \qquad (4)$$

$$O_f = G_F(G_T(I_t, I_s), G_B(I_s)), \tag{5}$$

where O_f is the output final image, $\theta = 10$.

4 Experiments

4.1 Datasets

Synthetic Dataset is synthesized by SynthText [5], containing 50,000 synthetic license plate images. The main idea is to select fonts, color, parameters of deformation randomly to generate styled text, then render it on the background image.

Yizhi2000 is a private license plate dataset containing 2,000 license plate images of good quality cropped from driving recorder images. They are resized to 150 × 48. The distribution of license plate data is unbalanced(the number of license plates in each province is extremely uneven). Besides, there are no data for some provinces, such as Qinghai, Tibet.

SUSY [20] is a public license plate dataset that contains all the 31 provinces in the Chinese mainland but without annotating the license plates. We extract the license plates with a YOLOv3 [13]. There are about 70 license plate images for each province.

GLPD is a generated license plate dataset we have released publicly, containing 1,000 license plates for each province, including all the 31 provinces of the Chinese mainland. To generate license plate images more effectively, we add SUSY to train the text substitution network to solve the data scarcity of some provinces.

4.2 Implementation Details

In our experiments, Adam [9] optimizer is adopted to train the model. We use the Synthetic Dataset to pretrain the background generation network, text substitution network, and license plate recognition network. We select 100 license plates from Yizhi2000 and erase the foreground text manually to finetune the background generation network. The initial learning rate is 5×10^{-4}, and the maximum iteration is 1,000. Afterward, we test the background generation network with Yizhi2000 and synthesize supervision data for the text substitution network. The input images of the text substitution network are resized to 300 × 96, and the batch size is set to 8. The learning rate is initially set to 1×10^{-4}, and the maximum iteration is 50,000. For the license plate recognition experiments in Sect. 4.5, we use SUSY to test the accuracy of different recognition models.

4.3 Evaluation Metrics

In this work, we use recognition accuracy (RA) and character recognition accuracy (CRA) to evaluate the effectiveness of generated data on the performance of the text recognition model [2]. Same with CycleWGAN [15], RA and CRA can be calculated as follows.

$$RA = \frac{Number\ of\ correctly\ recognized\ license\ plates}{Number\ of\ all\ license\ plates} \tag{6}$$

$$CRA = \frac{Number\ of\ correctly\ recognized\ characters}{Number\ of\ all\ characters} \tag{7}$$

Similar to RA and CRA, CRA-C is the recognition accuracy of the first character, namely the Chinese character, and CRA-NC is the character recognition accuracy of the last six characters, i.e., the letters and numbers. Besides, we also adopt other commonly used metrics to evaluate the image quality of the generated license plates.

- Fréchet Inception Distance (FID), which measures the distance between the distributions of synthesized images and real images;
- MSE, also known as l2 error;
- PSNR, which computes the ratio of peak signal to noise;
- SSIM, which computes the mean structural similarity index between two images.

A lower FID and MSE or higher SSIM and PSNR mean the generated images are more similar to ground truth.

4.4 Qualitative Experiments

As shown in Fig. 1, we compare some generated examples of the existing methods designed for license plate generation with our method visually. CycleWGAN [15], CylceWGAN-GP [16], and AsymCylceGAN [18] generate mottled background, ghosted, and blurred strokes. The images of Sun *et al.* [14] are better than the first three methods, but the texts are still unclear and hazy. Moreover, there is a big gap between the images generated by the four methods and the real license plate images on the real sense of overall image. The results indicate that the license plate images generated by our method have the best visual effect, and it is hard to distinguish them from the real license plate images.

Moreover, we reproduce pix2pix [8], CycleGAN [21], and SRNet [17] using the same dataset and training settings as our method. Figure 4 shows some examples generated by these methods with the same target text. Pix2pix can only generate some twisty numbers, and the foreground text and background are intertwined. CycleGAN performs better on letters and numbers but fails on the Chinese characters. Both pix2pix and CycleGAN have the mode collapse problem. These phenomena suggest that generating the whole license plate images can cause the mutual interference of the foreground text and background. The strokes of texts generated by SRNet are also blurred, and it cannot generate the Chinese characters with complex stroke skeleton. Finally, our methods can achieve better visual performance on the precise text strokes, background texture, and overall coordination and realism. Even for complex Chinese characters, such as the abbreviations of Jiangxi and Hubei, our method can generate precise strokes and skeletons. This experiment verifies that the license plates generated by our method are more homogeneous with the real license plates.

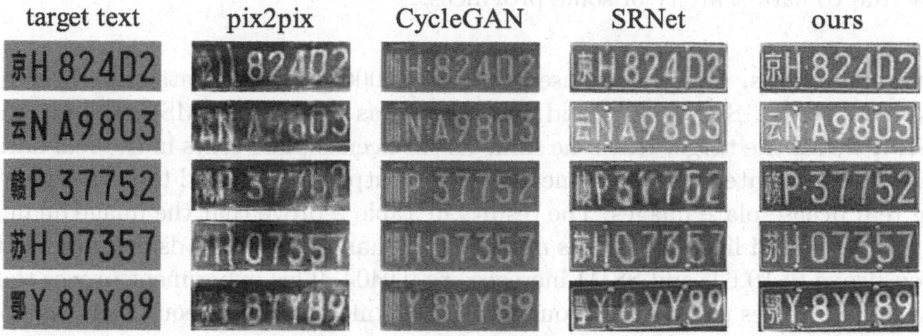

Fig. 4. Visual comparison of our method with pix2pix [8], CycleGAN [21], and SRNet [17]. The provinces of the five license plates are Beijing, Yunnan, Jiangxi, Jiangsu, Hubei (up to down).

4.5   Quantitative Experiments

Recognition Accuracy. We apply a text recognition model [2] to compare the effectiveness of different data generation methods for the LPR task. The total number of training sets is 30000 for all methods. Pix2pix, CycleGAN, SRNet, and ours are based on the same target texts. From Table 1, we can find that pretraining only makes the recognition model learn some letters and numbers. Pix2pix and CycleGAN are lower than traditional data augmentation methods on all four metrics because the generated images are much different from the real license plate images. Besides, CycleGAN cannot learn Chinese characters. SRNet also performs inadequately due to the gap between synthetic data and real data. Finally, even with a slight drop of CRA-NC, our method achieves

Table 1. The accuracy (%) of the text recognition model trained by different dataset. "pretrain" means training by the same synthetic dataset as GANs. "augmentation" means augmenting images with random crop, Gauss noise, etc.

Methods	RA	CAR	CRA-C	CRA-NC
Pretrain	6.4	73.1	22.8	79.3
Real data + augmentation	76.2	96.5	77.0	**99.8**
pix2pix [8]	55.9	93.0	60.7	98.1
CycleGAN [21]	6.4	74.0	17.3	81.1
SRNet [17]	58.5	93.4	66.2	97.8
Ours	**84.4**	**97.6**	**89.2**	98.9

the best RA, CRA, and CRA-C, especially for the CRA-C, which proves our method can significantly improve Chinese character recognition. In conclusion, this experiment validates the effectiveness of our proposed method to enhance license plate recognition performance. The four types of accuracy are generally low due to data scarcity of some provinces.

Other Metrics. For FID, we use the same 30,000 generated data of pix2pix [8], CycleGAN [21], SRNet [17], and our method as before. For MSE, PSNR, and SSIM, we set the target texts the same as the license plate texts in the real data, and then calculate these three metrics of the output images and the corresponding real license plate images. The results in Table 2 prove that the image quality of our generated license plates is much better than other methods. Notably, FID even drops to 10.64, and SSIM increases to 0.9404. This experiment proves that the license plates generated by our method are more homogeneous with the real license plates.

Table 2. Quantitative evaluation results on FID, MSE, PSNR, and SSIM.

Methods	FID	MSE	PSNR	SSIM
pix2pix [8]	192.43	0.5055	12.94	0.2238
CycleGAN [21]	110.43	0.3834	14.40	0.2566
SRNet [17]	48.13	0.1109	20.17	0.6221
Ours	**10.64**	**0.0222**	**27.77**	**0.9404**

5   Conclusion

In this work, we propose a robust Chinese license plate generation method by separating the foreground text and background of license plate images, improving the image quality of generated license plates. Our method can generate license plate images with the precise stroke and a real sense of the overall image. Besides, experiments on license plate recognition prove the effectiveness of our method for increasing LPR accuracy. Moreover, we release a generated license plate dataset with 1,000 images for each province, including all 31 provinces of the Chinese mainland.

In the future, we will try to solve inferior performance in some provinces due to data scarcity and explore to generate more diverse license plate data.

References

1. Arjovsky, M., Chintala, S., Bottou, L.: Wasserstein generative adversarial networks. In: Proceedings of the 34th International Conference on Machine Learning (ICML), vol. 70, pp. 214–223. PMLR, Sydney, NSW, Australia (2017)

2. Baek, J., et al.: What is wrong with scene text recognition model comparisons? dataset and model analysis. In: Proceedings of the International Conference on Computer Vision (ICCV), pp. 4715–4723. IEEE, Seoul, Korea (South) (2019)
3. Goodfellow, I.J., et al.: Generative adversarial networks. CoRR abs/1406.2661 (2014)
4. Gulrajani, I., Ahmed, F., Arjovsky, M., Dumoulin, V., Courville, A.: Improved training of wasserstein gans. In: Advances in Neural Information Processing Systems 30: Annual Conference on Neural Information Processing Systems, pp. 5767–5777. Long Beach, CA, USA (2017)
5. Gupta, A., Vedaldi, A., Zisserman, A.: Synthetic data for text localisation in natural images. In: Proceedings of the Conference on Computer Vision and Pattern Recognition (CVPR), pp. 2315–2324. IEEE, Las Vegas, NV, USA (2016)
6. He, K., Zhang, X., Ren, S., Sun, J.: Deep residual learning for image recognition. In: Proceedings of the Conference on Computer Vision and Pattern Recognition (CVPR), pp. 770–778. IEEE, Las Vegas, NV, USA (2016)
7. Huang, J., et al.: Research on vehicle license plate data generation in complex environment based on generative adversarial network. In: 11th International Conference on Digital Image Processing (ICDIP), vol. 11179, p. 1117932. International Society for Optics and Photonics (2019)
8. Isola, P., Zhu, J.Y., Zhou, T., Efros, A.A.: Image-to-image translation with conditional adversarial networks. In: Proceedings of the Conference on Computer Vision and Pattern Recognition (CVPR), pp. 1125–1134. IEEE, Honolulu, HI, USA (2017)
9. Kingma, D.P., Ba, J.: Adam: A method for stochastic optimization. In: 3rd International Conference on Learning Representations (ICLR), San Diego, CA, USA (2015)
10. Milletari, F., Navab, N., Ahmadi, S., V-net: Fully convolutional neural networks for volumetric medical image segmentation. In: 4th International Conference on 3D Vision (3DV), pp. 565–571. IEEE, Stanford, CA, USA (2016)
11. Mirza, M., Osindero, S.: Conditional generative adversarial nets. CoRR abs/1411.1784 (2014)
12. Radford, A., Metz, L., Chintala, S.: Unsupervised representation learning with deep convolutional generative adversarial networks. In: 4th International Conference on Learning Representations (ICLR), San Juan, Puerto Rico (2016)
13. Redmon, J., Farhadi, A.: Yolov3: An incremental improvement. CoRR abs/1804.02767 (2018)
14. Sun, M., Zhou, F., Yang, C., Yin, X.: Image generation framework for unbalanced license plate data set. In: Neural Information Processing - 26th International Conference (ICONIP), vol. 1143, pp. 127–134. Springer, Sydney, NSW, Australia (2019)
15. Wang, X., You, M., Shen, C.: Adversarial generation of training examples for vehicle license plate recognition. CoRR abs/1707.03124 (2017)
16. Wu, C., Xu, S., Song, G., Zhang, S.: How many labeled license plates are needed? In: Lai, J.-H., Liu, C.-L., Chen, X., Zhou, J., Tan, T., Zheng, N., Zha, H. (eds.) PRCV 2018. LNCS, vol. 11259, pp. 334–346. Springer, Cham (2018). https://doi.org/10.1007/978-3-030-03341-5_28
17. Wu, L., Zhang, C., Liu, J., Han, J., Liu, J., Ding, E., Bai, X.: Editing text in the wild. In: Proceedings of the 27th ACM International Conference on Multimedia, pp. 1500–1508. ACM, Nice, France (2019)
18. Zhang, L., Wang, P., Li, H., Li, Z., Shen, C., Zhang, Y.: A robust attentional framework for license plate recognition in the wild. CoRR abs/2006.03919 (2020)

19. Zhang, S., Liu, Y., Jin, L., Huang, Y., Lai, S.: Ensnet: ensconce text in the wild. In: Proceedings of the AAAI Conference on Artificial Intelligence, vol. 33, pp. 801–808. AAAI, Honolulu, Hawaii, USA (2019)
20. Zhao, Y., Yu, Z., Li, X., Cai, M.: Chinese license plate image database building methodology for license plate recognition. J. Electron. Imaging **28**(1), 013001 (2019)
21. Zhu, J.Y., Park, T., Isola, P., Efros, A.A.: Unpaired image-to-image translation using cycle-consistent adversarial networks. In: International Conference on Computer Vision (ICCV), pp. 2242–2251. IEEE, Venice, Italy (2017)

Towards Boosting Channel Attention for Real Image Denoising: Sub-band Pyramid Attention

Huayu Li[1], Haiyu Wu[2], Xiwen Chen[1], Hao Wang[1],
and Abolfazl Razi[1]([envelope])

[1] Northern Arizona University, Flagstaff, AZ 86011, USA
{hl459,xc53,hw328,Abolfazl.Razi}@nau.edu
[2] University of Notre Dame, Notre Dame, IN 46556, USA
hwu6@nd.edu

Abstract. Convolutional layers treat the Channel features equally with no prioritization. When Convolutional Neural Networks (CNNs) are used for image denoising in real-world applications with unknown noise distributions, particularly structured noise with learnable patterns, modeling informative features can substantially boost the denoising performance. Channel attentions in real-world image denoising tasks exploit dependencies between the feature channels; therefore, they can be viewed as a frequency-domain filtering mechanism. Existing channel attention modules typically use global statics as descriptors to learn inter-channel correlations. These methods deem inefficient in learning representative coefficients for re-scaling the channels at frequency level. This paper proposes a novel Sub-band Pyramid Attention (SPA) model based on wavelet transform to recalibrate the extracted features' frequency components in a more fine-grained fashion. Our method, in one sense, integrates the conventional frequency-domain filtering methods with deep learning architectures to achieve higher performance records. Experimental results show that ANNs equipped with the proposed attention module substantially improves upon the benchmark naive channel attention blocks. More specifically, we obtained a 3.97 dB gain compared to the best traditional algorithm, BM3D and a 1.87 dB to 0.18 dB gain over the DL-based methods in terms of denoising performance. Furthermore, our results show how the pyramid level affects the performance of the SPA blocks and exhibits favorable generalization capability for the SPA blocks.

Keywords: Deep learning · Attention model · Image denoising

This material is based upon work supported by the National Science Foundation under Grant 2008784.

H. Li and H. Wu—These authors contributed equally to this work.

Y. Peng et al. (Eds.): ICIG 2021, LNCS 12890, pp. 303–314, 2021.
https://doi.org/10.1007/978-3-030-87361-5_25

1 Introduction

Convolutional Neural Networks (CNN) have shown a remarkable performance in image denoising tasks compared to conventional filtering methods [4,22,32,33]. Mathematically, image denoising methods intend to recover a clean and high-quality target y from a corrupted low-quality observation x by eliminating noise, imaging artifacts, distortions, etc. In general, the overall impact of these undesired terms is modeled as a zero-mean Additive White Gaussian Noise (AWGN) with an arbitrary variance. Using the Gaussian noise model provides computational convenience. This model is backed by the central limit theorem that states that the normalized sum of independent and arbitrarily distributed random terms approach a normal distribution. Although appropriate for general and pure random noise modeling, the AWGN model is oversimplified for situations where the structured noise exhibits hidden patterns. For instance, image distortions due to cameras' loss of focus, lens scratch, dusty lens, camera shake, low illumination, and raindrops exhibit learnable patterns substantially different than a random noise [8].

Previous CNN-based methods [32–34] outperform the traditional methods [10,13] for image denoising due to the learning capacity of CNNs. However, they are mainly designed to deal with synthetic noise instead of real-world noise with more complicated and diverse compositions. Therefore, their performance might be suboptimal in real-world denoising tasks. Recently, new noise models [4,7,31,36] and new benchmark denoising methods [1,26] are proposed to tackle more realistic noise models. One popular way is using attention mechanisms to manage and quantify the interdependence between the extract feature maps. For instance, in RIDNet [4], a channel attention block [18] called feature attention was used for feature selection, which allows the network to focus on the feature channels of interest. Although feature attention methods obtain superior performance in real-world image denoising tasks, generating coarse feature descriptors based on the global pooling of the entire feature map is not optimal.

From the traditional image processing perspective, a natural image is composed of different frequency components, with high-frequency components representing the fine details and low-frequency components representing the global structure of the image; therefore, denoising is usually performed by smoothing and low-pass filtering. We re-think the DL-based denoising paradigm by leveraging traditional denoising concepts. Channel attention mechanisms can be regarded as an adaptive filter that suppresses the abundant frequency feature channels [35]. In most channel attention models, the feature maps' coarse statistics are generated by Global Average Pooling (GAP). Second-order channel attention was proposed in [14] for enriching the representation ability of the channel attention blocks. Nevertheless, these types of channel attention models are not flexible enough to deal with various frequency levels. In [5], Laplacian attention is proposed to integrate traditional methods and deep learning, adopting multiple convolutional layers with different receptive fields to model the frequency components of the input features. Despite the improvements obtained by this and similar methods, the following question remains open: Is there a better way of obtaining a representation for the frequency characteristics of the input image?

In this paper, a CNN architecture with an efficient and plug-and-play Sub-band Pyramid Attention (SPA) is proposed as an alternative approach for the existing channel attention models (Fig. 1). Based on the wavelet decomposition, the SPA module performs a more fine-grained frequency selection that weighs the sub-bands at different levels. The SPA module exhibits a restoration performance while preserving the detailed textures with a negligible increase in computational complexity. Experimental results on real image denoising confirm the superiority of the proposed method. We also review how the utilized pyramid level affects the denoising performance and the generalization capability of the SPA blocks. The proposed SPA method with a proven superior performance can replace the existing attention mechanisms and is readily applicable to DL networks with arbitrary structures. Our study reminds the fact that leveraging fundamental knowledge in image processing can improve DL methods' performance.

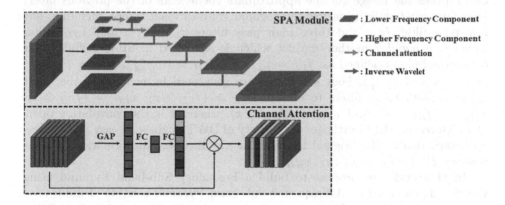

Fig. 1. The sub-band pyramid attention for frequency components selection.

2   Camera Noise vs Additive White Gaussian Noise

Most image denoising methods, such as [22,32,33] were trained based on image pairs $\{x_i, y_i\}_{i=1}^N$, where x_is are clean images easily available in large quantities, and $y_i = x_i + n$ are the artificial corrupted images by adding AWGN noise n with different standard deviations σ. While training a specific model for a certain noise level, the standard deviation σ for generating training and testing data is set to constant values $e.g.$, $\sigma = 15, 25, \ldots, 50$. For blind denoising, the models are trained under random noise levels and tested with unknown noise levels.

During camera imaging, a digital image goes through the sequential steps of photon-voltage conversion, analog amplification, and analog-to-digital conversion [19]. During these stages, multiple noise sources, including shot noise (photon noise, Gamma noise), read-out noise, and thermal noise, are involved [9].

We can roughly define the real noise model as a Poisson-Gaussian noise models [15, 19, 21] as $y = kP(\frac{x}{k}) + N(0, \sigma^2)$, where x and y are clean and noisy image pairs, k and σ are factors related to camera settings, and $P(\cdot)$ and $N(\cdot)$, respectively, denote the Poisson and Gaussian distributions. Unlike AWGN, real noise and image components are not independent that significantly limits the denoising performance. In addition to these noise terms, several other factors such as lens dirt and scratch, low light conditions, and natural air pollution can further distort the image.

3 Method

3.1 Frequency Sub-band Pyramid

The 2-D Discrete Wavelet Transform (DWT) is a powerful tool for analyzing image structures in spatial and frequency domains. At each layer, DWT decomposes the image (or the approximate coefficients of the previous layer) into four sub-bands using four orthogonal convolutional filters, including one low pass filter f_{LL}, and three high pass filters f_{LH}, f_{HL}, and f_{HH}. Haar wavelet, a popular mother wavelet which is also used in SPA, includes four orthogonal filters defined as: $f_{LL} = \begin{bmatrix} +1 & +1 \\ +1 & +1 \end{bmatrix}$, $f_{LH} = \begin{bmatrix} -1 & -1 \\ +1 & +1 \end{bmatrix}$, $f_{HL} = \begin{bmatrix} -1 & +1 \\ -1 & +1 \end{bmatrix}$, and $f_{HH} = \begin{bmatrix} +1 & -1 \\ -1 & +1 \end{bmatrix}$. Four sub-bands are generated by convolving the input image x with these filters to obtain: $x_{LL} = (f_{LL} \otimes x)$, $x_{LH} = (f_{LH} \otimes x)$, $x_{HL} = (f_{HL} \otimes x)$, and $x_{HH} = (f_{HH} \otimes x)$, where $\otimes$ is the convolution operator. Moreover, the bi-orthogonal property of DWT enables an easy and lossless reconstruction of the original image using the inverse transformation of Haar wavelet $IWT(x_{LL}, x_{LH}, x_{HL}, x_{HH})$.

In this work, we propose to build a Frequency Sub-band Pyramid using wavelet decomposition. A Frequency Sub-band Pyramid consists of multi-level frequency components of an image or its feature maps. Given an input x_0, DWT decomposes it into a set of detail coefficients $X_{1H} = [x_{1HH}, x_{1HL}, x_{1LH}]$ and approximate coefficients x_{1LL}. After further decomposition using multi-level DWT for n iterations, one low frequency component x_{nL} and n sets of high frequency components $X_{1H}, \ldots, X_{nH}$ are obtained. Stacking these components from the first to the last level forms a sub-band pyramid that represents the low-to-high frequency properties of the features to be modeled.

3.2 Sub-band Pyramid Attention

A channel attention [18] module is typically formulated as:

$$x^{'} = x * \sigma(f_2(ReLU(f_1(G_x)))) \tag{1}$$

for a 3D input $x \in C \times H \times W$, and a global descriptor $G_x \in C \times 1 \times 1$, which represents the statistics of each input map generated by the GAP. The functions f_1 and f_2 refer to two fully-connected layers activated by the Rectified Linear

Units $(ReLU)$ [24] and sigmoid function (σ). The channel attention module captures the channel dependencies from the global descriptor of the entire input, which is too coarse and may lead to information loss. The proposed SPA module exploits a more fine-grained channel-wise correlation with a new strategy of selective amplification of different spectral layers. Overall, the decomposition results $[x_nL, x_nH, \ldots, x_2H, x_1H]$ of an input x obtained by the Frequency Sub-band Pyramid are re-calibrated by the channel attention from lower to higher frequency levels as shown in Fig. 1. After being processed by the channel attention module, each lower frequency component is concatenated with its corresponding higher frequency component. The Inverse Wavelet Transform (IWT) is used to build the lower-frequency components layer by layer, starting from the top layer to the base layer until the entire feature map with the original size (i.e., the size of the input image) is reconstructed. The SPA module performs a more precise frequency selection mechanism than the naive channel attention approach by this operation. The SPA explicitly calibrates the dependencies between the feature channels while selecting the desired frequency component inside each feature map.

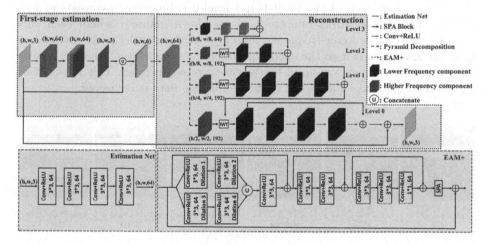

Fig. 2. The illustration of the entire network architecture: the network is divided into noise estimation and reconstruction stages. The noise estimation model is built by a plain CNN with SPA blocks. The reconstruction network is based on the sub-band pyramid, using a modified version of EAM [4], where we replaced the naive channel attention with SPA modules, and called it EAM+.

3.3 Network Architecture Overview

The network used in this work comprises two stages where the first stage performs the noise estimation, and the second stage performs the reconstruction, as shown in Fig. 2. For a noisy input $x \in C, H, W$, the first-stage F_e can be regarded as a pixel-wise noise level estimation $x' = F_e(x)$, where $x' \in C, H, W$ is the estimation of the noisy map of the input channels. The first-stage estimation includes four 64-channel convolutional layers followed by a ReLU activation, a SPA block, and a 3-channel convolutional layer. The filter size is 3×3 for each convolutional layer in the first-stage estimation. The SPA block is considered a frequency estimator to selectively suppress the redundant information from the extracted features. The estimation results are stacked with the input along the channels as $[x, x']$ and are fed to the second stage.

Similar to the SPA block, the reconstruction stage is also designed based on the wavelet pyramid. This network consists of two convolutional layers (the first and last layers) and four sub-networks. The first convolutional layer extracts shallow features from the input image and the estimated noisy map. A 3-levels wavelet pyramid of the feature is constructed. The level-3 to level-1 sub-networks process the low-pass sub-bands $x_{3LL}, x_{2LL}, x_{1LL}$, and the level-0 sub-networks processes the basis features x_{0LL}. The sub-networks are built based on the Enhancement Attention Modules (EAM) proposed in RIDNet [4]. We replace the channel attention blocks in EAM with the proposed SPA blocks and name the modules EAM+. Each of the level-3 and level-2 sub-networks consists of two EAM+, and each of the level-1 and level-0 sub-networks consists of four EAM+. The sub-networks operate in a top-down manner, where each sub-network receives the lower-frequency map x_{iLL} of the wavelet's current layer as its input and extends it to the entire map of this current layer, which is equivalent to the low-frequency map of the wavelet's previous layer. This information is passed to the next subnetwork until the full-size map is recovered.

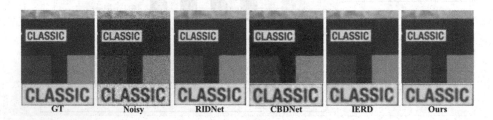

Fig. 3. A challenging example from SIDD dataset [1]. Our model exhibits a better color and edge preservation property.

4   Experiments

4.1   Experimental Setup

We use the Smartphone Image Denoising Dataset (SIDD) [1] and Darmstadt Noise Dataset (DnD) [26] for image denoising. The SIDD dataset provides 320 clean and noisy image pairs for training along with 1280 image pairs for validation. DnD dataset contains 50 pairs of real-world noisy and noise-free scenes. It provides bounding boxes of size 512 × 512 of 1000 Regions of Interests (ROIs) for 50 scenes for generating testing data. Our model was implemented by the Pytorch Framework [25] and trained with a Tesla P40 GPU. We equipped the network with level-3 SPA blocks. The hyper-parameters of the network are defined in Fig. 2. We used 512 × 512 patches cropped from the SIDD [1] training set to train our model and used the DnD [26] and validation set of the SIDD dataset to evaluate the reconstruction performance. Data augmentation by applying random rotations at 90, 180, and 270° and horizontal flipping was used in the training phase. Peak Signal-to-Noise Ratio (PSNR) is used as the evaluation metric, while Mean Absolute Error (MAE) is used as the loss function. The model is trained by the Adam optimizer [20] with an initial learning rate of $1e-4$. We trained the model at $2.5e5$ iterations and halved the learning rate for each of the $1e5$ iterations.

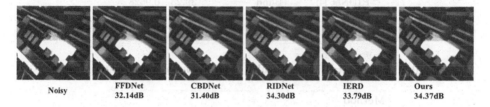

Fig. 4. Comparison of our method against some popular image denoising methods on DnD dataset.

4.2   Real Image Denoising

Table 2 represents the performances of the proposed method in terms of image denoising and reconstruction in comparison with several benchmark methods applied to the SIDD validation set. It can be seen that our method obtains remarkable results and outperforms the most commonly used DL-based denoising algorithms. Figure 3 presents an illustrative example, which shows that our method holds a competitive color and edge preservation property. Also, the results for the DnD dataset are summarized in Table 1. We compare the PSNR and SSIM [28] through the online evaluation system provided by the DnD [26] official website. The results show that the proposed method achieves a 3.97 dB gain compared to the best traditional algorithm, BM3D [13], while realizing a 1.87 to 0.18 dB gain over the DL-based methods [4,6,17,34]. Figure 4 shows the proposed method in restoring a noise-free image without over smoothing the details.

Table 1. PSNR and SSIM of the denoising methods evaluated on DnD [26] dataset.

Method	Blind/non-blind	PSNR	SSIM
CDnCNN-B [32]	Blind	32.43	0.7900
TNRD [12]	Non-blind	33.65	0.8306
LP [11]	Non-blind	34.23	0.8331
FFDNet [34]	Non-blind	34.40	0.8474
BM3D [13]	Non-blind	34.51	0.8507
WNNM [16]	Non-blind	34.67	0.8646
KSVD [3]	Non-blind	36.49	0.8978
MCWNNM [30]	Non-blind	37.38	0.9294
FFDNet+ [34]	Non-blind	37.61	0.9415
TWSC [29]	Non-blind	37.96	0.9416
CBDNet [17]	Blind	38.06	0.9421
RIDNet [4]	Blind	39.25	0.9528
IERD [6]	Blind	39.30	0.9531
Ours	Blind	**39.48**	**0.9580**

Table 2. The quantitative results (PSNR) for the SIDD dataset [1].

Method					
BM3D	FFDNet	CBDNet	RIDNet	IERD	Ours
30.88	29.20	30.78	38.71	38.82	**39.55**

4.3 Ablation Study

The major contribution of this work is proposing a novel implementation of the SPA attention module based on weighting wavelet layers. Although previous SPA-based attention mechanisms have already experienced remarkable performance, our approach offers a new perspective to this problem and answers new questions of "how does the pyramid level influence the denoising performance of the SPA blocks" and "if the SPA blocks can boost the performance of other networks with arbitrary architectures". Our results prove the superiority of the proposed SPA block compared to the naive channel attention block. At the same time, it also justifies the effect of different levels of SPA blocks. We also conducted an ablation study on the proposed network architecture. We test PSNR on the SIDD validation set for levels-0 to level-4. Notably, we define the naive channel attention as a level-0 pyramid (which means no pyramid). The second row of Table 3 shows that the higher pyramid level of the SPA blocks leads to a high PSNR and a better denoising performance. For evaluating the generalization of the SPA blocks, we conducted another ablation study by deploying SPA blocks at different levels in the RIDNet network as an alternative for its channel attention blocks. The third row of Table 3 shows the results of RIDNet when equipped with SPA blocks of different pyramid levels. The results show that the

SPA blocks generalize well in RIDNet while expecting to confirm that pyramids with more layers lead to better results.

Table 3. Investigation of effects of the pyramid level of SPA block and generalization on RIDNet.

Networks	Level	0	1	2	3	4
Ours	PSNR	39.24	39.33	39.47	39.55	39.57
RIDNet	PSNR	38.71	38.87	38.99	39.04	39.05

The proposed SPA attention is also generalized on the most commonly used AWGN model instead of only specific for real-world noise models. To investigate the AWGN noise, we use images with synthetic noise. We trained the blind denoising RIDNet and our network equipped with levels-0 to level-4 SPA attention on BSD500 [23] dataset with random AWGN (where the deviation σ varies between 5 to 55). The trained models were evaluated on BSD68 [27] dataset with noise level 15, 25, and 50. Table 4 compared the performance of each model. It consistently proves the generalizability.

Table 4. Comparisons on AWGN image denoising.

Noise levels	Method (RIDNet/Ours)			
	Level 1	Level 2	Level 3	Level 4
15	34.01/34.12	34.11/34.25	34.22/34.37	34.22/34.38
25	31.37/31.44	31.49/31.55	31.55/31.65	31.56/31.66
50	28.14/28.23	28.22/28.30	28.31/28.42	28.32/28.42

To further evaluate the performance of the proposed method, denoising is performed for Poisson-Gaussian noise model, which is defined as $y = P(x) + N(0, \sigma^2)$. This model includes Poisson-distribution $P(x)$ related to the clean image x, and followed by a Gaussian-distribution $N(0, \sigma^2)$. Here, we set the standard deviation σ to 15. We trained our network equipped with levels-0 to level-4 SPA attention on DIV2K [2] training set, and test them on DIV2K validation set. Table 5 presents the results of each level. The results show that the proposed SPA works better than naive channel attention (Level 0), and the performance gain still followed the obey the rules we observed in the previous experiments, that higher level pyramid brings more improvement.

Table 5. Comparisons on Poisson-Gaussian noise denoising.

Pyramid level	w/o CA	0	1	2	3	4
PSNR	31.11	31.52	32.21	32.57	33.04	33.06

Table 6. Comparisons on GPU runtime (seconds) and Model size (MB).

Level		w/o CA	0	1	2	3	4
Model size/GPU runtime	RIDNet	5.71/0.16	5.72/0.19	5.73/0.22	5.74/0.23	5.74/0.25	5.75/0.27
	Ours	17.11/0.22	17.13/0.24	17.16/0.29	17.18/0.32	17.21/0.35	17.23/0.41

4.4 Computational Overhead

As mentioned before, the SPA blocks improves the denoising performance while not adding considerable computational overhead. In this section, we compared the model sizes[1] when deployed different-level SPA blocks on both RIDNet and our network. It can be seen in Table 6 that the SPA blocks would not significantly increase the model size. Moreover, comparisons on average GPU runtime were conducted to show the proposed SPA module achieve a good trade-off between the calculation and performance. We fed images with a size of 512×512 for runtime evaluation. We tested each model 100 times and calculated the average runtime.

5 Conclusion

A novel channel attention module called Sub-band Pyramid Attention (SPA) is proposed in this work. The SPA blocks are built upon wavelet decomposition to realize a joint sub-band channel attention. The SPA is implemented as a plug-and-play module, hence can replace the naive channel attention in arbitrary deep learning networks. The proposed SPA block performs a more precise feature re-calibration that re-scales both the feature channels and the multi-level frequency components. The achieved gain for the proposed method over the conventional filtering methods and DL methods is considerable, ranging from 0.18 dB to 3.97 dB on the benchmark dataset of DnD. The generalization of the SPA blocks is verified by the ablation study, which suggests that the SPA module is compatible with other network architectures and can be widely used in other networks to boost image restoration performance.

References

1. Abdelhamed, A., Lin, S., Brown, M.S.: A high-quality denoising dataset for smartphone cameras. In: Proceedings of the IEEE Conference on Computer Vision and Pattern Recognition, pp. 1692–1700 (2018)

---

[1] Model size was calculated by torchsummary package (https://github.com/sksq96/pytorch-summary).

2. Agustsson, E., Timofte, R.: NTIRE 2017 challenge on single image super-resolution: dataset and study. In: Proceedings of the IEEE Conference on Computer Vision and Pattern Recognition Workshops, pp. 126–135 (2017)
3. Aharon, M., Elad, M., Bruckstein, A.: K-SVD: an algorithm for designing over-complete dictionaries for sparse representation. IEEE Trans. Sig. Process. **54**(11), 4311–4322 (2006)
4. Anwar, S., Barnes, N.: Real image denoising with feature attention. In: Proceedings of the IEEE International Conference on Computer Vision, pp. 3155–3164 (2019)
5. Anwar, S., Barnes, N.: Densely residual Laplacian super-resolution. IEEE Trans. Pattern Anal. Mach. Intell. (2020)
6. Anwar, S., Phuoc Huynh, C., Porikli, F.: Identity enhanced residual image denoising. In: Proceedings of the IEEE/CVF Conference on Computer Vision and Pattern Recognition Workshops, pp. 520–521 (2020)
7. Bao, L., Yang, Z., Wang, S., Bai, D., Lee, J.: Real image denoising based on multi-scale residual dense block and cascaded U-Net with block-connection. In: Proceedings of the IEEE/CVF Conference on Computer Vision and Pattern Recognition Workshops, pp. 448–449 (2020)
8. Boie, R.A., Cox, I.J.: An analysis of camera noise. IEEE Trans. Pattern Anal. Mach. Intell. **6**, 671–674 (1992)
9. Boyat, A.K., Joshi, B.K.: A review paper: noise models in digital image processing. arXiv preprint arXiv:1505.03489 (2015)
10. Buades, A., Coll, B., Morel, J.M.: A non-local algorithm for image denoising. In: 2005 IEEE Computer Society Conference on Computer Vision and Pattern Recognition, CVPR 2005, vol. 2, pp. 60–65. IEEE (2005)
11. Burger, H.C., Schuler, C.J., Harmeling, S.: Image denoising: can plain neural networks compete with BM3D? In: 2012 IEEE Conference on Computer Vision and Pattern Recognition, pp. 2392–2399. IEEE (2012)
12. Chen, Y., Pock, T.: Trainable nonlinear reaction diffusion: a flexible framework for fast and effective image restoration. IEEE Trans. Pattern Anal. Mach. Intell. **39**(6), 1256–1272 (2016)
13. Dabov, K., Foi, A., Katkovnik, V., Egiazarian, K.: Image denoising by sparse 3-D transform-domain collaborative filtering. IEEE Trans. Image Process. **16**(8), 2080–2095 (2007)
14. Dai, T., Cai, J., Zhang, Y., Xia, S.T., Zhang, L.: Second-order attention network for single image super-resolution. In: Proceedings of the IEEE Conference on Computer Vision and Pattern Recognition, pp. 11065–11074 (2019)
15. Foi, A., Trimeche, M., Katkovnik, V., Egiazarian, K.: Practical Poissonian-Gaussian noise modeling and fitting for single-image raw-data. IEEE Trans. Image Process. **17**(10), 1737–1754 (2008)
16. Gu, S., Zhang, L., Zuo, W., Feng, X.: Weighted nuclear norm minimization with application to image denoising. In: Proceedings of the IEEE Conference on Computer Vision and Pattern Recognition, pp. 2862–2869 (2014)
17. Guo, S., Yan, Z., Zhang, K., Zuo, W., Zhang, L.: Toward convolutional blind denoising of real photographs. In: Proceedings of the IEEE Conference on Computer Vision and Pattern Recognition, pp. 1712–1722 (2019)
18. Hu, J., Shen, L., Sun, G.: Squeeze-and-excitation networks. In: Proceedings of the IEEE Conference on Computer Vision and Pattern Recognition, pp. 7132–7141 (2018)
19. Jain, U.: Characterization of CMOS Image Sensor. Ph.D. thesis, MS Thesis, Delft University of Technology (2016)

20. Kingma, D.P., Ba, J.: Adam: A method for stochastic optimization. arXiv preprint arXiv:1412.6980 (2014)
21. Liu, X., Tanaka, M., Okutomi, M.: Practical signal-dependent noise parameter estimation from a single noisy image. IEEE Trans. Image Process. 23(10), 4361–4371 (2014)
22. Mao, X., Shen, C., Yang, Y.B.: Image restoration using very deep convolutional encoder-decoder networks with symmetric skip connections. In: Advances in Neural Information Processing Systems, pp. 2802–2810 (2016)
23. Martin, D., Fowlkes, C., Tal, D., Malik, J.: A database of human segmented natural images and its application to evaluating segmentation algorithms and measuring ecological statistics. In: Proceedings 8th IEEE International Conference on Computer Vision, ICCV 2001, vol. 2, pp. 416–423. IEEE (2001)
24. Nair, V., Hinton, G.E.: Rectified linear units improve restricted Boltzmann machines. In: ICML (2010)
25. Paszke, A., et al.: Automatic differentiation in PyTorch (2017)
26. Plotz, T., Roth, S.: Benchmarking denoising algorithms with real photographs. In: Proceedings of the IEEE Conference on Computer Vision and Pattern Recognition, pp. 1586–1595 (2017)
27. Roth, S., Black, M.J.: Fields of experts. Int. J. Comput. Vis. 82(2), 205 (2009)
28. Wang, Z., Bovik, A.C., Sheikh, H.R., Simoncelli, E.P.: Image quality assessment: from error visibility to structural similarity. IEEE Trans. Image Process. 13(4), 600–612 (2004)
29. Xu, J., Zhang, L., Zhang, D.: A trilateral weighted sparse coding scheme for real-world image denoising. In: Ferrari, V., Hebert, M., Sminchisescu, C., Weiss, Y. (eds.) ECCV 2018. LNCS, vol. 11212, pp. 21–38. Springer, Cham (2018). https://doi.org/10.1007/978-3-030-01237-3_2
30. Xu, J., Zhang, L., Zhang, D., Feng, X.: Multi-channel weighted nuclear norm minimization for real color image denoising. In: Proceedings of the IEEE International Conference on Computer Vision, pp. 1096–1104 (2017)
31. Zamir, S.W., et al.: CycleISP: real image restoration via improved data synthesis. In: Proceedings of the IEEE/CVF Conference on Computer Vision and Pattern Recognition, pp. 2696–2705 (2020)
32. Zhang, K., Zuo, W., Chen, Y., Meng, D., Zhang, L.: Beyond a Gaussian denoiser: residual learning of deep CNN for image denoising. IEEE Trans. Image Process. 26(7), 3142–3155 (2017)
33. Zhang, K., Zuo, W., Gu, S., Zhang, L.: Learning deep CNN denoiser prior for image restoration. In: Proceedings of the IEEE Conference on Computer Vision and Pattern Recognition, pp. 3929–3938 (2017)
34. Zhang, K., Zuo, W., Zhang, L.: FFDNet: toward a fast and flexible solution for CNN-based image denoising. IEEE Trans. Image Process. 27(9), 4608–4622 (2018)
35. Zhang, Y., Li, K., Li, K., Wang, L., Zhong, B., Fu, Y.: Image super-resolution using very deep residual channel attention networks. In: Ferrari, V., Hebert, M., Sminchisescu, C., Weiss, Y. (eds.) ECCV 2018. LNCS, vol. 11211, pp. 294–310. Springer, Cham (2018). https://doi.org/10.1007/978-3-030-01234-2_18
36. Zhao, Y., Jiang, Z., Men, A., Ju, G.: Pyramid real image denoising network. In: 2019 IEEE Visual Communications and Image Processing (VCIP), pp. 1–4. IEEE (2019)

Tiny Person Pose Estimation via Image and Feature Super Resolution

Jie Xu, Yunan Liu, Lin Zhao, Shanshan Zhang[✉], and Jian Yang

Key Laboratory of Intelligent Perception and Systems for High-Dimensional
Information of Ministry of Education, School of Computer Science and Engineering,
Nanjing University of Science and Technology, Nanjing 210094, China
{jiexu,liuyunan,linzhao,shanshan.zhang,csjyang}@njust.edu.cn

Abstract. Although great progress has been achieved on human pose
estimation in recent years, we notice the performance drops dramatically
when the scale of target person becomes small. In this paper, we start
with analysis on tiny person pose estimation and find that the failure is
mainly caused by blurriness and ambiguous edges in up-sampled images,
which are harmful for pose estimation. Based on the above analysis, we
propose to apply an additional super resolution network on top of an
existing pose estimation method to better handle tiny persons. Specifically, we propose three super resolution (SR) networks which apply on
image level, feature level and both levels, respectively. Furthermore, a
novel task-driven loss function tailored to pose estimation is proposed for
SR networks. Experimental results on the MPII and MSCOCO datasets
show that our proposed pose super resolution methods bring significant
improvements over the baseline for tiny persons.

Keywords: Pose estimation · Tiny pose estimation · Image super
resolution · Feature super resolution

1 Introduction

Human pose estimation is a basic task for interpreting people in images as the
provided locations of different body joints serve as important hints for human
body shape and action. It has been shown that pose estimation results are beneficial to some other human analysis tasks, including pedestrian detection [18],
human parsing [7],

The difficulty of tiny people pose estimation mainly lies in the missing image
details due to low resolution. The default choice of dealing with low resolution
images is to increase the resolution via some standard interpolation techniques,
for instance, bilinear or bicubic. However, those interpolation methods usually
induce blurriness, resulting in ambiguous borders among different body parts and
the background. As shown in Fig. 1, it is still very hard to estimate the poses of
tiny persons even after up-sampling by the bicubic interpolation method.

Y. Peng et al. (Eds.): ICIG 2021, LNCS 12890, pp. 315–327, 2021.
https://doi.org/10.1007/978-3-030-87361-5_26

Image   Simple   Ours   GT(Ground Truth)

Fig. 1. Qualitative comparison of Simple [17] and our PoseSR on tiny people pose estimation. Although the current state-of-the-art method Simple achieves good performance on public benchmarks, they fail at tiny person cases. It becomes more difficult to localize the human body joints when the persons are really small. The example images are upscaled by 8× for better visualization.

Encouraged by the notable progress in the field of natural image super resolution, we propose to use super resolution technics to deal with tiny person pose estimation. In contrast to image super resolution whose goal is to obtain high visual quality, we aim to achieve optimal pose estimation results. To this end, we consider using super resolution on both image and feature levels to close the performance gap between small and large scale persons. The image level super resolution helps to generate high resolution person images, which share similar visual quality with large ones, and thus enable the method to produce as good results as large scale persons. Alternatively, in a more straightforward way, the feature level super resolution is expected to improve the performance by enriching the representations of small scale persons.

In summary, the main contributions of this work are three-folds:

- We address the problem of tiny person pose estimation by using super resolution technics at both image and feature levels. To the best of our knowledge, this is one of the earliest work that studies tiny person pose estimation.
- We devise a pose oriented task-driven loss, enabling super resolution to facilitate pose estimation, and an end-to-end framework namely PoseSR.
- From the experimental results on MPII and MSCOCO datasets, the proposed PoseSR framework outperforms existing methods on tiny person pose estimation. The success is expected to push forward the applications of pose estimation in real world scenes.

2   Related Work

Human Pose Estimation. The problem of estimating positions of body parts has been extensively studied. Recent work exploit convolutional neural networks (CNN) to conduct human pose estimation. Deeppose [16] use a CNN in a iterative manner to regress human keypoints' positions directly. Hourglass [11] propose their stacked hourglass network to get multi-level feature information and capture feature at different scales, which becomes one of the most famous models for keypoints detection.

With the dramatic progress achieved on single person pose estimation by various excellent algorithms, researchers focus more on the problem of multi-person pose estimation. There are two pipelines to deal with multi-person pose estimation. One is the bottom-up methods which detect all possible joints in a crowded scene, and then the candidates are clustered into different people [5, 10, 12]. The other pipeline is top-down methods [1,3,6,13]. It detects all persons first and conducts single person pose estimation from the cropped image regions separately.

However, these successful work for human pose estimation all assume that input images have a sufficiently high resolution, and their performance can quickly slip into disappointment when the resolution of input images drops. To deal with the low resolution problem of tiny person pose estimation, [9] proposes an alternative probabilistic approach where a low resolution feature map is used to generate a dense field of Gaussian blobs, resulting in a rich continuous mixture model. Though, this method acquires some improvement on estimating the pose of tiny people, it suffers a decline in the accuracy of the estimated poses on normal persons. In this paper, we propose a method that is able to largely advance the performance of detecting tiny people's pose, while the estimation of persons in high resolution will not be affected or may also be improved.

Super Resolution. Single image super-resolution is a classical problem in low-level computer vision, which reconstructs a high-resolution (HR) image from a low-resolution (LR) image. Recently, inspired by the achievement of many computer vision tasks tackled with deep learning, neural networks have been a popular choice in SR and dramatic improvement has been achieved. [2] first exploit a three-layer convolution neural network, named SRCNN, to jointly optimize the feature extraction, non-linear mapping and image reconstruction stages in an end-to-end manner. Afterwards various convolution neural networks have been designed for image super-resolution.

Different from image super-resolution, feature super-resolution aims at directly enhancing the features extracted from a small size image for specific computer vision tasks. [14] propose a novel super-resolution technique called feature super-resolution (FSR) to improve the retrieval precision of small size images, and its performance is quite convincing. Inspired by this work, we try our hand at taking advantage of both image level and feature level super resolution to succeed in tiny person pose estimation.

Table 1. Results on MSCOCO [8] val 2017 dataset. The numbers are the mAP. ≤64 px represents the height of original input images are below 64 pixels. We compare the performance of two pose estimation methods with different model sizes at different scale ranges.

Model	Input size	≤64 px	≤128 px and ≥64 px	≥128 px	≥256 px	≥384 px	All
Simple [17]	256 × 192	0.589	0.688	0.750	0.776	0.778	0.725
	384 × 288	0.571	0.695	0.774	0.808	0.815	0.741
CPN [1]	256 × 192	0.562	0.677	0.738	0.760	0.772	0.712
	384 × 288	0.568	0.696	0.773	0.805	0.818	0.741

Table 2. Results of Simple [17] on MPII val dataset. The numbers are PCKh @0.5. The tiny person images are generated by down-sampling the original large images to 64 and 32 pixels in height.

Image size	Input size	Head	Shou	Elbow	Wrist	Hip	Knee	Ankle	Mean
256 × 256	256 × 256	96.351	95.329	88.989	83.176	88.420	83.960	79.594	88.532
64 × 64	256 × 256	93.281	90.880	81.405	73.103	81.738	75.478	71.398	81.837
32 × 32	256 × 256	76.774	74.083	58.105	47.406	63.095	52.508	48.886	61.585

3   Analysis on Tiny Person Pose Estimation

First of all, we observe how much the pose estimation performance drops when the target person becomes pretty small. We choose two state-of-the-art methods, namely Simple [17], CPN [1], and implement fine-grained evaluations for different scales on the MSCOCO val 2017 dataset. As shown in Table 1, for the method of Simple with a model input size of 256 × 192, the mAP drops by ~20 pp when the scale decreases from [256, inf] to [32,64]; similar finding for CPN. When we increase the model input size to 384 × 288 for both methods, the performance for large scale persons improves by ~4 pp for the scale range of [256, inf]; in contrast, the gain for the scale range of [32,64] is minimal (less than 1pp).

The above observations indicate that there is a huge gap between high resolution and low resolution images, and simply using a larger model does not help for tiny persons.

In order to understand the gap between high resolution and low resolution images, we first recall the data processing procedure used for pose estimation. For all existing pose estimation algorithms following the top-down pipeline, a common technique of data processing is to first crop out the person region and then scale it to the model input size, which is generally fixed for a given network. This becomes a default setting in the community for two reasons. On one hand, the model input size is usually set to a value much smaller than the original size of most images, so as to largely reduce the computational complexity. On the other hand, a model with a fixed input size is convenient for a large-batch training mode. Since the model input size is fixed, when the given image is larger than the fixed model input size, we need to down-sample the image to fit in; when the given image is smaller than the fixed model input size, we need to resize the image using methods like bi-linear up-sampling.

We assume the low performance for tiny persons is caused by the up-sampling procedure, which usually brings blurriness and artifacts. To study the impact of up-sampling factors on performance in a more specific way, we provide a comparison at different up-sampling factors. The experiments are conducted for the method of Simple on the MPII validation set, which generally consists of large scale images. And tiny persons images are generated by down-sampling the original large images to 64 and 32 pixels, respectively. From Table 2, we can see that compared to those images without up-sampling, the performance drops by ~7 pp when the factor is 4x, and the gap becomes even larger (~27 pp) when we further increase the factor to 8x.

From the above discussions, we conclude that the performance drop for tiny persons comes from inaccurate up-sampling methods. Therefore, in this paper we investigate to use super resolution techniques to enable better up-sampling, so as to enhance the pose performance for tiny persons. Please note that in this paper, we refer to a person whose upright height is less than 64 pixels in the original image as a tiny person.

4 Our Pose Super Resolution Approach

In this section, we will first briefly describe our proposed pose super resolution method (PoseSR) using both image and feature level super resolution; and then we will explain each component within the framework in more detail.

4.1 Overview

The flowchart of our proposed pose super resolution approach is shown in Fig. 2. On top of a basic pose estimation network, two additional super resolution networks are applied to better handle tiny persons. Right after the input image, an image super resolution network namely I-SRNet is applied to generate a high resolution image with high visual quality. Then the feature extraction module in PoseNet is used to extract shallow features, followed by a feature super resolution network namely F-SRNet is used to learn the mapping of better feature maps. Finally, two different levels of super resolution can be integrated into a fused framework, which is the overall structure shown in the Fig. 2.

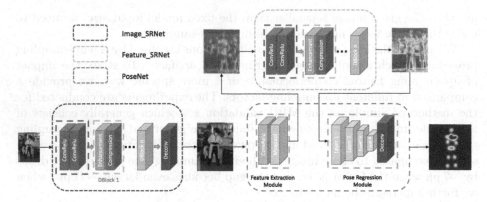

Fig. 2. The flowchart of our proposed pose super resolution approach. The whole architecture consists of three parts: Image_SRNet, Feature_SRNet and the PoseNet. Specifically, for a low-resolution input image, we enhance the image quality and the feature representations throughout the whole architecture, so we can get more accurate pose results for tiny persons.

4.2   Basic Pose Estimation Network

Current state-of-the-art methods for single person pose estimation follow the regression pipeline shown in the bottom right corner of Fig. 2. Basically, the PoseNet consists of two parts, one is shallow feature extraction module to process the input image, another part is the multi level or multi scale pose regression module to get the final heatmaps. Here, we use the Simple [17] as the basic PoseNet in our framework.

Generally, each input image is rescaled to a uniform size, and then goes through a CNN for feature extraction. Finally, the heatmaps for different body keypoints are predicted by the pose regression module. Specifically, for an input color image of $H \times W \times 3$, the dimension of predicted heatmaps is $\frac{H}{\delta} \times \frac{W}{\delta} \times K$, where K is the number of predefined human body keypoints and δ is a downsampling factor determined by the network stride, which is set as 4 in PoseNet.

4.3   Image-Level Pose Super Resolution

As we mentioned above, the existing human pose estimation algorithm is not competent for small people. Here, we introduce the proposed image-level pose super resolution framework to deal with tiny poses. Because lacking details in images of tiny people constitutes the main obstacle of detection, it is direct to think of enhancing the images by utilizing the technique of image super resolution. Recent years have witnessed remarkable progresses of image super resolution using deep learning. In this case, we expect to recover the HR image from the corresponding LR image of tiny people, following the process:

$$I^{SR} = \mathcal{S}_\mathcal{I}(I^{LR}; \theta_I) \tag{1}$$

where $\mathcal{S}_\mathcal{I}$ is the image super-resolution model and θ_I represents the model parameters.

The input and output of image super-resolution are both images, therefore, we can directly add it in front of the traditional human pose estimation framework, which makes the I-PoseSR network useful for tiny pose estimation. We illustrate the I-PoseSR framework in the bottom of Fig. 2. A general super resolution CNN can be utilized to generate high-resolution images as the input of the PoseNet. Our ultimate goal is to train a super resolution network to transfer the low resolution image input to super image quality similarly to those of high-resolution images. During the training progress, we freeze the PoseNet to ensure the normal pose prediction. Using this framework, we are able to improve the pose results of tiny people and maintain the performance on normal persons.

4.4 Feature-Level Pose Super Resolution

The CNNs have unique advantages in feature extraction, which is significantly better than manually designed features. The performance of PoseNet on different resolution images is mainly due to the difference in extracted features, so we design a feature super resolution network to make LR and HR images get the same or similar feature representations, so that tiny poses can be effectively solved as general poses.

The traditional pose network can be splitted into two parts, one is the part of feature extraction and the other is the pose regression module. Feature_level super resolution network is inserted between these two parts, which hopes to learn the mapping from low-resolution feature maps to high-resolution feature maps. Hence, the enhanced feature maps will be used for localizing keypoints. For the whole Feature_level PoseSR, The first block is to extract good representations for input images of I^{LR} and I^{HR}. In this work, we employ the pretrained previous two layers of PoseNet as the Feature Extraction Module to extract features, we do not use deeper level features because the higher level features is full with semantic information which is less helpful to recover details for low resolution features. We use paired F^{LR} and F^{HR} to denote the extracted feature of I^{LR} and I^{HR}, respectively.

After extracting representations, the feature super-resolution network $\mathcal{S}_\mathcal{F}$ transforms the raw poor features F^{LR} of input low-resolution images to highly discriminative ones, called super feature representations F^{SR}. It is defined as:

$$F^{SR} = \mathcal{S}_\mathcal{F}(F^{LR}; \theta_F), \tag{2}$$

where $\mathcal{S}_\mathcal{F}$ is the feature super-resolution model and θ_F represents the model parameters.

Based on the super resolution feature representation, the Pose Regression Module is used to predict the final heatmaps to get the pose of tiny person.

4.5 Fused-Level Pose Super Resolution

The two frameworks proposed above deal with the input image before the PoseNet and the features in the PoseNet. These two frameworks are able to be integrated into one framework that produces improvement at both image and feature levels. We refer to this integrated framework as IF-PoseSR. The input LR image is first processed by Image super-resolution in I-PoseSR, and then the recovered SR image is sent to F-PoseSR to get further enhancement on features and obtain the pose results finally.

4.6 Task-Driven Loss Function

In this sub-section, we introduce the proposed task-driven loss that makes PoseSR an end-to-end framework. For image super resolution, it is usual to use ground truth high resolution images to supervise the results. Therefore, the loss function used in super-resolution networks is a image reconstruction error from low-resolution to high-resolution, and it is commonly measured by the L1 distance between the two images. The image reconstruction error loss function is showed as below:

$$L_{re} = L_1(\mathcal{S}_\mathcal{I}(I^{LR}; \theta_I), I^{HR}), \tag{3}$$

where I^{LR} and I^{HR} represent the paired LR and HR images. Similarly, this loss function of the reconstruction error is also applicable to the feature super-resolution process.

Super-resolution with an image reconstruction error recovers high-frequency information of the image, such as edges and contours etc., while human pose estimation pays more attention on the details of the person, such as the features near the keypoints. Therefore, an image reconstruction error guided super resolution may not be able to recover information beneficial to pose estimation. In this paper, we propose to use a task-driven loss for driving super resolution to facilitate pose estimation. Whether super-resolution is done on the image or feature level, it serves for pose estimation. Thus, we come up the idea that the super resolution component can be trained together with the PoseNet in our PoseSR framework just using a general pose loss function. Comparing to the image-level or feature-level reconstruction loss, the use of pose loss for supervising the training of super-resolution can compel super resolution to recover details that are essential for pose estimation. Specifically, our task-driven loss function is to use high resolution heatmaps that are generated by using the HR images as the input of PoseNet to supervise the output of the corresponding LR input, the loss function is showed below:

$$L_{td} = MSE(H^{LR}, H^{HR}). \tag{4}$$

where H^{LR} is the output heatmaps of a LR input image, and H^{HR} represents the heatmaps generated by HR images.

5   Experiments

This section starts with some implementation details, followed by some ablation studies w.r.t. the choices of super resolution net and loss function. In the end, we will show some experimental results on the MPII and MSCOCO datasets.

5.1 Implementation Details

Datasets. We conduct our main experiments on the standard MPII human pose dataset. The MPII dataset contains about 25,000 images with over 40,000 annotated poses. We follow the same setting as in [15] to split training and validation sets. This dataset is very challenging as it covers daily human activities with large pose varieties. We also extend the experiment to MSCOCO. The MSCOCO dataset is a dataset with richer and more complex scene, including people of different sizes. But because the person which below 32 px at height is not labelled with human pose keypoints, we collect some tiny person to show the visualization results on real scene.

Training Details. All images on the MPII dataset are cropped and warped to the size of 256×256 as the HR images, and the LR images are of size 32×32 and 64×64 are obtained by down-sampling the HR images. We augment the training set by scaling each image with a random factor ranging in $[0.75, 1.25]$; besides, rotation ($\pm 30°$) and horizontal flipping are also used for data augmentation. The learning rate is set to 1×10^{-4} and 1×10^{-5} after 90 epochs, and train all frameworks 140 epochs. Mini-batch size is set to 32, and adam optimizer is used. Our whole framework is implemented in PyTorch. Specially, We train the PoseSR framework with the component of PoseNet fixed, because we want to make full use of the component of super resolution module(whether image_level or feature_level) to get better pose for tiny people without compromising the pose of high resolution images. For the PoseNet, the pretrained models on MPII can be directly utilized.

Testing Details. During testing, we crop the image with the given rough center location and scale of the person. The flipped image is used to obtain the final results by averaging the outputs.

Table 3. Comparison of task-driven loss and reconstruction loss on MPII validataion dataset at I_PoseSR and F_PoseSR. L_{re} represents the reconstruction loss, and L_{td} represents the task-driven loss. The second row shows the baseline results of LR input images.

Loss	Model	Head	Shou	Elbow	Wrist	Hip	Knee	Ankle	Mean
–	PoseNet	76.774	74.083	58.105	47.406	63.095	52.508	48.886	61.585
L_{re}	I-PoseSR	83.458	78.210	63.831	54.135	68.703	62.483	58.833	68.090
	F-PoseSR	79.400	69.192	53.554	43.823	61.745	54.109	51.109	59.883
L_{td}	I-PoseSR	89.734	84.188	71.280	60.597	75.818	66.451	61.880	**73.799**
	F-PoseSR	90.246	86.073	73.752	63.784	77.012	69.736	64.549	**75.883**

5.2   Ablation Study

We perform ablative analysis on loss functions, respectively. The experiments are conducted on the MPII validation set.

Loss Function. We first investigate the effectiveness of the proposed task-driven loss by comparing to the image reconstruction loss. When the reconstruction loss is used to train the SRNet, our PoseSR framework degenerates to a simple combination of an image SRnet and a Posenet. Table 3 presents the comparison results. Clearly, the performance of the proposed task-driven loss greatly surpasses the reconstruction loss, which demonstrates the advance of the task-driven loss that makes PoseSR an end-to-end framework. In the I-PoseSR framework, changing the image reconstruction loss to the task-driven loss, the mean PCKh@0.5 is increased from 68% to 73%. Also in the F-PoseSR framework, the performance of the task-driven loss is about 15% higher. This proves that the task-driven loss is able to drive the SRNet to recover helpful details for pose estimation.

5.3   Experimental Results on MPII

Based on the above ablation study, we choose IDN [4] as the SRNet and L_{td-HR} as the loss function to verify the efficacy of the proposed PoseSR framework on the MPII validation dataset. For comprehensiveness, we do the experiments both using the tiny people of size 32×32 and 64×64. Table 4 presents the results of the proposed three PoseSR frameworks. The baseline is the results of the PoseNet [17] that uses the same tiny people with our framework as the input. The results given by the PoseNet using HR images as the input make the upper bounds. Clearly, whether on the tiny people of size 32×32 or 64×64, all of the proposed PoseSR frameworks can largely improve the results of the baseline. Especially, when tiny people only have the size of 32×32, the performance of PoseNet significantly drops to 61.585% from 88.532%. However, the proposed IF-PoseSR can obtain a much more satisfying performance of 76.269%, which is about 15% higher than the baseline.

5.4   Extended Experiments on Real Tiny People

We evaluate the proposed framework on real tiny people without any annotations. We collect the tiny people from the MSCOCO dataset, since there is no keypoints annotation of tiny people whose height is below 32 px, we can only test such tiny people with the models trained on MPII dataset. The visual results are showed in Fig. 3. As can be seen from the visual effects, when the input samples of the network are relatively small, judging the specific pose of the person has certain difficulties for us, but for our model, we can get a relatively accurate posture which could help action recognition.

Table 4. Comparison on the downsampled MPII validation set. The numbers are PCKh. The PoseNet is fixed to Simple [17] in our proposed framework, and the SRNet in our all proposed PoseSR frameworks is fixed to IDN [4]. The results show that all of our proposed methods outperform the baseline results.

Tiny people size	Model	Head	Shou	Elbow	Wrist	Hip	Knee	Ankle	Mean
–	PoseNet_HR	96.351	95.329	88.989	83.176	88.420	83.960	79.594	88.532
32×32	PoseNet	76.774	74.083	58.105	47.406	63.095	52.508	48.886	61.585
	I-PoseSR	89.734	84.188	71.280	60.597	75.818	66.451	61.880	73.799
	F-PoseSR	90.246	86.073	73.752	63.784	77.012	69.736	64.549	75.883
	IF-PoseSR	**90.553**	**86.175**	**73.854**	**64.794**	**77.843**	**69.211**	**65.257**	**76.269**
64×64	PoseNet	93.281	90.880	81.405	73.103	81.738	75.478	71.398	81.837
	I-PoseSR	95.430	93.325	84.830	78.156	85.373	80.193	75.744	85.347
	F-PoseSR	95.362	93.461	84.540	78.224	85.200	80.374	75.413	85.301
	IF-PoseSR	**95.532**	**93.393**	**85.137**	**78.671**	**85.475**	**80.475**	**75.791**	**85.498**

Bicubic

I-PoseSR

F-PoseSR

IF-PoseSR

Fig. 3. Visualization of tiny person pose estimation results on the MSCOCO dataset. The input images are small ($\leq$ 32 pixels in height), so we upsample each of them by 8× for better visualization. We can see that our methods obtain more accurate pose estimation results by simply using bicubic upsampled images as inputs (the first row).

6   Conclusion

In this paper, we propose a novel PoseSR framework to tackle the tiny people pose estimation problem. Furthermore, a novel task-driven loss function is presented to make the proposed PoseSR more efficient to train. We evaluate the model performance on the famous pose estimation benchmarks MPII and MS-COCO, and great improvements on tiny person estimation are secured comparing to the current pose estimation methods.

Ackowledgments. This work was partially supported by the National Natural Science Foundation of China (Grant No. U1713208, 61802189), Funds for International Cooperation and Exchange of the National Natural Science Foundation of China (Grant No. 61861136011), Natural Science Foundation of Jiangsu Province, China (Grant No. BK20181299), the Fundamental Research Funds for the Central Universities (Grant No. 30920032201), National Key Research and Development Program of China (Grant No. 2017YFC0820601), China Postdoctoral Science Foundation (Grand No. 2020M681609).

References

1. Chen, Y., Wang, Z., Peng, Y., Zhang, Z., Yu, G., Sun, J.: Cascaded pyramid network for multi-person pose estimation. In: The IEEE Conference on Computer Vision and Pattern Recognition (CVPR), pp. 7103–7112 (2018)
2. Dong, C., Loy, C.C., He, K., Tang, X.: Learning a deep convolutional network for image super-resolution. In: Fleet, D., Pajdla, T., Schiele, B., Tuytelaars, T. (eds.) ECCV 2014. LNCS, vol. 8692, pp. 184–199. Springer, Cham (2014). https://doi.org/10.1007/978-3-319-10593-2_13
3. Fang, H.S., Xie, S., Tai, Y.W., Lu, C.: RMPE: regional multi-person pose estimation. In: The IEEE Conference on Computer Vision and Pattern Recognition (CVPR), pp. 2334–2343 (2017)
4. Hui, Z., Wang, X., Gao, X.: Fast and accurate single image super-resolution via information distillation network. In: The IEEE Conference on Computer Vision and Pattern Recognition (CVPR), pp. 723–731 (2018)
5. Insafutdinov, E., Pishchulin, L., Andres, B., Andriluka, M., Schiele, B.: DeeperCut: a deeper, stronger, and faster multi-person pose estimation model. In: Leibe, B., Matas, J., Sebe, N., Welling, M. (eds.) ECCV 2016. LNCS, vol. 9910, pp. 34–50. Springer, Cham (2016). https://doi.org/10.1007/978-3-319-46466-4_3
6. Sun, K., Xiao, B., Liu, D., Wang, J.: Deep high-resolution representation learning for human pose estimation. In: The IEEE Conference on Computer Vision and Pattern Recognition (CVPR), pp. 5693–5703 (2019)
7. Liang, X., Gong, K., Shen, X., Lin, L.: Look into person: joint body parsing & pose estimation network and a new benchmark. IEEE Trans. Pattern Anal. Mach. Intell. **41**, 871–885 (2019)
8. Lin, T.Y., et al.: Microsoft COCO: common objects in context. In: Fleet, D., Pajdla, T., Schiele, B., Tuytelaars, T. (eds.) ECCV 2014. LNCS, vol. 8693, pp. 740–755. Springer, Cham (2014). https://doi.org/10.1007/978-3-319-10602-1_48
9. Neumann, L., Vedaldi, A.: Tiny people pose. In: Asian Conference on Computer Vision (ACCV), pp. 558–574 (2018)
10. Newell, A., Huang, Z., Deng, J.: Associative embedding: end-to-end learning for joint detection and grouping. In: Advances in Neural Information Processing Systems (NeurIPS), pp. 2277–2287 (2017)
11. Newell, A., Yang, K., Deng, J.: Stacked hourglass networks for human pose estimation. In: Leibe, B., Matas, J., Sebe, N., Welling, M. (eds.) ECCV 2016. LNCS, vol. 9912, pp. 483–499. Springer, Cham (2016). https://doi.org/10.1007/978-3-319-46484-8_29

12. Pishchulin, L., et al.: DeepCut: joint subset partition and labeling for multi person pose estimation. In: The IEEE Conference on Computer Vision and Pattern Recognition (CVPR), pp. 4929–4937 (2016)
13. Su, K., Yu, D., Xu, Z., Geng, X., Wang, C.: Multi-person pose estimation with enhanced channel-wise and spatial information. In: The IEEE Conference on Computer Vision and Pattern Recognition (CVPR), pp. 5674–5682 (2019)
14. Tan, W., Yan, B., Bare, B.: Feature super-resolution: make machine see more clearly. In: The IEEE Conference on Computer Vision and Pattern Recognition (CVPR), pp. 3994–4002 (2018)
15. Tompson, J., Goroshin, R., Jain, A., LeCun, Y., Bregler, C.: Efficient object localization using convolutional networks. In: The IEEE Conference on Computer Vision and Pattern Recognition (CVPR), pp. 648–656 (2015)
16. Toshev, A., Szegedy, C.: DeepPose: human pose estimation via deep neural networks. In: The IEEE Conference on Computer Vision and Pattern Recognition (CVPR), pp. 1653–1660 (2014)
17. Xiao, B., Wu, H., Wei, Y.: Simple baselines for human pose estimation and tracking. In: Ferrari, V., Hebert, M., Sminchisescu, C., Weiss, Y. (eds.) ECCV 2018. LNCS, vol. 11210, pp. 472–487. Springer, Cham (2018). https://doi.org/10.1007/978-3-030-01231-1_29
18. Zhang, S., Yang, J., Schiele, B.: Occluded pedestrian detection through guided attention in CNNs. In: The IEEE Conference on Computer Vision and Pattern Recognition (CVPR), pp. 6995–7003 (2018)

Improved VIBE Shadow Elimination Method with Adaptive Threshold in the Environment of Tarmac Monitoring

Dong Zheng, Guowu Yuan$^{(\boxtimes)}$, Yang Wang, and Hao Zhou

School of Information Science and Engineering, Yunnan University, Kunming 650091, China
yuanguowu@sina.com

Abstract. The detection and counting of airport passengers and baggage is an important task of airport management. When passengers arrive at the aircraft docking area from the terminal building through a shuttle bus and boarding on foot, the counting of people and baggage based on airport surveillance video is often affected by complicated climate, Dynamic background, cast shadows and other factors, the paper improves the VIBE (Visual Background Extractor) foreground detection algorithm, adds a threshold adaptive mechanism, can accurately extract the foreground image under the dynamic background of the airport, and uses the pixel distribution histogram matching method to detect ghosts Finally, based on the Gaussian mixture model, the moving target is removed from the shadow, and the moving target is accurately counted on this basis. The experimental results show that the method proposed in the paper is better than the traditional shadow removal algorithm based on traditional VIBE in removing the shadow cast by passengers.

Keywords: Airport video surveillance · VIBE · Adaptive threshold · Pixel distribution histogram matching · Gaussian mixture model

1 Introduction

Counting airport passengers and luggage is an important task of airport management. When the boarding bridge is occupied or special air traffic control arrangements, in order to ensure the efficiency of airport operations and maximize airport resources, the airport allows passengers to reach the aircraft docking area from the terminal building through a shuttle bus and board the plane on foot. In this case, it is not easy to complete passenger and baggage counting through airport surveillance video, which is often affected by factors such as complex weather, dynamic background, and cast shadows.

This paper studies and analyzes the video clips of passengers boarding on foot after arriving at the aircraft parking area. It is found that in the process of passenger moving target detection, due to the influence of factors such as light, there is a shadow area, which leads to inaccurate moving target detection.

© Springer Nature Switzerland AG 2021
Y. Peng et al. (Eds.): ICIG 2021, LNCS 12890, pp. 328–340, 2021.
https://doi.org/10.1007/978-3-030-87361-5_27

2 Related Work

2.1 Introduction to the Apron Monitoring Environment

By analyzing the surveillance video of the airport apron, the key information of airport events is extracted, including: crew members boarding, passengers boarding, passengers leaving the aircraft, ground crews overhauling the aircraft, commanding tractors, etc. It is found that airport events generally have large background changes: for example, crew members usually board the aircraft at sunrise, and maintenance work is usually scheduled in the evening, and background mutations may also be encountered: such as changes in illumination at the moment of lighting lamp posts, rain, etc. Special weather conditions (Fig. 1).

Fig. 1. The apron surveillance video screen

Using the moving target tracking technology in the field of computer vision, crew members can board and clock in, count passenger flow information, determine whether the passenger boarding channel is crowded, whether the distance between the shuttle bus and the aircraft is reasonable after arriving at the station, and the position of the aircraft in emergencies Information alarm security personnel, etc. (Fig. 2).

Fig. 2. Shadow area generation

2.2 VIBE Algorithm

The ViBe algorithm was proposed by Olivier Barnich [1] and others. The foreground extraction algorithm based on background modeling has the characteristics of small amount of calculation and high speed. The VIBE algorithm adopts a random background update strategy. When dealing with changing background conditions, use the first frame of the real-time shooting video to establish a new background model, replace the old model, and complete the replacement of the background model, which can meet the requirements of real-time target detection on the apron. Use Vibe The flow chart of the algorithm for foreground detection is shown in Fig. 3:

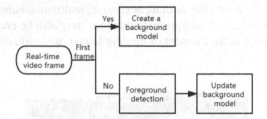

Fig. 3. VIBE algorithm foreground detection flowchart

The principle of the VIBE algorithm is to store the past pixels of the background pixel and the pixels in its neighborhood as a sample set, and compare it with the current input pixel value to determine whether the value belongs to the background point. It can be detailed into three steps:

Step 1: Initialize the background model

Random selection is used as the model sample value of the pixel, and 20 pixels are generally selected to form the sample set. When the video sequence is input, the VIBE algorithm uses its first frame to establish a background model. The background model of pixels can be expressed as:

$$U_{M^t} = f^t\left(x^i, y^j\right) \big| \left(x^i, y^j\right) \in W_D(x, y) \tag{1}$$

Let M and D be the pixel point set, $f^t\left(x^i, y^j\right)$ is the pixel value obtained by random selection, the superscripts of the horizontal and vertical coordinates represent the i-th and j-th random selection respectively, and $W_D(x, y)$ is the pixel value in the neighborhood, where the pixel point $\left(x^i, y^j\right)$ can be The number of selections is 1, 2, 3,..., N. This initialization method makes the model sensitive to noise and can deal with complex and changeable background conditions.

Step 2: Foreground detection

When the subsequent video sequence is input, the VIBE algorithm compares each pixel value of a single video frame with the sample set of the background model. Set this time as time t = k and the pixel value is $f^k(x, y)$, then the background model can be expressed as:

$$U_{M^{k-1}}\left(x^i, y^j\right) \tag{2}$$

Calculate the Euclidean distance between $f^k(x, y)$ and $W_D(x, y)$ pixels in the sample set. If the distance is less than the threshold R, then classify the pixels as approximate sample points:

$$f^k\left(x^i, y^j\right) = \begin{cases} U_{M^{k-1}}\left(x^i, y^j\right), , R, \text{ sample} \\ U_{M^{k-1}}\left(x^i, y^j\right) > R, \text{ foregound} \end{cases} \tag{3}$$

Step 3: Update the background model

In order to adapt to complex and changeable background conditions, it is necessary to update the background model. At the same time, considering the uncertainty of pixel changes, the random update strategy is adopted. In the process of processing the video frame by frame, not every sample set of the background model is It needs to be updated. The sample point W(x,y) obtained by random selection will be updated with a certain probability. The update probability is $1/\varphi$, where φ is the sampling parameter.

The foreground extraction result of the VIBE algorithm is shown in Fig. 4. Compared with the experimental results, in the foreground detection algorithm based on the background model, the VIBE algorithm has better performance in terms of extracting the completeness of the foreground and the effect of processing ghosts.

a)   Original image   b) Foreground extraction

Fig. 4. VIBE algorithm foreground detection flowchart

3   Improve VIBE Shadow Elimination Method

3.1   Build a Background Model

When a video sequence is input, the VIBE algorithm uses its first frame to build a background model, but when the first frame contains a moving target, the result of foreground detection will appear "ghost", which affects the result of the detection. In order to eliminate the "ghost" area, the idea of moving target detection using the inter-frame difference method is used. When the VIBE algorithm initializes the background model, the difference operation is performed on a specific frame sequence [2] to obtain a part of the background image, which is used to supplement VIBE The background information extracted by the algorithm, the specific operation process is as follows:

Step 1: Set input frame parameters: F_{k-1}, F_k, and F_{k+1} represent the k-1, k, and k + 1 frame image sequence respectively, where l represents the step length parameter, which is determined by the actual application environment.

Step 2: Set the video sequence i as the current input frame. When i = k, preprocess the F_{k-1}, F_k, and F_{k+1} image sequences, and then perform the difference operation to obtain the difference image S_k and the position information of the moving target in the current input frame, And extract the pixels of the non-moving target area in the current frame, which are part of the background image [3].

Step 3: Let i = i + 1, repeat the operation of step 2, that is, do the difference operation on the new F_{k-1}, F_k, and F_{k+1} image sequence to obtain the difference image S_i, and determine whether the pixels of the image can supplement the area of the moving target of S_k, If possible, add pixels and further determine whether S_k is complete, not complete or the differential image S_i cannot add S_k, then repeat step 3 until the background image S_k is complete.

3.2 Adaptive Radius Threshold

The radius threshold R is an important indicator for judging whether the approximate sample point is the former scenic spot. The value of R affects the foreground detection effect of the VIBE algorithm. When the background is static, only the foreground pixels are changing, and the radius threshold R may not be changed. In a dynamic background, a fixed radius threshold will cause the algorithm to classify background points as former scenic spots [4]. In the static background of the actual application scene, the radius threshold R should be set to a smaller value, on the contrary, in the dynamic background, it should be set to a larger value, so as to ensure the foreground detection effect.

Define $d_l(x)$ as the minimum Euclidean distance between pixel x and all background sample points $v_l(x)$, namely:

$$d_l(x) = \min\{(p_t(x) - v_1(x)), (p_t(x) - v_2(x)), \cdots (p_t(x) - v_n(x))\} \tag{4}$$

Calculate the average value $d_{\text{avg}}(x)$ of $d_l(x)$. Through analysis, the value of $d_{\text{avg}}(x)$ is proportional to the background change, that is, the greater the background change, the greater the value of $d_{\text{avg}}(x)$. According to this rule, the calculation formula of the adaptive radius threshold is obtained:

$$R_{\text{vad}}(x) = \begin{cases} R_{\text{var}}(x) \cdot \tau_c, & R_{\text{va}}(x) \le t \cdot d_{\text{avg}}(x) \\ R_{\text{var}}(x) \cdot \tau_d, & R_{\text{var}}(x) > t \cdot d_{\text{arg}}(x) \text{ and } R_{\text{var}}(x) \ge 15 \end{cases} \tag{5}$$

Among them, τ_c, τ_d, t are preset parameters. In order to prevent the radius threshold from being too low to cause false detection, the minimum value of the adaptive radius threshold $R_{\text{var}}(x)$ is set in the formula 5 [5].

3.3 Ghost Detection Method Based on Histogram Similarity

(1) Extract pixel distribution histogram

Firstly, formula (1) is used to model the background of the first frame of the input monitoring image, and then the foreground image is extracted by formula (3), and the result is morphologically processed to eliminate fine connections. Connect and label the foreground image to obtain the labeled foreground block $F_i(i = 1, 2, \ldots, n)$, where n represents the number of blocks, calculate the pixel distribution histogram $H_i(i = 1, 2, \ldots, n)$ of the n block area, and set the minimum bounding rectangle of the n block area as C_i, then the background image B_i can be expressed as:

$$B_i = C_i - F_i (i = 1, 2, \ldots, n) \tag{6}$$

The histogram of the pixel distribution of the background image is denoted as $N_i(i = 1, 2, \ldots, n)$ [6].

(2) Similarity matching

Divide the histogram $H_i(i = 1, 2, \ldots, n)$ of the foreground image and the histogram $N_i(i = 1, 2, \ldots, n)$ of the background image into 64 areas, each of which contains 4 consecutive gray levels, and accumulate the pixels of the area to obtain a 64-dimensional image vector. The purpose of the above operation is to convert pixels into vectors, and use the cosine similarity theorem combined with the Bhattacharyya distance to judge the matching degree of the histogram [7], where the angle of the vector tends to 0, the smaller the value of the Bhattacharyya distance (the matching is 0), the more similar. Assuming that two 64-dimensional image vectors are $a(x_1, x_2, \ldots, x_{64})$ and $b(x_1, x_2, \ldots, x_{64})$, the cosine value and Bhattacharyya distance D can be expressed as:

$$\cos(\theta) = \frac{\sum\limits_{i=1}^{64} a(x_i) \times b(x_i)}{\sqrt{\sum\limits_{i=1}^{64} a^2(x_i)} \times \sqrt{\sum\limits_{i=1}^{64} b^2(x_i)}} \tag{7}$$

$$D = \sqrt{1 - \sum\limits_{i=1}^{64} \frac{\sqrt{a(x_i) \cdot b(x_i)}}{\sum\limits_{i=1}^{64} a(x_i) \cdot \sum\limits_{i=1}^{64} b(x_i)}} \tag{8}$$

From formulas (8) and (9), the conditional formula for judging whether F_i it is a ghost image can be obtained:

$$F_i = \begin{cases} \text{ghost,} & M_{\cos\theta}(H_i, N_i) > T_1 \;\&\&\; M_D(H_i, N_i) < T_2 \\ \text{object,} & \text{otherwise} \end{cases} (i = 1, 2, \ldots, n) \tag{9}$$

Among them, $M_{\cos\theta}(H_i, N_i)$ and $M_D(H_i, N_i)$ respectively represent the cosine value and the Bhattacharyya distance of the pixel distribution histogram of the foreground image and the adjacent background area, and T_1 and T_2 are the angle and distance thresholds.

3.4 Shadow Elimination Based on Gaussian Mixture Model

Let $I_Y(x, y)$ represent the brightness component of the pixel (x, y) in the YCbCr color space, and similarly, the chromaticity components $I_{Cb}(x, y)$ and $I_{Cr}(x, y)$ of the pixel and the three components of the background image can be obtained. Set the differential component threshold T: Determine whether the pixel point is a shadow point by formula (10).

$$
\begin{aligned}
|I_Y(x, y) - B_Y(x, y)| &\le T_Y \\
|I_{Cb}(x, y) - B_{Cb}(x, y)| &\le T_{Cb} \\
|I_{Cr}(x, y) - B_{Cr}(x, y)| &\le T_{Cr}
\end{aligned}
\tag{10}
$$

The Gaussian mixture model is used for further verification. Establish K Gaussian models for shadow point L_t, and the probability density of L_t is represented by the weighted sum of K Gaussian model probability densities [8]. At time t, the probability that the pixel value obtained by L_t through calculation and determination belongs to the shaded area is:

$$
P(L_t) = \sum_{i=1}^{K} \omega_{i,t} \eta\left(L_t, \mu_{i,t}, \sum i, t\right)
\tag{11}
$$

Among them, $\omega_{i,t}$ represents the weight value, $\mu_{i,t}$ represents the mean value, $\sum i, t$ is the covariance matrix, and satisfies $\sum_{i=1}^{K} \omega_{i,t} = 1$ and $\sum_{i,t} = \sigma_{i,t}^2 I$, I is the identity matrix, and η represents the Gaussian probability density function. If the value of L_t at time t satisfies $|L_t - \mu_{i,t}| \le 2.5\sigma_{i,t}$, then the pixel point L_t matches the i-th Gaussian distribution [9]. When the matching is successful, the mean $\mu_{i,t}$ and the variance $\sigma_{i,t}^2$ are updated. If L_t does not meet the conditions, that is, when the matching fails, the $\omega_{i,t}$ value is minimized The Gaussian distribution of is in accordance with: the mean is L_t, and the standard deviation σ_0 is the update parameter.

3.5 Algorithm Steps

(1) Improve VIBE shadow removal process

Step 1: fill the background according to the difference idea to obtain a relatively complete background image, and use the first frame of the video to establish a background model according to the background modeling principle of the VIBE algorithm;

Step 2: Perform foreground detection on the input frame, and perform threshold segmentation operations on the detection results, including grayscale processing and binarization, and the results are shown in Fig. 5;

Step 3: Connected domain analysis, including morphological closing operations and removal of small areas. The main function of this step is to remove the influence of some noise and make the foreground image more accurate, as shown in Fig. 6:

Step 4: Perform neighborhood labeling on the foreground detection result, and then calculate the pixel distribution histogram of the foreground image and its neighborhood background pixel histogram respectively, compare the histogram similarity, determine whether the foreground image contains ghost images through the conditional formula, and finally All ghost area pixels are set to 0 and classified as background pixels.

Fig. 5. Foreground detection result

Fig. 6. Connectivity analysis

Step 5: Convert the foreground detection result after ghost removal and the background image with pixel classification from RGB color space to YCbCr color space, and determine whether the pixel is a shadow point by formula (10) (Fig. 7).

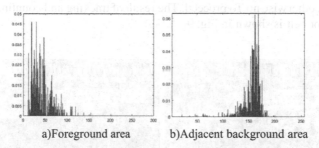

a)Foreground area   b)Adjacent background area

Fig. 7. Pixel distribution histogram

Step 6: Establish a mixed Gaussian shadow model to further verify the shadow area, and update the model parameters corresponding to the pixels that successfully match the Gaussian distribution.

Step 7: Sort the Gaussian distribution according to the ratio of the weight to the standard deviation from the largest to the smallest. If the sum of the weights of the first M Gaussian distributions is greater than the threshold T, determine the pixels that successfully match any Gaussian distribution within the M Gaussian distributions The point is a shadow point, and the pixel value of the shadow pixel is set to 0, otherwise the pixel is a foreground pixel.

Step 8: Obtain the foreground detection result of removing the shadow, and judge whether the input frame is the last frame, if it is, the tracking ends, otherwise skip to the second step (Fig. 8).

Fig. 8. Foreground detection result of removing shadows

(2) Principle of counting moving targets

The key of the counting algorithm is when the counter is + 1 and whether to execute + 1. The method used in this chapter is the feature threshold method, which classifies the foreground images extracted by the VIBE algorithm and counts the number of targets. In order to prevent the counting of small moving objects, such as floating leaves, flying birds, etc., a feature threshold is set, and feature extraction is performed on each part of the foreground image. When the relevant feature is greater than the threshold, the counter is + 1, otherwise no To proceed. The result of tracking and counting the luggage on the conveyor belt is shown in Fig. 9.

Fig. 9. Baggage count

4   Surveillance Video Simulation Experiment

4.1   Experimental Environment and Parameters

In this section, a total of 1200 frames of video footage of passengers boarding on foot and unloading their luggage from the aircraft after arriving at the aircraft parking area are carried by the ground crew to the conveyor carousel for experimentation. The relevant initialization parameters are shown in Table 1, where the auto-increment and auto-decrement parameters will change with the background change, thereby changing the adaptive radius threshold R (Fig. 10).

Table 1. Test parameters.

Shadow elimination	Improved VIBE algorithm
The number of Gaussian models K = 3	Number of pixels in sample set N = 20
Brightness component threshold $T_Y = 50$	Self-increasing parameter $\tau_c = 1.05$
Red chrominance component threshold $T_{Cb} = 20$	Self-decreasing parameter $\tau_d = 0.5$
Blue chrominance component threshold $T_{Cr} = 20$	Scale parameter t = 5

4.2 Experimental Results and Analysis

1. Shadow removal effect comparison

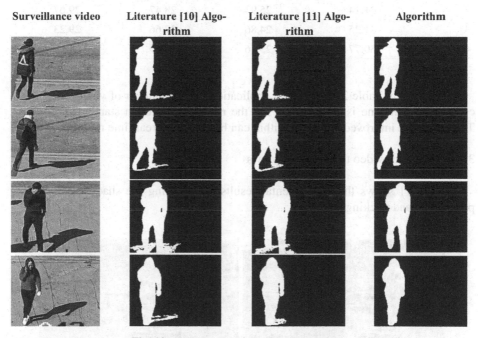

Surveillance video	Literature [10] Algorithm	Literature [11] Algorithm	Algorithm

Fig. 10. Shadow removal effect comparison

The shadow removal algorithm proposed in this article is based on the VIBE moving target tracking algorithm, which is as simple as possible and has a small amount of calculation. The idea of tracking and shadow elimination, the moving target is separated from the shadow. Using the ratio of the shadow pixel to the moving target pixel as a reference standard, the pixel ratio of literature 10 and literature 11 after shadow removal is about 0.23, and the algorithm proposed in this paper is better than the above 0.15.

2. Computing efficiency test

In order to test the computational efficiency of the algorithm proposed in this chapter, the "number of video frames processed per unit time" is used as an index to evaluate the efficiency of the algorithm, and the unit is frame/s. Test whether the traditional VIBE algorithm, the improved VIBE algorithm proposed in literature [10] and literature [11] and the algorithm proposed in this chapter meet the real-time detection standards. The algorithm to be tested performs target tracking on four video frame sequences containing shadow regions of moving targets.

Table 2. Algorithm processing speed comparison

Video number	VIBE algorithm	Literature [10] Algorithm	Literature [11] Algorithm	Algorithm
1	35.11	28.77	30.45	32.73
2	31.14	25.93	28.47	29.67
3	31.25	24.86	27.66	29.23
4	30.77	25.16	28.09	28.53

As shown in Table 2, in practical applications, if the number of video frames processed per unit time is greater than 25, the real-time detection standard is reached. Therefore, the improved VIBE algorithm can be applied to real-time monitoring.

3. Surveillance video to remove shadows

Figure 11 shows the experimental results of removing the shadow of boarding passengers and tracking counting.

Fig. 11. Passenger shadow elimination

5 Summary

This article mainly introduces an improved VIBE shadow elimination method with adaptive threshold. The first is to fill the background image with the difference idea to make the selection of the sample set in VIBE more complete when modeling the background. Then a threshold adaptive mechanism is added: the radius threshold will change with the change of the background, thus improving the robustness of the algorithm. The pixel distribution histogram matching method is used to remove the ghost image, and the ghost image area is judged by comparing the cosine value of the angle between the foreground image and the pixel distribution histogram of the adjacent background area and the Bhattacharyya distance and threshold. Finally, based on the Gaussian mixture model, the shadow of the moving target is detected and eliminated. First, the video frame sequence is converted from the RGB color space to the YCbCr color space, and then the component threshold comparison method is used to preliminarily determine the shadow points, and then create a mixture for the candidate shadow points The Gaussian shadow model, by sorting the Gaussian distributions corresponding to the candidate shadow points that meet the conditions in order of priority, determines that the candidate shadow points that successfully match the Gaussian distribution in a specific interval are the true shadow points, otherwise they are those of the previous scenic spot. Shadow points are eliminated. The number of video frames processed by the proposed algorithm in a unit event is higher than the improved VIBE algorithm proposed in [10] and [11], and slightly lower than the traditional VIBE algorithm. This is because the improved VIBE algorithm is After the foreground is extracted, ghost detection and shadow elimination are performed on the extraction result, which increases the cost of the algorithm.

Acknowledgement. This work is supported by the Natural Science Foundation of China (Grant No. 11663007, 62061049), the Application and Foundation Project of Yunnan Province (Grant No.202001BB050032, 2018FB100), the Commission for Collaborating Research Program of CAS Key Laboratory of Solar Activity, National Astronomical Observatories(Grant No.KLSA202115) and the Youth Top Talents Project of Yunnan Provincial "Ten Thousands Plan".

References

1. Barnich, O., Droogenbroeck, M.V.: ViBE: a powerful random technique to estimate the background in video sequences. In: 2009 IEEE International Conference on Acoustics, Speech and Signal Processing, pp. 945–948 (2009)
2. Yuan, G.: Research on Moving Target Detection and Tracking Algorithms in Intelligent Video Surveillance. Yunnan University (2012)
3. Guowu, Y., Zhiqiang, C., Jian, G., et al.: A moving target detection algorithm combining optical flow method and three-frame difference method. Small Microcomput. Syst. **34**(03), 668–671 (2013)
4. Gao, J., Zhu, H.: Moving object detection for video surveillance based on improved ViBe. In: 2016 Chinese Control and Decision Conference (CCDC), pp. 6259-6263 (2016)
5. Shao, X., Chen, X., Li, K., et al.: An improved moving target detection method based on vibe algorithm. Chinese Automation Congress (CAC) **2018**, 1928–1931 (2018)

6. Ren, M., Sun, H., Yang, J.: A general local pixel histogram construction method . In: China Association for Science and Technology 2000 Annual Conference, p.2 (2000)
7. Sengupta, M., Mandal, J.K.: Self authentication of color images through discrete cosine transformation (SADCT). In: 2011 International Conference on Recent Trends in Information Technology (ICRTIT), pp. 832-836 (2011)
8. Lin, P., Yen, H., Yu, C.: Gaussian distributive filtering in histogram equalization. In: 2010 International Conference on Broadband, Wireless Computing, Communication and Applications, pp. 544–549 (2010)
9. Zhang, J., Hong, X., Guan, S., et al.: Maximum gaussian mixture model for classification[C]. In: 2016 8th International Conference on Information Technology in Medicine and Education (ITME), pp. 587–591 (2016)
10. Chen, F., Zhu, B., Jing, W., et al. Removal shadow with background subtraction model ViBe algorithm[C]. In: 2013 2nd International Symposium on Instrumentation and Measurement, Sensor Network and Automation (IMSNA), pp. 264-269 (2013)
11. Lan, F., Fengqin, Y.: A vibe moving target detection algorithm for ghost and shadow removal. Progress Laser Optoelectr., 1–15 (2019)

Technological Development of Image Aesthetics Assessment

Ruoyu Zou[1]([✉]), Jiangbo Xu[1], and Ziyu Xue[1,2]

[1] State Key Laboratory of Media Convergence and Communication, Communication University of China, Beijing, China
xujiangbo@cuc.edu.cn
[2] Academy of Broadcasting Science (NRTA), Beijing, China
xueziyu@abs.ac.cn

Abstract. Quantitative research on aesthetics is a classic interdisciplinary research. With the rapid development of deep learning, various approaches have been made in image aesthetics assessment (IAA). Starting from the concept of image aesthetics, this report roughly follows the chronological sequence and first introduces the manual design of image aesthetic features. We divide IAA into generic image aesthetics assessment (GIAA) and personalized image aesthetics assessment (PIAA) to introduce separately in the deep learning part. Majority of approaches are GIAA, which purpose is to simulate general aesthetics. In this section, we separately reviewed representative studies of five assessment methods (aesthetic classification, aesthetic regression, aesthetic distribution, IAA with attributes, aesthetic description). Due to the subjectivity of aesthetics, human's aesthetics will more or less deviate from the generic value. PIAA aims to model the aesthetic preferences of specific user, and the research is of great value. We introduced this novel research in the fifth section. Finally, image aesthetic datasets of different uses are summarized. We hope this comprehensive survey can be helpful to researchers in the field of image and enhance the connection between computer and art.

Keywords: Image aesthetics assessment · Deep learning · Dataset

1 Introduction

The pursuit of beauty is human instinct. IAA can serve as guidance for tasks such as image enhancement, image cropping, image retrieval etc. In daily application scenarios, e-commerce websites use automatically generated IAA results as a guide to select product posters, and smart phones can use IAA to generate photo suggestions. At the same time, as the most widely used means of information recording, aesthetics assessment for images can also be applied in ecology [34], art

This work is supported by Research on Quality Evaluation Method of UHD Video based on Hevc (GJ181901).

Y. Peng et al. (Eds.): ICIG 2021, LNCS 12890, pp. 341–352, 2021.
https://doi.org/10.1007/978-3-030-87361-5_28

[10] and other fields. In view of the mass media resources and people's growing aesthetic needs, there will be more and more fields using IAA models in the future.

1.1 Image Quality Assessment (IQA)

IQA includes technical quality assessment and aesthetic quality assessment. The purpose of technical quality assessment is to simulate human eyes' perception of image distortion. For example, TID2013 [35] dataset for technical quality assessment contains 25 types of image distortion, such as artifact, noise, and blur. Aesthetic quality assessment also aims to achieve assessment that is close to subjective feelings. Treat technical quality as fidelity, aesthetic quality is artistic attribute based on that. Technical quality assessment uses objective grading to represent the distortion degree of images, while aesthetic quality assessment uses more complex and subjective evaluation results such as "beautiful" and "ugly".

Therefore, there is no perfect reference image for IAA, which means that IAA belongs to non-reference quality assessment. Talebi et al. [39] trained a CNN model with both technical quality dataset (TID2013 [35], LIVE [11]) and aesthetic quality dataset AVA [31], and verified that this model had good performance in both technical quality assessment and aesthetic quality assessment. To sum up, the study of IAA improves the requirement of image quality assessment from the basic technical quality to the more complex aesthetic level.

1.2 IAA Research

IAA research was launched less than 20 years, later than the development of machine learning and deep learning theory. Researchers usually adopt a data-driven method, the rise of large photography rating websites and mature subjective rating experiments provide sufficient resources for this method. IAA models mainly fall into two categories: extracting image features and inputting them into machine learning algorithms for decision making, and using neural network for end-to-end assessment (see Fig. 1)

In the first method, there are two ways of image feature extraction: manual design and feature extraction using CNN. Manual designed features often target the basic properties of the image, spatial layout, subject objects, and various photographic rules. Trained CNN can be used as feature extractor for image. Image features extracted by the deep learning model trained on other tasks are called generic deep features. The features extracted by the model trained with aesthetic data are called aesthetic deep features. In the decision making stage, machine learning algorithms such as KNN, SVM, random forest, linear regression and SVR can be used to classify or regress the aesthetic quality.

The end-to-end aesthetic assessment model benefits from the rapid development of deep learning and the establishment of large-scale image aesthetic dataset. Researchers designed different neural network models, calculated the loss between the output of last layer and training label by constructing loss function, and then iteratively updated the parameters of the model by back

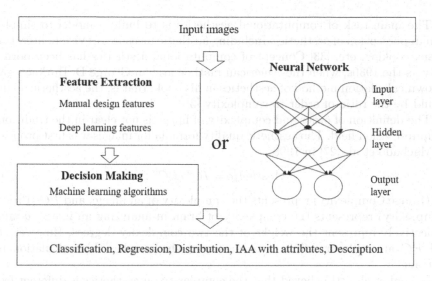

Fig. 1. Two general processes of IAA: Feature extraction and decision making, end-to-end assessment based on neural network.

propagation algorithm. The end-to-end assessment using neural network can be applied to all types of assessment: aesthetic classification, aesthetic regression, aesthetic distribution, IAA with attributes and aesthetic description.

Considering the abstraction of image aesthetics, this report intends to introduce the concept of image aesthetics in the Sect. 2 combining with the research on computational aesthetics. Then in the Sect. 3, we review the attempts of manual design features. IAA based on deep learning is divided into GIAA and PIAA, which are summarized in Sect. 4 and Sect. 5 respectively. There are various types of aesthetic datasets, and a new dataset is often accompanied with a novel research. We summarize the representative aesthetic datasets in Sect. 6. We also notice that IAA takes many forms and is developing. So this report mainly focuses on the research ideas rather than the performance of these models.

2   Inception of Image Aesthetics

Image aesthetics assessment (IAA) is a cross research direction of computational aesthetics, computer vision and psychology, which requires computer scientists to have a certain understanding of image aesthetics. The main difficulty of the study lies in the subjective and abstract aesthetic quality, as well as the variety of assessment methods.

In the field of art, artists tend to pay more attention to the emotions and ideas conveyed by their works than the aesthetic properties. Human's perception of aesthetics and emotion have something in common under some conditions. However, emotional impulses are completely subjective. Emotional responses shared between different people are hard to analyze.

The main task of computational aesthetics is to build a model to simulate human perception of aesthetics. Including aesthetic measures of vision, literature, music, cooking, etc. [33] Concept of computational aesthetics has been born as early as the 1930s, when the American mathematician George D. Burkhoff gave his own calculation method of aesthetics in his book, that is, the aesthetic quality should be the ratio of order to complexity [3].

The definition of order and complexity of image is not clear in the traditional computer vision field. The aesthetic quality formula for images was first proposed by Machado et al. [27] in 1998:

$$Aesthetic = IC^a/PC^b \qquad (1)$$

IC (Image Complexity) represents the complexity of an image, and PC (Process Complexity) represents the complexity of brain in analyzing an image. a and b respectively represent the weight of the two complexity degrees. However, IC and PC are still very difficult to measure, which makes this calculation too abstract.

Lakhal et al. [21] believed that the complexity on aesthetics is different from the information entropy used in the field of communication. They defined two kinds of complexity, namely, the entropy complexity representing the image information amount and a non-monotone increasing structural complexity.

Joshi et al. [17] discussed aesthetic and emotion in images from philosophy, photography, painting and other fields. They believed that computational framework based on machine learning is an essential method of computational aesthetics and analyzed image aesthetic data on the Internet.

With the development of computational aesthetics and definition of image aesthetic quality, calculation of image aesthetics has gradually changed from rule-driven method to data-driven method. Researchers are generally committed to designing an IAA model recognized by users with different cultural backgrounds and knowledge levels. These models have a wide range of applications although may be unconvincing for complex and abstract works of art.

3   Manual Designed Features

Researchers in the early stages of IAA adopted the method of manual design of aesthetic features. The development process of manual design features can be roughly summarized as the transformation from low-level image features to high-level aesthetic features. Low-level features of an image can reflect the basic attributes and technical quality, while the high-level aesthetic features are often based on photography rules and have a stronger ability of aesthetic expression.

In 2004, Tong et al. [40] took the lead in selecting the features of texture, color, shape and other concatenation into a 846-dimensional feature vector to classify the aesthetic quality of image. Then some researchers began to study the impact of global features on image aesthetic quality. Ke et al. [19] designed the spatial distribution of image edges, color distribution, hue, degree of blur, contrast and brightness. Aydin [2] uses five global features of sharpness, depth, clarity, hue and saturation. Since global features cannot fully represent the spatial structure and regional aesthetic properties in the image, researchers [7,25,43] tried to combine local features, features between regions and global features. Similarly, general image descriptors such as BOV, FV, and SIFT, can also be applied to IAA [30,44], but these features have limited performance due to the lack of attention to image aesthetics.

Images of different content usually have different aesthetic features. Aesthetic attributes can also be subdivided using evaluation criteria in the field of photography. Therefore, more complex and advanced aesthetic features are often targeted.

Luo et al. [25] divided images into seven categories: landscape, plant, animals, night, human, static, and architecture and designed different features for different types of images. Dhar et al. [8] designed 26 features to reflect the aesthetics and interest of the image through the classification of photos. Nishiyama et al. [32] uses the Moon-Spencer model to analyze color harmony in images. Jin et al. [16] summarized four types of lighting commonly used in portrait photography: Rembrandt, Paramount, Loop and Split, and used the stepwise feature pursuit algorithm to learn the contrast characteristics of the local lighting of photographic works.

Low-level features lack the ability to express image aesthetics. Complexity and abstraction of photography rules and the various types of pictures make the design of high-level aesthetic features a very complicated work. Therefore, IAA based on deep learning has become the mainstream research method at this stage. But we still believe in this time, manual design features have many practical applications in industry and can perform better in some area that have explicit aesthetics.

4   Generic Image Aesthetic Assessment (GIAA) Based on Deep Learning

GIAA model based on deep learning use neural network as a feature extractor or perform end-to-end IAA, which purpose is to model recognized aesthetics. This section introduces the research ideas according to the five types of IAA. We intersperses the analysis of five assessment types and datasets proposed in research during introduction.

4.1   Aesthetic Classify and Aesthetic Regression

Some studies use CNNs as feature extractors. In the early stage, Dong et al. [9] used image pyramid model to convert the original image into image blocks of different scales and same size and input them into AlexNet to extract features. In 2020, Sheng et al. [37] pointed out that the manipulation of image usually causes negative aesthetic effects. For this reason, they designed a novel self-supervised learning method to identify attributes like blur, camera shake and so on in the image. Then the features extracted by the recognition task were input into the linear classifier for aesthetic classification.

In 2013, the AVA dataset [31] containing 250,000 images was constructed and open sourced by Murray et al., which promoted end-to-end IAA as the mainstream algorithm.

In order to extract aesthetic features of different scales, many researchers have adopted the method of multi-column or multi-patches CNN models. In 2014, Lu et al. [23] designed the RAPID model, using two-column CNN to extract the features of global image and local image obtained by random cropping, and then splicing the global features and local features to classify aesthetic quality. Subsequently, Lu et al. [24] designed a multi-column neural network named DMA-Net with shared parameters. In order to extract detailed information in the image, multiple image patches of same size were randomly cropped from the original image for training. They also designed two feature fusion layers based on statistics and ranking to aggregate the output from multi-column network. Ma et al. [26] used a saliency detection method [45] to extract the salient areas of the image. The salient image blocks and the overall image were taken as vertices, and the spatial information between vertices were used as edges to construct an undirected attribute graph. The undirected attribute graph is converted into an one-dimensional vector and input to the network to extract composition information. In order to preserve the original size of image, Mai et al. [28] designed MNA-CNN. They designed an adaptive spatial pooling layer (ASP) that can output fixed-dimensional features. The model is a multi-column network using an ASP layer to extract aesthetic features of different scales. In addition, they trained a scene classification network to perform feature aggregation.

Kao et al. [18] believed that image semantic recognition is the key to assessing the aesthetics. The proposed model uses semantic recognition tasks to assist aesthetic quality evaluation under the framework of multi-task learning. The experiment found that some tags such as "Seascapes" are positively related to aesthetics, and some tags such as "Candid" are negatively related to aesthetics.

In 2018, Sheng et al. [38] applied attention mechanism to IAA. They randomly cropped out several image blocks, and then designed three attention mechanisms (average, minimum, and adaptive) to adjust the weight of image blocks during training. The experimental results show that the attention mechanism plays a positive role in the classification of image aesthetic.

4.2 Aesthetic Distribution

In the aesthetic distribution method, probability distribution is used to describe the possibility that an image is considered to belong to a certain aesthetic level, which reflects the subjectivity of IAA. Besides, distribution can be easily converted to classification and aesthetic score, which has been favored by many researchers.

Jin et al. [13] used kurtosis of image score histogram to measure the reliability of photos in AVA dataset, combined with the Jenson-Shannon divergence based on cumulative distribution as the loss function of aesthetic distribution task.

Hou et al. [12] found that EMD loss performs well on dataset that has inherent sorting among different categories. Subsequently, Talebi et al. [39] removed the last layer of MobileNet, Inception-v2 and VGG16 as the baseline model, after that they added a fully connected layer and a Softmax layer to output aesthetic distribution. They used EMD loss as loss function and made significant progress compared with other methods on AVA dataset. Cui et al. [6] combined the semantic information of image in the aesthetic distribution network, and chose a FCN to preserve the original size of input images.

4.3 IAA with Attributes

IAA with attributes means that the assessment results are generated for different aesthetic attributes. Combined with the other four decision making methods, it has a better ability to express aesthetic quality. IAA with attributes based on deep learning was first proposed in 2016 by Kong et al. [20]. They built AADB dataset containing about 10,000 pictures and open sourced. Photos in AADB have eleven aesthetic attributes (Rule of thirds, color harmony, interesting content, etc.) evaluated. Kong's model is trained using pictures in the AADB dataset and can output the quality of each attribute of the picture.

Malu et al. [29] adopted eight attributes in AADB. They used a multi-task neural network to extract features for these attributes, and used a visualization technology based on gradient back propagation to show the corresponding area of each attribute in the image. Jin et al. [15] uses a multi-task regression learning strategy to extract the general features and features of six attributes. The assessment result were displayed as an intuitive radar map.

4.4 Aesthetic Description

The research of aesthetic description is inspired by the task of image caption. Image caption is to generate a descriptive text for an image, while the task of aesthetic description is to generate aesthetic comment.

Aesthetic description is a more subjective assessment method, and often contains descriptions of one or more aesthetic attributes. Therefore, aesthetic descriptions are generally considered to be the highest level of IAA at the moment. It combines the research of computer vision and natural language processing. Limited by the scale and effectiveness of existing datasets, there are relatively few studies in this area.

The aesthetic description research started in 2017. Chang et al. [4] built PCCD containing image comments and aesthetic attributes. They proposed a novel model to generate aesthetic comments. Regarding the evaluation criteria of the generated aesthetic reviews, they pointed out that unlike the image captions datasets, the comments in PCCD have fewer synonymous sentences. Therefore, they believe that the SPICE [1] standard is more suitable for aesthetic description. In addition, Chang et al. also proposed a diversity index to measure the similarity between aesthetic reviews. Regrettably, PCCD has a small amount of data and has stopped updating.

Subsequently, Wang et al. [42] built a dataset called AVA-Reviews containing 52118 photos and 312708 reviews. Jin et al. [14] were inspired by PCCD dataset and crawled 330,000 pictures and comments of these pictures. After screening the content of the comments, 150000 pictures that have comments with one to five aesthetic attributes were retained. These photos helped them train a CNN-LSTM model combined with attention mechanism, which can generate five comments for different aesthetic attributes.

5   Personalized Image Aesthetic Assessment (PIAA)

PIAA is a challenging job and has great application prospects. GIAA can only reflect the aesthetics of a relatively small number of people in some controversial pictures. Unlike GIAA, PIAA is dedicated to learning aesthetic preferences that belong to specific users.

Constructing a personalized recommendation model for users is a problem that has been researched in the recommendation field. Because it is difficult to obtain effective and large amounts of user feedback in the field of IAA, traditional recommendation algorithms (collaborative filtering etc.) are not effective in PIAA tasks.

In 2017, Ren et al. [36] raised the issue of Personalized Image Aesthetics Assessment (PIAA). In order to link IAA with user's identity, he downloaded 40,000 images from the photography website Flickr and asked 210 workers to mark these images with 1 to 5 points on the online crowdsourcing survey platform, and finally built FLICKR-AES. They also built a dataset called REAL-CUR, consisting of 14 photo albums of real users with aesthetic ratings. Ren et al. proposed a PAM method that uses aesthetic bias of a single user to adjust the GIAA model to make it fit the user's aesthetic preferences, and an active PIAA method (Active-PAM) in order to reduce dependence on personalized data.

Li et al. [22] used personality characteristics to assist in the completion of GIAA and PIAA learning under the framework of multi-task learning. They used the PsychoFlickr dataset proposed in the research [5] to learn personality characteristics. The personality are The Big-Five (BF): Openness (O), Conscientiousness (C), Extroversion (E), Agreeableness (A), and Neuroticism (N). Trained GIAA model is fine-tuned using the aesthetic data of a single user in FLICKR-AES to generate PIAA model.

Zhu et al. [46] and Wang et al. [41] proposed methods based on meta-learning. The idea of meta-learning is considered "learning how to learn", and the purpose is to train a model that can quickly fit new tasks. In the training process of meta-learning, each user's aesthetics is treated as a single task and the aesthetic data is divided into a support set and a query set. Then the trained model is fine-tuned and tested on the test task. Experiments proved that meta-learning strategy performs well on PIAA tasks.

6   Aesthetic Datasets

IAA based on deep learning is a data-driven model. As a result of subjective assessment, aesthetic data is often accompanied by words even emoticons in daily life. Aesthetic data collection is much more complicated than other tasks such as image classification and saliency detection.

Looking back at the entire IAA development process, novel methods often accompanied with new datasets. A large-scale open source dataset can greatly promoted the development of IAA.

The above has briefly introduced some datasets and their built methods. This section intends to make a summary of some key information in the dataset. Table 1 is prepared for scale, assessment results, whether it contains aesthetic attributes, the identity of users, and whether it contains semantic information.

Table 1. Comparison of the properties of representative image aesthetics datasets

	CUHK-PQ [25]	AVA [31]	AADB [20]	FLICKR-AES [36]	PCCD [4]
Number of images	17690	255530	10000	40000	4235
Assessment type	Category	Distribution	Distribution	Distribution	Score
With attributes	No	No	Yes	No	Yes
Rater's ID	No	No	Yes	Yes	Yes
Semantic tags	No	Yes	No	No	No

7 Conclusion and Future Works

How does the brain perceive beauty? What are the characteristics of aesthetics? So far, IAA still has a lot of room for development. Research on aesthetic description and IAA with attributes are relatively small and not mature enough. In the near future, more advanced evaluation methods may be applied. There are also many problems need to be solved in PIAA.

This report reviews the development process of IAA roughly in chronological order, but those studies that are not yet popular are not worthless. IAA is a complex and huge subject. Different fields have different emphasis on aesthetics. For example, researches on composition and lighting can play a role in real-time shooting suggestions, and researches on color harmony can be used in the field of fashion etc.

Aesthetics datasets are complex and diverse. Many researchers choose to crawl photos from photography websites. Manipulation, technical quality and aesthetic value of photos are issues that researchers have to consider. How to value the multi-modality information on photography websites is also one of the works being researching.

This article reviews representative IAA approaches, We hope this report can help researchers who are engaged in or intend to engage in the work of IAA!

Acknowledgements. This work is supported by Training of Outstanding Talents in Beijing in 2017, Research on Quality Evaluation Method of UHD Video based on HEVC (GJ181901).

References

1. Anderson, P., Fernando, B., Johnson, M., Gould, S.: SPICE: semantic propositional image caption evaluation. In: Leibe, B., Matas, J., Sebe, N., Welling, M. (eds.) ECCV 2016. LNCS, vol. 9909, pp. 382–398. Springer, Cham (2016). https://doi.org/10.1007/978-3-319-46454-1_24
2. Aydın, T.O., Smolic, A., Gross, M.: Automated aesthetic analysis of photographic images. IEEE Trans. Vis. Comput. Graph. **21**(1), 31–42 (2014)
3. Birkhoff, G.D.: Aesthetic Measure. Harvard University Press (2013)
4. Chang, K.Y., Lu, K.H., Chen, C.S.: Aesthetic critiques generation for photos. In: Proceedings of the IEEE International Conference on Computer Vision, pp. 3514–3523 (2017)
5. Cristani, M., Vinciarelli, A., Segalin, C., Perina, A.: Unveiling the multimedia unconscious: Implicit cognitive processes and multimedia content analysis. In: Proceedings of the 21st ACM International Conference on Multimedia, pp. 213–222 (2013)
6. Cui, C., Liu, H., Lian, T., Nie, L., Zhu, L., Yin, Y.: Distribution-oriented aesthetics assessment with semantic-aware hybrid network. IEEE Trans. Multimedia **21**(5), 1209–1220 (2018)
7. Datta, R., Joshi, D., Li, J., Wang, J.Z.: Studying aesthetics in photographic images using a computational approach. In: Leonardis, A., Bischof, H., Pinz, A. (eds.) ECCV 2006. LNCS, vol. 3953, pp. 288–301. Springer, Heidelberg (2006). https://doi.org/10.1007/11744078_23
8. Dhar, S., Ordonez, V., Berg, T.L.: High level describable attributes for predicting aesthetics and interestingness. In: CVPR 2011, pp. 1657–1664. IEEE (2011)
9. Dong, Z., Shen, X., Li, H., Tian, X.: Photo quality assessment with DCNN that understands image well. In: He, X., Luo, S., Tao, D., Xu, C., Yang, J., Hasan, M.A. (eds.) MMM 2015. LNCS, vol. 8936, pp. 524–535. Springer, Cham (2015). https://doi.org/10.1007/978-3-319-14442-9_57
10. Elgammal, A., Liu, B., Elhoseiny, M., Mazzone, M.: CAN: Creative adversarial networks, generating "art" by learning about styles and deviating from style norms. arXiv preprint arXiv:1706.07068 (2017)
11. Ghadiyaram, D., Bovik, A.C.: Massive online crowdsourced study of subjective and objective picture quality. IEEE Trans. Image Process. **25**(1), 372–387 (2015)
12. Hou, L., Yu, C.P., Samaras, D.: Squared earth mover's distance-based loss for training deep neural networks. arXiv preprint arXiv:1611.05916 (2016)
13. Jin, X., et al.: Predicting aesthetic score distribution through cumulative Jensen-Shannon divergence. In: Proceedings of the AAAI Conference on Artificial Intelligence, vol. 32 (2018)
14. Jin, X., et al.: Aesthetic attributes assessment of images. In: Proceedings of the 27th ACM International Conference on Multimedia, pp. 311–319 (2019)
15. Jin, X., et al.: Predicting aesthetic radar map using a hierarchical multi-task network. In: Lai, J.H., et al. (eds.) PRCV 2018. LNCS, vol. 11257, pp. 41–50. Springer, Cham (2018). https://doi.org/10.1007/978-3-030-03335-4_4
16. Jin, X., Zhao, M., Chen, X., Zhao, Q., Zhu, S.-C.: Learning artistic lighting template from portrait photographs. In: Daniilidis, K., Maragos, P., Paragios, N. (eds.) ECCV 2010. LNCS, vol. 6314, pp. 101–114. Springer, Heidelberg (2010). https://doi.org/10.1007/978-3-642-15561-1_8
17. Joshi, D., et al.: Aesthetics and emotions in images. IEEE Sig. Process. Mag. **28**(5), 94–115 (2011)

18. Kao, Y., He, R., Huang, K.: Deep aesthetic quality assessment with semantic information. IEEE Trans. Image Process. **26**(3), 1482–1495 (2017)
19. Ke, Y., Tang, X., Jing, F.: The design of high-level features for photo quality assessment. In: 2006 IEEE Computer Society Conference on Computer Vision and Pattern Recognition, CVPR 2006, vol. 1, pp. 419–426. IEEE (2006)
20. Kong, S., Shen, X., Lin, Z., Mech, R., Fowlkes, C.: Photo aesthetics ranking network with attributes and content adaptation. In: Leibe, B., Matas, J., Sebe, N., Welling, M. (eds.) ECCV 2016. LNCS, vol. 9905, pp. 662–679. Springer, Cham (2016). https://doi.org/10.1007/978-3-319-46448-0_40
21. Lakhal, S., Darmon, A., Bouchaud, J.P., Benzaquen, M.: Beauty and structural complexity. Phys. Rev. Res. **2**(2), 022058 (2020)
22. Li, L., Zhu, H., Zhao, S., Ding, G., Lin, W.: Personality-assisted multi-task learning for generic and personalized image aesthetics assessment. IEEE Trans. Image Process. **29**, 3898–3910 (2020)
23. Lu, X., Lin, Z., Jin, H., Yang, J., Wang, J.Z.: RAPID: rating pictorial aesthetics using deep learning. In: Proceedings of the 22nd ACM International Conference on Multimedia, pp. 457–466 (2014)
24. Lu, X., Lin, Z., Shen, X., Mech, R., Wang, J.Z.: Deep multi-patch aggregation network for image style, aesthetics, and quality estimation. In: Proceedings of the IEEE International Conference on Computer Vision, pp. 990–998 (2015)
25. Luo, W., Wang, X., Tang, X.: Content-based photo quality assessment. In: 2011 International Conference on Computer Vision, pp. 2206–2213. IEEE (2011)
26. Ma, S., Liu, J., Wen Chen, C.: A-Lamp: adaptive layout-aware multi-patch deep convolutional neural network for photo aesthetic assessment. In: Proceedings of the IEEE Conference on Computer Vision and Pattern Recognition, pp. 4535–4544 (2017)
27. Machado, P., Cardoso, A.: Computing aesthetics. In: de Oliveira, F.M. (ed.) SBIA 1998. LNCS (LNAI), vol. 1515, pp. 219–228. Springer, Heidelberg (1998). https://doi.org/10.1007/10692710_23
28. Mai, L., Jin, H., Liu, F.: Composition-preserving deep photo aesthetics assessment. In: Proceedings of the IEEE Conference on Computer Vision and Pattern Recognition, pp. 497–506 (2016)
29. Malu, G., Bapi, R.S., Indurkhya, B.: Learning photography aesthetics with deep CNNs. arXiv preprint arXiv:1707.03981 (2017)
30. Marchesotti, L., Perronnin, F., Larlus, D., Csurka, G.: Assessing the aesthetic quality of photographs using generic image descriptors. In: 2011 International Conference on Computer Vision, pp. 1784–1791. IEEE (2011)
31. Murray, N., Marchesotti, L., Perronnin, F.: AVA: a large-scale database for aesthetic visual analysis. In: 2012 IEEE Conference on Computer Vision and Pattern Recognition, pp. 2408–2415. IEEE (2012)
32. Nishiyama, M., Okabe, T., Sato, I., Sato, Y.: Aesthetic quality classification of photographs based on color harmony. In: CVPR 2011, pp. 33–40. IEEE (2011)
33. Perc, M.: Beauty in artistic expressions through the eyes of networks and physics. J. R. Soc. Interface **17**(164), 20190686 (2020)
34. Polat, A.T., Akay, A.: Relationships between the visual preferences of urban recreation area users and various landscape design elements. Urban Forest. Urban Greening **14**(3), 573–582 (2015)
35. Ponomarenko, N., et al.: Color image database TID2013: peculiarities and preliminary results. In: European Workshop on Visual Information Processing (EUVIP), pp. 106–111. IEEE (2013)

36. Ren, J., Shen, X., Lin, Z., Mech, R., Foran, D.J.: Personalized image aesthetics. In: Proceedings of the IEEE International Conference on Computer Vision, pp. 638–647 (2017)
37. Sheng, K., et al.: Revisiting image aesthetic assessment via self-supervised feature learning. In: Proceedings of the AAAI Conference on Artificial Intelligence, vol. 34, pp. 5709–5716 (2020)
38. Sheng, K., Dong, W., Ma, C., Mei, X., Huang, F., Hu, B.G.: Attention-based multi-patch aggregation for image aesthetic assessment. In: Proceedings of the 26th ACM International Conference on Multimedia, pp. 879–886 (2018)
39. Talebi, H., Milanfar, P.: NIMA: neural image assessment. IEEE Trans. Image Process. **27**, 3998–4011 (2017)
40. Tong, H., Li, M., Zhang, H.-J., He, J., Zhang, C.: Classification of digital photos taken by photographers or home users. In: Aizawa, K., Nakamura, Y., Satoh, S. (eds.) PCM 2004. LNCS, vol. 3331, pp. 198–205. Springer, Heidelberg (2004). https://doi.org/10.1007/978-3-540-30541-5_25
41. Wang, W., Su, J., Li, L., Xu, X., Luo, J.: Meta-learning perspective for personalized image aesthetics assessment. In: 2019 IEEE International Conference on Image Processing (ICIP), pp. 1875–1879. IEEE (2019)
42. Wang, W., Yang, S., Zhang, W., Zhang, J.: Neural aesthetic image reviewer. IET Comput. Vis. **13**(8), 749–758 (2019)
43. Wong, L.K., Low, K.L.: Saliency-enhanced image aesthetics class prediction. In: 2009 16th IEEE International Conference on Image Processing (ICIP), pp. 997–1000. IEEE (2009)
44. Yeh, M.C., Cheng, Y.C.: Relative features for photo quality assessment. In: 2012 19th IEEE International Conference on Image Processing, pp. 2861–2864. IEEE (2012)
45. Zhang, J., Sclaroff, S., Lin, Z., Shen, X., Price, B., Mech, R.: Unconstrained salient object detection via proposal subset optimization. In: Proceedings of the IEEE Conference on Computer Vision and Pattern Recognition, pp. 5733–5742 (2016)
46. Zhu, H., Li, L., Wu, J., Zhao, S., Ding, G., Shi, G.: Personalized image aesthetics assessment via meta-learning with bilevel gradient optimization. IEEE Trans. Cybern. (2020)

Noise Robust Video Super-Resolution Without Training on Noisy Data

Fei Zhou[1,2,3,4], Zitao Lu[1,2,3,4], Hongming Luo[1,2,3,4], Cuixin Yang[1,2,3,4], and Bozhi Liu[1,2,3,4]($\boxtimes$)

[1] College of Electronics and Information Engineering, Shenzhen University, Shenzhen, China
[2] Peng Cheng Laboratory, Shenzhen, China
[3] Guangdong Key Laboratory of Intelligent Information Processing, Shenzhen, China
[4] Key Laboratory of Digital Creative Technology, Shenzhen, China

Abstract. Previous CNN-based video super-resolution (VSR) approaches can not be directly applied to noisy images, otherwise the noise
will be enhanced after super-resolution (SR) reconstruction models.
Some methods are robust to noise but all of them need to be trained
on specific noisy training datasets. In this paper, we propose a noise-
robust VSR network which only needs to be trained on the clean images.
That is, in our deep network for VSR, the model can appropriately super-
resolve noisy images without any training on noisy data. We put forward
a non-local spatio-temporal module, which not only achieves motion estimation and compensation, but also improves the robustness of our VSR
model to noise. A inter-frame fusion module is further presented to fuse
the complementary information from different frames. The experiments
conducted on both additive noise and multiplicative noise demonstrate
that the proposed method can generate visually and quantitatively high-
quality results, superior to state-of-the-art methods.

Keywords: Video · Super-resolution · Noise-robust

1 Introduction

Single image super-resolution (SISR) aims to recover a high-resolution (HR)
image from its corresponding low-resolution (LR) image, by exploring estimated
self-similarity; for video super-resolution (VSR), additional spatial information
across positions and temporal information between frames should be considered
to enhance details for a LR frame. The improved video frame quality could
be benefit to many computer vision tasks, such as object detection, semantic
segmentation. However, when the image is contaminated, the results of SR will
be very poor as demonstrated in Fig. 1. The capability of the proposed methods
that only trained on the clean images are still limited in dealing with noise
images and the noise will be amplified after the reconstruction model.

In this paper, we propose a video super-resolution deep learning framework
to achieve noise resilient video frames, which only need to be trained on the clean

© Springer Nature Switzerland AG 2021
Y. Peng et al. (Eds.): ICIG 2021, LNCS 12890, pp. 353–365, 2021.
https://doi.org/10.1007/978-3-030-87361-5_29

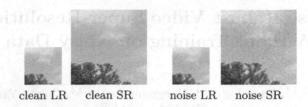

clean LR   clean SR   noise LR   noise SR

Fig. 1. Example of super-resolution with clean and noise input. Left: clean LR image and its corresponding Enhanced Deep Residual Networks for Single Image Super-Resolution (EDSR) [11] output. Right: LR image suffered from Speckle noise with 0.1 variance and its corresponding EDSR output.

training images. Specifically, we put forward a non-local spatio-temporal module to perform motion estimation and motion compensation on the neighboring frames. This will take advantage of the similarity of non-local spatio-temporal positions, and robust to noise. Finally we use inter-frame feature fusion module to fuse the video frame sequences to obtain complementary information of multiple frames. From the experiments shown, our method outperforms current state-of-the-art VSR methods, on PSNR, SSIM and visually.

2   Related Work

Single image super-resolution reconstruction methods can be roughly divided into two categories: (1) traditional methods, (2) learning-based methods.

Early SR methods include some well-known linear or non-linear filters, such as nearest-neighbor, bilinear, bicubic [20]. All of them are interpolation-based approaches. Due to their simple filtering kernels or weighting factors, these methods easily suffer from various artifacts. The rapid development of deep learning techniques greatly improved the performance of super resolution algorithms. Dong et al. [3] proposed a deep learning-based SR method (SRCNN) by firstly introducing a three layer convolutional neural network (CNN) for image SR. Inspired by this pioneering work, the residual network for training much deeper network architectures [7,8] was introduced and achieved superior performance. Later, MemNet in [14] have a persistent memory. These methods extract features from the interpolated LR images, which inevitably losses some details. To address this problem, several methods have been proposed, such as EDSR [11] and other methods [4,22–24], outperforming previous works by a large margin. Their solution is extracting features from the LR images and then upsampling at the network tail.

Single image super-resolution has achieved significant improvements over the last few years. Recently, more attentions have been shifted to video super-resolution. Video super-resolution aims to recover HR frames from a sequence of LR frames. Most video super-resolution methods consist of the following parts: motion estimation, motion compensation, fusion and upsampling.

Kappeler et al. [6] firstly put forward a video super-resolution with convolutional neural networks (VSRnet) which is based on SRCNN, where they shared the weights in a symmetrical way to handle the input frames. Several VSR methods use optical flow for explicit temporal alignment. These methods first estimate motions between the reference frame and each neighboring frame with optical flow and then warps the neighboring frame using the predicted motion map. However, it is difficult to obtain accurate flow when given a large motion. Besides, per-pixel motion estimation often suffers a heavy computation load. [2] is the first end-to-end video SR method that jointly trains optical flow estimation and spatial temporal networks. TDAN [15] uses deformable convolutions to align the input frames at the feature level without explicit motion estimation or image warping. Inspired by TDAN, EDVR [18] adopts deformable convolutions as a basic operation for alignment and achieve better performance. But the training process is unstable.

However, none of the above methods can be directly applied to noisy images without training on noise data. To super-resolve noisy LR images, in [9], a denoising procedure is performed at a middle resolution between LR and HR to prevent the residual noises from being boosted. In [5], the noise level of LR images is first estimated and then employed to determine the value of regularization parameter. Recently, the noise-robust iterative back-projection is presented in [21] for noisy image SR. But these methods required the datasets contain pairs of clean and noisy images. In this paper, we propose a novel neural network to obtain noise resilient image super-resolution, which only need to be trained on the clean training dataset. Experimental results demonstrate that our method outperforms the other state-of-the-art methods.

3 Methodology

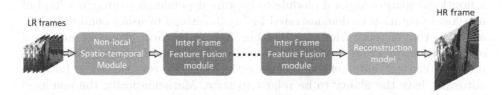

Fig. 2. The NRVSR framework.

3.1 Overview

The overview framework of the proposed Noise Robust Video Super-resolution (NRVSR) is shown in Fig. 2. We take $I_{[t-N:t+N]}$ low-resolution frames as input and generate a high-resolution output. We denote the middle frame I_t as the reference frame and $I_{[t-N:t-1,t+1:t+N]}$ as neighboring frames. Each neighboring frame is aligned to the reference frame by non-local spatio-temporal module. The inter-frame feature fusion module fuses image information of different frames. The fused features then pass through a reconstruction module. It is a feature-to-image mapping, which transforms fused multiple features of LR frames to an HR frame. It can be replaced by any other state-of-the-art SISR models. In this paper, we use Residual Feature Aggregation Network (RFAnet) [12] for reconstruction model.

3.2   Non-local Spatio-temporal Module

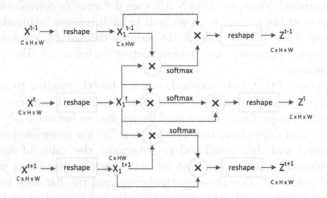

Fig. 3. Framework of the non-local spatial-temporal module. X^t represents the reference frame, X^{t-1} represents the neighboring frame. C denotes the number of channels. $\otimes$ denotes matrix multiplication.

It is a reasonable assumption that the noise is uncorrelated with the image information [1]. Therefore, in order to reduce the impact of noise, we propose a non-local spatio-temporal module to capture dependencies through a kind of non-local operation as demonstrated in Fig. 3. Instead of using non-local operation on the reference frame for filtering [25], we perform pixel-wise non-local operation on the reference frame and neighboring frame for information alignment. It can not only achieve motion estimation and compensation, but also naturally have the ability to be robust to noise. Mathematically, the non-local operation can be described as follows [17]:

$$\mathbf{z}_i = \frac{1}{\mathcal{H}(\mathbf{x})} \sum_{\forall j} f(\mathbf{x}_i, \mathbf{y}_j) g(\mathbf{y}_j). \qquad (1)$$

where x_i is the ith patch in reference frame, y_j are all possible patch (matching patch) in neighboring frame, z_i is the ith output patch in neighboring frame, which should be with the same size as x_i. The function $f(\cdot)$ calculates a scalar that represents the relationship between x_i and y_i. $g(\cdot)$ gives a representation of y_i and $\mathcal{H}(\mathbf{x})$ is used for normalization.

According to Wang et al. [17], they provided some options for function $f(\cdot)$ like Gaussian function, embedded Gaussian function and dot product function.

For simplicity, in this paper, the weight is calculated by the square of the Euclidean distance between two patches, defined as:

$$f(x_i, y_j) = e^{-\frac{\|x_i - y_j\|^2}{h^2}}. \tag{2}$$

Here $\|x_i - y_j\|^2$ represents the similarity of x_i and y_i, h is a adjustable scalar parameter that fixed in training. Here, we use the method in [18] to estimate the noise level and h is automatically adjusted during testing. The nomalization factor is set as $\mathcal{H}(\mathbf{x}) = \sum_{\forall j} f(\mathbf{x}_i, \mathbf{y}_j)$.

Taking the reference frame and previous frame for example as demonstrated in Fig. 3, X^t represents the reference frame, X^{t-1} represents the previous neighboring frame. We first reshape X^t to X_1^t and X^{t-1} to X_1^{t-1} to facilitate matrix multiplication. And then according to Formula (2), we calculate the similarity of X_1^t and X_1^{t-1} then through a softmax function and matrix multiplication with $g(X_1^{t-1})$:

$$Z^{t-1} = \left[softmax \left(\frac{2(X_1^t)^T X_1^{t-1} - (X_1^t)^T (X_1^t)^T - X_1^{t-1} X_1^{t-1}}{h^2} \right) \right] \cdot g(X_1^{t-1}). \tag{3}$$

The above softmax operation resemble the one to self-attention network [16]. The purpose of the latter reshape is to get an output of the same size as the input. The information in Z^{t-1} are totally derived from X_1^{t-1}. That is to say we make full use of intra information. In order to denoise better, we do the same operation on the reference frame. Since there is no noise during training, the value of h is very small so that this operation on the reference frame has no effect on the results of training. Through the non-local spatio-temporal module, we have achieved both motion estimation and motion compensation on the neighboring frames. At the same time, we take advantage of the similarity of the non-local position of the image, and perform weighted summation through self-attention to achieve robustness to noise.

3.3   Inter-frame Feature Fusion Module

In order to effectively make better use of spatio-temporal information among consecutive frames and fuse them, we propose a inter-frame feature fusion block (IFFFB) as demonstrated in Fig. 4. Taking the frame t as an example, we first adopt 3×3 convolutional layers, which can be described as:

$$F_1^t = Conv\_1 \left(F_0^t \right). \tag{4}$$

Where t represents the index of temporal dimension, $Conv\_1$ represents the first convolutional layer. F_0^t denotes the input feature and F_1^t denotes the extracted feature maps, which are supposed to contain information from each input feature. Inspired by the slow fusion and 3D convolution [13], the feature maps $\{F_1^{t-1}, F_1^t, F_1^{t+1}\}$ are concatenated:

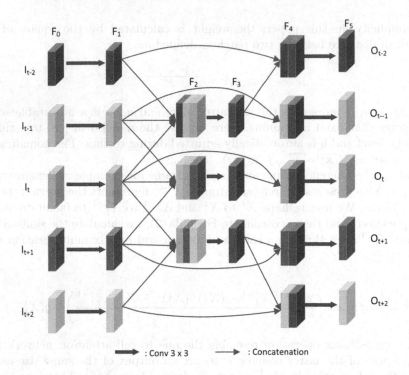

Fig. 4. The structure of one Inter-Frame Feature Fusion Block (IFFFB)

$$F_2^t = C\left\{F_1^{t-1}, F_1^t, F_1^{t+1}\right\}. \tag{5}$$

Where $C(\cdot)$ denotes concatenation. The front and back frames have closest information to the reference frame. That is to say, this aggregated deep feature map contains a large deal of the most similar temporal-correlated information. Then F_2^t will be through the second 3×3 convolutional layers:

$$F_3^t = Conv\_2\left(F_2^t\right). \tag{6}$$

The purpose of this convolution is to reduce dimensions and to have stronger representational capabilities. After that we concatenate the feature maps $\{F_3^t, F_1^t\}$:

$$F_4^t = C\left\{F_3^t, F_1^t\right\}. \tag{7}$$

Feature maps F_4^t contain two kinds of information now: self-independent spatial information and fully mixed temporal information. At last, we through the last 3×3 convolutional layers to ensure that input and output are the same dimension:

$$F_5^t = Conv\_3\left(F_4^t\right). \tag{8}$$

From Eq. (4)–Eq. (8), we can readily find that the output data dimension remains the same with input so we can set the number of IFFFB according to our needs. We can extract both intra-frame spatial correlations and inter-frame temporal correlations and fuse them iteratively.

4 Experiments and Analysis

4.1 Experiments Setup

Datasets. REDS consists of 240 training clips, 30 validation clips and 30 testing clips (each with 100 consecutive frames). Since the test ground truth is not available, we mix train set and validation set together and select 4 representative clips named REDS4 as our test set. The remaining training and validation clips are restricted as our training dataset.

Training Details. For training, we use the RGB input patches of size 48×48 from LR frames with the corresponding HR patches. It should be emphasized that the training pairs are clean HR-LR images. The network takes five consecutive frames as inputs. The training data is augmented with random horizontal flips and 90 rotations. We train our model with ADAM optimizer by setting β_1 = 0.9, β_2 = 0.999, and $\epsilon = 10^{-8}$. The learning rate is initialized as 10^{-4} and halved at every 2×10^5 minibatch updates. Mini-batch size is set to 32 and the channel size is set to 80. We train our networks using L1 loss instead of L2. The matching patch is set to 5×5 in non-local spatio-temporal module. We use 10 IFFFBs in the fusion model and use the RFANet [12] for SR reconstruction model. We implement our model with the PyTorch framework and train them using 2 NVIDIA 2080Ti GPUs.

Evaluation. Peak Signal-to-Noise Ratio (PSNR) and Structural Similarity Index (SSIM) are adopted to evaluate SISR or VSR performance of different methods. Mathematically, PSNR can be expressed as follows:

$$PSNR = 10 \times \log_{10}\left(\frac{(2^n - 1)^2}{MSE}\right),\tag{9}$$

$$MSE = \frac{1}{mn}\sum_{i=0}^{m-1}\sum_{j=0}^{n-1}\|Sr(i,j) - Gt(i,j)\|^2.\tag{10}$$

Here, $Sr(i, j)$ represents each pixel of the SR result, $Gt(i, j)$ represents each pixel of Ground True. In Formula (9), the value of n is 8. SSIM can be described as:

$$SSIM(X,Y) = L(X,Y) * C(X,Y) * S(X,Y),\tag{11}$$

$$L(X,Y) = \frac{2u_X u_Y + C_1}{u_X^2 + u_Y^2 + C_1},\tag{12}$$

$$C(X,Y) = \frac{2\sigma_X \sigma_Y + C_2}{\sigma_X^2 + \sigma_Y^2 + C_2},\tag{13}$$

$$S(X,Y) = \frac{\sigma_{XY} + C_3}{\sigma_X \sigma_Y + C_3}. \tag{14}$$

Here, X represents the SR output, Y represents the Ground True. u_X and u_Y represent the mean values of images X and Y respectively, σ_X and σ_Y represent the standard deviations of images X and Y respectively, and $\sigma_X * \sigma_X$ and $\sigma_Y * \sigma_Y$ respectively represent images X and Y Variance. σ_{XY} represents the image X and Y covariance. C_1, C_2 and C_3 are constants. Usually take $C_1 = (K_1 * L)^2$, $C_2 = (K_2 * L)^2$, $C_3 = C_2/2$, generally $K_1 = 0.01$, $K_1 = 0.03$, $L = 255$.

Instead of testing clean LR frames, in our experiments, we add different degrees of Gaussian noise (additive noise) to the testing clips of REDS. The variance is set to 0.01 and 0.05, respectively. We also add Speckle noise (multiplicative noise) to the testing clips. The variance is set to 0.05 and 0.1, respectively.

Comparisons with State-of-the-Art Methods. We compare the proposed method with 3 SISR approaches and 2 VSR approaches, including Bicubic, EDSR [11], ESRGAN [19], TDAN [15], EDVR [18] on REDS4. The quantitative results on RED4 with Speckle noise are shown in Table 2 and Table 3 while the results with Gaussian noise are shown in Table 1 and Table 4. We report the quantitative comparisons for scale x4. As shown in the tables, whether it is additive noise (Gaussian noise) or multiplicative noise (Speckle noise), NRVSR is significantly better than the state-of-the-art methods in PSNR and SSIM. Furthermore, our method can achieve better results under different noise levels. With Gaussian noise with a variance of 0.05 as shown in Fig. 5, the visual perception of Bicubic is very poor, this is partly due to images which are seriously contaminated. ESRGAN and EDSR restored the wrong information in the part of the window. The results of TDAN and EDVR are relatively blur. Compared

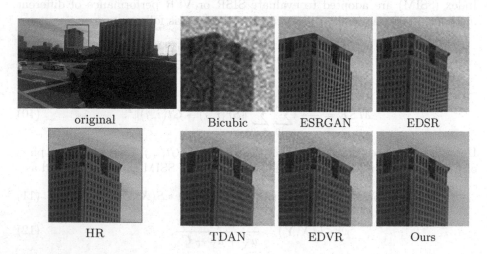

Fig. 5. Qualitative comparison on the REDS4 (clip015) with 0.05 Gaussian noise for 4× video SR. Zoom in for best view.

with the above method, our method is closer to the ground truth that with sharp edge and without noise and artifacts.

Table 1. Quantitative comparison (PSNR (dB) and SSIM) on REDS4 with 0.05 Gaussian noise.

Method	clip000	clip011	clip015	clip020	Average
Bicubic	20.16/0.32	20.70/0.32	21.33/0.30	20.44/0.35	20.66/0.32
EDSR	25.30/0.65	27.42/0.72	29.50/0.76	26.55/0.73	27.19/0.71
ESRGAN	25.37/0.65	27.53/0.73	29.48/0.76	26.64/0.74	27.25/0.72
TDAN	25.77/0.69	27.27/0.71	29.23/0.73	26.48/0.73	27.19/0.72
EDVR	26.07/0.69	27.54/0.72	29.66/0.76	26.79/0.73	27.51/0.72
Ours	**26.35/0.75**	**28.85/0.79**	**31.08/0.85**	**27.76/0.81**	**28.51/0.80**

Table 2. Quantitative comparison (PSNR (dB) and SSIM) on REDS4 with 0.1 Speckle noise.

Method	clip000	clip011	clip015	clip020	Average
Bicubic	20.16/0.32	20.70/0.32	21.33/0.30	20.44/0.35	26.02/0.75
EDSR	25.30/0.65	27.42/0.72	29.50/0.76	26.55/0.73	27.83/0.76
ESRGAN	25.37/0.65	27.53/0.73	29.48/0.76	26.64/0.74	27.96/0.77
TDAN	25.77/0.69	27.27/0.71	29.23/0.73	26.48/0.73	27.91/0.77
EDVR	26.07/0.69	27.54/0.72	29.66/0.76	26.79/0.73	28.33/0.78
Ours	**26.89/0.77**	**29.46/0.82**	**31.95/0.86**	**28.43/0.83**	**29.18/0.82**

original   Bicubic   ESRGAN   EDSR

HR   TDAN   EDVR   Ours

Fig. 6. Qualitative comparison on the REDS4 (clip000) with 0.1 Speckle noise for 4× video SR. Zoom in for best view.

For additive noise (Speckle noise) as shown in Fig. 6, our NRVSR outperforms the state-of-the-art methods by a large margin. For other comparison methods, whether SISR or VSR methods, the noise in the image is amplified. By contrast, it can be seen that our result have less noise and artifacts compared with other methods.

For relatively low noise levels, which are shown in Fig. 7 and Fig. 8, our performance also have advantages. The noise will be amplified after the super-resolution reconstruction model so their results will get worse. At the same time, our performance is clean and sharp.

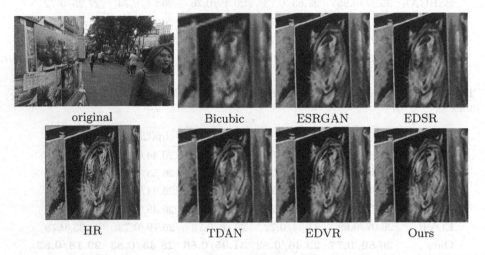

Fig. 7. Qualitative comparison on the REDS4 (clip020) with 0.01 Gaussian noise for 4× video SR. Zoom in for best view.

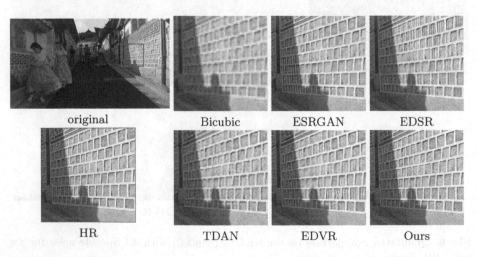

Fig. 8. Qualitative comparison on the REDS4 (clip011) with 0.05 Speckle noise for 4× video SR. Zoom in for best view.

Table 3. Quantitative comparison (PSNR (dB) and SSIM) on REDS4 with 0.05 Speckle noise.

Method	clip000	clip011	clip015	clip020	Average
Bicubic	24.51/0.66	26.01/0.73	28.43/0.79	25.36/0.74	26.08/0.73
EDSR	25.83/0.70	28.39/0.79	31.07/0.85	27.31/0.80	28.15/0.79
ESRGAN	25.92/0.70	28.63/0.80	31.40/0.85	27.46/0.81	28.35/0.79
TDAN	26.51/0.75	28.23/0.79	30.90/0.84	27.30/0.81	28.24/0.80
EDVR	26.87/0.75	28.68/0.80	31.60/0.86	27.79/0.81	28.74/0.80
Ours	**27.13/0.79**	**30.01/0.83**	**32.45/0.88**	**28.78/0.85**	**29.60/0.84**

Table 4. Quantitative comparison (PSNR (dB) and SSIM) on REDS4 with 0.01 Gaussian noise.

Method	clip000	clip011	clip015	clip020	Average
Bicubic	24.51/0.66	26.01/0.72	28.43/0.79	25.36/0.74	26.08/0.73
EDSR	25.87/0.71	28.55/0.79	31.06/0.85	27.33/0.80	28.20/0.79
ESRGAN	25.98/0.71	28.87/0.80	31.34/0.85	27.48/0.80	28.42/0.79
TDAN	26.55/0.76	28.33/0.79	30.88/0.84	27.30/0.81	28.26/0.80
EDVR	26.92/0.76	28.82/0.80	31.57/0.86	27.78/0.81	28.77/0.81
Ours	**27.14/0.80**	**30.15/0.84**	**32.38/0.88**	**28.78/0.85**	**29.61/0.84**

In summary, the proposed algorithm in this paper has a significant improvement in anti-noisy ability and restore details ability compared with other state-of-the-art algorithms.

5 Conclusion

In this work, we proposed a novel noise-robust deep neural VSR network which only need to be trained on the clean datasets. We put forward a non-local spatio-temporal module to achieve motion estimation and compensation and realize the robustness to noise. We also proposed a inter-frame feature fusion module to fuse complementary information.

Experimental results have shown that the proposed our algorithm achieves better performance in comparison with other state-of-the-art algorithms.

Acknowledgements. This work was in part by Guangdong Basic and Applied Basic Research Foundation with No. 2020A1515110884, and in part by Guangdong Basic and Applied Basic Research Foundation with No. 2021A1515011584. The authors would like to thank the editors and reviewers for their constructive suggestions on our work.

References

1. Buades, A., Coll, B., Morel, J.M.: Nonlocal image and movie denoising. Int. J. Comput. Vis. **76**(2), 123–139 (2008)
2. Caballero, J., et al.: Real-time video super-resolution with spatio-temporal networks and motion compensation. In: Proceedings of the IEEE Conference on Computer Vision and Pattern Recognition, pp. 4778–4787 (2017)
3. Dong, C., Loy, C.C., He, K., Tang, X.: Learning a deep convolutional network for image super-resolution. In: Fleet, D., Pajdla, T., Schiele, B., Tuytelaars, T. (eds.) ECCV 2014. LNCS, vol. 8692, pp. 184–199. Springer, Cham (2014). https://doi.org/10.1007/978-3-319-10593-2_13
4. Haris, M., Shakhnarovich, G., Ukita, N.: Recurrent back-projection network for video super-resolution. In: Proceedings of the IEEE/CVF Conference on Computer Vision and Pattern Recognition, pp. 3897–3906 (2019)
5. Huang, S., Sun, J., Yang, Y., Fang, Y., Lin, P., Que, Y.: Robust single-image super-resolution based on adaptive edge-preserving smoothing regularization. IEEE Trans. Image Process. **27**(6), 2650–2663 (2018)
6. Kappeler, A., Yoo, S., Dai, Q., Katsaggelos, A.K.: Video super-resolution with convolutional neural networks. IEEE Trans. Comput. Imaging **2**(2), 109–122 (2016)
7. Kim, J., Lee, J.K., Lee, K.M.: Accurate image super-resolution using very deep convolutional networks. In: Proceedings of the IEEE Conference on Computer Vision and Pattern Recognition, pp. 1646–1654 (2016)
8. Kim, J., Lee, J.K., Lee, K.M.: Deeply-recursive convolutional network for image super-resolution. In: Proceedings of the IEEE Conference on Computer Vision and Pattern Recognition, pp. 1637–1645 (2016)
9. Lee, O.Y., Lee, J.W., Kim, J.O.: Combining self-learning based super-resolution with denoising for noisy images. J. Vis. Commun. Image Represent. **48**, 66–76 (2017)
10. Lee, T.B., Heo, Y.S.: Single image super resolution using convolutional neural networks for noisy images. In: 2020 International Conference on Information and Communication Technology Convergence (ICTC), pp. 195–199. IEEE (2020)
11. Lim, B., Son, S., Kim, H., Nah, S., Mu Lee, K.: Enhanced deep residual networks for single image super-resolution. In: Proceedings of the IEEE Conference on Computer Vision and Pattern Recognition Workshops, pp. 136–144 (2017)
12. Liu, J., Zhang, W., Tang, Y., Tang, J., Wu, G.: Residual feature aggregation network for image super-resolution. In: Proceedings of the IEEE/CVF Conference on Computer Vision and Pattern Recognition, pp. 2359–2368 (2020)
13. Qiu, Z., Yao, T., Mei, T.: Learning spatio-temporal representation with pseudo-3D residual networks. In: Proceedings of the IEEE International Conference on Computer Vision, pp. 5533–5541 (2017)
14. Tai, Y., Yang, J., Liu, X., Xu, C.: MemNet: a persistent memory network for image restoration. In: Proceedings of the IEEE International Conference on Computer Vision, pp. 4539–4547 (2017)
15. Tian, Y., Zhang, Y., Fu, Y., Xu, C.: TDAN: temporally-deformable alignment network for video super-resolution. In: Proceedings of the IEEE/CVF Conference on Computer Vision and Pattern Recognition, pp. 3360–3369 (2020)
16. Vaswani, A., et al.: Attention is all you need. arXiv preprint arXiv:1706.03762 (2017)
17. Wang, X., Girshick, R., Gupta, A., He, K.: Non-local neural networks. In: Proceedings of the IEEE Conference on Computer Vision and Pattern Recognition, pp. 7794–7803 (2018)

18. Wang, X., Chan, K.C., Yu, K., Dong, C., Change Loy, C.: EDVR: video restoration with enhanced deformable convolutional networks. In: Proceedings of the IEEE/CVF Conference on Computer Vision and Pattern Recognition Workshops (2019)
19. Wang, X., et al.: ESRGAN: enhanced super-resolution generative adversarial networks. In: Leal-Taixé, L., Roth, S. (eds.) ECCV 2018. LNCS, vol. 11133, pp. 63–79. Springer, Cham (2019). https://doi.org/10.1007/978-3-030-11021-5_5
20. Yeganli, F., Nazzal, M., Ozkaramanli, H.: Super-resolution using multiple structured dictionaries based on the gradient operator and bicubic interpolation. In: 2016 24th Signal Processing and Communication Application Conference (SIU), pp. 941–944 (2016). https://doi.org/10.1109/SIU.2016.7495896
21. Yoo, J.S., Kim, J.O.: Noise-robust iterative back-projection. IEEE Trans. Image Process. **29**, 1219–1232 (2019)
22. Zhang, K., Gool, L.V., Timofte, R.: Deep unfolding network for image super-resolution. In: Proceedings of the IEEE/CVF Conference on Computer Vision and Pattern Recognition, pp. 3217–3226 (2020)
23. Zhang, Y., Li, K., Li, K., Wang, L., Zhong, B., Fu, Y.: Image super-resolution using very deep residual channel attention networks. In: Ferrari, V., Hebert, M., Sminchisescu, C., Weiss, Y. (eds.) ECCV 2018. LNCS, vol. 11211, pp. 294–310. Springer, Cham (2018). https://doi.org/10.1007/978-3-030-01234-2_18
24. Zhang, Y., Tian, Y., Kong, Y., Zhong, B., Fu, Y.: Residual dense network for image super-resolution. In: Proceedings of the IEEE Conference on Computer Vision and Pattern Recognition, pp. 2472–2481 (2018)
25. Zhou, F., Xia, S.T., Liao, Q.: Nonlocal pixel selection for multisurface fitting-based super-resolution. IEEE Trans. Circ. Syst. Video Technol. **24**(12), 2013–2017 (2014)

Shadow Detection and Removal Based on Multi-task Generative Adversarial Networks

Xiaoyue Jiang[1(✉)], Zhongyun Hu[1], Yue Ni[2], Yuxiang Li[1], and Xiaoyi Feng[1]

[1] Northwestern Polytechnical University, Xi'an, China
xjiang@nwpu.edu.cn
[2] China Academy of Launch Vehicle Technology, Beijing, China

Abstract. The existence of shadows is difficult to avoid in images. Also, it will affect object recognition and image understanding. But on the other hand, shadow can provide information about the light source and object shape. Therefore, accurate shadow detection and removal can contribute to many computer vision tasks. However, even the same object, its shadow will vary greatly under different lighting conditions. Thus it is quite challenging to detect and remove shadows from images. Recent research always treated these two tasks independently, but they are closely related to each other actually. Therefore, we propose a multi-task adversarial generative networks (mtGAN) that can detect and remove shadows simultaneously. In order to enhance shadow detection and shadow removal mutually, a cross-stitch unit is proposed to learn the optimal ways to fuse and constrain features between multi-tasks. Also, the combination weight of multi-task loss functions are learned according to the uncertainty distribution of each task, which is not set empirically as usual. Based on these multi-task learning strategies, the proposed mtGAN can jointly achieve shadow detection and removal tasks better than existing methods. In experiments, the effectiveness of the proposed mtGAN is shown.

Keywords: Shadow detection · Shadow removal · Multi-task learning · Adversarial generative network

1 Introduction

Even though shadow is a common physical phenomenon in nature, it brings great challenges for many computer vision algorithms. Shadows can break the continuity of original scenes or objects in images, which can confuse object detection or recognition algorithms. However, shadows also can provide information about the shape of the object [1], and the direction and intensity of light sources [2]. Therefore effective shadow detection and removal methods can improve the performance of computer vision systems.

Shadow detection and removal are challenging tasks. For the same object, the shape and intensity of the shadows may vary depending on the lighting

© Springer Nature Switzerland AG 2021
Y. Peng et al. (Eds.): ICIG 2021, LNCS 12890, pp. 366–376, 2021.
https://doi.org/10.1007/978-3-030-87361-5_30

conditions. Moreover, the intensity of the shadow is not uniform everywhere, which gradually changes from the edges to the inner area. For single image-based shadow detection, the color and texture constancy of object are always used. For example, shadow invariant color space [3], color distributions across shadow edges [4] and the color ratio of inside and outside shadow regions [5] are used to detect shadows. In addition, the intensity distribution of shadow and nonshadow also can be used to detect the existence of shadow [6]. Recently, deep learning based methods are applied to extract more complicated features for shadow regions. Shen et al. [7] applied deep neural networks to determine if an image patch contain shadow or not, and then the conditional random field method is applied to smooth the shadow edges. Khan et al. [8] setup two neural networks to extract feature from shadow region and shadow edge, respectively. Zheng et al. [9] integrate gradients of shadow region in CNN for shadow detection.

For shadow removal, classical works first do shadow detection and then shadow removal. In order to recovery the shadow region, some works recovery the gradient value of shadow regions to the same as related non-shadow regions [10]. Some works adjust intensity value, where Bayesian [8] or Random Forest [11] can be used to estimate the shadow matte. Qu et al. [12] propose a DeshadowNet, which contains three cooperative sub-deep networks to estimate the shadow matte in details. On the other hand, some works directly restore shadow free images without shadow detection. Some researchers apply intrinsic analysis methods [13,14] to recovery the reflectance map from images. Le et al. [15] design two networks to estimate relit image and shadow matte to help the final shadow removal. Fu et al. [16] created a series over exposure images and select the optimal one to fuse with the original image, and to remove the shadow. Recently, adversarial generative networks (GAN) has been also introduced for shadow removal. Wang et al. [17] propose to use two GANs, where one GAN is for shadow detection and the other GAN uses the detection results to create shadow free images. Ding et al. [18] proposed to combine shadow attention map with GAN for shadow removal. Liu et al. [19] proposed GANs to generate shadow and then remove shadow, where the generated false shadow region is constricted by the real shadow region in the discriminator.

Shadow detection and removal are always treated as two independent tasks, very few works consider the relationship between them. Actually, both shadow detection and removal are based on the features of shadow and nonshadow regions. Shadow detection focuses on the difference between them, while shadow removal cares about the intensity tendency between shadow and nonshadow. Thus, these two tasks share some common features. If these features are used properly, the two tasks can regularize and even improve each other. Therefore we propose a multi-task learning based GAN network for shadow detection and removal. Figure 1 shows the structure of the proposed network. The main contribution can be summarised as follows,

1. A GAN network is proposed for multi-task learning, which can implement shadow detection and removal simultaneously.

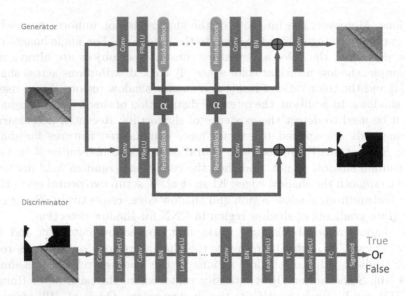

Fig. 1. The proposed multi-task GAN for shadow detection and removal. The number of output channels of the convolutional layer in the green part is 3, in the purple part is 2, and in the blue part is 64. Features are fused by the cross-stitch unit adaptively, the combination of losses from different tasks are learned as well. (Color figure online)

2. A cross-stitch module is proposed for the adaptive combination of features from shadow detection and shadow removal. Then the optimal way to regularize and enhance these two kinds of features mutually is learned during training
3. A loss function combination module is proposed for the optimal combination of loss functions. Through learning, the most suitable combination of loss function for shadow detection and removal tasks is obtained.

2   Related Works

Multi-task learning (MTL) has a rich history in machine learning, which refers to the application of several related subtasks to improve the learning of the overall model. In deep neural networks, MTL is widely used mainly in two different ways. The networks are shared by different tasks, including hard and soft parameter sharing.

Hard parameter sharing is to share some part of the network directly among tasks. Long et al. [20] proposed a deep relationship network, where different tasks share the same feature extractor and then are de-coded independently. Ranjan et al. [21] introduce a hyperface network to perform face detection, landmark localization, pose and gender recognition at the same time. These tasks also share the common feature extractor, and perform each specific task by different fully connected layers. For soft sharing, the combination of loss functions from different tasks is the main strategy. Cipollar et al. [22] introduce a multi-task loss function based on maximizing the Gaussian likelihood of task uncertainty.

Actually, for MTL, the core question is to find the optimal ways to share and boost information among tasks. Thus, the soft sharing strategy is more adaptive than the hard sharing. Accordingly, in the shadow detection and removal task, we propose to learn the optimal parameters of sharing the features, and also to learn the optimal ways to combine loss functions for the overall network, but not set empirically.

3   Multi-task GAN

We propose a multi-task GAN (mtGAN) for shadow detection and removal. In order to share common features and improve the learning procedure, the cross-stitch unit is applied. Also, an adaptive loss function is set to improve the learning furthermore. Besides the multi-task learning generator, the discriminator can judge the effect of created results which guarantees the performance of the generator.

3.1   Generator Based on Residual Learning

For shadow detection and removal, the result images have the same size as the input ones. U-Net is a classical structure used for pixel-wised segmentation, which is applied in stcGAN [17], but it is not suitable for our task actually. In U-Net, the spatial size of features are down-sampled in encoder then up-sampled in decoder, then a lot of details are lost. Therefore, we design a series of convolution layers to keep the spatial size of feature but not reduce their size as usual. Since the residual blocks [23] can simplify the learning tasks and make the entire network much deeper, they are used as the basic unit to construct the generator network for shadow detection and removal. Specifically, there are two convolution layers with a kernel size of $3 * 3$ and a channel size of 64, followed by the normalization layer [24], and use PReLU as the activation function. The network for shadow removal and shadow detection only differ slightly in the number of output channels, where there are two channels for shadow detection and three channels for shadow removal. This is because shadow detection is a binary classification problem, while shadow removal is a regression task to create a shadow free image with three color channels.

In order to enable two highly relevant tasks to fuse rich underlying features rather than just results, we propose a cross-stitch unit [25], as shown in Fig. 2. The cross-stitch unit tries to find the optimal way to regularize and fuse features from two related tasks, shadow detection and shadow removal. If the features from current layer are X_A and X_B, then through the cross-stitch unit, the output features $\tilde{X}_A$, $\tilde{X}_B$ can be combined as Eq. 1,

$$\begin{bmatrix} \tilde{X}_A \\ \tilde{X}_B \end{bmatrix} = \begin{bmatrix} \alpha_{AA} & \alpha_{AB} \\ \alpha_{BA} & \alpha_{BB} \end{bmatrix} \begin{bmatrix} X_A \\ X_B \end{bmatrix} \tag{1}$$

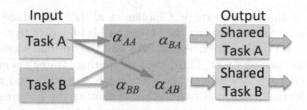

Fig. 2. Cross stitch unit linear combined input features.

The new features are the linear combination of features from two different tasks. α_{AA} and α_{BB} are the weight for the same task, while α_{AB} and α_{BA} are for different tasks. During back propagation training, these four coefficients will be optimized as well. Then with a series of cross-stitch units, features from two tasks are intertwisted together to achieve the optimal representation for each task. The shadow detection network and shadow removal network are shown as the generator in Fig. 1. The number of output channels of the convolutional layer in the green part is 3, in the purple part is 2, and in the blue part is 64.

3.2 Loss Functions

In addition to the generator, GAN also contains a discriminator that determines whether the created result is the same as the desired label. Through the competition between generator and discriminator, the best final result can be obtained. In our task, shadow detection and shadow removal results are used as input, the discriminator judge if these two images are a pair or not.

Generator Loss. In order to ensure that the final shadow detection and removal results not only achieve good visualization result but also high accuracy in quantitative evaluation, a combined generator loss function L_G is proposed, including uncertainty-based content loss L_E, adversarial loss L_A, and perceptual loss L_P as Eq. 2

$$L_G = L_E + \lambda_a L_A + \lambda_p L_P \tag{2}$$

where λ_a and λ_p are pre-defined weights for L_A and L_P respectively. If L_P is set to 0, the network will degenerate into a general generative countermeasure network. If L_A is set to 0, the network will degenerate into the structure proposed by [26].

In our task, the generator performs multi-task learning. Traditionally, the loss functions of different tasks are combined together empirically. But in fact, the weight of the loss function of each task will seriously affect the entire system. Thus, we propose to learn these combined weights for multi-task loss functions in L_E. Considering the uncertainty of each task [22], we find the optimal loss function by maximizing the likelihood of each task. For the regression task F_r, its uncertainty distribution can be written as Eq. 3

$$\log p(y|F_r(x), \sigma) \propto -\frac{1}{2\sigma^2} \|y - F_r(x)\| - \log \sigma \tag{3}$$

For classification task F_c, its uncertainty distribution can be set according to the Softmax classification function, and then written as Eq. 4

$$\log p(y = l_i | F_c(x), \sigma) = \frac{1}{\sigma^2} F_c^{l_i}(x) - \log \sum_i \exp(\frac{1}{\sigma^2} F_c^{l_i}(x)) \qquad (4)$$

where l_i is the ith class label. $F_c^{l_i}(x)$ is the ith value in F_c. For multi-task learning, the uncertainty of all the tasks can be considered as the sum of the uncertainty of each task as Eq. 5

$$\log p(Y | F_r, \sigma_1, F_c, \sigma_2) = \log p(y | F_r, \sigma_1) + \log p(y | F_c, \sigma_2) \qquad (5)$$

Then for shadow detection and removal tasks, minimizing the over loss function can be calculated by introducing Eq. 4 and Eq. 3 into Eq. 5. we can get

$$
\begin{aligned}
L_E &= -\log p(Y | F_r, \sigma_1, F_c, \sigma_2) \\
&= \frac{1}{2\sigma_1^2} L_1(x) + \frac{1}{\sigma_2^2} L_2(x) + \log \sigma_1 + \log \frac{\sum_{l_i} \exp\left(\frac{1}{\sigma_2^2} F_{l_1}^c(x)\right)}{\left(\sum_{l_i} \exp\left(F_{l_i}^c(x)\right)\right)^{\frac{1}{\sigma_2^2}}} \\
&\approx \frac{1}{2\sigma_1^2} L_1(x) + \frac{1}{\sigma_2^2} L_2(x) + \log \sigma_1 + \log \sigma_2
\end{aligned} \qquad (6)
$$

where $L_1(x) = \|y_1 - F_r(x)\|^2$ is the regression loss, i.e. shadow removal loss, and $L_2(x) = -\log softmax(y_2, F_C(x))$ is the classification loss, i.e. shadow detection loss. During training, the parameter σ_1 and σ_2 will be learned progressively to achieve an optimal representation.

L_A is the adversarial loss function is defined as:

$$L_A = \frac{1}{N} \sum_{n=1}^{N} \log(1 - D(y_{1n}, y_{2n})) \qquad (7)$$

where $D(y_{1n}, y_{2n})$ represents the judgment from the discriminator. If this value is near to 1 then the estimated results are the same as the labels.

L_P is the perception loss which is used to guarantee the similarity between estimated results and their labels in feature domain. Then results are not only similar to the label in intensity value but also similar in feature. VGG16, is used for the feature extractor, the perception loss is written as

$$L_P = \|V(G_1(x)) - V(y_1)\|^2 + \|V(G_2(x)) - V(y_2)\|^2 \qquad (8)$$

where G_1 and G_2 are the two generators for shadow detection and removal; V is the VGG16 model.

Discriminator Loss. It is set to judge the difference between results and the corresponding labels. For a set of N shadow detection and removal results, $\{y_{1n}, y_{2n}\}_{n=1}^{N}$, and their corresponding labels, $\{y'_{1n}, y'_{2n}\}_{n=1}^{N}$, the loss function of discriminator L_D is defined as Eq. 9,

$$L_D = -\frac{1}{N} \sum_{n=1}^{N} \log(D(y'_{1n}, y'_{2n})) + \log(1 - D(y_{1n}, y_{2n})) \qquad (9)$$

where D is the discriminator network.

4   Experiments

In order to train the proposed network, Adam algorithm is used to optimize the entire GAN. The learning rate is set to $1e-3$, the momentum factor is set to 0.9 and 0.999, ε is set to $1e-8$, and the weight attenuation term is set to 0. For the cross-stitch unit, α_{AA} and α_{BB} are the weight for the same task, while α_{AB} and α_{BA} are for different task. So, we use α_D instead of α_{AB}, α_{BA} and α_S instead of α_{AA}, α_{BB}. Then the same task weight is initialed as $\alpha_S = 0.9$, the different task weight is initialed as $\alpha_D = 0.1$. The gradient of cross-stitch module is too small compared with the backbone network, then its learning rate is set to a hundred times the backbone net.

The proposed multi-task GAN is trained on Image Shadow Triplets Dataset (ISTD) [17]. The dataset is the first large-scale dataset with shadow detection label and shadow removal results. It contains a training set of 1,330 images and a test set of 540 images.

We first compare the proposed multi-task learning framework with single task learning. In single task learning, the two generators for shadow detection and removal are independent to each other. Figure 3 shows the evaluation value in different training epochs. From the results, we can see the proposed mtGAN network performs better than single task learning, where it is about 0.4 lower in root mean square error (RSME). This is due to the regularization and improvement between two tasks by multi-task learning framework.

The results of shadow detection and shadow removal algorithms are shown in Tables 1 and 2, respectively. For shadow detection, the proposed mtGAN achieves the best detection results for non-shadow region and the overall region. Some sample images and their shadow detection results are shown in Fig. 4(a). Especially, in the $2nd$ row of Fig. 4(a), our methods, mtGAN, greatly improves the detection ability for non-shadow regions. That is mainly due to the propose GAN structures and the adaptive setting of loss functions, which can balance the

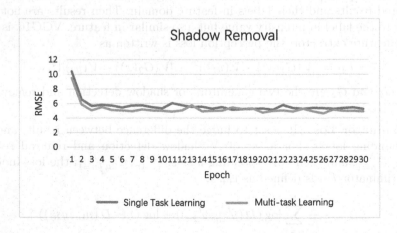

Fig. 3. Comparison between single task learning and multi-task learning

detection results in shadow and non-shadow regions. As a result, the proposed mtGAN can not only keep the precision for shadow regions but also for non-shadow regions.

For shadow removal results, the proposed mtGAN obtains the best results. From sample results in Fig. 4(b), we can see that our proposed mtGAN algorithm has better performance in maintaining the texture details and intensity consistency in the shadow removal results. Also, the proposed mtGAN completes shadow detection and removal at the same time, and obtains better results on both tasks compared with other single task learning of shadow detection or removal. The proposed cross-stitch units in the generator network fuse the features from shadow detection and removal optimally, and the two tasks mutually inspired the improvements. In addition, the discriminator judges the authenticity of the shadow detection and removal results, and further improves the results of the two tasks. At the same time, the adaptive combination of the loss function according to the uncertainty of the task also optimally guarantees the effectiveness of network training.

Table 1. Comparison of shadow detection (accuracy)

Methods	All	Non-shadow	Shadow
Guo et al. [27]	90.97%	90.77%	92.04%
Yang et al. [13]	91.15%	91.52%	89.19%
Gong et al. [28]	94.29%	93.82%	96.78%
stcGAN [17]	94.99%	94.45%	**97.86%**
mtGAN (proposed)	**95.78%**	**96.14%**	95.42%

Table 2. Comparison of shadow removal (RMSE)

Methods	All	Non-shadow	Shadow
Guo et al. [27]	9.3	7.46	18.95
Yang et al. [13]	15.63	14.83	19.82
Gong et al. [28]	8.53	7.29	14.98
stcGAN [17]	7.47	6.93	10.33
arGAN [18]	6.68	5.83	7.21
arGAN+SS [18]	5.89	5.41	6.65
mtGAN (proposed)	**4.86**	**4.58**	**6.18**

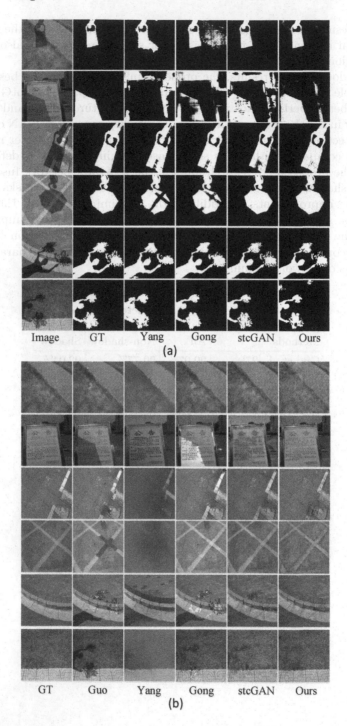

Fig. 4. Sample results. (a) shadow detection and (b) removal results. GT is the ground truth

5 Conclusion

Although shadows may interfere with object recognition or image understanding, they also provide some important information about the environment and the objects. Thus shadow detection and removal are always basic tasks for computer vision systems. Since shadow detection and shadow removal are related with each other deeply, we propose to combine these two tasks in a multi-task GAN network. In the proposed mtGAN, shadow detection and removal are not single tasks, these two tasks can stimulate and constrain each other so as to achieve the improvement of both tasks simultaneously. Within the network, the cross-stich units are proposed to learn the optimal way to fuse the feature of two tasks. In addition, content loss, adversarial loss and perceptual loss functions are proposed to guarantee the local and global consistency of shadow detection and removal results. Also the combination weight of different loss functions are learned as well in order to achieve the best performance. As a result, shadow detection and removal regularize and inspire each other mutually, and better results are obtained for both tasks.

Acknowledgement. This work is partly supported by the Key Research and Development Program of Shaanxi (Program Nos. 2020GY-050, 2021ZDLGY15-01, 2021ZDLGY09-04, 2021GY-004), and Shenzhen International Science and Technology Cooperation Project (No. GJHZ20200731095204013).

References

1. Benedek, C., Szirányi, T.: Bayesian foreground and shadow detection in uncertain frame rate surveillance videos. IEEE Trans. Image Process. **17**(4), 608–621 (2008)
2. Qi, M., Dai, J., Zhang, Q., Kong, J.: Cascaded cast shadow detection method in surveillance scenes. Optik-Int. J. Light Electron Opt. **125**(3), 1396–1400 (2014)
3. Finlayson, G.D., Hordley, S.D., Lu, C., Drew, M.S.: On the removal of shadows from images. IEEE Trans. Patt. Recogn. Mach. Intelli. **28**(1), 59–68 (2006)
4. Vazquez, E., Baldrich, R., De Weijer, J.V., Vanrell, M.: Describing reflectances for color segmentation robust to shadows, highlights, and textures. IEEE Trans. Pattern Recogn. Mach. Intell. **33**(5), 917–930 (2011)
5. Lalonde, J.-F., Efros, A.A., Narasimhan, S.G.: Detecting ground shadows in outdoor consumer photographs. In: Daniilidis, K., Maragos, P., Paragios, N. (eds.) ECCV 2010. LNCS, vol. 6312, pp. 322–335. Springer, Heidelberg (2010). https://doi.org/10.1007/978-3-642-15552-9_24
6. Jiang, X., Schofield, A.J., Wyatt, J.L.: Shadow detection based on colour segmentation and estimated illumination. In: British Machine Vision Conference (BMVC), pp. 1–11 (2011)
7. Shen, L., Chua, T.W., Leman, K.: Shadow optimization from structured deep edge detection. In: IEEE Conference on Computer Vision and Pattern Recognition (CVPR), pp. 2067–2074. IEEE (2015)
8. Khan, S.H., Bennamoun, M., Sohel, F., Togneri, R.: Automatic shadow detection and removal from a single image. IEEE Trans. Pattern Recogn. Mach. Intell. **3**, 431–446 (2016)
9. Zheng, Q., Qiao, X., Cao, Y., Lau, R.W.H.: Distraction-aware shadow detection. In: IEEE Conference on Computer Vision and Pattern Recognition (CVPR), pp. 5167–5176 (2019)

10. Finlayson, G.D., Hordley, S.D., Lu, C., Drew, M.S.: On the removal of shadows from images. IEEE Trans. Pattern Recogn. Mach. Intell. **28**(1), 59–68 (2006)
11. Gryka, M., Terry, M., Brostow, G.J.: Learning to remove soft shadows. ACM Trans. Graph. (TOG) **34**(5), 153 (2015)
12. Qu, L., Tian, J., He, S., Tang, Y., Lau, R.: DeshadowNet: a multi-context embedding deep network for shadow removal. In: IEEE Conference on Computer Vision and Pattern Recognition (CVPR), no. 2, p. 3 (2017)
13. Yang, Q., Tan, K.-H., Ahuja, N.: Shadow removal using bilateral filtering. IEEE Trans. Image Process. **21**(10), 4361–4368 (2012)
14. Barron, J.T., Malik, J.: Shape, illumination, and reflectance from shading. IEEE Trans. Pattern Recogn. Mach. Intell. **37**(8), 1670–1687 (2015)
15. Le, H., Samaras, D.: Shadow removal via shadow image decomposition. In: International Conference on Computer Vision (ICCV) (2019)
16. Fu, L., Zhou, C., Guo, Q., Juefei-Xu, F., Wang, S.: Auto-exposure fusion for single-image shadow removal. In: 2020 IEEE/CVF Conference on Computer Vision and Pattern Recognition (CVPR) (2021)
17. Wang, J., Li, X., Yang, J.: Stacked conditional generative adversarial networks for jointly learning shadow detection and shadow removal. In: IEEE Conference on Computer Vision and Pattern Recognition (CVPR), pp. 1788–1797 (2018)
18. Ding, B., Long, C., Zhang, L., Xiao, C.: ARGAN: attentive recurrent generative adversarial network for shadow detection and removal. In: International Conference on Computer Vision (ICCV) (2019)
19. Liu, Z., Yin, H., Wu, X., Wu, Z., Mi, Y., Wang, S.: From shadow generation to shadow removal. In: 2021 IEEE/CVF Conference on Computer Vision and Pattern Recognition (CVPR) (2021)
20. Long, M., Wang, J.: Learning multiple tasks with deep relationship networks. arXiv: Learning (2015)
21. Ranjan, R., Patel, V.M., Chellappa, R.: Hyperface: a deep multi-task learning framework for face detection, landmark localization, pose estimation, and gender recognition. IEEE Trans. Pattern Recogn. Mach. Intell. **41**(1), 121–135 (2019)
22. Cipolla, R., Gal, Y., Kendall, A.: Multi-task learning using uncertainty to weigh losses for scene geometry and semantics. In: IEEE Conference on Computer Vision and Pattern Recognition (CVPR), pp. 7482–7491 (2018)
23. He, K., Zhang, X., Ren, S., Sun, J.: Deep residual learning for image recognition. In: IEEE Conference on Computer Vision and Pattern Recognition (CVPR), pp. 770–778 (2016)
24. Ioffe, S., Szegedy, C.: Batch normalization: accelerating deep network training by reducing internal covariate shift. arXiv preprint arXiv:1502.03167D (2015)
25. Misra, I., Shrivastava, A., Gupta, A., Hebert, M.: Cross-stitch networks for multi-task learning. In: IEEE Conference on Computer Vision and Pattern Recognition (CVPR), pp. 3994–4003 (2016)
26. Johnson, J., Alahi, A., Fei-Fei, L.: Perceptual losses for real-time style transfer and super-resolution. In: Leibe, B., Matas, J., Sebe, N., Welling, M. (eds.) ECCV 2016. LNCS, vol. 9906, pp. 694–711. Springer, Cham (2016). https://doi.org/10.1007/978-3-319-46475-6_43
27. Guo, R., Dai, Q., Hoiem, D.: Single-image shadow detection and removal using paired regions. In: IEEE Conference on Computer Vision and Pattern Recognition (CVPR), pp. 2033–2040 (2011)
28. Gong, H., Cosker, D.: Interactive shadow removal and ground truth for variable scene categories. In: British Machine Vision Conference (BMVC) (2014)

A Multi-path Neural Network for Hyperspectral Image Super-Resolution

Jing Zhang[1,2,3(✉)], Zekang Wan[2], Minhao Shao[2], and Yunsong Li[1,2]

[1] State Key Laboratory of Integrated Service Network, Xidian University, Xi'an 710071, China
jingzhang@xidian.edu.cn, ysli@mail.xidian.edu.cn
[2] School of Telecommunications Engineering, Xidian University, Xi'an 710071, China
shaominhao@stu.xidian.edu.cn
[3] Guangzhou Institution of Technology, Xidian University, Guanzhou 510555, China

Abstract. The resolution of hyperspectral remote sensing images is largely limited by the cost and commercialization requirements of remote sensing satellites. Existing super-resolution methods for improving the spatial resolution of images cannot well integrate the correlation between spectral segments and the problem of excessive network parameters caused by high-dimensional characteristics. This paper studies a multipath-based residual feature learning method, which simplifies each part of the network into several simple and effective network modules to learn the spatial spectral features between different spectral segments. Through the designed multi-scale feature generation method based on wavelet transform and spatial attention mechanism, the non-linear mapping ability for features is effectively improved. The verification of three general hyperspectral data sets proves the superiority of this method compared with the existing hyperspectral SR methods.

Keywords: Super-resolution · Multi-path architecture · Attention mechanism · Hyperspectral image

1 Introduction

With the development of remote sensing technology, remote sensing satellites [1–4] can obtain a wide variety of hyperspectral images (HSI) with a mount of spectral bands. Researchers have achieved extensive and effective governance of the earth through HIS, such as land detection [5, 6], Urban Design [7], Road Planning [8], Agricultural Monitoring [9] and Disaster Prevention and Control [10]. Limited by the scale, bandwidth and stability of satellite imaging system, the spatial resolution of the obtained spectral image is low. Optimizing the imaging system through hardware optimization and process control not only brings huge challenges to engineering technology, but also increases equipment costs.

In the field of computer vision, starting from the perspective of image feature similarity, researchers obtain prior knowledge through complex linear and nonlinear models, and establish an mapping relations between low-resolution images (LR) and high-resolution

© Springer Nature Switzerland AG 2021
Y. Peng et al. (Eds.): ICIG 2021, LNCS 12890, pp. 377–387, 2021.
https://doi.org/10.1007/978-3-030-87361-5_31

images (HR).This kind of method can obtain high quality hyperspectral remote sensing images quickly and cheaply without changing the existing imaging environment, which has extremely high research significance and market prospect, and can also reduce the threshold for the development of commercial remote sensing satellites.

According to the difference in the theoretical basis of implementation, the image super-resolution method (SR) can be divided into three types: interpolation-based methods [11, 12], reconstruction-based methods [13], and learning-based methods [14–16]. In the interpolation-based method, the pixel value of the reconstructed pixel is only obtained by the weighted summation of its surrounding pixels. The reconstruction-based method briefly relies on the establishment of the image degradation model, such as Bayesian model [17], and learning the prior information of the existing image, which is applied to the reconstruction of the LR image. Although these two types of methods have improved the resolution of the image to a certain extent, they still have shortcomings in the reconstruction of image detail information.

The learning-based method optimizes the model through iterative training, which can reconstruct better image details. The application of convolutional neural network (CNN) in the field of image processing makes the performance of image SR method improved unprecedentedly. Only need to extract abstract features from the existing LR image and apply them to image reconstruction, apply the error between the result and HR image to the next round of learning, then we can get a general model that can reconstruct high quality images with tremendous real details. The classical SR methods include VDSR [18], EDSR [19], D-DBPN [20] and SAN [21]. Based on these methods, researchers began to seek SR methods suitable for HSI.

Different from natural images with only three channels, HIS has a large amount of spectral band information, and the adjacent bands have strong feature similarity, so the SR method for HIS generally uses 3D convolution to achieve non-linear mapping of features. Mei et al. [22] based on the basic network structure of FSRCNN [22], introduced 3D convolution to realize the multi-spectral reconstruction of HIS, and solved the problem of spectral distortion when traditional CNN performs SR on HIS. Li et al. [24] alternately used 2D units and 3D units in the model to achieve spatial feature information extraction, and the use of 2D units reduced the amount of network parameters which contributes to the lightweight of the HSI SR model. Based on the idea of spectral segment grouping, Xie et al. [25] divided the spectral segments into different sets, reconstructed the most important spectral segment of each subset, and guided the reconstruction of other spectral segments in the subset, and finally realized the SR of all spectral segments. Different from the starting point of spectral similarity, Hu et al. [26] designed a spectral difference module, a parallel convolution module and a fusion module for the reconstruction of spectral features and spatial spectral information from the difference between spectral segments. Li et al. [27] designed a hybrid convolution module based on 2D convolution and 3D convolution, and proposed MCNet, which can better extract the characteristic information of spectral information, but its 2D/3D conversion module does not substantially reduce the computational complexity of the network.

In this paper, we propose the Multi-Path Neural Network (MPNNet) for HIS SR. Combining the idea of depthwise separable convolution, we design an up and down sampling module using depthwise separable convolution, and based on this, propose the

Multi-Path Neural Block (MPNB). After that, the spatial attention mechanism based on wavelet transform is added to the multi-scale module to generate features with different gradient directions, and to reconstruct a clearer high-resolution hyperspectral image. A large number of experiments show that the proposed method is superior than existing methods.

2 Proposed Method

Different from the SR task of natural images, the SR method of HIS needs to reconstruct a large number of spectral segments with strong correlation, and the use of simple convolution to cascade is not able to fully mine the characteristic information between spectral segments. From the perspective of the receptive field, we designed a Multi-Path Neural Network based on multi-path feature fusion.

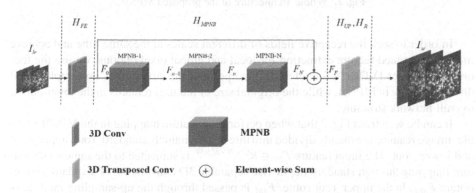

Fig. 1. Whole architecture of the proposed MPNNet.

It can be observed from the Fig. 1 that MPNNet is chiefly composed of three parts: Feature Extraction Network (H_{FE}), Feature Nonlinear Mapping Network (H_{MPNB}) and Image Reconstruction Network (H_{UP}).

Let $I_{LR} \in R^{H \times W \times B}$ denotes the low-resolution hyperspectral image, $I_{SR} \in R^{(\alpha \times H) \times (\alpha \times W) \times B}$ represent the reconstructed high-resolution hyperspectral image, where B is the number of frequency bands, H and W respectively denote the length and the width of the image block, and α denotes the sampling factor.

To preserve the geometric structure of the spectral image to the maximum extent, only 3D convolution is used in the H_{FE} to map the image features to a higher-dimensional feature space, which is the initial feature $F_0 \in R^{C \times B \times H \times W}$. In the H_{MPNB}, considering the up sampling and down sampling structure as the entry point, the cascaded MPNBs are used to realize the residual feature extraction of multiple receptive fields. Considering the characteristics of multi-spectral reconstruction in the H_{UP}, the 3D deconvolution is used to better capture the information of spatial spectral characteristics, and reconstruct the hyperspectral image by preserving rich details. More detailed information on MPNB is mentioned below.

2.1 Multi-path Feature Fusion

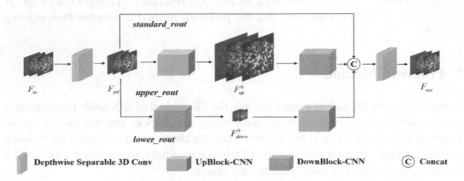

Fig. 2. Whole architecture of the proposed MPNB.

In order to seek the receptive fields of different scales at the same time and achieve more fine-grained feature extraction for local and global pixel regions, we use the theoretical basis of D-DBPN for reference and propose the structure of up sampling and down sampling in MPNB, while the original size of features remains in the longitudinal overall network structure.

It can be seen from Fig. 2 that when performing feature mapping in the MPNB module, image features are mainly divided into three paths, namely standard_rout, upper_rout and lower_rout. The input feature $F_{in} \in R^{C \times B \times H \times W}$ is subjected to the same-scale feature mapping through standard depthwise separable 3D convolution of standard_rout to obtain F_{std}. In the upper_rout route, F_{std} is passed through the up-sampling module to obtain the feature $F_{up}^0 \in R^{C \times B \times mH \times mW}$, and then the down-sampling module is used to change it back to the original size feature $F_{up} \in R^{C \times B \times H \times W}$, where m represents the scale factor. In the same way, in the lower_rout route, F_{std} is passed through the down-sampling module to obtain the feature $F_{down}^0 \in R^{C \times B \times \frac{H}{m} \times \frac{W}{m}}$, and then the up-sampling module is used to change it back to the original size feature $F_{down} \in R^{C \times B \times H \times W}$. Finally, the F_{std}, F_{up}, and F_{down} are cascaded, and the standard depthwise separable 3D convolution is used to perform the same-scale feature mapping of the down channel, and the output feature $F_{out} \in R^{C \times B \times H \times W}$ is obtained. The mathematical representation of the MSFMB module is shown below.

$$F_{std} = f[w_p * f(w_d * F_{in})] \tag{1}$$

$$F_{up} = g^{\downarrow}[g^{\uparrow}(F_{std})] \tag{2}$$

$$F_{down} = g^{\uparrow}[g^{\downarrow}(F_{std})] \tag{3}$$

$$F_{out} = f\{w_p * f[w_d * C(F_{std}, F_{up}, F_{down})]\} \tag{4}$$

where w_d represents the convolution kernel of depthwise convolution with a size of $3 \times 3 \times 3$, w_p represents the convolution kernel of a pointwise convolution with a size of $1 \times 1 \times 1$, f represents the LeakyReLU activation function, and $*$ represents the volume Product operation, $C(\cdot)$ stands for the concatenation operation, $g^{\downarrow}$ and $g^{\uparrow}$ stand for the up-sampling module and the down-sampling module.

2.2 Multi-scale Feature Transformation

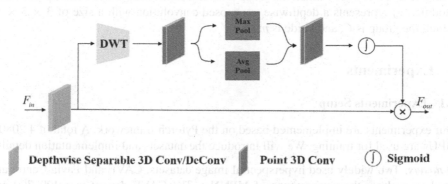

Depthwise Separable 3D Conv/DeConv   **Point 3D Conv**   ⓈSigmoid

Fig. 3. Whole architecture of the proposed UP/Down block with DWT spatial attention.

The design of the wavelet-based spatial self-attention mechanism is shown in Fig. 3. First, for the spectral feature $F_{in} \in R^{C \times B \times H \times W}$, the scale transformation with a sampling factor of m is performed through the depthwise separable convolution to obtain $F \in R^{C \times B \times mH \times mW}$, and then the four-layer image feature is obtained after the wavelet transformation is performed on F, which is F_{LL}, F_{LH}, F_{HL} and F_{HH}. Since the low-frequency information F_{LL} contains less detailed information, only F_{LH}, F_{HL} and F_{HH} are used for feature guidance when performing feature fusion. Since the spatial scales of the features obtained by DWT and the original features may be different, it is necessary to use interpolation to restore to the original size, and use standard 3D convolution for feature dimension fusion. The convolution kernel is $1 \times 1 \times 1$, and the output features are obtained. F_{Fusion}. After that, use Global Max Pooling and Global Average Pooling to obtain two single-layer feature maps $F_{avg}^w \in R^{1 \times B \times H \times W}$ and $F_{max}^w \in R^{1 \times B \times H \times W}$, and use standard convolution to fuse to obtain the final feature map. After the Sigmoid activation function, the coefficient feature map $M_w \in R^{1 \times B \times H \times W}$ is obtained, which is multiplied with F. After that, the final output feature map is obtained. The mathematical expression of the spatial attention sampling module based on wavelet transform can be expressed by the following formula:

$$F = f[w_p * f(w_d * F_{in})] \tag{5}$$

$$F_{LL}, F_{LH}, F_{HL}, F_{HH} = DWT(F) \tag{6}$$

$$F_{Fusion} = w_{3d1} * I[C(F_{LH}, F_{HL}, F_{HH})] \tag{7}$$

$$M_w(F) = \sigma[w_{3d1} * C(F_{avg}^w, F_{max}^w)] \otimes F$$
$$= \sigma\{w_{3d1} * C[AvgPool(F_{Fusion}), Maxpool(F_{Fusion})]\} \otimes F \qquad (8)$$

where $DWT(\cdot)$ stands for discrete wavelet transform, w_{3d1} denotes standard 3D convolution with a kernel size of $1 \times 1 \times 1$, I denotes the sampling operation to make the size of feature consistent with the spatial size of F, and $\otimes$ stands for matrix point multiplication. For the down-sampling module, w_d represents a depthwise convolution with a size of $3 \times 3 \times 3$, which the group is set to C, and stride is m. For the up-sampling module, w_d represents a depthwise transposed convolution with a size of $3 \times 3 \times 3$, which the group is C, and stride is m.

3   Experiments

3.1   Experiments Setup

Our experiments are implemented based on the Pytorch framework. A total of 4 2080ti GPUs are used for training. We will introduce the datasets and implementation details.

Datasets. Two widely used hyperspectral image datasets, CAVE and Pavia Centre are used to evaluate the performance of MPNNet. The CAVE dataset is a 400–700 nm hyperspectral dataset collected by Cooled CCD camera. There are 32 hyperspectral images with the size of $512 \times 512 \times 31$, among which 7 images are selected as the test set and the remaining 25 images are selected as the training set. The Pavia Center dataset is an image with a size of $715 \times 1096 \times 102$ obtained from the city of Pavia in northern Italy by ROSIS sensor, and we select the image with the size of $144 \times 144 \times 102$ in the upper left corner of the whole image as the test set, and the rest as the training set.

Implement Details. In MPNNet, we used a total of four MPNBs, and the sampling factor m in each MPNB module was set as 2. The L1 norm is applied to the network as a loss function for network training, and its mathematical expression is shown in the following formula:

$$L_{MAE}(I_{hr}, I_{sr}) = \frac{1}{N} \sum_{i=1}^{N} \left| I_{hr}^i - I_{sr}^i \right| \qquad (9)$$

Among them, I_{SR} represents the reconstructed spectral image, I_{hr} represents the original spectral image, and N represents the number of training samples.

The Adam method is used for the network optimization and update. In network training, the initial learning rate is set to 1e-4, the attenuation coefficient is 0.1 for every 120 rounds, and a total of 400 rounds are trained.

Evaluation Metrics. To qualitatively measure the MPNNet, four evaluation methods are employed to verify the effectiveness of the algorithm, including peak signal-to-noise ratio (PSNR), average peak signal-to-noise ratio (MPSNR), structural similarity (SSIM), and spectral angle mapping (SAM).

3.2 Experiments Results

We compare the proposed MPNNet with other 4 algorithms: Bicubic, VDSR, EDSR and MCNet. Table 1 and Table 2 shows the average PSNR, MPSNR, SSIM and SAM results of all methods. We can easily find that our method achieves the best performance among all the methods. Figure 4 and Fig. 5 shows the RGB image and erro image of" photo_and_face_ms" with a scale of 8 ×. Figure 6 and Fig. 7 shows the RGB image and erro image of Pavia Cetre with a scale of 4 ×.

Our method is superior to existing methods in terms of detail reconstruction and difference from HR. The results of SR using the Bicubic method will produce obvious artifacts. Our method can effectively reconstruct the dark details of human faces and the fine lines at street edges, while suppressing the generation of artifacts. According to the residual results in Fig. 5 and Fig. 7, the results generated by our method are cleaner, while other methods will show distortion and ambiguity that are significantly different from that of HR.

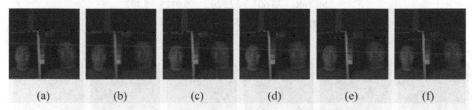

(a)   (b)   (c)   (d)   (e)   (f)

Fig. 4. The face image reconstruction results of various algorithms under the scale factor of 8. Reconstructed images of two test hyperspectral images in the CAVE dataset with spectral bands 26–17-9 as R-G-B. (a)HR, (b)Bicubic, (c)VDSR, (d)EDSR, (e)MCNet, (f)Ours.

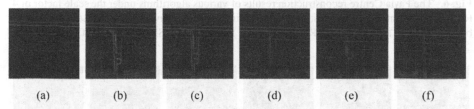

(a)   (b)   (c)   (d)   (e)   (f)

Fig. 5. The residual face image results of various algorithms under the scale factor of 8. (a)HR, (b)Bicubic, (c)VDSR, (d)EDSR, (e)MCNet, (f)Ours.

Table 1. Quantitative evaluation on the CAVE dataset of hyperspectral image SR algorithms: average PSNR/MPSNR/SSIM/SAM for scale factors 2, 4 and 8. The bold type represents the best result, and the underscore represents the second best result

Scale	Methods	PSNR↑	MPSNR↑	SSIM↑	SAM↓
	Bicubic	40.330	39.500	0.9820	3.311
	VDSR	44.456	43.531	0.9895	2.866

(*continued*)

Table 1. (*continued*)

Scale	Methods	PSNR↑	MPSNR↑	SSIM↑	SAM↓
× 2	EDSR	45.151	44.207	0.9907	2.606
	MCNet	45.878	44.913	0.9913	2.588
	Ours	**46.015**	**45.039**	**0.9917**	**2.497**
	Bicubic	34.616	33.657	0.9388	4.784
	VDSR	37.027	36.045	0.9591	4.297
× 4	EDSR	38.117	37.137	0.9626	4.132
	MCNet	38.589	37.679	0.9690	3.682
	Ours	**38.701**	**37.792**	**0.9694**	**3.679**
	Bicubic	30.554	29.484	0.8657	6.431
	VDSR	32.184	31.210	0.8852	5.747
× 8	EDSR	33.416	32.337	0.9002	5.409
	MCNet	33.607	32.520	0.9125	5.172
	Ours	**33.663**	**32.584**	**0.9131**	**5.093**

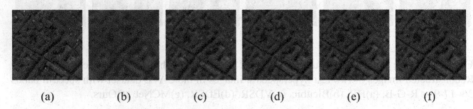

(a)   (b)   (c)   (d)   (e)   (f)

Fig. 6. The Pavia Centre reconstruction results of various algorithms under the scale factor of 4. Reconstructed images of two test hyperspectral images in the Pavia Centre dataset with spectral bands 60–31-12 as R-G-B. (a)HR, (b)Bicubic, (c)VDSR, (d)EDSR, (e)MCNet, (f)Ours.

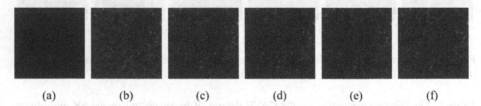

(a)   (b)   (c)   (d)   (e)   (f)

Fig. 7. The Pavia Centre residual image results of various algorithms under the scale factor of 4. (a)HR, (b)Bicubic, (c)VDSR, (d)EDSR, (e)MCNet, (f)Ours.

Table 2. Quantitative evaluation on the Pavia Centre dataset of hyperspectral image SR algorithms: average PSNR/MPSNR/SSIM/SAM for scale factors 2, 4 and 8. The bold type represents the best result, and the underscore represents the second best result

Scale	Methods	PSNR↑	MPSNR↑	SSIM↑	SAM↓
× 2	Bicubic	32.406	31.798	0.9036	4.370
	VDSR	35.392	34.879	0.9501	3.689
	EDSR	35.160	34.580	0.9452	3.898
	MCNet	35.124	34.626	0.9455	3.865
	Ours	**35.586**	**35.105**	**0.9501**	**3.701**
× 4	Bicubic	26.596	26.556	0.7091	7.553
	VDSR	28.328	28.317	0.7707	6.514
	EDSR	28.649	28.591	0.7782	6.573
	MCNet	28.791	28.756	0.7826	6.385
	Ours	**28.893**	**28.843**	**0.7831**	**6.058**
× 8	Bicubic	24.464	24.745	0.4899	7.648
	VDSR	24.526	24.804	0.4944	7.588
	EDSR	24.854	25.067	0.5282	7.507
	MCNet	24.877	25.096	0.5391	**7.429**
	Ours	**24.963**	**25.182**	**0.5422**	7.442

4 Conclusion

In this article, we propose a MPNNet method for super-resolution reconstruction of hyperspectral images. This method has shown outstanding performance and generalization ability on different data sets. MPNNet mainly designed several simple and effective networks to better learn the detailed information of the spectrum in HIS. To extract more spectral details from the perspective of multiple receptive fields, a multi-path feature mapping module is designed, which uses depthwise separable convolution to perform efficient feature scale transformation, and uses the attention mechanism based on wavelet transform to perform linear weighting to obtain detailed residual spectral characteristics. Based on the results of the experiments, the effectiveness of the proposed MPNNet method is proved. In subjective and objective experiments, our experimental performance is better than that of competitors.

Acknowledgments. This research was supported by the Natural Science Foundation of China under Grant 61801359, Grant 61571345 and the Pre-Research of the "Thirteenth Five-Year-Plan" of China Grant 305020903.

References

1. Son, S., Wang, M.: Ice detection for satellite ocean color data processing in the Great Lakes. IEEE Trans. Geosci. Remote Sens. **55**(12), 6793–6804 (2017)
2. Song, J., Jeong, J.H., Park, D.S., Kim, H.H., Seo, D.C., Ye, J.C.: Unsupervised denoising for satellite imagery using wavelet directional CycleGAN. IEEE Trans. Geosci. Remote Sens., 1–17 (2020)
3. Lee, J.H., Lee, S.S., Kim, H.G., Song, S.K., Kim, S., Ro, Y.M.: MCSIP net: multichannel satellite image prediction via deep neural network. IEEE Trans. Geosci. Remote Sens. **58**(3), 2212–2224 (2019)
4. Liu, X., Wang, M.: Super-resolution of VIIRS-measured ocean color products using deep convolutional neural network. IEEE Trans. Geosci. Remote Sens. **59**(1), 114–127 (2020)
5. Jalal, R., et al.: Toward efficient land cover mapping: an overview of the national land representation system and land cover map 2015 of Bangladesh. IEEE J. Selected Topics Appl. Earth Observ. Remote Sens. **12**(10), 3852–3861(2019)
6. Zhang, P., et al.: Monitoring of drought change in the middle reach of yangtze river. In: IGARSS 2018–2018 IEEE International Geoscience and Remote Sensing Symposium, pp. 4935–4938. IEEE (2018)
7. Goetzke, R., Braun, M., Thamm, H. P., Menz, G.: Monitoring and modeling urban land-use change with multitemporal satellite data. In: IGARSS 2008–2008 IEEE International Geoscience and Remote Sensing Symposium, Vol. 4, pp. IV-510. IEEE (2008)
8. Darweesh, M., Al Mansoori, S., AlAhmad, H.: Simple roads extraction algorithm based on edge detection using satellite images. In: 2019 IEEE 4th International Conference on Image, Vision and Computing, ICIVC, pp. 578–582. IEEE (2019)
9. Kussul, N., Shelestov, A., Yailymova, H., Yailymov, B., Lavreniuk, M., Ilyashenko, M.: Satellite agricultural monitoring in Ukraine at country level: world bank project. In: IGARSS 2020–2020 IEEE International Geoscience and Remote Sensing Symposium, pp. 1050–1053. IEEE (2020)
10. Di, Y., Xu, X., Zhang, G.: Research on secondary analysis method of synchronous satellite monitoring data of power grid wildfire. In: 2020 IEEE International Conference on Information Technology, Big Data and Artificial Intelligence, ICIBA, Vol. 1, pp. 706–710. IEEE (2020)
11. Hou, H., Andrews, H.: Cubic splines for image interpolation and digital filtering. IEEE Trans. Acoust. Speech Signal Process. **26**(6), 508–517 (1978)
12. Li, X., Orchard, M.T.: New edge-directed interpolation. IEEE Trans. Image Process. **10**(10), 1521–1527 (2001)
13. Dai, S., Han, M., Xu, W., Wu, Y., Gong, Y.: Soft edge smoothness prior for alpha channel super resolution. In: 2007 IEEE Conference on Computer Vision and Pattern Recognition, CVPR 2007, pp. 1–8. IEEE (2007)
14. Timofte, R., De Smet, V., Van Gool, L.: Anchored neighborhood regression for fast example-based super-resolution. In: Proceedings of the IEEE International Conference on Computer Vision, pp. 1920–1927 (2013)
15. Timofte, R., De Smet, V., Van Gool, L.: A+: Adjusted anchored neighborhood regression for fast super-resolution. In: Cremers, D., Reid, I., Saito, H., Yang, M.-H. (eds.) ACCV 2014. LNCS, vol. 9006, pp. 111–126. Springer, Cham (2015). https://doi.org/10.1007/978-3-319-16817-3_8
16. Yang, J., Wright, J., Huang, T.S., Ma, Y.: Image super-resolution via sparse representation. IEEE Trans. Image Process. **19**(11), 2861–2873 (2010)
17. Zheng, W., et al.: Image super-resolution reconstruction algorithm based on Bayesian theory. In: 2018 13th IEEE Conference on Industrial Electronics and Applications, ICIEA, pp. 1934–1938. IEEE (2018)

18. Kim, J., Lee, J.K., Lee, K.M.: Accurate image super-resolution using very deep convolutional networks. In: Proceedings of the IEEE conference on computer vision and pattern recognition, CVPR 2016, pp. 1646–1654 (2016)
19. Lim, B., Son, S., Kim, H., Nah, S., Mu Lee, K.: Enhanced deep residual networks for single image super-resolution. In: Proceedings of the IEEE Conference on Computer Vision and Pattern Recognition Workshops, CVPR 2017, pp. 136–144 (2017)
20. Haris, M., Shakhnarovich, G., Ukita, N.: Deep back-projection networks for super-resolution. In: Proceedings of the IEEE Conference on Computer Vision and Pattern Recognition, CVPR 2018, pp. 1664–1673 (2018)
21. Dai, T., Cai, J., Zhang, Y., Xia, S.T., Zhang, L.: Second-order attention network for single image super-resolution. In: Proceedings of the IEEE/CVF Conference on Computer Vision and Pattern Recognition, CVPR 2019, pp. 11065–11074 (2019)
22. Mei, S., Yuan, X., Ji, J., Wan, S., Hou, J., Du, Q.: Hyperspectral image super-resolution via convolutional neural network. In: 2017 IEEE International Conference on Image Processing, ICIP, pp. 4297–4301. IEEE (2017)
23. Dong, C., Loy, C.C., Tang, X.: Accelerating the super-resolution convolutional neural network. In: Leibe, B., Matas, J., Sebe, N., Welling, M. (eds.) ECCV 2016. LNCS, vol. 9906, pp. 391–407. Springer, Cham (2016). https://doi.org/10.1007/978-3-319-46475-6_25
24. Li, Q., Wang, Q., Li, X.: Exploring the relationship between 2D/3D convolution for hyperspectral image super-resolution. IEEE Trans. Geosci. Remote Sens. (2021)
25. Xie, W., Jia, X., Li, Y., Lei, J.: Hyperspectral image super-resolution using deep feature matrix factorization. IEEE Trans. Geosci. Remote Sens. 57(8), 6055–6067 (2019)
26. Hu, J., Jia, X., Li, Y., He, G., Zhao, M.: Hyperspectral image super-resolution via intrafusion network. IEEE Trans. Geosci. Remote Sens. 58(10), 7459–7471 (2020)
27. Li, Q., Wang, Q., Li, X.: Mixed 2D/3D convolutional network for hyperspectral image super-resolution. Remote Sens. 12(10), 1660 (2020)

Nighttime Thermal Infrared Image Colorization with Dynamic Label Mining

Fuya Luo(iD), Yijun Cao(iD), and Yongjie Li(✉)(iD)

School of Life Science and Technology, University of Electronic Science
and Technology of China, Chengdu 610054, China
liyj@uestc.edu.cn

Abstract. Translating a nighttime thermal infrared (NTIR) image into
a daytime color image, denoted as NTIR2DC, may be a promising
way to facilitate nighttime scene perception. Despite recent impressive
advances in the field of image-to-image translation, content distortion
in the NTIR2DC task remains under-addressed. Previous approaches
resort to annotated pixel-level labels to enforce semantic invariance during translation, which greatly limits their practicality. To ameliorate this
intractability, we propose a generative adversarial network with Dynamic
LAbel Mining called DlamGAN, which encourages a semantically consistent translation without requiring pixel-wise manual annotation. Specifically, a dynamic label mining strategy is proposed to extract the semantic cues of NTIR images online. The obtained cues are served as pseudo
labels to constrain the semantic consistency in the translation process. In
addition, an adaptive surrounding response integration module is introduced for adaptively integrating contextual information to reduce coding
ambiguity of NTIR images. Experimental results on FLIR and KAIST
datasets demonstrate the superiority of the proposed model in semantic
preservation.

Keywords: Thermal infrared image colorization · Image-to-image
translation · Nighttime scene perception

1 Introduction

In recent years, thermal infrared (TIR) cameras have been widely adopted in various applications requiring stable sensing of night or low visibility scenes, such
as security surveillance, autonomous driving and intelligent robotics. Compared
with visible cameras, TIR cameras are robust against illumination variations and
can capture objects in total darkness. However, the low contrast and monochromatic nature of TIR images hinders human interpretation and subsequent model
adaptation from visible spectrum. Therefore, it is of great significance to translate a nighttime TIR (NTIR) image to a reasonable daytime color (DC) image,

Supported by Key Area R&D Program of Guangdong Province (2018B030338001) and
National Natural Science Foundation of China (61806041, 62076055).

Y. Peng et al. (Eds.): ICIG 2021, LNCS 12890, pp. 388–399, 2021.
https://doi.org/10.1007/978-3-030-87361-5_32

which not only benefits the fast understanding of night scenes, but also narrows down the performance gap of computer vision tasks among different domains. In this paper, we aim to address the problem of NTIR image colorization by translating NTIR images to DC images (abbreviated as NTIR2DC).

Due to the difficulty of acquiring a large number of pixel-level aligned NTIR and DC image pairs, a possible solution is to utilize unsupervised image-to-image (I2I) translation methods to implement the NTIR2DC task. Witnessing the recent success of generative adversarial network (GAN) [6] on generating high-quality synthesized images, many studies have employed GANs for the I2I translation tasks [17,30]. Despite the impressive results, unsupervised I2I translation methods usually suffer from content distortion during the translation process. Many efforts have been made to ameliorate this intractable problem [15,23]. For example, AugGAN [9] and Sem-GAN [4] introduced additional segmentation branches to embed semantic information into the generator and constrain the segmentation masks of the translated images to be consistent with the labels. Although these methods can effectively reduce the content distortion in the translation process, the demand for pixel-level annotation greatly limits their practicality. In addition, the issue of content corruption in NTIR2DC tasks remains under-addressed.

To ensure semantic consistency without pixel-wise annotation, in this work, we proposed a GAN model with Dynamic LAbel Mining, namely DlamGAN. Specifically, we first predicted the segmentation masks of all DC images in the training set using a domain-adaptive semantic segmentation model [28], and used the intersection of the high-confidence regions therein and the predictions of the Detectron2 model [27] as pseudo-labels. Then, we introduced a pair of semantic segmentation networks in the GAN model for joint optimization with each component of the GAN network. Subsequently, the semantic segmentation branches of both domains were progressively trained by pseudo-labels of DC images, and a dynamic label mining strategy was proposed to extract the semantic cues of NTIR images online. The obtained cues were further used to encourage the semantic consistency of the translation process. Furthermore, inspired by the modulation effect of non-classical receptive fields (nCRF) [7,24], we designed an Adaptive Surrounding Response Integration (ASRI) module that uses surrounding long-range information to better encode local areas in NTIR images. Exhaustive experiments on FLIR [5] and KAIST [11] datasets demonstrate the superiority of the proposed method for content preservation on the NTIR2DC task. The main contributions of this paper can be summarized as:

- We proposed a new learning method to improve the semantic consistency of I2I translation without requiring pixel-wise manual annotation.
- We introduced an ASRI module to adaptively integrate contextual information to reduce the ambiguity of NTIR image encoding.
- Experimental results on the NTIR2DC task demonstrate that the proposed DlamGAN outperforms other state-of-the-art I2I translation methods in terms of semantic preservation.

2   Related Work

2.1   TIR Image Colorization

The purpose of TIR image colorization is to map a single-channel TIR image to a 3-channel RGB image, and maximize color rationality and maintain semantic invariance. In general, TIR image colorization approaches can be categorized into supervised and unsupervised approaches. The supervised methods achieve the colorization of TIR images by minimizing the distance between the translated RGB images and the ground truth. For example, Qayynm et al. [22] proposed a convolutional neural network with an encoder-decoder structure to achieve TIR image colorization. Berg et al. [2] proposed luminance and chromaticity losses to constrain the mapping of IR to visible RGB images. In contrast, without requiring paired samples, unsupervised colorization methods usually use GAN models to enforce that the distribution of the generated RGB images is similar to that of the real images. For example, Nyberg et al. [20] utilized the CycleGAN [30] to realize unpaired infrared-visible image translation. PearlGAN [18] introduced a structured gradient alignment loss to reduce geometric distortion in the NTIR2DC task. Despite the progress in TIR image colorzation, the semantic distortion problem in this field is still under-investigated.

2.2   Unpaired Image-to-Image Translation

Benefitting from the GAN model proposed by Goodfellow et al. [6], encouraging progress has been made in the field of unsupervised I2I translation in recent years [17,30]. For example, Zhu et al. [30] introduced the cycle-consistency loss to get rid of aligned image pairs on I2I translation. MUNIT [10] and DRIT++ [14] were proposed to improve the diversity of synthesized images. Anoosheh et al. designed multiple discriminators to improve the generation performance of night-to-day image translation task. U-GAT-IT [12] introduced an attention module to select specific regions for focused translation. Sem-GAN [4] utilized an additional semantic segmentation branch to encourage semantically invariant I2I translations. Zheng et al. [29] devised a fork-shape generator to boost multiple vision tasks in adverse weather conditions. Unlike previous methods, the proposed DlamGAN enhances the semantic consistency of the translation process without requiring manual annotation, which reduces the heavy burden of labeling the training samples.

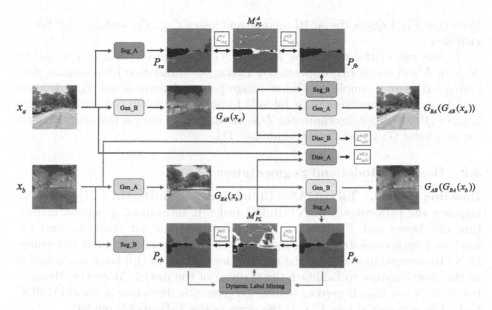

Fig. 1. The overall architecture of the proposed method. x_a and x_b respectively denote random images from daytime visible domain A and nighttime TIR domain B. The black arrows indicate the composition of the loss function, and the red and blue arrows correspond to the forward computation of domain A and domain B, respectively. The abbreviations for generator, discriminator and segmentation branch are Gen, Disc and Seg, respectively. Note that the proposed ASRI module is embedded into the generators, which is omitted for clearer visualization. (Color figure online)

3   Proposed Method

3.1   Overview and Problem Formulation

The overall framework is shown in Fig. 1. We choose the ToDayGAN-TIR [18] model as the baseline model, which consists of a pair of generators and discriminators with a total objective function including adversarial loss $\mathcal{L}_{adv}$, improved cycle-consistency loss $\mathcal{L}_{cyc}$, total variation (TV) loss $\mathcal{L}_{tv}$ and the additional structured gradient alignment (SGA) loss $\mathcal{L}_{sga}$. Then, we introduce two semantic segmentation networks S_A and S_B to predict the segmentation masks of the two domain images. The segmentation pseudo labels of the two domains, denoted as M_{PL}^A and M_{PL}^B, are obtained by the domain adaptation semantic segmentation model [28] and the proposed dynamic label mining module, respectively. Segmentation losses of translated images, denoted as $\mathcal{L}_{seg}^{fa}$ and $\mathcal{L}_{seg}^{fb}$, are used to encourage semantic consistency during translation. Moreover, the proposed ASRI module is embedded into the generators for adaptive selection of appropriate contextual information to reduce the ambiguity of NTIR image encoding.

Note that Fig. 1 omits the ASRI module and losses $\mathcal{L}_{cyc}$, $\mathcal{L}_{tv}$ and $\mathcal{L}_{sga}$ for better visibility.

In the rest of the paper, the DC and NTIR image sets will correspond to domain A and domain B, respectively. Taking the translation from domain A to domain B as an example, the input image pair of domain A and B is denoted as $\{x_a, x_b\}$, the generator G_{AB} intends to obtain plausible translation images $G_{AB}(x_a)$ to fool the discriminator D_B. Similarly, the inverse mapping includes the generator G_{BA} and the discriminator D_A.

3.2 Baseline Model and Segmentation Loss

Baseline Model. ToDayGAN-TIR modifies the ToDayGAN [1] model to improve the performance of NTIR2DC tasks. It introduced group normalization [26] layers and TV loss $\mathcal{L}_{tv}$ for eliminating color dot artifacts. And the improved cycle-consistency loss $\mathcal{L}_{cyc}$ is more sensitive to structural differences in NTIR images. In addition, the spectral normalization [19] layer is embedded in the discriminator to facilitate the training of the model. Moreover, the proposed SGA loss $\mathcal{L}_{sga}$ is used to reduce the geometric distortion in the NTIR2DC task. The adversarial loss $\mathcal{L}_{adv}$ is the same as the ToDayGAN model.

Segmentation Loss. Similar to Sem-GAN [4], we use semantic segmentation loss to enforce the semantic consistency of the I2I translation. The difference is that we do not require manual pixel-wise labels for both domains, but utilize pseudo labels of both domains to implement the model training. Specifically, the pseudo labels of DC and NTIR images (i.e., M_{PL}^A and M_{PL}^B) are obtained using the domain-adapted semantic segmentation model [28] and the dynamic label mining module, respectively. We first define the segmentation loss of real DC, real NTIR, fake DC and fake NTIR images as $\mathcal{L}_{seg}^{ra}$, $\mathcal{L}_{seg}^{rb}$, $\mathcal{L}_{seg}^{fa}$ and $\mathcal{L}_{seg}^{fb}$, respectively. We apply the pixel-wise cross-entropy loss as the segmentation loss. For example, $\mathcal{L}_{seg}^{ra}$ can be defined as:

$$\mathcal{L}_{seg}^{ra} = -\sum_{h=1}^{H}\sum_{w=1}^{W}\sum_{c=1}^{C} M_{PL}^A log(S_A(x_a)), \tag{1}$$

where H and W denote the height and the width of x_a, respectively, and C is the number of segmentation classes. Then we can obtain other segmentation loss (i.e., $\mathcal{L}_{seg}^{rb}$, $\mathcal{L}_{seg}^{fa}$ and $\mathcal{L}_{seg}^{fb}$) through Eq. (1). And the total segmentation loss can be defined as:

$$\mathcal{L}_{seg}^{all} = \lambda_{ra}\mathcal{L}_{seg}^{ra} + \lambda_{rb}\mathcal{L}_{seg}^{rb} + \lambda_{fa}\mathcal{L}_{seg}^{fa} + \lambda_{fb}\mathcal{L}_{seg}^{fb}, \tag{2}$$

where λ_{ra}, λ_{rb}, λ_{fa} and λ_{fb} are loss weights.

3.3 Dynamic Label Mining

Due to the lack of pixel-wise semantic labels for NTIR images, we propose a dynamic label mining module to extract the specific prediction regions of

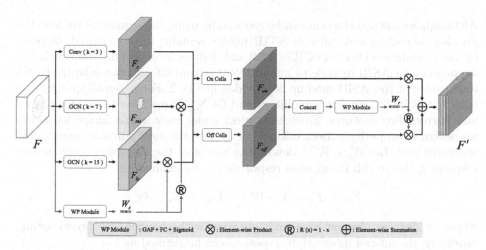

Fig. 2. Illustration of the proposed ASRI module. Conv, GCN, WP, GAP and FC denote convolution, global convolutional network [21], weight prediction, global averaged pooling and fully connected modules, respectively. The feature maps F_c, F_{ms} and F_{ls} represent the responses of the central, mid-range surrounding and long-range surrounding regions, respectively. Inspired by the dynamic nature of neuronal response [25], two weight vectors W_s and W_r are used to adaptively adjust the surrounding responses (i.e., F_{ms} and F_{ls}) and cellular responses (i.e., F_{on} and F_{off}).

segmentation networks as pseudo labels. We define $H^{rb} \in \mathbb{R}^{H \times W \times C}$ and $H^{fa} \in \mathbb{R}^{H \times W \times C}$ to denote the segmentation probability map for each position obtained by $S_B(x_b)$ and $S_A(G_{BA}(x_b))$, respectively. Then let $H^{rb}_{u,c}$ and $H^{fa}_{u,c}$ denote the probability of belonging to category c at position u for a real NTIR image x_b and fake DC image as input, respectively. Then, the category of the pseudo-label M^B_{PL} at position u is defined as:

$$
\left(M^B_{PL}\right)_u = \begin{cases} c_1 & H^{rb}_{u,c_1} \geq \theta_{bh}, c_1 = \arg\max_{c'} H^{rb}_{u,c'}, \\ c_2 & H^{rb}_{u,c_2} \geq \theta_{bl}, H^{fa}_{u,c_2} \geq \theta_a, c_2 = \arg\max_{c'} H^{fa}_{u,c'}, \\ unlabeled & otherwise. \end{cases} \quad (3)
$$

wherein θ_{bh} and θ_{bh} are the high and low thresholds of domain B, respectively. And θ_a is the threshold of domain A. In this way, we can mine the high-confidence region of the common predictions of the two network outputs as labels to reduce noisy annotations, which in turn can be used to encourage semantic consistency in translation process.

3.4 Adaptive Surrounding Response Integration Module

Due to the lack of rich texture and color information, as well as blurred boundaries between background categories (e.g., buildings and roads), category encoding of NTIR images without contextual information often falls into confusion.

Although semantic distortion can be reduced by using the segmentation loss, the problem of coding ambiguity in NTIR images remains to be explored. Inspired by the modulation effect of nCRF [7,24] and channel attention mechanism [8,16], we propose an ASRI module to integrate contextual information adaptively. An illustration of the ASRI module is provided in Fig. 2. For a given input feature map $F \in \mathbb{R}^{c \times h \times w}$, we use convolution and GCN [21] modules to extract central and surrounding features. Since the object scales vary across image locations, we design a competition mechanism to determine the most suitable surrounding receptive field. Let $W_s \in \mathbb{R}^{c \times 1}$ denote the weight of the long-range surrounding responses, the on-cell integration responses can be defined as:

$$F_{on} = F_c - (1 - W_s) \odot F_{ms} + W_s \odot F_{ls}, \tag{4}$$

where $\odot$ denotes element-wise multiplication with channel-wise broadcasting. Similarly, the off-cell integration responses can be defined as:

$$F_{off} = -F_c + (1 - W_s) \odot F_{ms} - W_s \odot F_{ls}. \tag{5}$$

Since the responses of the cells preferring to different features vary, we design a mechanism for adaptive integration of on–cell and off–cell responses. Let $W_r \in \mathbb{R}^{c \times 1}$ denote the weight of the on–cell responses, and the final fused responses can be defined as:

$$F' = W_r \odot F_{on} + (1 - W_r) \odot F_{off}. \tag{6}$$

By embedding the ASRI module into the generator, the model can adaptively exploit the long-range contextual information to reduce local coding ambiguity.

3.5   Objective Function and Training Process

In summary, the full objective function of DlamGAN can be written as:

$$\mathcal{L}_{all} = \mathcal{L}_{adv} + \lambda_{cyc}\mathcal{L}_{cyc} + \lambda_{tv}\mathcal{L}_{tv} + \lambda_{sga}\mathcal{L}_{sga} + \lambda_{seg}\mathcal{L}_{seg}^{all}, \tag{7}$$

where λ_{cyc}, λ_{tv}, λ_{sga} and λ_{seg} are loss weights. Referring to [18], λ_{cyc}, λ_{tv} and λ_{sga} are set to 10, 5 and 0.5, respectively. The value of λ_{seg} varies with the training phase.

The total training process can be divided into four stages. Let w_{sa} and w_{sb} denote the parameters of the segmentation network S_A and S_B, respectively. In stage I, λ_{seg} is set to 0 to ensure that the parameters of the generator and discriminator are fully learned. In stage II to IV, λ_{seg} is kept as 1 to progressively enforce the semantic consistency of the translation. Specifically, in stage II, λ_{ra} and λ_{fb} are set to 1, while λ_{rb} and λ_{fa} are kept at 0. Thus, the learning of w_{sa} and w_{sb} can be supervised by $\mathcal{L}_{seg}^{ra}$ and $\mathcal{L}_{seg}^{fb}$. In stage III, we fix w_{sa} and set the values of λ_{fb}, λ_{rb} and λ_{fa} to 1. The purpose of this stage is to fine-tune w_{sb} using $\mathcal{L}_{seg}^{rb}$ and $\mathcal{L}_{seg}^{fb}$. In stage IV, w_{sa} and w_{sb} are fixed together and we use $\mathcal{L}_{seg}^{fa}$ and $\mathcal{L}_{seg}^{fb}$ to reduce the semantic distortion during translation.

4   Experiments

4.1   Datasets and Evaluation Metrics

Datasets. Experiments are conducted on the FLIR and KAIST datasets. The FLIR Thermal Starter Dataset [5] provides an annotated TIR image set and non-annotated RGB image set for object detection tasks. The TIR and RGB images were acquired with a FLIR Tau2 imager and FLIR BlackFly imager, respectively. After separating the images from different time periods, we finally obtained 5447 DC images and 2899 NTIR images for the training of the NTIR2DC task. The KAIST Multispectral Pedestrian Detection Benchmark [11] provides somewhat aligned color and thermal image (640×512) pairs captured in day and night. After sampling to reduce the redundancy of images, the final training set consists of 1674 DC images and 1359 NTIR images.

Evaluation Metrics. In order to balance the evaluation of texture naturalness and semantic consistency, we first train a domain-adapted semantic segmentation model [28] using real DC images from the corresponding dataset. The obtained model is then used to predict the segmentation masks of the translated images, and the subsequent mIoU results between the masks and the groundtruth can be treated as a metric for image colorization.

4.2   Implementation Details

The proposed DlamGAN is implemented using PyTorch. We train the models using the Adam optimizer [13] with $(\beta_1, \beta_2) = (0.5, 0.999)$ on NVIDIA RTX 3090 GPUs. The batch size is set to one for all experiments. Learning rate begins at 0.0002, is constant for the first half of training and decreases linearly to zero during the second half. The total number of training epochs is 120. The thresholds θ_{bh}, θ_{bl} and θ_a in Eq. (3) are set to 0.95, 0.85 and 0.95, respectively. The number of training epochs at different stages (i.e., stage I to stage IV) is 30, 20, 30 and 40, respectively. The segmentation network consists of an encoder (i.e., the same structure as the encoder in the generator), a transposed convolutional layer, and an ASPP module [3]. The number of categories in segmentation losses is 19.

4.3   Experiments on FLIR Dataset

Figure 3 presents the translated results and corresponding segmentation outputs of various methods on FLIR dataset. Figure 3(a) is the reference nighttime visible color (NVC) image and its semantic segmentation output. Despite the differences in features and illumination, the domain-adapted semantic segmentation model [28] can obtain somewhat reasonable scene layout predictions on nighttime images. However, there are many errors in the identification of the sky area. In addition, as shown by the white dashed box in the segmentation

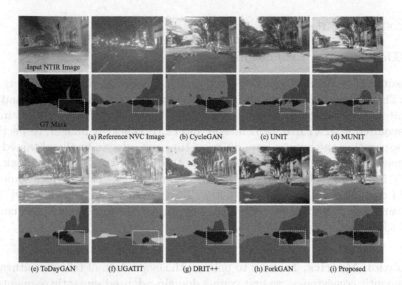

Fig. 3. The visual translation (the first row) and segmentation performance (the second row) comparison of different methods on FLIR dataset. The area covered by the white dotted box illustrates one of the regions that have big differences among different models. (Color figure online)

masks, UNIT, MUNIT, ToDayGAN and UGATIT all fail to generate plausible cars, and the translated images of DRIT++ and ForkGAN do not guarantee complete car prediction. In contrast, our method has a stronger ability to preserve scene content. Table 1 reports a quantitative comparison of the semantic consistency performance on the FLIR dataset. Due to the low contrast and the non-alignment with NTIR images, the mIoU of reference NVC images is only 35.6%. UGATIT and DRIT++ methods both fail to synthesize plausible outputs and thus obtain poor mIoU scores. As shown, the proposed method achieves the highest mIoU (47.7%) among all the methods, which demonstrates the superiority of the proposed approach in terms of semantic preservation. Note that due to the small number of samples containing trucks, buses and motorcycles in the training set, as well as the small area occupied by traffic signs, all methods have poor translation results for these four categories.

4.4   Experiments on KAIST Dataset

The qualitative translation and segmentation result comparisons on the KAIST dataset are presented in Fig. 4. Although NVC images can provide somewhat reasonable layout cues, small cars in the distance with strong lighting are extremely challenging for the segmentation model to identify. As shown in the white dashed box in the second row, UNIT, MUNIT, ToDayGAN, UGATIT, DRIT++ and ForkGAN fail to capture the characteristics of pedestrians. CycleGAN can make the segmentation model perceive pedestrians despite the lack of realistic struc-

Table 1. Semantic segmentation results of the translated images obtained by different translation methods on the FLIR dataset. All numbers are in %.

	Road	Building	Sign	Sky	Person	Car	Truck	Bus	Motorcycle	mIoU
NVC images	95.5	62.8	**6.4**	63.4	40.7	51.4	0.0	**0.4**	0.0	35.6
CycleGAN [30]	95.6	39.1	0.0	90.8	60.8	78.0	0.0	0.0	0.0	40.5
UNIT [17]	96.2	60.3	0.2	92.1	64.5	71.5	0.0	0.0	**14.6**	44.4
MUNIT [10]	96.0	27.5	0.0	92.8	49.6	64.3	0.0	0.0	0.0	36.7
ToDayGAN [1]	95.7	47.2	0.0	85.3	56.8	75.4	0.0	0.0	0.0	40.0
UGATIT [12]	94.3	18.4	0.0	89.0	23.7	59.0	0.0	0.0	0.0	31.6
DRIT++ [14]	**97.3**	29.4	0.0	78.4	28.0	78.9	0.0	0.0	0.0	34.7
ForkGAN [29]	94.4	55.1	0.0	90.7	60.5	76.1	0.0	0.0	0.0	41.9
Proposed	96.6	**78.5**	0.0	**94.0**	**72.6**	**87.3**	0.0	0.0	0.0	**47.7**

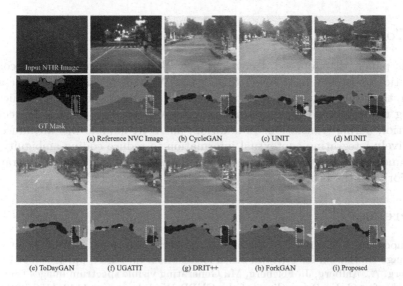

Fig. 4. The visual translation (the first row) and segmentation performance (the second row) comparison of different methods on the KAIST dataset. The area covered by the white dotted box illustrates one of the regions that have big differences among different models. (Color figure online)

ture. In contrast, the proposed DlamGAN can better maintain the pedestrian structure and perform a more reasonable translation. The quantitative comparison is listed in Table 2. Note that the proposed model achieves the highest mIoU among all the methods, and a significant improvement (i.e., +7.7%) compared with that on the real NVC images, which indicates that the proposed DlamGAN can facilitate nighttime scene perception while better preserving the scene layout. Similar to the experiments on the FLIR dataset, the poor performance in the translation of traffic signs and vehicles other than cars is due to the small number of samples available for learning.

Table 2. Semantic segmentation results of the translated images obtained by different translation methods on the KAIST dataset. All numbers are in %.

	Road	Building	Sign	Sky	Person	Car	Truck	Bus	Motorcycle	mIoU
NVC images	92.2	71.8	0.0	66.3	15.7	57.7	0.0	0.2	0.0	33.8
CycleGAN [30]	88.0	48.7	0.0	78.6	15.0	49.2	0.0	0.0	0.0	31.1
UNIT [17]	94.1	**73.9**	3.1	86.6	36.0	67.7	0.0	0.0	1.6	40.3
MUNIT [10]	88.7	34.5	0.2	81.0	7.8	46.2	0.0	0.0	0.6	28.8
ToDayGAN [1]	93.3	63.2	2.3	87.7	20.4	58.3	0.0	0.0	0.0	36.1
UGATIT [12]	90.0	52.2	1.3	73.3	16.7	53.0	0.0	0.0	0.0	31.8
DRIT++ [14]	91.2	71.5	0.0	73.8	5.1	56.2	0.0	0.0	0.0	33.1
ForkGAN [29]	93.9	54.3	0.9	87.0	22.7	66.2	0.0	0.0	2.9	36.4
Proposed	**94.4**	64.3	**4.0**	**89.3**	**43.1**	**68.3**	0.0	**5.8**	**4.0**	**41.5**

5 Conclusion

In this paper, we proposed a novel framework called DlamGAN to encourage semantic consistency in the NTIR2DC task. Without requiring semantic annotation, the semantic cues of NTIR images can be extracted by the dynamic label mining module. The obtained semantic cues were used to penalize the content distortion during translation. In addition, an ASRI module was introduced for adaptively integrating contextual information to reduce coding ambiguity. The experimental results on FLIR and KAIST datasets consistently demonstrate the superiority of the proposed model in semantic preservation.

References

1. Anoosheh, A., Sattler, T., Timofte, R., Pollefeys, M., Van Gool, L.: Night-to-day image translation for retrieval-based localization. In: ICRA, pp. 5958–5964 (2019)
2. Berg, A., Ahlberg, J., Felsberg, M.: Generating visible spectrum images from thermal infrared. In: Proceedings of the CVPR Workshops, pp. 1143–1152 (2018)
3. Chen, L.C., Papandreou, G., Kokkinos, I., Murphy, K., Yuille, A.L.: DeepLab: semantic image segmentation with deep convolutional nets, atrous convolution, and fully connected CRFs. IEEE Trans. Pattern Anal. Mach. Intell. **40**(4), 834–848 (2017)
4. Cherian, A., Sullivan, A.: Sem-GAN: semantically-consistent image-to-image translation. In: Proceedings of the WACV, pp. 1797–1806. IEEE (2019)
5. F.A. Group: FLIR thermal dataset for algorithm training. https://www.flir.co.uk/oem/adas/adas-dataset-form/, May 2019
6. Goodfellow, I.J., et al.: Generative adversarial nets. In: Proceedings of the NeurIPS (2014)
7. Grigorescu, C., Petkov, N., Westenberg, M.A.: Contour detection based on non-classical receptive field inhibition. IEEE Trans. Image Process. **12**(7), 729–739 (2003)
8. Hu, J., Shen, L., Sun, G.: Squeeze-and-excitation networks. In: Proceedings of the CVPR, pp. 7132–7141 (2018)
9. Huang, S.W., Lin, C.T., Chen, S.P., Wu, Y.Y., Hsu, P.H., Lai, S.H.: AugGAN: cross domain adaptation with GAN-based data augmentation. In: Proceedings of the ECCV, pp. 718–731 (2018)

10. Huang, X., Liu, M.Y., Belongie, S., Kautz, J.: Multimodal unsupervised image-to-image translation. In: Proceedings of the ECCV, pp. 172–189 (2018)
11. Hwang, S., Park, J., Kim, N., Choi, Y., So Kweon, I.: Multispectral pedestrian detection: benchmark dataset and baseline. In: Proceedings of the CVPR, pp. 1037–1045 (2015)
12. Kim, J., Kim, M., Kang, H., Lee, K.H.: U-GAT-IT: unsupervised generative attentional networks with adaptive layer-instance normalization for image-to-image translation. In: Proceedings of the ICLR (2019)
13. Kingma, D.P., Ba, J.: Adam: a method for stochastic optimization. arXiv preprint arXiv:1412.6980 (2014)
14. Lee, H.Y., et al.: Drit++: diverse image-to-image translation via disentangled representations. Int. J. Comput. Vis. **128**(10), 2402–2417 (2020)
15. Li, P., Liang, X., Jia, D., Xing, E.P.: Semantic-aware grad-GAN for virtual-to-real urban scene adaption. arXiv preprint arXiv:1801.01726 (2018)
16. Li, X., Wang, W., Hu, X., Yang, J.: Selective Kernel networks. In: Proceedings of the CVPR, pp. 510–519 (2019)
17. Liu, M.Y., Breuel, T., Kautz, J.: Unsupervised image-to-image translation networks. In: Proceedings of the NeurIPS (2017)
18. Luo, F., Li, Y., Zeng, G., Wang, G., Li, Y.: Thermal infrared image colorization for nighttime driving scenes with top-down guided attention. arXiv preprint arXiv:2104.14374 (2021)
19. Miyato, T., Kataoka, T., Koyama, M., Yoshida, Y.: Spectral normalization for generative adversarial networks. arXiv preprint arXiv:1802.05957 (2018)
20. Nyberg, A., Eldesokey, A., Bergstrom, D., Gustafsson, D.: Unpaired thermal to visible spectrum transfer using adversarial training. In: Proceedings of the ECCV (2018)
21. Peng, C., Zhang, X., Yu, G., Luo, G., Sun, J.: Large Kernel matters-improve semantic segmentation by global convolutional network. In: Proceedings of the CVPR, pp. 4353–4361 (2017)
22. Qayynm, U., Ahsan, Q., Mahmood, Z., Chcmdary, M.A.: Thermal colorization using deep neural network. In: Proceedings of the IBCAST, pp. 325–329 (2018)
23. Roy, P., Häni, N., Chao, J.J., Isler, V.: Semantics-aware image to image translation and domain transfer. arXiv preprint arXiv:1904.02203 (2019)
24. Vinje, W.E., Gallant, J.L.: Natural stimulation of the nonclassical receptive field increases information transmission efficiency in v1. J. Neurosci. **22**(7), 2904–2915 (2002)
25. Weinberger, N.M.: Dynamic regulation of receptive fields and maps in the adult sensory cortex. Annu. Rev. Neurosci. **18**, 129 (1995)
26. Wu, Y., He, K.: Group normalization. In: Proceedings of the ECCV, pp. 3–19 (2018)
27. Wu, Y., Kirillov, A., Massa, F., Lo, W.Y., Girshick, R.: Detectron2. https://github.com/facebookresearch/detectron2 (2019)
28. Zheng, Z., Yang, Y.: Unsupervised scene adaptation with memory regularization in vivo. In: Proceedings of the IJCAI (2020)
29. Zheng, Z., Wu, Y., Han, X., Shi, J.: ForkGAN: seeing into the rainy night. In: Proceedings of the ECCV (2020)
30. Zhu, J.Y., Park, T., Isola, P., Efros, A.A.: Unpaired image-to-image translation using cycle-consistent adversarial networks. In: Proceedings of the ICCV, pp. 2223–2232 (2017)

SA-GNN: Stereo Attention and Graph Neural Network for Stereo Image Super-Resolution

Huiling Li[1,2], Qiong Liu[1,2](✉), and You Yang[1,2]

[1] School of Electronic Information and Communications, Huazhong University
of Science and Technology, Wuhan 430074, China
q.liu@hust.edu.cn
[2] Wuhan National Laboratory for Opto-electronics, Wuhan 430074, China

Abstract. The goal of the stereoscopic image super-resolution (SR) is
to reconstruct a pair of high-resolution (HR) images from corresponding low-resolution (LR) images. The existing stereo SR methods based on
convolutional neural network (CNN) benefit from additional information
from a different viewpoint to some extent. However, they cannot make
good use of the complementary information from the different viewpoint,
resulting in a lack of textures and details. The unevenly distributed features from left and right images were treated equally. To overcome the
above difficulties, we put forward a stereo attention graph neural network
(SA-GNN), which can extract reliable priors non-locally and fuse consistent contents adaptively cross different viewpoints. SA-GNN contains
a series of stereo graph neural networks (SGNN), which alternate iteratively between in-view graph and cross-view graph under the aggregation and update mechanism of graph neural networks (GNN) to enhance
SR performance. The comparison experiment results on four public
datasets demonstrate that our SA-GNN outperforms the state-of-the-art
methods.

Keywords: Stereo image super-resolution · Graph neural network

1 Introduction

With the rapid development of binocular camera, left and right stereoscopic
images have become more and more popular in many applications such as automatic driving, remote sensing and mobile phones. At the same time, with the
updating of hardware devices such as GPUs, the need for higher-quality stereo
images is increasing, bringing about the demand for stereo super-resolution
technology.

This work was supported in part by the National Natural Science Foundation of China
under Grant 91848107, and in part by the National Key Research and Development
Program of China under Grant 2020YFB2103501.

Y. Peng et al. (Eds.): ICIG 2021, LNCS 12890, pp. 400–411, 2021.
https://doi.org/10.1007/978-3-030-87361-5_33

Single image super-resolution (SISR) is a classic ill-posed problem. Therefore, SISR methods based on deep learning have achieved promising performance in recent years. Dong et al. first introduced CNN into the super-resolution problem of a single image in 2014 and proposed the SRCNN framework [1]. Since then, SR networks have become deeper and more complex, allowing more useful information to be mined from a single viewpoint. Lim et al. proposed an EDSR network using both local and residual connections [9]. Zhang et al. combined residual connection [3] with dense connection [5], and proposed a residual dense network to fully use hierarchical feature representations for SISR [25].

Different from single-image super-resolution(SISR), the target of the stereoscopic image SR is to reconstruct high-resolution images from a pair of low-resolution images. The stereo SR can extract additional complementary information of the corresponding pixels from the other viewpoint. Thus, the most challenging problem in the stereo images SR is how to make full use of this complementary information to enhance the final SR performance.

Jeon et al. first proposed a StereoSR network for stereo images SR in 2018 [6]. The right LR viewpoint was moved towards different parallax shifts to align with the left LR viewpoint to estimate parallax priors. However, StereoSR has the defects that it cannot handle a large parallax more than 64 pixels and the parallax is also a fixed value. Wang et al. proposed PASSRnet in 2019, introducing a parallax attention mechanism that searches along the epipolar line to estimate the parallax of the stereo images. It eliminates the limitation of the parallax range [18]. But it cannot fully utilize the spatial information within the viewpoint as SISR does. In 2020, Ying et al. inserted the same parallax attention mechanism into two identical pre-trained SISR networks which depended on the performance of SISR frameworks [22]. In 2021, Wang et al. proposed a iPASSR to address occlusion and illuminance problem based on PASSRnet [21]. However, the unevenly distributed information from left and right images were treated equally in above methods. Song took the complementarity of the left and right images into account [17]. But only the fixed weight of the overall features of different viewpoints is considered, which had difficulties in adaptively excavating the distribution of complementary information.

The existing CNN-based methods of stereo SR deal equally with the non-uniform complementary information of different viewpoints, resulting in incorrect textures and fuzzy details. Instead, graph neural network is an iterative reasoning module, which can integrate non-local spatial information adaptively. Recently, there are many applications of GNN on computer vision [4,13]. Contrary to above CNN-based methods, non-local neural networks [19] can capture long-range dependencies and perform self-attention weighting in some image restoration tasks [24]. Thus, it can look for correlation between cross-view information in stereo images. However, all nodes in non-local network are fully connected, which contains high computational complexity. To reduce the computation, gathering k nearest neighboring nodes is applied in image restoration rather than full connection [12,26]. For example, in [4], He et al. proposed a MV-GNN for compression artifacts reduction task, which built a K-neighbor graph on each pixel to aggregate multi-view information.

The current challenge for stereo SR is how to adaptively utilize complementary information from two different viewpoints to obtain more reliable priors and to recover more accurate high-frequency details. In order to address the issues raised above, we take advantage of GNN mechanisms, which mainly adopt neighborhood aggregation framework for representation learning. Relative to forementioned GNN methods used for image restoration, we build and update alternately two K-nearest graphs on different viewpoints. On the one hand, it adaptively distinguishes the consistent priors from different viewpoints. On the other hand, it increases the depth of GNN to enhance the representation capability. Moreover, the nodes of graphs are patch-wise rather than pixel-wise inspired by [26], which is easier to discover self-similarity at texture or edges.

In this paper, we put forward a GNN-based method, namely, stereo attention graph neural network(SA-GNN) for stereo SR task to adaptive fuse complementary information cross viewpoints. In our proposed method, a pair of LR images is firstly input to feature extraction net and generate initial features. After warping different viewpoints to the same one, we construct two K-neighbor graphs in this viewpoint and cross viewpoints based on the features similarity. Then we alternate iteratively between propagating in-view graph and cross-view graph. Later, two kinds of residual information are fused over the proposed residual features fusion module. One is residual features between different viewpoints, the other is between high and low resolution features. The fused features are fed to the reconstruction net, and then transformed to the image space.

There are two main contributions of this paper:

1) We propose a GNN-based network named as SA-GNN for the stereo SR problem. A stereo graph neural network(SGNN) is proposed to adaptively utilize the uneven prior information from cross viewpoints to improve stereo images SR performance.
2) A residual features fusion module is proposed to fuse two kinds of residual information, which are the cross-view and high-low resolution residual information respectively. It works to preserve more high frequency details.

2   Stereo Attention Graph Neural Network (SA-GNN)

In this section, we will introduce the proposed method in details. In subsequent sections, the left and right stereo low resolution images are denoted as $I_{LR}^l \in \mathbb{R}^{H \times W \times 3}$ and $I_{LR}^r \in \mathbb{R}^{H \times W \times 3}$, while the stereo high resolution images are denoted as $I_{HR}^l \in \mathbb{R}^{sH \times sW \times 3}$ and $I_{HR}^r \in \mathbb{R}^{sH \times sW \times 3}$. The notation s is used to denote the upscaling factor (e.g., 2, 4).

In this work, our goal is to take the LR stereo images I_{LR}^l and I_{LR}^r as inputs and generate super-resolved stereo images $I_{SR}^l \in \mathbb{R}^{sH \times sW \times 3}$ and $I_{SR}^r \in \mathbb{R}^{sH \times sW \times 3}$ and to restore as much details and textures as possible. The framework of SA-GNN is depicted in Fig. 1, which consists of three sub-networks: a feature extraction net, a stereo view interaction net and a reconstruction net.

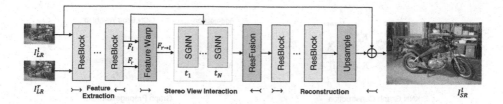

Fig. 1. An overview of our SA-GNN network.

Firstly, a pair of images I^l_{LR} and I^r_{LR} is respectively input to the weight-shared feature extraction net based on stacked residual blocks [3] to generate initial features. Then the stereo view interaction network better excavates the rich cross-view information. Finally, the fused features are fed to the reconstruction net, and then transformed to the image space. Next, we further introduce the components of the network in the following sections.

2.1 Stereo View Interaction Net

In stereo view interaction net, reliable cross-view information is extracted and fused. This net consists of three parts: feature warp module, stereo graph neural network module, residual feature fusion module. After being warped in the feature warp module, initial features are filterd and updated under the guidance of the stereo graph neural network module. In the end, the residual feature fusion module extracts high frequency information from cross-view and high-low resolution residual features.

Feature Warp. The initial features $F_l, F_r \in \mathbb{R}^{H \times W \times C}$ obtained after feature extraction need to be warped to the same viewpoint, for example the left viewpoint. Inspired by parallax-attention mechanism [18], the feature warp process can be formulated as Eq. (1):

$$F_{r \to l} = M_{r \to l} \otimes F_r \tag{1}$$

where $M_{r \to l} \in \mathbb{R}^{H \times W \times W}$ denotes a parallax attention map learned from F_l, F_r, $\otimes$ denotes batch-wise matrix multiplication, and $F_{r \to l}$ denotes features warped from the right viewpoint to the left viewpoint.

Stereo Graph Neural Network (SGNN). As showed in Fig. 1, we propose iterative SGNN layers to adaptively utilize the uneven prior information of cross viewpoints. Details of each SGNN layer are exhibited in Fig. 2.

Graph Construction. In order to choose and take advantage of complementary cross-view priors non-locally, we construct two graphs $G_{in} = \{V^{in}, E^{in}\}$, $G_{cross} = \{V^{cr}, E^{cr}\}$ within the reference viewpoint(e.g., the left viewpoint) and

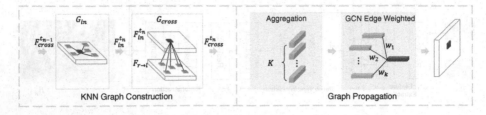

Fig. 2. Construction and Propagation of SGNN.

cross viewpoint respectively. We take each 3×3 pixels patch from the reference viewpoint as the query patch denoted as q_0. In graph G_{in}, all 3×3 pixels patches in a window centered on q_0 in reference viewpoint are nodes candidates. The correlation between each node candidate q_c and q_0 is measured in the feature domain f_{q_0}, f_{q_c} by the Euclidean distance, which can be formulated as $\|f_{q_0} - f_{q_c}\|^2$. The main node q_0 is only connected to the most correlative K nodes. Meanwhile, the accompanying edge is defined as the difference $\|f_{q_0} - f_{q_c}\|$ between each node and node q_0.

Similarly, in graph G_{cross}, we regard patches of $F_{in}^{t_n}$ from the former G_{in} as the query and then find the most correlative K nodes in the other warping viewpoint (e.g.,$F_{r \to l}$).

Graph Propagation. We alternate between computing graph G_{in} and graph G_{cross} for t_N layers, obtaining features $F_{in}^{t_N}$ in the viewpoint as well as $F_{cross}^{t_N}$ cross the viewpoint from the final SGNN layer. Inspired by graph propagation model in [4,10,15,26], the propagation model aggregates K nearest neighbor nodes and updates the main node after graph construction. For each connected node $q_c \in \{q_1, ..., q_K\}$, we first aggregate their features. Then the update process is based on graph convolutional network (GCN) to turn each edge into weights $\{w_1, ..., w_K\}$. The update function can be defined as Eq. (2):

$$f'_{q_0} = \frac{1}{C(f_q)} \sum w_c \cdot f_{q_c}, c \in 1, ..., K \tag{2}$$

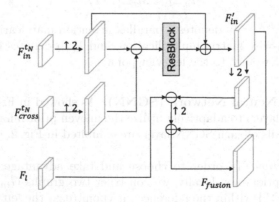

Fig. 3. Structure of ResFusion

The factor $\frac{1}{C(f_q)}$ is used for normalization. In this way, our proposed SGNN is good at propagating message adaptively and updating nodes.

Residual Features Fusion (ResFusion). The structure of ResFusion is depicted in Fig. 3. Also,the fusion equation is defined as follows:

$$F'_{in} = \text{ResBlock}\left(F_{in}^{t_N} \uparrow 2 - F_{\text{cross}}^{t_N} \uparrow 2\right) + F_{in}^{t_N} \uparrow 2 \tag{3}$$

$$F_{fusion} = (F'_{in} \downarrow 2 - F_l) \uparrow 2 + F'_{in} \tag{4}$$

The operator $\downarrow 2, \uparrow 2$ represent down-sampling $\times 2$ and up-sampling $\times 2$ composed of convolution and deconvolution [23] operations, respectively. Equation (3) computes the residual features of $F_{in}^{t_N}$ and $F_{\text{cross}}^{t_N}$ to pay more attention to complementary information across viewpoints. In addition, Eq. (4) computes the residual features of F'_{in} and initial features F_l to extract more high frequency information. Besides, this step helps to low resolution features to be transformed to $F_{fusion} \in \mathbb{R}^{2H \times 2W \times C}$.

2.2   Reconstruction Net and Loss Function

In the end, the fused features go through the stacked residual module and the up-sampling module composed of deconvolution operations to attain super-resolved image. At last, bicubic up-sampled images from input I_{LR}^l at certain scale factor is added to generate I_{SR}^l.

We use two loss functions to constrain the network training. The conventional mean square error(MSE) loss function can be defined as Eq. (5):

$$L_{MSE} = \left\| I_{HR}^l - I_{SR}^l \right\|^2 \tag{5}$$

To alleviate over smoothing caused by MSE loss, L1 perceptual loss [7] is utilized as Eq. (6):

$$L_{per} = \frac{1}{C_j W_j H_j} \sum_{c=1}^{C_j} \sum_{w=1}^{W_j} \sum_{h=1}^{H_j} \left(\left\| \phi_j \left(I_{SR}^l \right) - \phi_j \left(I_{HR}^l \right) \right\|_1 \right) \tag{6}$$

where C_j, W_j, H_j denote channel, width, height of the features $\phi_j()$ of the output j-th layer of vggnet [16]. Thus, the formulation of the total loss is defined as Eq. (7):

$$L_{total} = L_{MSE} + \lambda L_{per} \tag{7}$$

where λ is a hyper-parameter weighing the two loss functions. λ is set to be 0.1 during experiments.

3   Experiment and Discussion

In this section, we first introduce the details of the training and testing set, as well as experiment settings. Next, we conduct an ablation study. Then, the performance of SA-GNN was evaluated in terms of quantitative scoring and visual qualitative quality on the benchmark datasets.

3.1   Image Datasets and Implementation Details

Following the experimental setting of iPASSR [21], the training set contains 800 images of Flickr1024 dataset [20] and 60 images of the Middlebury dataset [14]. Meanwhile, the testing set has 5 images from the Middlebury dataset [14], 20 images from the KITTI 2012 dataset [2] and 20 images from the KITTI 2015 dataset [11], 112 images from the Flickr1024 dataset [20].

Bicubic interpolation was used to preprocess the HR images with scale factors of 2 and 4 by down-sampling, and then the down-sampling images were clipped into 30×90 image patches as the LR input for training. Their HR counterparts were cropped accordingly.

Our network was implemented in PyTorch using Ubuntu18.04 system with a Nvidia RTX 1080Ti GPU. All models were optimized using the Adam method with $\beta_1 = 0.9, \beta_2 = 0.999$ and a batch size of 2. The initial learning rate was set to 1×10^{-4}. The training was stopped after 80 epochs.

Table 1. Quantitative results achieved by different methods on different datasets. Mean PSNR/SSIM values achieved on the left images are listed here. The best results are in bold.

Dataset	Scale	Single Image SR		Stereo Image SR		
		Bicubic	EDSR	PASSRnet	iPASSR	Ours
Middlebury	×2	30.46/0.897	34.84/**0.948**	34.13/0.942	34.41/0.945	**34.98**/0.938
KITTI2012	×2	28.44/0.880	30.83/0.919	30.68/0.916	30.97/0.921	**33.49/0.936**
KITTI2015	×2	27.81/0.881	29.94/0.923	29.81/0.919	30.01/0.923	**34.14/0.948**
Flickr1024	×2	24.94/0.818	28.66/0.908	28.38/0.904	28.60/**0.910**	**28.71**/0.882
Middlebury	×4	26.27/0.755	29.15/0.838	28.62/0.823	29.16/0.837	**30.64/0.843**
KITTI2012	×4	24.52/0.731	26.26/0.795	26.26/0.792	26.56/0.805	**28.69/0.839**
KITTI2015	×4	23.79/0.707	25.38/0.781	25.42/0.777	26.32/0.808	**28.46/0.834**
Flickr1024	×4	21.82/0.629	23.46/0.728	23.19/0.720	23.44/**0.729**	**24.78**/0.719

3.2   Comparison to the State-of-the-Arts

In this section, we compare our proposed SA-GNN to the conventional bicubic interpolation [8] and several state-of-the-art method, including a SISR method EDSR [9], two stereo image SR methods(e.g., PASSRnet [18], iPASSR [21]).

Quantitative Results. The quantitative results of above four test sets are shown in Table 1. We take peak signal-to-noise ratio(PSNR) and structural similarity index measure(SSIM) as main metrics. It can be seen that SA-GNN has the highest PSNR for all scale factors on all datasets, and the SSIM is the highest on the KITTI 2012 dataset [2] and the KITTI 2015 dataset [11]. Our SA-GNN catches up with the performance of EDSR which is one of typical SISR methods. For 4× SR experiments, the results on the KITTI 2015 dataset [11] show that the average PSNR of the SA-GNN method is at least 2.14dB higher than other methods. For 2× SR experiments, the results on the KITTI 2015 dataset [11] show that the average PSNR of the SA-GNN method is at least 4.13dB higher than other methods.

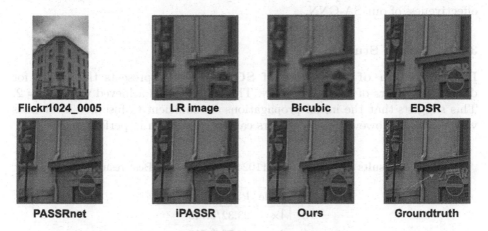

Fig. 4. Visual comparative results for 4× stereo SR.

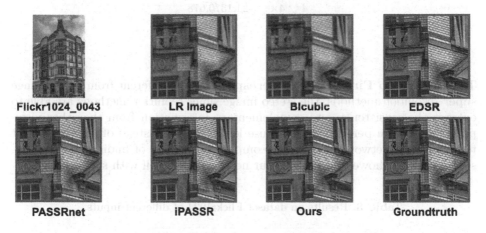

Fig. 5. Visual comparative results for 2× stereo SR.

Qualitative Results. Figure 4 and Fig. 5 show the qualitative results of ×4 and ×2 SR, respectively. The enlarged red areas show that our proposed SR method can restore sharper edges. For ×4 SR, the results of these benchmarks are not only over smoothing, but also lack clear details. Our method can restore clearer letters of Flckr1024-0005. For ×2 sr, we can clearly restore the texture of walls of Flckr1024-0043.

The SISR methods that only utilize spatial information for SR cannot reliably recover degenerated details. In contrast, our SA-GNN can use the supplementary cross-view information provided by the stereo image to select the details that are reliable to be preserved. These qualitative results evidently prove the effectiveness of our SA-GNN.

3.3 Ablation Study

Determination of t_N Layers of SGNN. Table 2 presents the results for different numbers of layers of SGNN. The best result is achieved when $t_N = 2$. This suggests that the initial propagations are sufficient to fuse non-local cross view features. However, deeper layers cause degradation in performance.

Table 2. Results on dataset Flickr1024 of different t_N.Best result is in bold.

t_N	Scale	PSNR/SSIM
0	4×	23.32/0.713
1	4×	24.76/0.716
2	4×	**24.78/0.719**
3	4×	24.13/0.679
4	4×	24.13/0.678

The Ability to Find Stereo Correspondence. Different from single image super resolution methods, the stereo image super reolution methods are able to extract the consistency and complementary information from the other viewpoint to improve performance. We use left-left input instead of left-right input to retrain the network in order to compare the ability of finding stereo correspondence. As showed in Table 3, our network deals well with stereo images.

Table 3. Results on dataset Flickr1024 of different inputs.

Input	Scale	PSNR/SSIM
Left-left	4×	24.73/0.718
Left-right	4×	24.78/0.719
Improvement	4×	0.05/0.001

The Effectiveness of Resfusion Module and Perceptual Loss. We retrained our network with different settings as showed in Table 4. To validate the effectiveness of Resfusion module, we remove it from the stereo view interaction net. Then, the average PSNR suffers a decrease of 0.05dB. Also, we removed perceptual loss to retrain the whole network, resluting in a decrease of 0.01dB of the average PSNR.

Table 4. Results on dataset Flickr1024 to validate the effectiveness of Resfusion and perceptual loss. Best result is in bold.

Models	Scale	PSNR
SA-GNN w/o ResFusion	4×	24.73
SA-GNN w/o Perceptual loss	4×	24.77
SA-GNN	4×	**24.78**

4 Conclusion

In this paper, we propose a stereo attention graph neural network to for stereo image SR. In our method, we focus on how to adaptive fuse complementary information cross-view priors. In our proposed method, a pair of images is firstly input to feature extraction net consisting of stacked residual blocks and generate initial features. Followed by a stereo view interaction net, two K-neighbor graphs are designed in and cross the viewpoint based on the feature similarity. Then we alternate iteratively between updating and propagating graph in view and graph cross view. Later, Residual features between different viewpoints, and between high-low resolution features are utilized to restore high frequency details. The fused features are fed to the reconstruction net, and then transformed to SR image space. Experimental results show that our method outperforms other methods on four benchmark datasets both in average PSNR gain. At the same time, better qualitative performance has been achieved by our SA-GNN. In our future work, we will focus on designing a GNN with stronger ability to distinguish the validity of cross-view features for stereo image SR task.

References

1. Dong, C., Loy, C.C., He, K., Tang, X.: Learning a deep convolutional network for image super-resolution. In: Fleet, D., Pajdla, T., Schiele, B., Tuytelaars, T. (eds.) ECCV 2014. LNCS, vol. 8692, pp. 184–199. Springer, Cham (2014). https://doi.org/10.1007/978-3-319-10593-2_13
2. Geiger, A., Lenz, P., Urtasun, R.: Are we ready for autonomous driving? The KITTI vision benchmark suite. In: 2012 IEEE Conference on Computer Vision and Pattern Recognition, pp. 3354–3361. IEEE (2012)

3. He, K., Zhang, X., Ren, S., Sun, J.: Deep residual learning for image recognition. CoRR abs/1512.03385 (2015). http://arxiv.org/abs/1512.03385
4. He, X., Liu, Q., Yang, Y.: MV-GNN: multi-view graph neural network for compression artifacts reduction. IEEE Trans. Image Process. **29**, 6829–6840 (2020)
5. Huang, G., Liu, Z., Van Der Maaten, L., Weinberger, K.Q.: Densely connected convolutional networks. In: Proceedings of the IEEE Conference on Computer Vision and Pattern Recognition, pp. 4700–4708 (2017)
6. Jeon, D.S., Baek, S.H., Choi, I., Kim, M.H.: Enhancing the spatial resolution of stereo images using a parallax prior. In: Proceedings of the IEEE Conference on Computer Vision and Pattern Recognition, pp. 1721–1730 (2018)
7. Johnson, J., Alahi, A., Fei-Fei, L.: Perceptual losses for real-time style transfer and super-resolution. In: Leibe, B., Matas, J., Sebe, N., Welling, M. (eds.) ECCV 2016. LNCS, vol. 9906, pp. 694–711. Springer, Cham (2016). https://doi.org/10.1007/978-3-319-46475-6_43
8. Keys, R.: Cubic convolution interpolation for digital image processing. IEEE Trans. Acoust. Speech Signal Process. **29**(6), 1153–1160 (1981)
9. Lim, B., Son, S., Kim, H., Nah, S., Lee, K.M.: Enhanced deep residual networks for single image super-resolution. In: Proceedings of the IEEE Conference on Computer Vision and Pattern Recognition Workshops, pp. 136–144 (2017)
10. Mei, Y., Fan, Y., Zhou, Y., Huang, L., Huang, T.S., Shi, H.: Image super-resolution with cross-scale non-local attention and exhaustive self-exemplars mining. In: Proceedings of the IEEE/CVF Conference on Computer Vision and Pattern Recognition, pp. 5690–5699 (2020)
11. Menze, M., Geiger, A.: Object scene flow for autonomous vehicles. In: Proceedings of the IEEE Conference on Computer Vision and Pattern Recognition, pp. 3061–3070 (2015)
12. Plötz, T., Roth, S.: Neural nearest neighbors networks. Adv. Neural. Inf. Process. Syst. **31**, 1087–1098 (2018)
13. Qi, X., Liao, R., Jia, J., Fidler, S., Urtasun, R.: 3D graph neural networks for RGBD semantic segmentation. In: Proceedings of the IEEE International Conference on Computer Vision, pp. 5199–5208 (2017)
14. Scharstein, D., et al.: High-resolution stereo datasets with subpixel-accurate ground truth. In: Jiang, X., Hornegger, J., Koch, R. (eds.) GCPR 2014. LNCS, vol. 8753, pp. 31–42. Springer, Cham (2014). https://doi.org/10.1007/978-3-319-11752-2_3
15. Simonovsky, M., Komodakis, N.: Dynamic edge-conditioned filters in convolutional neural networks on graphs. In: Proceedings of the IEEE Conference on Computer Vision and Pattern Recognition, pp. 3693–3702 (2017)
16. Simonyan, K., Zisserman, A.: Very deep convolutional networks for large-scale image recognition. arXiv preprint arXiv:1409.1556 (2014)
17. Song, W., Choi, S., Jeong, S., Sohn, K.: Stereoscopic image super-resolution with stereo consistent feature. In: Proceedings of the AAAI Conference on Artificial Intelligence, vol. 34, pp. 12031–12038 (2020)
18. Wang, L., et al.: Learning parallax attention for stereo image super-resolution. In: Proceedings of the IEEE/CVF Conference on Computer Vision and Pattern Recognition, pp. 12250–12259 (2019)
19. Wang, X., Girshick, R., Gupta, A., He, K.: Non-local neural networks. In: Proceedings of the IEEE Conference on Computer Vision and Pattern Recognition, pp. 7794–7803 (2018)
20. Wang, Y., Wang, L., Yang, J., An, W., Guo, Y.: Flickr1024: a large-scale dataset for stereo image super-resolution. In: Proceedings of the IEEE/CVF International Conference on Computer Vision Workshops (2019)

21. Wang, Y., Ying, X., Wang, L., Yang, J., An, W., Guo, Y.: Symmetric parallax attention for stereo image super-resolution. arXiv preprint arXiv:2011.03802 (2020)
22. Ying, X., Wang, Y., Wang, L., Sheng, W., An, W., Guo, Y.: A stereo attention module for stereo image super-resolution. IEEE Signal Process. Lett. **27**, 496–500 (2020)
23. Zeiler, M.D., Taylor, G.W., Fergus, R.: Adaptive deconvolutional networks for mid and high level feature learning. In: 2011 International Conference on Computer Vision, pp. 2018–2025. IEEE (2011)
24. Zhang, Y., Li, K., Li, K., Zhong, B., Fu, Y.: Residual non-local attention networks for image restoration. arXiv preprint arXiv:1903.10082 (2019)
25. Zhang, Y., Tian, Y., Kong, Y., Zhong, B., Fu, Y.: Residual dense network for image super-resolution. In: Proceedings of the IEEE Conference on Computer Vision and Pattern Recognition, pp. 2472–2481 (2018)
26. Zhou, S., Zhang, J., Zuo, W., Loy, C.C.: Cross-scale internal graph neural network for image super-resolution. arXiv preprint arXiv:2006.16673 (2020)

Ground-to-Aerial Image Geo-Localization with Cross-View Image Synthesis

Jiaqing Huang and Dengpan Ye[✉]

Key Laboratory of Aerospace Information Security and Trusted Computing,
Ministry of Education, School of Cyber Science and Engineering, Wuhan University,
Wuhan, China
yedp@whu.edu.cn

Abstract. The task of ground-to-aerial image geo-localization can be achieved by matching a ground view query image to aerial images with geographic labels in a reference database. It remains challenging due to the drastic change in viewpoint. In this paper, we propose a new cross-view image synthesis conditional generative adversarial networks (cGAN) called Crossview Sequential Fork (CSF) to generate ground images from aerial images. CSF achieves a more detailed synthesis effect by the generation of segmentation maps and edge detection images. And the synthesis ground images are input to the image matching framework Cross View Synthesis Net (CVS-Net) to assist geo-localization, the distance between the descriptors of source ground image and synthesis ground image is calculated to assist the training of the network. CVS-Net is leveraged on the Siamese architecture to do metric learning for the matching task. Moreover, we introduce SARE loss as part of the training procedure and improve it by our data entry form which greatly improves the convergence rate and image retrieval accuracy compared to traditional triplet loss. Experimental results demonstrate the effectiveness and superiority of our proposed method over the state-of-the-art method on two benchmark datasets.

Keywords: Siamese network · Image geo-localization · Image synthesis

1 Introduction

Geo-localization task refers to determining the real-world geographic location (e.g. GPS coordinates) for each query image. It can be applied for image localization in social media, unmanned driving, navigation, and augmented reality. With the development of these applications, the accuracy and stability of image geo-localization methods are increasingly required. Traditional geo-localization approaches deal with satellite and aerial imagery that usually involve different image sensing platforms and require accurate sensor modeling and pixel-wise geo-reference image, e.g. digital ortho-quad (DOQ) [31] and Digital Elevation

© Springer Nature Switzerland AG 2021
Y. Peng et al. (Eds.): ICIG 2021, LNCS 12890, pp. 412–424, 2021.
https://doi.org/10.1007/978-3-030-87361-5_34

Map (DEM). It's hard for this kind of method to generally applicate in the real world due to the high demand for sensing platforms and image quality. In recent years, with the development of deep learning technology, more and more classical model and framework in image classification are applied in image geo-location [27–30], GAN and relative models [7,18] especially bring a lot of motivation and improvement to the field. These methods achieve remarkable results on benchmark datasets [27,30].

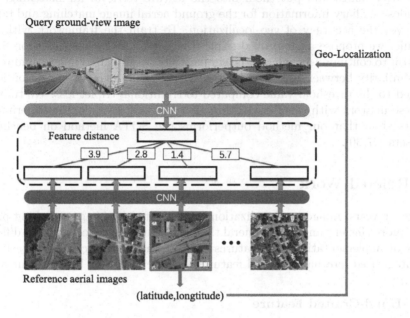

Fig. 1. Ground-to-Aerial Image Geo-Localization. Given a ground-view image as a query, the goal of geo-localization is to determine its geo-location by matching it with a reference database of aerial images with geographic labels.

The mainstream of image geo-localization method based on deep learning is implemented by image retrieval which achieves the effect of geolocation on the query images through the matching between the unknown images and the images with geolocation labels. Existing ground image datasets [8,20] are mostly biased towards famous tourist areas and the geo-localization always fails in the area without matching images. In contrast, aerial image is taken from devices with bird's eye view, e.g.satellites and drones, densely cover the Earth with strict geo-label. Therefore, the matching of ground image and aerial image has gradually become the mainstream of geo-localization approaches. However the difference of shooting angles between aerial images and ground images also brings challenges to the matching of images, this causes the traditional handcrafted features of cross-view matching such as SIFT [17] to fail. In this context, many works apply deep learning technology framework [4,10,23,25,27] to end-to-end image matching and use convolutional neural network for representation learning between ground images and aerial images. Vo and Hays [27] use an additional network branch to estimate the orientation and utilize multiple possible orientations of the aerial images to find the best angle for matching across the two views. By embedding Netvlad layer [2] on the top of CNN, CVM-NET ensures that CNN is stable to the change of perspective when extracting descriptors.

In this paper, we propose an auxiliary cGAN module CSF to predict the corresponding ground image from the aerial image, and then combine it with the source image and put them into the feature retrieval for matching. This provides auxiliary information for the ground-aerial image matching and further improves the accuracy of geo-localization. To train the framework with CSF module, we propose an improved triple SARE (T-SARE) loss based on SARE loss [16] to continuously enlarge the similarity between paired images and reduce the similarity between unpaired images, so that the model optimization is not limited to the threshold value compared to traditional triplet loss. We train the siamese network with the T-SARE function and CSF module, the experimental results show that our method outperforms the SOTA method on benchmark datasets [27, 30].

2 Related Work

In recent years, image geo-localization implemented by image matching proves to be more efficient and more general than other methods. According to different kinds of implementation, the features used in image geo-localization tasks can be categorized into hand-crafted features and deep learning based features.

2.1 Hand-Crafted Feature

Manual features based on computer vision were widely used in the field of cross-view image matching in the early stage [3, 8, 17, 26]. Due to the huge differences in the perspective, there are significant differences between the aerial image and ground view image in the same place. Bansal et al. [3] extracted the oblique aerial image to see the building facade, and then matched the building facade for geo-localization patches. Viswanathan et al. [26] improved the matching performance of local feature descriptors by converting the ground image into a top-down view. Due to the rich difference in appearance caused by different viewing angles, hand-crafted features always fail to generalize in different situations and reach poor accuracy in practical application.

2.2 Deep Learning Based Feature

With the introduction of deep learning into the field of cross-view image matching and retrieval, end-to-end image geo-localization frameworks are established and features based on deep learning prove to be more robust and more accurate [4, 10, 13, 21, 23]. Based on VLAD descriptor in [11], ArandJelovic et al. [2] proposed the learnable layer of Vlad, i.e. Netvlad, which can be embedded into the end-to-end deep network training superior to multiple fully connected layers, Max Pooling and Vlad. [15] proposed the first deep learning method to realize ground-aerial geo-localization based on two Siamese CNNs (i.e., WHERE-CNN and WHERE-CNN-DS). Comparative experiments demonstrated significant improvement in its performance with the handcrafted descriptor. Workman et al. [29] introduced A deep learning method to learn the semantic representation of aerial images. They also proposed a CNN model to integrate the semantic features of different spatial scales. Their work demonstrated that features trained from cross-view image pairs were significantly superior to off-the-shelf CNN features. Hu et al. proposed CVM-NET [10], which used the Netvlad module [2] to aggregate the CNN feature unit to generate the representation of discriminant images. They also manually distribute weight to the soft-margin triplet loss to speed up training. [4] proposed a lightweight attention module (FCAM) and integrated it into a basic residual network to form a Siamese network, which achieved better performance than the plain model (without FCAM). [23] proposed the GeoCapsNet based on the capsule network, the capsule layer encoded the features extracted from images to model the spatial feature hierarchies and enhance the representation power.

2.3   Image Retrieval Loss

The selection of loss function is very important in deep learning-based image retrieval tasks. The most widely used loss function in the early stage is the max-margin triplet loss, which forces the distance between positive pairs to be less than negative pairs. [9] pointed out that the selection of margin value in loss has a great influence on experimental performance. [27] proposed a soft margin triplet loss to solve this problem, and CVM-NET [10] continued to improve on this basis and proposed a weighted soft marginal triplet loss to accelerate the convergence speed of training.Due to the lack of constraints on uncorrelated pairs, triplet loss will decrease inter-class variance when reducing intra-class variance, which is alleviated in the quadruplet [5] loss. SARE loss [16] normalized the matching distance and expressed in the way of probability distribution to avoid the influence of threshold in the triplet loss, which is proved to be effective and more robust.

3   Proposed Method

In this section, we introduce the CSF module to process the cross-view synthesis of aerial images firstly, then integrate it with the Siamese framework of image matching and improve the SARE loss [16] to train the framework appropriately.

3.1   CSF Module

The mapping of ground images to aerial images using cGAN can be regarded as a process of visual domain adaptation. Zhai gets semantic images by transforming the VGG features of images and then transfers ground images to aerial images based on the semantic images [30]. Krishna Regmi proposed X-fork and X-seq structures to generate a segmentation map with the help of cGAN to assist in the cross-view conversion of images [19]. Our model is mainly based on the improvement of X-fork and X-seq, as shown in the Fig. 2:

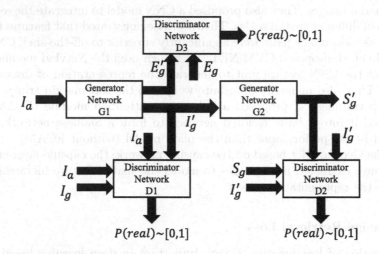

Fig. 2. Our proposed cross-view image synthesis model CSF: a sequence of two cGANs, G1 synthesizes target view image that is used by G2 for segmentation map synthesis in corresponding view and edge detection image. I_a and I_g are real images in aerial and ground views respectively. E_g is the ground truth edge detection image obtained by Canny algorithm. S_g is the ground-truth segmentation map in street-view obtained using pre-trained RefineNet. I_g', E_g' and S_g' are synthesized ground image, edge detection image and segmentation map in ground view.

We propose the CSF structure, in which the first network generates cross-view ground images and the corresponding edge detection images, and the second network gets ground images from the first generator as input to generate a segmentation map. The whole system is end-to-end trained so that both cGANs are trained simultaneously. segmentation map is used to help the transform of view. Compared with the X-Seq framework in [19], we add edge detection images of ground images in G1 to participate in the training. As artifacts often appear in the segmentation map, buildings fail to be generated, and objects with rich details tend to be generated with fewer details. Therefore, edge detection images are used to generate more details by contour information of images. Edge detection image is realized by Canny edge detection algorithm. Generate more details including buildings, trees, etc. The purpose of the low-level visual features is to generate more effective image descriptors to achieve better performance of image feature retrieval, although more details often lead to certain chaos in the image, extended experiment proves that it's worthy for the trade.

Referring to the loss function of traditional cGAN, we obtain the equivalent expressions for losses of cross-view cGAN network in this architecture. For G2the ground images generated by G_1 are considered as conditioning inputs. We now express the cGAN loss for this network as:

$$\min_{G_2} \max_{D3} L_{cGAN}(G_2, D_2) = E[logD_2(S_g', I_g')]$$

$$+ E[log(1 - logD_2(S_g', I_g'))] \qquad (1)$$

where, $I_g' = G_1(I_a)$ and $S_g' = G_2(I_g')$, The L1 loss for the G_2 is

$$\min_{G_2} L_{L1}(G_2) = E[|||S_g - S_g'||_1] \qquad (2)$$

Correspondingly, replacing the relevant symbol in the above equation by G_1, we can obtain $L_cGAN(G_1, D_1), L_cGAN(G_1, D_2)$, we express the loss of G_1 as:

$$L_{cGAN}(G_1) = L_{cGAN}(G_1, D_1) + \lambda_1 L_{cGAN}(G_1, D_2) \qquad (3)$$

$$L_{L1}(G_1) = ||I_g - I_g'||_1 + \lambda_1 ||E_g - E_g'||_1 \qquad (4)$$

The overall objective function for the CSF network is:

$$L_{X-fork-seq} = L_{cGAN}(G_1) + \lambda_2 L_{L1}(G_1) + L_{cGAN}(G_2, D_2) + \lambda_2 L_{L1}(G_2) \qquad (5)$$

Equation 5 is optimized during the training to learn the parameters of G_1, D_1, G_2, D_2, D_3.

3.2 Network Achitecture

The proposed overall framework of CVS-NET is shown in the Fig. 3, which follows the Siamese network structure with two identical networks in parallel, the input of both are ground image and aerial image respectively. Firstly, we extract the local features of the image through the fully convolutional network (FCN) f^L and get $U_i = f^L(I_i, \theta_i^L)$, where is,g represents a ground image or aerial branch, I_i represents the corresponding image, and θ_i^L represents the corresponding FCN network parameters. In this paper, we choose VGG16 as f^L. The local feature vector U_i is input to the NetVLAD layer [2] to obtain the global descriptor. The global descriptor of an image can be formally represented as $v_i = f^G(U_i, \theta_i^G)$. The two branches of the network framework adopt completely independent parameters. The ground images transformed by the CSF module are input into the ground branch as independent data, and the distance between the generated global descriptors and the corresponding ground images will be added to the loss of the overall network framework optimization.

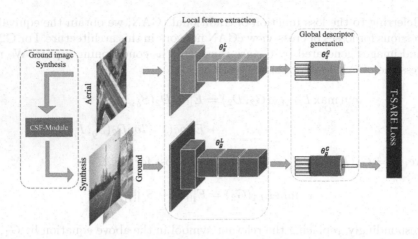

Fig. 3. Overview of our proposed CVS-Net. The parallel deep networks and NetVLADs are used to pool the images from different views into a common space, the CSF module is used for ground image synthesis and provides auxiliary information.

3.3 T-SARE Loss

The triple loss is a classical loss function in the image retrieval task, the simplest triplet loss is the max-margin triplet loss: $L_{max} = max(0, m + d_{pos} - d_{neg})$, where d_{pos} and d_{neg} respectively represent the distance between the positive and negative example in the selected tuple. The distance is always calculated by the Euclidian distance of the image global descriptors. M is the margin and has been proved in [9] that margin should be carefully selected manually to get good results. The principle of the loss is that the distance between the global descriptors of the positive examples is greater than the distance between the global descriptors of the negative examples through training so that the correct results can be obtained when searching images according to the distance. In order to avoid the influence of manually selected margin, the soft margin triplet loss is proposed in [27]:

$$L_{soft} = In(1 + e^d) \qquad (6)$$

The main disadvantage of soft margin triple loss is that the slow convergence rate, and when the distance difference between the positive example and the negative example is small, the loss fails to continue declining, so the accuracy is limited for the image retrieval task. In our work, SARE loss proposed in [16] is modified and applied to the image geo-localization task to avoid this limitation. SARE loss calculates the probability of correct and wrong image matching by distance:

$$L_\theta (q, p, n) = h_{p|q} \log \left(\frac{h_{p|q}}{c_{p|q}} \right) + h_{n|q} \log \left(\frac{h_{n|q}}{c_{n|q}} \right) \qquad (7)$$

where $h_{(p|q)}$, $h_{(n|q)}$ is the corresponding probability distribution of positive and negative cases, they can be approached by the matching correct probability of

$c_{(p|q)}$ and matching error probability $c_{(n|q)}$. Since the optimization is carried out by approaching the global probability, SARE loss will not stop after converging to a certain threshold and is not easily limited to the local optimal situation. $c_{(p|q)}$ and $c_{(n|q)}$ is calculated as below:

$$c_{p|q} = \frac{\exp\left(-d_{pos}\right)}{\exp\left(-d_{pos}\right) + exp\left(-d_{neg}\right)} \qquad (8)$$

$$c_{n|q} = 1 - c_{p|q} \qquad (9)$$

We improve the SARE loss according to the proposed model structure as below:

$$c_{p|q} = \lambda_3 c_{p_a|q} + (1 - \lambda_3) c_{p_g|q} \qquad (10)$$

where $c_{(p_a|q)}$ represents the matching correct probability of aerial image and $c_{(p_g|q)}$ represents the matching correct probability of synthesis ground image. The above equation respectively weights $c_{(p_a|q)}$ and $c_{(p_g|q)}$ to get the total result, and then uses the equation of SARE to get the specific loss value. The Eqn is our correction of SARE loss function based on CVS-NET, which is called T-SARE loss in the extended experiment.

4   Experiments and Discussions

4.1   Dataset

We evaluate our proposed CVS-Net framework on two existing cross-view datasets – CVUSA [27] and Vo and Hays [30]. The CVUSA dataset contains 35532 image pairs for training and 8884 image pairs for testing, all ground images are panoramas. The Vo and Hays dataset contains more than 1 million cross-view image pairs from 9 different cities. All ground images are cropped from panoramic images to a fixed size 230×230. We randomly chose 9 cities from the dataset and 8 of which are used to train the network, and the 9th is for testing. Fig shows a few examples from the datasets.

To pretrain our CSF module for the synthesis of ground images, the source segmentation maps are required (edge detection image is calculated by Canny algorithm). The CVUSA dataset has annotated segmentation maps for ground view images, but for Vo and Hays dataset such information is not available. To compensate, we use one of the leading semantic segmentation methods, known as the RefineNet [14].

4.2   Implementation Details

For the CVS-Net architecture, we use the VGG16 [22] pre-trained on ImageNet [12] to extract local features, and the number of clusters for NetVLAD to generate the global descriptors is set to 64. The net architecture in cGAN module is set as same as [19]. We set $_1 = 1$, $_2 = 0.8$, $_3 = 0.5$ for the training of CSF and T-SARE loss. All the parameters in NetVLAD and fully connected layers are randomly initialized. CVS-Nets are implemented by Tensorflow and trained using Adam optimizer with a learning rate of 10–5 and dropout(=0.9) for all fully connected layers. We feed pairs of corresponding aerial and ground images into our Siamese architecture. We have a total of $2M \times 2(M - 1)$ triplets for M positive pairs of ground-to-aerial images. This is because for each ground or aerial image in M positive pairs, there are $M - 1$ corresponding negative pairs from all the other images, and for each aerial, there is a corresponding generated ground image to double the pair.

4.3 Comparative Results

Evaluation Metric. Follow Vo and Hays [27], and workman et al. [29]. Our networks are evaluated by the recall accuracy at top 1%. For a query ground view image, the localization is considered to be successful if the corresponding aerial image is ranked within the top 1% of the retrieval results in the whole dataset which are calculated by feature distances.

Comparison to Existing Approaches. We compare our proposed CVS-Nets to six state-of-the-art methods [4,10,23,27,29,30] on two benchmark datasets [27,30]. Table 1 shows the top 1% accuracies of our model and other methods. It can be seen that our CVS-Net trained with T-SARE loss achieves competitive results on CVUSA dataset [30], and outperforms all the other approaches on Vo and Hays dataset [27]. The results show that our auxiliary cGAN module makes little progress for panoramas to improve the geo-localization performance, this is mainly caused by the diversity of information and the complexity of structure contained in panoramic pictures. With the progress compared to CVM-Net, we can see that the auxiliary information does not disturb the precision of geo-localization, which means we can still expect better results with the development of the cross-view transform model. And for the ordinary ground image in Vo and Hays [27], the extraordinary result proves that the ground images generated by CSF improve the accuracy in the geo-localization task greatly. Figure 4 plots the

Table 1. Comparison of top 1% on our CVS-Nets with other existing approaches.

	Recall @top1%	
	Vo and Hays	CVUSA
Workman et al. [29]	15.40%	34.30%
Vo and Hays [27]	59.90%	63.70%
Zhai et al. [30]	–	43.20%
CVM-Net [10]	67.90%	91.40%
GeoCapsNet [23]	69.59%	96.52%
Siam-FCANet [4]	71.50%	98.30%
CVS-Net	77.03%	92.30%

Top-K (from 1 to 80) recall accuracy of our CVS-Nets with other approaches on Vo and Hays dataset. It illustrates that our proposed architecture outperforms all the other SOTA approaches.

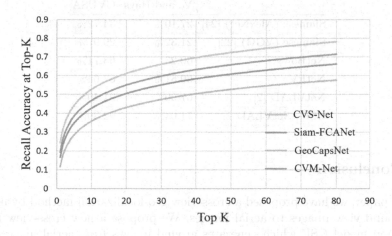

Fig. 4. Comparasion of our method and other existing approaches [4,10,23]; All models are trained on Vo and Hays [27].

Cross-View Methods Comparision. In order to prove the superiority of cGAN over traditional single image descriptors based matching, we select several classic image descriptors in the image retrieval task: VLAD [11], Fisher Vectors [1] and Bag of Words [6]. Following the NetVLAD in [2], we propose the NetFV and NetBOW network layer based on Fisher Vectors and Bag of Words descriptors. The new layer is used to generate global descriptors in the image retrieval task and put on the top of the Siamese network framework. The experimental results are shown in Table 2. The results prove the significance to add the descriptors generation layer to the network in the image geo-localization task. The above methods can all improve the effect in cross-view matching, among which NetVLAD layer [2] is the most significant one. Our cGAN auxiliary module obviously enhances the accuracy and stability of image geolocation by adding external auxiliary information on the basis of internal image feature extraction.

Table 2. Performance of different image descriptors in image matching Siamese framework on two benchmark datasets [27,30].

	Recall @top1%	
	Vo and Hays	CVUSA
Siamese (AlexNet) [24]	27.10%	34.72%
Siamese (VGG) [22]	21.32%	29.97%
NetBow	60.23	63.71%
NetFV	60.51%	67.64%
NetVLAD [2]	67.90%	91.40%
CSF+NetVLAD	71.03%	92.30%

5 Conclusion

In this paper, we have proposed a cross-view geo-localization method by matching ground view images to aerial images. We propose a new cross-view transformation model CSF which generates ground images from aerial images, and the generated images are input to the image matching framework to assist geo-localization in our CVS-Net architecture. Besides, we introduce SARE loss to improve the defect of triple loss, and T-SARE loss is improved base on the input form of CVS-Net. We test our method on two benchmark datasets, experimental results demonstrate the effectiveness and superiority of our proposed method over the state-of-the-art method.

Acknowledgement. This work was partially supported by the National Natural Science Foundation of China NSFC [grant numbers 62072343, U1736211]. The National Key Research Development Program of China [grant numbers 2019QY(Y)0206].

References

1. Image classification with the fisher vector: Theory and practice. Int. J. Comput. Vis. (IJCV) **105**(3), 222–245 (2013)
2. Arandjelovic, R., Gronat, P., Torii, A., Pajdla, T., Sivic, J.: NetVLAD: CNN architecture for weakly supervised place recognition. IEEE Trans. Patt. Anal. Mach. Intell. (2017)
3. Bansal, M., Sawhney, H.S., Cheng, H., Daniilidis, K.: Geo-localization of street views with aerial image databases. In: Proceedings of the 19th ACM International Conference on Multimedia, pp. 1125–1128. MM 2011. Association for Computing Machinery, New York, NY, USA (2011). https://doi.org/10.1145/2072298.2071954
4. Cai, S., Guo, Y., Khan, S., Hu, J., Wen, G.: Ground-to-aerial image geo-localization with a hard exemplar reweighting triplet loss. In: International Conference on Computer Vision (ICCV) (2019)
5. Chen, W., Chen, X., Zhang, J., Huang, K.: Beyond triplet loss: a deep quadruplet network for person re-identification. IEEE (2017)

6. Galvez-Lpez, D., Tardos, J.D.: Bags of binary words for fast place recognition in image sequences. IEEE Trans. Rob. **28**(5), 1188–1197 (2012)
7. Goodfellow, I.J., et al.: Generative adversarial networks. Adv. Neural. Inf. Process. Syst. **3**, 2672–2680 (2014)
8. Hays, J., Efros, A.A.: IM2GPS: estimating geographic information from a single image. In: IEEE Conference on Computer Vision and Pattern Recognition(CVPR) (2008)
9. Hermans, A., Beyer, L., Leibe, B.: In defense of the triplet loss for person re-identification (2017)
10. Hu, S., Feng, M., Nguyen, R., Lee, G.H.: CVM-Net: cross-view matching network for image-based ground-to-aerial geo-localization. In: Computer Vision and Pattern Recognition (CVPR) (2018)
11. Jegou, H., Douze, M., Schmid, C., Perez, P.: Aggregating local descriptors into a compact image representation. In: 2010 IEEE Conference On Computer Vision and Pattern Recognition (CVPR) (2010)
12. Jia, D., Wei, D., Socher, R., Li, L.J., Kai, L., Li, F.F.: ImageNet: a large-scale hierarchical image database. In: Proceedings of IEEE Computer Vision and Pattern Recognition, pp. 248–255 (2009)
13. Li, Y., Wang, S., He, H., Meng, D., Yang, D.: Fast aerial image geolocalization using the projective-invariant contour feature. Remote Sensing **13**(3), 490 (2021)
14. Lin, G., Milan, A., Shen, C., Rcid, I.: RefineNet: multi-path refinement networks for high-resolution semantic segmentation. In: 2017 IEEE Conference on Computer Vision and Pattern Recognition (CVPR) (2017)
15. Lin, T.Y., Cui, Y., Belongie, S., Hays, J.: Learning deep representations for ground-to-aerial geolocalization. IEEE (2015)
16. Liu, L., Li, H., Dai, Y.: Stochastic attraction-repulsion embedding for large scale image localization. In: 2019 IEEE/CVF International Conference on Computer Vision (ICCV) (2020)
17. Lowe, D.G.: Distinctive image features from scale-invariant keypoints. Int. J. Comput. Vis. (IJCV) **60**(2), 91–110 (2004)
18. Mirza, M., Osindero, S.: Conditional generative adversarial nets. Comput. Sci. 2672–2680 (2014)
19. Regmi, K., Borji, A.: Cross-view image synthesis using conditional GANs. IEEE (2018)
20. Sattler, T., Havlena, M., Schindler, K., Pollefeys, M.: Large-scale location recognition and the geometric burstiness problem. In: 2016 IEEE Conference on Computer Vision and Pattern Recognition (CVPR) (2016)
21. Shi, Y., Yu, X., Liu, L., Zhang, T., Li, H.: Optimal feature transport for cross-view image geo-localization. In: Proceedings of the AAAI Conference on Artificial Intelligence, vol. 34(7), pp. 11990–11997 (2020)
22. Simonyan, K., Zisserman, A.: Very deep convolutional networks for large-scale image recognition. Comput. Sci. (2014)
23. Sun, B., Chen, C., Zhu, Y., Jiang, J.: GEOCAPSNET: aerial to ground view image geo-localization using capsule network. IEEE (2019)
24. Technicolor, T., Related, S., Technicolor, T., Related, S.: ImageNet classification with deep convolutional neural networks
25. Tian, Y., Chen, C., Shah, M.: Cross-view image matching for geo-localization in urban environments. In: 2017 IEEE Conference on Computer Vision and Pattern Recognition (CVPR) (2017)
26. Viswanathan, A., Pires, B.R., Huber, D.: Vision based robot localization by ground to satellite matching in GPS-denied situations (2005)

27. Vo, N.N., Hays, J.: Localizing and orienting street views using overhead imagery. In: European Conference on Computer Vision (ECCV) (2016)
28. Workman, S., Jacobs, N.: On the location dependence of convolutional neural network features. In: 2015 IEEE Conference on Computer Vision and Pattern Recognition Workshops (CVPRW) (2015)
29. Workman, S., Souvenir, R., Jacobs, N.: Wide-area image geolocalization with aerial reference imagery. IEEE (2015)
30. Zhai, M., Bessinger, Z., Workman, S., Jacobs, N.: Predicting ground-level scene layout from aerial imagery. In: 2017 IEEE Conference on Computer Vision and Pattern Recognition (CVPR) (2017)
31. Zitova, B., Flusser, J.: Image registration methods: a survey. Image Vis. Comput. **21**(11), 977–1000 (2003)

Self-supervised Hyperspectral and Multispectral Image Fusion in Deep Neural Network

Jianhao Gao[1], Jie Li[1(✉)], Qiangqiang Yuan[1], Jiang He[1], and Xin Su[2]

[1] School of Geodesy and Geomatics, Wuhan University,
Wuhan, People's Republic of China
aaronleecool@whu.edu.cn
[2] School of Remote Sensing and Information Engineering, Wuhan University,
Wuhan, People's Republic of China

Abstract. Hyperspectral and multispectral image fusion is to obtain high-resolution hyperspectral images from low-resolution hyperspectral images and high-resolution multispectral images. In recent years, many studies have applied deep learning methods to complete the fusion task. However, the function of deep learning-based methods is enslaved to the size and quality of training dataset, constraining the application of deep learning to the situation where training dataset is not available. In this paper, we introduce a new fusion algorithm, which operates in a self-supervised manner without training datasets. The proposed method obtains high-resolution hyperspectral images with the constraint of low-resolution hyperspectral image and a traditional fusion method. Several simulation and real-data experiments are conducted with remote sensing hyperspectral data under the condition where training datasets are unavailable. Quantitative and qualitative results indicates that the proposed method outperforms those traditional methods by a large extent.

Keywords: Deep neural network · Hyperspectral and multispectral fusion · Self-supervised optimization

1 Introduction

Hyperspectral remote sensing images can reflect not only the color information but also the physical property of ground objects, which contributes a lot to Earth tasks such as ground object classification [30], and environment monitoring [17]. However, due to the signal-to-noise ratio, spatial resolution of hyperspectral images cannot be as high as that of multispectral images. One mainstream strategy to obtain high-resolution hyperspectral optical images is the hyperspectral and multispectral image fusion. According to [28], traditional hyperspectral and multispectral image fusion methods can be roughly classified into three families: 1) component substitution-based methods (CS-based methods) [3,6,12,13]; 2)

© Springer Nature Switzerland AG 2021
Y. Peng et al. (Eds.): ICIG 2021, LNCS 12890, pp. 425–436, 2021.
https://doi.org/10.1007/978-3-030-87361-5_35

multiresolution analysis-based methods (MRA-based methods) [2,7,15,20]; 3) variation model-based methods (VM-based methods) [4,5,11,14,27,29].

CS-based methods are the most traditional fusion methods. These methods include Gram-Schmidt transformation (GS) [13], Adaptive Gram-Schimidt transformation (GSA) [3]. General CS-based methods can obtain high-resolution hyperspectral images with sharp edges but cannot obtain feature maps perfectly matching the spectral information of multispectral images. MRA-based methods are another most classic hyperspectral and multispectral fusion methods. Representative methods include Generalized Laplacian Pymarid family (GLP) [7], the decimated wavelet transform (DWT) [20] and smoothing filter-based intensity modulation (SFIM) [15]. However, MRA-based methods often suffer from the blurry spatial presentation. VM-based methods are more novel methods. They treat the fusion of hyperspectral and multispectral images as an ill-posed inverse problem. Equations are first established by observation model [31] and then constrained by many handcraft priors. Popular priors contain the sparse prior [4,5,11] and low-rankness prior [26,32]. VM-based methods can acquire fusion results with better balance between spatial and spectral accuracy. However, it is hard to determine the most suitable parameters.

Recent studies focus on introducing deep learning methods to the fusion of hyperspectral and multispectral fusion, which can be classified as the fourth kind of methods (DL-based methods). For example, [10] proposed a Unet-style network for the hyperspectral and multispectral image fusion task. [16] introduced 3D convolution layers into the hyperspectral and multispectral image fusion fusion task. Despite the success of DL-based methods in the hyperspectral and multispectral image fusion, their performance depends heavily on the size and quality of datasets. So DL-based methods are not as flexible as those traditional methods under the situation of limited dataset. It is of great value to explore how to obtain fusion results by strong fitting ability of deep neural network without dataset in a self-supervised manner.

In order to obtain high-quality fusion results with the help of strong fitting ability of deep neural network and operate in self-supervised manner without datasets, we introduce one arbitrary traditional method as constraint for the hyperspectral and multispectral image fusion . We summarize our contribution as follow:

- We introduce a strategy for self-supervised fusion of hyperspectral and multispectral images. The proposed strategy can work in the network, making use of the strong fitting abilty and not considering the size and even the existence of training dataset.
- An arbitrary traditional method is introduced as the reference to constrain the spatial accuracy of fusion results. Two simple but effective optimization terms are proposed as constraint to guarantee the spectral and spatial accuracy of fusion results.
- Several simulation and real-data experiments are conducted with some popular hyperspectral datasets. Fusion results outperform those of state-of-the-art traditional methods, testifying the superiority of the proposed strategy.

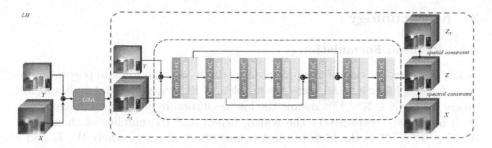

Fig. 1. Framework of the proposed method.

2 Related Work

2.1 Image Optimization Based on Deep Neural Network

Due to the strong fitting and representation ability, deep neural network are introduced by some studies [9,19,21,23] to some interesting applications where training datasets are unnecessary. These application includes style transfer [9], super-resolution and inpainting [23]. For example, given a style image and a content image, [9] extracts style representation of the style image and content representation of the content image in the VGG network and combines them to optimize the input map. Finally, a style-transferred image is acquired until optimizing to the optimal. A similar work is that given a texture image, [8] can generate images in a VGG network with similar but different texture from reference image. [23] finds that the deep neural network itself can be viewed as a prior. With the random noise as input of network and the known degradation model, the network can complete many low-level vision tasks including super-resolution, inpainting and denoising. Despite the success of these image optimization studies based on deep neural network, they have not been applied to the spatial-spectral fusion tasks such as hyperspectral and multispectral fusion.

2.2 Image Optimization

Some studies [1,24,25] introduce initializaed CNN to image optimization work. For example, given a trained GAN model, two latent codes and their corresponding output images from GAN, [1] interpolates the two latent codes in the input layer to obtain an output image whose features are between those of two original output images. The output of network has the internal visual effects between those of two original networks. Recently, [24] has made use of VGG network to obtain the high-level feature maps of the given two images. Then they interpolate the two feature maps and back-propagate the new feature maps to the image space. The acquired image share the internal features with the two given images.

3 Methodology

3.1 Problem Formulation

Before the introduction of the proposed methods, we give some important notations for simplification and state the problem of hyperspectral and multispectral image fusion. $X \in \mathbb{R}^{w \times h \times C}$ means the low-resolution hyperspectral image where w, h and C are respectively the width, height and the number of channels of X. $Y \in \mathbb{R}^{W \times H \times c}$ is the high-resolution multispectral image where W, H and c respectively mean the width, height and band number of Y. We aim to obtain $Z \in \mathbb{R}^{W \times H \times C}$ which shares the same spatial resolution with Y and the same spectral resolution with X. Specificly, the width and height of Y are much larger than those of X while the channel number of X is much larger than that of Y ($W \gg w$, $H \gg h$, $C \gg c$).

It is well accepted that X and Y are two degradation results of Z. On the one hand, X can be viewed as the product of down-sampling Z by some spatial down-sampling algorithm D_s such as bicubic and bilinear algorithm. On the other hand, Y is thought to be obtained by dowm-sampling Z in the spectral dimension by some spectral down-sampling algorithm D_ϕ. The two degradation processes are illustrated in Eq. 1 and 2. The target high-resolution hyperspectral image can be obtained by solving the Eq. 3 which is the weighted adding of Eq. 1 and 2:

$$X = D_s(Z) \tag{1}$$

$$Y = D_\phi(Z) \tag{2}$$

$$Z^* = \arg\min(\|X - D_s(Z)\|_1^1 + \|Y - D_\phi(Z)\|_1^1) \tag{3}$$

For the spectral degradation model D_ϕ, existing studies all select linear regression model or spectral response function which is also a linear model. However, given the situation where spectral response function cannot accurately reflect the relation between Z and Y, the results may not be satisfying. We will reflect this phenomenon in the real experiment.

3.2 Optimization Process

We complete the whole process in a deep neural network G and denote the traditional fusion method we use as T. As is mentioned before, results of traditional methods have either high spatial accuracy or high spectral accuracy due to the trade-off between the two. So one traditional method, which can well restore the spatial information, is selected to constrain our model and this traditional method can be one of GSA [3], GLP [2], CNMF [29] and so on. We select GSA in the paper.

First, X is up-sampled to meet the size of Y and then concatenated with Y as the input of network G. An initial output Z is obtained from G.

$$Z = G(X, Y) \tag{4}$$

To constrain the spectral accuracy of Z, we construct the spectral optimization term directly with X and Z:

$$\mathcal{L}_{spatial} = \|X \uparrow_n - Z_1 \downarrow_n \uparrow_n\|_1^1 \tag{5}$$

where $\downarrow_n$ is the operation of down-sampling by n times and $\uparrow_n$ is the operation of up-sampling by n times. n is the spatial resolution ratio between Y and X. Although down-sampling operation can well represent the spectral information of Z, here we add the up-sampling operation to the constraint term to further strengthen the spatial information of Z. Then we make use of the selected traditional fusion method T to get a reference high-resolution hyperspectral image Z_T:

$$Z_T = T(X, Y) \tag{6}$$

The spatial optimization term is constructed between Z_T and Z to constrain the spatial accuracy of output:

$$\mathcal{L}_{spectral} = \|Z - Z_T\|_1^1 \tag{7}$$

In the previous self-supervised methods, they often construct the spatial optimization term or spatial relationship directly between Z and Y in a linear manner. Acutally, the relationship between the natural multispectral image and hyperspectral image is not linear. So establishing a linear relationship may lead to severe spectral distortion. To handle the drawback, the proposed method diffuses the spatial information of multispectral image to all bands of low-resolution hyperspectral image. On the one hand, this operation can enhance the spatial constraint. On the other hand, compared with Y, their spectral information is close to the ground truth and easier to correct in spite of potential spectral distortion. So Z_T more suitable than Y to be the spatial constraint.

The spatial and spectral optimization terms are added by weight to get the total optimization term which is described in Eq. 8:

$$\mathcal{L}_{total} = \mathcal{L}_{spatial} + \lambda\mathcal{L}_{spectral} \tag{8}$$

It is worth mentioning that the whole process needs no training dataset and operate in an self-supervised manner. In general, the two optimization terms are constructed by hyperspectral images with different spatial and spectral accuracy. Actually, the proposed method can also be viewed as the process of spectral information correction of Z_T.

3.3 Network Structure

We design a U-net-style deep neural network to complete the whole task. For the sake of practical application, the depth of network is set as 7. In each of the first six layers, there exists a convolution operation, a batch-normalization operation and a non-linear activation operation. For the last layer, there are only a convolution operation and a non-linear activation operation. To avoid the gradient vanishing phenomena, two skip connection operations are used. One operates between the first layer and the fifth layer; another is added between the second and the fourth layer. Detailed parameters are listed in Fig. 1.

4 Experiments

4.1 Experiment Settings

Datasets. We apply three popular hyperspectral datasets to evaluate the proposed method. They are respectively Pavia University dataset, Washington DC dataset and Houston 2018 dataset. Pavia University dataset is obtained by ROSIS sensor. We crop a patch with the size of $280 \times 280 \times 103$ from the dataset as the high resolution hyperspectral image. Washington DC dataset whose size is $1208 \times 307 \times 191$, is an aerial hyperspectral image acquired by the Hydice sensor. We select a patch with the size of $280 \times 280 \times 191$ as the high resolution hyperspectral image. Houston 2018 dataset is the dataset originally used in the competition of 2018 IEEE GRSS Data Fusion, consisting of 14 pairs of hyperspectral images and natural high-resolution multispectral images. Hyperspectral images have a size of 601×596 and totally 48 bands. In the experiment, we select 8 pairs of hyperspectral and multispectral images to testify the effectiveness of the proposed method. We follow the Wald's protocol and downsample the hyperspectral images by 8 times of obtain the low-resolution hyperspectral images. In the first two dataset, the multispectral images are simulated by linear spectral response function. In the third dataset, the multispectral images are natural images.

Comparison Methods. We select six state-of-the-art fusion methods from different kinds of fusion methods. They are respectively Adaptive Gram-Schmidt method (GSA) [2], Coupled Nonnegative Matrix Factorization (CNMF) [29], Coupled Spectral Unmixing (ICCV15) [14], Generalized Laplacian Pyramid for HyperSharpening (GLPHS) [18], Hyperspectral Subspace regularization (HySure) [22] and Smoothing Filter-based Intensify Modulation for HyperSharpening (SFIMHS) [15].

Evaluation Methods. Four commonly used indexes are used to evaluate the fusion results of the proposed and the comparison methods. They are respectively peak-signal-to-noise ratio (PSNR), Structure similarity index (SSIM), Correlation Coefficient (CC), Spectral Angle Mapper (SAM).

4.2 Experiments with Simulated Multispectral Images

Washington DC Dataset. We visualize the fusion results of the proposed method and six comparison methods on Washington DC dataset in Fig. 2. To

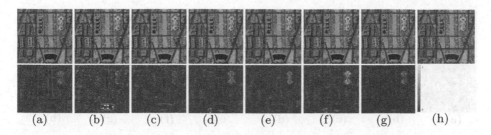

Fig. 2. Results and their residual maps on Washington DC dataset. (a) GSA; (b) SFIMHS; (c) GLPHS; (d) CNMF; (e) ICCV15; (f) HySure; (g) Ours; (h) Ground Truth

Table 1. Quantitative results on Wahshington DC dataset.

Method	PSNR	SSIM	SAM	CC
GSA	<u>38.6088</u>	0.9839	1.9482	<u>0.9932</u>
SFIMHS	36.4287	0.9817	2.2033	0.9924
GLPHS	38.3836	<u>0.9857</u>	<u>1.8832</u>	0.9929
HySure	36.9171	0.9696	2.2603	0.9767
CNMF	37.5585	0.9763	2.1159	0.9750
ICCV15	37.5309	0.9805	1.9879	0.9901
Ours	**39.1793**	**0.9871**	**1.6910**	**0.9937**

more intuitively compare the results of all methods, we further display their residual difference maps from the ground truth in Fig. 2. It can be observed that the result of the proposed method has the least residual information. We also compare the proposed method with other six methods quantitatively in Table 1 which lists the four indexes mentioned above. The proposed method achieves the highest scores in all five indexes and outperform the method with the second highest score by a large extent.

Pavia University Dataset. The fusion results of patches from Pavia University dataset obtained by the seven methods are displayed in Fig. 3. Figure 3 also presents the residual information of results from all methods compared with the ground truth. The proposed method has the less residual information in the fusion result than the other methods. We also compare the fusion results with quantitative evaluation in Table 2. The evaluation results with the highest scores are marked in bald and those with the second highest scores are marked with underline. Again the proposed method achieves the highest scores in all five evaluation indexes, indicating that the result of the proposed method is the most accurate in both spatial and spectral details.

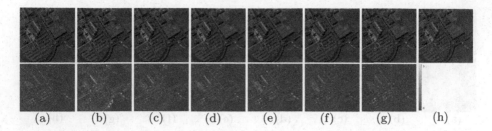

(a)   (b)   (c)   (d)   (e)   (f)   (g)   (h)

Fig. 3. Results and their residual maps on Pavia University dataset. (a) GSA; (b) SFIMHS; (c) GLPHS; (d) CNMF; (e) ICCV15; (f) HySure; (g) Ours; (h) Ground Truth

Table 2. Quantitative results on Pavia University dataset.

Method	PSNR	SSIM	SAM	CC
GSA	38.0679	0.9721	3.6394	0.9337
SFIMHS	35.8753	0.9651	4.0605	0.9343
GLPHS	37.6781	0.9720	3.6576	0.9335
HySure	38.3872	0.9737	3.3430	0.9220
CNMF	37.6992	0.9742	3.3215	0.9178
ICCV15	35.7145	0.9676	3.6405	0.9215
Ours	**38.7378**	**0.9749**	**3.2758**	**0.9345**

4.3   Experiment with Real Multispectral Images

The experiments presented above assume that multispectral images can be simulated by adding the channels of corresponding hyperspectral images linearly according to the spectral response function. However, according to [28], the actual relationship between hyperspectral images and multispectral images obtained physically is far from linear but non-linear. The performance on this dataset reflects the practicability of the methods. We also attempt to obtain hyperspectral images with spatial resolution 8 times higher than low-resolution hyperspectral images by the process of fusion in this experiment.

We display the fusion results of the proposed method and the comparison method in Fig. 4. From Fig. 4, we observe that all comparison methods cannot acquire results with sharp spatial details and spectral information at the same time. Compared with these methods, results of the proposed method have accurate spectral and spatial information. We also display the residual information maps of ground truth and results from all methods in Fig. 4. The proposed method has the least residual information in the fusion results compared with the other six methods in Houston 2018 dataset. That means the proposed method does not rely on the accuracy of spectral response function and can well perform in real situations. The quantitative evaluation scores of fusion results from all

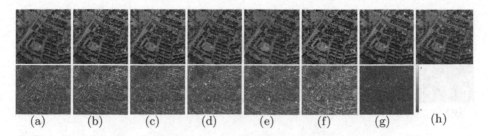

Fig. 4. Results and their residual maps on Houston 2018 dataset. (a) GSA; (b) SFIMHS; (c) GLPHS; (d) CNMF; (e) ICCV15; (f) HySure; (g) Ours; (h) Ground Truth

Table 3. Quantitative results on Houston 2018 dataset.

Method	PSNR	SSIM	SAM	CC
GSA	24.2119	0.5682	9.4216	0.9995
SFIMHS	22.6962	0.5431	11.0776	0.9996
GLPHS	24.4170	0.5633	8.0521	0.9996
HySure	18.8145	0.3710	18.2986	0.9961
CNMF	24.6457	0.5935	8.5538	0.9990
ICCV15	23.6509	0.5699	8.0248	0.9994
Ours	**27.1092**	**0.6767**	**7.5355**	**0.9997**

methods are listed in Table 3. The proposed method acquires the highest scores in all indexes and outperforms the comparison methods by a large extent.

4.4 Discussions

As is mentioned before, the constraint terms in the proposed method are respectively the low resolution hyperspectral images and the pseudo high resolution hyperspectral images, in which the pseudo high resolution hyperspectral images are obtained from the traditional fusion methods. In the proposed method, we introduce the initial fusion results of GSA as the pseudo high resolution hyperspectral images. In fact, the selection of traditional fusion methods is not that important and we can acquire the final results with high accuracy with arbitrary traditional fusion methods.

We select four traditional fusion methods, which are respectively GSA, CNMF, ICCV15 and SFIMHS, and make use of their fusion results as constraint. The comparison experiment is conducted on the Houston 2018 dataset. We display the visual results in Fig. 5. Figure 5(e–h) are results of our method with corresponding results of GSA, CNMF, ICCV15 and SFIMHS as reference. We can observe from Fig. 5 that although the results of those traditional methods including GSA, CNMF, ICCV15 and SFIMHS have very different spectral information from each other, the fusion results of the proposed method are almost

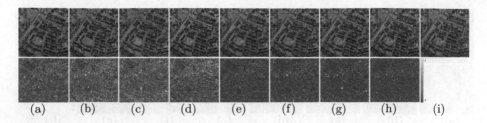

(a)   (b)   (c)   (d)   (e)   (f)   (g)   (h)   (i)

Fig. 5. Results and their residual maps on Houston 2018 dataset. (a) GSA; (b) CNMF; (c) ICCV15; (d) SFIMHS; (e) GSA as reference; (f) CNMF as reference; (g) ICCV15 as reference; (h) SFIMHS as reference

Table 4. Quantitative results with different traditional methods.

Method	PSNR	SSIM	SAM	CC
GSA	24.2119	0.5682	9.4216	0.9995
GSA as reference	**27.1092**	0.6767	**7.5355**	0.9997
SFIMHS	22.6962	0.5431	11.0776	0.9996
SFIMHS as reference	27.0676	0.6830	7.8998	0.9997
CNMF	24.6457	0.5935	8.5538	0.9990
CNMF as reference	27.0754	**0.6838**	7.6375	0.9997
ICCV15	23.6509	0.5699	8.0248	0.9994
ICCV15 as reference	26.8140	0.6780	7.6650	**0.9997**

the same. We further present their residual information maps from the ground truth in Fig. 5. Although different traditional methods have residual information in their results in different degrees, when they serves as the constraint terms in the proposed method, the corresponding results will have the similar degree of residual information. Table 4 lists the quantitative evaluation scores of results from four methods and corresponding results from the proposed method. We can find that the quality of results improves a lot from the results of corresponding traditional methods. Although the four traditional methods have evaluation results with different levels, their corresponding results have similar quantitative evaluation scores, indicating the flexibility of the proposed method.

5   Conclusion

In this paper, we introduce a self-supervised strategy, which makes use of a traditional fusion methods as spatial constraint, to the hyperspectral and multispectral image fusion task. The spatial information of target is constrained by the initial high-resolution hyperspectral image obtained by the traditional method and the spectral accuracy is constrained by the low-resolution hyperspectral image. A simple deep neural network is used to complete the optimization process. We conduct several simulation and real-data experiments on some popular hyperspectral datasets to compare the proposed method with other state-of-the-art methods. Quantitative and qualitative results confirm the outperformance and higher accuracy of the proposed methods compared with other fusion methods.

References

1. Abdal, R., Qin, Y., Wonka, P.: Image2StyleGAN: how to embed images into the stylegan latent space? In: Proceedings of the IEEE/CVF International Conference on Computer Vision, pp. 4432–4441 (2019)
2. Aiazzi, B., Alparone, L., Baronti, S., Garzelli, A., Selva, M.: MTF-tailored multiscale fusion of high-resolution MS and pan imagery. Photogramm. Eng. Remote Sens. **72**(5), 591–596 (2006)
3. Aiazzi, B., Baronti, S., Selva, M.: Improving component substitution Pansharpening through multivariate regression of MS + pan data. IEEE Trans. Geosci. Remote Sens. **45**(10), 3230–3239 (2007)
4. Akhtar, N., Shafait, F., Mian, A.: Sparse spatio-spectral representation for hyperspectral image super-resolution. In: Fleet, D., Pajdla, T., Schiele, B., Tuytelaars, T. (eds.) ECCV 2014. LNCS, vol. 8695, pp. 63–78. Springer, Cham (2014). https://doi.org/10.1007/978-3-319-10584-0_5
5. Akhtar, N., Shafait, F., Mian, A.: Bayesian sparse representation for hyperspectral image super resolution. In: Proceedings of the IEEE Conference on Computer Vision and Pattern Recognition, pp. 3631–3640 (2015)
6. Carper, W., Lillesand, T., Kiefer, R.: The use of intensity-hue-saturation transformations for merging spot panchromatic and multispectral image data. Photogramm. Eng. Remote. Sens. **56**(4), 459–467 (1990)
7. Chavez, P., Sides, S.C., Anderson, J.A., et al.: Comparison of three different methods to merge multiresolution and multispectral data- Landsat TM and SPOT panchromatic. Photogramm. Eng. Remote. Sens. **57**(3), 295–303 (1991)
8. Gatys, L.A., Ecker, A.S., Bethge, M.: Texture synthesis using convolutional neural networks. arXiv preprint arXiv.1505.07376 (2015)
9. Gatys, L.A., Ecker, A.S., Bethge, M.: Image style transfer using convolutional neural networks. In: Proceedings of the IEEE Conference on Computer Vision and Pattern Recognition, pp. 2414–2423 (2016)
10. Han, X.H., Zheng, Y., Chen, Y.W.: Multi-level and multi-scale spatial and spectral fusion CNN for hyperspectral image super-resolution. In: Proceedings of the IEEE/CVF International Conference on Computer Vision Workshops (2019)
11. Iordache, M.D., Bioucas-Dias, J.M., Plaza, A.: Sparse Unmixing of hyperspectral data. IEEE Trans. Geosci. Remote Sens. **49**(6), 2014–2039 (2011)
12. Kwarteng, P., Chavez, A.: Extracting spectral contrast in Landsat thematic mapper image data using selective principal component analysis. Photogramm. Eng. Remote. Sens. **55**(1), 339–348 (1989)
13. Laben, C.A., Brower, B.V.: Process for enhancing the spatial resolution of multispectral imagery using pan-sharpening. US Patent 6,011,875, 4 Jan 2000
14. Lanaras, C., Baltsavias, E., Schindler, K.: Hyperspectral super-resolution by coupled spectral unmixing. In: Proceedings of the IEEE International Conference on Computer Vision, pp. 3586–3594 (2015)
15. Liu, J.: Smoothing filter-based intensity modulation: a spectral preserve image fusion technique for improving spatial details. Int. J. Remote Sens. **21**(18), 3461–3472 (2000)

16. Palsson, F., Sveinsson, J.R., Ulfarsson, M.O.: Multispectral and hyperspectral image fusion using a 3-D-convolutional neural network. IEEE Geosci. Remote Sens. Lett. **14**(5), 639–643 (2017)
17. Plaza, A., Du, Q., Bioucas-Dias, J.M., Jia, X., Kruse, F.A.: Foreword to the special issue on spectral unmixing of remotely sensed data. IEEE Trans. Geosci. Remote Sens. **49**(11), 4103–4110 (2011)
18. Selva, M., Aiazzi, B., Butera, F., Chiarantini, L., Baronti, S.: Hyper-sharpening: a first approach on SIM-GA data. IEEE J. Selected Topics Appl. Earth Observations Remote Sens. **8**(6), 3008–3024 (2015)
19. Shaham, T.R., Dekel, T., Michaeli, T.: SinGAN: learning a generative model from a single natural image. In: Proceedings of the IEEE/CVF International Conference on Computer Vision, pp. 4570–4580 (2019)
20. Shahdoosti, H.R., Javaheri, N.: Pansharpening of clustered MS and pan images considering mixed pixels. IEEE Geosci. Remote Sens. Lett. **14**(6), 826–830 (2017)
21. Shocher, A., Bagon, S., Isola, P., Irani, M.: InGAN: capturing and retargeting the "DNA" of a natural image. In: Proceedings of the IEEE/CVF International Conference on Computer Vision, pp. 4492–4501 (2019)
22. Simoes, M., Bioucas-Dias, J., Almeida, L.B., Chanussot, J.: A convex formulation for hyperspectral image superresolution via subspace-based regularization. IEEE Trans. Geosci. Remote Sens. **53**(6), 3373–3388 (2014)
23. Ulyanov, D., Vedaldi, A., Lempitsky, V.: Deep image prior. In: Proceedings of the IEEE Conference on Computer Vision and Pattern Recognition, pp. 9446–9454 (2018)
24. Upchurch, P., et al.: Deep feature interpolation for image content changes. In: Proceedings of the IEEE Conference on Computer Vision and Pattern Recognition, pp. 7064–7073 (2017)
25. Wang, X., Yu, K., Dong, C., Tang, X., Loy, C.C.: Deep network interpolation for continuous imagery effect transition. In: Proceedings of the IEEE/CVF Conference on Computer Vision and Pattern Recognition. pp. 1692–1701 (2019)
26. Yang, S., Zhang, K., Wang, M.: Learning low-rank decomposition for pan-sharpening with spatial-spectral offsets. IEEE Trans. Neural Networks Learn. Syst. **29**(8), 3647–3657 (2017)
27. Yasuma, F., Mitsunaga, T., Iso, D., Nayar, S.K.: Generalized assorted pixel camera: postcapture control of resolution, dynamic range, and spectrum. IEEE Trans. Image Process. **19**(9), 2241–2253 (2010)
28. Yokoya, N., Grohnfeldt, C., Chanussot, J.: Hyperspectral and multispectral data fusion: a comparative review of the recent literature. IEEE Geosci. Remote Sensing Mag. **5**(2), 29–56 (2017)
29. Yokoya, N., Yairi, T., Iwasaki, A.: Coupled nonnegative matrix factorization unmixing for hyperspectral and multispectral data fusion. IEEE Trans. Geosci. Remote Sens. **50**(2), 528–537 (2011)
30. Zhang, F., Du, B., Zhang, L.: Scene classification via a gradient boosting random convolutional network framework. IEEE Trans. Geosci. Remote Sens. **54**(3), 1793–1802 (2015)
31. Zhang, L., Shen, H., Gong, W., Zhang, H.: Adjustable model-based fusion method for multispectral and panchromatic images. IEEE Trans. Syst. Man Cybern. Part B (Cybern.) **42**(6), 1693–1704 (2012)
32. Zhou, Y., Feng, L., Hou, C., Kung, S.Y.: Hyperspectral and multispectral image fusion based on local low rank and coupled spectral unmixing. IEEE Trans. Geosci. Remote Sens. **55**(10), 5997–6009 (2017)

Degradation Reconstruction Loss: A Perceptual-Oriented Super-Resolution Framework for Multi-downsampling Degradations

Zongyao He[1] , Zhi Jin[1(✉)] , Xiao Xu[2] , and Lei Luo[3]

[1] Sun Yat-sen University, Shenzhen 518107, China
hezy28@mail2.sysu.edu.cn, jinzh26@mail.sysu.edu.cn
[2] Technical University of Munich, Munich, Germany
xiao.xu@tum.de
[3] Chongqing University of Posts and Telecommunications, Chongqing, China
luolei@cqupt.edu.cn

Abstract. Recent years have witnessed the great success of deep learning-based single image super-resolution (SISR) methods. However, most of the existing SR methods assume that low-resolution (LR) images are purely bicubic downsampled from high-resolution (HR) images. Once the actual degradation is not bicubic, their outstanding performance is hard to maintain. Although several SR methods have super-resolved LR images with multiple blur kernels and noise levels, they still follow the bicubic downsampling assumption. To address this issue, we propose a novel degradation reconstruction loss (DRL) to capture the degradation-wise differences between HR images and SR images based on a degradation simulator. By involving the proposed degradation simulator and the loss, a perceptual-oriented SR framework for multi-downsampled images is formed. Extensive experimental results demonstrate that our method outperforms the state-of-the-art perceptual-oriented SR methods on both multi-downsampled datasets and bicubic downsampled datasets.

Keywords: Image super-resolution · Degradation reconstruction loss · Multiple downsampling degradations · Generative adversarial network

1 Introduction

Single image super-resolution (SISR) aims to reconstruct a high-resolution (HR) image from a single low-resolution (LR) image. Since the pioneering work that adopts a convolutional neural network (CNN) for super-resolution [6], deep learning-based SR methods have used various network architectures and training strategies to continuously improve the SR performance, i.e., peak signal-to-noise

This work was supported in part by the National Natural Science Foundation of China (No. 62071500, No. 61701313).

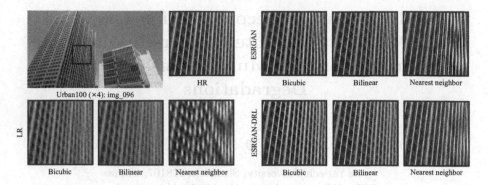

Fig. 1. The SR comparison results for multi-downsampling degradations with scale factor 4. "Bicubic", "Bilinear", and "Nearest neighbor" indicate the LR images are obtained by the corresponding downsampling degradation. Both the models are trained on a multi-downsampled dataset.

ratio (PSNR) and structure similarity (SSIM) [24]. These methods are regarded as PSNR-oriented SR methods. However, PSNR-oriented SR methods are fundamentally inconsistent with the subjective evaluation of human observers [23]. Therefore, perceptual-oriented SR methods, such as SRGAN [17] and ESRGAN [23] have been proposed to improve the overall visual quality of SR results. To achieve this goal, perceptual loss [13] is adopted during the generative adversarial network (GAN) [7] training process.

The aforementioned SR methods dedicated to pure bicubic downsampling degradation, lack the scalability of using a single model to handle multiple degradations. To better implement SR methods applicable to real-world images, we should first understand the degradation process of HR images to LR images. An LR image is obtained from an HR image through the following degradation model:

$$y = (x \otimes k) \downarrow_s + n. \tag{1}$$

where y is the LR image, $x \otimes k$ represents the convolution operation between the HR image x and the blur kernel k, $\downarrow_s$ represents the downsampling method with a scale factor s, and n is the noise level.

Based on the image degradation model, several SR methods for multiple degradations have been proposed. SRMD [26] takes the provided blur kernel and noise level as a prior input of the SR network. Instead of using the provided blur kernel, IKC [8] iteratively estimates a blur kernel at test time. If the blur kernel is close to reality, IKC achieves satisfactory performance. However, most SR methods for multiple degradations still follow the assumption of bicubic downsampling degradation.

The most commonly used downsampling methods are bicubic, bilinear, and nearest neighbor. It can be observed from Fig. 1 that LR images with bicubic, bilinear, and nearest neighbor downsampling degradation suffer from different information loss. To address the aforementioned problem of the existing SR methods, we are the first to focus on the impact of multi-downsampling degradations. We propose a degradation reconstruction loss to measure the degradation-wise differences between HR images and SR images using the degradation simulator. The degradation simulator models the degradation process with multi-downsampling by generating LR images using HR images and estimated degradation maps. By involving the degradation simulator and the loss, a perceptual-oriented SR framework for multi-downsampled images is formed.

The main contributions of this paper are as follows:

- We propose a degradation simulator to model the degradation process of HR images to LR images. The degradation simulator provides satisfactory results in modeling multi-downsampling degradations.
- We propose a degradation reconstruction loss to capture the degradation-wise differences between HR images and SR images for multi-downsampling degradations. Our method assisted by the loss outperforms the state-of-the-art perceptual-oriented SR methods.
- We are the first to investigate the SISR task with multi-downsampling degradations. Hopefully, this work can narrow the gap between manually downsampled LR images and real-world LR images.

2   Related Work

For several decades, SISR has remained an active research topic, and plenty of approaches have been proposed in the literature. These approaches can be classified into PSNR-oriented SR methods [5,6,8,12,16,18,21,26–28] and perceptual-oriented SR methods [4,13,17,22,23]. Our work is inspired by these two aspects and their adopted losses.

2.1   PSNR-Oriented SR Methods and Adopted Losses

PSNR-oriented SR methods are defined as adopting pixel loss to reduce the differences in pixel space, thereby improving the objective indexes (e.g., PSNR and SSIM) of SR results. Dong et al. [6] proposed SRCNN, which is a pioneer work of deep learning-based SR methods. Later on, the field has witnessed a variety of network architectures, such as Laplacian pyramid structure [16], residual blocks [17], densely connected network [21], residual dense network [28], and multipath recursive residual network [12]. Specifically, Lim et al. [18] modified SRResNet [17] to construct a more in-depth and broader residual network denoted as EDSR. Zhang et al. [27] proposed RCAN, which improves the SR performance by introducing the residual-in-residual network architecture and channel attention mechanism. The aforementioned methods assume that LR images are purely bicubic downsampled from HR images, therefore lack the scalability to handle multiple degradations. Aiming at this problem, Zhang et al. [26] proposed SRMD, which uses the degradation map stretched from the real blur kernel as a prior input for blind SR. Later, Gu et al. [8] proposed IKC, which iteratively corrects the estimated blur kernel to make it more accurate. Bulat et al. [5] firstly trained a High-to-Low GAN to learn how to degrade HR images and then trained a Low-to-High GAN to super-resolve LR images using the output of High-to-Low GAN. Li et al. PSNR-oriented SR methods generally adopt mean absolute error (MAE) or mean square error (MSE) loss in pixel space to assist the network to converge towards a good PSNR performance. Therefore, the corresponding outputs are often over-smoothed and lack high-frequency details.

2.2 Perceptual-Oriented SR Methods and Adopted Losses

Compared with PSNR-oriented SR methods, perceptual-oriented SR methods aim to generate more human-vision-friendly results. Johnson et al. [13] introduced the perceptual loss, which is based on differences in high-level features extracted from a pre-trained classification network, e.g., VGG16 or VGG19. Based on the idea of being close to perceptual similarity [4], the perceptual loss is used to improve the visual quality of SR images by minimizing the error in feature space instead of pixel space. Ledig et al. [17] proposed SRGAN, which first applies GAN and perceptual loss to the SISR task to generate realistic images. Wang et al. [23] further proposed ESRGAN, which utilizes the residual-in-residual dense block (RRDB) as the backbone of the generator and introduces a relativistic discriminator to learn sharper edges and more detailed textures compared to SRGAN. Wang et al. [22] proposed SFT-GAN, which employs semantic segmentation maps as categorization prior inputs for recovering realistic textures. Perceptual-oriented SR methods usually adopt a combination of adversarial loss, perceptual loss, and pixel loss to achieve better visual quality but lower PSNR and SSIM compared with PSNR-oriented SR methods.

3 Method

3.1 Multiple Downsampling Degradations

Downsampling degradations include the nearest neighbor, bilinear, bicubic, Lanczos interpolation, etc. Different from the previous SR methods, our degradation model can handle multi-downsampling degradations simultaneously. We use Frobenius inner products [10] between HR image pixels and downsampling kernels to model the degradation process without blur and noise. A downsampling kernel k_i^d performs the Frobenius inner product with the HR pixels x_i in the downsampling neighborhood i to generate an LR pixel y_i:

$$y_i = \langle x_i, k_i^d \rangle_F, \tag{2}$$

Since the downsampling kernel and the downsampling neighborhood are the same size, the downsampling kernels form a degradation map of the same size as the HR image. Therefore, downsampling can be modeled by a downsampler $\downarrow_s$ and the Hadamard product [10] between the HR image x and the degradation map m:

$$y = (x \circ m) \downarrow_s, \tag{3}$$

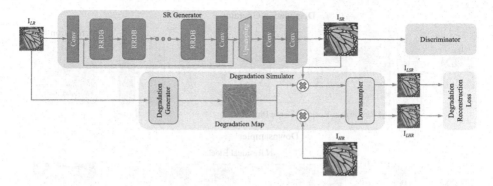

Fig. 2. The perceptual-oriented SR framework for multi-downsampling degradations using the degradation reconstruction loss.

Specifically, given a degradation map m_e under any downsampler $\downarrow_s^e$, we can find a degradation map m_f under a fixed downsampler $\downarrow_s^f$ by solving the following problem:

$$m_f = \arg\min_{m_f} \|(x \circ m_f) \downarrow_s^f - (x \circ m_e) \downarrow_s^e \|. \tag{4}$$

Therefore, given an LR image with any downsampling degradation, we can estimate a degradation map from the LR image, and then use this degradation map and a fixed downsampler to re-produce the LR image by degrading the corresponding HR image.

3.2 Proposed SR Framework

The proposed SR framework, as illustrated in Fig. 2, consists of two parts: the SR generator and discriminator, and the degradation simulator. We retain the high-level architectural design of the SR generator and discriminator as ESRGAN. Therefore, the SR generator uses 23 RRDBs as basic blocks. The discriminator is a relativistic average discriminator [14] which predicts the probability of whether a real image is relatively more realistic than a fake one. The degradation simulator receives the LR image and the HR image to output an estimated LR image, called the HR generated LR image I_{LHR}. Similarly, the LR image generated by the input LR image and the SR image is called the SR generated LR image I_{LSR}.

3.3 Degradation Simulator

By solving the problem in Eq. 4, we propose a degradation simulator (Fig. 3) to model multi-downsampling degradations. The degradation simulator is pretrained to learn to generate I_{LHR} that estimates the real LR image with any downsampling degradation. After training, the degradation simulator parameters are fixed when training the SR generator.

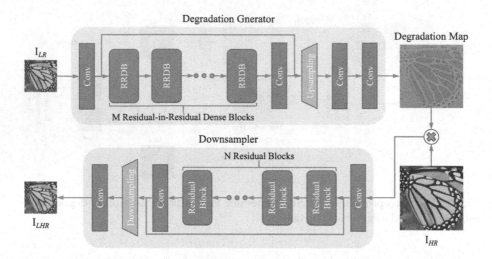

Fig. 3. Network architecture of the degradation simulator.

The degradation simulator consists of a degradation generator and a downsampler. The degradation generator receives an LR image as the input to output a degradation map that carries the degradation information. We utilize 6 RRDBs to form the backbone of the degeneration generator, where most computations are done in the LR feature space. The resolution of the input is increased by two deconvolution layers. The downsampler receives the Hadamard product between the HR image and the degradation map as the input and outputs an estimated LR image. The downsampler is modified from SRResNet [17], with the sub-pixel convolutional layers being replaced by a 4-stride convolutional layer to decrease the resolution. Hence, most of the computations are done with 10 residual blocks (RBs) in the HR feature space.

3.4   Degradation Reconstruction Loss

To accurately calculate the proposed degradation reconstruction loss for the SR generator, we first pre-train an effective degradation simulator with the loss function defined as:

$$L_{deg} = L_{per} + \alpha L_{pix}, \tag{5}$$

where L_{deg} is the total loss for the degradation simulator D, L_{per} is the perceptual loss, L_{pix} is the pixel loss, and α is the coefficient to balance these two loss terms.

The pixel loss L_{pix} is calculated by mean absolute error (MAE) between I_{LHR} and the real LR image in pixel space:

$$L_{pix} = \frac{1}{N} \sum_{i=1} \|I_i^{LR} - D(I_i^{LR}, I_i^{HR})\|_1, \tag{6}$$

The perceptual loss L_{per} represents the feature differences between I_{LHR} and the LR image extracted from the pre-trained VGG19 network ϕ [20], which is formulated as:

$$L_{per} = \frac{1}{N} \sum_{i=1} \|\phi(I_i^{LR}) - \phi(D(I_i^{LR}, I_i^{HR}))\|_1. \tag{7}$$

Using the pre-trained degradation simulator, we improve on SRGAN and ESRGAN to design a loss for the SR generator, which can be formulated as:

$$L_G = L_{Per} + \alpha L_{Pix} + \beta L_{Adv} + \gamma L_{Deg}, \tag{8}$$

where L_G is the total loss for the SR generator G, and L_{Deg} is the degradation reconstruction loss. The perceptual loss L_{Per} and pixel loss L_{Pix} have similar forms to the L_{per} and L_{pix} in Eq. 5, but calculate the differences between SR images and HR images. The adversarial loss L_{Adv} is calculated with a relativistic average discriminator, which can be referred to [14]. α, β, γ are the coefficients to balance the loss terms.

The degradation reconstruction loss L_{Deg} captures the degradation-wise differences between the SR image and the HR image based on the degradation simulator D. The degradation-wise differences are defined as the differences between I_{LSR} and I_{LHR} in pixel space and feature space. Hence, the degradation reconstruction loss is formulated as:

$$L_{Deg} = \frac{1}{N} \sum_{i=1} (\|\phi(D(I_i^{LR}, G(I_i^{LR}))) - \phi(D(I_i^{LR}, I_i^{HR}))\|_1$$
$$+ \alpha \|D(I_i^{LR}, G(I_i^{LR})) - D(I_i^{LR}, I_i^{HR})\|_1). \tag{9}$$

4   Experiments

4.1   Implementation and Training Details

Training Dataset. Similar to ESRGAN, we use 800 HR images from DIV2K [1] as the training dataset. We train our models on the multi-downsampled DIV2K800 dataset. Therefore, each HR image is downsampled using the MAT-LAB bicubic, bilinear, and nearest neighbor kernel functions to obtain three corresponding LR images. The spatial size of the cropped HR patch is 128×128 and the LR patch is with size 32×32. We train our models in RGB channels and utilize data argumentation including random horizontal flips and 90-degree rotations.

Training Details. We first train the degradation simulator for 3×10^5 iterations (50 epochs) using the loss function in Eq. 5 with $\alpha = 1 \times 10^{-2}$. The learning rate is set to 1×10^{-4} and decayed by a factor of 2 every 6×10^4 iterations.

The SR generator is trained in two stages. First, we pre-train a PSNR-oriented SR model with MAE pixel loss for 3×10^5 iterations. The learning

Table 1. The comparison results (PSNR↑/PI↓/FID↓) for multi-downsampling degradations with scale factor 4 on four benchmark datasets. All of the models are trained on the multi-downsampled DIV2K800 dataset. "DRL" indicates to train a model with the proposed degradation reconstruction loss. The best results are highlighted in **bold**.

Dataset	Bicubic	SRGAN	SRGAN-DRL	ESRGAN	ESRGAN-DRL
Set5 Bic	26.70/7.369/-	27.09/3.711/-	27.27/**3.314**/-	28.20/3.793/-	**28.77**/3.800/-
Set5 Bil	25.88/7.649/-	27.81/4.232/-	28.05/3.673/-	28.17/3.684/-	**28.70**/**3.608**/-
Set5 Nea	25.23/6.453/-	24.37/3.560/-	24.96/**3.345**/-	24.91/3.517/-	**25.40**/3.891/-
Set14 Bic	24.09/7.027/-	24.26/2.983/-	24.29/**2.764**/-	24.76/2.957/-	**25.17**/2.888/-
Set14 Bil	23.65/7.336/-	24.83/3.158/-	25.02/2.925/-	24.94/2.951/-	**25.28**/**2.884**/-
Set14 Nea	**22.76**/6.519/-	21.77/2.769/-	22.11/**2.763**/-	22.07/2.930/-	22.70/2.921/-
BSD100 Bic	23.88/7.044/134.94	23.37/**2.379**/65.47	23.39/2.389/68.70	23.96/2.507/60.96	**24.21**/2.495/**60.73**
BSD100 Bil	23.56/7.356/138.82	24.12/2.714/66.12	24.19/2.609/69.27	24.13/2.558/63.87	**24.30**/**2.534**/**61.58**
BSD100 Nea	**22.83**/6.541/163.75	21.36/2.565/91.13	21.76/**2.438**/95.43	21.80/2.598/84.01	22.31/2.594/**81.86**
Urban100 Bic	21.04/7.006/81.38	21.43/**3.553**/34.52	21.63/3.622/32.11	22.21/3.762/29.43	**22.38**/3.705/**26.72**
Urban100 Bil	20.63/7.165/86.15	21.83/3.589/35.10	22.03/**3.556**/32.74	22.34/3.694/29.24	**22.53**/3.645/**26.50**
Urban100 Nea	19.30/6.689/113.75	18.61/**3.399**/67.63	19.09/3.654/62.38	18.95/3.664/51.92	**19.49**/3.576/**50.29**

rate is set to 2×10^{-4} and halved at [60k, 120k, 180k, 240k] iterations. Then, we employ the pre-trained SR model as an initialization for the SR generator. The SR generator is trained for 3×10^5 iterations using the loss function in Eq. 8 with $\alpha = 1 \times 10^{-2}$, $\beta = 5 \times 10^{-3}$, and $\gamma = 10$. The learning rate is initialized as 1×10^{-4} and halved at [60k, 120k, 180k, 240k] iterations. We use Adam [15] and alternately update the SR generator and discriminator network until the network converges.

Evaluation. We evaluate our models on four public benchmark datasets – Set5 [2], Set14 [25], BSD100 [19], and Urban100 [11]. Similar to the existing SR methods, we use PSNR as the objective criteria for fair comparison. For perceptual-wise evaluation, we use perceptual index (PI) [3] and fréchet inception distance (FID) [9].

4.2 Results and Evaluation

Quantitative Results. We compare our proposed ESRGAN-DRL with bicubic interpolation and the state-of-the-art perceptual-oriented SR methods, i.e., SRGAN and ESRGAN on four public benchmark datasets with multi-downsampling degradations. The quantitative results, which are summarized in Table 1, confirm that the SR methods assisted by the degradation reconstruction loss outperform the reference SR methods in PSNR, PI, and FID on the benchmark datasets. The degradation reconstruction loss can improve the SR performance for multi-downsampling degradations, with a huge improvement on seriously degraded (nearest neighbor) datasets. Meanwhile, the comparison results confirm that the degradation reconstruction loss can be a plug-and-play loss to improve the existing perceptual-oriented SR methods.

Table 2. The comparison results (PSNR↑/PI↓/FID↓) for pure bicubic degradation with scale factor 4 on four benchmark datasets. The models are trained on the bicubic downsampled DIV2K800 dataset. The best results are highlighted in **bold**.

Dataset	ESRGAN	ESRGAN-DRL
Set5	28.18/3.540/-	**28.19/3.458/-**
Set14	24.52/2.852/-	**24.69/2.814/-**
BSD100	23.76/**2.459/58.50**	**23.84**/2.468/58.85
Urban100	22.15/3.734/26.51	**22.32/3.715/24.38**

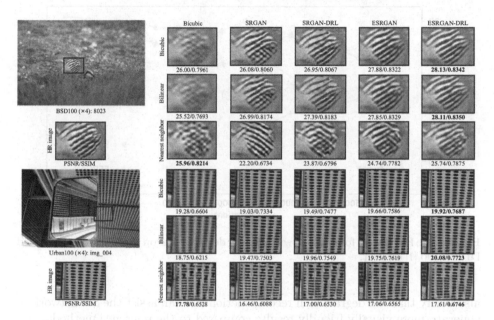

Fig. 4. The qualitative comparison results for multi-downsampling degradations with scale factor 4.

We train ESRGAN-DRL and ESRGAN on the bicubic downsampled DIV2K800 dataset for pure bicubic downsampling degradation comparison. As illustrated in Table 2, although ESRGAN-DRL is proposed for multi-downsampling degradations, the results indicate that ESRGAN-DRL outperforms ESRGAN on bicubic downsampled datasets, as well.

Qualitative Results. The qualitative results for multi-downsampling degradations are illustrated in Fig. 4. It can be observed that ESRGAN-DRL provides the best visual quality in both structures and details. The SR results of ESRGAN-DRL have better color balance, more pleasant textures, and fewer artifacts. Moreover, ESRGAN-DRL provides a greater improvement in more severely degraded images. The qualitative results of ESRGAN-DRL and SRGAN-DRL

Table 3. Ablation study for components in ESRGAN-DRL. Each column represents a model with its configurations. The improvements are highlighted in **bold**. The evaluation results are evaluated on the multi-downsampled DIV2K100dataset.

Configuration	1st	2nd	3rd	4th
DRL	×	✓	✓	✓
Feature Domain	×	LR + LR	**LR + HR**	LR + HR
Degradation Generator	×	6 RRDBs	6 RRDBs	**6 RRDBs**
Downsampler	×	10 SFT-RRDBs	10 SFT-RBs	**10 RBs**
PSNR↑/SSIM↑/FID↓	24.93/0.6917/23.01	24.82/0.6874/23.15	24.95/0.6910/22.41	**25.33/0.7068/21.75**

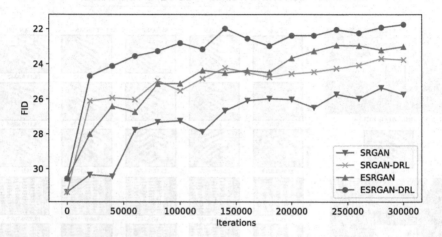

Fig. 5. The FID curves for multi-downsampling degradations on the multi-downsampled DIV2K100 [1] dataset.

also verify that the degradation reconstruction loss can assist the SR network to generate more visually friendly results compared to the reference methods.

Training Process. The FID training curves for multi-downsampling degradations are illustrated in Fig. 5. The experiments demonstrate that the degradation reconstruction loss significantly helps the convergence of SRGAN-DRL and ESRGAN-DRL. Moreover, the training of SRGAN-DRL and ESRGAN-DRL is fast and not sensitive to the learning rate.

4.3   Ablation Study

We gradually modify our model to study the effects of each component in the proposed ESRGAN-DRL. The overall comparison is summarized in Table 3. We utilize 23 RRDBs as the SR generator in all models of Table 3.

We train the model with degradation reconstruction loss since the 2nd column of Table 3. However, the initial degradation reconstruction loss in the 2nd column does not enhance our model due to the unsatisfactory performance of the degradation simulator. Therefore, we modify the degradation simulator in the following columns to achieve better SR performance. The feature domain "LR + LR" in the 2nd column indicates that both the degradation generator and the downsampler are extracting features in the LR feature space. The SFT-RRDBs in the 2nd column are RRDBs using spatial feature transform (SFT) layers [8] to receive the degradation map input. In the 3rd column, the downsampler of the degradation simulator is modified from 10 SFT-RRDBs to 10 SFT-RBs and extracts features in the HR feature space. This modification makes an improvement in PSNR, SSIM, and FID results. We further modify the degradation generator and the downsampler to consist of 6 RRDBs and 10 RBs, respectively. This modification in the 4th column provides the best evaluation results. Therefore, we adopt the model in the 4th column as our proposed method.

5 Conclusion

We propose a perceptual-oriented SR framework for multi-downsampling degradations by involving the proposed degradation simulator and degradation reconstruction loss. Different from the existing SR methods for multiple degradations, we propose a degradation simulator to model the image degradation process with multi-downsampling degradations. Extensive experimental results demonstrate that the proposed degradation reconstruction loss based on the degradation simulator can well guide our method to recover LR images from low-quality factors. The SR results of our method have fewer artifacts, better color balance, and superior overall visual quality. Moreover, the experiments demonstrate that the degradation reconstruction loss can be plug and play to improve the existing perceptual-oriented SR methods. In our future work, we will explore the use of degradation reconstruction loss for more complex degradations.

References

1. Agustsson, E., Timofte, R.: NTIRE 2017 challenge on single image super-resolution: dataset and study. In: CVPRW, pp. 126–135 (2017)
2. Bevilacqua, M., Roumy, A., Guillemot, C., Alberi-Morel, M.L.: Low-complexity single-image super-resolution based on nonnegative neighbor embedding (2012)
3. Blau, Y., Mechrez, R., Timofte, R., Michaeli, T., Zelnik-Manor, L.: The 2018 PIRM challenge on perceptual image super-resolution. In: ECCV (2018)
4. Bruna, J., Sprechmann, P., LeCun, Y.: Super-resolution with deep convolutional sufficient statistics. arXiv preprint arXiv:1511.05666 (2015)
5. Bulat, A., Yang, J., Tzimiropoulos, G.: To learn image super-resolution, use a GAN to learn how to do image degradation first. In: Ferrari, V., Hebert, M., Sminchisescu, C., Weiss, Y. (eds.) ECCV 2018. LNCS, vol. 11210, pp. 187–202. Springer, Cham (2018). https://doi.org/10.1007/978-3-030-01231-1_12

6. Dong, C., Loy, C.C., He, K., Tang, X.: Learning a deep convolutional network for image super-resolution. In: Fleet, D., Pajdla, T., Schiele, B., Tuytelaars, T. (eds.) ECCV 2014. LNCS, vol. 8692, pp. 184–199. Springer, Cham (2014). https://doi.org/10.1007/978-3-319-10593-2_13

7. Goodfellow, I., et al.: Generative adversarial nets. In: NIPS, pp. 2672–2680 (2014)

8. Gu, J., Lu, H., Zuo, W., Dong, C.: Blind super-resolution with iterative kernel correction. In: CVPR, pp. 1604–1613 (2019)

9. Heusel, M., Ramsauer, H., Unterthiner, T., Nessler, B., Hochreiter, S.: GANs trained by a two time-scale update rule converge to a local Nash equilibrium. In: NIPS, pp. 6626–6637 (2017)

10. Horn, R.A., Johnson, C.R.: Matrix Analysis. Cambridge University Press, Cambridge (2012)

11. Huang, J.B., Singh, A., Ahuja, N.: Single image super-resolution from transformed self-exemplars. In: CVPR, pp. 5197–5206 (2015)

12. Jin, Z., Iqbal, M.Z., Bobkov, D., Zou, W., Li, X., Steinbach, E.: A flexible deep CNN framework for image restoration. IEEE Trans. Multimedia **22**, 1055–1068 (2019)

13. Johnson, J., Alahi, A., Fei-Fei, L.: Perceptual losses for real-time style transfer and super-resolution. In: Leibe, B., Matas, J., Sebe, N., Welling, M. (eds.) ECCV 2016. LNCS, vol. 9906, pp. 694–711. Springer, Cham (2016). https://doi.org/10.1007/978-3-319-46475-6_43

14. Jolicoeur-Martineau, A.: The relativistic discriminator: a key element missing from standard GAN. arXiv preprint arXiv:1807.00734 (2018)

15. Kingma, D.P., Ba, J.: Adam: a method for stochastic optimization. arXiv preprint arXiv:1412.6980 (2014)

16. Lai, W.S., Huang, J.B., Ahuja, N., Yang, M.H.: Deep Laplacian pyramid networks for fast and accurate super-resolution. In: CVPR, pp. 624–632 (2017)

17. Ledig, C., et al.: Photo-realistic single image super-resolution using a generative adversarial network. In: CVPR, pp. 4681–4690 (2017)

18. Lim, B., Son, S., Kim, H., Nah, S., Mu Lee, K.: Enhanced deep residual networks for single image super-resolution. In: CVPRW, pp. 136–144 (2017)

19. Martin, D., Fowlkes, C., Tal, D., Malik, J.: A database of human segmented natural images and its application to evaluating segmentation algorithms and measuring ecological statistics. In: ICCV, pp. 416–423 (2001)

20. Simonyan, K., Zisserman, A.: Very deep convolutional networks for large-scale image recognition. arXiv preprint arXiv:1409.1556 (2014)

21. Tai, Y., Yang, J., Liu, X., Xu, C.: MemNet: a persistent memory network for image restoration. In: ICCV, pp. 4539–4547 (2017)

22. Wang, X., Yu, K., Dong, C., Change Loy, C.: Recovering realistic texture in image super-resolution by deep spatial feature transform. In: CVPR, pp. 606–615 (2018)

23. Wang, X., et al.: ESRGAN: enhanced super-resolution generative adversarial networks. In: Leal-Taixé, L., Roth, S. (eds.) ECCV 2018. LNCS, vol. 11133, pp. 63–79. Springer, Cham (2019). https://doi.org/10.1007/978-3-030-11021-5_5

24. Wang, Z., Bovik, A.C., Sheikh, H.R., Simoncelli, E.P.: Image quality assessment: from error visibility to structural similarity. IEEE Trans. Image Process. **13**(4), 600–612 (2004)

25. Zeyde, R., Elad, M., Protter, M.: On single image scale-up using sparse-representations. In: ICCS, pp. 711–730 (2010)

26. Zhang, K., Zuo, W., Zhang, L.: Learning a single convolutional super-resolution network for multiple degradations. In: CVPR, pp. 3262–3271 (2018)

27. Zhang, Y., Li, K., Li, K., Wang, L., Zhong, B., Fu, Y.: Image super-resolution using very deep residual channel attention networks. In: Ferrari, V., Hebert, M., Sminchisescu, C., Weiss, Y. (eds.) ECCV 2018. LNCS, vol. 11211, pp. 294–310. Springer, Cham (2018). https://doi.org/10.1007/978-3-030-01234-2_18

28. Zhang, Y., Tian, Y., Kong, Y., Zhong, B., Fu, Y.: Residual dense network for image super-resolution. In: CVPR, pp. 2472–2481 (2018)

Auto-calibration of Exit Pupils for Autostereoscopic Display with the Eye Tracker

Min Li, Xicai Li, Bangpeng Xiao, Jie Liu, and Yuanqing Wang[✉]

School of Electronic Science and Engineering, Nanjing University, Nanjing 210023, China
yqwang@nju.edu.cn

Abstract. In order to solve the pseudo stereoscopic problem in the auto-stereoscopic display, a program is proposed to automatically determine the mapping relationship between the human eyes position and the exit pupil modes. This scheme enables the best viewing position to move accurately with the human eyes, and the stereoscopic viewing range can be continuously extended to the entire viewable range of the display. In this paper, a monocular camera and a black-and-white exit pupil fringe are used to detect the above mapping relationship. Innovatively, an automatic calibration method based on horizontal and vertical gray histograms is proposed, and a method based on straight line detection of image edges is proposed for mutual verification. The experimental results show that the proposed method can accurately calculate the slope and the period of the exit pupil and derive the complete mapping relationship. It is more accurate and automated than the traditional way. When the exit pupil mode is adjusted, the image brightness change rate is less than 3.3%, which can basically realize seamless switching.

Keywords: Pseudo stereoscopic · Auto-calibration technology · Seamless switching

1 Introduction

In recent years, with the progress of science and technology, more and more people seek to a more realistic display, and the stereoscopic display technology [1–4] is beginning to attract much attention. The main principle of the parallax method in the stereoscopic display is to use special optical equipment to project the left and right parallax images to the positions of the viewer's left and right eyes, so that the viewer's left and right eyes can see two images with different viewing angles respectively. Therefore, autostereoscopic display needs to know the position of the observer's eyes [5]. Generally speaking, the spatial distribution of adjacent viewpoint images formed by autostereoscopic display technology is fixed. The movement of the viewer's head may cause the left eye to see the right image and the right eye to see the left image, which will cause the appearance of "pseudo-stereoscopic", and the viewer may have symptoms such as dizziness and nausea [6].

© Springer Nature Switzerland AG 2021
Y. Peng et al. (Eds.): ICIG 2021, LNCS 12890, pp. 450–462, 2021.
https://doi.org/10.1007/978-3-030-87361-5_37

In order to eliminate this phenomenon, it is necessary to use eye tracking technology to adjust the exit pupil mode in time when human eyes are moving, and we should always keep the left eye seeing the left image and the right eye seeing the right image. To achieve the above effect, the key point is to accurately locate the position of the exit pupil area corresponding to various modes in the camera used for human eyes detection. At present, a common method is to use dual cameras to calculate the depth information of the human eyes and use geometric relations to calculate the sub-pixel movement corresponding to the human eyes' movement [7–9]. However, the disadvantage of this method is that the calibration of the dual camera is very complicated, and it is difficult to determine the initial position. In view of the above-mentioned shortcomings, we innovatively propose an automatic calibration method for specific display parameters. This method only needs to use one monocular camera, by shooting black and white exit pupil fringes and then performing related calculations, the corresponding relationship between the exit pupil area at the best viewing position and its position in the camera can be measured. In this way, the exit pupil mode corresponding to the position of human eyes in the camera can be directly and accurately determined, and continuous and real-time stereoscopic viewing effects can be realized.

2   Stereoscopic Display Related Principles

2.1   Stereoscopic Display and Exit Pupil Modes

The autostereoscopic display discussed in this article can project a stereoscopic image into two periodic left and right views through the internal optical structure. When the light of the left view only appears in the L area of the best viewing position, and the light of the right view only appears in the R area, the viewer can see the normal stereoscopic effect, otherwise, the pseudo-stereoscopic phenomenon will appear, which means that the convex ones are regarded as concave, and the concave ones are regarded as convex as shown in Fig. 1 where L refers to the left view area and R refers to the right view area.

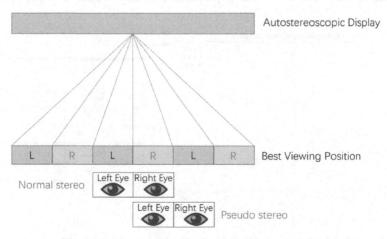

Fig. 1. Schematic diagram of auto-stereoscopic display

The "pseudo-stereoscopic" phenomenon occurs because the left eye sees the right image, and the right eye sees the left image. When human eyes are fixed at this time and the exit pupil is translated in one direction, so that the left eye sees the left image and the right eye sees the right image, the "pseudo-stereoscopic" phenomenon will disappear. However, in this solution, the exit pupil is shifted after the occurrence of "pseudo-stereoscopic", and the stereogram seen by the viewer will "jump" due to the large change in brightness, and the stereoscopic effect is discontinuous. Therefore, we propose to divide the exit pupils of the left eye and right eye into 3 equal parts, which are recorded as $L_1, L_2, L_3, R_1, R_2, R_3$, a total of six regions [10], as shown in Fig. 2. We follow the movement of human eyes through eye tracking program, and move the exit pupil before human eyes reach the "pseudo-stereoscopic" area. When the human eyes position is in the area L_2, R_2, the exit pupil is not changed. When it moves to the area L_1, R_1 or the area L_3, R_3, the exit pupil is shifted by $\frac{1}{6}$ of a period.

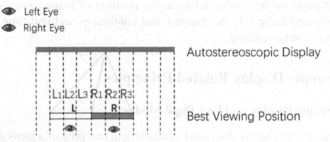

Fig. 2. Schematic diagram of the exit pupil mode zone

2.2 The Relationship Between the Camera and the Position of Human Eyes

In order to cover any area, the exit pupil needs to be moved six times. We call the exit pupil after each movement an "exit pupil mode", so there are six "exit pupil modes".

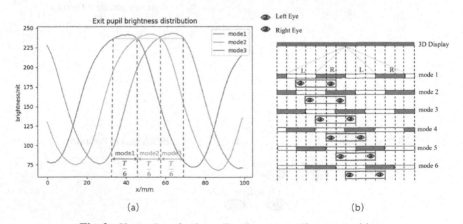

(a)   (b)

Fig. 3. Six modes of exit pupil and corresponding eye positions

Taking modes 1, 2, and 3 as examples, the brightness distribution of each exit pupil mode is shown in Fig. 3(a). In order to make the brightness of the exit pupil always greater than 95% of the maximum brightness, the exit pupil mode should be switched where two adjacent exit pupil modes intersect. The width occupied by each mode is $\frac{1}{6}$ of a period, so that the viewer will not feel the change of brightness at all. The exit pupil of each mode and the position of human eyes in this mode are shown in Fig. 3(b). The eye tracking program will detect the eye position of viewers in real time, query the correspondence table of the eye position and the exit pupil mode and determine which exit pupil mode should be used at this time according to the eye position, and then adjust the auto-stereoscopic display.

In order to determine the correspondence relationship table between the position of human eyes and exit pupil modes, we select the test chart with the left view image being completely black and the right view image being completely white. Besides, the stereo display, the monocular camera and the exit pupil image receiving board shall be placed in the form of Fig. 4. The exit pupil image of the black and white test chart is an evenly spaced black and white fringe image.

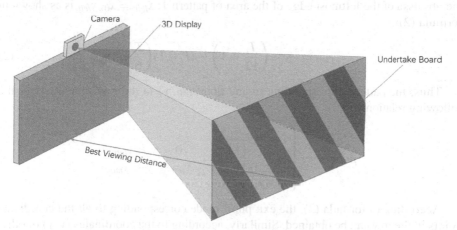

Fig. 4. Schematic diagram of experimental shooting scene

3 Correspondence Between the Human Eyes Position and Exit Pupil Modes

3.1 The Principle of Correspondence Relationship Calculation

In this article, we use a monocular camera for measurement and calculation. The specific measurement steps are as follows:

The scene is shown in Fig. 4. Assuming that the exit pupil mode is P at this time, the schematic diagram of the enlarged black and white stripes on the bearing plate is shown in Fig. 5(a). The movement period T of the exit pupil of the six modes is the width of a pair of black and white stripes, so the widths of L_1, L_2, L_3, R_1, R_2 or R_3 are all $\frac{T}{6}$.

Our eye tracking program chooses to track the position of the left eye, so at this time the L2 area (the area with a width of $\frac{T}{6}$ centered on the reference point C (x_0, y_0) in the middle of the white stripe) should be mode P. The L1 area on the left is the mode P-1 (when P = 1, P-1 = 6), the L3 area is the mode P + 1 (when P = 6, P + 1 = 1), and so on.

Next the analysis of the calculation of the correspondence between human eyes coordinates and the exit pupil modes will be discussed. As shown in Fig. 5(a), if the coordinates (x_0, y_0) of the middle point C of a certain line of L2, the slope k of the stripes and the period T of the black and white stripes are known, then any point (x, y) on the line with a slope of k where the midpoint C is located satisfies formula (1):

$$\begin{cases} y - y_0 = k(x - x_0) \\ y = k(x - x_0) + y_0 \end{cases} \tag{1}$$

According to the slope k and the coordinates of point C, the coordinates of all points on the straight line can be obtained. Then we can calculate the mode distribution of the entire row where point C is located. As shown in Fig. 5(b), if the pattern of point C is P, the abscissa of the leftmost edge of the area of pattern 1: $x_{left} = x_0$, y_{left} is as shown in formula (2):

$$y_{left} = y_0 - \left(\frac{T}{12} - 1\right) - (P - 1)\left(\frac{T}{6}\right) \tag{2}$$

Thus, the pattern corresponding to any point (x_0, y) in the row should satisfy the following relationship:

$$pattern = \begin{cases} 6 - \dfrac{|y_{left}-y|\%T}{\left(\frac{T}{6}\right)} & 0 < y < y_{left} \\ \dfrac{|y_{left}-y|\%T}{\left(\frac{T}{6}\right)} + 1 & y_{left} \leq y < y_{max} \end{cases} \tag{3}$$

According to formula (3), the exit pupil mode corresponding to all the coordinate points in the row can be obtained. Similarly, according to the coordinates (x, y) of other

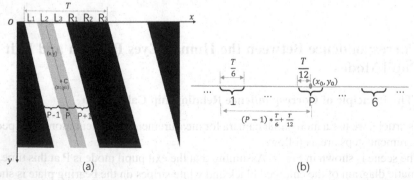

Fig. 5. Black and white exit pupil fringe corresponding to exit pupil mode P and mode calculation of other coordinate points in the line of point C

points on the straight line with the slope of k where the center point C is obtained, all the exit pupil modes corresponding to the coordinate points within the resolution range of the camera are displayed can be obtained row by row.

In a word, as long as we can determine the coordinates (x_0, y_0) of point C (a certain midpoint of the white stripes), the black and white stripe period T, the stripe slope k, and the currently displayed picture mode P, we can find the complete correspondence between human eyes coordinates and exit pupil modes.

3.2 Solve the Attributes of the Exit Pupil Using the Gray Histogram

As shown in Fig. 7(a), due to the continuous switching of black and white stripes in the image, when the pixel sequence of a certain line in the image is taken out by line, it can be found that the sequence has obvious sinusoidal characteristics. Therefore, we can use this feature to analyze the gray histogram by reducing the dimensions from the horizontal and vertical directions. The specific principle is shown in Fig. 6. At the beginning, we select a certain row y_0, and solve the gray peak points of this row, denoted as $P_0(x_0, y_0)$ and $P_1(x_1, y_0)$. Then we analyze the grayscale data of the x_0 column and solve the vertical grayscale peak point $P_2(x_0, y_2)$ above the P_0 point and the period T and the slope k of the fringe will satisfy the formula (4). So, we only need to solve the three points P_0, P_1 P_2 to get the slope and period, and to calculate the complete correspondence relationship table based on the coordinates of $P_0(x_0, y_0)$ and the corresponding mode number of the exit pupil.

$$\begin{cases} T = x_1 - x_0 \\ k = \frac{dy}{dx} = \frac{(y_0-y_2)}{(x_1-x_0)} \end{cases} \tag{4}$$

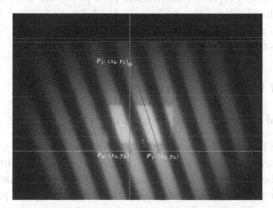

Fig. 6. Schematic diagram of period and slope solution.

The specific method of solving the three points is divided into the following steps:

(1) Image preprocessing

The original exit pupil fringe has low contrast, and the border is not obvious, so we need to preprocess the image to better highlight the fringe structure [11]. Firstly, we convert the three-channel RGB image into a single-channel grayscale image. Then we use the grayscale transformation to stretch the image to map the grayscale value to the range of [0,255]. Considering that we are interested in the edge part of the striped image, we need to use the Laplacian operator to perform convolution operations for image sharpening or edge enhancement.

(2) Solve the lateral peak point

After determining the row of y_0, it is necessary to smooth the grayscale data of this row to eliminate the repeated peaks caused by a part of the jagged data. In this paper, we use mean filter for smoothing. After that, the peak detection is performed. The peak detection in this article uses local peak detection, which is to find the maximum value within the peak radius settled independently, instead of the maximum value that is only compared with the left value and the right value in the traditional sense. Finally, we use a similar method for peak screening. The middle element selected from the remaining peak points is marked as $P_0(x_0, y_0)$, and the peak point to the right of P_0 is marked as $P_1(x_0, y_1)$.

(3) Solve the longitudinal peak point

According to the point x_0 obtained in the previous step, the column of gray data is also smoothed by mean filter. However, the sinusoidal characteristic of the longitudinal gray value distribution is not obvious. It can be seen that the longitudinal gray peak points have shifted. For peak detection, the calculated coordinate point will not correspond to the center of the white stripe, but $\frac{1}{2}$ of the sum of the coordinates of the two valley points can be used to accurately represent the middle peak point. We use the same method to find the local gray-level valley value of the gray-level data and filter it. Finally, the center position of the two adjacent estimates is marked as the peak value. Then we mark the peak point with coordinates less than y_0 as $P_2(x_0, y_2)$.

4   Experiment Results and Discussion

4.1   Experimental Results of Gray Histogram Method

We carried out the horizontal gray-scale peak detection according to the above steps, and the result is shown in Fig. 7, where the peak point is marked with " +". As shown in Fig. 7(a), it can be seen that after the mean filtering, the spikes in the original data are removed. However there are still many consecutive repeated peak points during peak detection as shown in Fig. 7(c). But the redundant peak points are accurately removed after the filtering algorithm as shown in Fig. 7(d).

The result of vertical grayscale peak detection is shown in Fig. 8. The peak point is marked with "+" and the bottom point is marked with "+". In order to obtain the most accurate peak point, the method of finding the valley value before finding the midpoint of the adjacent valley value is used for peak detection, so it can be seen from the figure that the peak point does not appear in the place where the gray value is the largest.

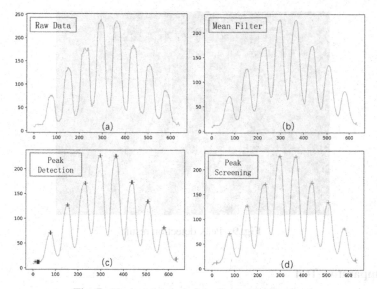

Fig. 7. Horizontal peak detection and screening

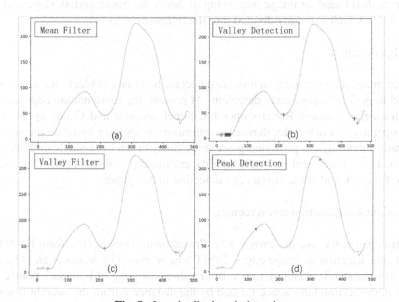

Fig. 8. Longitudinal peak detection

Finally, we use OpenCV to draw the three points P_0, P_1, P_2 and the two-by-two connection on the original image, as shown in Fig. 9. It can be seen that the two peak detections are very accurate, and the connection line of P_1 and P_2 is basically parallel to the fringe.

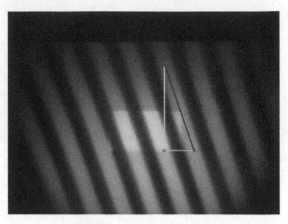

Fig. 9. Peak detection result

4.2 Comparative Test

In order to compare with the above detection results and verify each other, we adopted another method based on image processing to detect the fringe period, slope and point $C:P_0(x_0, y_0)$, which is mainly divided into the following steps:

(1) Edge detection

After image preprocessing, in order to detect the boundary of black and white stripes, we need to perform image edge detection. At present, the more mature edge detection operators mainly include Roberts operator, Sobel operator and Canny operator. The Canny operator is a first-order derivative optimization operator based on the signal-to-noise ratio criterion, the positioning accuracy criterion and the single-edge response criterion. Its accuracy and anti-noise ability are more prominent [12], which is very suitable for black and white stripe edge detection in this paper.

(2) Straight line detection and screening

In this paper, we use the Progressive Probabilistic Hough Transform (PPHT) for straight line detection of fringe edges. PPHT was proposed by Matas et al. [13], and it is based on the standard Hough transform, random sampling of boundary points. Then it votes in the accumulator space formed by the distance ρ from the straight line to the origin and the straight-line angle θ $(0 \sim \pi)$. When the threshold is reached, we think there is a straight line in this place. This method is not like the standard Hough transform to retrieve all the boundary points, it only performs partial sampling, which greatly reduces the calculation time and the amount of calculation [14][14]. The effect of straight -line detection is shown in Fig. 10(a). It can be seen that under the lower limit conditions, there are too many straight lines detected, and screening is required.

Firstly, we should remove the straight horizontal edge caused by the exit pupil receiving plate and it can be removed by limiting the slope range of the straight line. The limiting condition in this article is: the straight line whose slope satisfies $-0.1 < k < 0.1$ is the horizontal straight line that needs to be deleted. In addition, we also need to remove redundant lines that are too close. The specific method is to sort the intercept size of the line on the horizontal axis in ascending order, and then set a threshold and subtract adjacently. If it is found that the difference between the horizontal intercepts of adjacent lines is less than the threshold, it is considered to be a redundant line that is too close to each other. After deleting the repeated lines, the remaining straight line is shown in Fig. 10(b). It can be seen that the edge straight line detected by this method is very accurate.

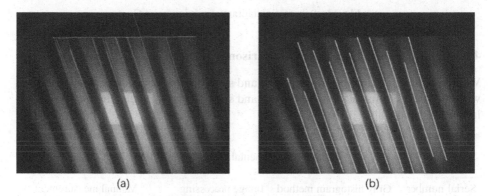

(a)   (b)

Fig. 10. Straight line detection and screening effect chart

(3) Solve for pupil fringe slope, period and C point

The stripe slope is the average of the slopes of the remaining straight lines in Fig. 10(b). The period is twice the average of the difference between the horizontal intercepts of these adjacent straight lines. For the convenience of calculation, we set point C as a point on the middle line of a white stripe and is relatively close to the center of the image. The schematic diagram of solving point C is shown in Fig. 11, where y_0 can be selected as half of the number of image rows. The solving steps are as follows:

(1) Calculate the midpoint of the intercept of the adjacent horizontal axis in the remaining straight lines, record it as $(x_1, 0)$, and save it into the array b
(2) Take the middle element of the array b and find the point (x_0, y_0) on the same straight line as it according to the slope
(3) Determine whether the gray value of (x_0, y_0) is within the brightness range of the white stripes. If yes, mark this point as point C, otherwise take the right adjacent element of the middle element of array b, and perform step (2)(3) again.

After solving the above data, the entire correspondence relationship table can be obtained row by row according to the above principle, which can be mutually verified with the data obtained by the gray histogram method.

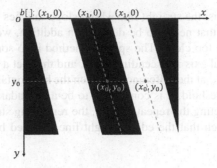

Fig. 11. Schematic diagram of solving point C

4.3 Experimental Result Data Comparison

We compared the exit pupil fringe period and slope obtained by the above two methods with the results of manual measurement, and selected six representative data as shown in the following Table 1:

Table 1. Experimental data comparison

Serial number	Gray histogram method		Image processing method		Manual measurement	
	Slope (k)	Period (T)	Slope (k)	Period (T)	Slope (k)	Period (T)
1	3.12	71	3.02	73	3	69
2	2.93	70	2.93	72	2.97	68
3	2.85	69	2.99	72	2.89	71
4	2.95	70	3.04	71	3	70
5	3.04	68	2.96	72	2.89	70
6	3.06	68	2.91	73	2.96	70

The solved part of the correspondence relationship table is shown in Fig. 12. It is in the form of txt, which can be read by subsequent programs. The fusion mode corresponding to human eye coordinates (x_0, y_0) is the number corresponding to row of y_0 and column of x_0 in the table. After actual testing, the correspondence table is very accurate, and can accurately return the correct fusion mode number according to the position of the human eyes.

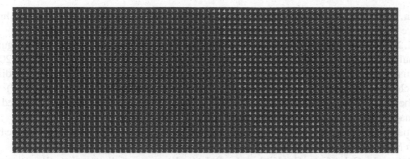

Fig. 12. Screenshot of the solved correspondence table

5 Conclusion

In this article, a program to automatically determine the mapping relationship between human eyes position and the exit pupil modes is proposed. In this way, we can query the correspondence table and use the eye position to get the exit pupil mode that should be set to the stereoscopic display and the best stereoscopic viewing position will accurately move with the human eye, and at the same time, the brightness jump phenomenon that occurs during mode switching will be reduced, and further, the pseudo-stereoscopic problem of the auto-stereoscopic display will be solved. In this paper, we innovatively propose an automatic calibration method based on the horizontal grayscale histogram, and a method based on image edge line detection to verify each other.

Experimental results show that the proposed method can accurately calculate the slope and period of the exit pupil and can deduce the complete mapping relationship. The method used in this paper is more accurate and automated than the traditional method. When the exit pupil mode is adjusted, the image brightness change rate is less than 3.3%, which can realize the effect of seamless switching.

References

1. Wu, F., Lv, G.J., Deng, H., Zhao, B.C., Wang, Q.H.: Dual-view integral imaging three-dimensional display using polarized glasses. Appl. Opt. **57**(6), 1447–1449 (2018)
2. Rohwer, K., Jorke, H., Neubert, T., Vergöhl, M.: Optische Interferenzfilter auf Polymerfolien: Spektrale Kanaltrennung in der 3D-Projektion nach dem Wellenlängenmultiplex-Verfahren. Vak. Forsch. Prax. **30**(1), 30–34 (2018)
3. Shi, L., Srivastava, A.K., Tam, A.M.W., Chigrinov, V.G., Kwok, H.: S: 2D–3D switchable display based on a passive polymeric lenticular lens array and electrically suppressed ferroelectric liquid crystal. Opt. Lett. **42**(17), 3435–3438 (2017)
4. Zhuang, Z., et al.: Addressable spatial light modulators for eye-tracking autostereoscopic three-dimensional display using a scanning laser. Appl. Optics **57**(16), 4457–4466 (2018).
5. Lee, S., et al.: Autostereoscopic 3D display using directional subpixel rendering. Opt. Express **26**(16), 20233 (2018)
6. Qin, K.H., Luo, J.L.: Autostereoscopic display technology and its development. J. Image Graphics A **14**(10), 1934–1941 (2009)
7. Lin, D.K., Liang, W.T., Liang, H.W., et al: Study on spatiotemporal seamless naked eye 3D display technology based on face tracking. Television Technol. **39**(05), 70- 73+77 (2015)

8. Jin, S.W., Yang, Q., Li, J.J.: Stereoscopic video combining image fusion algorithm and human eye tracking. Comput. Syst. Appl. **09**, 112–117 (2014)
9. Li, X.C., Wu, Q.Q., Xiao, B.P., Liu, X.Y., Wang, Y.Q.: High speed and robust infrared-guiding multiuser eye localization system for autostereoscopic display. Appl. Optics **59**(14) (2020)
10. Huang, J.P., Huang, K.C., Wang, Y.Q., et al.: Research on 3D content fusion display technology based on human eye tracking. Electron. Devices **40**(6), 1534–1538 (2017)
11. Zheng, H.B., Shi, H., Du, Y.C., et al.: Fast extraction method of fringe from structured light image with uneven illumination. Comput. Sci. **46**(5), 272–278 (2019)
12. Huang, F.H., Liu, Q.F., Ji, J.F.: Research on the edge detection operator of digital image based on MATLAB. Mech. Eng. Autom. **4**, 48–50 (2011)
13. Matas, J., Galambos, C., Kittler, J.: Robust detection of lines using the progressive probabilistic hough transform. Comput. Vis. Image Underst. **78**(1), 119–137 (2000)
14. Diao, Y., Wu, C., Luo, H., et al.: Straight line detection optimization algorithm based on improved probability Hough transform. Acta Optica Sinica **38**(8), 0815016 (2018)

Computer Graphics and Visualization

Semantic and Optical Flow Guided Self-supervised Monocular Depth and Ego-Motion Estimation

Jiaojiao Fang◉ and Guizhong Liu(✉)◉

Xi'an Jiaotong University, Xi'an 710049, China
liugz@xjtu.edu.cn

Abstract. The self-supervised depth and camera pose estimation methods are proposed to address the difficulty of acquiring the densely labeled ground-truth data and have achieved a great advance. As the stereo vision could constrain the predicted depth to a real-world scale, in this paper, we study the use of both left-right pairs and adjacent frames of stereo sequences for self-supervised semantic and optical flow guided monocular depth and camera pose estimation without real pose information. In particular, we explore (i) to construct a cascaded structure of the depth-pose and optical flow for well-initializing the optical flow, (ii) a cycle learning strategy to further constrain the depth-pose learning by the cross-task consistency, and (iii) a weighted semantic guided smoothness loss to match the real nature of a depth map. Our method produces favorable results against the state-of-the-art methods on several benchmarks. And we also demonstrate the generalization ability of our method on the cross dataset.

Keywords: Self-supervised learning · Monocular depth estimation · Camera pose estimation · Stereo vision

1 Introduction

Scene understanding is a crucial yet challenging problem in robotics and autonomous driving. One goal is to recognize and analyze the 3D scene structure and camera pose information from monocular 2D images. Traditional methods fail to model the ability of humans to infer the 3D geometric structure of a scene from a monocular image. Whereas with the rise of deep learning, several methods [5, 15] try to understand a scene in a supervised manner by large amounts of densely labeled data. But these methods are based primarily on the assumption that a plentiful of densely labeled ground-truth data is available which is costly and time-consuming [29].

Hence, some researchers attempt to address this problem by self-supervised learning from either stereo pairs [9] or video sequences [23] based on the scene structure re-projection error [10, 23] and multi-view geometric consistency [16]. Learning a mapping from a monocular image to a depth map in a self-supervised manner is challenging due to the high dimensions densely continuous-valued outputs, so more constraints are

© Springer Nature Switzerland AG 2021
Y. Peng et al. (Eds.): ICIG 2021, LNCS 12890, pp. 465–477, 2021.
https://doi.org/10.1007/978-3-030-87361-5_38

needed to solve this problem. The self-supervised optical flow methods have achieved excellent access, as it is easier than the 3D scene understanding. Existing methods import the deep learning-based optical flow for depth-pose learning, and achieve competitive performance [2, 19, 22]. The deep learning-based optical flow extraction is expensive in space and time, while the iterative optimization-based TVNet [6] achieves competitive accuracy with the fastest feature extraction time. Furthermore, the depth values of the pixels within an object always be close and relative, and significant changes occurred at the boundary of an object. To improve the reliability of the depth-pose estimation and imitate the learning process of humans, semantic segmentations are introduced for multi-task learning to mutually positive transfer between semantic segmentation and depth estimation [1, 12, 31, 34]. While they always treat the foreground objects, i.e. cars, and the background equally, which is not squared with the factual scene structure. Thus the different depth distribution of each class should be treated differently. The scale-ambiguity issue is common in self-supervised monocular depth estimation, existing methods mainly incorporate the stereo information into the monocular videos-based methods by given the stereo relations of two image planes.

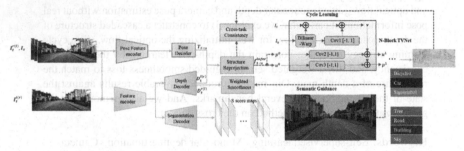

Fig. 1. An overview of the proposed pipeline for self-supervised depth and camera poses estimation. The depth network and pose network are learned collaboratively with the TVNet optical flow and guided by semantic segmentation.

In this paper, we propose a novel framework that jointly learns the semantic and optical flow-guided self-supervised monocular depth and camera pose from stereo video sequences. An overview of our proposed framework has been depicted in Fig. 1. Specifically, our main contributions are as follows:

1) We incorporate the structure of predicting the stereo views' disparity maps only based on a monocular image into the structure-from-motion (SfM) based self-supervised depth-pose learning framework, which takes full advantage of the constraints from spatial and temporal image pairs to improve upon prior art on monocular depth estimations. Our method can solve the scale ambiguity problem by stereo pairs without pose supervision.

2) We introduce the interpretable and simple optical flow, TVNet, into the self-supervised depth and pose learning framework to construct a cascaded structure with an end-to-end cycle learning strategy for well initializing the TVNet and better facilitating the depth-pose learning. Thus, the mismatching problem can be significantly alleviated, and the TVNet can be well-initialized.

3) As we always know that pixels labeled as 'sky' must accompany very large depth values and the depth values of the road are gradually increasing while the depth values of the pedestrian are almost the same. In this paper, we jointly train the depthpose and the semantic segmentation tasks and construct a weighted semantic guided region-aware smoothness loss to treat each class differently and make the predicted depth map closer to the real values.

2 Related Work

There are substantial studies on monocular depth estimation, including geometry-based methods [35] and learning-based methods [5]. In this paper, however, we concentrate only on the self-supervised depth-pose learning and semantic-guided depth estimation, which is highly related to the research topic of this paper.

Self-supervised depth estimation. Self-supervised methods enable learning the depth and pose networks from unlabeled images by substituting the direct ground-truth supervision with the new views synthesis loss. Godard et al. [9] and Garg et al. [7] proposed the stereo vision-based self-supervised methods, then Zhou et al. [23] proposed a self-supervised structure-from-motion-based learning framework that jointly learns the depth and camera pose from monocular video sequences. Based on this framework, a large corpus of works were proposed to promote self-supervised learning performance from different aspects. For more robust self-supervision signals, Mahjourian et al. [16] proposed a 3D geometric consistency loss which directly measured the whole structure of a scene, Shen et al. [32] introduced the epipolar geometry to measure the matching error, another kind of methods leveraged auxiliary tasks such as the optical flow [19, 22] to strengthen depth supervision via cross-task consistency. To deal with the dynamic objects, selective masks were used to filter out the unreliable information during training. Prior works generated the mask by the auto-learning network [23], while the recent methods produced the mask by geometric error guidance [10, 24, 26], which were proved to be more effective. Guizilini et al. [11] proposed a novel depth network architecture to improve the estimation performance. There also exist other methods trying to enhance the network performance with traditional SfM [3], which offer pseudo labels for depth estimation. Poggi et al. [18] focused on the uncertainty estimation for self-supervised monocular depth estimation. And recently some methods were proposed to solve the scale ambiguity problem [26, 32].

Semantic guided Depth estimation. Semantic information had been shown to provide positive effects on monocular depth estimation [1, 31]. The methods could be classified into two categories by the manner of using semantic information. One group of the methods used the outputs of semantic labels directly to guide the depth learning. Chen et al. [1] constrained the depth maps by leveraging the semantic labels of the scene. Klingner et al. [30] and Casser et al. [25] addressed the dynamic moving objects issues by the indication of the semantic map. The other group of methods enhanced the depth feature representation by semantic feature guidance [12, 27] proposed a segmentation-like loss term for depth estimation. Li et al. [28] fused these two manners and proposed an individual semantic network for better scene representation.

3   The Proposed Method

3.1   Cascaded Structure and Cycle Learning Strategy

Monocular depth, optical flow, and ego motion are coupled by the nature of 3D scene geometry. A reasonable combination of these tasks would improve the prediction performance. It contains two stages, the rigid 3D structure reasoning stage and the optical flow iterating stage. The first stage to infer scene structure is made up of two sub-networks, i.e. the DepthNet and the PoseNet. The depth maps and camera poses are regressed respectively and combined to produce the rigid scene flow. And the second stage is to feed the rigid scene flow into the TVNet based optical flow to form a cascaded structure for iterating the optical flow from these initial values. The TVNet [6] is obtained by imitating and unfolding the iterative optimization process of the TV-L1 method [34] and formulates the iterations as customized layers of a neural network. Thus it can be naturally connected with other related networks to form an end-to-end trainable architecture. It is not necessary to carefully design a complex network structure with unknown interpretability or to store the optical-flow features anymore. Since the Taylor expansion is applied in TVNet to linearize the brightness difference, the initial flow field should be close to the real field to ensure a smaller approximation error. Thus it is proper to construct a cascaded structure for depth-pose and optical flow learning. Furthermore, we constrain the cross-task geometric consistency check during training, which significantly enhances the coherence of the predictions and achieves impressive performance.

Our first stage aims to reconstruct the rigid scene structure with robustness towards non-rigidity and outliers. The DepthNet takes a single image $I_t^{l(r)} \in R^{H \times W \times 3}$ as input to regress a pair of pixel-wise stereo depth maps $(D_t^{l(r)}, D_t^{r(l)})$ and exploits accumulated scene priors for depth prediction. Similar to [9], our model does not require the relative pose between the stereo pair. The PoseNet takes the concatenated adjacent views $[I_t, I_s] \in R^{H \times W \times 6}$ as input to regress the relative 6DoF camera poses $T_{t \to s} = [R, t]$ from the target view I_t to the source views I_s, where $s \in \{t - 1, t + 1\}$. With the estimated depth and pose, the reprojected scene flow from the target image I_t to the source image I_s can be represented by

$$f_{t \to s}^{\inf er} = p - KT_{t \to s}D_t^{l(r)}(p)K^{-1}p \tag{1}$$

where $K \in R^{3 \times 3}$ denotes the camera intrinsic and p denotes homogeneous coordinates of a pixel in the frame I_t. Here the estimated optical flow of the TVNet-15 [6] is represented as $f_{t \to s}^{pre}$ and can be optimized by the loss as follows:

$$L_{op} = \min_{u(p)} \sum (|u_1(p)| + |u_2(p)| + \lambda \rho(u(p))) \tag{2}$$

where $u(p) = (u_1(p), u_2(p))$ denotes the displacement of the position p from time t to the next frame $t + 1$ of each iteration process and $\rho(u(p))$ is defined to penalize the brightness difference of adjacent time. The more implementation details are recommended to see the literature TVNet [6]. Instead of setting the initial value $u^0(p) = (0, 0)$, here we use the $u^0(p) = f_{t \to s}^{\inf er}(p)$ as the initial value of the TVNet.

As we all know that stereo view reconstruction can achieve more reliable results due to it is less affected by the illumination variation. In this paper, we adopt the minimum error among source views and a per-pixel binary auto-mask μ proposed by [10] to construct the photometric loss of the adjacent views as $L_{vs} = \mu \min_s pe(I_t, I_{s \to t})$, where $pe(,)$ is a mixture of L1-Norm and structural similarity (SSIM) difference.

We also use the left-right disparity consistency loss L_{lr} and the stereo image reconstruction losses L_{ap} introduced by [9] to constrain the depth maps. Thus the total reconstruction loss of our method can be expressed as:

$$L_{syth} = L_{vs} + \lambda_a L_{ap} + \lambda_c L_{lr} \tag{3}$$

where λ_a and λ_c are the weightings for the left-right image reconstruction loss and the left-right disparity consistency loss, respectively. The cross-task consistency on the depth-pose and optical flow estimation can further constrain the depth-pose learning procedure. Like other methods [26, 32], we compute a binary mask $M(p)$ based on the distribution of the consistency difference between $f_{t \to s}^{pre}(p)$ and $f_{t \to s}^{\inf er}(p)$ to filter out the outliers. The binary mask can be computed by:

$$M(p) = \{ \begin{array}{ll} 1, & Percentile(|f_{t \to s}^{pre}(p) - f_{t \to s}^{\inf er}(p)|) < T_M \\ 0, & Otherwise \end{array} \tag{4}$$

Where pixel positions whose geometry consistency loss is above a percentile threshold T_M are filtered out. Thus the optical flow-guided depth and pose learning loss can be reformulated as:

$$L_{pf} = \sum_r \sum_s \sum_p M(p)|f_{t \to s}^{pre}(p) - f_{t \to s}^{\inf er}(p)|. \tag{5}$$

Where r indexes over different feature scales of the image, s indexes over source images, and p indexes over all pixels.

3.2 Semantic Guided Depth Estimation

The existing depth estimation methods generally focus on pixel-wise disparity estimation and regard all pixels within an image as spatial homogeneity, which would lead to unfavorable disparity estimation along object boundaries. To overcome the limitation, we perform disparity estimation by leveraging semantic information to improve the quality of the depth maps. The semantic segmentation is derived by a neural network that implements a non-linear mapping between an input image I_t and the output scores $y_t \in R^{H \times W \times S}$ for all pixel indexes p and classes s. We thus define the semantic segmentation loss L_{seg} as:

$$L_{seg} = \omega_s CE(s_{GT}, s) \tag{6}$$

where $\omega_s CE()$ indicates the weighted cross-entropy loss, ω_s are the weights of each semantic class, $s \in S$ is the predicted semantic labels of each pixel p from a set of classes $S = \{1, 2, \cdots, S\}$ and s_{GT} denotes the ground truth labels from an additional disjoint dataset. To approximate the real distribution of the depth map, we proposed a region-aware smoothness loss function to constrain the depth values belonging to the same objects to be closer with their nearby pixels, while making a difference between the foreground objects and the background. $S_t = \varphi(y_t)$ is the operation that sets the maximum value along each channel as 1 and sets the remaining values as 0. Then the weighted region-aware disparity smoothness term is defined as:

$$L_{sm} = \Sigma_p(|\partial_x D_t^{l(r)}(p)| + |\partial_y D_t^{l(r)}(p)|) \odot \omega_{sf}(1 - S_t) \tag{7}$$

where $\partial_x(\cdot)$ and $\partial_y(\cdot)$ are the gradients of disparity in horizontal and vertical direction respectively $\odot$ denotes element-wise multiplication, S_t is the gradients of the segmentation map in each channel which mean the edges of all classes, and $\omega_{sf} \in R^S$ is the smoothness weights of all semantic classes. Thus the weighted semantic guided smooth factor is low (close to zero) on the boundary regions of the objects, high (close to one) on the foreground objects' central regions, and smaller on the background regions. The depth value of the nearby pixels within the edge of one semantic object should be almost the same for the foreground objects, while just be closer and gradually changed for the background of the nearby pixels. Thus the smoothness degree of each class should be different during training. The second term $1 - \nabla S_t$ is an edge detector operation to identify edges of the segmentation map.

Thus our final loss function becomes:

$$L_{final} = L_{syth} + \lambda_s L_{sm} + \lambda_f L_{pf} + \lambda_o L_{op}. \tag{8}$$

Where λ_s and λ_f are the weightings for the depth smoothness loss and the geometry consistency loss, respectively.

4 Experiments

In this section, we evaluated the quantitative and qualitative performance of our method, and compared it with the state-of-the-arts methods mainly on the KITTI dataset [8] for a fair comparison. We also evaluated the cross dataset generalization ability on the Make3D dataset [21].

4.1 Implementation Details

Parameters setting. The algorithm was implemented in the PyTorch [17] framework. For all the experiments, we set the weighting of the different loss components as $\lambda_s = 0.01$, $\lambda_f = 0.001$, $\lambda_a = 0.5$ and $\lambda_c = 0.5$. We trained our model for 40 epochs with the Adam [14] optimizer, Gaussian random initialization, and mini-batch size of 6. The learning rate was initially set to 0.0001 for the first 30 epochs and then dropped to 0.00001 for the reminder. The network took almost 28 h to train on a single Titan Xp for 20 epochs.

Network architecture. Our networks are based on SGDepth [30], where an encoder-decoder architecture with skip connections is employed. To ensure comparability to

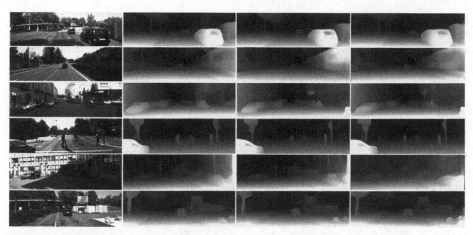

Fig. 2. The qualitative results of the proposed method on the KITTI dataset. The left, middle, and right columns show respectively input images, the state-of-the-art predicted depth maps Godard et al. [10], Klingner et al. [30] and the depths maps obtained by ours. Our method predicts sharper boundaries and fine-grained details on distant objects.

existing work [10, 12, 30], we choose the ResNet18 [13] pretrained on Imagenet [20] as encoder. The shared encoder was trained according to [30]. The depth head has two channels at each output layer and has 4 different spatial scales of the outputs. A sigmoid output σ is used to ensure the predicted depth to be within a reasonable range, which is converted to a depth map by $1/a\sigma + b$, where a and b are chosen to constrain the depth values within the range [0.1, 100]. For simplicity, the segmentation decoder uses the same architecture as the depth decoder, except for the last layer having S channels feature maps, whose elements are converted to class probabilities by a softmax function. The pose network's architecture is the same as in [30].

Datasets. We utilized one dataset to learn the semantic segmentation and another one for the self-supervised depth-pose and optical flow training. For training the semantic segmentation we utilized the Cityscapes dataset [4] while at the same time we use the KITTI dataset [8] for training the depth estimation. Similar to other state-of-the-art approaches we trained our model on the Eigen split dataset [5] which excluded 679 images from the KITTI dataset for testing and remove static frames following [23]. All the experiments were performed with image sequences captured by color cameras with fixed focal length. We resized images to 640 × 192 during training, but the network can be tested with arbitrary input image size, due to the depth and pose networks were all with the fully convolutional structure.

Augmentation and processing. We performed horizontal flips and the following data augmentations during training, with 50% chance: random brightness, contrast, saturation, and hue jitter with respective ranges of ±0.2, ±0.2, ±0.2, and ±0.1 as in [10]. All the images fed to the pose and depth networks are performed with the same augmentations. For results trained in stereo image pairs, we did not perform median scaling as the scale has to be learned by the stereo vision.

Table 1. Results on the KITTI dataset [8] using the Eigen split [5] compared with the state-of-the-art methods by the authors' report. 'S' and 'M' refer to stereo images and monocular images self-supervision, respectively. 'Inst' and 'Sem' indicate the instance or semantic information.

Method	Train	Error (lower is better)				Accuracy (higher is better)		
		Abs Rel	Sq Rel	RMSE	RMSE log	$\delta < 1.25$	$\delta < 1.25^2$	$\delta < 1.25^3$
Zhou et al. [23]	M	0.183	1.595	6.709	0.270	0.734	0.902	0.959
Godard et al. [9]	S	0.133	1.142	5.533	0.230	0.830	0.936	0.970
Vid2Depth [16]	M	0.163	1.240	6.220	0.250	0.762	0.916	0.968
Yin et al. [22]	M	0.149	1.060	5.567	0.226	0.796	0.935	0.975
Chen et al. [1]	S	0.118	0.905	5.096	0.211	0.839	0.945	0.977
Godard et al. [10]	M	0.115	0.903	4.863	0.193	0.877	0.959	0.981
Godard et al. [10]	MS	0.106	0.818	4.750	0.196	0.874	0.957	0.979
Casser et al. [25]	M+Inst	0.141	1.026	5.291	0.215	0.816	0.945	0.979
Bian et al. [26]	M	0.137	1.089	5.439	0.217	0.830	0.942	0.975
Xue et al. [32]	M	0.113	0.864	4.812	0.191	0.877	0.960	0.981
Guizilini et al. [12]	M+Sem	0.117	0.854	4.714	0.191	0.873	0.963	0.981
ṇKlingner et al. [30]	M+Sem	0.113	0.835	4.693	0.191	0.879	0.961	0.981
Ours	MS+Sem	0.105	0.801	4.631	0.189	0.881	0.962	0.982

4.2 Main Results

In this section, we start by the comparison to multiple state-of-the-art methods, followed by an analysis of how the single components of our method improve the estimation results.

Depth Estimation Results on KITTI. We first provided a comparison with the state-of-the-arts self-supervised methods on the monocular depth evaluation by the Eigen split in Table 1. To be fair for all methods, we used the same crop manner as [10] and evaluated the prediction with the same resolution as the input image. The evaluation metrics conformed to the one used in [10], and the depth value was capped to 80 m during evaluation. Our method outperforms all comparable baselines, where we compare to methods that use only video sequences as supervision on the KITIT dataset. As the resolution of the input image highly dependent on the estimation performance, we reported the results at the middle resolutions 640 × 192 for a fair comparison. Due to fairness, we do not compare against results with online refinement [1] or employing a more efficient network architecture [11], as such techniques can improve any methods. Qualitative results were shown in Fig. 2. We could observe that our method was able to reconstruct small objects such as traffic signs and could achieve the state-of-the-art performance.

Depth Estimation Results on Make3D. To illustrate the generalization ability of our method, we evaluated our model trained only on the KITTI dataset on the Make3D test set of [21]. Make3D consists of only RGB/Depth pairs and without stereo image. Qualitative results were shown in Fig. 3, note that our model is only trained on the KITTI dataset, and directly tested on Make3D. These results would be further improved with more relevant training data.

Table 2. Odometry results on the KITTI [8] odometry dataset. Results show the average absolute trajectory error, and standard deviation, in meters.

Methods	Sequence 09	Sequence 10	# frames
Garg et al. [7]	0.013 ± 0.010	0.012 ± 0.011	3
Zhou et al. [23]	0.021± 0.017	0.020 ± 0.015	5
Mahjourian et al. [16]	0.013± 0.010	0.012 ± 0.011	3
GeoNet [22]	0.012± 0.007	0.012 ± 0.009	5
Ranjan et al. [19]	0.012± 0.007	0.012 ± 0.008	5
Monodepth2 [10]	0.017± 0.008	0.015 ± 0.010	2
SGDepth [30]	0.019± 0.010	0.016 ± 0.010	2
Ours	0.011 ± 0.007	0.012 ± 0.008	2

Fig. 3. Illustration of examples of depth predictions on the unseen Make3D dataset [21].

Pose Estimation Results on KITTI Odometry. While we mainly concentrated on better depth estimation, we also compared our pose networks with competing methods on the KITTI odometry dataset since the two tasks are inter-dependent. The KITTI odometry dataset contains 11 driving sequences with ground-truth poses available (and 11 sequences without ground-truth). We evaluated the pose error on sequences 09 and 10. Competing methods typically feed more frames to their pose network for improving their performance. We had observed that with the joint optical flow learning, the result of visual odometry would be improved. We measured the Absolute Trajectory Error (ATE) over N-frame snippets (N = 3 or 5), as measured in [10]. As showed in Table 2, our method outperformed other state-of-the-art approaches.

Table 3. Ablation studies. Results for different variants of our model trained on KITTI 2015 [8] using the Eigen split.

Method	Error (lower is better)				Accuracy (higher is better)		
	Abs Rel	Sq Rel	RMSE	RMSE log	$\delta < 1.25$	$\Delta < 1.25^2$	$\Delta < 1.25^3$
Baseline	0.115	0.903	4.863	0.193	0.877	0.959	0.977
+Stereo	0.113	0.863	4.767	0.192	0.875	0.957	0.980
+Cascaded-cycle learning	0.106	0.842	4.723	0.191	0.877	0.959	0.979
+ Weighted Semantic guidance	0.105	0.801	4.631	0.189	0.881	0.962	0.982

4.3 Ablation Studies

To verify how each component of our model contributed to the overall performance, we performed ablation studies by changing various components of our model based on and listed the results in Table 3. The study was performed on the Eigen split for better comparison. We see that each component of our model could promote the estimation performance of the baseline model [10], and all our components combined lead to a significant improvement. As expected, integrating stereo information into a monocular model could increase accuracy.

Benefits of the cascaded structure by cycle learning strategy for depth estimation. We also compared our only depth estimation model with the jointly depth-pose and TVNet learning framework with zero initialization. Our method performed better than the model that simply jointed training three networks together on the KITTI Eigen split dataset. We further verified that the cycle learning could address the mismatching problem which could be reflected by the end-to-end point error.

Effect of the weighted semantic guided smoothness loss. We saw that the weighted semantic guided smoothness loss could not only achieve improvement of the quantitative results than the edge-aware first order smooth loss and the second-order smooth loss, the qualified results could also be better improved. Semantic information could improve depth estimation in all cases.

More specifically, we applied the exact network architecture of Godard et al. [9] that predicted the disparity maps for stereo views from a monocular image by randomly using the left or right view as input instead of only using the left image as input, which would solve the problem of unawareness of structural information from the other view, and promoted the depth and pose estimation.

5 Conclusions

In this paper, we have presented a self-supervised semantic and optical flow-guided depth-pose learning pipeline from stereo sequences with an unknown stereo pose. This framework takes full advantage of the constraints on the unlabeled stereo and temporal image pairs by predicting stereo disparity maps from a monocular image. Furthermore, we import the explainable TVNet into the self-supervised depth-pose learning and construct a cascaded structure with a cycle learning strategy for better depth-pose and optical flow learning. Finally, we propose a weighted semantic guided smoothness loss to treat the foreground objects and background region differently for predicting more natural and reasonable depth maps. Experiments show that our method can exceed the existing self-supervised method, and can generalize well to the unseen dataset.

References

1. Chen, P., Liu, A.H., Liu, Y., Wang, Y.F.: Towards scene understanding: Unsupervised monocular depth estimation with semantic-aware representation. In: Proceedings of the IEEE Conference on Computer Vision and Pattern Recognition, pp. 2624–2632 (2019)
2. Chen, Y., Schmid, C., Sminchisescu, C.: Self-supervised learning with geometric constraints in monocular video: connecting flow, depth, and camera. In: Proceedings of the IEEE International Conference on Computer Vision, pp. 7063–7072 (2019)
3. Zhan, H., Weerasekera, C.S., Bian, J., Reid, I.: Visual odometry revisited: What should be learnt?. In: IEEE International Conference on Robotics and Automation, pp. 4203–4210 (2020)
4. Cordts, M., et al.: The cityscapes dataset for semantic urban scene understanding. In: Proceedings of the IEEE Conference on Computer Vision and Pattern Recognition, pp. 3213–3223 (2016)
5. Eigen, D., Puhrsch, C., Fergus, R.: Depth map prediction from a single image using a multiscale deep network. In: Advances in Neural Information Processing systems, pp. 2366–2374 (2014)
6. Fan, L., Huang, W., Gan, C., Ermon, S., Gong, B., Huang, J.: End-to-end learning of motion representation for video understanding. In: Proceedings of the IEEE Conference on Computer Vision and Pattern Recognition, pp. 6016–6025 (2018)

7. Garg, R., Kumar, B,G.V., Carneiro, G., Reid, I.: Unsupervised CNN for single view depth estimation: geometry to the rescue. In: European Conference on Computer Vision, pp. 740–756 (2016)
8. Geiger, A., Lenz, P., Urtasun, R.: Are we ready for autonomous driving? The kitti vision benchmark suite. In: 2012 IEEE Conference on Computer Vision and Pattern Recognition, pp. 3354–3361 (2012)
9. Godard, C., Mac Aodha, O., Brostow, G.J.: Unsupervised monocular depth estimation with left-right consistency. In: Proceedings of the IEEE Conference on Computer Vision and Pattern Recognition, pp. 270–279 (2017)
10. Godard, C., Mac Aodha, O., Firman, M., Brostow, G.J.: Digging into self-supervised monocular depth estimation. In: Proceedings of the IEEE International Conference on Computer Vision, pp. 3828–3838 (2019)
11. Guizilini, V., Ambrus, R., Pillai, S., Raventos, A., Gaidon, A.: 3D packing for self-supervised monocular depth estimation. In: IEEE/CVF Conference on Computer Vision and Pattern Recognition (2020)
12. Guizilini, V., Hou, R., Li, J., Ambrus, R., Gaidon, A.: Semantically-guided representation learning for self-supervised monocular depth. In: International Conference on Learning Representations (2020)
13. He, K., Zhang, X., Ren, S., Sun, J.: Deep residual learning for image recognition. In: Proceedings of the IEEE Conference on Computer Vision and Pattern Recognition, pp. 770–778 (2016)
14. Kingma, D.P., Ba, J.: Adam: a method for stochastic optimization. arXiv preprint arXiv:1412.6980 (2014)
15. Laina, I., Rupprecht, C., Belagiannis, V., Tombari, F., Navab, N.: Deeper depth prediction with fully convolutional residual networks. In: International Conference on 3D Vision, pp. 239–248 (2016)
16. Mahjourian, R., Wicke, M., Angelova, A.: Unsupervised learning of depth and ego-motion from monocular video using 3D geometric constraints. In: Proceedings of the IEEE Conference on Computer Vision and Pattern Recognition, pp. 5667–5675 (2018)
17. Paszke, A., et al.: PyTorch: An imperative style, high-performance deep learning library. In: Proceedings of NeurIPS, Vancouver, BC, Canada, pp. 8024–8035 (2019)
18. Poggi, M., Aleotti, F., Tosi, F., Mattoccia, S.: On the uncertainty of self-supervised monocular depth estimation. In: IEEE/CVF Conference on Computer Vision and Pattern Recognition (CVPR) (2020)
19. Ranjan, A., et al.: Competitive collaboration: Joint unsupervised learning of depth, camera motion, optical flow and motion segmentation. In: Proceedings of the IEEE Conference on Computer Vision and Pattern Recognition, pp. 12240–12249 (2019)
20. Russakovsky, O., et al.: Imagenet large scale visual recognition challenge. Int. J. Comput. Vis. **115**(3), 211–252 (2015)
21. Saxena, A., Sun, M., Ng, A.Y.: Make3D: learning 3D scene structure from a single still image. IEEE Trans. Pattern Anal. Mach. Intell. **31**(5), 824–840 (2009)
22. Yin, Z., Shi, J.: Geonet: Unsupervised learning of dense depth, optical flow and camera pose. In: Proceedings of the IEEE Conference on Computer Vision and Pattern Recognition, pp. 1983–1992 (2018)
23. Zhou, T., Brown, M., Snavely, N., Lowe, D.G.: Unsupervised learning of depth and ego-motion from video. In: Proceedings of the IEEE Conference on Computer Vision and Pattern Recognition, pp. 1851–1858 (2017)
24. Wang, G., Wang, H., Liu, Y., Chen, W.: Unsupervised learning of monocular depth and ego-motion using multiple masks. In: IEEE 2019 International Conference on Robotics and Automation (ICRA), pp. 4724–4730 (2019)

25. Casser, V., Pirk, S., Mahjourian, R., Angelova, A.: Depth prediction without the sensors: leveraging structure for unsupervised learning from monocular videos. Proc. AAAI Conf. Artif. Intell. **33**, 8001–8008 (2019)
26. Bian, J., et al.: Unsupervised scale-consistent depth and ego-motion learning from monocular video. Adv. Neural Inf. Process. Syst. 35–45 (2019)
27. Choi, J., Jung, D., Lee, D., Kim, C.: Safenet: Self-supervised monocular depth estimation with semantic-aware feature extraction. In: Workshops at the 34th Conference on Neural Information Processing Systems (2020)
28. Li, R., He, X., Zhu, Y., Li, X., Sun, J., Zhang, Y.: Enhancing self-supervised monocular depth estimation via incorporating robust constraints. In: Proceedings of the 28th ACM International Conference on Multimedia, pp. 3108–3117 (2020)
29. Uhrig, J., Schneider, N., Schneider, L., Franke, U., Brox, T., Geiger, A.: sparsity invariant CNNs. In: International Conference on 3D Vision (2017)
30. Klingner, M., Termohlen, J., Mikolajczyk, J., Fingscheidt, T.: Self-supervised monocular depth estimation: Solving the dynamic object problem by semantic guidance. In: European Conference on Computer Vision, (2020)
31. Meng, Y., et al.: SIGNet: semantic instance aided unsupervised 3D geometry perception. In: Proceedings of CVPR, Long Beach, CA, USA, pp. 9810–9820, June 2019
32. Shen, T., Luo, Z., Zhou, L., et al.: Beyond photometric loss for self-supervised ego-motion estimation. In: International Conference on Robotics and Automation, pp. 6359–6365 (2019)
33. Xue, F., Zhuo, G., Huang, Z., Fu, W., Wu, Z., Ang, Jr.: Toward hierarchical self-supervised monocular absolute depth estimation for autonomous driving applications. In: IEEE/RSJ International Conference on Intelligent Robots and Systems (IROS) (2020)
34. Zach, C., Pock, T., Bischof, H.: A duality based approach for realtime TV-L1 optical flow. Pattern Recogn. 214–223 (2007)
35. Schonberger, J.-L., Frahm, J.-M.: Structure-from-motion revisited. In: Proceedings of the IEEE Conference on Computer Vision and Pattern Recognition, pp. 4104–4113 (2016)

Frequency Transfer Model: Generating High Frequency Components for Fluid Simulation Details Reconstruction

JingYuan Zhu[1], HuiMin Ma[2(✉)], TianYu Hu[2], and Jian Yuan[1]

[1] Tsinghua University, Beijing 100084, China
jy-zhu20@mails.tsinghua.edu.cn, jyuan@tsinghua.edu.cn
[2] University of Science and Technology Beijing, Beijing 100083, China
{mhmpub,tianyu}@ustb.edu.cn

Abstract. In this paper, a novel method is proposed for data-driven high frequency components generation of velocity fields in fluid simulation. It targets on fluid simulation based on N-S Equation which may suffer from details missing because of low simulation grid resolution and other reasons causing energy dissipation. A frequency transfer model structured with deep learning methods is designed to generate high frequency components with low frequency components as inputs. Considering that high frequency components cannot be inferred from lower ones exactly, our model provides another freedom to adjust the ratio of low frequency and high frequency components in velocity fields to obtain results with diversity and reality. A series of evaluations and results are presented to show our model's effectiveness in generating high frequency components from low frequency components without improving grid simulation to alleviating energy and dissipation and reconstruct details in fluid simulation.

Keywords: Frequency transfer model · Frequency components · Details reconstruction · Fluid simulation

1 Introduction

Fluid motion is one of the most common natural phenomena in our daily life. High dimensionality of variables and equations used by humans to describe fluid systems decide the complexity of fluid simulation. Fluid motion is nonlinear and non-stationary in most cases. Velocity fields play important roles in simulation process since they would interact with other physical fields. In general, velocity fields consist of different frequency components. Lower frequency components describe larger scale motions that would decide basic motion and global distributions of fluid. Higher frequency components originate from fluid viscosity

Supported by National Natural Science Foundation of China (No. U20B2062, No. 61673237); Beijing Municipal Science and Technology Project (No. Z191100007419001); Beijing National Research Center for Information Science and Technology.

© Springer Nature Switzerland AG 2021
Y. Peng et al. (Eds.): ICIG 2021, LNCS 12890, pp. 478–489, 2021.
https://doi.org/10.1007/978-3-030-87361-5_39

and describe smaller scale motions like local vortexes and turbulent flows which would improve realism and visual effect of fluid simulation results. Lack of high frequency components in velocity field is the main reason for the details missing phenomenon as illustrated in Fig. 1.

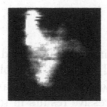

Fig. 1. Lack of high frequency components in velocity fields results in details missing like local vortex in fluid simulation.

All kinds of numerical methods were proposed to realize vorticity confinement and reconstruct details in fluid simulation, most of which generate high frequency components with higher grid resolution, more iterations and additional terms for refinements resulting in large calculation quantity. In recent years many works have proved deep learning methods competitive alternatives compared with traditional methods in fields such as parameterized generation, temporal prediction, super-resolution, and so on. Successes in super-resolution researches of fluid flow proved it possible to realize details generation with deep learning methods. We handle this problem from a different view with a novel frequency transfer model based on deep learning instead of relying on analytical or numerical methods to realize high frequency components generation without increasing grid resolution. Our approach is aimed at physical fields which contain more information than images used in super-resolution researches of fluid flow.

Taking complexity and large freedoms of fluid systems into account, the frequency transfer model first made use of multilayer convolutional neural networks (CNN) to transfer information from a large simulation space to a relatively smaller latent space. Then the second part in the transfer model including fully connected (Dense) and long short-term memory (LSTM) layers generate latent codes including high frequency components information with latent codes encoded from low frequency components as inputs. The final part of thr frequency transfer model is a multilayer deconvolutional neural network which is symmetrical with the first one. It plays the role of transferring latent codes back to real physics fields in simulation space. Through a series of evaluations, we proved the frequency transfer model's effectiveness in generating high frequency components of velocity fields in fluid simulation. The specific contributions of this work are:

- an end-to-end frequency transfer model based on neural networks to improve the reality of fluid simulation through generating high frequency components of velocity fields from low frequency components without increasing grid resolution,

- an additional freedom in frequency transfer model, through which the ratio of generated high frequency components and original low frequency components could be adjusted to obtain results with diversity,
- a scaling method to guarantee the validity of frequency transfer model could be trained appropriately in spite of simulation data's value size.

2   Related Work

Despite that machine learning methods had been proposed for a long time [1], widely research and application of neural networks take place in recent years. As for computer graphics, approaches based on machine learning were proposed even later but has already produced impressive results in topics including style transfer [2], temporal prediction [3] and super-resolution problems [4].

Physics-Based Deep Learning (PBDL) represents the field of methods with combinations of deep learning techniques and physical modeling. Researches in PBDL proved deep learning techniques could be competitive alternatives in comparison with traditional methods in solving physical problems. Thuerey et al. [5] investigated the accuracy of deep learning models for Reynolds-Averaged Navier-Stokes solutions and obtained a mean relative pressure and velocity error of less than 3% across a range of previously unseen airfoil shapes which shows the potential capability of deep learning methods to solving physical systems. Similar approaches also perform well in generating desired implicit surfaces [6] and droplet formation [7] with data-driven models. Convolutional neural networks were used to extract features and generate descriptors from fluid data to track deformable fluid regions [8]. Hennigh et al. compressed Lattice Boltzmann fluid simulation with Lat-Net based on deep neural networks. [9] Deep residual recurrent neural network (DR-RNN) was applied for subsurface multi-phase flow problems to model the evolution of dynamical systems [10]. Kim et al.'s work demonstrated that complex parameterization of fluid flow could be handled in reduced spaces to improve simulation speed significantly compared with traditional numerical methods [11]. Morton et al. presented a method for learning the forced and unforced dynamics directly from CFD data [12]. Their model based on Koopman theory could produce stable dynamic models over extended time horizons. Similar works leverage deep learning to discover representations of Koopman eigenfunctions from data [13]. S. Wiewel et al. demonstrated for the first time that 3D space and time functions of physics system can be predicted within latent spaces of neural networks [14]. Later they proposed an end-to-end trained neural network architecture to predict the complex dynamics fluid flows system robustly with high temporal stability [15]. Not only for data in forms of Euler representation [16], deep learning methods could learn stable and temporally coherent feature spaces from data in forms of Lagrangian representation [17] like points clouds that change over time as well [18].

Further application includes larger-scale problems including global weather conditions predictions with data-driven methods [19]. Generative Adversarial Networks (GAN) became highly successful in image generation tasks [20]. Previous researches have proved GAN to be useful in the generation of fluid simulation as well. TempoGAN, a temporally coherent generative model which was able to infer more realistic high-resolution details was proposed to address the super-resolution problems for fluid flows [21]. Multi-Pass GAN decomposed generative problems on Cartesian field functions into multiple smaller sub-problems so that they can be learned more efficiently [22]. While many of the works mentioned above share the same goal to generate details for fluid simulation, they view the process as a super-resolution problem and improve the reality of fluid simulation through promoting grid resolution. Our work demonstrates that it is possible to generate high frequency components to realize details reconstruction without improving grid resolution for fluid flows including liquid and gas.

3   Method

The network architecture of our end-to-end frequency transfer model is shown in Fig. 2. It is briefly divided into three parts. The first part represents an encoder to reduce the dimensionality of the original input velocity fields and improve the calculation efficiency of the whole model by transferring velocity fields to latent codes. The second part is a transfer module for latent codes including dense layers and LSTM layers for generating high frequency components with latent codes of lowers frequency components as inputs. The last part shares a symmetrical structure with the encoder in the first part. However, it should be emphasized that even if structures of encoder and decoder are symmetrical, their functions are not. The encoder transfers lower frequency components of velocity field inputs to latent codes, while the decoder transfers latent codes generated by the latent transfer module to velocity fields containing both low and high frequency components.

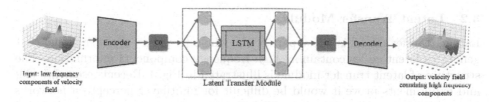

Input: low frequency
components of velocity
field

Latent Transfer Module

Output: velocity field
containing high frequency
components

Fig. 2. Architecture overview of frequency transfer network. Our model is basically divided into three parts including encoder, latent transfer module and decoder.

3.1   Encoding and Decoding Model

Our central goal is to generate high frequency components of velocity field in fluid simulation without expanding grid resolution. Considering large scale of original velocity data, our model first reduce dimensionality of this frequency transfer problem with an encoding model. We employ function f_e and f_d to represent encoder which transfers low frequency components of velocity fields

($\mathbf{v}_0$) to latent codes ($\mathbf{c}_0$) of lower dimensions with mapping $f_e(\mathbf{v}_0) = \mathbf{c}_0$ and decoder which transfers generated latent codes ($\mathbf{c}$) from latent transfer module to complete velocity fields with mapping $f_d(\mathbf{c}) = \mathbf{v}_{gen}$. Symmetrical structures of encoders and decoders are illustrated in Fig. 3.

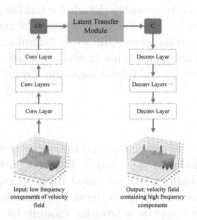

Fig. 3. Architecture of encoder and decoder. The encoder consists of a sequence of convolutional layers, decoder consists of a sequence of deconvolutional layers in correspondence.

Unlike autoencoders used in Latent Space Physics [14] and other works, which would train encoders and corresponding decoders at the same time, the encoder and decoder should be trained with latent transfer module in the end-to-end frequency transfer model together to simplify the whole training process.

3.2 Latent Transfer Module

Latent transfer model is a key part of the whole frequency transfer model that generates latent codes containing high frequency components information. The structure of latent transfer module is illustrated in Fig. 4. Recent researches [23] and experiments prove it would be difficult for multilayer perceptron networks to learn high frequency functions. Therefore, latent transfer module is designed to be a combination of Dense layers and LSTM layers. We employ function f_t to represent latent transfer module which realize high frequency components generation through mapping $f_t(\mathbf{c}_0) = \mathbf{c}$. Considering encoder and decoder share symmetrical structures, latent transfer module only change values but not change the size of latent codes.

As for generation tasks, the mean squared error (MSE) loss function is normally used in order to lead the model to generate more accurate results. In our model, we also made use of MSE loss (Eq. 1) to guarantee generation fields would be close to ground truth.

$$L_{mse} = MSE(f_d(f_t(f_e(\mathbf{v}_0))) - \mathbf{v}) \tag{1}$$

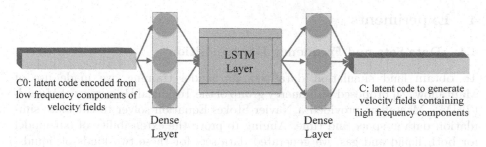

CO: latent code encoded from low frequency components of velocity fields

C: latent code to generate velocity fields containing high frequency components

Dense Layer   Dense Layer

Fig. 4. Detailed architecture of latent transfer module. Latent transfer module takes latent codes encoded from low frequency components as inputs and generates latent codes for decoder to reconstruct complete velocity fields containing high frequency components.

With MSE loss function frequency transfer model would generate velocity field distribution that would be close to ground truth on average. As for fluid simulation data, it would be normal for velocity fields or density fields to form uneven distributions. In addition, information of high frequency components doesn't totally exist in lower frequency components. Therefore it is impossible to obtain a one-to-one mapping between low and high frequency components. Taking that into account, we add another freedom to adjust the frequency transfer model's tendency for generating velocity fields close to ground truth equally in the whole field or generating velocity fields close to ground truth, especially in extreme values. Weight loss function (Eq. 2) is proposed to improve weights in positions that have larger values in ground truth by weight function $\omega_{\mathbf{v}}$ which is positively correlated to the absolute value of velocity. The addition of weight loss would lead the frequency transfer model to generate velocity fields more accurately in positions of extreme values. Since the calculation of weight loss function needs the value of ground truth, it is only available in training.

$$L_{weight} = MSE((f_d(f_t(f_e(\mathbf{v_0}))) - \mathbf{v})\omega_{\mathbf{v}}) \tag{2}$$

To take advantage of both MSE loss function and weight loss function, we provide another freedom through a hyperparameter α to realize weighted addition. So the minimization problem solved in the frequency transfer model has the form:

$$min_{\theta_e,\theta_t,\theta_d}(\alpha L_{mse} + (1 - \alpha)L_{weight}) \tag{3}$$

Here, $\theta_e, \theta_t, \theta_d$ denote parameters in encoder, latent transfer module and decoder. The larger value of α represents a more obvious tendency to generating results with equal weights in the whole velocity fields. In contrast, smaller values would lead the model to obtain results closer to velocity fields in positions of extreme values.

4   Experiments

4.1   Data Sets and Frequency Decomposition

To obtain fluid simulation data sets for model training, we made use of
Mantaflow [24] proposed by Thuerey group of the Technical University of Munich
(TUM). Mantaflow provided a Navier-Stokes Equation solver to calculate sim-
ulation data in space and time. Aiming to prove the extensibility of our model
for both liquid and gas, we generated data sets for these two kinds of liquids.
Detailed information of data sets are listed in Table 1.

Table 1. Data sets generated from Mantaflow used in frequency transfer model training. As for liquid simulation, 50 time steps were skipped to obtain stable simulation
results.

Data type	gas64	gas128	liquid64	liquid128
Scenes	1000	1000	1000	1000
Time steps skipped	0	0	50	50
Time steps	100	100	100	100
Resolution	64	128	64	128

To obtain different frequency components of velocity fields, what should be
done first is to decompose velocity fields into low and high frequency components. There exists many frequency decomposition such as fast fourier transform
(FFT), wavelet transform and Empirical Mode Decomposition (EMD) [25,26].
EMD methods decompose the signal into a small number of intrinsic mode
functions (IMFS) Compared with FFT and wavelet transforms, EMD methods
show higher computation complexity. Considering that grid resolution needs to
be maintained during the decomposition and reconstruction process, we finally
choose FTT to decompose training data. Figure 5 shows an example of velocity
field decomposition through FFT.

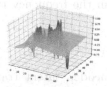 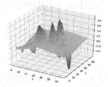

Fig. 5. Decomposition examples of velocity fields in fluid simulation through FFT.
Original velocity fields are shown on the left, low frequency components are shown on
the right correspondingly.

4.2 Scaling Method and Model Convergence

Fluid simulation shows great diversity in data distribution and value size, frequency transfer model cannot always be trained appropriately. For example, sometimes it would be hard for the model to deal with training data of relatively smaller values. To deal with such situations, we proposed a scaling method to improve the model's training results with linear transformations applied to the input data to guarantee their value is suitable for training. The scaling method avoids neural networks to deal with extremely small gradients and improve calculation accuracy in model training. Comparison in frequency transfer model training with and without scaling method is displayed in Fig. 6. Apparently, the scaling method takes significant effects and leads to improvement in both visual effects and numerical error. Similar convergence to the example shown in Fig. 7 could be achieved for both liquid and gas training data with appropriate scaling methods.

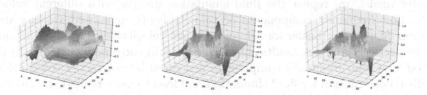

Fig. 6. Comparison of frequency transfer model's output between data with and without scaling method. Results without scaling method are shown on the left, results with scaling method is shown are the middle. Ground truth is shown on the right.

5 Results

The frequency transfer model is applied to data sets listed in Table 1 to prove its validity. Results generated from the model trained with MSE loss based on liquid data and gas data are shown in Fig. 8. As our model is self-adaptive for data resolution, it can be applied to data sets with different resolutions. Results generated from the model trained with simulation data of higher resolution could

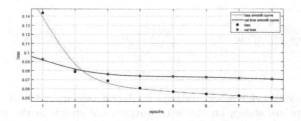

Fig. 7. Loss and validation loss in the frequency transfer model's training process.

486   J. Zhu et al.

be found in Fig. 9, including both liquid and gas. Generation results show that the frequency transfer model trained with MSE loss could reconstruct velocity fields similar to ground truth with high frequency components addition. More accurate evaluation with PSNR value is shown in Table 2. It is shown that our model could reach a PSNR value higher than 30 for all of the four data sets.

Table 2. Evaluations for our model's outputs with data sets of different kind of fluid and resolution. ($\alpha = 0.5$)

PSNR	64×64	128×128
Liquid	34.18	34.81
Gas	35.58	31.36

To further evaluate high frequency components generated by our frequency transfer model, we repeat the fluid simulation process with different velocity fields. Low frequency components of velocity fields, generated velocity fields with our frequency transfer model, and original velocity fields are used to simulate respectively and get results shown in Fig. 10 in correspondence. It's further proved that high frequency components generated by our model could achieve details reconstruction for fluid simulation and lead to more realistic results compared with those in lack of high frequency components.

Besides, we trained models with different values of α to verify our model's capability to generate velocity fields with different ratios of low frequency and high frequency components. Results are shown in Fig. 11. Compared with results generated with MSE loss, it's obvious that with a smaller value of α, the frequency transfer model performs better in extreme values reconstruction. With different values of α, the ratio of low frequency and high frequency components becomes controllable.

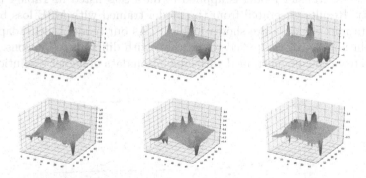

Fig. 8. Frequency transfer model outputs for liquid velocity fields of resolution 64×64. Model inputs are shown on the left. Outputs are shown in the middle. Ground truth is shown on the right. Figures in two rows show velocity fields of liquid and gas respectively.

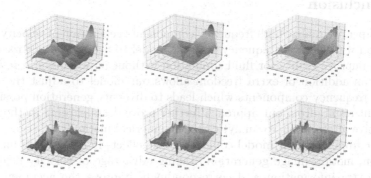

Fig. 9. Frequency transfer model outputs for velocity fields of resolution 128 × 128. Model inputs are shown on the left. Outputs are shown in the middle. Ground truth is shown on the right. Figures in two rows show velocity fields of liquid and gas respectively.

Fig. 10. Comparison of density fields generated with different velocity fields used in the simulation. Low frequency components of velocity fields (left), generated velocity fields from our model (middle) and ground truth (right) are displayed correspondingly.

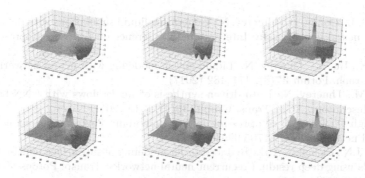

Fig. 11. Comparison of frequency transfer model outputs trained with different α. In the upper row, model input, model output with MSE loss, and ground truth are displayed in order. In the lower row, model output with alpha values 0.3, 0.5, and 0.7 are displayed from left to right.

6 Conclusion

In this paper, we realize high frequency components generation of velocity in fluid simulation with a novel frequency transfer model to achieve details reconstruction and improve reality for fluid simulation without improving grid resolution. Besides, an addition of extra freedom allows our model to adjust the ratio of different frequency components which leads to diversity generation possibilities. Significant results from our approach further prove deep learning methods to be competitive alternatives to analytical and numerical methods.

Apart from that, our model could also take effects in other fields like super-resolution, motion image generation. Taking advantage of velocity fields could provide extra information and correspondingly improve the accuracy of generation results and visual effects. Future researches will be concentrated on more widely applications in related fields and improving transfer accuracy and rationality.

References

1. Rumelhart, D.E., Hinton, G.E., Williams, R.J.: Learning representations by back-propagating errors. Nature **323**, 533–536 (1986)
2. Luan, F., Paris, S., Shechtman, E., Bala, K.: Deep photo style transfer. In: Proceedings of the IEEE Conference on Computer Vision and Pattern Recognition, pp. 4990–4998 (2017)
3. Flynn, J., Neulander, I., Philbin, J., Snavely, N.: DeepStereo: learning to predict new views from the world's imagery. In: Proceedings of the IEEE Conference on Computer Vision and Pattern Recognition, pp. 5515–5524 (2016)
4. Lai, W.S., Huang, J.B., Ahuja, N., Yang, M.H.: Deep Laplacian pyramid networks for fast and accurate super-resolution. In: Proceedings of the IEEE Conference on Computer Vision and Pattern Recognition, pp. 624–632 (2017)
5. Thuerey, N., Weißenow, K., Prantl, L., Hu, X.Y.: Deep learning methods for Reynolds-averaged Navier-Stokes simulations of airfoil flows. AIAA J. **58**(4), 25–36 (2019)
6. Prantl, L., Bonev, B., Thuerey, N.: Generating liquid simulations with deformation-aware neural networks. In: International Conference on Learning Representations (2017)
7. Um, K., Hu, X., Thuerey, N.: Liquid splash modeling with neural networks. Comput. Graph. Forum **37**(8), 171–182 (2017)
8. Chu, M., Thuerey, N.: Data-driven synthesis of smoke flows with CNN-based feature descriptors. ACM Trans. Graph. **36**(4), 1–14 (2017)
9. Hennigh O.: Lat-net: compressing lattice Boltzmann flow simulations using deep neural networks. arXiv:1705.09036 (2017)
10. Kani, J.N., Elsheikh, A.H.: Reduced-order modeling of subsurface multi-phase flow models using deep residual recurrent neural networks. Transp. Porous Media **126**, 713–741 (2019)
11. Kim, B., Azevedo, V.C., Thuerey, N., Kim, T., Gross, M., Solenthaler, B.: Deep fluids: a generative network for parameterized fluid simulations. Comput. Graph. Forum **38**(2), 59–70 (2019)
12. Morton, J., Witherden, F.D., Jameson, A., Kochenderfer, M.J.: Deep dynamical modeling and control of unsteady fluid flows. In: Advances in Neural Information Processing Systems 31 (2018)

13. Lusch, B., Kutz, J.N., Brunton, S.L.: Deep learning for universal linear embeddings of nonlinear dynamics. Nat. Commun. **9**, 1–10 (2018). Article no. 4950
14. Wiewel, S., Becher, M., Thuerey, N.: Latent-space physics: towards learning the temporal evolution of fluid flow. Comput. Graph. Forum **38**(2), 71–82 (2018)
15. Wiewel, S., Kim, B., Azevedo, V.C., Solenthaler, B., Thuerey, N.: Latent space subdivision: stable and controllable time predictions for fluid flow. Comput. Graph. Forum **39**, 15–25 (2020)
16. Tompson, J., Schlachter, K., Sprechmann, P., Perlin, K.: Accelerating Eulerian fluid simulation with convolutional networks. In: Proceedings of the 34th International Conference on Machine Learning 70, pp. 3424–3433 (2017)
17. Ummenhofer, B., Prantl, L., Thuerey, N., Koltun, V.: Lagrangian fluid simulation with continuous convolutions. In: International Conference on Learning Representations (2020)
18. Prantl, L., Chentanez, N., Jeschke, S., Thuerey, N.: Tranquil clouds: neural networks for learning temporally coherent features in point clouds. arXiv:1907.05279 (2020)
19. Rasp, S., Ducbon, P.D., Scher, S., Weyn, J.A., Mouatadid, S., Thuerey, N.: WeatherBench: a benchmark data set for data-driven weather forecasting. J. Adv. Model. Earth Syst. **12**(11), e2020MS002203 (2020)
20. Goodfellow, I.J., et al.: Generative adversarial networks. In: Advances in Neural Information Processing Systems, vol. 3, pp. 2672–2680 (2014)
21. Xie, Y., Franz, E., Chu, M., Thuerey, N.: TempoGAN: a temporally coherent, volumetric GAN for super-resolution fluid flow. ACM Trans. Graph. **37**(4CD), 1–14 (2018)
22. Werhahn, M., Xie, Y., Chu, M., Thuerey, N.: A multi-pass GAN for fluid flow super-resolution. In: Proceedings of the ACM on Computer Graphics and Interactive Techniques, vol. 2, no. 2 (2019)
23. Tancik, M., et al.: Fourier features let networks learn high frequency functions in low dimensional domains. arXiv:2006.10739 (2020)
24. Thuerey, N., Pfaff, T.: MantaFlow (2018). http://mantaflow.com
25. Huang, N.E., et al.: The empirical mode decomposition and the Hilbert spectrum for nonlinear and non-stationary time series analysis. Proc. Math. Phys. Eng. Sci. **454**(1971), 903–995 (1998)
26. Gao, Y., Li, C.F., Ren, B., Hu, S.M.: View-dependent multiscale fluid simulation. IEEE Trans. Visual Comput. Graph. **19**(2), 178–188 (2012)

Low Crosstalk Multi-view 3D Display Based on Parallax Barrier with Dimmed Subpixel

Xueling Li and Yuanqing Wang[✉]

School of Electronic Science and Engineering, Nanjing University, No. 163 Xianlin Avenue,
Qixia District, Nanjing 210023, China
yqwang@nju.edu.cn

Abstract. Multi-view three-dimentional display system stands out for its easy realization and flexible viewing effect among all kinds of autostereoscopic display techniques. However, traditional multi-view display system suffers from severe crosstalk. Here a five-view display system with dimmed subpixel is presented to reduce crosstalk, and at the same time ensures fine viewing experience. The dimmed subpixel is arranged interlocked to make sure that the full color formation is intact and also to balance the distribution of the exit pupil. The crosstalk is reduced from 16% to 12.5%. There are three synthetic modes. Incorporated with the eye tracking device, the main viewer is able to get the best viewing experience by changing the image synthetic mode according to the viewer's position.

Keywords: Autostereoscopic display · Multi-view · Low crosstalk

1 Introduction

Autostereoscopic display technique holds great advantages over traditional 2-dimentional (2D) display, for its authentic viewing experience and practical application in many fields [1–14]. It is generally believed that 3-dimentional (3D) display is the ultimate visual media. There are several categories of 3D display technique, such as binocular parallax display [1–10], integral display [11], light field display [12, 13] and volumetric display [14]. Among the mentioned techniques, integral imaging, volumetric imaging and light field display are capable of providing both vertical and horizontal parallax. However, they suffer from more than one of the disadvantages below: intricate and sophisticated structure, large volume and computational complexity. Hence, binocular parallax display stands out among them, for its low cost and easy assembly.

Binocular parallax display system usually contains a parallax barrier or a lenticular lens array. Between these two optical components, parallax barrier based autostereoscopic display system is easier to be embodied with lower cost than lenticular lens based display system, even though it suffers from some degree of brightness loss [3–5]. Parallax barrier is employed to form 3D images in the spatial domain. In order to realize fine motion parallax and large viewing angle, multiple viewing zones are formed in the viewing plane, and therefore, the resolution of each viewing zone is reduced. Furthermore, the vertical and horizontal resolution is unbalanced due to the increase of viewing

Y. Peng et al. (Eds.): ICIG 2021, LNCS 12890, pp. 490–500, 2021.
https://doi.org/10.1007/978-3-030-87361-5_40

zones. Researches are conducted by many scholars to balance the resolution [3], but it either requires high refreshing rate of liquid crystal (LC) panel, or sacrifices the brightness of the system. Besides that, the crosstalk of parallax barrier based 3D display is inevitable. Because the vertical columns of subpixels have the same basic color [15], slanted parallax barrier is used to make up a pixel, which brings about crosstalk between adjacent viewing zones. In [3], a multi-view 3D display based on dual parallax barriers has the crosstalk of about 16%. Last but not least, the viewing positions are fixed, so in some particular areas, the viewer either gets pseudostereoscopy or completely blurred images.

To overcome the problems above as much as possible, we propose a five-view autostereoscopic display system based on parallax barrier with a unique subpixel adjustment approach. The system consists of a direct backlight, a liquid crystal display (LCD) panel, a parallax barrier, an image processing module, as well as an eye tracking device. The image processing module fuses the input five-view image. Then, the parallax barrier project the image into the viewing area that forms viewing zones. There are 3 synthetic modes for our system. The eye tracking device is able to detect the main viewer's eye position, and sends the signal to the image processing module to change the synthetic mode, so that the main viewer can perceive the best viewing experience. To verify our idea, a prototype is set up and experiments are carried out to evaluate the performances. For each viewing zone, the system displays image resolution of 1152*1440. Also a system of traditional multi-view display without dimmed subpixel is set up for comparison. Average crosstalk for each viewing zone is about 12.5% in the proposed method, obviously lower than 16% of traditional method.

2 Structure and Principle

2.1 Structure Configuration

Figure 1 illustrates the major structure of the proposed multi-view system. In Fig. 1, the LCD provides synthetic images input from the image processing module. Synthetic image is modulated by the slanted parallax barrier and forms viewing zones in the viewing plane. The distribution of the viewing zones can be clearly seen in Fig. 1, where only horizontal distribution is considered. Among the viewing zones, parallax is continuous between neighboring zones, except the 5th viewing zone and the 1th viewing zone.

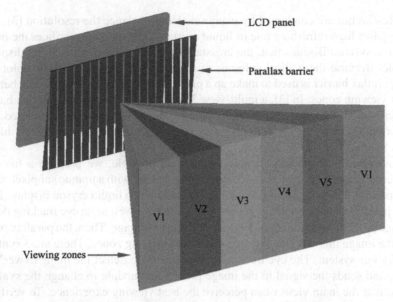

Fig. 1. The optical structure of the proposed system.

2.2 Resolution

The proposed method of multi-view synthetic image is shown in Fig. 2. Every two adjacent subpixels contribute to one viewing zone. In order to realize full color, red, green and blue subpixels are required, as shown in Fig. 2. The black dashed rectangular circles out one sub-cycle that is composed of 10 columns × 3 rows subpixels. A complete cycle consists 30 columns × 30 rows, which is 30 sub-cycles. For different sub-cycles, the full color composition is slightly different, but the pattern is similar. According to the full color composition, the resolution of each viewing zone can be determined. Suppose the overall resolution of the display panel is M (horizontal) × N (vertical). For each viewing zone, the resolution m (horizontal) × n (vertical) can be determined by Eq. (1):

$$\begin{cases} m = \frac{M \times 3}{10} = \frac{3M}{10} \\ n = \frac{2N}{3} \end{cases} \qquad (1)$$

Fig. 2. Subpixel arrangement of the multi-view system.

The proportion of horizontal and vertical resolution is $m : n = 9M : 20N$.

2.3 Parameter Calculation

To form viewing zones in the specific area, the period of the parallax barrier needs to be determined. As shown in Fig. 3, d is the distance between the LCD panel and the parallax barrier, p is the period of the parallax barrier, t is the width of a subpixel, L is the viewing distance, and e is the width of one exit pupil. According to geometric optics, d and p can be determined by Eq. (2) and (3):

$$d = L * \frac{2t}{e} \tag{2}$$

$$p = \frac{L}{L+d} * 10t \tag{3}$$

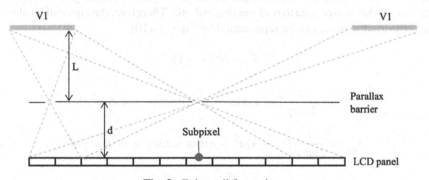

Fig. 3. Exit pupil formation.

2.4 Crosstalk Reduction

However, due to the characteristic of slanted parallax barrier, crosstalk between adjacent viewing zones is inevitable and rather huge, jeopardizing viewing experience. So, a new subpixel adjustment method is proposed, that can reduce the crosstalk significantly. The subpixel adjustment method is shown in Fig. 4. Take viewing zone 3 as an example. The image information that can be perceived by the viewer through slanted parallax barrier is demonstrated in Fig. 4(a). The yellow slanted dashed lines are the edges of the viewing zone. It is obvious that the image information for the respective viewing zone is contributed by the intended view image and the unintended view images, which cause crosstalk. The colored area between the dashed lines are the intended image information, and the gray areas are the unintended image information. The crosstalk evaluation based on area is represented by Eq. (4)–(6).

$$S_u = \frac{1}{2tan\gamma} \times [(a - 3t \times tan\gamma)^2 + a^2] \tag{4}$$

$$S_i = 6t^2 - S_u \tag{5}$$

$$CT_a = \frac{S_u}{S_i} \tag{6}$$

In Eq. (4), S_u is the calculated area of the unintended image information as shown in Fig. 4(a) ① and ②, t is the width of the subpixel, and normally the height of the subpixel is $3t$, γ is the angle of the slanted parallax barrier, a is the width of the intersection. In Eq. (5), S_i is the area of intended image information. In Eq. (6), CT_a is the crosstalk evaluation based on area. It is obvious that with the decrease of S_u, CT_a decreases as well, therefore the viewing experience is better.

Hence, to reduce crosstalk, it takes the effort either to increase the intended image area (or its light intensity), or to reduce the unintended image area (or its light intensity). Clearly, the easiest way to achieve that goal is by reducing the unintended image light intensity, as shown in Fig. 4(b). Supposing the light intensity of the unintended image is reduced to α ($\alpha \leq 1$) of the original light intensity. It equals to reducing the contribution of the unintended image area to α of the original one. Therefore, the crosstalk evaluation of the improved method can be represented by Eq. (7)–(10).

$$S' = 3t^2(\alpha + 1) \tag{7}$$

$$S'_{u1} = \frac{1}{2tan\gamma}[(\alpha + 1)a^2 - 6ta \times tan\gamma + 9t^2tan^2\gamma] \tag{8}$$

$$S'_{u2} = \frac{1}{2tan\gamma}[(\alpha + 1)a^2 - \alpha(6ta \times tan\gamma - 9t^2tan^2\gamma)] \tag{9}$$

$$CT'_a = \frac{S'_{u1}}{S' - S'_{u1}} \text{ or } \frac{S'_{u2}}{S' - S'_{u2}} \tag{10}$$

In Eq. (7)–(10), S' is the equivalent adjusted total image area, S'_{u1} and S'_{u2} are the equivalent unintended image area of two different scenarios, CT'_a is the crosstalk evaluation based on area. S'_{u1} and S'_{u2} represent that area ① or area ② is the dimmed subpixel respectively. Similarly, with the decrease of α, the crosstalk decreases as well, when other parameters are set. The dimmed subpixel is arranged interlocked for two purposes. The first is to make sure the full color formation is intact. The second purpose is to balance the distribution of the exit pupil, so that the light distribution of exit pupil is symmetrical.

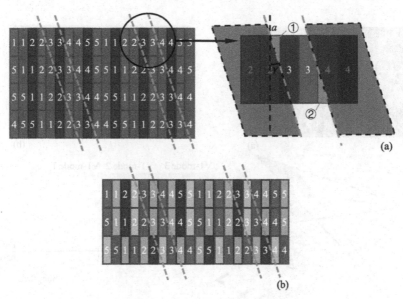

Fig. 4. Crosstalk evaluation based on area. (a) Traditional subpixel arrangement. (b) Subpixel adjustment through interlocked dimmed subpixel to reduce crosstalk.

2.5 Changeable Synthetic Mode

There are three synthetic modes in our system. Figure 4(a) illustrated one of the synthetic modes. The corresponding viewing zone distribution is shown in Fig. 5(c). When the viewer's eyebrow center is located at the black check mark, he/she gets correct image; however, when the viewer's eyebrow center is located at the red cross, he/she gets either completely blurred image or pseudostereoscopic image. To overcome this problem, the synthetic mode is supposed to change according to the viewer's position. Another synthetic mode is shown in Fig. 5(a), which is able to overcome the problem of blurry. There is a distance of $e/2$ between the same viewing zone of the first and the second modes, as shown in Fig. 5(d). Figure 5(b) is the third synthetic mode, that solves the problem of pseudostereoscopy, and that all viewing zones are moved e based on the first synthetic mode, as shown in Fig. 5(d). In general, when there is only one viewer, the synthetic image can be adjusted according to the position of the viewer acquired by the eye tracking device, so that he/she can perceive the best viewing experience. When there are multiple viewers, the synthetic mode is determined by the main viewer, who is the closest to the middle of the viewing plane.

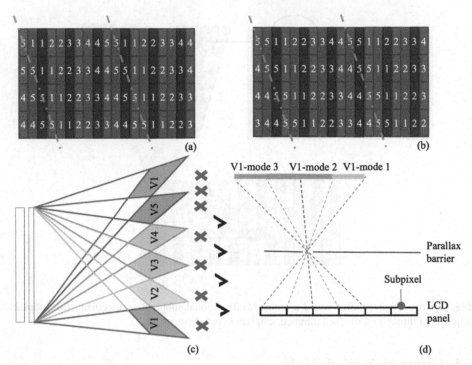

Fig. 5. Changeable synthetic mode. (a) The second mode of pixel arrangement. (b) The third mode of pixel arrangement. (c) Viewing zone distribution. (d) Exit pupil movement of the three modes.

3   Experiments and Results

The proposed idea is a 5-view autostereoscopic display system, that adopts special subpixel adjustment method to reduce crosstalk, and can also provide better viewing experience by three modes of synthetic image. To evaluate our idea, a prototype is set up, and a series of experiments are carried out.

The prototype employs a 27 inches LCD panel, and the model information of the LCD is summarized in Table 1.

Table 1. Characteristic of the display panel

Screen diagonal	685.65mm (27.0″)	Pixel H*V	1920(*3) *1080
Active area	597.6(H)*336.15(V)mm	Contrast ratio	1000(Typ.)
Response time	5ms (Typ. on/off)	Display mode	TN mode, normally white

Figure 6(a) shows the outlook of the prototype. The width of one subpixel is 0.0518mm, and according to Eq. (2) and (3), the period of the parallax barrier is 0.5157mm, which is shown in Fig. 6(b). The parallax barrier has the same slant angle as

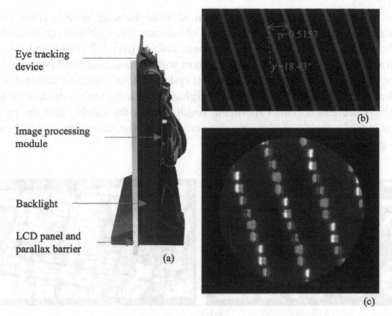

Fig. 6. Information about the prototype. (a) Outlook of the prototype. (b) Parallax barrier under the microscope. (c) Subpixel arrangement under the microscope.

the subpixel arrangement illustrated in Fig. 6(c), which is the subpixel arrangement of one viewing zone displaying pure white information. At the same time, the brightness of the subpixel next to another perspective is dimmed, as in $\alpha = 0.65$. The dimmed subpixel is changed alternately row by row, to make sure the exit pupil distribution is symmetrical, instead of leaning to one direction. When the viewing distance is 900 mm, the displaying effect of the five viewing zones is shown in Fig. 7.

At the best viewing distance, when the viewer/camera moves along the horizontal plane, he/she/it perceives different image information, as illustrated from (a) to (e), and the parallax between adjacent viewing zones is continuous, except for V1 and V5. According to the previous analysis, the resolution of one perspective is 1152 * 1440.

Crosstalk is the most important parameter for autostereoscopic display. For the proposed 5-view system, the crosstalk can be calculated by Eq. (11).

$$CT_i = \frac{\sum_{j \neq i} I_j}{I_i} \tag{11}$$

In the equation, CT_i ($i = 1 \sim 5$) is the crosstalk for the ith viewing zone, I_i is the brightness intensity for the ith viewing zone. The crosstalk for the ith viewing zone is contributed by the image information leakage from all the other viewing zones. The brightness distribution of the five viewing zones is measured and recorded in Fig. 8. Figure 8(a) is the brightness distribution with dimmed subpixel, and Fig. 8(b) is the brightness distribution without dimmed subpixel. They are measured by displaying the corresponding view pure white image and the rest views pure black images. Pure white image has subpixel value 255 and dimmed subpixel value 165.75, in the case that $\alpha =$

0.65. As we can see, the distance between adjacent viewing zone is about 60 mm, which is the average interpupillary distance of humans. The minimum crosstalk for V3 is 11.3%, which is mainly caused by brightness leakage from V2, 0.047, and V4, 0.066. The average crosstalk for the proposed system with dimmed subpixel is about 12.5%, while the average crosstalk for the traditional system without dimmed subpixel is about 16%. Clearly, with dimmed subpixel, the brightness contribution to adjacent view zone is effectively decreased. This experiment result verifies the validity that the proposed system is indeed capable of reducing crosstalk, and at the same time, the 3D viewing effect is guaranteed.

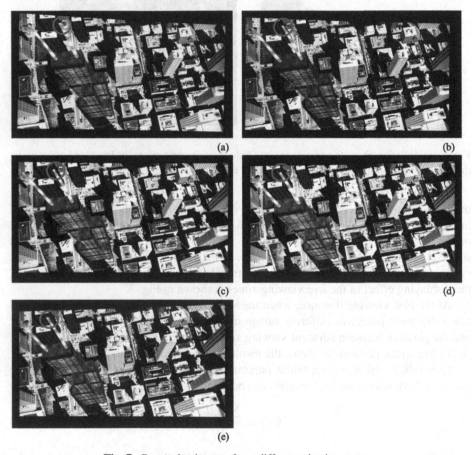

(a)

(b)

(c)

(d)

(e)

Fig. 7. Perceptive images from different viewing zones.

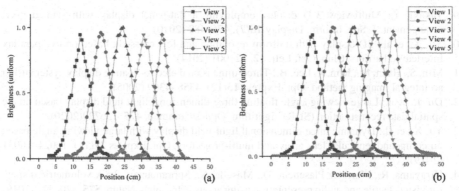

Fig. 8. Brightness distribution of the 5-view system. (a) Brightness distribution with dimmed subpixel. (b) Brightness distribution without dimmed subpixel.

4 Conclusion

In this paper, we propose a five-view autostereoscopic display system. Considering the traditional multi-view system suffers from severe crosstalk that deteriorate viewing experience, we adopted dimmed subpixel to reduce crosstalk. The dimmed subpixel is placed interlocked to balance the color and the distribution of exit pupil. Eye tracking device is able to detect the position of the main viewer, so that the synthetic mode of image can be adapted to provide the best viewing effect. Three synthetic modes are required in our system that can solve the problems of blurry and pseudostereoscopy. The average crosstalk of the improved system is 12.5%, lower than that of the traditional approach.

References

1. Luo, J., Wang, Q., Zhao, W., Li, D.: Autostereoscopic three-dimensional display based on two parallax barriers. Appl. Opt. **50**(18), 2911–2915 (2011)
2. Qi, L., Wang, Q., Luo, J., Zhao, W., Song, C.: An autostereoscopic 3D projection display based on a lenticular sheet and a parallax barrier. J. Disp. Technol. **8**(7), 397–400 (2012)
3. Lv, G., Wang, J., Zhao, W., Wang, Q.: Three-dimensional display based on dual parallax barriers with uniform resolution. Appl. Opt. **52**(24), 6011–6015 (2013)
4. Lv, G., Wang, Q., Wang, J., Zhao, W.: Multi-view 3D display with high brightness based on a parallax barrier. Chin. Opt. Lett. **11**(12), 121101 (2013)
5. Lv, G., Zhao, W., Wang, J., Wang, Q.: Shared pixel based parallax barrier 3D display with high brightness. Optik **125**(8), 1984–1986 (2014)
6. Lv, G., Wang, Q., Zhao, W., Wang, J.: 3D display based on parallax barrier with multiview zones. Appl. Opt. **53**(7), 1339–1342 (2014)
7. Ki-Hyuk, Y., Heongkyu, J., Hyunkyung, K., Inkyu, P., Sung-Kyu, K.: Diffraction effects incorporated design of a parallax barrier for a high-density multi-view autostereoscopic 3D display. Opt. Express **24**(4), 4057–4075 (2016)
8. Qi, L., Wang, Q., Luo, Y., Wang, A., Liang, D.: Autostereoscopic 3D projection display based on two lenticular sheets. Chin. Opt. Lett. **10**(1), 32–34 (2012)

9. Takaki, Y.: Multi-view 3-D display employing a flat-panel display with slanted pixel arrangement. J. Soc. Inform. Display **18**(7), 476–482 (2010)

10. Yu, X., et al.: 3D display with uniform resolution and low crosstalk based on two parallax interleaved barriers. Chin. Opt. Lett. **12**, 121001 (2014)

11. Min, S., Hahn, M., Kim, J., Lee, B.: Three-dimensional electro-floating display system using an integral imaging method. Opt. Express **13**(12), 4358–4369 (2005)

12. Du, J., et al.: Large viewing angle floating three-dimensional light field display based on the spatial data reconstruction (SDR) algorithm. Optics Commun. **475**, 126229(2020).

13. Yu, X., et al.: Dynamic three-dimensional light-field display with large viewing angle based on compound lenticular lens array and multi-projectors. Opt. Express **27**(11), 16024–16031 (2019)

14. Hirayama, R., Martinez Plasencia, D., Masuda, N., Subramanian, S.: A volumetric display for visual, tactile and audio presentation using acoustic trapping. Nature **575**, 320–323 (2019)

15. Lv, G., Wang, Q., Zhao, W., Wu, F.: Special subpixel arrangement-based 3D display with high horizontal resolution. Appl. Opt. **53**(31), 7337–7340 (2014)

DRLFNet: A Dense-Connection Residual Learning Neural Network for Light Field Super Resolution

Congrui Fu[1,3], Xin Ma[1], Yao Liu[1], Junhui Hou[2], and Hui Yuan[3(✉)]

[1] School of Information Science and Engineering, Shandong University, Jinan, China
[2] City University of Hong Kong, Hong Kong, Hong Kong
[3] School of Control Science and Engineering, Shandong University, Jinan, China
huiyuan@sdu.edu.cn

Abstract. Light field records both spatial and angular information of light rays. By using light field cameras, 3D scenes can be reconstructed easily for further virtual reality applications. Limited by the sensor size, there is a trade-off between the spatial and angular resolution. To address this problem, we propose a dense-connection residual learning neural network, namely DRLFNet, to super resolve light field images in spatial domain. The dense-connection residual learning is implemented based on the proposed dense-connection residual block (DResBlock) that is used to efficiently exploit the joint spatial and angular features and the hierarchical features in different layers. Experimental results demonstrate that the proposed method out-performs other state-of-the-art methods by a large margin in both visual and numerical evaluations.

Keywords: Light field images · Super-resolution · Dense-connection · Residual learning

1 Introduction

Light field (LF) imaging has attracted more and more attention in both industry and academia in recent years, especially with the emergence of commercial LF cameras [1] and the dedication in Virtual Reality (VR) [2]. Different from conventional cameras, the light field cameras can not only record the light intensity distribution, but also record the incident angle of the light rays, as shown in Fig. 1 [18]. That is to say the LF cameras can simultaneously capture the position and angle information of the light in the space. The light field image (LFI) can effectively improve the performance of some computer vision hotspot problems, such as image segmentation [3], depth estimation [4], 3D reconstruction,

This work was supported in part by the National Natural Science Foundation of China under Grants 62172259, the open project program of state key laboratory of virtual reality technology and systems, Beihang University, under Grant VRLAB2021A01, the Major Scientific and Technological Innovation Project of Shandong Province under Grant 2020CXGC010109, and the OPPO Research Fund.

© Springer Nature Switzerland AG 2021
Y. Peng et al. (Eds.): ICIG 2021, LNCS 12890, pp. 501–510, 2021.
https://doi.org/10.1007/978-3-030-87361-5_41

target recognition, and saliency detection [5]. Due to the limitation of sensor size, there is a trade-off between spatial resolution and angular resolution in LFIs. Therefore, LF super-resolution (SR) is a key technology for the extensive application of LF cameras. In this paper, we focus on the spatial SR of LFIs.

SR is to obtain the high resolution (HR) image from one or several low-resolution (LR) images. For LF image SR, the Bayesian SR restoration framework is commonly adopted, with Lambertian and textual prior assumptions, e.g., the Gaussian mixture model [6] and the variational models [7,8]. Recently, with the help of convolutional neural networks (CNN), great achievements have been achieved in SR. Dong et al. [9] first proposed an end-to-end CNN that is called as SRCNN for single image super resolution (SISR). Based on the framework of SRCNN, Kim et al. [10] proposed a very deep super resolution (VDSR) neural network in which residual learning and high learning rates were used to optimize the network for fast convergence. Lai et al. [11] proposed a neural network, namely LapSRN, that adopts the Laplacian pyramid to progressively reconstruct the sub-band residuals of HR images. For more recent work about SISR, refer to [12].

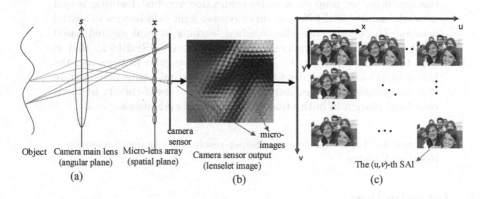

Fig. 1. Light field imaging. (a) Schematic structure of a microlens-based LF camera; (b) The camera sensor output image that is lenslet image; (c) sub-aperture images (SAIs).

The SISR methods can be directly used for LFIs, but the inherent characteristics of LFIs are ignored. For example, the neighboring SAIs are also helpful for the SR of the current SAI. For LFIs, Yoon et al. [13] first proposed a CNN-based SR framework, namely LFCNN. The network concatenated the spatial SR network and the angular SR network to enhance the spatial and angular resolution simultaneously. In its successor [14], the authors shared some portions of the convolutions in angular SR network to reduce the number of parameters. Gul et al. [15] proposed a spatial and angular resolution enhancement network with two separate CNNs. The network was applied directly on the lenslet images of LF, rather than the SAIs. Wang et al. [16] proposed a multi-scale fusion scheme to accumulate contextual information from multiple scales using bidirectional recurrent CNN for LF spatial SR, namely LFNet. Farrugia et al. [17] used low-rank prior and deep CNN to perform spatial SR for LFIs. Yeung et al. [18] proposed a spatial-angular separable (SAS) convolution module to efficiently extract and exploit spatial and angular features for LF spatial SR. Zhang et al. [29] proposed a learning-based method using residual convolutional networks in which the inherent structure information of LFIs is explored by different network branches, namely resLF. Jin et al. [30] proposed a novel learning-based LF spatial SR framework LFSSR which explored the complementary information among views by combinatorial geometry embedding and training over a structure-aware loss function.

To improve the performance of LF spatial SR, we propose a dense-connection residual learning CNN based on the SAS convolution block [18], namely DRLFNet. In the proposed method, we treat the LFI spatial SR problem as the combination of upsampling and quality enhancement. The proposed network consists four modules: simple upsampling, shallow feature extraction, deep feature extraction and reconstruction. To extract the deep feature efficiently, we propose a dense-connection residual block (DResBlock) as the basis.

The remainder of this paper is organized as follows. The principle of LF imaging and representation is briefly introduced in Sect. 2. Then, the proposed network structure is described in detail in Sect. 3. Experimental results and conclusions are presented in Sect. 4 and 5, respectively.

2   Light Field Imaging and Representation

2.1   LF Imaging

LF imaging is one of the most representative theories in the field of computational photography. There are three ways of acquiring light field, i.e., camera array [19], LF camera based on encoding mask [20] and LF camera based on microlens array [2,21]. At present, the most commonly used method is to capture the LF by the microlens array-based LF camera, e.g. Lytro [21] and RayTrix [2]. Compared to traditional cameras, the LF camera includes an additional microlens array in front of the camera main lens to capture the light coming from different directions as shown in Fig. 1(a). The initial output of the camera sensor is called as lenslet image, as shown as Fig. 1(b). The lenslet image is composed by a lot of macro images that are further composed by a few pixels. Each pixel in a macro image denotes a light ray coming from a certain direction. After rearranging, the pixels coming from the same direction are ordered together to generate an SAI, as shown in Fig. 1(c).

2.2   4D LF Representation

The two-plane parameterization model [22] is usually adopted to represent a LF, as shown in Fig. 2, in which a light ray $L_F(x, y, u, v)$ is determined by its interactions with the two parallel planes uv (for angular dimensions) and xy (for spatial dimensions). In this paper, we use (H, W, M, N) to represent the resolution of the four dimensions, i.e., the spatial super resolution is $H \times W$ and the angular resolution is $M \times N$.

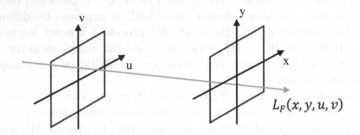

Fig. 2. Two-plane parameterization model for LF representation.

3   Proposed Method

3.1   Overview

Given a low resolution 4D LF image $LF^{lr}(x, y, u, v)$ with a resolution of (H, W, M, N), the goal of LFSR is to reconstruct its high-resolution counterpart $LF^{hr}(x, y, u, v)$ with the resolution of $(\alpha H, \alpha W, \beta M, \beta N)$,

$$LF^{lr}(x, y, u, v) \xrightarrow{LFSR} LF^{hr}(x, y, u, v), \tag{1}$$

where α and β are the upsampling factors for spatial and angular dimensions, respectively. Because only the LF spatial SR is focused on in this paper, we have $\alpha > 1, \beta = 1$.

As shown in Fig. 3, the proposed DRLFNet includes four modules: simple upsampling, shallow feature extraction, deep feature extraction and reconstruction.

(a) *Simple upsampling:* this module is to use a simple interpolation filter to increase the resolution. In the proposed method, we adopt the bicubic filter for its low complexity and performance.
(b) *Shallow feature extraction:* this module consists of a 2D spatial convolutional layer and a Leaky rectified linear unit (Leaky ReLU). The input LFI $LF_0 \in \mathbb{R}^{\alpha H \times \alpha W \times M \times N}$ is non-linearly transformed into the feature $F_0 \in \mathbb{R}^{\alpha H \times \alpha W \times K \times M \times N}$, where K is the number of 2D spatial filters.
(c) *Deep feature extraction:* in this module, the joint spatial and angular features are extracted efficiently by the SAS block and cascaded hierarchically by dense-connection to extract sophisticated features for further reconstruction. Detailed description of this module will be given in *part B* of this section.

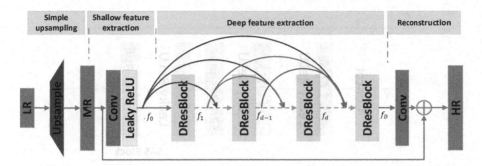

Fig. 3. Proposed DRLFNet network structure. The network consists four main modules: simple upsampling, shallow feature extraction, deep feature extraction and reconstruction.

(d) *Reconstruction:* the goal of this module is to reconstruct the super resolved LFIs. First the residual features extracted from the previous module are integrated by a 2D convolution layer to learning the high frequency detail of the HR LFI. Then, the input LF_0 is used as a low frequency compensation to finally reconstruct the HR LFI.

Given the reconstructed HR LFI $\hat{Y}$ and the original HR as Y, the loss function of proposed network is defined as

$$\mathrm{loss}(Y, \hat{Y}) = \sqrt{(\hat{Y} - Y)^2 + \varepsilon^2}, \tag{2}$$

where $\mathcal{E}$ is set to 10^{-3}.

3.2 Deep Feature Extraction

The deep feature extraction module consists of N DResBlocks, as shown in Fig. 3. The output of the n-th DResBlock can be represented as

$$\begin{aligned} f_n &= F_{\mathrm{DResBlock,n}} \left(\{f_{n-1}, f_{n-2}, \cdots, f_0\} \right) \\ &= F_{\mathrm{SAS}} \left(F_{\mathrm{reduce}} \left([f_{n-1}, f_{n-2}, \cdots, f_0] \right) \right) + f_{n-1}, \end{aligned} \tag{3}$$

where $n \in \{1, \cdots, N\}$, $F_{\mathrm{DResBlock,n}}$ denotes the feature extraction operator of the DResBlock, $\{f_{n-1}, f_{n-2}, \cdots, f_0\}$ and f_n are the input and the output feature of the DResBlock, $[:, :, :]$ denotes the concatenation operator, F_{reduce} denotes the 1×1 convolutional layer followed by a Leaky ReLU activation operation. F_{SAS} is the SAS convolution operator.

As shown in Fig. 4, the deep feature is extracted by the proposed DResBlock. In the DResBlock, we propose to use dense connection to concatenate the previous features so that the long-term features can be reserved hierarchically. The 1×1 convolutional layer with Leaky ReLU is used to reduce the dimension of the extracted features to ensure that the number of features fed into the SAS block

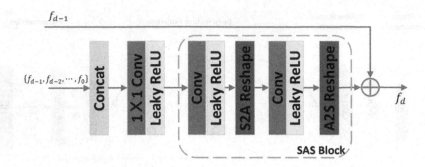

Fig. 4. The structure of the proposed DResBlock.

is the same in each DResBlock. The SAS block in which alternative angular and spatial 2D convolutions are performed is utilized to extract the joint spatial and angular feature efficiently [18].

4 Experimental Results and Analyses

4.1 Datasets and Training

We adopted two public real-world LFIs datasets, i.e., Stanford Lytro Light Field Archive [23] and the LF image data set created by Kalantar [24], for train and test. In the original LFIs (with angular resolution of 14×14), the boundary SAIs are usually dark and blurry or even black, therefore only the eight views in the middle region are used in the experiments. Accordingly, the resolution of original LFIs is $541 \times 376 \times 8 \times 8$.

From the datasets, we chose 130 LFIs for training and 57 LFIs for testing. The color space of LFIs was first transformed from RGB to YUV, and only the Y (luminance) channel was used for training. We first randomly cropped the LFIs into patches with resolution of $\alpha s \times \alpha s \times 8 \times 8$ to generate the ground truth labels. Then each patch was spatially burred and spatially down sampled to generate the network inputs with the resolution of $s \times s \times 8 \times 8$. In the experiments, we set s to be 16.

It should be noted that the proposed neural network was only used for luminance component. For the chrominance (i.e., U and V) components, only the bicubic interpolation were performed. Then the super resolved YUV components were inverse converted to the RGB color space. The average PSNR and SSIM of all the SAIs of a LFI is used to evaluate the SR performance.

The proposed model was implemented on MATLAB platform with MatConvNet toolbox [25] and trained by a graphical card with 1080Ti GPU. The convolution layers denoted by "Conv" in Fig. 3 and 4 are composed of 64 filters with the size of 3×3, except for the last convolution layer that only includes a single filter with the size of 3×1. The convolution layers denoted by "1×1 Conv" in Fig. 4 are composed of 64 filters with the size of 1×1. The MSRA initialization method [26] was used to initialize filter weights, and the biases were initialized to be zeros. The learning rate was initialized as $3e - 6$ with a dropping factor of 0.5 for every four hundred iterations.

4.2 Effect of the Number of DResBlocks

The proposed DResBlock is the most important basis in the proposed network. To verify the performance of the DResBlock, we experimentally investigated the influence of the number of DResBlocks, as shown in Table 1. We can see that the reconstructed quality increases with the number of DResBlocks. But more DResBlocks will expend more computational cost. To balance the computational complexity and the performance, we used 7 DResBlocks for further comparison.

Table 1. Influence of the number of DResBlocks.

Scale	Metric	Number of DResBlocks		
		3	5	7
$\alpha = 2$	PSNR(dB)	39.81	40.37	**40.63**
	SSIM	0.974	0.977	**0.978**
$\alpha = 3$	PSNR(dB)	36.44	36.96	**37.09**
	SSIM	0.948	0.951	**0.959**

4.3 Compared with State-of-the-art Methods

To verify the superiority of the proposed neural network, the single-image based methods, e.g., bicubic interpolation, VDSR [10] and LapSRN [11], and the LFI spatial SR methods, e.g. graph optimization based (GO) [27] method, linear subspace projection-based (LSP) [28] method and the CNN-based methods [14,18,29] (denoted as LFCNN, SAS and resLF, respectively), were used for comparison. Although the LFCNN is able to super-resolve LFIs in both spatial and angular dimensions, we only compared its spatial SR results. From Table 2, we can see that the proposed method performs the best in both PSNR and SSIM. Compared to the state-of-the-art SAS [18], an average 0.26 dB PSNR gain and 0.001 SSIM increment can be achieved by the proposed method on scale 2.

Figure 5 shows the visual comparison of the reconstructed LFIs. We can see that the proposed method is better in edges, which are more faithful to the ground truth.

Table 2. PSNR and SSIM comparisons between the proposed method and the State-of-the-art Method.

Scale	Metric	Bicubic	VDSR [10]	LapSRN [11]	GO [27]	LSP [28]	LFCNN [14]	resLF [29]	SAS [18]	Our
$\alpha = 2$	PSNR(dB)	34.63	36.78	36.67	35.52	34.18	35.51	38.76	40.37	**40.63**
	SSIM	0.935	0.955	0.953	0.944	0.927	0.945	0.956	0.977	**0.978**
$\alpha = 3$	PSNR(dB)	31.23	32.98	32.84	31.97	31.18	32.51	35.87	37.00	**37.09**
	SSIM	0.868	0.900	0.897	0.887	0.847	0.882	0.939	0.955	**0.959**

Fig. 5. Visual comparison of different methods for spatial super resolution. The top is 2×spatial super resolution. The bottom is 3×spatial super resolution. The super-resolved images are shown, where the corresponding PSNR and SSIM values are illustrated below. The zoom-in of the framed patches are provided. Zoom in the figure for better viewing.

5   Conclusion

We treat the LF spatial SR problem as a combination of naive upsampling and sophisticated quality enhancement, and proposed a dense-connection residual learning neural network for the LF spatial SR by fully exploiting the hierarchical features in layers and the joint spatial and angular features in neighboring SAIs. The proposed neural network is composed of four modules, i.e., simple upsampling, shallow feature extraction, deep feature extraction and reconstruction. To extract the deep features efficiently, the DResBlock was proposed based on the SAS block. Experimental results show that the proposed neural network is effective.

References

1. Ng, R., Levoy, M., Bredif, M., Duval, G., Horowitz, M., Hanrahan, P.: Light field photography with a hand-held plenoptic camera. Comput. Sci. Tech. Rep. Stanford Univ. **2**(11), 1–11 (2005)
2. https://www.raytrix.de/
3. Xu, Y., Nagahara, H., Shimada, A., Taniguchi, R.: TransCut2: transparent object segmentation from a light-field image. IEEE Trans. Comput. Imaging **5**(3), 465–477 (2019)
4. Zhang, S., Sheng, H., Li, C., Zhang, J., Xiong, Z.: Robust depth estimation for light field via spinning parallelogram operator. Comput. Vis. Image Underst. **145**, 148–159 (2016)
5. Li, N., Ye, J., Ji, Y., Ling, H., Yu, J.: Saliency detection on light field. IEEE Trans. Pattern Anal. Mach. Intell. **39**(8), 1605–1616 (2017)
6. Mitra, K., Veeraraghavan, A.: Light field denoising, light field superresolution and stereo camera based refocussing using a GMM light field patch prior. In: Proceedings of the IEEE Conference on Computer Vision and Pattern Recognition Workshops, pp. 22–28 (2012)
7. Sven, W., Goldluecke, B.: Spatial and angular variational super-resolution of 4D light fields. In: Proceedings of the 12th European Conference on Computer Vision (2012)
8. Zhou, S., Yan, Y., Su, L., Ding, X., Wang, J.: Multiframe super resolution reconstruction method based on light field angular images. Opt. Commun. **404**, 189–195 (2017)
9. Dong, C., Loy, C.C., He, K., Tang, X.: Image super-resolution using deep convolutional networks. IEEE Trans. Pattern Anal. Mach. Intell. **38**(2), 295–307 (2016)
10. Kim, J., Lee, J.K., Lee, K.M.: Accurate image super-resolution using very deep convolutional networks. In: Proceedings IEEE Conference on Computer Vision and Pattern Recognition (CVPR), pp. 1646–1654 (2016)
11. Lai, W., Huang, J., Ahuja, N., Yang, M.: Deep laplacian pyramid networks for fast and accurate super resolution. In: Proceedings IEEE Conference on Computer Vision and Pattern Recognition (CVPR), pp. 5835–5843 (2017)
12. Yang, W., Zhang, X., Tian, Y., Wang, W., Xue, J., Liao, Q.: Deep learning for single image super-resolution: a brief review. IEEE Trans. Multimedia **21**(12), 3106–3121 (2019)
13. Yoon, Y., Jeon, H., Yoo, D., Lee, J., Kweon, I.S.: Learning a deep convolutional network for light-field image super-resolution. In: Proceedings of the IEEE Conference on Computer Vision and Pattern Recognition Workshops (ICCVW), pp. 57–65 (2015)
14. Yoon, Y., Jeon, H., Yoo, D., Lee, J., Kweon, I.S.: Light-field image super-resolution using convolutional neural network. IEEE Sig. Process. Lett. **24**(6), 848–852 (2017)
15. Gul, M.S.K., Gunturk, B.K.: Spatial and angular resolution enhancement of light fields using convolutional neural networks. IEEE Trans. Image Process. **27**(5), 2146–2159 (2018)
16. Wang, Y., Liu, F., Zhang, K., Hou, G., Sun, Z., Tan, T.: LFNet: a novel bidirectional recurrent convolutional neural network for light-field image super-resolution. IEEE Trans. Image Process. **27**(9), 4274–4286 (2018)
17. Farrugia, R.A., Guillemot, C.: Light field super-resolution using a low-rank prior and deep convolutional neural networks. IEEE Trans. Pattern Anal. Mach. Intell. **42**(5), 1162–1175 (2020)

18. Yeung, H.W.F., Hou, J., Chen, X., Chen, J., Chen, Z., Chung, Y.Y.: Light field spatial super-resolution using deep efficient spatial-angular separable convolution. IEEE Trans. Image Process. **28**(5), 2319–2330 (2019)
19. Wilburn, B., Joshi, N., Vaish, V., Talvala, E., Antunez, E.R., Barth, A., et al.: High performance imaging using large camera arrays. ACM Trans. Graph. **24**(3), 765–776 (2005)
20. Veeraraghavan, A., Raskar, R., Agrawal, A.: Dappled photography: mask enhanced cameras for heterodyned light fields and coded aperture refocusing. ACM Trans. Graph. **26**(3), 69 (2007)
21. https://www.lytro.com/
22. Levoy, M., Hanrahan, P.: Light field rendering. In: Computer Graphics (Proceedings of SIGGRAPH 1996), pp. 31–42 (1996)
23. Raj, A.S., Lowney, M., Shah, R., Wetzstein, G.: Stanford Lytro Light Field Archive. Accessed: Mar. 2017. [Online]. Available: http://lightfields.stanford.edu/
24. Kalantari, N.K., Wang, T.-C., Ramamoorthi, R.: Learning-based view synthesis for light field cameras. ACM Trans. Graph. **35**(6), 193 (2016)
25. Vedaldi, A., Lenc, K.: MatConvNet: convolutional neural networks for MATLAB. In: Proceedings of ACM International Conference on Multimedia (MM), pp. 689–692 (2015)
26. He, K., Zhang, X., Ren, S., Sun, J.: Delving deep into rectifiers: surpassing human-level performance on imageNet classification. In: Proceedings 2015 IEEE International Conference on Computer Vision (ICCV), pp. 1026–1034 (2015)
27. Rossi, M., Frossard, P.: Geometry-consistent light field super-resolution via graph-based regularization. IEEE Trans. Image Process. **27**(9), 4207–4218 (2018)
28. Farrugia, R.A., Galea, C., Guillemot, C.: Super resolution of light field images using linear subspace projection of patch-volumes. IEEE J. Sel. Top. Sig. Process. **11**(7), 1058–1071 (2017)
29. Zhang, S., Lin, Y., Sheng, H.: Residual networks for light field image super-resolution. In: IEEE/CVF Conference on Computer Vision and Pattern Recognition (CVPR), vol. 2019, pp. 11038–11047 (2019)
30. Jin, J., Hou, J., Chen, J., Kwong, S.: Light field spatial super-resolution via deep combinatorial geometry embedding and structural consistency regularization. In: 2020 IEEE/CVF Conference on Computer Vision and Pattern Recognition (CVPR), Seattle, WA, USA, pp. 2257–2266 (2020)

PSF Estimation of Simple Lens Based on Circular Partition Strategy

Hanxiao Cai, Weili Li, Maojun Zhang, Zheng Zhang, and Wei Xu(✉)

College of Systems Engineering, National University of Defense Technology,
Changsha, China
weixu@nudt.edu.cn

Abstract. Recently, single-lens computational imaging has gradually become a new research direction of computational photography, which combines the front-end simple optical imaging equipment with the late image restoration algorithm to obtain high-quality images. Single lens computational imaging is essentially a problem of image restoration. The estimation accuracy of point spread function (PSF) will directly affect the quality of image restoration. Existing spatially variant PSF estimation methods usually divide images into rectangular blocks. Considering the imaging characteristics of single lens, a PSF estimation method based on a circular partition strategy is proposed in this paper. Experimental results show that this segmented method can achieve better PSF estimation accuracy and improve image restoration quality.

Keywords: Computational photography · Simple lens imaging · Point spread function · Circular partition strategy

1 Introduction

Single lens optics often suffer from optical aberration, the deviation between a real and idealized optical system, which always includes certain effects such as geometric distortion, chromatic aberration, spherical aberration and coma [11], especially the single lens with spherical surfaces. These aberrations make single lens unable to be directly used for high quality photography. Modern camera optics design is becoming increasingly complicated to compensate aberrations with the requirement of high-quality images. However, optical aberrations are inevitable, and the design of lenses always involves a trade-off among various parameters. Such sophisticated combinations aim to optimize the light efficiency of the optical system while correcting the optical aberrations mentioned previously. Modern lens design has improved geometric imaging properties, but also face the high cost and weight problems of camera objectives, as well as increased lens flare [2].

Heide [2] and Schuler [15] utilized a simple lens system with an image deconvolution method to achieve the image effect of single lens reflex(SLR) cameras. Their work provides a solution to the contradiction between image quality

© Springer Nature Switzerland AG 2021
Y. Peng et al. (Eds.): ICIG 2021, LNCS 12890, pp. 511–522, 2021.
https://doi.org/10.1007/978-3-030-87361-5_42

and the complexity of imaging equipment. However, the methods presented by Schuler and Heide require a complex calibration process to estimate the PSF, and the image restoration method is time-consuming, concerning which are impractical in actual implementation.

Traditional image restoration is generally considered that point spread function (PSF) is spatially invariant, but the actual optical system suffering from various optical aberrations cannot be strictly linear space invariant. Non-blind or blind deconvolution algorithms of image restoration based on spatially varying PSF gradually show their superiority. These algorithms divide an image into M*N cells, like a checkerboard, and then estimate the PSF by each cell. However, this partition strategy is not consistent with the blurring characteristics of single lens optics so that the image restoration accuracy is not high enough.

Real optical systems suffer from dispersion in the lens elements, leading to the blurred edge known as spherical aberration. The spherical aberrations of single lens are severe, since the focal point of the light rays at the edge of the convex lens is closer to the optical center of the lens than the focal point of the light rays near the axis, the monochromatic large aperture beam emitted by the object point on the axis cannot converge to a point after refraction through the lens, which means it cannot produce a conjugate image point, but will obtain an extended image spot. When spherical aberration exists, there is no ideal image point at any position. The image of the object point is always a dispersion circle. With regard to spherical aberration, we directly use a non-blind deconvolution method to estimate the PSF according to the blur extent of every circular part around the image center. After the PSF is estimated, a simple non-blind deconvolution method is used to obtain a clear image (Fig. 1).

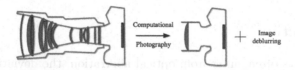

Fig. 1. Computational imaging through single lens.

Our work proves the possibility to acquire high-quality images with the combination of single lens design and image restoration method. We proposed a circular partition strategy that can get a higher accuracy of image restoration compared with traditional methods. Future camera lenses can be simpler, lighter, cheaper, and more compact. Simple lens imaging is potentially meaningful in many scientific applications, such as astronomical imaging, remote sensing, medical imaging, consumer photography, and computational photography.

2   Related Work

2.1   Single Lens Imaging

Single lens computational imaging is a relatively new research direction in recent years. This idea of simple optics with computationally-corrected aberrations was proposed by Schuler in 2011 [15]. His simple lens camera had a single lens equipped with Canon 5D MKII (Fig. 2(a)). The single-lens imaging system designed by Heide et al. [2] is shown in Fig. 2(b). Heide [2] improved simple lens imaging based on the research of Schuler. This lens of the single-lens imaging system is a zoom lens with a focal length of 130 mm and an aperture of F4.5. The single lens imaging system designed by Tao et al. [20] is shown in Fig. 2(c). They divided the key modules in the compensation algorithm of transversal mirror difference into forwarding convolution and backward convolution. The single-lens imaging system designed by Cui et al. [3] is shown in Fig. 2(d). The focal length of the lens is 35 mm and the aperture is F2.4. They use the sparse representation based method to process the image blurring caused by the aberration of the single-lens imaging system. Peng et al. [13] designed a wide-angle imaging system based on an aspheric Fresnel lens, as shown in Fig. 2(e), the focal length of their single lens is 43 mm.

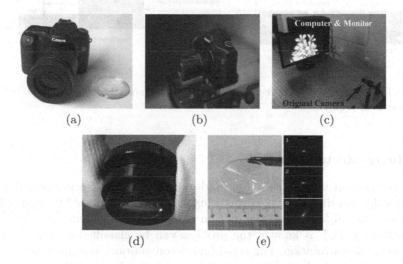

(a)   (b)   (c)

(d)   (e)

Fig. 2. Current single lens imaging system. [2,3,13,15,20]

2.2   PSF Estimation

In the early, PSF estimated from the image restoration algorithm is spatially-invariant, which means the form and extent of blur are the same throughout the image. Later Levin [7] found that the blur caused by camera shake is different in different areas of the image so that spatially-invariant PSF is not accurate

enough to describe the blur extent of an image. So the spatially-variant PSF
estimation has become the focus of image restoration research in recent years.
For blur in dynamic scenes, Kim et al. [4] used the image partitioning method to
obtain spatially-variant PSF before a complex nonlinear PSF estimation through
scene segmentation. On that basis, Kim and Lee et al. [5] tried to approximate
PSF by the local linear method. In the previous work [21], we use the corner
detection method to estimate the PSF of the self-made single lens imaging system, as shown in Fig. 3. Firstly, the checkerboard image and clear noise image
are displayed on the computer screen. Then, the computer screen is directly pho-
tographed by single lens imaging system. After corner detection, color adjustment, mapping and clipping, the clear noise image and blur noise image pairs are
obtained to estimate spatially-variant PSF of single lens imaging system with
non-blind deconvolution method. To estimate spatially-variant PSF, the clear
noise image and blur noise image were divided into 3×4 rectangular sub image
blocks, which is a commonly used segmentation method in spatially-variant PSF
estimation.

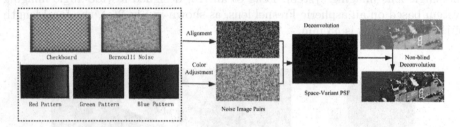

Fig. 3. The overview of PSF estimation framework and the enhancement achieved
using our measured PSF.

2.3   Image Restoration

Image restoration is a longstanding and challenging problem in computational
photography and digital image processing. Image blur is caused by atmospheric
turbulence, out-of-focus, and the motion of the camera or scene [16]. According
to whether the PSF is known, the problem can be classified as non-blind and
blind image deconvolution. For non-blind deconvolution, the most basic image
deconvolution methods include frequency-space division and the Wiener filter
[18], this method deals poorly with frequencies that are suppressed by the PSF.
Richardson Lucy (RL) algorithm [10,14] is a traditional iterative image deconvolution method, which was proposed to compensate for blur in optical systems
that are insufficiently corrected for aberrations. The basic RL algorithm has been
extended in many ways, such as the residual deconvolution method [9] and the
bilateral RL method [19] proposed by Yuan. Blind image deconvolution can be
classified into separative methods and jointly methods [16]. For separative methods, the PSF is identified first, and then used to restore the clear image with

non-blind deconvolution. For joint methods, the original clear image and PSF are identified simultaneously. Popular blind deconvolution methods in recent years include those based on maximum a posteriori [17], variational Bayesian [6], and edge prediction [8].

3   Methods

3.1   Circular Partition Strategy

As mentioned above, the image blur caused by the monochromatic aberration and chromatic aberration of the single lens itself is similar to the defocus blur in shape, both of which are disk-like rings and gradually spread uniformly from the middle part to the surrounding areas. However, traditional PSF estimation methods based on rectangular partition strategy Fig. 4(a) mix parts with different blur extent, which descended the PSF estimation accuracy.

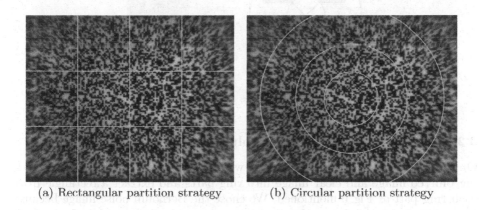

(a) Rectangular partition strategy   (b) Circular partition strategy

Fig. 4. .

In order to make the PSF closer to the characteristics of the single lens imaging system, we proposed a method that divides images into ring blocks to make the blur extent within each block more uniform and similar, as shown in Fig. 4(b). After estimating four PSFs from four pairs of ring blocks by using the non-blind deconvolution method [21], we can get four clear images by non-blind deconvolution. Each image has a ring part that is matched with one PSF so we joint these four parts and get our final clear image. The process is shown in Fig. 5.

Considering that the calculation process is time-consuming and more suitable for rectangle image patches, we extracted four rectangles from one ring and jointed them into a larger rectangle to take the place of the ring so as to simplify the process, as shown in Fig. 6.

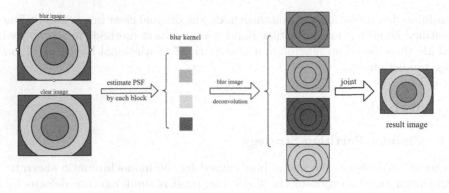

Fig. 5. Process of Block Deconvolution.

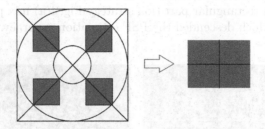

Fig. 6. Extract rectangles from ring image patch.

3.2 PSF Estimation and Deconvolution

On the circular partition strategy basis, we divided a pair of noise images including blurred image and clear image into ring parts and extract a rectangle from each ring part as Fig. 6 mentioned. We chose the Bernoulli noise image because the spectral characteristics of noise images are more abundant which can lead to a more accurate PSF. Then we use the non-blind deconvolution method to estimate the PSF while replacing the original l_1 regularization of k with a Gaussian regularization to improve the accuracy of PSF estimation (Fig. 7). Once the PSF k for the finest level has been estimated, a variety of non-blind image deconvolution methods are employed to recover the sharp image x from y. One of the simplest methods is RL. However, this method is sensitive to wrong PSF estimates, which result in ringing artifacts in x. Krishnan chose to use the non-blind deconvolution method from [7], because it is fast and robust with small PSF errors. This algorithm uses a continuation method to solve the following cost function:

$$\min_x \quad \lambda \|x \otimes k - y\|_2 + \|\nabla_{x'} x\|_\alpha + \|\nabla_{y'} y\|_\alpha \tag{1}$$

where $\nabla_{x'}$ and $\nabla_{y'}$ are the derivative filters to generate the high-frequency version $y = [\nabla_{x'} y, \nabla_{y'} y]$. We use $\lambda = 3000$, $\alpha = 0.8$ for all results. As it mentioned in [7], Eq. 3 is minimized by alternating two sub-problems some times before

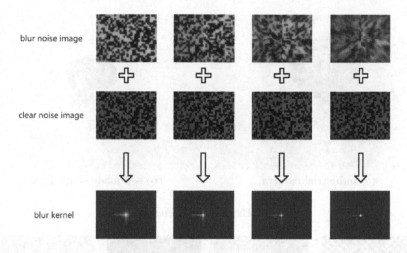

Fig. 7. PSF Estimation From Noise Images.

increasing the value of β and repeating. β is a weight that varies during the optimization. Starting with some small value β_0, it's scaled by a factor β_{Inc} until it exceeds the fixed value β_{Max}. We use $\beta_0 = 1$, $\beta_{Inc} = 2\sqrt{2}$ and $\beta_{Max} = 256$ in the experiment.

4   Experiments

In this section, we present a detailed comparison of single lens aberration correcting deconvolution methods with different partition strategies. Figure 8 shows our self-made simple lens of f/35 mm and Hikvision camera MV-CA013-21UC respectively.The real test images were all obtained with auto exposure and auto gain. We implemented our algorithm and conducted experiments in MATLAB. All experiments were performed on one core of an Intel Core 4 Quad CPU with 2.11 GHz and 16 GB RAM.

4.1   Image Restoration Model Experiments

To test the feasibility of the image restoration model mentioned above, first, we generate four images including a checkerboard image, a noise image, a pure white, and a pure black image. These four images are shown on the computer screen in turn. Second, we collect these four pictures taken from a single lens. Figure 9(a) is a checkerboard that is used to perform corner detection before projection relationship from the original image to the captured image. Figure 9(b) is a noise image to estimate PSF. Figure 9(c) and (d) are used to adjust the color of the image.

(a) industrial camera   (b) self-made single lens

Fig. 8. Experimental Facilities

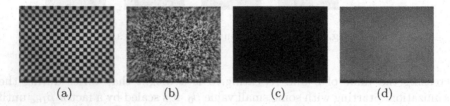

(a)   (b)   (c)   (d)

Fig. 9. Pictures taken from single lens

We find the pixel coordinate correspondence between the checkerboard image taken from a single lens and the original checkerboard image generated from Matlab by using the Harris corner detection algorithm [1]. After getting two corner coordinates matrix Mat1 and Mat2 with Harris' algorithm , we can calculate the coordinate correspondence between the two images. Due to the reflection of the computer screen, the uneven illumination in the room and the influence of the parameters of the webcam, the tone of the noise image is not consistent with that of the noise image generated by MATLAB. If directly with PSF estimation, the two images will affect the estimation precision of the PSF, which affects the follow-up results of the image restoration algorithm. Therefore, it is necessary to adjust the color of the noise image based on pure black image and pure white image. Finally, a restored image is generated after PSF estimation and deconvolution (Fig. 10).

(a) Blur image   (b) Image restoration result   (c) Blur image   (d) Image restoration result

(e) Details in blur image   (f) Details in restored image

(g) Details in blur image   (h) Details in restored image

Fig. 10. Image restoration results.

4.2 Circular Partition Effect

PSF estimated in the Subsect. 4.1 is spatially invariant, but the degree of blur obtained by a single lens imaging system is not consistent. So in this section we compared circular partition strategy with grid partition strategy based on the image restoration by visual intuition and measuring Blind Image Quality Index(BIQI).

Compare Images by Visual Intuition. Figure 11 show some difference that Fig. 11(a) shows a more obvious ringing effect while Fig. 11(b) looks more smooth due to a more accurate PSF. We can find more noise in Fig. 11(e) which makes the image darker and cause serious distortion. Figure 11(g) and (h) also show the same characteristic.

(a) Grid partition (b) Circular partition (c) Grid partition (d) Circular partition

(e) Details in grid partition   (f) Details in circular partition

(g) Details in grid partition   (h) Details in circular partition

Fig. 11. Different partition strategy results.

Compare Images by BIQI. The framework for calculation of BIQI is as follows [12]. Given a distorted image, the algorithm first estimates the presence of a set of distortions in the image. The amount or probability of each distortion in the image is gauged and denoted as p_i. The first stage is essentially a classification stage. The second stage evaluates the quality of the image along each of these distortions. Let q_i represent the quality scores from each of the five quality assessment algorithms(corresponding to the five distortions). The quality of the image is then expressed as a probability-weighted summation:

$$BIQI = \sum_{i=1}^{5} p_i \cdot q_i \qquad (2)$$

For BIQI, the smaller value means better image quality. Table 1 shows the BIQI of the test result. All the index values were computed by averaging the scores of a set of images including different sceneries. From the value of Table 1,

Table 1. Image evaluation index BIQI of single lens camera.

Image	BIQI
Blurred image	*95.6559*
Restoration with spatially invariant PSF	*39.6201*
Restoration with grid partition PSF	*33.9139*
Restoration with circular partition PSF	**26.0487**

we can see that, all values show that, with the PSF estimated by the proposed method, the image restoration results with circular partition strategy are the best.

5 Conclusions

In this study, we improved that a simple non-blind image deconvolution method was applied to estimate the PSF of the optical system, instead of complicated PSF calibration process. Then a fast non-blind image deconvolution method combined with the estimated PSF was used to restore the clear image. To further improve the PSF estimation accuracy, we found a better partition strategy that is more consistent with the blurring characteristics of single lens optics than previous work.

In the future, further improvement can be developed by estimating space-variant PSF. In addition, more information about the lens can be explored and added to the PSF estimation process.

Acknowledge. This research was partially supported by National Basic Enhancement Research Program of China under key basic research project, National Natural Science Foundation (NSFC) of China under project No. 61906206, 62071478.

References

1. Harris, J.R., Battiste, D.R., Bertus, B.J.: Cracking catalysts comprising pillared clays (1988)
2. Heide, F., Rouf, M., Hullin, M.B., Labitzke, B., Kolb, A.: High-quality computational imaging through simple lenses. ACM Trans. Graph. **32**(5), 149 (2013)
3. Cui, J., Huang, W.: Optical aberration correction for simple lenses via sparse representation. Optics Commun. **401**, 201–213 (2018). (A Journal Devoted to the Rapid Publication of Short Contributions in the Field of Optics & Interaction of Light with Matter)
4. Kim, T.H., Ahn, B., Lee, K.M.: Dynamic scene deblurring. In: IEEE International Conference on Computer Vision (2013)
5. Kim, T.H., Lee, K.M.: Segmentation-free dynamic scene deblurring. In: Computer Vision & Pattern Recognition (2014)
6. Lee, S., Cho, S.: Recent advances in image deblurring. In: Siggraph Asia, pp. 1–108 (2013)

7. Levin, A., Weiss, Y., Durand, F., Freeman, W.T.: Understanding and evaluating blind deconvolution algorithms. IEEE (2009)
8. Li, X., Zheng, S., Jia, J.: Unnatural l0 sparse representation for natural image deblurring. In: IEEE Conference on Computer Vision & Pattern Recognition (2013)
9. Lu, Y., Jian, S., Long, Q., Shum, H.Y.: Image deblurring with blurred/noisy image pairs. ACM Trans. Graph. 26(3), 1 (2007)
10. Lucy, L.B.: An iterative technique for the rectification of observed distributions. Astron. J. 79(6), 745 (1974)
11. Mahajan, V.N.: Aberration theory made simple. Books in Canada (2011)
12. Moorthy, A.K., Bovik, A.: A two-step framework for constructing blind image quality indices. IEEE Sig. Process. Lett. 17, 513–516 (2010)
13. Peng, Y., Sun, Q., Xiong, D., Wetzstein, G., Heide, F.: Learned large field-of-view imaging with thin-plate optics. ACM Trans. Graph. 38(6), 1–14 (2019)
14. Richardson, W.H.: Bayesian-based iterative method of image restoration. J. Opt. Soc. Am. 62, 55–59 (1972)
15. Schuler, C.J., Hirsch, M., Harmeling, S., Schlkopf, B.: Non-stationary correction of optical aberrations. In: IEEE International Conference on Computer Vision, ICCV 2011, Barcelona, Spain, 6–13 November, 2011 (2011)
16. Smith, B., Lysenko, M.: Image deblurring (2009)
17. Stockham, T.G., Cannon, T.M., Ingebretsen, R.B.: Blind deconvolution through digital signal processing. Proc. IEEE 63(4), 678–692 (1975). https://doi.org/10.1109/PROC.1975.9800
18. Wiener, N.: The extrapolation, interpolation and smoothing of stationary time series, with engineering applications. J. R. Statist. Soc. A (General) 113(3), 413 (1950)
19. Yuan, L., Sun, J., Quan, L., Shum, H.Y.: Progressive inter-scale and intra-scale non-blind image deconvolution. ACM Trans. Graph. 27(3), 1–10 (2008)
20. Yue, T., Suo, J., Xiao, Y., Zhang, L., Dai, Q.: Image quality enhancement using original lens via optical computing. Opt. Express 22(24), 29515–30 (2014)
21. Zhan, D., Li, W., Yin, X., Niu, C., Liu, J.: PSF estimation method of simple-lens camera using normal sinh-arcsinh model based on noise image pairs. IEEE Access 9, 49338–49353 (2021)

Photometric Stereo Based on Multiple Kernel Learning

Yinuo Wang[1]([✉]), Yu Guo[2], Xiaoxiao Yang[2], Xuetao Zhang[1], and Fei Wang[1]

[1] Institute of Artificial Intelligence and Robotics, Xi'an Jiaotong University,
Xi'an, China
wynkingdom@stu.xjtu.edu.cn, {xuetaozh,wfx}@xjtu.edu.cn
[2] School of Software Engineering, Xi'an Jiaotong University, Xi'an, China
yu.guo@xjtu.edu.cn, yangxiaoxiao@stu.xjtu.edu.cn

Abstract. Photometric stereo is a widely used surface reconstruction method which can estimate surface normals of an object from its images captured under different lighting conditions by a fixed camera. To deal with non-Lambertian reflections efficiently, kernel regression based photometric stereo has been proposed and achieved promising results. However, in practice, different data-sets often require different kernels, and the existing methods need selecting and tuning the predefined kernel manually. This is not user-friendly since it's hard to find the best kernel for different data-sets. Furthermore, an improper kernel is very likely to degrade the performance. In this work, we adopt multiple kernel learning to handle this problem. The proposed method learns an optimal consensus kernel from multiple predefined kernels by automatically assigning the most suitable weights for different base kernels. The proposed method is tested on various data-sets, and the experiment results show that our multiple kernel based model outperforms the single kernel based method.

Keywords: Photometric stereo · Surface reconstruction · Multiple kernel learning

1 Introduction

Photometric stereo is a popular 3D reconstruction method which is capable of estimating surface normals of an object using only one camera [18]. It has the advantage of high accuracy and low cost. The traditional photometric stereo is strictly under Lambertian reflection assumption, where only three images in different lighting conditions are sufficient for surface normal estimation. However, Lambertian reflection assumption is nearly impossible to satisfy in practice due to the influence of specularities and shadows. Thus, dealing with non-Lambertian

Supported by National Major Science and Technology Projects of China (No. 2019ZX01008101), Xi'an Science and Technology Innovation Program (No. 201809162CX3JC4), Natural Science Foundation of Shaanxi Province (CN) (2021JQ-05).

© Springer Nature Switzerland AG 2021
Y. Peng et al. (Eds.): ICIG 2021, LNCS 12890, pp. 523–532, 2021.
https://doi.org/10.1007/978-3-030-87361-5_43

reflection conditions is an important task in photometric stereo. There are mainly two ways to solve such problem. The first is to treat specularity and shadow pixels as outliers, and after removing these outliers using statistical methods, one can still reconstruction the surface using models formed under Lambertian reflection assumption. The second is to use bidirectional reflectance distribution function (BRDF) based models to estimate the surface normals.

The methods based on Lambertian reflection are well studied [2, 4, 8, 11–13, 19–21]. Though some objects may have some specularity pixels, Lambertian reflection can still be approximated. Cook-Torrance model is one typical Lambertian reflection based method. This model treat surface reflection as the sum of Lambertian reflection part and specularities or shadows part. In this way, the specularity and shadow pixels can be handled as outliers. Base on such assumption, extra light sources are adopted, with a total number of four, to detect specularities and shadows [4], based on which, color information is added to further improve the model [2]. However, in more complex scenes, four light sources are far from enough, so more light sources are added in following studies, such as RANSAC based models [13] and median based models [11]. Some optimization framework based methods are also proposed to detect outliers. For example, the observed intensity can be formulated as the sum of a low-rank diffusive model and a sparse error matrix which accounts for the corruption by shadows and specularities. By using L1-norm regularization term to ensure the sparsity of the error matrix, such model can achieve high reconstruction accuracy [19]. Moreover, a hierarchical Bayesian approximation can be adopted to estimate the surface normals while simultaneously separating the non-Lambertian corruptions, which can also achieve satisfying accuracy [8]. In order to ensure the sparsity of the shadows and specularities, the methods mentioned above usually require many images, and their performance degenerates greatly when dealing with complex reflectance.

The methods based on BRDF do not follow Lambertian assumption, instead, they seek more complex models to handle non-Lambertian conditions [1, 3, 5–7, 9, 10, 15, 16]. Some use parametric reflectance models. For example, bipolynomial reflectance model is proposed so that the low-frequency component of reflectance can be precisely represented [16]. Models that exploit reflectance properties are also proposed. An improved sparse Bayesian regression based method that utilizes monotonicity of BRDF can achieve better results [9]. Consensus photometric stereo based on assumptions of monotonicity, visibility, and isotropy of surface normals can work without knowing the camera response function [7]. Photometric stereo based on reflection sparsity modeling models the general characteristics of different reflection components, and a second order cone programming problem is formulated to solve the model [6]. Models mentioned above are able to achieve higher accuracy than those based on Lambertian assumption, but they have the disadvantage of high computational expense.

By formulating the photometric stereo problem as kernel regression, surface normal can be efficiently solved in closed form, photometric stereo based on kernel regression can achieve high accuracy while maintaining better efficiency [14]. Kernel functions can map the light direction to an infinite dimensional space, which is appropriate in representing the variety of reflectance. In practice, however, the optimal kernel function for different scenes are often different, and a less proper kernel will even degrade the performance. The existing kernel based photometric stereo model uses a single predefined kernel that requires parameter searching and fine-tuning. Such model is not user-friendly and it's hard to find the optimal kernel.

In this work, we propose a photometric stereo model based on multiple kernel learning. The proposed model learns an optimal consensus kernel from multiple predefined kernels by automatically assigning the most suitable weights for different base kernels. Such method avoids kernel selecting and fine-tuning, resulting in a more suitable kernel function for different scenes.

The proposed model is tested on various data-sets, and the experiment results show that our multiple kernel based model outperforms the single kernel based method.

2   Photometric Stereo Based on Multiple Kernel Learning

2.1   Photometric Stereo Using Kernel Regression

Given a surface point, the relation among the surface normal n, the light source from the direction l and the observed intensity $q(n, l)$ can be model as

$$q(n, l) = \sigma(n, l) n^\top l \tag{1}$$

where $\sigma(n, l)$ is the reflectance of the point related to the light direction and surface normal. Similar as [6], by letting $\hat{t}(n, l) = 1/\sigma(n, l)$, we can rewrite (1) as

$$\hat{t}(n, l) = \frac{n^\top l}{q(n, l)} \tag{2}$$

when surface normal n is given, (2) becomes

$$\hat{t}(l) = \frac{n^\top l}{q(l)}. \tag{3}$$

Due to the complex nature of general BRDFs, $\hat{t}(l)$ is a highly nonlinear reflectance function. Kernel function can be introduced to deal with the nonlinearity. Given a kernel function $\phi(\cdot) : \mathbb{R}^3 \rightarrow \mathcal{H}$, we can represent $\hat{t}(l)$ as $\hat{t}(l) = \phi(l)^\top w$. Then, (3) can be written as

$$\phi(l)^\top w = \frac{n^\top l}{q(l)}. \tag{4}$$

(4) can be represented in matrix form as

$$\boldsymbol{\Phi} w = n^\top L \tag{5}$$

where $\boldsymbol{\Phi} = [\phi(l_1), \phi(l_2), \dots, \phi(l_N)]^\top$, $\boldsymbol{L} = [\frac{l_1}{q(l_1)}, \frac{l_2}{q(l_2)}, \dots, \frac{l_N}{q(l_N)}]$. Then, the following optimization problem can be formed to solve n and w,

$$\min_{n,w} \left\| \boldsymbol{n}^\top \boldsymbol{L} - \boldsymbol{\Phi} \boldsymbol{w} \right\|_2^2 + \delta \boldsymbol{w}^\top \boldsymbol{w}$$

$$\text{s.t.} \quad \boldsymbol{n}^\top \boldsymbol{n} = 1. \tag{6}$$

The dual problem is as follows,

$$\min_{n,\alpha} \left\| \boldsymbol{n}^\top \boldsymbol{L} - \boldsymbol{G} \boldsymbol{\alpha} \right\|_2^2 + \delta \boldsymbol{\alpha}^\top \boldsymbol{G} \boldsymbol{\alpha}$$

$$\text{s.t.} \quad \boldsymbol{n}^\top \boldsymbol{n} = 1. \tag{7}$$

where $\boldsymbol{\alpha} = \delta^{-1} \left(\boldsymbol{n}^\top \boldsymbol{L} - \boldsymbol{\Phi} \boldsymbol{w} \right)$, $\boldsymbol{w} = \boldsymbol{\Phi}^T \boldsymbol{\alpha}$ and $\boldsymbol{G} = \boldsymbol{\Phi} \boldsymbol{\Phi}^\top$ is Gram matrix with entries

$$\boldsymbol{G}_{ij} = \langle \phi(l_i), \phi(l_j) \rangle, i, j = 1, \dots, N. \tag{8}$$

2.2 Photometric Stereo Based on Multiple Kernel Learning

In our model, instead of using one single kernel, an optimal consensus kernel is learned from multiple predefined kernels.

Given k predefined kernels, of which the corresponding Gram matrix is denoted as $\boldsymbol{G}_i$, and the optimal consensus kernel denoted as $\boldsymbol{G}^*$, the propose model can be formed by the following optimization problem,

$$\min_{n,\alpha,b,G^*} \left\| \boldsymbol{n}^\top \boldsymbol{L} - \boldsymbol{G}^* \boldsymbol{\alpha} \right\|_2^2 + \delta \boldsymbol{\alpha}^\top \boldsymbol{G}^* \boldsymbol{\alpha} + \epsilon \left\| \boldsymbol{G}^* - \sum_{i=1}^k b_i \boldsymbol{G}_i \right\|_F^2$$

$$\text{s.t.} \quad \boldsymbol{n}^\top \boldsymbol{n} = 1, \ b \geq 0, \ \sum_{i=1}^k b_i = 1 \tag{9}$$

where b_i is the weight for the i th kernel. In this work, we use Gaussian kernel as follows,

$$G(l_i, l_j) = \exp(-\gamma \|l_i - l_j\|_2^2). \tag{10}$$

2.3 Optimization for Problem (9)

Observing optimization problem (9), we can see that though (9) is not jointly convex with respect to n, α, b and $\boldsymbol{G}^*$, it is convex with respect to every one of them while holding others fixed. Thus, we can apply alternating optimization approach to solve the problem.

Update n while G^*, α and b are given: The sub-problem for updating n is equivalent to (7). According to previous work by Shen H.L. et al. [14], n can be obtained by solving an eigen decomposition problem. First, compute $\boldsymbol{Q}$ as follows,

$$\boldsymbol{Q} = \delta \boldsymbol{L} (\boldsymbol{G} + \delta \boldsymbol{I})^{-1} \boldsymbol{L}^\top \tag{11}$$

Algorithm 1: Photometric Stereo Based on Multiple Kernel Learning

---

Input: Light directions $\{l_i\}_{i=1}^N$, predefined kernel functions $\{G_i\}_{i=1}^k$, observed intensity $q(l_i)$

Output: Optimal consensus kenrel function G^*, surface normal n

1 **Initialization:** $G^* = \sum_{i=1}^k G_i/k$, $b_i = 1/k$, $L = [\frac{l_1}{q(l_1)}, \frac{l_2}{q(l_2)}, \ldots, \frac{l_N}{q(l_N)}]$;

2 **while** *not converges* **do**

3   Calculate Q according to (11);

4   Update n as the eigenvector corresponding to the minimum eigenvalue of Q;

5   Update G^* according to (14);

6   Update b by solving (16);

7 **end**

---

then, n is the eigenvector corresponding to the minimum eigenvalue of Q.

Update G^* and α while n and b are given: Note that we have $w = \Phi^\top \alpha$, $\Phi w = L^\top n$ and $G^* = \Phi \Phi^\top$, and it can be deduced that

$$\alpha = G^{*-1} L^\top n. \tag{12}$$

Setting the derivative of (9) with respect to G^* as zero, we have

$$2\left(G^* \alpha - L^\top n\right) \alpha^\top + \delta \alpha \alpha^\top + 2\delta \left(G^* - \sum_{i=1}^k b_i G_i\right) = 0. \tag{13}$$

Then, we can get a closed-form solution for G^* as

$$G^* = \frac{1}{2}\left(\alpha \alpha^\top + \delta I\right)^{-1}\left(\sum_{i=1}^k b_i G_i + \delta \alpha \alpha^\top + 2L^\top n \alpha^\top\right) \tag{14}$$

Update b while n, α and G^* are given: The sub-problem for updating b is equivalent to

$$\min_b \epsilon \left\| G^* - \sum_{i=1}^k b_i G_i \right\|_F^2$$

$$\text{s.t.} \quad b \geq 0, \ \sum_{i=1}^k b_i = 1. \tag{15}$$

We can rewrite (15) as follows,

$$\min_b \epsilon b^\top M b - a^\top b$$

$$\text{s.t.} \quad b \geq 0, \ \sum_{i=1}^k b_i = 1. \tag{16}$$

where $a = \epsilon \operatorname{Tr}(G^* G_i)/2$ and $M_{ij} = \epsilon \operatorname{Tr}(G_i G_j)$. It can be seen that (16) is a quadratic programming problem with linear constraints, which can be easily solved with existing packages.

By repeating the above mentioned process, we can obtain the optimal kernel, and a more accurate surface reconstruction. The complete algorithm is as in Algorithm 1.

3 Experiments

3.1 Data-Set Description

In this work, DiLiGenT data-set proposed by Shi B et al. [17] is used to test the performance of our proposed model. This data-set focuses on non-Lambertian methods and contains calibrated directional lightings, objects of general reflectance, and ground truth shapes (normals). DiLiGenT contains 10 different objects with various textures, and the details are shown in Table 1.

Table 1. Objects in DiLiGenT and their textures.

Object	Texture
CAT	Diffuse
POT1	Rough
BALL	Sparse specular
READING	Sparse specular
BEAR	Broad specular
BUDDA	Soft specular
POT2	Spatially-varying
GOBLET	Spatially-varying
COW	Metallic paint
HARVEST	Spatially-varying/Metallic paint

Besides DiLiGenT, we also use textures provided by MERL BRDF database to render Bunny, as shown in Fig. 1. The proposed model is also tested on this data-set.

3.2 Experiment Settings

Our proposed model is compared with least square based photometric stereo (LS-PS) [18] and single kernel based photometric stereo (Kernel-PS) [14].

Angular error is used to evaluate the models, which is

$$\text{Error} = \frac{\arccos(N \cdot N_{gt})}{n} \times \frac{180}{\pi} \tag{17}$$

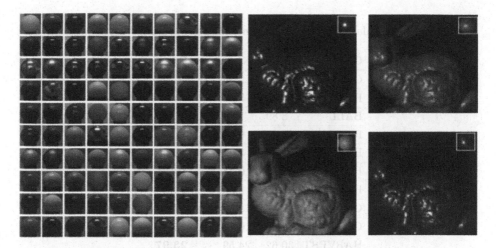

Fig. 1. Bunny rendered with different textures in MERL BRDF database.

where $N \in \mathbb{R}^{n \times 3}$ is the estimated surface normals, while $N_{gt} \in \mathbb{R}^{n \times 3}$ is the ground truth surface normals.

The hyper-parameters in all evaluated models are decided using grid search method. The predefined kernels in the proposed methods are five Gaussian kernels with $\gamma = \{0.25, 0.30, 0.35, 0.40, 0.45\}$.

3.3 Experiment Results

The tested angular errors in DiLiGenT data-set are listed in Table 2. A visualization of reconstruction errors of Cat, Reading and Goblet in DiLiGenT is shown in Fig. 2. It can be seen that our proposed model has the lowest reconstruction error among all tested models. From the visualization result, we can easily see that the least square photometric stereo model has low robustness against objects with complex textures. Though the kernel based photometric stereo model has much less error compared with the least square model, it still performs poorly in some complex spots, e.g. the complex region in Reading. And our proposed multiple kernel based model can performs very well dealing with various textures, meaning the proposed model has better robustness compared with single kernel based model.

To further evaluate the performance of our proposed multiple kernel based model, we compare it with the single kernel based model on MERL Database. The results are shown in Fig. 3. Where Kernel-PS with three different kernels are tested, which are kernels with $\gamma = 10^{-1}$, $\gamma = 10^{-1.2}$ and $\gamma = 10^{0.6}$. Those are the kernels that have been tested to have good performance in most data-sets. It can be seen that compared with single kernel based method, our model has the lowest reconstruction error, and the error fluctuates less on objects with different textures, meaning the proposed method is a more general framework that can deal with complex reflections.

Table 2. Angular errors of different models tested in DiLiGenT data-set.

Object	LS-PS	Kernel-PS	Proposed
CAT	4.10	2.25	**2.03**
POT1	8.41	5.63	**5.26**
BALL	8.89	7.28	**7.09**
READING	8.39	6.68	**6.46**
BEAR	14.65	8.52	**8.26**
BUDDA	14.92	10.64	**10.24**
POT2	18.50	12.30	**10.23**
GOBLET	19.80	13.50	**12.13**
COW	25.60	16.79	**15.16**
HARVEST	30.62	24.59	**23.97**

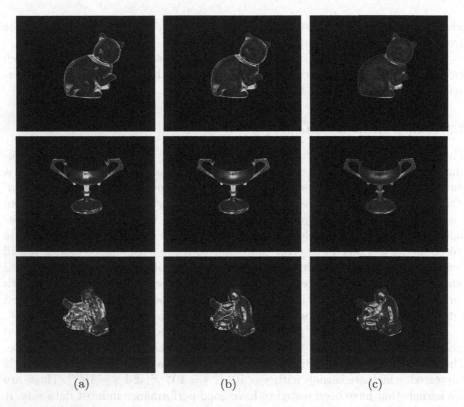

(a)   (b)   (c)

Fig. 2. A visualization of reconstruction errors of Cat, Reading and Goblet in DiLi-GenT with (a) LS-PS (b) Kernel-PS (c) Proposed Model, where the brighter pixel means greater reconstruction error.

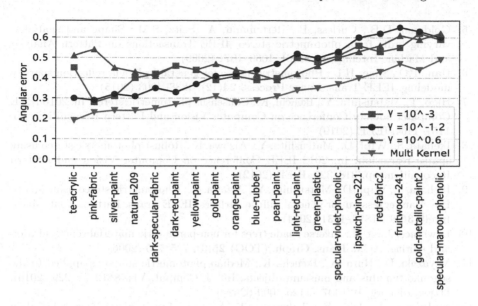

Fig. 3. Angular errors of the proposed model and Kernel PS on surface reconstruction of different textures.

4 Conclusions

In this work, a novel framework of photometric stereo based on multiple kernel learning is proposed. The proposed model can learn an optimal consensus kernel from multiple predefined kernels by automatically assigning the most suitable weights for different base kernels. This overcomes the disadvantage of selecting and tuning the kernel parameters in single kernel based models. Experiment results of the lowest construction errors show that our proposed method is more robust when dealing with different kinds of textures.

References

1. Alldrin, N., Zickler, T., Kriegman, D.: Photometric stereo with non-parametric and spatially-varying reflectance. In: 2008 IEEE Conference on Computer Vision and Pattern Recognition, pp. 1–8. IEEE (2008)
2. Barsky, S., Petrou, M.: The 4-source photometric stereo technique for three-dimensional surfaces in the presence of highlights and shadows. IEEE Trans. Pattern Anal. Mach. Intell. **25**(10), 1239–1252 (2003)
3. Chung, H.S., Jia, J.: Efficient photometric stereo on glossy surfaces with wide specular lobes. In: 2008 IEEE Conference on Computer Vision and Pattern Recognition, pp. 1–8. IEEE (2008)
4. Coleman, E.N., Jr., Jain, R.: Obtaining 3-dimensional shape of textured and specular surfaces using four-source photometry. Comput. Graph. Image Process. **18**(4), 309–328 (1982)

5. Goldman, D.B., Curless, B., Hertzmann, A., Seitz, S.M.: Shape and spatially-varying brdfs from photometric stereo. IEEE Transactions on Pattern Analysis and Machine Intelligence **32**(6), 1060–1071 (2009)
6. Han, T.Q., Shen, H.L.: Photometric stereo for general brdfs via reflection sparsity modeling. IEEE Trans. Image Process. **24**(12), 4888–4903 (2015)
7. Higo, T., Matsushita, Y., Ikeuchi, K.: Consensus photometric stereo. In: 2010 IEEE Computer Society Conference on Computer Vision and Pattern Recognition, pp. 1157–1164. IEEE (2010)
8. Ikehata, S., Wipf, D., Matsushita, Y., Aizawa, K.: Robust photometric stereo using sparse regression. In: 2012 IEEE Conference on Computer Vision and Pattern Recognition, pp. 318–325. IEEE (2012)
9. Ikehata, S., Wipf, D., Matsushita, Y., Aizawa, K.: Photometric stereo using sparse Bayesian regression for general diffuse surfaces. IEEE Trans. Pattern Anal. Mach. Intell. **36**(9), 1816–1831 (2014)
10. Lawrence, J., et al.: Inverse shade trees for non-parametric material representation and editing. ACM Trans. Graph. (TOG) **25**(3), 735–745 (2006)
11. Miyazaki, D., Hara, K., Ikeuchi, K.: Median photometric stereo as applied to the segonko tumulus and museum objects. Int. J. Comput. Vis. **86**(2–3), 229 (2010). https://doi.org/10.1007/s11263-009-0262-9
12. Mukaigawa, Y., Ishii, Y., Shakunaga, T.: Analysis of photometric factors based on photometric linearization. JOSA A **24**(10), 3326–3334 (2007)
13. Ngan, A., Durand, F., Matusik, W.: Experimental analysis of BRDF models. Rendering Techniques **2005**(16th), 2 (2005)
14. Shen, H.L., Han, T.Q., Li, C.: Efficient photometric stereo using kernel regression. IEEE Trans. Image Process. **26**(1), 439–451 (2016)
15. Shi, B., Tan, P., Matsushita, Y., Ikeuchi, K.: A biquadratic reflectance model for radiometric image analysis. In: 2012 IEEE Conference on Computer Vision and Pattern Recognition, pp. 230–237. IEEE (2012)
16. Shi, B., Tan, P., Matsushita, Y., Ikeuchi, K.: Bi-polynomial modeling of low-frequency reflectances. IEEE Trans. Pattern Analysis Mach. Intell. **36**(6), 1078–1091 (2013)
17. Shi, B., Wu, Z., Mo, Z., Duan, D., Yeung, S.K., Tan, P.: A benchmark dataset and evaluation for non-lambertian and uncalibrated photometric stereo. In: Proceedings of the IEEE Conference on Computer Vision and Pattern Recognition, pp. 3707–3716 (2016)
18. Woodham, R.J.: Photometric method for determining surface orientation from multiple images. Opt. Eng. **19**(1), 191139 (1980)
19. Wu, L., Ganesh, A., Shi, B., Matsushita, Y., Wang, Y., Ma, Y.: Robust photometric stereo via low-rank matrix completion and recovery. In: Kimmel, R., Klette, R., Sugimoto, A. (eds.) ACCV 2010. LNCS, vol. 6494, pp. 703–717. Springer, Heidelberg (2011). https://doi.org/10.1007/978-3-642-19318-7_55
20. Wu, T.P., Tang, K.L., Tang, C.K., Wong, T.T.: Dense photometric stereo: a Markov random field approach. IEEE Trans. Pattern Anal. Mach. Intell. **28**(11), 1830–1846 (2006)
21. Yu, C., Seo, Y., Lee, S.W.: Photometric stereo from maximum feasible Lambertian reflections. In: Daniilidis, K., Maragos, P., Paragios, N. (eds.) ECCV 2010. LNCS, vol. 6314, pp. 115–126. Springer, Heidelberg (2010). https://doi.org/10.1007/978-3-642-15561-1_9

Hair Salon: A Geometric Example-Based Method to Generate 3D Hair Data

Qiaomu Ren[1], Haikun Wei[1], and Yangang Wang[1,2(✉)]

[1] School of Automation, Southeast University, Nanjing, China
yangangwang@seu.edu.cn
[2] Shenzhen Research Institute of Southeast University, Shenzhen, China

Abstract. Due to the complex geometry and wide shape variations of hair, it is difficult to collect 3D hair data for deep learning applications of hair modeling. This paper introduces a geometric example-based method to generate 3D hair data. Our key idea is to generate new hair data according to a reference hair model automatically. The reference hair model is first aligned with the most widely used parametric human model. We then edit individual strand by an offset function and generate full hair with Perlin Noise. Finally, smoother results without hair-body penetration are obtained by optimizing the moving direction. Our method can be used to generate sufficient data for deep learning applications of hair modeling and human digitization with detailed hair strands. The results demonstrate the effectiveness of our method.

Keywords: Hair generation · Geometry processing

1 Introduction

Hairstyle is an important part in modeling human characters and a crucial factor in determining personal impression. However, compared with human face [3,9], hand [24] and body [2,18,22] which are easily parameterizable, hair can be highly complex and has wide shape variations, which makes hair modeling one of today's most challenging problems in computer graphics. [5,12,16,31] can generate high-quality 3D hair, but they require specialized hardware setups or computationally-heavy refinement. With the recent development of deep learning, many works [25,32,35] used neural networks to model or reconstruct 3D hair models. Zhou et al. [35] proposed the first deep neural network to generate dense hair geometry from a single-view image. Satio et al. [25] adopted a variational auto-encoder structure to generate 3D hair. Zhang et al. [32] grew hair strands from the scalp guided by 3D orientation volume generated by GANs.

This work was supported in part by Shenzhen Fundamental Research Program under Grant JCYJ20180306174459972, Natural Science Foundation of Jiangsu Province under Grant BK20180355 and the Fundamental Research Funds for the Central Universities.

Y. Peng et al. (Eds.): ICIG 2021, LNCS 12890, pp. 533–544, 2021.
https://doi.org/10.1007/978-3-030-87361-5_44

The major issue of such learning-based approaches is the requirement of sufficient data. Hu et al. [13] built a public accessible 3D hair dataset [1] which contains 343 hair models and most of them are created manually by artists. [25,32,35] built their datasets in a similar way. But compared with 3D human [14,17,33] or hand [10,34] datasets, available hair datasets are negligible both in the quantity and size, due to the highly complex geometry and wide shape variations of hair.

To solve this problem, we propose a geometric method to generate new 3D hair data according to a given example. Our key idea is to generate a new hair model according to a given example automatically, which can generate sufficient data for deep learning applications of hair modeling and human digitization. To make full use of the existing hair dataset [1] which treats hair as a collection of strands, we select the hair model from USC-HairSalon [1] or other hair strand model as a reference hair model. The reference hair model is aligned with the Skinned Multi-Person Linear model (SMPL) [18] and has a fixed number of hair roots through rigid alignment, parameterization and interpolation, which benefits human digitization with detailed hair. To generate more hair models which have natural appearance, we edit hair strands by an offset function and apply the method of editing a single strand to the entire hair model with a pseudo-noise function. Besides, to obtain a smoother result without penetration, we optimize the moving direction when avoiding hair-body penetration.

The main contributions of this work are summarized as follows.

- We propose a method to generate new hair data with natural appearance based on the reference hair model, which can be used to generate sufficient data for hair modeling.
- We align hair models with the SMPL model and all of them have 15,412 uniform roots, which benefits human digitization with detailed hair strands at the same time.
- We construct a synthetic hair dataset, which helps future research for hair modeling.

2   Related Works

Hair Digitization. Hair digitization has been a hot topic in recent years, due to its importance in human digitization. Many efforts have been made in computer graphics and computer vision. We only review the literature related to ours. For a more detailed introduction, please refer to a comprehensive survey [30] of hair modeling.

Yu [31] developed a hairstyling system according to the relationship between vector fields and hair strands. Kim et al. [16] proposed a multi-resolution hair modeling system to form clusters at multiple scales. Wang et al. [29] presented an example-based approach to hair modeling using traditional 2D texture synthesis techniques. Masayuki et al. [20] were the first who used multiple images to reconstruct a 3D hair model. Paris et al. [21] proposed a novel method to compute the image orientation of the hairs from their anisotropic behavior. The image orientation is raised into a 3D orientation by analyzing the light reflected by the hair fibers. Chai et al. [7] first introduced single-view hair modeling techniques. They proposed a plausible strand-based 3D hair model adequate for portrait manipulation. Hu et al. [13] built the first hair modeling system based on a database of complete hairstyles. Chai et al. [6] introduced the first fully automatic method for 3D hair modeling from a single portrait image.

With the recent success of deep learning, deep neural networks were widely used in hair modeling. Zhou et al. [35] proposed the first deep neural network to generate dense hair geometry according to a single-view image. They inferred 3D hair strands from a 2D orientation map directly using a deep neural network. Satio et al. [25] adopted a variational auto-encoder structure to decode the occupancy field and flow field from the volumetric latent space. The input images can be encoded to the hair coefficients which are aligned to the volumetric latent space using networks. Zhang et al. [32] proposed the architecture of GANs to generate 3D orientation volume and grew hair strands from the scalp guided by 3D orientation volume.

Human Digitization. The parametric models [2,18] of human were widely used for human digitization. But the methods [4,8,11,17,22,36] which used parametric models can only generate a naked human body, even if some [8,22,36] of them wanted to capture a full body. Besides, some template-free methods [26,28] used a voxel representation or an implicit representation to generate a detailed human body with hair. But none of these methods can directly generate hair represented as strands.

Hair Dataset. Compared with 3D human [14,17,33] or hand [10,34] datasets, available hair datasets are negligible both in the quantity and size. Hu et al. [13] built a publicly accessible 3D hair dataset [1] which contains 343 hair models and most of these hair models are created manually by artists. Similar to Hu et al. [13], Zhou et al. [35] collected 340 hair models from online resources and combined hair models to construct a synthesis hair dataset. Satio et al. [25] collected 816 hair models using a hair modeling method and 343 hair models from USC-HairSalon [1]. Zhang et al. [32] trained Hari-GANs using a hair dataset of 303 hair models following [13]. To the best of our knowledge, only USC-HairSalon [1] is available among the datasets used by [25,32,35].

3   Method

Our method can be applied to hair model represented as a collection of strands. The whole pipeline of our method is shown in Fig. 1. We take a hair model from USC-HairSalon [1] as a reference hair model. We then align the roots of this reference model to the SMPL model [18] and generate a new hair model with 15,412 uniform roots by parameterization, interpolation and penetration avoidance. To produce more natural-looking results, we add an offset to each hair point in the strands and apply this method to the entire hair model by a pseudo-random noise function. The details are described in the following subsections.

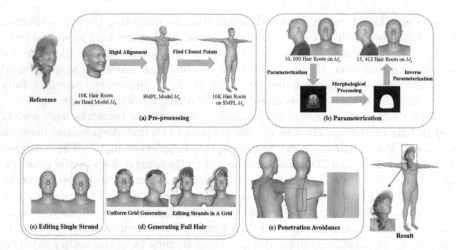

Fig. 1. Overview: (a) The reference hair model is first aligned with the SMPL model (in Sect. 3.1). (b) We use parameterization to define the scalp surface on the SMPL model and generate 15,412 uniform hair roots on this scalp (in Sect. 3.2). (c) We edit single hair strand by an offset function (in Sect. 3.3). (d) To generate full hair, we apply the method of editing single strand to the whole hair (in Sect. 3.4). (e) To obtain a smoother result without hair-body penetration, we optimize the moving direction before updating hair points (in Sect. 3.5).

3.1 Pre-processing

Since the hair model in USC-HairSalon is aligned with a fixed head model which is denoted as M_h, some key points (such as eyes, nose, ears, etc.) are chosen to align M_h with the SMPL model, which is denoted as M_s:

$$min \sum_i \left\| s * (p_h^i + t) - p_s^i \right\| \tag{1}$$

where $p_h^i \in R^3$ and $p_s^i \in R^3$ are the corresponding key points on the head model M_h and the SMPL model M_s, $s \in R^1$ and $t \in R^3$ are the coefficients to be solved which respectively represent scale and translation.

When M_h is aligned with M_s, the hair roots on M_h should also be transferred to M_s. Each hair root on M_h should find a closest point p_c on the surface of M_s. The iteration is repeated until all triangle faces on M_s have been traversed. The above problem can be broken down into the following sub-problems:

- Given a root point p and a mesh M, find the closest point p^i on each triangle face $F^i \in M$ and its corresponding distance d^i
- Find the point among p^i which has the smallest distance d^i

$$p_c = p^{argmin \, d^i} \tag{2}$$

To find the closes point p^i on each triangle face, we can refer to the method [19] of ray-triangle intersection. After the above steps, the corresponding hair roots on the surface of M_s are created.

3.2   Parameterization

A scalp surface represents the region to grow hair strands, which is similar to a hemisphere. We use parameterization [29] to define the scalp surface on M_S. We first transform the world coordinates of 10,000 hair roots on M_s to a scalp space (u, v). In this way, we can get a UV map (see UV map A in Fig. 2(a)). Based on this UV map, we use morphological processing methods such as expansion and erosion to obtain a smooth UV map (see UV map B in Fig. 2(b)).

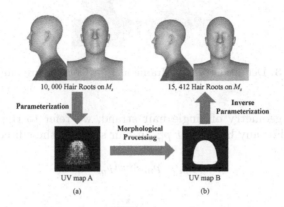

Fig. 2. Parameterization and inverse parameterization: 10,000 hair roots (red points) on M_s are transformed to UV map A using parameterization; UV map B is generated by morphological processing methods according to UV map A; 15,412 uniform hair roots (blue points) are generated based on UV map B using inverse parameterization. (Color figure online)

Each white pixel both in UV map A and B has a corresponding point on the surface of M_s. Inverse parameterization is used to transform the white pixels in UV map B to the world coordinates (x, y, z). Finally, there are 15,412 hair roots on the SMPL model (see blue points on M_s in Fig. 2(b)). Because not every root in the hair models of USC-HairSalon has hair strands and the morphological operation on the UV map increases the number of hair roots, we should ensure that each of the 15,412 roots has a hair strand growing from it. To achieve this goal, we use nearest-neighbor interpolation.

3.3   Editing Single Hair Strand

Hair strands are represented as polylines, and each strand has a fixed number of points (100 in USC-HairSalon and our method) from the root to the end. Given the hair strands from the previous steps, we need to edit them which will produce a wider variety of results. Similar to [31], we need to establish a local frame for any hair point in hair strands. For any hair point $p_m^i (i = 0, ..., 99; m = 0, ..., 15411)$, the z-axis of its local frame is the tangential direction (blue line in

Fig. 3) at p_m^i and a Up vector (bright blue line in Fig. 3) is the vector from the centroid of the scalp (purple point in Fig. 3) to p_m^i. We can get the x-axis (red line in Fig. 3) and y-axis (green line in Fig. 3) by cross product according to the z-axis and the Up vector.

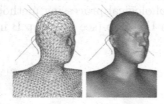

Fig. 3. Definition of local frame at p_m^i. (Color figure online)

To edit the geometry of single hair strand, we refer to the offset function defined in [31]. For any hair point p_m^i in hair strands, the edited hair point $\bar{p}_m^i$ can be written as:

$$\bar{p}_m^i = p_m^i + \psi(p_m^i) \tag{3}$$

$$\psi(p_m^i) = \phi(t), t = \sum_{n=1}^{i} \left\| p_m^n - p_m^{n-1} \right\| \tag{4}$$

$$\phi(t) = \theta(t)sin(2\pi(Rt + P_0)t + \phi_0) + Bias \tag{5}$$

$$\theta(t) = A + Bte^{-\alpha t} + C(1 - e^{-\beta t} + De^{\gamma(t-t_0)}) \tag{6}$$

where $\|\cdot\|$ represents the L2 norm and $\sum_{n=1}^{i} \left\| p_m^n - p_m^{n-1} \right\|$ is the accumulated arc length; R, P_0, ϕ_0, $Bias$, A, B, C, D, α, β, γ and t_0 are all constant parameters. As shown in Fig. 4, we can change above constant parameters to obtain the different edited results of hair strands.

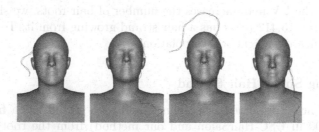

Fig. 4. The edited results of single hair strand: red curve represents the original hair strand and blue curve represents the edited hair strand. (Color figure online)

3.4   Generating Full Hair

In the previous subsection, we only consider the method of editing a single hair strand and cannot set constant parameters for each hair strands. Considering that hair strands whose root positions are close may have a similar geometric shape, these hair strands should have the same parameters in Eq. (5) and Eq. (6). The scalp is similar to a hemisphere, so a polar coordinate system is used to generate grids on the surface of the scalp. 15,412 roots can first be expressed as a position in the polar coordinate system. We divide the polar coordinate space into uniform grids and each hair root will belong to a corresponding grid according to its position in the polar coordinate system (see Fig. 5). We can control the parameters of the uniform division to generate grids of different scales (please compare the results of (a) and (b) in Fig. 5).

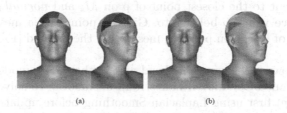

(a)   (b)

Fig. 5. Uniform grid generation: hair roots with the same color are in the same grid and have the same parameters in Eq. (5) and Eq. (6); compared with the grids in (a), the grids in (b) has finer granularity.

After the generation of the grids, we can use the same set of parameters for the hair strands in the same grid. As shown in Fig. 6, original hair strands (Fig. 6(a)) can be modified by Eqs. (3, 4, 5 and 6) and we can get more curvy hair strands (Fig. 6(b)).

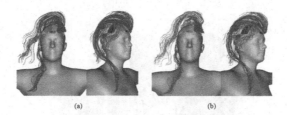

(a)   (b)

Fig. 6. Original hair strands and corresponding edited hair strands in the front and side view.

To achieve natural appearance, we need to set parameters in Eq. (5) and Eq. (6) for hair strands in all grids and adjacent grids should have similar parameters to ensure a smooth transition of shapes. Similar to [31], we use Perlin Noise [23] to generate smoothly varying random parameters in Eq. (5) and Eq. (6).

3.5 Penetration Avoidance

Due to the difference in topology between M_h and M_s, hair strands may penetrate M_s. We judge whether each point in hair strands is inside or on the surface of M_s, and if so, these points need to be moved out of the mesh. Given any point p which need to be moved, we compute the distance $dis(p)$ and moving direction $dir(p)$:

$$dis(p) = \begin{cases} D(p) + d, & p \; inside \; M_s \\ d, & p \; on \; M_s \end{cases} \tag{7}$$

$$dir(p) = \begin{cases} \nabla p, & p \; inside \; M_s \\ normal_p, & p \; on \; M_s \end{cases} \tag{8}$$

where $D(p)$ is the distance from p to the closest point on M_s and d is a constant; ∇p is the gradient to the closest point of p on M_s and $normal_p$ is the normal vector of the face which p belongs to. Given a point and a mesh, we can find the closes point of the given point on mesh using the method [19] of ray-triangle intersection.

Due to the low resolution of the head part in the SMPL model, $dir(p)$ is not smooth which causes the moved hair strand unsmooth. To solve this problem, we smooth $dir(p)$ first using Laplacian Smoothing before updating hair points. After getting the smoothed directions $dir^s(p)$, Eq. (7) is updated as:

$$dis^s(p) = \begin{cases} D^s(p) + d, & p \; inside \; M_s \\ d, & p \; on \; M_s \end{cases} \tag{9}$$

where $D^s(p)$ is the distance from a point p to the surface of M_s along the direction of $dir^s(p)$ and d is a constant. By using Eq. (10), we can avoid the hair-body penetration and get a smooth result (see Fig. 7).

$$p_{new} = p + dis^s(p) * dir^s(p) \tag{10}$$

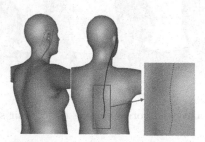

Fig. 7. Avoiding penetration: red points represent the hair points in the raw hair strand, which may penetrate the mesh M_s; blue points represent the moved points; green lines represent the moving directions. (Color figure online)

As shown in Fig. 8, hair models in (a) and (d) are selected from USC-HairSalon, the hair models in (b) and (c) are the edited results based on the model in (a); the hair models in (e) and (f) are the edited results based on the model in (d). The edited result is similar to the original hair model, but they are different in detail. Because we just give small offsets to hair strands in the original hair model, the edited result still has natural appearance.

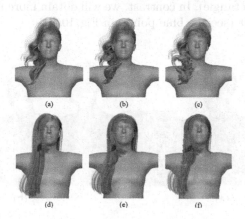

Fig. 8. Modified results: (a) and (d) are the original hair models in USC-HairSalon, (b) and (c) are the modified full results based on (a); (e) and (f) are the modified full results based on (d).

4   Results

4.1   Implementation Details

In our method, we select a hair model from USC-HairSalon [1] or other hair model, which is represented as a collection of strands, as a reference hair model. Our implementation runs on a system with an Intel Core i7-9700k, 32 GB memory. Besides, hair rendering is not the focus of this paper. But to achieve the results close to the natural visual effects, we render the final results refer to [15,27]. More results can be found in Fig. 9.

Fig. 9. Overview of the results.

4.2 Ablation Study

Smoothing Moving Direction. In Subsect. 3.5, we smooth the moving direction before updating the position of hair points. If we don't smooth the moving direction $dir(p)$, we will obtain hair strands that have unnatural appearance.

As shown in Fig. 10(a), green lines which represent moving directions are messy so that the updated hair points have unnatural appearance (see the blue points in the red rectangle). In contrast, we will obtain more natural appearance and smoother result (see the blue points in Fig. 10(b)).

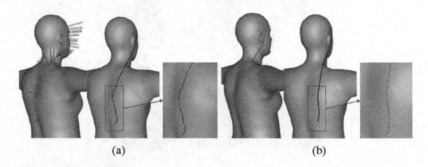

(a)   (b)

Fig. 10. Smoothing moving direction: red points represent the points in the raw hair strand; blue points represent the moved points; green lines represent the moving directions in (a) and the smoothed moving directions in (b). (Color figure online)

5 Conclusion

In this paper, we propose a method to generate more hair data with natural appearance, based on a reference hair model. By editing the reference hair model with manually selected parameters, we can produce more hair data which can be used to generate sufficient data for deep learning applications of hair modeling. In addition, generated hair models all have a fixed number of uniform roots and are aligned with the most widely used parametric human model which benefits human digitization with detailed hair strands at the same time.

References

1. Usc-hairsalon: A 3D hairstyle database for hair modeling. http://www-scf.usc.edu/~liwenhu/SHM/database.html
2. Anguelov, D., Srinivasan, P., Koller, D., Thrun, S., Rodgers, J., Davis, J.: Scape: shape completion and animation of people. In: ACM SIGGRAPH 2005 Papers, pp. 408–416 (2005)
3. Blanz, V., Vetter, T.: A morphable model for the synthesis of 3D faces. In: Proceedings of the 26th Annual Conference on Computer Graphics and Interactive Techniques, pp. 187–194 (1999)

4. Bogo, F., Kanazawa, A., Lassner, C., Gehler, P., Romero, J., Black, M.J.: Keep it SMPL: automatic estimation of 3D human pose and shape from a single image. In: Leibe, B., Matas, J., Sebe, N., Welling, M. (eds.) ECCV 2016. LNCS, vol. 9909, pp. 561–578. Springer, Cham (2016). https://doi.org/10.1007/978-3-319-46454-1_34

5. Bruderlin, A.: A method to generate wet and broken-up animal fur. J. Vis. Comput. Anim. **11**(5), 249–259 (2000)

6. Chai, M., Shao, T., Wu, H., Weng, Y., Zhou, K.: Autohair: fully automatic hair modeling from a single image. ACM Trans. Graph. **35**(4) (2016)

7. Chai, M., Wang, L., Weng, Y., Yu, Y., Guo, B., Zhou, K.: Single-view hair modeling for portrait manipulation. ACM Trans. Graph. (TOG) **31**(4), 1–8 (2012)

8. Choutas, V., Pavlakos, G., Bolkart, T., Tzionas, D., Black, M.J.: Monocular expressive body regression through body-driven attention. In: Vedaldi, A., Bischof, H., Brox, T., Frahm, J.-M. (eds.) ECCV 2020. LNCS, vol. 12355, pp. 20–40. Springer, Cham (2020). https://doi.org/10.1007/978-3-030-58607-2_2

9. Gerig, T., et al.: Morphable face models-an open framework. In: 2018 13th IEEE International Conference on Automatic Face & Gesture Recognition (FG 2018), pp. 75–82. IEEE (2018)

10. Gomez-Donoso, F., Orts-Escolano, S., Cazorla, M.: Large-scale multiview 3D hand pose dataset. Image Vis. Comput. **81**, 25–33 (2019)

11. Guan, P., Weiss, A., Balan, A.O., Black, M.J.: Estimating human shape and pose from a single image. In: 2009 IEEE 12th International Conference on Computer Vision, pp. 1381–1388. IEEE (2009)

12. Hadap, S., Magnenat-Thalmann, N.: Interactive hair styler based on fluid flow. In: Computer Animation and Simulation 2000, pp. 87–99. Springer (2000). https://doi.org/10.1007/978-3-7091-6344-3_7

13. Hu, L., Ma, C., Luo, L., Li, H.: Single-view hair modeling using a hairstyle database. ACM Trans. Graph. (ToG) **34**(4), 1–9 (2015)

14. Joo, H., et al.: Panoptic studio: a massively multiview system for social interaction capture. IEEE Trans. Pattern Anal. Mach. Intell. **41**(1), 190–204 (2017)

15. Kajiya, J.T., Kay, T.L.: Rendering fur with three dimensional textures. ACM Siggraph Comput. Graph. **23**(3), 271–280 (1989)

16. Kim, T.Y., Neumann, U.: Interactive multiresolution hair modeling and editing. ACM Trans. Graph. (TOG) **21**(3), 620–629 (2002)

17. Lassner, C., Romero, J., Kiefel, M., Bogo, F., Black, M.J., Gehler, P.V.: Unite the people: closing the loop between 3D and 2D human representations. In: Proceedings of the IEEE Conference on Computer Vision and Pattern Recognition, pp. 6050–6059 (2017)

18. Loper, M., Mahmood, N., Romero, J., Pons-Moll, G., Black, M.J.: Smpl: a skinned multi-person linear model. ACM Trans. Graph. (TOG) **34**(6), 1–16 (2015)

19. Möller, T., Trumbore, B.: Fast, minimum storage ray-triangle intersection. J. Graph. Tools **2**(1), 21–28 (1997)

20. Nakajima, M., Ming, K.W., Takashi, H.: Generation of 3D hair model from multiple pictures. IEEE Comput. Graph. Appl. **12** (1999)

21. Paris, S., Briceno, H.M., Sillion, F.X.: Capture of hair geometry from multiple images. ACM Trans. Graph. (TOG) **23**(3), 712–719 (2004)

22. Pavlakos, G., et al.: Expressive body capture: 3D hands, face, and body from a single image. In: Proceedings of the IEEE/CVF Conference on Computer Vision and Pattern Recognition, pp. 10975–10985 (2019)

23. Perlin, K.: An image synthesizer. ACM Siggraph Comput. Graph. **19**(3), 287–296 (1985)

24. Romero, J., Tzionas, D., Black, M.J.: Embodied hands: modeling and capturing hands and bodies together. ACM Trans. Graph. (ToG) **36**(6), 1–17 (2017)
25. Saito, S., Hu, L., Ma, C., Ibayashi, H., Luo, L., Li, H.: 3D hair synthesis using volumetric variational autoencoders. ACM Trans. Graph. (ToG) **37**(6), 1–12 (2018)
26. Saito, S., Huang, Z., Natsume, R., Morishima, S., Kanazawa, A., Li, H.: Pifu: pixel-aligned implicit function for high-resolution clothed human digitization. In: Proceedings of the IEEE/CVF International Conference on Computer Vision, pp. 2304–2314 (2019)
27. Sintorn, E., Assarsson, U.: Hair self shadowing and transparency depth ordering using occupancy maps. In: Proceedings of the 2009 Symposium on Interactive 3D Graphics and Games, pp. 67–74 (2009)
28. Varol, G., et al.: Bodynet: volumetric inference of 3D human body shapes. In: Proceedings of the European Conference on Computer Vision (ECCV), pp. 20–36 (2018)
29. Wang, L., Yu, Y., Zhou, K., Guo, B.: Example-based hair geometry synthesis. In: ACM SIGGRAPH 2009 Papers, pp. 1–9 (2009)
30. Ward, K., Bertails, F., Kim, T.Y., Marschner, S.R., Cani, M.P., Lin, M.C.: A survey on hair modeling: styling, simulation, and rendering. IEEE Trans. Vis. Comput. Graph. **13**(2), 213–234 (2007)
31. Yu, Y.: Modeling realistic virtual hairstyles. In: Proceedings Ninth Pacific Conference on Computer Graphics and Applications. Pacific Graphics 2001, pp. 295–304. IEEE (2001)
32. Zhang, M., Zheng, Y.: Hair-GAN: recovering 3D hair structure from a single image using generative adversarial networks. Vis. Inform. **3**(2), 102–112 (2019)
33. Zhang, T., Huang, B., Wang, Y.: Object-occluded human shape and pose estimation from a single color image. In: Proceedings of the IEEE/CVF Conference on Computer Vision and Pattern Recognitio,. pp. 7376–7385 (2020)
34. Zhao, Z., Wang, T., Xia, S., Wang, Y.: Hand-3D-studio: a new multi-view system for 3D hand reconstruction. In: ICASSP 2020–2020 IEEE International Conference on Acoustics, Speech and Signal Processing (ICASSP), pp. 2478–2482. IEEE (2020)
35. Zhou, Y., et al.: Hairnet: single-view hair reconstruction using convolutional neural networks. In: Proceedings of the European Conference on Computer Vision (ECCV), pp. 235–251 (2018)
36. Zhou, Y., Habermann, M., Habibie, I., Tewari, A., Theobalt, C., Xu, F.: Monocular real-time full body capture with inter-part correlations. arXiv preprint arXiv:2012.06087 (2020)

Single Scene Image Editing Based on Deep Intrinsic Decomposition

Hao Sha[1], Yue Liu[1,2(✉)], Kai Lu[1], Chenguang Lu[1], Hengrun Chen[1], and Yongtian Wang[1]

[1] Beijing Engineering Research Center of Mixed Reality and Advanced Display, School of Optics and Photonics, Beijing Institute of Technology, Beijing 100081, China
liuyue@bit.edu.cn

[2] Beijing Film Academy, Advanced Innovation Center for Future Visual Entertainment, Beijing 100088, China

Abstract. Intrinsic decomposition is an inherent problem in computer graphics and computer vision, which decomposes an image into a reflectance image and a shading image. Through the processing of reflectance and shading, it can achieve the image scene editing effect consistent with the vision of the real scene, which endows application potentials to augmented reality. In this paper, we propose a convolutional neural network structure that includes shared and independent encoder to the independent decoder as well as several different loss functions for training based on the assumption of intrinsic decomposition and differences in datasets. To address the shortcomings of the existing synthetic dataset, we reconstruct the new synthetic data and train our network on the synthetic and real datasets in sequence. We quantitatively and qualitatively evaluate our intrinsic decomposition results on the IIW dataset, and the result shows that they outperform those of existing methods. We also perform image editing based on our deep intrinsic decomposition on images of real different scenes and obtain satisfactory visual results.

Keywords: Computer graphics · Computer vision · Intrinsic decomposition

1 Introduction

Intrinsic decomposition is an inherent problem in computer graphics and computer vision, which decomposes images at the physical level and is of significant help in computer vision tasks such as scene understanding. It also has important applications in image relighting [3, 4], retexturing [5, 6] and material recoloring [7, 8]. The intrinsic image decomposition was first proposed by Barrow et al. [1], who represented image formation as a pixel-by-pixel multiplication of the reflectance layer R and the shading layer S based on the common Lambertian assumption:

$$I = R \bullet S \qquad (1)$$

Y. Peng et al. (Eds.): ICIG 2021, LNCS 12890, pp. 545–556, 2021.
https://doi.org/10.1007/978-3-030-87361-5_45

The reflectance layer represents the reflectance of the material surface in the scene, which determines the color texture and other information, and the shading layer represents the appearance of the scene after the effect of light, which is expressed as geometry, shadow and lighting effects.

Although reflectance and shading are different at the illumination level, they both represent intrinsic information of the same scene, so they have shared and independent information in scene understanding. In this paper we propose an encoder-to-decoder CNN structure containing independent and shared weights. The front part of this network consists of an encoder with shared weights for reflectance and shading, and the second part consists of two decoders that are independent of each other. The feature scales of the encoder and decoder are symmetric to each other. After each scale convolutional layer of the encoder, there are two skip layer structures that flow into different decoders, and this skip layer structure is equipped with feature-compressed convolutional layers that serve as separate decoder structures for reflectance and shading respectively. We first train our network on a CGI dataset with reflectance ground truth in a supervised way, it is worth noting that the original CGI dataset only contains rendered images and reflectance, the dynamic range of shading obtained according to the method in [18] is too large for the network to converge well, so we make a new shading for the dataset and resynthesize the dataset to improve the convergence of the network. To enhance the performance of our model on real data, we also train and test the model on the IIW dataset, and obtain competitive results. We introduce multiple physical and prior-based loss functions in the network training and add an image-based filtering method to enhance the overall prediction. Finally, we use the decomposition results to edit different images and obtain satisfactory visual results in different scene modes (Fig. 1).

The rest of this paper is organized as follows. In Sect. 2, we review the works related to this paper. In Sect. 3, we describe in detail the deep intrinsic decomposition method. In Sect. 4, we show the quantitative and qualitative experimental results of intrinsic decomposition and ablation study. In Sect. 5, we implement image editing based on intrinsic decomposition, and in Sect. 6, we conclude the paper.

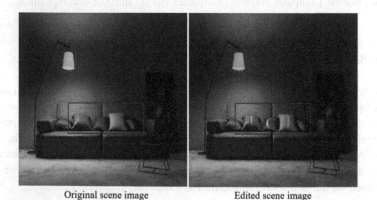

Original scene image   Edited scene image

Fig. 1. Single scene image editing effects based on our method.

2 Related Work

2.1 Optimization Based Intrinsic Decomposition

The classical approaches of intrinsic decomposition are usually based on the relationship between pixels and some prior cognitions [9–11]. For example, the reflectance of a scene is usually constant in segments, and the number of reflectance in a scene is fixed. The discrete and constant nature of the reflectance creates a highly variable material boundary in the appearance of the scene. The shading image reflects more geometric information such as scene shape, occlusion and rich lighting information such as smooth shadow, high frequency lighting. These methods input the image priors into the optimization model and obtain the intrinsic image by iteratively solution [2, 20–22]. Although a priori-based optimization methods can achieve good results in specific scenes [9], they pose high restrictions on the scene and cannot be generalized well. Moreover, most of the priors exist only for simple single-object scene images, it is difficult to extract such information for complex scene images. There are also many methods to improve the quality of decomposition by the incorporation of the additional image scene information [12] or other additional cues such as depth [23], but such methods have even lower applicability and cannot be applied to a wide range of image editing tasks. Some prior constraint methods based solely on pixel relationships again ignore the physical information contained in the scene, and thus are also subject to higher errors.

2.2 Learning Based Intrinsic Decomposition

In recent years, convolutional neural networks have shown excellent performance on many scene understanding tasks, such as semantic segmentation of scenes [13], depth prediction of scenes [14], etc. However, the intrinsic decomposition differs from the above tasks in that the intrinsic ground truth of real images cannot be obtained, so most CNN-based methods use synthetic datasets instead of real datasets for supervised learning of the network. However, it has been found in practice that networks trained by synthetic datasets often perform poorly when being tested on real images, and for this reason many methods incorporate manually judged sparse reflection labeled datasets IIW [16] and shadow labeled datasets SAW [19] into the network training as well to enhance the generalization performance of the network on real data. [15] used the synthetic MPI Sintel dataset and the MIT intrinsic dataset for joint training of the network, and although they successfully decomposed A and S, the quality of their dataset limited its decomposition on real data. [18] synthesized a large high-quality indoor scene dataset CGI to train CNNs, but such a high-quality dataset also suffers from shortcomings when being tested on real data. Therefore, most current end-to-end learning methods train the network on synthetic datasets and then transfer the pre-trained network to real datasets for unsupervised or semi-supervised training [24–26]. There are also some methods that improve the intrinsic decomposition by adding information such as normal, which in turn reduces artifacts in reflectance and shading [27–29]. The essence of convolutional neural networks aims at extracting similar features of the data, but ignores the specificity of each image, so when the test data is too far from the training data, unsatisfactory results often occur.

3   Deep Intrinsic Decomposition

3.1   Dataset

Although the CGI dataset is a high-quality synthetic intrinsic dataset, the original dataset contains only RGB images and their reflectance, so we need to solve for the ground truth of the shading of the input image based on the relationship of the intrinsic images. However, we find that the color information contained in the shading is lost after converting the shading from Eq. 1 to a single channel, resulting in inconsistency between the reconstructed image and the original input image, as shown in the second column of Fig. 2. Second, the dynamic range of the generated shading is too large, and the overall dark shading leads to a darker reconstructed image, which increases the difficulty of fitting the network and increases the difference between the synthesized data and the real data. Therefore, in order to keep the shading within the dynamic range of the input image, we solve for the intensity of the input image and use it as the new shading, then reduce the dynamic range of the reflectance to generate a new reflectance, and finally reconstruct the new input image with the processed reflectance and shading as shown in the third column of Fig. 2. Our newly synthesized data set not only satisfies Eq. 1 of the intrinsic image assumption, but is also visually closer to the real image. Finally, the CGI dataset used for training has a total of 18k pairs of images, and in order to conduct the comparison, we also choose the original CGI reconstructed dataset of the same scene to train the network.

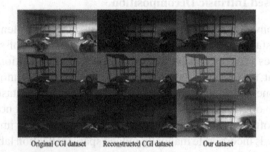

Original CGI dataset   Reconstructed CGI dataset   Our dataset

Fig. 2. Comparison of the CGI dataset and our reconstructed dataset.

To enhance the decomposition of our network on real datasets, we select the IIW dataset [16] for transfer training of our pre-trained network. the IIW dataset contains 5k real photos with a total of 872161 sparse pairwise artificial judgments of reflectance, and we perform training following the previous work by using 1/4 of the images for testing and the others for training.

3.2   Network Architecture

As shown in Fig. 3, our network mainly consists of shared encoders (blue blocks), independent encoders (green blocks) and independent decoders (red blocks).

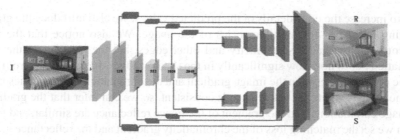

Fig. 3. Our network architecture. (Colour online figure)

The input RGB image is first convolved by a layer of convolution to expand the features of the input image, which is then fed to the encoder network. Because reflectance and shading are identical in terms of image content but independent at the physical level, our encoder network adds independent encoder layers after each shared encoding layer to connect to the symmetric scale decoder layer. After passing through the encoder, the input features are fed to the decoder, which progressively up-samples the features from the encoder by convolution and deconvolution and finally recovers them to the input image size. The final output features are recovered to reflectance and shading by a layer of 1*1 convolution of the feature map, and the number of features in each layer of the network is shown in Fig. 3. The detailed network structures are as follows.

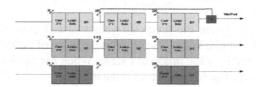

Fig. 4. The decoding layer and the encoding layer.

As shown in the first row of Fig. 4, the head of our shared encoding layer is a convolutional layer, followed immediately by a residual block, and the tail is a maximum pooling layer, with all convolutional layers consisting of a 3*3 convolution, Leaky-ReLu, and BN. As shown in the second row of Fig. 4, the head of our independent encoding layer is a convolutional layer, followed by a convolutional layer with features reduced to half, and the tail is connected to a convolutional layer with features increased by a factor of 2. The structure of the convolutional layer is the same as that of the shared coding layer. As shown in the third row of Fig. 4, the head of our independent decoding layer is a convolutional layer with the same structure as the first two layers, and the tail is connected to an up-sampling layer consisting of a 2*2 deconvolution, ReLu and BN.

3.3 Loss Function

For the synthetic dataset containing dense ground truth, we compute the scale-invariant error L_{lsv} of the predicted values with respect to the ground truth pixel by pixel[18]. In order to increase the edge details of the predicted values, we also introduce the gradient matching loss L_{grad} for multiple scales of the image. We also notice that the image gradient contains shadows, geometry and other edges, but the gradient of the image chromaticity does not show significantly in the shadow edges. It can be seen from Fig. 5 that the difference between the image gradient and the chromaticity gradient lies mainly in some regions where the reflectance is consistent, so we can infer that the gradient of the image chromaticity and the gradient of the image reflectance are similar, and for this reason we set the matching loss of the chromaticity gradient and the reflectance gradient $L_{chromagrad}$. Finally, we set the reconstruction error based on the physical assumptions of the image L_{recon}, where

$$L_{lsv} = \frac{1}{N} \sum_{i=1}^{N} \|R_i - R_i^*\|_2 - \|\frac{1}{N} \sum_{i=1}^{N} R_i - \frac{1}{N} \sum_{i=1}^{N} R_i^*\|_2 +$$
$$\frac{1}{N} \sum_{i=1}^{N} \|S_i - S_i^*\|_2 - \|\frac{1}{N} \sum_{i=1}^{N} S_i - \frac{1}{N} \sum_{i=1}^{N} S_i^*\|_2 \tag{2}$$

$$L_{grad} = \sum_{l=1}^{L} \frac{1}{N_l} \sum_{i=1}^{Ni} \|\nabla R_{l,i} - \nabla R_{l,i}^*\|_2 + \|\nabla S_{l,i} - \nabla S_{l,i}^*\|_2 \tag{3}$$

$$L_{chromagrad} = \frac{1}{N} \sum_{i=1}^{N} \|\nabla R_i - \nabla C_i^*\|_2 \tag{4}$$

$$L_{recon} = \frac{1}{N} \sum_{i=1}^{N} \|R_i * S_i - I_i^*\|_2 \tag{5}$$

$R_{l,i}(R_{l,i}^*)$ and $S_{l,i}(S_{l,i}^*)$ are the predicted values of reflectance (ground truth) and shading (ground truth) at pixel i and l scale, I_i^* is the value of the input image at pixel i, N_l is the number of pixels of the image at l scale. When l is equal to 1, the image is in the original scale space. The loss on the CGI dataset is:

$$\mathrm{L_{CGI}} = \lambda_1 * L_{lsv} + \lambda_2 * L_{grad} + \lambda_3 * L_{chromagrad} + \lambda_4 * L_{recon} \tag{6}$$

The IIW dataset contains sparse manually judged labels, for which we first set the order loss of IIW [18], where $L_{ord} \cdot = \sum_{(i,j)} e_{i,j}(R)$

$$e_{(i,j)}(R) = \begin{cases} w_{i,j}(R_i - R_j)^2, & J_{i,j} = 0 \\ w_{i,j}(t - R_i + R_j)^2, & J_{i,j} = +1 \\ w_{i,j}(t - R_j + R_i)^2, & J_{i,j} = -1 \end{cases} \tag{7}$$

and $J_{i,j}$ is the pixel relationship of IIW, indicating that point i is darker (-1), point j is darker ($+1$) or both have the same reflectance, $w_{i,j}$ comes from the confidence weights in the dataset judgment. We also set the smoothing loss on local reflectance [18]:

$$L_{rs} = \sum_{l=1}^{L} \frac{1}{N_l l} \sum_{i=1}^{Ni} \sum_{j \in N(Li)} v_{l,i,j} \|R_{l,i} - R_{l,j}\|_2 \tag{8}$$

where $N(l, i)$ denotes the 8-connected neighborhood of the pixel at position i and scale l. The reflectance weight, $v_{l,i,j} = \exp\left(-\frac{1}{2}(\mathbf{f}_{l,i} - \mathbf{f}_{l,j})^T M^{-1}(\mathbf{f}_{l,i} - \mathbf{f}_{l,j})\right)$ and the feature vector $\mathbf{f}_{l,i}$ are defined as $[p_{l,i}, I_{l,i}, c_{l,i}^1, c_{l,i}^2]$, where $p_{l,i}$ and $I_{l,i}$ are the spatial position and image intensity respectively, and $c_{l,i}^1$, $c_{l,i}^2$ are the first two elements of chromaticity. M is a covariance matrix defining the distance between two feature vectors. The total loss on the IIW dataset is:

$$L_{IIW} = \lambda_1 * L_{ord} + \lambda_2 * L_{rs} + \lambda_3 * L_{chromagrad} + \lambda_4 * L_{recon} \tag{9}$$

RGB image — Gradient of RGB — Gradient of chromaticity — Error of gradient

Fig. 5. Comparison of different gradients.

3.4 Training Details

We implement our approach on pytorch [30]. For CGI dataset, we train our network using the Adam [31] optimizer, with initial learning rate of 0.00001 and mini-batch size of 4, The weights of the loss function are 2.0,0.25,2.0,1.0 respectively. For the IIW dataset, we load the pre-trained model from the CGI dataset for fine-tune using the Adam optimizer, with initial learning rate of 0.00001 and mini-batch size of 1, The weights of the loss function are 2.0, 1.0,1.0,2.0, respectively.

4 Experimental Results

4.1 Evaluation on the IIW Dataset

We evaluate our intrinsic decomposition results on the IIW dataset. Quantitative comparisons of Weighted Human Disagreement Rate (WHDR) [16] and qualitative comparisons between our method and other methods are shown in Fig. 6.

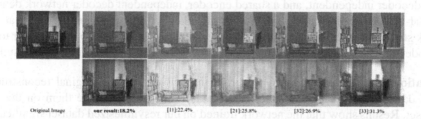

Original Image   our result:18.2%   [11]:22.4%   [21]:25.8%   [32]:26.9%   [33]:31.3%

Fig. 6. Quantitative and qualitative comparisons on IIW.

It can be seen from Fig. 6 that our method obtains the lowest WHDR score (lower is better) in the quantitative evaluation compared to the other methods, and it can also be seen from the qualitative results that our results are visually better, which is evident in our predicted smoother reflectance and better performance in terms of detail. It is worth noting that WHDR is only an evaluation of reflectance, but in terms of the visual effect of shading, our predicted shading is clearly better than other methods, especially in terms of shading details, smoothness of shadows and changes in lighting.

4.2 Ablation Study

We train on synthetic and real datasets sequentially with a shared and independent encoder to independent decoder network structure, setting all the loss functions proposed in Sect. 3.3 to obtain our best results. A quantitative comparison of our ablation study is shown in Table 1, where the first column indicates the method used and the second column indicates the increase in WHDR compared to the best results.

Table 1. Ablation study with different network structures and parameter settings.

Method	Increase value of WHDR
The best result	0%
ID-net	1.14%
SH-net	0.92%
Original reconstruction CGI Dataset	2.89%
Without IIW dataset	**3.25%**
L_1	0.82%
L_2	0.88%
$L_{chromagrad}$	0.74%
With the bilateral filter	−2.21%

Ablation Study of the Network Structure. To explore the effect of the network architecture on our results, we set up a network structure denoted as ID-net with both encoder and decoder independent, and a shared encoder, independent decoder network denoted as SH-net. We train both networks with all other settings the same as the final network structure, and the results show that the use of a shared independent encoder to the decoder-independent network structure improves the intrinsic decomposition results.

Ablation Study on the Dataset. We train the network on the original reconstructed CGI dataset and our reconstructed CGI dataset, and then evaluate them on the IIW dataset. Results show that the network trained on our resynthesized dataset significantly improves decomposition results, demonstrating that the processing on the dataset is effective and viable. We also compare the results of training directly on the synthetic data and transfer training by adding the real IIW dataset, and it can be found that adding the real dataset significantly reduces the value of WHDR and improves the decomposition of the network on the real data. Moreover, in real image editing applications, the decomposed reconstructed real image has deviations compared to the original image because of the deviations between the synthetic and real datasets, and we have to fine-tune the pre-trained network on the real dataset to enhance the performance of the network on the real data.

Ablation Study of the Loss Function. The loss function used in our best results is based on the scale invariant loss of L_2 parametric, and we compare it with the training framework based on L_1 parametric and L_2 parametric, and the experimental results show that the scale invariant loss can make the network fit better and improve the final results. We also study the ablation of the chromatic gradient matching loss, and the experimental results show that the chromatic gradient matching loss also improves the prediction effect.

The Ablation Study of the Filter Introduction. We add bilateral filters to filter the predicted results and find that the introduction of filters would significantly improve the quantitative metrics in the IIW dataset. As for the visual appearance, the introduction of bilateral filters would blur many due details and not necessarily bring the actual benefit on the intrinsic decomposition as it should as shown in Fig. 7. This reflects that the evaluation metrics of the IIW dataset are not fully representative of the quality of the intrinsic decomposition and it has some limitations, so we do not filter the predicted reflectance in practical applications.

Predicted reflectance R   Reflectance after filter RF   Details of R   Details of RF

Fig. 7. Comparison of reflectance before and after the filter.

5 Application in Image Editing

Based on our deep intrinsic decomposition model, we implement realistic editing of a single image. Figure 8 shows our overall framework, where we input the image into our deep intrinsic decomposition model, process the output intrinsic image by re-texturing the reflectance, and then reconstruct the edited intrinsic image to obtain the final result. Compared to previous realistic image editing [34], our method does not require huge rendering calculations, it only requires the pixel multiplication of reflectance and shading, which significantly saves time and computational resources. Our method produces realistic image editing results as shown in Fig. 9, in which we compare editing directly on the image with editing based on our method. It can be seen from Fig. 9 that the image editing based on our method is different from editing directly on the image level, which endows the newly inserted character with the lighting changes and textures from the original scene, as if the scene were edited directly on the 3D level.

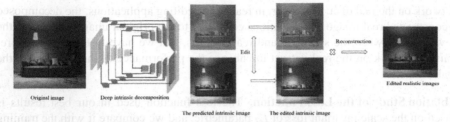

Fig. 8. Our overall image editing framework.

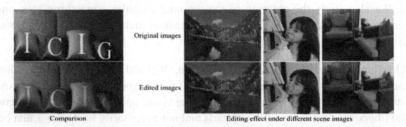

Fig. 9. Image editing effects for different scenes.

To demonstrate the generalizability of our method on different scenes, we conduct the proposed image editing approach on outdoor images, portraits and indoor images respectively. As shown in the first column of Fig. 9, we repaint the outdoor scene by repainting some dead leaves with green color to turn winter into spring. As shown in the second column of Fig. 9, we re-makeup the portrait and apply a new lipstick with a realistic appearance to the girl in the photo. In the third row of Fig. 9, we replace the material and insert virtual objects into the indoor scene, replacing the fabric of the sofa on the left with a frosted brown fabric and overlaying a cartoon pattern on the cushion on the right. All these effects prove that our approach demonstrates excellent capabilities in a range of scenarios.

6   Conclusion

In this paper, we propose a deep neural network architecture based on physical assumptions to solve the decomposition problem of intrinsic images. We make modifications to previous synthetic datasets and propose the new loss function to further improve the quality of intrinsic image decomposition. We also use our architecture to complete the image editing task for several different scenes, and the results show that our framework can produce good quality images in different scenes. However, our approach has some limitations because the intrinsic image assumptions are based on white illumination and scenes with diffuse reflections, and our results tend to perform poorly when facing specular reflections or colored illumination. Our future work will focus on proposing new models to solve such problems.

Acknowledgement. This work was supported by the Key-Area Research and Development Program of Guangdong Province (No.2019B010149001) and the 111 Project (B18005) and the National Natural Science Foundation of China (No.61960206007).

References

1. Barrow, H., et al.: Recovering intrinsic scene characteristics. Comput. Vis. Syst. **2**, 3–26 (1978)
2. Land, E.H., John J.M.: Lightness and retinex theory. JOSA **61**(1), 1–11(1971)
3. Beigpour, S., Van De Weijer, J.: Object recoloring based on intrinsic image estimation. In: International Conference on Computer Vision 2011, pp. 327–334. IEEE (2011)
4. Duchêne, S., et al.: Multiview intrinsic images of outdoors scenes with an application to relighting. ACM Trans. Graph. **34**(5), 164 (2015)
5. Bousseau, A., Sylvain, P., Frédo, D.: User-assisted intrinsic images. In: ACM SIGGRAPH Asia 2009 Papers, pp. 1–10 (2009)
6. Shen, J., et al.: Re-texturing by intrinsic video. Inf. Sci. **281**, 726–735 (2014)
7. Ye, G., et al.: Intrinsic video and applications. ACM Trans. Graph. (ToG) **33**(4), 1–11 (2014)
8. Meka, A., et al.: Live intrinsic video. ACM Trans. Graph. (TOG) **35**(4), 1–14 (2016)
9. Barron, J.T., Malik, J.: Shape, illumination, and reflectance from shading. IEEE Trans. Pattern Anal. Mach. Intell. **37**(8), 1670–1687 (2014)
10. Bi, S., Xiaoguang, H., Yizhou, Y.: An l 1 image transform for edge-preserving smoothing and scene-level intrinsic decomposition. ACM Trans. Graph. (TOG) **34**(4), 1–12 (2015)
11. Shen, L., Yeo, C.: Intrinsic images decomposition using a local and global sparse representation of reflectance. In: CVPR 2011, pp. 697–704. IEEE (2016)
12. Chen, Q., Koltun, V.: A simple model for intrinsic image decomposition with depth cues. In: Proceedings of the IEEE International Conference on Computer Vision, pp. 241–248. IEEE (2013)
13. Badrinarayanan, V., Alex K., Roberto, C.: Segnet: a deep convolutional encoder-decoder architecture for image segmentation. IEEE Trans. Pattern Anal. Mach. Intell. **39**(12), 2481–2495 (2017)
14. Eigen, D., Fergus, R.: Predicting depth, surface normals and semantic labels with a common multi-scale convolutional architecture. In: Proceedings of the IEEE International Conference on Computer Vision, pp. 2650–2658. IEEE (2015)
15. Narihira, T., Maire, M., Yu, S.X.: Direct intrinsics: Learning albedo-shading decomposition by convolutional regression. In: Proceedings of the IEEE International Conference on Computer Vision, p. 2992. IEEE (2015)
16. Bell, S., Kavita, B., Noah, S.: Intrinsic images in the wild. ACM Trans. Graph. (TOG) **33**(4), 1–12 (2014)
17. Grosse, R., Johnson, M.K., Adelson, E.H., Freeman, W.T.: Ground truth dataset and baseline evaluations for intrinsic image algorithms. In: 2009 IEEE 12th International Conference on Computer Vision, pp. 2335–2342. IEEE (2009)
18. Li, Z., Snavely, N.: Cgintrinsics: better intrinsic image decomposition through physically-based rendering. In: Proceedings of the European Conference on Computer Vision (ECCV), pp. 371–387. IEEE (2009)
19. Kovacs, B., Bell, S., Snavely, N., Bala, K.: Shading annotations in the wild. In: Proceedings of the IEEE Conference on Computer Vision and Pattern Recognition, pp. 6998–7007. IEEE (2017)
20. Rother, C., et al.: Recovering intrinsic images with a global sparsity prior on reflectance. Adv. Neural Inf. Process. Syst. **24**, 765–773 (2011)

21. Zhao, Q., et al.: A closed-form solution to retinex with nonlocal texture constraints. IEEE Trans. Pattern Anal. Mach. Intell. **34**(7), 1437–1444 (2012)
22. Shen, L., Yeo, C.: Intrinsic images decomposition using a local and global sparse representation of reflectance. In: CVPR 2011, pp. 697–704. IEEE (2011)
23. Barron, J.T., Malik, J.: Intrinsic scene properties from a single RGB-D image. In: Proceedings of the IEEE Conference on Computer Vision and Pattern Recognition, pp. 17–24. IEEE (2013)
24. Liu, Y., Li, Y., You, S., Lu, F.: Unsupervised learning for intrinsic image decomposition from a single image. In: Proceedings of the IEEE/CVF Conference on Computer Vision and Pattern Recognition, pp. 3248–3257. IEEE (2020)
25. Nestmeyer, T., Gehler, P.V.: Reflectance adaptive filtering improves intrinsic image estimation. In: Proceedings of the IEEE Conference on Computer Vision and Pattern Recognition, pp. 6789–6798. IEEE (2017)
26. Qian, Y., Shi, M., Kamarainen, J.K., Matas, J.: Fast Fourier intrinsic network. In: Proceedings of the IEEE/CVF Winter Conference on Applications of Computer Vision, pp. 3169–3178. IEEE (2021)
27. Sheng, B., et al.: Intrinsic image decomposition with step and drift shading separation. IEEE Trans. Vis. Comput. Graph. **26**(2), 1332–1346 (2018)
28. Zhou, H., Yu, X., Jacobs, D.W.: Glosh: Global-local spherical harmonics for intrinsic image decomposition. In: Proceedings of the IEEE/CVF International Conference on Computer Vision, pp. 7820–7829. IEEE (2019)
29. Luo, J., et al.: NIID-Net: adapting surface normal knowledge for intrinsic image decomposition in indoor scenes. IEEE Trans. Vis. Comput. Graph. **26**(12), 3434–3445 (2020)
30. Pytorch. (2016). http://pytorch.org
31. Kingma, D.P., Jimmy, B.: Adam: a method for stochastic optimization. arXiv preprint arXiv: 1412.6980 (2014)
32. Garces, E., Munoz, A., Lopez-Moreno, J., Gutierrez, D.: Intrinsic images by clustering. Comput. Graph. Forum **31**(4), 1415–1424 (2012)
33. Bonneel, N., et al.: Interactive intrinsic video editing. ACM Trans. Graph. (TOG) **33**(6), 1–10 (2014)
34. Zhou, Z., Meng, M., Zhou, Y.: Massive video integrated mixed reality technology. ZTE Technol. J. **23**(06), 10–13 (2017)

3A2A: A Character Animation Pipeline for 3D-Assisted 2D-Animation

Oscar Dadfar$^{(\boxtimes)}$ and Nancy Pollard

Carnegie Mellon University, Pittsburgh, PA 15213, USA
{odadfar,npollard}@andrew.cmu.edu

Abstract. 2D hand-drawn character animation requires a substantial amount of time and drawing experience, turning away many interested in the field based on their lack of drawing ability. In an effort to make this type of animation more accessible to new creators without drawing experience, we provide a pipeline that creates hand-drawn character keyframes from stick figures. Our 2D interface allows users to draw and edit stick figures in 3D space that are then used to pose and toon-shade any 3D character model. We give these reference images a hand-drawn effect by applying a sketch-like filter to the cel-shaded output and compose it with a painted shading effect. We evaluate our work on multiple animation cycles and various models, demonstrating the program's ease-of-use for individuals with or without drawing experience. This strategy helps non-artists create 2D hand-drawn human character animations by reducing the entire hand-drawn character pipeline to simply drawing stick figures. We believe that if anyone can draw stick figures, then anyone can animate.

Keywords: Human-centered computing · Graphical user interfaces · Fine arts

1 Introduction

Since Disney's release of Snow White and the Seven Dwarfs in 1937, traditional hand-drawn animation gained momentum as one of the most entertaining and inspiring mediums of creativity and storytelling of its time. A few decades later, many animation studios have yet to put out any hand-drawn animation films, with Disney having no plans for releasing any 2D animation films in the future [28]. The cost and skill associated with drawing out every frame, a practice originally done on cel-sheet paper due to the lack of technology, was too expensive compared to its computer-generated counterpart that requires no drawing experience. As easier 3D tools became more widely accessible, more novice content creators would avoid the art of hand-drawn animations in favor of 3D animation, citing that they do not have the necessary drawing skills to create traditional animations [1].

A few notable qualities make hand-drawn animation more favorable compared to its 3D counterpart. Traditional animation has a human-like touch,

Y. Peng et al. (Eds.): ICIG 2021, LNCS 12890, pp. 557–568, 2021.
https://doi.org/10.1007/978-3-030-87361-5_46

Fig. 1. Our program computes the joint angles of a set of key body joints to pose any 3D model. The posed model is toon-shaded and sketched over to help give a hand-drawn animation. Bottom row of frames were sketched and colored using the middle row reference keyframes.

where every stroke is carefully thought out rather than interpolated. Characters are not limited to human constraints and can bend and rotate limbs in any fashion. Yet in order to create such character animations, individuals need to know how to draw characters accurately (per frame) and consistently (across frames), putting forth a high artistic barrier for those interested in the field.

In order to alleviate the high requirements of 2D animation, we developed an animation pipeline that does not require any artistic ability from the user when creating hand-drawn animations. While previous work explores 3D animation from 2D sketches, our pipeline is the first of its kind to use 3D models to help go from stick figures to a 2D character animation. We can model realistic body turns and proper object perspectives that are otherwise difficult for 2D character animators to draw, giving beginner animators an easy way to generate and stylize characters in a toon-like fashion. We demonstrate the program's ease-of-use in creating several different hand-drawn animation cycles applied to various character models and evaluate the system on a number of individuals with and without traditional artistic backgrounds. The final pipeline allows anyone to, regardless of artistic ability, create 2D hand-drawn animations, encouraging individuals without artistic backgrounds to create hand-drawn animations despite their lack of drawing experience.

2   Related Works

Making 2D animation easier has been a persistent challenge, pushing creators to spend more time dreaming and less time drawing. Disney Research's Mender was developed as a vector/raster hybrid interface for computing in-betweens quickly [33] and Adobe's Flash Professional software integrated a similar pen tool to vectorize brush strokes, but both approaches suffered from the same artifacts when trying to adjust to complex geometries like face and body turns. Researchers at Autodesk added "Motion Amplifiers" that apply a set of transformations on a vector to model the motions found in the 12 Principles of Animation [17,30], although the resulting vector still suffers from its inability to exhibit 3D rotations. 2D sketches can also be used to to pose 2D vectored characters [27], but this is limited in viewpoint as we cannot consider 3D rotations.

We can edit 3D motions to obey the 12 Principles by applying filters or convolutions to exaggerate [18,34] or squash and stretch [19] these 3D motions, making them look more 2D like. While these filters are a step in the right direction, the viewer can often see that the results were generated by a filter and not by hand animation, thus leading the viewer to loose interest in the work. An alternative to this is to use inverse kinematics on the joint angles [20,21] or bone segments [3] to pose the characters in the exaggerated ways we see in 2D animation. One solver in particular attempts to use 2D sketches in the model's 3D environment as a basis for 3D character posing using inverse kinematics [24], making 3D character posing and animating a 2D constrained problem, given that all target movements lie along the same plane. We use this mechanism of editing 3D data along the 2D camera plane as a part of the backbone of our drawing interface, as it provides a way to pose 3D characters from 2D-constrained sketches.

State-of-the-art research in this area focuses on 2D-assisted 3D animation from rough 2D skeletons [7,9,12] and from detailed artist drawings [15]. Converting 2D sketches to 3D posing data is an under-constrained problem, leading to many possible poses per 2D sketch. Rather than querying the user to pick the best pose from a sketch or searching for similar 3D poses from a database [23,29], we attempt to properly constrain the problem by drawing 2D stick figures in 3D space. These 3D interfaces for 2D sketches have been used previously for iterative character re-posing [24] and to define spatial trajectories of character motions [10,11,31]. These same 3D drawing environments can also be used for creating 3D human character models [25] or various other 3D models [5,35,36] from 2D sketches. They provide an interface for drawing within 3D space that leads to a fully-constrained conversion between sketch and 3D posing, and rotations in these 3D sketch spaces can be achieved by easily computing the quaternion rotations [16] between joints. While intuitive, these models are used for 3D animation rather than 2D. We combine these 3D spaces with 2D rendering techniques to provide the first accurate 3D animation interface for 2D rendering.

Toon Shading is a non-photorealistic rendering style that helps give 3D animation a 2D cartoon-like look [4,13] by thresholding on the shader's color value to give a render high-contrast shading effects that we see in 2D imaging and paintings. Hand-drawn shading is an alternative that integrates sketch-like strokes around the contours of an image to give it a more natural, hand-drawn feel [6,22,26,32]. When rasterizing 3D-posed reference frames, we can apply these hand-drawn shading styles to the contours of our exported 3D character animation sequence to help make it look more like a 2D sketch while also introducing the stochasticity and roughness of human sketches that we see between frames.

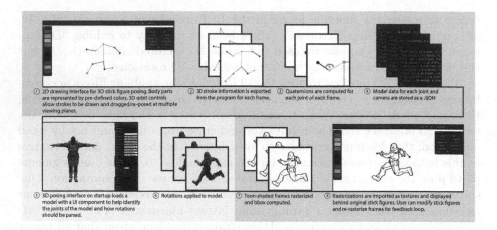

Fig. 2. Block diagram of the interface. Blue regions refer to the sketch interface while orange regions refer to the posing interface. The joint rotations of the sketch in 3D space are used to pose a user-imported 3D model. These model frames are toon-shaded and cropped before being loaded behind the original stick figure, providing a live feedback-loop. (Color figure online)

3   Approach

Figure 2 shows a high-level description of the animation interface segmented into two parts: 2D and 3D. The 2D drawing interface is the user side that is responsible for gathering the joint vectors that comprise the stick figure. This data is sent to the 3D interface where these rotations are computed and applied to a rigged character model that is toon-shaded and rasterized before being sent back to the 2D interface. The user has a chance to make any corrections and re-pose any frames they are not happy with. Once done with their animation cycle, users can sketch their character animation using these frames as keyframe reference or can use the hand-drawn program we discuss in the paper to algorithmically give the character a sketch-like feel.

2D Interface. We construct a 2D interface that can sketch multi-color strokes in 3D space. The different stroke colors refer to different body parts, including the back, left-leg, left-ankle, right-leg, right-ankle, left-shoulder, left-arm, right-shoulder, and right-arm. The user can draw on the plane parallel to the current camera's view and drag endpoints of existing stokes parallel to the same camera plane. We install an orbital camera to view the stick figure from different angles and to help redraw/drag existing strokes. This mechanism allows users to draw in the native xy-plane that they are used to drawing in 2D on pen and paper while still allowing the user to modify depths of strokes in the z-pane. If the user draws a stroke that already exists on the current frame, the previously existing stroke is cleared, allowing for only one instance of each body part per frame.

Fig. 3. 3D posing interface with configurable parameters. The user specifies the joint mappings between the joints in the 2D setting with the joint names for the specific model.

The interface's provided timeline coupled with the onion skinning tool allows for drawing in-betweens with ease after drawing the main keyframes.

The user can link together joints, where the program attaches strokes if they share a common joint. Some common joints include the shoulder connected by the back and left/right-shoulder or the knee connected by the left/right-leg and left/right ankle. This way, the user does not have to make sure strokes connect when drawing them, but can auto-connect joints afterwards.

The rotational data of the joints are used to pose and display a toon-shaded rasterization of the user-selected model behind the user's stick figure for each frame. This allows the user to see in full perspective how their posing looks and allows them to edit their stick figures in realtime.

3D Interface. Each joint maps to a base vector and end vector, where we seek to obtain the rotation transforming a joint along the base vector to the end vector. For each joint, we fetch the initial base vector of the model before any transformations are applied. This helps us compute the quaternion rotation from the base's rest vector to the current base vector [8,14]. We apply the inverse of this quaternion to the base and end vectors for the current joint, allowing us to reset the base vector to its rest position before computing the current joint's quaternion rotation from base to end in its initial space. This is because we will be applying the quaternion rotation to each joint from it's rest position, so we want to compute quaternions when the base vector is aligned with it's rest position.

Each quaternion can be broken into a pitch, yaw, and roll. Because we do not define orientations for our joints, the roll is left undefined when computing the quaternion. This can lead to random rotations that affect the child joint, offsetting target rotations by some amount along the roll of the parent joint. To fix this, we remove the roll component from each joint's parent quaternion. We compute the current axis as the child joint's roll axis and the target axis as the world-space end vector of the child joint and attempt to minimize the dot

Algorithm 1. Joint Rotations

```
for (curJoint, parentJoint) in jointMap do
    Vec3 base = normalize( curJoint.base )
    Vec3 end = normalize( curJoint.end )
    Vec3 initBase = normalize( modelInit[curJoint.id].base )
    //reset base/end to init orientation
    Quat q0 = quaternionFromUnitVec( base, initBase );
    Vec3 baseR = base.rotateByQuaternion( q0.inv() );
    Vec3 endR = end.rotateByQuaternion( q0.inv() );
    Quat q = quaternionFromUnitVec( endR, baseR );
    curJoint.rotateQuaternion( q );
    //remove rollAxis rotation from parent
    Vec3 current = curJoint.rollAxis;
    Vec3 target = end;
    Vec3 axis = target.cross( current );
    float angle = acos( target.dot( current ));
    parentJoint.rotateAxisAligned( parentJoint.rollAxis, angle );
end for
```

product between these two vectors. We can compute the rotation angle between the current and target axis, and apply an axis-aligned rotation onto the parent joint's roll axis for the computed rotation angle. This effectively removes the roll component of the parent's quaternion and correctly aligns the child joint to its target location.

The user can import any rigged 3D model to pose using their stick-figure joint rotations. Since the model joint names and rotations differ from model to model, our interface traverses the model's scene graph and provides a list of all joint names to the user. The user can then configure which local joints map to which model joints. Because these are model-specific parameters, they only need to be computed once per model as shown in Fig. 3.

When rasterizing the frames, we use toon-shading where we extrude the geometry of back-facing normals that are shaded black to give it an outline effect. We interpolate the vertex normals of the model along the faces to create smooth normals that we can threshold on in order to compute hard shadows for our figure. We combine this with a movable directional light to give it a flat-shading effect. For each frame, we pose the model using the quaternions computed per joint and then rasterize the frames and save them to the device (Fig. 4).

We can search for the rasterized frames on the device and compute the bounding box of the toon-shaded image in order to crop the image and display it as a texture behind the bounding box of the stick figure. This allows the user to see in real-time how the frame posing aligns with their stick-figure and allows them to make quick edits to body parts and re-rasterize frames if they need to. This iterative process helps users experiment and refine their animations cycles.

Fig. 4. Applying the same joint rotations to multiple toon-shaded models

Fig. 5. Computing the hand-drawn and paint details separately before compositing them. A displacement map sampled from perlin noise is used on the paint details to give them additional temporal inconsistency.

Sketch Effect. We can generate a hand-drawn feeling along the contours from the backface shading of each frame by applying rough sketch strokes to these contours. Each sketch is comprised of a bezier curve of several nearby points. We generate a random point along the contour of the frame and search for the next point within a given radius of the previous point using uniform rejection sampling, making sure the next point falls within the contour of the frame as well. To help remove extraneous strokes that cut across non-outline regions, we also verify the midpoint between every two points also lies along the contours. We can generate N random strokes in the bounding box of the frame or generate N/C strokes per cell in a $C \times C$ uniform grid to promote the uniformity of strokes distributed.

We can separate the shading components from our toon-shaded models and run a thresholded convolution filter that bins colors into either a light or a shaded color depending on which color the average of the convolution is closer to per pixel. This provides blotchier, smoother details that replicate hand-painted effects for shading. We can apply both light and dark shadows by duplicating the blotchy shading and apply a choke convolution that narrows the region, creating darker shadows in more concentrated regions. We finish by adding a displacement map to the shading, where the displacements are read from a perlin noise texture to provide smooth jittery distortions to the shading per frame to give shading a slight temporal inconsistency, similar to what would be found in hand-painted frames. The results are composited with the stroke effect in Fig. 5 to provide both hand-drawn strokes and shading.

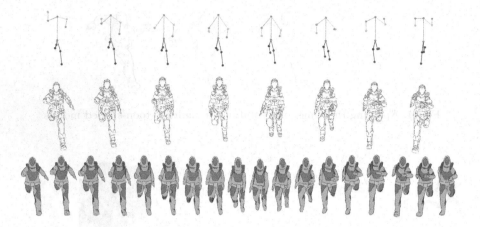

Fig. 6. Front-view run cycles. Bottom row colored-in by novice user.

4 Results

Of the 5 participants we selected to evaluate our system, 1 participant had traditional drawing abilities, 1 participant had vector-art abilities but no drawing abilities, and the remaining 3 participants had no prior art experience. We aim to measure the effects of the pipeline along a diverse set of backgrounds but focus primarily on individuals without art backgrounds.

We evaluated our system on several core animations cycles, such as jumping-jacks and run cycles, which can be seen in Fig. 1, Fig. 6 and Fig. 7. Models were provided by Adobe Mixamo [2], allowing us to configure the joint rotations once in order for the rotations to work for most models. Our comprehensive demo of video animations can be found here.

Participants without drawing experience were asked to sketch over the resulting edge-detected run-cycle frames in Fig. 1 and Fig. 6 to give them a more hand-drawn feel. These participants found that sketching over the reference frames was simple and required no previous drawing experience, yet mentioned that drawing over every frame can take a long time. Because of this, these participants preferred using our sketching algorithm on the contour frames to generate quick automatic sketches of these animation cycles in Fig. 7, requiring no additional sketching and saving users a substantial amount of time.

5 Discussion

The Run, Walk, and Kick cycles in Table 1 were generated by the 2 artist participants while all other cycles were from non-artist participants. Participants without prior art experience were able to create fluid animation cycles, primarily because the animation interface required them to draw rough stick figures. In some cycles in Table 1 the drawing time was substantially longer than the editing time. This happened in cycles such as run and kick that were visually more

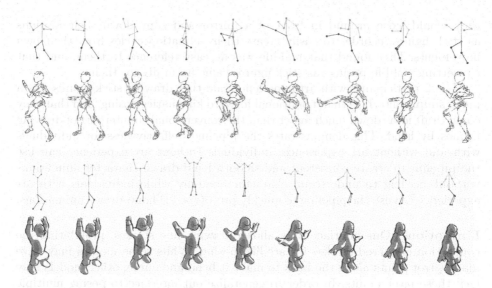

Fig. 7. Participant-generated stick figure animations and the resulting posed output. Top uses edge detection while bottom uses our sketch-painting algorithm with N=1,500 and C=5.

challenging to think and draw the posings for. Most cycles had lower editing times, mainly because it is easier for users to see and edit in-betweens of primitive color-coded stick figures using onion skinning than of larger, more complex 3D character rigs, allowing users to quickly identify and edit changes to their work whenever they noticed a temporal inconsistency in the motion.

Table 1. Animation cycle timed (in mins)

Cycle	Frames	Drawing	Editing	Cycle	Frames	Drawing	Editing
Run	24	16.4	9.4	Kick	17	10.2	4.0
Run (Side)	25	16.4	9.4	Stretch	9	7.3	5.2
Walk	11	7.3	8.9	Dab	9	5.1	2.2
Jump	10	4.2	2.2	Warrior	8	6.2	2.5
Jump (Side)	11	8.19	7.1	Tree Pose	20	8.3	6.3

Following the study, users were asked about their impressions about the pipeline. Non-artist users found it easy to think about their animations as stick figures rather than individual joint rotations when producing their character animation cycles, as stick figure drawings were ubiquitous in their pre-school and elementary school periods. When asking about their thought process during the animation stage, these individuals without art or posing experience said they would move around in front of a mirror and copy down their motions as stick figures in order to easily create their animation cycles from their own movements. They found that real-life was an easy reference to them, and that converting real-life posings as stick figures came naturally for them.

The 2 participants with art experience said that drawing stick figures was a much simpler interface than traditional forward kinematics posing, and that they could draft ideas down much faster than the conventional counterpart of drawing frames by hand. This demonstrates the pipeline's effectiveness for individuals with and without art experience. Individuals without art experience can use the pipeline to create consistent and smooth hand-drawn character animations without needing to understand character anatomy while individuals with art experience can use the pipeline to quickly prototype 2D hand-drawn animations.

Limitations. Our interface only allows drawing line strokes, prohibiting the generation of curved strokes for arc-like posing. While some models may have many pivot points along the back to make it bend and curve, other models may lack these pivot points. In order to generalize our interface to posing multiple models, we use line strokes, not worrying about curved or arc-like body parts.

When computing joint angles, the stick figure from the 2D interface is only concerned with aligning body parts in the 3D model to match their stick figures. Yet this is still an under constrained problem, since our algorithm does not account for the fact that users should be able to rotate joints around themselves that do not change the character pose, but change body part orientations. A common example is twisting an arm around itself. These body part orientations are not specified in the original 2D interface. Future work could explore adding a normal to each stroke to help visualize the orientation, and moving this normal around would change the orientation. When computing joint angles, this changes our alignment strategy from aligning vectors to aligning planes since each joint is described by their unique direction and normal. In this case, there always exists a unique rotation between two planes.

Future work could also look into adding in support for head rotations as well. Most artists represent heads in basic sketches as circle with a cross, where the cross intersection represents where the nose is oriented. Our program would analyze where this point is relative to the center of the circle, as well as whether the cross is bent inwards or outwards to denote whether the nose is facing towards or away from the camera. This information would be enough to construct a unit vector from the center of the face to the cross point and compute the quaternion rotation of the vector from its rest position.

6   Conclusion

Our implementation bridges a 2D drawing interface with a 3D posing and rendering interface in order to assist with the process of creating 2D hand-drawn animations. We also introduce a novel toon-based shading scheme that builds on classic cel-shading to create hand-drawn effects and shading. We believe that with our interface, if anyone can draw stick-figures, then anyone can animate.

References

1. Why we're seeing less 2D animated movies and why they probably won't make a comeback. Bloop Animation (2019)
2. Adobe: Mixamo (2021). https://www.mixamo.com/
3. Aristidou, A., Lasenby, J.: Graphical Models, pp. 243–260 (2011)
4. Bénard, P., Hertzmann, A.: Line drawings from 3D models. CoRR http://arxiv.org/abs/1810.01175 (2018)
5. Chen, B.Y., Ono, Y., Nishita, T.: Character animation creation using hand-drawn sketches. Vis. Comput. **21**, 551–558 (2005). https://doi.org/10.1007/s00371-005-0333-z
6. Curtis, C.: Loose and sketchy animation (1998). http://otherthings.com/uw/loose/sketch.html
7. Davis, J., Agrawala, M., Chuang, E., Popović, Z., Salesin, D.: A sketching interface for articulated figure animation. In: Proceedings of the 2003 ACM SIGGRAPH/Eurographics Symposium on Computer Animation, pp. 320–328 (2003)
8. Day, M.: Extracting Euler angles from a rotation matrix (2014)
9. Dvorožňák, M., Sýkora, D., Curtis, C., Curless, B., Sorkine-Hornung, O., Salesin, D.: Monster mash: a single-view approach to casual 3D modeling and animation. ACM Trans. Graph. **39**(6), 1–12 (2020)
10. Guay, M., Ronfard, R., Gleicher, M., Cani, M.P.: Adding dynamics to sketch-based character animations. In: Proceedings of the Workshop on Sketch-Based Interfaces and Modeling, pp. 27–34 (2015)
11. Guay, M., Ronfard, R., Gleicher, M., Cani, M.P.: Space-time sketching of character animation. ACM Trans. Graph. **34**(4), 1–10 (2015). https://doi.org/10.1145/2766893
12. Hecker, R., Perlin, K.: Controlling 3D objects by sketching 2D views. In: Sensor Fusion V, pp. 46–48 (1992). https://doi.org/10.1117/12.131636
13. Hudon, M., Pagés, R., Grogan, M., Ondrej, J., Smolic, A.: 2D shading for cel animation. Expressive 2018 (2018). https://doi.org/10.1145/3229147.3229148
14. Hughes, N.: Quaternion to/from euler angle of arbitrary rotation sequence and direction cosine matrix conversion using geometric methods (2017)
15. Jain, E., Sheikh, Y., Hodgins, J.: Leveraging the talent of hand animators to create three-dimensional animation. In: Proceedings of the 2009 ACM SIGGRAPH/Eurographics Symposium on Computer Animation, pp. 93–102 (2009). https://doi.org/10.1145/1599470.1599483
16. Jia, Y.B.: Quaternions and rotations (2013). http://graphics.stanford.edu/courses/cs348a-17-winter/Papers/quaternion.pdf
17. Kazi, R.H., Grossman, T., Umetani, N., Fitzmaurice, G.: Motion amplifiers: sketching dynamic illustrations using the principles of 2D animation. In: Proceedings of the 2016 CHI Conference on Human Factors in Computing Systems, pp. 4599–4609 (2016). https://doi.org/10.1145/2858036.2858386
18. Kwon, J.Y., Lee, I.K.: Rubber-like exaggeration for character animation. In: Pacific Graphics, pp. 18–26 (2007). https://doi.org/10.1109/PG.2007.25
19. Kwon, J.Y., Lee, I.K.: The squash-and-stretch stylization for character motions. IEEE Trans. Vis. Comput. Graph. **18**, 488–500 (2011). https://doi.org/10.1109/TVCG.2011.48
20. Lander, J.: Making kine more flexible. Game Developer Mag. **1**, 15–22 (1998)
21. Lander, J.: Oh my god, i inverted kine! Game Developer Mag. **9**, 9–14 (1998)

22. Liu, D., Nabail, M., Hertzmann, A., Kalogerakis, E.: Neural contours: learning to draw lines from 3D shapes. In: Computer Vision and Pattern Recognition (2020)
23. Lv, P., et al.: A suggestive interface for sketch-based character posing. Comput. Graph. Forum **34**(7), 111–121 (2015). https://doi.org/10.1111/cgf.12750
24. Mahmudi, M., Harish, P., Le Callennec, B., Boulic, R.: Artist-oriented 3D character posing from 2D strokes. Comput. Graph. **57**, 81–91 (2016). https://doi.org/10.1016/j.cag.2016.03.008
25. Mao, C., Qin, S.F., Wright, D.: A sketch-based approach to human body modelling. Comput. Graph. **33**(4), 521–541 (2009). https://doi.org/10.1016/j.cag.2009.03.028
26. Muhammad, U.R., Yang, Y., Song, Y., Xiang, T., Hospedales, T.M.: Learning deep sketch abstraction. CoRR http://arxiv.org/abs/1804.04804 (2018)
27. Pan, J., Zhang, J.: Sketch-based skeleton-driven 2D animation and motion capture. Trans. Edutainment **6**, 164–181 (2011). https://doi.org/10.1007/978-3-642-22639-7-17
28. Stein, M.: Will disney ever return to making hand-drawn animated films? The Mickey Mindset (2016)
29. Tang, Z., Xiao, J., Feng, Y., Yang, X., Zhang, J.: Human motion retrieval based on freehand sketch. Comput. Anim. Virtual Worlds **25**(3–4), 271–279 (2014). https://doi.org/10.1002/cav.1602
30. Thomas, F.: The illusion of life: Disney animation. (1995)
31. Thorne, M., Burke, D., van de Panne, M.: Motion doodles: an interface for sketching character motion. ACM Trans. Graph. **23**(3), 424–431 (2004). https://doi.org/10.1145/1015706.1015740
32. Tong, Z., Chen, X., Ni, B., Wang, X.: Sketch generation with drawing process guided by vector flow and grayscale. Trans. Edutainment (2020)
33. Whited, B., Daniels, E., Kaschalk, M., Osborne, P., Odermatt, K.: Computer-assisted animation of line and paint in disney's paperman. In: Proceedings of the 2012 ACM SIGGRAPH/Eurographics Symposium on Computer Animation (2012). https://doi.org/10.1145/2343045.2343071
34. Wu, T.T.: Character rigs for motion exaggeration (2006)
35. Yang, R., Wünsche, B.: Life-sketch - a framework for sketch-based modelling and animation of 3D objects. In: Conferences in Research and Practice in Information Technology Series, vol. 106 (2010)
36. Yonemoto, S.: A sketch-based skeletal figure animation tool for novice users. In: 2012 Ninth International Conference on Computer Graphics, Imaging and Visualization, pp. 37–42 (2012). https://doi.org/10.1109/CGIV.2012.18

Motion and Tracking

A Detection and Tracking Combined Network for Long-Term Tracking

Hao Zeng, Zhengning Wang$^{(\boxtimes)}$, Deming Zhao, Yijun Liu, and Yi Zeng

University of Electronic Science and Technology of China, Chengdu 611731, China
zhengning.wang@uestc.edu.cn

Abstract. Long-term tracking algorithms need to track targets stably in long videos. Compared with short-term tracking, long-term tracking faces more complex challenges. Such as the background brightness distributed in the entire gray level, wide range of target scale changes, more frequent motion blur and occlusion and other challenges. Existing long-term tracking algorithms cannot solve these challenges well, and easily cause tracking box drift, which significantly decrease the accuracy and robustness of the algorithms. In this paper, we design a detection and tracking combined network that can implement a global instance search for the tracked target. We integrate deformable convolution into the siamese network to solve the target deformation problem during long-term tracking. Besides, guided anchor is adopted in RPN to generate more sparse and accurate proposals, which can decrease the interference of the background. We design the cascaded RCNN with template information to filter out proposals and refine coordinates. And finally, select the highest confidence proposal as the final tracking box. Experiments show that our method has a stronger discriminative ability and can get more accurate tracking boxes compared with other advanced trackers. On several long-term tracking benchmarks, our method has achieved excellent performance.

Keywords: Deep learning · Long-term tracking · Deformable convolution · Guided anchor · Cascaded RCNN

1 Introduction

Visual object tracking is an important research interest in computer vision, and it has a wide range of applications in video surveillance, behavior analysis, unmanned driving and other fields. Since long-term tracking contains longer video sequences, it faces more complex challenges, such as background brightness distributed throughout the gray level, wide range of target scale changes, and frequently occured motion blur. In addition, the tracked target in the camera field of view will frequently disappear and reappear, which requires the long-term tracking network to have the ability to re-track. Compared with short-term tracking, long-term tracking has a wider range of practical applications and has greater research significance.

© Springer Nature Switzerland AG 2021
Y. Peng et al. (Eds.): ICIG 2021, LNCS 12890, pp. 571–582, 2021.
https://doi.org/10.1007/978-3-030-87361-5_47

Long-term tracking algorithms consist of two kinds of algorithms, including correlation filtering based algorithms and deep learning based algorithms. The TLD algorithm proposed by Kalal et al. [1] is the first to apply the correlation filtering method to long-term tracking. The algorithm uses an optical flow-based matcher for local search and a set of weak classifiers for global re-detection. Inspired by TLD, Ma et al. [2] developed a long-term correlation tracker (LCT), using the KCF [3] method as a local tracker and a random fern classifier as a detector. However, the early correlation filtering methods use traditional features, resulting in low tracking robustness and accuracy. Due to the development of deep learning, deep features have also been applied to correlation filtering methods in recent years. ATOM [4] tracks the target through sequential classification and estimation, and iteratively optimizes the rough initial position of the target obtained by classification to perform accurate detection box estimation. This method achieves higher accuracy, but multiple random initialization and iterative refinement of the detection box per frame greatly reduce the speed of the algorithm.

Since deep learning has achieved good performance on many tasks, researchers have also introduced deep learning into target tracking. Long-term tracking algorithms based on deep learning originate from SiamFC [5], which uses the siamese network to extract the corresponding features of the template frame and the search frame, and then performs cross-correlation operations on the two features to find the position with the strongest response of the search frame. On the basis of SiamFC, Li et al. [6] propose SiamRPN, which combines the RPN mechanism of target detection with the target tracking algorithm based on the siamese network. Zhu et al. [7] analyze SiamRPN and find that the unbalanced distribution of non-semantic backgrounds and backgrounds containing distractors in the training set affect the performance of the model. So, they propose the DaSiamRPN model. In the training phase, the original detection dataset is introduced to expand the positive sample pairs and enhance the generalization of the model. At the same time, the difficult negative sample pairs are further expanded to improve the anti-interference ability of the tracker. Li et al. [8] analyze that the training method of the siamese tracking model represented by SiamFC destroys the translation invariance of the network. Therefore, the target is placed offset in the data preprocessing stage to reduce the impact of pixel padding on the translation invariance.

After 2019, the academic community has proposed large-scale long-term tracking data sets such as LaSOT [9] and GOT10K [10]. Since the SiamRPN++ model has a large number of hyperparameters, its generalization ability is insufficient. In 2020, Huang et al. [11] propose the long-term tracking baseline algorithm GlobalTrack, which combines the siamese network with Faster RCNN [12], and regards the tracking task as a template-guided global instance detection problem. Compared with other advanced trackers, GlobalTrack achieves higher accuracy and stronger robustness on long-term tracking data sets. However, according to the characteristics of long-term tracking data sets, GlobalTrack still has many areas for improvement. In this paper, we analyze and improve the

GlobalTrack algorithm, and propose a long-term tracking network that combines detection and tracking.

(1) The target tracking network based on global instance search uses the conventional ResNet50 as the siamese network. The standard convolution unit in the siamese network is a rectangle. The use of this geometric structure to model large and unknown-shaped targets has inherent shortcomings. The feature extraction is not accurate and sufficient. In this paper, we introduce deformable convolution [13] into the siamese network to solve the problem of target deformation in long-term tracking.

(2) The use of traditional regional proposal network (RPN) in long-term tracking scenarios will bring about two problems. One is that the target area occupies a small proportion of the image, resulting in most anchors belonging to negative samples. Negative samples will cause the tracking algorithm to drift. The other is that the preset anchors cannot cover the various extreme aspect ratios of the target, and it will also cause the tracker to lose the target. In response to these problems, we introduce the guided anchor [14] into the RPN to generate sparse and high-quality proposals.

(3) The target tracking network based on global instance search uses a single-stage regional convolutional neural network (RCNN). The single-stage RCNN will cause the distribution of the proposals input to the coordinate regressor in the training phase and the inference phase to be different, resulting in unbalanced matching problem. After the RPN with guided anchor, we design a cascaded template-guided RCNN structure. Experiments show that our method has a stronger discriminative ability and can get more accurate tracking boxes compared with other advanced trackers. On several long-term tracking benchmarks, our method has achieved excellent performance.

2   Method

Our network consists of three parts, including a robust siamese network, a RPN with guided anchor, and a cascaded RCNN. We improve the siamese network to fully extract features, and adopt the RPN with guided anchor to generate sparse and accurate proposals. Besides, cascaded RCNN is used to filter out proposals and refine coordinates. Experiments show that our method has a stronger discriminative ability and get more accurate tracking boxes compared with other state-of-the-art trackers on the long-term tracking benchmarks. So, the algorithm has reached an advanced level. The overall structure of our network is shown in Fig. 1.

2.1   Robust Siamese Network

In the long-term tracking data set, the shape of the tracked target will undergo various changes, such as the change in the aspect ratio of the target caused by the

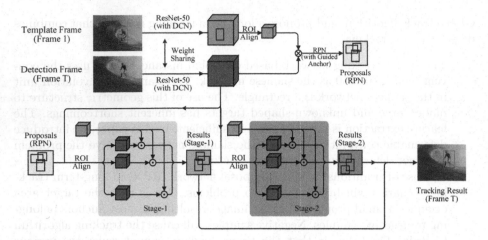

Fig. 1. Proposed long-term tracking framework.

different shooting distance of cameras, and the change in the shape of the target itself. In addition, the low refresh rate of cameras and motion blur will cause the tracking algorithm to drift. In response to these problems, we replace the standard convolution in the siamese network with deformable convolution. Deformable convolution (DCN) adds an extra offset to the spatial sampling position during feature extraction, and adaptively adjusts the receptive field of the convolution, which can improve the ability to model the deformation of the tracked target.

2.2   High-Quality Proposal Generation

Let z denotes the ROI (Region-Of-Interest) features of the template instance, x represents the search image features. Use z to perform cross-correlation operations on x to encode the template's information on x, and the generated feature map $\hat{x}$ contains the correlation between z and x, as shown in formula (1). Then we use the guided anchor on $\hat{x}$ to generate sparse and high-quality proposals x_i.

$$\hat{x} = f_{out}(f_x(x) \otimes f_z(z))\{z \in R^{k \times k \times c}; x, \hat{x} \in R^{h \times w \times c}\} \tag{1}$$

where h, w, and k represent the size of the feature, $\otimes$ represents the convolution operation, and f_z, f_x, and f_{out} are used to change the size of the corresponding feature and change the number of channels. The classification loss L_{cls} and localization loss L_{loc} are binary cross-entropy and smoothing L1, respectively. The total loss of RPN is defined as:

$$L_{rpn}(z, x) = L_{rpn}(\hat{x}) = \frac{1}{N_{cls}} \sum_i L_{cls}(p_i, p_i^*) + \lambda \frac{1}{N_{loc}} \sum_i p_i^* L_{loc}(s_i, s_i^*) \tag{2}$$

where N_{cls} and N_{loc} are the number of proposals used for classification and coordinate regression, p_i and s_i are the predicted score and location of the i-th proposal, while p_i^* and s_i^* are groundtruths. λ is a weight for balancing the classification and localization losses.

2.3   Multi-Stage Refinement

After the RPN with guided anchor, a multi-stage template-guided RCNN is used. Each RCNN structure combines the features of the template as the guided information. Specifically, the ROI Align operation is uniformly performed on the proposal x_i generated in the RPN, and the size of x_i after the ROI Align is the same as z. Given the ROI features of z and the i-th proposal x_i, feature modulation is performed in RCNN to encode their correlation, as shown in formula (3).

$$\hat{x}_i = h_{out}(h_x(x_i) \odot h_z(z))\{x_i, z \in R^{k \times k \times c}\} \tag{3}$$

where $\odot$ denotes the Hadamard production, h_z, h_x, and h_{out} are used to change the size of the corresponding feature and change the number of channels. After feature modulation, classification and coordinate regression are performed on $\hat{x}_i$. Then re-select the corresponding refined proposals from x, and perform feature modulation with z to obtain the second-stage proposals. Finally, sort the proposals output from the two stages, and select the proposal with the highest confidence as the tracking area in the current frame. During training, we use binary cross-entropy and smoothing L1 as classification and localization losses to optimize the model. The total loss of RCNN is formulated as:

$$L_{rcnn}(z, x) = \frac{1}{N_{prop}} \sum_i L_{rcnn}(\hat{x}_i) \tag{4}$$

$$L_{rcnn}(\hat{x}_i) = L_{cls}(p_i, p_i^*) + \lambda p_i^* L_{loc}(s_i, s_i^*) \tag{5}$$

where N_{prop} is the proposal number, p_i and s_i are the estimated confidence and location (center and scale offsets), while p_i^* and s_i^* are groundtruths. λ is a weight for balancing different losses.

3   Experiments

In this section, we first introduce the parameter setting and evaluation indicators. Then, we analyze the results of the experiment. The results include the comparison experiment of RCNN order and the ablation study of each substructure improved in this paper. Finally, we compare our method with the state-of-the-art trackers on four benchmarks. And visualize our tracking results on a part of the test set.

3.1   Implementation Details

Parameter. We set the number of output channels of f_z, f_x, f_{out}, h_z, h_x, and h_{out} to 256, and λ in both RPN and RCNN is 1. We use a combination of COCO [15], GOT-10K [10], and LaSOT [9] datasets for training our model, where the sampling probabilities of the three datasets are 0.4, 0.4 and 0.2. We use stochastic gradient descent with a batch size of 4 pairs to train our model. The momentum and weight decay are set to 0.9 and 1×10^{-4}. The program is trained on 4 GTX 1080TI GPUs.

Evaluation Indicator. To show the effectiveness of our method, we evaluate four large-scale long-term tracking benchmarks, including LaSOT, GOT10K, TLP [16], and OxUvA [17]. Since the long-term tracking benchmarks are produced by different institutions, the corresponding test indicators are not exactly the same. We use the indicators corresponding to each data set for testing and comparison.

3.2 Quantitative Evaluation

RCNN Order Comparison. We set up two-order, third-order, and fourth-order RCNN structures on the baseline network. The training is performed under the same hardware configuration and parameters. The comparison plot on the LaSOT test set is shown in Fig. 2. The LaSOT dataset [9] is one of the most recent large-scale datasets with high-quality annotations. It contains 1400 challenging sequences (1120 for training and 280 for testing) with 70 tracking categories, with average of 2500 frames per sequence. In this work, we follow the one-pass evaluation (success and precision) to evaluate different trackers on the test set of LaSOT. In Fig. 2, the B and Baseline represent the baseline network (GlobalTrack). Compared to the baseline, the cascaded 2nd, 3rd, and 4th order RCNN structures significantly improve the overall performance of the tracking algorithm. In addition, the cascaded second-order RCNN has the best performance, increasing precision and success value by 7.4% and 5.6% respectively. So, we adopt the cascaded second-order RCNN structure on the baseline.

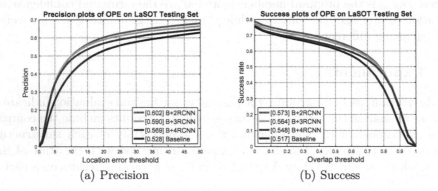

(a) Precision   (b) Success

Fig. 2. The comparison of RCNN order on the test set of LaSOT.

Ablation Study. We test the influence of deformable convolution and guided anchor on the LaSOT test set, as shown in Fig. 3. B and Baseline represent the baseline network (GlobalTrack), DCN represents the deformable convolution, and GA represents the guided anchor. After adding deformable convolution to B+2RCNN, the precision and success value are increased by 1.6% and 1.4%, respectively. Taking B+2RCNN+DCN as the baseline, after adding the guided anchor to the baseline, the precision and success value are improved by 0.9% and 0.6% respectively. The above results express the effectiveness of every sub-structure.

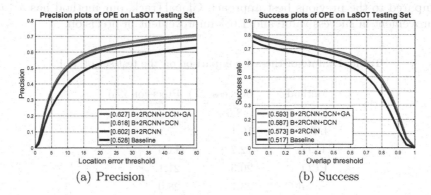

(a) Precision   (b) Success

Fig. 3. Ablation study on the test set of LaSOT.

Evaluation on LaSOT. Figure 4 is the success and precision plots of our method and several state-of-the-art algorithms, including SPLT [18], C-RPN [19], SiamRPN++ [8], ATOM [4], DaSiamRPN [7], GlobalTrack [11], LTMU [20], DIMP [21]. Compared to the previous best approach DIMP, the precision and success value of our method have been improved by 6.4% and 3.3%, respectively, indicating the advantage of our method.

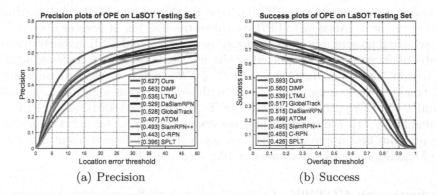

(a) Precision   (b) Success

Fig. 4. State-of-the-art comparison on the test set of LaSOT.

Evaluation on TLP. The TLP dataset [16] contains 50 HD videos from real-world scenarios, with an average of 13500 frames per sequence. We follow the one-pass evaluation (success and precision) to evaluate different trackers on the TLP dataset, including KCF [3], LCT [2], TLD [1], ECO [22], SiamFC [5], MDNet [23], SPLT [18], GlobalTrack [11]. The experimental results are shown in Table 1. Compared to the previous best approach GlobalTrack, our method has a 1.6% improvement in success value and 1.6% improvement in precision.

Table 1. State-of-the-art comparison on the test set of TLP.

Method	Success (%)	Precision (%)
KCF	8.6	6.3
LCT	10.1	7.1
TLD	12.2	11.6
ECO	20.5	21.1
SiamFC	23.7	28.0
MDNet	37.2	38.1
SPLT	41.6	40.3
GlobalTrack	52.0	55.6
Ours	**53.6**	**57.2**

Evaluation on OxUvA. The OxUvA dataset [17] contains 366 object tracks in 337 videos. Each video in this dataset lasts for average 2.4 min, which is much longer than other commonly used short-term datasets (such as OTB2015). In the OxUvA dataset, three criteria are adopted to evaluate different trackers, including true positive rate (TPR), true negative rate (TNR) and maximum geometric mean (MaxGM). TPR measures the fraction of present objects that are reported present as well as the location accuracy, and TNR gives the fraction of absent frames that are reported as absent. MaxGM makes a trade-off between TPR and TNR (i.e., $MaxGM = \sqrt{TPR \cdot TNR}$), which is used to rank different trackers. We compare our tracker with several recent algorithms, including SiamFC [5], ECO [22], MDNet [23], LCT [2], TLD [1], MBMD [24], SPLT [18], GlobalTrack [11], the experimental results are shown in Table 2. Compared to the previous best approach SPLT, our method has an improvement of 1.1% on the MaxGM and an improvement of 16.2% on the TPR.

Evaluation on GOT10K. GOT10K [10] is a challenging large-scale dataset which contains more than 10,000 videos of moving objects in real-world. It is also challenging in terms of zero-class-overlap between the provided training subset and testing subset. In the GOT10K dataset, two criteria are adopted to evaluate different trackers, including average overlap rate (AO) and success rate (SR). AO means the average of overlap rates between tracking results and groundtruths over all frames. SR means the percentage of successfully tracked frames where overlap rates are above a threshold. According to the different thresholds, SR consists of SR0.50 and SR0.75. We compare our tracker with several recent algorithms, including MDNet [23], ECO [22], SiamFC [5], DaSiamRPN [7], ATOM [4], SiamFC++ [25], D3S [26], DIMP [21], the experimental results are shown in Table 3. Compared to the previous best approach DIMP, our method achieves a 2.8% improvement in the AO and a 10.2% improvement in the SR0.75.

Table 2. State-of-the-art comparison on the test set of OxUvA.

Method	MaxGM (%)	TPR (%)	TNR (%)
SiamFC	31.3	39.1	0.0
ECO	31.4	39.5	0.0
MDNet	34.3	47.2	0.0
LCT	39.6	29.2	53.7
TLD	43.1	20.8	**89.5**
MBMD	54.4	60.9	48.5
GlobalTrack	60.3	57.4	63.3
SPLT	62.2	49.8	77.6
Ours	**63.3**	**66.0**	60.6

Table 3. State-of-the-art comparison on the test set of GOT10K.

Method	AO (%)	SR0.50 (%)	SR0.75 (%)
MDNet	29.9	30.3	9.9
ECO	31.6	30.9	11.1
SiamFC	34.8	35.3	9.8
DaSiamRPN	44.4	53.6	22.0
ATOM	55.6	63.5	40.2
SiamFC++	59.5	69.5	47.9
D3S	59.7	67.6	46.2
DIMP	61.1	71.7	49.2
Ours	**63.9**	**71.7**	**59.4**

3.3   Qualitative Analysis

Figure 5 is partial sequences selected from the LaSOT test set, in which the red bounding box represents the tracking result of our method, and the green bounding box represents the tracking result of the baseline GlobalTrack. Through the visualization results in different scenes, we can see that our method can regress the position of the tracked target more accurately and track the target robustly. Our method has a stronger ability to discriminate against background interference.

The first row in Fig. 5 is the *bottle* video sequence in LaSOT. The main challenges are the scale change and motion blur of the target. Compared with the baseline algorithm, our method has obvious advantages for motion blur, and can accurately regress the coordinates of the tracking box. The second row in Fig. 5 is the *dog* video sequence in LaSOT. The main challenge is the deformation of the target. The baseline algorithm is easy to drift to other interference targets. Compared with the baseline algorithm, our method has higher robustness to deformation and can track the target stably. The third row in Fig. 5 is the *truck* video sequence in LaSOT. The main challenges are the problem of small targets and background interference. Compared with the baseline algorithm, our method has a stronger discriminative ability.

Fig. 5. Partial sequences visualization of LaSOT.

4 Conclusion

In order to achieve long-term tracking more effectively, we propose a long-term tracking network that combines detection and tracking. For each search frame, the template frame is used to search on it to eliminate accumulated errors, thereby avoiding tracking algorithm drift. Aiming at the severe deformation and motion blur of the target in long-term tracking, we apply deformable convolution to the siamese network to avoid the drift of the tracking algorithm. In the RPN, the guided anchor is used to generate sparse and accurate proposals to decrease the interference of the background. The cascaded template-guided RCNN filter out proposals and refines coordinates. Experiments show that our method has a stronger discriminative ability and get more accurate tracking boxes compared with other state-of-the-art trackers on the long-term tracking benchmarks. So, the algorithm has achieved excellent performance.

References

1. Kalal, Z., Mikolajczyk, K., Matas, J.: Tracking-learning-detection. IEEE Trans. Pattern Anal. Mach. Intell. **34**(7), 1409–1422 (2011)
2. Ma, C., Yang, X., Zhang, C., et al.: Long-term correlation tracking. In: IEEE Conference on Computer Vision and Pattern Recognition, pp. 5388–5396 (2015)
3. Henriques, F., Caseiro, R., Martins, P., et al.: High-speed tracking with kernelized correlation filters. IEEE Trans. Pattern Anal. Mach. Intell. **37**(3), 583–596 (2014)
4. Danelljan, M., Bhat, G., Khan, S., et al.: Atom: accurate tracking by overlap maximization. In: IEEE Conference on Computer Vision and Pattern Recognition, pp. 4660–4669 (2019)
5. Bertinetto, L., Valmadre, J., Henriques, J.F., Vedaldi, A., Torr, P.H.S.: Fully-convolutional Siamese networks for object tracking. In: Hua, G., Jégou, H. (eds.) ECCV 2016. LNCS, vol. 9914, pp. 850–865. Springer, Cham (2016). https://doi.org/10.1007/978-3-319-48881-3_56
6. Li, B., Yan, J., Wu, W., et al.: High performance visual tracking with Siamese region proposal network. In: IEEE Conference on Computer Vision and Pattern Recognition, pp. 8971–8980 (2018)
7. Zhu, Z., Wang, Q., Li, B., et al.: Distractor-aware Siamese networks for visual object tracking. In: European Conference on Computer Vision (ECCV), pp. 101–117 (2018)
8. Li, B., Wu, W., Wang, Q., et al.: Siamrpn++: evolution of Siamese visual tracking with very deep networks. In: IEEE Conference on Computer Vision and Pattern Recognition, pp. 4282–4291 (2019)
9. Fan, H., Lin, L., Yang, F., et al.: Lasot: a high-quality benchmark for large-scale single object tracking. In: IEEE Conference on Computer Vision and Pattern Recognition, pp. 5374–5383 (2019)
10. Huang, L., Zhao, X., Huang, K.: GOT-10k: a large high-diversity benchmark for generic object tracking in the wild. arXiv preprint arXiv:1810.11981 (2018)
11. Huang, L., Zhao, X., Huang, K.: Globaltrack: a simple and strong baseline for long-term tracking. In: AAAI Conference on Artificial Intelligence, pp. 11037–11044 (2020)

12. Ren, S., He, K., Girshick, R., et al.: Faster R-CNN: towards real-time object detection with region proposal networks. IEEE Trans. Pattern Anal. Mach. Intell. **39**(6), 1137–1149 (2016)

13. Dai, J., Qi, H., Xiong, Y., et al.: Deformable convolutional networks. In: IEEE International Conference on Computer Vision, pp. 764–773 (2017)

14. Wang, J., Chen, K., Yang, S., et al.: Region proposal by guided anchoring. In: IEEE Conference on Computer Vision and Pattern Recognition, pp. 2965–2974 (2019)

15. Lin, T.-Y., et al.: Microsoft COCO: common objects in context. In: Fleet, D., Pajdla, T., Schiele, B., Tuytelaars, T. (eds.) ECCV 2014. LNCS, vol. 8693, pp. 740–755. Springer, Cham (2014). https://doi.org/10.1007/978-3-319-10602-1_48

16. Moudgil, A., Gandhi, V.: Long-term visual object tracking benchmark. arXiv preprint arXiv:1712.01358 (2017)

17. Valmadre, J., Bertinetto, L., Henriques, J. F., et al.: Long-term tracking in the wild: a benchmark. In: European Conference on Computer Vision (ECCV), pp. 670–685 (2018)

18. Yan, B., Zhao, H., Wang, D., et al.: 'Skimming-Perusal' Tracking: a framework for real-time and robust long-term tracking. In: IEEE International Conference on Computer Vision, pp. 2385–2393 (2019)

19. Fan, H., Ling, H.: Siamese cascaded region proposal networks for real-time visual tracking. In: IEEE Conference on Computer Vision and Pattern Recognition, pp. 7952–7961 (2019)

20. Dai, K., Zhang, Y., Wang, D., et al.: High-performance long-term tracking with meta-updater. In: IEEE Conference on Computer Vision and Pattern Recognition, pp. 6298–6307 (2020)

21. Bhat, G., Danelljan, M., Gool, L.V., et al.: Learning discriminative model prediction for tracking. In: IEEE International Conference on Computer Vision, pp. 6182–6191 (2019)

22. Danelljan, M., Bhat, G., Shahbaz, Khan, F., et al.: Eco: efficient convolution operators for tracking. In: IEEE Conference on Computer Vision and Pattern Recognition, pp. 6638–6646 (2017)

23. Nam, H., Han, B.: Learning multi-domain convolutional neural networks for visual tracking. In: IEEE Conference on Computer Vision and Pattern Recognition, pp. 4293–4302 (2016)

24. Zhang, Y., Wang, D., Wang, L., et al.: Learning regression and verification networks for long-term visual tracking. arXiv preprint arXiv:1809.04320 (2018)

25. Xu, Y., Wang, Z., Li, Z., et al.: Siamfc++: towards robust and accurate visual tracking with target estimation guidelines. In: AAAI Conference on Artificial Intelligence, pp. 12549–12556 (2020)

26. Lukezic, A., Matas, J., Kristan, M.: D3S-A discriminative single shot segmentation tracker. In: IEEE Conference on Computer Vision and Pattern Recognition, pp. 7133–7142 (2020)

Scale Adaptive Target Tracking Based on Kernel Correlation Filter and Residual Network

Xue Zhang[1], Dong Hu[1,2,3]($\boxtimes$), and Ting Zhang[1]

[1] Jiangsu Province's Key Lab of Image Procession and Image Communications,
Nanjing University of Posts and Telecommunications, Nanjing 210003, China
{1219012710,hud,1218012403}@njupt.edu.cn
[2] Education Ministry's Engineering Research Center of Ubiquitous Network and Heath Service,
Nanjing, China
[3] Education Ministry's Key Lab of Broadband Wireless Communication and Sensor Network
Technology, Nanjing, China

Abstract. In this paper, a scale adaptive target tracking algorithm based on deep residual network and kernel correlation filter is proposed. Although kernel correlation filter is a fast and effective target tracking algorithm, its tracking effect is not ideal in the case of the occlusion, blur and scale change caused by the fast moving target in the real environment. To deal with these problems, corresponding measures are integrated in the proposed new algorithm. Firstly, the structure of the ResNet50 network was adjusted and trained. The deep residual network was used to extract target features and integrate the kernel correlation filter algorithm to carry out adaptive response graph fusion to find the target location. Then, we add the scale estimation module, and use the HOG feature to replace the original deep feature training scale filter. Based on the structure of binary sort tree, binary search is carried out on the scale, and the scale discriminant index is used to judge whether the target has reached the appropriate scale. Experimental results show that our proposed algorithm can achieve scale adaptation of target tracking, and the tracking performance is further improved.

Keywords: Target tracking · Residual network · Kernel correlation filter · Scale adaptation · Binary sort tree

1 Introduction

Object tracking is a basic computer vision task with wide application. However, the target tracking algorithm still faces many challenges because of the complex scenes in the real tracking. In order to adapt to the actual application scenario and ensure the accuracy and robustness of the target tracking, efforts have been paid in theoretical research and applications.

So far, the development of target tracking technique has experienced three stages. Correlation filtering is one of the two popular technologies for target tracking. Bolme et al. [1] proposed simplest object tracking method with the idea of correlation filter in 2010. Later, Henriques proposed the Scale Adaptive Kernel Correlation Filter (SAKCF)

© Springer Nature Switzerland AG 2021
Y. Peng et al. (Eds.): ICIG 2021, LNCS 12890, pp. 583–595, 2021.
https://doi.org/10.1007/978-3-030-87361-5_48

[2] algorithm which exhibited amazing tracking performance. Li et al. put forward SAMF [3] method which uses multi-scale spatial sampling based on KCF towards scale adaptation. Meanwhile, Danelljan et al. took the lead in using the integration of translational filter and scale filter to implement Discriminative Scale Space Tracking (DSST) [4] method to achieve scale adaptation. With the rapid development and success in image processing, deep learning has been introduced in target tracking, especially, the combination and integration of these two technologies has attracted research interests. Convolutional neural network (CNN) [5] has been applied to target tracking. Ma et al. proposed the Hierarchical Convolutional Features (HCF) [6] algorithm, which extracted the features from different convolutional layers and fused them into the correlation filter to obtain the final target position. Zhang et al. proposed a Scale Adaptive HCF (SAHCF) [7] algorithm, which used a pre-trained VGGNet [8] to extract features for kernel correlation filter.

In this paper, the tracking problems in complex environment are studied in depth. We apply the deep residual network (ResNet) [9] to extract the network features and integrate the KCF algorithm. The binary search is carried out on the scale based on the structure of binary sort tree to achieve the tracking target scale adaptation. The rest of this paper is organized as follows. The second section introduces the technical analysis of KCF and CNN. Section 3 discusses the proposed algorithm details, namely, the scale adaptive target tracking method which integrates the KCF with the ResNet to extract features. Section 4 provides a discussion concerning the result of experiment and comparisons with several known advanced algorithms. Finally, the summary is delivered in Sect. 5.

2   Related Work

2.1   Kernel Correlation Filter

On account of the kernel correlation filter, object tracking is to use an image with certain feature to train the filter, and then model the target as a whole. Typically, specify the target center tracking frame to select the target at first, then associate with the subsequent frame search boxes filter to perform convolution operations. The new position of the target depends on the maximum value of the output convolution result, and filter is constantly updated on the basis of the tracking result.

The kernel correlation filter has ridge regression of cyclically shifted samples. It can use Fast logarithmic Fourier Transform (FFT). The training purpose of the algorithm is to achieve an objective function minimizing the error function (1):

$$\min_{w} \sum_i (f(x_i) - y_i)^2 + \lambda ||w||^2 \tag{1}$$

Where x_i is the image sample, y_i is the regression result of the sample, and $\lambda ||w||^2$ is the regularization term. The tracking target area is the tracking position which corresponds to the maximum probability value. Details of KCF can refer [10].

2.2 Convolutional Neural Network

Convolutional Neural Network (CNN) consists of one or more convolutional layers and a full connectivity layer, and also includes associative weighting and pooling layers. It can extract robust features with invariance of rotation, translation and deformation. Automatic extracting relevant features from the initial image data layer by layer is more effective and accurate. Since AlexNet [11], complicated CNNs which is supported by GPU have continuously won in large-scale visual recognition competitions [12], such as VGGNet, ResNet and so on. Consequently, the application of CNNs in object tracking has a rapid increase and becomes more flexible.

In this paper, we use ResNet50 to extract image features. ResNet mainly has the following characteristics: it uses the jumping way to solve the problem of network performance degradation as the depth deepens. Also, it is very flexible. The specific number of layers of the network is determined according to different tasks to achieve the effect of balancing network complexity and performance. Compared with VGGNet, ResNet transfers shallow convolutional feature information to deep network through identity mapping. Deep feature integrates shallow feature information, contains more detailed target information, and has stron14ger robustness to illumination changes and target shielding in tracking. Furthermore, ResNet50 adopts the bottleneck structure, which can reduce the number of network parameters, greatly improve the training efficiency of network model and promote the real-time tracking. Therefore, the network model selected in this paper is ResNet50, which is used to extract image features after adjusting its network structure.

3 Proposed Method

Figure 1 presents the block diagram of proposed algorithm. It is a general structure of scale adaptive target tracking which is based on Kernel Correlation Filter and Residual Network. The key points of the algorithm, such as network adjustment and training for feature extraction, position estimation by multi-channel feature fusion, scale adaptation, as well as model update are introduced in the following.

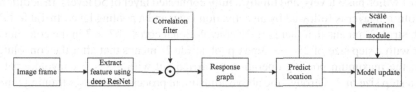

Fig. 1. Block diagram of proposed algorithm

3.1 Network Adjustment and Training

ResNet50 is used to extract image features in this paper. In order to speed up the feature extraction process, this paper makes corresponding adjustments to the Residual network in the following ways: compared with the initial network structure, the number of filters in the convolutional layer is adjusted to one half of the original number, so that the number of channels extracted from the convolutional layer will be reduced by half with the same scale. The specific structure is shown in Table 1.

Table 1. The adjusted ResNet50 network structure

Network Name	Convolutional layer parameters	Output dimension
Conv1_x	7 × 7, 32, stride 2 3 × 3 max pool, stride 2	112 × 112
Conv2_x	$\begin{bmatrix} 1 \times 1, 32 \\ 3 \times 3, 32 \\ 1 \times 1, 128 \end{bmatrix} \times 3$	56 × 56
Conv3_x	$\begin{bmatrix} 1 \times 1, 64 \\ 3 \times 3, 64 \\ 1 \times 1, 256 \end{bmatrix} \times 4$	28 × 28
Conv4_x	$\begin{bmatrix} 1 \times 1, 128 \\ 3 \times 3, 128 \\ 1 \times 1, 512 \end{bmatrix} \times 6$	14 × 14
Conv5_x	$\begin{bmatrix} 1 \times 1, 256 \\ 3 \times 3, 256 \\ 1 \times 1, 1024 \end{bmatrix} \times 3$	7 × 7

The depth of the deep residual network is 50, including 5 groups of convolutional layers. It starts with a 7 × 7 convolution, which then passes through 16 building blocks, each of which has 3 levels, and finally a fully connected layer of 50 levels. In addition, the convolution layer is followed by an activation layer and a pooling layer. In Table 1, "7 × 7, 32, stride2" means that there are 32 convolutional cores of 7 × 7 in the convolutional layer with a step size of 2; "3 × 3max pool, stride 2" means that after the convolutional layer, the maximum pooling operation is carried out with a 3 × 3 convolutional core with a step size of 2. Through the above adjustment process, the image training time can be effectively reduced and the efficiency of depth feature extraction can be improved.

ResNet50 is used in this paper to extract image features. The model is trained on ILSVRC2012 large data set, which contains more than 1000 types of images and has a very wide range of applications. Firstly, the data set is preprocessed in this paper. In order to improve the training speed, the size of the input image is uniformly cut and scaled to 224 × 224 in this paper.

Next, the specific training process of the deep residual network is introduced. Specifically, the corresponding layer of the adjusted ResNet50 network is randomly initialized during training, and the stochastic gradient descent (SGD) [13] algorithm is used for optimization. The training samples of equal batch size are used to update the model parameters. The batch size is set to 64 and the momentum is set to 0.9. The size of learning rate has a crucial influence on the speed of weight updating in the training process and controls the learning process of the network model. Besides, the initial learning rate is set as 10^{-2}, and the number of rounds is slowed down by adopting the strategy. When the total number of rounds is 0.4 and 0.8, the learning rate decays to one tenth of the original one. In order to improve the generalization performance of the model, L2 regularization was adopted after the loss function, and the regularization parameter was set as 7×10^{-5}. In addition, to prevent the occurrence of overfitting and improve the training efficiency of the model, the packet loss rate used is set to 0.5.

3.2 Target Position Estimation

In feature extract module of Fig. 1, two convolutional layers Conv3 and Conv4 of ResNet50 network are used to extract the multi-channel features of the target in the video sequence for training the kernel correlation filter.

Suppose a multi-channel high-dimensional feature x is extracted from the target feature graph of the current frame, where x represents the eigenvector with the size of M $\times$ N $\times$ D on the l-th layer, M, N, D denotes the width, height and number of characteristic channels, $x \in R^{M \times N \times D}$. The virtual sample obtained by cyclic displacement of the target sample feature $\mathbf{X}$ along the M and N directions is used as the training sample. Each cyclic shift sample is $x(i, j) \in \{0, 1, ..., M-1\} \times \{0, 1, ..., N-1\}$. Learn the optimal correlation filter by solving the following minimization problem:

$$w^* = \arg \min_{w} \sum_{i,j} ||w \cdot x(i, j) - y(i, j)||^2 + \lambda ||w||_2^2 \tag{2}$$

Where, λ represents the regularization parameter ($\lambda \geq 0$). The linear product defined by $w \cdot x(i, j) = \sum_{d=1}^{D} w^d x^d (i, j), (d \in \{1, ..., D\})$ represents different characteristic channels. $y(i, j) \in R^{M \times N}$ represents a two-dimensional Gaussian function of the target image block:

$$y(i, j) = e^{-\frac{(i-M/2)^2 + (j-N/2)^2}{2\sigma^2}} \tag{3}$$

Where σ is the Gaussian kernel bandwidth. The minimization problem in Eq. (2) is transformed from time domain to frequency domain for solution:

$$W^* = \arg \min_{W} \sum_{i,j} || \sum_{d=1}^{D} W^d \odot \overline{X}^d - Y||^2 + \lambda \sum_{d=1}^{D} ||W^d||_2^2 \tag{4}$$

Where, X, Y, and W are the Fourier transforms of $x(i, j), y(i, j)$, and w respectively. $\overline{X}$ represents the complex conjugate of X, and the operator, $\odot$ represents the multiplication of the corresponding elements. Assuming that x_l represents the image features extracted by the l-th layer convolution layer, then for d ($d \in \{1, ..., D\}$) channels in the frequency domain, the best filter is:

$$W_l^d = \frac{Y_l \odot \overline{X}_l^d}{\sum_{d=1}^{D} X_l^d \odot \overline{X}_l^d + \lambda} \tag{5}$$

Given an image block in a frame, assume $z_l (z_l \in R^{M \times N \times D})$ represents the feature vector of M × N × D on the l-th layer, then the correlation response graph of the correlation filter and sample image block can be calculated by the following formula:

$$f_l(z) = F^{-1}(\sum_{d=1}^{D} W_l^d \odot \overline{Z}_l^d) \tag{6}$$

Where the operator F^{-1} represents the inverse Fourier transform. By looking for the position with the maximum response value on the correlative response graph $f(z)$ with the size of M × N, the target position of the l-th convolutional layer is estimated. Then a tracking confidence evaluation index is proposed, which gives more weight to the response graph with higher confidence and less weight to the response graph with lower confidence, and adaptively fuses the response graph with the index. The average peak correlation energy (APCE) [14] is used to measure the confidence of target tracking as shown in formula (7).

$$APCE = \frac{F_{\max} - F_{\min}}{\text{mean}\left(\sum_{\min} (F_{x,y} - F_{\min})^2\right)} \tag{7}$$

Where $F_{\max}$ and $F_{\min}$ represent the peak and minimum values in the output response respectively, $F_{x,y}$ represents the response of the target at position (x, y). APCE value describes the fluctuation degree of target response. The larger the value is, the higher the tracking confidence is. Otherwise, the poorer the tracking confidence is.

In the target tracking video, the target and background of two adjacent frames are continuously changing, and the correlation filtering responses obtained by them are also relatively similar. Therefore, the consistency of correlation filtering response (CCFR) between two adjacent frames is defined to describe the tracking stability as below.

$$CCFR = ||f^t(x, y) - f^{t-1}(x - \Delta x, y - \Delta y)||_2^2 \tag{8}$$

Where $f'(x, y)$ represents the relevant response graph of the target at frame, and Δx, Δy represent the relative change of the position of the target between two adjacent frames. The smaller the CCFR value, the higher the similarity of response graph between two adjacent frames, and the stronger the tracking stability. Otherwise, the tracking stability is weak. Through the above analysis, APCE and CCFR are combined here to define a more reliable target tracking confidence evaluation function for weighting allocation of response graph. The new confidence value is evaluated by (9).

$$conf(APCE, CCFR) = \frac{APCE}{CCFR + \varepsilon} \tag{9}$$

Where, ε is a constant tending to 0.

As described above, the kernel correlation filter is first trained by Conv3 and Conv4 of ResNet50, then the correlation response of each layer is calculated, so the confidence of the l-th layer is calculated:

$$conf_l = \frac{APCE_l}{CCFR_l + \varepsilon} \tag{10}$$

Then, according to the tracking confidence evaluation function obtained, the adaptive weight distribution of response graph of each layer is carried out, and the final fused response graph is as follows:

$$f(z) = \frac{conf_l}{\sum\limits_{l=3,4} conf_l} f_l(z) \tag{11}$$

The position of the maximum value of the resulting response graph is the estimated position of the target:

$$(x, y) = \arg\max_{i,j} f(z) \tag{12}$$

3.3 Target Scale Adaptation

Although the position correlation filter is trained by extracting the depth features of the image above to predict the position of the target, the scale of the target is still the scale of the target in the previous frame. Therefore, it is necessary to train a scale filter to accurately estimate current target scale.

It is assumed that the size of the target image tracked by the position filter is $M \times N$ at the time of a frame t. s different scales are constructed to estimate the image targets centering on the middle of every image. s samples of different sizes to be tested were extracted to obtain the HOG features of each sample, and then the D-dimensional feature x_t^d was obtained in series to form a feature vector x^s. Finally, filter training samples of different scales in the S layer were constituted to conduct the training of scale filter w^s. The error term is minimized by the following equation:

$$\varepsilon = ||g - \sum_{l=1}^{d} w^s * x^s||^2 + \lambda \sum_{s=1}^{d} ||w^s||^2 \tag{13}$$

Where λ is the regularization coefficient, g is usually the expected Gaussian response, and g, w^s and x^s have the same dimension and size. Convert it to Fourier domain for solution, and the filter is as follows:

$$W^s = \frac{\overline{G}^s}{\sum\limits_{s=1}^{d} \overline{X}^s X^s + \lambda} = \frac{A^s}{B^s} \tag{14}$$

Where, capital letters are the discrete Fourier transform of the corresponding quantity.

In view of the problem that most current target tracking algorithms have redundancy or fixed scale when dealing with scale change, we propose a fast scale evaluation method, which adopts a search strategy. First of all, a simple scale pool S is defined as shown in Formula (14), and candidate targets of different scales are obtained from this scale pool for each frame of the video. we use 1 as the size of the initial scale template, δ as the scale of change, and $1-\delta, 1+\delta$ represent the scale of reduction and expansion of the original image respectively.

$$S = \{1 - \delta, 1, 1 + \delta\} \tag{15}$$

At frame t, the position filter outputs the position of the target image, performs estimation of S scales on the image sample Z and extracts feature Z^s. Then, the maximum correlation response of y_t^s at frame t is obtained by training with the formula (16):

$$y_t^s = \arg\max \mathcal{F}^{-1} \left\{ \frac{\sum_{s=1}^{d} \overline{A}_{t-1}^s Z_t^s}{B_{t-1}^s + \lambda} \right\} \tag{16}$$

Where A_{t-1}^s and B_{t-1}^s are the filter coefficients at frame t -1 respectively. The maximum position of s scale response graphs can be obtained by the following equation:

$$y_{t\,max} = \arg\max_{s} \left(y_t^1, y_t^2, ..., y_t^s \right) \tag{17}$$

The maximum value of the scale response graph is not enough to evaluate the effectiveness of the target scale, so a more confident scale discriminant index is proposed. First, the Euclidean distance between the response graph and the expected output response is used as the maximum reliability of the response graph, namely:

$$E_t^s = \exp\left(-\|y_t^s - g\|^2\right) \tag{18}$$

Where g is the Gaussian expected output, and E_t^s is the error weight. Then, the scale discrimination index T_t^s is obtained with (19):

$$T_t^s = E_t^s \cdot y_{t\,max} \tag{19}$$

The maximum value max $\{ T_t^s \}$ was obtained by calculating their scale discriminant indexes through S scales respectively, and the scale at this time was the optimal scale of the target in S scales. In this section, the search direction of the current frame candidate scale is quickly found by establishing a simple scale pool. Based on the advantage of binary sort tree in data search, a binary search strategy based on tree structure is proposed. In the target scale estimation module, the original simple scale pool is sorted into a rough search in the form of binary tree sort tree. After that, the scale is divided in each parent node according to the initial scale change value, and the scale is amplified and reduced respectively, so as to realize the scale search from rough to fine. The specified operation is shown in Fig. 2.

Firstly, the above simple scale pool was arranged into a binary sort tree, namely the first and second floors in Fig. 2. Equation (9) was used to calculate the scale discrimination index T_t^s of the three scales, and the maximum value was obtained to determine the direction of finding the target candidate scales. Then, scale dichotomy is carried out on the determined search direction. In the example above, the scale of A2 in the second layer is enlarged and reduced by $\delta/2$ respectively, that is to say, the scale of B1 in the third layer is $1+\delta - \delta/2$, and the scale of B2 is $1+\delta+\delta/2$.Similarly, when the scale changes to the $n(n \geq 2)$ layer, the scale of the left and right child nodes is respectively enlarged and reduced on the basis of the scale of the current parent node $\delta/2^{n-2}$, at this time, the whole search structure still maintains the structure of binary sort tree. When the scale discriminant index T_f calculated from the parent node is greater than the scale discriminant index T_l at the left child node and the scale discriminant index T_r at the right child node, dichotomy of scale is stopped in the tree structure, that is, the scale s at the parent node is the optimal scale for the target candidate position.

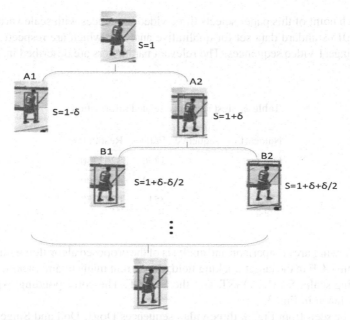

Fig. 2. Diagram of target scale estimation based on tree search strategy

3.4 Model Update

During the tracking process, the appearance of the target will undergo changes such as rotation, deformation, occlusion and so on. In order to adapt to the change of target appearance during tracking, model update strategy is usually introduced into tracking algorithm to update the appearance in real time, so as to obtain more accurate tracking results.

Set A_t^s and B_t^s to represent their molecular and denominator items in frame T, then the model update strategy of scale correlation filter W^s is as follows:

$$A_t^s = (1 - \eta_s)A_{t-1}^s + \eta_s Y \odot \overline{X}_t^s \tag{20}$$

$$B_t^s = (1 - \eta_s)B_{t-1}^s + \eta_s \sum_{k=1}^{K} X_t^k \odot \overline{X}_t^k \tag{21}$$

$$W_t^s = \frac{A_t^s}{B_t^s + \lambda_s} \tag{22}$$

Where, η_s is the learning rate of the scale correlation filter.

4 Experiments

4.1 Qualitative Experiment Verification

The research point of this paper selects three video sequences with scale variation from the OTB-2015 standard data set for qualitative analysis, which are respectively Dog1, Doll and Singer1 video sequences. The relevant parameters are described in Table 2 for details:

Table 2. Test sequence related information

Name of the sequence	Frames	Resolution
Dog1	1350	320*240
Doll	3872	400*300
Singer1	351	624*352

The following are comparison and analysis of the proposed algorithm with the classical algorithm HCF in the target tracking field, the current mainstream tracking algorithm of processing scale, SAMF, DSST, and the SAHCF. The corresponding experimental results are shown in Fig. 3.

As can be seen from Fig. 3, three video sequences Dog1, Doll and Singer1 all have obvious scale changes. For the Dog1 video sequence, the target gradually approached the lens from the 355 to 954 frames, and gradually moved away from the lens from the 954 to the 1322 frames. The tracking frame size of the HCF algorithm was fixed, but due to the change of the target scale, the tracking of the video sequence failed at the 1322 frames. Although SAMF algorithm, DSST algorithm and SAHCF algorithm are able to track the target, the tracking frame has appeared a large drift by 1322 frame. The algorithm proposed by this OURS can accurately detect the change of the target scale, accurately locate the target, and realize the self-adaptation of the scale. The consistent results can be seen for Doll and Singer1 sequences also have similar phenomena.

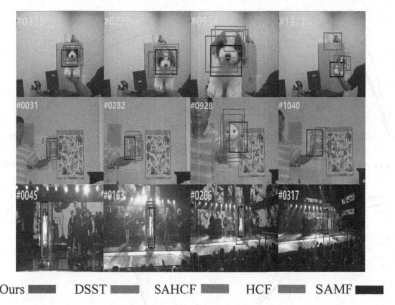

Ours ▬▬▬ DSST ▬▬▬ SAHCF ▬▬▬ HCF ▬▬▬ SAMF ▬▬▬

Fig. 3. Comparison of results of scale adaptation of out method with DSST, SAHCF, HCF and SAMF.(Tracking sequence from top to bottom: Dog1 sequence, Doll sequence, Singer1 sequence)

4.2 Quantitative Experiment Verification

Figure 4 shows the accuracy curve and success rate curve of our algorithm in comparison with SAHCF, HCF, SAMF and DSST in 100 video sequences and 37 scaling factors of OTB2015, respectively.

As can be seen from Fig. 4(a), compare with the other four algorithms, the average accuracy of our algorithm improved by 4.5%, 12.7%, 16.6% and 19.6% respectively. In Fig. 4(b), the success rate is increased by 5.7 percent, 9.8 percent, 20.5 percent and 22.3 percent, respectively. Under the condition of scale change, the proposed algorithm still maintains high accuracy and precision. As can be seen from Fig. 4(c), the accuracy of our algorithm is 4.6%, 14.2%, 17.1% and 21.6% higher respectively. In Fig. 4(d), the success rate of our algorithm under the interference of scale change is 63.6%. 11, while for SAHCF, HCF, SAMF and DSST, the success rate is 5.8%, 10.4%, 20.7% and 23.2%, respectively.

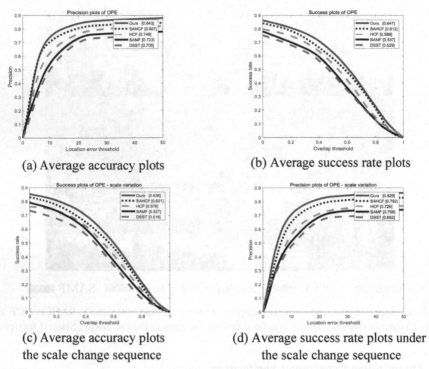

(a) Average accuracy plots

(b) Average success rate plots

(c) Average accuracy plots
the scale change sequence

(d) Average success rate plots under
the scale change sequence

Fig. 4. Average accuracy curve and success rate curve of our method and SAHCF, HCF, SAMF and DSST.

5   Conclusion

In this paper, a novel target tracking algorithm is proposed, which fuses the deep residual network into the kernel correlation filter framework to achieve accurate target location. At the meanwhile, a fast scale adaptive target tracking method based on tree search strategy is incorporated, which solves the problem of mesoscale variation of target tracking and improves the accuracy and robustness of target tracking.

References

1. Bolme, D.S., Beveridge, J.R., Draper, B.: Visual object tracking using adaptive correlation filters. In: IEEE Conference on Computer Vision and Pattern Recognition, pp. 2400–2416 (2010)
2. Henriques, J.F., Caseiro, R., Martins, P.: Exploiting the circulant structure of tracking-by-detection with kernels. In: European Conference on Computer Vision, pp. 702–715 (2012)
3. Li, Y., Zhu, J.: A scale adaptive kernel correlation filter tracker with feature integration, pp. 254–265 (2015)
4. Danelljan, M., Häger, G., Khan, F.S., et al.: Accurate scale estimation for robust visual tracking. In: British Machine Vision Conference (2014)
5. Jürgen, S.: Deep learning in neural networks. Neural Netw. **61**, 85–117 (2014)

6. Ma, C., Huang, J.-B., Yang, X., et al.: Hierarchical convolutional features for visual tracking. In: Proceedings of the IEEE International Conference on Computer Vision, pp. 3074–3082 (2015)
7. Zhang, J., Hu, D., Zhang, B., et al.: Hierarchical convolution feature for target tracking with kernel- correlation filtering. In: International Conference on Image and Graphics, pp. 297–306 (2019)
8. Chen, P.H., Lin, C.J., Schölkopf, B.: A tutorial on ν-support vector machines. Stoch. Models Bus. Ind. **21**, 111–136 (2005)
9. He, K., Zhang, X., Ren, S.: Deep residual learning for image recognition. IEEE Trans. Syst. **1**, 267–275 (2015)
10. Wen, S.P., Huang, T.W., Yu, X.H., Chen, M.Z.Q., Zeng, Z.G.: Aperiodic sampled-data sliding-mode control of fuzzy systems with communication delays via the event-triggered method. IEEE Trans. Fuzzy Syst. **24**(5), 1048–1057 (2016)
11. Simonyan, K., Zisserman, A.: Very deep convolutional networks for large-scale image recognition Computer Science, pp. 569–577 (2014)
12. Wen, S.P., Zeng, Z.G., Chen, M.Z.Q., Huang, T.W.: Synchronization of switched neural networks with communication delays via the event-triggered method IEEE Trans. Neural Netw. Learn. Syst. **28**(10), 2334–2343 (2017)
13. Bordes, L.B., Gallinari, P.: SGD-QN: careful quasi-Newton stochastic gradient descent. J. Mach. Learn. Res. **10**, 1737–1754 (2009)
14. Wang, M., Liu, Y., Huang, Z.: Large margin object tracking with circulant feature maps. In: 2017 IEEE Conference on Computer Vision and Pattern Recognition (CVPR). IEEE (2017)

Adaptive Gaussian-Like Response Correlation Filter for UAV Tracking

Junjie Chen[1], Tingfa Xu[1,2(✉)], Jianan Li[1(✉)], Lei Wang[1], Ying Wang[1], and Xiangmin Li[1]

[1] Image Engineering and Video Technology Laboratory, School of Optics and Photonics, Beijing Institute of Technology, Beijing 100081, China
{ciom_xtf1,lijianan}@bit.edu.cn
[2] Beijing Institute of Technology Chongqing Innovation Center, Chongqing 401120, China

Abstract. Existing Discriminative Correlation Filters (DCF) based methods usually use a heatmap with a two-dimensional Gaussian distribution to represent the foreground probability map on the search image plane and regularize tracker's response map in every frame. However, in many real-world scenarios, there often exist non-zero correlation responses in background regions due to the existence of distractors that have similar appearance as the target. In such cases, forcing the output response map to be ideally Gaussian-distributed will lead to contradictory constrains on representation learning, thus hurting performance. To alleviate this, we propose a novel tracker, named Gaussian-like response Correlation Filter (GLCF), which constructs expected response maps by assigning non-zero values to the locations of distractors adaptively depending on their similarity with the target, and thus maintains inter-object consistency and improves robustness. Extensive experiments on four benchmarks well demonstrate the superiority of the proposed method over both DCF and deep based trackers. Specifically, our method achieves new state-of-the-art performance on UAVDT dataset while running at a speed of 28.9 FPS on a single CPU.

Keywords: UAV tracking · Discriminative correlation filters · Adaptive Gaussian-like function

1 Introduction

Given a target object specified by a bounding box in the first frame, visual object tracking aims to determine the exact location of the target in subsequent frames, which serves as a fundamental task in the computer vision community. Recently, increasing attention has been paid to Unmanned Aerial Vehicle (UAV) tracking [13,17,24,26] due to its promising applications in the field of geomatics [33], agroforestry [37,42], transportation [18] and mid-air aircraft tracking [21].

Current object tracking methods can be mainly divided into two streams: Discriminative Correlation Filter (DCF) based and deep based. Considering the

© Springer Nature Switzerland AG 2021
Y. Peng et al. (Eds.): ICIG 2021, LNCS 12890, pp. 596–609, 2021.
https://doi.org/10.1007/978-3-030-87361-5_49

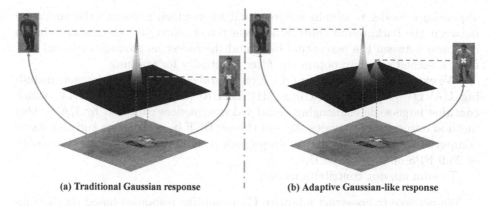

(a) Traditional Gaussian response   (b) Adaptive Gaussian-like response

Fig. 1. Target response maps for filter optimization. Traditional tracking methods apply a heat map with a two-dimensional Gaussian distribution peaked at the target centre as ground-truth response map, which ignores distractors in background regions. In contrast, our method measures the similarity between the content in background regions and the target, and adjusts the ground-truth response value at background locations accordingly, producing an adaptive Gaussian-like response map for more effective filter optimization.

fact that UAVs provide only limited power capacity and computational resources on-board, deep trackers are less effective due to low inference speed and high computational overheads. In contrast, DCF based trackers enable computation in Fourier frequency domain and are more computationally efficient, providing ideal solutions to real-time UAV tracking.

Traditional DCF based methods use a heat map with a two-dimensional Gaussian distribution as ground-truth response map for a search image. The peak of the Gaussian-shaped map is centered on the ground-truth location of the target, and the expected response values for all background regions remain zero. Such a Gaussian-shaped response map works properly when only a single target exists in the search image. However, in most real-world scenarios, especially in UAV tracking, distractors that are very similar to the target often co-exist in background regions, which will naturally produce high response values, as inllustrated in Fig. 1. In such cases, simply regularizing the predicted response map to be Gaussian-shaped and forcing responses for all distractors to be zero, which largely ignores the fact that distractors share similar appearance as the target, could empirically disturb representation learning and lead to model degradation.

In light of this, we propose a novel Gaussian-like response Correlation Filter (GLCF) tracker, which adaptively constructs Gaussian-like shaped response map to meet the demand in real-world scenarios. Concretely, unlike conventional solutions that manually construct multi-Gaussian response [3], we introduce a new regularization term into objective function, and implement two rounds of optimization to obtain an adaptive Gaussian-like response and thus a robust tracker. In the first round, we use the ideal Gaussian distribution and the target appearance model to obtain a perceptual filter which measures the similarity between the background content and the target. Next, we use the correlation response between the perceptual filter and the target as ground-truth and perform a second solver to obtain the filter eventually for tracking.

We extensively evaluate our GLCF on several commonly used datasets including UAVDT [11], UAV123@10fps [31], DTB70 [22] and VisDrone [44], which contains large-scale challenging aerial video sequences captured by UAVs. Our method outperforms previous state-of-the-art DCF based trackers and also shows competitive results compared to deep trackers, while reaching a real-time speed of 28.9 FPS on a single CPU.

To sum up, our contributions are:

- We propose to construct adaptive Gaussian-like responses based on the similarity between the background content and the target, which effectively improves model's robustness.
- We are the first to design an adaptive Gaussian-like response map for efficient optimization of DCF trackers.
- Our model establishes new state-of-the-art on UAVDT dataset.

2   Related Works

2.1   Discriminative Correlation Filter

Discriminative Correlation Filter (DCF) based methods have been widely applied to visual tracking due to high computational efficiency. Bolme et al. [4] proposed Minimum Output Sum of Squared Error (MOSSE) filter and were the first to apply correlation filter to object tracking. Henriques et al. [16] introduced circulant matrix to produce sufficient samples for training and detection while maintaining a fast tracking speed. However, the resulting periodic repetitions at boundary positions limit the discriminative capability of trackers. To mitigate this issue, various regularization terms have been introduced. Danelljan et al. [8] adopted a spatial regularization term which penalizes the filter coefficients for background regions to enforce the tracker to focus more on target center. Galoogahi et al. [14] applied a binary matrix to generate real positive and negative samples for model training, which shows promise in lifting the discriminative ability of trackers.

2.2   Adaptive Gaussian-Like Function

After MOSSE [4] pioneered the use of correlation filter for object tracking, it became a conventional approach to use the Gaussian distribution as desired target response output. Mueller et al. [3] were the first to investigate the effect of designing an adaptive target response for CF tracking to improve performance. However, they only changed the peak of the Gaussian function and constructed a multi-peaked Gaussian based on the response values at the center of the target and at several nearby locations within fixed distances. In contrast, we automatically compute a Gaussian-like response from the objective function that takes both the similarity between the background content and the target and target's aspect ratio into account, which effectively improves the performance of the tracker.

3   Method

This section describes our model in detail.

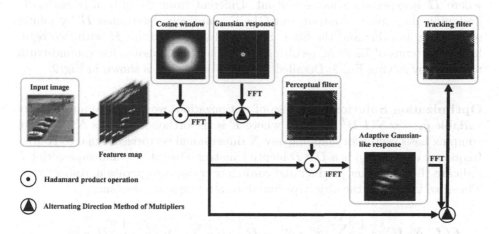

Fig. 2. The workflow of our GLCF tracker. We first use ADMM algorithm to compute a perceptual filter that generates adaptively varying Gaussian-like response based on the target aspect ratio and background content in the current frame, and then use the Gaussian-like labels to optimize tracking filter to locate the target in the next frame.

3.1   Adaptive Gaussian-Like Response Correlation Filter

The objective function of our baseline method (BACF) can be formulated as:

$$E(f_k) = \frac{1}{2} \left\| \sum_{d=1}^{D} (Bx_k^d * f_k^d) - y \right\|_2^2 + \frac{1}{2} \sum_{d=1}^{D} \|f_k^d\|_2^2, \tag{1}$$

where $x_k^d, f_k^d \in \mathbb{R}^T$ denote the d-th channel of the vectorized image and filter of frame k, respectively. D is the total channel number. $y \in \mathbb{R}^T$ is the expected response (with Gaussian distribution). $*$ indicates convolution operator. $B \in \mathbb{R}^{M \times N}$ is a cropping matrix to select central M elements in x_k^d, N is the length of x. Usually $N >> M$.

Though the cropping matrix B makes the tracker focus more on the target and well mitigates boundary effect, using an ideal Gaussian distribution as expected output limits further improvements in tracking performance due to the neglect of non-zero correlation responses in background regions. To alleviate this, we present a novel object function by introducing a new regularization term:

$$E(f_k, H) = \frac{1}{2} \left\| \sum_{d=1}^{D} (Bx_k^d * f_k^d) - H \right\|_2^2 + \frac{1}{2} \sum_{d=1}^{D} \left\| f_k^d \right\|_2^2 + \frac{1}{2} \left\| H - y \right\|_2^2, \quad (2)$$

where H is expected response output. Different from [3], instead of manually designing the expected output, our GLCF adaptively determines H by jointly optimizing its value and the filter. Specifically, we constrain H with two regularization terms of L2 form, resulting in an adaptive Gaussian-like ground-truth response by solving Eq. 2. Detailed model optimization is shown in Fig. 2.

Optimization Solution. For ease of optimization, we introduce an auxiliary variable $\hat{g}_k = \sqrt{N}(FB^T \otimes I_D)f_k$, where F is the orthonormal $N \times N$ matrix of complex basis vector for mapping any N dimensional vectorized signal to Fourier frequency domain. I_D is a $D \times D$ identity matrix. Operator $\otimes$ and superscript T indicate the Kronecker product and conjugate transpose operation, respectively. Thus, we transform the objective function into frequency domain:

$$E(f_k, \hat{g}_k^d, \hat{H}) = \frac{1}{2} \left\| \sum_{d=1}^{D} (\hat{x}_k^d * \hat{g}_k^d) - \hat{H} \right\|_2^2 + \frac{1}{2} \sum_{d=1}^{D} \left\| f_k^d \right\|_2^2 + \frac{1}{2} \left\| \hat{H} - \hat{y} \right\|_2^2. \quad (3)$$

We use Alternating Direction Method of Multipliers (ADMM) algorithm to minimize Eq. 3 to achieve a local optimal solution. The augmented Lagrangian form of the equation can be formulated as:

$$L_k(f_k, \hat{g}_k^d, \xi^T, \hat{H}) = E(f_k, \hat{g}_k^d, \hat{H}) + \hat{\xi}^T(\hat{g}_k - \sqrt{N}(FB^T \otimes I_D)f_k) \\ + \frac{\rho}{2} \left\| \hat{g}_k - \sqrt{N}(FB^T \otimes I_D)f_k \right\|_2^2, \quad (4)$$

where $\hat{\xi}^T = [\hat{\xi}_1^T, \hat{\xi}_2^T, ..., \hat{\xi}_D^T]$ is the $1 \times DN$ Lagrangian vector in Fourier domain, ρ is a penalty factor. Then, ADMM is applied by alternately solving the following sub-problems:

Solution to Sub-problem $\hat{g}_{k+1}$. The sub-problem $\hat{g}_{k+1}$ can be formulated as:

$$\hat{g}_{k+1} = argmin\frac{1}{2} \left\| \sum_{d=1}^{D} (\hat{x}_k^d \odot \hat{g}_k^d) - \hat{H} \right\|_2^2 + \hat{\xi}^T(\hat{g}_k - \sqrt{N}(FB^T \otimes I_D)f_k)$$
$$+ \frac{\rho}{2} \left\| \hat{g}_k - \sqrt{N}(FB^T \otimes I_D)f_k \right\|_2^2, \tag{5}$$

which is too complex to solve directly. Given the fact that x_k is sparse banded, each element of $\hat{y}(\hat{y}(t), t = 1, 2, ..., N)$ is dependent only on each $x_k(t) = [x_k^1(t), x_k^2(t), ..., x_k^D(t)]^T$ and $\hat{g}_k(t) = [conj(\hat{g}_k^1(t)), conj(\hat{g}_k^2(t)), ..., conj(\hat{g}_k^D(t))]^T$, $conj(.)$ denotes the complex conjuate operation. So we divide the vectorized image x_k into N elements and solve the problem by N smaller and independent problems, over $t = [1, 2, ..., N]$:

$$\hat{g}_{k+1}(t) = argmin\frac{1}{2} \left\| \hat{x}_k^T(t) \odot \hat{g}_k(t) - \hat{H}(t) \right\|_2^2$$
$$+ \hat{\xi}^T(\hat{g}_k(t) - \sqrt{N}(FB^T \otimes I_D)f_k(t)) + \frac{\rho}{2} \left\| \hat{g}_k(t) - \sqrt{N}(FB^T \otimes I_D)f_k(t) \right\|_2^2, \tag{6}$$

where $f_k(t) = [f_k^1(t), f_k^2(t), ...f_k^D(t)]$, $\hat{x}_k^T(t)$ is the discrete Fourier transformation of $x_k^T(t)$. Each smaller problem can be calculated efficiently to achieve the solution of Eq. 6:

$$\hat{g}_{k+1}(t) = \frac{\hat{H}(t)\hat{x}(t) - N\xi^T + N\rho\hat{f}_k(t)}{\hat{x}(t)\hat{x}(t)^T + N\rho I_D}. \tag{7}$$

We use Sherman-Morrison formula to accelerate inverse operation:

$$(M + uv^T)^{-1} = M^{-1} - M^{-1}uv^TM^{-1}(1 + v^TM^{-1}u). \tag{8}$$

Hence, Eq. 7 can be reformulated as:

$$\hat{g}_{k+1}(t) = \frac{1}{\rho N}(I - \frac{\hat{x}(t)\hat{x}(t)^T}{\rho N + \hat{x}(t)\hat{x}(t)^T})(\hat{H}(t)\hat{x}(t) - N\xi^T + N\rho\hat{f}_k(t)). \tag{9}$$

Solution to Subproblem f_k. The subproblem f_k can be written as:

$$f_{k+1} = argmin\frac{1}{2} \sum_{d=1}^{D} \left\| f_k^d \right\|_2^2 + \hat{\xi}^T(\hat{g}_k - \sqrt{N}(FB^T \otimes I_D)f_k)$$
$$+ \frac{\rho}{2} \left\| \hat{g}_k - \sqrt{N}(FB^T \otimes I_D)f_k \right\|_2^2, \tag{10}$$

which can be easily solved as follows:

$$f_{k+1} = \frac{\xi^T N + \rho N g_{k+1}}{1 + \rho N}. \tag{11}$$

Solving $\hat{H}$. If $\hat{g}_{k+1}, f_{k+1}, \hat{\xi}$ are fixed, the closed-form solution regrading $\hat{H}$ can be determined as:

$$\hat{H} = \underset{\hat{H}}{argmin} \frac{1}{2} \left\| \sum_{d=1}^{D} (\hat{x}_k^d \odot \hat{g}_k^d) - \hat{H} \right\|_2^2 + \frac{1}{2} \left\| \hat{H} - \hat{y} \right\|_2^2$$

$$= \frac{\sum_{d=1}^{D} (\hat{g}_k^d * \hat{x}_k^d) + \hat{y}}{2}. \tag{12}$$

In practice, we utilize an additional ADMM solver to obtain H for better convergence.

Update of Lagrangian Parameter. We update Lagrangian multipliers as:

$$\xi^{i+1} = \xi^i + \rho(g_{k+1}^{i+1} - f_{k+1}^{i+1}), \tag{13}$$

where i denotes iteration number. g_{k+1}^{i+1} and f_{k+1}^{i+1} indicate the solution of subproblem g_{k+1} and f_{k+1}, respectively. The coefficient ρ (initially equals 1) is computed as:

$$\rho^{i+1} = min(\rho_{max}, \beta\rho^i), \tag{14}$$

where β and ρ_{max} are set as 10 and 10,000 respectively.

3.2 Appearance Model Update

The appearance model $\hat{x}_k^{model}$ is updated as follows:

$$\hat{x}_k^{model} = (1 - \eta)\hat{x}_{k-1}^{model} + \eta\hat{x}_k, \tag{15}$$

where η is the learning rate of the appearance model.

4 Experiments

In this section, we first compare our GLCF with prior state-of-the-arts on four challenging UAV datasets. Then, we provide experimental analysis to validate our design choices.

4.1 Implementation Details

All experiments are performed using MATLAB R2018a on a computer with Intel i5-6500 CPU@3.2 GHz, 8 GB RAM. We set $\eta = 0.017$. The iteration number of ADMM is 2. We extract Histogram of Oriented Gradients (HOG) [6] and Color Names (CN) [9] features for input images.

We use two widely-used metrics, including precision plot and success plot to describe the performance of all trackers through One-Pass Evaluation (OPE). Precision plot computes the percentages of frames in which the estimated target location is within a given distance threshold to the ground-truth. We use the score at the threshold of 20 pixels for ranking trackers. Success plot measures the fractions of successful frames in which the Intersection over Union (IoU) between the predicted bounding box and ground-truth is greater than a certain threshold varied from 0 to 1. We use the Area Under Curve (AUC) of success plots to rank all trackers.

4.2   Comparing with State-of-the-Arts

We compare our GLCF with eleven state-of-the-art deep trackers, i.e., MCCT [41], SiamFC [2], CFNet [38], HCF [29], C-COT [10], UDT [40], MDNet [32], ASRCF [5], TADT [23], CREST [36], IBCCF [20], and fourteen hand-crafted trackers including AutoTrack [26], STRCF [19], ECO-HC [7], CSR-DCF [27], MCCT-H [41], ARCF-H [17], BACF [14], DSST [28], fDSST [30], SRDCF [8], Staple [1], SAMF [25], CN [9] and KCF [35].

UAVDT Dataset. UAVDT [11] is selected from over 10 h of videos taken by an UAV at different locations in urban areas. The targets are mainly vehicles with additional attributions such as weather conditions, flying altitude and camera view. For a comprehensive evaluation, we add default trackers in UAVDT(i.e., GOTURN [15], HDT [34], MCPF [43], PTAV [12]) for comparison as well. Figure 3(a) provides comparisons of top twenty trackers on UAVDT benchmarks. To the best of our knowledge, despite the fact that GLCF uses only hand-crafted features, it is the best performing tracker on UAVDT, in both success and precision.

VisDrone2018-test-dev Dataset. VisDrone2018-test-dev [44] contains 35 sequences captured by various UAV platforms at over 14 different cites in China, featuring a diverse real-world scenarios. Figure 3(b) shows the overall performance of top twenty trackers. It is worth noting that our GLCF outperforms all trackers that use hand-crafted features.

UAV123@10fps Dataset. We also conduct experiments on UAV123@10fps [31] dataset, which consists of 123 challenging sequences with 12 different attributes. All sequences are temporally down-sampled to 10 FPS to simulate challenging large target displacements between two consecutive frames. Figure 3(c) shows the overall performance of top twenty trackers. Our method shows competitive performance, even surpassing some deep trackers.

DTB70 Dataset. DTB70 [22] comprises of 70 sequences covering different types of UAV movements including rapid translation and rotation. The targets include human, animals and rigid objects. Figure 3(d) shows the overall performance of top twenty trackers. Our method improves the performance of the baseline method (BACF) very well, both in terms of precision and success rate.

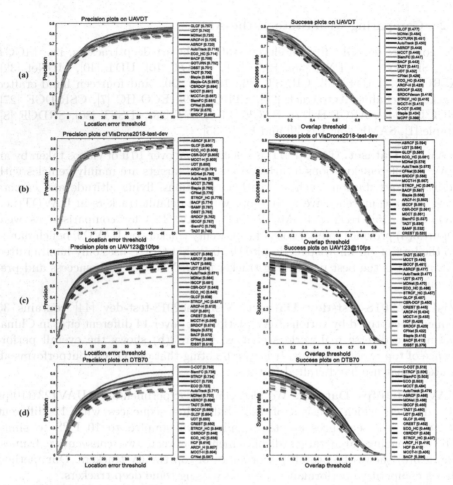

Fig. 3. Performance comparisons on (a) UAVDT, (b) VisDrone2018-test-dev, (c) UAV123@10fps dataset and (d) DTB70. Precision plots (left) and success plots (right) are given.

4.3 Attribute-Based Evaluation

Figure 4 provides the success plots of nine attributes on UAVDT dataset. Notably, GLCF performs the best in most attributes, even better than some deep trackers, such as TADT [23], MDNet [32], MCCT [41], UAT [40], CREST [36].

4.4 Qualitative Evaluation

Figure 5 illustrates some qualitative results of GLCF and other trackers. One can see that GLCF shows superiority compared to other trackers in handling challenging tracking situations, including but not limited to quick deformation, low resolution, partial occlusion, and lost from view.

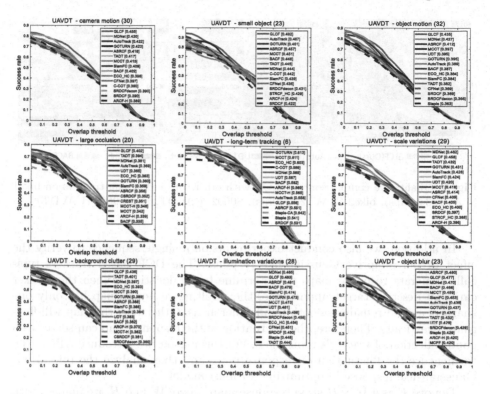

Fig. 4. Attribute-based evaluation. Success plots on 9 attributes-based comparisons between GLCF and other 14 state-of-the-art trackers on UAVDT dataset.

Table 1. Ablation analysis on UAVDT, VisDrone2018-test-dev, UAV123@10fps and DTB70.

	UAVDT		VisDrone2018-test-dev		UAV123@10fps		DTB70	
	Precision	Success	Precision	Success	Precision	Success	Precision	Success
Baseline	0.722	0.455	0.801	0.580	0.631	0.457	0.651	0.446
GLCF	0.757	0.477	0.809	0.583	0.638	0.457	0.664	0.455

4.5 Ablation Study of Gaussian-Like Response in Training

To validate the effect of our Gaussian-like response on model training, we design a baseline method that has the same feature extraction and scale estimation strategies as our GLCF, except for using a Gaussian distribution as ground-truth response map.

We compare our GLCF with the baseline method on four datasets. Table 1 clearly shows that, thanks to the proposed adaptive Gaussian-like response, tracking performance has been improved on all four datasets, in both precision and success plot.

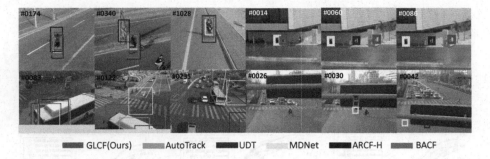

GLCF(Ours)   AutoTrack   UDT   MDNet   ARCF-H   BACF

Fig. 5. Qualitative comparison of GLCF with other top performing trackers on bike1 (UAV123@10fps), bike2 (UAV123@10fps), S0602 (UAVDT) and S0601 (UAVDT).

In addition, we also conduct experiments on a single sequence to verify the effect of our adaptive Gaussian-like response. The DCF based trackers typically generate response maps to determine target location. When the tracker can well describe target appearance, the resulting response map has only one sharp peak and remains smooth in all other areas. Otherwise, the map will fluctuate drastically. Therefore, the fluctuation of the response map can server as a good reflection of tracker's robustness. For this reason, we introduce APCE [39] to measure the fluctuation of response maps and thus analyze the role of our Gaussian-like response in optimizing a robust model.

Denote F as a $W \times H$ sized response map, where W and H are map's width and height in pixels, respectively. F_{max} and F_{min} is the maximum and minimum value of F, respectively. APCE is calculated as:

$$APCE = \frac{1}{WH} \cdot \frac{|F_{max} - F_{min}|^2}{\sum_{i=1}^{N} \sum_{j=1}^{H} (F_{i,j} - F_{min})^2}. \tag{16}$$

Figure 6 shows the effect of our adaptive Gaussian-like response. As one can see, benefiting from adaptive Gaussian-like response, the tracker is more robust and thus produces an ideal response map to better locate targets.

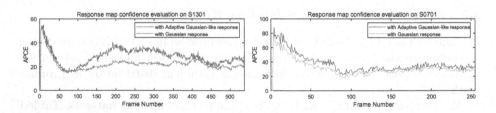

Fig. 6. Effect of adaptive Gaussian-like response in training.

5 Conclusion

In this paper, we propose a novel tracker called Adaptive Gaussian-like Response Correlation Filter (GLCF) for UAV visual tracking. Specifically, we introduce a Gaussian-like response as the ground-truth output based on the similarity between the background content and the target in each frame. Compared to traditional CF trackers that use a single bandwidth Gaussian as the ground-truth response, GLCF allows for the presence of non-zero correlation responses in the background and takes into account the aspect ratio of the target, which makes the tracker more versatile. Comprehensive experiments on four widely used UAV datasets show that the GLCF achieves significant performance improvements over the baseline (BACF) approach and is comparable to other state-of-the-art trackers, even achieving the best performance on the UAVDT dataset. In addition, our GLCF is able to run in real time (28.9 FPS) on a single CPU, which has great potential for application on the limited computational resources of UAVs.

Acknowledgment. This work was supported by the Key Laboratory Foundation under Grant TCGZ2020C004 and Grant 202020429036.

References

1. Bertinetto, L., Valmadre, J., Golodetz, S., Miksik, O., Torr, P.H.S.: Staple: complementary learners for real-time tracking. In: CVPR (2016)
2. Bertinetto, L., Valmadre, J., Henriques, J.F., Vedaldi, A., Torr, P.H.S.: Fully-convolutional Siamese networks for object tracking. In: Hua, G., Jégou, H. (eds.) ECCV 2016. LNCS, vol. 9914, pp. 850–865. Springer, Cham (2016). https://doi.org/10.1007/978-3-319-48881-3_56
3. Bibi, A., Mueller, M., Ghanem, B.: Target response adaptation for correlation filter tracking. In: Leibe, B., Matas, J., Sebe, N., Welling, M. (eds.) ECCV 2016. LNCS, vol. 9910, pp. 419–433. Springer, Cham (2016). https://doi.org/10.1007/978-3-319-46466-4_25
4. Bolme, D., Beveridge, J., Draper, B., Lui, Y.M.: Visual object tracking using adaptive correlation filters. In: CVPR (2010)
5. Dai, K., Wang, D., Lu, H., Sun, C., Li, J.: Visual tracking via adaptive spatially-regularized correlation filters. In: CVPR (2019)
6. Dalal, N., Triggs, B.: Histograms of oriented gradients for human detection. In: CVPR (2005)
7. Danelljan, M., Bhat, G., Shahbaz Khan, F., Felsberg, M.: Eco: efficient convolution operators for tracking. In: CVPR (2017)
8. Danelljan, M., Häger, G., Khan, F., Felsberg, M.: Learning spatially regularized correlation filters for visual tracking. In: ICCV (2015)
9. Danelljan, M., Khan, F., Felsberg, M., van de Weijer, J.: Adaptive color attributes for real-time visual tracking. In: CVPR (2014)
10. Danelljan, M., Robinson, A., Shahbaz Khan, F., Felsberg, M.: Beyond correlation filters: learning continuous convolution operators for visual tracking. In: Leibe, B., Matas, J., Sebe, N., Welling, M. (eds.) ECCV 2016. LNCS, vol. 9909, pp. 472–488. Springer, Cham (2016). https://doi.org/10.1007/978-3-319-46454-1_29

11. Du, D., et al.: The unmanned aerial vehicle benchmark: object detection and tracking. In: ECCV (2018)
12. Fan, H., Ling, H.: Parallel tracking and verifying: a framework for real-time and high accuracy visual tracking. In: ICCV (2017)
13. Fu, C., Lin, F., Li, Y., Chen, G.: Correlation filter-based visual tracking for UAV with online multi-feature learning. Remote. Sens. **11**, 549 (2019)
14. Galoogahi, H.K., Fagg, A., Lucey, S.: Learning background-aware correlation filters for visual tracking. In: ICCV (2017)
15. Held, D., Thrun, S., Savarese, S.: Learning to track at 100 FPS with deep regression networks. In: Leibe, B., Matas, J., Sebe, N., Welling, M. (eds.) ECCV 2016. LNCS, vol. 9905, pp. 749–765. Springer, Cham (2016). https://doi.org/10.1007/978-3-319-46448-0_45
16. Henriques, J.F., Caseiro, R., Martins, P., Batista, J.: Exploiting the circulant structure of tracking-by-detection with kernels. In: Fitzgibbon, A., Lazebnik, S., Perona, P., Sato, Y., Schmid, C. (eds.) ECCV 2012. LNCS, vol. 7575, pp. 702–715. Springer, Heidelberg (2012). https://doi.org/10.1007/978-3-642-33765-9_50
17. Huang, Z., Fu, C., Li, Y., Lin, F., Lu, P.: Learning aberrance repressed correlation filters for real-time UAV tracking. In: ICCV (2019)
18. Karaduman, M., Eren, H.: UAV traffic patrolling via road detection and tracking in anonymous aerial video frames. J. Intell. Robot. Syst. **95**(2), 675–690 (2019)
19. Li, F., Tian, C., Zuo, W., Zhang, L., Yang, M.H.: Learning spatial-temporal regularized correlation filters for visual tracking. In: CVPR (2018)
20. Li, F., Yao, Y., Li, P., Zhang, D., Zuo, W., Yang, M.H.: Integrating boundary and center correlation filters for visual tracking with aspect ratio variation. In: ICCV Workshops (2017)
21. Li, R., Pang, M., Zhao, C., Zhou, G., Fang, L.: Monocular long-term target following on UAVs. In: CVPR Workshops (2016)
22. Li, S., Yeung, D.Y.: Visual object tracking for unmanned aerial vehicles: a benchmark and new motion models. In: AAAI (2017)
23. Li, X., Ma, C., Wu, B., He, Z., Yang, M.H.: Target-aware deep tracking. In: CVPR (2019)
24. Li, Y., Fu, C., Huang, Z., Zhang, Y., Pan, J.: Keyfilter-aware real-time UAV object tracking. In: ICRA (2020)
25. Li, Y., Zhu, J.: A scale adaptive kernel correlation filter tracker with feature integration. In: Agapito, L., Bronstein, M.M., Rother, C. (eds.) ECCV 2014. LNCS, vol. 8926, pp. 254–265. Springer, Cham (2015). https://doi.org/10.1007/978-3-319-16181-5_18
26. Li, Y., Fu, C., Ding, F., Huang, Z., Lu, G.: Autotrack: towards high-performance visual tracking for UAV with automatic spatio-temporal regularization. In: CVPR (2020)
27. Lukežič, A., Vojíř, T., Čehovin Zajc, L., Matas, J., Kristan, M.: Discriminative correlation filter with channel and spatial reliability. In: CVPR (2017)
28. Danelljan, M., Hager, G., Khan, F., Felsberg, M.: Accurate scale estimation for robust visual tracking. In: BMVC (2014)
29. Ma, C., Huang, J.B., Yang, X., Yang, M.H.: Hierarchical convolutional features for visual tracking. In: ICCV (2015)
30. Danelljan, M., Hager, G., Khan, F.S., Felsberg, M.: Discriminative scale space tracker. IEEE Trans. Pattern Anal. Mach. Intell. **39**(8), 1561–1575 (2017)
31. Müller, M., Smith, N., Ghanem, B.: A benchmark and simulator for UAV tracking. In: ECCV (2016)

32. Nam, H., Han, B.: Learning multi-domain convolutional neural networks for visual tracking. In: CVPR (2016)
33. Nex, F., Remondino, F.: UAV for 3D mapping applications: a review. Appl. Geomatics **6**, 1–15 (2014)
34. Qi, Y., et al.: Hedged deep tracking. In: CVPR (2016)
35. Caseiro, R., Martins, P.J., Batista, J.: High-speed tracking with kernelized correlation filters. IEEE Trans. Pattern Anal. Mach. Intell. **37**(3), 583–596 (2015)
36. Song, Y., Ma, C., Gong, L., Zhang, J., Lau, R., Yang, M.H.: Crest: convolutional residual learning for visual tracking. In: ICCV (2017)
37. Torresan, C., et al.: Forestry applications of UAVs in Europe: a review. Int. J. Remote Sens. **38**, 2427–2447 (2017)
38. Valmadre, J., Bertinetto, L., Henriques, J., Vedaldi, A., Torr, P.H.S.: End-to-end representation learning for correlation filter based tracking. In: CVPR (2017)
39. Wang, M., Liu, Y., Huang, Z.: Large margin object tracking with circulant feature maps. In: CVPR (2017)
40. Wang, N., Song, Y., Ma, C., Zhou, W., Liu, W., Li, H.: Unsupervised deep tracking. In: CVPR (2019)
41. Wang, N., Zhou, W., Tian, Q., Hong, R., Wang, M., Li, H.: Multi-cue correlation filters for robust visual tracking. In: CVPR (2018)
42. Zhang, C., Kovacs, J.: The application of small unmanned aerial systems for precision agriculture: a review. Precision Agric. **13**, 693–712 (2012)
43. Zhang, T., Xu, C., Yang, M.H.: Multi-task correlation particle filter for robust visual tracking. In: CVPR (2017)
44. Zhu, P., Wen, L., Bian, X., Ling, H., Hu, Q.: Vision meets drones: a challenge. In: ECCV (2018)

Online Scene Text Tracking
with Spatial-Temporal Relation

Yan Xiu, Hong-Yang Zhou, Shu Tian[✉], and Xu-Cheng Yin

University of Science and Technology Beijing, Beijing, China
{shutian,xuchengyin}@ustb.edu.cn

Abstract. Scene texts in video are not fixed in color, size, format and are easily confused with the background, which imposes significant challenges in video scene text tracking. The trajectories are often be fragmented caused by these. Most tracking methods focus on the matching of the appearance features and the temporal information across frames, treating each text as a separate object. However, the relations among all texts are also important cues. In this paper, we propose a novel online video scene text tracking approach with the spatial-temporal relation module utilizing multiple cues, i.e. appearance, geometry and temporal. The spatial-temporal relation module enhances appearance features by modeling the relations between texts with each other in the same frame, which can avoid the influence of bad detection results, and track text stably and consistently. We achieved more tracked texts and more complete trajectories on IC15 with the spatial-temporal relation module.

Keywords: Spatial-temporal relation · Scene text tracking · Multiple object tracking

1 Introduction

Scene text in videos often contains rich semantic information and plays an important role in many practical applications of computer vision tasks, such as semantic-based video analysis and automated driving systems. Text detection and recognition are usually done frame by frame. Affected by the blurred frame, illumination, occlusion, etc., the performance of text detection and recognition is not so well, missing detection and false detection often occur.

The previous methods follow tracking-by-detection paradigm, which firstly localizes the text in every single frame and associates them across the frame. Most of them focus on the similarity of appearance features between the trajectories and detection results. Each text instance is regarded as an individual object, while the texts are not isolated but affected each other. Especially in video, the relations between two texts in consecutive frames are very similar. As illustrated in Fig. 1, the text instances in frame t-1 show the spatial relation. The relative localization of each text to the text "ROLEX" is similar in two consecutive frames, so we use CNN to learn the spatial relations of each pair of

© Springer Nature Switzerland AG 2021
Y. Peng et al. (Eds.): ICIG 2021, LNCS 12890, pp. 610–622, 2021.
https://doi.org/10.1007/978-3-030-87361-5_50

text instances. Moreover, when the "ROLEX" is missed in the frame t, it will be reinforced in the appearance features as we utilize temporal information by transferring the location relation among texts in frame t-1 to frame t.

frame t-1   **frame t**

Fig. 1. To cope with low quality detection results, the spatial-temporal relation module utilizes several cues, such as localization, appearance and temporal information.

Inspired by relation network [7], we propose an online scene text tracking method, introducing the spatial-temporal relation to simultaneously encode various cues. The spatial relation encodes the location information of all texts in one single frame, and the spatial relation of each text with other texts in the previous frame is utilized as the temporal relation to tracking them in the current frame. Enhanced features are obtained by integrating the appearance features with the relation features that encoding localization information and temporal information.

The spatial-temporal relation module integrates various information, such as appearance, localization and temporal information. The features enhanced by relations benefit our tracker to maintain those missed detections or blurred texts that may easily be classified as background, and improve the completeness of trajectories. The experiment on IC15 demonstrates that our method effectively improves the number of tracked text and predicts more complete trajectories.

2   Related Work

Multiple Object Tracking (MOT). The goal of multiple object tracking (MOT) is to locate objects in adjacent frames and gain their trajectories over time. Despite the vast literature on multi-object tracking [14,29], multiple object tracking still remains a challenging problem, inaccurate detection results, occlusion between objects, especially in crowded environments where occlusions and false detection are common.

Most MOT methods [4,16,23,27,31] follow the tracking-by-detection paradigm, getting detection results and associating them across frames, thus easily suffering from occlusions or noisy detection in crowded scenes. Recently, the newly raised joint object and tracking paradigm has drawn increasing attention, for its high efficiency and simple architecture. Tracktor [1] utilizing the object detector's full capabilities, predicting the location of objects by regression of the detector. JDE [22] adds an embedding branch to predict the embedding features for the estimation of similarity. Chained Tracker [17] converts the challenging cross-frame association problem into a pair-wise object detection problem, it takes frame pairs as input and tracking objects by regress paired bounding boxes that appear in this frame pairs. These methods are simple, but tracking accuracy is not satisfying unless some re-identification module is introduced.

Video Scene Text Tracking. Scene text tracking faces more challenges than multi-object tracking, such as low contrast between text and background, text deformation caused by camera motion. Tracker should also pay attention to the unique characteristic of text, such as text usually in the same color, font and the relative position between characters is fixed.

The traditional text tracking methods that using template matching [8,15], partial filtering [5] were popular in the past, but these methods can not identify the same text that disappears for a few frames and then reappear. Tracking-by-detection paradigm can easily solve text re-initialization problem, Zuo et al. [32] and Tian et al. [19] propose to tracking with multiple tracking algorithms(tracking-by-detection, spatial-temporal context learning, linear prediction). Motion model and optical flow reflect the movement of the text and benefit tracker much. Wu et al. [24] tracking text based on motion prediction and optical flow estimation. Similarly, Yang et al. [26] proposed a tracking method based on median flow tracker to recall some missed text in detection. Wang et al. [20] making use of the temporal correlation of text and enhance detection results by tracking. Wang et al. [21] attempt to utilize the layout constraint of text regions to generate trajectories. Yu et al. [30] proposed an end-to-end video text detection and online tracking model, associate text with an appearance-geometry descriptor with memory mechanism and tracking text robust. Cheng et al. [3] proposed a unified detection, tracking and recognition model, extracts text features by text re-identification network, and trains it to learn a suitable distance function to estimate the similarity between texts. The tracking methods above only focus on the temporal information between frames when tracking and data association with appearance features, while they ignore the cues among texts in the single frame.

Text Detection and Multi-oriented Object Detection The core of arbitrary orientations and quadrilateral shapes text detection is extracting features that can distinguish text from background. Liao et al. [13] proposed a differentiable binarization module (DB) to detect scene text based on segmentation in real-time, and are widely used in text detection domain, for example, Mask-TextSpotter V3 [12] build the Segmentation Proposal Network based on DB. Some multi-oriented object detection using rotated bounding boxes or quadrangles to present the locations of object. The performance is heavily influenced by angle prediction, especially for long oriented objects, such as scene text. Gliding vertex [25] proposed a two-stage multi-oriented object detection network, which predicts four length ratios $(\alpha_1, \alpha_2, \alpha_3, \alpha_4)$ and obliquity factor r based on the horizontal bounding box.

3   Method

3.1   Overview

The proposed method follows the online joint detection and tracking paradigm [1], which simultaneously detects and tracks text across frames. Most joint detection and tracking methods ignore the relation among objects in the single frame. In contrast, we aim to utilize the geometry and appearance relation among texts as spatial relation and the relation comes from the previous frame as temporal relation, so as to enhance the appearance feature and minimize the impact of missing detection and low-quality frame. To this end, we proposed an online joint detection and tracking method with spatial-temporal relation module, tracking texts by the appearance features encoding with the geometry cues and temporal cues.

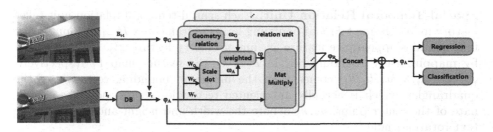

Fig. 2. The online joint detection and tracking pipeline for scene text tracking with spatial-temporal relation module. At each time step t, DB extracts the fused appearance feature map F_t. The spatial-temporal relation module enhances the appearance features of each text with the geometry cues and temporal cues among all bounding boxes B_{t-1}, and then the localization of each trajectory on current frame is predicted by regression.

Formally, let I_t be the t-th frame in the input video, the bounding boxes of texts in I_t can be defined as a set $B_t = \{b_t^{i_1}, b_t^{i_2}, ...\}$, where the i-th bounding box b_t^i represented as an arbitrary oriented and quadrilateral shapes by four corner vertices coordinates. Each trajectory consists of a series of bounding boxes $T^i = \{b_{t_1}^i, b_{t_2}^i, ...\}$, the trajectories of N texts form the trajectory set $T = \{T^1, T^2, ..., T^N\}$.

Our tracking pipeline is illustrated in Fig. 2, given the current frame I_t and the bounding boxes of tracklets in the previous frame B_{t-1} as input, the appearance features of each text φ_A are extracted and enhanced by the spatial-temporal relation module. The spatial-temporal relation module computes the geometry weights from the geometry embedding of all texts, and weights the appearance features by them. Then the localization of trajectories in the current frame are regressed on these features. The identification of each trajectory is transmitted from frame to frame through the regression, the trajectories of all texts can be obtained after tracking across all frames in the video.

3.2   Spatial-Temporal Relation Module

Inspired by the object relation module [7], we introduce object relation module to scene text tracking. Under the assumption that the movement of text between video frames is small, we extend the object relation module to spatial-temporal domain by taking the text bounding boxes of trajectories in frame t-1 and feature map in frame t as input. Furthermore, as we tracking text in arbitrary orientations and quadrilateral shapes, we adopt the spatial-temporal relation model to arbitrary rectangle forms.

The spatial relation encodes the position cues among all texts in one single frame, while our extended spatial-temporal relation encodes the temporal cues and position cues at the same time, the position cues in the previous frame can reduce the impact comes from occlusion or low-quality detection results.

Spatial-Temporal Relation Unit. Each spatial-temporal relation unit takes feature map of frame t F_t and bounding boxes in frame t-1 B_{t-1} as input. Each text contains appearance feature φ_A^i and geometry feature φ_G^i. φ_A^i is obtained by mapping each bounding box in B_{t-1} to the feature map F_t respectively. $\varphi_G^i = (x_i, y_i, w_i, h_i, \theta_i)$ comes from the minimum bounding rectangle of the quadrangles, which is actually an oriented rectangle. x_i, y_i denote the coordinate of the center point, w_i, h_i denote the width and height and θ_i denote the text rotation angle.

The spatial-temporal relation encodes the appearance features and the geometry features with temporal information. The spatial-temporal relation unit firstly obtained appearance weight ω_A^{ji} and geometry weight ω_G^{ji}, and then ω_A^{ji} and ω_G^{ji} are used to weight the appearance features as spatial-temporal relation.

The geometry weight ω_G^{ji} is computed based on a high-dimensional representation of each pair of text geometry features, by projecting the 5-dimensional relative geometry feature to the high-dimensional space. The relative geometry feature is defined as $\left(log \left(\frac{|x^j - x^i|}{w^j} \right), log \left(\frac{|y^j - y^i|}{h^j} \right), log \left(\frac{w^i}{w^j} \right), log \left(\frac{h^i}{h^j} \right), |\frac{\theta^j - \theta^i}{90}| \right)^T$, each item represents the difference in size, position and ratio between the pair bounding boxes. In this way, the relation module can encode the text position, size and ratio information into the appearance feature by geometry weight.

Meanwhile, the appearance features of texts are computed appearance weight the same as query, key and values in Scaled Dot-Product Attention. The appearance weight measures the similarity between each appearance feature φ_A^i with other appearance feature φ_A^j. The appearance weight is computes as

$$\omega_A^{ji} = \frac{dot\left(W_K \varphi_A^j, W_Q \varphi_A^i\right)}{\sqrt{d_k}}. \tag{1}$$

The relation weight ω^{ji} represents the weight of the j-th text to current i-th text. When computing the relation weight, geometry weight is used to weight appearance weight as

$$\omega^{ji} = \frac{\omega_G^{ji} \cdot exp\left(\omega_A^{ji}\right)}{\sum_k \omega_G^{ki} \cdot \left(\omega_A^{ki}\right)}. \tag{2}$$

The weighted relation feature $\varphi_R(i)$, that denotes the i-th text with other texts, is computed as

$$\varphi_R(i) = \sum_j \omega^{ji} \cdot \left(W_V \cdot \varphi_A^j\right). \tag{3}$$

Spatial-Temporal Relation Module. The whole relation module consists of N_r relation unit, each relation unit encodes different relations. The input text's appearance feature is finally augmented by adding N_r concatenated relation features on it. The output appearance feature can be formulated as

$$\varphi_A^i = \varphi_A^i + Concat\left[\varphi_R^1(i), ..., \varphi_R^{N_r}(i)\right], \tag{4}$$

where i indicates each text in frame.

3.3   Tracking with Relation

In this paper, we propose a method based on joint detection and tracking methods with the relation module extended into spatial-temporal domain. Strengthen the text's appearance feature by aggregating the relations with other texts in the previous frame. The overall tracking process is shown in Algorithm 1.

Tracking Pipeline. Given the current frame I_t, detection results in frame t D_t and the bounding boxes of tracklets in previous frame B_{t-1} as input, the tracker computes feature map F_t of current frame. Each bounding box is mapped to the feature map to obtain the corresponding appearance feature φ_A and are fed into relation regression module. In spatial-temporal relation module, all bounding boxes are considered as geometry features φ_G. φ_G together with appearance features are calculated a variety of different relation features φ_R, which contain spatial-temporal information and can be added to appearance features. The weighted appearance features are then used for predicting the accurate location and classifying each tracklet in current frame. The identification of each trajectory is transmitted from frame t-1 to frame t through the regression of each bounding box. The trajectories of all texts can be obtained after tracking across all frames in the video. The initialization, termination and reactivation of trajectories are described as follows.

Algorithm 1: Tracking algorithm

Input: frame t I_t.
Output: trajectories T.

foreach *video frame I_t* **do**
  $\varphi_A = Spatial - Temporal\ relation\,(DB\,(I_t, B_{t-1})\,, B_{t-1})$
  $box\_score, reg\_box = regress\_track(\varphi_A, T)$
  if $box\_score^i < \lambda_{reg}$ **then**
  | inactive T^i
  else
  | T^i update it's position with reg_box^i
  update trajectories' features in reid model
  get the detection result D_t in current frame
  foreach *trajectory T^i and all detection results D_t* **do**
    compute $IoU = \{IoU^1\,(b_t^i, d_t^1)\,, IoU^2\,(b_t^i, d_t^2)\,, ..., IoU^k\,(b_t^i, d_t^k)\}$
    if $IoU^k > \lambda_{init}$ **then**
      if $similarity(d_t^k, T_{inactive}^q) > \lambda_{reid}$ **then**
      | T^q update it's position with D_t^k
      else
      | $T = T \cup T^k$

Trajectory Initialization and Termination. Predicting the location of text in the current frame through regression can only maintain and predict the trajectories that already exist, so tracker also needs detection results to initialize new trajectories. In each time step t, after the prediction of trajectories' location, tracker computes the IoU of detection result D_t and all existing trajectories in current frame B_t. A detection d_t^k is a new text when it's IoU with all trajectories are lower than a threshold λ_{init}, which means this text didn't belong to any trajectory.

Trajectories end when the text leaves the frame or is occluded by something. In these cases, the classification score will be small, indicates that it is unlikely to be a text. So tracker terminates the trajectory when its score is lower than λ_{reg}, and turns its state to inactivate.

Trajectory Reactivation. Furthermore, in order to recognize reappeared text, we trained a re-identification model on the dataset generated from icdar "text in videos". Tracker saves the terminated trajectories for some frames. Once a new detection bounding box d^k is found, the tracker computes the similarity between d^k with all inactivate trajectories $T_{inactivate}$. If the similarity of d^k with $T_{inactivate}^q$ is greater than λ_{reid}, d^k will be considered belongs to $T_{inactivate}^q$. The q-th inactivate trajectory will be reactivated in the tracker.

3.4 Loss Function

The proposed method involves loss for regression and classification stage, and can be formulated as $L = L_{cls} + L_{reg}$. The classification loss L_{cls} is the same as Faster R-CNN [18]. The regression loss contains three terms for horizontal box regression loss L_h, length ratio regression loss L_α and obliquity factor regression loss L_r:

$$L_{reg} = \lambda_1 L_h + \lambda_2 L_\alpha + \lambda_3 L_r, \tag{5}$$

where $\lambda_1, \lambda_2, \lambda_3$ are the hyperparameters that balance the three terms, which are the same as gliding vertex [25].

4 Experiment

4.1 Implement Details

We implement our network with PyTorch platform and all experiments are run on the GeForce GTX 1080 Ti. In training stage, we set *batch size* = 2 and learn the network by adopting SGD with the fixed *learning rate* = 10^{-4}, the loss weight are all set to 1. We tried different sets of tracking thresholds, and chose the best tracking thresholds based on the best MOTA. In testing stage, we set the tracking thresholds $\lambda_{reg} = 0.8, \lambda_{init} = 0.3, \lambda_{reid} = 2.0$.

Network Architecture. In the case of tracking text, our feature extracting network is based on text detection network DB [13] with a ResNet-50 backbone, the regression and classification module are based on gliding vertex [25] which can regress bounding box in multi-orientations and quadrilateral shapes. Both DB and the regression and classification module are fine-tuned on video training set IC15, all video frames with ground-truth are regenerated as 9598 images and gts, and are fed into the network training the detector. In order to improve the regression ability, we exchange the extracted proposals to the ground-truth bounding boxes in previous frame, only train the regression and classification module with and without the relation module by freezing the parameters of the feature extractor network.

4.2 Dataset and Evaluation Protocols

Dataset. We evaluate our method on video scene text dataset: ICDAR 'text in videos' 2013 dataset (IC13) [10] and 2015 dataset (IC15) [9]. IC15 contains 25 videos (13450 frames) for training and 24 videos (14374 frames) for testing, which are collected by the organizers in different countries, using 4 different cameras, covering different scripts and languages. All videos correspond to 7 high-level tasks, which can represent real-life outdoors and indoor applications. IC13 is the subset of IC15, which contains 13 videos for training and 15 videos for testing.

Evaluation Metrics. For quantitative tracking performance, we evaluate the proposed framework with the CLEAR MOT Metrics [2], i.e., the multiple object tracking accuracy (MOTA), the multiple object tracking precision (MOTP) and IDF1 score. In addition, we also use the metrics defined in [11], including the percentage of mostly tracked targets (MT), the percentage of mostly lost targets (ML) and the percentage of partially tracked targets (PT).

4.3 Ablation Study

We present the result of ablation study on IC15 for tracking performance and IC13 for detection performance.

Table 1. Ablation study about spatial-temporal relation module on IC15. Ours (w/o relation) denotes our method without relation module. Ours denotes our method with spatial-temporal relation module.

Model	MOTA	MOTP	IDF1	MT	PT	ML
Ours (w/o relation)	19.28	68.00	48.24	768	561	587
Ours	**33.09**	**71.04**	**51.44**	**864**	**509**	**543**

Table 2. Detection performance on IC13. Detection denotes the performance of text detector. Ours(w/o relation) denotes our method without relation module. Ours denotes our method with spatial-temporal relation module.

Model	Precision	Recall	F-score
Detection	50.07	27.70	35.67
Ours (w/o relation)	70.25	43.71	53.89
Ours	**81.63**	**48.04**	**60.48**

Table 1 verifies the effectiveness of spatial-temporal relation module in improving the tracking performance. Both models are fine-tuned on IC15. By applying the spatial-temporal relation, we can get more tracked trajectories and more precise trajectories. There is a significant improvement of MOTA, which increases from 19.28% to 33.09% and MOTP also increases from 68.00% to 71.04%.

We also compare the detection performance before and after tracking on IC13. As shown in Table 2, compared with the performance of detection result, the model without relation enhances detection performance on precision, recall and F-score, due to tracking recovers more missed texts and suppresses false detection results. Our method achieves the best performance on detection by adding the spatial-temporal relation that can integrate more temporal information and spatial information. The improvement proves that we can get more accurate bounding boxes by applying spatial-temporal relation.

Table 3. Tracking performance evaluation on IC15.

Model	MOTA	MOTP	IDF1	MT	PT	ML
h&h lab	**53.74**	**76.92**	**65.51**	**874**	**536**	**506**
FREE [3]	43.16	76.78	57.92	702	364	850
SRC-B-TextProcessingLab	23.09	68.51	39.40	274	481	1161
AJOU [6]	16.44	72.71	36.07	271	458	1187
USTB_TexVideo II-2 [28]	12.29	71.78	21.93	92	439	1385
Ours	33.09	71.04	51.44	864	509	543

4.4 Benchmark Evaluations

We compare our method with other text tracking methods on IC15 in Table 3. All results are cited from the ICDAR official website[1]. There are no corresponding papers for the methods in the first and third lines. Our method achieves competitive performance on mostly tracked, partially tracked and mostly lost, which proves the effectiveness of spatial-temporal relation among texts in track-

Fig. 3. Visualization of our tracking results on two sequences of IC15 test set. w/o relation denotes the trajectories generated by the model without spatial-temporal relation module, ours denotes the trajectories generated with spatial-temporal relation.

---

[1] https://rrc.cvc.uab.es/.

ing. As illustrated in Fig. 3, the trajectories of our method are more complete while miss more texts without the spatial-temporal relation.

Our method uses a good scene text detector that can detect more text bounding boxes than those in ground truth. Hence, our false positive is much higher than other methods, which leads to the drop of MOTA. Our method can precisely track text with low speed, such as the videos taken with a hand-held camera. While our method do not perform so good on the videos shoot beside highway, in which the movements of text are in high speed. The regression in this situation is not very precise and caused a lower MOTP.

5   Conclusion

In this paper, we propose an online scene text tracking network with spatial-temporal relation, focusing on exploiting the relations among texts to track texts more robust. In future, we'll further explore the spatial-temporal relation in text re-identification to improve the accuracy of maintaining the identity information in tracking process.

Acknowledgement. The research is supported by National Key Research and Development Program of China (2020AAA09701), National Natural Science Foundation of China (61806017, 62006018) and Fundamental Research Funds for the Central Universities (FRF-NP-20-02).

References

1. Bergmann, P., Meinhardt, T., Leal-Taixe, L.: Tracking without bells and whistles. In: Proceedings of the IEEE/CVF International Conference on Computer Vision. pp. 941–951 (2019)
2. Bernardin, K., Stiefelhagen, R.: Evaluating multiple object tracking performance: the clear mot metrics. EURASIP J. Image Video Process. **2008**, 1–10 (2008)
3. Cheng, Z., et al.: Free: a fast and robust end-to-end video text spotter. IEEE Trans. Image Process. **30**, 822–837 (2020)
4. Chu, P., Ling, H.: Famnet: joint learning of feature, affinity and multi-dimensional assignment for online multiple object tracking. In: Proceedings of the IEEE/CVF International Conference on Computer Vision, pp. 6172–6181 (2019)
5. Goto, H., Tanaka, M.: Text-tracking wearable camera system for the blind. In: 2009 10th International Conference on Document Analysis and Recognition. pp. 141–145. IEEE (2009)
6. Henriques, J.F., Caseiro, R., Martins, P., Batista, J.: Exploiting the circulant structure of tracking-by-detection with kernels. In: European Conference on Computer Vision, pp. 702–715. Springer (2012)
7. Hu, H., Gu, J., Zhang, Z., Dai, J., Wei, Y.: Relation networks for object detection. In: Proceedings of the IEEE Conference on Computer Vision and Pattern Recognition, pp. 3588–3597 (2018)
8. Huang, W., Shivakumara, P., Tan, C.L.: Detecting moving text in video using temporal information. In: 2008 19th International Conference on Pattern Recognition, pp. 1–4. IEEE (2008)

9. Karatzas, D., et al.: Icdar 2015 competition on robust reading. In: 2015 13th International Conference on Document Analysis and Recognition (ICDAR), pp. 1156–1160. IEEE (2015)
10. Karatzas, D., et al.: Icdar 2013 robust reading competition. In: 2013 12th International Conference on Document Analysis and Recognition, pp. 1484–1493. IEEE (2013)
11. Li, Y., Huang, C., Nevatia, R.: Learning to associate: hybridboosted multi-target tracker for crowded scene. In: 2009 IEEE Conference on Computer Vision and Pattern Recognition, pp. 2953–2960. IEEE (2009)
12. Liao, M., Pang, G., Huang, J., Hassner, T., Bai, X.: Mask textspotter v3: segmentation proposal network for robust scene text spotting. arXiv preprint arXiv:2007.09482 (2020)
13. Liao, M., Wan, Z., Yao, C., Chen, K., Bai, X.: Real-time scene text detection with differentiable binarization. In: Proceedings of the AAAI Conference on Artificial Intelligence, vol. 34, pp. 11474–11481 (2020)
14. Luo, W., Xing, J., Milan, A., Zhang, X., Liu, W., Kim, T.K.: Multiple object tracking: a literature review. Artificial Intelligence, p. 103448 (2020)
15. Na, Y., Wen, D.: An effective video text tracking algorithm based on sift feature and geometric constraint. In: Pacific-Rim Conference on Multimedia, pp. 392–403. Springer (2010)
16. Pang, B., Li, Y., Zhang, Y., Li, M., Lu, C.: Tubetk: adopting tubes to track multi-object in a one-step training model. In: Proceedings of the IEEE/CVF Conference on Computer Vision and Pattern Recognition, pp. 6308–6318 (2020)
17. Peng, J., et al.: Chained-tracker: chaining paired attentive regression results for end-to-end joint multiple-object detection and tracking. In: European Conference on Computer Vision, pp. 145–161. Springer (2020)
18. Ren, S., He, K., Girshick, R., Sun, J.: Faster r-cnn: towards real-time object detection with region proposal networks. arXiv preprint arXiv:1506.01497 (2015)
19. Tian, S., Pei, W.Y., Zuo, Z.Y., Yin, X.C.: Scene text detection in video by learning locally and globally. In: IJCAI, pp. 2647–2653 (2016)
20. Wang, L., Wang, Y., Shan, S., Su, F.: Scene text detection and tracking in video with background cues. In: Proceedings of the 2018 ACM on International Conference on Multimedia Retrieval, pp. 160–168 (2018)
21. Wang, X., Feng, X., Xia, Z.: Scene video text tracking based on hybrid deep text detection and layout constraint. Neurocomputing 363, 223–235 (2019)
22. Wang, Z., Zheng, L., Liu, Y., Wang, S.: Towards real-time multi-object tracking. arXiv preprint arXiv:1909.12605 2(3), 4 (2019)
23. Wu, J., Cao, J., Song, L., Wang, Y., Yang, M., Yuan, J.: Track to detect and segment: an online multi-object tracker. arXiv preprint arXiv:2103.08808 (2021)
24. Wu, L., Shivakumara, P., Lu, T., Tan, C.L.: A new technique for multi-oriented scene text line detection and tracking in video. IEEE Trans. Multimed. 17(8), 1137–1152 (2015)
25. Xu, Y., et al.: Gliding vertex on the horizontal bounding box for multi-oriented object detection. IEEE Trans. Pattern Analysis Mach. Intell. 43, 1452–1459 (2020)
26. Yang, X.H., He, W., Yin, F., Liu, C.L.: A unified video text detection method with network flow. In: 2017 14th IAPR International Conference on Document Analysis and Recognition (ICDAR), vol. 1, pp. 331–336. IEEE (2017)
27. Yin, J., Wang, W., Meng, Q., Yang, R., Shen, J.: A unified object motion and affinity model for online multi-object tracking. In: Proceedings of the IEEE/CVF Conference on Computer Vision and Pattern Recognition, pp. 6768–6777 (2020)

28. Yin, X.C., Pei, W.Y., Zhang, J., Hao, H.W.: Multi-orientation scene text detection with adaptive clustering. IEEE Trans. Pattern Anal. Mach. Intell. **37**(9), 1930–1937 (2015)

29. Yin, X.C., Zuo, Z.Y., Tian, S., Liu, C.L.: Text detection, tracking and recognition in video: a comprehensive survey. IEEE Trans. Image Process. **25**(6), 2752–2773 (2016)

30. Yu, H., Huang, Y., Pi, L., Zhang, C., Li, X., Wang, L.: End-to-end video text detection with online tracking. Pattern Recogn. **113**, 107791 (2021)

31. Zhu, J., Yang, H., Liu, N., Kim, M., Zhang, W., Yang, M.H.: Online multi-object tracking with dual matching attention networks. In: Proceedings of the European Conference on Computer Vision (ECCV), pp. 366–382 (2018)

32. Zuo, Z.Y., Tian, S., Pei, W.Y., Yin, X.C.: Multi-strategy tracking based text detection in scene videos. In: 2015 13th International Conference on Document Analysis and Recognition (ICDAR), pp. 66–70. IEEE (2015)

Equivalence of Correlation Filter and Convolution Filter in Visual Tracking

Shuiwang Li[2,3], Qijun Zhao[1,2(✉)], Ziliang Feng[1,2], and Li Lu[2]

[1] National Key Laboratory of Fundamental Science on Synthetic Vision,
Sichuan University, Chengdu, China
[2] College of Computer Science, Sichuan University, Chengdu, China
{qjzhao,fengziliang,luli}@scu.edu.cn
[3] Guilin University of Technology, Guilin, China

Abstract. (Discriminative) Correlation Filter has been successfully applied to visual tracking and has advanced the field significantly in recent years. Correlation filter-based trackers consider visual tracking as a problem of matching the feature template of the object and candidate regions in the detection sample, in which correlation filter provides the means to calculate the similarities. In contrast, convolution filter is usually used for blurring, sharpening, embossing, edge detection, etc. in image processing. On the surface, correlation filter and convolution filter are usually used for different purposes. In this paper, however, we prove, for the first time, that correlation filter and convolution filter are equivalent in the sense that their minimum mean-square errors (MMSEs) in visual tracking are equal, under the condition that the optimal solutions exist and the ideal filter response is Gaussian and centrosymmetric. This result gives researchers the freedom to choose correlation or convolution in formulating their trackers. It also suggests that the explanation of the ideal response in terms of similarities is not essential.

Keywords: Correlation filter · Convolution filter · Visual tracking

1 Introduction

Visual tracking is a fundamental and challenging task in the field of computer vision, which has applications in numerous fields, e.g., disaster response [44], intelligent traffic [4] and wildlife protection [37], etc. However, visual tracking is still confronting with onerous challenges, e.g., object deformation, illumination variation, background clutter, motion blur, occlusion, visual angle and scale change, and real-time requirement, etc. [19]. Given its broad range of real-world applications, a number of large-scale benchmark datasets have been established, on which considerable methods have been proposed and demonstrated with significant progress in recent years. Two currently predominant approaches are discriminative correlation filter (DCF)-based methods and deep learning (DL)-based methods. Deep learning has been intensively studied and demonstrated remarkable success in a wide range of computer vision areas, such as image

© Springer Nature Switzerland AG 2021
Y. Peng et al. (Eds.): ICIG 2021, LNCS 12890, pp. 623–634, 2021.
https://doi.org/10.1007/978-3-030-87361-5_51

classification, object detection, image caption and semantic segmentation, etc. [1,22,45]. Inspired by deep learning breakthroughs in these fields, DL-based methods have attracted considerable interest in the visual tracking community and witness rapid development and great advances in recent years. And thanks to available large-scale datasets for training, DL-based trackers have achieved and are achieving state-of-the-art tracking performance and outperform DCF-based trackers significantly in terms of precision and accuracy. Despite deep learning-based approaches have achieved great success and are promising in dealing with the challenges in visual tracking [2,8,27,41], its efficiency is unsatisfactory in the scenarios where computational resources is limited while real-time requirement is strict. One such real-world scenario is unmanned aerial vehicle (UAV)-based tracking where video sequences are captured by cameras mounted on board UAVs. Equipped with visual tracking algorithms, UAV has been wildly used in various applications, e.g., target following [40] aircraft refueling [42], disaster response [44], autonomously landing [33], and wildlife protection [37], etc. Compared with general tracking scenes, UAV tracking faces more onerous challenges [13], in particular due to the limitations of onboard computing resources, battery capacity and maximum load of UAV, the deployment of DL-based tracking algorithms in UAV is still not feasible because deep neural networks usually need large storage space and computing resource, which are often difficult to meet in such small platforms as generic UAVs. DL-based tracking methods may be also not suitable for other samll platforms, for instance, mobile phone, handheld computer device and micro robot, etc., where resources are very limited. For this reason, DCF-base tracking algorithms because of their high CPU speed, which though are not as good as the DL-based tracking algorithms in terms of precision and accuracy, still attract a lot of attention of researchers and engineers, especially in the field of UAV tracking [16,20,25,30–32]. That is why the study of DCF-based tracking algorithms still has important value and application prospect.

DCF-based trackers [7,14,17,26,30] are among the most efficient tracking algorithms for the time being [13]. These tracking algorithms consider object tracking as a problem of matching the feature template of the object and candidate regions in the detection sample, in which correlation filter provides the means to calculate the similarities. The candidate region with the highest similarity is usually taken as the new state of the object. According to the Parseval theorem and the correlation theorem, the correlation filters can be solved in the frequency domain efficiently and the correlation operation can be evaluated in an efficient way as well through the FFT (fast Fourier transform) algorithm. In contrast, convolution filter are usually used for blurring, sharpening, embossing, edge detection, etc. in image processing [38]. On the surface, correlation filter and convolution filter are usually used for different purposes. In this paper, for the first time we prove that correlation filter and convolution filter are equivalent in the sense that their minimum mean-square error (MMSE) in visual tracking are equal, under the condition that the optimal solutions exist and the ideal filter response is Gaussian and centrosymmetric. Moreover, according to the Parseval theorem and the convolution theorem convolution filters can be solved in the frequency domain as well. This result gives researchers the freedom to choose correlation or convolution in formulating their trackers. It also suggests that the explanation of the ideal response in terms of similarities is not essential. In fact, current state-of-the-art DL-based methods are basically all Siamese trackers [5,23,24,43], which all employ a correlation operator to predict a target confidence at each spatial position in a dense and efficient sliding-window manner in order to localize the target, based upon which different heads may be used for either classification or regression or even other tasks. Therefore, our result also poses a question on whether the correlation operator could be replaced by the convolution operator and, furthermore, whether the similarity learning-based explanation of Siamese trackers is essential.

2   Related Works

The correlation filter first appeared in the field of signal processing, and later was applied to visual tracking, now known as the discriminative correlation filter (DCF). Below we provide a brief review on DCF-based trackers. Bolme et al. [3] first used correlation filter for visual tracking and proposed the minimum output sum of squared error (MOSSE) filter, which is considered the first DCF-based tracker. They considered the visual tracking as the problem of matching the initial object template and the candidate sub-images in the detection sample using correlation filter, and they proposed to efficiently solved the filter in the frequency domain. From the perspective of using cyclic sampling to obtain training samples for learning a linear regressor, the CSK tracker proposed by Henriques et al. [18] actually obtained the same discriminant correlation filter, which were latter improved by the KCF [17] tracker with kernel tricks and multi-channel features. By that time, DCF-based tracking algorithms not only showed good performance in various complex scenes, but also ran much faster than other types of tracking algorithms. Afterwards, DCF-based methods developed rapidly and increasingly achieved great improvements. For instance, to reduce boundary effects caused by the periodic assumption of DCF Danelljan et al. [9] proposed spatially regularized DCF (SRDCF) for tracking. On the basis of SRDCF, Daneljan et al. further proposed the C-COT tracker [11] and the ECO tracker [7] successively. C-COT uses the VGG neural network to extract features and extends the feature maps of different resolutions to a continuous spatial domain through interpolation, and learns continuous convolution operators for visual tracking. The ECO tracker aims to simultaneously improve both speed and performance. It designs a factorized convolution operator which drastically reduces the number of parameters in the model, and a compact generative model of the training sample distribution that significantly reduces memory and time complexity. In addition, it uses a conservative model update strategy to improve robustness and to further reduce complexity. Lukezic et al. [34] introduced the concept of channels and spatial reliabilities to DCF tracking in order to overcome the limitations related to the rectangular shape representation of the object. Mueller et al. [36] proposed context-aware DCF to incorporate global context to deal with fast motion, occlusion or background clutter on the grounds that conventional DCF trackers are learned locally. By introducing temporal regularization to SRDCF, Li et al. [26] proposed spatial-temporal regularized correlation filters (STRCF) to achieve more robust appearance models. In order to online automatically and adaptively learn spatio-temporal regularization , Li et al. [30] proposed an automatic spatio-Temporal regularization approach (Auto-Track). As for feature representation, the DCF-based approaches were initially restricted to a single feature channel and later extended to multi-channel feature maps [11,15], such as HOG [6] and color names [10] and deep CNN features [11,21,35,39]. To efficiently model how both the foreground and background of the object varies over time, Galoogahi et al. [14] proposed the backgroundaware correlation filter (BACF), which extracts patches densely from background using a cropping matrix and can be learned very efficiently. By enforcing restriction to the rate of alteration in response maps generated in the detection phase, Huang et al. [20], based upon the BACF tracker, proposed the aberrance repressed correlation filters (ARCF) to repress aberrances happening during the tracking process. Following BACF and ARCF, in order to improve the convergence properties and the wildly adopted discriminative scale estimation in DCF-based trackers, Li et al. [29] proposed the residue-aware correlation filter (RACF) for UAV tracking in particular. BACF, ARCF and RACF all in fact can be thought of as asymmetric discriminative correlation filters proposed by Li et al. [28], which have some theoretical advantages for visual tracking.

3   Proof of the Equivalence of Correlation Filter and Convolution Filter in Visual Tracking

3.1   Correlation Filter in Visual Tracking

A DCF-based tracker aims to learn a multi-channel convolution filter f from a set of training samples $\{x_k\}_{k=1}^t$, where each training sample x_k consists of d feature maps with x_k^l denoting the l_{th} one. The the coordinate of the maximum value of y represents the center position of the object to be tracked. The filter f consists of d 2-D correlation filter $\{f^l\}_{l=1}^d$. Each f^l and x_k^l will be conducted the correlation operation, producing the correlation filter response. Let $x_k^l \in R^{m \times n}, f^l \in R^{m \times n}, N = mn$. Suppose m and n are even numbers to simplify our discussion. Then the correlation filter response of f to x_k is

$$R(x_k; f) = \sum_{l=1}^d x_k^l \odot f^l, \tag{1}$$

where $\odot$ denotes the circular correlation operator. The general objective function of correlation filter-based tracker is as follows,

$$\arg\min_f \sum_{k=1}^t \alpha_k \|R(x_k; f) - y\|^2 + \lambda \sum_{l=1}^d \|f^l\|^2, \tag{2}$$

where y, defined by a 2-D centrosymmetric Gaussian function, is the ideal filter response, t is the current frame number, $\alpha_k \geqslant 0$ decides the weight of each sample x_k, λ is the penalty coefficient of the regularization. The matrix norm $\|\cdot\|$ is just the Frobenius norm, defined by

$$\|f^l\| = \left(\sum_{i=1}^{m}\sum_{j=1}^{n}|f(i,j)|^2\right)^{\frac{1}{2}} = \|\vec{f}^l\|, \tag{3}$$

where $\vec{f}^l$ denotes the vectorized f^l. It is worthy of note that the special case where $k = t$ and $\alpha_k = 1$ is frequently used, when the objective function is more simple as follows [12],

$$\arg\min_{f}\ \|R(x_k;f) - y\|^2 + \lambda\sum_{l=1}^{d}\|f^l\|^2. \tag{4}$$

Now, we discuss solving the problem (2). Substituting (1) into (2) we have

$$\arg\min_{f}\ \sum_{k=1}^{t}\alpha_k\|\sum_{l=1}^{d}x_k^l \odot f^l - y\|^2 + \lambda\sum_{l=1}^{d}\|f^l\|^2. \tag{5}$$

According to the Parseval's theorem and the correlation theorem, (5) is equivalent to

$$\arg\min_{\hat{f}}\ \sum_{k=1}^{t}\alpha_k\|\sum_{l=1}^{d}\mathrm{conj}(\hat{x}_k^l) \odot \hat{f}^l - \hat{y}\|^2 + \lambda\sum_{l=1}^{d}\|\hat{f}^l\|^2, \tag{6}$$

where $\hat{z}$ denotes the Fourier transform of z, conj represents the operation of conjugate. It is obvious that (6) is equivalent to the following vectorized form,

$$\arg\min_{\vec{\hat{f}}}\ \sum_{k=1}^{t}\alpha_k\|\sum_{l=1}^{d}\mathrm{conj}(\vec{\hat{x}}_k^l) \odot \vec{\hat{f}}^l - \vec{\hat{y}}\|^2 + \lambda\sum_{l=1}^{d}\|\vec{\hat{f}}^l\|^2. \tag{7}$$

Let $\hat{\mathbf{X}}_k = [\mathrm{diag}(\vec{\hat{x}}_k^1)^{\mathrm{H}}, ..., \mathrm{diag}(\vec{\hat{x}}_k^d)^{\mathrm{H}}]$, $\hat{\mathbf{f}} = [(\vec{\hat{f}}^1)^{\mathrm{H}}, ..., (\vec{\hat{f}}^d)^{\mathrm{H}}]^{\mathrm{H}}$, $\hat{\mathbf{y}} = \vec{\hat{y}}$, where ^{H} represents the conjugate transpose. Then (7) is equivalent to

$$\arg\min_{\hat{\mathbf{f}}}\ \sum_{k=1}^{t}\alpha_k\|\hat{\mathbf{X}}_k\hat{\mathbf{f}} - \hat{\mathbf{y}}\|^2 + \lambda\|\hat{\mathbf{f}}\|^2. \tag{8}$$

This is a linear least square problem whose optimal solution $\hat{\mathbf{f}}_*$ (if exists) satisfies the following system of linear equations:

$$[(\sum_{k=1}^{t}\alpha_k\hat{\mathbf{X}}_k^{\mathrm{H}}\hat{\mathbf{X}}_k) + \lambda\mathbf{I}_{dN}]\hat{\mathbf{f}}_* = \sum_{k=1}^{t}\alpha_k\hat{\mathbf{X}}_k^{\mathrm{H}}\hat{\mathbf{y}}, \tag{9}$$

where $\mathbf{I}_{dN}$ is a identity matrix of size $dN \times dN$. If $[(\sum_{k=1}^{t}\alpha_k\hat{\mathbf{X}}_k^{\mathrm{H}}\hat{\mathbf{X}}_k) + \lambda\mathbf{I}_{dN}]$ is invertible, then

$$\hat{\mathbf{f}}_* = [(\sum_{k=1}^{t}\alpha_k\hat{\mathbf{X}}_k^{\mathrm{H}}\hat{\mathbf{X}}_k) + \lambda\mathbf{I}_{dN}]^{-1}(\sum_{k=1}^{t}\alpha_k\hat{\mathbf{X}}_k^{\mathrm{H}}\hat{\mathbf{y}}). \tag{10}$$

When $d = 1$, $[(\sum_{k=1}^{t} \alpha_k \hat{\mathbf{X}}_k^{\mathrm{H}} \hat{\mathbf{X}}_k) + \lambda \mathbf{I}_{dN}]$ reduces to a diagonal matrix. If it is invertible, $\hat{\mathbf{f}}$ can be easily obtained. But when $d \neq 1$, the inversion of $[(\sum_{k=1}^{t} \alpha_k \hat{\mathbf{X}}_k^{\mathrm{H}} \hat{\mathbf{X}}_k) + \lambda \mathbf{I}_{dN}]$ becomes much complicated. In fact, Li et al. [28] proved, under general conditions, that $[(\sum_{k=1}^{t} \alpha_k \hat{\mathbf{X}}_k^{\mathrm{H}} \hat{\mathbf{X}}_k) + \lambda \mathbf{I}_{dN}]$ is a block matrix with each block is a diagonal matrix if $d \neq 1$.

3.2   Convolution Filter in Visual Tracking

In this paper, the filter constructed by the convolution operator is called the convolution filter to distinguish it from the correlation filter, although no distinction is made between them in some literature [7,9,11]. Replacing the circular correlation operator in the objective function (5) by the circular convolution operator results in the objective function of convolution filter-based tracker as follows,

$$\underset{f}{\arg\min} \ \sum_{k=1}^{t} \alpha_k \| \sum_{l=1}^{d} x_k^l \circledast f^l - y \|^2 + \lambda \sum_{l=1}^{d} \| f^l \|^2. \tag{11}$$

According to the Parseval theorem and the convolution theorem, (11) is equivalent to

$$\underset{\hat{f}}{\arg\min} \ \sum_{k=1}^{t} \alpha_k \| \sum_{l=1}^{d} \hat{x}_k^l \odot \hat{f}^l - \hat{y} \|^2 + \lambda \sum_{l=1}^{d} \| \hat{f}^l \|^2. \tag{12}$$

And (12) is obviously equivalent to the following vectorized formulation:

$$\underset{\vec{f}}{\arg\min} \ \sum_{k=1}^{t} \alpha_k \| \sum_{l=1}^{d} \vec{\hat{x}}_k^l \odot \vec{\hat{f}}^l - \vec{\hat{y}} \|^2 + \lambda \sum_{l=1}^{d} \| \vec{\hat{f}}^l \|^2. \tag{13}$$

Let $\hat{\mathbf{X}}'_k = [\mathrm{diag}(\vec{\hat{x}}_k^1), ..., \mathrm{diag}(\vec{\hat{x}}_k^d)]$, $\hat{\mathbf{f}}' = [(\vec{\hat{f}}^1)^{\mathrm{H}}, ..., (\vec{\hat{f}}^d)^{\mathrm{H}}]^{\mathrm{H}}$, $\hat{\mathbf{y}} = \vec{\hat{y}}$, then (12) is equivalent to

$$\underset{\hat{\mathbf{f}}'}{\arg\min} \ \sum_{k=1}^{t} \alpha_k \| \hat{\mathbf{X}}'_k \hat{\mathbf{f}}' - \hat{\mathbf{y}} \|^2 + \lambda \| \hat{\mathbf{f}}' \|^2. \tag{14}$$

The optimal solution $\hat{\mathbf{f}}'_*$ of (14) (if exists) satisfies the following system of linear equations:

$$[(\sum_{k=1}^{t} \alpha_k \hat{\mathbf{X}}'_k^{\mathrm{H}} \hat{\mathbf{X}}'_k) + \lambda \mathbf{I}_{dN}] \hat{\mathbf{f}}'_* = \sum_{k=1}^{t} \alpha_k \hat{\mathbf{X}}'_k^{\mathrm{H}} \hat{\mathbf{y}}. \tag{15}$$

If $[(\sum_{k=1}^{t} \alpha_k \hat{\mathbf{X}}'_k^{\mathrm{H}} \hat{\mathbf{X}}'_k) + \lambda \mathbf{I}_{dN}]$ is invertible, then

$$\hat{\mathbf{f}}'_* = [(\sum_{k=1}^{t} \alpha_k \hat{\mathbf{X}}'_k^{\mathrm{H}} \hat{\mathbf{X}}'_k) + \lambda \mathbf{I}_{dN}]^{-1} (\sum_{k=1}^{t} \alpha_k \hat{\mathbf{X}}'_k^{\mathrm{H}} \hat{\mathbf{y}}). \tag{16}$$

3.3   Proof of the Equivalence

Let

$$
\hat{\mathbf{s}}(\{\hat{\mathbf{G}}_k(\vec{x}_k^1, ..., \vec{x}_k^d)\}_{k=1}^t; \{\alpha_k\}_{k=1}^t, \hat{\mathbf{y}})
$$

$$
= [(\sum_{k=1}^t \alpha_k \hat{\mathbf{G}}_k^{\mathrm{H}}(\vec{x}_k^1, ..., \vec{x}_k^d)\hat{\mathbf{G}}_k(\vec{x}_k^1, ..., \vec{x}_k^d)) + \lambda \mathbf{I}_{dN}]^{-1}(\sum_{k=1}^t \alpha_k \hat{\mathbf{G}}_k^{\mathrm{H}}(\vec{x}_k^1, ..., \vec{x}_k^d)\hat{\mathbf{y}}),
$$

$$
\hat{\mathbf{G}}_k(\vec{x}_k^1, ..., \vec{x}_k^d) = [\mathrm{diag}(\vec{x}_k^1), ..., \mathrm{diag}(\vec{x}_k^d)].
$$

(17)

If the optimal solution of the correlation filter-based tracker defined by (7) and that of the convolution filter-based tracker defined by (12) are considered as functions of $\{\hat{x}_k\}_{k=1}^t$, then the optimal solutions given in (10) and (16) respectively satisfy the following equations:

$$
\hat{\mathbf{f}}_*(\vec{x}_k^1, ..., \vec{x}_k^d) = \hat{\mathbf{s}}(\{\hat{\mathbf{G}}_k(\mathrm{conj}(\vec{x}_k^1), ..., \mathrm{conj}(\vec{x}_k^d))\}_{k=1}^t; \{\alpha_k\}_{k=1}^t, \hat{\mathbf{y}})
$$
$$
\hat{\mathbf{f}}'_*(\vec{x}_k^1, ..., \vec{x}_k^d) = \hat{\mathbf{s}}(\{\hat{\mathbf{G}}_k(\vec{x}_k^1, ..., \vec{x}_k^d)\}_{k=1}^t; \{\alpha_k\}_{k=1}^t, \hat{\mathbf{y}}).
$$

(18)

Therefore, it follows that

$$
\hat{\mathbf{f}}_*(\{\vec{x}_k^1, ..., \vec{x}_k^d\}_{k=1}^t) = \hat{\mathbf{f}}'_*(\{\mathrm{conj}(\vec{x}_k^1), ..., \mathrm{conj}(\vec{x}_k^d)\}_{k=1}^t)
$$
$$
\hat{\mathbf{f}}'_*(\{\vec{x}_k^1, ..., \vec{x}_k^d\}_{k=1}^t) = \hat{\mathbf{f}}_*(\{\mathrm{conj}(\vec{x}_k^1), ..., \mathrm{conj}(\vec{x}_k^d)\}_{k=1}^t).
$$

(19)

Since y is a 2-D centrosymmetric Gaussian function, the Fourier transform of y is also a Gaussian function. Therefore, $\hat{y}$ is real valued. So we have $\mathrm{conj}(\hat{\mathbf{y}}) = \hat{\mathbf{y}}$. Thus,

$$
\mathrm{conj}(\hat{\mathbf{f}}'_*(\{\vec{x}_k^1, ..., \vec{x}_k^d\}_{k=1}^t)) = \mathrm{conj}(\hat{\mathbf{s}}(\{\hat{\mathbf{G}}_k(\vec{x}_k^1, ..., \vec{x}_k^d)\}_{k=1}^t; \{\alpha_k\}_{k=1}^t, \hat{\mathbf{y}}))
$$

$$
= \mathrm{conj}([(\sum_{k=1}^t \alpha_k \hat{\mathbf{G}}_k^{\mathrm{H}}(\vec{x}_k^1, ..., \vec{x}_k^d)\hat{\mathbf{G}}_k(\vec{x}_k^1, ..., \vec{x}_k^d)) + \lambda \mathbf{I}_{dN}]^{-1}(\sum_{k=1}^t \alpha_k \hat{\mathbf{G}}_k^{\mathrm{H}}(\vec{x}_k^1, ..., \vec{x}_k^d)\hat{\mathbf{y}}))
$$

$$
= [(\sum_{k=1}^t \alpha_k \hat{\mathbf{G}}_k^{\mathrm{H}}(\mathrm{conj}(\vec{x}_k^1), ..., \mathrm{conj}(\vec{x}_k^d))\dot{\mathbf{G}}_k(\mathrm{conj}(\vec{x}_k^1), ..., \mathrm{conj}(\vec{x}_k^d))) + \lambda \mathbf{I}_{dN}]^{-1}
$$

$$
(\sum_{k=1}^t \alpha_k \hat{\mathbf{G}}_k^{\mathrm{H}}(\mathrm{conj}(\vec{x}_k^1), ..., \mathrm{conj}(\vec{x}_k^d))\hat{\mathbf{y}})
$$

$$
= \hat{\mathbf{f}}'_*(\{\mathrm{conj}(\vec{x}_k^1), ..., \mathrm{conj}(\vec{x}_k^d)\}_{k=1}^t)
$$

$$
= \hat{\mathbf{f}}_*(\{\vec{x}_k^1, ..., \vec{x}_k^d\}_{k=1}^t).
$$

(20)

Note that $\mathrm{conj}(\hat{\mathbf{G}}_k(\vec{x}_k^1, ..., \vec{x}_k^d)) = \hat{\mathbf{G}}_k(\mathrm{conj}(\vec{x}_k^1), ..., \mathrm{conj}(\vec{x}_k^d))$ was used in the derivation of (20). Denote the time domain expressions of the optimal solutions $\hat{\mathbf{f}}_*$ and $\hat{\mathbf{f}}'_*$ by f_* and f'_* respectively. For a given detection sample $x_{k'}$ the filer responses corresponding to f_* and f'_*, respectively, are $R(x_{k'}; f_*) =$

$\sum_{l=1}^{d} x_{k'}^{l} \odot f_{*}^{l}$ and $R'(x_{k'}; f'_{*}) = \sum_{l=1}^{d} x_{k'}^{l} \circledast f''_{*}$. Since $\hat{\mathbf{X}}_{k'}(\vec{x}_{k'}^{1}, ..., \vec{x}_{k'}^{d}) = [\text{diag}(\vec{x}_{k'}^{1})^{\text{H}}, ..., \text{diag}(\vec{x}_{k'}^{d})^{\text{H}}]$ and $\hat{\mathbf{X}}'_{k'}(\vec{x}_{k'}^{1}, ..., \vec{x}_{k'}^{d}) = [\text{diag}(\vec{x}_{k'}^{1}), ..., \text{diag}(\vec{x}_{k'}^{d})]$, it follows that

$$\hat{\mathbf{X}}_{k'}(\vec{x}_{k'}^{1}, ..., \vec{x}_{k'}^{d}) = \text{conj}(\hat{\mathbf{X}}'_{k'}(\vec{x}_{k'}^{1}, ..., \vec{x}_{k'}^{d})). \tag{21}$$

Therefore,

$$
\begin{aligned}
R(x_{k'}; f_{*})[i, j] &= (\sum_{l=1}^{d} x_{k'}^{l} \odot f_{*}^{l})[i, j] \\
&= \mathbf{F}^{-1}\{\text{vec}^{-1}[\hat{\mathbf{X}}_{k'}(\vec{x}_{k'}^{1}, ..., \vec{x}_{k'}^{d})\hat{\mathbf{f}}_{*}(\{\vec{x}_{k}^{1}, ..., \vec{x}_{k}^{d}\}_{k=1}^{t})]\}[i, j] \\
&= \mathbf{F}^{-1}\{\text{vec}^{-1}[\text{conj}(\hat{\mathbf{X}}'_{k'}(\vec{x}_{k'}^{1}, ..., \vec{x}_{k'}^{d}))\text{conj}(\hat{\mathbf{f}}'_{*}(\{\vec{x}_{k}^{1}, ..., \vec{x}_{k}^{d}\}_{k=1}^{t}))]\}[i, j] \\
&= \mathbf{F}^{-1}\{\text{vec}^{-1}[\text{conj}\left(\hat{\mathbf{X}}'_{k'}(\vec{x}_{k'}^{1}, ..., \vec{x}_{k'}^{d})\hat{\mathbf{f}}'_{*}(\{\vec{x}_{k}^{1}, ..., \vec{x}_{k}^{d}\}_{k=1}^{t})\right)]\}[i, j] \\
&= \mathbf{F}^{-1}\{\text{conj}(\mathbf{F}\{R'(x_{k'}; f'_{*})\})\}[i, j] \\
&= \text{conj}(R'(x_{k'}; f'_{*})[-i, -j]) \\
&= R'(x_{k'}; f'_{*})[-i, -j], \quad i \in [-\frac{m}{2}, \frac{m}{2}], j \in [-\frac{n}{2}, \frac{n}{2}],
\end{aligned}
\tag{22}
$$

where $\mathbf{F}^{-1}$ denotes the inverse Fourier transform, vec^{-1} is the inverse operation of the vectorization. Additionally, $y[i, j] = y[-i, -j]$ since y is a centrosymmetric Gaussian function. Therefore,

$$
\begin{aligned}
&\|R(x_{k'}; f_{*})] - y\|^{2} \\
&= \sum_{i=-\frac{m}{2}}^{\frac{m}{2}} \sum_{j=-\frac{n}{2}}^{\frac{n}{2}} \text{conj}(R(x_{k'}; f_{*})[i, j] - y[i, j])(R(x_{k'}; f_{*})[i, j] - y[i, j]) \\
&= \sum_{i=-\frac{m}{2}}^{\frac{m}{2}} \sum_{j=-\frac{n}{2}}^{\frac{n}{2}} \text{conj}(R'(x_{k'}; f'_{*})[-i, -j] - y[i, j])(R(x_{k'}; f_{*})[i, j] - y[i, j]) \\
&= \sum_{i=-\frac{m}{2}}^{\frac{m}{2}} \sum_{j=-\frac{n}{2}}^{\frac{n}{2}} (R'(x_{k'}; f'_{*})[-i, -j] - y[i, j])(R(x_{k'}; f_{*})[i, j] - y[i, j]) \\
&= \sum_{i=-\frac{m}{2}}^{\frac{m}{2}} \sum_{j=-\frac{n}{2}}^{\frac{n}{2}} (R'(x_{k'}; f'_{*})[-i, -j] - y[i, j])(\text{conj}(R'(x_{k'}; f'_{*})[-i, -j]) - y[i, j]) \\
&= \sum_{i=-\frac{m}{2}}^{\frac{m}{2}} \sum_{j=-\frac{n}{2}}^{\frac{n}{2}} (R'(x_{k'}; f'_{*})[-i, -j] - y[-i, -j])(\text{conj}(R'(x_{k'}; f'_{*})[-i, -j]) - y[-i, -j])
\end{aligned}
\tag{23}
$$

$$= \sum_{i=-\frac{m}{2}}^{\frac{m}{2}} \sum_{j=-\frac{n}{2}}^{\frac{n}{2}} (R'(x_{k'}; f'_*)[i,j] - y[i,j])(\mathrm{conj}(R'(x_{k'}; f'_*)[i,j]) - y[i,j])$$

$$= \sum_{i=-\frac{m}{2}}^{\frac{m}{2}} \sum_{j=-\frac{n}{2}}^{\frac{n}{2}} (R'(x_{k'}; f'_*)[i,j] - y[i,j])\mathrm{conj}(R'(x_{k'}; f'_*)[i,j] - y[i,j]) \tag{24}$$

$$= \|R'(x_{k'}; f'_*) - y\|^2.$$

If $[(\sum_{k=1}^{t} \alpha_k \hat{\mathbf{X}}_k^H \hat{\mathbf{X}}_k) + \lambda I_{dN}]$ is invertible, then $[(\sum_{k=1}^{t} \alpha_k \hat{\mathbf{X}}'_k{}^H \hat{\mathbf{X}}'_k) + \lambda I_{dN}]$ is also invertible and vice versa, because they are conjugated. Based on the above deductions, the following conclusions can be drawn.

Proposition 1. *If the optimal solution* $\hat{\mathbf{f}}_*(\{\vec{\tilde{x}}_k^1, ..., \vec{\tilde{x}}_k^d\}_{k=1}^t)$ *in (5) exists, then the optimal solution* $\hat{\mathbf{f}}'_*(\{\vec{\tilde{x}}_k^1, ..., \vec{\tilde{x}}_k^d\}_{k=1}^t)$ *in (11) exists as well, and vice versa. Moreover, if y is a 2-D centrosymmetric Gaussian function, then*

$$\hat{\mathbf{f}}_*(\{\vec{\tilde{x}}_k^1, ..., \vec{\tilde{x}}_k^d\}_{k=1}^t) = \mathrm{conj}(\hat{\mathbf{f}}'_*(\{\vec{\tilde{x}}_k^1, ..., \vec{\tilde{x}}_k^d\}_{k=1}^t)). \tag{25}$$

Meanwhile, given a detection sample $x_{k'}$, *the correlation filter response of* $f_* = \mathrm{vec}^{-1}[F^{-1}\{\hat{\mathbf{f}}_*\}]$ *and the convolution filter response of* $f'_* = \mathrm{vec}^{-1}[F^{-1}\{\hat{\mathbf{f}}'_*\}]$, *respectively, to* $x_{k'}$ *satisfy the following equations:*

$$\|R(x_{k'}; f_*)] - y\|^2 = \|R'(x_{k'}; f'_*) - y\|^2, \tag{26}$$

$$R(x_{k'}; f_*)[i,j] = R'(x_{k'}; f'_*)[-i, -j], \quad i \in [-\frac{m}{2}, \frac{m}{2}], j \in [-\frac{n}{2}, \frac{n}{2}]. \tag{27}$$

Proposition (1) in fact shows that in visual tracking the correlation filter and the convolution filter are equivalent in the sense of equal minimum mean-square error of estimation, under the condition that the ideal filter response is a 2-D centrosymmetric Gaussian function and the optimal solutions exist. More specifically,

* As long as the optimal solution of one of the filters is known, the optimal solution of the other can be obtained immediately;
* The mean-square errors of the filter responses of the two optimal solutions to a given detection sample are equal;
* The filter responses of the two optimal solutions to a given detection sample are symmetric about the origin. Intuitively, assuming there is only one maximal value in the filter response of either the optimal solution to a given detection sample, when the coordinate of the maximal value of the filter response of one of the filters is estimated correctly, the other is also estimated correctly; when the coordinate of the maximal value of one of the filters deviates from the correct position, the coordinate of the maximal value of the other deviates from the correct position in the opposite direction, but their distances from the correct position are equal.

4   Conclusion

In this paper, for the first time we prove that correlation filter and convolution filter are equivalent in the sense that their minimum mean-square errors (MMSEs) in visual tracking are equal, under the condition that the optimal solutions exist and the ideal filter response is a 2-D centrosymmetric Gaussian function. This result gives researchers the freedom to choose correlation or convolution in formulating their trackers. It also suggests that the explanation of the ideal response in terms of similarities is not essential.

Acknowledgment. This work is supported by the National Natural Science Foundation of China (No. 61773270, 61971005, 62066042).

References

1. Amirian, S., Rasheed, K., Taha, T.R., Arabnia, H.R.: Automatic image and video caption generation with deep learning: a concise review and algorithmic overlap. IEEE Access **8**, 218386–218400 (2020)
2. Bhat, G., Danelljan, M., Gool, L.V., Timofte, R.: Know your surroundings: Exploiting scene information for object tracking. In: ECCV, no. 23, pp. 205–221 (2020)
3. Bolme, D.S., Beveridge, J.R., Draper, B.A., Lui, Y.M.: Visual object tracking using adaptive correlation filters. In: 2010 IEEE Computer Society Conference on Computer Vision and Pattern Recognition, pp. 2544–2550. IEEE (2010)
4. Bota, S., Nedevschi, S.: Tracking multiple objects in urban traffic environments using dense stereo and optical flow. In: 2011 14th International IEEE Conference on Intelligent Transportation Systems (ITSC), pp. 791–796 (2011)
5. Chen, Z., Zhong, B., Li, G., Zhang, S., Ji, R.: Siamese box adaptive network for visual tracking. In: 2020 IEEE/CVF Conference on Computer Vision and Pattern Recognition (CVPR), pp. 6668–6677 (2020)
6. Dalal, N., Triggs, B.: Histograms of oriented gradients for human detection. In: 2005 IEEE Computer Society Conference on Computer Vision and Pattern Recognition (CVPR'05), vol. 1, pp. 886–893 (2005)
7. Danelljan, M., Bhat, G., Khan, F.S., Felsberg, M.: Eco: efficient convolution operators for tracking. In: 2017 IEEE Conference on Computer Vision and Pattern Recognition (CVPR), pp. 6931–6939 (2017)
8. Danelljan, M., Gool, L.V., Timofte, R.: Probabilistic regression for visual tracking. In: 2020 IEEE/CVF Conference on Computer Vision and Pattern Recognition (CVPR), pp. 7183–7192 (2020)
9. Danelljan, M., Hager, G., Khan, F.S., Felsberg, M.: Learning spatially regularized correlation filters for visual tracking. In: 2015 IEEE International Conference on Computer Vision (ICCV), pp. 4310–4318 (2015)
10. Danelljan, M., Khan, F.S., Felsberg, M., van de Weijer, J.: Adaptive color attributes for real-time visual tracking. In: CVPR '14 Proceedings of the 2014 IEEE Conference on Computer Vision and Pattern Recognition, pp. 1090–1097 (2014)
11. Danelljan, M., Robinson, A., Khan, F.S., Felsberg, M.: Beyond correlation filters: learning continuous convolution operators for visual tracking. In: 14th European Conference on Computer Vision (ECCV), Amsterdam, The Netherlands, 11–14 October 2016, vol. 9909, pp. 472–488 (2016)

12. Fu, C., Li, B., Ding, F., Lin, F., Lu, G.: Correlation filter for uav-based aerial tracking: a review and experimental evaluation. arXiv preprint arXiv:2010.06255 (2020)
13. Fu, C., Lin, F., Li, Y., Chen, G.: Correlation filter-based visual tracking for uav with online multi-feature learning. Remote Sens. **11**(5), 549 (2019)
14. Galoogahi, H.K., Fagg, A., Lucey, S.: Learning background-aware correlation filters for visual tracking. In: 2017 IEEE International Conference on Computer Vision (ICCV) (2017)
15. Galoogahi, H.K., Sim, T., Lucey, S.: Multi-channel correlation filters. In: 2013 IEEE International Conference on Computer Vision, pp. 3072–3079 (2013)
16. He, Y., Fu, C., Lin, F., Li, Y., Lu, P.: Towards robust visual tracking for unmanned aerial vehicle with tri-attentional correlation filters. arXiv preprint arXiv:2008.00528 (2020)
17. Henriques, J.F., Caseiro, R., Martins, P., Batista, J.: High-speed tracking with kernelized correlation filters. IEEE Trans. Pattern Anal. Mach. Intell. **37**(3), 583–596 (2015)
18. Henriques, J.F., Caseiro, R., Martins, P., Batista, J.: Exploiting the circulant structure of tracking-by-detection with kernels. In: ECCV'12 Proceedings of the 12th European conference on Computer Vision, vol. Part IV, pp. 702–715 (2012)
19. Hu, W., Xie, N., Li, L., Zeng, X., Maybank, S.: A survey on visual content-based video indexing and retrieval. Syst. Man Cybern. **41**(6), 797–819 (2011)
20. Huang, Z., Fu, C., Li, Y., Lin, F., Lu, P.: Learning aberrance repressed correlation filters for real-time uav tracking. In: 2019 IEEE/CVF International Conference on Computer Vision (ICCV), pp. 2891–2900 (2019)
21. Kart, U., Lukezic, A., Kristan, M., Kamarainen, J.K., Matas, J.: Object tracking by reconstruction with view-specific discriminative correlation filters. In: 2019 IEEE/CVF Conference on Computer Vision and Pattern Recognition (CVPR), pp. 1339–1348 (2019)
22. Khan, A., Sohail, A., Zahoora, U., Qureshi, A.S.: A survey of the recent architectures of deep convolutional neural networks. Artif. Intell. Rev. **53**(8), 5455–5516 (2020). https://doi.org/10.1007/s10462-020-09825-6
23. Li, B., Wu, W., Wang, Q., Zhang, F., Xing, J., Yan, J.: Siamrpn++: evolution of siamese visual tracking with very deep networks. In: 2019 IEEE/CVF Conference on Computer Vision and Pattern Recognition (CVPR), pp. 4282–4291 (2019)
24. Li, B., Yan, J., Wu, W., Zhu, Z., Hu, X.: High performance visual tracking with siamese region proposal network. In: 2018 IEEE/CVF Conference on Computer Vision and Pattern Recognition, pp. 8971–8980 (2018)
25. Li, F., Fu, C., Lin, F., Li, Y., Lu, P.: Training-set distillation for real-time uav object tracking. In: 2020 IEEE International Conference on Robotics and Automation (ICRA), pp. 9715–9721 (2020)
26. Li, F., Tian, C., Zuo, W., Zhang, L., Yang, M.H.: Learning spatial-temporal regularized correlation filters for visual tracking. In: 2018 IEEE/CVF Conference on Computer Vision and Pattern Recognition, pp. 4904–4913 (2018)
27. Li, P., Chen, B., Ouyang, W., Wang, D., Yang, X., Lu, H.: Gradnet: gradient-guided network for visual object tracking. In: 2019 IEEE/CVF International Conference on Computer Vision (ICCV), pp. 6162–6171 (2019)
28. Li, S.W., Jiang, Q.B., Zhao, Q.J., Lu, L., Feng, Z.L.: Asymmetric discriminative correlation filters for visual tracking. Front. Inf. Technol. Electron. Eng. **21**(10), 1467–1484 (2020)
29. Li, S., Liu, Y., Zhao, Q., Feng, Z.: Learning residue-aware correlation filters and refining scale estimates with the grabcut for real-time uav tracking (2021)

30. Li, Y., Fu, C., Ding, F., Huang, Z., Lu, G.: Autotrack: towards high-performance visual tracking for uav with automatic spatio-temporal regularization. In: 2020 IEEE/CVF Conference on Computer Vision and Pattern Recognition (CVPR), pp. 11923–11932 (2020)
31. Li, Y., Fu, C., Ding, F., Huang, Z., Pan, J.: Augmented memory for correlation filters in real-time uav tracking. arXiv preprint arXiv:1909.10989 (2019)
32. Li, Y., Fu, C., Huang, Z., Zhang, Y., Pan, J.: Keyfilter-aware real-time uav object tracking. In: 2020 IEEE International Conference on Robotics and Automation (ICRA), pp. 193–199 (2020)
33. Lin, S., Garratt, M.A., Lambert, A.J.: Monocular vision-based real-time target recognition and tracking for autonomously landing an uav in a cluttered shipboard environment. Auton. Robots 41(4), 881–901 (2016)
34. Lukezic, A., Vojir, T., Zajc, L.C., Matas, J., Kristan, M.: Discriminative correlation filter with channel and spatial reliability. In: 2017 IEEE Conference on Computer Vision and Pattern Recognition (CVPR), pp. 4847–4856 (2017)
35. Ma, C., Huang, J.B., Yang, X., Yang, M.H.: Hierarchical convolutional features for visual tracking. In: 2015 IEEE International Conference on Computer Vision (ICCV), pp. 3074–3082 (2015)
36. Mueller, M., Smith, N., Ghanem, B.: Context-aware correlation filter tracking. In: 2017 IEEE Conference on Computer Vision and Pattern Recognition (CVPR), pp. 1387–1395 (2017)
37. Olivares-Mendez, M., et al.: Towards an autonomous vision-based unmanned aerial system against wildlife poachers. Sensors 15, 31362–31391 (2015)
38. Pratt, W.K.: Introduction to Digital Image Processing (2013)
39. Sun, Y., Sun, C., Wang, D., He, Y., Lu, H.: Roi pooled correlation filters for visual tracking. In: 2019 IEEE/CVF Conference on Computer Vision and Pattern Recognition (CVPR), pp. 5783–5791 (2019)
40. Vanegas, F., Campbell, D., Roy, N., Gaston, K.J., Gonzalez, F.: Uav tracking and following a ground target under motion and localisation uncertainty. In: 2017 IEEE Aerospace Conference (2017)
41. Wang, Q., Zhang, L., Bertinetto, L., Hu, W., Torr, P.H.: Fast online object tracking and segmentation: A unifying approach. In: 2019 IEEE/CVF Conference on Computer Vision and Pattern Recognition (CVPR), pp. 1328–1338 (2019)
42. Yin, Y., Wang, X., Xu, D., Liu, F., Wang, Y., Wu, W.: Robust visual detection-learning-tracking framework for autonomous aerial refueling of uavs. IEEE Trans. Instrum. Meas 65(3), 510–521 (2016)
43. Yu, Y., Xiong, Y., Huang, W., Scott, M.R.: Deformable siamese attention networks for visual object tracking. In: 2020 IEEE/CVF Conference on Computer Vision and Pattern Recognition (CVPR), pp. 6728–6737 (2020)
44. Yuan, C., Liu, Z., Zhang, Y.: Aerial images-based forest fire detection for firefighting using optical remote sensing techniques and unmanned aerial vehicles. J. Intell. Rob. Syst. 88, 635–654 (2017)
45. Zhao, Z.Q., Zheng, P., Xu, S.T., Wu, X.: Object detection with deep learning: a review. IEEE Trans. Neural Netw. 30(11), 3212–3232 (2019)

LSNT: A Lightweight Siamese Network Based Tracker

Xuezhen Dong, Zhangjin Huang[✉], Lu Zou, Fangjun Wang,
and Zonghui Zhang

University of Science and Technology of China, Hefei 230026, Anhui, China
zhuang@ustc.edu.cn

Abstract. Trackers based on the Siamese network have achieved remarkable advancements in accuracy and robustness, yet the trackers suffer from enormous computation and memory storage cost, which hinder their rapid inference, making it difficult to deploy in calculation-constrained and memory storage-constrained scenarios. Moreover, a general depthwise correlation attempts to process the entire feature map indiscriminately, which cannot extract more robust features. In this paper, we presented a Lightweight Siamese Network based Tracker (LSNT) to tackle the above issues. In the tracking head part, an extremely efficient module is adopted to simplify the network, so as to maintain a balance with the backbone network in parameter quantity. Furthermore, a novel Spatial-Channel Attention based Depthwise (SCAD) correlation is introduced to enhance the ability of the feature fusion module. Compared with the baseline tracker, LSNT has fewer parameters and calculations, but experiments conducted on the GOT-10k benchmark demonstrate that it achieves comparable performance in terms of accuracy and robustness, thus confirming its efficiency and effectiveness.

Keywords: Siamese networks · Lightweight networks · Feature fusion

1 Introduction

In vision applications such as video surveillance, human-computer interaction, and autonomous driving, the demand for visual object tracking algorithms continues to grow. The trackers based on the modern Siamese network [7,12,13,23,25] are resource intensive and require a lot of calculation and memory storage to achieve the excellent tracking performance, which make them difficult to apply to a wide range of industrial production or life needs. Therefore, it is very necessary to study how to lighten the tracker based on the Siamese network and accelerate its inference speed on devices with limited computing power and memory storage without significantly reducing the tracking accuracy and robustness.

From the perspective of network structure, the Siamese network based trackers can be divided into three parts, namely the backbone part, the feature fusion

© Springer Nature Switzerland AG 2021
Y. Peng et al. (Eds.): ICIG 2021, LNCS 12890, pp. 635–646, 2021.
https://doi.org/10.1007/978-3-030-87361-5_52

part and the tracking head part. In the backbone part, most current trackers tend to employ huge classification networks (e.g., ResNet-50 [8] and GoogLeNet [21]), which are responsible for extracting features of both template image and search image patch. This process inevitably requires a lot of calculation and memory storage cost. In the tracking head part, the state-of-the-art trackers use general convolutional layers to form a heavy tracking head, which also introduces a lot of parameters and calculations. Previous work [17] in object detection demonstrates that the capability of the backbone and detection head should match. Specifically, the small-backbone-large-head design will lead to weak features from the lightweight backbone network, and the powerful tracking head will become redundant. It inspires us to think: *Can we design a small-backbone-small-head tracking network to avoid this problem?*

Therefore, inspired by the recent developments of lightweight image classification networks [19] that can significantly reduce the number of parameters and computation, we design an efficient tracking head using some inverted residual blocks [19], which has roughly the same number of parameters in the backbone and the tracking head.

In the feature fusion part, the state-of-the-art trackers usually adopt one of coarse naive correlation [2,22] and depthwise correlation [3,7,12] for correlation operation. The coarse naive correlation simply regards the template feature as a convolution kernel, which results in only one response map required, so it is difficult to accurately predict the bounding box of the tracking target. The depthwise correlation uses each channel of the template feature map as a convolution kernel, and calculates the correlation with the corresponding channel of the search image feature map. However, these cross-correlation methods fail to pay more attention to tracking targets, resulting in irrelevant features that affect tracking accuracy. In order to reduce the influence of irrelevant information, we design a new spatial-channel attention based depthwise correlation, which optimizes the intermediate response map in the spatial and channel dimensions.

In this article, we use SiamCAR as our baseline tracker, and our goal is to lighten this tracker without severely degrading the performance. The main contributions of this work are summarized as follows:

- We propose a lightweight Siamese network based tracker, termed LSNT, which is a small-backbone-small-head model.
- We presente a better feature fusion module called SCAD, which enhances the features of the target and weakens the features of background.
- Experiment results conducted on the GOT-10k benchmark demonstrate that this lightweight tracker with SCAD module can achieve comparable performance compared with the baseline tracker, which proves its effectiveness and efficiency.

2   Related Work

The current single object tracking methods are mainly divided into the correlation filter based methods [4,9,22] and the Siamese network based methods [7,12,13,23,25]. The obvious disadvantage of the correlation filter based method is that it can only learns relatively simple models. Therefore, we mainly focus on the Siamese network based methods and their feature fusion module.

2.1 Siamese Network Based Tracking

With the rapid development of deep learning, trackers based on the Siamese network have also been extensively developed. SiamFC [2] takes the lead in using a Siamese network as a feature extractor, and trains the similarity metric between the target image and the search image patch. Encouraged by its success, researchers propose many trackers based on the Siamese network [3,7,12,13,23]. CFNet [22] extends SiamFC [2] with a differentiable correlation filter layer and performs online tracking to improve accuracy. FlowTrack [26] proposes using optical flow to update the target template online, which gets a higher accuracy score on popular benchmarks, but the tracking speed is slower than CFNet. However, all these methods require multi-scale testing to cope with the scale changes, and cannot handle the aspect ratio changes caused by the target appearance changes.

In order to strike a balance between accuracy and efficiency, SiamRPN [13] introduces the Regional Proposal Network [18] to avoid time-consuming multi-scale estimation steps. SiamRPN++ [12] and SiamDW [25] explore the reason why deep neural network could not achieve better results in the tracker based on the Siamese network. The above methods are anchor-based trackers, which can effectively handle changes in scale and aspect ratio, but the hyperparameters of the anchor box must be carefully designed. It is usually need to be adjusted heuristically, which involves many skills, and finally good performance can be achieved.

Subsequent works are dedicate to eliminating the negative effects of anchors. Researchers propose more and more anchor-free trackers, such as SiamBAN [3] and SiamCAR [7], which achieve superior performance than the previous anchor-based trackers. SiamBAN [3] designes a box adaptive network that avoids setting hyperparameters related to candidate boxes and makes the tracker more flexible and versatile. SiamCAR [7] proposes a new classification and regression framework for visual tracking. The framework does not need to set anchor boxes in advance, which greatly reduces the number of hyperparameters. However, these trackers usually contain a large number of parameters and calculations, which limits their application in practical scenarios.Therefore, we need a lightweight and effective network in the tracker.

2.2 Feature Fusion

Feature fusion is the core operation of the tracker based on the Siamese network, which is responsible for fusing the features of the template image and search image patch. Fusion methods can be divided into two categories: coarse naive correlation [2] and depthwise correlation [3,7,9,12].

SiamFC [2] employs coarse naive correlation to embed features from the two branches of the Siamese network. Specifically, the template feature is used as the kernel to directly perform a convolution operation on the search image features to obtain a single channel response map used for target position prediction. However, this correlation method can only get one response map, so it cannot effectively solve the problem of scale change. Therefore, we have to employ the strategy of multi-scale search, which is time-consuming and has limited impact on the final tracking performance.

In order to achieve more effective feature fusion, some trackers including SiamRPN++ [12], SiamCAR [7] and SiamBAN [3] use depthwise correlation to enhance cross-correlation and generate multiple response maps with different semantics. However, depthwise correlation indiscriminately deals with the template features and the feature detector, which makes the unimportant background features have a great impact on the tracking results. Attention mechanism [1,14,24] is a good strategy to solve the above problem. Therefore, we introduce an auxiliary attention module to refine the feature fusion process.

3   Proposed Method

In this section, we describe the proposed lightweight tracker framework. As shown in Fig. 1, this tracker consists of three parts: Siamese network backbone, feature fusion module and tracking head. The Siamese network backbone is leveraged to extract the convolutional feature maps of the template image and the search image patch. It is worth noting that we use 1.0x instead of 1.4x MobileNetV2 as the backbone to further lighten the tracker, which is different from other trackers [3,12]. Then, an attention based depthwise correlation, called SCAD, is developed to improve the ability of the feature fusion module. Finally, we employ the inverted residual block [19] to further lighten the tracking head.

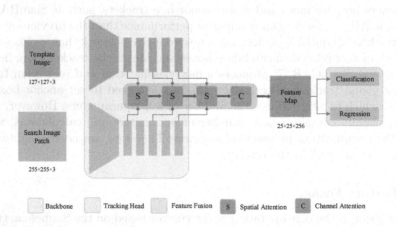

Fig. 1. Illustration of our proposed framework. Given a pair of template images and search image patches, the network predict the bounding box of the tracking target in the search image patches.

3.1 Spatial-Channel Attention Based Depthwise Correlation

Since the general depthwise correlation processes the features of the entire template and the feature detectors indiscriminately, the response maps cannot efficiently integrate the features of the specific tracking target. Therefore, we first use the spatial attention module to selectively focus on the features of the tracking target, and then we use the channel attention module to explore the relationship between the channels of the feature map, which puts more attention on the feature extractor related to the tracking target. Figure 2 shows the detailed information of SCAD, including spatial attention module and channel attention module.

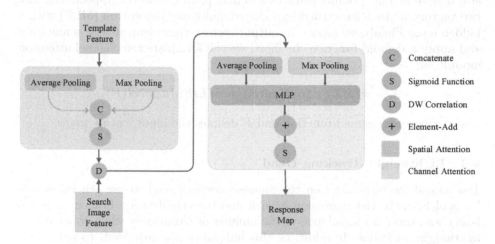

Fig. 2. Illustration of our proposed feature fusion module SCAD. The left part is spatial attention based depthwise correlation, and the right part is channel attention module.

Similar to the spatial attention module in CBAM [24], we first apply average pooling and max pooling operations along the channel axis on the template feature map to generate two 2D maps: $F_{avg}^s \in R^{1 \times H \times W}$ and $F_{max}^s \in R^{1 \times H \times W}$, representing the average pooling feature and the maximum pooling feature, respectively. Then, we concatenae the two 2D maps to form a more effective descriptor. Finally, we use a convolutional layer on the descriptor, which purpose is to generate a spatial attention map $A_s \in R^{H \times W}$. In order to clearly illustrate this process, we formulate the spatial attention module as:

$$A_s = \sigma(Conv([AvgPool(F), MaxPool(F)]))$$

where σ represents the sigmoid function and F denotes the input feature maps. We use the template features processed by the spatial attention module to perform the depthwise correlation with the search image features.

It is noteworthy that visual tracking requires rich representations that span levels from low to high, scales from small to large, and resolutions from fine to coarse. Therefore, we need to compound and aggregate different deep layers to enhance the ability of feature representation. In addition, we use the same spatial attention module for different deep layers.

We concatenate the outputs of the spatial attention module, and then input them into the channel attention module. Different from spatial attention, channel attention focuses on searching for the most attractive object in the response maps. First, we aggregate the spatial information of the feature maps by using the average pooling operation and the max pooling operation, which generate two different spatial context vectors: $F_{avg}^c \in R^{C \times 1 \times 1}$ and $F_{max}^c \in R^{C \times 1 \times 1}$, which also denote average pooling features and max pooling features respectively. The two vectors are then forwarded to a shared multilayer perceptron (MLP) with a hidden layer. Finally, we merge the output vectors using element-wise summation and apply a sigmoid function. In short, we can formulate the channel attention module as:

$$A_c = \sigma(MLP(AvgPool(F)) + MLP(MaxPool(F)))$$

where σ denotes sigmoid function and F denotes the input feature maps.

3.2 Lightweight Tracking Head

Traditional trackers based on the Siamese network tend to use general convolutional layers in the regression branch and the classification branch. It is too heavy and cause an imbalance in the number of parameters when coupled to a lightweight backbone. In addition, this imbalance not only leads to redundant calculations, but also increases the risk of overfitting.

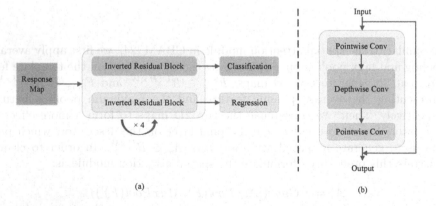

Fig. 3. (a) Illustration of our proposed lightweight tracking head. Similar to SiamCAR, it contains two branches of classification and regression. (b) Inverted residual block [19]. It is the core component of the lightweight tracking head.

In order to solve this problem, we propose an efficient tracking head that can lighten the network by replacing the general convolutional layers with the inverted residual blocks [19]. As shown in Fig. 3(a), we leverage the classification-regression head network from SiamCAR as the tracking head. The classification branch predicts category information (target or background), and the regression branch predicts the bounding box of the target at each position. The details of the inverted residual block [19] are shown in Fig. 3(b), we first use point-wise convolution to expand the channels of the input feature map, and then use depthwise convolution followed by a sigmoid function. Finally, we employ pointwise convolution to reduce the channels and use shortcuts directly between bottlenecks.

In addition, we observe that setting the expansion factor to 2 can effectively improve the performance without introducing many parameters. By using a lightweight tracking head, we reduce the number of parameters by half, which is roughly the same as those of the backbone network.

4   Experiments

4.1   Implementation Details

Training. The proposed tracker is implemented in Python with PyTorch and trained on an RTX 3090 card. We first pretrain the backbone network on ImageNet, and then transfer it to the tracking network. Our tracker is trained by Stochastic Gradient Descent (SGD), with 64 pairs per batch. The network is trained with 20 Epochs. For the first 10 epochs, we first train the feature fusion module and the tracking head module, while the parameters of the backbone are frozen. In the last 10 epochs, all parameters in the backbone network will be unfrozen and trained together with the subsequent modules. It should be noted that we only use the GOT-10k training dataset to train our tracker.

Tracking. For offline models, visual tracking follows the same protocol as in SiamCAR [7]. The feature map of the template image is extracted only in the first frame, and then it is continuously matched with the subsequent search image patchs. Since the size and aspect ratio of the bounding box generally do not vary much in consecutive frames, we use spatio-temporal consistency to supervise the tracking. Therefore, we refer to the strategy introduced in SiamRPN [13] to suppress large displacements and large changes in size and ratio by setting the hyperparameters of the cosine window and the scale change penalty.

4.2   Dataset and Evaluation Metrics

GOT-10k [10] is a large-scale, high-diversity benchmark for general object tracking, which contains more than 10,000 videos of moving objects in the real world. To ensure a fair comparison of these trackers, all models use the same training and testing dataset. We automatically obtain the analysis results through the official website after uploading the tracking results. The evaluation metrics provided include success plot, average overlap (AO) and success rate (SR). AO represents the average overlap between all estimated bounding boxes and ground truth boxes. $SR_{0.5}$ represents the rate of successful tracking frames whose overlap exceeds 0.5, and $SR_{0.75}$ represents frames whose overlap exceeds 0.75.

4.3 Representative Visual Results

In this section, we analyze the results from a qualitative perspective. Figure 4 provides an illustration of the tracking process of the proposed LSNT, SiamCAR and ECO performed on the GOT-10k benchmark. Figure 4(a) shows that our tracker can accurately track the target even if the target is severely occluded. We find that, as shown in Fig. 4(b), our tracker can cope with large-scale changes well. Figure 4(c) shows that our tracker has the ability to retrieve the lost targets. In addition, the performance of our tracker is still good when encountering an interference scenario similar to that shown in Fig. 4(d).

Fig. 4. The proposed LSNT and two baseline trackers including SiamCAR [7] and ECO [4] are qualitatively evaluated on four challenging sequences. Our tracker handles various challenges, such as *occlusion, large-scale changes, loss, and background confusion*, achieving results comparable to SiamCAR [7] and far superior to ECO [4].

4.4 Evaluation on GOT-10k

We further evaluate the proposed tracker from a quantitative perspective and compare it with the benchmark trackers including SiamCAR [7], SiamRPN [13], SPM [23], SiamFC [2] and some methods based on correlation filters. Table 1 and

Fig. 5(a) shows the results on the GOT-10k testing dataset. It can be found that the performance of the proposed tracker is comparable to SiamCARand better than other baseline trackers. We get the best $SR_{0.5}$ score (0.684), the second best AO score (0.574) and $SR_{0.75}$ score (0.392).

Table 2 further compares the number of parameters, GFLOPs and FPS between LSNT and SiamCAR. It can be seen that LSNT reduces a lot of parameters and computation compared with SiamCAR. In addition, we separately

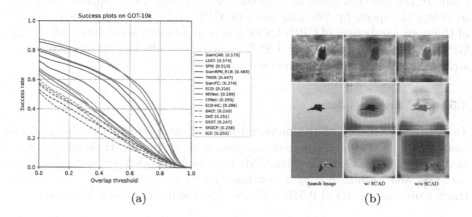

(a)   (b)

Fig. 5. (a) Comparisons on GOT-10k. Our LSNT has comparable performance compared to SiamCAR and is superior to other methods. (b) SCAD visualization results. SCAD enhances the features of the target and weakens the features of background.

Table 1. The evaluation on GOT-10k. **Red** and *Blue* fonts indicate the top-2 results.

Tracker	AO	$SR_{0.5}$	$SR_{0.75}$
KCF [9]	0.203	0.177	0.065
SRDCF [6]	0.236	0.227	0.094
DSST [5]	0.247	0.223	0.081
DAT [16]	0.251	0.242	0.048
BACF [11]	0.260	0.262	0.101
ECO-HC	0.286	0.276	0.096
CFNet [22]	0.293	0.265	0.087
MDNet [15]	0.299	0.303	0.099
ECO [4]	0.316	0.309	0.111
SiamFC [2]	0.374	0.404	0.144
THOR [20]	0.447	0.538	0.204
SiamRPN [13]	0.483	0.581	0.270
SPM [23]	0.513	0.593	0.359
SiamCAR [7]	**0.579**	*0.677*	**0.437**
LSNT (Ours)	*0.574*	**0.684**	*0.392*

Table 2. Comparison on models.

Tracker	Parameters(M)				GFLOPs	FPS(GPU)	FPS(CPU)
	Backbone	Feature fusion	Head	All			
SiamCAR	45.528	0.919	4.737	51.381	118.549	52.27	1.2
LSNT	1.813	0.387	2.167	4.366	7.826	77.57	10.3

evaluate the speed of these two trackers on GPU and CPU. Specifically, LSNT increases the speed by 48% and 858% on GPU and CPU, respectively. Because of the poor parallelism of CPU, LSNT has more obvious acceleration effect than GPU. These results show that LSNT is extremely efficient in computing constrained and memory constrained scenarios.

4.5   Ablation Studies

To verify the efficacy of the proposed method, we perform a component-wise analysis on GOT-10k benchmark, as presented in Table 3. It should be noted that we replace ResNet50 in SiamCAR with MobileNetV2 [19] as the backbone network, and formulate it as a new baseline for fair comparison. The baseline tracker obtains an AO of 0.516, $SR_{0.5}$ of 0.605 and $SR_{0.75}$ of 0.312 (Table 3).

Table 3. Ablation studies on GOT-10k dataset.

	Components	AO	$SR_{0.5}$	$SR_{0.75}$
(a)	Baseline	0.516	0.605	0.312
(b)	+ lightweight detection head	0.547	0.640	0.368
(c)	+ channel attention module	0.551	0.652	0.360
(d)	+ spatial attention module	0.574	0.684	0.392

Discussion on Lightweight Tracking Head. In order to study the impact of lightweight tracking head, we train two models on the GOT-10k training dataset. One uses a general tracking head for training, and the other uses a lightweight tracking head for training. As shown in Table 3(b), the lightweight tracking head significantly improves AO by 3.1%, $SR_{0.5}$ by 3.5% and $SR_{0.75}$ by 5.6%, which shows that the small-backbone-small-head is better than the small-backbone-big-head.

Discussion on SCAD Correlation. We evaluate the SCAD correlation on the GOT-10k benchmark to analyze the impact of the spatial attention module and the channel attention module, respectively. Figure 5(b) visualizes the response map, which shows that SCAD effectively enhances the features of the tracking target and weakens the features of the background. As shown in Table 3(c), adding the channel attention module can bring improvements of 0.4% on AO and

1.2% on $SR_{0.50}$, but $SR_{0.75}$ decreases by 0.8%. Finally, we further add the spatial attention module to the tracker. As shown in Table 3(d), the spatial attention module can also bring improvements of 2.3% on AO, 3.2% on $SR_{0.5}$, and 3.2% on $SR_{0.75}$. These results prove the effectiveness of the SCAD correlation.

5 Conclusion

In this article, we introduce a lightweight Siamese network based tracker, termed LSNT, which performs accurate and fast tracking on the GOT-10k benchmark. In the tracking head part, we analyze the shortcomings of existing trackers and propose a lightweight tracking head. In the feature fusion part, we use an efficient cross-correlation called SCAD, which includes a spatial attention module and a channel attention module. Based on the above design, our tracker achieves comparable tracking effect as the baseline tracker, while greatly reducing the cost of calculation and memory storage.

Acknowledgements. This work was supported in part by the National Key R&D Program of China (No. 2018YFC1504104), the National Natural Science Foundation of China (Nos. 71991464/71991460, and 61877056), and the Fundamental Research Funds for the Central Universities of China (No. WK5290000001).

References

1. Ba, J., Mnih, V., Kavukcuoglu, K.: Multiple object recognition with visual attention. arXiv preprint arXiv:1412.7755 (2014)
2. Bertinetto, L., Valmadre, J., Henriques, J.F., Vedaldi, A., Torr, P.H.S.: Fully-convolutional siamese networks for object tracking. In: Hua, G., Jégou, H. (eds.) ECCV 2016. LNCS, vol. 9914, pp. 850–865. Springer, Cham (2016). https://doi.org/10.1007/978-3-319-48881-3_56
3. Chen, Z., Zhong, B., Li, G., Zhang, S., Ji, R.: Siamese box adaptive network for visual tracking. In: Proceedings of the IEEE/CVF Conference on Computer Vision and Pattern Recognition, pp. 6668–6677 (2020)
4. Danelljan, M., Bhat, G., Shahbaz Khan, F., Felsberg, M.: Eco: efficient convolution operators for tracking. In: Proceedings of the IEEE Conference on Computer Vision and Pattern Recognition, pp. 6638–6646 (2017)
5. Danelljan, M., Häger, G., Khan, F., Felsberg, M.: Accurate scale estimation for robust visual tracking. In: British Machine Vision Conference, Nottingham, 1–5 September 2014. BMVA Press (2014)
6. Danelljan, M., Hager, G., Shahbaz Khan, F., Felsberg, M.: Learning spatially regularized correlation filters for visual tracking. In: Proceedings of the IEEE International Conference on Computer Vision, pp. 4310–4318 (2015)
7. Guo, D., Wang, J., Cui, Y., Wang, Z., Chen, S.: Siamcar: siamese fully convolutional classification and regression for visual tracking. In: Proceedings of the IEEE/CVF Conference on Computer Vision and Pattern Recognition, pp. 6269–6277 (2020)
8. He, K., Zhang, X., Ren, S., Sun, J.: Deep residual learning for image recognition. In: Proceedings of the IEEE Conference on Computer Vision and Pattern Recognition, pp. 770–778 (2016)

9. Henriques, J.F., Caseiro, R., Martins, P., Batista, J.: High-speed tracking with kernelized correlation filters. IEEE Trans. Pattern Anal. Mach. Intell. **37**(3), 583–596 (2014)
10. Huang, L., Zhao, X., Huang, K.: Got-10k: a large high-diversity benchmark for generic object tracking in the wild. IEEE Trans. Pattern Anal. Mach. Intell. **1**(1), 1–17 (2019)
11. Kiani Galoogahi, H., Fagg, A., Lucey, S.: Learning background-aware correlation filters for visual tracking. In: Proceedings of the IEEE International Conference on Computer Vision, pp. 1135–1143 (2017)
12. Li, B., Wu, W., Wang, Q., Zhang, F., Xing, J., Yan, J.: Siamrpn++: evolution of siamese visual tracking with very deep networks. In: Proceedings of the IEEE/CVF Conference on Computer Vision and Pattern Recognition, pp. 4282–4291 (2019)
13. Li, B., Yan, J., Wu, W., Zhu, Z., Hu, X.: High performance visual tracking with siamese region proposal network. In: Proceedings of the IEEE Conference on Computer Vision and Pattern Recognition, pp. 8971–8980 (2018)
14. Mnih, V., Heess, N., Graves, A., Kavukcuoglu, K.: Recurrent models of visual attention. arXiv preprint arXiv:1406.6247 (2014)
15. Nam, H., Han, B.: Learning multi-domain convolutional neural networks for visual tracking. In: Proceedings of the IEEE Conference on Computer Vision and Pattern Recognition, pp. 4293–4302 (2016)
16. Pu, S., Song, Y., Ma, C., Zhang, H., Yang, M.H.: Deep attentive tracking via reciprocative learning. arXiv preprint arXiv:1810.03851 (2018)
17. Qin, Z., et al.: Thundernet: towards real-time generic object detection on mobile devices. In: Proceedings of the IEEE/CVF International Conference on Computer Vision, pp. 6718–6727 (2019)
18. Ren, S., He, K., Girshick, R., Sun, J.: Faster r-cnn: towards real-time object detection with region proposal networks. arXiv preprint arXiv:1506.01497 (2015)
19. Sandler, M., Howard, A., Zhu, M., Zhmoginov, A., Chen, L.C.: Mobilenetv 2: inverted residuals and linear bottlenecks. In: Proceedings of the IEEE Conference on Computer Vision and Pattern Recognition, pp. 4510–4520 (2018)
20. Sauer, A., Aljalbout, E., Haddadin, S.: Tracking holistic object representations. arXiv preprint arXiv:1907.12920 (2019)
21. Szegedy, C., Vanhoucke, V., Ioffe, S., Shlens, J., Wojna, Z.: Rethinking the inception architecture for computer vision. In: Proceedings of the IEEE Conference on Computer Vision and Pattern Recognition, pp. 2818–2826 (2016)
22. Valmadre, J., Bertinetto, L., Henriques, J., Vedaldi, A., Torr, P.H.: End-to-end representation learning for correlation filter based tracking. In: Proceedings of the IEEE Conference on Computer Vision and Pattern Recognition, pp. 2805–2813 (2017)
23. Wang, G., Luo, C., Xiong, Z., Zeng, W.: Spm-tracker: series-parallel matching for real-time visual object tracking. In: Proceedings of the IEEE/CVF Conference on Computer Vision and Pattern Recognition, pp. 3643–3652 (2019)
24. Woo, S., Park, J., Lee, J.Y., Kweon, I.S.: Cbam: convolutional block attention module. In: Proceedings of the European Conference on Computer Vision (ECCV), pp. 3–19 (2018)
25. Zhang, Z., Peng, H.: Deeper and wider siamese networks for real-time visual tracking. In: Proceedings of the IEEE/CVF Conference on Computer Vision and Pattern Recognition, pp. 4591–4600 (2019)
26. Zhu, Z., Wu, W., Zou, W., Yan, J.: End-to-end flow correlation tracking with spatial-temporal attention. In: Proceedings of the IEEE Conference on Computer Vision and Pattern Recognition, pp. 548–557 (2018)

A Virtual Mouse Based on Parallel Cooperation of Eye Tracker and Motor Imagery

Zeqi Ye, Yingxin Liu, Yang Yu$^{(\boxtimes)}$, Lingli Zeng, Zongtan Zhou, and Fengyu Xie

College of Intelligence Science and Technology, National University of Defense Technology, Changsha, China

Abstract. It has become a reality for paralyzed patients to use independent BMI-based assistive application to facilitate their lives. However, it was still a problem to switch among applications, if applications like typing and wheelchair-control were integrated in a device. In order to solve this problem, this paper realized a virtual mouse by combining eye tracker and MI, hoping to help patients to switch BMI applications independently and conveniently. The improved VT filter proposed in this paper solved the stable validity problem of the cursor. During the 2000 ms for MI, the time when the mouse stabilized in the valid area of the file can reach 94%. Asynchronous MI was realized in this paper through sliding window to enhance the flexibility of the system. The classification accuracy of left hand and right hand was 92.36%, that of left hand and idle state was 90.28%, and that of right hand and idle state was 90.63%. The final results were obtained by voting, which reached 91.33%. The results proved that the decoding of MI data would not be impacted during the control of eye tracker, which meant that the parallel control mechanism toward multi-cognitive modality proposed in this paper was feasible. This multi-cognitive modality based parallel control mechanism is in line with cognitive habits of human beings, and promising in improving the performance of human-machine fusion systems, in the future.

Keywords: Parallel control · Multi-cognitive modality · Virtual mouse · Eye tracker · Motor imagery

1 Introduction

Brain machine interface (BMI) is a kind of interactive system built between humans and machines. Since the German doctor Hans Berger collected brain waves on a human skull in 1924 [1], BMI has been well developed as one of the major technologies for human-machine interactions [2–8] nowadays, especially in the field of neurorehabilitation and disability assistance [7, 8]. One of the most classic applications is the P300 Speller proposed by Farewell and Donchin in 1988 [9] in which BMI acted as a virtual keyboard. However, only typing function is not enough to support paralyzed patients to use computers independently, which means that it is of great significance to explore a technology that can realize the functions of mouse.

In order to realize the functions of mouse through BMI, many researchers at home and abroad have carried out a series of studies in the past decades. In 2002, Serruya

© Springer Nature Switzerland AG 2021
Y. Peng et al. (Eds.): ICIG 2021, LNCS 12890, pp. 647–658, 2021.
https://doi.org/10.1007/978-3-030-87361-5_53

et al. proved that motor cortex neurons can be decoded to control the position of a computer cursor [10]. And, in 2008, Kim et al. realized neural control of computer cursor velocity by decoding motor cortical spiking activity [11]. Furthermore, in 2011, Simeral et al. successfully realized neural control of cursor trajectory and click by a human with tetraplegia [12]. Recently, in 2020, Degenhart et al. explored the stability of BMI for neural controlled computer cursor [13]. So far, controlling the movement of the computer cursor through motor neurons has reached a certain height. However, whether it can directly control the cursor without the neuron discharge when seeing the target, just as BMI omits the muscular movements and directly controls external devices through neurons? The answer can be found from the eye tracker.

Depending on the characteristics of eye movement tracks when humans process visual information, the eye tracker has been widely used in researches of psychology and cognitive field such as attention and regions of interest (ROI) in recent years [14–16]. With the maturity and popularization of the technology, the position of the computer cursor can be definitely controlled by the eye tracker instead of motor cortex neurons, which can be called dimensional reduction attack. Problems that are difficult in one area may be easy for another technology, such as road sign recognition in the field of unmanned car. In the future, if the road sign designed for humans is replaced with a QR code that is convenient for unmanned car recognition, the problem of road sign recognition would be easily bypassed. But this is not a negation of previous studies. Road sign recognition promoted the development of machine vision technology, and neural controlled computer cursors promoted the intention recognition of motor cortex neurons.

In fact, the lack of function keys also limited the application of the eye tracker. Many eye tracker involved games still require a hand-eye coordination mechanism [17–19]. While function keys happen to be suitable for neural control. So, to complement each other, multiple cognitive components interacting with machines in parallel may be better than BMI alone. There were previous studies involving hybrid BMI that integrated information from motor imagery (MI) and eye tracker [20–22]. But most of these studies extracted the eye gaze as attention feedback to assist MI. Differently, in this paper, eye tracker and MI work in parallel according to the mechanism of division of labor and cooperation. Thus, a virtual mouse that is more convenient and more in line with humans' operating habits is realized.

2 Experiments

2.1 Design and Procedure

The purpose of this experiment was to evaluate the performance of a duo-mode parallel control system. The experimental tasks were set up as practical as possible. Firstly, subjects were asked moving the virtual mouse cursor to aim at a file on the desktop through eye tracker, and triggering the right click of the virtual mouse through the right-hand MI to pop up the menu bar. Secondly, moving the virtual mouse cursor to aim at the open button in the menu bar, and triggering the left click of the virtual mouse through the left-hand MI to open the file, as shown in Fig. 1a. Thirdly, moving the virtual mouse cursor to aim at the red cross located on the top right corner of the interface and triggering

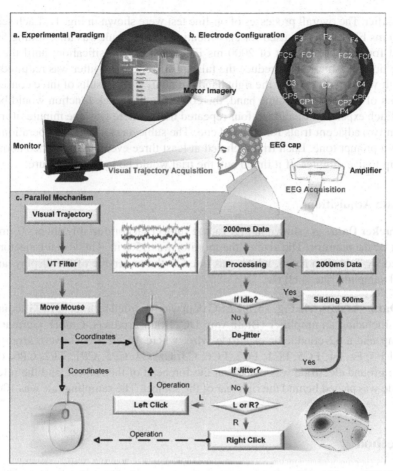

Fig. 1. Duo-mode parallel system. a, Experimental paradigm. The position of the eye tracker was relatively fixed with the monitor and located in an appropriate position to ensure that the visual trajectory of the subjects can be collected completely. Subjects were required to control the mouse movement by the eye tracker, at the same time, imagine a right-hand movement to pop-up the menu, and then imagine a left-hand movement to open a file on the desktop. **b,** Electrode configuration. **c,** Parallel mechanism. On the branch line of the eye tracker, visual trajectory was mainly processed by a series of filters like VT (Velocity Threshold) filter to obtain valid and stable visual coordinates. On the branch line of the EEG, asynchronous MI data can be decoded into control instructions in real time by sliding window, and the reliability can be guaranteed with the help of de-jitter. Finally, the movement and the click operation were integrated to control the mouse.

the left click through left-hand MI to close the application. The above three steps were defined as a trial. It should be noted that the MI data was required to be identified as idle state during no operation.

Before each experiment, the subjects were required to calibrate the eye tracker and perform several trials of left-hand and right-hand MI tasks according to cues to train the classifier. The overall processes of on-line test were shown in Fig. 1c. Each segment of 2000 ms EEG data was used for classification. If the result was idle, sliding 500 ms forward for another segment of 2000 ms EEG data for classification, until the result became non-idle. In order to reduce the false positive rate, de-jitter was required when the result was the left hand or the right hand, i.e., only if the results of three consecutive segments of data were the same hand, the corresponding click function would be triggered. Each experiment included four repeated trials. There was one minute of interval between two adjacent trials for rest and cue. The subjects can start the operations after hearing a prompt tone. Each trial included at least three events as described above and lasted up to five minutes. If it timed out, the trial would be judged as failure.

2.2   Data Acquisition

Eye Tracker Data. As shown in Fig. 1a, the subject sat comfortably about 60 cm away in front of the monitor. The size of the monitor was 15.6 in. The visual trajectory was recorded by Tobii Pro Nano, which was fixed to the underside of the display, and the original sampling rate is 60 Hz.

EEG Data. As shown in Fig. 1b, the EEG data was recorded by a set of EEG acquisition device, including an amplifier (BrainAmp DC, Brain Products, GmbH, Germany), an EEG cap and a 32-conductor electrode wire, where 16 electrodes were arranged on channel F3, Fz, F4, FC5, FC1, FC2, FC6, C3, Cz, C4, CP5, CP1, CP2, CP6, P3 and P4. The ground electrode was placed on the forehead of the subject, and the reference electrode was placed behind the right ear of the subject. The sampling rate was 1000 Hz.

3   Method

3.1   VT Filter of Eye Tracker

It is in accordance with the habits of the subjects that the vision stays on the operated object during the operation, which means that cognitive processes occur mainly during gaze but not saccade. So VT filter, firstly proposed by A Olsen in 2012 [23], was introduced to eliminate saccades and reduce cursor wobbles in the gaze area. VT filter is an algorithm used to eliminate saccade based on velocity. The core idea is to calculate the velocity between two sampling points of eye tracker signal and set a threshold to pick out sampling points that are larger than the threshold as saccade. In order to improve the real-time performance of the virtual mouse, the actual used equation of velocity was simplified as

$$V = \frac{\sqrt{(X_{t_1} - X_{t_2})^2 + (Y_{t_1} - Y_{t_2})^2}}{|t_1 - t_2|} \tag{1}$$

Where V is velocity. X_{t_1} and Y_{t_1} are the coordinates of the eye tracker signal at t_1. Similarly, X_{t_2} and Y_{t_2} are the coordinates at t_2. The unit is pixels per second.

In addition, what different from the proposed VT filter was that not only the upper threshold, but also the lower threshold was set in this paper to reduce the negative impact to the operation caused by cursor swaying around the target. Because in previous studies, VT filter used to be utilized for offline analyzing about region of interesting (ROI), which cared less about the precision. But precision is an important evaluation indicator for control.

3.2 EEG Processing

The EEG processing mainly included Artifact Subspace Reconstruction (ASR), Empirical Mode Decomposition (EMD) and Common Spatial Patterns (CSP).

ASR. ASR is an automatic and effective method for on-line artifacts rejection. It mainly contains three steps, i.e., reference data extraction, artifact thresholds determination, artifacts rejection and clean data reconstruction. Before ASR, the original EEG signal was filtered by 5–40 Hz bandpass filter to reduce the effect of noise on sensorimotor rhythms (SMRs) including μ(8–12 Hz) and β(12–30 Hz), and 48–52 Hz notch filter to eliminate power line interference. ASR can be implemented by aligning the data format with the input interface of the open-source function clean_rawdata in EEGlab [24].

EMD. EMD is a kind of time-frequency processing method [25], which can decompose the EEG signals into several components that satisfy the conditions of intrinsic mode functions (IMFs) [26]. Compared with CSP alone, it is more scientific for EMD and CSP to give weights to the influence of each sub-band signal on the result. Suppose that the original data $X(t) \in R^{C \times N}$, where C is the number of channels, N is the number of sampling points. After EMD, the original data was divided into M main $IMFs \in R^{M \times C \times N}$, where M is the max integer less than $log_2(N)$. Each $IMF \in R^{C \times N}$ was separately put into CSP filter.

CSP. The event-related desynchronization (ERD) induced by left-hand and right-hand MI tasks is a kind of spatial feature [27]. And CSP happens to be a spatial filter, which can improve the spatial distinguishability between samples [28]. The whitened covariance matrixes of two categories of data were decomposed by eigenvalue decomposition, and subsequently the eigenvalue diagonal matrixes were arranged in descending and ascending order respectively, so as to improve the distinguishability of the two categories of data. With the help of spatial filter $W \in R^{C \times C}$, the *pth* IMF can be extracted as $Z_p \in R^{C \times N}$. Finally, the spatial features $F_p \in R^{1 \times N}$ can be obtained by further calculating the variance of Z_p, and magnifying the difference by logarithm.

$$Z_p = W_p \cdot IMF_p, p \in [1, M] \qquad (2)$$

$$F_p = \log(\text{var}(Z_p)) \qquad (3)$$

After integrating the spatial features of all the IMFs, the dimension of F becomes $M \times N$. Furthermore, stepwise linear discriminant analysis (SWLDA) was used for feature dimensionality reduction and classification.

3.3 MI Classification

CSP is only suitable for two-category classification. Hence, in order to realize three-category classification, three two-category classifiers were adopted, a left-hand/idle classifier, a right-hand/idle classifier and a left-hand/right hand classifier. Each classifier was implemented through SWLDA. SWLDA can analyze each component of the feature matrix one by one, and use the t-test to analyze the contribution of each component to the classification, so as to eliminate the features that have no significant contribution, and retain the significant components [29, 30]. After the classifier parameter ω was obtained by training, the score of each sample could be calculated

$$score = \omega^T \cdot F \tag{4}$$

The higher the score, the greater the probability that the sample belonged to the positive category of the corresponding classifier. And the final result was obtained by voting with three classifiers.

3.4 MI De-jitter

After the first 2000 ms was satisfied, each 500 ms EEG data would output a result, which may be a left hand, a right hand or an idle. The de-jitter counter would restart

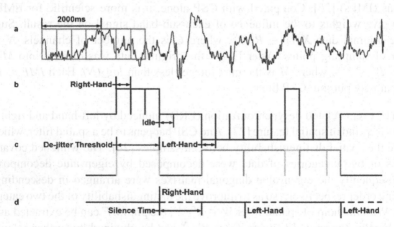

Fig. 2. Processes of De-jitter. a, Schematic diagram of sliding window for asynchronous MI. Each colorful window was the smallest processing unit, which contained a piece of 2000 ms EEG data. The interval between two adjacent windows with different color was 500 ms. **b,** Preliminary identification results of each segment of data. Each upward rectangular wave indicates that the recognition result was the right hand, oppositely, each downward rectangular wave represented that the recognition result was the left hand, and the rest were idle. **c,** Schematic diagram of de-jitter. Each de-jitter threshold required three consecutive non-idle recognition results. The cyan rectangle represented that the recognition result was the right hand, and the magenta rectangle represented that the recognition result was the left hand. **d,** The result of the final output. The positive pulse meant the right hand, and the negative pulses meant the left hands. Dotted lines represented silene periods lasting 1500 ms, during which output nothing.

counting whenever the recognition result changes to a non-idle state that was different from the current one. As the first magenta rectangle and the first cyan rectangle showed in the Fig. 2c, three consecutive occurrences with the same non-idle result would trigger the functions. And once the function was triggered, the counter would be cleared to zero. However, as the second cyan rectangle showed in the Fig. 2c, any change in the recognition result after the counting would cause the counter to return to zero, and the output would be forcibly converted to idle. The three recognition cycles after each function were silence periods, as shown by the dotted lines in the Fig. 2d. And this was why the second magenta rectangle in the Fig. 2c outputs nothing when the counting threshold was met.

4 Results

In most of previous researches on eye tracker, only high thresholds were set for VT Filter, i.e. only the sampling points whose speed below the threshold were considered valid. The VT Filter with a high threshold used to be used to eliminate saccade components, which was useful for finding ROI. However, for gaze data (Fig. 3e), the effect of VT Filter with a high threshold was not obvious, that can only eliminate some severe high-speed noise caused by blinking as shown in Fig. 3c, but can hardly improve the stability of the valid value as shown in Fig. 3f and Fig. 3d. For the 200 sampling points in Fig. 3f,

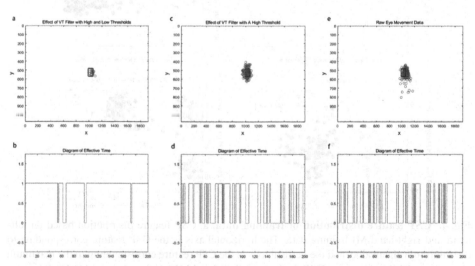

Fig. 3. Gaze effect comparison diagram of VT Filter. a, Effect of VT Filter with high and low thresholds. The orange rectangle indicated where the target folder with a valid area of 76 times 88 pixels was displayed on a 1920 times 1080 monitor. Blue circles were the trajectory of the mouse controlled by eye tracker. **b,** Effective diagram of the VT Filter with high and low thresholds. For a certain moment, if the position of the mouse, i.e. blue circle, fell within the valid area, i.e. orange rectangle, the valid value was set to 1 at this moment. Otherwise, the valid value was set to 0. The diagram showed the results of 200 consecutive sampling points. **c,** Effect of VT Filter with only a high threshold. **d,** Effective diagram of the VT Filter with only a high threshold. **e,** Raw gaze data. **f,** Effective diagram of raw gaze data. (Color figure online)

the sampling points falling in the valid area accounted for 40% of the total, while for the 200 sampling points in Fig. 3d, the valid rate was improved to 53%. But it was far from enough for the virtual mouse that required the cursor remaining valid during MI. The low-speed target-centered jitter made the cursor switch between valid and invalid rapidly, which had a great negative impact on the operability of the system. With many kinds of attempts, in fact, the problem can be simply and effectively solved if only adding a low threshold to the VT Filter. As shown in Fig. 3a, since the noise of the low-speed jitter would not trigger the mouse movement, almost all the sampling points fell within the valid area. And from the result in Fig. 3b, the valid time stably reached 94% in the duration of 200 sampling points, that satisfied the requirement of the virtual mouse.

As can be seen from the Fig. 4abc, the three two-category CSPs of left-right, left-idle and right-idle all had good spatial characteristics. Specifically, the classification accuracy of left hand and right hand was 92.36%, that of left hand and idle state was 90.28%, and that of right hand and idle state was 90.63%. In addition, it seemed that the results of substituting idle state training data into CSP parameters trained by right-hand

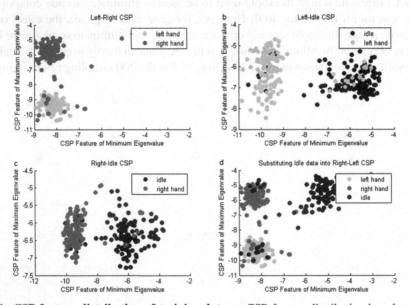

Fig. 4. CSP feature distribution of training data. a, CSP feature distribution based on left-hand and right-hand MI training data. The horizontal axis is the CSP feature corresponding to the minimum eigenvalue, and the vertical axis is the CSP feature corresponding to the maximum eigenvalue. Blue points were CSP features of right-hand MI training data, and red points were CSP features of left-hand MI training data. **b**, CSP feature distribution based on left-hand and idle state MI training data. Black points were CSP features of idle state MI training data, and red points were CSP features of left-hand MI training data. **c**, CSP feature distribution based on right-hand and idle state MI training data. Black points were CSP features of idle state MI training data, and blue points were CSP features of right-hand MI training data. **d**, The training data of idle state was substituted into CSP features trained by left-hand and right-hand MI training data. Black points were CSP features of idle state MI training data, blue points were CSP features of right-hand MI training data and red points were CSP features of left-hand MI training data. (Color figure online)

and left-hand training data could also be well separated from right hand dataset and left-hand dataset, as shown in Fig. 4d. The final recognition results could be obtained by voting within three classifiers and the accuracy reached 91.33%, which meant that all three classifiers could work effectively, and the addition of eye tracker did not cause a great negative impact on the classification of MI.

5 Conclusion

This paper proposed a parallel control mechanism toward multi-cognitive modality to realize a virtual mouse aiming at facilitating the application switching of the BMI system, furthermore, improving the practicability and flexibility of the BMI system. The experimental results showed that the improvement proposed in this paper can effectively help the eye tracker to stabilize the cursor in the valid region during the MI. It was because the difficulty of guaranteeing stable validity that, in previous studies, the eye tracker was mainly used to analyze cognitive state of subject, but seldomly in the field of cognitive control engineering. This paper provided an effective method to achieve stable validity, which was expected to help the eye tracker to be more widely used in the human-machine fusion control field in the future. What's more, the experimental results proved that the decoding of MI data would not be impacted during the control of eye tracker, i.e. the brain can encode observation and motor imagery in parallel. This multi-cognitive modality based parallel control mechanism is in line with cognitive habits of human beings, and promising in improving the performance of human-machine fusion systems.

6 Discussion

It has become a reality for paralyzed patients to use independent BMI-based assistive application to facilitate their lives. However, it was still a problem for paralyzed patients to switch among applications, if applications like typing and wheelchair-control were integrated in a device. In the daily life of healthy users, the operation of switching applications was usually achieved by manipulating the mouse. So, this paper realized a virtual mouse hoping to help paralyzed patients to switch applications independently and conveniently.

Limited information transfer rate caused that BMI was more suitable for switch control, i.e. controlling of functions, than continuous control, i.e. controlling of movement. The reason for using MI instead of steady-state visual evoked potential or event-related potential was that the induced EEG technology needed to take up the eyes of users. The induced EEG technology and the eye tracker can only share the right to use the user's eyes by polling, which will greatly reduce the efficiency of the system. While the spontaneous EEG technology, i.e. MI, can coexist well with the eye tracker, realizing the parallelism rather than the concurrency.

The reason why the eye tracker was considered to be more suitable for mouse position control than EEG technology was that the eye tracker can save the operation time after locking the target and directly control the position of the mouse, just like BMI technology could save the time of control command transmission in muscles and directly change the environment. However, it is hard for eye tracker to realize switch controls. For example, the function of magnifying the ROI could be achieved by a long gaze, but after zooming in, how to zoom out would be a problem.

Therefore, after integrating the advantages of the eye tracker and BMI, this paper adopted a parallel method of division of labor to make them enhance their strengths and avoid weaknesses, so as to achieve a high-performance virtual mouse. It should be noticed that this collaborative mechanism was different from Hybrid BMI, which mainly aimed at improving the performance of BMI through other cognitive components. However, similar to the working mechanism of human senses, the components of this mechanism worked in parallel based on the idea of division of labor and cooperation.

Next step, we are going to use the data recorded by eye tracker to synchronously analyze the cognitive state of the subjects as a feedback to build a closed-loop system while control the cursor, which would make the eye tracker itself parallelism. In addition, we are going to use the data in silence period to detect error-related potentials (Errp) [31] as a feedback to save the cost caused by error recognition. In the future, according to the characteristics of different cognitive components, perhaps more components, e.g. auditory evoked potential (AEP) [32] and smelling [33] will be able to integrate together in some way to enhance the performance of some special applications. In conclusion, human-computer interaction should not only be limited to BMI. The parallel interaction among multiple cognitive components and the environment may also be a good way of realizing human-computer interaction.

Acknowledgement. This work was supported by the National Natural Science Foundation of China (62006239).

References

1. Berger, H.I.: Über das Elektrenkephalogramm des Menschen. Eur. Arch. Psychiatry Clin. Neurosci. **87**, 527–570 (1928)
2. Liu, Y., Habibnezhad, M., Jebelli, H.: Brain-computer interface for hands-free teleoperation of construction robots. Autom. Constr. **123** (2021)
3. B., et al.: Noninvasive neuroimaging enhances continuous neural tracking for robotic device control. Sci. Robot. **4**(31), eaaw6844 (2019)
4. Han, X., et al.: A novel system of SSVEP-based human-robot coordination. J. Neural Eng. **16**(1), 016006 (2019)
5. Kuhner, D., et al.: A service assistant combining autonomous robotics, flexible goal formulation, and deep-learning-based brain–computer interfacing. Robot. Auton. Syst. **116**, 98–113 (2019)
6. Xu, Y., et al.: Shared control of a robotic arm using non-invasive brain–computer interface and computer vision guidance. Robot. Auton. Syst. **115**, 121–129 (2019)
7. Hochberg, L.R., et al.: Reach and grasp by people with tetraplegia using a neurally controlled robotic arm. Nature **485**(7398), 372–375 (2012)
8. Wessberg, J., et al.: Real-time prediction of hand trajectory by ensembles of cortical neurons in primates. Nature **408**(6810), 361–365 (2000)
9. Farwell, L.A., Donchin, E.: Talking off the top of your head: toward a mental prosthesis utilizing event-related brain potentials. Electroencephalogr. Clin. Neurophysiol. **70**(6) (1988)

10. Serruya, M.D., et al.: Instant neural control of a movement signal. Nature (2002)
11. Kim, S.P., et al.: Neural control of computer cursor velocity by decoding motor cortical spiking activity in humans with tetraplegia. J. Neural Eng. **5**(4), 455–476 (2008)
12. Simeral, J.D., et al.: Neural control of cursor trajectory and click by a human with tetraplegia 1000 days after implant of an intracortical microelectrode array. J. Neural Eng. **8**(2), 025027 (2011)
13. Degenhart, A.D., et al.: Stabilization of a brain–computer interface via the alignment of low-dimensional spaces of neural activity. Nature Biomed. Eng. **4**(7), 1–14 (2020)
14. Egovnik, T., et al.: An analysis of the suitability of a low-cost eye tracker for assessing the cognitive load of drivers. Appl. Ergon. **68**, 1–11 (2018)
15. Fabio, R.A., et al.: Longitudinal cognitive rehabilitation applied with eye-tracker for patients with Rett Syndrome. Res. Dev. Disabil. **111**(1), 103891 (2021)
16. Daniela, V., et al.: Visual exploration patterns of human figures in action: an eye tracker study with art paintings. Front. Psychol. **6**, 1636 (2015)
17. Chen, Y., Tsai, M.J.: Eye-hand coordination strategies during active video game playing: an eye-tracking study. Comput. Hum. Behav. **51**(OCT.), 8–14 (2015)
18. Tchalenko, J.: Eye-hand coordination in portrait drawing (2001)
19. Gonzalez, D.A., Niechwiej-Szwedo, E.: The effects of monocular viewing on hand-eye coordination during sequential grasping and placing movements. Vis. Res. **128**, 30–38 (2016)
20. Wang, H., et al.: Hybrid gaze/EEG brain computer interface for robot arm control on a pick and place task. In: 2015 37th Annual International Conference of the IEEE Engineering in Medicine and Biology Society (EMBC) (2015)
21. Dong, X., et al.: Hybrid Brain Computer Interface via Bayesian integration of EEG and eye gaze. In: 2015 7th International IEEE/EMBS Conference on Neural Engineering (NER) (2015)
22. Doherty, D.O., et al.: Exploring gaze-motor imagery hybrid brain-computer interface design. In: The IEEE International Conference on Bioinformatics and Biomedicine (BIBM) (2015)
23. Olsen, A.: The Tobii I-VT fixation filter: algorithm description (2012)
24. Delorme, A., Makeig, S.: EEGLAB: an open source toolbox for analysis of single-trial EEG dynamics including independent component analysis. J. Neurosci. Methods **134**(1), 9–21 (2004)
25. Wu, Z., Huang, N.E.: Ensemble empirical mode decomposition: a noise-assisted data analysis method. Adv. Adapt. Data Anal. **1**(1) (2009)
26. Huang, N.E., et al.: The empirical mode decomposition and the Hilbert spectrum for nonlinear and non-stationary time series analysis. Proc. Roy. Soc. Lond. Ser. A: Math. Phys. Eng. Sci. **454**(1971), 903–995 (1998)
27. Müller-Gerking, J., Pfurtscheller, G., Flyvbjerg, H.: Designing optimal spatial filters for single-trial EEG classification in a movement task. Clin. Neurophysiol. **110**(5), 787–798 (1999)
28. Ramoser, H., Muller-Gerking, J.: Optimal spatial filtering of single trial EEG during imagined hand movement. IEEE Trans. Rehabil. Eng. **8**, 441–446 (2000)
29. Johnson, G.D., Krusienski, D.J.: Ensemble SWLDA classifiers for the P300 speller. In: Jacko, J.A. (ed.) HCI 2009. LNCS, vol. 5611, pp. 551–557. Springer, Heidelberg (2009). https://doi.org/10.1007/978-3-642-02577-8_60
30. Krusienski, D.J., et al.: Toward enhanced P300 speller performance. J. Neurosci. Methods **167**(1), 15–21 (2008)
31. Zeyl, T., et al.: Adding real-time Bayesian ranks to error-related potential scores improves error detection and auto-correction in a P300 speller. IEEE Trans. Neural Syst. Rehabil. Eng. **24**(1), 46–56 (2016)

32. Behroozmand, R., Korzyukov, O., Larson, C.R.: Effects of voice harmonic complexity on ERP responses to pitch-shifted auditory feedback. Clin. Neurophysiol. **122**(12), 2408–2417 (2011)

33. Kim, K., et al.: Odor habituation can modulate very early olfactory event-related potential. Sci. Rep. **10**(1), 18117 (2020)

A Monocular Reflection-Free Head-Mounted 3D Eye Tracking System

Shihao Cao[1], Xinbo Zhao[1,3]([✉]), Beibei Qin[1], Junjie Li[1], and Zheng Xiang[2]

[1] School of Computer Science, Northwestern Polytechnical University,
Xi'an 710129, China
{caoshihao,2019262385,2019202143}@mail.nwpu.edu.cn
[2] School of Software, Northwestern Polytechnical University, Xi'an 710129, China
zxiang@mail.nwpu.edu.cn
[3] Ningbo Institute of Northwestern Polytechnical University, Ningbo 315103, China
xbozhao@nwpu.edu.cn

Abstract. Head-mounted eye tracking has significant potential for gaze baesd application such as consumer attention monitoring, human-computer interaction, or virtual reality (VR). Existing methods, however, either use pupil center-corneal reflection (PCCR) vectors as gaze directions or require complex hardware setups and use average physiological parameters of the eye to obtain gaze directions. In view of this situation, we propose a novel method which uses only a single camera to obtain gaze direction by fitting a 3D eye model based on the motion trajectory of pupil contour. Then a 3D to 2D mapping model is proposed based on the fitting model, so the complex structure of hardware and the use of average parameters for the eyes are avoided. The experimental results show that the method can improve the gaze accuracy and simplify the hardware structure.

Keywords: 3D gaze estimation · Single camera · Head-mounted device · Pupil contour · Mapping model

1 Introduction

Over the past decades, eye tracking systems have become a widely used tool in fields such as marketing research [1], psychological studying [2,3] and human-computer interaction [4,5]. Recently, eye tracking has also been applied to virtual reality and augmented reality devices for control [6] and panoramic rendering [7,8]. Currently, commercially available head-mounted eye-tracking devices are expensive such as tobii and Google Glasses, thus designing a head-mounted eye-tracking system with simple hardware structure and low cost is of great significance to researchers for research in related fields.

Typically, the methods of head-mounted eye tracking systems are divided into 2D and 3D according to the features of eye movement changes used, and the 2D methods are simpler in hardware structure compared to the 3D methods. The

© Springer Nature Switzerland AG 2021
Y. Peng et al. (Eds.): ICIG 2021, LNCS 12890, pp. 659–672, 2021.
https://doi.org/10.1007/978-3-030-87361-5_54

2D approachs use 2D eye movement features as input to construct a mapping model to obtain the location of the human eye gaze point. Takemura et al. [9] and Carlos et al. [10] use a camera and an infrared light source to obtain the pupil center and spot to form a pupil center-corneal refection vector, which was fitted by a polynomial to obtain the gaze position. Their method is the most common method for head-mounted eye tracking systems because of its good accuracy and relatively simple hardware structure, but their method has poor accuracy at non-calibrated points. Arar et al. [11] used four fixed infrared lights to extract the pupil center as well as four light spots to obtain the location of the gaze point based on the geometric principle of cross-ratio invariance. Their method requires four infrared light sources in order to obtain the reflected position of the corneal spot, which makes the hardware structure complex and has poor practicality. Moreover, the common disadvantage of the 2D methods is that the 2D features used do not make full use of the information of gaze direction changes, and therefore have poor accuracy at non-calibrated points.

In contrast to the 2D methods, the 3D methods directly obtain gaze direction and calculate the intersection with the scene to estimate the gaze point location based on the structural characteristics of the eye. However, most 3D methods rely on measurement information that is calibrated in advance such as light source position coordinates, camera position coordinates, screen position coordinates, and other information, causing great inconvenience to the use of eye tracking systems. Shih et al. [12] used two cameras and two light sources to calculate the human optics axis direction directly, avoiding the system calibration process and calibration errors. Nevertheless, this method requires multiple cameras to be calibrated and the position of the light sources need to be pre-set. Roma et al. [13] constructed a 3D eye model by considering the pupil and the radius of the eye as known quantities, and the direction of the line from the center of the eye to the center of the pupil as the visual axis. Their method ignores the physiological differences between different users. Zhu Z et al. [14] used two cameras and two infrared light sources to calculate corneal and pupillary parameters to obtain the direction of human eye gaze. Their method has the same disadvantages with Shih's [12].

In summary, for head-mounted eye tracking systems, existing methods are usually 2D methods using pupil center-corneal reflection vectors for interpolation or 3D methods using three-dimensional eye models. The disadvantage of the 2D method is that pupil center-corneal reflection vectors as a feature does not take full advantage of the information on the change in line of sight, resulting in poor accuracy on non-calibration. The disadvantage of the 3D method is that it usually requires advance calibration of the position relationship of the camera, IR light source or uniform modeling of the eye ignoring individual differences. Moreover, it has a complex hardware structure and high production cost. Hence, we need a lightweight head-mounted eye tracker. Swirski et al. [15] proposed a method to recover 3D eyeball from a monocular, but they only evaluated the model for synthetic eye images in a simulation environment, and the realistic performance of eye-to-scene camera has never been quantified. In order to solve the problems of existing head-mounted eye tracking systems, this paper proposes a monocular reflection-free head-mounted 3D eye tacking system. Compared with existing methods, our method requires only one camera, does not use the average physiological parameters of the eye, and is able to improve accuracy at non-calibrated points.

The contributions of this work are threefold. First, an eye model is proposed that is more applicable to real-time human eye videos captured by eye cameras rather than just synthetic images in a simulation environment. Secondly, a mapping model from the 3D gaze direction vectors to the 2D plane is proposed, using the gaze direction angle instead of the PCCR to do the interpolation. Experimental results show that the method proposed in this paper has better accuracy. Finally, this paper designs a low-cost, simple hardware structure head-mounted eye-tracking system, which provides great convenience for research in related fields.

2   3D Eye Model

2.1   Computational Model of Eye Center

The model proposed by Swirski et al. [15] is based on two assumptions: (1) the apparent pupil contour in 2D eye image is a perspective projection of a 3D pupil circle P which is tangent to the eyeball of fixed radius, R. (2) the center of the eyeball is stationary over time. In their model, the gaze direction varies with the motion of the 3D pupil circle P on the eyeball surface. At each time point, the state of the eye model is determined by eye center c and the 3D pupil circle P.

Given a set of N eye images, recorded over a period of time, pupil contours are extracted from each image by means of an automatic pupil extraction algorithm [16–18], leading to sets of two-dimensional contour edges $c_i = \{e_{ij}, j = 1, ..., M_i\}$. Firstly, the edges ε_i of the contours on each image are fitted to ellipses l_i. Next, assuming a pinhole camera model for perspective projection, the inverse projection of the pupil ellipse produces two 3D circles when fixing an arbitrary size of radius r [19]. Two 3D circles can be obtained by unprojection, and these two circles are denoted as:

$$\left(p^+, n^+, r\right), \left(p^-, n^-, r\right) \tag{1}$$

where p^+ and p^- denote the centers of the circles and n^+ and n^- denote the normals of the circles. For the two circles obtained by unprojection of each pupil ellipse, Swirski et al. [15] removed the ambiguity by projecting the 3D vectors into the 2D image space. Because the normal of two circles in the image space are parallel:

$$\tilde{n}_i^+ \propto \tilde{n}_i^- \tag{2}$$

Similarly, the line between $\tilde{p}_i^+$ and $\tilde{p}_i^-$ is parallel to $\tilde{n}_i^\pm$. The Eq. (3) can be derived:

$$\exists s, t \in R \cdot \tilde{p}_i^+ = \tilde{p}_i^- + s\tilde{n}_i^+ = \tilde{p}_i^- + t\tilde{n}_i^- \tag{3}$$

which means that you can choose either one of the two circles for this stage and calculate the projection of eyeball center $\tilde{c}$ by computing the intersection of the normal vectors. These vectors may have numerical or measurement errors and therefore will almost never intersect at a single point. Thus we can find the point with the smallest sum of distances from each line by the least squares method.

$$\tilde{c} = \left(\sum_i \left(I - \tilde{n}_i \tilde{n}_i^T \right) \right)^{-1} \cdot \left(\sum_i \left(I - \tilde{n}_i \tilde{n}_i^T \right) \tilde{p}_i \right) \tag{4}$$

The limitation of this approach is that only the eye model is fitted on the synthetic image sequence, while the situation in the real-time video will be more complex compared to the synthetic image.

There are two differences between performing pupil detection on video frames captured by an eye camera and pupil detection on a synthetic image: (1) The pupil outline on the synthetic image is distinct, while in the video frame the pupil outline may be blurred due to motion blur. (2) The pupil contour on the synthetic image is complete, whereas on the video frame it may be incomplete due to blinking, eyelash occlusion, or excessive eye rotation. In this case, the pupil contour may be partially or even completely obscured, resulting in low accuracy of the fitted ellipse.

Swirski et al. [17] obtained the projection of eyeball center by projecting the normal vector of the circle into the image space and then solving for the intersection of clusters of lines using least squares. In their method all projections of the normal vector are used to calculate $\tilde{c}$. However, when excessive eye rotation or incomplete pupil contours are encountered, the distance between the normal vector of the ellipse and $\tilde{c}$ may be too large, as in Fig. 1. Thus, this paper proposes an optimization algorithm to calculate the position of the center of the eye c.

We can calculate N lines from N images by Eq. ((3)), denoted as L^N. Then M line are randomly selected from L^N to obtain L^M, Eq. ((4)) can be rewritten as ((8)) for this stage.

$$L^N = \{ \tilde{n}_i, i = 1, \ldots, N \} \tag{5}$$

$$\{M\} = \text{random}(\{N\}) \tag{6}$$

$$L^M = \{ \tilde{n}_j, j = 1, \ldots, M \} \tag{7}$$

$$\tilde{c}_m = \left(\sum_j \left(I - \tilde{n}_j \tilde{n}_j^T \right) \right)^{-1} \cdot \left(\sum_j \left(I - \tilde{n}_j \tilde{n}_j^T \right) \tilde{p}_j \right) \tag{8}$$

where $\tilde{c}_m$ is the coordinates of eye center in the image space calculated by the iterative algorithm. Then we count the number of lines whose distance from $\tilde{c}_m$ is within the given threshold, repeat Eqs. (6)–(8) and select the intersection with the largest number of lines among all results. We calculate the intersection points again for those lines whose obtained results are within the threshold condition and compare them with the original results until the results are not changing. We then unproject $\tilde{c}_m$ to find 3D eyeball center c by fixing the z coordinate of c.

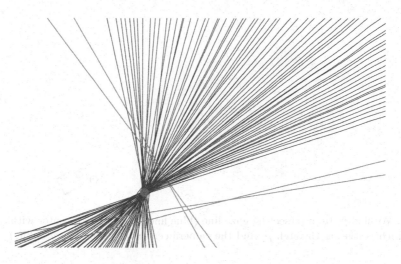

Fig. 1. The green point is the theoretical projection position of the center of the eye. The orange line is the normal vector projection when the eye is overrotated or the pupil contour is incomplete. (Color figure online)

2.2   Calculating the Radius of the Eye

Once we obtain the coordinates of eyeball center c, we note that the normal n_i of each pupil has to point away from eyeball center c:

$$n_i \cdot (p_i - c) > 0 \tag{9}$$

Therefore, when projected into the image space, $\tilde{n}_i$ has to point away from the projected center $\check{c}$:

$$\tilde{n}_i \cdot (\tilde{p}_i \quad \tilde{c}) > 0 \tag{10}$$

The pupil is tangent to the eye in the assumptions of Sect. 2.1, and the eye radius R can be estimated after obtaining the correct pupil projection. Since the unprojection of pupil has a distance ambiguity, we cannot use p_i directly to calculate R. Thus, we consider a candidate location $\hat{p}_i$ for the pupil center that is different from p_i, which is another possible unprojection of p_i at a different distance. This means that $\hat{p}_i$ is on the line passing through camera center and p_i, meanwhile the pupil circle is tangent to the eye, the line passing through c and parallel to n_i must pass through $\hat{p}_i$. The position of $\hat{p}_i$ can be obtained by calculating the intersection of these two lines, as in Fig. 2. Since two lines hardly ever intersect in space, the least squares method is used here to calculate the intersection point.

We then obtain the radius R of the eye by calculating the mean value of the distance between $\hat{p}_i$ and c.

$$R = \frac{1}{M} \sum_{i=1}^{M} (\hat{p}_i - c) \tag{11}$$

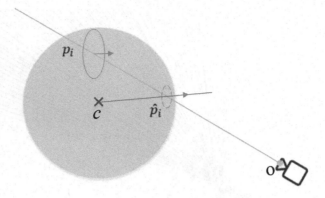

Fig. 2. We find $\hat{p}_i$ by intersecting gaze line (blue line) from eyeball center with orange line which is passing through p_i and the camera center o. (Color figure online)

2.3 Calculating Gaze Direction

In the assumptions of Sect. 2.1 each pupil center is on the surface of the eye and its projection is $\tilde{p}_i$. Due to the ambiguity of the distance, the p_i obtained by unprojection calculation can hardly lie exactly on the surface of the eye. However, in the normal case, the line passing through the center of the camera and p_i is intersected by the eye. Therefore, A new pupil center p_i' can be determined by calculating the intersection of the line passing through the center of the camera and p_i with the eye (c, R). In order to calculate the position of the intersection point, the magnitudes of d_1 and L are first calculated.

$$
\begin{aligned}
d_1^2 &= R^2 - d_2^2 \\
&= R^2 - \left(\|c - o\|^2 - L^2 \right) \\
&= R^2 + L^2 - \|c - o\|^2
\end{aligned}
\tag{12}
$$

$$
L = (c - o) \cdot \frac{(p_i - o)}{\|p_i - o\|}
\tag{13}
$$

As can be seen by Fig. 3, normally, the line $o - p_i$ will have two intersections with the eye (c, R), and the closest intersection is chosen here.

$$
d_{\min} = L - d_1
\tag{14}
$$

$$
p_i' = d_{\min} \cdot \frac{(p_i - o)}{\|p_i - o\|}
\tag{15}
$$

After obtaining the new pupil center position, n_i is discarded in favor of using $n_i' = p_i' - c$ as gaze direction.

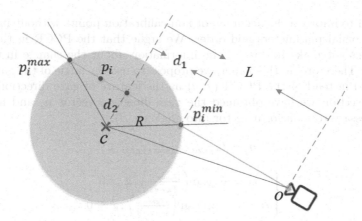

Fig. 3. We use the average radius of the eye R to recalculate the spatial position of the pupil p_i^{min}.

3   System Design and Implementation

In any head posture, with the eye looking at different positions, the pupil center will be presented in a different position in the image. Therefore, it is often assumed that the movement of the pupil center can be used as a feature of the change in vision. The most common PCCR method uses the vector between the pupil center and the reflected light spot on the cornea to represent the feature of gaze direction. Assuming that the head-mounted device remains fixed relative to the head, the position of light source's reflected spot on the cornea is fixed. The spot does not change with eye movement, so the PCCR vector only changes with the movement of the pupil center. Then the pupil corneal vector (x, y) in the eye camera image is mapped to the pixel point (X, Y) on the scene image or screen by the interpolation formula.

$$X = \sum_{k=0}^{n-1} a_k x^i y^j, i \in [0, k], j \in [0, k] \tag{16}$$

This method is more accurate when looking at the calibration points, but less accurate when looking at the non-calibrated points. The reason for this phenomenon is that annotating the calibration points corresponds to bringing the interpolated nodes into the interpolation formula, while annotating the non-calibrated points corresponds to bringing the non-interpolated nodes into the interpolation formula. A deeper reason is that the polynomial chosen does not fit well the correspondence between the gaze points and the PCCR, or that there is no corresponding polynomial relationship between the two. The usual solution to this problem is to increase the order of the polynomial to improve the accuracy of the fit, but this results in more parameters and increases the complexity of the calibration procedure. Moreover, when the order is high enough, the Runge Phenomenon may occur. To address this problem this paper proposes a solution to improve the accuracy of non-calibration points without increasing the polynomial parameters and order. We argue that the PCCR in the ocular image does not make full use of the information about the change in the gaze direction. Therefore, in this paper, we propose to use the angle of the gaze direction (α, β) instead of the PCCR (x, y) as the feature of gaze direction. In the previous section we have obtained the gaze direction vector n_i' and here it is only necessary to transform vector into angle (α, β).

$$n_i' = (x_{\text{gaze}}, y_{\text{gaze}}, z_{\text{gaze}}) \tag{17}$$

$$\begin{cases} \alpha = \arctan\left(\frac{|z_{\text{gaze}}|}{x_{\text{gaze}}}\right), x > 0 \\ \alpha = \pi - \arctan\left(\frac{|z_{\text{gaze}}|}{|x_{\text{gaze}}|}\right), x \leq 0 \end{cases} \tag{18}$$

$$\begin{cases} \beta = \arctan\left(\frac{|z_{\text{gaze}}|}{y_{\text{gaze}}}\right), y > 0 \\ \beta = \pi - \arctan\left(\frac{|z_{\text{gaze}}|}{|y_{\text{gaze}}|}\right), y \leq 0 \end{cases} \tag{19}$$

The mapping between the gaze direction angle (α, β) and the scene image coordinates (X, Y) is then modelled by a polynomial. Then Eq. ((20)) can be rewritten as

$$X = \sum_{k=0}^{n-1} a_k \alpha^i \beta^j, i \in [0, k], j \in [0, k] \tag{20}$$

A comparison of Eq. (20) with Eq. (16) shows that the system designed in this paper uses the same number of parameters as the traditional pupil-corneal vector method. In contrast to the PCCR method, the system is designed to use the angle of the gaze direction instead of PCCR vector, thus improving the use of the variation in visual information. A 3D to 2D mapping model is used to avoid advance calibration between the camera and the headset and to reduce the hardware architecture requirements.

4   Experiments

We use a head-mounted eye-tracking device made in our laboratory, in which the image resolution of the scene camera and the eye infrared camera are both 640×480 pixels. The acquisition frame rate is 60 FPS. The development environment is Qt Creator 4.7 + OpenCV 3.0. In order to ensure the fairness of the experimental results, our experiments use the same head-mounted device to test the experimental results of the PCCR method and the method proposed in this paper (Fig. 4).

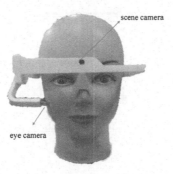

Fig. 4. The head-mounted eye tacker made by our laboratory with a scene camera and a eye camera.

4.1 Calibration

In the experiment, we use a nine-point calibration for both our method and the PCCR method respectively. Then the subjects gazed at the calibrated and non-calibrated points and collected the distribution of their respective gazing points. The polynomial used in the calibration process was the second order polynomial proposed by Cerrolaza et al. [20]:

$$X = a_0 + a_1 x + a_2 x^2 + a_3 y \\ + a_4 y^2 + a_5 xy \tag{21}$$

$$Y = b_0 + b_1 x + b_2 x^2 + b_3 y \\ + b_4 y^2 + b_5 xy \tag{22}$$

4.2 Data Collection

We invited 6 subjects to participate in this experiment. Every subject sits at a position approximately 0.7 m in front of the screen and adjusts the head posture to ensure that all calibration points on the screen are present in the scene image. The head posture is kept fixed during the calibration. Firstly, the markers on the screen are looked at in turn and the angle of vision or pupil-corneal vector is recorded for each calibration point. Secondly, the subject looks at a set of dots on the calibration target after the calibration is completed, and for each dot we collect 20 consecutive frames of data as a result of the experiment. Finally, significant shifts caused by involuntary eye movements such as nystagmus are removed. The distribution of the results of our method and PCCR method on calibration points are shown in Fig. 5 and Fig. 6.

In order to further evaluate the accuracy of the proposed method and the PCCR method at non-calibrated points, 16 test points different from the calibrated points were experimentally fixed on the target for evaluation. The distribution of the results of our method and PCCR method on test points are shown in Fig. 7 and Fig. 8.

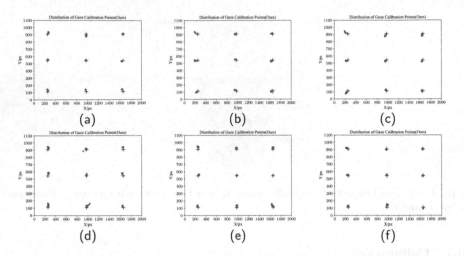

Fig. 5. Distribution of gaze calibration points (Ours).

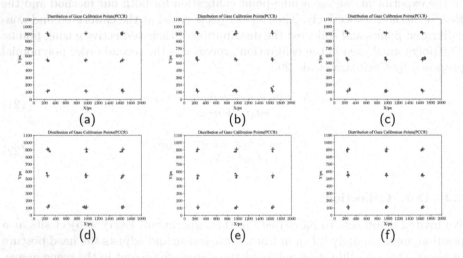

Fig. 6. Distribution of gaze calibration points (PCCR).

The crosses in Fig. 5, 6, 7 and Fig. 8 represent the calibration points on the calibration target and the cluster of points represent the real gaze points collected during the experiment. Once the data for the gaze points have been collected, Eq. (23) is used to calculate the angular error.

$$\bar{\alpha}_l = \frac{\sum_{j=0}^{N} \arctan\left(\sqrt{(x_{ij} - X_i)^2 + (y_{ij} - Y_i)^2}/L\right)}{N} \tag{23}$$

where N is the number of qualified samples, (x_{ij}, y_{ij}) is the position of the j-th data corresponding to the i-th gaze point collected, and (X_i, Y_i) is the position

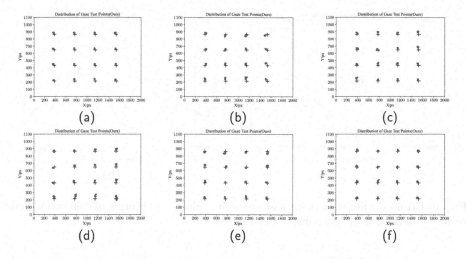

Fig. 7. Distribution of gaze test points (Ours).

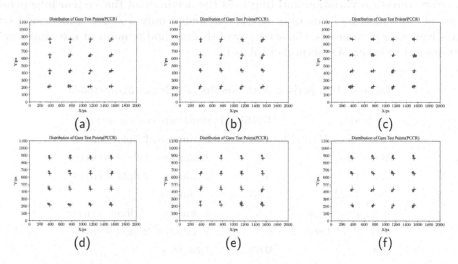

Fig. 8. Distribution of gaze test points (PCCR).

of the i-th reference gaze point. Figure 9 give the angular errors for each point when observing both calibrated and non-calibrated points for both our methods and the PCCR method.

According to the experimental data in Fig. 9, the errors of our method and the PCCR method are 0.56° and 0.60° respectively for the annotated calibration points, and 0.63° and 0.94° respectively for the annotated non-calibrated points. The experimental results show that the errors of the two methods are close to each other at the calibration points, and the accuracy of our method is improved at the non-calibrated points. Figure 9 show that using gaze direction

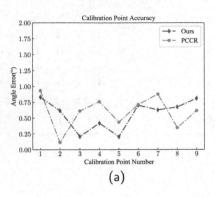 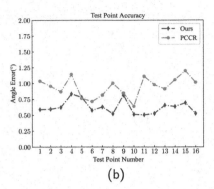

(a)   (b)

Fig. 9. Error of calibration point and test point results. (a) is error of calibration point results; (b) is error of test point results.

angles instead of PCCR vectors as features makes better use of the information on gaze direction variation and improves the accuracy of the system in general and at non-calibrated points in particular. Using only a single camera and no eye-averaging parameters, the accuracy of this method remains at the same level compared to other 3D methods (Table 1).

Table 1. Comparison of the results of different 3D methods.

Method	RMSE(°)	Hardware configuration
Shih Sheng-Wen [12]	0.8	2 cameras, 1 light sources
Zhu Z [14]	1.6	2 cameras, 1 light sources
Liu [21]	3.7	2 cameras, 2 light sources
Wen Q [22]	3.45	1 cameras
Tobii Pro Glasses 3	0.5	4 cameras, 16 light sources
Diskablis Glasses 3	0.3	2 cameras, 2 light sources
Ours	0.63	1 camera

5   Conclusion

Based on the features of the pupil's motion trajectory, we propose a single-camera head-mounted 3D eye tracking system. The number of cameras is reduced by analyzing the pupil motion trajectory to obtain the 3D gaze direction. By using the mapping model from the gaze direction to the scene, the advance calibration of the hardware structure is avoided. Moreover, the results show that the method in this paper has better accuracy at non-calibrated points compared to the PCCR method when using the same hardware equipment. The complexity of the hardware structure is greatly reduced while ensuring accuracy.

Acknowledgment. This work was supported by the National Natural Science Foundation of China under Grants nos. 61871326, and Ningbo Natural Science Foundation under Grants nos. 202003N4367.

References

1. van Reijmersdal, E.A., Rozendaal, E., Hudders, L., Vanwesenbeeck, I., Cauberghe, V., van Berlo, Z.M.: Effects of disclosing influencer marketing in videos: an eye tracking study among children in early adolescence. J. Interact. Market. **49**, 94–106 (2020)
2. Steindorf, L., Rummel, J.: Do your eyes give you away? A validation study of eye-movement measures used as indicators for mindless reading. Behav. Res. Methods **52**(1), 162–176 (2020)
3. Bergman, M.A., et al.: Is a negative attentional bias in individuals with autism spectrum disorder explained by comorbid depression? An eye-tracking study. J. Autism Dev. Disord. 1–14 (2021). https://doi.org/10.1007/s10803-021-04880-6
4. Bozomitu, R.G., Păsărică, A., Tărniceriu, D., Rotariu, C.: Development of an eye tracking-based human-computer interface for real-time applications. Sensors **19**(16), 3630 (2019)
5. Rahal, R.M., Fiedler, S.: Understanding cognitive and affective mechanisms in social psychology through eye-tracking. J. Exp. Soc. Psychol. **85**, 103842 (2019)
6. Matthews, S., Uribe-Quevedo, A., Theodorou, A.: Rendering optimizations for virtual reality using eye-tracking. In: 2020 22nd Symposium on Virtual and Augmented Reality (SVR), pp. 398–405. IEEE (2020)
7. Pohl, D., Zhang, X., Bulling, A.: Combining eye tracking with optimizations for lens astigmatism in modern wide-angle HMDs. In: 2016 IEEE Virtual Reality (VR), pp. 269–270. IEEE (2016)
8. Mikhailenko, M., Kurushkin, M.: Eye-tracking in immersive virtual reality for education: a review of the current progress and applications (2021)
9. Takemura, K., Takahashi, K., Takamatsu, J., Ogasawara, T.: Estimating 3-D point-of-regard in a real environment using a head-mounted eye-tracking system. IEEE Trans. Hum. Mach. Syst. **44**(4), 531–536 (2014)
10. Morimoto, C.H., Mimica, M.R.: Eye gaze tracking techniques for interactive applications. Comput. Vis. Image Underst. **98**(1), 4–24 (2005)
11. Arar, N.M., Gao, H., Thiran, J.P.: Towards convenient calibration for cross-ratio based gaze estimation. In: 2015 IEEE Winter Conference on Applications of Computer Vision, pp. 642–648. IEEE (2015)
12. Shih, S.W., Liu, J.: A novel approach to 3-D gaze tracking using stereo cameras. IEEE Trans. Syst. Man Cybern. Part B (Cybern.) **34**(1), 234–245 (2004)
13. Urano, R., Suzuki, R., Sasaki, T.: Eye gaze estimation based on ellipse fitting and three-dimensional model of eye for "intelligent poster". In: 2014 IEEE/ASME International Conference on Advanced Intelligent Mechatronics, pp. 1157–1162. IEEE (2014)
14. Zhu, Z., Ji, Q.: Novel eye gaze tracking techniques under natural head movement. IEEE Trans. Biomed. Eng. **54**(12), 2246–2260 (2007)
15. Swirski, L., Dodgson, N.: A fully-automatic, temporal approach to single camera, glint-free 3D eye model fitting. In: Proceedings of PETMEI, pp. 1–11 (2013)

16. Li, Z., Miao, D., Liang, H., Zhang, H., Liu, J., He, Z.: Efficient and accurate iris detection and segmentation based on multi-scale optimized mask R-CNN. In: Zhao, Y., Barnes, N., Chen, B., Westermann, R., Kong, X., Lin, C. (eds.) ICIG 2019. LNCS, vol. 11902, pp. 715–726. Springer, Cham (2019). https://doi.org/10.1007/978-3-030-34110-7_60

17. Świrski, L., Bulling, A., Dodgson, N.: Robust real-time pupil tracking in highly off-axis images. In: Proceedings of the Symposium on Eye Tracking Research and Applications, pp. 173–176 (2012)

18. Santini, T., Fuhl, W., Kasneci, E.: Pure: robust pupil detection for real-time pervasive eye tracking. Comput. Vis. Image Understand. **170**, 40–50 (2018)

19. Safaee-Rad, R., Tchoukanov, I., Smith, K.C., Benhabib, B.: Three-dimensional location estimation of circular features for machine vision. IEEE Trans. Robot. Autom. **8**(5), 624–640 (1992)

20. Cerrolaza, J.J., Villanueva, A., Villanueva, M., Cabeza, R.: Error characterization and compensation in eye tracking systems. In: Proceedings of the Symposium on Eye Tracking Research and Applications, pp. 205–208 (2012)

21. Liu, M., Li, Y., Liu, H.: 3D gaze estimation for head-mounted eye tracking system with auto-calibration method. IEEE Access **8**, 104207–104215 (2020)

22. Wen, Q., Bradley, D., Beeler, T., Park, S., Xu, F.: Accurate real-time 3D gaze tracking using a lightweight eyeball calibration. Comput. Graph. Forum **39**(2), 475–485 (2020)

Video Analysis and Understanding

Coding and Quality Evaluation
of Affordable 6DoF Video Content

Pan Gao[1,2]($\boxtimes$), Ran Wei[2], Yingjie Liu[2], and Manoranjan Paul[3]

[1] College of Computer Science and Technology, Nanjing University of Aeronautics
and Astronautics, Nanjing 211106, China
Pan.Gao@nuaa.edu.cn
[2] Science and Technology on Electro-Optic Control Laboratory, Luoyang, China
[3] Charles Sturt University, Bathurst, NSW 2795, Australia

Abstract. We present a coding and quality evaluation method for Six
Degrees of Freedom (6DoF) video content. Firstly, the 6DoF video content is generated using an affordable capturing setup, and represented as
the commonly used 6DoF format 3-D mesh. To overcome the difficulty in
exploiting the temporal redundancy in mesh with different connectivity
at every frame, we transform the mesh sequence into colored point clouds
for compression, which saves the bit budget for connectivity while keeping the photo-realistic characteristics of the 3-D object. We compress the
point cloud sequence using MPEG video-based point cloud compression
structure, which can achieve the bit rate close to common media format.
We also conduct projection-based and point-based quality evaluation
to examine the compression distortion effect. Particularly, we employ
PCA to find the representative viewing perspective for projection. We
will release some data set and source codes to foster further research in
this area.

Keywords: Six Degrees of Freedom · Coding and quality evaluation ·
3-D mesh · Point clouds

1 Introduction

With advancement in virtual/augmented reality hardware, interest in Six
Degrees of Freedom (6DoF) video has overwhelmingly proliferated recently [7].
6DoF video allows the users to not only look around, but also move around
the virtual world. In 6DoF, a 3-D geometry model is generally created from
photo-realistic graphics or multi-view video of real-world scene, and then 6DoF
video is photo-realistically displayed to the users by rendering the model in the
sequence with texture information being mapping to it. The goal of 6DoF video
is to allow the user to interactively choose an arbitrary viewpoint of the dynamic
scene with both translational and rotational movements. To enable interactiv-
ity for the user at the receiver, an end-to-end chain involving the acquisition

© Springer Nature Switzerland AG 2021
Y. Peng et al. (Eds.): ICIG 2021, LNCS 12890, pp. 675–686, 2021.
https://doi.org/10.1007/978-3-030-87361-5_55

of multi-view video, geometry extraction, coding of 3-D geometry model, and quality evaluation for 6DoF video is thus needed.

To create 6DoF video content, there is a number of algorithms that have been developed. A well-known and useful algorithm for geometry extraction is shape-from-silhouette (SfS) [4], which creates 3-D volume from the segmented silhouette videos. To enhance details of visual hull, several SfS variants have been proposed, e.g., feature correspondence refined SfS [18], shading variations based SfS [22], etc. With the convergence of computer vision and computer graphics, another common 3D reconstruction method is multiview stereo (MVS), where the stereo correspondence is used to reconstruct the scene geometry [9]. Considering the larger volume of video content creation methods, in this work, we focus on compression and quality evaluation of 6DoF video. In particular, we are interested more in the contents generated by an affordable capturing setup, such as using a sparse set of RGB cameras or hand-held cameras. Due to the limited number of cameras used, such generated 6DoF video contents are commonly represented as 3-D polygonal mesh, in which high-quality 3-D models can be provided by specifying both the geometry and topology [8].

For compression and quality evaluation of 3-D mesh-based 6DoF content, to the best of our knowledge, there is few works specifically designed for natural scene. All the efforts have been devoted in developing algorithms for compressing the mesh-based 3-D animation sequence [11,12], and [10]. Generally speaking, these algorithms can be roughly divided into two categories, i.e., static mesh coding and dynamic mesh coding, both of which include geometry coding and connectivity coding. In static mesh coding, vertex coordinates of geometry are usually uniformly quantized, and, then, during compression, the position of the encoded vertex is predicted by the already-encoded neighbors. The connectivity is entropy-coded by using a predefined traverse scheme for mesh elements. In contrast to individually coding each mesh frame, dynamic mesh coding explores the temporal redundancy between vertex coordinates across frames. However, this geometry redundancy removal is performed with the condition that the vertex count and the connectivity are constant across frames, with only vertex coordinates varied. If geometry, vertex count and the connectivity vary across frames, which is usually the case in reconstructed 3-D natural scene as we investigated in this work, exploitation of temporal redundancy in geometry and connectivity would become very difficult. This is because, there is no one-to-one correspondence between vertexes across frames.

The first work that can be considered as compression and quality evaluation for 6DoF content of natural scene is [17], in which SfS is used for geometry extraction, and a view-dependent texture mapping algorithm is developed for photo-realistic rendering. In this paper, the authors used H.264/AVC to compress dynamic textures, i.e., the video sequences of all the cameras. In [20], a model-based free viewpoint video system of human actors is developed. This approach applied a model-based marker-less human motion capture algorithm to reconstruct FVV from multiview video footage, and the rendering of the moving person from arbitrary perspectives is achieved by using a texture atlas, a parameterization function, which maps the surface of the 3-D model into the 2D domain.

The texture atlas is then predictively encoded by using a shape-adaptive wavelet algorithm. In [13], the authors proposed a pipeline for 3-D tele-immersion with live-reconstructed geometry. To speed up the encoding of mesh, a pattern-based connectivity coding scheme is proposed. However, in those 6DoF video systems, 3-D geometry model is encoded using static mesh coding method, which is not sufficiently efficient for transmission. In order to make 6DoF content more compressible and accessible, the authors of [2] developed an end-to-end solution to encode FVV as a compact data stream, where a dense set of RGB and IR video cameras are used to record the scene. Inspired by the concepts of I and P frames in video coding, this solution splits the mesh sequence into keyframes and predictive frames. The keyframes contain geometry and connectivity information, while the predictive frames contain only delta geometry information. In order to make the surface geometry and tessellation (i.e., texture atlas) coherent between consecutive frames, a mesh tracking algorithm is proposed to fit the keyframe meshes to neighboring frames. However, obtaining the minimum set of keyframes that can register all other frames within some constraints is NP-hard, and the normal matrix used for registration can occasionally be ill-conditioned. Further, projection-based quality evaluation for compressed 3-D mesh is not conducted.

In this work, in order to close the gap between content creation and compression, we further investigate how to efficiently compress and evaluate the 6DoF video content. We choose the 6DoF content, i.e., 3-D polygonal mesh, generated by inexpensive acquisition devices and computing machines. Due to the difficulty and complexity in making vertex number and connectivity constant and atlas texture consistent between frames in compression of time-varying dynamic mesh, we convert 3-D mesh sequences to point cloud sequences with color information for each vertex, and compress them using the MPEG point cloud coding standard, i.e., TMC2 [6], which saves the bit consumption for connectivity. Further, since TMC2 encodes the point cloud by using geometry video and texture video, the point number does not require to be constant and the atlas textures also do not require to be strictly consistent between successive frames. After decoding and rendering point cloud, we conduct principle component analysis (PCA) assisted projection-based and 3-D point-based quality evaluation for 6DoF content.

The rest of the paper is organized as follows. We detail the compression steps in Sect. 2. The proposed PCA-assisted projection method and quality evaluation methods is presented in Sects. 3, followed by point-based quality evaluation method in Sect. 4. Finally, concluding remarks are given in Sect. 5.

2 Compression of 6DoF Video Content

To have a high-quality moving-around viewing experience, we use the 6DoF video content created by the method in [15], which uses an affordable camera setup to capture the scene. We choose three sequences for validation of our compression and quality evaluation method here, namely, "Rafa", "Medieval man", and "Matis", [23] which are presented in Fig. 1 for illustration. In contrast

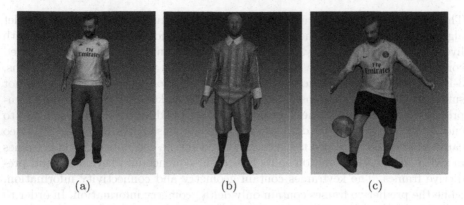

(a)   (b)   (c)

Fig. 1. Screen-shot of the created 3-D mesh sequences using the method proposed in [15]. (a) "Rafa" sequence. (b) "Medieval man" sequence. (c) "Matis" sequence.

to synthetic animation sequence, the above produced 3D meshes are generally time-varying dynamic, i.e., the vertex number and connectivity are not constant across frames. For ease of compression, one can use the template-based approach to amend the triangulation to produce spatiotemporally coherent meshes. However, the atlases still cannot be guaranteed to be temporally coherent. The illustration of inconsistent parameterization in texture is shown in Fig. 2. Inconsistent atlas, also means that, for a same face in two successive frames, different texture coordinates are needed for texture mapping. Since the connectivity contains both vertex coordinate indexes and texture coordinate indexes, exploiting temporal redundancy in connectivity in a dynamic mesh is extremely difficult without atlas consistency. The authors of [2] proposed a mesh tracking method to make tessellation coherent. However, selecting the keyframes covering a continuous frame range is a rather challenging task, and performing registration for predictive frames is quite expensive. Further, the compression ratios may be influenced by the size of the group of frames that is variable in the sequence. In this work, for high compression performance, we convert the textured mesh to point cloud sequence with color attribute for each point, and then use the latest point cloud compression standard to compress them.

2.1 Preprocessing Steps

We apply a midpoint-based surface subdivision scheme [16] to iteratively refine mesh, where every edge is splitted on its midpoint, and each triangle is thus substituted with four smaller triangles. Then, we generate color information for each point by transferring the texture atlas to vertex using corresponding texture coordinates. Finally, we removed all the faces in the mesh. We generate four different vertex count point cloud sequences for each mesh sequence, i.e., 62K, 127K, 250K, 495K, which are used to represent the point cloud resolutions in this work. Considering that the point cloud codec compresses the point cloud sequence by generating planar video and requires the point position to be integer,

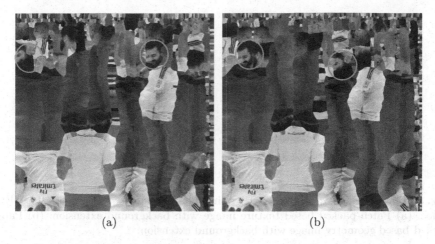

(a)   (b)

Fig. 2. Illustration of the temporally inconsistent parameterization. (a) The 133*th* texture atlas frame of the "Rafa" mesh sequence. (b) The 134*th* texture atlas frame of the "Rafa" mesh sequence.

a scaling is thus performed for vertex coordinates of each point cloud sequence, and the point cloud models are translated to the origin (0,0,0) of the bounding box of the original points. The point position (x_i, y_i, z_i) in the frame coordinate transformed from the original world coordinate $(x_i^{world}, y_i^{world}, z_i^{world})$ can be expressed as in (1), where (t_x, t_y, t_z) and s are the translation and scaling parameters. These parameters can be derived by the bounding cube of the input point locations. The source codes for these preprocessing steps can be found at the link[1].

$$(x_i, y_i, z_i) = \left((x_i^{world}, y_i^{world}, z_i^{world}) - (t_x, t_y, t_z) \right) s \qquad (1)$$

2.2 Compression for Point Cloud Sequence

We compress point cloud sequence using the video-based point cloud compression framework, i.e., Test Model Category 2 (TMC2) [1], which is the latest standard reference software for volumetric video compression and achieves the start-of-the-art performance. To have a wide range of reconstructed point cloud qualities, four different geometry and texture Quantization Parameter (QP) pairs are employed, i.e., $\{(17, 20), (30, 35), (37, 43), (41, 48)\}$. TMC2 firstly generates patches from point cloud with clustering, where six oriented planes are defined in terms of the normal and each point is associated with the plane that has the closest normal [5]. The minimum number of points for a connected component to be retained as a patch is set to 16. The extracted patches are then packed onto the 2D grid images. Two video sequences are generated, geometry video and texture video, both of which are then encoded with the HEVC codec separately [19]. At the

---

[1] https://github.com/I2MLab/Translation-and-Scaling-for-geometry-cooridnates-of-point-clouds.

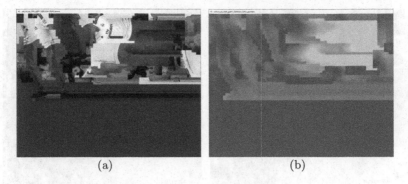

(a)   (b)

Fig. 3. Planar images generated from point cloud frame to be fed into the HEVC codec. (a) Patch-packed based texture image with background extension. (b) Patch-packed based geometry image with background extension.

decoder, the texture video, geometry video, occupancy map, and auxiliary patch information are decoded in parallel. The 3-D geometry positions of the points are computed by leveraging the auxiliary patch information and the geometry images, while the color values of the points are directly read from the texture images. The generated patch-based texture and geometry images are shown as in Fig. 3.

3   PCA-Assisted Projection and Quality Evaluation

In this section, we use the projection-based method to evaluate the quality of the point clouds compressed by the above method. We firstly project the point cloud to the planar images, and then use the image-based quality metric (i.e., PSNR and SSIM [21]) to examine the quality. As the 2-D images the point cloud is projected to can be arbitrary, we use PCA to determine the representative viewing perspectives. With the aim of obtaining the planar images from the 3-D coordinate the point cloud resides, we divide the destination projection planes into three categories, i.e., X-Y plane, X-Z plane, and Y-Z plane. Figure 4 shows the three eigenvectors (directions) found by using PCA on the "Medieval man", along which the point cloud model can be projected into 2-D images without deformation. In the following, we use the projection to X-Y plane as an example to elaborate on the PCA-assisted projection method.

To project the point cloud into the X-Y plane, we use PCA to find the viewing perspectives around Y-axis. We apply PCA on the geometry coordinates of X and Z axes, and obtain two eigenvectors (these two vectors are the same length, but point in perpendicular directions), which represent the dominate viewing directions. Assume that the one of the eigenvectors for projecting the point clouds to X-Y plane is denoted as $<a, b>$, which is the most representative viewing direction. Thus, the rotation angle θ around the Y-axis can be derived as follows

$$\theta = \arctan(b/a) \qquad (2)$$

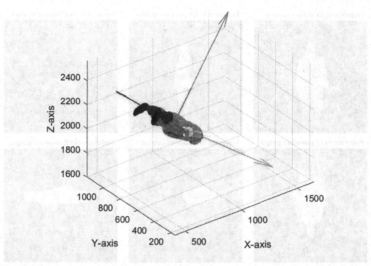

Fig. 4. Illustration of the three projection perspectives found by employing PCA on the point cloud content "Medieval man".

With the rotation angle of X-Z axes in 2-D space indicating the principle viewing perspective, we can use it for 3-D rotation of the point cloud accordingly. The homogeneous geometry coordinate $\mathbf{p_i}$ of the point cloud after 3-D rotation can be represented as

$$\mathbf{p_i} = \begin{bmatrix} \cos\theta & 0 & \sin\theta & 0 \\ 0 & 1 & 0 & 0 \\ -\sin\theta & 0 & \cos\theta & 0 \\ 0 & 0 & 0 & 1 \end{bmatrix} \begin{bmatrix} x_i \\ y_i \\ z_i \\ 1 \end{bmatrix} \tag{3}$$

For the image observed from the perspective determined by the first eigenvector, we orthogonally project the point cloud to the X-Y plane forming an image, i.e.,

$$\begin{bmatrix} \tilde{x}_i \\ \tilde{y}_i \\ 1 \end{bmatrix} = \begin{bmatrix} 1 & 0 & 0 & 0 \\ 0 & 1 & 0 & 0 \\ 0 & 0 & 0 & 1 \end{bmatrix} \mathbf{p_i} \tag{4}$$

where $\tilde{x}_i$ and $\tilde{y}_i$ are 2D coordinates of the projected image. When there exists multiple points project into a same position in the 2D image, we only keep the point with the smallest depth value, i.e., z_i. Then, the color information for the 2D image is filled with the corresponding color information of the point cloud. Assume that $\tilde{\mathbf{T}}$ and $\mathbf{T}$ are the three-column vectors representing the color information for the 2D image and point cloud, respectively, then $\tilde{\mathbf{T}}$ can be represented as follow

$$\tilde{\mathbf{T}}[\tilde{x}_i, \tilde{y}_i] = \mathbf{T}[x_i, y_i] \tag{5}$$

Similarly, we can obtain the projection images in X-Y planes for the other eigenvector from PCA.

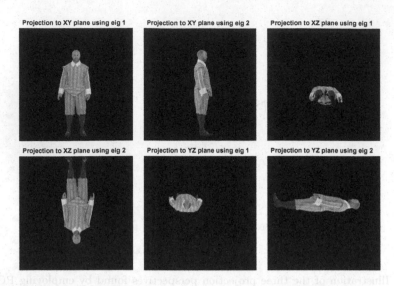

Fig. 5. Projection of the point cloud to the planar X-Y, X-Z, and Y-Z planes. For each plane, two eigenvectors are employed for projection, which are represented as eig 1, and eig 2, respectively.

For the projection images in the X-Z and Y-Z planes, we employ the PCA on the geometry coordinates of Y-Z and X-Y axes, respectively, and then project the point cloud to those planes using the associated eigenvectors. Figure 5 illustrates the projected 2D images for these three planes, where only the first two eigenvectors are used for each plane projection.

Table 1 summarize the average PSNR and SSIM values for the various projection images of the sequence "Medieval man" compressed by different geometry and color QP pairs. As can be observed, for a same used QP pair, the PSNRs and SSIMs for the eig 1 projected image in the X-Y plane and the eig 2 projected image in the X-Z plane are generally lower than those of others. This is due to that, the projected areas that can be observed from those perspectives for the point cloud are larger than other perspectives, and thus they are distorted more by the compression noises. For a same plane, PSNR and SSIM may exhibit different quality modeling characteristics for different eigenvector-assisted projection images. For instance, in the YZ plane at QP of (37,43), the PSNR for the first eigenvector projected image is lower than that of the second eigenvector. However, in terms of SSIM, the quality of first eigenvector projected image is better than that of the second eigenvector. As the QPs for geometry and color increase, both PSNR and SSIM for all the perspective projected images tend to decrease, which confirms that the quality of the projected images from the point cloud is also inversely proportional with the QP values.

Table 1. PSNR and SSIM measured for the projection images of the sequence "Medieval man" compressed by various geometry and color QP pairs.

Metric	Perspective	QPs for geometry and color			
		(17,20)	(30,35)	(37,43)	(41,48)
PSNR	XY (eig 1)	37.89	35.33	33.93	32.69
	XY (eig 2)	39.89	36.90	35.60	34.15
	XZ (eig 1)	40.04	37.53	35.39	34.14
	XZ (eig 2)	37.81	35.13	33.72	32.35
	YZ (eig 1)	40.78	37.26	34.71	33.31
	YZ (eig 2)	39.82	36.67	34.97	33.25
SSIM	XY (eig 1)	0.974	0.959	0.946	0.937
	XY (eig 2)	0.985	0.976	0.967	0.961
	XZ (eig 1)	0.987	0.978	0.969	0.963
	XZ (eig 2)	0.976	0.960	0.947	0.938
	YZ (eig 1)	0.990	0.983	0.977	0.973
	YZ (eig 2)	0.986	0.976	0.968	0.961

4   3-D Point-Based Quality Evaluation

In this section, we conduct 3-D point-based objective quality evaluation for decoded point cloud sequences. That is, unlike the projection-based quality evaluation, we separately measure the geometry and color quality for the point cloud. We use the MPEG 3DG group newly-developed point2plane metric to measure the geometry distortion caused by point cloud compression, which has been demonstrated to be better aligned with perceptual quality of point clouds compared to the point2point metric [3]. For the quality of the color attribute of the point cloud, we measure the luminance PSNR of the points, which is calculated between the distorted points and the nearest points in the reference point cloud [14]. Further, the bit rate for the point cloud-based 6DoF video is computed with the frame rate of 30 fps.

The results of the objective quality evaluation for decoded point clouds are shown in Fig. 6. As can be observed, as the bit rate increases, both geometry and color distortions decrease for all the sequences at different resolutions. When comparing the results among different resolutions of a sequence, we found a very interesting phenomenon. That is, at the same bit rate, the geometry errors of the low resolution point cloud are higher than that of the high resolution point cloud, while, the color errors of the low resolution point cloud are lower than that of the high resolution point cloud, especially in the case of high bit rate. The substantial reason can be explained as follows. For geometry error induced by compression, it is calculated by the coordinates of the distorted point and the nearest neighboring point in the original point cloud. When the point count of the original point cloud is larger, there are more available points that can better match the distorted point in the sense of geometry position, which results in less geometry distortion. On the other hand, for color distortion induced by compression, it is calculated with the luminance of the points. The higher the point count in the point cloud, the less bits assigned to the color of each point will be, which means that the more distortion would be possibly introduced to the color attribute of each point of a higher resolution point cloud.

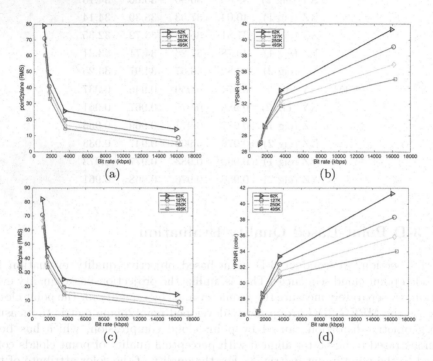

Fig. 6. Objective quality evaluation for decoded point clouds. (a) point2plane versus bit rate measured for geometry attribute of "Matis" sequence. (b) YPSNR versus bit rate measured for color attribute of "Matis" sequence. (c) point2plane versus bit rate measured for geometry attribute of "Rafa" sequence. (d) YPSNR versus bit rate measured for color attribute of "Rafa" sequence.

5   Conclusion

In this paper, we propose an integrated capture and processing pipeline for 6DoF video system. Two key components, i.e., compression and quality evaluation, are introduced to transform 6DoF content to a compressible and accessible data format. We choose the watertight 3-D mesh sequences produced by affordable capturing configuration as the 6DoF input content. Then, we convert the 3-D mesh sequences into colored point clouds, which can be compressed as an MPEG video bit stream. Projection-based objective quality evaluation demonstrates coding efficiency, in which six primary projected images are derived from various viewing perspectives. In addition, point-based quality assessment are also conducted to reveal the respective geometry and color qualities affected by compression noise. This work addresses the challenge of an end-to-end content delivery chain for realistic 6DoF video, and establishes ground for further improvement. Future work may include the optimization of the video-based point cloud coder and the investigation of a more perceptually-related quality metric for 6DoF video.

Acknowledgements. This work is supported in part by Aeronautical Science Foundation of China under Grant 201951052001, the Natural Science Foundation of Jiangsu Province under Grant BK20170806, and the Natural Science Foundation of China under Grant 61701227. The authors would like to thank Prof. A. Smolic, Dr. E. Zerman, and Dr. C. Ozcinar for their guidance and helpful advice on various technical issues examined in this paper. The authors also would like to thank Volograms Ltd. For making their created holograms accessible.

References

1. Point cloud compression category 2 reference software, TMC2 v7.0. http://mpegx. intevry.fr/software/MPEG/PCC/TM/mpeg-pcc-tmc2.git. Accessed Mar 2020
2. Collet, A., et al.: High-quality streamable free-viewpoint video. ACM Trans. Graph. (TOG) **34**(4), 69 (2015)
3. Tian, D., Ochimizu, H., Feng, C., Cohen, R., Vetro, A.: Evaluation metrics for point cloud compression. ISO/IEC JTC1/SC29/WG11 MPEG2016/M39966, Geneva, CH (2017)
4. Eisert, P., Steinbach, E., Girod, B.: Multi-hypothesis, volumetric reconstruction of 3-D objects from multiple calibrated camera views. In: 1999 IEEE International Conference on Acoustics, Speech, and Signal Processing (ICASSP), 1999. Proceedings, vol. 6, pp. 3509–3512 (1999)
5. Hoppe, H., DeRose, T., Duchamp, T., McDonald, J., Stuetzle, W.: Surface reconstruction from unorganized points. In: ACM SIGGRAPH 1992 Proceedings, pp. 71–78 (1992)
6. Mammou, K.: PCC Test Model Category 2 v0. ISO/IEC JTC1/SC29 WG11 Doc. N17248, Macau, China (2017)
7. Krichenbauer, M., Yamamoto, G., Taketom, T., Sandor, C., Kato, H.: Augmented reality versus virtual reality for 3D object manipulation. IEEE Trans. Visual. Comput. Graph. **24**(2), 1038–1048 (2018)
8. Kubota, A., Smolic, A., Magnor, M., Tanimoto, M., Chen, T., Zhang, C.: Multiview imaging and 3DTV. IEEE Signal Process. Mag. **24**(6), 10–21 (2007)
9. Liu, Y., Dai, Q., Xu, W.: A point-cloud-based multiview stereo algorithm for freeviewpoint video. IEEE Trans. Visual. Comput. Graph. **16**(3), 407–418 (2010)
10. Maglo, A., Lavoué, G., Dupont, F., Hudelot, C.: 3D mesh compression: survey, comparisons, and emerging trends. ACM Comput. Surv. **47**(3), 44 (2015)
11. Mamou, K., Zaharia, T., Prêteux, F.: FAMC: the MPEG-4 standard for animated mesh compression. In: 15th IEEE International Conference on Image Processing, 2008. ICIP 2008, pp. 2676–2679. IEEE (2008)
12. Mamou, K., Zaharia, T., Prêteux, F.: TFAN: a low complexity 3D mesh compression algorithm. Comput. Anim. Virtual Worlds **20**(2–3), 343–354 (2009)

13. Mekuria, R., Sanna, M., Izquierdo, E., Bulterman, D.C., Cesar, P.: Enabling geometry-based 3-D tele-immersion with fast mesh compression and linear rateless coding. IEEE Trans. Multimedia **16**(7), 1809–1820 (2014)
14. Muja, M., G. Lowe, D.: Fast approximate nearest neighbors with automatic algorithm configuration. In: VISAPP International Conference on Computer Vision Theory and Applications, pp. 331–340 (2009)
15. Pagés, R., Amplianitis, K., Monaghan, D., Ondřej, J., Smolić, A.: Affordable content creation for free-viewpoint video and VR/AR applications. J. Vis. Commun. Image Represent. **53**, 192–201 (2018)
16. Peters, J., Reif, U.: Subdivision Surfaces. Springer, Heidelberg (2008). https://doi.org/10.1007/978-3-540-76406-9
17. Smolic, A., et al.: Free viewpoint video extraction, representation, coding, and rendering. In: IEEE International Conference on Image Processing, 2004. ICIP 2004, vol. 5, pp. 3287–3290 (2004)
18. Starck, J., Hilton, A.: Surface capture for performance-based animation. IEEE Comput. Graph. Appl. **27**(3), 21–31 (2007)
19. Sullivan, G.J., Ohm, J.R., Han, W.J., Wiegand, T., et al.: Overview of the high efficiency video coding (HEVC) standard. IEEE Trans. Circuits Syst. Video Technol. **22**(12), 1649–1668 (2012)
20. Theobalt, C., Ziegler, G., Magnor, M., Seidel, H.P.: Model-based free-viewpoint video: acquisition, rendering, and encoding. In: Proceedings of Picture Coding Symposium, San Francisco, USA, pp. 1–6 (2004)
21. Wang, Z., Bovik, A.C., Sheikh, H.R., Simoncelli, E.P.: Image quality assessment: from error visibility to structural similarity. IEEE Trans. Image Process. **13**(4), 600–612 (2004)
22. Wu, C., Varanasi, K., Liu, Y., Seidel, H.P., Theobalt, C.: Shading-based dynamic shape refinement from multi-view video under general illumination. In: 2011 IEEE International Conference on Computer Vision (ICCV), pp. 1108–1115 (2011)
23. Zerman, E., Gao, P., Ozcinar, C., Smolic, A.: Subjective and objective quality assessment for volumetric video compression. In: IS&T Electronic Imaging, Image Quality and System Performance XVI (2019)

Adaptive Self-supervised Depth Estimation in Monocular Videos

Julio Mendoza[iD] and Helio Pedrini[✉][iD]

Institute of Computing, University of Campinas, Campinas, SP 13083-852, Brazil
helio@ic.unicamp.br

Abstract. In this work, we develop and evaluate two adaptive strategies to self-supervised depth estimation methods based on view reconstruction. First, we propose an adaptive consistency loss that extends the usage of minimum re-projection to enforce consistency on the pixel intensities, structure, and feature maps. Moreover, we evaluate two approaches to use uncertainty to weigh the error contribution in the input frames. Finally, we improve our model with a composite visibility mask. The results show that the adaptive consistency loss can effectively combine photometric, structure and feature consistency terms. Moreover, weighting the error contribution using uncertainty can improve the performance of a simpler version of the model, but cannot improve them model when all improvements are considered. Finally, our combined model achieves competitive results when compared to state-of-the-art methods.

Keywords: Depth estimation · View synthesis · Monocular videos

1 Introduction

Dense depth maps are useful representations of a scene that have been used in several computer vision applications, such as 3D reconstruction, virtual and augmented reality, robot navigation, scene interaction and autonomous driving. Depth maps can be obtained with sensors. However, in some scenarios, it is unfeasible to rely solely on them. Such demand has increased the interest in the development of effective methods, and recently it has motivated the development of approaches based on deep learning.

The existing data sets for depth estimation have enabled training deep models in a supervised approach. However, the size, quality and availability of labeled data sets are becoming a barrier for supervised approaches. Researchers use complex and costly procedures to collect ground truth and the available data sets are smaller than the ones used in other computer vision tasks.

In recent years, various self-supervised approaches have been proposed to learn depth maps from monocular videos. These methods rely on appearance and geometric consistency among nearby frames on videos, to reconstruct a reference frame with the intensities of another frame and to use the reconstruction error as a supervisory signal. Thus, these methods can learn dense depth maps without

© Springer Nature Switzerland AG 2021
Y. Peng et al. (Eds.): ICIG 2021, LNCS 12890, pp. 687–699, 2021.
https://doi.org/10.1007/978-3-030-87361-5_56

labeled data sets and can take advantage of the vast amount and rich variability of video data available.

One of the main challenges of self-supervised approaches based on reconstruction is that some pixels in frame cannot be explained from other frames because of occlusion, specular reflection, textureless regions among other reasons. Several approaches deal with these challenges excluding or attenuating the influence of pixels based on priors or adaptive approaches that leverage the availability of multiple frames neighboring a target frame to explain their pixels.

In this work, we develop and evaluate two adaptive strategies to improve the robustness of self-supervised depth estimation approaches with pixels that violate the assumptions of view reconstruction. Initially, we develop an adaptive consistency loss that extends the usage of minimum re-projection to enforce consistency on 3D structure and feature maps, in addition to the photometric consistency. Moreover, we evaluate the usage of uncertainty as loss attenuation mechanism, where the uncertainty is learned by modeling predictions as Laplacian, smooth-L1 or Cauchy probability distributions. Finally, we improve our model with a composite visibility mask.

2   Related Work

View Reconstruction Based Depth Estimation. Deep learning approaches based on view reconstruction leverage the correspondence between the pixels of two views of the same scene. This correspondence could be computed with the relative pose between cameras that captures both views, and a depth map of a single view. This principle was used by Garg et al. [5], where a stereo pair provides the views, the parameters of the device give the relative pose, and a depth network predicts the depth map. Similarly, Zhou et al. [28] proposed a method where the relative pose and the depth map are estimated with deep networks.

These approaches have been improved, for example, to deal with occluded regions that cannot be reconstructed using geometric priors [15,17], to deal with moving objects, which violate the static assumption of view reconstruction, using optical flow [9,26] or segmenting and estimating the motion of moving objects [2,14,23], and to improve the learning signal by enforcing consistency between several representations of the scene [3,17,26]. Our approach improves the learning signal enforcing consistency between 3D coordinates, feature maps, and color information of the views.

Consistency Constraints. The availability of a correspondence between the pixels on the source and target views allows supervision by enforcing consistency on representations, in addition to the pixel intensities. For example, we can enforce consistency between forward and backward optical flows [16,26], predicted and projected depth maps [7,16], 3D coordinates [17], and feature maps [20,27]. However, we cannot enforce consistency in the entire image because some regions do not have valid correspondences, for example, occluded regions produced by the motion of the camera or objects, or regions with specular reflection where the color is inconsistent with the structure of the scene, and also due to multiple correspondences for single pixels at homogeneous regions do not provide supervision. Approaches that exclude or attenuate the error contribution of these regions have been proposed in the literature. For example, learning an explainability mask [28], excluding pixels that are projected out of the field of view [17], excluding pixels with high inconsistencies on optical flows or depth maps [26], excluding stationary pixels [8], excluding occluded pixels using to geometric cues [9], attenuating the error using similar criteria [18]. Another approach leverage the availability of correspondences from multiple source frames [8] or estimated from different models [3], considering only the correspondences with minimum photometric error. Our approach extends the minimum re-projection error on other consistency constraints in addition to photometric consistency.

Adaptive Losses Based on Uncertainty. The importance of quantifying the uncertainty on predictions has motivated research endeavors in several problems on computer vision, such as robust regression [1], representation learning [22], object detection [11], image de-raining [25], optical flow [12] and depth estimation [13,19,21,24]. Researchers have explored approaches that leverage uncertainty information for depth estimation, for instance, a method that leverages existing uncertainty estimation techniques [21] and an approach that predicts the uncertainty using a neural network [13,19,24]. A recent work explored approaches to estimate epistemic uncertainty and aleatoric uncertainty on an unsupervised monocular setting [19]. In this work, we explore several probability functions to predict aleatoric uncertainty to improve depth estimation.

3   Method

Figure 1 illustrates the main components of our method. In this section, we provide an overview of our baseline system. Moreover, we introduce two adaptive strategies to improve the robustness of our approach. Finally, we explore additional constraints.

3.1   Preliminaries

Approaches that use view reconstruction as main supervisory signal require to find correspondences between pixel coordinates on frames that represent views of the same scene. These correspondences can be computed using multi-view geometry. Given a pixel coordinate x_t in a target frame $\mathbf{I_t}$, we can obtain its coordinate x_s in a source frame $\mathbf{I_s}$ by back-projecting x_t to the camera coordinate system of the $\mathbf{I_t}$ using its depth value $\mathbf{D_t}(x_t)$, and the inverse of its intrinsic matrix $\mathbf{K}^{-1}$. Then, the relative motion transformation $\mathbf{T_{t \to s}}$ is applied to project the coordinates form the coordinate system of the $\mathbf{I_t}$ to the coordinate system of $\mathbf{I_s}$. Finally, the coordinates are projected onto the image plane in the source

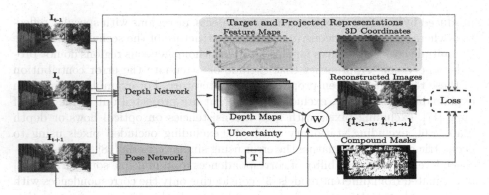

Fig. 1. Overview of our method. The depth network is used to predict the depth maps for the target $\mathbf{I_t}$ and source images $\mathbf{I_s} \in \{\mathbf{I_{t-1}}, \mathbf{I_{t+1}}\}$. The pose network predicts the Euclidean transformation between the target and source camera coordinate systems $\mathbf{T_{t \to s}}$.

frame. We express this correspondence in Eq. 1. We refer the reader to [28] for a detailed explanation.

$$x_s \sim \mathbf{K T_{t \to s} D_t}(x_t) \mathbf{K}^{-1} x_t \tag{1}$$

Once we know the projected coordinates and, therefore, the pixel intensities in the source image plane for each pixel x_t in the target image, we reconstruct the target frame $\hat{\mathbf{I}}_{\mathbf{s \to t}}(x_t) = \mathbf{I_s}(x_s)$. This process is known as image warping. This approach requires the dense depth map $\mathbf{D_t}$ of the target image, which we aim to reconstruct, the Euclidean transformation $\mathbf{T_{t \to s}}$, and camera intrinsics $\mathbf{K}$. Our model predicts the depth maps and the Euclidean transformation using convolutional neural networks and assumes that the camera intrinsics are given. The networks are trained using the reconstruction error as supervisory signal.

3.2   Adaptive Consistency Loss

Consistency could be enforced on representations of the scene such as 3D structure and feature maps. We propose an *adaptive consistency loss* that, in addition to the photometric consistency, also considers 3D structure and feature consistency constraints. This idea leverages the robustness of the min-reprojection error to pixels with high reconstruction error that could potentially be outliers. The adaptive consistency loss is defined as follows:

$$\mathcal{L}_{ac} = \sum_{x_t \in \mathbf{I_t}} \min_{\mathbf{I_s}} \Big(M_o(x_t) \Big(\rho_{pc}\big(\mathbf{I_t}(x_t), \hat{\mathbf{I}}_{\mathbf{s \to t}}(x_s)\big)$$
$$+ \lambda_{sc}\rho_{sc}\big(\mathbf{C_{s \to t}}(x_t), \hat{\mathbf{C}}_{\mathbf{s \to t}}(x_s)\big) + \lambda_{fc}\rho_{fc}\big(\mathbf{\Phi_t}(x_t), \hat{\mathbf{\Phi}}_{\mathbf{s \to t}}(x_s)\big) \Big) \Big) \tag{2}$$

where ρ_{pc} measures the photometric consistency between pixels on the original $\mathbf{I_t}$ and reconstructed images $\hat{\mathbf{I}}_{\mathbf{s \to t}}$, ρ_{sc} measures the structure consistency between the 3D-coordinates of the target image projected to the camera coordinate system of the source image $\mathbf{C}_{s \to t}$, and the 3D-coordinates of the source image in its own camera coordinate system $\hat{\mathbf{C}}_{s \to t}$, and ρ_{fc} measure the feature dissimilarity between the feature vectors for all pixels, and obtained from the target $\mathbf{\Phi}_t$, and the warped source feature maps $\hat{\mathbf{\Phi}}_{s \to t}$. The feature maps are extracted from the decoder part of the depth network. M_o is a visibility mask that excludes pixels that lie out the field-of-view on the source frame [17].

Our photometric error function ρ_{pc} is a combination of an $L1$ distance and the structure similarity index metric (SSIM), with a trade-off parameter α. This function is shown in Eq. 3.

$$\rho_{pc}(p, q) = ||p - q||_1 + \alpha \frac{1 - \text{SSIM}(p, q)}{2} \tag{3}$$

Our structure error function ρ_{sc} is the average of a normalized absolute difference of the coordinates as follows:

$$\rho_{sc}(x, y) = \frac{1}{3} \sum_{i=1}^{3} \frac{|x_i - y_i|}{|x_i| + |y_i|} \tag{4}$$

Our feature dissimilarity function ρ_{sc} measures the squared L_2 distance of the L_2 normalized feature vectors $\hat{f}_s = f_s / ||f_s||_2$ and $\hat{f}_t = f_t / ||f_t||_2$, with $f_s = \hat{\mathbf{\Phi}}_{s \to t}(x_s)$ and $f_t = \mathbf{\Phi}_t(x_t)$.

$$\rho_{fc}(f_s, f_t) = ||\hat{f}_s - \hat{f}_t||_2^2 \tag{5}$$

The total loss is the sum of the adaptive consistency loss and depth smoothness loss term [7] for the defined output scales $\mathcal{S}$.

$$\mathcal{L}_{total} = \sum_{i \in \mathcal{S}} \mathcal{L}_{ac}^{(i)} + \mathcal{L}_{ds}^{(i)} \tag{6}$$

3.3 Error Weighting Using Uncertainty

The adaptive consistency loss can handle cases in which at least one the source images can provide the information to reconstruct each pixel. However, several cases might break this condition, for instance, homogeneous regions and regions with specular reflection. Therefore, we aim to find other mechanisms to handle pixels with large error on these cases.

An approach is to allow the model to learn the uncertainty about the depth estimates, and leverage this information to attenuate the effect of pixels with large errors on the overall error. We can do that by placing a probability distribution function over the outputs of the model. The predicted depth values $\mathbf{D}_t(x_t)$ are modeled as corrupted with additive random noise sampled from a PDF with a scale parameter σ_{x_t} that is predicted by depth network. σ_{x_t} quantifies the uncertainty of the model on the predictions. The model is trained to minimize the negative log-likelihood.

First, we assume that noise comes from a Laplacian distribution, then the error function is the negative log-likelihood of this distribution. Equation 7 shows the error function.

$$\rho_{Laplacian}(p_t, p_s) = \frac{|\rho_{pc}(p_t, p_s)|}{\sigma_{x_t}} + \log(2\sigma_{x_t}) \tag{7}$$

where $p_t = \mathbf{I_t}(\mathbf{x_t})$, $p_s = \hat{\mathbf{I}}_{\mathbf{s} \to \mathbf{t}}(x_s)$, ρ_{pc} is the photometric error function, and σ_{x_t} is the predicted uncertainty for the pixel x_t.

We can observe that the first term in Eq. 7 attenuates the error when the uncertainty is high. Then, the second term discourages the model to predict high uncertainty values for all pixels. Thus, in order to minimize the function, the model is encouraged to predict high uncertainty values for pixels with large errors, attenuating the influence of large error in the overall error.

In order to explore the space of probability functions, we also evaluate our approach on the smooth-L1 functions and the Cauchy functions [1]. We define the probability distribution associated to the smooth-L1 function using the family of probability distributions defined in [1]. Equation 8 shows the negative log-likelihood associated to the smooth-L1 function.

$$\rho_{smooth-L1}(p_t, p_s) = \sqrt{\left(\frac{\rho_{pc}(p_t, p_s)}{\sigma_{x_t}}\right)^2 + 1} - 1 + \log(Z(1)) \tag{8}$$

where $Z(1)$ is a normalization factor for smooth-L1 function. We refer the reader to [1] for a detailed explanation. Finally, Eq. 9 shows the negative log-likelihood associated with the Cauchy distribution.

$$\rho_{Cauchy}(p_t, p_s) = \log\left(\frac{1}{2}\left(\frac{\rho_{pc}(p_t, p_s)}{\sigma_{x_t}}\right)^2 + 1\right) + \log(\sqrt{2\pi}\sigma_{x_t}) \tag{9}$$

Similarly, we propose to attenuate the error contribution in the scale of the images. This is a single uncertainty σ_t is predicted by each image. In the training process, the uncertainty is optimized to match to the distribution of errors for all the pixels of each image.

3.4   Exploring Visibility Masks

We combine several strategies to filter out pixels that are likely to be outliers. We mask the pixels on the target image that lie out of the field-of-view on the source image, also known as principled mask [26], the pixels that belong to homogeneous regions and do not change their appearance, even when the camera is moving [8], and the target pixels that are occluded in the source view [9]. The resulting composite mask is applied to our adaptive consistency loss at each scale.

3.5   Implementation Details

The depth network is a convolutional encoder-decoder network with skip connections. We used a ResNet18 as backbone for the encoder part of the depth network. The decoder network is composed of deconvolutional layers that upsample the bottleneck representation in order to upscale the feature maps to the input resolution. For uncertainty estimation, we add a channel on the output of the depth network. In order to predict uncertainty pixel values, the extra channel is used as uncertainty map. On the other hand, when we aim to predict a single uncertainty value for image, we use spatial average pooling over the uncertainty map. The motion network predicts the relative motion between two input frames. The relative camera motion has a 6-DoF representation that corresponds to 3 rotation angles and the translation vector. The motion network is composed of the first five layers of the ResNet18 architecture, followed by a spatial average pooling and four 1×1 convolutional layers.

4   Experiments

In this section, we show the experiments conducted to evaluate each component of our system separately, as well the complete system with the proposed components.

4.1   Experiments Setup

Dataset. We use the KITTI benchmark [6]. It was created to reduce the bias and to complement available benchmarks with real-world data. It is composed of video sequences with 93 thousand images acquired through high-quality RGB cameras captured by driving on rural areas and highways of a city. We used the Eigen split [4] with 45023 images for training and 687 for testing. Moreover, we partitioned the training set on 40441 for training, 4582 for validation. For result evaluation, we used the standard metrics [4].

Training. Our networks are trained using ADAM optimization algorithm with a learning rate of $2e - 5$, $\beta_1 = 0.9$, $\beta_2 = 0.999$, $\epsilon = 10^{-8}$. We used the batch size of 12 snippets. Each snippet is a 3-frame sequence. The frames are resized to a resolution of 416×128 pixels.

4.2   Adaptive Consistency Loss

Table 1 shows the performance of the baseline model improved by considering the spatial and feature consistency loss terms individually, as well as combined using average and minimum re-projection. The first rows shows the results of our baseline model that only considers the photometric consistency and depth smoothness loss terms. Then, we evaluate the performance of the model including structure and feature consistency terms individually and jointly by using average or minimum re-projection. As other works in the literature [7,16,17,20,27], we show that including structure and feature consistency terms is beneficial. The results indicate that our implementations of structure and feature consistency can improve the performance of the model individually, in most of the metrics. Furthermore, we show that both terms are complementary and, together, can improve the performance with average and minimum re-projection losses. We obtained better results with minimum re-projection error.

Table 1. Ablation study. We evaluate the performance of structure and feature consistency terms with average re-projection, and the adaptive consistency loss, which uses minimum re-projection error.

Avg.	Min.	SC	FC	↓ Lower is better				↑ Higher is better		
				Abs Rel	Sq Rel	RMSE	Log RMSE	$\delta < 1.25$	$\delta < 1.25^2$	$\delta < 1.25^3$
				0.1116	0.8905	4.7177	0.1840	0.8717	0.9564	0.9817
✓		✓		0.1113	1.0024	4.6312	0.1807	0.8797	0.9595	0.9823
✓			✓	0.1104	<u>0.8747</u>	4.6005	0.1800	0.8785	0.9587	0.9825
✓		✓	✓	<u>0.1096</u>	1.0134	<u>4.5476</u>	<u>0.1776</u>	**0.8838**	<u>0.9611</u>	<u>0.9828</u>
	✓	✓	✓	**0.1059**	**0.7520**	**4.4537**	**0.1737**	<u>0.8834</u>	**0.9620**	**0.9848**

4.3 Error Weighting Using Uncertainty

We evaluate the usage of uncertainty to weigh the error contribution when the uncertainty values are predicted by pixel and by image.

Error Weighting by Pixel. Table 2 shows that predicting uncertainty to weight the error contribution by pixel improves the performance of the baseline model using smooth-L1 probability function. However, the variants of the model that use the Laplacian and Cauchy distribution degrade the results.

We observe that the model predicts incorrect depth values on regions where the pixel intensities vary. This variation occurs because the predictive uncertainty is formulated on the photo-metric consistency term (Eq. 7).

Table 2. Using uncertainty to weigh the error contribution by pixel.

Method	↓ Lower is better				↑ Higher is better		
	Abs Rel	Sq Rel	RMSE	Log RMSE	$\delta < 1.25$	$\delta < 1.25^2$	$\delta < 1.25^3$
Baseline-L1	0.1894	4.1497	5.9739	0.2433	**0.8111**	0.9228	0.9599
Laplacian	0.1987	4.4033	6.0675	0.2481	0.8034	0.9216	0.9593
Smooth-L1	**0.1810**	**3.0795**	**5.6726**	**0.2386**	0.8027	**0.9245**	**0.9634**
Cauchy	0.1968	3.2513	5.9439	0.2540	0.7836	0.9147	0.9565

Error Weighting by Image. Table 3 shows the effect of predictive uncertainty by image to weight the error contribution of images using the Laplacian, Smooth-L1, and Cauchy probability functions. The first row shows our baseline, which use an L1 distance between pixel intensities to measure photometric consistency and depth smoothness.

Our results indicate that the Smooth-L1 function improves the performance of the baseline and outperforms the approaches that assume other distributions. However, using uncertainties predicted through Laplacian and Cauchy functions does not improve the performance. Qualitative results are illustrated in Fig. 2.

Table 3. Using uncertainty to weigh the error contribution by image.

Method	↓ Lower is better				↑ Higher is better		
	Abs Rel	Sq Rel	RMSE	Log RMSE	$\delta < 1.25$	$\delta < 1.25^2$	$\delta < 1.25^3$
Baseline-L1	0.1894	4.1497	5.9739	0.2433	0.8111	0.9228	0.9599
Laplacian	0.1928	4.4074	5.9921	0.2472	**0.8153**	0.9234	0.9598
Smooth-L1	**0.1561**	**1.3712**	**5.3931**	**0.2239**	0.8018	**0.9286**	**0.9683**
Cauchy	0.1976	3.3892	6.0628	0.2530	0.7846	0.9160	0.9600

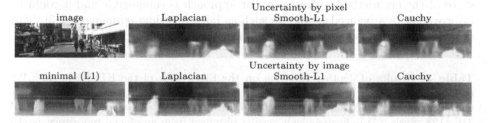

Fig. 2. Qualitative results of error weighting approach with uncertainty. The first column shows a target image and its depth maps predicted with the minimal model. The remaining columns show the results for the error weighting approaches for the PDF associated to Laplacian, Smooth-L1 and Cauchy functions. For each function, the first and second rows show the result of considering an uncertainty value by pixel and by image, respectively.

4.4 Visibility Masks

We performed ablation studies with visibility masks to filter out inconsistent pixels. We used model trained with the adaptive consistency loss as baseline. Table 4 shows that every mask improves the error metrics, as well as the thresholded accuracy metrics. Moreover, the model trained with all mask formulations achieved better results. Qualitative results are illustrated in Fig. 3.

Table 4. Ablation study of additional masks. We considered the Field-of-View masks (FOV), Auto mask (AM), Geometric mask (GM).

			↓ Lower is better				↑ Higher is better		
FOV	AM	GM	Abs Rel	Sq Rel	RMSE	Log RMSE	$\delta < 1.25$	$\delta < 1.25^2$	$\delta < 1.25^3$
✓			<u>0.1059</u>	**0.7520**	4.4537	0.1737	0.8834	0.9620	**0.9848**
✓	✓		0.1063	0.8071	4.5570	0.1779	0.8829	0.9612	0.9831
✓		✓	0.1073	0.9355	**4.4135**	<u>0.1734</u>	<u>0.8877</u>	**0.9629**	<u>0.9840</u>
✓	✓	✓	**0.1015**	<u>0.7692</u>	<u>4.4297</u>	**0.1719**	**0.8890**	<u>0.9622</u>	0.9839

Fig. 3. Qualitative results. Depth prediction using our final model.

4.5   Comparison with the State of the Art

Table 5 shows that our method achieved competitive results when compared to state-of-the-art methods. Moreover, our approach is compatible and it could be improved with advanced strategies such as inference-time refinement [2,3], joint depth and optical flow estimation [3], and effective architecture designs [10].

Table 5. Results of depth estimation on the Eigen split of the KITTI dataset. We compared our results against several methods of the literature. In order to allow a fair comparison, we report the results of competitive methods trained with a resolution of 416×128 pixels. (*) indicates newly results obtained from an official repository. (-ref.) indicates that the online refinement component is disabled.

Method	↓ Lower is better				↑ Higher is better		
	Abs Rel	Sq Rel	RMSE	Log RMSE	$\delta < 1.25$	$\delta < 1.25^2$	$\delta < 1.25^3$
Zhou et al. [28]*	0.183	1.595	6.709	0.270	0.734	0.902	0.959
Mahjourian et al. [17]	0.163	1.240	6.220	0.250	0.762	0.916	0.967
Ying et al. [26]*	0.149	1.060	5.567	0.226	0.796	0.935	0.975
Casser et al. [2] (-ref.)	0.141	<u>1.026</u>	5.290	0.215	0.816	0.945	<u>0.979</u>
Chen et al. [3] (-ref.)	0.135	1.070	5.230	<u>0.210</u>	0.841	0.948	**0.980**
Gordon et al. [9]	<u>0.129</u>	**0.959**	5.230	0.213	0.840	0.945	0.976
Ours	0.131	1.037	<u>5.173</u>	**0.204**	<u>0.846</u>	<u>0.952</u>	**0.980**
Godard et al. [8]	**0.128**	1.087	**5.171**	**0.204**	**0.855**	**0.953**	0.978

5   Conclusions

In this work, we show that minimum re-projection can be used to jointly enforce consistency on photometric, 3D structure, and feature representations of frames. This approach reduces the influence of pixels without valid correspondences on other consistency constraints, in addition to photometric consistency.

Moreover, our results suggest that the error weighting approaches based on predictive uncertainty at pixel and image levels can be beneficial when the model is minimal, when the model does not implement additional strategies to handle invalid correspondences and when the outputs are assumed to follow the probability distribution derived from the smooth-L1 function. Further exploration could be done to leverage uncertainty to improve the performance of self-supervised depth estimation methods that consider several priors to handle invalid correspondences.

Acknowledgments. The authors are thankful to National Council for Scientific and Technological Development (CNPq grant #309330/2018-1) and São Paulo Research Foundation (FAPESP grants #17/12646-3 and #2018/00031-7) for their financial support.

References

1. Barron, J.T.: A general and adaptive robust loss function. In: IEEE Conference on Computer Vision and Pattern Recognition, pp. 4331–4339 (2019)
2. Casser, V., Pirk, S., Mahjourian, R., Angelova, A.: Depth prediction without the sensors: leveraging structure for unsupervised learning from monocular videos. In: AAAI Conference on Artificial Intelligence, vol. 33, pp. 8001–8008 (2019)
3. Chen, Y., Schmid, C., Sminchisescu, C.: Self-supervised learning with geometric constraints in monocular video: connecting flow, depth, and camera. In: IEEE International Conference on Computer Vision, pp. 7063–7072 (2019)
4. Eigen, D., Puhrsch, C., Fergus, R.: Depth map prediction from a single image using a multi-scale deep network. In: Advances in Neural Information Processing Systems, pp. 2366–2374 (2014)
5. Garg, R., B.G., V.K., Carneiro, G., Reid, I.: Unsupervised CNN for single view depth estimation: geometry to the rescue. In: Leibe, B., Matas, J., Sebe, N., Welling, M. (eds.) ECCV 2016. LNCS, vol. 9912, pp. 740–756. Springer, Cham (2016). https://doi.org/10.1007/978-3-319-46484-8_45
6. Geiger, A., Lenz, P., Stiller, C., Urtasun, R.: Vision meets robotics: the KITTI dataset. Int. J. Robot. Res. **32**(11), 1231–1237 (2013)
7. Godard, C., Mac Aodha, O., Brostow, G.J.: Unsupervised monocular depth estimation with left-right consistency. In: IEEE Conference on Computer Vision and Pattern Recognition, pp. 270–279 (2017)
8. Godard, C., Mac Aodha, O., Firman, M., Brostow, G.J.: Digging into self-supervised monocular depth prediction. In: International Conference on Computer Vision (ICCV), October 2019
9. Gordon, A., Li, H., Jonschkowski, R., Angelova, A.: Depth from videos in the wild: unsupervised monocular depth learning from unknown cameras. arXiv preprint arXiv:1904.04998 (2019)

10. Guizilini, V., Ambrus, R., Pillai, S., Raventos, A., Gaidon, A.: 3D packing for self-supervised monocular depth estimation. In: IEEE/CVF Conference on Computer Vision and Pattern Recognition, pp. 2485–2494 (2020)

11. He, Y., Zhu, C., Wang, J., Savvides, M., Zhang, X.: Bounding box regression with uncertainty for accurate object detection. In: IEEE Conference on Computer Vision and Pattern Recognition, pp. 2888–2897 (2019)

12. Ilg, E., et al.: Uncertainty estimates and multi-hypotheses networks for optical flow. In: Ferrari, V., Hebert, M., Sminchisescu, C., Weiss, Y. (eds.) ECCV 2018. LNCS, vol. 11211, pp. 677–693. Springer, Cham (2018). https://doi.org/10.1007/978-3-030-01234-2_40

13. Klodt, M., Vedaldi, A.: Supervising the new with the old: learning SFM from SFM. In: Ferrari, V., Hebert, M., Sminchisescu, C., Weiss, Y. (eds.) ECCV 2018. LNCS, vol. 11214, pp. 713–728. Springer, Cham (2018). https://doi.org/10.1007/978-3-030-01249-6_43

14. Lee, M., Fowlkes, C.C.: CeMNet: self-supervised learning for accurate continuous ego-motion estimation. In: IEEE Conference on Computer Vision and Pattern Recognition Workshops, pp. 1–8 (2019)

15. Li, R., Wang, S., Long, Z., Gu, D.: UnDeepVO: monocular visual odometry through unsupervised deep learning. In: IEEE International Conference on Robotics and Automation, pp. 7286–7291. IEEE (2018)

16. Luo, C., et al.: Every pixel counts++: joint learning of geometry and motion with 3D holistic understanding. arXiv preprint arXiv:1810.06125 (2018)

17. Mahjourian, R., Wicke, M., Angelova, A.: Unsupervised learning of depth and ego-motion from monocular video using 3D geometric constraints. In: IEEE Conference on Computer Vision and Pattern Recognition, pp. 5667–5675 (2018)

18. Mendoza, J., Pedrini, H.: Self-supervised depth estimation based on feature sharing and consistency constraints. In: 15th International Joint Conference on Computer Vision, Imaging and Computer Graphics Theory and Applications, Valletta, Malta, pp. 134–141, February 2020

19. Poggi, M., Aleotti, F., Tosi, F., Mattoccia, S.: On the uncertainty of self-supervised monocular depth estimation. In: IEEE/CVF Conference on Computer Vision and Pattern Recognition, pp. 3227–3237 (2020)

20. Shi, Y., Zhu, J., Fang, Y., Lien, K., Gu, J.: Self-supervised learning of depth and ego-motion with differentiable bundle adjustment. arXiv preprint arXiv:1909.13163 (2019)

21. Tonioni, A., Poggi, M., Mattoccia, S., Di Stefano, L.: Unsupervised domain adaptation for depth prediction from images. IEEE Trans. Pattern Anal. Mach. Intell. 42(10), 2396–2409 (2019)

22. Wiles, O., Sophia Koepke, A., Zisserman, A.: Self-supervised learning of class embeddings from video. In: IEEE/CVF International Conference on Computer Vision Workshops, pp. 1–8 (2019)

23. Xu, H., Zheng, J., Cai, J., Zhang, J.: Region deformer networks for unsupervised depth estimation from unconstrained monocular videos. arXiv preprint arXiv:1902.09907 (2019)

24. Yang, N., von Stumberg, L., Wang, R., Cremers, D.: D3VO: deep depth, deep pose and deep uncertainty for monocular visual odometry. arXiv preprint arXiv:2003.01060 (2020)

25. Yasarla, R., Patel, V.M.: Uncertainty guided multi-scale residual learning-using a cycle spinning CNN for single image de-raining. In: IEEE/CVF Conference on Computer Vision and Pattern Recognition, pp. 8405–8414 (2019)

26. Yin, Z., Shi, J.: GeoNet: unsupervised learning of dense depth, optical flow and camera pose. In: IEEE Conference on Computer Vision and Pattern Recognition, pp. 1983–1992 (2018)
27. Zhan, H., Garg, R., Saroj Weerasekera, C., Li, K., Agarwal, H., Reid, I.: Unsupervised learning of monocular depth estimation and visual odometry with deep feature reconstruction. In: The IEEE Conference on Computer Vision and Pattern Recognition, pp. 340–349 (2018)
28. Zhou, T., Brown, M., Snavely, N., Lowe, D.G.: Unsupervised learning of depth and ego-motion from video. In: IEEE Conference on Computer Vision and Pattern Recognition, pp. 1851–1858 (2017)

Drowning Detection Based on Video Anomaly Detection

Xinyu He[1,2], Fei Yuan[1,2], and Yi Zhu[1,2(✉)]

[1] Key Laboratory of Underwater Acoustic Communication and Marine Information Technology, Xiamen University, Ministry of Education, Xiamen, China
zhuyi@xmu.edu.cn
[2] Department of Communication Engineering, School of Information, Xiamen University, Xiamen, China

Abstract. People are always trouble with drowning problems and want a drowning detection method. Almost existing methods extract simulated drowning features for supervised classification, but drowning events are rare abnormal events that are difficult to really simulate. In this paper, an unsupervised video anomaly detection method is proposed to detect pool drowning events. At first, we make a new dataset of pool scenes. Drowning events are only in the test set and the train set only includes pool normal events. Pool dataset is preprocessed and a neural network modified from ResNet is proposed to reconstruct input video frames. The differences between reconstructed frames and ground truth frames are compared to detect anomalous events not in the training set. Experiments show that proposed method is more applicable to video anomaly detection in pool scenes than existing methods and it is feasible that methods based on video anomaly detection for drowning detection.

Keywords: Drowning detection · Anomaly detection · Pool dataset

1 Introduction

Swimming is one of the most popular sports in summer. But drowning problems caused by swimming are perplexing people. Every year, many people lose their lives due to drowning and drowning is a global public problem. Most swimming pools are equipped with professional lifeguards in order to reduce the mortality rate of drowning accidents, but it is difficult for lifeguards to stay focused for a long time to observe swimmers. Therefore, drowning detection in pools is necessary for guaranteeing the safety of swimmers.

Traditional drowning detection algorithms mainly use improved traditional image processing algorithms to extract low-level semantic features. These methods lack robustness. Moreover, most of studies extract simulated drowning features for supervised classification to distinguish normal behaviors and drowning

Y. Peng et al. (Eds.): ICIG 2021, LNCS 12890, pp. 700–711, 2021.
https://doi.org/10.1007/978-3-030-87361-5_57

behaviors, but drowning behaviors are rare abnormal behaviors that are difficult to really simulate. The most representative early drowning detection system is the "Poseidon" drowning alarm system [1] produced by Vision IQ, which monitors the swimmer's activity position in real time through infrared lenses and RGB cameras installed above and inside the pool wall, and determines whether drowning has occurred based on the swimmer's standing time under the water. The drowning early warning system is proposed by the DEWS group at Nanyang Technological University [2]. They use a camera on the swimming pool as a monitoring device and develops a module containing data fusion and Hidden Markov Models to learn unique features of different swimming behaviors to identify early drowning behaviors after foreground detection of swimmers. Nasrin Salehi et al. through a camera erected above the pool, use HSV thresholding mechanism and a contour detection feature for target identification and tracking of swimmers, and the system alerts if a previous tracked swimmer disappears for some time [3].

An unsupervised video detection is proposed to detect drowning events in pool scenes in this work. Video anomaly detection is a challenging task in computer vision. In general, an event is identified as an abnormal event when it occurs rarely or unexpectedly. Therefore, it is difficult to obtain many samples of abnormal events and anomaly detection is not a typical classification problem. Now video anomaly detection algorithms based on unsupervised deep learning perform optimally. Research in this domain usually follows the idea that normal patterns is learned from training sets containing only normal events, and the abnormal events deviating from this representation are detected. Drowning events rarely occur, so they are abnormal events. The video data of normal events including swimming and treading can be collected relatively easily. Therefore, video anomaly detection can also be applied for drowning detection.

The major contributions of our work are summarized as follows: 1) Unsupervised video anomaly detection algorithms are applied in drowning detection for the first time in this paper. 2) We make a new dataset of pool scenes for training neural networks and evaluating this drowning detection algorithm. The dataset contains underwater videos of crowds swimming, treading and simulating drowning. 3) The impact of underwater image preprocessing techniques on the performance of the underwater video anomaly detection algorithm is compared and analyzed. 4) According to the crowd characteristics of pool scenes, a new neural network is proposed for video anomaly detection in pool scenes and compared with other anomaly detection methods, it is shown that the proposed anomaly detection algorithm is reliable and more suitable for pool drowning detection.

2   Related Work

Abnormal events in videos are usually caused by unexpected appearances and motions. There are various methods for video anomaly detection. Extracting spatial and temporal features of videos is the most important step. Previously, some low-level semantic manual features were designed to model the features of videos, but all these manual features lack robustness and good generalization performance in complex scenes. Gradient histograms [4] and optical flow histograms [5] have been widely used. In [6], Markov Random Fields (MRF) are applied to model the normal pattern of the video to detect abnormal events. The mixed dynamic textures (MDT) are used to model normal crowd behavior [7]. A hybrid representation of the local optical flow pattern by a probabilistic PCA (MPPCA) model is used [8]. Normal patterns are then defined by this representation and MRF. In addition to these statistical models, sparse coding or dictionary learning is a popular approach to encode normal patterns [9–11], which assume that any regular pattern can be linearly represented as a linear combination based on a dictionary.

In recent years, deep learning methods have also achieved great success in video anomaly detection tasks. Deep learning methods can extract spatial and temporal features of videos more effectively and obtain high-level semantic features of videos and they have better robustness in complex scenes. However, these methods adopt U-Net structure in neural networks to generate frames, which are susceptible to unstable backgrounds. In [12], D. Xu et al. design a multi-layer autoencoder to learn the features. In another work, M. Hasan et al. propose a convolutional autoencoder to learn video features and to detect anomalies based on reconstruction errors [13]. The spatial-temporal convolutional neural network is designed to capture video features in both spatial and temporal dimensions [14]. Instead of detecting anomalous events by minimizing the reconstruction error of the training data, the new anomaly detection method based on future frame prediction is proposed with multiple constraints and generative adversarial networks to generate high-quality future frame images [15]. Ionescu R T et al. first detect objects on the video and then leverage convolutional autoencoder to extract features for motion objects. They also propose a classification method based on normal clustering of training samples to distinguish normal events and abnormal events [16]. Because powerful convolutional neural networks may be able to reconstruct anomalous video frames well, the augmented memory modules are applied in some recent works [17,18], which attenuate the representation power of convolutional neural networks. In one new work [19], the self-training deep ordinal regression technique is applied to video anomaly detection.

In this paper, the U-Net structure isn't applied for reducing the impact of background information. The proposed network further boosts the robustness of anomaly detection.

3   The Pool Anomaly Detection Dataset

Drowning detection is a difficult problem because the features of drowning are not well defined. The idea of this work is to accomplish the drowning detection task through an unsupervised video anomaly detection algorithm. To train neural networks and evaluate the performance of the video anomaly detection algorithm in pool scenes, this work provides a pool dataset in which drowning events are considered as abnormal events. Currently, two publicly anomaly detection datasets are widely used. They are the CUHK Avenue dataset [11] and the UCSD Pedestrian dataset [7]. The normal patterns in these datasets are relatively homogeneous, such as walking. In addition, they have almost no change of light in the background and the size of the moving objects does not change much. This pool dataset is obtained from an underwater surveillance camera installed on the wall of the pool. The size of a standard pool is 50 m * 21 m, so we choose to first install two cameras in a small area of 12.5 m * 10.5 m to capture according to the size of the pool and the parameters of the underwater cameras. The location of the underwater cameras is shown in Fig. 1. In normal patterns, the posture of the crowd in the video contains a variety of swimming and treading. The drowning event is then simulated by volunteers. The background brightness of the video in this dataset changes, the crowd density changes from sparse to crowded, and the size of the moving object varies widely. In addition, underwater videos are blurry.

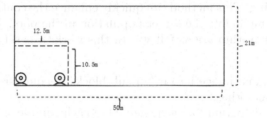

Fig. 1. The location of the underwater camera.

The dataset contains two pool scenes. One is acquired by the left underwater camera and the other is acquired by the right underwater camera. This dataset includes 16 training video clips and 9 test video clips. For each test video clip, the correct annotation includes a binary flag to indicate the presence of anomalies in the frame. This dataset can also be provided for future anomaly detection algorithms. Some samples of the dataset are shown in Fig. 2. The captured underwater videos of normal behavior in the pool contain a variety of scenes, such as standing and swimming. The crowd in the sample include both male and female. The swimming postures include breaststroke, backstroke, freestyle, and other swimming postures. The pool abnormal behavior video also contains single drowning, double drowning, swimming and drowning at the same time.

4 Underwater Image Preprocessing

Due to the complexity of the underwater environment, water produces absorption and scattering effects on light. The phenomenon of color degradation, low contrast and blurred details appear in underwater images acquired by optical vision systems. Therefore, we first enhance acquired underwater frames to

Normal   Abnormal

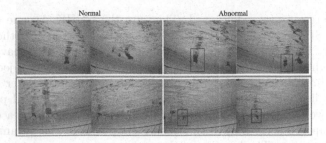

Fig. 2. Some samples including normal and abnormal frames in the Pool datasets are illustrated. Red boxes denote anomalies in abnormal frames. (Color figure online)

enhance the information in the region of interest that is most relevant to the current task and suppress the information in the region of disinterest. Here Contrast-Limited Adaptive Histogram Equalization (CLAHE) is applied for underwater image preprocessing. This method can quickly enhance the contrast of the underwater image and highlights the target population in the pool. The specific steps of the CLAHE algorithm are as follows. In this work, n is set to 8 and c is set to 4.

1. Divide the original image into n * n sub-blocks of equal size and not superimposed on each other.
2. Calculate the histogram for each channel of each sub-block.
3. Calculate the cropping amplitude T with the following formula.

$$T = c * \frac{n_x\, n_y}{K} \tag{1}$$

where n_x and n_y are the number of pixels per sub-block in the x and y directions, K is the number of gray levels and c is the crop factor.
4. Each histogram is cropped using the threshold T. The number of pixels cropped off is reallocated to the corresponding sub-block histogram.
5. Do histogram equalization on the reassigned sub-block histograms and the grayscale mapping function of each sub-block is derived.

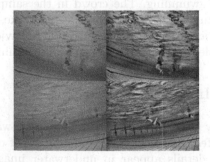

Fig. 3. Some results of underwater image preprocessing. Left: raw image. Right: CLAHE.

6. The bilinear interpolation algorithm is applied to calculate the grayscale values of the corresponding pixels of each sub-block, and the image enhanced by CLAHE algorithm are obtained.

5   Video Anomaly Detection

We first preprocess underwater images and propose a new neural network with a codec structure. The proposed network is mainly used to extract spatial features and temporal features of the video.

Network Architecture. Deep neural networks have been performing well in image and video processing tasks and can extract the features of images and videos well. Therefore, a deep neural network is designed for extracting features of normal behavior. Because the training set in the video anomaly detection task only contains video frames with normal events, a coded and decoded neural network structure is often designed to reconstruct video frames and compare the reconstructed video frames with the ground truth for video anomaly detection.

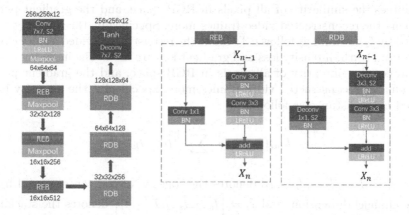

Fig. 4. Left: The architecture of our proposed network. Middle: The detailed architecture of REB (residual encoding block). Right: The detailed architecture of RDB (residual decoding block). S2 denotes stride 2 in the convolution layer.

The encoder usually extracts video frame features and the decoder usually recovers video frames. ResNet is often used in image classification tasks [20], and we modify ResNet and change it into a codec image generation network for video anomaly detection tasks. The encoder mainly consists of one convolutional layer, three max pooling layers and three residual coding base modules. The decoder mainly consists of three residual decoding base modules and one deconvolution layer. The residual coding module and the residual decoding module are modified from the base module in ResNet. The residual connection can alleviate the gradient disappearance problem to a certain extent, which is conducive to learning features to further improve the network performance. Compared with other networks, this network also has a larger receptive field and is more suitable for crowd targets in swimming pools. The structure of the network is shown in Fig. 4. We use a 7×7 convolutional kernel with a step size of 2×2 in the first convolutional layer. Batch normalization is applied for each convolutional layer. Leaky ReLU is then applied as the activation function after batch normalization. The size and step of the kernels for all max pooling layers are set to 2×2.

In most classical convolutional networks for image recognition, the input data is a single image with three channels. However, in video anomaly detection networks, the input data is a video clip consisting of multiple frames and the anomaly detection is performed on each frame to determine whether anomalies occur. This task requires only short-time motion features and the human action in this scene is highly variable. So to extract motion features and spatial features, this method stacks t frames in the channel dimension and inputs them into the network, where t is set to 4.

Objective Function. To make the reconstructed video frames close to the ground truth, intensity loss and gradient loss are used. The intensity penalty guarantees the similarity of all pixels in RGB space, and the gradient penalty sharpens the reconstructed video frames more. Specifically, the intensity loss is defined by ℓ_2 distance as follows. To make the reconstructed video frames close to the ground truth, intensity loss and gradient loss are used. The intensity penalty guarantees the similarity of all pixels in RGB space, and the gradient penalty sharpens the reconstructed video frames more. Specifically, the intensity loss is defined by ℓ_2 distance as follows.

$$L_{int}(\widehat{x}_t, x_t) = \sum_{k=t-3}^{t} \left\| \widehat{I}_k - I_k \right\|_2^2 \tag{2}$$

where $x_t = [I_{t-3}, I_{t-2}, I_{t-1}, I_t]$ denotes the stacking of real consecutive 4 frames in the channel dimension, and $\widehat{x}_t = \left[\widehat{I}_{t-3}, \widehat{I}_{t-2}, \widehat{I}_{t-1}, \widehat{I}_t\right]$ denotes the stacking of the reconstructed consecutive 4 frames in the channel dimension. The gradient loss of the network is defined as follows.

$$L_{\text{gd}}(\widehat{x}_t, x_t) = \sum_{k=t-3}^{t} l_{gd}(\widehat{I}_k, I_k) \tag{3}$$

where l_{gd} is a gradient loss calculation function defined as follows.

$$l_{gd}(\widehat{I}, I) = \sum_{i,j} \left\| \left| \widehat{I}_{i,j} - \widehat{I}_{i-1,j} \right| - \left| I_{i,j} - I_{i-1,j} \right| \right\|_1$$
$$+ \left\| \left| \widehat{I}_{i,j} - \widehat{I}_{i,j-1} \right| - \left| I_{i,j} - I_{i,j-1} \right| \right\|_1 \tag{4}$$

where i,j represents the spatial coordinates of the video frame.

We combine these constraints regarding intensity, gradient and structural similarity into our objective function. The objective function is defined by:

$$L = \lambda_{int}L_{int}(\widehat{x}_t, x_t) + \lambda_{gd}L_{gd}(\widehat{x}_t, x_t) \tag{5}$$

To train the network, all frames are normalized to $[0, 1]$ and the size of each frame is resized to 256×256. The network is trained using the optimizer Adam with a learning rate of 0.0002 and a batch size of 32. Here, $\lambda_{int} = 1$ and $\lambda_{gd} = 1$.

Regularity Score. Normal events can be well reconstructed. Therefore, we are able to compare the difference between the reconstructed sequences and the ground truth for anomaly detection. Here we use the Euclidean distance to represent the reconstruction error defined as follows.

$$e(t) = \frac{1}{4} \sum_{i=t-3}^{t} \left\| I_i - \widehat{I}_i \right\|_2^2 \tag{6}$$

After calculating the reconstruction error for each frame of each test video, we regularize the reconstruction error of all frames in a test video to the range $[0,1]$, and then calculate the standard score for each frame by using the following equation:

$$S(t) = \frac{e(t) - \min_t e(t)}{\max_t e(t) - \min_t e(t)} \tag{7}$$

The threshold corresponding to the point with the largest difference between FPR and TPR can be found to achieve the best detection effect.

6   Experiments

In this section, we evaluate the proposed method as well as other different video anomaly detection methods in the pool dataset and also demonstrate the effectiveness of underwater images preprocessing and video anomaly detection algorithms to accomplish drowning detection.

6.1   Evaluation Metric

The proposed method is evaluated by the common evaluation metrics in video anomaly detection tasks. ROC curves are produced by varying the threshold and calculating true positive rate (TPR) and false positive rate (FPR). The average area under the ROC curve (AUC) is then calculated, and the AUC represents the binary classification performance of the algorithm. In addition, we also use the equal error rate (EER) to evaluate the performance and it represents the probability of misclassification when the false positive rate equals the false negative rate. Higher AUC values and lower EER values indicate that the algorithm indicated better anomaly detection performance.

Table 1. The AUC and EER of different methods in the pool dataset

Methods	Without underwater image preprocessing		With underwater image preprocessing	
	AUC ↑	EER ↓	AUC ↑	EER ↓
Ano-Pred [15]	72.54%	32.00%	77.87%	28.88%
Conv-AE [13]	77.19%	30.90%	75.26%	32.27%
STAE [21]	77.91%	32.50%	77.03%	28.17%
MNAD [18]	63.93%	40.44%	75.17%	33.33%
The proposed method	**81.07%**	**24.22%**	**83.94%**	**22.16%**

6.2 Comparison with Existing Methods and Impact of Underwater Image Preprocessing

In this section, the proposed method is compared with other state-of-the-art video anomaly detection methods. Then we continue to compare the various methods with and without underwater image preprocessing. The AUC values and EER values of the various methods are listed in Table 1, and the ROC curves of the various methods after underwater image preprocessing are also provided in Fig. 5. For comparison. The figure and the table show that the proposed method outperforms all the existing methods, which proves the effectiveness of the proposed method and shows that the proposed network is more suitable for video anomaly detection in swimming pool scenes, and the performance of various methods increase to some extent after underwater image preprocessing,

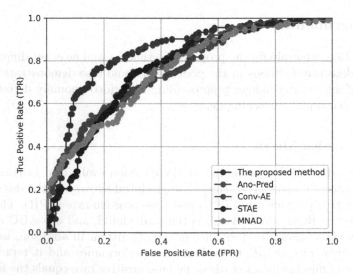

Fig. 5. ROC comparison with existing methods in Pool dataset.

which indicates that underwater image preprocessing is helpful for underwater video anomaly detection.

6.3   Qualitative Results

The quality results of the proposed method in Pool dataset are shown in Fig. 6. It shows one of the input frames, one of the output frames and the error map. The figure shows that the water surface region always produces large errors in the water surface due to irregular fluctuations of water and light. However, the errors in the water surface region are always present in the normal and abnormal frames, so they can cancel out when comparing with each other and they do not have a large effect on the results of detecting abnormal frames. The error map shows that when a person does normal behavior, the error in the corresponding region is relatively small. When a person does abnormal behavior of drowning, the error of the corresponding region increases significantly and is highlighted in the Fig. 6.

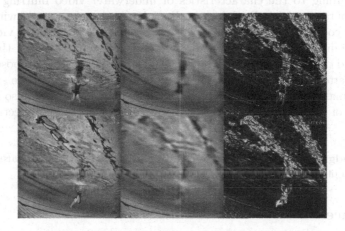

Fig. 6. Qualitative normal results and qualitative abnormal results from the proposed method. The top is the normal results, the bottom is abnormal results. One of input frame stacks (left); One of reconstructed frame stacks (middle); Error heat map (right).

6.4   Running Time

Our framework is implemented with NVIDIA GeForce GTX 1080Ti GPUs and Pytorch. The average running time is about 90 fps. We also show the running time of various methods in Pool dataset in Table 2. It can show that the proposed method is very fast and it can meet the real-time requirements.

Table 2. The inference time of different methods in pool dataset

Methods	Inference time
Ano-Pred	27 FPS
Conv-AE	21 FPS
STAE	14 FPS
MNAD	23 FPS
The proposed method	**90 FPS**

7   Conclusion

Because abnormal events of drowning rarely occur and normal events in pools including swimming and treading can be relatively easy to collect a lot of video data, a new video anomaly detection method is proposed for pool drowning detection in this paper. At first, we produce a pool anomaly detection dataset. Then according to the characteristics of underwater video blurring and large variation of target size in Pool dataset, Pool dataset is preprocessed with CLAHE and a new codec structured neural network is designed to mark the video frames with large differences between reconstructed frames generated by the network and ground truth as anomalies. The experiments show that the proposed method is much better than the current anomaly detection methods, more suitable for video anomaly detection in pool scenes and also fast. This work also proves the feasibility of video anomaly detection algorithms for drowning detection in pool scenes.

Acknowledgment. The authors would like to thank the National Natural Science Foundation of China (61771412, 61871336 and 62071401).

References

1. Meniere, J.: System for monitoring a swimming pool to prevent drowning accidents. US Patent 6,133,838, 17 October 2000
2. Eng, H.-L., Toh, K.-A., Yau, W.-Y., Wang, J.: Dews: a live visual surveillance system for early drowning detection at pool (2008)
3. Salehi, N., Keyvanara, M., Amirhassan Monadjemmi, S.: An automatic video-based drowning detection system for swimming pools using active contours. Int. J. Image Graph. Signal Process. **8**(8), 1 (2016)
4. Dalal, N., Triggs, B.: Histograms of oriented gradients for human detection. In: 2005 IEEE Computer Society Conference on Computer Vision and Pattern Recognition (CVPR 2005), vol. 1, pp. 886–893. IEEE (2005)
5. Dalal, N., Triggs, B., Schmid, C.: Human detection using oriented histograms of flow and appearance. In: Leonardis, A., Bischof, H., Pinz, A. (eds.) ECCV 2006. LNCS, vol. 3952, pp. 428–441. Springer, Heidelberg (2006). https://doi.org/10.1007/11744047_33

6. Zhang, D., Gatica-Perez, D., Bengio, S., McCowan, I.: Semi-supervised adapted HMMS for unusual event detection. In: 2005 IEEE Computer Society Conference on Computer Vision and Pattern Recognition (CVPR 2005), vol. 1, pp. 611–618. IEEE (2005)

7. Mahadevan, V., Li, W., Bhalodia, V., Vasconcelos, N.: Anomaly detection in crowded scenes. In: 2010 IEEE Computer Society Conference on Computer Vision and Pattern Recognition, pp. 1975–1981. IEEE (2010)

8. Kim, J., Grauman, K.: Observe locally, infer globally: a space-time MRF for detecting abnormal activities with incremental updates. In: 2009 IEEE Conference on Computer Vision and Pattern Recognition, pp. 2921–2928. IEEE (2009)

9. Cong, Y., Yuan, J., Liu, J.: Sparse reconstruction cost for abnormal event detection. In: CVPR 2011, pp. 3449–3456. IEEE (2011)

10. Zhao, B., Fei-Fei, L., Xing, E.P.: Online detection of unusual events in videos via dynamic sparse coding. In CVPR 2011, pp. 3313–3320. IEEE (2011)

11. Lu, C., Shi, J., Jia, J.: Abnormal event detection at 150 fps in matlab. In: Proceedings of the IEEE International Conference on Computer Vision, pp. 2720–2727 (2013)

12. Xu, D., Ricci, E., Yan, Y., Song, J., Sebe, N.: Learning deep representations of appearance and motion for anomalous event detection. arXiv preprint arXiv:1510.01553 (2015)

13. Hasan, M., Choi, J., Neumann, J., Roy-Chowdhury, A.K., Davis, L.S.: Learning temporal regularity in video sequences. In: Proceedings of the IEEE Conference on Computer Vision and Pattern Recognition, pp. 733–742 (2016)

14. Zhou, S., Shen, W., Zeng, D., Fang, M., Wei, Y., Zhang, Z.: Spatial-temporal convolutional neural networks for anomaly detection and localization in crowded scenes. Signal Process. Image Commun. **47**, 358–368 (2016)

15. Liu, W., Luo, W., Lian, D., Gao, S.: Future frame prediction for anomaly detection-a new baseline. In: Proceedings of the IEEE Conference on Computer Vision and Pattern Recognition, pp. 6536–6545 (2018)

16. Tudor Ionescu, R., Shahbaz Khan, F., Georgescu, M.-I., Shao, L.: Object-centric auto-encoders and dummy anomalies for abnormal event detection in video. In: Proceedings of the IEEE/CVF Conference on Computer Vision and Pattern Recognition, pp. 7842–7851 (2019)

17. Gong, D., et al.: Memorizing normality to detect anomaly: memory-augmented deep autoencoder for unsupervised anomaly detection. In: Proceedings of the IEEE/CVF International Conference on Computer Vision, pp. 1705–1714 (2019)

18. Park, H., Noh, J., Ham, B.: Learning memory-guided normality for anomaly detection. In: Proceedings of the IEEE/CVF Conference on Computer Vision and Pattern Recognition, pp. 14372–14381 (2020)

19. Pang, G., Yan, C., Shen, C., van den Hengel, A., Bai, X.: Self-trained deep ordinal regression for end-to-end video anomaly detection. In: Proceedings of the IEEE/CVF Conference on Computer Vision and Pattern Recognition, pp. 12173–12182 (2020)

20. He, K., Zhang, X., Ren, S., Sun, J.: Deep residual learning for image recognition. In: Proceedings of the IEEE Conference on Computer Vision and Pattern Recognition, pp. 770–778 (2016)

21. Chong, Y.S., Tay, Y.H.: Abnormal event detection in videos using spatiotemporal autoencoder. In: Cong, F., Leung, A., Wei, Q. (eds.) ISNN 2017. LNCS, vol. 10262, pp. 189–196. Springer, Cham (2017). https://doi.org/10.1007/978-3-319-59081-3_23

NBA Basketball Video Summarization for News Report via Hierarchical-Grained Deep Reinforcement Learning

Naye Ji[1,2] , Shiwei Zhao[1,3], Qiang Lin[1,2], Dingguo Yu[1,2], and Youbing Zhao[1,2(✉)]

[1] Intelligent Media Institute, Communication University of Zhejiang, Hangzhou, China
{jinaye,qiang_lin,yudg,zyb}@cuz.edu.cn
[2] Key Lab of Film and TV Media Technology of Zhejiang Province, Hangzhou, China
[3] School of Software Technology, Zhejiang University, Hangzhou, China
21751129@zju.edu.cn

Abstract. At present, the demand for short video generation is increasing, especially for sports news report, which urgently needs automatic video summarization methods to reduce time and labor cost. This paper focuses on NBA basketball videos and seeks for the actual needs of news report on sports video summarization. We propose a hierarchical-grained deep reinforcement learning framework to generate short basketball video. For a long basketball game video, we propose a hierarchical-grained subshot segmentation algorithm, which takes into account both semantics and objective factors, and preserves spatiotemporal consistency. Then we select candidate frames through a news element enhanced deep reinforcement learning framework. On this basis, a news report oriented video summarization algorithm based on probability sampling is implemented with the fusion of multi-game and multi-news elements. Experimental results on the NBA dataset newly collected by us demonstrate the effectiveness of the proposed framework. Moreover, the proposed method is able to highlight the video content including well preserved news elements.

Keywords: Video summarization · News report · Reinforcement learning

1 Introduction

Recently, with the rapid development of big data and artificial intelligence technology, in the media industry, journalists no longer focus solely on news events and the news scene itself. They start to explore the usage of big data and artificial intelligence technology to report news, further promoting the development of popular data news. Nowadays, video is an important manifestation of data news since it is a popular media type for information dissemination. However,

© Springer Nature Switzerland AG 2021
Y. Peng et al. (Eds.): ICIG 2021, LNCS 12890, pp. 712–728, 2021.
https://doi.org/10.1007/978-3-030-87361-5_58

with the explosive growth of video data, a series of problems and challenges have been brought to the applications of video browsing, storage, retrieval and so on. Compared with the raw long video, the short video is concise in content and distinctive in theme, which is more in line with the current fast-paced reading habits. At the same time, due to the popularity and development of mobile Internet, the news market of mobile terminals has expanded greatly. Therefore, for data news reports, the need of fast short video generation is especially urgent.

Furthermore, when the Asian Games, the Olympic Games and other large-scale sports events are held, there will be many sports events to be reported. In order to better report data news, sports event videos need to be processed as short videos to meet the needs of news reporting. Converting the raw sports event videos to required short videos automatically is a short video generation problem which generally can be divided into three stages: video abstraction stage, video comprehension stage and video creation stage [18,21].

In the video abstraction stage, the short video is generated by selecting the key frames that can reflect the main information in the original video to summarize the video content. At this stage, the short video generation technology mainly focuses on the selection of key frames [5,7,9,11,15,29,33,34], that is, the representative video frames. In the next stage, i.e., video comprehension stage, short video generation focuses more on sequence features and semantic information of video. At this point, the selection is no longer limited to static key frames, but a series of representative video clips or key sub-shots [3,4,12,17,19,24,38]. Further, during the creation stage, short video generation combines the information behind the video content to create short video with new storyline [13,14,26,27], which can enrich the form of expression. For example, Yu et al. [32] presents a fine-grained video captioning method for sports narrative.

So far, current short video generation work is typically based on a general-purpose video, and the duration of the raw video typically does not exceed 10 min. In contrast, sports videos have their own characteristics and faces the following challenges in serving the demand for news report. First, a raw sport video from the TV station often takes a long time and has lots of noises (e.g. including advertisements, narratives) which leads to the lack of sports video database. Secondly, a sport video contains distinct spatiotemporal events which are important for news report. How to both avoid spatial variation and keep temporal processing is an obstacle of video summarization. Finally, a sport video involves many dynamic entities, such as a quick-moving ball or interacting persons. The generated short video should contain the important activities of dynamic entities and keep the movement continuous. In this paper, we try to solve the problem of short sports video generation for news reports from the above challenges. We focus on NBA basketball video because basketball video is one of the most challenging videos among all the sports videos, i.e., it involves multiple people, details of motions, and even outside interference.

We propose an NBA video summarization framework oriented for news report. First, in order to solve the existence of news semantic and motion complexity in NBA videos, we propose a hierarchical-grained subshot segmentation approach as shown in Fig. 1 (part-1). The hierarchical-grained subshot segmentation make the long duration video well decomposed with spatiotemporal effectiveness. However, the number of segmented frames is still huge, causing supervised methods difficult to implement. Thus, we adopted deep reinforcement learning to select candidate frames according to required news elements. The composed diversity and representativeness reward function assists to select candidate frames. Furthermore, we construct a candidate's library consisted of various news elements, i.e. overall, highlight, sidelight. Using our proposed probability sampling, we can obtain the optimized video frame sequence for news report summarization.

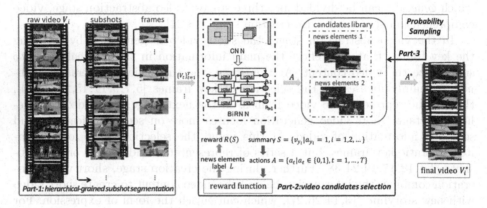

Fig. 1. Overview of our NBA video summarization framework oriented for news report

To the best of our knowledge, this paper is the first work on such long duration and HD sports video summarization. Due to the deficiency of good sports videos for experiment, we introduce a new database, which contains 100 NBA basketball HD 1080p videos from online websites. Each video has been removed of advertisements and are about 20 min duration. We conduct experiments on three datasets, our NBA dataset, SumMe [9] and TVSum [24], to evaluate our method. The quantitative results show that our method can solve the NBA video summarization well, especially for a satisfactory time cost on both long duration and high-quality raw video. In addition, the qualitative results illustrate that our framework can better identify news element related frames from NBA videos.

The main contributions of this paper are summarized as follows: (1) an effective framework of NBA basketball video summarization oriented for news report; (2) a hierarchical-grained subshot segmentation approach which preserves spatiotemporal information well; (3) a deep reinforcement learning model to discover appropriate video candidates based on given news elements; (4) a new video database of 100 HD NBA video parts with about 20 min duration for video tasks.

The remainder of this paper is organized as follows. Section 2 reviews the related video generation methods. Section 3 introduces the proposed NBA video summarization framework and details of our approaches. Section 4 presents the experimental results and analysis. Finally, conclusions and future work are provided in Sect. 5.

2 Related Work

The short video generation problem in this paper includes video abstraction and video comprehension stage, which can be referred as a video summarization problem. Broadly speaking, video summarization has been studied over two decades in the literature. Early methods pay more attention to the low-level visual features of video, including two major research directions: key frame selection methods and subshot selection methods. For recent years, by introducing high-level deep features, deep architectures dominate video summarization research. In the following subsections, we will introduce their related work in detail.

Key Frame Based Video Summarization. Key frame based methods select a subset of frames to form a summary, and typically use low-level features like optical flow [29] or image differences [33]. Recent work also injects high-level information such as object tracks [15] or predict object and event salience [5]. Key frame selection criteria for summaries are often taken as a score prediction problem, typically estimating visual interestingness on various level features as in [9]. Considering the local correlation of video frames, Vidal et al. [6] employs Locality-constrained Linear Coding (LLC) to preserve the locality. Later, some other strategies for key-frame based video summarization aims to find correlative, diverse and representative frames through subset selection methods [7,34] or clustering algorithms [11]. Similarly, Li et al. [12] designs four criteria functions and proposes a general framework for edited video and raw video summarization.

Key Subshot Based Video Summarization. In contrast, key subshots based techniques first segment the input into subshots using shot boundary detection. The summary then consists of a selected set of representative subshots, or takes user input to generate a storyboard [1,28], or performs a temporal segmentation into semantically-consistent subshots [19]. In [3], a video is summarized by finding shots that co-occur most frequently across videos collected using a topic keyword. Furthermore, some dictionary learning methods [4,17,38] seeks to find a few representative subshots to form the summary, which can be viewed as the dictionary elements. In this case, the video summary is selected by sparse coding.

Unsupervised vs. Supervised Summarization. Whatever the above choices, existing methods are unsupervised and supervised from the perspective of the learning model for video summarization. Unsupervised approaches dominate the field of video summarization for a long time. They are generally designed to make the summarization meets the desired properties, such as conciseness, representativeness, and informativeness. Thus, the corresponding selection criteria for summaries include content frequency [2,11], coverage [4,38], relevance [24], and user's attention [5], etc. Moreover, [20] presents an approach that learns to generate optimal video summaries by learning from unpaired data. Recently, supervised video summarization approach has also received much research focus. It takes videos and their human labeled summaries as training data to explicitly learn how human would summarize videos. For example, Gong et al. [26] treat video summarization as a supervised subset selection problem, and present a probabilistic model called sequential Determinantal Point Process (seqDPP) to learn how a diverse and representative subset is selected from the training set. Potapov et al. [19] train a set of SVM classifiers to score each segment in a video with an importance score, and those segments with higher scores constitute a video summary.

Deep Architectures for Video Summarization. More recently, deep learning based approaches are gaining increasing attention. In this kind of works, video summarization tasks are defined as different target problems, and the deep network architecture is used to construct and train the model. The corresponding research work has achieved good results: objective function optimization purpose solved by CNN or RNN [22,30,31], end-to-end model transformation purpose solved by LSTM and DPP-LSTM [16,25,35], video structure affects purpose solved by hierarchical RNN [37] or bidirectional LSTM [36]. Furthermore, reinforcement learning (RL) is also effective in video summarization tasks. Song et al. [23] applies RL to train a summarization network for selecting category-specific key frames. Their learning framework requires key frame labels and category information of training videos. Later, in the way that labels or user interactions are not required at all during the learning process, the summarization method [39] can be fully unsupervised and is more practical to be deployed for large-scale video summarization.

3   Our Approach

As shown in Fig. 1, our proposed NBA video summarization framework include three parts. The first part is to segment long raw videos into spatiotemporal retained subshots. And the second part is to choose useful candidates through news elements driven deep reinforcement learning. Finally, we generate short videos from constructed candidates' library by probability sampling.

3.1   Hierarchical-Grained Subshot Segmentation Approach

We propose a hierarchical-grained subshot segmentation approach for NBA match video's subshot segmentation task, which combined temporal and spatial dimension of video subshots. The temporal dimension shot segmentation approaches are mainly based on the temporal dimension, and the segmentation granularity is more delicate. It is suitable for subjective subshot segmentation. However, due to the global optimization, the time complexity of the temporal dimension algorithm depends heavily on the size of the data, and there will be performance problems in the large-scale data environment. On the other hand, the spatial dimension subshot segmentation approaches are mainly based on the spatial dimension, and the segmentation granularity is coarse. It is suitable for objective subshot segmentation. The time complexity of the spatial dimension algorithm is independent of the size of the data, and it is suitable for large-scale data environment. However, in the task of NBA game video's subshot segmentation, subjective shots belong to the subsets of objective subshots. Therefore, we use the result sets of objective subshot segmentation for subjective subshot segmentation, which can reduce the optimization interval and improve the efficiency of the algorithm.

The specific process of hierarchical-grained subshot segmentation approach is as follows (Fig. 2). Firstly, the coarse-grained segmentation of original video is performed by using Detect-Content algorithm [8]. Secondly, based on the coarse segmentation result, KTS algorithm [19] is used for fine-grained segmentation. Finally, by integrating the segmentation results of the above steps, we can achieve the best subshot segmentation results for NBA match video's subshot segmentation task. The proposed hierarchical-grained subshot segmentation approach can solve the performance problem of data scale dependence to a great extent, and ensures a good segmentation effect in both the coarse and fine dimensions of video subshot. Besides, the proposed approach can segment subjective and objective shots well at the same time. The specific flow of the hierarchical-grained shot segmentation algorithm is shown in Algorithm.1.

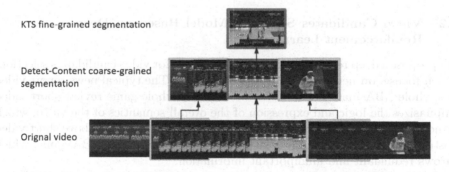

Fig. 2. Hierarchical-grained subshot segmentation process

Algorithm 1. Hierarchical-grained shot segmentation algorithm

---

Input: video frame sequence $V = \{v_i | i = 1, \cdots, n\}$
Output: shot transition point $S = \{v_i | v_i \in V, i = 0, \cdots, |S|\}$
1: initialize the final segment collection empty, $S \leftarrow \emptyset$
2: initialize the coarse-grained segment collection empty, $C \leftarrow \emptyset$
3: initialize the fine-grained segment collection empty, $F \leftarrow \emptyset$
4: **for all** $v_i \in V, i \leq n - 1$ **do**
5:    $h_i \leftarrow compute\_HSV\_histogram(v_i)$
6:    $h_{i+1} \leftarrow compute\_HSV\_histogram(v_i)$
7:    $x_2 \leftarrow 0$
8:    **for** $t = 1, k$ **do**
9:      **if** $(h_i(t)! = 0 || h_{i+1}! = 0)$ **then**
10:       $x^2 \leftarrow \frac{(h_i(t) - h_{i+1}(t))^2}{\max(h_i(t), h_{i+1}(t) + x^2)}$
11:      **else**
12:       $x^2 \leftarrow x^2$
13:      **end if**
14:      **if** $x^2 > 0$ **then**
15:        add v_i to C
16:      **else**
17:        **continue**
18:      **end if**
19:    **end for**
20: **end for**
21: **for all** $v_j \in C, j \leq |C| - 1$ **do**
22:    add $compute\_KTS(\{v_j | j \leq i \leq j + 1\})$ to F
23: **end for**
24: $S = C \cup F$
25: **return** S;

3.2   Video Candidates Selection Model Based on Deep Reinforcement Learning

We propose a deep reinforcement learning method for video candidate's selection, which focuses on news reports of an NBA match. The typical news report video is a whole NBA match review short video. The whole game review short video emphasizes the logic and expression of the overall semantics of the video, which is more dependent on the temporal and causal dimension. The above short video abstraction is an abstraction of high-level abstraction of an NBA game, which throws redundant and unimportant information.

In the proposed method, we adopt deep summarization network (DSN) [39] to predict the probability of each video frame in the original video that to be selected. In detail, we first use the encoder of a convolutional neural network (CNN) to extract the visual features of a video V. The video is decomposed into T frame, and the extracted features of the tth video frame can be denoted as $\{x_t\}_{t=1}^{T}$. Then, we use the features $\{x_t\}_{t=1}^{T}$ as input to the decoder part of DSN to discover the hidden state $\{h_t\}_{t=1}^{T}$. Here, the decoder part of DSN is a bidirectional recurrent neural network (Bi-RNN). Through the Bi-RNN, each hidden state h_t is associated with a forward hidden state forward $h_t^{froward}$ and a backward hidden state backward $h_t^{backward}$, which contains information about the future and past of the tth video frame. The output of Bi-RNN is a full connection via a sigmoid activation function as Eq. 1:

$$p_t = \sigma(Wh_t),$$
$$a_t \sim Bernoulli(p_t).$$
(1)

where σ represents the sigmoid activation function, $a_t \in \{0, 1\}$ is used to determine whether the tth video frame is selected as a candidate according to the predicted probability p_t. The ultimate selected video frame sequence set is $A = \{a_t | a_t \in \{0, 1\}, t = 1, \cdots, T\}$. Accordingly, we can obtain the candidate video frames of a video, that is $S = \{v(y_i) | a(y_i) = 1, i = 1, 2, \cdots\}$. These candidate video frames make up the abstract sequence of the original NBA game video.

In order to generate high quality abstraction of the NBA match video, we need to maximize the expectation of the reward function $R(S)$. That means we need to optimize $R(S)$ to evaluate the quality of selected short video candidates during the training process of DSN. Therefore, high-quality candidates should satisfy both diversity and representativeness in order to keep the complete information in the original video to a maximum extent. In order to achieve the above target, we adopt Diversity-Representativeness Reward function to measure the diversity and representativeness of short video candidates. The reward function $R(S)$ consists of the diversity function R_{div} and the representativeness function R_{rep}:

$$R(S) = R_{div} + R_{rep}.$$
(2)

The full learning process for the video candidate's selection model is shown as part-2 of Fig. 1. For an NBA match video V, the video is firstly divided into T video frames $\{V_t\}_{t=1}^T$. Then, for the extracted features x_t of the frame V_t, we calculate the difference between selected video frames in feature space to assess the extent of diversity R_{div}. Afterwards, the mean of the pairwise dissimilarities among the selected frames can be obtained. Let all the selected video frames be $y = \{y_i | a_{y_i} = 1, i = 1, \cdots, |y|\}$, R_{div} can be represented as Eq. 3:

$$R_{div} = \frac{1}{|y|(|y| - 1)} \sum_{t \in y} \sum_{t' \in y, t' \neq t} d(x_t, x_{t'}),$$

$$d(x_t, x_{t'}) = 1 - \frac{x_t^T x_{t'}}{\|x_t\|_2 \|x_{t'}\|_2}.$$
(3)

In this equation, $d(\cdot, \cdot)$ indicates the dissimilarity function. On the other hand, the representativeness reward R_{rep} ensures the content and topic orientation of short video candidates. R_{rep} measures how well the generated summary can represent the original video. The function can be defined as:

$$R_{rep} = \exp(-\frac{1}{T} \sum_{t=1}^{T} \min_{t' \in y} \|x_t - x_{t'}\|_2). \qquad (4)$$

3.3 Probability Sampling Short-Video Generation Method

Based on the above selected short video materials, we proposed a probability sampling short-video generation method to create the final NBA match short videos. First, we make up the corresponding results of video materials and organize storage processing. On this basis, through the way of probability sampling, the video materials of different matches and various news elements are sampled and fused. Eventually, a short video of the NBA match oriented for news report is obtained, which combines multiple matches and multiple news elements.

Video Materials Organization. The selected video materials have been scored by importance in Sect. 3.2 according to the news elements. In order to cover a variety of news elements, we need to predict importance scores of all the video frames from the original video. As shown in Fig. 3, the original video frames are mapped according to the results of subshot segmentation and the indexes of the sampled video frames. The average of the predicted importance score of all video frames belonging to the same subshot is used as the final score to complete the predicted importance score of all the original video frames. The result complement algorithm is shown in detail as Algorithm 2. After that, we adopt H5 file format to store the selected video candidates into a candidate's library for better organization.

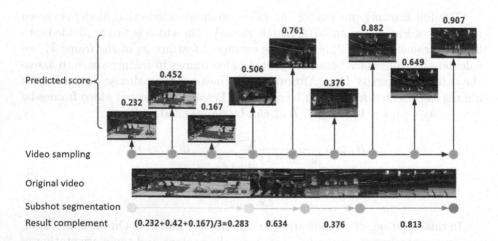

Fig. 3. Result complement process

Algorithm 2. Result complement algorithm

Input:

  original video frame sequence $V = \{v_i | i = 1, \cdots, n\}$

  sampling video frame sequence $P = \{p_i | p_i \in V, i = 0, \cdots, P\}$

  score sequence of sampling video frame $R = \{r_i | i = 0, \cdots, |R|\}$

  shot transition point sequence $S = \{v_i | v_i \in V, i = 0, \cdots, |S|\}$

Output: score sequence of all the original video frames $A = \{a_i | i = 0, \cdots, |V|\}$

1: initialize the result collection with zeros,

2: **for all** $a_i \in A$ **do**

3:   $a_i \leftarrow 0$

4: **end for**

5: **for all** $s_i \in S, i \leq |S| - 1$ **do**

6:   $score \leftarrow 0$

7:   $num \leftarrow 0$

8:   **for all** $P_j \in P, j \leq |P| - 1$ **do**

9:     **if** $i \leq j \leq i + 1$ **then**

10:       $score \leftarrow score + r_j$

11:       $num \leftarrow num + 1$

12:     **else**

13:       **continue**

14:     **end if**

15:   **end for**

16:   $avg\_score \leftarrow score/num$

17:   **for all** $a_j \in A, j \leq |V| - 1$ **do**

18:     **if** $i \leq j \leq i + 1$ **then**

19:       $a_j \leftarrow avg\_score$

20:     **else**

21:       **continue**

22:     **end if**

23:   **end for**

24: **end for**

25: **return** A

Probability Sampling. In order to better generate the final short video, we introduce several customized parameters to assemble the above-mentioned stored video materials. The customized parameters include the range of the material files, the proportion of news elements, the duration and format of the video. On this basis, we retrieve the material resources through probability sampling which meet video summarization requirements. In detail, we search the video materials according to their indexes and types from the material library. Then we count the number and score distribution of all video materials. Next, we sample each material according to the proportion of the news elements in order from high score to low score. At the same time, we sample all the materials evenly according to the duration parameters. Finally, we output the final short video file according to the format, frame number and other parameters. The specific probability sampling algorithm for short video generation is shown in Algorithm 3.

Algorithm 3. Probability sampling for short video generation algorithm

---

Input: original candidate's video frame sequence $V = \{v_i | i = 1, \cdots, n\}$ results of
    candidate's video frame sequence $R^k = \{r_i^k | k \in \{1, 2, 3\}, i = 0, \cdots, n\}$
    ratio of news elements $ratio^k$, duration t

Output: selected candidate's video frame sequence $A = \{a_i | a_i \in \{0, 1\}, i = 0, \cdots, |V|\}$

 1: initialize the result collection with zeros,
 2: **for all** $a_i \in A$ **do**
 3:    $a_i \leftarrow 0, \ time \leftarrow 0$
 4: **end for**
 5: **for** $k = 1, 3$ **do**
 6:    $sort(R^k)$ by DESC
 7:    $R^k \leftarrow get\_top(ratio^k, R^k)$
 8:    $time \leftarrow compute\_time(R^k) + time$
 9:    **if** $time > t$ **then**
10:        $ratio \leftarrow t/time$
11:        **for** $k = 1, 3$ **do**
12:           $sort(R^k)$ by DESC
13:           $R^k \leftarrow get\_top(ratio^k, R^k)$
14:        **end for**
15:    **else**
16:        **continue**
17:    **end if**
18: **end for**
19: **for** $k = 1, 3$ **do**
20:    **for all** $r_i^k \in R^k, i \leq |R^k|$ **do**
21:        **if** $r_i^k > 0$ **then**
22:           $a_i \leftarrow 1$
23:        **else**
24:           **continue**
25:        **end if**
26:    **end for**
27: **end for**
28: **return** A

---

4   Experimental Results and Analysis

We evaluate the experimental results of hierarchical-grained subshot segmentation and video candidate's selection separately. The hierarchical-grained subshot segmentation experiment is tested on our NBA dataset. Then, the video candidates selection experiment is evaluated on three datasets, including our NBA dataset, SumMe [9], TVSum [24].

4.1   NBA Dataset Collection

We collect 20 original NBA HD game video from online websites. Then, we remove advertisements manually and split them into 100 parts. Each video part corresponds to a section of the NBA game; thus, the duration is about 20 min.

All the videos are of high quality with 25fps and 1980 * 1080 resolution. The dataset has been published on Github[1].

4.2 Hierarchical-Grained Subshot Segmentation Experiment

We compare our hierarchical-grained subshot segmentation method with KTS method and Detect-Content method from two aspects. One is the time cost experiment; the other is the segmentation effect experiment. The experiment data is the raw NBA videos of our NBA dataset (with fps = 25).

Time Cost Experiment. We select 10 groups of videos with duration of 2 min, 5 min, 10 min, 15 min, and 20 min, respectively. The time cost experiment is done on the computer with an Intel i7 8700 6-core CPU, 32 GB memory and NVIDIA GTX 1080 graphics card. Table 1 shows the mean time cost (lower is better) of different methods. Meanwhile, we compare the time difference of the three methods more intuitively with the curve graph shown in Fig. 4. The time cost and the video duration increase rate of the proposed hierarchical-grained subshot segmentation method is between the two approaches. The hierarchical-grained method is slightly higher than the Detect-Content method, but it is still much smaller than KTS method. The experimental results show that our algorithm has obvious optimization effect.

Table 1. Results of time cost on variant video duration for different subshot segmentation approaches

Method	2 min	5 min	10 min	15 min	20 min
KTS(s)	132.123	212.998	802.340	2821.232	6185.504
Detect-content(s)	6.269	14.969	37.267	117.632	182.722
Hierarchical-grained(s)	34.475	67.241	184.010	382.321	673.676

Segmentation Effect Experiment. For segmentation effect evaluation, we select 10 groups of videos with duration of 5 min, 10 min, and 20 min, respectively. We compared our proposed Hierarchical-Grained method with KTS and Detect-Content Method within the allowable fault tolerance range (± 25 fps, ± 75 fps, ± 125fps). The performance measures are average F-Score for segmentation (higher is better). From Table 2, we can see the subshot segmentation effect of Detect-Content and Hierarchical-Grained is obviously better than that of KTS in each video scale. In contrast, the Detect-Content algorithm can achieve good segmentation effect in a smaller error range. Moreover, by introducing semantic subshot segmentation based on Detect-Content method, the overall segmentation effect of Hierarchical-Grained method has been obviously improved. For news report, the results of the proposed Hierarchical-Grained method are the best, which meet the segmentation requirements of NBA match videos.

---

[1] https://github.com/conniemy/BasketballVideo.

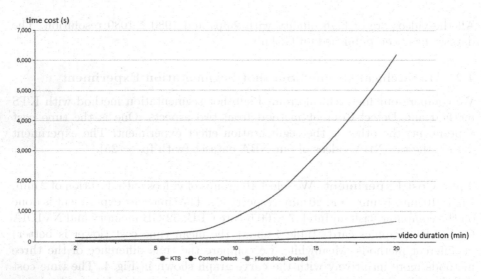

Fig. 4. Time cost on variant video duration for different subshot segmentation approaches

Table 2. Results of different subshot segmentation approaches on NBA match videos

Duration	FPS	KTS	Detect-content	Hierarchical-grained
5 min	±25	0.451	0.884	0.914
	±75	0.732	0.915	0.923
	±125	0.904	0.936	0.964
10 min	±25	0.432	0.871	0.901
	±75	0.636	0.904	0.911
	±125	0.874	0.924	0.945
20 min	±25	0.414	0.843	0.893
	±75	0.607	0.894	0.908
	±125	0.847	0.907	0.927

4.3   Video Candidates Selection Experiment

The experiment data is derived from the raw NBA videos of our NBA dataset. The duration of each video varies from 20 to 30 min. We construct the NBA Datasets through subshot segmentation, video frames extraction and sampling (with fps = 2). We evaluate our methods on NBA Dataset, SumMe [9] and TVSum [24]. For each dataset, we choose 100 videos for experiment, and divide the training set and the test set by the proportion 8:2 randomly. For fair comparison with other approaches, we follow the commonly used protocol [35] to compute F-Score as the metric to assess the similarity to measure the effectiveness of summaries.

In detail of DSN, we adopt the GoogLeNet Inception V3 version [10] as the CNN model to extract the visual features in training process. In the decoder part, we verify the effectiveness of the diversity-representative reward function of reinforcement learning model for video candidate's selection. The model trained with the diversity and representative rewards jointly is denoted by DR-DSN. We compare the DR-DSN model with the ones trained with diversity reward function only and representative reward function only, which are denoted by D-DSN and R-DSN, respectively.

Table 3. Results of different variants of our method on SumMe and TVSum.

Model	NBA Datasets	SumMe	TVSum
D-DSN	0.386	0.405	0.562
R-DSN	0.381	0.407	0.569
DR-DSN	0.398	0.414	0.576

Table 3 reports the results of different variants of our method on NBA Datasets, SumMe and TVSum. We can see DR-DSN demonstrates that by using diversity and representative rewards collaboratively. We can better teach DSN to produce high-quality summaries that are diverse and representative. Moreover, we provide qualitative results for an exemplar video of our NBA Datasets in Fig. 5. In general, our method produces high-quality summaries that include key information during an NBA match. To span the temporal structure, only small variations in some frames are observed. The peak regions of ground truth are almost captured.

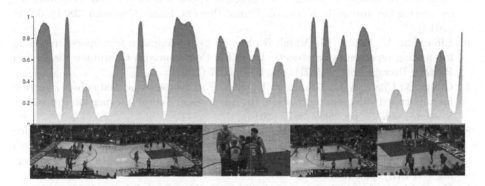

Fig. 5. Video candidates selection results generated of our approach for a video in NBA Datasets. The line area represents the result score of the video frame sequence predicted by the corresponding short video candidate material selection model. The darker the color area, the higher the score, that is, the higher the probability of being selected as the candidate material. The bottom area shows the five image frames with the highest score selected by our candidate selection algorithm.

5   Conclusion

In this paper, we propose a framework of NBA video summarization aiming at news report. Since the dataset we collected is long HD video, we propose a hierarchical-grained algorithm to segment videos to subshots with both segmentation and time effectiveness. Then, to tackle unsupervised video summarization, we adopt a label free reinforcement learning approach to find candidate frames with added news elements. By probability sampling from candidate library, we implement the video summarization algorithm based on the fusion of multi-game and multi-news elements for sports news report. The efficiency of our framework is verified on three datasets, including our NBA database.

Acknowledgments. This work was funded by the Key Research and Development Plan of Zhejiang Province (No. 2019C03131) and the Basic Public Welfare Research Project of Zhejiang Province (No. LGF21F020004).

References

1. Almeida, J., Leite, N.J., Torres, R.d.S.: Vison: video summarization for online applications. Pattern Recogn. Lett. **33**(4), 397–409 (2012)
2. Avila, S., Lopes, A., Luz, A.D., Araújo, A.: VSUMM: a mechanism designed to produce static video summaries and a novel evaluation method. Pattern Recogn. Lett. **32**(1), 56–68 (2011)
3. Chu, W.S., Song, Y., Jaimes, A.: Video co-summarization: video summarization by visual co-occurrence. In: IEEE Conference on Computer Vision and Pattern Recognition (CVPR), pp. 3584–3592 (2015)
4. Cong, Y., Yuan, J., Luo, J.: Towards scalable summarization of consumer videos via sparse dictionary selection. IEEE Trans. Multimedia **14**(1), 66–75 (2012)
5. Ejaz, N., Mehmood, I., Baik, S.W.: Efficient visual attention based framework for extracting key frames from videos. Signal Process. Image Commun. **28**(1), 34–44 (2013)
6. Elhamifar, E., Sapiro, G., Vidal, R.: See all by looking at a few: sparse modeling for finding representative objects. In: IEEE Conference on Computer Vision and Pattern Recognition (CVPR), pp. 1600–1607 (2012)
7. Gong, B., Chao, W.L., Grauman, K., Sha, F.: Diverse sequential subset selection for supervised video summarization. In: Advances in Neural Information Processing Systems, vol. 27, pp. 2069–2077 (2014)
8. Gruzman, I.S., Kostenkova, A.S.: Algorithm of scene change detection in a video sequence based on the three dimensional histogram of color images. In: 2014 12th International Conference on Actual Problems of Electronics Instrument Engineering (APEIE), p. 1 (2014)
9. Gygli, M., Grabner, H., Riemenschneider, H., Van Gool, L.: Creating summaries from user videos. In: Fleet, D., Pajdla, T., Schiele, B., Tuytelaars, T. (eds.) ECCV 2014. LNCS, vol. 8695, pp. 505–520. Springer, Cham (2014). https://doi.org/10.1007/978-3-319-10584-0_33
10. Ji, Z., Xiong, K., Pang, Y., Li, X.: Video summarization with attention-based encoder-decoder networks (2018)

11. Kuanar, S.K., Panda, R., Chowdhury, A.S.: Video key frame extraction through dynamic delaunay clustering with a structural constraint. J. Vis. Commun. Image Represent. **24**(7), 1212–1227 (2013)
12. Li, X., Zhao, B., Lu, X.: A general framework for edited video and raw video summarization. IEEE Trans. Image Process. **26**(8), 3652–3664 (2017)
13. Lin, J.C., Wei, W.L., Wang, H.M.: Automatic music video generation based on emotion-oriented pseudo song prediction and matching. In: ACM International Conference on Multimedia, pp. 372–376 (2016)
14. Lin, J.C., Wei, W.L., Yang, J., Wang, H.M., Liao, H.Y.M.: Automatic music video generation based on simultaneous soundtrack recommendation and video editing. In: ACM International Conference on Multimedia, pp. 519–527 (2017)
15. Liu, D., Hua, G., Chen, T.: A hierarchical visual model for video object summarization. IEEE Trans. Pattern Anal. Mach. Intell. **32**(12), 2178–2190 (2010)
16. Mahasseni, B., Lam, M., Todorovic, S.: Unsupervised video summarization with adversarial LSTM networks. In: 2017 IEEE Conference on Computer Vision and Pattern Recognition (CVPR), pp. 2982–2991 (2017)
17. Mei, S., Guan, G., Wang, Z., Wan, S., He, M., Feng, D.D.: Video summarization via minimum sparse reconstruction. Pattern Recogn. **48**(2), 522–533 (2015)
18. Money, A.G., Agius, H.: Video summarisation: a conceptual framework and survey of the state of the art. J. Vis. Commun. Image Represent. **19**(2), 121–143 (2008)
19. Potapov, D., Douze, M., Harchaoui, Z., Schmid, C.: Category-specific video summarization. In: Fleet, D., Pajdla, T., Schiele, B., Tuytelaars, T. (eds.) ECCV 2014. LNCS, vol. 8694, pp. 540–555. Springer, Cham (2014). https://doi.org/10.1007/978-3-319-10599-4_35
20. Rochan, M., Wang, Y.: Video summarization by learning from unpaired data. In: IEEE/CVF Conference on Computer Vision and Pattern Recognition (CVPR), pp. 7902–7911 (2019)
21. Sebastian, T., Puthiyidam, J.J.: A survey on video summarization techniques. Int. J. Comput. Appl **132**(13), 30–32 (2015)
22. Sigurdsson, G.A., Chen, X., Gupta, A.: Learning visual storylines with skipping recurrent neural networks. In: Leibe, B., Matas, J., Sebe, N., Welling, M. (eds.) ECCV 2016. LNCS, vol. 9909, pp. 71–88. Springer, Cham (2016). https://doi.org/10.1007/978-3-319-46454-1_5
23. Song, X., et al.: Category driven deep recurrent neural network for video summarization. In: 2016 IEEE International Conference on Multimedia Expo Workshops (ICMEW), pp. 1–6 (2016)
24. Song, Y., Vallmitjana, J., Stent, A., Jaimes, A.: TVSum: summarizing web videos using titles. In: IEEE Conference on Computer Vision and Pattern Recognition (CVPR), pp. 5179–5187 (2015)
25. Szegedy, C., et al.: Going deeper with convolutions. In: 2015 IEEE Conference on Computer Vision and Pattern Recognition (CVPR), pp. 1–9 (2015)
26. Tang, T., Jia, J., Mao, H.: Dance with melody: an LSTM-autoencoder approach to music-oriented dance synthesis. In: ACM International Conference on Multimedia, pp. 1598–1606 (2018)
27. Wang, L., Ho, Y.S., Yoon, K.J., et al.: Event-based high dynamic range image and very high frame rate video generation using conditional generative adversarial networks. In: IEEE/CVF Conference on Computer Vision and Pattern Recognition(CVPR), pp. 10081–10090 (2019)
28. Wang, M., Hong, R., Li, G., Zha, Z.J., Yan, S., Chua, T.S.: Event driven web video summarization by tag localization and key-shot identification. IEEE Trans. Multimedia **14**(4), 975–985 (2012)

29. Wolf, W.: Key frame selection by motion analysis. In: IEEE International Conference on Acoustics, Speech, and Signal Processing Conference, vol. 2, pp. 1228–1231 (1996)

30. Yang, H., Wang, B., Lin, S., Wipf, D., Guo, M., Guo, B.: Unsupervised extraction of video highlights via robust recurrent auto-encoders. In: 2015 IEEE International Conference on Computer Vision (ICCV), pp. 4633–4641 (2015)

31. Yao, T., Mei, T., Rui, Y.: Highlight detection with pairwise deep ranking for first-person video summarization. In: 2016 IEEE Conference on Computer Vision and Pattern Recognition (CVPR), pp. 982–990 (2016)

32. Yu, H., Cheng, S., Ni, B., Wang, M., Zhang, J., Yang, X.: Fine-grained video captioning for sports narrative. In: IEEE Conference on Computer Vision and Pattern Recognition (CVPR), pp. 6006–6015 (2018)

33. Zhang, H.J., Wu, J., Zhong, D., Smoliar, S.W.: An integrated system for content-based video retrieval and browsing. Pattern Recogn. 30(4), 643–658 (1997)

34. Zhang, K., Chao, W.L., Sha, F., Grauman, K.: Summary transfer: exemplar-based subset selection for video summarization. In: IEEE Conference on Computer Vision and Pattern Recognition (CVPR), pp. 1059–1067 (2016)

35. Zhang, K., Chao, W.-L., Sha, F., Grauman, K.: Video summarization with long short-term memory. In: Leibe, B., Matas, J., Sebe, N., Welling, M. (eds.) ECCV 2016. LNCS, vol. 9911, pp. 766–782. Springer, Cham (2016). https://doi.org/10.1007/978-3-319-46478-7_47

36. Zhao, B., Li, X., Lu, X.: HSA-RNN: hierarchical structure-adaptive RNN for video summarization. In: 2018 IEEE/CVF Conference on Computer Vision and Pattern Recognition (CVPR), pp. 7405–7414 (2018)

37. Zhao, B., Li, X., Lu, X.: Hierarchical recurrent neural network for video summarization (2019)

38. Zhao, B., Xing, E.P.: Quasi real-time summarization for consumer videos. In: 2014 IEEE Conference on Computer Vision and Pattern Recognition (CVPR), pp. 2513–2520 (2014)

39. Zhou, K., Qiao, Y., Xiang, T.: Deep reinforcement learning for unsupervised video summarization with diversity-representativeness reward. In: Thirty-Second AAAI Conference on Artificial Intelligence, pp. 7582–7589. AAAI (2018)

Efficient Unsupervised Monocular Depth Estimation with Inter-Frame Depth Interpolation

Min Zhang and Jianhua Li[✉]

Dalian University of Technology, No. 2 Linggong Road, Ganjingzi District,
Dalian, Liaoning, China
jianhual@dlut.edu.cn

Abstract. To alleviate the need of expensive depth annotations, some existing works resort to unsupervised learning methods for depth estimation using monocular videos. To improve the accuracy of the prediction with the relationship of the inter-frame, we present a new unsupervised learning algorithm for monocular depth estimation. In contrast to most existing works, our method predicts depth maps for both target and source frames in each iteration. An inter-frame depth interpolation module is designed, which learns to infer the depth map of the target frame based on those of the source frames. A temporal consistency loss is also proposed to penalize the discrepancy of the predicted depth maps across frames, which not only enforces the coherence of video depth prediction but also provides supervision to source view depth estimation. Similar to the idea of the mutual learning, our method takes full advantages of both target and source views for depth estimation learning. Each module of our proposed method is differentiable, allowing end-to-end training of the whole system. Experiments on the popular KITTI dataset have been conducted and shown that our method performs favorably against state-of-the-art approaches.

Keywords: Depth estimation · Supervised · Another keyword

1 Introduction

Monocular depth estimation aims to reconstruct the depth information from a single input image. Its accuracy strongly influences the downstream applications, including robotics, autonomous driving, 3D reconstruction, *etc.*. However, since the problem of depth estimation from a single view itself is under-determined and ill-posed, it is still a very challenging task nowadays to design accurate and robust monocular depth estimation algorithms. With the rapid development of deep learning techniques, deep convolutional neural network (CNN) based approaches have recently achieved significant progress in depth estimation. Nevertheless,

Supported by the National Natural Science Foundation of China 61771088.

Y. Peng et al. (Eds.): ICIG 2021, LNCS 12890, pp. 729–741, 2021.
https://doi.org/10.1007/978-3-030-87361-5_59

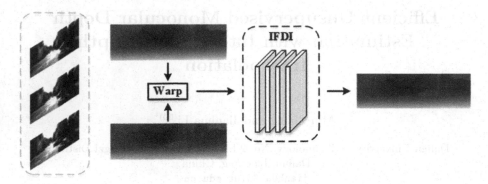

Fig. 1. The training sample of the whole network is three continuous images. The depth prediction network estimates depth from the RGB image. Our IFDI module takes the warped source depth maps estimated by the depth prediction network as inputs and infers the target depth.

training a deep CNN with sophisticated architectures entails large scale training data with ground truth depth annotations which are expensive to achieve or still very rare in terms of scene diversities. To address the above drawbacks, some recent works explore unsupervised network training with geometric constraints using monocular videos. Existing unsupervised depth estimation methods using monocular videos operate under the structure-from-motion (SfM) setting and leverage geometric consistency as supervision. They typically take one target and multiple source frames as an input training sample, and consist of a depth model that predicts a depth map for each pixel in the target frame and a pose model that estimates the relative camera pose translation between the target and source frames. During the training stage, the depth model can only learn from the target frame within one training iteration, while the source frames are mostly used for target view synthesis. In order to optimize the depth model on extra frames (*e.g.*, the source frames), either enlarging the training batch size or performing additional forward-backward training iterations is required, leading to inefficient depth network training with increased GPU memory and computational overhead. Besides, it does not change the nature of predicting depth from the single frame.

To mitigate the above issue, we propose an efficient unsupervised learning algorithm for monocular depth estimation using unlabeled videos. Unlike prior work, our method is able to optimize depth prediction for both target and source frames within one training iterations. To this purpose, we propose a trainable IFDI module which is used to infer the depth for the target frame by learning to capture the underlying pattern of depth variations between adjacent frames, see Fig. 1. The IFDI module adopts a different formulation by taking the depth maps of adjacent source frames as input to generate that of the target frame. The IFDI performs in a per-pixel basis, which enables more flexibility in manipulating non-rigid object regions. More importantly, the IFDI is fully differentiable, allowing end-to-end training of the entire system.

Motivated by the idea of mutual learning [21], we further investigate a temporal consistency loss to minimize the differences between the target depth maps predicted by the depth estimation network and IFDI module, respectively. For one thing, since the monocular depth estimation network and IFDI module employ different form of depth estimation, their predictions may be complementary. The temporal consistency loss encourages these two models to learn from each other in a mutually beneficial manner, providing additional supervisions for training depth estimation from source frames. For another, since the inference of IFDI module highly relies on the depth predictions of source images, the temporal consistency loss as well as its gradients are computed and back-propagated across adjacent frames, enforcing temporally more consistent depth prediction results.

In summary, the contribution of this paper is at least twofold. First, we propose a new unsupervised learning framework for depth estimation with monocular videos, which takes full advantages of source frames for learning depth estimation, thus considerably improves network training efficiency. Second, we design an inter-frame depth interpolation (IFDI) module and a temporal consistency loss. Their collaboration allows the monocular depth estimation network as well as the IFDI module to be learned in a mutually beneficial and temporal consistent manner. The proposed method sets new state-of-the-art unsupervised learning performance on a widely adopted depth estimation benchmark.

2   Method

In this section, we present the details of our proposed unsupervised monocular depth estimation method. We first briefly review the principles of geometric view synthesis based unsupervised learning framework in Sect. 2.1 to introduce the notations used in our algorithm. Section 2.2 and 2.3 elaborate on the proposed inter-frame depth interpolation module and consistency boost loss, respectively. Finally, Sect. 2.5 presents the overall network architecture and implementation details.

2.1   View Synthesis for Unsupervised Learning

The basic idea of most existing unsupervised monocular video depth estimation methods is to explore geometric view synthesis as supervision to jointly train a depth estimation and a pose estimation model.

Mathematically, we can denote the depth estimation model as $\mathcal{F}_D : \mathbf{I}_t \rightarrow \mathbf{D}_t$ that maps an input target frame $\mathbf{I}_t$ to its depth map $\mathbf{D}_t$, the pose estimation model as $\mathcal{F}_T : (\mathbf{I}_t, \mathbf{I}_s) \rightarrow \mathbf{T}_{t \rightarrow s}$ that predicts the camera pose translation $\mathbf{T}_{t \rightarrow s}$ from the target frame $\mathbf{I}_t$ to the source frame $\mathbf{I}_s$. The homogeneous coordinates $\mathbf{p}_t$ of a pixel in the target frame can be reprojected to the source frame as follows,

$$\mathbf{p}_s = \mathbf{K}\mathbf{T}_{t \rightarrow s}\mathbf{D}_t(\mathbf{p}_t)\mathbf{K}^{-1}\mathbf{p}_t, \tag{1}$$

Where $\mathbf{K}$ denotes the camera intrinsics matrix; $\mathbf{D}_t(\mathbf{p}_t)$ represents the predicted depth of pixel $\mathbf{p}_t$, and $\mathbf{p}_s$ indicates the reprojected coordinates in the source view. With all these reprojected coordinates, we can then reconstruct the target depth map using source frame as $\mathbf{I}'_t(\mathbf{p}_t) = \mathbf{I}_s\langle\mathbf{p}_s\rangle$ with $\langle\rangle$ indicating the bilinear sampling. Since the coordinate reprojection and sampling operations are both differentiable, the depth and pose estimation models can then be trained by minimizing the photometric errors between the reconstructed and the original target frames. A widely-adopted loss function in the literature combines the L1 loss and the SSIM measurement as follows.

$$L_p(\mathbf{I}_t, \mathbf{I}'_t) = \frac{\lambda}{2}(1 - SSIM(\mathbf{I}_t, \mathbf{I}'_t)) + (1 - \lambda)\|\mathbf{I}_t - \mathbf{I}'_t\|_1, \tag{2}$$

The hyperparameter λ is set to 0.9 to emphasize the impact of the SSIM similarity.

2.2 Inter-Frame Depth Interpolation

One drawback of the above unsupervised learning framework is that the input source images are mainly used for view synthesis to provide depth supervision, while the depth estimation network can only be trained on the single image during one training iteration, leading to an inefficient network training process and insufficient scene feature. We circumvent these issues by proposing an IFDI module, which allows us to learn depth estimation from both target and source images within one iteration. Rather than using source view synthesis as supervision to train source depth prediction, we propose to transform the source depth to the target view. Consequently, the depth estimation network can be supervised by measuring the consistency between target and source depth predictions.

On the physical, when the observer O is moving in a certain direction, the distance $\mathbf{D}_t$ between the observed S and O will change continuously in a certain rule. If the rules are grasped, given the distance in $\mathbf{D}_{t'}, t' \in \{t - 1, t + 1\}$, we can infer the distance of t-th frame D_t. In our case, O is the camera, and the distance between O and S is the depth value that we want to figure out.

Another problem that needs to be solved is how to find the matching pixels belonging to the same point in the real world from different frames. Because of the motion of the camera, points at the same position in different RGB images do not necessarily represent the same point in the real world. As mention in Sect. 2.1 the reprojected coordinates on the reference view $\mathbf{p}_{t'}$ warps the reference image into the target view. We apply it to the depth domain:

$$\mathbf{D}'_{t'} = \mathbf{D}_{t'} < \mathbf{p}_{t'} > \tag{3}$$

The $\mathbf{D}'_{t'}$ and the $\mathbf{D}_t$ are calibrated in pixel coordinate system of the target view, but the value of each pixel in $\mathbf{D}'_{t'}$ is the depth value of the matched pixels in the reference view.

In order to make full use of the reference frames by inferring depth map in the target view from the variation the reference ones, we choose the middle frame of the video clip as the target frame, $t' \in \{t-1, t+1\}$ as the reference ones to find the supervised relationship as much as possible. With a limited range of the perspective, the camera can not capture the observed S that out of view field, and relative pixels will be inevitably out of the view due to the motion of the camera. We can mask out these pixels by complying with the following rules:

$$\mathbf{D}'_{t'} \begin{cases} = 0, & \mathbf{p}_{t'} \notin [-1, 1] \\ \neq 0, & \mathbf{p}_{t'} \in [-1, 1] \end{cases}$$

If the $\mathbf{p}_{t'}$ is out of the filed of camera vision in t'-th frame, we can not find the matching points in one of the target frames. $\mathbf{D}'_{t'}$ will disable those points that out of lens view.

Based on the above observation, the IFDI module is designed to capture the depth variations across frames with a linear transformation. Specifically, given the predicted depth maps $\{\mathbf{D}_{t-1}, \mathbf{D}_t, \mathbf{D}_{t+1}\}$ of three consecutive frames with the t-th frame as the target frame, we first warp source depth prediction $\mathbf{D}_{t-1}$ and $\mathbf{D}_{t+1}$ to the target view denoted as $\mathbf{D}'_{t-1}$ and $\mathbf{D}'_{t+1}$, respectively, such that the depth values of warped depth maps $\mathbf{D}'_{t-1}$ and $\mathbf{D}'_{t+1}$ are spatially aligned with those of the target depth map $\mathbf{D}_t$. The IFDI module then takes the warped depth maps $\mathbf{D}'_{t-1}$ and $\mathbf{D}'_{t+1}$ as input, and produces two corresponding weight maps $\mathbf{W}_{t-1}$ and $\mathbf{W}_{t+1}$.

The IFDI module predicts $\{\mathbf{M}_{t'}, t' \in \{t-1, t+1\}\}$ for each matched points in depth video. For the points that successfully reprojected to the reference camera pose, the value of the $\mathbf{M}_{t'}(\mathbf{p}_{t'})$ will indicate the linear transformation from the reference perspective to the target one. Ideally, if the observer O is in uniform linear motion and the observed S is in stationary, $\mathbf{M}_{t'}(\mathbf{p}_{t'})$ is constant for each pixel. The ideal assumption is hard to reach, and the reality is much more complicated. For example, the $\mathbf{M}_{t'}(\mathbf{p}_{t'})$ of the moving object and the still object is disparate. There are discontinuity at the edge of the object. It is also different in the camera motion in the different shot intervals. Thus the IFDI outputs the $\mathbf{M}_{t'}(\mathbf{p}_{t'})$ in pixel level. The inferred target depth map of the IFDI module is computed by:

$$\hat{\mathbf{D}}_t = \mathbf{M}_{t-1}\mathbf{D}'_{t-1} + \mathbf{M}_{t+1}\mathbf{D}'_{t+1} \tag{4}$$

2.3   Consistency Boost Loss

The monocular depth estimation captures the depth information from the size of the object in the scene, while the IFDI module infers depth from the multi-view information. These two forms of data provide complementary features of a high-level semantic level. Therefore the output of the IFDI module and the monocular depth network are expected to be the same. In consideration of the scale of depth values, the relative error is the suitable choice. We design a consistency boost loss function, see Formula 5, and reach a good performance.

$$L_c = \max(\frac{\hat{\mathbf{D}}_t}{\mathbf{D}_t}, \frac{\mathbf{D}_t}{\hat{\mathbf{D}}_t}) - \min(\frac{\hat{\mathbf{D}}_t}{\mathbf{D}_t}, \frac{\mathbf{D}_t}{\hat{\mathbf{D}}_t}) \tag{5}$$

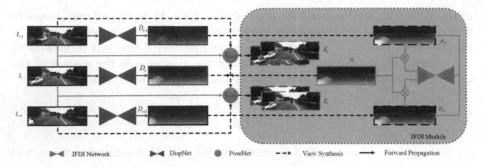

IFDI Network ▶◀   DispNet ▶◀   PoseNet ●   View Synthesis ‑‑▶   Forward Propagation ⟶

Fig. 2. The architecture of our method. The video frames are inputted to the DispNet in turn and acquire the corresponding estimated depth maps. The reference depth maps $\mathbf{D}_{t-1}$ and $\mathbf{D}_{t+1}$ is warped to the target view represented as $\mathbf{D}'_{t'}$ which is calibrated to the coordinates of the target frame but the value of each pixel is the depth value of the matching points in reference views. $\{\mathbf{D}'_{t'}, t' \in \{t-1, t+1\}\}$ are then fed to the IFDI module. The Consistency Boost Loss computes the difference between the two depth maps in target views, denoted in the solid blue border $\mathbf{D}_t$ and solid green border $\hat{\mathbf{D}}_t$. The per-pixel minimum Reprojection Photometric error computes the difference between the target RGB image $\mathbf{I}_t$ and the warped RGB images $\mathbf{I}'_t$. The warped denoted in the dotted blue border and the dotted blue border is respectively warped based on predicted depth results of the DispNet and the IFDI Module. (Color figure online)

Where $\hat{D}_t$ indicates the reprojected depth map of the IFDI module and D_t is the predicted depth map of the monocular depth estimator.

2.4   Loss Function

Our final loss function becomes:

$$L_{final} = L_{p\_min}(\mathbf{D}_t) + L_{p\_min}(\hat{\mathbf{D}}_t) + \beta L_{smooth}(\mathbf{D}_t) + \beta L_{smooth}(\hat{\mathbf{D}}_t) + \gamma L_c \quad (6)$$

where $\beta = 1e - 3$, and $\gamma = 1$.

As for the reprojection photometric loss, Formula 2 simply gathers the error of all the reconstructed ones from the reference view together. In practice, there is a case that some pixels in the target frame can be matched in one reference frame but not in another. If we just compute the reprojection photometric loss as the Formula 2, even the depth value is predicted correctly, the loss value will not accurately reflect the difference between the predicted result and the actual value. [7] proposed per-pixel minimum reprojection loss. Instead of taking all the reprojection photometric loss into account, they use the minimum of the reprojection photometric loss among all the reference frames for each pixel.

$$L_{p\_min} = \min_{t'}(L_p(\mathbf{I}'_{t'}, \mathbf{I}_t)) \quad (7)$$

We compute reprojection photometric error in this way for the warped image based the predicted depth results of the IFDI module and the DispNet respectively, represented by the $L_{p\_min}(\mathbf{D}_t)$ and $L_{p\_min}(\hat{\mathbf{D}}_t)$. In order to guarantee the continuous change of the depth value and keep the discontinuity at the edge of the RGB image, we use the edge-aware smoothness loss function [6]:

$$L_{smooth} = |\partial_x \mathbf{D}_t| e^{-|\partial_x \mathbf{I}_t|} + |\partial_y \mathbf{D}_t| e^{-|\partial_y \mathbf{I}_t|} \tag{8}$$

2.5 Network Architecture

Our module involves three learnable convolutional neural networks: the DispNet, the PoseNet, the IFDI Network. The DispNet inputs the single RGB image and outputs the corresponding disparity map. We adopt the architecture proposed in [11]. It is an encoder-decoder style based on the resnet-18 as the backbone with skip connection, and outputs in multi-scale manner, $1, 1/2, 1/4, 1/8$ of the original size. The predicted disparity maps can be converted to the depth maps by: $1/(10 * sigmoid(disp) + 0.01)$. We use a resnet-18 followed by two fully connected layers as the PoseNet. It takes the paired target RGB image and the reference image as the input and outputs estimated camera pose in 6-DoF. The IFDI module takes two adjacent predicted depth maps as input, and outputs the masks for each reference depth frames. It consists of a resnet-18 and 4 series of upconvolution layers with skip-connection to recover the same resolution as original size of the input image. The whole architecture is shown in Fig. 2.

3 Experiment

In this section, we investigate the effectiveness of each component by adding them into the baseline and we compare our method with the former works on KITTI dataset [5]. To demonstrate the generalization capability of our model, we test on the Make3D dataset [15] without any finetune after trained on the KITTI dataset.

3.1 Unsupervised Monocular Depth Estimation

To prove the effectiveness of our method, we compare it with other methods on the KITTI dataset. As shown in Table 1, our method achieves the state-of-the-art result on the KITTI dataset. Our method even outperforms some supervised method [3,8,9] and someones trained on the stereo videos or image pairs [4,12, 13,20]. Compared with the multi-task methods [17–19,23], our model gets better performance with less computing resources. More importantly, there are no extra efforts applied to seek for the non-rigid area with even better performance.

The qualitative experimental results are shown in Fig. 3. We compared with three different methods to verify the advantages of our method. The depth maps predicted by our method have a pretty desirable visual effect. Our method is sensitive to the edge of the object, which is considered to be related to the IFDI module and the per-pixel minimum reprojection photometric loss. It is hard to figure the object that moves in front of the camera in the same direction as the observer, e.g. the car in the image in 9-th line in Fig. 3, but our model performs

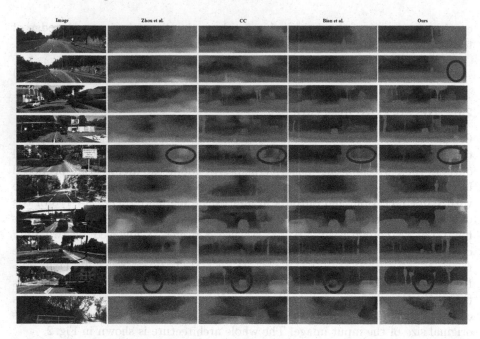

Fig. 3. Qualitative depth predictions of our module and some other works. (Color figure online)

Table 1. Depth Estimation on the KITTI Dataset in Eigen's split. S: methods in a supervised manner. Stereo: trained with the stereo image pairs in an unsupervised way. U: Unsupervised monocular depth estimation. * denotes the shape of the input image is 128*416.

Methods	Supervision	AbsRel	SqRel	RMSE	RMSE_log	$\delta < 1.25$	$\delta < 1.25^2$	$\delta < 1.25^3$
Eigen [3]	S	0.203	1.548	6.307	0.282	0.702	0.890	0.890
Liu [9]		0.201	1.584	6.471	0.273	0.680	0.898	0.967
Klodt [8]		0.166	1.490	5.998	–	0.778	0.919	0.966
Garg [4]	Stereo	0.152	1.226	5.849	0.246	0.784	0.921	0.967
Zhan [20]		0.144	1.391	5.869	0.241	0.803	0.928	0.969
Mehta [12]		0.128	1.019	5.403	0.227	0.827	0.935	0.971
Poggi [13]		0.129	0.996	5.281	0.223	0.831	0.939	0.974
Zhou [22]	U	0.198	1.836	6.565	0.275	0.718	0.901	0.960
Yang [18]		0.182	1.481	6.501	0.267	0.725	0.906	0.963
Mahjourian [10]		0.163	1.240	6.220	0.250	0.762	0.916	0.968
LEGO [17]		0.162	1.352	6.267	0.252	–	–	–
GEONet [19]		0.155	1.296	5.857	0.233	0.793	0.931	0.973
DDVO [16]		0.151	1.257	5.583	0.228	0.810	0.936	0.974
DFNet [23]		0.150	1.124	5.507	0.223	0.806	0.933	0.973
Casser [2]		0.141	1.026	5.291	0.215	0.816	0.945	0.979
CC [14]		0.140	1.070	5.326	0.217	0.826	0.941	0.975
Bian [1]		0.137	1.089	5.439	0.217	0.830	0.942	0.975
Ours*		**0.128**	**0.937**	5.092	<u>0.210</u>	<u>0.846</u>	<u>0.948</u>	**0.978**
Ours		**0.118**	**0.838**	**4.850**	**0.203**	**0.867**	**0.955**	**0.979**

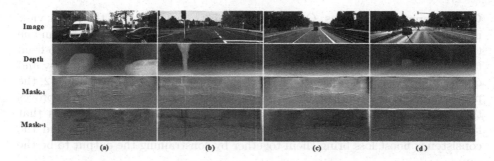

Fig. 4. The 1-th row are the target images and the 2-th are the reconstructed depth maps of the IFDI module. The 3-th and 4-th denote the masks predicted by the IFDI module for each warped reference depth maps.

well on such case which is thought to be owing to take the reference frames into account. Besides, our method can also evaluate the depth of the tiny object against the complex backgrounds accurately, see the traffic lights and handrail in red circle in Fig. 3.

3.2 Ablation Study

The IFDI Module. The IFDI module takes reference depth maps as input, and outputs two masks for them respectively. For the demands of the three adjacent RGB frames, we choose 653 test images that exists front and back RGB images from the Eigne's split for the ablation experiments. The IFDI module significantly improves the performance, see first two lines in Table 2. The visualization of the output is shown in Fig. 4. Just as expected, α tends to fit in nearly the same value in object area, and has a significant variation against the surrounding region in the occluded and motion area, e.g. the moving car in Fig. 4 (a) (d), the edge of the traffic signal (c), some occlusion area (b). The obvious large or small pixels in the border of the images is the unmatched area because of the camera motion. It dynamically preserves the more accurate set of the two reprojection relationships in the format of weighted masks.

Table 2. Comparisons of the proposed components. *Ref* denotes the IFDI Module. $-$ denotes the output does not exist. I denotes the output of the DispNet. R is the prediction of the IFDI module. If there is no special annotation the output is trained in multi-scale, and s in a single-scale. Except for special notes, the training is conducted with images of $128 * 416$ and l denotes $256 * 832$.

	AbsRel		SqRel		RMSE		RMSE_log		$\delta < 1.25$		$\delta < 1.25^2$		$\delta < 1.25^3$	
	I	R	I	R	I	R	I	R	I	R	I	R	I	R
Base	0.145	$-$	1.099	$-$	5.614	$-$	0.227	$-$	0.806	$-$	0.938	$-$	0.975	$-$
Base + Ref	0.138	0.136	0.983	0.975	5.480	5.440	0.217	0.216	0.818	0.822	0.942	0.943	0.977	0.978
Base + Ref + $L_c(s)$	0.130	0.131	0.976	0.966	5.146	5.111	0.211	0.208	0.842	0.840	0.947	0.948	0.977	0.979
Base + Ref + L_c	0.129	0.130	0.934	0.931	5.090	5.071	0.207	0.205	0.841	0.839	0.949	0.949	0.976	0.980
Base + Ref + $L_c(l)$	0.118	0.121	0.835	0.832	4.843	4.826	0.202	0.199	0.867	0.860	0.955	0.955	0.979	0.981

Consistency Boost Loss. Our method predicts depth maps of the target view in different ways. The output of the DispNet learns the relationships from the target image to its depth map, while the IFDI module infers the depth map from the reference frames. The predictions of the two modules are unsatisfactory and quite different with the absence of the consistency boost loss. From Table 2, the participation of the consistency boost loss reduces the discrepancy and improves the performance of both two predicted results. We think the reason is that the features extracted from different input data are complementary, and the consistency boost loss bring them together by constraining the output to be the same.

Generalization. We select Make3D dataset to verify the generalization ability of our model that trained on KITTI without any finetune and get pleasant qualitative and quantitative results. The qualitative and quantitative results are shown in Fig. 5 and Table 3. **Others**

Table 3. Quantitative results on Make3D dataset. All of the methods mentioned in the table are trained on KITTI and test on Make3D directly without any finetune. − denotes the matrix is not released in the paper.

Method	AbsRel	SqRel	RMSE	RMSE_log
Godard [6]	0.544	10.94	11.76	0.193
Zhou [22]	0.383	5.321	10.47	0.478
CC [14]	0.320	−	−	−
Bian [1]	**0.312**	−	−	−
Ours	0.347	**4.390**	**9.687**	**0.427**

To the effective backward of the gradient and convergence of the optimal solution, the multi-scale output is widely used in the pixel-level tasks. We also experiment with multi-scale and the single-scale outputs. The experiments show that if we use all the scales of the output to compute the per-pixel minimum reprojection photometric loss, the network will converge to a better result than the single-scale nearly 3 epochs faster. Following [1,14], we also train the network with images of two different resolutions, 128 * 416 and 256 * 832. All the quantitative results are listed in Table 2.

Image	Annotation	Prediction

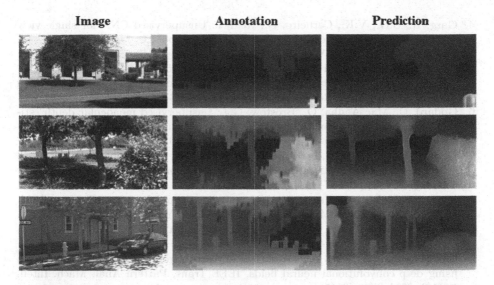

Fig. 5. Some qualitative results of our methods on the Make3D dataset.

4   Conclusion

We propose an efficient unsupervised monocular depth estimation model that truly makes use of the monocular video to be adequate and accurate training samples. Our core contribution is a IFDI module that firstly infers a depth map in target view from the adjacent ones. It provides additional supervision by learning of the mapping from the RGB images to corresponding depth maps. As far as we know, it is the first work to infer the depth from the variations of the adjacent depth frames. Inspired by the multal learning, the consistency loss confirms the network update parameters in appropriate directions by automatically learning additional cues from depth maps obtained in different ways. Experiments prove that all the proposed parts can effectively improve the performance, and achieve state-of-the-art results on the KITTI dataset.

References

1. Bian, J.W., et al.: Unsupervised scale-consistent depth and ego-motion learning from monocular video. In: Thirty-Third Conference on Neural Information Processing Systems (NeurIPS), pp. 35–45 (2019)
2. Casser, V., Pirk, S., Mahjourian, R., Angelova, A.: Depth prediction without the sensors: leveraging structure for unsupervised learning from monocular videos. In: Proceedings of the AAAI Conference on Artificial Intelligence, pp. 8001–8008 (2019)
3. Eigen, D., Puhrsch, C., Fergus, R.: Depth map prediction from a single image using a multi-scale deep network. In: Advances in Neural Information Processing Systems, vol. 27, pp. 2366–2374 (2014)

4. Garg, R., B.G., V.K., Carneiro, G., Reid, I.: Unsupervised CNN for single view depth estimation: geometry to the rescue. In: Leibe, B., Matas, J., Sebe, N., Welling, M. (eds.) ECCV 2016. LNCS, vol. 9912, pp. 740–756. Springer, Cham (2016). https://doi.org/10.1007/978-3-319-46484-8_45
5. Geiger, A., Lenz, P., Stiller, C., Urtasun, R.: Vision meets robotics: the kitti dataset. Int. J. Robot. Res. (IJRR) **32**(11), 1231–1237 (2013)
6. Godard, C., Mac Aodha, O., Brostow, G.J.: Unsupervised monocular depth estimation with left-right consistency. In: The IEEE Conference on Computer Vision and Pattern Recognition (CVPR), pp. 6602–6611 (2017)
7. Godard, C., Oisin, M.A., Firman, M., Brostow, G.J.: Digging into self-supervised monocular depth estimation. In: The IEEE International Conference on Computer Vision (ICCV), pp. 3827–3837 (2019)
8. Klodt, M., Vedaldi, A.: Supervising the new with the old: learning SFM from SFM. In: Ferrari, V., Hebert, M., Sminchisescu, C., Weiss, Y. (eds.) ECCV 2018. LNCS, vol. 11214, pp. 713–728. Springer, Cham (2018). https://doi.org/10.1007/978-3-030-01249-6_43
9. Liu, F., Shen, C., Lin, G., Reid, I.: Learning depth from single monocular images using deep convolutional neural fields. IEEE Trans. Pattern Anal. Mach. Intell. **38**(10), 2024–2039 (2015)
10. Mahjourian, R., Wicke, M., Angelova, A.: Unsupervised learning of depth and ego-motion from monocular video using 3D geometric constraints. In: The IEEE Conference on Computer Vision and Pattern Recognition (CVPR), pp. 5667–5675 (2018)
11. Mayer, N., et al.: A large dataset to train convolutional networks for disparity, optical flow, and scene flow estimation. In: The IEEE Conference on Computer Vision and Pattern Recognition (CVPR), pp. 4040–4048 (2016)
12. Mehta, I., Sakurikar, P., Narayanan, P.: Structured adversarial training for unsupervised monocular depth estimation. In: 2018 International Conference on 3D Vision (3DV), pp. 314–323 (2018)
13. Poggi, M., Tosi, F., Mattoccia, S.: Learning monocular depth estimation with unsupervised trinocular assumptions. In: 2018 International Conference on 3D Vision (3DV), pp. 324–333 (2018)
14. Ranjan, A., et al.: Competitive collaboration: joint unsupervised learning of depth, camera motion, optical flow and motion segmentation. In: The IEEE Conference on Computer Vision and Pattern Recognition (CVPR), pp. 12232–12241 (2019)
15. Saxena, A., Sun, M., Ng, A.Y.: Make3D: learning 3D scene structure from a single still image. IEEE Trans. Pattern Anal. Mach. Intell. **31**(5), 824–840 (2008)
16. Wang, C., Miguel Buenaposada, J., Zhu, R., Lucey, S.: Learning depth from monocular videos using direct methods. In: The IEEE Conference on Computer Vision and Pattern Recognition (CVPR), pp. 2022–2030 (2018)
17. Yang, Z., Wang, P., Wang, Y., Xu, W., Nevatia, R.: LEGO: learning edge with geometry all at once by watching videos. In: The IEEE Conference on Computer Vision and Pattern Recognition (CVPR), pp. 225–234 (2018)
18. Yang, Z., Wang, P., Xu, W., Zhao, L., Nevatia, R.: Unsupervised learning of geometry from videos with edge-aware depth-normal consistency. In: Proceedings of the Thirty-Second AAAI Conference on Artificial Intelligence, pp. 7493–7500 (2018)
19. Yin, Z., Shi, J.: GeoNet: unsupervised learning of dense depth, optical flow and camera pose. In: The IEEE Conference on Computer Vision and Pattern Recognition (CVPR), pp. 1983–1992 (2018)

20. Zhan, H., Garg, R., Saroj Weerasekera, C., Li, K., Agarwal, H., Reid, I.: Unsupervised learning of monocular depth estimation and visual odometry with deep feature reconstruction. In: The IEEE Conference on Computer Vision and Pattern Recognition (CVPR), pp. 340–349 (2018)
21. Zhang, Y., Xiang, T., Hospedales, T.M., Lu, H.: Deep mutual learning. In: CVPR, pp. 4320–4328 (2018)
22. Zhou, T., Brown, M., Snavely, N., Lowe, D.G.: Unsupervised learning of depth and ego-motion from video. In: The IEEE Conference on Computer Vision and Pattern Recognition (CVPR), pp. 6612–6619 (2017)
23. Zou, Y., Luo, Z., Huang, J.-B.: DF-Net: unsupervised joint learning of depth and flow using cross-task consistency. In: Ferrari, V., Hebert, M., Sminchisescu, C., Weiss, Y. (eds.) ECCV 2018. LNCS, vol. 11209, pp. 38–55. Springer, Cham (2018). https://doi.org/10.1007/978-3-030-01228-1_3

Video Playback Quality Evaluation Based on User Expectation and Memory

Shuyi Ji[1], Liqun Lin[1], Yiwen Xu[1], Weiling Chen[1], Nan Chen[1], and Tiesong Zhao[1,2(✉)]

[1] Fujian Key Lab for Intelligent Processing and Wireless Transmission of Media Information, Fuzhou University, Fuzhou 350108, China
`t.zhao@fzu.edu.cn`
[2] Peng Cheng Laboratory, Shenzhen, China

Abstract. The Video Quality Assessment (VQA) has been attracting attentions of image processing community due to its applications in evaluation and optimization of user experience during video playback. Until now, the researches on VQA mainly focus on short video sequences less than 10 s that have similar quality representations to images. In this work, we propose a VQA model for the medium-length video sequences by considering the user perception, expectation and memory. Firstly, we aggregate the popular perception-based VQA metrics to develop a hybrid metric with high consistency to subjective scores. Secondly, we exploit the impact of user expectation on quality evaluation and further utilize it to refine our model. Thirdly, the exponential decay law of user memory is introduced to generate the final model, namely, Expectation and Memory-based VQA (EM-VQA). Experimental results show that the proposed model achieves superior performance than the state-of-the-art VQA models.

Keywords: Video quality assessment (VQA) · User experience · Perception · Memory

1 Introduction

In recent years, there has been a tremendous growth in video communications, the user demand on perceived quality also increases. Since network throughput is unstable and difficult to predict, video quality fluctuation events often occur, which affect the subjective experience of users [1]. To provide a better user experience during video playback, many successful studies have been developed. Duanmu et al. [2] proposed a Quality of Experience (QoE) prediction approach that considers the video presentation quality and playback stalling events, which is consistent with subjective opinion. In [3], a series of subjective experiments were carried out to understand human QoE behaviors in the multi-dimensional adaptation space. The experimental results show that the quality deviation introduced by quality adaptation is related to adaptive intensity, adaptive type, inherent video quality and content. However, these studies were conducted with short

© Springer Nature Switzerland AG 2021
Y. Peng et al. (Eds.): ICIG 2021, LNCS 12890, pp. 742–752, 2021.
https://doi.org/10.1007/978-3-030-87361-5_60

video sequences of less than 10 s. Therefore, it cannot reflect the actual video playback process, where users are used to viewing videos for a long time.

Although the current researches mainly focus on short video sequences, some experts have also studied medium-length video sequences. In [4], several temporal pooling strategies were conducted on the short videos and longer videos, and the current temporal pooling methods are mostly effective on short videos. Chen et al. [5] proposed a Hammerstein–Wiener model for predicting the time-varying subjective quality of rate-adaptive videos. Shen et al. [6] proposed a QoE model to evaluate QoE of adaptive streaming services, which can accurately assess the users' feeling. The researches of long video sequences are based on stalling events, rebuffering evaluation and compression artifacts, and take less account of the influence factors of users themselves. As a result, we will consider three aspects of QoE influence factors, including user perception, expectation and memory, to construct a VQA model for the medium-length video sequences.

Since the Human Visual System (HVS) is the ultimate recipient of videos, an effective VQA methods needs to measure and optimize video quality with respect to visual perception. However, the visual information contained in a video is complex and diverse, and many VQA methods are only applicable to one video distortion type. Thus, it is hard to design a general VQA method. A feasible approach is to combine all metrics into a fusion metric to generate the final quality scores. For example, papadopoulos et al. [7] presented a method for combining a number of existing video quality metrics. Compared with other objective metrics, this method has better perceived quality correlation at the block level. In [8], Li et al. proposed a practical quality metric that fuses two metrics and motion information, and shows higher correlation with subjective quality. Motivated by it, we consider combining several perception-based VQA metrics based to develop a hybrid metric, which is more consistent with user perception.

In addition, user psychological characteristics play a significant role in subjective QoE, such as expectation and memory. User expectation comes from the accumulation of daily viewing habits. Some scholars have done some work on user expectation. Hosek et al. [9] designed a subjective assessment methodology on mobile YouTube QoE. The results show that subjects have higher QoE expectations from the tablet than from smartphone. Deora et al. [10] proposed a quality of service management framework based on user expectation, which reflects the correlation between user expectation and MOS in terms of news update frequency. Memory is a kind of psychological phenomenon, which means that the past conditions and user experience have an impact on current perceived quality [11]. Some experts have utilized memory effect to study the characteristics of video perception. Ghadiyaram et al. [12] proposed a continuous-time video QoE predictor, which can accurately predict the instantaneous QoE of the user by modeling the hysteresis effect and other influence factors. In [13], Bampis et al. continuously predicted the QoE of streaming video through a dynamic network, and considered the impact of recency effect on QoE. Through the above research, it can be found that user expectation and memory are highly correlated with subjective experience, which can be used to better understand and simulate user evaluation behavior.

In this paper, we propose an Expectation and Memory-based VQA (EM-VQA) model for the medium-length, which estimates the video quality by considering user perception, expectation and memory. We summarize the major contributions of this work as follows.

1) Proposing a hybrid metric that aggregates multiple perception-based VQA metrics, which is highly consistent with the subjective quality scores.
2) Modeling the user expectation that reflects the impact of expectation on perceived video quality. By conducting subjective experiments, we obtain the user expectation of different video, which can be utilize to refine our model.
3) Proposing an expectation and memory-based model for the medium-length video sequences by considering the user perception, expectation and memory. The results indicate that the proposed model achieves the superior performance than the state-of-the-art VQA models.

The rest of this paper is organized as follows. Section 2 describes the proposed model. The experimental results are reported in Sect. 3, where extensive performance comparison is made. Finally, we summarize our work in Sect. 4.

2 Proposed Model

In this section, we present our proposed EM-VQA model and show its framework in Fig. 1. As shown in Fig. 1, multiple perception-based metrics are used to compare the perceptual features between the distorted video V_D and the reference video V_R to generate the quality score, respectively. Then, we adopt the regression module to obtain the hybrid quality score Q_{PH} of the distorted video. Considering that user expectation is highly correlated with subjective perceived quality, a subjective experiment was conducted to capture the impact of user expectation during video playback. Through experiment, we can get the expectation Q_E of each user, and further utilize it to refine our model. Finally, the exponential decay temporal pooling function of user memory is introduced to generate the final quality score Q_{EM}.

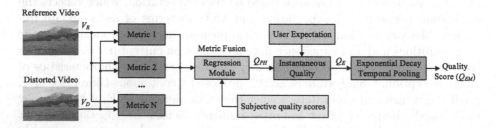

Fig. 1. Framework of the proposed EM-VQA model.

2.1   Hybrid Modeling of Perceptual Metrics

For the distorted video V_D, we can calculate its quality scores vector, which is denoted by q_i, where $i = 1, 2, ..., N$ denote the metric index. The quality score vector q_i of each video to be trained can be expressed as

$$q_i = f_i(V_R, V_D), \quad i = 1, 2, ..., N, \tag{1}$$

where V_R and V_D are the reference video and distorted video, $f_i(.)$ is a mapping function. Then, we input the quality score vector $q = [q_1, ..., q_N]^T$ into the regression module, namely Support Vector Regression (SVR) [14] to obtain the hybrid quality score Q_{PH}, which can be defined as

$$Q_{PH} = wq + b, \tag{2}$$

where $w = [w_1, ..., w_N]$ is a weight vector and b is a bias term. The goal of the training phase is to find the unknown w and b that minimize the difference between hybrid quality score Q_{PH} and the subjective Mean Opinion Score (MOS). Finally, we adopt formula (2) to determine the hybrid quality score Q_{PH} of each distorted video, and utilize the 5-fold cross validation method to reflect the performance results of the hybrid metric.

2.2   Expectation Modeling and Impact

Different users often have different expectations for video quality during video playback, and their MOS tend to correlate closely with their expectations [10]. In VQA, the formation of user expectation comes from the accumulation of daily viewing habits. For example, users who are used to watching low-quality video, providing low-quality videos is enough to meet his expectation. Conversely, low-quality videos cannot meet the expectation of users who often watch high-quality videos. Therefore, the accumulation of viewing habits will have an impact on user expectation, thus affecting the perceived quality of videos. For users, the average of the video quality that users are accustomed to viewing is defined as the user expectation, which can be obtained by

$$E = \frac{1}{M} \sum_{j=1}^{M} V_j, \tag{3}$$

where E represents the user expectation for video quality, M denotes the number of videos viewed by users, and V_j is the objective quality of the j-th video. Since user expectation is related to subjective quality scores, we utilize it to improve the prediction value Q_{PH} of the hybrid metric, which form is

$$Q_E = w \begin{bmatrix} Q_{PH} \\ E \end{bmatrix} + b, \tag{4}$$

where Q_E denotes the perceived quality of video affected by user expectation, Q_{PH} represents the hybrid quality score, E characterizes the user expectation. The weight vector w and the bias term b can be determined by SVR.

2.3   Memory Modeling and Impact

Due to the impact of memory, the perceived quality of users not only depends on the video quality at the current moment, but also affected by the video quality at the earlier stage. To characterize the memory during video playback, we introduced the exponential decay temporal pooling model [15] to simulate the forgetting curve of human perception, which can be defined as

$$Q_{EM}(k) = \gamma Q_{EM}(k-1) + (1-\gamma)Q_E(k), \tag{5}$$

where $Q_{EM}(k)$ represents the perceived quality under the impact of expectation memory, k denotes a video segment, γ characterizes the memory strength, $Q_E(k)$ is the instantaneous quality of video segment k, which can be calculated by using the perception and expectation based metric in Sect. 2.2.

In practical application, we consider a video playback process u with k video segments. The quality score vector of these video segments is expressed by $Q_E = [Q_E^{(u)}(1), Q_E^{(u)}(2), ..., Q_E^{(u)}(k), 1]$. Expand formula (5) to get the prediction value $\tilde{Q}_{EM}(k)$ of perceived quality, which is of the form as follows

$$\tilde{Q}_{EM}(k) = \sum_{i=1}^{k} \gamma^{k-1}(1-\gamma)Q_E(i) + \gamma^k Q_{EM}(0)$$
$$= Q_E[\gamma^{k-1}(1-\gamma), ..., \gamma^0(1-\gamma), \gamma^k Q_{EM}(0)]^T. \tag{6}$$

Suppose there is a series of video playback processes u to be tested, which has the same initial state, and known the subjective user ratings. The prediction value $\tilde{Q}_{EM}$ can be estimated by a linear model, which form is

$$\tilde{Q}_{EM} = [Q_E^{(1)}, Q_E^{(2)}, ..., Q_E^{(u)}]^T [z_0, z_1, ..., z_k]^T, \tag{7}$$

where $Q_E^{(u)}$ represents the quality score vector of the u-th playback process, which contains the instantaneous quality of each video segment. $z_0, z_1, ..., z_k$ are the parameters to be solved. Since the quality scores vector Q_E and subjective user ratings $\hat{Q}_{EM}$ of each playback process are known, the value of $z_0, z_1, ..., z_k$ can be obtained by the least square method. According to formula (6), the optimized γ can be derived by

$$\gamma = \frac{1}{k} \sum_{i=1}^{k} \frac{z_{i-1}}{z_i}, \tag{8}$$

where k represents the number of video segment, z_i is the obtained parameter, and γ characterizes the memory strength. By substituting γ into formula (6), we can obtain the prediction value Q_{EM} affected by user expectation and memory.

3   Experimental Results

In this section, we show the experimental results of the proposed EM-VQA model. The comparison experiments were conducted based on the QADS database [16] and the medium-length video database developed by us to verify the validity and accuracy of the proposed model.

3.1   Experimental Setups

1) Dataset for training: During video playback, the viewing resolution is usually fixed, which means that videos with different resolutions will be scaled to the same resolution for users to view. Therefore, it is unreasonable to use the video quality before up-sampling to measure the actual perceived quality of users. To capture the impact of scaling distortion on user perception, we train video frames on the QADS database, which contains 60 low-resolution videos at different images and the corresponding 980 high-resolution images of different quality.

2) Dataset for testing: To verify the test performance of the proposed hybrid metric and EM-VQA model, we conducted experiments on 90 medium-length test video sequences. The snapshots of video sequences are shown in Fig. 2. As shown in Fig. 3, each test video sequence is composed of three 15-second segments with different spatial resolution. Nine playback modes are utilized to simulate the fluctuation of video quality during video playback.

Fig. 2. Snapshots of test video sequences.

3.2   Performance of Hybrid Metric

The six metrics described in Table 1 are selected for aggregation, which are two widely used Full-Reference (FR) metrics (SSIM [17], PSNR), three common No-Reference (NR) metrics (DIIVINE [18], HOSA [19], BRISQUE [20]) and one Super-Resolution (SR) metric (LNQM [16]). These metrics can extract the naturalness, texture, structure and other features contained in a video, which can better reflect the human perceptual characteristics. Pearson Linear Correlation Coefficient (PLCC), Kendall Rank-Order Correlation Coefficient (KROCC) and Spearman Rank-Order Correlation Coefficient (SROCC) are selected to compare the performance of the proposed hybrid metric with other existing state-of-the-art VQA metrics.

Table 1. Six quality metrics used for aggregation.

Metric Index	F1	F2	F3	F4	F5	F6
Metric Name	SSIM [17]	PSNR	DIIVINE [18]	HOSA [19]	BSRQUE [20]	LNQM [16]

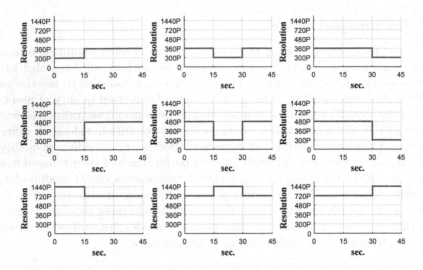

Fig. 3. Nine video playback modes.

The experimental results are shown in Table 2, where the best performance metric is highlighted in bold. Clearly, the performance of the proposed metric is superior to other existing metrics. In addition, Table 3 provides the performance results for the different number of VQA metrics, and the number of metrics increases in turn. The PLCC trend is also demonstrated in Fig. 4 for comparison. From Table 3 and Fig. 4, we observed that the performance of hybrid metric improved significantly when the number of metrics was increased to three, and the best performance was achieved when the number of metrics was the maximum. However, there is little improvement in performance when the number of metrics exceeds three.

Table 2. Performance comparision among 7 quality metrics.

Metric used	PLCC	KROCC	SROCC
SSIM [17]	0.6239	0.4447	0.6249
PSNR	0.6955	0.4617	0.6409
DIIVINE [18]	0.5866	0.4162	0.5801
HOSA [19]	0.8044	0.5766	0.7898
BSRQUE [20]	0.7210	0.4872	0.6590
LNQM [16]	0.8289	0.5846	0.7824
Q_{PH}	**0.8492**	**0.6161**	**0.8037**

Table 3. Performance measure for hybrid metric.

No.of Metric used	PLCC	KROCC	SROCC
1(F1)	0.6239	0.4447	0.6249
2(F1~F2)	0.6318	0.4512	0.6336
3(F1~F3)	0.8101	0.5881	0.7854
4(F1~F4)	0.8346	0.5931	0.7923
5(F1~F5)	0.8404	0.6076	0.8005
6(F1~F6)	0.8492	0.6142	0.8037

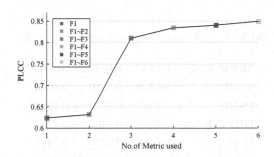

Fig. 4. PLCC performance for hybrid metric.

3.3 Performance of Expectation-Based Method

To obtain the user expectation of the test video sequences, we conducted a user expectation subjective experiment. The source video of the medium-length video sequences are used to construct the test sequences of user expectation. As shown in Fig. 5, each test sequence of user expectation is composed of five 15-s video segments with different resolution: 400× 300, 640 × 360, 720 × 480, 1280 × 720 and 2560 × 1440. Users need to watch a total of ten test sequences of user expectation.

400×300	640×360	720×480	1280×720	2560×1440

Fig. 5. Test sequence of user expectation.

All subjective tests were conducted according to ITU-R BT. 500-13 [21]. Since the resolution of the source videos are 3840 × 2160, all the test sequences need to be enlarged for viewing. A total of 20 subjects participated in the subjective experiment, including 10 males and 10 females, aged between 20 and 35. Visual acuity and color vision are confirmed from each subject before the test. The Single Stimulus (SS) methodology [21] is adopted in the experiment.

In the experiment, subjects are requested to watch 10 test sequences. During video playback, if subjects believe that the current video quality can meet their expectations and can be used for daily viewing, the resolution corresponding to the current video frame will be recorded.

Then, SVR was adopted to train the expectation of subjects and the hybrid quality score Q_{PH}, which are obtained in the subjective experiment and Sect. 3.2, to minimize the difference between the prediction values Q_E and subjective quality scores. Finally, the correlation between the prediction values and subjective test scores is calculated to measure performance. The experimental results are shown in Table 4. It can be found that the performance of Q_E is better than other metrics.

Table 4. Performance of memory based model.

Metric used	PLCC	KROCC	SROCC
SSIM [17]	0.6389	0.4520	0.6260
PSNR	0.7362	0.5026	0.7063
DIIVINE [18]	0.7413	0.5407	0.7242
HOSA [19]	0.8283	0.5926	0.7481
BSRQUE [20]	0.7586	0.5072	0.6571
LNQM [16]	0.8350	0.5975	0.7897
Q_E	**0.8547**	**0.6077**	**0.7914**

3.4   Performance of EM-VQA Model

We tested the performance of the proposed EM-VQA model on the test video sequences. First, we used the Q_E obtained in Sect. 3.3 to calculate the instantaneous quality of the EM-VQA model. Then, 5-fold cross validation strategy is performed to verify the performance of the model. 90 test video sequences are randomly divided into five groups. In each group, the unselected sequences are used for training. Since the MOS for each test sequence is known, we can calculate the memory strength γ according to formula (8). The trained γ will then be substituted into formula (6) to predict the video quality, and the values of γ obtained by different models are shown in Table 5. The performance results are shown in the Table 6. It can be found that the performance of the proposed EM-VQA model is better than Q_{PH}, Q_E and other state-of-the-art VQA models, and can well predict the perceived quality of users during video playback.

Table 5. The value of memory strength (γ).

Metric used	SSIM [17]	PSNR	DIIVINE [18]	HOSA [19]	BRISQUE [20]	LNQM [16]	EM-VQA
γ	0.6579	0.8645	0.8655	1.0235	0.4918	0.5980	0.8747

Table 6. Performance of EM-VQA model.

Metric used	PLCC	KROCC	SROCC
SSIM [17]	0.7835	0.5919	0.7456
PSNR	0.8198	0.6106	0.7434
DIIVINE [18]	0.7964	0.5411	0.7274
HOSA [19]	0.8584	0.5901	0.7567
BSRQUE [20]	0.8414	0.5668	0.7440
LNQM [16]	0.8553	0.6061	0.7441
EM-VQA	**0.8621**	**0.6154**	**0.7685**

4 Conclusion

In this paper, we propose an EM-VQA model for the medium-length video sequences by considering the user perception, expectation and memory. Multiple perception-based VQA metrics were aggregated, including structural similarity, natural scene statistics, high-order statistical aggregation and other metrics, to develop a hybrid metric with high consistency to subjective scores. Then, we analyze the impact of user expectation on quality evaluation and further utilize it to refine our model. Finally, the exponential decay law of user memory is introduced to generate the final model. Experimental results confirmed that the proposed model is superior to the existing state-of-the-art VQA models. As future work, we plan to further improve the model with respect to human psychological characteristics.

Acknowledgments. This work is partially supported by grants from Natural Science Foundation of China (No. 62001404) and Fujian Provincial Education Department (No. JAT200024).

References

1. Eswara, N., Ashique, S., Panchbhai, A., Chakraborty, S., Sethuram, H.P.: Streaming video QoE modeling and prediction: a long short-term memory approach. IEEE Trans. Circ. Syst. Video Technol. **30**(3), 661–673 (2019)
2. Duanmu, Z., Zeng, K., Ma, K., Rehman, A., Wang, Z.: A quality-of-experience index for streaming video. IEEE J. Sel. Top. Signal Process. **11**(1), 154–166 (2017)
3. Duanmu, Z., Rehman, A., Wang, Z.: A quality-of-experience database for adaptive video streaming. IEEE Trans. Broadcast. **64**(2), 474–487 (2018)
4. Seufert, M., Slanina, M., Egger, S., Kottkamp, M.: "to pool or not to pool": a comparison of temporal pooling methods for http adaptive video streaming. In: International Workshop on Quality of Multimedia Experience (QoMEX), pp. 52–57 (2013)
5. Chen, C., Choi, L.K., de Veciana, G., Caramanis, C., Heath, R.W., Bovik, A.C.: Modeling the time-varying subjective quality of http video streams with rate adaptations. IEEE Trans. Image Process. **23**(5), 2206–2221 (2014)

6. Shen, Y., Liu, Y., Liu, Q., Yang, D.: A method of QoE evaluation for adaptive streaming based on bitrate distribution. In: IEEE International Conference on Communications Workshops (ICC), pp. 551–556 (2014)
7. Papadopoulos, M.A., Katsenou, A.V., Agrafiotis, D., Bull, D.R.: A multi-metric approach for block-level video quality assessment. Signal Process. Image Commun. **78**, 152–158 (2019)
8. Li, Z., Aaron, A., Manohara, M.: Toward a practical perceptual video quality metric (2016). http://techblog.netflix.com/2016/06/toward-practical-perceptual-video.html
9. Hosek, J., Ries, M., Vajsar, P., Nagy, L., Penizek, R.: User's happiness in numbers: Understanding mobile youtube quality expectations. In: International Conference on Telecommunications and Signal Processing (TSP), pp. 607–611 (2015)
10. Deora, V., Shao, J., Gray, W., Fiddian, N.: A quality of service management framework based on user expectations. In: International Conference on Service-Oriented Computing (ICSOC), pp. 104–114 (2003)
11. Yu, S., Tao, R., Hou, Y.: Modeling for short-form http adaptive streaming considering memory effect. In: International Conference on Broadband and Wireless Computing, Communication and Applications (BWCCA), pp. 82–87 (2015)
12. Ghadiyaram, D., Pan, J., Bovik, A.C.: Learning a continuous-time streaming video QoE model. IEEE Trans. Image Process. **27**(5), 2257–2271 (2018)
13. Bampis, C., Li, Z., Bovik, A.C.: Continuous prediction of streaming video QoE using dynamic networks. IEEE Signal Process. Lett. **24**(7), 1083–1087 (2017)
14. Smola, A., Schölkopf, B.: A tutorial on support vector regression. Stat. Comput. **14**, 199–222 (2004)
15. Xue, J., Zhang, D.Q., Yu, H., Chen, C.W.: Assessing quality of experience for adaptive http video streaming. In: IEEE International Conference on Multimedia and Expo Workshops (ICMEW), pp. 1–6 (2014)
16. Ma, C., Yang, C.Y., Yang, X., Yang, M.H.: Learning a no-reference quality metric for single-image super-resolution. Comput. Vision Image Underst. **158**, 1–16 (2017)
17. Wang, Z., Bovik, A.C., Sheikh, H.R., Simoncelli, E.P.: Image quality assessment: from error visibility to structural similarity. IEEE Trans. Image Process. **13**(4), 600–612 (2004)
18. Moorthy, A.K., Bovik, A.C.: Blind image quality assessment: from natural scene statistics to perceptual quality. IEEE Trans. Image Process. **20**(12), 3350–3364 (2011)
19. Xu, J., Ye, P., Li, Q., Du, H., Liu, Y.: Blind image quality assessment based on high order statistics aggregation. IEEE Trans. Image Process. **25**(9), 4444–4457 (2016)
20. Mittal, A., Moorthy, A.K., Bovik, A.C.: No-reference image quality assessment in the spatial domain. IEEE Trans. Image Process. **21**(12), 4695–4708 (2012)
21. BT. 500–13, I.R.: Methodology for the subjective assessment of the quality of television pictures (2012)

Talking Face Video Generation
with Editable Expression

Luchuan Song[1], Bin Liu[1,2](✉), and Nenghai Yu[1,2]

[1] University of Science and Technology of China, Hefei, China
slc0826@mail.ustc.edu.cn,{flowice,ynh}@ustc.edu.cn
[2] Key Laboratory of Electromagnetic Space Information,
Chinese Academy of Science, Hefei, China

Abstract. In rencent years, the convolutional neural network have been proved to be a great success in generating talking face. Existing methods have combined a single face image with speech to generate talking face video. The challenge with these methods is that only the lips change in the video, lacking other facial expressions such as blinking and eyebrow movements. In order to solve this problem, this paper propose a embedding system to tackle the task of talking face video generation by using a still image of a person and an audio clip containing speech. We can modify some of the natural expressions through high-level structure, *i.e.*, the facial landmarks. Compared with the direct audio-to-image method, our approach avoids spurious correlations between audio-visual signals that were unrelated to the speech content. In addition, to generate the face of the network, a face sequence generation method based on single sample learning is designed.

Keywords: Talking face video generation · Facial expression · Embedding system

1 Introduction

The talking face generation problem aims to synthesize natural expressions in talking face video with a still facial image and a piece of audio clip. Aside from topics of academic, it is widely used in communication systems, such as face animation, teleconference, computer aided instruction and other applications.

There are some methods of lip tampering based on computer graphics [10,17]. Given a source image, 3DMM or 3D mesh can be obtained and used to model both the driving and source faces [19]. The estimated 3D is used to transform the expression of the source face to match that of the driving face. However, it requires additional steps to transfer the hidden regions and 3D modeling of faces. Instead of solving the problem of talking face generation from the perspective of 3D model, this paper lies on GAN and style transformation to manage this problem.

Subject independent approaches have been proposed to convert audio features directly into video frames. Most of these methods restrict the problem to

Y. Peng et al. (Eds.): ICIG 2021, LNCS 12890, pp. 753–764, 2021.
https://doi.org/10.1007/978-3-030-87361-5_61

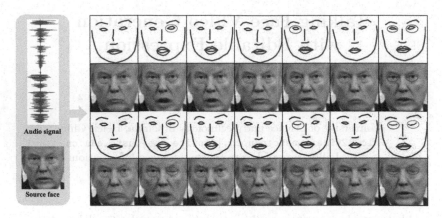

Fig. 1. The faces generated by the existing methods ATVGNet [3] (first and second row), with no expression. Our method edit the eye landmark to produce results (third and fourth row) which have blink action. The differences between the two methods are highlighted in red. (Color figure online)

generating only the mouth. There are also attempts to modify the mouth of the speaker in the video [11]. However, the face generated by these methods has certain limitations. For example, Chen *et al.* [3] proposed a method to produce lips that accurately match to speech, but it lacks the natural expression of the face. Kumar *et al.* [11] could have tampered with the lip shapes in Obama's speech videos, but the method based on image translation [9] requires a large number of public figures' video like Obama. However, for non-public figures, it is hard to get lots of video for training.

Compared with these approaches, in this paper we present a system for creating talking face video from single face image. The talking face synthesized by our method use deep ConvNets through a sequence of convolutional operations. Therefore, we can obtain the posture of the human face by modifying the high-level semantic information related to the posture. Inspired by the method of audio generating landmark [11,17], we generate the mouth landmark from the given speech, and then modify the eye and head position landmarks to get a natural expression (as shown in Fig. 1). The face corresponding to the landmark is generated through the network under the condition of single source face and landmark, so as to obtain the talking face video containing expressions. Furthermore, to improve the quality of the generated frames and save computing resources, we design a warping-based method to ensure the quality of the generated hair, beard, wrinkles and other details. In summary, the key highlights of the work is as following:

1) A novel method is proposed to solve the problem of the expression in talking face generation based on a single face photograph.
2) A fusion algorithm based on classic warping is designed to further enhance the generated face and optimize the details of facial wrinkles and hair.

3) The experimental results compared with the state-of-the-art methods, our method has improved both in quantitative and qualitative measurement.

2   Related Work

Traditional talking face generation methods can be classified into the two categories: 1) model-based methods, 2) feed-forward-based methods.

Model-based Methods. The main goal is to establish the relationship between 3D models and faces. It typically contains three steps: **i)** Capture face movement [10,18,19]. **ii)** Fit the movement of the face into a parametric space or 3D model [10]. By changing the parameters of the model, the attitude of the corresponding face can be changed directly. **iii)** Rerender new video [18,19]. Because different 3D models are required for diverse faces, the robustness of these methods for universal faces is defective. In this paper, GAN-based method is used to solve the problem of audio-to-visual.

Feed-forward Methods. These methods have a similar pipeline to model-based methods but replace the third rerender step with a neural network generator. For example, Kim et al.[10] took 3D rendering results, illumination and the expression as inputs to generate a near-real quality image. Here, we focus on a single image as input to reconstruct a set of images. Wu et al.[25] took only the boundary information as input to achieve a competitive result and they trained an encoder-decoder structure to get the connection between a real face and boundary latent spaces. Chang et al.[2] proposed manipulation methods that support single face input. But they only alter the appearance of facial components and face difficulty in handling large shape and pose changes. Some models such as body generator [6] and street view generator [15,24] can implement single face generation problem but these methods are confronted with identity shift or coarse details of face when adopted to generate face image directly and fails to enable single face reenactment with continuous pose representation, due to the challenge in large shape changes, the complexity of pose and expression. To address this challenge, we design a new cascade method to solve the problem of identity and face details during generation.

3   Methodology

Overview. Figure 2 illustrates the pipline of our method, φ is used to convert the audio signal $a_{1:T}$ into landmark $m_{1:T}$.

$$m_{1:T} = \varphi(a_{1:T}), \tag{1}$$

Then we remove the lip landmark of p_p and map the lip generated by Audio2Landmark (pretrain model of keypoint generation network [11]).

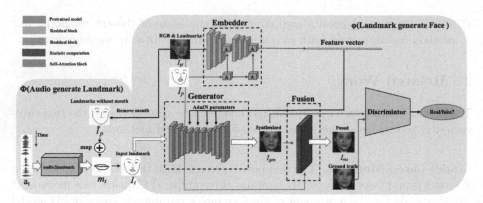

Fig. 2. Overview of the proposed method. The φ transfers audio signal to lip landmark representation, and the ϕ generates video frames based on the proposed generator and embedder.

$$I_{1:T} = \hat{I}_p \oplus m_{1:T}, \tag{2}$$

We add the $m_{1:T}$ to the I_{gt} by overlay addition ($\oplus$ in formula). In the ϕ, we take I_{gt} and spatial information I_p as reference input, and then enter them into the embedder to get the AdaIN [7] parameters. The generator uses the relevant parameters to generate the real face from the target pose $I_{1:T}$ and ensure that the identity is consistent with I_{gt}. The discriminator learn to distinguish the generated face and ground truth at different image scales to ensure the quality of the generated results. To ensure the details of results, I_{gt} and I_{gen} are fused by the fusion block.

$$I_{gen} = \phi(I_{1:T}, I_p, I_{gt}), \tag{3}$$

During training, we only need to train the generator, embedder and discrimintor, where the generator and embedder are jointly trained.

We assume that the face landmarks' locations (we use face alignment code [1] to obtain them) for all frames are available. Landmarks are rasterized into three-channel images using blue line segments to connect certain landmarks.

3.1 Landmark2Face

The blue part in Fig. 2 shows the overview of the proposed talking face generation model. In order to make our network have the generalization ability for general face, we adopt the method of style transfer, $i.e.$, driving the generation of real target face through one or more reference face information combined with the target's landmark.

Embedder. The main role of embedder network is to transform 2D image to AdaIN [7] parameters and use them to predict results of the generator. It receives style information I_{gt}, the corresponding landmark I_p at the same time. To fuse this two domains, we utilize self-attention block [26] to learn a mapping function $\Omega\colon \theta \Rightarrow (\alpha, \beta)$ where affine transformation parameters are obtained by condition θ as $(\alpha, \beta) = \Omega(\theta)$. After obtaining α, β, the self-attention block [26] perform feature-wise modulation on feature map Υ as $\alpha \odot \Upsilon + \beta$, and $\odot$ refers similarity calculation. Here we obtain the prior condition θ from the features of I_{gt} and feature map Υ from I_p and generate δ_i, σ_i as following:

$$\delta_i, \sigma_i = Embedder(I_{gt}, I_p), \tag{4}$$

where δ_i, σ_i are the affine parameters containing the style information. In our network, there are two (δ_i, σ_i) pairs, which are the inputs for each of the self-attention blocks [26], and (δ_i, σ_i) correspond to (α, β). To transfer the style information to the target landmark, we use adaptive instantiation (AdaIN) [7] on residual blocks z_i (green residual block in Fig. 2) in generator. The AdaIN [7] operation is defined as:

$$AdaIN(z_i, \delta_i, \sigma_i) = \delta_i(\frac{z_i - \mu(z_i)}{\sigma(z_i)}) + \sigma_i, \tag{5}$$

which is similiar to *Instance Normalization (IN)* [20], but replaces the affine parameters from *IN*. The embedder consists of residual downsampling and upsampling blocks and insert 64×64 spatial resolution self-attention block [26].

Generator. The sequence generator is defined as G, where:

$$I_{gen} = G(Embedder(I_{gt}, I_p), I_{1:T}), \tag{6}$$

It is used to generate synthesized face I_{gen} with target pose $I_{1:T}$ and the results of embedder. The proposed generator network is based on the image-to-image translation architecture [22], but replaces downsampling and upsampling layers with residual blocks, and all the convolutional layers in generator are followed by *Instance Normalization* [20] layers.

Discrimintor. It has the same structure as the discrimintor of Markovian discriminator [22] and adjust the input size as appropriate. It receives a synthetic face, a real one and learns to distinguish between them.

3.2   Face Detail Fusion Algorithm

Although the generator is very effective in generating the target face, it is difficult to ensure that the face wrinkles, hair texture and background. To reduce the size of the network and ensure consistency in the details of the inner face, the fusion algorithm is based on warping method which has an advantage in generating facial details. However, the traditional facial fusion has two problems: 1) facial color shift and 2) discontinuous image background. To address these

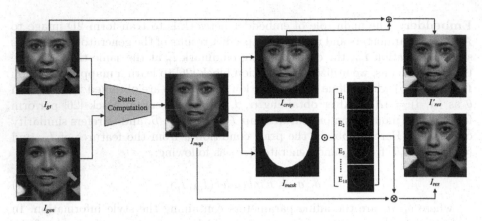

Fig. 3. The fusion process of the generated face I_{gen} and the reference face I_{gt}. The I_{gen} and I_{gt} have different facial expressions and backgrounds (shown in red box). We obtain I_{map} by static pixel mapping, which solves the color shift, but the background is still different from the I_{gt}. The $\otimes$ represents the progressive fusion method in Eq. 7, the $\oplus$ is directly put the face of the crop I_{crop} on the reference face I_{gt} and the $\odot$ is the gradually corroded edge extractor (shown in Algorithm 1). From the red arrows of I'_{res} and I_{res}, it can be found that the results of our method has a smoother boundary than the results without fusion. (Color figure online)

problems, we design a fusion algorithm as shown in Fig. 3. The fusion algorithm is divided into two steps, warp-based facial pixel transformation and progressive facial fusion. We take into account that there is a slight color shift between the generated face and the reference face (yellow arrows in I_{gen} and I_{gt} of Fig. 3), and we introduce the warp-based fusion block (grey part in Fig. 3). The details of the warp-based fusion block shown in Fig. 4. The mask of the reference face I_{gt} and the mask of generated face I_{gen} are calculated by the landmark which is detected by the face detector [1] and have unary relational operation between pixels and record relationship between the pixels to form a new mask. We record the pixel-position corresponding to each position (i, j) on the mask of the reference face. For the generated faces of different position, (i, j) is converted to the position of (i', j'). We adopt the rigid transformation parameters of the face as a priori to calculate such a mapping function: $\mathcal{F}(i, j) \Rightarrow (i', j')$. Our warp-based fusion method is able to deal with exaggerated mouth and head actions.

For the background, we adopt a progressive fusion method in Algorithm 1. The main idea of fusion is to calculate different levels of pixels for the reference inner face and the generated inner face region (the order is determined by the face mask), and the degree of fusion is controlled by the following formula:

$$I_{res} = I_{gt} * (1 - I_{mask}) + \sum E_i * (I_{gen} * \frac{i}{N} + I_{gt} * \frac{N - i}{N}), \qquad (7)$$

the E_i is the ith edge map of the I_{mask} (shown in Fig. 3) and the N is the adjustable parameters, we set the $N = 10$ in our experiment.

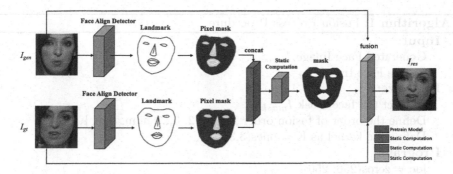

Fig. 4. The details of the face pixel location mapping method. The reference face mask and generated face mask are introduced to record the pixel-position of the two different face. The pixel correspondence between different masks is used to guide the changes of pixels of the RGB face image.

4   Experiments

4.1   Experiment Settings

Datasets. Experiments of the proposed method are done at LRW dataset [5] and Voxceleb2 datasets [4]. We split the training set and evaluation set as the original dataset.

Metrics. Multiple comparison metrics are used to evaluate photo realism and identity preservation of generated images. Specifically, we use PSNR and structured similarity (SSIM) [23] to evaluate the quality of the synthesized face. Besides image quality evaluation, we also evaluate identity (Id) preserving capability by measuring the recognition accuracy with a fixed model [21]. At the video-level , we adopt the Video Multi-Method Assessment Fusion (VMAF) [13] which was proposed by Netflix to approximate human perception of video quality. Although our method is based on a single image generation, the fusion algorithm greatly guarantees the temporal of the generated faces. The USER in the score of the user study, the details of the user study shown in the Sect. 4.3.

Implementation Details. For landmark2face, Adam optimizer is used with $\beta_1 = 0.5$, $\beta_2 = 0.999$ where $\beta1$ is for generator and $\beta2$ is for discriminator. And the learning rate of generator and discriminator are 2e-4 and 5e-5, respectively. The losses of our framework are as follows, **1) Style loss:** L_{Style} constrain the mean and variance of the global color between the reference face image and the generated face image, and it similar to [12]. **2) Lab loss:** L_{Lab}, RGB color space converted to Lab color space and calculate Euclidean distance between generated face and reference face on **a** and **b** dimensions of Lab color space to ensure the same skin color unaffected by light. **3) Id loss:** L_{Id} is the pixel-loss between activations of $Conv1, 6, 11, 18, 25$ VGGFace [16] layers for ground truth and generated images, and the purpose is to ensure that the generated face is consistent with the real face on the identity. **4) Perceptual loss:** L_{Perce}

Algorithm 1: Fusion Process Procedure

Input:
  Generated Face Image I_{gen},
  Source Face Image I_{gt}
Initialize:
  Extract the face mask I_{mask},
  Define the order of fusion order i $\in$ {1, 2, 3,..., num_grad },
  Define the kernel as K = ones(3,3)
Program:
  loc = zeros(256, 256),
  lob = 1 - I_{mask},
  nlob = lob,
  for i = 1, ..., num_grad+1 :
    nloc1 = 1 - lob,
    nlob = Filter2D(nlob, -1, K),
    nloc2 = 1 - nlob,
    E_i = nloc1 - nloc2,
    $E_i[E_i(x,y)! = 0]$ = 1, $(x,y) \in (256, 256)$,
    $pa_0 = I_{gt} * E_i$,
    $pa_1 = I_{gen} * E_i$,
    pa = i/num_grad * pa_1 + (num_grad - i)/num_grad * pa_0,
    $I = I_{gen} - I_{gen} * E_i + pa$,
    $I_{res} = I + I_{gt} * (1 - I_{mask})$
Output:
  I_{res}

---

is the perceptual loss [22] between the generated face and ground truth after resampling. **5) GAN loss:** L_{Gan} is the multi-scale GAN loss [22]. The total loss function is:

$$L_{total} = \lambda_1 L_{Style} + \lambda_2 L_{Lab} + \lambda_3 L_{Id} + \lambda_4 L_{Perce} + \lambda_5 L_{Gan}, \tag{8}$$

where $\lambda_1 = 5$, $\lambda_2 = 0.03$, $\lambda_3 = 1$, $\lambda_4 = 1$ and $\lambda_5 = 1$ in our experiments as the empirical values.

4.2   Comparison with State-of-the-Art Methods

We compare our framework with several state-of-the-art methods that support single input generation. Since there are few single input face models, we also compare our model with single input generation models in other domains: 1) X2face [24]: a network that drive face reconstruction through posture, we adopt the pretrained model provide by the authors. 2) CycleGAN [27]: a translation model between different image domains with unsupervised conversion, we retrain it on our datasets. 3) MUNIT [8]: a very powerful method in the sketch-to-image, we follow the official code and retrain on our datasets. 4) VU-net [6]: which synthesized images of objects conditioned on shape information by using VAE, we

Table 1. Quantitative results of different methods on LRW dataset and VoxCeleb2 dataset.

Method(T)	PSNR↑	SSIM↑	Id%↑	VMAF↑	USER↓
LRW [5]					
X2face [24]	23.9	0.54	43.9	43.1	0.87
CycleGAN [27]	30.0	**0.62**	72.7	51.9	**0.57**
MUNIT [8]	22.1	0.52	52.1	58.4	0.72
VU-net [6]	24.4	0.54	40.1	51.0	0.74
Ours w/o Fusion	29.4	0.56	66.4	60.7	0.66
Ours	**32.1**	0.60	**77.9**	**69.5**	0.60
VoxCeleb2 [4]					
X2face [24]	29.7	0.58	40.8	41.7	0.81
CycleGAN [27]	33.6	**0.62**	72.0	55.9	0.60
MUNIT [8]	19.7	0.43	55.6	66.0	0.73
VU-net citech61esser2018variational	21.9	0.51	42.1	53.9	0.71
Ours w/o Fusion	30.8	0.54	65.8	63.2	0.64
Ours	**33.9**	0.59	**79.1**	**70.2**	**0.59**

follow the authors guide and reproduce on our datasets. 5) The proposed model without fusion. Figure 5 shows the qualitative results of all methods and the proposed framework. CycleGAN [27] performs well on inner face components but with mostly static pose, and it can not handle all mouth movements. Despite the high-quality image generation in other domains, MUNIT [8] are confronted with the identity problem. Vanilla VU-net [6] and X2face [24] generate blurred inner face, and face the identity shift problem as well. The proposed method can simultaneously modify the mouth movements of the inner face and the whole head pose while still preserving the face identity. Table 1 summarizes all quantitative results. Table 1 shows the quantitative results of the methods in Fig. 5. From the Table 1, we learn that our method has the best PSNR and acceptable SSIM compared to other methods, which demonstrates that the facial details generated by our method are more adequate. Compared with other methods, our method has the best ability to maintain identity and produces the smallest identity deviation. Thanks to the facial fusion module, although our method is an image-based generation method, the temporal and quality of the generated videos (VMAF) are the best compared to other methods.

4.3 User Study

We perform a user study to evaluate the realism of the results as seen by the human respondents. We show 50 people the triplets of images of the same person on three different video sequences (two real and one fake) and ask the user to

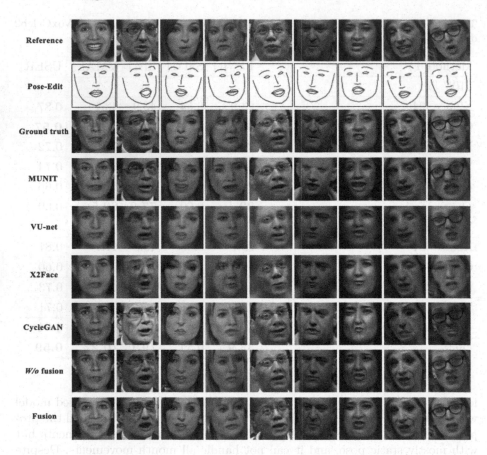

Fig. 5. Qualitative comparison with state-of-the-art single image generation methods.

find the fake image. The user accuracy (success rate, between 0 and 1) is the metric USER. The results are shown in the last column of Table 1. Our method has a best USER score compared to other methods.

4.4   Ablation Study

With/Without **Fusion.** We compare the differences caused by the method with/without fusion, and the results are shown in Table 1 and Fig. 5. Compared with no fusion, the fusion method leads to better face image quality and realism.

Loss Concat Weight. For the loss function, we can decompose it into the parts related to the embedder and parts related to the generator. Specifically, if the loss function's variables contain reference face (ground truth), we assume that this part is related to embedder or generator. Thus we reconstruct the loss function as:

$$L_{total} = L_{generator} + \alpha L_{embedder},$$
$$L_{embedder} = L_{Style} + 0.06 L_{Lab}, \qquad (9)$$
$$L_{generator} = L_{Id} + L_{Perce} + L_{Gan}.$$

We investigate the contribution of the concatenation between the generator and embedder, and the influence of α, the embedder loss weight. Table 2 provides the ablation study results in terms of identity preserving metric values. We can see that concatenation boosts identity preservation performance significantly, and an overly large α will cause overfitting on training data.

5   Conclusion

To bypass the complex computer graphics-based method for talking face generation, we propose a novel method using only a single face and audio clip. By adopting style transfer, the face landmark can be utilized to real facial expressions and guarantee the details of the generated face. In the future work, we will consider to use the optical flow to solve the problem of video jitter between the upper and lower frames and make the generated video more realistic.

Table 2. The identity preserving performance under different setting of generator and embedder on the same reference face test data.

α	0	3	5	10	20	50
Id%	29.6	54.0	**85.7**	59.0	43.1	31.7

References

1. Bulat, A., Tzimiropoulos, G.: How far are we from solving the 2d & 3d face alignment problem?(and a dataset of 230,000 3d facial landmarks). In: CVPR, pp. 1021–1030 (2017)
2. Chang, H., Lu, J., Yu, F., Finkelstein, A.: Pairedcyclegan: asymmetric style transfer for applying and removing makeup. In: CVPR, pp. 40–48 (2018)
3. Chen, L., Maddox, R.K., Duan, Z., Xu, C.: Hierarchical cross-modal talking face generation with dynamic pixel-wise loss. In: CVPR, pp. 7832–7841 (2019)
4. Chung, J.S., Nagrani, A., Zisserman, A.: Voxceleb2: deep speaker recognition. arXiv preprint arXiv:1806.05622 (2018)
5. Chung, J.S., Zisserman, A.: Lip reading in the wild. In: Lai, S.-H., Lepetit, V., Nishino, K., Sato, Y. (eds.) ACCV 2016. LNCS, vol. 10112, pp. 87–103. Springer, Cham (2017). https://doi.org/10.1007/978-3-319-54184-6_6
6. Esser, P., Sutter, E., Ommer, B.: A variational u-net for conditional appearance and shape generation. In: CVPR, pp. 8857–8866 (2018)
7. Huang, X., Belongie, S.: Arbitrary style transfer in real-time with adaptive instance normalization. In: ICCV, pp. 1501–1510 (2017)

8. Huang, X., Liu, M.Y., Belongie, S., Kautz, J.: Multimodal unsupervised image-to-image translation. In: Proceedings of the European Conference on Computer Vision (ECCV), pp. 172–189 (2018)
9. Isola, P., Zhu, J.Y., Zhou, T., Efros, A.A.: Image-to-image translation with conditional adversarial networks. In: CVPR, pp. 1125–1134 (2017)
10. Kim, H., et al.: Deep video portraits. ACM TOG **37**(4), 1–14 (2018)
11. Kumar, R., Sotelo, J., Kumar, K., de Brébisson, A., Bengio, Y.: Obamanet: photo-realistic lip-sync from text (2017). arXiv preprint arXiv:1801.01442
12. Li, Y., Wang, N., Liu, J., Hou, X.: Demystifying neural style transfer (2017). arXiv preprint arXiv:1701.01036
13. Li, Z., Aaron, A., Katsavounidis, I., Moorthy, A., Manohara, M.: Toward a practical perceptual video quality metric. Netflix Tech. Blog. **6**, 2 (2016)
14. Ma, L., Jia, X., Sun, Q., Schiele, B., Tuytelaars, T., Van Gool, L.: Pose guided person image generation. In: Advances in Neural Information Processing Systems, pp. 406–416 (2017)
15. Park, T., Liu, M.Y., Wang, T.C., Zhu, J.Y.: Semantic image synthesis with spatially-adaptive normalization. In: CVPR, pp. 2337–2346 (2019)
16. Parkhi, O.M., Vedaldi, A., Zisserman, A.: Deep face recognition (2015)
17. Suwajanakorn, S., Seitz, S.M., Kemelmacher-Shlizerman, I.: Synthesizing obama: learning lip sync from audio. ACM TOG **36**(4), 95 (2017)
18. Thies, J., Zollhöfer, M., Nießner, M., Valgaerts, L., Stamminger, M., Theobalt, C.: Real-time expression transfer for facial reenactment. ACM Trans. Graph. **34**(6), 183–1 (2015)
19. Thies, J., Zollhofer, M., Stamminger, M., Theobalt, C., Nießner, M.: Face2face: real-time face capture and reenactment of rgb videos. In: CVPR, pp. 2387–2395 (2016)
20. Ulyanov, D., Vedaldi, A., Lempitsky, V.: Instance normalization: the missing ingredient for fast stylization (2016). arXiv preprint arXiv:1607.08022
21. Wang, F., et al.: Residual attention network for image classification. In: CVPR, pp. 3156–3164 (2017)
22. Wang, T.C., Liu, M.Y., Zhu, J.Y., Tao, A., Kautz, J., Catanzaro, B.: High-resolution image synthesis and semantic manipulation with conditional gans. In: CVPR, pp. 8798–8807 (2018)
23. Wang, Z., Bovik, A.C., Sheikh, H.R., Simoncelli, E.P.: Image quality assessment: from error visibility to structural similarity. IEEE TIP **13**(4), 600–612 (2004)
24. Wiles, O., Koepke, A.S., Zisserman, A.: X2face: a network for controlling face generation using images, audio, and pose codes. In: ECCV, pp. 670–686 (2018)
25. Wu, W., Zhang, Y., Li, C., Qian, C., Loy, C.C.: Reenactgan: learning to reenact faces via boundary transfer. In: ECCV, pp. 603–619 (2018)
26. Zhang, H., Goodfellow, I., Metaxas, D., Odena, A.: Self-attention generative adversarial networks (2018). arXiv preprint arXiv:1805.08318
27. Zhu, J.Y., Park, T., Isola, P., Efros, A.A.: Unpaired image-to-image translation using cycle-consistent adversarial networks. In: Proceedings of the IEEE International Conference on Computer Vision, pp. 2223–2232 (2017)

Protecting Encrypted Video Stream Against Information Leak Using Adversarial Traces

Ziwei Zhang and Dengpan Ye[✉]

Key Laboratory of Aerospace Information Security and Trusted Computing,
Ministry of Education, School of Cyber Science and Engineering,
Wuhan University, Wuhan, China
yedp@whu.edu.cn

Abstract. TLS protocol encryption hides the specific packet content but not the network characteristics. The adversary can determine the relevant information of the video through traffic analysis by using convolutional neural networks. In this paper, we propose a new novel defense mechanism that injects dummy packets into the video stream by pre-computing adversarial traces. Moreover, to deal with different network conditions, we offer two adversarial methods. 1) When the network condition is relatively single, applying traditional adversarial examples will play a good role in the effect with a small amount of bandwidth overhead. 2) When the network condition becomes more complex, we have no prior knowledge about upcoming network packets. Therefore, the traditional adversarial sample method that needs entire stream traces to calculate cannot be applied. To solve this problem, we take advantage of adversarial patches' input-agnostic and location-agnostic properties to generate "universal" adversarial traces. We experimentally demonstrate that our defense methods are promising solutions in the underlying scenarios.

Keywords: Encrypted video stream · Adversarial examples ·
Adversarial patches · Traffic analysis

1 Introduction

With the gradual popularization of SSL/TLS, more and more studies [1–6] focus on encrypted traffic analysis. They use the corresponding algorithm to breach users' sensitive information by analyzing the feature of the metadata(packet size, timings, etc.), such as website fingerprint attack which adversary learn from patterns of encrypted traffic to/from known web pages, and classify unidentified traffic with reasonable accuracy.

MPEG-DASH is a video streaming standard that enables high-quality streaming of media content over the Internet delivered from conventional HTTP web servers. TLS encrypts video stream content, but encryption does not change its own network characteristics. Recent advance [7] demonstrated that the packet

© Springer Nature Switzerland AG 2021
Y. Peng et al. (Eds.): ICIG 2021, LNCS 12890, pp. 765–776, 2021.
https://doi.org/10.1007/978-3-030-87361-5_62

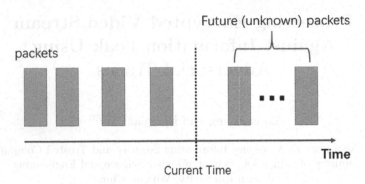

Fig. 1. Traditional adversarial example needs to know the entire video stream traces.

burst patterns of the video stream would be its fingerprint. What's more, they build a CNN model called the identification model to classify these finger-prints from YouTube, Netflix, Amazon, and Vimeo with very high accuracy. For instance, their techniques identified YouTube videos (from a small dataset of 18 videos) with 0 false positives and 0.988 recall.

Against this solid deep-learning-based attack, adversarial example [9] is a natural method to turn to for confusing a DL model, so we explore how to create adversarial examples for the video stream and implement them in the real world. Firstly, we use the traditional adversarial example method(FGSM) to generate adversarial traces. And successfully reduce the accuracy of the classification model. The experimental results show that the success rate of applying FGSM to defeat the identification model is more than 90% with only 8% bandwidth over-head. In addition, we test the effect of FGSM on other non-DL models(SVM, Logistic Regression, RandomForest). The results show that FGSM also has a good effect on other non-DL classification models.

However, when we implement FGSM in the real world, we find another prob-lem we have to face: The network condition is variable. That means when network conditions become complex due to congestion or other issues, we will have no prior knowledge about upcoming network packets as shown in the Fig. 1. How-ever, FGSM or other traditional adversarial example methods need the entire video stream traces to generate an adversarial input. To solve this problem, we propose a practical and effective defense to calculate "universal" adversarial traces against the identification model. The key insight of our defense is derived from the concept of adversarial patch [10]. Adversarial patch can cause misclas-sifications when applied to a wide range of input values. It is input-agnostic and location-agnostic. These properties meet our need to generate "universal" adversarial traces.

Contributions. In this paper, the key contributions of this work are as follows:

– We evaluate the effectiveness of traditional adversarial example methods against the traffic(video stream) analysis model.

- We find that both traditional adversarial example methods and other defensive strategies, including the state-of-art method, will be ineffective when loss the prior knowledge of upcoming packets.
- We propose a practical defense to calculate "universal" adversarial traces which adapt to various network conditions and achieve a significant effect.

2 Related Work

There has been a great deal of good work in different fields of traffic analysis defense; our job is both inspired and separate from them.

Defenses Against Side-Channel Attacks. At present, there are some defense strategies against side-channel attacks. They perturb time characteristic into the series [11–14] or add noise to shared resources [15, 16]. Chiefly, Xiao et al.'s [17], who use the d* algorithm to mitigate storage side channels attack in the Linux OS. Their work has played a good role in preventing information leakage. But their scene is different from ours, every packet series were certain before injecting, and the defender knows precisely when and how the adversary observes the metadata. However, we need to generate adversarial traces under a scenario which has no prior knowledge about upcoming network packets. A recent research [18] proposes to defend video stream using adversarial examples and differential privacy, but they do not consider the complexity of the network situation.

Defenses Against Website Fingerprint Attacks. The scenario and challenge for defending against website fingerprint attacks are very similar to our work. Adversary get sensitive information about websites such as domain or page content by analyzing network characteristics. It used to be realized by the traditional machine learning method, but now the deep learning method is gradually emerging. Nowadays more and more studies have been proposed to defeat website fingerprint attacks. Some research focus on the application layer [3,19,20], defenders change the routing algorithm or confuse HTTP requests to make adversary touch real traffic as little as possible. Application-layer defense strategies are often difficult to implement in reality. Because the premise of their implementation is very harsh, such as target websites only had HTTP protocols. And these methods against deep-learning-based attack effect is inferior, with less than 60% protection success rate. Other research focus on the network layer, defenders aim to fool the classification model by inserting dummy packets. In the earlier studies [21–23], they use constant rate padding to reduce information leakage caused by time intervals and traffic volume. However, these methods always require high bandwidth overhead($> 150\%$). Recent study find that inserting packages between two packets with a large time gap will reduce the bandwidth overhead. (WTF-PAD [6]) or by focusing on the front end of the trace (the front end that has been shown to contain the most information

Front [2]). They also show useless when applying in against deep-learning-based attack(only achieve 9% and 28% protection success rate). Finally, there is a supersequence defense method [24–26] which committee to find a longer package trace that contains subsequences of different website traces. One of the representative methods, called Walkie-talkie, only gets 50% protection success rate against DNN attacks. In general, no method can maintain a high success rate with a small amount of bandwidth overhead.

3   Method

In this section, we will introduce the specific details of the two adversarial methods under different network conditions.

3.1   Target Model

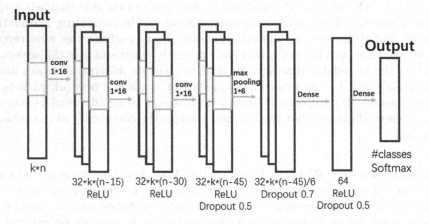

Fig. 2. Target model architecture. k denotes the number of feature types taken. n is the recording time in seconds divided by the time-series sampling rate.

Firstly, we need to introduce what we are defending against. We reconstructed the idea in Schuster et al. [7] to perform fingerprinting attacks of 200 Youtube videos using a set of four classifiers. It consists of three convolutional layers, one max pooling layer, and two dense layers. Figure 2 shows the entire CNN architecture. The inputs of the target model are features we extract from the video stream, including down/up/all bytes per second (BPS), down/up/all packet per second (PPS), down/up/all average packet length (PLEN), and burst. A burst is a sequence of points in a time series $(ti; yi)$ such that $t_i - t_{i-1} < I$ for some I (we used $I = 0.5$). To take a first look at the performance of our reconstructed attack model, we choose 5-fold cross-validation method, which means each time there is a different 20% of the traces for testing while the remaining 80% are for training. As shown in Table 1, SVM, LR and RF achieve 0.81, 0.82, and 0.76 classification accuracy; meanwhile CNN model has the highest accuracy of 0.94.

Table 1. Classification accuracy with one standard deviation.

Index	SVM	LR	RF	CNN
Average accuracy	0.81	0.82	0.76	0.94
Standard deviation	0.064	0.061	0.049	0.004

3.2 The Traditional Adversarial Approach

we generate adversarial samples using Fast Gradient Sign Method(FGSM) proposed by Goodfellow et al. [9] as following formula:

$$x^* = x + \eta \, \text{sign} \left(\nabla_x L(g(x; \theta), y) \right) \tag{1}$$

x is the original input sample, $g(x; \theta)$ presents the model parameterized by θ. y is the label corresponding to the x, and the $L(g(x; \theta), y)$ is the loss function of the classifier. η could control the degree of added noise. ∇_x is the gradient of the given loss L, which means the direction where the loss increases the most.

If we control the η larger, the added noise will be more effective but is also easier to detect by human eyes or machine classifiers. On the contrary, if we control the η smaller, it is less effective but is harder to be detected.

In experiment, we use $LinfFastGradientAttack()$ in $FoolBox$ [8] python library. And control the noise level from small to large increase. And then, we feed these adversarial samples to the CNN classifier, which is mentioned above. We find that the CNN classifier's success rate of detection is greatly reduced. This result tells us that the traditional adversarial samples are very effective against this identification model. The complete experimental results will be described in the following section.

3.3 Adversarial Patches for Video Stream

Adversarial patch is firstly introduced by Tom B. Brown et al. [10]. They create universal and robust image patches in the physical world to fool deep-learning based model. And existing work [27–29] expand this idea to bypass facial recognition classifiers. The main advantage of adversarial patch is both input-agnostic and location-agnostic. That means no matter what the input image is, no matter where the adversarial patch is, the patch will all fool the deep-learning based model. In other words, adversarial patches were universal and robust which can be pre-computed without full knowledge of the input.

For a given DNN model ($\mathbb{F}$), a targeted adversarial patch p_{adv} is computed via the following optimization:

$$p_{adv} = \text{argmin}_p \, \mathop{\mathbb{E}}_{x \in \mathcal{X}, l \in L} \text{loss} \left(\mathbb{F}(\Pi(p, x, l)), y_t \right) \tag{2}$$

X presents the set of training images, L is a distribution of locations in the image, y_t is the target label, and Π is a function that makes the patch to a random location in an image. By optimizing on all the training set images, the patch will gain strong transferability across images.

To inject adversarial patches into the video stream and implement in the real world, we should consider the scenario that user u visits to video V on youtube or other platforms. We need to inject an adversarial patch $p_{V,T}$ to u's live traffic, and meanwhile attacker is analyzing user's traffic, stealing privacy. Our goal is to make attacker's model classification result from V to T. In order to generate such a patch that achieves the above purposes, our method inspects the input space under constraint and searches for the potential adversarial patches that transfer the result which user visits V to the user visits T. The above optimization can be formulated as follows:

$$p_{V,T} = \operatorname{argmin}_p \mathbb{E}_{x \in X_V, s \in S} \operatorname{loss}\left(\mathbb{F}(\Pi(p, x, s)), y_T\right)$$
$$\text{subject to } |p| \leq p_{\text{bandwidthMax}} \tag{3}$$

The differences between Eq. (2) and Eq. (3) we must explain clearly. where $p_{\text{bandwidthMax}}$ defines the maximum bandwidth overhead, and S defines the schedule function that we inject a patch into live traffic which we will expand in subsequent chapters.

The Schedule of Patch Injection. If we implement adversarial patches in the real world, the block size of injected dummy packets will be the fixed pattern. Adversary can easily detect and recognize the "fingerprint" of our adversarial patch. To tackle this challenge, We introduce the schedule function S. We break patch p into many segments of equal size Mp called "small patch". Every small patch could protect a segment of x, which size is Mx. Using the patches' property of location-agnostic, they will produce the same effect no matter where it is. Thus, S defines all possible sets of small patch locations. $\Pi(p, x, s)$ which we called injection function in Eq. (3) defines a randomly selected location for each small patch in a segment of X.

The Process of Patch Optimization. We use Stochastic Gradient Descent (SGD) to solve the patch optimization problem defined by Eq. (3). As we all know, variables must be continuous values in SGD optimization. So we need to allow the constraints on $p_{W,T}$ to lie in $[-1, 1]^n$. And once the optimization process ends, we change any negative value to -1 and any non-negative value to $+1$. It's a prevalent method to solve discrete optimization problems, appears in many domains like natural language processing [30–32] and malware classification [33].

4   Experiments

In this section, we perform a systematic evaluation of our defense method under a variety of scenarios. Specifically, we described the process of collecting dataset, evaluate our traditional adversarial example method and adversarial patches effects against various attack methods under various bandwidth overhead, evaluate the effect of adversarial patches under the different platforms, compare the effect of adversarial patches with state-of-art method under different feature input.

4.1   Dataset Collection

We randomly collected 50 different videos on each of four different platforms (200 videos in total), and ensured their length no less than 20 min. Each video was visited 100 times and collected all the traces(200*100). We recorded the timestamps and sizes of all corresponding packets of the first 2 min of network traffic. The whole process is accomplished through automated scripts under two win 10 computer. Meanwhile in order to feed model with the same length, we put the raw data into 0.25-s bins, thus Each 2-min video stream was decomposed as an array of 480 bins.

4.2   The Effect of Traditional Adversarial Example Method

To test the performance of FGSM against the video stream identification model, we used the initial noise(bandwidth overhead = 2%) and fed them to the CNN classifier. Figure 3 shows the success rate of CNN classifier is reduced to 56% with only 2% bandwidth overhead. This result tells us that the traditional adversarial samples are very effective against this identification model.

To test the effect of FGSM on other non-DL models, including Support Vector Machine (SVM), Logistic Regression (LR), Random Forest (RF). We use the different degree noise to generate adversarial examples. Figure 4 shows that although FGSM has an effect on the non-DL model, it is not as significant as the DL model.

4.3   The Effect of Adversarial Patches

When network conditions become complex due to congestion or other problems, we don't have prior knowledge about upcoming network packets. However, FGSM or other traditional adversarial example methods need the entire video stream traces to generate an adversarial input. So we have proposed "universal" adversarial traces derived from adversarial patches. Firstly, we test the effect of adversarial patches against various attack methods under various bandwidth overhead. Figure 5 shows that adversarial patches are more effective than FGSM and have strong transferability; It also reduced the success rate of the non-DL model down to 40% with 2% bandwidth overhead.

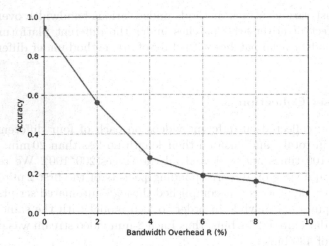

Fig. 3. Test FGSM effect against video stream identification model. Each data point is the result of a 5-fold cross-validation.

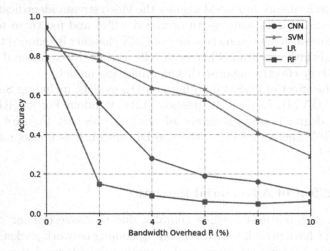

Fig. 4. Test FGSM effect against four different attack methods including DL model and non-DL model.

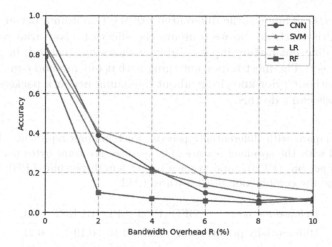

Fig. 5. Test adversarial patches effect against four different attack methods including DL model and non-DL model.

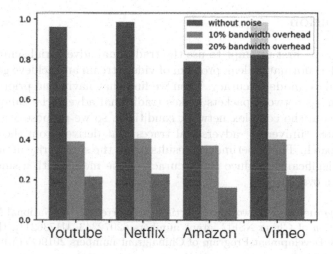

Fig. 6. Test adversarial patches effect under different platform(Youtube, Netflix, Amazon, and Vimeo).

The Effect Under Different Platform. We also evaluate adversarial patches' effect under different platforms (Youtube, Netflix, Amazon, and Vimeo). Figure 6 shows that our adversarial patches are effective against video streaming attacks on every video platform. This result also indicates that the defense of the major video platforms against this attack is still not implemented.

Compare with the State-of-art Method. To our best knowledge, the state-of-art method to defend video stream traffic-analysis was proposed by Xiaokuan

Zhang et al. [18]. They use the differential privacy to obtain a better result with less bandwidth overhead. So we compare the effect of adversarial patches with them under different feature inputs. Table. 2 shows our method, in general, get the better effect. The most important thing is that our method can achieve better results without prior knowledge about upcoming network packets. However, other methods can't do this.

Table 2. Compare with differentially private, Each column represents the accuracy when trained with the specified feature. The features are total bytes per bin (BPB), total packets per bin (PPB), total average packet length per bin (LPB), total bursts (BURST), and the combination of all features (ALL).

Defense method	BPB	PPB	LPB	BURST	ALL
Differentially private	0.22	0.20	0.16	0.19	0.21
Adversarial patches	**0.17**	0.21	0.18	**0.14**	**0.20**

5 Conclusion

In this paper, we first attempt to use the traditional adversarial sample method to address the information leak problem of video stream and achieve good performance to reduce model accuracy. Then we find that having no prior knowledge about upcoming network packets makes traditional adversarial samples unable to be applied in the complex network conditions, so we propose a new defense that calculates "universal" adversarial traces that derives from the concept of adversarial patch. The experimental results prove the superiority of our method, which can significantly reduce the accuracy of the model with a small amount of bandwidth overhead.

Acknowledgement. This work was partially supported by the National Natural Science Foundation of China NSFC [grant numbers 62072343, U1736211]. the National Key Research Development Program of China[grant numbers 2019QY(Y)0206].

References

1. Hayes, J., Danezis, G.: k-fingerprinting: a robust scalable website fingerprinting technique. In: USENIX Security Symposium (2016)
2. Gong, J., Wang, T.: Zero-delay lightweight defenses against website fingerprinting. In: 29th USENIX Security Symposium. USENIX Association, Boston (2020)
3. de la Cadena, W., et al.: Trafficsliver: fighting website fingerprinting attacks with traffic splitting. In: Proceedings of CCS (2020), pp. 1971–1985 (2020)
4. T. Wang, X. Cai, R. Nithyanand, R. Johnson, and I. Goldberg, "Effective attacks and provable defenses for website fingerprinting," in USENIX Security Symposium, 2014

5. Hou, C., Gou, G., Shi, J., Fu, P., Xiong, G.: Wfgan: Fighting back against website fingerprinting attack using adversarial learning. In: Proceedings of ISCC (2020), pp. 1–7. IEEE (2020)
6. Juarez, M., Imani, M., Perry, M., Diaz, C., Wright, M.: Toward an efficient website fingerprinting defense. In: Askoxylakis, I., Ioannidis, S., Katsikas, S., Meadows, C. (eds.) ESORICS 2016. LNCS, vol. 9878, pp. 27–46. Springer, Cham (2016). https://doi.org/10.1007/978-3-319-45744-4_2
7. Schuster, R., Shmatikov, V., Tromer, E.: Beauty and the burst: remote identification of encrypted video streams. In: USENIX Security Symposium (2017)
8. Rauber, J., Brendel, W., Bethge, M.: Foolbox: a python toolbox to benchmark the robustness of machine learning models. In: 34th International Conference on Machine Learning, Reliable Machine Learning in the Wild Workshop (2017). https://arxiv.org/abs/ 1707.04131
9. Goodfellow, I., Shlens, J., Szegedy, C.: Explaining and harnessing adversarial examples. arXiv preprint arXiv:1412.6572v3 (2014)
10. Brown, T.B., Mane, D., Roy, A., Abadi, M., Gilmer, J.: Adversarial patch. arXiv preprint ' arXiv:1712.09665 (2017)
11. Li, P., Gao, D., Reiter, M.K.: Mitigating access-driven timing channels in clouds using stopwatch. In: 2013 43rd Annual IEEE/IFIP International Conference on Dependable Systems and Networks (DSN). IEEE (2013)
12. Liu, W., Gao, D., Reiter, M.K.: On-demand time blurring to support side-channel defense. In: Foley, S.N., Gollmann, D., Snekkenes, E. (eds.) ESORICS 2017. LNCS, vol. 10493, pp. 210–228. Springer, Cham (2017). https://doi.org/10.1007/978-3-319-66399-9_12
13. Martin, R., Demme, J., Sethumadhavan, S.: Timewarp: rethinking timekeeping and performance monitoring mechanisms to mitigate sidechannel attacks. In: ACM SIGARCH Computer Architecture News (2012)
14. Vattikonda, B.C., Das, S., Shacham, H.: Eliminating fine grained timers in xen. In: Proceedings of the 3rd ACM Workshop on Cloud Computing Security Workshop. ACM (2011)
15. Brickell, E., Graunke, G., Neve, M., Seifert, J.-P.: Software mitigations to hedge aes against cache-based software side channel vulnerabilities. IACR Cryptology ePrint Archive (2006)
16. Keramidas, G., Antonopoulos, A., Serpanos, D.N., Kaxiras, S.: Non deterministic caches: a simple and effective defense against side channel attacks. In: Design Automation for Embedded Systems (2008)
17. Xiao, Q., Reiter, M.K., Zhang, Y.: Mitigating storage side channels using statistical privacy mechanisms. In: Proceedings of the 22nd ACM SIGSAC Conference on Computer and Communications Security. ACM (2015)
18. Zhang, X., Hamm, J., Reiter, M.K., Zhang, Y.: Statistical privacy for streaming traffic. In: Proceedings of NDSS 2019 (2019)
19. Cherubin, G., Hayes, J., Juarez, M.: Website fingerprinting defenses at the application layer. PoPETS 2017(2), 186–203 (2017)
20. Henri, S., Garcia-Aviles, G., Serrano, P., Banchs, A., Thiran, P.: Protecting against website fingerprinting with multihoming. PoPETS 2020(2), 89–110 (2020)
21. Cai, X., Nithyanand, R., Johnson, R.: Cs-buflo: a congestion sensitive website fingerprinting defense. In: Proceedings of WPES, pp. 121–130 (2014)
22. Cai, X., Nithyanand, R., Wang, T., Johnson, R., Goldberg, I.: A systematic approach to developing and evaluating website fingerprinting defenses. In: Proceedings of CCS, pp. 227–238 (2014)

23. Dyer, K.P., Coull, S.E., Ristenpart, T., Shrimpton, T.: Peek-a-boo, i still see you: why efficient traffic analysis countermeasures fail. In: Proceedings of IEEE S&P, pp. 332–346. IEEE (2012)

24. Nithyanand, R., Cai, X., Johnson, R.: Glove: a bespoke website fingerprinting defense. In: Proceedings of WPES, pp. 131–134 (2014)

25. Wang, T., Cai, X., Nithyanand, R., Johnson, R., Goldberg, I.: Effective attacks and provable defenses for website fingerprinting. In: Proceedings of USENIX Security, pp. 143–157 (2014)

26. Wang, T., Goldberg, I. Walkie-talkie: an efficient defense against passive website fingerprinting attacks. In: Proceedings of USENIX Security, pp. 1375–1390 (2017)

27. Song, D., et al.: Physical adversarial examples for object detectors. In: Proceedings of WOOT (2018)

28. Wallace, E., Feng, S., Kandpal, N., Gardner, M., Singh, S.: Universal adversarial triggers for attacking and analyzing nlp. arXiv preprint arXiv:1908.07125 (2019)

29. Wu, Z., Lim, S.-N., Davis, L., Goldstein, T. Making an invisibility cloak: real world adversarial attacks on object detectors. arXiv preprint arXiv:1910.14667 (2019)

30. Papernot, N., Mcdaniel, P., Swami, A., Harang, R.: Crafting adversarial input sequences for recurrent neural networks. In: Proceedings of MILCOM, pp. 49–54. IEEE (2016)

31. Ren, S., Deng, Y., He, K., Che, W.: Generating natural language adversarial examples through probability weighted word saliency. In: Proceedings of ACL, pp. 1085–1097 (2019)

32. Wang, X., Jin, H., He, K.: Natural language adversarial attacks and defenses in word level. arXiv preprint arXiv:1909.06723 (2019)

33. Kolosnjaji, B., et al.: Adversarial malware binaries: evading deep learning for malware detection in executables. In: Proceedings of EUSIPCO, pp. 533–537. IEEE (2018)

Adaptive Spatio-Temporal Convolutional Network for Video Deblurring

Fengzhi Duan and Hongxun Yao[✉]

Harbin Institute of Technology, Harbin, China
h.yao@hit.edu.cn

Abstract. Video deblurring is a challenging task due to the spatially variant blur caused by camera shake, object motions, and depth variations, etc. However, for the blurred area in the current video frame, the corresponding pixels of its neighboring video frames are often clear. Based on this observation, we propose an Adaptive Spatio-Temporal Convolutional Network (ASTCN) to compensate for blurry pixels in the current frame by using clear pixels in adjacent frames. In order to use the spatial information of adjacent frames in the current frame, the video frames must be aligned first. Existing methods usually estimate optical flow in the blurry video to align consecutive frames. However, they tend to generate artifacts when the estimated optical flow is not accurate. In order to overcome the limitations of optical flow estimation, we use deformable convolution in ASTCN to complete multi-scale adjacent frame alignment at the feature level. Secondly, we propose an adaptive spatio-temporal feature fusion module based on dynamic filters, which uses the features of the clear regions of adjacent frames to perform adaptive feature transformation on the intermediate frame to remove the blur. Extensive experimental results show that the proposed algorithm has shown superior performance on the benchmark datasets as well as real-world videos.

Keywords: Video deblurring · Pixel quality compensation · Dynamic filter

1 Introduction

1.1 Research Background

Video deblurring is a basic problem in the field of computer vision, which aims to recover clear frames from blurred video sequences. In recent years, with the explosion of short videos and the widespread popularity of handheld and airborne video capture devices, this issue has received active attention and research from related professionals. The blur in the video is usually caused by target motion, camera shake, and depth changes. This kind of blur is a spatial change blur, that is, different frames in a video sequence and different areas of the same frame have different degrees of blur. Therefore, the use of a globally unified fuzzy kernel cannot eliminate this spatial change blur. Blurred video will not only lead to the degradation of the human visual sensory experience, but also hinder some advanced visual tasks, such as target detection, visual tracking and SLAM. Therefore, it is very meaningful to study an effective video deblurring algorithm.

© Springer Nature Switzerland AG 2021
Y. Peng et al. (Eds.): ICIG 2021, LNCS 12890, pp. 777–788, 2021.
https://doi.org/10.1007/978-3-030-87361-5_63

Furthermore, in order to allow non-professionals to use the algorithm and improve the portability and ease of use of the algorithm, it is necessary to develop a video deblurring system based on the algorithm.

1.2 Image Deblurring

The task of image deblurring is to output the restored clear image for the input blurred image. However, due to different reasons and different types of image blur in the real world, it is difficult to use a unified model or algorithm to deal with all blurs. Recent algorithms try to deal with the spatial change blur caused by camera shake, high-speed target movement, and depth changes in dynamic scenes. Most of these methods are based on the following image degradation models:

$$B = L \otimes K + N \tag{1}$$

B, L, and N represent blurred image, clear image and additional noise, respectively, and K is the fuzzy kernel, which represents the convolution operation.

Finding the blur kernel for each pixel is a highly ill-conditioned problem. Traditional methods try to model the fuzzy model by making a priori assumptions about the fuzzy source. [1, 2] assume that the blur is only caused by 3D camera movement. However, in dynamic scenes, due to the presence of multiple moving objects and camera movement, kernel estimation is more challenging. [3] proposed a dynamic scene deblurring method. However, the estimation of these blur kernels is still inaccurate, especially in the case of sudden object movement and severe camera shake. This erroneous blur kernel estimation directly affects the quality of the latent image, resulting in ringing artifacts in the restored image.

In recent years, CNN has been applied to image processing problems and has shown good results [4–7]. Since there is no real blurred image in the real world and the clear image of its corresponding label can be used for supervised learning, related researchers usually use the fuzzy kernel to convolve the clear image to generate the corresponding blurred image. [4, 5, 7] use blurry images with unified blur kernel synthesis for training. Since the advent of image deblurring data set [8, 9], by directly estimating the deblurring output without kernel estimation, an end-to-end learning method [8, 10, 11] has been proposed. These end-to-end methods only need to input the blurred image, and after the model is processed, the final clear image after deblurring can be obtained.

1.3 Video Deblurring

Early research on video deblurring only regarded it as a simple extension of image deblurring, and the redundant information between video frames was not fully utilized. Recent research divides the video restoration task into four parts: feature extraction, adjacent frame alignment, feature fusion, and feature reconstruction through a more complex process, making full use of the spatial information of the video between frames. Recent methods have made significant progress due to the use of clearer areas from adjacent frames [12, 13] or optical flow from consecutive frames [14, 15] to compensate the quality of intermediate video frames. However, directly using the clear area of adjacent frames to compensate for the area corresponding to the intermediate frame usually produces obvious artifacts because the adjacent video frames are not completely aligned. Most existing methods [16–18] perform alignment by explicitly estimating the optical flow field between the reference frame and its adjacent frames. However, the optical flow estimation has a large amount of calculation and is difficult to be accurate, which often causes artifacts in the reference frame.

In recent years, with the successful application of CNN in the field of image processing, video deblurring methods based on deep neural networks have been extensively studied by relevant personnel. These methods utilize the timing relationship between input frames in various ways. DBN [9] stacks 5 consecutive frames in the channel dimension, and the convolutional neural network aggregates spatiotemporal information between adjacent frames. KIM [19] et al. used a deep loop network to connect multiple frame features to restore the current image. But these methods all perform adjacent frame alignment through optical flow estimation. Another research area achieves implicit motion compensation through dynamic filtering [20] or deformable convolution [21], which achieves a better alignment effect. It can perform the alignment of adjacent frames well without requiring a large amount of calculation, and the accuracy is higher than that of the optical flow estimation method.

1.4 ASTCN

To overcome the above limitations, we propose an Adaptive Spatio-Temporal Convolutional Network (ASTCN) for video deblurring. ASTCN includes three modules: a multi-scale deformable convolution alignment module, an adaptive spatiotemporal feature fusion module, and a feature reconstruction module. The input of the model is N consecutive video frames, and the output is the reconstructed intermediate frame.

The main contributions are summarized as follows:

- We propose a multi-scale adjacent frame alignment module based on deformable convolution, which overcomes the large and inaccurate problems of traditional optical flow estimation for alignment.
- We propose an adaptive spatiotemporal feature fusion module based on dynamic filters, which performs pixel-level feature transformation on the intermediate frame.
- We quantitatively and qualitatively evaluated our network on the benchmark dataset and proved its superior performance.

2 Related Work

2.1 Single-Image Deblurring

Recently, researchers have proposed many end-to-end CNN models [8, 10, 23, 24] for image deblurring. In order to obtain a large receptive field for processing large blur, a multi-scale strategy is used in the literature [8, 10]. In order to deal with the non-uniform blur of the dynamic scene, Zhang et al. used the spatial variant RNN [25] to eliminate the blur by using the RNN weights generated by the neural network in the feature space.

In order to generate clear images with more details, the adversarial loss is used in the literature [8, 24] to train the network, so that the restored images are more in line with human visual perception.

2.2 Video Deblurring

Unlike single image deblurring, video deblurring methods can utilize redundant spatial information that exists across adjacent frames. Therefore, CNN-based methods usually use multiple consecutive frames in the video sequence as model input to restore the intermediate video frame.

[26] proposed a quality enhancement method MFQE for compressed video. The core idea is to compensate poor quality (blurred) frames with good quality (clear) frames: First, MFQE uses a classifier to find the good quality frames in the video. For each bad frame, use its adjacent two frames. A good frame for quality enhancement. Before the quality is enhanced, the two adjacent good frames need to be motion compensated to align to the state of the bad frame at the moment. This method achieves better performance and improves the recovery effect of poor quality frames in a video sequence. But there are two problems at the same time: (1) MEQE relies on accurate motion compensation (optical flow estimation). If the motion compensation is not accurate, subsequent quality enhancement methods will fail. (2) Different adjacent frames and different areas of the same video frame have different degrees of blur, so while MFQE uses good quality frames to make up for poor quality frames, it may also introduce blurred areas in good quality frames. Therefore, good quality areas in adjacent frames should be used at the pixel level to compensate for the corresponding poor quality areas in the current frame.

In the NTIRE 2019 Video Enhancement Challenge, [27] proposed the EDVR algorithm. To compensate for the quality of adjacent frames, the EDVR algorithm uses a spatio-temporal attention fusion module to assign pixel-level aggregation weights on each video frame, so that the same area of different adjacent frames and different areas of the same video frame contribute to the recovery of intermediate frames All are different. However, the algorithm has too many parameters and a large amount of calculation, which leads to a long model reasoning time, which is difficult to apply to actual production.

STFAN [22] proposed a filter adaptive convolution layer, which applies an element-wise convolution kernel to the video frame that needs to be restored, and it adaptively transforms the features of the video frame at the pixel level according to the input. Adjacent frame alignment and deblurring are both spatial mutation tasks, because the blur in a dynamic scene is non-uniform blur. STFAN uses the proposed filter adaptive convolution layer, and regards the two processes of alignment and deblurring as two filter adaptive convolutions in the feature domain. STFAN integrates adjacent frame alignment and deblurring into the same frame without the need for displayed motion estimation.

3 Proposed Algorithm

In this section, we first give an overview of our algorithm in Sec. 3.1. Then the three components of the algorithm are explained in Sect. 3.2–3.4: multi-scale deformable convolution alignment module, adaptive spatiotemporal feature fusion module and feature reconstruction module.

3.1 Overview

As shown in Fig. 1, ASTCN consists of three parts: a multi-scale deformable convolution alignment module, an adaptive spatio-temporal feature fusion module and a feature reconstruction module. The model uses five consecutive frames as input to recover a clear intermediate frame. The intermediate frame of five consecutive frames is represented as a reference frame, and the remaining frames are represented as adjacent frames.

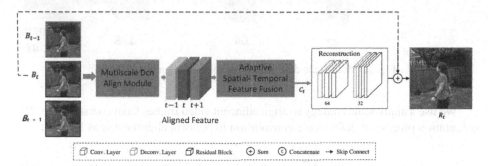

Fig. 1. Proposed network structure.

3.2 Multi-scale Deformable Convolution Alignment Module

Since the adjacent video frames in the video sequence have a certain amount of jitter, it is necessary to align the adjacent frames before the spatio-temporal feature fusion in order to use the clear areas in the adjacent frames to make up for the corresponding fuzzy areas in the reference frame. Compensate to the state of the reference frame at the moment. Traditional alignment methods are based on motion estimation, such as optical flow estimation. This type of method requires a large amount of calculation, and the optical flow estimation is difficult to be accurate, especially when there is a large jitter between adjacent video frames. Inaccurate motion estimation may introduce artifacts in the recovered video frames, seriously affecting the performance of the network.

Because there are different degrees of jitter between different adjacent frames and reference frames, and CNN has limitations in geometric transformation modeling due to its fixed convolution kernel configuration, so it is impossible to use CNN to handle this different degree of jitter. [15] proposed a deformable convolution operation to enhance the geometric transformation modeling capabilities of conventional CNN. Later [21] applied the deformable convolutional network to the task of video super-resolution reconstruction to align adjacent frames. Inspired by [21, 29], we proposed a multi-scale adjacent frame alignment module based on deformable convolutional network as shown in Fig. 2.

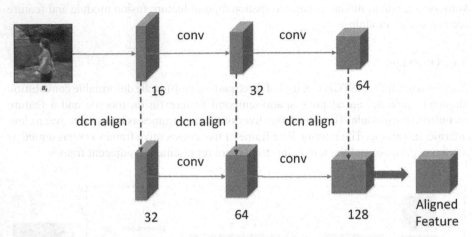

Fig. 2. Multi-scale deformable convolution alignment module

We use a multi-scale strategy to align adjacent video frames from coarse to fine. The calculation process of deformable convolution to perform alignment is as follows:

$$Ft + i(x, y) = \sum_{k=1}^{K} wk \bullet Ft + i(p + pk + offsetk) \bullet maskk \qquad (2)$$

Where mask is the spatial mask of size H × W × 1. Spatial mask is obtained by multiplying the occlusion mask and the pixel quality mask. The value of the mask is a hard value of 0 or 1. 0 represents the occluded area in adjacent frames which has no effect on compensating for intermediate frames. The pixel quality mask reflects the clarity of pixels at different spatial positions of adjacent video frames. Its value is soft and lies between 0 and 1. The higher the value, the better the pixel quality. Spatial mask realizes pixel compensation in the spatial domain and solves the occlusion problem of adjacent video frames. Finally, we get the aligned features as the input of the adaptive spatiotemporal feature fusion module.

3.3 Adaptive Spatio-Temporal Feature Fusion Module

In the video deblurring task, alignment and feature fusion are the two most critical parts. How to efficiently fuse the spatio-temporal features of the aligned consecutive frames is the core of this part. Because the blur in the dynamic scene is non-uniform blur, the degree of blur is different at different spatial positions.

Motivated by the Kernel Prediction Network (KPN) [28], which applies the generated spatially variant filters to the input image, we propose the adaptive spatio-temporal

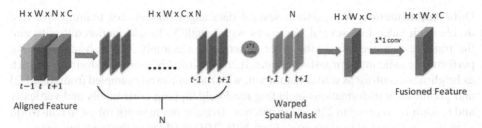

Fig. 3. Adaptive spatio-temporal feature fusion module

feature fusion module which applies generated element-wise convolutional filters to the aligned features, as shown in Fig. 3.

This module conforms to the dynamic filter architecture and includes two branches: filter generation module and dynamic filter convolution module. The filter generation module warps the Spatial Mask of each video frame with optical flow to get the warped spatial mask. The dynamic filter convolution module performs convolution operations on the generated warped spatial mask and aligned feature. So the convolution kernel here has no parameters to learn, but the intermediate calculation results. The parameters that the model needs to learn are greatly reduced, and the model inference speed is accelerated. The last 1×1 convolution is an ordinary convolution operation, the purpose is to merge the feature information of different channels on the features of the transformed intermediate frame. Finally, we get the fused feature map of intermediate frame.

3.4 Feature Reconstruction Module

The feature reconstruction network is responsible for reconstructing the features transformed by the spatio-temporal feature fusion module into a residual image with the same resolution as the intermediate frame, and finally adding the reconstructed residual image and the intermediate frame to obtain a clear frame that is restored.

The reconstruction network is composed of two deconvolution modules, and each deconvolution module is composed of a deconvolution layer and two residual blocks. The deconvolution layer up-samples the input features, and the residual module can well prevent the network from disappearing due to the depth of the gradient. The deformable convolution alignment module and the feature reconstruction network as a whole are an Encoder-Decoder structure, which itself is conducive to image enhancement tasks such as image denoising.

4 Experiments

4.1 Implementation Details

Dataset. In our experiments, we train the proposed network using the video deblurring dataset from [9]. It contains 71 videos (6,708 blurry-sharp pairs), splitting into 61 training videos (5,708 pairs) and 10 testing videos (1,000 pairs).

Data Augmentation. We perform several data augmentations for training. We first divide each video into several sequences with length 5. To add motion diversity into the training data, we reverse the order of sequence randomly. For each sequence, we perform the same image transformations. It consists of chromatic transformations such as brightness, contrast as well as saturation, which are uniformly sampled from [0.8, 1.2] and geometric transformations including randomly flipping horizontally and vertically and randomly cropping to 256 × 256 patches. To make our network robust in real-world scenarios, a Gaussian random noise from N(0, 0.01) is added to the input images.

Loss Function. To effectively train the proposed network, we use the mean squared error (MSE) loss that measures the differences between the restored frame R and its corresponding sharp ground truth S:

$$\mathcal{L}_{mse} = \frac{1}{CHW} \|R - S\|^2, \tag{3}$$

where C, H, W are dimensions of image, respectively; R and S respectively denote the restored image and the corresponding ground truth.

Experimental Settings. We use the Xavier initialization method to initialize the ASTCN network and use the Adam optimizer to train it, where $\beta 1 = 0.9$ and $\beta 2 = 0.999$. Since the alignment module is unstable in the process of learning feature offset, the initial learning rate of the multi-scale deformable convolution alignment module is set to a small 1e-6, and the initial learning rate of the remaining modules is set to 1e-4, and the entire network is trained end-to-end together. The learning rate of all modules decays by 0.1 times every 400 k iterations, and the ASTCN network finally converges after 850 k iterations. We use the Pytorch framework to implement the network, and train and test it on NVIDIA GeForce 2080Ti.

4.2 Experimental Results

Quantitative Evaluations. In order to evaluate the performance of the ASTCN algorithm, we compared it with the video deblurring algorithm in recent years on the DVD [9] data set (the running results of the remaining algorithms are from the original paper). In the experiment, PSNR and SSIM are used as evaluation indicators, and Time (sec) represents the time required for each algorithm to process a video frame. Params (M) is the parameter quantity of the model, and its unit is millions. PSNR and SSIM reflect the accuracy of each algorithm, and Time (sec) and Params (M) reflect the efficiency of the algorithm. It can be seen from Table 1 that ASTCN is superior to the latest algorithm Pan [30] in terms of performance and efficiency. Although Kupyn [24] and STFAN [22] have less processing time and model parameters, their deblurring effect is far worse than that of ASTCN. It can be said that this algorithm takes into account both performance and efficiency, and can efficiently process blurred videos.

Qualitative Evaluations. In order to further verify the generalization ability of the ASTCN algorithm, we conducted a qualitative evaluation on the real fuzzy video

Table 1. Quantitative evaluation on the video deblurring dataset [36], in terms of PSNR, SSIM, running time (sec) and parameter numbers ($\times 10^6$) of different networks.

Method	Kupyn [24]	Nah [8]	Su [9]	STFAN [22]	Pan [30]	Ours
PSNR	26.78	29.51	30.05	31.15	32.13	32.15
SSIM	0.848	0.912	0.920	0.905	0.927	0.928
Time(sec)	0.22	4.78	6.88	0.15	0.87	0.53
Params(M)	11.38	11.38	16.67	5.37	16.19	13.16

Fig. 4. Unprocessed real blurred image

sequence in the DVD [9] dataset. As shown in the Figs. 4, 5, 6, ASTCN recovers the detailed information in the blurred image, which can powerfully handle the unknown real blur in the dynamic scene, which further proves the superiority of the algorithm.

Fig. 5. Image processed by ASTCN

Fig. 6. Blurred image (left) and deblurred image (right) in the same area detail comparison

5   Conclusion

We have proposed a novel adaptive spatio-temporal network for video deblurring based on deformable convolution and dynamic filters. The entire model is end-to-end, and you only need to input a blurred video sequence to get the deblurred video. Our proposed multi-scale deformable convolution alignment module can perform the alignment of adjacent frames well without displaying the motion estimation, and solves the problem of large and inaccurate alignment of traditional optical flow estimation. The adaptive spatio-temporal feature fusion module adaptively performs pixel-level feature transformation on the reference frame according to the input continuous video frames, which greatly improves the efficiency of feature fusion and shortens the model inference time. The experimental results demonstrate the effectiveness of the proposed method in terms of accuracy, speed as well as model size.

References

1. Gupta, A., Joshi, N., Zitnick, C.L., et al.: Single image deblurring using motion density functions. In: European Conference on Computer Vision, vol. 68, no. 1, pp. 562-573 (2010). https://doi.org/10.1007/978-3-642-15549-9_13

2. Whyte, O., Sivic, J., Zisserman, A., Ponce, J.: Non-uniform deblurring for shaken images. In: International Journal of Computer Vision, vol. 98, no. 2, pp. 168–186 (2012)
3. Kim, T.H., Ahn, B., Lee, K.M.: Dynamic scene deblurring. In: International Conference on Computer Vision, vol. 53, no. 2, 065–074 (2013)
4. Xu, L., Ren, J.S., Liu, C., Jia, J.: Deep convolutional neural network for image deconvolution. In: Advances in Neural Information Processing Systems, vol. 46, no. 1, pp. 1790–1798 (2014)
5. Schuler, C.J., Hirsch, M., Harmeling, S., Sch¨olkopf, B.: Learning to deblur. In: IEEE Transactions on Pattern Analysis and Machine Intelligence, vol. 38, no. 7, pp. 1439–1451 (2016)
6. Sun, J., Cao, W., Xu, Z., Ponce, J.: Learning a convolutional neural network for non-uniform motion blur removal. In: IEEE Conference on Computer Vision and Pattern Recognition, vol. 63, no. 1, pp. 769–777 (2015)
7. Leibe, B., Matas, J., Sebe, N., et al.: A neural approach to blind motion deblurring. 221–235 (2016). https://doi.org/10.1007/978-3-319-46487-9.(Chapter 14)
8. Nah, S., Kim, T.H., Lee, K .M.: Deep multi-scale convolutional neural network for dynamic scene deblurring. In: IEEE Conference on Computer Vision and Pattern Recognition, vol. 13, no. 1, pp. 623–634 (2017)
9. Su, S., Delbracio, M., Wang, J., et al.: Deep video deblurring for hand-held cameras. In: IEEE Conference on Computer Vision and Pattern Recognition, vol. 86, no. 7, pp. 130–139 (2017)
10. Tao, X., Gao, H., Wang, Y., et al.: Scale-recurrent network for deep image deblurring. 20(4), 231–240 (2018)
11. Zhang, Y, Tian, Y., Kong, Y., Zhong, B., Fu, Y.: Residual dense network for image super-resolution. In: The IEEE Conference on Computer Vision and Pattern Recognition, vol. 35, no. 8, pp. 302–312 (2018)
12. Matsushita, Y., Ofek, E., Ge, W., Tang, X., Shum, H.-Y.: Full-frame video stabilization with motion inpainting. IEEE Trans. Pattern Anal. Mach. Intell. 28(7), 1150–1163 (2006)
13. Cho, S., Wang, J., Lee, S.: Video deblurring for hand-held cameras using patch-based synthesis. ACM Trans. Graph. 31(4), 64 (2012)
14. Hyun Kim, T., Mu Lee, K.: Generalized video deblurring for dynamic scenes. In: IEEE Conference on Computer Vision and Pattern Recognition, vol. 16, no. 1, pp. 323–334 (2012)
15. Ren, W., Pan, J., Cao, X., Yang, M-H.: Video deblurring via semantic segmentation and pixelwise non-linear kernel. In: International Conference on Computer Vision, vol. 12, no. 3, pp. 32–41 (2017)
16. Caballero, J., et al.: Realtime video super-resolution with spatio-temporal networks and motion compensation. In: The IEEE Conference on Computer Vision and Pattern Recognition, vol. 27, no. 2, 372–382 (2018)
17. Xue, T., Chen, B., Wu, J., et al.: Video enhancement with task-oriented flow. Int. J. Comput. Vision 10(3), 23–32 (2017)
18. Kim, T.H., Sajjadi, M.S.M., Hirsch, M., Schölkopf, B.: Spatio-temporal transformer network for video restoration. In: Ferrari, V., Hebert, M., Sminchisescu, C., Weiss, Y. (eds.) ECCV 2018. LNCS, vol. 11207, pp. 111–127. Springer, Cham (2018). https://doi.org/10.1007/978-3-030-01219-9_7
19. Kim, T.H., Mu Lee, K., Scholkopf, B., Hirsch, M.: Online video deblurring via dynamic temporal blending network. In: Conference on Computer Vision and Pattern Recognition, vol. 45, no. 2, pp. 120–129 (2017)
20. Jo, Y., Oh, S.W., Kang, J., et al.: Deep video super-resolution network using dynamic upsampling filters without explicit motion compensation. In: IEEE, vol. 13, no. 1, pp. 13–21 (2018)
21. Tian, Y., Zhang, Y., Fu, Y., et al.: TDAN: temporally deformable alignment network for video super-resolution. 13(1), 23–33 (2018)

22. Zhou, S., Zhang, J., Pan, J., et al.: Spatio-temporal filter adaptive network for video deblurring. 35(1), 36–47 (2019)

23. Zhang, J., et al.:. Dynamic scene deblurring using spatially variant recurrent neural networks. In: Conference on Computer Vision and Pattern Recognition, vol. 15, no. 1, pp. 78–89 (2018)

24. Kupyn, O., Budzan, V., Mishkin, D., Matas, J.: Deblurgan: blind motion deblurring using conditional adversarial networks. In: Conference on Computer Vision and Pattern Recognition, vol. 25, no. 2, pp. 78–89 (2018)

25. Liu, S., Pan, J., Yang, M.-H.: Learning recursive filters for low-level vision via a hybrid neural network. In: Leibe, B., Matas, J., Sebe, N., Welling, M. (eds.) ECCV 2016. LNCS, vol. 9908, pp. 560–576. Springer, Cham (2016). https://doi.org/10.1007/978-3-319-46493-0_34

26. Yang, R., Xu, M., Wang, Z., et al.: Multi-frame quality enhancement for compressed video. In: IEEE vol. 19, no. 2, 765–773 (2018)

27. Wang, X., Chan, K.C.K., Yu, K., et al.: EDVR: video restoration with enhanced deformable convolutional networks. 21(5), 5563–5575 (2019)

28. De Brabandere, B., Jia, X.: Dynamic filter networks. 23(2), 980–993 (2016)

29. Dai, J., Qi, H., Xiong, Y., et al.: Deformable convolutional networks. 27(2), 213–224 (2017)

30. Pan, J., Bai, H., Tang, J.: Cascaded deep video deblurring using temporal sharpness prior. 18(2), 1534–1542 (2020)

Ts-Unet: A Temporal Smoothed Unet for Video Anomaly Detection

Zhiguo Wang[1,2], Zhongliang Yang[1], Yujin Zhang[1], Nan Su[1,2], and Guijin Wang[1,2(✉)]

[1] Department of Electronic Engineering, Tsinghua University, Beijing, China
wangguijin@tsinghua.edu.cn
[2] Beijing National Research Center for Information Science and Technology, Beijing, China

Abstract. A Temporal-Smoothed Unet (TS-Unet) to detect video anomalies is proposed in this paper. The model is trained on regular videos to predict future frames, and uses prediction errors of test videos to detect anomalies. In addition to constraining model's prediction result, particularly, a temporal-smooth loss is presented to force time-continuous feature maps changing smoothly in the latent space. By utilizing the temporal-smooth loss, the model learns more videos' temporal regularity information; and achieve better anomaly detection performances. Experiments on multiple datasets show the superiority and validate the effectiveness of the proposed model.

Keywords: Anomaly detection · Video analysis · Temporal-smooth · Generative model

1 Introduction

Video anomaly detection plays an important role in social security guards. It is a challenging task because of the scarcity, diversity and scenario dependency of abnormal events.

Recently, generation-error based methods have drawn lots of attention [1–10]. They train a generative model to generate regular frames, then judge the frames with large generation-errors as anomalous. The generation-error based methods can be separated into two branches: long-short-term-memory (LSTM) branch, and non-LSTM branch.

In LSTM branch, methods combine an encoder and LSTM layers to map video frames to feature-maps in the hidden space; and then decode feature-maps to generate new frames. Chong et al. [1] utilized LSTM-autoencoder (LSTM-AE) to reconstruct a sequence of frames to detect anomalies. Lee et al. [2] utilized a bidirectional LSTM to predict a video clip's middle frame to detect anomalies. Song et al. [3] proposed an adversarial attention-based LSTM-AE to detect anomalies. The advantage of LSTM-branch methods is that the LSTM-layer enables models to learn videos' spatial-temporal information. However, at the same time, the LSTM-layer slows down data processing, because the LSTM-layer process the input-data frame by frame, in a serial manner.

© Springer Nature Switzerland AG 2021
Y. Peng et al. (Eds.): ICIG 2021, LNCS 12890, pp. 789–798, 2021.
https://doi.org/10.1007/978-3-030-87361-5_64

In non-LSTM branch, methods first encode video frames to feature maps in hidden space, then directly decode these feature maps to generate new frames [4–10]. Hasan et al. [4] employed AE to reconstruct input frames. To achieve better generation results, Liu et al. [5] leveraged U-net as the generator and applied multiple generative losses to constrain the generated results. Ravanbakhsh et al. [9] used a cross-channel generative manner to prevent model learn meaningless information. Gong et al. [6] augmented AE with a memory module to constrain the model's generalization ability. Zhou et al. [7] constructed an attention map to alleviate the foreground-background imbalance problem. Wang et al. [10] proposed a block-level process to solve different crowding-levels' influences on anomaly detection. The advantage of this branch's methods is its processing speed, because they process the input-data in parallel. The disadvantage is that the feature maps in hidden space cannot capture videos' temporal regularity information well [1].

In order to enable non-LSTM methods to learn more temporal regularity information, this paper proposes a Temporal-Smoothed Unet (TS-Unet) model. The model is trained to predict future frames for input clips. In addition to utilizing multiple generative losses to constrain the model's prediction result, a temporal-smooth loss is presented to constrain the model's latent space. The contents of video frames change smoothly across time, hence feature maps of time-continuous frames should also change smoothly in the latent space. Thus, the proposed temporal-smooth loss would force time-continuous feature maps to change smoothly in the latent space. In this way, the model learns videos' temporal regularity information: the videos' temporal-smooth property, and thus achieve better anomaly detection performances.

Experiments are carried out on multiple datasets. A new state-of-the-art performance is achieved, which shows the superiority and proves the proposed model's effectiveness.

2   Related Works

The development of video anomaly detection algorithms can be roughly divided into two stages: the traditional machine learning stage [11] and deep learning stage [12]. Recently, most of works [1–10, 13–16] focus on deep-learning- based methods. According to the manners of calculating anomaly scores, the deep-learning methods can be further classified into three categories: cluster-based methods, generative adversarial network (GAN)-based methods, and generation-error based methods.

Cluster-based methods judged samples that lie away from regular samples' clusters as anomalous. Fan et al. [13] grouped video frames into different clusters in the latent space, and judged video frames whose feature map do not belong to any existing clusters as anomalies.

GAN-based methods judged samples with low distribution probabilities as anomalies. They [14–16] trained a GAN network to generate fake frames; and trained discriminator to identify fake and real frames. Thereby, the discriminator can learn regular frames' distribution and output distribution probabilities for input frames. Thus, the trained discriminator can be used to detect anomalies.

Generation-error based methods judged samples which deviate from regular samples' manifold distribution as anomalous. They [1–10] trained a generative network to generate regular frames. In this way, the model learned the manifold distribution of regular samples. The generation-errors were used to measure samples' distances from the manifold. Thereby, frames with large generation-errors were judged as anomalies.

3   The Proposed TS-Unet

The framework of the proposed TS-Unet is shown in Fig. 1. In the training stage, k time-continuous clips $\{clip_0, clip_1, \ldots, clip_k\}$ are feed to the model. For each $clip_t$, the model generates a future frame $\hat{I}_t$ for it, whose ground truth is I_t. There are two kinds of losses used to constrain the model: generative loss and temporal-smooth loss.

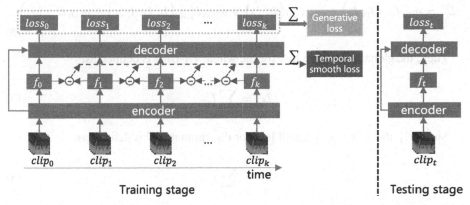

Fig. 1. The framework of the proposed TS-Unet. The model predicts future frames for input video clips. In addition to utilizing generative losses to constrain the prediction results, a temporal-smooth loss is presented to force time-continuous feature maps to change smoothly in the latent space. In the testing stage, the prediction error is utilized to detect anomalies, where only one clip is needed to detect a single frame.

3.1   Generative Loss

In this paper, all the losses used to constrain model's generation result are generative losses. In the proposed model, for each $clip_t$, there are four generative losses: pixel intensity loss L_{int}^t, gradient loss L_{gd}^t, optical flow loss L_{flow}^t, and adversarial loss L_{adv}^t. They are defined as:

$$L_{int}^t\left(I_t, \hat{I}_t\right) = \|\hat{I}_t - I_t\|_2 \tag{1}$$

$$L_{gd}^t\left(I_t, \hat{I}_t\right) = \sum_{i,j} \begin{array}{l} \left\| \left|\hat{I}_{t,i,j} - \hat{I}_{t,i-1,j}\right| - \left|I_{t,i,j} - I_{t,i-1,j}\right| \right\|_1 + \\ \left\| \left|\hat{I}_{t,i,j} - \hat{I}_{t,i,j-1}\right| - \left|I_{t,i,j} - I_{t,i,j-1}\right| \right\|_1 \end{array} \tag{2}$$

$$L_{flow}^t\left(I_t, \hat{I}_t, I_{t-1}\right) = \left\|\mathcal{F}\left(\hat{I}_t, I_{t-1}\right) - \mathcal{F}(I_t, I_{t-1})\right\|_1 \tag{3}$$

$$L_{adv}^t\left(\hat{I}\right) = \frac{1}{2}\sum_{i,j}\left(\mathcal{D}\left(\hat{I}_t\right)_{i,j} - 1\right)^2 \tag{4}$$

where $\mathcal{F}$ indicates the Flow-net [17], which is utilized to generate flow maps; $\mathcal{D}$ indicates a discriminator trained in an adversarial manner with the TS-Unet. The loss of $\mathcal{D}$ is defined as:

$$L_{\mathcal{D}}^t\left(I_t, \hat{I}_t\right) = \frac{1}{2}\sum_{i,j}\left(\mathcal{D}(I_t)_{i,j} - 1\right)^2 + \frac{1}{2}\sum_{i,j}\left(\mathcal{D}\left(\hat{I}_t\right)_{i,j}\right)^2 \tag{5}$$

For $clip_t$, its global generative loss can be expressed as:

$$L_{\mathcal{G}}^t = \omega_{int}L_{int}^t\left(I_t, \hat{I}_t\right) + \omega_{gd}L_{gd}^t\left(I_t, \hat{I}_t\right) + \omega_{flow}L_{flow}^t\left(I_t, \hat{I}_t, I_{t-1}\right) + \omega_{adv}L_{adv}^t\left(\hat{I}_t\right) \tag{6}$$

Then, the global generative loss for the whole TS-Unet is defined as:

$$L_{\mathcal{G}} = \sum_{t=0}^{k} L_{\mathcal{G}}^t \tag{7}$$

Similarly, the global adversarial loss for discriminator $\mathcal{D}$ is defined as:

$$L_{\mathcal{D}} = \sum_{t=0}^{k} L_{\mathcal{D}}^t \tag{8}$$

3.2 Temporal-Smooth Loss

The contents of video frames change smoothly across time. Therefore, time-continuous frames' feature maps should also change smoothly in the hidden space. However, utilizing the generative loss is not enough to enable a model to learn this temporal information well. Hence, a temporal-smooth loss is proposed in this paper to force time-continuous feature maps to change smoothly in the latent space.

Euclidean distance is adopted to measure the distance between two feature maps. In a sequence of time-continuous feature maps, the distances between every two time-neighbouring feature maps are calculated. The sum of these distances is used to measure the feature-map-sequence's temporal smoothness and thus used as the temporal-smooth loss for this sequence. By minimizing the temporal-smooth loss, feature maps are forced to change smoothly in the latent space.

Let $\{f_0, f_1, \ldots, f_k\}$ represent k time-continuous feature maps for $\{clip_0, clip_1, \ldots, clip_k\}$. In the latent space, the temporal-smooth loss L_{temp} can be defined as follows:

$$L_{temp} = \sum_{i=1}^{k-1} \|f_{i+1} - f_i\|_2 \tag{9}$$

3.3 Objective Function

Combining generative loss L_G and temporal-smooth loss L_{temp}, the objective function for TS-Unet is defined as:

$$L_{TS\_unet} = L_G + \omega_{temp} L_{temp} \tag{10}$$

When training $\mathcal{D}$, the loss function in Eq. (8) is adopted as the objective function.

3.4 Anomaly Detection

TS-Unet is trained on regular videos. It cannot predict anomalies well. Therefore, its prediction error can be used to detect anomalies. It is worth noting that, when detecting a frame, only a single clip is needed. That means: when testing, comparing with the baseline Unet [5], any additional computational burden is not added, which maintains the advantages of computing speed of non-LSTM methods. Considering that, anomalies usually occur locally in the scene, the maximum of block-level generation-errors on a frame is used to detect anomalies. The anomaly score of the frame I_t is represented as:

$$S(t) = max\left(mean_{bl\_size}\left(\sum_c \|\hat{I}_{t,i,j} - I_{t,i,j}\|_2 \right) \right) \tag{11}$$

where c indicates the number of channels of a frame; $mean_{bl\_size}$ indicates a mean filter operation with kernel size bl_size. In this paper, bl_size is set to 30, which is foreground target-size level; $max()$ indicates a max-pooling operation used to get the maximum of block-level prediction errors on a frame.

There are two manners when normalizing anomaly scores: normalization processed on each video segment's frames (norm-each), normalization processed on all the video segments' frames (norm-whole). Considering that, norm-each will cause alarms in every video segment, even though there is no anomaly. Therefore, the norm-whole manner is utilized here, which is defined as:

$$S_{norm}(t) = \frac{S(t) - min(S)}{max(S) - min(S)} \tag{12}$$

where $max(S)$ and $min(S)$ indicate the maximum and minimum values of $S(t)$ in all the testing videos. Based on the anomaly scores, one can set a threshold to determine whether a frame is anomalous or not.

4 Experiments

In this section, the performances of TS-Unet is evaluated and analyzed.

4.1 Datasets

The datasets used in the experiments are briefly introduced here. Some samples are shown in Fig. 2. **USCD ped2 dataset** [18] contains 16 training and 12 testing videos. Anomalous events include cycling, skateboarding, crossing lawns, cars, etc. **CUHK Avenue dataset** [19] contains 16 training videos and 21 testing videos. Anomalous events include running, throwing objects etc.

Fig. 2. Some normal and abnormal samples in Ped2 and Avenue datasets.

4.2 Evaluation Metric

The most commonly used evaluation metric is the Receiver Operation Characteristic (ROC) curve and the Area Under this Curve (AUC). A higher AUC value indicates better anomaly detection performance. Following the work [5], the frame-level AUC is adopted to evaluate the anomaly detection performances.

4.3 Implementation Details

The structures of the Unet module and D are the same as the baseline [5]. In the experiments, all video frames are resized to 256×256, and pixel values are normalized to [-1, 1]. Each clip contains 4 consecutive frames; every two time-neighbouring clips have 3 overlapped frames. In the training process, the temporal-smooth size k is set to 5, ω_{temp} is set to 10, the mini-batch size is 2. In generative losses, the weights for multiple child generative losses are set as: $\omega_{int} = 1$, $\omega_{gd} = 1$, $\omega_{flow} = 2$, $\omega_{adv} = 0.05$. Adam [20] is used as the optimizer. The TS-Unet's and the discriminator's learning rates are [1e-4,1e-5] and [1e-5,1e-6] respectively, whose boundaries are both 40000. The model is trained for 25000 iterations on Ped2 and 100000 iterations on Avenue dataset.

4.4 Experimental Results

Table 1 shows the frame-level AUC performances of TS-Unet comparing with state-of-the-art methods. As shown in the table, TS-Unet achieves a new state-of-the-art performance, which demonstrates the effectiveness of the proposed model.

Table 1. Frame-level AUCs of different methods on the Ped2 and Avenue datasets.

	Ped2	Avenue
Narrowed cluster [21], 2018	94.4	87.8
Future Predict [5], 2018	95.4	85.1
Stan [2], 2018	96.5	87.2
sRNN-AE [22], 2019	92.21	83.48
Attention-driven [7], 2019	96.0	86.0
VRNN [23], 2019	96.06	85.75
MemAE [6], 2019	94.1	83.3
Deep-OC [24], 2019	96.9	83.5
ST-Cascade [25], 2020	92.9	83.5
GMFC-VAE[13],2020	92.2	83.4
Integrate [15], 2020	96.3	85.1
TS-Unet (proposed)	**97.81**	**88.38**

4.5 Ablation Study

In this section, the effectiveness of the proposed temporal-smooth loss is analyzed, the impacts of temporal-smooth size k and weight ω_{temp} to anomaly detection are explored.

Effectiveness of Temporal-Smooth Loss.
In Fig. 3, (a)(b) compared the temporal-smooth losses of TS-Unet and Unet; (c)(d)

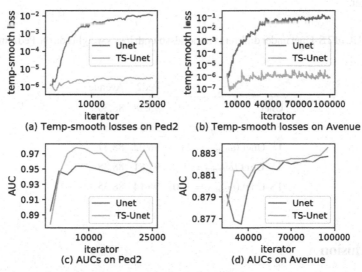

(a) Temp-smooth losses on Ped2   (b) Temp-smooth losses on Avenue

(c) AUCs on Ped2   (d) AUCs on Avenue

Fig. 3. Temporal-smooth losses and anomaly detection AUCs on Ped2 and Avenue datasets. (a) and (c) come from the same process; (b) and (d) come from the same process.

compared the AUCs of TS-Unet and Unet. As shown in the figure, by applying the temporal-smooth constraint, TS-Unet's temporal-smooth losses are smaller than that in the baseline Unet, and TS-Unet's anomaly detection performances are better than that in the Unet. That proves the effectiveness of temporal-smooth loss to improving anomaly detection performances.

Impact of Different Temporal-Smooth Sizes.
In Table 2, the impact of different temporal-smooth sizes k to anomaly detection is explored. As shown in the table, the larger the k, TS-Unet tends to achieve better performances. Therefore, $k = 5$ is applied in this paper.

Table 2. AUC of TS-Unet under different temporal-smooth sizes on the Ped2 and Avenue datasets.

	Ped2	Avenue
Unet	95.98	88.30
TS-Unet ($k = 3$)	96.25	88.33
TS-Unet ($k = 4$)	96.43	88.32
TS-Unet ($k = 5$)	**97.81**	**88.37**

Impact of Different Temporal-Smooth Weights.
In Table 3, the impact of different temporal-smooth weights ω_{temp} to anomaly detection is explored. As shown in the table, when ω_{temp} changes across magnitudes, TS-Unet achieves different performances, but all the performances are better than the Unet. When $\omega_{temp} = 10$, TS-Unet achieves the best performances. Therefore, $\omega_{temp} = 10$ is applied in this paper.

Table 3. AUC of TS-Unet under different temporal-smooth loss's weights on the Ped2 and Avenue datasets.

	Ped2	Avenue
Unet	95.98	88.30
TS-Unet ($\omega_{temp} = 0.1$)	96.54	88.37
TS-Unet ($\omega_{temp} = 1$)	96.02	88.37
TS-Unet ($\omega_{temp} = 10$)	**97.81**	**88.38**
TS-Unet ($\omega_{temp} = 100$)	96.14	88.35

5   Conclusion

This paper proposes a TS-Unet to detect video anomalies. The model utilizes prediction error to detect anomalies. In addition to constraining the prediction result, it utilizes a temporal-smooth loss to force time-continuous feature maps to change smoothly in hidden space. In this way, the model learns more temporal-regularity information and achieves better performances. Experimental results show the superiority and approve the effectiveness of the proposed model.

Acknowledgements. This work was supported by the Sichuan Science and Technology Program (2020GZYZF0006). Furthermore, we are grateful for Huachuang Aima Information Technology (Chengdu) Co., Ltd.

References

1. Chong, Y.S., Tay, Y.H.: Abnormal event detection in videos using spatiotemporal autoencoder. In: Advances in Neural Networks - ISNN 2017, pp. 189–196 (2017)
2. Lee, S., Kim, H.G., Ro, Y.M.: STAN: Spatio-temporal adversarial networks for abnormal event detection. In: 2018 IEEE International Conference on Acoustics, Speech and Signal Processing (ICASSP), pp. 1323–1327 (2018)
3. Song, H., Sun, C., Wu, X., Chen, M., Jia, Y.: Learning normal patterns via adversarial attention-based autoencoder for abnormal event detection in videos. IEEE Trans. Multimed. **22**(8), 2138–2148 (2020)
4. Hasan, M., Choi, J., Neumann, J., Roy-Chowdhury, A.K., Davis, L.S.: Learning temporal regularity in video sequences. In: 2016 IEEE Conference on Computer Vision and Pattern Recognition (CVPR), pp. 733–742 (2016)
5. Liu, W., Luo, W., Lian, D., Gao, S.: Future frame prediction for anomaly detection-a new baseline. In: 2018 IEEE/CVF Conference on Computer Vision and Pattern Recognition, pp. 6536–6545 (2018)
6. Gong, D., et al.: Memorizing normality to detect anomaly: memory-augmented deep autoencoder for unsupervised anomaly detection. In: 2019 IEEE/CVF International Conference on Computer Vision (ICCV), pp. 1705–1714 (2019)
7. Zhou, J.T., Zhang, L., Fang, Z., Du, J., Peng, X., Yang, X.: Attention-driven loss for anomaly detection in video surveillance. IEEE Trans. Circuits Syst. Video Technol. **30**(12), 4639–4647 (2020)
8. Wang, T., et al.: Generative neural networks for anomaly detection in crowded scenes. IEEE Trans. Inf. Forensics Secur. **14**(5), 1390–1399 (2019)
9. Ravanbakhsh, M., Nabi, M., Sangineto, E., Marcenaro, L., Regazzoni, C., Sebe, N.: Abnormal event detection in videos using generative adversarial nets. In: 2017 IEEE International Conference on Image Processing (ICIP), pp. 1577–1581 (2017)
10. Wang, Z., Yang, Z., Zhang, Y.J.: A promotion method for generation error-based video anomaly detection. Pattern Recognit. Lett. **140**(12), 88–94 (2020)
11. Popoola, O.P., Wang, K.: Video-based abnormal human behavior recognition—a review. IEEE Trans. Syst. Man Cybern. Part C Appl. Rev. **42**(6), 865–878 (2012)
12. Kiran, B., Thomas, D., Parakkal, R.: An overview of deep learning based methods for unsupervised and semi-supervised anomaly detection in videos. J. Imaging **4**(2), 36 (2018)
13. Fan, Y., Wen, G., Li, D., Qiu, S., Levine, M.D., Xiao, F.: Video anomaly detection and localization via Gaussian mixture fully convolutional variational autoencoder. Comput. Vis. Image Underst. **195**(102920), 1–12 (2020)
14. Sabokrou, M., Khalooei, M., Fathy, M., Adeli, E.: Adversarially learned one-class classifier for novelty detection. In: 2018 IEEE/CVF Conference on Computer Vision and Pattern Recognition, pp. 3379–3388 (2018)

15. Tang, Y., Zhao, L., Zhang, S., Gong, C., Li, G., Yang, J.: Integrating prediction and reconstruction for anomaly detection. Pattern Recognit. Lett. **129**(18), 123–130 (2020)
16. Ravanbakhsh, M., Sangineto, E., Nabi, M., Sebe, N.:Training adversarial discriminators for cross-channel abnormal event detection in crowds. In: 2019 IEEE Winter Conference on Applications of Computer Vision (WACV), pp. 1896–1904 (2019)
17. Dosovitskiy, A. et al.: FlowNet: learning optical flow with convolutional networks. In: 2015 IEEE International Conference on Computer Vision (ICCV), pp. 2758–2766 (2015)
18. Mahadevan, V., Li, W., Bhalodia, V., Vasconcelos, N.: Anomaly detection in crowded scenes. In: 2010 IEEE Computer Society Conference on Computer Vision and Pattern Recognition, pp. 1975–1981 (2010)
19. Lu, C., Shi, J., Jia, J.: Abnormal event detection at 150 FPS in MATLAB. In: 2013 IEEE International Conference on Computer Vision, pp. 2720–2727 (2013)
20. Kingma, D.P., Ba, J.: Adam: a method for stochastic optimization. In: International Conference on Learning Representations, pp. 1–15 (2015)
21. Ionescu, R.T., Smeureanu, S., Popescu, M., Alexe, B.: Detecting abnormal events in video using narrowed normality clusters. In: 2019 IEEE Winter Conference on Applications of Computer Vision (WACV), pp. 1951–1960 (2019)
22. Luo, W., et al.: Video anomaly detection with sparse coding inspired deep neural networks. IEEE Trans. Pattern Anal. Mach. Intell. **43**(3), 1070–1084 (2021)
23. Lu, Y., Kumar, K.M., Nabavi, S.S., Wang, Y.: Future frame prediction using convolutional VRNN for anomaly detection. In: 2019 16th IEEE International Conference on Advanced Video and Signal Based Surveillance (AVSS), pp. 1–8 (2019)
24. Wu, P., Liu, J., Shen, F.: A deep one-class neural network for anomalous event detection in complex scenes. IEEE Trans. Neural Networks Learn. Syst. **31**(7), 1–14 (2019)
25. Li, N., Chang, F., Liu, C.: Spatial-temporal cascade autoencoder for video anomaly detection in crowded scenes. IEEE Trans. Multimed. **23**(16), 203–215 (2021)

DBAM: Dense Boundary and Actionness Map for Action Localization in Videos via Sentence Query

Weigang Zhang[1]($\boxtimes$), Yushu Liu[1], Jianping Zhong[1], Guorong Li[2], and Qingming Huang[2]

[1] School of Computer Science and Technology, Harbin Institute of Technology, Weihai, China
wgzhang@hit.edu.cn
[2] School of Computer Science and Technology, University of Chinese Academy of Sciences, Beijing, China

Abstract. Action localization in videos via sentence query remains a very challenging problem because of the semantic misalignment and the structural misalignment. With the observation that activities should be localized with both the local keywords of query sentence and the global information of whole video, we propose a novel method named Dense Boundary and Actionness Map (DBAM). This method trains a self-attention model to evaluate the importance of each word in the query sentence. Then it constructs a two-dimensional visual feature map for each candidate moment after video encoding. The visual feature map is cross-modal concatenated with the semantic feature and then DBAM directly performs convolution over the feature map to predict two-dimensional actionness map, starting map and ending map for candidate moments. The three maps are fused to generate proposals. We evaluate DBAM on the two challenging public benchmarks Charades-STA and TACoS and it outperforms the state-of-the-art by a large margin.

Keywords: Video understanding · Cross-modal retrieval · Action localization

1 Introduction

With the technology advancement of network infrastructure, the ubiquity of video-capturing devices, and the development of social media, the amount of video data is continuously booming. Manually searching for a specific visual event of interest from these videos is inefficient. In order to tackle this problem, many computer vision algorithms focus on temporally localizing activities in videos. Although impressive improvement has been made in temporal action localization [1–3], these algorithms are limited to a predefined set of simple activities, such as running, jumping, etc. In the real-world applications, activities are more complex than atomic actions, such as "running up the stairs", in which case the localization of "running" may not uniquely identify the moment. An intuitive way is to localize activities via natural language sentence query, which aims at localizing a moment in the video which semantically corresponds to the given description

© Springer Nature Switzerland AG 2021
Y. Peng et al. (Eds.): ICIG 2021, LNCS 12890, pp. 799–810, 2021.
https://doi.org/10.1007/978-3-030-87361-5_65

as shown in Fig. 1. Using natural language, this kind of localization not only supports unconstrained activities, but also adds specific constraints including objects and their properties as well as relations.

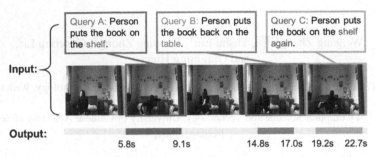

Fig. 1. Illustration of action localization in videos via sentence query. a robust model needs to overcome both the semantic misalignment (on the shelf/on the table) and the structural misalignment (again).

To tackle the task of action localization in videos via sentence query, anchor-based methods [4–8] train a binary classifier and a regressor on a set of predefined-scale anchors or sliding windows whereas anchor-free methods such as ABLR [9] outputs the temporal boundaries of each action, and SAP [10] thresholds on the temporal attention sequence of the video to obtain the result proposals. However, this task is still challenging. For example, as shown in Fig. 1, the only difference between query A "person puts the book on the shelf" and query B "person puts the book back on the table" is the place to put the book, and a robust model needs to distinguish these visually similar moments (overcome the semantic misalignment). What's more, for query C "person puts the book on the shelf again", the model also needs to scan the whole video and compare the video context to find the second occurrence of "person puts the book on the shelf" (overcome the structural misalignment).

We argue that activities should be localized with the local keywords of query sentence and the global information of whole video. Although CTRL [4] samples several frames before and after the action to include the temporal context information, context should be content-adaptive rather than manually pre-defined. With the above observation, in this work, we propose Dense Boundary and Actionness Map (DBAM) for action localization in videos via sentence query in a simple way without prior information or complex postprocess. We train a self-attention model to evaluate the importance of each word in the query sentence and construct a two-dimensional cross-modal feature map for each candidate moment in the video. And then we directly perform two-dimensional convolution over the map to generate an actionness map to evaluate the confidence score for candidate moments and two boundary maps to refine their temporal boundaries. Our Rank1@tIoU = 0.7 reaches 24.57% (4.03 percentage point improvement over the state-of-the-art) on the Charades-STA [4] dataset and Rank1@tIoU = 0.5 reaches 26.28% on the TACoS [11] dataset.

2 Related Works

Action localization in videos via sentence query aims at determining the starting and ending time of the temporal region that best corresponds to the given verbal description. As a pioneer work, MCN [11] embeds the feature of the video and the query sentence into a joint space and measures their distance, then it thresholds on the distance sequence to obtain the result proposals. The cross-modal fusion proposed by MCN is relatively too simple to capture complex interaction between these two modalities thus many recent works focus on tackling this issue from the following respects:

(1) Adding prior information in the feature extraction stage. ACL-K [12] extracts the verb-obj pairs from the query sentence to enhance the information of complex activities. DORi [13] adds the object relationships to the extracted video visual feature via object detection algorithm.
(2) Improving the way of proposals generation. CTRL [4], VAL [5], SLTA [6] etc. sample candidate video clips of different scales with sliding-windows. These algorithms evaluate the similarity between each window and the query sentence, and then adjust the boundaries of these windows. TGN [7], QSPN [8] etc. train a binary classifier and a regressor on a set of predefined anchors for each temporal step. The difference between this method and the sliding-windows based methods is that this method is able to process the whole video in a single stream while sliding-windows based methods process each window separately. Recent works also focus on proposal-free methods. ABLR [9] discovers the temporal boundaries in video of each query sentence. SM-RL [14] and TripNet [15] use reinforcement learning to simulate the human perception procedure of localizing action.
(3) Removing redundant proposals in the postprocessing stage. MAN [16] uses graph convolution network to model the relationships among candidate moments to re-rank them.

Our work generates proposals with the anchor-based strategy and focuses on processing the whole video directly with convolution on the two-dimensional feature map. Meanwhile, our work aims at tackling the task of action localization in videos via sentence query with a simple way without prior information or complex postprocess, which can reduce the labor-intensive manual labeling and increase the computation speed.

3 Approach

3.1 Problem Formulation

Given a long untrimmed video $V = \{f_i\}_{i=1}^{N_f}$, as well as a query sentence $S = \{w_i\}_{i=1}^{N_w}$, where f_i is the ith frame of V, N_f is the total number of frames, w_i is the ith word in S, and N_w is the total number of words. The main goal of this task is to identify temporal boundaries of the visual content that S refers to. Specifically, each training video is annotated with a set of temporal annotations $A = \{S_i, t_{is}, t_{ie}\}_{i=1}^{N_a}$, where S_i denotes the ith sentence description of a video segment from t_{is} to t_{ie} and N_a is the total number of annotations. This task aims at generating a set of proposals $P = \{t_{is}, t_{ie}\}_{i=1}^{N_p}$ according to $\{S_i\}_{i=1}^{N_a}$ to cover the ground truth. Figure 2 illustrates the framework of our approach. Our work aims at simultaneously focusing on the local information of query sentence and global information of whole video with two-dimensional convolution and feature map.

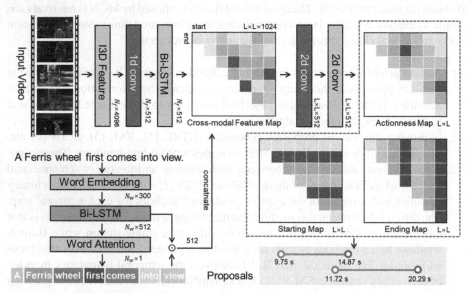

Fig. 2. The framework of our approach. We construct a 2D cross-modal feature map for each candidate moment after encode both the video and the query sentence respectively. We directly perform 2D convolution over the feature map to generate the possibility map for actionness, starting and ending. The three maps are fused to generate proposals.

3.2   Multi-modal Feature Encoding

Sentence Encoding. For each word w_i in S, we use the GloVe word2vec model [17] to generate the embedding vector e_i. The vector is then fed into a two-layer Bi-directional LSTM to encode the whole query sentence as $H = \{h_i\}_{i=1}^{N_w}$. Next, we train a one-dimensional CNN to predict the attention score $A = \{a_i\}_{i=1}^{N_w}$ for each word w_i and the original feature H is weighted by A to construct the attentive representation of S as $F_S = \sum_{i=1}^{N_w} a_i \times h_i$. The above sentence encoding process can be formulated as:

$$
\begin{cases}
e_i = Embedding(w_i) \\
h_i^{fw} = LSTM^{fw}\left(e_i, h_{i-1}^{fw}\right) \\
h_i^{bw} = LSTM^{bw}\left(e_i, h_{i-1}^{bw}\right) \\
h_i = \left[h_i^{fw}, h_i^{bw}\right] \\
a_i = F(W_S \times h_i + b_S) \\
F_S = \sum_{i=1}^{N_w} a_i \times h_i
\end{cases}
\tag{1}
$$

Video Encoding. Similar to prior methods, the input video is partitioned into a sequence of non-overlapping clips $C = \{c_i\}_{i=1}^{N_c}$ by a regular frame interval δ, where $N_c = N_f/\delta$. We use the I3D network [18] pre-trained on the Kinetics dataset [19] to extract visual feature of these clips. We also train a one-dimensional CNN and a two-layer Bi-directional LSTM to encode these clips with sufficient temporal context information. The above video encoding process can be formulated as:

$$
\begin{cases}
f_{Vi} = I3D(ci) \\
f_{Vi} = F(W_V \times f_{Vi} + b_V) \\
h_i^{fw} = LSTM^{fw}\left(f_{Vi}, h_{i-1}^{fw}\right) \\
h_i^{bw} = LSTM^{bw}\left(f_{Vi}, h_{i-1}^{bw}\right) \\
f_{Vi} = \left[h_i^{fw}, h_i^{bw}\right] \\
F_V = \{f_{Vi}\}_{i=1}^{N_c}
\end{cases}
\tag{2}
$$

3.3   Cross-Modal Feature Map for Prediction

We uniformly partitioned the duration of V into T non-overlapping temporal regions. Then we reconstruct a feature map $M_F^{T \times T \times D}$, in which the first two dimensions T indicate the starting time and ending time respectively and D represents the feature dimension. For each temporal region $[T_i, T_j]$ in this feature map, we perform max-pooling over the feature of clips within this region to compute the element $m_{fi,j}$ in M_F. In this way, all corresponding candidate moments are obtained. Next, we extract cross-modal feature based on both F_S and M_F as: $M_F = M_F || F_S$, where $||$ denotes the concatenation operation. We train a two-layer two-dimensional CNN over M_F to get a more compact representation, and generate the actionness possibility map M_a, the starting possibility map M_s, and the ending possibility map M_e for each moment candidate.

3.4   Training and Inference

Training. Each training data consists of a query sentence S, an input video V, and the ground truth moment (t_s, t_e). We define the actionness region as $[t_s, t_e]$, the starting region as $[t_s - \frac{d}{10}, t_s + \frac{d}{10}]$ and the ending region as $[t_e - \frac{d}{10}, t_e + \frac{d}{10}]$, where $d = t_e - t_s$. We calculate the temporal Intersection-over-Union (tIoU) between the moment candidates and these three ground truth regions to form the label for the actionness map, the starting map, and the ending map. During training, we adopt the sum of weighted binary logistic regression loss L_{bl} for the three labels as:

$$
L_{bl} = \lambda L_{bl}^a + L_{bl}^s + L_b^e
\tag{3}
$$

For example, L_{bl}^a is defined as:

$$
L_{bl}^a = \left(\alpha^+ \bullet b_i \bullet log(M_a) + \alpha^- \bullet (1 - b_i) \bullet log(1 - M_a)\right)
\tag{4}
$$

where $b_i = sign(tIoU^a - 0.5)$ is a two-value function that convert $tIoU^a$ map from continuous values to $\{0,1\}$. We denote $l^+ = \sum b_i$ and $l^- = T \times T - l^+$, then the weighted parameters $\alpha^+ = \frac{T \times T}{l^+}$ and $\alpha^- = \frac{T \times T}{l^-}$ to balance the positive and negative samples. L_{bl}^s and L_{bl}^e is calculated in the same way. Especially, we only consider L_{bl} for moment candidates with ending time larger than starting time.

Inference. We average boundary probabilities of these moment candidates sharing the same starting or ending location to make the boundaries smooth and robust:

$$m_{s_{i,j}}' = \frac{1}{T} \sum_{k=1}^{T} m_{s_{i,k}}, m_{e_{i,j}}' = \frac{1}{T} \sum_{k=1}^{T} m_{e_{k,j}} \tag{5}$$

where $m_{s_{i,j}}, m_{e_{i,j}}, m_{s_{i,j}}', m_{e_{i,j}}'$ is the element in M_s, M_e, M_s' and M_e', respectively. We predict the final confidence score map of moment candidates by multiplying three maps as: $score = M_a \times M_s' \times M_e'$. We retrieve candidates when the ending time is longer than the starting time according to the score map. Afterwards, the top n proposals in each video are obtained.

4 Experiments

4.1 Dataset and Evaluation Metrics

Following the convention, we conduct experiments on two publicly accessible datasets: Charades-STA [4] and TACoS [11]. Each dataset consists of videos as well as their associated temporally annotated sentences.

Charades-STA: This dataset is built based on Charades, which focuses on indoor activities. The original Charades dataset [20] only provides a paragraph description for each video. Gao et al. [11] constructed temporal annotation for sentences in a semi-automatic way including sentence decomposition, keyword matching, and human check. In total, there are 12408 moment-query pairs for training and 3720 moment-query pairs for testing. Videos are 30 s long on average and query sentences have 6 words on average.

TACoS: This dataset has 127 videos about cooking scenarios. There are 10146, 4589 and 4083 moment-query pairs for training, validation and testing respectively. Videos are 5 min long on average and query sentences have 8 words on average.

Evaluation Metrics: We adopt Rank n @ tIoU = m to measure the action localization performance of our model. The metric is defined as the percentage of top n proposals whose tIoU with ground truth is larger than m.

4.2 Comparisons with State-Of-The-Arts

We compare our DBAM with recent state-of-the-art methods, including:

(1) Sliding windows-based methods: MCN [11], CTRL [4], ACRN [21], ROLE [22], ACL-K [12], VAL [5], SLTA [6].
(2) Anchor-based methods: TGN [7], QSPN [8], CMIN [24], MAN [16].
(3) Reinforcement Learning-based Methods: SM-RL [14], TripNet [15].
(4) Other Methods: CBP [23], ABLR [9], SAP [10].

Table 1. Performance comparisons on Charades-STA.

Method	Rank1@		Rank5@	
	tIoU = 0.5	tIoU = 0.7	tIoU = 0.5	tIoU = 0.7
Random	8.51	3.03	37.12	14.06
MCN [11]	17.46	8.01	48.22	26.73
TGN [7]	18.90	–	31.02	–
ACRN [21]	20.26	7.64	71.99	27.79
ROLE [22]	21.74	7.82	70.37	30.06
SLTA [6]	22.81	8.25	72.39	31.46
VAL [5]	23.12	9.16	61.26	27.98
CTRL [4]	23.63	8.89	58.92	29.52
ABLR [9]	24.36	9.01	–	–
SM-RL [14]	24.36	11.17	61.25	32.08
SAP [10]	27.42	13.36	66.37	38.15
ACL-K [12]	30.48	12.20	64.84	35.13
QSPN [8]	35.60	15.80	79.40	45.40
CBP [23]	36.80	18.87	70.94	35.74
TripNet [15]	38.29	16.07	–	–
MAN [16]	41.24	20.54	**83.21**	51.85
Ours (DBAM)	**42.98**	**24.57**	77.96	**53.41**

Table 1 shows the performance comparison on Charades-STA. DBAM outperforms above methods across most of the criteria. It is worth noting that DBAM performs extremely well with top 1 results and surpasses the state-of-the-art MAN [16] with 4.03 percentage point and with 1.74 percentage point in terms of Rank1@ tIoU = 0.7 and Rank1@ tIoU = 0.5, respectively. Table 2 shows the performance comparison on TACoS. It can be seen that DBAM outperforms the state-of-the-art by a large margin. All these results demonstrate that the proposed two-dimensional feature map can effectively

Table 2. Performance comparisons on TACoS.

Method	Rank1@			Rank5@		
	tIoU = 0.1	tIoU = 0.3	tIoU = 0.5	tIoU = 0.1	tIoU = 0.3	tIoU = 0.5
Random	3.28	1.81	0.83	15.09	7.03	3.57
MCN [11]	14.42	–	5.58	37.35	–	10.33
ABLR [9]	34.70	19.50	9.40	–	–	–
ROLE [22]	20.37	15.38	9.94	45.45	31.17	30.13
SLTA [6]	23.13	17.07	11.92	46.52	32.90	20.86
CTRL [4]	24.32	18.32	13.30	48.73	36.69	25.42
ACRN [21]	24.22	19.52	14.62	47.42	34.97	24.88
VAL [5]	25.74	19.76	14.74	51.87	38.55	26.52
QSPN [8]	25.31	20.15	15.23	53.21	36.72	25.30
SM-RL [14]	26.51	20.25	15.95	50.01	38.47	27.84
CMIN [23]	32.48	24.64	18.05	62.13	38.46	27.02
SAP [10]	31.15	–	18.24	53.51	–	28.11
TGN [7]	41.87	21.77	18.90	53.40	39.06	31.02
TripNet [15]	–	23.95	19.17	–	–	–
ACL-K [12]	31.64	24.17	20.01	57.85	42.15	30.66
CBP [24]	–	27.31	24.79	–	43.64	37.40
Ours (DBAM)	**45.46**	**32.60**	**26.28**	**69.89**	**47.93**	**38.22**

model the dependency between moment candidates and thus can perceive more context information from neighboring moment candidates.

4.3 Ablation Studies

We conduct the ablation studies on Charades-STA as shown in Table 3. Base + A + M_a + M_s + M_e is the full implement of our DBAM. In Base + A + M_a we generate result proposals only according to the actionness possibility map while in Base + A + M_s + M_e we generate result proposals based on the starting and ending possibility maps. And in Base + M_a, we remove the self-attention model for the query sentence and average the feature of each word to form the sentence feature. The self-attention model can distinguish the most relevant words to filter noisy information of the query sentence, which leads to a better performance. Although the boundary matching strategy is efficient in temporal action detection, in this task of action localization via sentence query, a video may contain a series of activities and there are not obvious temporal boundaries of the visual information, and thus using the single boundary possibility maps to localize actions is insufficient and challenging. However, the ablation studies verify that the boundary possibility maps can indeed assist to localize actions with more accurate boundaries.

Table 3. Ablation studies on Charades-STA.

Method	Rank1@		Rank5@	
	tIoU = 0.5	tIoU = 0.7	tIoU = 0.5	tIoU = 0.7
Base + M_a	40.78	22.44	73.95	47.66
Base + A + M_a	41.02	23.33	75.70	47.98
Base + A + M_s + M_e	31.80	14.22	65.03	39.70
Base + A + M_a + M_s + M_e	**42.98**	**24.57**	**77.96**	**53.41**

4.4 Qualitative Results

We visualize the ground-truth tIoU map as well as M_a, M_s' and M_e' in Fig. 3. We uniformly partitioned each video from Charades-STA into 16 non-overlapping temporal regions, thus the dimension of each map is 16×16. The possibility maps are reliably predicted for videos with either single or two query sentences. In the first two cases, M_a accurately pinpoints the ground-truth location, while in the last case, the proposals generated by M_a are refined with the assistance of matching M_s' and M_e'.

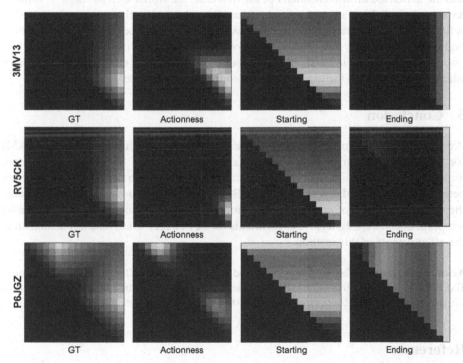

Fig. 3. Visualization of the ground truth and three types of possibility maps generated on Charades-STA. Each row represents the ground truth, the possibility map for actionness, starting and ending, respectively. Bright color means higher value.

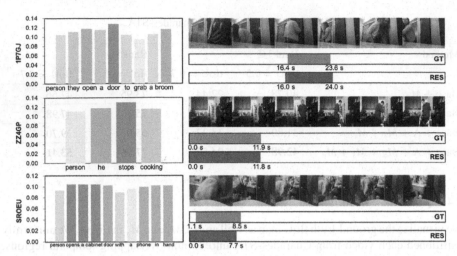

Fig. 4. Visualization of the attention weight of each word and the action localization results on Charades-STA.

In Fig. 4, we also visualize the attention weight of each word in the query sentence and the action localization results. For the first case, the words such as "door", "broom" have a relatively high attention weight. Identifying these pivotal nouns can improve the action localization performance. For the last two cases, the appearance of the frames is highly similar without shot change, while our model can focus on the modifiers such as "stops" and "a phone in hand". All of these results verify that our model is capable of adaptively identifying the useful words from the query sentence.

5   Conclusion

We present a novel method named Dense Boundary and Actionness Map (DBAM) for action localization in videos via sentence query. DBAM directly performs two-dimensional convolution over the cross-modal feature map to model the dependency between moment candidates. Then the DBAM outputs an actionness map to evaluate the confidence score of each candidate moment and two boundary maps to refine its temporal boundaries. Extensive experiments on the two real-world datasets demonstrate the effectiveness of this method.

Acknowledgements. This work was supported in part by the Italy-China Collaboration Project TALENT under Grant 2018YFE0118400; in part by the National Natural Science Foundation of China under Grant 61976069, Grant 61620106009, Grant 61772494 and Grant 61931008.

References

1. Lin, T., Zhao, X., Su, H., Wang, C., Yang, M.: BSN: Boundary sensitive network for temporal action proposal generation. In: Proceedings of the European Conference on Computer Vision, pp. 3–19 (2018)

2. Xu, M., Zhao, C., Rojas, D.S., Thabet, A., Ghanem, B.: G-TAD: sub-graph localization for temporal action detection. In: Proceedings of the Conference on Computer Vision and Pattern Recognition, pp. 10156–10165 (2020)

3. Lin, C., et al.: Fast learning of temporal action proposal via dense boundary generator. In: Proceedings of the AAAI Conference on Artificial Intelligence, pp. 11499–11506 (2020)

4. Gao, J., Sun, C., Yang, Z., Nevatia, R.: Tall: temporal activity localization via language query. In: Proceedings of the International Conference on Computer Vision, pp. 5267–5275 (2017)

5. Song, X., Han, Y.: VAL: visual-attention action localizer. In: Pacific Rim Conference on Multimedia, pp. 340–350 (2018)

6. Jiang, B., Huang, X., Yang, C., Yuan, J.: Cross-modal video moment retrieval with spatial and language-temporal attention. In: Proceedings of the International Conference on Multimedia Retrieval, pp. 217–225 (2019)

7. Chen, J., Chen, X., Ma, L., Jie, Z., Chua, T.-S.: Temporally grounding natural sentence in video. In: Proceedings of the Conference on Empirical Methods in Natural Language Processing, pp. 162–171 (2018)

8. Xu, H., He, K., Plummer, B.A., Sigal, L., Sclaroff, S., Saenko, K.: Multilevel language and vision integration for text-to-clip retrieval. In: Proceedings of the AAAI Conference on Artificial Intelligence, pp. 9062–9069 (2019)

9. Yuan, Y., Mei, T., Zhu, W.: To find where you talk: temporal sentence localization in video with attention based location regression. In: Proceedings of the AAAI Conference on Artificial Intelligence, pp. 9159–9166 (2019)

10. Chen, S. Jiang, Y.-G.: Semantic proposal for activity localization in videos via sentence query. In: Proceedings of the AAAI Conference on Artificial Intelligence, pp. 8199–8206 (2019)

11. Anne Hendricks, L., Wang, O., Shechtman, E., Sivic, J., Darrell, T., Russell, B.: Localizing moments in video with natural language. In: Proceedings of the International Conference on Computer Vision, pp. 5803–5812 (2017)

12. Ge, R., Gao, J., Chen. K., Nevatia, R.: Mac: mining activity concepts for language-based temporal localization. In: Proceedings of the Winter Conference on Applications of Computer Vision, pp. 245–253 (2019)

13. Rodriguez-Opazo, C., Marrese-Taylor, E., Fernando, B., Li, H., Gould, S.: DORi: discovering object relationships for moment localization of a natural language query in a video. In: Proceedings of the Winter Conference on Applications of Computer Vision, pp. 1079–1088 (2021)

14. Wang, W., Huang, Y., Wang, L.: Language-driven temporal activity localization: a semantic matching reinforcement learning model. In: Proceedings of the Conference on Computer Vision and Pattern Recognition, pp. 334–343 (2019)

15. Hahn, M., Kadav, A., Rehg, J.M., Graf, H.P.: Tripping through time: efficient localization of activities in videos. arXiv preprint arXiv:1904.09936 (2019)

16. Zhang, D., Dai, X., Wang, X., Wang, Y.-F., Davis, L.S.: Man: moment alignment network for natural language moment retrieval via iterative graph adjustment. In: Proceedings of the Conference on Computer Vision and Pattern Recognition, pp. 1247–1257 (2019)

17. Pennington, J., Socher, R., Manning, C.D.: Glove: global vectors for word representation. In: Proceedings of the Conference on Empirical Methods in Natural Language Processing, pp. 1532–1543 (2014)

18. Carreira, J., Zisserman, A.: Quo vadis, action recognition? a new model and the kinetics dataset. In: Proceedings of the Conference on Computer Vision and Pattern Recognition, pp. 6299–6308 (2017)

19. Kay, W., et al.: The kinetics human action video dataset. arXiv preprint arXiv:1705.06950 (2017)

20. Sigurdsson, G.A., Varol, G., Wang, X., Farhadi, A., Laptev, I. Gupta, A.: Hollywood in homes: crowdsourcing data collection for activity understanding. In: Proceedings of the European Conference on Computer Vision, pp. 510–526 (2016)

21. Liu, M., Wang, X., Nie, L., He, X., Chen, B., Chua, T.-S.: Attentive moment retrieval in videos. In: Proceedings of the International ACM SIGIR Conference on Research and Development in Information Retrieval, pp. 15–24 (2018)

22. Liu, M., Wang, X., Nie, L., Tian, Q., Chen, B., Chua, T.-S.: Cross-modal moment localization in videos. In: Proceedings of the ACM International Conference on Multimedia, pp. 843–851 (2018)

23. Zhang, Z., Lin, Z., Zhao, Z., Xiao, Z.: Cross-modal interaction networks for query-based moment retrieval in videos. In: Proceedings of the International ACM SIGIR Conference on Research and Development in Information Retrieval, pp. 655–664 (2019)

24. Wang, J., Ma, L., Jiang, W.: Temporally grounding language queries in videos by contextual boundary-aware prediction. In: Proceedings of the AAAI Conference on Artificial Intelligence, pp. 12168–12175 (2020)

A Deep Transfer Learning-Based Object Tracking Algorithm for Hyperspectral Video

Tang Yiming[1], Liu Yufei[1,2], Huang Hong[1(✉)], Zhang Chao[3], and Yuan Li[1]

[1] Key Laboratory of Optoelectronic Technology and Systems of the Education Ministry of China, Chongqing University, Chongqing 400044, China
hhuang@cqu.edu.cn
[2] Collaborative Innovation Center for Brain Science, Chongqing University, Chongqing 400044, China
[3] Beijing Institute of Spacecraft Environment Engineering, Beijing 100094, China

Abstract. Deep convolutional neural networks (CNNs) have been proved effective in color video visual tracking task. Compared with color video, hyperspectral video contains abundant spectral and material-based information which increases the instance-level discrimination ability. Therefore, hyperspectral video has huge potential for improving the performance of visual tracking task. However, deep trackers based on color video need a large number of samples to train a robust model, while it is difficult to train a hyperspectral video-based CNN model because of the lack of training samples. To tackle with this problem, a novel method is designed on basic of transfer learning technique. At first, a mapping convolutional operation is designed to embed high dimensional hyperspectral video into three channels as color video. Then, the parameters of CNN model learned on color domain are transferred into hyperspectral domain through fine-tuning. Finally, the fine-tuned CNN model is used for hyperspectral video tracking task. The hyperspectral tracker is evaluated on hyperspectral video dataset and it outperforms many state-of-the-art trackers.

Keywords: Visual tracking · Hyperspectral video · Transfer learning · Convolutional neural network

---

Y. Tang—Methodology, Validation, Data duration, Writing-review, Writing-original draft
Y. Liu—Supervision, Investigation, Methodology, Validation, Formal analysis, Writing-review & editing
H. Huang—Methodology, Formal analysis, Validation, Writing-review
C. Zhang—Methodology, Formal analysis, Validation, Writing-review
Y. Li—Validation, Writing-review

Y. Peng et al. (Eds.): ICIG 2021, LNCS 12890, pp. 811–820, 2021.
https://doi.org/10.1007/978-3-030-87361-5_66

1   Introduction

Visual object tracking is a fundamental task in the field of computer vision, and it aims to locate a particular object in subsequent frames while the location and size of the target in the first frame are known [1]. It can be furtherly used for behavioral analysis or motion prediction, and also can serve for more advanced applications, including video surveillance, unmanned aerial vehicles, military precision guidance and human-computer interaction [2]. Compared with tasks in computer vision [3], such as semantic segmentation, image classification and super-resolution reconstruction, instance-level discrimination ability possesses deeper significance.

Hyperspectral video has drawn more attentions in visual tracking due to its good instance-level discrimination ability [4–6]. In contrast to traditional color video, hyperspectral video provides abundant optical information, which reflects the underlying material characteristics of targets [7–9]. Consequently, several hand-craft hyperspectral tracking algorithms have been proposed based on correlational filter [10]. However, hand-craft feature has its limits in representing the deep semantic information of targets.

Deep CNN models have been proved effective in color video-based visual tracking in recent years. Many robust tracking frameworks are proposed with well-designed CNN architectures such as VGGNet [11] and ResNet [12]. In [13], CNNs are pre-trained through a multi-domain strategy (MDNet) on color videos and the tracking task is regarded as binary classification problem. For Siamese network-based trackers [14], training samples are paired and offline trained to optimize a correlation function, then the target is estimated by finding the location with maximum output response. In [15], visual tracking is divided into classification and regression branches, and the model is trained with large amounts of samples. Deep learning techniques such as attention mechanism [16] and meta-learning [17] are introduced to improve the robustness of deep trackers. To further enhance the robustness of hyperspectral video trackers, we try to develop a more powerful tracker based on deep model.

For deep trackers on color video, abundant training samples are provided to learn a generic representation of targets in the training process. When it comes to hyper-spectral tracking, the main challenge for constructing a deep model is the lack of training samples. In order to address this issue, transfer learning [18] technique is introduced in this paper, which can transfer well-learned knowledge from source domains into target domains.

Since videos in color domain are quite different with those in hyperspectral domain, it is important to find a way to effectively embed high-dimensional hyperspectral data into CNN models. Therefore, we design a mapping convolutional operation (MCO) to eliminate the difference between source domain (color domain) and target domain (hyperspectral domain), the MCO is a convolutional layer which is connected ahead of the convolutional layers with transferring parameters, and all weights are optimized in the transfer learning process. Then, a new CNN model is constructed and pre-trained with limited hyperspectral videos, which transfers learned knowledge into hyperspectral domain through fine-tuning. The MCO is connected ahead of the transfer convolutional layers, and fully connection (FC) layers are connected behind the transfer convolutional layers in the CNN model. In tracking process, we adopt the same strategy in MDNet to estimate the state of targets. The proposed transfer learning-based hyperspectral tracker (TLHT) can effectively exploit the hierarchical features of hyperspectral video and it shows good performance compared with both color trackers and hyperspectral trackers.

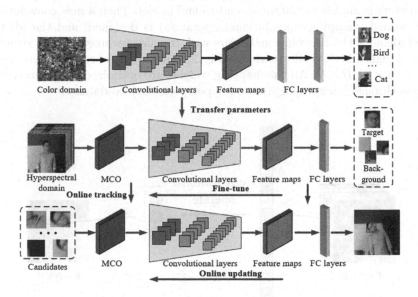

Fig. 1. Overall framework of TLHT.

2   Proposed Method

The overall framework of the proposed TLHT method is shown in Fig. 1. The designed MCO is connected with the transfer convolutional layers obtained from the pre-trained VGGNet, FC layers are also added behind the transfer convolutional layers as a binary classifier. Then the deep model is fine-tuned on hyperspectral videos to transfer the parameters into target domain. After that, the transferred model is adopted to accomplish the hyperspectral tracking task.

2.1   Mapping Convolutional Operation

Well-designed CNN models have shown good performance in varies of computer vision fields. Those pre-trained CNN models can obtain generic representations of color images and videos. For example, features in shallow layers can represent the blobs, corners and edges of images while features in deep layers contain sematic information of images [18]. The generic discriminative information is also important to hyperspectral videos. Therefore, transferring CNN models into hyperspectral domain can be useful. Unfortunately, images in hyperspectral videos contain hundreds of bands while color images contain three channels, causing huge difficulty for transfer learning.

Let $T \in R^{W \times H \times B}$ be an image in hyperspectral video, $W \times H$ denotes the spatial size while B denotes the number of spectral bands, then image with the same spatial size as in color videos can be denoted as $I \in R^{W \times H \times 3}$. In order to achieve the transformation, we expected to embed hyperspectral images with B channels into 3 channels with mapping parameters, and we also expect these parameters learnable to obtain an end-to-end model. Then a new convolutional layer named (mapping convolutional operation) is designed, and the MCO is added ahead of the convolutional layers with transfer parameters. The structure of the designed MCO is illustrated in Fig. 2, and the size of convolutional kernel is set as $1 \times 1 \times B \times 3$. All the mapping weights are optimized in the fine-tuning process through backpropagation on hyperspectral video dataset.

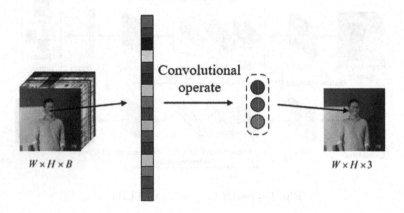

Fig. 2. Illustration of the mapping convolutional operation.

2.2   Transfer Learning Process

Transfer learning aims to improve the performance of target task with learned parameters in source task when there are insufficient training samples in target domain. To transfer learned generic information from color domain into hyperspectral domain, the architectures and weights obtained from the convolutional layers of pre-trained VGG-M network are fine-tuned. Before fine-tuning, those convolutional layers are connected with one MCO ahead and three FC layers behind, while the last FC layer is a binary classifier. Weights in additional FC layers and MCO are initialized randomly. Then images collected from hyperspectral videos are divided into positive samples and negative samples with respect to targets and backgrounds, respectively. In the process of fine-tuning, those samples are resized and put into CNN model for training, soft-max cross-entropy loss function is used to calculate the loss and SGD method is used for backpropagation, all weights are preserved when the network is converged or reaches the predefined max iterations number. After fine-tuning, the CNN model with optimal weights is applied for online tracking.

2.3 Online Tracking Process

The online tracking process in our framework adopts the same strategy in MDNet. To track an arbitrary object, target and background samples are generated to fine-tune the CNN model in the first frame for a particular task. When tracking, predicted candidates generated from the location of the object in previous frame are put into the CNN model, and the positive scores of candidates are output to estimate the location in current frame, the optimal state of the object is obtained by finding the candidate with the maximum positive score. Besides, bounding box regression is adapted to find a tight bounding box enclosing the object. After this, the CNN model is updated with samples collected in a short-term tracking period.

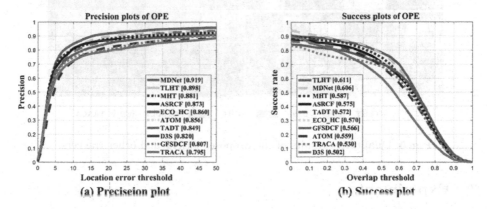

Fig. 3. Precision and success plots of trackers on hyperspectral videos or false-color videos.

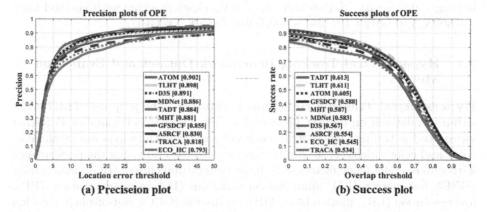

Fig. 4. Precision and success plots of trackers on hyperspectral videos or color videos.

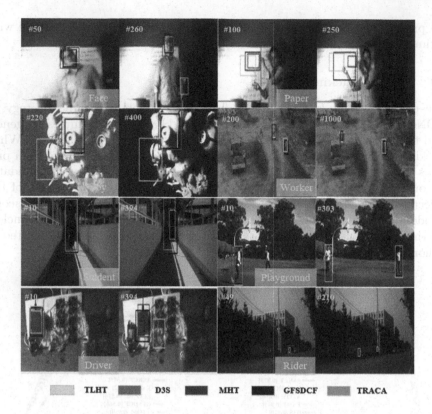

Fig. 5. Qualitative results of the proposed TLHT and other trackers.

3   Experiment

The proposed TLHT method is trained on hyperspectral tracking dataset, and it is compared with both hyperspectral trackers and color trackers. The algorithm is programmed with Matlab and runs on Windows machine with an Intel Core i7-7800X 3.50 GHz CPU and a NIVIDIA TITAN Xp GPU.

3.1   Hyperspectral Tracking Benchmark Dataset and Evaluation Metrics

Hyperspectral Tracking Benchmark Dataset. The proposed TLHT algorithm is validated on dataset presented in [10]. The dataset contains 35 testing videos and 40 training videos while each video is formed into hyperspectral, false-color and color videos. 11 attributes are involved for evaluating the performance with different challenge factors, which are background clutter (BC), deformation (DEF), fast motion (FM), illumination variations (IV), in-plane rotation (IPR), low resolution (LR), motion blur (MB), occlusions (OCC), out-of-plane rotation (OPR), out-of-view (OV), scale variations (SV).

Evaluation Metrics. Success and precision plots are curved to report the results of trackers. Success plots present the average success rate exceeding a certain overlap ratio ranging from 0 to 1 with ground-truth, and area under curve (AUC) is calculated to evaluate the performance. Precision plots present the average distance precision (DP) within a certain center pixel distance to ground-truth, and the DP within 20 pixels (DP@20) is calculated to evaluate the performance.

Table 1. The attributed AUC scores of trackers on hyperspectral videos or color videos. The best two results are marked in red and blue fonts.

Attributes	THLT	MHT	TADA	MDNET	ECO_HC	GFSDCF	ATOM	D3S	TRACA	ASRCF
BC	0.659	0.607	0.645	0.639	0.532	0.593	0.654	0.622	0.552	0.597
DEF	0.691	0.664	0.646	0.676	0.656	0.618	0.672	0.704	0.572	0.626
FM	0.562	0.541	0.659	0.624	0.588	0.560	0.602	0.612	0.521	0.660
IPR	0.702	0.670	0.691	0.694	0.583	0.670	0.680	0.658	0.638	0.619
IV	0.506	0.480	0.514	0.433	0.531	0.571	0.470	0.445	0.484	0.452
LR	0.489	0.477	0.488	0.516	0.476	0.495	0.553	0.492	0.365	0.581
MB	0.592	0.560	0.683	0.619	0.615	0.631	0.652	0.614	0.391	0.685
OCC	0.552	0.564	0.573	0.576	0.533	0.548	0.593	0.545	0.527	0.537
OPR	0.699	0.644	0.693	0.695	0.597	0.672	0.675	0.671	0.608	0.625
OV	0.427	0.395	0.662	0.509	0.501	0.513	0.673	0.605	0.459	0.657
SV	0.611	0.576	0.599	0.584	0.555	0.606	0.582	0.551	0.502	0.536

Table 2. The attributed DP@20 scores of trackers on hyperspectral videos or color videos. The best two results are marked in red and blue fonts.

Attributes	THLT	MHT	TADA	MDNET	ECO_HC	GFSDCF	ATOM	D3S	TRACA	ASRCF
BC	0.925	0.901	0.937	0.902	0.776	0.888	0.955	0.960	0.802	0.890
DEF	0.985	0.908	0.888	0.987	0.892	0.873	0.977	0.942	0.839	0.872
FM	0.841	0.774	0.920	0.884	0.761	0.757	0.920	0.995	0.752	0.914
IPR	0.987	0.940	0.942	0.982	0.778	0.919	0.962	0.941	0.906	0.866
IV	0.820	0.801	0.795	0.811	0.848	0.861	0.763	0.786	0.856	0.762
LR	0.803	0.819	0.838	0.921	0.815	0.833	0.903	0.910	0.698	0.904
MB	0.846	0.839	0.953	0.884	0.844	0.851	0.999	1.000	0.551	1.000
OCC	0.825	0.813	0.843	0.803	0.753	0.774	0.806	0.888	0.820	0.798
OPR	0.083	0.893	0.046	0.078	0.800	0.025	0.965	0.942	0.864	0.875
OV	0.692	0.679	0.906	0.769	0.688	0.702	0.997	1.000	0.691	1.000
SV	0.912	0.872	0.870	0.906	0.812	0.606	0.860	0.865	0.791	0.806

3.2 Comparison Experiments

The proposed TLHT algorithm is compared with some state-of-the-art tracking algorithms, including MHT [10], MDNet [13], ECO_HC [19], TRACA[20], ATOM [21], TADT [22], D3S [23], ASRCF [24] and GFSDCF [25].

Hyperspectral trackers TLHT and MHT are tested on hyperspectral videos, the other trackers are tested on false-color videos generated from hyperspectral videos and color videos.

Quantitative Comparison. In this part, the overall performance of TLHT is compared with the mentioned trackers. The precision and success plots are presented in Figs. 3 and 4. Compared with hyperspectral tracker MHT, hand-craft feature-based trackers ECO_HC and GFSDCF, the proposed method achieves higher AUC and DP@20 scores benefiting from the transferred CNN model. It approves that deep models can effectively improve the accuracy of hyperspectral tracker. Besides, the proposed TLHT tracker achieves competitive results compared with state-of-the-art deep trackers. As shown in Figs. 3 and 4, deep trackers TADT and ATOM perform the best AUC and DP@20 scores on color videos, respectively. For false-color videos, MDNet obtains best DP@20 score of 0.919 while TLHT obtains the best AUC score of 0.611. Most color tackers produce worse results on false-color videos because those color-based models are not adaptive to false-color videos, which come from hyperspectral videos and contain more hyperspectral information. In general, the proposed TLHT achieves competitive results compared with color trackers, it demonstrates that the proposed method can effectively transfer the knowledge learned from color domain into hyperspectral domain, and the discriminative hyperspectral information is preserved through the training process. Furthermore, it also illustrates that hyperspectral video can improve the robustness of visual tracking due to its instance-level discrimination ability.

Attributed Comparison. In this part, the results of different attributes are evaluated with trackers on hyperspectral videos or color videos. The AUC and tab2DP@20 scores of each attribute are shown in Tables 1 and 2, the best two scores are described in red and blue fonts. The results show that TLHT ranks the first for AUC scores on attributes of BC, IPR, OPR and SV while ranks the second on the attribute of DEF. For DP@20 scores, the TLHT algorithm ranks the first on attributes of IPR, OPR and SV, while ranks the second on the attribute of DEF. The TLHT tracker also obtains good scores in most attributes except OV and LR, that is because incorrect candidate samples are generated when the target is out of view(OV) and the lack of spatial details when the resolutions of samples are too low(LR). Above all, the results indicate that the TLHT algorithm is robust in handling with different challenge factors.

Qualitative Evaluation. We report qualitative evaluations of TLHT and four state-of-the-art trackers, including MHT, GFSDCF, D3S and TRACA. The qualitative results are visualized in Fig. 5. In Student and Rider, scale variation is the main challenge factor. In Toy, Playground and Paper, target rotates and there are similar objects in background, where instance-level discriminative ability is much important. In Worker and Face, the targets deforms over times. In Toy and Driver, the background clusters result in severe drifting for trackers. In Toy, the evident illumination variation also affects the robustness of trackers. The results intuitively demonstrate that TLHT can handle well with those situations while other trackers drift.

4   Conclusion

To exploit the strong ability of deep CNN models on hyperspectral tracking task, this paper presents a robust hyperspectral tracker based on transfer learning technique. A mapping convolutional operation (MCO) is designed to mitigate the difference between color videos and hyperspectral videos. In addition, the architecture and weights in CNN model, which is pre-trained in color domain, are transferred into hyperspectral domain through fine-tuning. Finally, the transferred CNN model is adopted to tracking task with the same strategy used in MDNet. Extensive experiments demonstrate the effectiveness of TLHT, the comparison results also reveal the potential of CNN model in hyperspectral visual tracking. In the future, we expect to optimize the TLHT algorithm by using more deep learning techniques such as attention mechanism and meta-learning.

Acknowledgments. Thanks to the National Natural Science Foundation of China under Grant 42071302, the Fundamental Research Funds for the Central Universities under Grant 2020CDCGTM002, the Basic and Frontier Research Programmes of Chongqing under Grant cstc2018jcyjAX0093, and the Innovation Program for Chongqing Overseas Returnees under Grant cx2019144 for funding this work. We would also like to thanks to NIVIDIA Corporation for the support of GPU device.

Conflict of Interest. The authors declare that they have no known competing financial interests or personal relationships that could have appeared to influence the work reported in this paper.

References

1. Li, P.X., Wang, D., et al.: Deep visual tracking: review and experimental comparison. Pattern Recogn. **76**, 323–338 (2018)
2. Tang, Y.M., Liu, Y.F., Huang, H., et al.: A scale-adaptive particle filter tracking algorithm based on offline trained multi-domain deep network. IEEE Access **8**, 31970–31982 (2020)
3. Tan, Y.H., Luo, H.Q., Wang, X.P., Liu, M.: Convolutional neural network cascade based neuron termination detection in 3d image stacks. In: 2018 IEEE International Conference on Image Processing, pp. 4048–4052. IEEE, Athens (2018)
4. Li, Z.Y., Huang, H., Duan, Y.L., Shi, G.Y.: DLPNet: a deep manifold network for feature extraction of hyperspectral imagery. Neural Netw. **129**, 7–18 (2020)
5. Xu, K.J., Huang, H., Deng, P.F., Li, Y.: Deep feature aggregation framework driven by graph convolutional network for scene classification in remote sensing. IEEE Trans. Neural Netw. Learn. Syst. (2021). https://doi.org/10.1109/TNNLS.2021.3071369
6. Xu, K.J., Huang, H., Deng, P.F.: Remote sensing image scene classification based on globalClocal dual-branch structure model. IEEE Geosci. Remote Sens. Lett. (2021). https://doi.org/10.1109/LGRS.2021.3075712
7. Uzair, M., Mahmood, A., Mian, A.: Hyperspectral face recognition with spatiospectral information fusion and PLS regression. IEEE Trans. Image Process. **24**, 1127–1137 (2015)

8. Pu, C.Y., Huang, H., Luo, L.Y.: Classification of hyperspectral image with attention mechanism-based dual-path convolutional network. IEEE Geosci. Remote Sens. Lett. **9**, 1–5 (2021)
9. Duan, Y.L., Huang, H., Tang, Y.X.: Local constraint-based sparse manifold hypergraph learning for dimensionality reduction of hyperspectral image. IEEE Trans. Geosci. Remote Sens. **59**(1), 613–628 (2021)
10. Xiong, F.C., Zhou, J., Qian, Y.T.: Material based object tracking in hyperspectral videos. IEEE Trans. Image Process. **29**, 3719–3733 (2020)
11. Simonyan, K., Zisserman, A.: Very deep convolutional networks for large-scale image recognition. In: 2015 International Conference on Learning Representation, pp. 1–14. VenueSan Diego (2015)
12. He, K., Zhang, X., Ren, S., Sun, J.: Deep residual learning for image recognition. In: 2016 IEEE Conference on Computer Vision and Pattern Recognition, pp. 770–778. IEEE, Las Vegaso (2016)
13. Nam, H., Han, B.: Learning multi-domain convolutional neural networks for visual tracking. In: 2016 IEEE Conference on Computer Vision and Pattern Recognition, pp. 4293–4302. IEEE, Las Vegaso (2016)
14. Li, B., Wu, W., Wang, Q., et al.: SiamRPN plus plus: evolution of siamese visual tracking with very deep networks. In: 2019 IEEE Conference on Computer Vision and Pattern Recognition, pp. 4277–4286. IEEE, Salt Lake City (2019)
15. Bhat, G., Danelljian, M., et al.: Learning discriminative model prediction for tracking. In: 2019 IEEE International Conference on Computer Vision, pp. 6181–6190. IEEE, Seoul (2019)
16. Wang, Q., Teng, Z., et al.: Learning attentions: residual attentional siamese network for high performance online visual tracking. In: 2018 IEEE Conference on Computer Vision and Pattern Recognition, pp. 4854–4863. IEEE, Long Beach (2018)
17. Choi, J., Kwon, J., Lee, K.M.: Deep meta learning for real-time target-aware visual tracking. In: 2019 IEEE International Conference on Computer Vision, pp. 911–920. IEEE, Seoul (2019)
18. He, X., Chen, Y.S., Ghamisi, P.: Heterogeneous transfer learning for hyperspectral image classification based on convolutional neural network. IEEE Trans. Geosci. Remote Sens. **58**, 3246–3263 (2020)
19. Danelljian, M., Bhat, G., Khan, F.S., Felsberg, M.: ECO: efficient convolution operators for tracking. In: 2017 IEEE Conference on Computer Vision and Pattern Recognition, pp. 6638–6646. IEEE, Hawaii (2017)
20. Choi, J., Chang, H.J., et al.: Context-aware deep feature compression for high-speed visual tracking. In: 2018 IEEE Conference on Computer Vision and Pattern Recognition, pp. 479–488. IEEE, Long Beach (2018)
21. Danelljian, M., Bhat, G., et al.: ATOMAccurate tracking by overlap maximization. In: 2019 IEEE International Conference on Computer Vision, pp. 4655–4664. IEEE, Seoul (2019)
22. Li, X., Ma, C., et al.: Target-aware deep tracking. In: 2019 IEEE International Conference on Computer Vision, pp. 1369–1378. IEEE, Seoul (2019)
23. Lukežič, A., Matas, J., Kristan, M.: Target-aware deep tracking. In: 2019 IEEE International Conference on Computer Vision, pp. 1369–1378. IEEE, Seoul (2019)
24. Dai, K.N., Wang, D., et al.: Visual tracking via adaptive spatially-regularized correlation filters. In: 2019 IEEE Conference on Computer Vision and Pattern Recognition, pp. 4665–4674. IEEE, Salt Lake City (2019)
25. Xu, T.Y., Feng, Z.H., et al.: Joint group feature selection and discriminative filter learning for robust visual object tracking. In: 2019 IEEE International Conference on Computer Vision, pp. 7949–7959. IEEE, Seoul (2019)

Author Index

Printed in the United States
by Baker & Taylor Publisher Services